UMI is committed to providing Christians with materials ... of God's Word. By completing the following survey, you will help us to better serve yo ... for your feedback and for purchasing this edition of *Precepts I* ...

Teachers: If you want to belong to the *Precepts For Liv* ... nministries.com.

1. How did you receive this copy of *Precepts*?
   ❒ Purchased by Church ❒ Purchased for Self ❒ Promotional Copy

2. How is it being used?
   ❒ Weekly Sunday School Curriculum ❒ Midweek Bible Study ❒ Personal Study
   ❒ Lesson Preparation ❒ Other: ______________________________

3. You are (check all that apply):
   ❒ Sunday School/Bible Study Teacher ❒ Sunday School/Group Study Student ❒ Pastor
   ❒ Sunday School Superintendent/Director of Christian Education ❒ Bible Student in Home

4. On a scale of 1–5, please rate the following features of your *Precepts For Living®* book.

1 (Not Very Helpful) to 5 (Extremely Helpful)

Quarter At-a-Glance	1	2	3	4	5	N/A
Quarterly Engaging the Theme Essay	1	2	3	4	5	N/A
Quarterly Christian Education in Action Essay	1	2	3	4	5	N/A
Quarterly Perspective Essay	1	2	3	4	5	N/A
Quarterly Heritage Profile	1	2	3	4	5	N/A
Weekly Focal Verses: King James Version	1	2	3	4	5	N/A
Weekly Focal Verses: *New Living Translation*	1	2	3	4	5	N/A
Weekly In Focus Story	1	2	3	4	5	N/A
Weekly The People, Places, and Times	1	2	3	4	5	N/A
Weekly Background	1	2	3	4	5	N/A
Weekly In Depth Commentary	1	2	3	4	5	N/A
Weekly Search the Scriptures	1	2	3	4	5	N/A
Weekly Discuss the Meaning	1	2	3	4	5	N/A
Weekly Lesson in Our Society	1	2	3	4	5	N/A
Weekly Make It Happen	1	2	3	4	5	N/A
Weekly More Light on the Text (Greek/Hebrew)	1	2	3	4	5	N/A
Daily Bible Readings	1	2	3	4	5	N/A
Precepts CD-ROM	1	2	3	4	5	N/A

If you use the CD-ROM, which are your favorite electronic resources available in your *Precepts* CD-ROM Library?

____

5. Does your church use UMI materials other than *Precepts For Living®*?
   ❒ Sunday School ❒ Vacation Bible School ❒ Other: ______________

6. For Bible Study, rank the order of your preferred Bible translation. Place a "1" next to your first choice, "2" next to your second choice, "3" next to your third choice, and "4" next to your fourth choice. Leave blank if you do not use a particular translation.

____ King James Version (KJV) ____ *New King James Version* (NKJV)
____ *New International Version* (NIV) ____ *New Living Translation* (NLT)
____ Other: ______________________________

7. What could UMI do to make this product better or easier to use?

____

____

BUSINESS REPLY MAIL

FIRST-CLASS MAIL PERMIT NO. 92609 CHICAGO IL

POSTAGE WILL BE PAID BY ADDRESSEE

MARKETING DEPARTMENT
UMI
P O BOX 436987
CHICAGO IL 60643-9809

--- fold here ---

8. Who made the decision to purchase this copy of *Precepts*? ❒ I did. ❒ Someone else (Skip to #11).

9. What influenced your decision?

	1 (Not Very Helpful) to 5 (Extremely Helpful)				
Received advertisement/catalog	1	2	3	4	5
Received a promotional copy	1	2	3	4	5
Previewed at a conference/convention	1	2	3	4	5
Recommendation of Pastor	1	2	3	4	5
Recommendation of Other	1	2	3	4	5
Other: ____________________	1	2	3	4	5

10. How did you purchase: ❒ Bookstore ❒ Direct from UMI ❒ Other: ________________

11. What other commentary/curricula did you use, if any, before *Precepts*? ____________________________

____

Profile Info:
12. Gender: ❒ Male ❒ Female

13. Age: ❒ Under 20 ❒ 20–34 ❒ 35–49 ❒ 50–64 ❒ 65+

14. Denomination: ❒ AME ❒ AMEZ ❒ Baptist
❒ CLG ❒ CME ❒ COGIC ❒ Full Gospel
❒ Nondenominational ❒ NPBC ❒ Pentecostal ❒ PNBC
❒ United Methodist ❒ Other:________________________________

15. City/State: ____
16. Name: ____
17. E-mail: ____

Please send any additional comments or feedback to precepts@urbanministries.com!

Deacon Larinzo D. Clayton

UMI ANNUAL COMMENTARY

PRECEPTS FOR LIVING®

MISSION STATEMENT

We are called of God to create, produce, and distribute quality Christian education products; to deliver exemplary customer service; and to provide quality Christian educational services, which will empower God's people, especially within the Black community, to evangelize, disciple, and equip people for serving Christ, His kingdom, and church.

UMI ANNUAL COMMENTARY

***PRECEPTS FOR LIVING*® 2008–2009**

INTERNATIONAL SUNDAY SCHOOL LESSONS

VOLUME 11

UMI (URBAN MINISTRIES, INC.)

Melvin Banks Sr., Litt.D., Founder and Chairman

C. Jeffrey Wright, J.D., President and CEO

Item No.: 1-2009. ISBN-13: 978-1-60352-329-5. ISBN-10: 1-60352-329-4. Publisher: UMI (Urban Ministries, Inc.), Chicago, IL 60643-6987. To place an order, call us at 1-800-860-8642 or visit our website at www.urbanministries.com.

CONTRIBUTORS

Editor
Vincent E. Bacote, Ph.D.

Vice President of Editorial
Cheryl P. Clemetson, Ph.D.

Developmental Editor & Staff Writer
Evangeline Carey

Copy Editor
Megan Bell

Product Manager
Vicki Frye

Designer
Trinidad D. Zavala

Bible Illustrator
Fred Carter

Contributing Writers Essays/In Focus Stories
Luvell Anderson
Evangeline Carey
Francis Morkeh
Nathan Smith
Dr. Louis H. Wilson

Bible Study Guide Writers
Luvell Anderson
Lisa Crayton
Rukeia Draw
Darcy Ingraham
Jennifer King
Vanessa Lovelace
LaTonya Mason
Keyonn Pope
Amy Rognlie
Frederick Thomas
Faith Waters
Charlesetta Watson-Holmes
Jimmie Wilkerson-Chaplin
Barbara Williams

More Light on the Text Writers
J. Ayodeji Adewuya, Ph.D.
Moussa Coulibaly, Ph.D.
Clay Daniels
Richard Gray
Ransome Merith
Francis Morkeh
Nathan Munn
Anthony Myles
James Rawdon
Raedorah Stewart
Reuben Unaegbu, Ph.D.
Dr. Louis H. Wilson

UMI®

Dear *Precepts* Customer,

We are thrilled to bring you the 2008–09 *Precepts For Living®*. As you engage God's Word through the lessons presented in *Precepts For Living®*, we know that you will continue to find this a valuable Bible study tool!

Along with the *Precepts For Living® Personal Study Guide* (the workbook) and the CD-ROM version of *Precepts,* we continue to offer *Precepts* in large print. You will also notice that the biblical text for each lesson continues to include the *New Living Translation* in addition to the King James Version, which is a great way to illumine your understanding of the text through side-by-side comparison. In conjunction, we are also proud to offer our aid to teachers with a section entitled "Creative Teaching."

On our Christian journey, *Precepts For Living®* not only serves as a witness through our learning and sharing more of the Bible but it also helps us develop new tools and other innovative ways to move toward a deeper understanding and practice of God's Word. As Paul admonishes Timothy to "Study to shew thyself approved" (2 Timothy 2:15), Christians today are given the same responsibility. Challenging ourselves to learn and grow more as teachers and in our understanding of God's Word prepares us to be stronger Christians and to witness to others about the saving power of Jesus Christ.

During your course of study for this year, you have the opportunity to discover or expand your understanding and knowledge through the following themes: "The New Testament Community," "Human Commitment," "New Creation in Christ," and "Call Sealed with a Promise." Each year of continued study holds immense promise for your Christian walk.

Precepts For Living® will continue to evolve and develop in an effort to meet our customers' needs. We appreciate your comments and feedback, and this year we are including a survey that you can complete by hand or online. Your response is valuable to us. If you have other questions or suggestions, please e-mail us at precepts@urbanministries.com or mail your comments to UMI, *Precepts For Living®*, P.O. Box 436987, Chicago, IL 60643-6987.

We pray that God will edify and encourage you and others through this book.

Yours in Christ,

Dr. Vincent E. Bacote

Dr. Vincent E. Bacote,
Editor

Uncovering the Benefits of Precepts

It is a great privilege to participate in Christian Education and play a significant role in the spiritual formation of fellow Christians in our churches. *Precepts For Living*® is a resource that is designed to help you lead others toward greater knowledge and practice of following Jesus Christ. To that end, I would like to help you to uncover the benefits of the resources provided to you in this year's commentary.

From the standpoint of your vocation as a teacher, it is very important to be aware of the great responsibility that goes along with your position. James 3:1 reminds us that we have such a great opportunity in front of us that we run the risk of greater judgment if we are derelict in our duties; this is a strong word to us that helps us understand the great influence we have when we help our students to learn about God's Word. To be a teacher means that we are participating in one of the church's greatest tasks, one that the ancient church called "catechesis." While this word is often associated with particular denominations and with a form of teaching that relies upon a systematic question and answer format, the central meaning of the word is "teaching," and it carries with it the idea of teaching the entirety of the faith to Christians. While many Sunday School teachers might not be familiar with this word, the truth is that every time any of us helps others to learn about God's Word and ways, we are participating in this great task of the church that has been with us from the beginning. Our participation in catechesis is central to the life of the church, and at times, this function of the church gets lost in the midst of other concerns. As a teacher, you have an opportunity to energize and/or revitalize this aspect of your church's ministry. Are you up for the challenge?

What is the goal when you are using *Precepts For Living*® to open up the riches of the Bible to your students? It is more than merely the acquisition of "spiritual data." Certainly we want our students to grow in knowledge, but the knowledge we seek to pass on is not merely Bible facts but a larger sense of knowledge where the information and doctrine conveyed is oriented toward a faithful life of discipleship. The People, Places, and Times; Background; In Depth; and More Light on the Text sections are there to help you with providing insight and understanding of the text. But the lesson is about more than simply compiling information. In each lesson, you will also see that we have In Focus stories and the Lesson in Our Society and Make It Happen sections. These sections are there to serve as catalysts for bringing the biblical text to our life situations. It is very important that we, as teachers, pass on knowledge that will enable our students to not only deepen their devotion to God in an "upward" focus but also will help them to better embody that devotion in a way that makes their lives a living witness to the world. In each lesson, our goal should be one of helping our students become better at being living examples of the Scriptures, as their lives may be the only Bible some people ever read.

In order to best uncover the benefits of this commentary, you will find it beneficial to utilize the essays that highlight notable African Americans, highlight quarterly themes, and also help you to become a better teacher by providing insight on enhancing the classroom experience and providing ways to convey the lesson across a range of learning styles. We believe that this commentary is a great tool that can help the church form fully devoted followers of Christ, and we invite you to take advantage of the variety of resources provided here. May God be glorified as you play your part in this great task of the church!

Creative Teaching

• **Energizing the Class.** If the class does not seem as enthusiastic or energy is low, after you open with prayer, have everyone stretch to the sky or outward. Then tell the class to shake off the low energy, and open up their hands to receive the love of God that is right there. You can always have a 30-second meet and greet time. This usually helps to wake people up so that you can begin class on a higher energy level.

• **Two Teachers in One Class—Bring Out the Best in Both.** Taking turns works in some classes, but in others it creates tension and favorites. Encourage teachers to study together, and then divide the segments of the lesson. Perhaps one will teach the introduction while the other teaches a section of the text. Encourage them to also become a true team with each contributing throughout the lesson.

• **Remember.** Everyone cannot read or write on the same level. Use different teaching techniques and styles when teaching. How you learn affects how you teach, so be open and willing to learn and teach through various mediums.

• **Avoid Study in Isolation.** People often "get it" when they are involved with more than talking about the lesson. Why not allow the class to see the connections themselves. Try using a chart to have adult students work in pairs or groups to compare and contrast Bible persons such as David and Solomon or Ruth and Orpah, Naomi's daughters-in-law. To help the students get started, suggest specific categories for comparisons such as lifestyles, families, or public ministry. As class members search the Scriptures, they will learn and remember much more than if you had told them about either person.

• **Group Studies.** Break the class into groups, and have each group read the Scripture lesson and a section of the Background for the text. Have each group create a two-minute skit about the Scripture to share with the class. Encourage the groups to use their imaginations and energy. You may want to have at least one "leader" in a group if you have more than two or three reserved persons in your class.

• **Volunteers.** Many classes begin with reading the lesson. When class members have studied, this activity is more "bringing minds" together than about the actual lesson. Still some classes can benefit from dramatic and creative reading of Bible passages at any point in the lesson. When the passage under study lends itself, assign volunteers parts. This need not be formal—standing up isn't even critical. This strategy works best in passages that have a story such as the conversation between Moses and his father-in-law, Jethro, or Paul confronting the merchants in Thessalonica. Assign one person to each speaking character in the Bible text. Feel free to be creative with giving the class roles as "the crowd." Make sure to assign a narrator who will read the parts not spoken. It is fun, it is fast, and it makes for memorable Bible reading.

• **Alternatives.** Select one or two persons from the class to read the Scripture lesson with enthusiasm and drama. Ask a few persons to develop a newspaper or magazine headline with a brief story that explains the headlines. Have another group write the headlines and a story that will be used in a cell phone video. (Let the class know that they should bring their cell phones—with video recording—so that most people can share in this activity. Presently, there is technology available for cell phone videos.)

• **Materials.** You may want to have large sheets of paper, markers, glue or tape, newspapers, and magazines available on a weekly basis for the various activities.

• **Additional Methods.** Write the theme on a large poster board or sheet of paper, and ask each person to write a word or draw a picture that best describes the theme. Read the themes aloud, and discuss any of the pictures before you begin your class discussion or activities. If you have a very large class or time is limited, only select a few words and/or pictures for discussion. The discussion can be led by you, or you can invite the class to have a brief dialogue with you.

• **Websites.** Log on to our website: www.urbanministries.com. E-mail us at precepts@urbanministries.com, and send us some of your favorite Teaching Tips for ages 18 and over that you want to share with others. If yours is selected, we will post them under our Teaching Tips sections for *Precepts*. If you have ice breaker activities, please indicate this as well. Your submissions should be no longer than 125 words.

• **Closing.** At the end of the lesson, give your class the assignment of looking for scenes from films or television, advertisements, or parts of songs that either demonstrate the coming week's In Focus story, Lesson in Our Society section, or Make It Happen section. Encourage them to be creative and to come up with an explanation of how their contribution helps make the truth of the lesson come to life.

• **Prayer.** Have a Prayer Request Board for persons to write their prayer requests on each Sunday. You may want to make this a weekly activity that someone reads the prayer request and the class decided which prayer requests they will pray for during the week. One Sunday School teacher has his class write their prayer requests on sheets of paper and place them in the middle of the floor once a year. He then shares with the class that he will write them all down in a prayer journal that he keeps and prays over them at least once a week. Be creative and create your own prayer journal or prayer tradition(s) within your class.

Possible Questions Related to the Heritage Profiles:

1. Why are some people chosen over others to be recognized for their achievements?

2. When reading the Heritage Profiles, what contemporary person comes to mind? A family member or friend can be a part of your decision.

3. Have you ever been recognized for a special achievement? How did you feel, and who have you lifted up to receive a special award in your church, community, or family? Why?

4. List three things that you believe are important that someone else knows.

5. What similarities do you see between the historical figure and your life? If there are none, share some ways that the person's life may have impacted your life and for future generations.

6. List three characteristics that stand out about the Heritage Profiles that you think are either positive or negative. List three characteristics about your life that you believe are either positive or negative. Compare the lists and write a short paragraph about the similarities and/or differences.

Remember that creative teaching can maximize your students' learning experience.

TABLE OF CONTENTS

TABLE OF CONTENTS

Fall Quarter 2008

THE NEW TESTAMENT COMMUNITY

LESSONS

Unit 1: The Birth of a New Community

SEPTEMBER

Unit 2: The Development and Work of the New Community

OCTOBER

Unit 3: The New Community Faces Growth Pains

NOVEMBER

Winter Quarter 2008–2009

HUMAN COMMITMENT

LESSONS

Unit 1: Commitment to the Messiah

DECEMBER

Unit 2: Old Testament People of Commitment

JANUARY

FEBRUARY

CYCLE OF 2007–2010

Arrangement of Quarters According to the Church School Year, September through August

	FALL	WINTER	SPRING	SUMMER
Year One 2007–08	**Creation** God Created a People (Genesis)	**Call** God's Call to the Christian Community (Luke)	**Covenant** God, the People, and the Covenant (1 and 2 Chronicles, Ezra, Nehemiah, Daniel, Haggai)	**Christ** Images of Christ (Gospels, Hebrews)
Year Two 2008–09	**Community** The New Testament Community (Matthew, Mark, Acts, 2 Corinthians, Ephesians, Philippians, 2 Timothy)	**Commitment** Human Commitment (Joshua, Judges, 2 Samuel, 2 Kings, Esther, Isaiah, Luke)	**Creation** New Creation in Christ (Ezekiel, Luke, Acts, Ephesians)	**Call** Call Sealed with a Promise (Exodus, Leviticus, Numbers, Deuteronomy)
Year Three 2009–10	**Covenant** Covenant Communities (Joshua, Judges, Ezra, Nehemiah, Mark, 1 and 2 Peter)	**Christ** Christ the Fulfillment (Matthew)	**Community** Teachings on Community (Ruth, John, New Testament)	**Commitment** Christian Commitment in Today's World (Philippians, 1 and 2 Thessalonians)

The Church of the Living God—The New Community

by Evangeline Carey

In the next four quarters of our *Precepts For Living® Annual Commentary,* before you begin to explore further biblical venues, we hope that you will pause to once again reflect on the cover. From the image of the sky and those majestic mountains, we want you to get a vivid vision of what God, the Creator, has done, is doing, and is going to do for His people. Look—truly see with spiritual eyes—and appreciate that man can invent, but only Almighty God can create.

There are two arguments that tell us that even if we did not know that there is a God we could look at the universe and know that Someone bigger than you and me does exist. Our universe tells us, then, that Someone externally created the cosmos. These arguments contend that since we cannot get something from nothing when we look at our vast, complex universe, all of the entities point to this Someone. This is the "Cosmological Argument." Genesis 1–2 tells us that a living, sovereign God—a God who is in control of His universe and never out of control of it—is that Someone. He is the external, adequate cause to which the universe owes its existence and greatness.

The "Teleological Argument" hits the nail on the head when it tells us that the order and purpose in the universe imply that there must be an "orderer" or "a designer." Look at that sky and the mountains on the cover and see if you do not agree. That Orderer or Designer is God

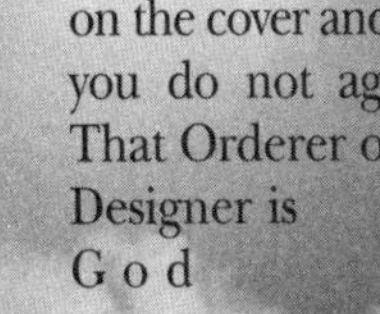

(Genesis 1–2). He is the intelligent Designer, the uncaused Cause, the unmoved Mover, who created something from nothing. No one created Him, but He created everything. Thus, from God's hand in nature, we see the hand and creativity of this intelligent Designer, who is God.

Subsequently, from the beauty of the sky on this cover and the complexities of the mountains, we should know that there is a God and that He is worthy to be worshiped and praised. As Psalm 90:2 declares, "Before the mountains were brought forth, or ever thou hadst formed the earth and the world, even from everlasting to everlasting, thou art God." In other words, we don't have to worry about our God disappearing on us. Forever and ever, He will be God, and He will exist. Psalm 19:1 proclaims, "The heavens declare the glory of God; and the firmament sheweth his handywork." On the cover, you are looking at some of the handiwork of Almighty God. Use this picture to help you not only meditate on God's creation and God's holy, inerrant Word but also on the sinfulness of man and God's forgiveness.

This same God, who created the heavens and the earth, also created the "new community"—His church. This holy, just, pure God built His church on the rock, which is Jesus, the Son of the Living God. He is the foundation upon which the new community—the church—resides. We unapologetically contend that she is God's church, and He has not given up the reins to anyone. He allows ministers or pastors/elders to be her overseers, but He is the Head of His church (Colossians 1:18). He owns her.

Mark 12:10 declares that, "The stone which the builders rejected is become the head of the corner." Jesus' own people (the Jews) rejected Him, but He is the head or cornerstone of His church, made up of Jews and Gentiles. He is the foundation upon which His church is built. God is her refuge. God is her shield. God is her present help in time of trouble. God is her all in all!

As students of God's holy, reliable, trustworthy, inerrant Word, we know that the church is not a building. It is a people—those who have believed on the Lord Jesus Christ, God's one and only Son, and are saved from eternal separation from a holy (set apart from sin) God. The church—the new community—therefore, is made up of believers who are "a great multitude, which no man could number, of all nations, and kindreds, and people, and tongues" (Revelation 7:9).

According to the New Testament, "eight figures represent the relationship of Christ to His church" (Wycliffe 1998):

- **Christ is the Shepherd**—the church is the sheep or the flock (John 10:1–30; Acts 20:28; Hebrews 13:20).
- **Christ is the Vine**—the church is the branches (John 15:1–17).
- **Christ is the Cornerstone or Foundation**—the church is made of the stones of a holy temple (Ephesians 2:20–22; 1 Corinthians 3:9–17; 1 Peter 2:4–8).
- **Christ is the High Priest**—the church is a kingdom of priests (Hebrews 5:1–10; 6:13–8:6; 1 Peter 2:5, 9; Revelation 1:6).
- **Christ is the Head**—the church is the many-membered body (Ephesians 1:22–23; 4:4, 12, 15; 1 Corinthians 12:12–27; Colossians 1:18).
- **Christ is the Bridegroom**—the church is the bride (John 3:29; 2 Corinthians 11:2; Ephesians 5:25–33; Revelation 19:7–8).
- **Christ is the Firstborn or Firstfruits among many brethren**—the church is the many brethren (Romans 8:29; 1 Corinthians 15:20, 23; Revelation 1:5).
- **Christ is Master**—the church is the slave, servant (Ephesians 6:5–9; Colossians 3:22–4:1; 1 Corinthians 7:22–23; Romans 6:18, 22; Philippians 1:1).

God loves His church. He loves His people so much that He sent His one and only Son to die for us. The height and depth of that love is captured in Romans 5:8: "But God commendeth his love toward us, in that, while we were yet sinners, Christ died for us." In essence, before we even loved Him, He died for you and for me. Isaiah 53:5 says, "But he was wounded for our transgressions, he was bruised for our iniquities: the chastisement of our peace was upon him; and with his stripes we are healed." Then Peter informs us in 1 Peter 2:21–24 that "because Christ also suffered for us, leaving us an example, that ye should follow his steps: Who did no sin, neither was guile found in His mouth: Who, when he was reviled, reviled not again; when he suffered, he threatened not; but committed himself to him that judgeth righteously: Who his own self bare our sins in his own body on the tree, that we, being dead to sins, should live unto righteousness: by whose stripes ye were healed."

Indeed, Christ is our example, and we should follow in His steps. Even though He never sinned or deceived anyone, He died for your sins and mine. He did not even retaliate when He was insulted by those who hated Him. He did not threaten to get even with those who heaped so much hurt upon Him. Instead, He knew that He was in good hands because He was in the hands of God, the Father.

As we survey portions of God's Word through the lens of community—the new community that God birthed, nurtures, grows, and disciplines—contemplate the awesome love of God that brought His wonderful salvation to His church. In fact, Jesus is coming the second time to reign over and live with her—His bride—forever and ever. Until He comes, she has her battles to fight, her problems to solve, her tears to shed; but thank God, she never has to do so alone.

God is always there for the sheep of His pasture!

Source:

Pfeiffer, Charles F., Howard F. Vos, John Rea, eds. *Wycliffe Bible Dictionary*. Peabody, Mass.: Hendrickson Publishers, Inc., 1998.

***Evangeline Carey** is a staff writer and the developmental editor of* Precepts For Living® *for UMI. Evangeline has also been an adult Sunday School teacher for more than 25 years.*

September 2008
Quarter At-A-Glance

The New Testament Community

The focus of this quarter is a survey of the New Testament, through the lens of the Christian community—the new community that Jesus birthed found, built, and nourishes, and is the Head of.

UNIT 1 • THE BIRTH OF A NEW COMMUNITY

In these four lessons, we will explore the beginnings of the Christian community. The lessons examine the core values and teaching of this new community and their commission for ministry as given to them by Jesus, Himself.

Lesson 1: September 7, 2008
A New Community
Mark 1:1–8; Matthew 3:1–3

John the Baptist was called by God to not only announce that the Messiah (God's one and only Son) would come but prepare the listeners for the baptism with the Holy Spirit that Jesus would bring. Therefore, John's baptism of repentance set the stage for the coming of our Lord and Saviour, Jesus Christ.

Lesson 2: September 14, 2008
The Birth of a New Community
Matthew 1:18–25; 2:13–15

Matthew, one of Jesus' disciples, revealed who Jesus is in relation to the Hebrew Scripture. The central theme to his complete gospel is of Emmanuel (God with us). Matthew also explained that Joseph (Jesus' step-father) had a link in the Davidic line. Therefore, Jesus is the God-man, sent to save humanity from their sins, and His coming fulfills Old Testament prophesy.

Lesson 3: September 21, 2008
Core Values of the New Community
Matthew 5:1–16

In the Beatitudes that Jesus presented at the Sermon on the Mount, Matthew spelled out the core values of Jesus Christ and His new community. He told of how the kingdom of God is built on God's righteousness. Consequently, members of God's community should follow God's lead by walking in and teaching these values.

Lesson 4: September 28, 2008
Creating a Community of Servants
Matthew 20:17–28

James and John's mother asked Jesus to give her sons important positions in His kingdom. This request showed a lack of understanding of Jesus' purpose and mission.

Jesus taught that greatness, in His kingdom, is the result of serving others.

UNIT 2 • THE DEVELOPMENT AND WORK OF THE NEW COMMUNITY

In these four lessons, the work and ministry of the new community is explored. The lessons focus on the empowerment and expansion of the Christian community as well as some key witnesses and their commission for ministry.

Lesson 5: October 5, 2008
Empowered to Be a Community
Acts 2:1–17

Pentecost was originally an Old Testament festival that occurred 50 days after Passover. The coming of the Holy Spirit, at Pentecost, was the fulfillment of a promise Jesus had made to His disciples. When He came, God empowered His community to do many powerful and persuasive acts that amazed people so much that they wanted to become a part of God's new community—the church. The Holy Spirit, then, came and indwelled the people of the new community so that they could do what God wanted them to do—so that they could go and make disciples by spreading the Good News.

Lesson 6: October 12, 2008
Expansion of the Community
Acts 6:1–5, 8–15

There was a long tradition of caring for the poor within the synagogue, and Christians continued this practice. In the early church, the Hellenists, Greek-speaking Jews, felt that their widows were being neglected in the daily distribution of goods. The apostles appointed deacons and delegated responsibilities. By appointing deacons, the apostles instituted a model of shared leadership in the community of faith.

Lesson 7: October 19, 2008
Transformed to Witness to the Community
Acts 9:1–11, 16–19

This passage describes the powerful and immediate experience of the presence of Christ for Saul (Paul). This study not only includes his Damascus Road conversion, where he saw a vision of Jesus Christ, but the gifts of hospitality (at the house of Judas) and healing (at the hands of Ananias). The story of Saul's conversion, from a persecutor to a preacher, provides the faith community with a positive example of transformation in Christ.

Lesson 8: October 26, 2008
Commissioned by the Community
Acts 13:1–12

With the commissioning of Barnabas and Saul (Paul), the Christian community spread primarily among Gentiles. In fact, the church at Antioch served as a major center for the early Christian church. After fasting and praying, leaders laid hands on these two missionaries and sent them on their way to do the work that God had called them to do.

UNIT 3 • THE NEW COMMUNITY FACES GROWTH PAINS

These five lessons focus on the early struggles of the Christian community. It explores four aspects of the community members—how they were equipped for ministry, how they handled conflict, their witness in the world, and the persecution they faced.

Lesson 9: November 2, 2008
Fitting into the Community
Ephesians 4:1–16

Paul's letter to the church at Ephesus challenges us to use our diverse identities and gifts to build up the Christian community. God gives every member of His church gifts that are to be used to edify or bless the body, to enhance the unity of the church and the work of Christ. In this lesson, Paul affirms the diversity of gifts and gives guidelines as to how and when the gifts are to be used.

Lesson 10: November 9, 2008
Conflict in the Community
Galatians 2:11–21

Through writing and example, Paul admonished believers that our acceptance before God comes not by following the rules but through living faithfully to Christ.

Because of division in the early church between Jewish and Gentile Christians, Paul taught that there are unifying factors that should be in the forefront of every believer's mind. These factors include the fact that Christ lives in every believer, through His Holy Spirit, and the link between Christ's death and resurrection and every believer's own death and resurrection from sin.

Lesson 11: November 16, 2008
Communion with God in the Midst of Struggle
Philippians 3:17–4:9

Paul exhorted the Philippians to follow examples of those who worked together for the common good and rejoiced together. He noted that the Christian community will have struggles and that God's church needs the peace of God to guard each and every heart and mind, in Christ Jesus.

Lesson 12: November 23, 2008
Witness of the Community
2 Timothy 2:1–3; 4:1–5

Paul admonished Timothy to prepare others, just as Paul had prepared him for discipleship, ministry, and service. He knew that the new community will be a witness for or against Christ, depending on their conduct.

Lesson 13: November 30, 2008
Persecution within the Community
2 Corinthians 11:17, 21–30; 12:9–10

Paul boasted about his suffering. His boasts were prompted by challenges from others in the Corinthian church who thought they had it rough. Paul said their complaints were no match for the suffering he had known. Paul was a mature believer and taught the Corinthians that there were going to be many challenges to the new community that would come from within. He said that, through his own weaknesses, he found strength in the grace of God and they could, too.

A New Community

by Evangeline Carey

The church of God—the new community—is not the brick and mortar of our various multimillion-dollar worship centers. It is not the opulent, ornate, stained-glass windows that remind us of certain Scriptures in the Bible. It is not the cutting-edge technical tools, which we use to teach and preach the Word of God. The New Community—the church of the Living God—is people who are made in God's image. They are also fallible (weak, frail, imperfect) people who needed a Saviour, acknowledged that need, and accepted the gift of their salvation through God's one and only Son, Jesus Christ.

God made Jesus to be both Lord and Messiah over His church (Acts 2:36). All humanity has to do is accept the gift that God has given them by believing on the Lord Jesus Christ as their personal Saviour (John 3:16). Those who accept God's gift are a part of the church of the Living God. Hence, believers are no longer estranged from a Holy God because of their sins, but have been reconciled to God by the death of His Son (Romans 5:10; 2 Corinthians 5:18). Consequently, the new community's relationship and friendship with God have been restored. Its members are a part of His family. We are the sheep of His pasture. We are His flock.

In Greek, the word "church" is *ekklesia* (**ek-klay-SEE-ah**), "which never refers to a place of worship but has in view an assembly of people. In the overwhelming majority of cases, *ekklesia* indicates a local company of believers" (Pfeiffer, Vos, and Rea 1998). The Word of God states emphatically that:

- "For [God] has rescued [His church—the new community] from the kingdom of darkness and transferred us into the Kingdom of his dear Son [Jesus]" (Colossians 1:13, NLT).
- God has called us out of sin and death (eternal damnation—eternal separation from a holy God) to a new community—a community of acceptance, forgiveness, unconditional love, and repentance (Acts 2:38; 1 Corinthians 13:1; 1 John 1:7, 9; 4:11–12).
- God has set us apart (sanctified us) for His kingdom where He will reign as King of kings and Lord of lords forever and ever (Revelation 19:16).

As depicted in a wonderful vintage hymn entitled "O Church of God," the family of God—the new community—has special attributes. According to its writer, Charles W. Naylor:

> The church of God one body is, One Spirit dwells within;
> And all her members are redeemed, And triumph over sin.
> Divinely built, divinely ruled, To God she doth submit;
> His will her law, His truth her guide, Her path is glory lit.
> God set her members each in place, According to His will
> Apostles, prophets, teachers, all, His purpose to fulfill.
> In beauty stand, O church of God, With righteousness arrayed;
> Put on thy strength and face thy foes with courage undismayed.

Accordingly, the new community helps God to build His kingdom (carry out the Great Commission) and at Jesus' Second Coming, she will dwell with Him. All believers will see Christ, the One who paid our sin debt in full. At that time, we will behold Him face-to-face (Revelation 21).

The Scriptures also give voice to the fact that:

- The church—the new community—is made up of "every kindred, and tongue, and people, and nation" (Revelation 5:9). Therefore, it is both local and universal.
- In addition, the church—the new community—is made up of only those whose sins have been forgiven because they accepted the gift of God's wonderful salvation through Jesus Christ. In essence, they have acknowledged Jesus Christ as Lord and Saviour. According to God's Word, believers have confessed with their mouth the Lord Jesus, and believed in their hearts that God has raised Him

from the dead. Therefore, they are saved. They know that they are the children of God (Christians) because they have God's Spirit living and operating within them (Romans 8:9; 10:9).

• The church—the new community—is metaphorically the "bride of Christ," the Lamb's (Jesus Christ's) wife (Revelation 21:2, 9–10).

• The church—the new community—is united by common links: "One Lord, one faith, one baptism, One God and Father of all, who is above all, and through all, and in you all" (Ephesians 4:5–6).

• The church—the new community—has the indwelling of the Holy Ghost (the third person of the Trinity—Father, Son, and Holy Spirit) within her to help lead, guide, and teach her God's will and His ways (Romans 8:9).

• As the church—the new community—seeks to walk worthy in what God has called them to do (help build His kingdom), the Holy Spirit also directs believers and energizes their community life so that they can dwell together in unity (Matthew 28:18–20).

• The church—new community—is joined to Christ by His Spirit (1 Corinthians 6:17). The power of her life is the Holy Spirit, who gives her not only strength; but authority, boldness, confidence, courage, and discernment (insight) (Acts 4:23–31; 5:12–16; 9:29).

• As commanded by the Word of God, the true church—the new community—is longsuffering in dealing with one another, as well as patient. Her members deal with one another in love (John 13:34; Ephesians 4:1–3; 1 John 4:7–10).

• Thus, Jesus Christ is the rock, or foundation, on which God built His church—the new community. He is the cornerstone. He was rejected by His own people (the Jews), but became the cornerstone of His own new building—the church—His new community, which is made up of both Jews and Gentiles (21:42–43).

• Therefore, Jesus Christ is the "head of the body, the church" (Colossians 1:18).

• Jesus Christ came the first time as the Messiah, the Suffering Servant. However, He is coming the second time as Judge. His judgment will begin with the household of God—the church—the new community (1 Peter 4:17).

God's church is indeed unique and special because she is birthed, loved, nurtured, disciplined, grown, and rewarded for her work for God by God, Himself—the Creator of the universe. Are you identified with Christ and His church? Is your name recorded in heaven? Your answers will determine where you will spend *all* eternity.

Sources:

Alexander, Desmond T., et.al, eds. *New Dictionary of Bible Theology*. Downers Grove, Ill.: InterVarsity Press, 2000.

Bromiley, Geoffrey W., ed. *International Standard Bible Encyclopedia*. Grand Rapids, Mich.: Wm. B. Eerdmans Publishing Company, 1979.

Naylor, Charles W. "O Church of God." *Worship the Lord/Hymnal of the Church of God*. Anderson, Ind.: Warner Press, Inc., 1989.

Pfeiffer, Charles F., Howard F. Vos, John Rea, eds. *Wycliffe Bible Dictionary*. Peabody, Mass.: Hendrickson Publishers, Inc., 1998.

***Evangeline Carey** is a staff writer and the developmental editor of* Precepts For Living® *for UMI. Evangeline has also been an adult Sunday School teacher for more than 25 years.*

Christian Education in Action

Building a New Testament Community: Conceptions and Misconceptions

by Francis Morkeh

God is the originator and developer of true community life. His intentions and purposes can be traced and validated in the Scriptures, human history, and contemporary experiences of life. There are many specific topics and in-depth issues that can be explored in regard to true community in the New Testament era. Space does not allow for an exhaustive treatment here, but we can survey some of the general trends of God's perspective on community life.

First, God lives and functions in a holy and everlasting community with the Son (Jesus Christ) and the Holy Spirit. The biblical account shows that the triune God has functioned in unity of purpose in creation, redemption, and working toward *shalom,* or peace (Genesis 1:1–3, 26–28; 12:1–4).

Second, God created the first human being, Adam, and placed him in a community of family—with Eve and his children. God intended that humans would live in a family situation, which is supportive because they love, nurture, and care for each other. It is also transformative because they instruct, discipline, and guide people toward godly values. God intended that individuals live not in complete isolation or autonomy, but in community relationships that promote holistic productivity and progress based on a biblical worldview.

Third, a critical study of the general revelations of life and the special revelations of Scripture shows that God purposefully created all the rich diversities of elements and structures in our environment. He also created the different varieties of life that are found in creation. Animal and plant species, ethnic groups, and all kinds of social and cultural diversities in our world give testimony to God's wonderful handiwork. These rich diversities work together to bring glory to God's name. His vision and values of *shalom* mean that all creation is to live in justice, harmony, excellence, and dignity.

According to theologian Cornelius Plantinga, these are evidences of God's commitment to let all of creation work together. However, Scripture teaches that after the Fall in the Garden of Eden, God's original plans for authentic community life were defied and perverted (Genesis 3:14–21). Although humankind still possessed a deep inner desire to continue with the process of community-building on many fronts—in both secular and religious dimensions—the processes that have sometimes been employed to accomplish this purpose lack a sound biblical/theological foundation.

The New Testament community, inaugurated by God's redemptive act through Christ, opened the door for God's new and living way. As religion scholar Albert Wolters has noted, "God's act of redemption, through Jesus Christ, restored and reconciled humankind and the entire creation back to God. Through this divine act, God's original purpose for a true human community was reestablished" (Wolters 1985). The rationale behind God's purpose for establishing a new order, modeled by the New Testament community, is to bring people into repentance so that they can know God. They are also to experience a transformed life and live out the values of God's kingdom as exemplified in Jesus Christ. Christ demonstrated love toward everyone, identified with and brought restoration to the oppressed, and transformed the life situations of people. The purpose for these activities was to build a new community of people who would represent and demonstrate His kingdom values on Earth and bring glory to His name. God desires that His people will find true joy, peace, and love based on His ultimate purpose. He also desires that His people will bring about experiences of transformation in lives and societies.

Understanding the Core Values of God's Community

Many theological educators have debated what should be the core values and standards of excellence exemplified by a New Testament community of believers. There is no unanimous agreement on all points. Yet there seems to be a common concern by most evangelical Christians regarding the core values necessary to express God's idea of a true community. It is worthy, at this point, to mention just two of these core values: (1) The New Testament community exists to represent Christ on Earth. (2) It is a community created by God to help bring about transformation of lives and society.

The first underlying value for God's people as His representatives on Earth is to help others realize the significance of God's unconditional love toward all humankind (Romans 5:7–8; John 3:16). The heartbeat of Christianity is to bring about reconciliation to broken relationships and to foster holistic restoration of people's broken lives. This means that the value of the New Testament community is not an attempt to reinforce ethnocentric mind-sets of one ethnic/tribal group against the other. Nor is it a way to devise strategies by which one community or family can monopolize and manipulate others in order to achieve a hidden agenda of oppression and suppression. Instead, God's idea is to build a worthy community of people who will truly represent Him on Earth by demonstrating and exemplifying the love of Christ. This love seeks to graciously share restoration, reconciliation, and transformation, which promotes love, equality, and justice for all humankind.

The second underlying value involves holistic change. As God's vessels of transformation, believers must be equipped to help people realize their true identity and vocation in God through the redemptive work of Christ. It is important to develop theological/biblical foundations that help people understand that God's idea of transformation is not centered on mere behavioral changes—God wants true change of hearts, minds, attitudes, worldviews, and lifestyles. We should also refrain from conforming uncritically to cultural standards that encourage ungodly existential and ideological worldviews that undermine sound Christian principles. Man's inclination to forge political, economic, and social bonds in order to protect a particular self-interest is nothing new. Historically, attempts at social transformation from a purely humanist perspective have resulted in men and women being treated like mere commodities, objects, and tools. Social and political theoretical models developed by people such as Karl Marx and Frederick Engels support this line of thinking.

While there may be a few good lessons that can be learned from aspects of these social theories, the values of the New Testament community are derived from a biblical worldview. The community of Jesus Christ on Earth is shaped by eternal principles based on God's ultimate purpose for His creation. The central message that informs God's representatives on Earth includes an understanding that human beings must not be treated as mere objects or tools. This is the idea of *imago Dei* (Genesis 1:26–28)—all people are valuable because they are created in the image of God. To become a true New Testament community that conforms to God's perspective and changes society, we must always keep these core principles in focus.

Implications for Christian Spirituality and Service

1. In our desire to carry out God's purpose on Earth and to extend the core values of the kingdom of God to all people, our approach and strategy must be defined by love and humility.

2. Our vision to transform the political, social, and economic structures of this world to conform to God's idea of *shalom* should always focus on putting the needs of human beings at the center of our policies and agendas. Any attempt to holistically transform the lives of broken people should have at its roots the words and lifestyle that Jesus Christ modeled on Earth. Christ loves all people unconditionally. He sacrificially died for the world in order to build a true community.

3. The New Testament community must learn from the example of Christ. He was intentional about identifying with the weak, marginalized, and poor in order to empower them to realize their true identity and vocation in God.

4. We should not discriminate against people just because their social positions in life do not fit our preconceived frameworks. People will open themselves up to our message of the Cross when we love them without condemnation or judgment.

5. God's ways of accomplishing His purposes on Earth, through us, require that we develop solid theological foundations that are geared toward achieving *shalom*.

6. It is not enough to build an inward-looking community of believers who are satisfied staying within the walls of church and focusing on internal church issues. A true community that represents Christ purposefully reaches out to touch people beyond church walls and cultural divides.

Sources:

Farganis, James. *Readings in Social Theory: The Classic Tradition to Post-Modernism.* New York: McGraw-Hill Companies, 1996.

Plantiga Jr., Cornelius. *Not the Way It's Supposed to Be: A Breviary of Sin.* Grand Rapids, Mich.: Wm. B. Eerdmans Publishing Company, 1995.

Walsh, Brian, and Richard Middleton. *The Transforming Vision: Shaping a Christian Worldview.* Downers Grove, Ill.: InterVarsity Press, 1984.

Wolters, Albert. *Creation Regained: Biblical Basics for a Reformational View.* Grand Rapids, Mich.: Wm. B. Eerdmans Publishing Company, 1985.

Francis Morkeh *holds a B.A. in biblical studies from Central University College, Ghana, and an M.A. in educational ministries from Wheaton College, where he is a Ph.D. candidate.*

Perspective

From Shame to Community

by Nathan Smith

I sat at the table, surrounded by Indian brothers and sisters from all over the subcontinent. As I listened to each of the leaders share about their struggles and concerns, we seemed to zero in on one topic—the "nets." What is a net, you may ask, and what does it have to do with the New Testament community? Let me give a little more context.

I was participating in a Christian teen event in the city of Hyderabad, India. Approximately 300 Christian teenagers from all over the country had come together (some from as far as 48 hours away) for a week of fun, teaching, worship, music, and mayhem. The conference was in its seminal stages, and each year it had attracted more and more teenagers from around India. Amidst the cauldrons of curry, rivers of rice, and the hottest heat of the year, we uncovered a much hotter topic. The "nets," or accountability and fellowship groups that these teens were being encouraged to form, were not working so well. They had begun to ask our leaders to place them in a "net" that did not include people from their home city but with another group of teens from a different city.

At first, we were confused. The whole idea of shaping these "nets," with other teens from their home, was so that they could continue meeting once they descended from our mountaintop experience and settled back into reality. The strategy was to provide them with a Christian community that would help them to "make it" back in the real world. Then it came to us. We discovered that, in their opinion, a "net" would not be a safe place for them to share honestly, if it involved friends from their hometown. In many Eastern cultures, shame and honor are the currencies of the day. For centuries, these cultures have avoided any encounter with shame as much as possible. Shame is such a piercing issue for them that they could not bear the idea of someone else from their community, even a close friend, knowing about what was really going on in their hearts and lives. For them, the idea of community is very different from what we experience in the West. The people of the Eastern cultures, from which the Hebrew and Christian Scriptures originated, possessed similar feelings about community and shame.

If we go back to Genesis, we see that Adam and Eve, after disobeying the Lord, attempted fruitlessly to cover their "shame" with leaves (Genesis 3:7). Yet, if there had been no community between each other or with God, where would their shame have been directed? How would they have felt it? The communities that they were created into provided them with the dynamics to sense this shame. We, too, are invited into the communities of the Trinity (Father, Son, and Holy Spirit) as well as of the redeemed. But, instead of God condemning Adam and Eve to die, we find Him covering their shame with an animal skin— therefore, requiring the death and the shedding of that animal's blood (v. 21). We all share in this breaking of community, the image of God being stained and broken as we, along with Adam and Eve, struggle in isolating ourselves from each other and from God. Yet, this fast-forwards us to the death and resurrection of our Lord Jesus Christ.

How, then, can we encourage these young Indian people to form their "nets" and to have open and honest accountability with each other.

The late Mike Yaconelli gave us an insight in his book, *Messy Spirituality*. He told about a recovering alcoholic, who was struggling with both alcoholism and a decision. His lifelong battle with the bottle had been mostly unsuccessful. When his weary wife finally gave him an ultimatum, before the community of faith, with tears in his eyes, he chose his wife over alcohol. The church community encouraged and helped him in the battle.

Something inside of us yearns for a community like this, a community that not only challenges us to make the right decisions but also allows for us to safely share our real life with them—even our shame. I have heard one friend teach that God needs us to "zero out" before He can begin to "zero in." Before it can be fully realized and our true struggles dealt with, part of zeroing out has to be done in community. We need the redeemed in our process of transformation and they need us. No one can do it on his own; we are not created to do so.

Stanley Grenz, in his volume *Theology for the Community of God*, speaks of Christians as being made in the image of God. This image is a signpost of God's design for us to be in community as the Father, Son, and Holy Spirit are in community with each other. After God created Adam, He made sure that we would read that though Adam was in perfect fellowship with God and creation he still needed someone. So God created the first human community with Eve. Thus began the eternal fellowship among the Trinity, the community of man, and finally of creation. Adam and Eve, however, eventually decided to isolate themselves from the Trinity, as well as each other and the creation, when they chose to disobey. Thus, they broke the "image of God" that held them in unity with God and creation (Genesis 3:7, 10, 15, 17–19). Grenz explains that sin is actually "the lack of and loss of community." We still bear the image of God, but not perfectly; therefore, we suffer in our broken communities. Christ came to restore fellowship with the triune God and with creation but accomplished this as a human. He became the new Adam, thus enabling those who believed in Him to be reunited into the unbroken fellowship of God, humanity, and creation.

Grenz says, "According to the New Testament, Christ is the image of God" (2 Corinthians 4:4; Colossians 1:15; Hebrews 1:3). As the church, therefore, we are Christ's body and share in Christ's calling to be this new "image of God." As a result, Paul states that we are being transformed in the image of God in Christ (1 Corinthians 15:49; 2 Corinthians 3:18; Colossians 3:10). In order to embrace transformation, we are continuously called away from isolation and into community, away from hiding our shame and into communing with the redeemed and with God, Himself. This is only possible if we are covered by the blood of the Lamb. We look to Revelation 7:9–10 (NIV) and read the words of John as he wrote, "After this I looked and there before me was a great multitude that no one could count, from every nation, tribe, people and language, standing before the throne and in front of the Lamb. They were wearing white robes and were holding palm branches in their hands. And they cried out in a loud voice: 'Salvation belongs to our God, who sits on the throne, and to the Lamb.'"

With all the heartache, disappointment, frustration, rebellion, and so many other difficulties that overwhelm communities of faith, is it worth it? Is it worth it to keep going, to continue loving, forgiving, simply meeting together, etc.? With churches splitting, pastors falling into sin, and generations not understanding each other, sometimes it seems easier to follow Jesus alone, instead of with a bunch of Christians. Yet, the passage in Revelation points us to a different reality taking place in heaven. One day we will stand as the community of God before Him, worshiping and in complete unity, yet from all different walks, languages, and generations. That day shapes and forms what we do today as we read the Lord's Prayer, "your kingdom come, your will be done on earth as it is in heaven" (Matthew 6:10, NIV). What do we do until then?

I remember sitting at that same youth conference in Hyderabad, India, with a leader from the U.S., picking his brain for what he thought would be the central principles of effective cross-cultural youth ministry. After politely listening to him, I finally got to the point of why I was asking and proudly spilled out my "insight." I said that teenagers need mentoring, meaningful service, significant leadership opportunities, and a place to unwind their foolishness. He pursed his chin and nodded in agreement but then added, "I would include one more thing—belonging. They need belonging."

What does belonging mean for us today? How do we create it for our own lives and also the life of our church? Does it mean condoning sin or redefining what sin is so that some won't feel uncomfortable? I don't think so. Though we don't condone sin, as a New Testament community we invite the sinner into the transforming community of God—the Father, Son, and Holy Spirit. We do this by following the example that Christ left for us, through His life, and by learning from the communities of faith that followed Christ's ascension.

We all need to belong, to be known and still accepted. We all need a God who meets us where we are and accepts us but doesn't leave us there. As the church, we are called to be in the world but not of the world and then to invite the world to experience God's love and community. At times, it may mean allowing them to see the messiness of our lives, where we experience shame and doubt, the real stuff of life. It may, at other times, mean engaging them amid the mess of their lives where they don't want anyone—especially God. We have the privilege, though, of taking Him with us wherever we go. We may need to invite ourselves, as Christ did with Zacchaeus (Luke 19:1–10). There is a need for them to be met by us where they are, as Christ would meet them. We call them into the brokenness of our community, proclaiming that God is transforming us and that He can transform them, too. This all starts with us being the community of God, connected to the triune God, and in constant communion with each other and creation. When a lost world sees that kind of community, they will come to Jesus and experience the hospitality of heaven.

Sources:

Grenz, Stanley J. *Theology for the Community of God.* Grand Rapids, Mich.: Wm. B. Eerdmans Publishing Company, 2000.

Yaconelli, Mike. *Messy Spirituality: God's Annoying Love for Imperfect People.* Grand Rapids, Mich.: Zondervan, 2002.

Nathan Smith *has a bachelor's degree in church history and historical theology from Moody Bible Institute and is currently pursuing an M.Div. at Trinity Evangelical Divinity School in Deerfield, Illinois. He has served as a youth pastor as well as an overseas missionary with Operation Mobilization.*

September 2008
Heritage Profile

Phillis Wheatley

(1753–1784)
Poet

Phillis Wheatley overcame the adverse conditions of slavery to become a world-renowned poet. Ms. Wheatley was born in Africa—most sources say Senegal—around 1753. When she was 7 or 8 years old, she was kidnaped and sold to John and Susannah Wheatley of Boston. Because the ship's captain didn't think she would live long, she was sold for a cheap price on the Boston dock.

The Wheatleys were impressed with the young slave girl's ability to learn quickly and taught her English, Latin, and Greek. She mastered the English language a short while after her arrival in America, and she was able to read the Bible and quickly comprehended its teachings. The Wheatley family was reportedly a Christian family, and they introduced their slave girl to Christ. The Wheatleys paid special attention to young Phillis and treated her much like a family member. Yet, although they were Christians, they did not free her or renounce slavery.

The intelligent young girl, who was frail and sickly looking, received international attention when she wrote "On the Death of the Rev. Mr. George Whitefield, 1770." The poem was an elegy for the famous evangelical preacher. It caught the attention of English noblewoman and philanthropist Selina Hastings, countess of Huntingdon. The countess supported Phillis's work and helped fund her book *Poems on Various Subjects, Moral and Religious* in 1773. The book, a collection of 39 poems, contained an opening note certifying that a young Negro slave girl had written the poems, signed by a group of prominent Boston citizens who had examined the young Phillis. She was also granted her freedom from the Wheatleys in 1773.

The theme of salvation ran throughout many of her works. She said every person, regardless of race, was in need of salvation. She connected Christian freedom and beliefs to racial freedom for Blacks. She wrote about the irony of Christians owning slaves and supporting the degrading institution of slavery. Phillis included biblical characters in many of her poems, such as "Goliath of Gath." She wrote a poem that honored George Washington, who later met with her and commended her on her work.

Mrs. Wheatley, named Phillis after the slave ship on which she arrived in Boston, married John Peters in 1778. Mr. Peters was a free Black man from Boston. Their children died as babies, and Phillis died while in her early 30s. Despite her fame, she died in complete poverty.

However, her work lived on. Abolitionists used her poetry and ideas to campaign against the institution of slavery, and she is now credited with beginning both the Black American writing tradition and the Black American women's writing tradition. She served as an example of how humans could overcome tragic life situations.

Sources:

http://www.earlyamerica.com/review/winter96/wheatley.html

Women in History. Phillis Wheatley biography. Lakewood Public Library. http://www.lkwdpl.org/wihohio/whea-phi.htm

TEACHING TIPS

September 7
Bible Study Guide 1

1. Words You Should Know

A. Way (Mark 1:2) *hodos* (Gk.)—Refers to a path, way, or road that is traveled. Jesus had to follow a God-ordained spiritual path, which John the Baptist was instrumental in making passable.

B. Remission (v. 4) *aphesis* (Gk.)—Forgiveness; a release from sin.

C. Repent (Matthew 3:2) *metanoia* (Gk.)—Implies a voluntary change of mind or heart, usually from worse to better, evil to good, sin to righteousness.

2. Teacher Preparation

Unifying Principle—Repentance Leads to Community. People look for a place where they can belong. What kind of community fosters a sense of belonging? The new community, of which John the Baptist spoke and to which Jesus called people, was a community of love, acceptance, repentance, and forgiveness.

A. Pray for the students in your class. Ask God to help them embrace the principles in the AIM for Change.

B. Read and study the Focal Verses, especially in the context of the challenges and joys of belonging to new communities, especially communities of faith.

C. Brainstorm some of the new beginnings that you have experienced in the past year, and come prepared to discuss these.

3. Starting the Lesson

A. Ask one student to open the class with prayer using the Keep in Mind verse as a guide.

B. Then emphasize the AIM for Change learning goals.

C. Have volunteers read the Keep in Mind verse and Focal Verses. Discuss.

4. Getting into the Lesson

A. Write the phrases "new birth" and "new beginnings" on the board. Ask the students what positive and negative images these phrases evoke. Write down some of these comments.

B. Ask a few students to pick one word or phrase shared, and discuss how it related to a recent experience they had.

C. Share one of your new birth experiences, noting adjustments you made.

5. Relating the Lesson to Life

A. Ask a volunteer to share the In Focus story.

B. Engage the students in a discussion on how the story relates to the idea of "new community."

6. Arousing Action

A. Allow time for volunteers to share one "new birth" area that they or a family member is adjusting to. Allow the students to offer solutions to any problems that they may be experiencing.

B. Encourage the students to commit that area to prayer throughout this entire unit.

C. Close the class with prayer, welcoming any petitions related to today's lesson.

Worship Guide

For the Superintendent or Teacher
Theme: A New Community
Theme Song: "Turn Your Eyes upon Jesus"
Devotional Reading: 1 Peter 2:1–10
Prayer

A NEW COMMUNITY

SEPT 7th

Bible Background • MARK 1:1–8; MATTHEW 3:1–12
Printed Text • MARK 1:1–8; MATTHEW 3:1–3 Devotional Reading • 1 PETER 2:1–10

AIM for Change

By the end of the lesson, we will:
EXPLORE the beginnings of a new community that was announced by John and pioneered by Jesus;
RECOGNIZE that the community of faith is a place where we belong or fit in; and
IDENTIFY ways that we can be involved in this community and commit ourselves to take action.

Keep in Mind

"Repent ye: for the kingdom of heaven is at hand" (from Matthew 3:2).

Focal Verses

KJV **Mark 1:1** The beginning of the gospel of Jesus Christ, the Son of God;

2 As it is written in the prophets, Behold, I send my messenger before thy face, which shall prepare thy way before thee.

3 The voice of one crying in the wilderness, Prepare ye the way of the Lord, make his paths straight.

4 John did baptize in the wilderness, and preach the baptism of repentance for the remission of sins.

5 And there went out unto him all the land of Judaea, and they of Jerusalem, and were all baptized of him in the river of Jordan, confessing their sins.

6 And John was clothed with camel's hair, and with a girdle of a skin about his loins; and he did eat locusts and wild honey;

7 And preached, saying, There cometh one mightier than I after me, the latchet of whose shoes I am not worthy to stoop down and unloose.

8 I indeed have baptized you with water: but he shall baptize you with the Holy Ghost.

Matthew 3:1 In those days came John the Baptist, preaching in the wilderness of Judaea,

2 And saying, Repent ye: for the kingdom of heaven is at hand.

3 For this is he that was spoken of by the prophet Esaias, saying, The voice of one crying in the wilderness, Prepare ye the way of the Lord, make his paths straight.

NLT **Mark 1:1** This is the Good News about Jesus the Messiah, the Son of God. It began

2 just as the prophet Isaiah had written: "Look, I am sending my messenger ahead of you, and he will prepare your way.

3 He is a voice shouting in the wilderness, 'Prepare the way for the LORD's coming! Clear the road for him!'"

4 This messenger was John the Baptist. He was in the wilderness and preached that people should be baptized to show that they had repented of their sins and turned to God to be forgiven.

5 All of Judea, including all the people of Jerusalem, went out to see and hear John. And when they confessed their sins, he baptized them in the Jordan River.

6 His clothes were woven from coarse camel hair, and he wore a leather belt around his waist. For food he ate locusts and wild honey.

7 John announced: "Someone is coming soon who is greater than I am—so much greater that I'm not even worthy to stoop down like a slave and untie the straps of his sandals.

8 I baptize you with water, but he will baptize you with the Holy Spirit!"

Matthew 3:1 In those days John the Baptist came to the Judean wilderness and began preaching. His message was,

2 "Repent of your sins and turn to God, for the Kingdom of Heaven is near."

3 The prophet Isaiah was speaking about John when he said, "He is a voice shouting in the wilderness, 'Prepare the way for the LORD's coming! Clear the road for him!'"

In Focus

From a hidden position, Quentin secretly watched his band practice for an upcoming gig. They were good—really good. However Quentin's concern wasn't about their ability, but about the attitude of the group's drummer, Adrian.

Adrian, the band's self-proclaimed "show dog," liked being the center of attention. His antics increasingly diminished the band's ability to minister to crowds. Even after occasional reprimands, Adrian continued to act outrageously, onstage and offstage.

If today's practice went as usual, Quentin would have to drop Adrian from the Festival of Arts event and maybe even the band itself.

"Adrian, you're drowning us out," Michelle yelled again from her position at the mike. Oblivious to Michelle's rising frustration, Adrian continued to drum fast and loud.

"You're too loud," Michelle said again. She walked over to the electrical outlet and yanked the plugs to Adrian's drum set.

"What's the problem?" Adrian asked, bewildered.

"You are," Michelle said, angrily placing her hands on her hips. "I'm tired of you always needing to be the center of attention. I quit!"

"Oh, no you don't!" Quentin called, rapidly walking onstage. "I need you and the band needs you. You're a wonderful psalmist."

He looked at Adrian. "I'm sorry, but you can't play at the festival gig."

"But w–w–why?" Adrian stammered. "You know I'm the best drummer this group has ever had. And the crowds love me."

"I know," Quentin said, "but that doesn't change the fact that you seem unaware of the difference between ministry and performance. I don't need backup musicians who think their skills are more important than sharing God's love with people."

"What you really mean is that you can't have a drummer who gets more attention than *you*, Mr. Christian Artist of the Year," Adrian sneered.

"You're out of line," Quentin warned. "Need I remind you that the *real* reason we minister through music is to prepare the way for people to receive Christ? I want you in the band, and I want you to play at the festival event, but your attitude has to change. Starting now. What do you say?"

"Say?" Adrian said, glaring at Quentin and the other band members. "I say this is bogus. I quit!" Throwing down his drumsticks, he stormed out. A half-hour later he returned just as the band finished praying.

Adrian addressed Quentin and the rest of the group. "I was wrong. Please forgive me. What we do is really not about me. It's about being a 'voice in the wilderness,' like John the Baptist was. May I have another chance?"

Over the cheers of the others, Adrian just barely heard Quentin's "You bet," before being engulfed in a group hug.

Adrian learned and we, too, must learn that fitting into any community requires commitment to community purposes, guidelines, and leaders. It also requires a willingness to repent when we are wrong. In today's lesson, we learn similar principles as we study John the Baptist's attitudes and actions during his public ministry, as he helps to build a new community—the church.

The People, Places, and Times

Mark. John Mark is the full name of this companion and student of the apostle Peter. When Peter escaped from jail with the assistance of an angel (Acts 12:1–17), he went to the home of Mark's mother but was not initially let in because the believers were too discouraged to accept that it was him. Mark penned his Gospel to convey information he had gleaned from Peter. Mark also served alongside the apostles Paul and Barnabas but was barred from doing so again after he returned home before the mission was completed. This sparked a rift between those church leaders. Despite this, Mark later regained favor with Paul, who noted he was "profitable. . .for the ministry" (2 Timothy 4:11).

John the Baptist. The story of John's conception and release into ministry is a familiar one to many Christians. John was a miracle child, born to childless, elderly parents—the priest Zacharias and his wife Elisabeth (Luke 1:5–25). Both were descendants of Aaron, a bloodline that would have been a source of joy had it not been for their childless state. Initially Zacharias doubted the angel's announcement of the promised child. As a result, he was unable to speak until John's dedication and naming. While still pregnant, Elisabeth received a visit from her cousin Mary, who also had been divinely chosen to bear a child—Jesus. The baby jumped in Elisabeth's womb when she heard Mary's voice (Luke 1:41).

Filled with the Holy Spirit from conception, John was the prophesied forerunner of Jesus. John preceded Jesus in public ministry. Public reception of John's ministry was tremendous: "And there went out unto him all the land of Judaea, and they of Jerusalem, and were all baptized of him in the river of Jordan, confessing their sins" (Mark 1:5). More so, they ventured into the wilderness—or desert—to hear him (v. 4; Matthew 3:1)! John took no credit for the response to his preaching but properly relegated himself to the role of messenger, rather than saviour.

Wilderness. In the Old and New Testaments, the wilderness served as a place God chose to meet with, chastise, and revive His children. The wilderness was also the place where Jesus endured a 40-day fast, encountered Satan, and overcame temptation (Matthew 4:1–11). Because John did not initially venture into the cities to preach, people had to come out of those cities into the wilderness to hear him. In many respects, their action showed the opposite of a scriptural truth: It is often necessary to leave the wilderness of sin in order to receive and follow Christ.

Background

The book of Mark is an "as-told-to" version of material found in the other Gospels. Like an Old Testament scribe, Mark recorded on scrolls what he gleaned from his mentor, the apostle Peter.

Mark reveals the "beginning of the gospel of Jesus Christ, the Son of God" (Mark 1:1). The word "Christ" in Greek is *Christos* (**khris-TOS**), meaning "anointed." In the Old Testament, generally the priests, and especially the high priest, were anointed with oil as a visible symbol of the acceptance and furtherance of their spiritual service. But in the New Testament, "Christ" refers specifically to Jesus to denote His status as the only person God has *anointed*—and appointed—as "high priest" and Saviour of mankind. Mark further notes that Jesus' public ministry actually began with John the Baptist's ministry (v. 2). In verse 3, he quotes Old Testament prophecy to prove this (Isaiah 40:3).

For centuries, the "word of the Lord" was scarce in Israel, due in large part to three factors: (1) the nation's rampant, continual sin; (2) its disregard for God's warnings through the prophets; and (3) its ill treatment of God's servants, the prophets. Equally scarce were events that fulfilled prophecy, such as the births and ministries of John the Baptist and Jesus.

Beginning with John the Baptist, prophetic fulfillment was at hand. Isaiah prophesied that a messenger would serve as a "voice," paving the way for Israel's reception of the coming Messiah—Jesus. That messenger—or forerunner—was John the Baptist (Mark 1:2).

At-A-Glance

1. In the Beginning (Mark 1:1)
2. A Messenger of Hope (vv. 2–4; Matthew 3:1–3)
3. The People's Response to the Message (Mark 1:5)
4. A New Community (vv. 6–8)

In Depth

1. In the Beginning (Mark 1:1)

At the onset, Mark makes it clear that the information he will impart will have two characteristics. It will start at the beginning and proceed from there, and it will be limited, focusing solely on the "gospel of Jesus Christ."

2. A Messenger of Hope (vv. 2–4; Matthew 3:1–3)

John the Baptist was a messenger from God. The term "messenger," from the Greek word *aggelos* (**ANG-el-os**), relates to the position of one who announces, proclaims, or delivers a message, and is the same word used to describe the function of angels. Here it refers to John, who fulfilled the Old Testament prophecies in Malachi, and Isaiah, as a forerunner who prepared people for Jesus' message and ministry.

John the Baptist's purpose was "to turn the hearts of the fathers to the children, and the disobedient to the wisdom of the just; to make ready a people prepared for the Lord" (Luke 1:17). He was to focus on matters of the heart. He preached that individual repentance and cleansing, not ceremonial washing, was crucial for reconnecting with God. John's message was, therefore, designed to move people toward reconciliation by encouraging the repentance of sins.

Repentance would benefit John's hearers in two ways. First, repentance would lead to reconciliation with God, cleansing of their consciences, and the joy of renewed fellowship with Him. Second, once they were free from the burden of sin, community members could enjoy improved interpersonal relationships.

Further, John's preaching made it apparent that membership in the new community would be faith-based, not works-based. In a society in which people had become too comfortable with skirting the Law, John's message was uncompromisingly strong, simple, and forthright.

3. The People's Response to the Message (Mark 1:5)

Every preacher anticipates both reception and rejection of his or her message. But not even John the Baptist could have expected the overwhelmingly positive and fruitful response his message received. It was spontaneous. "The whole Judean countryside and all the people of Jerusalem went out to him. Confessing their sins, they were baptized by him in the Jordan River" (v. 5, NIV).

This "new community" was birthed by repentance, forgiveness, and love. Community unity was forged by the act of baptism, which provided a foundation for new believers to share common ground as they waited for the imminent appearance of the Messiah, of whom John the Baptist hinted (vv. 7–8).

Imagine the scene at the river's edge as person after person waited to be baptized. Even with help, such community baptism would have taken quite some time. And imagine the jubilation that rippled through the crowd once the new believers realized that their divine appointment in the desert had result in a new, right relationship with God.

To top it all off, John the Baptist promised that the best was yet to come. "There cometh one mightier than I after me," he said, "the latchet of whose shoes I am not worthy to stoop down and unloose. I indeed have baptized you with water: but he shall baptize you with the Holy Ghost" (v. 8).

4. A New Community (vv. 6–8)

John ushered in the beginning of a new community structure—whose foundation was Christ—that put everyone on the same playing field. He preached a message of repentance; then he baptized hearers who favorably responded. The sequence of events was important to the nation known for its ceremonial acts. The nation needed to know the divine order of restored relationship with God: first repentance and second any ceremonial act (like baptism) affirming that relationship. By baptizing people from all walks of life, John revealed a God-centric society that modeled God's love, forgiveness, healing, and acceptance. Soon, only one criterion would be necessary for membership: faith. Only one attitude would be lauded: servanthood. And only one social rule mattered: the Golden Rule.

By drawing attention toward faith and away from works, John the Baptist prepared a new community of believers to rely more on God than on tradition. In many respects, therefore, John the Baptist was a "minister of reconciliation." He led people back to God, which enabled them to reconcile with each other. All of this was possible, in part, because John modeled what it meant to be an ideal citizen of the new community. He was concerned about the welfare of others. He did not take advantage of others. He respected the authority of the Saviour to come after him, and turned others to Jesus' authority. And he willingly stepped into the shadows when it was time to do so.

Search the Scriptures

1. What was John the Baptist's purpose in life (Mark 1:1–4)?

2. Why do you think it was a good idea to immediately baptize the new believers (v. 4–5)?

3. What did John preach that made people realize the urgency of his message (Matthew 3:2)?

4. Prophecy "validated" John's ministry (Matthew 3:1–3; Mark 1:2–3). Explain.

Discuss the Meaning

1. In what ways could baptism help the community draw closer together?

2. Why do you think John made such a big deal about repentance (Matthew 3:2)?

3. What did John mean by "Prepare ye the way of the Lord, make his paths straight" (v. 3)?

Lesson in Our Society

The experience of birthing any new thing is often a mixed bag. Birth, by its very nature, provides opportunities for us to embrace new challenges, connect with new communities (such as a new place of employment, church, or neighborhood), and use dormant gifts and talents. (Praise God!) At the same time, they stir up our "nests," shake our sense of belonging, and compel us to reposition ourselves in order to fit in. (Lord, help!) Since change is inevitable, we cannot avoid birth experiences, but we can learn to thrive during them. One key to keep in mind is that change is temporary. So stop fretting and begin trusting God. Then ask God to help you show compassion and mercy in the future to family, friends, and coworkers when they are in the midst of their birthing seasons.

Make It Happen

Sometimes, in new settings, we suffer feelings of isolation because we don't open ourselves to new people or experiences. Other times we may feel isolated simply because people don't know we are interested in certain areas of ministry or we remain silent when the call goes out for volunteers. Do these situations sound familiar to you, or is there another root cause for any isolation you have experienced in the past? Ask God to deliver you from these hindering influences. This week, read Romans 8:28 daily, and then use it as a foundation for each day's prayer petitions. If needed, refer back to today's AIM for Change section to glean specific areas about which you may want to pray.

Follow the Spirit

What God wants me to do:

____

____

Remember Your Thoughts

Special insights I have learned:

____

____

More Light on the Text

Mark 1:1–8; Matthew 3:1–3

This lesson begins a four-lesson survey of the beginning of the Christian faith. The first lesson focuses on the beginning of the beginning. The passages from the gospels of Mark and Matthew record how God's new and clear-cut revelation of Himself in Jesus began with one person whom we know as John the Baptist. Nothing in these passages or elsewhere in the New Testament indicates that he was highly educated, socially influential, or wealthy. To the contrary, John the Baptist was none of these. However, God used him to start a new understanding of God and of human life that would spread across the world and bring about a new community. This study reminds Bible students of the difference God can make through a single person who is willing to entrust everything to Him.

1 The beginning of the gospel of Jesus Christ, the Son of God;

Although this verse begins with the word "the" in the English translations of the Bible, such as the King James and the New International versions, originally Mark did not include the word. The "beginning" Mark was referring to was the beginning of Jesus, not of Mark's writing. Mark used "gospel" (Gk. *euaggelion,* **yoo-ang-GHEL-ee-on**) to mean "good news," especially important news such as the birth of a new king or a military victory.

Jesus Christ is the name of the Son of God. Jesus is the Greek form of the name Joshua, which in Hebrew meant "Jehovah saves." It was the earthly name Mary and Joseph had given Him at the angel Gabriel's instruction (Matthew 1:21; Luke 1:31). Christ (Gk. *Christos,* **khris-TOS**) was originally a title for someone anointed with oil to a holy position. By combining the two names, Mark highlighted Jesus' role as God's chosen one and pointed toward His nature as both human and divine.

2 As it is written in the prophets, Behold, I send my messenger before thy face, which shall prepare thy way before thee. 3 The voice of one crying in the wilderness, Prepare ye the way of the Lord, make his paths straight.

In Mark 1:2–3, Mark quoted two prophets regarding John the Baptist. In verse 2, Mark quoted from the prophet Malachi (Malachi 3:1). In verse 3, Mark quoted from Isaiah (Isaiah 40:3). Both verses give identical instructions for hearers to *prepare* the Lord's way.

When the Greek New Testament was translated into the English King James Version in 1611, the earliest and oldest manuscripts of Mark's gospel were not available. Instead of the phrase "as it is written in the prophets" found at the beginning of verse 2, those earliest copies of the gospel of Mark read "in the book of the prophet Isaiah." This shows that Mark followed the custom of grouping similar quotations from different Old Testament writings together and identifying them with the better-known prophet. In this verse, the better-known prophet was Isaiah. Someone later copying Mark's gospel wrote "in the prophets," thinking that made the Gospel more accurate, since two prophets were cited (Lightfoot 1979).

Malachi clearly mentioned a forerunner, a "messenger." The Greek word used here is *aggelos* (**AHN-**

gel-os), and is most often translated "angel," when referring to a heavenly messenger. Mark quoted Malachi first, but since Isaiah, the better-known prophet, had foretold a century earlier how the way for God's new work should be prepared, Mark identified him as the original speaker. Both Matthew and Luke quoted the same prophecy from Isaiah (see Matthew 3:3; Luke 3:4). Most Bible scholars today accept that Matthew and Luke used Mark as a source in writing their Gospels, which is why the first three Gospels are called the Synoptic Gospels. *Synoptic* means "to see with one eye."

It was a great honor whenever a king chose to travel into a region of his realm. In preparation for a royal arrival, workers would go ahead on the route he would take to clear away any obstacles. They would remove any trees that had fallen across the road, fill in any washouts, level any steep ascents, or straighten any detours that would slow the king's journey. "Prepare ye the way" meant to leave nothing to stumble over. Mark quoted Isaiah's prophecies to show how John the Baptist, as Jesus' forerunner, fulfilled his role in preparing for Jesus' arrival on the scene (cf. Isaiah 62:10).

The word "crying" (Heb. *qara'*, **kaw-RAW**) meant to proclaim the truth as in court, to call for people's attention, or to summon people to you. The word "crying" might make a reader think of expressing pain or sadness, or possibly calling for help. However, crying in verse 3 simply meant to speak loudly or to shout, such as shouting for joy.

The first statement in verse 2 says the messenger will be sent "before thy face." That can mean "ahead of you" but it can also mean "in plain view." John the Baptist was not timid. He wanted to get people's attention and wanted them to hear what he had to say.

Although some modern translations identify the forerunner's location as "in the desert" (NIV), "in the wilderness" in the KJV and NLT is more accurate. Although the Jordan River valley is bounded by the Arabian Desert on the east and the Dead Sea to the south, the word "wilderness" (Gk. *eremos*, **ER-ay-mos**) referred to an uninhabited area or pastureland, a place away from any city. In other words, John called people to come away from home or work to examine their relationship with God.

4 John did baptize in the wilderness, and preach the baptism of repentance for the remission of sins.

Baptism was not a new practice, but the way John applied it was new. Mark said John preached "a baptism of repentance for the remission of sins." "Repentance" (Gk. *metanoia*, **met-AN-oy-ah**) described a total transformation of a person's life. Some scholars interpret that John was saying the baptism was part of the person's sin being forgiven; others understand it as meaning baptism was done in acknowledgement of having been forgiven. The difference comes as a result of the Greek word *eis* (**ice**) or "for."

The word is used both ways. In Matthew 12:41, Jesus told some Pharisees, "The men of Nineveh... repented at (*eis*) the preaching of Jonah." They repented because of Jonah's preaching. In Luke 5:4, Jesus told Peter "let down your nets for (*eis*) a catch." Peter was told to let down his nets *in order to* catch some fish. Whichever way it is understood, John the Baptist told people they should be baptized after they had confessed their sin and their need for forgiveness.

The parable of the Prodigal Son (Luke 15:11–20) gives a clear example of what John the Baptist meant by repentance. "When he came to his senses" (v. 17, NIV), he saw himself in a new and regretful way. As a result, "he got up and went to his father" (v. 20, NIV). More was involved than regret over past wrongs or evil acts; repentance meant a change of behavior.

5 And there went out unto him all the land of Judaea, and they of Jerusalem, and were all baptized of him in the river of Jordan, confessing their sins.

According to religious scholars, three features of John's baptism differed from regular Jewish baptism. First, whereas only Gentile converts to the Jewish religion were baptized, John called for all Jews to admit their sinfulness and their need for God's forgiveness. This verse shows that not only common people came from all over the province of Judea, but also religious leaders and priestly officials from the temple came from Jerusalem. John declared they were all under God's judgment, needed His forgiveness, and should be baptized.

Second, people did not baptize themselves. In Judaism, a person who was baptized immersed himself or herself. John's baptism, more than taking a moral bath, required yielding oneself to another's control.

Third, John's baptism wasn't cleansing from a defiling Gentile past, but cleansing from admitted sins that required God's forgiveness. That forgiveness was then confirmed and symbolized by submission to baptism.

When Mark said that all kinds of people "went out" (Gk. *ekporeuomai*, **ek-por-YOO-om-ahee**) from the largest city of Judea into the countryside to hear John preach, he was not describing a quick process or a one-time event. The form of the words "went out" indicates a repeated act. The same holds for the words "were baptized." It implies that a steady stream of people kept going out to John, so they could be baptized. Every day they came to admit their sins, receive forgiveness, and be baptized. With John's preaching and baptizing, a special time had begun in which the Gospel would reach out to the whole world.

All three Synoptic Gospels—Matthew, Mark, and Luke—use the same word for "confessing" (Gk. *exomologeo*, **ex-om-ol-og-EH-o**). Without the Greek preposition *ex*, the word means "to confess or admit." With *ex* added, it means the same except stronger, "to confess out," or "to admit openly." It was not enough just to come for baptism; owning up to one's sin was a necessary first step.

6 And John was clothed with camel's hair, and with a girdle of a skin about his loins; and he did eat locusts and wild honey;

Was John the Baptist strange? To modern readers this verse may make him appear so, especially when Mark mentioned eating locusts. Although that may sound disgusting, John's diet would not have been unusual for someone living a simple life out in the Judean wilderness. Mark was not trying to present John as eccentric. Rather, John ate what was available to someone living out in the wilderness.

John's robe of camel hair, held closed with a leather belt, matched that of Elijah, who was prophesied to announce the arrival of the Messiah (see 2 Kings 1:8; Malachi 4:5). Later Jesus told His followers that John the Baptist's coming fulfilled that prophecy (see Matthew 11:13–14).

7 And preached, saying, There cometh one mightier than I after me, the latchet of whose shoes I am not worthy to stoop down and unloose.

Did Mark begin this verse using two words when one would have been enough? No, he used two words to make clear not only what John said but how he said it. "Preached" (Gk. *kerusso*, **kay-ROOS-so**) meant to make a public announcement. The word was commonly used to describe a royal representative who was sent out into a kingdom to announce a new decree by the king. That was exactly what John the Baptist understood as his task.

Once again, as in verses 3 and 5, Mark emphasized that John the Baptist called people to come and be part of a new community as the people of God. He was not timid in announcing people's need to repent or God's new revelation that was coming soon. To the contrary, he proclaimed it boldly.

However, John the Baptist avoided making himself the center of his preaching. Instead he minimized his status while maximizing that of Jesus. He placed his role as of less value than a menial servant untying the sandals of a guest before his feet were washed.

8 I indeed have baptized you with water: but he shall baptize you with the Holy Ghost.

John saw his baptism as only a first step in responding to God's revelation in Christ. He presented it not as an end, but as the beginning of participation in a new community of faith. The repentance that John's baptism indicated was the first step in turning *from* something *to* something or Someone else. The goal was to turn *from* sin *to* God. As Paul later wrote, praising the Thessalonian Christians, "you turned to God from idols to serve the living and true God" (1 Thessalonians 1:9, NIV).

Both John the Baptist and Jesus were insistent that the road back to God began with repentance (Matthew 3:2; 4:17). John stressed that living for God requires more than the will to repent; it requires the empowerment of God's Spirit, which would come through Holy Spirit (John 16:7; 20:22). As Eduard Schweizer commented, "Only God's coming to men…makes it possible for men to come to God."

Matthew 3:1 In those days came John the Baptist, preaching in the wilderness of Judaea, 2 And saying, Repent ye: for the kingdom of heaven is at hand.

In both Mark's and Matthew's gospels, John the Baptist appeared suddenly with no introduction. John the Baptist began preaching out in the uninhabited wilderness along the Jordan River, away from the distractions of everyday life. During 40 years of wandering in the Sinai wilderness, south of where John the Baptist preached, God had first begun to reveal His will to the Israelites. North of there at Mt. Carmel, God had proven His greatness through Elijah over the pagan god, Baal, and his

450 prophets (1 Kings 18:17–40). Now in the Judean wilderness of the Jordan River bottom, John the Baptist called the Jews to turn to God in repentance and baptism and experience His forgiveness anew.

"At hand" (Gk. *eggizo,* **eng-ID-zo**) means "close by." The apostle Paul used the same word in Philippians 2:30 when he explained that their representative, Epaphroditus, had been "nigh unto death," indicating that it had been very close.

Matthew used the perfect tense, "is at hand," which indicated a past event that has continuing effect in the present. Since time began, God has been Creator and absolute Master of the universe. This is true for the past, the present, and the future. John the Baptist declared that God's eternal mastery would soon break into human history and that He would reveal Himself in a new and complete way.

3 For this is he that was spoken of by the prophet Esaias saying, The voice of one crying in the wilderness, Prepare ye the way of the Lord, make his paths straight.

Matthew did not include the parallel saying from Malachi, but he, like all the Gospel writers, quotes Isaiah 40:3. Isaiah spoke of preparing to return, by God's help, from exile in Babylon through the Arabian Desert. John the Baptist declared the place to prepare was in their individual lives, through repentance, which was then confirmed by baptism.

Going through the motions was not enough. John the Baptist spurned mere regret (Luke 3:8–14). Repenting and regretting were not the same. Much later, the apostle Peter summarized beginning the Christian life by laying aside all known sin in a person's life (1 Peter 2:1). Again and again God commissioned prophets—from Moses to Malachi—to call God's chosen people to turn back to Him. Lightfoot called John the Baptist's preparatory service for God "the very gate and entrance...of the gospel."

Sources:

Filson, Floyd V. *The Gospel According To St. Matthew.* Peabody, Mass.: Hendrickson Publishers, 1987.

Green, Michael. *Matthew for Today: Expository Study of Matthew.* Dallas, Tex.: Word Publishing, 1988.

Hobbs, Herschel H. *An Exposition of the Four Gospels, Vol. 1. The Gospel of Matthew.* Grand Rapids, Mich.: Baker Book House, 1965.

———. *An Exposition of the Four Gospels, Vol. 2. The Gospel of Mark.* Grand Rapids, Mich.: Baker Book House, 1970.

Lightfoot, John. *A Commentary on the New Testament from the Talmud and Hebraica, Vol. 2. Matthew—I Corinthians.* Grand Rapids, Mich.: Baker Book House. (Reprinted from 1859 edition), 1979.

Nineham, D. E. T*he Gospel of St. Mark.* New York: Penguin Books, 1977.

Schweizer, Eduard. *The Good News According to Mark.* Atlanta: John Knox Press, 1970.

———. *The Good News According to Matthew.* Atlanta: John Knox Press, 1975.

Daily Bible Readings

M: God's Coming Messenger
Malachi 3:1–5
T: Preparing the Way
Isaiah 40:1–5
W: A Voice Crying Out
Isaiah 40:6–11
T: Proclaiming Good New
Matthew 3:4–10
F: Pointing to Christ
Matthew 3:11–19
S: You Are God's People
1 Peter 2:1–10
S: John Prepares the Way
Mark 1:1–8; Matthew 3:1–3

NOTES

TEACHING TIPS

September 14
Bible Study Guide 2

1. Words You Should Know

A. Appeared (Matthew 1:20) *phaino* (Gk.)—Means "to appear" and refers to the deliberate appearing of someone as the angel of the Lord in Joseph's dream.

B. Conceived (v. 20) *genna* (Gk.)—Means "to be born."

C. Raised (v. 24) *diegeir* (Gk.)—Means "to be awakened or aroused from sleep."

2. Teacher Preparation

Unifying Principle—A Humble Beginning. What community offers value and significance to those who, in the world's eyes, may seem insignificant? The new community, as exemplified in Jesus, provides a place where all people have value and significance.

A. Read Micah 5:2 and Matthew 2:5–6 for background of the significance of Jesus' birthplace.

B. Read the Focal Verses in both the King James Version (KJV) and *New Living Translation* (NLT).

C. Research a few famous individuals who have had humble, insignificant beginnings.

D. Be prepared to discuss, from your own life, how God's greatest gifts to us often appear as big things in small packages.

3. Starting the Lesson

A. Using the AIM for Change section, lead the class in prayer.

B. Write the phrase "New Community" on the board.

C. Introduce these concepts: the "New Community" is the church of the living God, the church is God's people and not a building; and the church had humble beginnings.

4. Getting into the Lesson

A. Ask for "humble beginnings" examples and engage in discussion.

B. Share the "humble beginnings" of some of the famous individuals you researched.

C. Explain to the students that "humble beginnings" do not necessarily mean failure in life but can spell success and appreciation of God's blessings.

D. Now, have volunteers read the Focal Verses. Engage in discussion.

5. Relating the Lesson to Life

A. Have the students assemble in groups of up to six people to share what the "new community"—the church—means to them and how it has impacted their lives.

B. Gather the class, asking for one representative of the group to share one overriding principle that seems to rise out of the discussion.

C. Discuss how these experiences encourage a divine perspective on the gifts and talents God gives us and their use in diverse settings.

6. Arousing Action

A. Have the students examine the Make It Happen section. Discuss salient points.

B. Challenge the students to choose one talent they have withheld because it seemed insignificant, and pray for guidance on ways to use it in their church and community.

C. Close the class with prayer.

Worship Guide

For the Superintendent or Teacher
Theme: The Birth of a New Community
Theme Song: "O Church of God"
Devotional Reading: Hosea 11:1–4
Prayer

THE BIRTH OF A NEW COMMUNITY

Bible Background • MATTHEW 1:18–2:23
Printed Text • MATTHEW 1:18–25; 2:13–15 Devotional Reading • HOSEA 11:1–4

AIM for Change

By the end of the lesson, we will:
REVIEW the story of Jesus' birth as the beginning of the new community;
CONSIDER our value and significance in the community of faith;
and IDENTIFY our unique gifts and use them in service to others.

Keep in Mind

"And thou Bethlehem, in the land of Juda, art not the least among the princes of Juda: for out of thee shall come a Governor, that shall rule my people Israel" (Matthew 2:6).

Focal Verses

KJV **Matthew 1:18** Now the birth of Jesus Christ was on this wise: When as his mother Mary was espoused to Joseph, before they came together, she was found with child of the Holy Ghost.

19 Then Joseph her husband, being a just man, and not willing to make her a publick example, was minded to put her away privily.

20 But while he thought on these things, behold, the angel of the LORD appeared unto him in a dream, saying, Joseph, thou son of David, fear not to take unto thee Mary thy wife: for that which is conceived in her is of the Holy Ghost.

21 And she shall bring forth a son, and thou shalt call his name JESUS: for he shall save his people from their sins.

22 Now all this was done, that it might be fulfilled which was spoken of the Lord by the prophet, saying,

23 Behold, a virgin shall be with child, and shall bring forth a son, and they shall call his name Emmanuel, which being interpreted is, God with us.

24 Then Joseph being raised from sleep did as the angel of the Lord had bidden him, and took unto him his wife:

25 And knew her not till she had brought forth her firstborn son: and he called his name JESUS.

2:13 And when they were departed, behold, the angel of the Lord appeareth to Joseph in a dream, saying, Arise, and take the young child and his mother, and flee into Egypt, and be thou there until I bring thee word: for Herod will seek the young child to destroy him.

NLT **Matthew 1:18** This is how Jesus the Messiah was born. His mother, Mary, was engaged to be married to Joseph. But before the marriage took place, while she was still a virgin, she became pregnant through the power of the Holy Spirit.

19 Joseph, her fiancé, was a good man and did not want to disgrace her publicly, so he decided to break the engagement quietly.

20 As he considered this, an angel of the Lord appeared to him in a dream. "Joseph, son of David," the angel said, "do not be afraid to take Mary as your wife. For the child within her was conceived by the Holy Spirit.

21 And she will have a son, and you are to name him Jesus, for he will save his people from their sins."

22 All of this occurred to fulfill the Lord's message through his prophet:

23 "Look! The virgin will conceive a child! She will give birth to a son, and they will call him Immanuel, which means 'God is with us.'"

24 When Joseph woke up, he did as the angel of the Lord commanded and took Mary as his wife.

25 But he did not have sexual relations with her until her son was born. And Joseph named him Jesus.

2:13 After the wise men were gone, an angel of the Lord appeared to Joseph in a dream. "Get up! Flee to Egypt with the child and his mother," the angel said. "Stay there until I tell you to return, because Herod is going to search for the child to kill him."

14 That night Joseph left for Egypt with the child and Mary, his mother,

14 When he arose, he took the young child and his mother by night, and departed into Egypt:

15 And was there until the death of Herod: that it might be fulfilled which was spoken of the Lord by the prophet, saying, Out of Egypt have I called my son.

15 and they stayed there until Herod's death. This fulfilled what the Lord had spoken through the prophet: "I called my Son out of Egypt."

In Focus

Jean hummed as she carefully pinned the decorative silk flower to her choir robe. Looking at herself in the mirror in the church's foyer, she smiled at how nicely the flower matched both her robe and the barrette she had pinned in her hair.

"Simply perfect," said a voice that was very near. Jean jumped at the words. She hadn't realized Mother Juanita had walked up.

"Thank you," said Jean, leaning over to kiss the woman's cheek. "I like looking nice, and different," she added, eyeing other choir members lining up near the sanctuary doors.

"So do I," Mother Juanita countered, "but because of the nurses' board's strict uniform-only policy, I leave my Sunday best for weeks I'm not on duty. Plus, members and visitors need to be able to quickly spot me in an emergency."

Mother Juanita lowered her voice to a whisper. "Want to know a secret?" She paused until Jean leaned in closer to hear. "The real reason I don't mind looking like other members on the nurses' board is because I feel it is an honor to wear my uniform. It lets God and people know that I am here to serve."

Jean returned to the mirror as Mother Juanita walked away. She slowly began removing the flashy barrette and flower pin. *It is an honor to wear this uniform, too,* she said to herself. She hurried to find her place in the alto section of the choir's line.

Belonging to a community necessitates changes in the way we act and think. We prove our commitment when we repent of any actions that hinder personal or community advancement.

The People, Places, and Times

Egypt. To save Jesus' life, Joseph and Mary fled to the very place that once represented bondage and oppression to the Hebrews. By doing so, they fulfilled Hosea's prophecy (Hosea 11:1). Herod's death should have signaled the end of the threat to Jesus' life, but Joseph's fear and another dream confirmed that this was not the case. As a result, the family relocated to Galilee.

Bethlehem. To eliminate confusion, Scripture makes it clear that Jesus was born in Bethlehem, Judea (Judaea, KJV), to distinguish it from a town called Bethlehem in Galilee. Because of its rich fields, used for sheep grazing and for growing wheat and barley, the name means "house of bread" or "house of food."

Angels. God created these invisible beings to serve Him (Satan and his cohorts rebelled against serving God and were punished for that rebellion). One way they do so is by serving as messengers sent from God to Earth for specific purposes. Whether by their power or God's, angels can become visible to humans as needed. In recent years, stories of angelic encounters have sparked renewed interest in angels. Christians should be wary. God never intended us to worship angels, and any activity that promotes praying to or seeking after angels should be avoided.

Dreams. Throughout Bible times, God used dreams to communicate with people about imminent good or harm. These messages of God caught people's attention. Sometimes God allowed individuals to understand the meanings behind their own dreams. Other times, because dreams are often full of symbolism, it was necessary to seek out someone with the gift of dream interpretation. This was not always easy, as God limited this ability to certain people, like prophets. The prophet Daniel, for example, once revealed the contents of a troubling dream King Nebuchadnezzar had forgotten along with its meaning. Before doing so, however, Daniel made it clear that the ability to do both came from God (Daniel 2). Finally, God often thwarted the efforts of would-be dream interpreters.

Source:

Beers, V. Gilbert. *The Victor Handbook of Bible Knowledge.* Wheaton, Ill.: Victor Books, 1981.

Background

The disciple Matthew (Levi) is said to be the writer of the book of Matthew. Before Jesus called him to be one of His disciples, Matthew was a hated tax collector for the Roman Empire. However, he responded immediately to Jesus' call and invited many friends to his home to meet the Christ.

Matthew wrote the gospel of Matthew to prove that Jesus is indeed the long-awaited Messiah. He wrote especially to the Jews. His Gospel forms the connecting link between the Old and New Testaments and emphasizes the fulfillment of prophecy.

For centuries the "word of the Lord" was scarce in Israel, due in large part to three factors: (1) the nation's rampant, continual sin; (2) its disregard for God's prophetic warnings; and (3) its ill-treatment of God's servants, the prophets. Equally scarce were events like the births and ministries of John the Baptist and Jesus, which fulfilled prophecy.

Prophetic fulfillment was now at hand. "In those days came John the Baptist, preaching in the wilderness of Judaea, And saying, Repent ye: for the kingdom of heaven is at hand" (Matthew 3:1–2).

At-A-Glance

1. Divine Conception (Matthew 1:18)
2. Divine Correction (vv. 19–25)
3. Divine Selection (2:13–15)

In Depth

1. Divine Conception (Matthew 1:18)

For Mary, there were grave risks associated with getting involved in the divine conception, which sparked a new community of faith. Those risks included: (1) loss of relationship—Mary could lose her opportunity to get married; (2) loss of reputation—if it was known she was carrying a child that was not Joseph's, she could be labeled as an adulterous woman; and (3) public embarrassment and punishment—by law Mary could be severely punished for her supposed sin.

Despite these risks, Mary embraced the opportunity to serve God in such an astonishing way. She joyfully exclaimed, "Behold the handmaid of the Lord; be it unto me according to thy word" (Luke 1:38). From that moment, her role in the divine conception was sealed—as was that of Joseph.

2. Divine Correction (vv. 19–25)

Scripture doesn't say how Joseph learned of Mary's pregnancy, but his reaction was understandable. He wanted to end their relationship, albeit quietly. "But while he thought on these things, behold, the angel of the LORD appeared unto him in a dream" (Matthew 1:20). The dream imparted three key things. First, Joseph was reassured that Mary had not been unfaithful: "that which [was] conceived in her is of the Holy Ghost" (v. 20). Second, Joseph was told the baby's sex and what he was to be named. Third, he was told the baby's divine purpose: "he shall save his people from their sins" (v. 21). Heeding the angel's instruction, Joseph married Mary.

From an outsider's perspective, the new community of faith may seem to have had a rocky beginning. Not so. Through it, we see clear signs of God's purpose, and of the rescue and deliverance that ultimately would result from Jesus' ministry. God never makes mistakes. He didn't pick just any virgin or any carpenter—and there were likely thousands of both in Nazareth. Instead, God chose the couple who would, individually and together, place His will above all else. Their individual and collective actions paved the way for the new community that would be known as one that fosters belonging and acceptance.

3. Divine Selection (2:13–15)

Jesus' hometown was an unassuming village with somewhat of a negative reputation. After meeting Jesus, Philip told Nathanael "we have found him, of whom Moses in the law, and the prophets, did write, Jesus of Nazareth, the son of Joseph" (John 1:45). Nathanael responded, "Can there any good thing come out of Nazareth?" (v. 46). The comment seemed to imply that God would never consider bringing a Messiah out of Nazareth, yet it was there that Jesus grew to adulthood.

That God chose a carpenter and a young woman of little social status, from a town with a less-than-reputable image, to jump-start His plan of salvation cements the truth that "God is no respector of persons"—ever (Acts 10:34). To God, every individual is a candidate for an intimate relationship with Him. Everyone has value and significance, despite any perceived humble beginnings. Everyone has value and gifts (seen and unseen) that can make a positive impact on community life. Indeed, while others may have overlooked Mary and Joseph as stewards of great treasures, God gave them the opportunity to steward Earth and heaven's greatest treasure: the baby who would one day prove to be Saviour of the world.

It is important that we keep this in mind during the selection processes in our communities of faith. In particular, we should not show partiality when determining who should be the focus of evangelistic outreaches but rather freely share the Gospel with people from all walks of life. Further, instead of using material possessions or some other status symbol as a criterion for selecting candidates for special training or ministry positions, we should allow everybody an equal chance to use their gifts and talents for God's glory.

God also chose the place where the couple should go to escape from Herod and be safe. He chose Egypt and told Joseph in a second dream. In their early history, the Israelites had been in slavery in Egypt for more than 400 years. Yet Joseph was to go to Egypt to protect the child's life. Even though Joseph was not Jesus' biological father (that role was filled by the Holy Spirit), Joseph was responsible for Jesus' safety and well-being. Being a godly man, Joseph obeyed God to the letter and protected Jesus.

God shows in this account that indeed He is sovereign. He is in charge of His salvation plan. He is in charge of the new community—the church. The Messiah, Jesus Christ, had come to save God's people, the new community—the church—from their sins. God was in control of keeping Jesus safe, and He used Joseph and Mary to carry out His plans.

Search the Scriptures

1. What was the primary reason Joseph did not want to put Mary away (Matthew 1:19)?

2. What reason did the angel provide to show that Mary had not been unfaithful (vv. 20–21)?

3. What was Joseph's response to the angelic visitation (v. 24)?

Discuss the Meaning

1. Why was timing essential for the visitation of the angel?

2. Why do you think is it important to know that Joseph did not have intimate relations with Mary until after Jesus was born (Matthew 1:25)?

3. Jesus was Mary's firstborn son. What does the term imply?

4. What lessons can be learned from Nazareth's status in God's eyes, versus in people's eyes?

Lesson in Our Society

Governmental leaders worldwide are often chosen based on a system of elitism. Preferred candidates are those with long pedigrees, wealth, and status. That same thinking has permeated many churches. But God would have us remember that "in every nation he that feareth him, and worketh righteousness, is accepted with [God]" (Acts 10:35).

Make It Happen

When was the last time you chose a political candidate or ministry candidate based on what they materially have, rather than on a clear leading from God that this person would be best? Perhaps peer pressure or information overload from the "best candidate for the spots" camp influenced your decision. Starting today, make the commitment to follow the inner urgings and promptings from the Lord when making such decisions.

Follow the Spirit

What God wants me to do:

____

____

Remember Your Thoughts

Special insights I have learned:

____

____

More Light on the Text

Matthew 1:18–25; 2:13–15

18 Now the birth of Jesus Christ was on this wise: When as his mother Mary was espoused to Joseph, before they came together, she was found with child of the Holy Ghost.

"Birth" (Gk. *genesis*, **JGHEN-es-is**) is the translation of the same word used for the first book in the Old Testament. This is the story of how God began to make possible a new world and a new life through Jesus (see 2 Corinthians 5:17).

Matthew said Mary was "espoused" (Gk. *mnesteuo*, **mnace-TYOO-o**, meaning "to be promised in marriage, to be betrothed") to Joseph. This was not the same as being engaged, though it was similar. In Jesus' day, Jewish marriage consisted of three stages. First came engagement, which was usually arranged (sometimes when the boy and girl were still children) by the parents or a marriage broker. When they were old enough to marry, a formal commitment, to which the man and woman agreed, was made. It required the confirmation of two witnesses. The betrothal agreement, the requirement of witnesses, and a betrothal period indicated intention and deliberation for marrying, not necessity.

Once the couple was betrothed, or espoused, they were referred to as husband and wife—note Joseph is "her husband" and Mary is "thy wife" (vv. 19–20). After that agreement, the couple were considered married, though they did not begin living together until after a wedding ceremony: the third stage. That often came about a year later. Dissolving a betrothal required divorce, not annulment, and sexual unfaithfulness during the betrothal period was considered adultery, not promiscuity, for which the penalty was death by stoning (see Deuteronomy 22:23–24).

How was Mary "found with child" and by whom? Was she showing? We don't know, and the Bible doesn't say. How did Joseph find out? Again, the Bible doesn't tell us. However, when Joseph learned of Mary's pregnancy, he made the logical assumption that she had been unfaithful to him with another man.

19 Then Joseph her husband, being a just man, and not willing to make her a publick example, was minded to put her away privily.

Jesus' criticism of many Jews, especially their leaders, was that though they kept the Mosaic Law, technically they often failed to obey its intention. Likely the reason God chose Joseph to be Jesus' earthly stepfather was that he was not a legalistic Jew. He obeyed God's laws literally, but also, and just as importantly, spiritually.

That's what Matthew meant when he called Joseph "just" in verse 19. "Just" (Gk. *dikaios,* **dik-AH-yoce**) didn't mean Joseph was kind or fair-minded toward others, although he may have been. "Just" here means that Joseph was faithful to God as expressed by his obedience to the Mosaic Law. Several modern Bible versions express this fact more clearly by describing Joseph as "just and upright" (*Amplified Bible*), "righteous" (NRSV, NIV) and "a man of principle" (REB).

For Joseph, being faithful to God meant faithfully obeying the Mosaic Law. That presented Joseph with two choices. He could publicly disgrace Mary by exposing her infidelity at the door of her father's house (see Deuteronomy 22:20–22) or he could present her with a bill of divorcement (Deuteronomy 24:1), which the Talmud, the commentary of Jewish religious practice, called for upon taking two witnesses. Joseph didn't want to expose Mary to public shame, or as the King James Version (KJV) says "make her a publick example" (Gk. *paradeigmatizo,* **par-ad-igue-mat-ID-zo**), so he chose the second course.

Joseph decided to divorce Mary. He decided to "put her away" (Gk. *apoluo,* **ap-ol-OO-o**, which means "to set free, let go, or dismiss"). In other words, Joseph discovered something about Mary that made her unacceptable to a faithful Jew. Therefore, his intent was to divorce her "privily" (Gk. *lathra,* **LATH-rah**), meaning he decided to handle the situation as gently and privately as possible, with as few people as possible knowing about it.

Again Scripture reveals why God chose Joseph to serve as Jesus' earthly father. His planned treatment of Mary mirrored Paul's description of Christlike behavior: "As God's chosen people, holy and dearly loved, clothe yourselves with compassion, kindness, humility, gentleness and patience" (Colossians 3:12, NIV).

20 But while he thought on these things, behold, an angel of the LORD appeared unto him in a dream, saying, Joseph, thou son of David, fear not to take unto thee Mary thy wife: for that which is conceived in her is of the Holy Ghost.

The angel addressed Joseph according to his genealogy: "thou son of David." Prophecy had foretold that a "son," a descendant of David, would lead the Hebrew people to freedom and glory (Isaiah 11:1–10; Jeremiah 23:5–6). Since the gospel of Matthew was addressed primarily to Christians from a Jewish background, Joseph's Davidic ancestry needed to be clearly shown.

The angel told Joseph that God's instructions for him were to accept Mary as his wife, which meant going ahead with the wedding and taking her into his home as his bride. The angel also warned him not to let fear overcome him. Fear of gossip, disdain, rejection, as well as fear of disobeying God's law, though natural, should not concern them. The baby that was growing inside of Mary began from a holy source, not a sinful failing.

21 And she shall bring forth a son, and thou shalt call his name JESUS: for he shall save his people from their sins.

The angel told Joseph that Mary would give birth

to a son. The angel directed Joseph that when the baby boy arrived, he should give Him the name Jesus. Jesus (Gk. *Iesous,* **ee-ay-SOOCE)** is the Greek form of the Hebrew name Joshua (Heb. *Yehowshuwa`*, **yeh-ho-SHOO-ah**). Jesus' divinely dictated name explained the purpose of God's mission for Him. It combined two Hebrew words meaning "God saves."

Jesus was an often-used name for boys then, so Jesus' name not only communicated God's spiritual purpose for Him but at the same time identified Him with the sinful humanity that needed God's forgiveness. God sent Jesus to Earth and, in obedience, Jesus came to fulfill His name. Many Jews wanted, and most expected, a Messiah who would set them free politically from Roman domination to become a powerful nation again. What made Jesus unique and brought about His rejection was that God's purpose for Him was to set people free spiritually from domination by sin.

22 Now all this was done, that it might be fulfilled which was spoken of the Lord by the prophet, saying, 23 Behold, a virgin shall be with child, and shall bring forth a son, and they shall call his name Emmanuel, which being interpreted is, God with us.

Matthew explained God's purposes by quoting a prophecy from Isaiah 7:14. Chapters 7–9 of Isaiah tell how King Ahaz of Judah was threatened with invasion by the kings of Israel, the northern Hebrew kingdom, and Aram (Syria). The prophet Isaiah urged Ahaz to seek a sign of God's will or His help, but Ahaz refused. He chose instead to contact the king of Assyria for protection. That request signaled Judah's weakness and invited invasion by a nation with a larger, more powerful army than those by whom he was being threatened. When Ahaz refused to seek God's will and help, Isaiah delivered the prophecy that Matthew quoted in verse 23: "Behold, a virgin shall conceive, and bear a son, and shall call his name Immanuel" (Isaiah 7:14). John Lightfoot interpreted the prophecy as an allegory, almost a joke. Israel was as likely to invade Judah as a virgin was to give birth to a son.

The word Isaiah used for "virgin" (Heb. *`almah,* **al-MAW**) wasn't the term generally used for a woman who had not had sexual relations (Heb. *bethuwlah,* **beth-oo-LAW**). The word Isaiah used meant "a young, unmarried woman of marriageable age." Such a woman would be assumed to be a virgin. The nearly identical word in a language closely related to Hebrew is used as a synonym for its word for "virgin." When the Hebrew Old Testament was translated into Greek, *`almah* was rendered with the word *parthenos,* Greek for "virgin" (**par-THEN-os**). Matthew, quoting Isaiah 7:14 from the Greek translation, applied it to Jesus and showed that He was the literal fulfillment of Isaiah's prophecy.

While Jesus' birth from a virgin is a basic truth of the Christian faith, Matthew's main emphasis here was on who Jesus was and is—"God with us"—rather than how He was conceived and born. Nowhere in Acts or in any of Paul's letters is the nature of Jesus' birth mentioned, but God's presence with us, guiding and strengthening us, is spoken about again and again. *That in no way denies the reality of Jesus' virgin birth.* Instead it shows that it was not a primary emphasis in the preaching or teaching of the first century church. Dr. Eduard Schweizer wrote that for Matthew the important factor was "Jesus' life, not his birth."

24 Then Joseph being raised from sleep did as the angel of the Lord had bidden him, and took unto him his wife:

When Matthew said Joseph "took" Mary as his wife, that simple word says so much. First it means he accepted her as his wife. Second, he abandoned any suspicion about infidelity by Mary. Third, although the Scripture gives no specifics, Joseph likely went ahead with the wedding and the Jewish traditions that went with beginning a marriage. Fourth—and most important—he became indispensable in preparing for the Saviour's life during Mary's pregnancy.

Joseph "did as the angel…had bidden him" sounds like Joseph consented to a request by the angel. The *New International Version* (NIV) conveys Matthew's meaning better. It says Joseph "did what the angel of the Lord had commanded." The Greek word for "bidden" is *prostasso* (**pros-TAS-so**). Joseph obeyed God's command—no discussion, no argument, no debate.

Joseph's obedience was vital to the fulfillment of God's purposes for Mary as Jesus' virgin mother. When he "took"—accepted—Mary as his wife, he accepted her pregnancy as his own. He accepted the gossip of neighbors about Mary's early delivery, only a few months after their wedding. He accepted the possibility that the "stigma of fornication," as Dr. Herschel Hobbs termed it, would be associated with his wife. (The Jewish Talmud claimed that Jesus was conceived after Mary had sexual relations with a Roman soldier.) By accepting Mary as his wife, Joseph inserted himself between Mary and whatever rumors of infidelity or promiscuity arose as a result of her giving birth to Jesus. God chose Joseph as Jesus' foster father as deliberately as He chose Mary to be Jesus' mother.

25 And knew her not till she had brought forth her firstborn son: and he called his name JESUS.

Although no divine command prevented it, Joseph did not engage in marital intimacy with Mary until after she gave birth to Jesus. "Till" and "firstborn" suggest that their marriage followed a customary course, after Jesus was born. The naming of additional brothers and sisters in Matthew 13:55–56 and Mark 6:3 support that reasoning.

Joseph did nothing that might interfere with or potentially confuse what God alone had begun. His abstinence from sexual intimacy with Mary in no way indicates a lack of desire. The tense of the verb "knew" suggests the opposite. "Knew" (Gk. *ginosko, **ghin-OCE-ko***) is in the Greek imperfect tense. That indicates a repeated action in the past meaning that Joseph repeatedly resisted his desire to have sex with Mary, until after Jesus' birth.

Naming a child, especially a son, was a father's responsibility (Luke 1:62). Once again, in naming Jesus, we see Joseph's faithful obedience to the angel's instructions from God.

2:13 And when they were departed, behold, the angel of the Lord appeareth to Joseph in a dream, saying, Arise, and take the young child and his mother, and flee into Egypt, and be thou there until I bring thee word: for Herod will seek the young child to destroy him.

The people who departed were the Magi (astrologers) from the east, traditionally known as the wise men (Matthew 2:1). Dr. Hobbs proposed that their gifts for Jesus (Matthew 2:11) may have financed Joseph's flight with Mary and the Baby Jesus from Bethlehem into Egypt.

For the second time, an angel appeared in Joseph's dreams with a message from God. Five times in the first two chapters of Matthew's gospel (1:20; 2:12, 13, 19, 22) God speaks through dreams. God ordered Joseph to get up and "flee into Egypt." "Flee" can mean to escape or to disappear. God wanted the infant Jesus where Herod couldn't find Him.

Herod was a brilliant, personable leader as well as a ruthlessly ambitious one. He repeatedly led troops to confront and defeat those who planned to control Jerusalem, which earned him the grudging confidence of Jewish leaders. Although Herod was Jewish only by marriage, he built the enormous Jerusalem temple, which was considered one of the marvels of the ancient world.

Although Herod came from the minor desert province of Idumea, he went to Rome and charmed Octavius Caesar and Mark Antony into making him the governor over all Judea. Later Idumea, Samaria, and Galilee were put under his control, after he persuaded Marc Antony to make his major rival disappear, leaving him as king over territory from north of the Sea of Galilee to the south end of the Dead Sea and from the Mediterranean coast to the east side of the Jordan River.

God foresaw Herod's coming brutality. No viciousness was beyond Herod when it came to protecting his own interests. During more than 30 years as governor and king, he killed his wife, two sons, and his father-in-law, plus dozens of others who had no close personal relationship to him. Slaughtering all baby boys born in the Bethlehem area who were two years old or younger is not improbable or unbelievable of Herod (Matthew 2:16).

14 When he arose, he took the young child and his mother by night, and departed into Egypt:

Of the three stories involving Joseph that Matthew relates (1:18–25; 2:13–15, 19–22), this one defines him best. Joseph was asleep when the angel appeared and delivered God's instructions. The angel warned him to go to Egypt, which was more than 200 miles away, mostly through desert. Apparently the dream startled Joseph awake, because he didn't go back to sleep. Joseph got up and took off—"during the night" (NIV)—disappearing into Egypt with Jesus and Mary. Those three words make clear that Joseph didn't wait around or think about it. God's instructions were clear, "so he got up…and left for Egypt" (NIV).

This illustrates why Joseph's obedience was so vital. He gave prompt, diligent care and protection to Mary and Jesus. He set a living example for Jesus of how to respond to God's commands. His example remains as a model of the importance of church members for each other and for Christian parents before their children.

Like many Christians attending Bible classes, Sunday School, church group meetings, or worship services, Joseph wasn't a "big talker." Rather, he was the classic example of a man of few words. He let his actions speak for him, even before the Saviour of the world. The example of those who don't say much can still be vitally important if they let their behavior show their commitment to God and Christlike values (Matthew 5:16; 1 Peter 2:21; 3:15–16).

15 And was there until the death of Herod: that it might be fulfilled which was spoken of the Lord by the prophet, saying, Out of Egypt have I called my son.

Many Bible scholars have remarked that Matthew's gospel is patterned on the first five books of the Old Testament (the Pentateuch, or Torah, or the Law), which were the heart of Judaism in Jesus' day. The central figure in them is Moses, who led the Hebrew people out of Egypt and slavery to the Promised Land in Canaan. When the prophet Hosea says, "Out of Egypt I have called my son," he first of all meant Moses, but also the Hebrew people. The next verse, Hosea 11:2, shows this because God speaks of "my son" as "they."

Like Moses, God sent Jesus to lead us to freedom—not just social freedom, vocational freedom, or political freedom, but spiritual freedom. God wants us to know the fullness of freedom. In Galatians 5:1 (NIV), Paul wrote, "It is for freedom that Christ has set us free. Stand firm, then, and do not let yourselves be burdened again by a yoke of slavery." Too often, instead of following Jesus to the freedom God wants for us, we allow ourselves to be burdened down by jobs, by hobbies, by destructive habits, and sometimes even by positive activities that lead us away from God's freedom of spirit, rather than into it.

Sources:

Baab, O. J. "Virgin," *Interpreters Dictionary of the Bible.* Vol. 4. R–Z. Nashville, Tenn.: Abingdon Press, 1962.

Filson, Floyd V. *The Gospel According to St. Matthew.* Peabody, Mass.: Hendrickson Publishers, 1987.

Green, Michael. *Matthew for Today: Expository Study of Matthew.* Dallas, Tx.: Word Publishing, 1988.

Hobbs, Herschel H. *An Exposition of the Four Gospels,*Vol. 1. The Gospel of Matthew. Grand Rapids, Mich.: Baker Book House, 1965.

Lightfoot, John. *A Commentary on the New Testament from the Talmud and Hebraica.* Matthew–1 Corinthians. Vol. 2. Matthew–Mark. Grand Rapids, Mich.: Baker Book House, 1979. (Reprinted from 1859 edition.)

Schweizer, Eduard. *The Good News According to Matthew.* Atlanta: John Knox Press, 1975.

Daily Bible Readings

M: God's Care for God's People
Hosea 11:1–7

T: To All Who Receive Christ
John 1:10–14

W: Consider Your Call
1 Corinthians 1:26–31

T: Gifted by God's Spirit
1 Corinthians 12:4–13

F: Members of the Body
1 Corinthians 12:14–27

S: The Kingdom of God's Son
Colossians 1:9–14

S: God Is with Us
Matthew 1:18–25; 2:13–15

NOTES

TEACHING TIPS

September 21
Bible Study Guide 3

1. Words You Should Know

A. Blessed (Matthew 5:3–11) *makarios* (Gk.)—Denotes being fully satisfied (spiritually and naturally) independent of circumstances.

B. Merciful (v. 7) *eleemon* (Gk.)—Showing mercy, compassion. The mercy seat in the temple was a visible reminder that God does not deal with us according to our sin, but according to His tender compassion for us.

C. Rejoice (v. 12) *chairo* (Gk.)—A word used to express the joy related to God's grace.

D. Glorify (v. 16) *doxazo* (Gk.)—To magnify, praise, or extol God.

2. Teacher Preparation

Unifying Principle—Finding True Happiness. People search for happiness in many places, but they often find the opposite due to their wrong choices. Who teaches us to know true and lasting happiness? Through His teachings, Jesus described how to find true happiness.

A. Read the Focal Verses from both the KJV and NLT. Write down some common "keys to happiness" that people rely on.

B. Gather 8 ½ x 11" sheets of colored paper and cut in quarters, cutting enough for each student to have two. Leave one blank for each student's use. On the other, draw a key and write one word from your "keys to happiness" list. You can use your words more than once if needed. Place the "keys" in a paper bag, and keep the blank papers in a stack for use separately.

C. Pray for your students' understanding of true keys to happiness, as exemplified in the core values found in the Focal Verses.

3. Starting the Lesson

A. Using the AIM for Change, open with prayer.

B. Read the Keep in Mind verse in unison.

C. Read the AIM for Change in unison.

4. Getting into the Lesson

A. Summarize the Focal Verses. Discuss.

B. Then, have each student draw a "key to happiness" from the paper bag. Ask for volunteers to share specific keys, and any related insight they can from personal experience with that key.

C. Ask the students to share a few examples of the problems associated with lost keys.

D. Explain how these are similar to the wrong choices people make that often lead them to lose the very keys they believe bring happiness.

5. Relating the Lesson to Life

A. Refer to the Focal Verses.

B. Lead a discussion on the differences between the eternal core values and the temporal keys.

C. Using the Focal Verses, share a few examples of how students can exchange a specific key for a related core value.

6. Arousing Action

A. Distribute blank colored squares.

B. Have a volunteer read the Make It Happen section.

C. Have the students write one core value they would like to develop in their lives, and how they plan to do so.

D. Close the class with prayer.

Worship Guide

For the Superintendent or Teacher
Theme: Core Values of the New Community
Theme Song: "I Want to Be a Follower of Christ"
Devotional Reading: Numbers 6:22–27
Prayer

CORE VALUES OF THE NEW COMMUNITY

Bible Background • MATTHEW 5:1–7:28
Printed Text • MATTHEW 5:1–16 Devotional Reading • NUMBERS 6:22–27

AIM for Change

By the end of the lesson, we will:
REVIEW Jesus' teachings about happiness;
EXPRESS our understanding of Jesus' teachings; and
IDENTIFY one of Jesus' teachings and DECIDE how and when to put it into practice.

Keep in Mind

"Seek ye first the kingdom of God, and his righteousness; and all these things shall be added unto you" (Matthew 6:33).

Focal Verses

KJV **Matthew 5:1** And seeing the multitudes, he went up into a mountain: and when he was set, his disciples came unto him:

2 And he opened his mouth, and taught them, saying,

3 Blessed are the poor in spirit: for theirs is the kingdom of heaven.

4 Blessed are they that mourn: for they shall be comforted.

5 Blessed are the meek: for they shall inherit the earth.

6 Blessed are they which do hunger and thirst after righteousness: for they shall be filled.

7 Blessed are the merciful: for they shall obtain mercy.

8 Blessed are the pure in heart: for they shall see God.

9 Blessed are the peacemakers: for they shall be called the children of God.

10 Blessed are they which are persecuted for righteousness' sake: for theirs is the kingdom of heaven.

11 Blessed are ye, when men shall revile you, and persecute you, and shall say all manner of evil against you falsely, for my sake.

12 Rejoice, and be exceeding glad: for great is your reward in heaven: for so persecuted they the prophets which were before you.

13 Ye are the salt of the earth: but if the salt have lost his savour, wherewith shall it be salted? it is thenceforth good for nothing, but to be cast out, and to be trodden under foot of men.

14 Ye are the light of the world. A city that is set on a hill cannot be hid.

15 Neither do men light a candle, and put it

NLT **Matthew 5:1** One day as he saw the crowds gathering, Jesus went up on the mountainside and sat down. His disciples gathered around him,

2 and he began to teach them.

3 "God blesses those who are poor and realize their need for him, for the Kingdom of Heaven is theirs.

4 God blesses those who mourn, for they will be comforted.

5 God blesses those who are humble, for they will inherit the whole earth.

6 God blesses those who hunger and thirst for justice, for they will be satisfied.

7 God blesses those who are merciful, for they will be shown mercy.

8 God blesses those whose hearts are pure, for they will see God.

9 God blesses those who work for peace, for they will be called the children of God.

10 God blesses those who are persecuted for doing right, for the Kingdom of Heaven is theirs.

11 "God blesses you when people mock you and persecute you and lie about you and say all sorts of evil things against you because you are my followers.

12 Be happy about it! Be very glad! For a great reward awaits you in heaven. And remember, the ancient prophets were persecuted in the same way.

13 "You are the salt of the earth. But what good is salt if it has lost its flavor? Can you make it salty again? It will be thrown out and trampled underfoot as worthless.

14 "You are the light of the world—like a city on a hilltop that cannot be hidden.

under a bushel, but on a candlestick; and it giveth light unto all that are in the house.

16 Let your light so shine before men, that they may see your good works, and glorify your Father which is in heaven.

15 No one lights a lamp and then puts it under a basket. Instead, a lamp is placed on a stand, where it gives light to everyone in the house.

16 In the same way, let your good deeds shine out for all to see, so that everyone will praise your heavenly Father.

In Focus

Monday morning, Cheri hardly tasted her breakfast of cereal and fruit. Her mind kept wandering to her pastor's sermon yesterday. A flood had wiped out a major section of a neighboring city, killing residents and causing millions of dollars in property damage. Her church was responding with donations of money, food, and clothing. The church especially asked for business and casual clothing for men. Cheri could not contribute money or food, but she could send clothes—lots of them.

She left the kitchen and headed to her bedroom, stopping at the walk-in closet she had avoided since her husband died six months ago. She flipped on the light and eyed the designer clothing. Her Samuel did not always dress so fancy, especially when they were first married. Back then they survived off of "peanut-butter love," scrimping and saving to afford some of the nice things they wanted, like a home in a safe neighborhood where they could raise children. Today would have been their thirtieth anniversary. She was thankful for God's many blessings, but she'd trade all of their fancy possessions for one peanut butter sandwich and a kiss from Samuel. "I love you, honey," she said, heading for the row of starched shirts.

Many people place high value on material blessings, which they think bring true happiness. But as today's lesson shows, true happiness can only be found in a relationship with Jesus.

The People, Places, and Times

Matthew. Matthew was a tax collector. These professionals were also known as publicans. They were especially hated because of their propensity to extort higher taxes than were necessary. Publicans were usually Roman, but Jews like Matthew were also allowed to hold lower-ranking positions within the profession. Matthew's career put him at odds with his fellow Jews, who did not appreciate their brother stealing from them. He was at work one day when Jesus walked by and called him into full-time ministry (Matthew 9:9–13). By calling Matthew into service, Jesus confirmed once again that God accepts every individual who is willing to serve Him.

Matthew "left all" to follow Jesus and accept the call to full-time service. Thus, he joined the other original disciples who later were appointed apostles. Grateful for the call to service, Matthew—also called Levi—"made him a great feast in his own house: and there was a great company of publicans and of others that sat down with them" (Luke 5:29). That dinner angered the scribes and Pharisees (the religious leaders of the day), who questioned why Jesus would eat with such individuals. With his friends insulted and community leaders angry, Matthew could easily have reconsidered the decision to serve Jesus, but he did not. He remained steadfast, serving Jesus for his entire three-year ministry, then serving the church as one of its first apostles.

Taxes. Jews had to pay multiple taxes to the Romans. The taxes were particularly burdensome because they covered nearly every aspect of life. Taxes were imposed, for example, on real estate, at seaports, on sales of good and services, and even on animals. Stiff penalties were imposed for failure to pay taxes. Because taxes were such a hot-button issue, Jewish leaders unsuccessfully tried to trick Jesus into admitting that He favored taxes.

Multitudes. The term dually refers to the diversity of people groups represented, as well as the huge number of people who flocked to Jesus seeking healing, or to hear him teach and preach.

Sermon on the Mount. Jesus' deliverance of the Beatitudes is popularly referred to as the Sermon on the Mount. The exact location is unknown, which may have been intentional. Because it describes how to find true happiness, Matthew wanted readers to focus more on the content of Jesus' sermon, rather than on the significance of the place where He delivered it.

Beatitudes. The Beatitudes are guidelines for true happiness. Bible scholar V. Gilbert Beers notes that "as God gave the Law to Moses on Mount Sinai to guide His people's conduct and service, so Jesus gave His disciples the Sermon on the Mount to guide their conduct and service to Him and His Father."

Source:

Beers, V. Gilbert. *The Victor Handbook of Bible Knowledge.* Wheaton, Ill.: Victor Books, 1981.

Background

The book of Matthew is the first book of the New Testament. Matthew begins his Gospel with the genealogy of Jesus, to provide proof that Jesus was the Jews' hoped-for Messiah. He also includes material not found in the three other Gospels—10 of the 15 parables and 3 of the 20 miracles Matthew records are not found in the other books.

Jesus, surrounded by the multitudes, took the opportunity to share the keys to true happiness. By having a relationship with Jesus, these keys become operational. The Beatitudes are outcomes of that relationship. Thus, they are of more eternal significance than the temporal healings people fervently sought.

Source:

Zodhiates, Spiros, ed. *Hebrew Greek Key Study Bible, King James Version.* Chattanooga, Tenn.: AMG Publishers, 1984.

At-A-Glance

1. Free for All (Matthew 5:1–2)
2. True Happiness (vv. 3–12)
3. Visible Impact (vv. 13–16)

In Depth

1. Free for All (Matthew 5:1–2)

Jesus' ministry was in full swing, with amazing results. He "went about all Galilee, teaching in their synagogues, and preaching the gospel of the kingdom, and healing all manner of sickness and all manner of disease among the people" (Matthew 4:23). His fame swiftly spread to Syria, until suddenly "there followed him great multitudes of people from Galilee, and from Decapolis, and from Jerusalem, and from Judaea, and from beyond Jordan" (v. 25).

Thousands of people, including unbelievers, followed Jesus. They represented different socioeconomic backgrounds, but they all had one thing in common: They wanted the broken areas of their lives fixed. They sought physical and psychological wholeness. So "they brought unto him all sick people that were taken with divers diseases and torments, and those which were possessed with devils, and those which were lunatick, and those that had the palsy; and he healed them" (v. 24). Many would have been content with these blessings, but Jesus was not through. He delivered a memorable sermon that today still shows people the keys to true happiness.

2. True Happiness (vv. 3–12)

People relentlessly pursue happiness, only to find disappointment because of wrong decisions they make. Some of those decisions include choosing the wrong friends, spouse, or career. Other wrong decisions include poor choices in how they spend their time, talent, or treasure. Without Christ, people will continue to make wrong choices. Jesus explained the proper way to find so-called "happiness" is through a relationship with God, and adhering to God's guidelines for our service to Him and behavior toward others.

All told, Jesus shared eight kinds of spiritual blessings that stem from that relationship. Moreover, the term "blessed" preceding each Beatitude translates as "fully satisfied." Thus, it denotes a condition much deeper than the world's definition of happiness. Believers who take each Beatitude to heart, and apply it to their lives, will experience life-altering satisfaction that enables them to triumph over any situation. For example, the "poor in spirit," or spiritually helpless individuals, will gain access to the "kingdom of heaven" (v. 3). Those who "mourn"—or deeply grieve—the fact that sin's power is difficult to overcome will be comforted by *the* Comforter, the Holy Ghost (v. 4). Believers who consistently "hunger and thirst for righteousness" will be filled by Living Water and the Bread of Life—Jesus, Himself (v. 6). Those who are "persecuted for righteousness' sake" and suffer related physical harm will find "the kingdom of heaven" a safe haven (v. 10).

Further rewards await believers who are merciful, pure in heart, or make peace. The Beatitudes are encouraging because they paint a realistic picture of

Christian life and service. Unlike some would have us believe, the Christian life is not trial-free. Perhaps this is why Jesus did not shy away from addressing common emotional and physical issues or dangers people face. At the same time, the Sermon on the Mount confirmed Jesus' approach to sickness and disease. Ailments, whether physical or emotional, should not be treasured, but rather dealt with to ensure believers' overall well-being.

Finally, Jesus alluded to the fact that God's design for our happiness centers on core values that are opposite to the world's values. For this reason, believers cannot follow the world's system of doing things and expect Christlike results or the manifestation of the fruit of the Spirit in their lives. This is another reason why spiritual maturity is essential. As Christians, we must be able to distinguish God's will from our desires. We must be able to see His hand in our trials, even when He is not the cause of those trials. We must be willing to develop Christlike characteristics that enable us to enjoy true happiness.

3. Visible Impact (vv. 13–16)

True happiness always involves serving God and others. Therefore Jesus appropriately concludes the Sermon on the Mount with an emphasis on community service. Jesus reminded the believers, among the multitudes, that they were the "salt of the earth" (v. 13) and "light of the world (v. 14). Listeners immediately understood the reference to salt, which served essential purposes in their lives. They used different types of salt for different purposes. Among other things, they used salt to flavor and preserve food. In spiritual terms, salt was a phrase used to denote the covenant God had with the Israelites.

Christians are to have the same visible impact as salt. We are to bring a "Christlike" savor and flavor to the communities we serve by using our time, talent, and treasure to meet varied needs. We also are to help preserve lives by sharing the Gospel with the unsaved, allowing them the privilege of receiving eternal life.

For maximum impact, salt needs to be fully absorbed into everything it touches. It is not enough for us to "sprinkle" ourselves around, barely coming into contact with people. No, we must "rub" shoulders with the saved and unsaved, helping to provide a glimpse of Jesus to others. We are to use our special gifts and talents, pouring them out at home, in the workplace, at church, and wherever we find we are needed. However, we are not to mingle with the other "flavors" around us so that we lose our flavor. Instead, as we are "in the world, and not of it," we can visibly help steer people away from sin and toward Christ.

Being a "light" in the community also serves the same function. We can be the beacon that shines and shows people to the path of righteousness. We can be a shining example of disadvantaged individuals, allowing them to see that "with God all things are possible" (Matthew 19:26). We can be the light that pushes back the darkness of drug use in our neighborhood. But that will not happen if we cloak our lights behind closed doors, unwilling to get involved and make a difference. And it will not happen if people do not know we are Christians. We must be willing to make "our calling and election sure" (2 Peter 1:10).

Search the Scriptures

1. What condition enables one to inherit the kingdom of heaven (Matthew 5:3)? Explain.

2. When we mourn, of what can we be assured (v. 4)?

3. What blessings are available to the persecuted (vv. 10–12)?

4. Why is it important for our lives to shine (vv. 14–16)?

Discuss the Meaning

1. Why does God's way of living contradict the world's standards?

2. Why are the Beatitudes a standard of conduct for believers?

3. How is "being blessed" different from "being happy"?

4. How are the blessings promised in the Beatitudes inherently for the community and not just the individual?

Lesson in Our Society

Many people claim Bible promises and wonder why those promises are never fulfilled. They forget that the prerequisite is faith in Jesus Christ. Other promises are conditional, so we need to make sure we fulfill any condition before expecting the promise to manifest. What promise of God are you standing on today? Are you sure you fully understand the promise in context of the surrounding Scriptures? Or are you "naming and claiming" a portion of Scripture that you don't fully understand? This week, reread one or more Bible promises that you have claimed, but are still awaiting the outcome(s). Ensure that you understand each and that you have fulfilled any conditions that God has placed on that promise. If you have not, ask God for His power to help you fulfill your part, so that He can do His part. If you desire, team up with an accountability partner to help.

Make It Happen

What condition are you facing that fits into one of the areas Jesus mentioned in the Sermon on the Mount? Identify one of the related teachings, and decide how and when to put it into practice. Record your choice and intended action in your journal or Bible study notebook, asking God for help to keep it before your eyes.

Follow the Spirit

What God wants me to do:

____

____

Remember Your Thoughts

Special insights I have learned:

____

____

More Light on the Text

Matthew 5:1–16

As God first began to reveal Himself and His will for humanity through Moses, He gave Israel what we call the Ten Commandments. They are 10 basic principles to guide His people toward God's fulfillment for their lives. When God set about revealing Himself finally and perfectly, He delivered a set of basic principles for finding life at its fullest through Jesus. Those eight spiritual principles are called the Beatitudes. The word "beatitude" is from the Latin word *beatus*, meaning "blessed."

As the Ten Commandments, the Jewish Law from Moses, are the heart of God's first revelation, the Beatitudes are the heart of the Sermon on the Mount given by Jesus, God's perfect revelation of Himself. They differ from the Ten Commandments in that they are promises, rather than laws or rules. These aren't rules for getting into God's kingdom of heaven. Instead they are eight promises for how a person, who has decided to become Jesus' disciple, can find the quality of life that fits that commitment.

The Beatitudes focus on developing a character that allows Jesus' follower to enjoy that heavenly relationship more fully. They aren't eight promises to eight different kinds of people. Rather, they are eight steps toward progressively becoming a full-fledged citizen of God's kingdom, "the ethics of discipleship," as one Bible scholar calls them.

Each Gospel was written to reach a particular group of people. Matthew's audience was primarily Christians from a Jewish background. They constantly fought off feelings of unfaithfulness to God for not observing the ritual laws from Moses. Recognizing this, Matthew repeatedly shows that following Jesus and His teaching weren't abandoning the Law of Moses, but fulfilling it (Matthew 5:17).

None of the Beatitudes are completely new. Each has its beginning in the Old Testament. For instance, in the third Beatitude Jesus supported the promise "blessed are the meek" by quoting Psalm 37:11, "the meek shall inherit the earth." Many Bible scholars see in Isaiah 61:1–7 an early form of the truths Jesus organized in the Beatitudes. Mention is made there of "good tidings unto the meek" and "comfort to all who mourn."

The Beatitudes follow the pattern seen in the Ten Commandments. Jesus started with principles for a right relation to God; after them follow principles for a relationship with others.

1 And seeing the multitudes, he went up into a mountain: and when he was set, his disciples came unto him:

These first words, "seeing the multitudes" confirm what Matthew, the other Gospel writers, and the whole New Testament affirm about God's love for all people (John 3:16). Seeing the spiritually needy multitudes prompted Jesus to teach them how their deepest needs for purpose and fulfillment could be satisfied.

The mountain location tells us more than just where Jesus taught. At three other key moments in Jesus' time on Earth, Matthew mentions a mountain, at Satan's greatest temptation (Matthew 4:8), at His transfiguration (Matthew 17:1–2), and at His delivery of His Great Commission (Matthew 28:16–20). A practical reason for ascending onto the mountainside was so He could be better heard by any of the multitude who wanted to listen.

"And seeing the multitudes, he went up into a mountain: and when he was set, his disciples came unto him" (Matthew 5:1).

2 And he opened his mouth and taught them, saying,

Sitting rather than standing was the customary Jewish posture for teaching. Matthew indicated Jesus' speech in three ways in only nine words, opened, taught, and saying. In this way he signals his readers that this time was intended as important formal teaching.

3 Blessed are the poor in spirit: for theirs is the kingdom of heaven.

All eight Beatitudes begin with the word "blessed" (Gk. *makarios,* **mak-AR-ee-os**). It describes someone who was "fortunate or to be congratulated." Dr. Floyd Filson says Matthew is using it as an exclamation, "O the happiness of…!"

Poor described being completely broke, destitute, in utter poverty, not someone of merely limited means. When Jesus added the words "in spirit" he meant a person lacking any spiritual resources, someone who was spiritually powerless. In Judea (Judaea, KJV) and Galilee, under Roman rule, many ordinary people were physically poor. After centuries of oppression by the Assyrians, the Babylonians, the Syrians, and now the Roman Empire, "the poor" was a fitting description for many Jews who felt they had been ground underfoot by social and political forces. Widespread poverty and lack of influence made them targets for exploitation by those with wealth and power. Both foreigners and other Jews took advantage of their weakness. Jesus said those who recognized they were in spiritual poverty were fortunate. He said that was the starting place for becoming a citizen of God's kingdom. Only when a person recognized and admitted his or her spiritual need for God was that person ready to enter God's kingdom. This fits the simple statement that both Jesus and John the Baptist used to begin their preaching to the crowds: "repent: for the kingdom of heaven is at hand" (Matthew 3:2; 4:17). Matthew almost always says "kingdom of heaven" rather than "kingdom of God" because Jews avoided using the word "God" for fear of misusing God's name.

4 Blessed are they that mourn: for they shall be comforted.

"To mourn" (Gk. *pentheo,* **pen-THEH-o**) means "to be consumed by grief." Here, Jesus' promise does not apply to the person grieving over everyday tragedies of life, such as car wrecks, earthquakes, or house fires. The mourning Jesus referred to here was over spiritual poverty, both of a person's own moral failure and its effect, and the effect of sin in the world as a whole.

When Jesus promised that those who mourned would be "comforted" (Gk. *parakaleo,* **par-ak-al-EH-o**), it was nearly identical to the word He used for the Holy Spirit (Gk. *parakletos,* **par-AK-lay-tos**) in John 14:16 and 16:7. Paul would later expand on Jesus' promise in 2 Corinthians 7:10 (NLT): "For the kind of sorrow God wants us to experience leads us away from sin and results in salvation. There's no regret for that kind of sorrow. But worldly sorrow, which lacks repentance, results in spiritual death."

5 Blessed are the meek: for they shall inherit the earth.

How many people have heard this Beatitude and snorted in disgust because they thought *meek* meant weak? Nothing could be farther from what Jesus meant. Jesus used the word "meek" (Gk. *praus,* **prah-OOCE**) to describe Himself, "I am meek and lowly in heart" (Matthew 11:29). However being meek did not prevent Him from confronting the most influential and powerful people of His day, standing up to their brutality, and voluntarily enduring crucifixion. Obviously meek did not mean cowardly or timid.

J. Wallace Hamilton, in his book *Ride the Wild Horses,* uses a horse to explain what Jesus meant by "meek." He says that neither a wild horse nor a dead horse is of any use. A wild horse might be useful someday, but a dead horse never will. The only horse of any value is a meek horse, a bridle-wise horse. Once a horse is broken and has been gentled, its strength can be directed in useful ways for travel as transportation, for entertainment, or for relaxation.

"Meek" contained the idea of gentleness, kindness, or humility. It was the exact opposite of arrogant, ruthless, or aggressive. Michael Green writes that it was the opposite of "bigheaded." Although the word "meek" never occurs in the epistle of James, the book warns against failing to be meek. "You want something, but don't get it. You kill and covet, but you cannot have what you want. You quarrel and fight" (James 4:2, NIV). Keep in mind that as its first verse shows, the epistle of James was written to Christians! James was reminding his readers that Christians must guard against being drawn into seeking their own advantage (see also Ephesians 4:1–3; Philippians 2:3–9).

James 4:7–8 (NIV) describes the value in being meek: "Submit yourselves, then, to God. Resist the Devil, and he will flee from you. Come near to God and He will come near to you. Wash your hands, you sinners, and purify your hearts, you double-minded." The meek person understands that although God is eternal, they are destined to die. Where God is all-powerful, they are prone to sickness and injury. And while God is all-knowing, they are ignorant and often confused.

Robert Mounce explains how the meek will inherit the earth this way: "The aggressive are unable to enjoy their ill-gotten gains. Only the meek have the capacity to enjoy in life all those things that provide genuine and lasting satisfaction."

The apostle Paul served as a good example. While living free in Ephesus as a missionary spreading the message of Jesus, he wrote to the church in Rome, "everything belongs to you—whether…the world, or life and death, or the present and the future. Everything belongs to you, and you belong to Christ, and Christ belongs to God" (1 Corinthians 3:21–23, NLT). He added in a second letter to Corinth, "We own nothing, and yet we have everything" (2 Corinthians 6:10, NLT). Later he affirmed, from a prison cell in Rome, that what he had written in better times still applied in hard times, "I have learned how to be content with whatever I have. I know how to live on almost nothing or with everything. I have learned the secret of living in every situation" (Philippians 4:11–12, NLT).

6 Blessed are they which do hunger and thirst after righteousness: for they shall be filled.

Hunger and thirst are common symbols for strong desire. Matthew used a form of both words that indicates a constant desire to know, not a passing fancy or a brief craving (Psalm 42:2). Jesus promised that the deepest needs of those who continually seek God's purposes will be fulfilled. In Philippians 4:19, Paul assured the poor and tiny Christian body at Philippi that "my God shall supply all your need according to his riches in glory by Christ Jesus."

Six hundred years before Christ, Theognis, the Greek poet from near Corinth, defined "righteousness" (Gk. *dikaiosune*, **dik-ah-yos-OO-nay**) as "the sum of all the best character qualities." An ongoing pursuit of God's righteous will is important because a person's spiritual need affects every part of life, from family concerns and social affairs to work duties or political activities.

A follower of Jesus must recognize his or her ruined spiritual condition, mourn its effects on our lives and on the world, and humbly accept our reliance on God's grace. This Beatitude shows that a life of steadfast discipleship should not mean a life of constant depression. Jesus' promise was that pursuing God's goal for our lives will result in complete fulfillment (John 15:5, 7). The secret of total satisfaction in life is to maintain a single-minded desire to live up to God's best.

7 Blessed are the merciful: for they shall obtain mercy.

The Ten Commandments began by focusing on a right relation to God. Jesus followed the same pattern in the first four Beatitudes to show His disciples how they should understand their relation to God. In the fifth Beatitude, He showed how His followers should practice a right relation to other people.

Many times the Gospels record that people came to Jesus pleading "have mercy on me," or begging Him to have mercy on a son or a daughter (Matthew 15:22; 20:30). To be merciful is much more than feeling sorry for people with problems. Dr. Herschel Hobbs called mercy "active pity." Active is correct, but pity was not exactly what Jesus meant.

Mercy is something Jesus expects Christians to *do*, not something we should *feel*. Bob Pierce, founder of World Vision, used to say, "Pity looks and turns away, but compassion has to help." Compassion is what Jesus called for.

Everyone needs mercy sometimes. It arises the more we get in touch with our spiritual and mortal neediness and our universal need of forgiveness (Romans 3:21–23). When we deny our human weakness and guilt, traits rise in us that are the opposites of mercy—cruelty, brutality, and vengefulness. Christians must constantly guard against letting those responses crowd out mercy. Mercy was the course Paul was urging in Ephesians 4:2 (NIV): "Be completely humble and gentle; be patient, bearing with one another in love."

8 Blessed are the pure in heart: for they shall see God.

A pure heart has moral purity, unmixed motives, and loyalty to God's will, regardless of the circumstances. During Jesus' days on Earth, the heart was considered to drive the will more than the emotions. Strong feelings were associated primarily with the kidneys, the intestines, or the bowels. The heart was thought of as the center of physical, mental, and spiritual life.

As an example in 2 Corinthians 9:7 (NLT), Paul used the same word Matthew uses here when he wrote, "You must each decide in your own heart (Gk. *kardia*, **kar-DEE-ah**) how much to give." Jesus' promise is that a single-minded devotion to God will allow His followers access to God's guidance and grace (Hebrews 4:14–16).

9 Blessed are the peacemakers: for they shall be called the children of God.

A peacemaker worked to solve conflicts between people and restore acceptance. Such a person was the opposite of someone with a hostile, fault-finding attitude. Psalm 34:14 (NLT) urged God's people to "search for peace, and work to maintain it."

Michael Green judges from this Beatitude that "those who reconcile the estranged are doing something which is just like God." After Jesus had given Himself as a sacrifice for our sins, Paul wrote that God has commissioned Christians to work to bring peace between people and God (2 Corinthians 5:18). This is not a promise to people who take a pleasant, passive attitude toward those they disagree with. As William Cutler and Richard Peace wrote in *Examining Your Lifestyle*, "this Beatitude calls for active involvement in reconciliation between those in conflict." Jesus' final Beatitude shows that can be costly, dangerous, and even deadly.

10 Blessed are they which are persecuted for righteousness' sake: for theirs is the kingdom of heaven.

Only in the first and last Beatitudes did Jesus state that His promise could be experienced immediately. As soon as a person is willing to accept his or her spiritual poverty, that person enters into the realm of God's kingdom of love and grace. When commitment to God's ways becomes costly and Jesus' followers are still willing to accept the price of obedience, they have entered fully into God's kingdom.

11 Blessed are ye, when men shall revile you, and persecute you, and shall say all manner of evil against you falsely, for my sake. 12 Rejoice, and be exceeding glad: for great is your reward in heaven: for so persecuted they the prophets which were before you.

Although Jesus begins this statement with the word "blessed," this is not one of the Beatitudes. Instead this is instruction for His disciples on how to apply them personally. This was His challenge for them to live by. Notice in verse 11, Jesus changed from saying blessed are *they* to saying blessed are *you.*

Jesus confronted them with the reality that turning from sin and self was hard. Living a life in keeping with God's purposes was not easy. Those who commit themselves to pursuing God's best for themselves and God's world can make themselves a target for persecution.

Jesus described three forms that persecution may take: insults, harassment, and lies. Some faithful followers of Jesus have endured all three kinds of persecution. "Revile" (Gk. *oneidizo,* **on-i-DID-zo**) meant "to heap insults onto a person, to be buried under an avalanche of them, not merely taunted with a single offensive remark." Early Christians were wrongly accused of being atheists because they did not believe in the gods of Greek mythology. Because the bread and wine of the Lord's Supper was described as the body and blood of Christ, they were falsely called cannibals.

Jesus urged His disciples to make such persecution a source of pleasure. This is exactly what Paul and Silas did when they were thrown in jail, after first being stripped and beaten. Acts 16:25 (NLT) reads, "Around midnight Paul and Silas were praying and singing hymns to God, and the other prisoners were listening." Their behavior confirmed that they were citizens of God's kingdom.

13 Ye are the salt of the earth: but if the salt have lost his savour, wherewith shall it be salted? it is thenceforth good for nothing, but to be cast out, and to be trodden under foot of men.

A common debate among Bible scholars is whether Jesus meant salt as a flavoring or as a preservative. It was used both ways, to flavor food and to preserve it—especially meat—which would spoil quickly in that time without refrigeration. Many people still enjoy salt-cured ham today.

Since Jesus mentioned salt's "savour," His first thought was apparently the flavor salt adds to food. That is also the comparison Paul makes in Colossians 4:6 (NIV) where he says, "Let your conversation be always full of grace, seasoned with salt." All sacrifices at the temple were to be salted first (Leviticus 2:13). Jesus wanted His followers to understand that living by the principles in the Beatitudes would give life its most satisfying flavor.

A little boy once described salt as "that stuff that makes food taste bad if you leave it out." Jesus didn't intend for living by His example and teachings to make Christians wimpy, boring people. Pure salt never loses its flavor. Salt can remain in a shaker for months, even years. Yet when sprinkled on food, it instantly adds flavor.

When Jesus mentioned salt losing its savor, he was probably referring to the piles of white mineral deposits that collected along the Dead Sea as water evaporated, which contained large amounts of salt. However, when it rained, the salt content in the mineral deposits was dissolved and washed away, leaving a white powder. That white powder was useless as salt but was still white like salt. Its only use was to be scattered on footpaths to harden as people walked on them.

Salt was essential to life in Jesus' day. A part of a Roman legionnaire's salary included a ration of salt. In fact the word "salary" derives from the practice of including a portion of salt in a Roman soldier's pay. Likewise, Jesus wanted living by God's good purposes to add a pleasing savor to living, not to make life tasteless and boring.

14 Ye are the light of the world. A city that is set on an hill cannot be hid. 15 Neither do men light a candle, and put it under a bushel, but on a candlestick; and it giveth light unto all that are in the house.

When Jesus compared His presence and teaching to light shining from a city on a hill, He emphasized that when He had the top place in a person's life, it would be obvious. Jesus says that a candle gives light to everyone in a house. Most houses of Jesus' day consisted of a single big room. Light makes life better in both large and small situations. Light can make it possible to see dangers that darkness would conceal. Light can guide us to good things.

Light doesn't work by force. It simply enters where an opening exists and darkness disappears. Light has no use except to shine. The idea of lighting an oil lamp and then covering it with a basket was nonsense. Jesus' point was that there was no such thing as a secret follower. Both salt and light functioned by penetration, inwardly in food, outwardly in the home or outside world. God's presence was meant to make a difference not just in a person's life, but also in the lives of those about them.

16 Let your light so shine before men, that they may see your good works, and glorify your Father which is in heaven.

In English, we use one word when addressing other people. The word is "you," whether we mean you as an individual or you as a group. The language in which Matthew wrote was not like that. Through all eight Beatitudes (vv. 3–10) and in the six verses in which Jesus challenged His disciples to live by them (vv. 11–16), not once does He address them as individuals. The poor, the meek, the merciful, and the pure in heart all are in the plural form. Likewise, when Jesus says, "ye are the salt...[and] the light... [and] your light," each time He uses the plural.

Why is that? Certainly not because our individual lives aren't important to God—because they are. Jesus came to save us from sin and inaugurate God's kingdom. His plan is to include His church in His kingdom. Therefore, we should make the Beatitudes our core values and implement them as a community of servants.

Sources:

Clements, R. E. *The New Century Bible Commentary, Isaiah 1–39.* Grand Rapids, Mich.: Wm. B. Eerdmans Publishing Company, 1980.

Cutler, William and Peace, Richard. *Sermon on the Mount: Examining Your Lifestyle.* Littleton, Co.: Serendipity House, 1995.

Filson, Floyd V. *The Gospel According To St. Matthew.* Peabody, Mass.: Hendrickson Publishers, 1987.

Green, Michael. *Matthew for Today: Expository Study of Matthew.* Dallas, Tx.: Word Publishing, 1988.

Hamilton, J. Wallace. *Ride the Wild Horses.* Nashville, Tenn.: Abingdon Press, 1980.

Hobbs, Herschel H. *An Exposition of the Four Gospels,* Vol. 1. The Gospel of Matthew. Grand Rapids, Mich.: Baker Book House, 1965.

Lightfoot, John. *A Commentary on the New Testament from the Talmud and Hebraica Matthew–I Corinthians.* Vol. 2. Matthew–Mark. Grand Rapids, Mich.: Baker Book House, reprinted from 1859 edition, 1979.

Schweizer, Eduard. *The Good News According to Matthew.* Atlanta: John Knox Press, 1975.

Daily Bible Readings

M: Asking for God's Blessing
Numbers 6:22–27

T: Blessed by the Father
Matthew 25:31–40

W: Acting on Jesus' Words
Matthew 7:24–29

T: Returning Evil with Good
Romans 12:9–13

F: Living in Harmony with Others
Romans 12:14–21

S: Inheriting a Blessing
1 Peter 3:8–15

S: Blessing for God's People
Matthew 5:1–16

NOTES

TEACHING TIPS

September 28
Bible Study Guide 4

1. Words You Should Know

A. Princes (Matthew 20:25) *archon* (Gk.)—Rulers, chiefs.

B. Minister (v. 26) *diakonos* (Gk.)—A servant or minister; denotes voluntary rather than paid service.

C. Ransom (v. 28) *lutron* (Gk.)—A price paid for setting free a captive.

2. Teacher Preparation

Unifying Principle—Serving Others. Everyone yearns to be recognized as important in the eyes of others. How does one achieve greatness? Jesus taught that if we wish to be great, we must become a servant and follow His example of service to others.

A. Purchase (or design on computer labels) "smiley face" stickers, enough to distribute one per student. Bring in play money (or cut strips of green paper).

B. Create a list of "service with a smile" factors—those things that make or break a "service encounter" (such as a meal at a restaurant or a welcome to a new church).

C. Read the Focal Verses and Devotional Reading.

3. Starting the Lesson

A. Open with prayer.

B. Ask the students to read the Focal Verses. Discuss.

C. Have volunteers read the Keep in Mind verse. Discuss.

4. Getting into the Lesson

A. Ask the students to name some community servants they encounter daily.

B. Invite volunteers to role-play (five minutes each) two community servants from the list (for example, nice cop/tough cop or rude waitress/attentive waitress). Distribute "play money" to remaining students, allowing them to participate by responding appropriately to service rendered (for example, to give tips, speak words of thanks).

C. Ask the students, "Which of the servants would you consider great? Why?" Allow time for discussion.

5. Relating the Lesson to Life

SEPT 28th

A. Have a volunteer read the Devotional Reading.

B. Remind the students that they serve multiple communities daily (at home, work, school, etc.). Provide examples of internal and external barriers that hinder them from serving with "the mind of Christ."

C. Give them a few minutes to develop a plan to serve one of these communities this week (some examples include devoting 15 minutes each day to help a struggling coworker brush up on computer skills; running errands for an elderly neighbor; participating in a church-run service activity).

6. Arousing Action

A. Distribute "smiley face" stickers. Tell the students that these are to encourage them to have the mind of Christ in all they humbly offer "service with a smile."

B. Remind them to act upon their service plan. Invite them to offer specific prayer requests.

C. Close with prayer.

Worship Guide

For the Superintendent or Teacher
Theme: Creating a Community of Servants
Theme Song: "Lift Him Up"
Devotional Reading: Philippians 2:1–11
Prayer

CREATING A COMMUNITY OF SERVANTS

Bible Background • MATTHEW 20:1–28; MARK 10:35–45
Printed Text • MATTHEW 20:17–28 Devotional Reading • PHILIPPIANS 2:1–11

AIM for Change

By the end of the lesson, we will:
RETELL the teaching of Jesus about greatness;
RECOGNIZE the responsibility and value of being a servant; and
DEVELOP and ACT on a plan to serve others, while EXPRESSING our understanding of Jesus' teachings.

Keep in Mind

"The Son of man came not to be ministered unto, but to minister, and to give his life a ransom for many" (from Matthew 20:28).

Focal Verses

KJV **Matthew 20:17** And Jesus going up to
Jerusalem took the twelve disciples
apart in the way, and said unto them,
18 Behold, we go up to Jerusalem; and the Son of
man shall be betrayed unto the chief priests and unto
the scribes, and they shall condemn him to death,
19 And shall deliver him to the Gentiles to mock,
and to scourge, and to crucify him: and the third day
he shall rise again.
20 Then came to him the mother of Zebedees
children with her sons, worshipping him, and desiring a certain thing of him.
21 And he said unto her, What wilt thou? She saith
unto him, Grant that these my two sons may sit, the
one on thy right hand, and the other on the left, in
thy kingdom.
22 But Jesus answered and said, Ye know not what
ye ask. Are ye able to drink of the cup that I shall
drink of, and to be baptized with the baptism that I
am baptized with? They say unto him, We are able.
23 And he saith unto them, Ye shall drink indeed
of my cup, and be baptized with the baptism that I am
baptized with: but to sit on my right hand, and on my
left, is not mine to give, but it shall be given to them
for whom it is prepared of my Father.
24 And when the ten heard it, they were moved
with indignation against the two brethren.
25 But Jesus called them unto him, and said, Ye
know that the princes of the Gentiles exercise dominion over them, and they that are great exercise
authority upon them.
26 But it shall not be so among you: but whosoever
will be great among you, let him be your minister;

NLT **Matthew 20:17** As Jesus was going up
to Jerusalem, he took the twelve disciples aside privately and told them what was going to
happen to him.
18 "Listen," he said, "we're going up to Jerusalem,
where the Son of Man will be betrayed to the leading
priests and the teachers of religious law. They will sentence him to die.
19 Then they will hand him over to the Romans
to be mocked, flogged with a whip, and crucified. But
on the third day he will be raised from the dead."
20 Then the mother of James and John, the sons
of Zebedee, came to Jesus with her sons. She knelt
respectfully to ask a favor.
21 "What is your request?" he asked. She replied,
"In your Kingdom, please let my two sons sit in places
of honor next to you, one on your right and the
other on your left."
22 But Jesus answered by saying to them, "You
don't know what you are asking! Are you able to
drink from the bitter cup of suffering I am about to
drink?" "Oh yes," they replied, "we are able!"
23 Jesus told them, "You will indeed drink from
my bitter cup. But I have no right to say who will sit
on my right or my left. My Father has prepared those
places for the ones he has chosen."
24 When the ten other disciples heard what
James and John had asked, they were indignant.
25 But Jesus called them together and said, "You
know that the rulers in this world lord it over their
people, and officials flaunt their authority over those
under them.
26 But among you it will be different. Whoever
wants to be a leader among you must be your servant,

27 And whosoever will be chief among you, let him be your servant:

28 Even as the Son of man came not to be ministered unto, but to minister, and to give his life a ransom for many.

27 and whoever wants to be first among you must become your slave.

28 For even the Son of Man came not to be served but to serve others and to give his life as a ransom for many."

In Focus

Jimmy, First Church's short-term missions director, stood up and waved at the 15 church members sitting in rows behind him on the packed airplane. They were all exhausted but excited about the week-long missions trip that had ended the previous evening, especially the members who had never served on such a trip before. Each had expressed feelings of inadequacy when told the outreach would include construction projects, kids' activities, crafts, sports, and other activities designed to attract various age groups.

"I warn you," said Carla, an accountant for a government agency, "putting me on the construction team would be ugly—real ugly." She opted for girls' basketball duty, but during the week she ended up also sanding and painting walls.

"Trust me, you don't want me to sing," 19-year-old Josiah joked about the VBS-styled kids' outreach. Assigned to the construction team, he was also a hit as Jo-Jo, the singing clown.

By week's end, Carla and Josiah not only served in familiar areas but also helped in those they vowed were not for them. Their willingness to come out of their comfort zones contributed to a successful missions trip that dramatically improved the quality of many lives and homes.

The average person does not associate greatness with servanthood. To Jesus, though, servants are the truly "great" people in the world. If you want to be great, serve others. If you want to see God's power as you serve, come out of your comfort zone.

The People, Places, and Times

Sons of Zebedee. The two men (James and John) were working on their family's fishing boat when called to ministry (Matthew 4:21). Immediately, they left their father and family business to serve Jesus, who nicknamed them "sons of thunder" (Mark 3:17). For three years, they watched Jesus' miracles, emulated His works, and endured hardships. Now, according to the mother's request, they wanted to assure that their sacrifice would pay off when Jesus came into His real kingdom. Their mother specifically requested that they hold important positions.

Background

Jesus often used stories called "parables" to illustrate spiritual truths. Prior to His last visit to Jerusalem, He shared with the disciples a community-service related parable (Matthew 20:1–16). In it, a landowner hires a group of workers to work in his vineyard for an agreed-upon salary. He then, over the course of 11 hours, invites three other sets of individuals to "work," but only promises to give them "whatsoever is right." At the end of the day, everybody received the same amount of money. This miffed the first group, who had worked the longest—12 grueling hours. When they complained, the landowner rebuked them for their attitude.

The parable shows differences between "workers" and "servants" in several key areas:

Expectations. Workers "hire" out their services, and thus expect and demand pay. Servants volunteer or work without expectation of specific reward (monetary or otherwise).

Attitude. Unhappy workers focus on what others receive (vv. 10–12). Servants do not (we can assume this as Jesus did not mention any negative attitudes of the servants).

Rewards. Workers receive exactly what they ask for (a salary). Servants receive money (if applicable) and much more (joy in helping others). Jesus promises, "he that reapeth receiveth wages, and gathereth fruit unto life eternal: that both he that soweth and he that reapeth may rejoice together" (John 4:36).

The point? Jesus is looking for "servants" who will trust Him—those who will faithfully and joyfully labor in His kingdom without complaining and without expecting rewards for each act of service completed. In other words, God is looking for servants who will not "nickel and dime" Him.

Ironically, Matthew places the next story on the heels of this parable. James and John's mother requested a place of prominence for her sons, when Jesus "comes into his kingdom." Clearly, the men missed the point of the parable of the laborers. Nonetheless, Jesus did not rebuke the family. He did, however, explain that God alone apportions positions in the kingdom of heaven. Shortly afterward, He chided the other 10 disciples, who were indignant when they heard about the request made by James and John's mother. It is possible that Jesus did so because their indignation hinted at their own secret expectations.

At-A-Glance

1. Service: Duration (Matthew 20:17–19)
2. Service: Expectations (vv. 20–23)
3. Service: Competition (vv. 24–26)
4. Service: Attitudes (vv. 27–28)

In Depth

1. Service: Duration (Matthew 20:17–19)

The window of opportunity to serve varies. For the workers in the parable of the laborers, it was measured in hours. For Jesus, it was measured in years. Sometimes the duration of service is known as in a short-term missions trip or a leadership role for a church ministry. Other times, such as an unexpected encounter with a stranger, it is unknown. Because duration can vary, it is essential that Christians maximize service opportunities.

Jesus was ever mindful of the window of opportunity He had to reach the multitudes and of trainable community servants who could emulate and surpass His works. He exhorted the disciples to do the same: "Say not ye, There are yet four months, and then cometh harvest? behold, I say unto you, Lift up your eyes, and look on the fields; for they are white already to harvest" (John 4:35).

When Jesus could no longer take the sickle to the harvest, He had no regrets. He had completed the work given to Him. He could discuss the pending crucifixion, without preceding discourses beginning with "I wish...." Likewise, we sidestep the valley of regret when we make the most of every opportunity.

God has ordained works of service for every Christian. In order to have no regrets upon completion of them, we must be certain we have single-mindedly done the will of God while embracing every evangelistic and discipleship opportunity. At the same time, we must be willing to step aside and let others serve when our service duration draws to a close. Only then can we link arms with God, creating communities of servants who "turn the world upside down" (Acts 17:6).

2. Service: Expectations (vv. 20–23)

The trip to Jerusalem would be Jesus' last. Before entering the city, He took the disciples aside for a last-minute reminder of the betrayal and death He knew would occur. Matthew records only one immediate reaction to this announcement: a visit from James, John, and their mother. She came worshiping, but her real goal was to request a position of honor for her sons.

The request was inappropriate for three reasons. First, it ignored the fact that Jesus had just announced what should have been the worst news the disciples could receive about their mentor. Second, it lacked understanding of Jesus' purpose and mission during the years spent training the 12 disciples. Third, it revealed the family's unrealistic service expectations.

Jesus' response teaches the importance of evaluating service expectations. Left unchecked, improper expectations can undermine the ability to effectively serve. Furthermore, allowing family members to speak for us is inappropriate. Always, it can lead to unhealthy attitudes that impact us and those we serve with. Therefore, serve without expectations. As you do, "let nothing be done through strife or vainglory; but in lowliness of mind let each esteem other better than themselves" (Philippians 2:3).

3. Service: Competition (vv. 24–26)

What started out as a seemingly simple request for a leadership position ended up being a source of division among the disciples. Once the other 10 disciples heard of the request, they were "moved with indignation against the two brethren" (Matthew

20:24). Jesus rebuked all the disciples, explaining the importance of having an attitude that surpassed that of the Gentiles. And in a heated moment when the men were jockeying for position, He noted, "whoever wants to become great among you must be your servant" (v. 26, NIV). In other words, "Stop jockeying for position. Be humble!"

Humility is the cornerstone of Christian service. It promotes, not hinders, unity. A spirit of competition, on the other hand, can destroy it. Many churches, ministries, and communities have been destroyed because of infighting between individuals who were called to serve, not reign. If any Christian endeavor is to succeed, it must be bathed in humility and have servanthood as its foundation. Each "servant" must emulate Jesus, "Who, being in the form of God, thought it not robbery to be equal with God: But made himself of no reputation, and took upon him the form of a servant" (Philippians 2:6–7).

4. Service: Attitudes (vv. 27–28)

As the parable of the laborers revealed, attitude plays a role in service effectiveness. Jesus was the epitome of a "public servant." He served well and without regard to personal sacrifice or gain. Furthermore, He did not allow others to distract him. When declining food on one occasion, Jesus explained his inner satisfaction by saying, "My meat is to do the will of him that sent me, and to finish his work" (John 4:34).

Embracing the work of God requires embracing a spirit of teamwork. Christian servants are not "lone rangers," but members of the body of Christ. Each member is needed, and each must properly function in order for the body of Christ to be whole, healthy, and effective. "For as the body is one, and hath many members, and all the members of that one body, being many, are one body: so also is Christ" (1 Corinthians 12:12).

Teamwork works—all the time. We serve the fairest Master any servant could have. Thus, there is no need to "sweat the small stuff." Instead, allow God to take care of the details. As we do, like the laborers who only worked one hour, we will be community servants who are pleasantly surprised at the natural and supernatural rewards we receive.

Search the Scriptures

1. The worried mother asked Jesus, "________ that these my two sons may ________, the one on thy ____________ ____________, and the other on the ____________, in thy ________" (Matthew 20:21).

2. Jesus responded, "Ye ____________ not what ye ____________" (v. 22).

3. "It ________ be ________ to ________ for ________ it is ____________ of my ________" (v. 23).

4. "____________ will be ________ among you, let him ________ your ____________" (v. 26).

Discuss the Meaning

1. Why was timing and essence of the mother's request inappropriate?

2. God seeks a community of servants. Explain.

3. Who should be our model for service? Why? How?

Lesson in Our Society

"Service with a smile" is the motto of many organizations. Company executives realize that since quality of service is directly related to customer satisfaction, they must ensure that employees understand corporate service goals and objectives. These must be effectively communicated and backed by relevant training. Employees who seek to excel will engage in a variety of activities to keep their skills sharp and their attitudes right. What about you? Are you in need of a service checkup? Is it time for you to sharpen the skills necessary to serve those God has called you to serve? If so, ask God to steer you to the right church, community, or workplace resources. Then humble yourself and request whatever is needed to get you back on the service track.

Make It Happen

The Good News is all about serving others. If you are not actively involved in at least one ministry of your church, what is holding you back? Do you feel inadequate to serve? Or have you allowed nonessential activities to crowd your schedule? God needs you. Your church and community need you. Make a commitment to get involved. If desired, seek out those opportunities that allow your entire family to serve together.

Follow the Spirit

What God wants me to do:

____

____

Remember Your Thoughts

Special insights I have learned:

____

____

More Light on the Text

Matthew 20:17–28

In only 11 verses, Matthew records four episodes that show how difficult it was for Jesus to win those closest to Him to His way of living. He had just informed them again of His coming execution in Jerusalem, when the mother of James and John asked Jesus that her sons be given the highest leadership positions in Jesus' coming kingdom. That was followed by the fury of the other 10 disciples, who were enraged by James and John's desire for positions of power. Jesus then explained to them all God's way to importance and status.

17 And Jesus going up to Jerusalem took the twelve disciples apart in the way, and said unto them,

When Matthew said Jesus was "going up" to Jerusalem, it was both figuratively and literally true. Jesus and His company were somewhere near Jericho. The site of the temple in Jerusalem was considered an exalted and holy place, the City of God. In the 15-mile journey to Jerusalem, the road would ascend nearly 4,000 feet, so they would truly be "going up."

As they trudged toward Jerusalem, Jesus drew aside the 12 men to whom He planned to entrust His revelation when He returned to His Father. The *Good News* translation adds the word "again," indicating that Jesus did this more than once. Note that our text calls these 12 "disciples" (Gk. *mathetes*, **math-ay-TES**), which meant pupils, students, or learners. Their teaching of Jesus' principles, after His ascension, would be the basis for the new Christian community; but they had to learn them first. As these four incidents show, that did not happen quickly or easily.

18 Behold, we go up to Jerusalem; and the Son of Man shall be betrayed unto the chief priests and unto the scribes, and they shall condemn him to death, 19 And shall deliver him to the Gentiles to mock, and to scourge, and to crucify him: and the third day he shall rise again.

This made the third time Jesus had declared He was going to be killed while He was in Jerusalem (Matthew 16:21; 17:22–23). This was not the last time He tried to make them understand the purpose of His death in God's plan (26:1–2).

Each time He mentioned His coming death, He explained what lay ahead for Him more fully. At first He merely said He would suffer many things, the Jewish leaders would reject Him as Messiah, and that He would be killed (Mark 8:31). Luke 9:45 (NLT) says that "they didn't know what he meant. Its significance was hidden from them." The next time, He added that He would be betrayed (Mark 9:31; Luke 9:44).

At this third announcement, before arriving in Jerusalem, He explained three more details. Not only would the priests and lay leaders reject Him but they would condemn Him. After that, they would hand Him over to their Roman oppressors, the very people they expected the Messiah to deliver them from. Lastly, He named His form of execution as crucifixion. He would not be stoned as a fake Messiah, but executed as a common criminal. Until this time, He had simply said that He would be killed. But all three times, He had included that on the third day He would rise from the dead.

He also added that the Romans would not only execute Him, they would "mock" (Gk. *empaizo*, **emp-AHEED-zo**) Him, which meant "to play with something." When applied to a person, it meant "to make fun of someone, to ridicule or to humiliate the person." In addition, they would "scourge" Him, meaning beat Him with whips, to weaken Him before crucifixion. Sometimes criminals died from the scourging, but sometimes they hung on the cross for two or three days before finally dying. Crucifixion was the most painful and degrading form of Roman execution.

20 Then came to him the mother of Zebedees children with her sons, worshipping him, and desiring a certain thing of him.

This verse begins with Matthew's favorite word—"then" (Gk. *tote*, **TOT-eh**). He used it 90 times in his Gospel, more than all other New Testament writers combined. Both the *New International Version* and the *New Living Translation* render it the same as the King James Version. However, it didn't mean sometime after the event just mentioned, but immediately after.

Matthew said that Jesus halted His procession to Jerusalem to inform His disciples in detail how He was going to be executed when He got there.

"The Son of man came not to be ministered unto, but to minister" (from Matthew 20:28).

Immediately after that, apparently ignoring that grave announcement, Zebedee's wife approached Jesus asking Him for a favor. Her two sons, James and John, two of Jesus' closest disciples, accompanied her. Bible scholars mostly agree that her name is Salome, one of three women at the crucifixion who went to Jesus' empty tomb on Sunday morning (Matthew 27:56; Mark 15:40).

Dr. Herschel Hobbs asks a good question in his commentary: "Why was she so bold?" Only Matthew mentions her. Was she simply a mother aggressive for her sons' welfare? Or had her sons pressured their mother into putting the question to Jesus? Since Mark tells this incident as though James and John put the request to Jesus directly, that seems to be the likely explanation.

When she came to Jesus, our text says she was "worshipping" (Gk. *proskuneo,* **pros-koo-NEH-o**) Him. The literal meaning of the word is "to kiss toward." It originally meant to get down on one's knees and kiss the feet of the king. In Jesus' day, it meant to bow down in worship or honor of someone, which is what Salome did. Her presence, at that time and later, show that women were actively and intimately involved in Jesus' earthly mission (Mark 15:40–41; Luke 8:1–3).

21 And he said unto her, What wilt thou? She saith unto him, Grant that these my two sons may sit, the one on thy right hand, and the other on the left, in thy kingdom.

This verse shows that, although Jesus' disciples failed to grasp the kind of Messiah God wanted Him to be, Salome and her sons were fully convinced that He was the Messiah. Believing that, she asked Jesus to designate her sons to the top two positions in His kingdom, apparently over Peter. She and her sons may have believed that Peter had disqualified himself for leadership because of Jesus' criticism of him at Bethsaida (Matthew 16:22–23).

Salome asked Jesus to "grant" her sons the positions of authority. The *New Living Translation* words her request with "Promise that...." The request was for Jesus to tell her that He would do so.

22 But Jesus answered and said, Ye know not what ye ask. Are ye able to drink of the cup that I shall drink of, and to be baptized with the baptism that I am baptized with? They say unto him, We are able. 23 And he saith unto them, Ye shall drink indeed of my cup, and be baptized with the baptism that I am baptized with: but to sit on my right hand, and on my left, is not mine to give, but it shall be given to them for whom it is prepared of my Father.

When Jesus replied, it was not to Salome. "Ye," in the medieval English, is the plural for "you." If Jesus was replying to Salome, He would have said "you." Obviously, His reply was to James and John, who had given their mother the task of asking the favor of Jesus.

Having her make the request of Jesus was a shrewd strategy. It would give the appearance that she was asking for the favor and not directly reveal the ambition of her sons. Perhaps it even seemed like an "innocent" request from an older woman who loved her children.

In Jesus' reply, "Ye know not what ye ask," "ask" is in the middle voice, which meant Jesus was saying, you don't know what you're asking *for yourselves.* Modern slang might be, "you don't know what you're getting yourselves into."

A cup could represent something of great joy or benefit as when Psalm 23:5 exults, "My cup runneth over" or Psalm 116:13 (NIV) rejoices, "I will lift up the cup of salvation." A cup could also signify great sorrow as when Jesus prayed, "O my Father, if it be possible, let this cup pass from me" (Matthew 26:39). That is what Jesus meant here that the brothers did not grasp. In spite of His just telling his disciples that He was going to experience a horrific death, the brothers' ambition prevented them from seeing the costly price of identifying with Jesus.

Jesus' mention of baptism suggested being swamped by or overwhelmed by some condition. When Jesus asked if they could withstand the great difficulty that lay ahead, they said that they could. To their credit, neither man shrank from the challenge when their time came. James became leader of the church in Jerusalem when Peter's replacement was needed, a position of prominence that led to his beheading by Herod (Acts 12:1–2). A number of traditions record that his brother John suffered persecution and imprisonment because of his commitment to the risen Jesus.

This took place, however, only after they met the resurrected Jesus. Only then did all of Jesus' patient teaching break into their understanding, even then with difficulty (Mark 16:14). In spite of professing "we are able," James and John ran away and hid along with all of Jesus' other disciples on the night of His arrest (Matthew 26:31, 56).

In spite of His longstanding closeness to James and John, Jesus replied that what they had asked of Him was not possible. It was as though He said, "You will indeed suffer rejection, persecution, and death because of your relationship to Me, but My Father determines positions of leadership in His kingdom, not Me."

24 And when the ten heard it, they were moved with indignation against the two brethren.

Matthew doesn't say how, but the other 10 of Jesus' closest disciples learned what James and John had done. They were incensed and "insulted" (Gk. *aganakteo,* **ag-an-ak-TEH-o**) that the cousins had used their family connections in this way. They may have been angry with themselves for not taking the initiative, as James and John had done. In the past they had all discussed status within God's kingdom among themselves and with Jesus (Matthew 18:1–5; Mark 9:33–35).

Even though their beliefs and expectations for the Messiah were incorrect, James and John's request was not necessarily wrong. Since they had known Jesus so well and so long, they may well have assumed they were best fitted to be in charge.

All of the 12 understood that someone had to lead and take charge of securing God's purposes. The New Testament teaches that leadership is important. Paul referred to "he that ruleth" (Romans 12:8) as one of God's spiritual gifts, and a proper role in His church. First Timothy 3:1 describes the responsibilities of those who "desire the office of bishop."

25 But Jesus called them unto him, and said, Ye know that the princes of the Gentiles exercise dominion over them, and they that are great exercise authority upon them.

The emphasis here is between the top rulers, such as Caesars and kings, and the people under them, such as governors, who are given power to enforce the use of their rulers' powers. Both words begin with the addition of the Greek preposition *kata* (**kat-AH**), which indicates using downward force toward people under them.

This verse shows Jesus' patience in teaching. He does not criticize or condemn James and John's request. Why then did He mention the nature of Gentile authorities? It seems to be a warning against dealing harshly with one another. Paul followed his mention of spiritual oversight by saying, "Love each other with genuine affection, and take delight in honoring one another" (Romans 12:10, NLT).

26 But it shall not be so among you: but whosoever will be great among you, let him be your minister; 27 And whosoever will be chief among you, let him be your servant:

The fourth word in this sentence is *not* (Gk. *ouch,* **ookh**). Jesus was insisting that this should not be the type of leadership used among them. Paul would later support Jesus' instruction in Philippians 2:3–4 when he wrote, "Let nothing be done through strife or vainglory; but in lowliness of mind let each esteem other better than themselves. Look not every man on his own things, but every man also on the things of others." Peter specifically counseled congregational leaders against the authoritarian style of Gentiles, "Don't lord it over the people assigned to your care, but lead them by your own good example" (1 Peter 5:3, NLT).

Jesus did not downgrade a desire for leadership here. "Whosoever will be great" (v. 26) means "whoever wishes, wants or desires to be great." The same applies in verse 27. Jesus didn't call people who had no ambition. To the contrary, Jesus endorsed the ambition for leadership and excellence. Jesus presented them with a different way of achieving their desire for purpose and fulfillment, a way that is opposite from the way the world customarily pursues.

Several words indicate that difference. The first word to notice is "minister" (Gk. *diakonos*, **dee-AK-on-os**), which did not refer to a church official, although it is the same word that's translated as deacon later in the New Testament. Its basic meaning was a servant who was given menial tasks, such as rinsing dust off the feet of guests as they arrived. Jesus took that task at His final meal with these disciples as an example of the shape their leadership should take (John 13:3–5, 12–15). The second word is "servant" (Gk. *doulos*, **DOO-los**). Although the New Testament often uses the word to mean "servant," the most common meaning of the word is "slave," a person considered as property by another person. The two words make clear that serving is how Jesus defined greatness in God's kingdom. To become great or number one in God's estimate calls for putting the interests of others on an equal footing with, or ahead of, your own.

Both verses quote Jesus as speaking of "*your* minister" and "*your* servant." In English the word "your" can refer to a single person or a group. That's not the case in the Greek language. Both times Matthew uses the plural form. Then at the end of each description of service, Jesus said to provide the service "among you." Matthew uses the plural form of "you," meaning a group, not just one person. The group that "your" servant or slave applies to and the "you" both mean the church. Jesus was saying that His followers are to be a community of servants to each other and to the world that God made, and that Jesus loved enough to die for.

28 Even as the Son of man came not to be ministered unto, but to minister, and to give his life a ransom for many.

Jesus did not call as His closest disciples people who wanted little from life. Instead, He called those who wanted a lot from life. He promised them a lot from life, if they followed Him (John 10:10). His own life and death were offered as our best model for fulfillment through service (1 Corinthians 11:1). Jesus urged James, John, and the other 10 disciples to abandon the desire to be served and, as He did, trust in God's wise, fatherly care.

Our example, as we serve one another and the world that Jesus loves, is to be wholehearted in our service. Jesus described the service of His life and death as a "ransom" (Gk. *lutron*, **LOO-tron**), the payment required to buy a slave's freedom. Therefore, in the kingdom of God, greatness is not about who we can rule over or order about, but who can endure hard times and injustice, and still be a great witness for God.

Daily Bible Readings

M: The Humility of Christ
Philippians 2:1–11
T: The Greatest in the Kingdom
Matthew 18:1–5
W: Serving and Following Jesus
John 12:20–26
T: Serving Fearlessly
Matthew 10:24–33
F: Serving in God's Strength
1 Peter 4:7–11
S: The Last Will Be First
Matthew 20:1–16
S: The Serving Son of Man
Matthew 20:17–28

NOTES

TEACHING TIPS

October 5
Bible Study Guide 5

1. Words You Should Know

A. Pentecost (Acts 2:1) *pentekoste* (Gk.)—A Christian feast that marks the beginning of harvest activities. It began on the 50th day, following the Passover.

B. Holy Ghost (v. 4) *pneuma hagios* (Gk.)—The third person of the Holy Trinity.

C. Prophesy (v. 17) *propheteuo* (Gk.)—Revelatory speech from God, including the foretelling of future events; one of the gifts of the Spirit.

2. Teacher Preparation

Unifying Principle—United by the Spirit. The "new community"—the church—is made up of people of all nationalities, ethnic groups, and racial backgrounds. They are all who believe on the Lord Jesus Christ as their Saviour. Because of this diversity, it is the Holy Spirit who unites them around the agenda of God—building His kingdom and church.

A. Prayerfully, read Acts 2:1–17 and Ephesians 2:11–22.

B. Read some of the cross-references to make sure you have a clear understanding of the text.

C. Prayerfully read Bible Study Guide 5.

D. Consider how we can perpetuate a life led by the Holy Spirit.

E. Consider how a holier life better equips us for sharing the Gospel.

F. Complete lesson 5 in the *Precepts For Living® Personal Study Guide.*

3. Starting the Lesson

A. Pray with your students.

B. Ask each student to read a Focal Verse.

C. Briefly emphasize portions of key verses to spark the students' interest.

D. Review the Words You Should Know section.

4. Getting into the Lesson

A. Ask a volunteer to read In Focus.

B. Invite the students to share similar experiences.

C. Read and discuss The People, Places, and Times.

D. Discuss the Background section.

E. Ask the students if they believe that Pentecost was the beginning of the Christian church and to briefly explain their point of view.

F. Allow the students a few minutes to complete the Search the Scriptures questions.

G. Now discuss the Search the Scriptures questions and corresponding verses, and ask them to share their answers.

5. Relating the Lesson to Life

A. Allow the students a few minutes to complete the Discuss the Meaning questions.

B. Ask for volunteers to read a Discuss the Meaning question and a corresponding verse and to share their answers.

C. Now read and discuss the Lesson in Our Society section.

D. Ask the students to share their thoughts and insights on that section.

6. Arousing Action

A. Ask a volunteer to read the Make It Happen section.

B. Ask the students to think about the accomplishments of different activists and to consider what the consequences would have been had they done nothing at all.

C. Encourage the students to review the Focal Verses and key sections of the lesson throughout the week.

D. Encourage the students to write down any questions they might have.

E. Close with prayer.

Worship Guide

For the Superintendent or Teacher
Theme: Empowered To Be a Community
Theme Song: "Holy Spirit, Truth Divine"
Devotional Reading: Ephesians 2:11–22
Prayer

EMPOWERED TO BE A COMMUNITY

Bible Background • ACTS 2:1–47
Printed Text • ACTS 2:1–17 Devotional Reading • EPHESIANS 2:11–22

AIM for Change

By the end of the lesson, we will:
DISCUSS the events surrounding the coming of the Holy Spirit on the Day of Pentecost;
IMAGINE the effects that the coming of the Holy Spirit had on those who were gathered; and
SPREAD the Gospel through the power of the Holy Spirit.

Keep in Mind

"And they were all filled with the Holy Ghost, and began to speak with other tongues, as the Spirit gave them utterance" (Acts 2:4).

Focal Verses

KJV **Acts 2:1** And when the day of Pentecost was fully come, they were all with one accord in one place.

2 And suddenly there came a sound from heaven as of a rushing mighty wind, and it filled all the house where they were sitting.

3 And there appeared unto them cloven tongues like as of fire, and it sat upon each of them.

4 And they were all filled with the Holy Ghost, and began to speak with other tongues, as the Spirit gave them utterance.

5 And there were dwelling at Jerusalem Jews, devout men, out of every nation under heaven.

6 Now when this was noised abroad, the multitude came together, and were confounded, because that every man heard them speak in his own language.

7 And they were all amazed and marvelled, saying one to another, Behold, are not all these which speak Galilaeans?

8 And how hear we every man in our own tongue, wherein we were born?

9 Parthians, and Medes, and Elamites, and the dwellers in Mesopotamia, and in Judaea, and Cappadocia, in Pontus, and Asia,

10 Phrygia, and Pamphylia, in Egypt, and in the parts of Libya about Cyrene, and strangers of Rome, Jews and proselytes,

11 Cretes and Arabians, we do hear them speak in our tongues the wonderful works of God.

12 And they were all amazed, and were in doubt, saying one to another, What meaneth this?

NLT **Acts 2:1** On the day of Pentecost all the believers were meeting together in one place.

2 Suddenly, there was a sound from heaven like the roaring of a mighty windstorm, and it filled the house where they were sitting.

3 Then, what looked like flames or tongues of fire appeared and settled on each of them.

4 And everyone present was filled with the Holy Spirit and began speaking in other languages, as the Holy Spirit gave them this ability.

5 At that time there were devout Jews from every nation living in Jerusalem.

6 When they heard the loud noise, everyone came running, and they were bewildered to hear their own languages being spoken by the believers.

7 They were completely amazed. "How can this be?" they exclaimed. "These people are all from Galilee,

8 and yet we hear them speaking in our own native languages!

9 Here we are—Parthians, Medes, Elamites, people from Mesopotamia, Judea, Cappadocia, Pontus, the province of Asia,

10 Phrygia, Pamphylia, Egypt, and the areas of Libya around Cyrene, visitors from Rome

11 (both Jews and converts to Judaism), Cretans, and Arabs. And we all hear these people speaking in our own languages about the wonderful things God has done!"

12 They stood there amazed and perplexed. "What can this mean?" they asked each other.

13 Others mocking said, These men are full of new wine.

14 But Peter, standing up with the eleven, lifted up his voice, and said unto them, Ye men of Judaea, and all ye that dwell at Jerusalem, be this known unto you, and hearken to my words:

15 For these are not drunken, as ye suppose, seeing it is but the third hour of the day.

16 But this is that which was spoken by the prophet Joel;

17 And it shall come to pass in the last days, saith God, I will pour out of my Spirit upon all flesh: and your sons and your daughters shall prophesy, and your young men shall see visions, and your old men shall dream dreams:

13 But others in the crowd ridiculed them, saying, "They're just drunk, that's all!"

14 Then Peter stepped forward with the eleven other apostles and shouted to the crowd, "Listen carefully, all of you, fellow Jews and residents of Jerusalem! Make no mistake about this.

15 These people are not drunk, as some of you are assuming. Nine o'clock in the morning is much too early for that.

16 No, what you see was predicted long ago by the prophet Joel:

17 'In the last days,' God says, 'I will pour out my Spirit upon all people. Your sons and daughters will prophesy. Your young men will see visions, and your old men will dream dreams.

In Focus

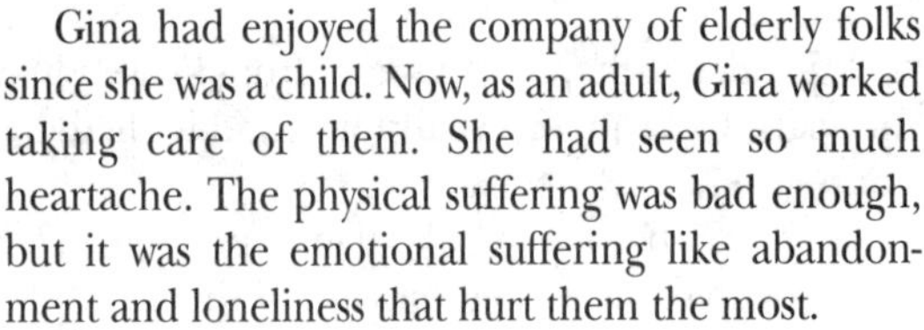

Gina had enjoyed the company of elderly folks since she was a child. Now, as an adult, Gina worked taking care of them. She had seen so much heartache. The physical suffering was bad enough, but it was the emotional suffering like abandonment and loneliness that hurt them the most.

In the past year, there had been several elderly folks in Gina's church who had succumbed to poor health and were no longer able to attend services. Gina genuinely missed seeing their faces in church on Sunday morning. She began to pray for the folks she missed, and the more she prayed, the greater her burden became. Her burden began to expand beyond the boundaries of her church and extended to the elderly folks who needed to hear the Gospel of Jesus Christ.

The Holy Spirit was at work in Gina's heart. Surely she wasn't the only one in her church who saw the need for outreach in this area. Gina spoke with her pastor, and with his prayer and support, she launched a visitation and outreach program for the elderly in her community. The outreach team found that some of the elderly folks wanted to hear nothing about a Saviour or the gift of salvation. They began to pray that the Holy Spirit would soften those hardened hearts and that He would empower them in their ministry. One by one, lost souls were led to Christ—not only the elderly, but their family members and caregivers as well.

Today's story illustrates how the empowerment of the Holy Spirit, at work in one faithful heart, can reach out to lost, hurting souls and unite a community.

The People, Places, and Times

Pentecost. The origin of Pentecost precedes the birth, death, and resurrection of Jesus Christ. It's one of the seven feasts of Jehovah and one of the three major Pilgrimage Feasts. Pentecost is celebrated 50 days after Passover, on the Sabbath, and was also called the "Feast of Harvest" and the "Feast of First Fruits." God presented these holy feasts to Moses and it was required that the Children of Israel observe them annually (Leviticus 23:5–21). Pentecost is symbolically related to the Jewish holiday Shavuot or the Feast of Weeks, which celebrates Moses receiving the Ten Commandments on Mount Sinai. In the New Testament, Pentecost takes on yet another meaning. Christians celebrate Pentecost as a commemoration of the descent of the Holy Spirit and the outpouring of the gifts of the Spirit. The parallel between Shavuot and Pentecost is interesting. Shavuot also represents the Jews being freed from slavery to Egypt, while Pentecost represents humankind being freed from slavery to sin.

Source:

Pfeiffer, Charles F., Howard F. Vos, John Rea, eds. *Wycliffe Bible Dictionary.* Peabody, Mass.: Hendrickson Publishers, Inc., 1998.

Background

The celebration of Pentecost, as depicted in the New Testament (Acts 2:1–21), was prophesied in the

Old Testament in Joel 2:28–32. Some believe that the Day of Pentecost marked the beginning of the Christian church. The celebration united Jews from many nations; 14 are mentioned. Filled with and empowered by the Holy Spirit, the apostles, who were Galileans, preached the Gospel to the Jewish nations in their native languages.

At-A-Glance

1. Manifestation of the Holy Spirit (Acts 2:1–3)
2. Filled with the Holy Spirit (vv. 4–5)
3. Empowered by the Holy Spirit (vv. 6–12)
4. Doubting the Holy Spirit (v. 13)
5. Prophesying by the Holy Spirit (vv. 14–17)

In Depth

1. Manifestation of the Holy Spirit (Acts 2:1–3)

There are two important factors that existed on the Day of Pentecost: (1) the apostles were all gathered together in one place, and (2) they were all of one accord. They knew beforehand what was going to happen and they were in complete agreement with it. Compliance with the Holy Spirit and with each other was necessary for the success of the events that were about to unfold.

Imagine you are part of a baseball team that's about to play the tie-breaker in the World Series. This is the moment you've worked for and anticipated. When you arrive at the stadium, you find that your team's pitcher and catcher didn't show up. The team players that are present are panicking and bickering among themselves. Can this team play a winning game? Are they going to win the support of their fans? No, of course not.

The apostles were also a team, and Jesus was their leader. It was vital that God's team be of one accord in body, mind, and spirit on this history-making Day of Pentecost. The manifestation of the Holy Spirit was not a quiet, natural affair. It was rather an audacious, supernatural event. The Holy Spirit arrived with a loud sound, like that of a strong gush of wind. It was a sound so loud that it filled the place where they were sitting. Its mighty force was heard and felt by everyone there. It's likely that the surrounding area also heard the arrival of the Holy Spirit. However, to signify that this was a supernatural event, the fixation was on this particular place.

There was also visible evidence of the presence of the Holy Spirit in the form of what appeared to be flames that lit upon all of them—not consuming flames, but gentle flames.

2. Filled with the Holy Spirit (vv. 4–5)

When a person receives the gift of salvation, they also receive the indwelling of the Holy Spirit (Romans 8:9). However, to have the indwelling of the Holy Spirit and to be filled with the Spirit are two different things. After Jesus' death and resurrection, the apostles received the Holy Spirit (John 20:22), but the filling or indwelling of the Spirit would take place on Pentecost. Upon being filled with the Spirit, the apostles spoke in tongues (Acts 2:4), and it caught the attention of a multitude of Jewish people from many lands who had come for the festival. It was especially strange to them because they all heard their own languages being spoken.

The Holy Spirit guides us in our spiritual walk (John 16:13). The more we seek and follow the direction of the Holy Spirit in our life, the more devout we become. The fullness of the Holy Spirit is necessary for us to reach the pinnacle of sanctification. The idea of being filled with the Spirit is one of allowing God to have control. It is as though instead of holding on to the steering wheel, you handed God the keys to the car and agreed to go along for the ride. To be filled with the Spirit requires us to be in submission to God so He can direct our lives and transform us.

3. Empowered by the Holy Spirit (vv. 6–12)

When the apostles were filled with the Holy Spirit, it was then that He empowered them with the gifts of the Spirit. Gifts of the Spirit should not be confused with the fruit of the Spirit. Gifts of the Spirit enable us to serve others. The fruit of the Spirit develops and grows throughout our life. It is measured by the quality of our Christian walk. The more we delve into God's Word and apply its teachings to our lives, the more spiritual growth we experience. The more we grow, the more evident the fruit of the Spirit becomes in our life. The fruit of the Spirit is love, joy, peace, longsuffering, gentleness, goodness, faith, meekness, and temperance (Galatians 5:22–23).

On the Day of Pentecost, the apostles were graced with the gift of speaking in tongues. In this event, these Galileans preached the Gospel of Jesus

Christ in the native languages of the Jewish people. This was a miracle, an unexplainable and unlikely event, that amazed and confused the crowd and led them to inquire about this strange occurrence. Perhaps we can compare it to the experience of hearing the performance of a musical savant. A savant may have the mentality of a young child, but he can play the piano like an accomplished composer. When we witness such a thing, we are amazed and confounded. It is simply beyond our human comprehension. It's a miracle. So it was on the Day of Pentecost.

4. Doubting the Holy Spirit (v. 13)

Have you ever heard the saying, "there's one in every crowd"? Well, on the Day of Pentecost, there was more than one. Much like today's hecklers, the doubters in the crowd mocked the whole affair. They sought to undermine the miracle they were witnessing and explain it away by claiming that the apostles were drunk. The mockers were probably as amazed and confused as everyone else. Possibly to hide their own lack of understanding, they tried to explain a supernatural event as a human occurrence.

5. Prophesying by the Holy Spirit (vv. 14–17)

Peter countered the mocking with great boldness. He declared in a very loud, clear voice that the hecklers were wrong. It was only nine o'clock in the morning and they were not drunk.

In today's society, an activist for any cause is driven by conviction. When one declares his convictions or his truth, he is not timid. What if Dr. Martin Luther King Jr. had been timid in his activism? If he were afraid to ruffle a few feathers, what would he have accomplished? In all likelihood, he wouldn't have accomplished much. Peter and his fellow apostles were also activists. They were activists for the cause of Christ, and they declared their convictions and the truth with a boldness that could not be ignored.

The apostles knew exactly what was taking place. They knew this Day of Pentecost was the fulfillment of Old Testament prophecy. Long before Jesus was even born, Joel had prophesied this day. The apostles were privy to that fact. Peter quoted the prophecy of Joel as written in Joel 2:28–32 to the crowd.

Search the Scriptures

1. What was the second miracle that indicated the presence of the Holy Spirit (Acts 2:3)?

2. When they heard the apostles speaking in different languages, what were the feelings of the Jewish people (vv. 6–7)?

3. In an attempt to explain away the miracle, what did the mockers in the crowds say about the apostles (v. 13)?

4. Who was the Old Testament prophet that prophesied this Day of Pentecost (v. 16)?

Discuss the Meaning

1. Why do you think the Holy Spirit made such a grand entrance (Acts 2:2–3)?

2. Do you think the miracle of tongues, on the Day of Pentecost, was in the apostles speaking in different languages or in the Jews hearing the Gospel in their own languages (vv. 4–6)?

3. Peter quoted Joel's Old Testament prophecy to the crowd (vv. 16–17). What impact do you think this had on the people present?

4. In today's In Focus story, we see how the Holy Spirit at work in one heart can reach out to many for the cause of Christ. Gina could have ministered to the elderly on her own, rather than share her burden with the pastor and other members of her church. How successful would the ministry have been had she chosen to go it alone? Which way would you have done it and why?

Lesson in Our Society

There are so many hurting people in today's world. Homelessness, poverty, illness, addiction, violence, injustice, and loneliness are just a few of the problems that plague our society. Even Christians can be overwhelmed when we look around and see all the suffering and all the need. It would be easier to stick our heads in the sand and let someone else deal with it, and many people do just that.

Recently, in the news, there was a story about a man who was beaten by a gang of kids because he witnessed them committing a crime. The man pulled in to a convenience store across the street. The gang of kids, probably fearful that he was going to call the police, beat him, causing serious injury. There were witnesses to this violent attack, but no one did a thing. No one intervened. No one even called the police. The man crawled into his car and drove home and was later admitted to the hospital with serious injuries. No arrests were made.

Remember that the Holy Spirit empowers us to come out of our comfort zones and to reach out and help others. If you had witnessed that crime, what would you have done? Would you have intervened or called the police? Why? Why not?

Make It Happen

When you look around your community, what do you see? Who is hurting, who needs help, and who needs to hear the Gospel of Jesus Christ? There are so many. Are you going to answer the Holy Spirit's call to action or are you going to leave the burden for someone else?

Follow the Spirit

What God wants me to do:

____

____

Remember Your Thoughts

Special insights I have learned:

____

____

More Light on the Text

Acts 2:1–17

1 And when the day of Pentecost was fully come, they were all with one accord in one place.

The Greek word for Pentecost is *pentekoste* (**pen-tay-kos-TAY**), and it literally means "50th." The Day of Pentecost was given this name because it fell on the 50th day after the Passover. This day was also referred to as the Feast of Weeks and as "the day of firstfruits" (Numbers 28:26). At the Passover feast, a sheaf from the coming grain harvest was presented, and then, at Pentecost, two leavened loaves of the harvest were presented to the Lord as the firstfruits of the completed grain harvest. In later Jewish tradition, it became associated with the giving of the law of Moses at Mount Sinai, 50 days after the exodus from Egypt.

The place where they were together is referred to as "the house" in verse 2. Perhaps this is the same place as that mentioned in 1:13, though there is no way of concluding that definitively.

2 And suddenly there came a sound from heaven as of a rushing mighty wind, and it filled all the house where they were sitting.

The Greek word for "mighty" is *biaios* (**BEE-ah-yos**) and means "violent, forcible." We are not left in doubt as to the origin of the mighty rushing wind of verse 2. It is from heaven. The Greek word for "wind" is *pnoe* (**pno-AY**) and is also translated as "breath." Thus, what took place that day was not from man; it was a supernatural and sovereign act of God. Wind is often used in the Bible in reference to the Holy Spirit, who, in light of Jesus' promise in 1:8, is represented here as the mighty rushing wind that fills the whole house. The Spirit had come indeed to grant Christ's people what He promised, power to be His witnesses in Judea (Judaea, KJV), Samaria, and to the uttermost parts of the earth.

The fact that He came on Pentecost gives further significance to the event. Since God already knows the full number of those who are His in Christ, these believers and those who will later believe as a result of their witness are appointed a kind of firstfruits of the full harvest of believers gathered to Christ.

3 And there appeared unto them cloven tongues like as of fire, and it sat upon each of them.

The coming of the Holy Spirit on these early Christians was both audible (the sound of a mighty rushing wind) and visible (appeared as divided tongues of fire). It must have been an amazing experience. The tongues rested on each one of them. No one who was in the house was excluded from this experience. As He is given to all who believe in the Lord Jesus Christ, the Spirit was given to them all.

4 And they were all filled with the Holy Ghost, and began to speak with other tongues, as the Spirit gave them utterance.

Filling with the Spirit, a repeated experience, is to be distinguished though not disconnected from the baptism of the Spirit, a one-time experience. In the Scriptures, when people were filled with the Spirit, they were enabled to carry out special ministry tasks from the Lord. Here, the filling with the Spirit led to the ability of those gathered in the house to speak with "other tongues." Verse 4 does not tell us the nature of these tongues, whether they were ecstatic or not. However, the context would suggest that they were known languages, since verse 6 reports that the people heard them speaking in their own languages. That the disciples were able to speak in these other languages was no less amazing, however, than if they had been speaking in a prayer language, since the implication of the verse is that

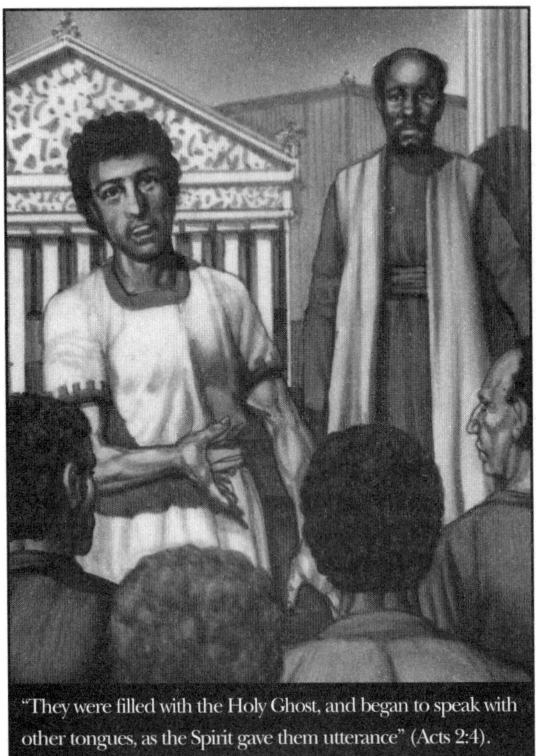
"They were filled with the Holy Ghost, and began to speak with other tongues, as the Spirit gave them utterance" (Acts 2:4).

the disciples did not have knowledge of these languages of themselves, but spoke in them by the power of the Holy Spirit.

5 And there were dwelling at Jerusalem Jews, devout men, out of every nation under heaven. 6 Now when this was noised abroad, the multitude came together, and were confounded, because that every man heard them speak in his own language. 7 And they were all amazed and marvelled, saying one to another, Behold, are not all these which speak Galilaeans? 8 And how hear we every man in our own tongue, wherein we were born? 9 Parthians, and Medes, and Elamites, and the dwellers in Mesopotamia, and in Judaea, and Cappadocia, in Pontus, and Asia, 10 Phrygia, and Pamphylia, in Egypt, and in the parts of Libya about Cyrene, and strangers of Rome, Jews and proselytes, 11 Cretes and Arabians, we do hear them speak in our tongues the wonderful works of God. 12 And they were all amazed, and were in doubt, saying one to another, What meaneth this?

These Jews dwelling at Jerusalem were devout men of every nation under heaven. In the Greek, "devout" is *eulabes* (**yoo-lab-ACE**) and means "reverencing God; pious; religious." Thus, many of the Jews present, during this event, were pilgrims from other nations who had come to Jerusalem to celebrate Pentecost. That they were from every nation under heaven is a way of saying that they were from many different places. Verses 9–10 gives us some of the names of those places. Also there were proselytes in the groups, Gentiles who had been converted to Judaism. Those who were gathered were amazed to hear these people speaking in their own languages, especially in light of the fact that the speakers were all Galileans and not from any of the lands whose languages they spoke. They heard these believers speaking the mighty acts of God, which no doubt included His former acts of old and His new ones accomplished in the person and work of Jesus Christ. Such an amazing miracle needed an explanation. Thus the amazed and perplexed bystanders ask, "What does this mean?"

13 Others mocking said, These men are full of new wine.

In the Greek, the word "mocking" is *chleuazo* (**khlyoo-AD-zo**) and means "to deride, jeer." No matter how amazing the miracle, there are always skeptics, always those who question the veracity of God's acts, always those who ridicule God's work. So it was in this case. There were those who jeered at or derided the event, attributing God's miracle to the effects of alcohol. They accused those whom God had filled with the Spirit as being filled with new wine.

14 But Peter, standing up with the eleven, lifted up his voice, and said unto them, Ye men of Judaea, and all ye that dwell at Jerusalem, be this known unto you, and hearken to my words: 15 For these are not drunken, as ye suppose, seeing it is but the third hour of the day.

Peter, who had been in many ways a leader and often the most outspoken of the Twelve, addressed the crowd who had gathered to witness this amazing miracle of God. It should be noted that even though Peter gave the address, the text says he stood with the 11. He spoke as representative of the Twelve. He spoke with their support.

Before he explained what the miracle was all about, he took time first to refute the ridiculous and absurd claim that their ability to speak in other languages was the result of drunkenness. He said, "Be this known unto you and hearken to my words." In the Greek, "hearken" is *enotizomai* (**en-o-TID-zom-ahee**), meaning "to receive into the ear, to give ear to, listen." He told them to listen to his words, because what they believed was not so. Those in the Upper Room were not drunk as some would claim. After all, Peter humorously suggested, "It is too early in the morning to get drunk."

16 But this is that which was spoken by the prophet Joel; 17 And it shall come to pass in the last days, saith God, I will pour out of my Spirit upon all flesh: and your sons and your daughters shall prophesy, and your young men shall see visions, and your old men shall dream dreams:

Peter attributed the event instead to the prophecy of Joel 2:28–32. There, Joel spoke of the coming "day of the Lord." Joel used the term "thereafter" to refer to the timeframe of his prophecy, while Luke used a more precise phrase: "in the last days." Joel noted that the sign of the day of the Lord would be the coming of the Spirit upon all flesh. In Greek, the word "flesh" is *sarx* (**sarx**) and means "the body, the body of a man."

The original context of Joel's prophecy called for repentance and prophesied the forgiveness that would come as a result. Peter saved this part for the conclusion of his sermon. Here the emphasis was upon the coming of the Spirit, which those gathered in the house had just experienced and witnessed. Yet, it is important to say that this pouring out of the Spirit at Pentecost was not the conclusion, but the beginning of God's promise. The pouring out of the Spirit on 120 Jews could not possibly fulfill a prophecy that has in view people from every tribe, tongue, and nation.

Daily Bible Readings

M: Fellowship with God and Jesus
1 John 1:1–4
T: Living in Hope
Acts 2:22–35
W: Living in Fellowship
Acts 2:37–47
T: Receive the Holy Spirit
John 20:19–23
F: One Body in Christ
Romans 12:3–8
S: The Coming of the Holy Spirit
Acts 2:1–13
S: Living in the Last Days
Acts 2:1–21

NOTES

TEACHING TIPS

October 12

Bible Study Guide 6

1. Words You Should Know

A. Grecians (Acts 6:1) *hellenistes* (Gk.)—One who imitates the manners and customs or the worship of the Greeks, and use the Greek tongue (language).

B. Of honest report (v. 3) *martureo* (Gk.)—Bear witness, testify, bear record, or have a good report.

C. Full of faith (v. 5) *pistis* (Gk.)—"Assurance," the conviction that God exists and is the Creator and Ruler of all things, the Provider and Bestower of eternal salvation, through Christ.

D. Libertines (v. 9) *libertinos* (Gk.)—A group of Jews who once lived in Rome, now liberated and allowed to return to Palestine.

2. Teacher Preparation

Unifying Principle—Discerning Gifts for Leadership. In the "new community"—the church—there are many jobs to be done (many responsibilities). For the church to carry out her role in a lost and dying world, there needs to be a division of labor. Therefore, the church has to learn what gifts each member possesses and use those gifts to God's glory.

A. Prayerfully read Acts 6 in the King James Version (KJV) and at least one other translation.

B. Read some of the cross-references to make sure you have a clear understanding of the text.

C. Prayerfully read Bible Study Guide 6.

D. Consider the dynamics of the church and how, through the delegation of duties, the church runs more smoothly.

E. Complete lesson 6 in the *Precepts For Living® Personal Study Guide.*

3. Starting the Lesson

A. Pray with your students.

B. Have volunteers read the Focal Verses.

C. Briefly emphasize portions of key verses to spark your students' interest.

D. Review the Words You Should Know section.

4. Getting into the Lesson

A. Ask a volunteer to read the In Focus section.

B. Invite the students to share similar stories.

C. Ask a volunteer to read The People, Places, and Times.

D. Read and discuss the Background section.

E. Ask the students if they think the apostles made a wise decision in choosing seven Hellenists or if they think the outcome would have been different had they chosen both Hellenists and Hebrews to oversee the food distribution.

F. Allow the students a few minutes to complete the Search the Scriptures questions. Discuss.

5. Relating the Lesson to Life

A. Allow the students a few minutes to complete the Discuss the Meaning questions.

B. Read and discuss the Discuss the Meaning questions and corresponding verses.

C. Then read and discuss the Lesson in Our Society section.

6. Arousing Action

A. Share insights on the Make It Happen section.

B. Then discuss a hypothetical situation of conflict within the church, and ask volunteers to share how they would solve the problem fairly.

C. Encourage the students to review the Focal Verses and key sections of the lesson throughout the week.

D. Also encourage the students to write down any questions they might have.

E. Close with prayer.

Worship Guide

For the Superintendent or Teacher
Theme: Expansion of the Community
Theme Song: "Tell It to Jesus"
Devotional Reading: Acts 1:3–11
Prayer

EXPANSION OF THE COMMUNITY

Bible Background • ACTS 6:1–15; 8:1–8
Printed Text • ACTS 6:1–5, 8–15 Devotional Reading • ACTS 1:3–11

AIM for Change

By the end of the lesson, we will:
INVESTIGATE the cause of the Hellenists' complaint regarding the neglect of their widows;
REFLECT on the rationale and motive used by the Twelve to have the community of disciples address the issue; and
DEVELOP tools for defusing potentially divisive conflict within the church.

Keep in Mind

"The word of God increased; and the number of the disciples multiplied in Jerusalem greatly" (from Acts 6:7).

Focal Verses

KJV **Acts 6:1** And in those days, when the number of the disciples was multiplied, there arose a murmuring of the Grecians against the Hebrews, because their widows were neglected in the daily ministration.

2 Then the twelve called the multitude of the disciples unto them, and said, It is not reason that we should leave the word of God, and serve tables.

3 Wherefore, brethren, look ye out among you seven men of honest report, full of the Holy Ghost and wisdom, whom we may appoint over this business.

4 But we will give ourselves continually to prayer, and to the ministry of the word.

5 And the saying pleased the whole multitude: and they chose Stephen, a man full of faith and of the Holy Ghost, and Philip, and Prochorus, and Nicanor, and Timon, and Parmenas, and Nicolas a proselyte of Antioch:

6:8 And Stephen, full of faith and power, did great wonders and miracles among the people.

9 Then there arose certain of the synagogue, which is called the synagogue of the Libertines, and Cyrenians, and Alexandrians, and of them of Cilicia and of Asia, disputing with Stephen.

10 And they were not able to resist the wisdom and the spirit by which he spake.

11 Then they suborned men, which said, We have heard him speak blasphemous words against Moses, and against God.

12 And they stirred up the people, and the elders, and the scribes, and came upon him, and caught him, and brought him to the council,

NLT **Acts 6:1** But as the believers rapidly multiplied, there were rumblings of discontent. The Greek-speaking believers complained about the Hebrew-speaking believers, saying that their widows were being discriminated against in the daily distribution of food.

OCT 12th

2 So the Twelve called a meeting of all the believers. They said, "We apostles should spend our time teaching the word of God, not running a food program.

3 And so, brothers, select seven men who are well respected and are full of the Spirit and wisdom. We will give them this responsibility.

4 Then we apostles can spend our time in prayer and teaching the word."

5 Everyone liked this idea, and they chose the following: Stephen (a man full of faith and the Holy Spirit), Philip, Procorus, Nicanor, Timon, Parmenas, and Nicolas of Antioch (an earlier convert to the Jewish faith).

6:8 Stephen, a man full of God's grace and power, performed amazing miracles and signs among the people.

9 But one day some men from the Synagogue of Freed Slaves, as it was called, started to debate with him. They were Jews from Cyrene, Alexandria, Cilicia, and the province of Asia.

10 None of them could stand against the wisdom and the Spirit with which Stephen spoke.

11 So they persuaded some men to lie about Stephen, saying, "We heard him blaspheme Moses, and even God."

13 And set up false witnesses, which said, This man ceaseth not to speak blasphemous words against this holy place, and the law:

14 For we have heard him say, that this Jesus of Nazareth shall destroy this place, and shall change the customs which Moses delivered us.

15 And all that sat in the council, looking stedfastly on him, saw his face as it had been the face of an angel.

12 This roused the people, the elders, and the teachers of religious law. So they arrested Stephen and brought him before the high council.

13 The lying witnesses said, "This man is always speaking against the holy Temple and against the law of Moses.

14 We have heard him say that this Jesus of Nazareth will destroy the Temple and change the customs Moses handed down to us."

15 At this point everyone in the high council stared at Stephen, because his face became as bright as an angel's.

In Focus

RISE AND SHINE!
Rise and shine, O Christian!
The world is dark with pain,
Shine the light of God's love,
Bless in this storm of rain.
Rise and shine, O Christian!
Let others see Jesus in you!
People are crying all around,
They need a life brand new.
Rise and shine, O Christian!
Come now into the fray,
God wants to use you,
To show someone the way!
—Evangeline Carey

In today's study, we find that God needs His family to work together in His vineyard—to be merciful and compassionate toward each other as they carry out the Great Commission, bringing lost souls to Christ. The world should know the church not only because of their love for these lost souls, but also because of their love for each other.

The People, Places, and Times

Hellenists. The Hellenists, also called Grecians, were Jews who spoke the Greek language and followed Greek customs but were not of Greek ancestry. They were not from Judea, but probably came to attend the festivals. Some of the Hellenists were from African cities: Cyrene, Alexandria, and Cilicia, "the area of Southeast Asia Minor between Pamphylia on the West, the Amanus Mountains on the East, Lycaonia and Cappadocia on the North, and the Mediterranean on the South" (Pfeiffer, Vos, and Rea 1998).

Hebrews. Hebrews were native Jews who spoke the Hebrew language of the Old Testament. These Jews were proud that they dwelt in the land promised to their forefathers. They also lived near the temple and regularly took part in the ceremonies and rituals. It probably made them feel dignified and a step above the Hellenists.

Sources:

Barnes, Albert. *Barnes' Notes On The New Testament.* WORDsearch Corp. 2004.

Pfeiffer, Charles F., Howard F. Vos, John Rea, eds. *Wycliffe Bible Dictionary.* Peabody, Mass.: Hendrickson Publishers, Inc., 1998.

Background

During this time, the church had experienced a growth spurt. The Jerusalem Chruch had a mixture of Christians from different countries, of different classes, and converts from other religions (also called proselytes).

The Hebrews' feelings of superiority likely increased the feelings of unrest amongst the Hellenists. They were well aware of how the Hebrews felt, and knowing that, they expected to be treated unfairly. As a result, the Hellenists became suspicious. When they thought their widows were being treated unfairly, they voiced their grievances.

Sources:

Barnes, Albert. *Barnes' Notes on the New Testament.* Grand Rapids, Mich.: Kregel Classics, 1962.

Clark, Adam. *Adam Clark's Commentary on the New Testament.* Nashville, Tenn.: Nelson Reference, 1997.

At-A-Glance

1. The Challenge of Discrimination (Acts 6:1–5)
   A. The Problem (v. 1)
   B. The Solution (vv. 2–5)
2. The Challenge of False Accusations (6:8–15)

In Depth

1. The Challenge of Discrimination (Acts 6:1–5)

A. The Problem (Acts 6:1)

Undoubtedly, due to the converts to Christianity at Pentecost, the church had experienced notable growth. Also, the preaching of the Gospel seemed to prompt controversy, and that seemed to attract more people rather than turn them away. Previously, they were of one accord; now we find them knee-deep in discord. As a result of the growth, the church was both blessed and stressed. It's easier to keep harmony within a smaller group. However, when you mix ethnic groups and classes, it's a given that there will be differences of opinions and the possibility of the favoritism or neglect based on group identity. This is what happened here between the Hellenists, who were not natives of Jerusalem, and the Hebrews, who were.

Have you ever moved to a different city or state and become a new member in a church? On a Christian level, one would rightfully assume that a new church member would be welcomed with open arms into the local family of God. You would expect to be treated fairly and with the same respect as any other member. However, at an outreach meeting, you find that your suggestions are not appreciated and are met with negativity, even though you were involved with several outreach programs in your previous church. Some are bold enough to suggest that while they appreciate your interest, you are new to the community and the church, so you can't possibly know what would work. This is your first experience with discrimination, and you leave feeling hurt and defeated.

In the early church, caring for the widows among them was very important. There was a daily distribution of food, and the Hellenists believed that their widows were being slighted. They already felt inferior, and now they believed they were being discriminated against as well.

B. The Solution (vv. 2–5)

The apostles called a meeting to address the problem of discrimination against the Hellenist widows. Their duty was to pray and preach the Gospel, and they couldn't justify neglecting that duty in order to handle the matter at hand. Did they think the job of distributing food was beneath them? No, it was a matter of priorities in ministry.

Do we expect our pastor to organize our church suppers? Not usually, unless maybe he's a chef and a pastor. We all have different duties within the church according to our spiritual gifts or the fruits of the Spirit.

Suppose you're building your dream house. Would you have the plumber run the wiring and hook up the electricity? No, of course not. Although your new home will need plumbing and electricity, the jobs are delegated to the ones who are trained to do that particular type of work. It's the same within the church. Jobs should be delegated according to God-given gifts (1 Corinthians 12:8–10), fruits of the Spirit (Galatians 5:22–23), and talents. This was also the point the apostles were trying to make.

As sanctioned by the apostles, seven men were to be appointed by the church. Perhaps with the church responsible for appointing these men, the apostles could not be accused of partiality or improper use of the church alms (money). It was further decided that the seven men to be chosen should have certain qualities of Christian character. They were to be honest, wise, and live a Spirit-led life. Honesty was obviously an important quality. Wisdom likely meant both fair and frugal handling of money. Men who lived by the Spirit would be respected, trusted, and less likely to make wrong decisions that would lead to even more dissension in the church.

Even in secular, charitable organizations, people in any position should be chosen based on such qualities. No organization should appoint a treasurer who is a known gambler or thief. Often, when someone is appointed to a position such as this and it's found later that the appointed person has a history of dishonest or questionable activities, they are quickly relieved of their position.

The men who were appointed by the church were Stephen, Philip, Prochorus, Nicanor, Timon, Parmenas, and Nicolas. All of these men were Hellenist Jews. The Hellenists were the ones who felt their widows were being discriminated against.

The appointing of representatives from the same group was likely to silence the complaints.

2. The Challenge of False Accusations (6:8–15)

Once again, even after the appointment of the seven, the arguing commenced. A group of men consisting of Libertines, Cyrenians, Alexandrians, and men from Cilicia and Asia began arguing with Stephen. Rumor or gossip had it that Stephen was saying things that were disrespectful toward Moses and God. What probably started as an inquiry into the gossip escalated into a more heated argument. Rumors have a habit of causing problems such as this.

Have you ever played the gossip game? You whisper something in a person's ear and that person whispers into the next person's ear and around the room it goes. By the time it gets to the last person, what was originally said has changed into something completely different. In a game the results can be funny, but in real life the results of rumors or gossip can cause great harm. Person by person, the truth is stretched and twisted in its retelling until it's as far from the truth as you can get. Unfortunately, the results can ruin a person's formerly unblemished character.

The men causing all the rumors didn't have a leg to stand on against Stephen's impeccable Christian character and Spirit-led life, so they took it a step further.

Stephen's accusers stirred up people against him and had him brought before the council of Jewish elders. In addition, they convinced witnesses to pervert the truth of Stephen's doctrines so that he could be falsely accused of blasphemy. The accusers said that they heard Stephen say Jesus of Nazareth would destroy them and change their practices.

In those days, Moses and his laws were highly respected. Any suggestion of changing them would be considered blasphemy. The Jews considered God as giver of the laws (God gave the laws to Moses); therefore, anyone changing or altering the laws for any reason would be considered blasphemous. While Jesus taught that the Gentiles would destroy that place, there was no evidence of Stephen ever having said that.

In verse 15, we read that the council was focused on Stephen and that his face was like an angel's. Similarly, in Exodus 34:29–30 we read that Moses' face shone when he came down from Mount Sinai and that Aaron and the others were afraid to go near him. Why was Stephen's face shining? Stephen's face shone with the confidence of one found to be faithful to Christ.

Sources:

Barnes, Albert. *Barnes' Notes on the New Testament.* Grand Rapids, Mich.: Kregel Classics, 1962.

Clark, Adam. *Adam Clark's Commentary on the New Testament.* Nashville, Tenn.: Nelson Reference, 1997.

Henry, Matthew. *Commentary on the Whole Bible, Complete and Unabridged.* Peabody, Mass.: Hendrickson Publishers, 1991.

Search the Scriptures

1. What was the apostles' reason for not personally handling the distribution of food (Acts 6:2)?
2. What were the criteria for choosing the first deacons (Acts 6:3)?
3. Of the seven men chosen, which one was the proselyte (v. 5)?
4. What was Stephen accused of (v. 11)?
5. What did the witnesses accuse Stephen of saying (vv. 13–14)?

Discuss the Meaning

1. What are the negative results of discrimination?
2. What is the importance of strong Christian character?
3. Why do people tell lies about their fellow man?

Lesson in Our Society

In today's fast-paced society, people are always searching for new ways to handle the stress in their lives. Bookstores are filled with books on the subject, popular psychologists offer endless advice and still we are searching for the one method that really works. Even in the secular world, most experts agree that the key to handling the everyday stresses of life is inner peace. Although they might be on the right track, inner peace does not come from daily meditation or yoga. The search for a solution continues.

We should remember, however, that the only way we can gain inner peace and handle stress successfully is by living a Spirit-led life in Christ. Other things may work for a while, but they are doomed to fail. Because people bring their stresses with them to the worship services, believers have to be mindful of others' pain and reach out and touch them. We have to look past their faults and see their needs. We should not be so quick to gossip and talk about someone because they are withdrawn or isolating themselves from the church community. Instead, try to be an encourager in Christ.

Make It Happen

The apostles chose seven men to handle the daily food distribution. Today's churches also delegate responsibilities. Many churches ask for volunteers to help in different areas. Consider the gifts God has given you and what fruit of the Spirit He has given you. Is there an area in your church where you can volunteer to serve?

Follow the Spirit

What God wants me to do:

____

____

Remember Your Thoughts

Special insights I have learned:

____

____

More Light on the Text

Acts 6:1–5, 8–15

1 And in those days, when the number of the disciples was multiplied, there arose a murmuring of the Grecians against the Hebrews, because their widows were neglected in the daily ministration.

Just after Jesus' resurrection, the early church experienced tremendous growth. In Acts 2, we read of more than 3,000 who joined the church. A few chapters later, 5,000 men, not including women and children, were added to the church. A rough estimate would put the Jerusalem church somewhere in the neighborhood of about 20,000 believers. It was a growing church, and with growth came challenges.

A complaint arose between the Hellenists and the Hebrews. Both groups were Jewish. The Hellenists were most likely Jews from surrounding nations whose native language was Greek while the Hebrews were from Palestine and spoke Aramaic. Thus the Hellenists likely attended synagogues where Greek was spoken and the Septuagint (Greek Translation of the Old Testament Scriptures) was used, while the Hebrews attended synagogues where Aramaic was spoken and the original Hebrew Scriptures were used. The Hellenists, though remaining loyal to Judaism, had absorbed some of Greek culture. This led to some cultural and social differences between the Hellenists and the Hebrews.

The dispute between the two groups was practical and not theological. It was over daily ministration. In the Greek, "ministration" (*diakonia,* **dee-ak-on-EE-ah**) means "ministry, service, ministering, especially of those who execute the commands of others."

In Acts 4, we are told about a common fund created by the growing community into which the wealthier members of the community placed the proceeds of recent property sales. The fund was used to support the needs of the poorer members of the community. The dispute in chapter 6 centers on the Hellenists' complaint that the funds were not being distributed properly. They felt that their widows were at a disadvantage. Given the division that already existed between the two groups, failure to resolve this conflict could have divided the church.

2 Then the twelve called the multitude of the disciples unto them, and said, It is not reason that we should leave the word of God, and serve tables. 3 Wherefore, brethren, look ye out among you seven men of honest report, full of the Holy Ghost and wisdom, whom we may appoint over this business. 4 But we will give ourselves continually to prayer, and to the ministry of the word.

The disciples decided that it was time for a congregational business meeting. They gathered the full number of the disciples, the whole church, and gave their decision on the resolution of the issue. They decided that it was not their responsibility to "wait tables" (Gk. *diakoneo trapeza,* **dee-ak-on-EH-o TRAP-ed-zah**). The word for tables has a double meaning. It is a word that can be used for the tables of money changers or the table used to serve meals. It was not theirs to manage finances and serve meals. Their God-given responsibility was the ministry of the Word and prayer.

In this particular passage, "to the ministry" in the Greek is also *diakonia,* but this time it refers to those who by the command of God proclaim and promote religion among men. Therefore, they charged the community to select from among them seven men and not just any seven. The men to be chosen had to possess good character. In the Greek "of honest report" is *martureo* (**mar-too-REH-o**) and means "to bear witness, testify, and bear record." They had to be filled with God's Spirit. In the Greek, "of the holy" is *hagios* (**HAG-ee-os**) and means "a saint."

"The word of God increased; and the number of the disciples multiplied in Jerusalem greatly" (from Acts 6:7).

"Ghost" is *pneuma* (**PNYOO-mah**) and refers to the Spirit (of God). They also had to possess godly wisdom. "Wisdom" in the Greek is *sophia* (**sof-EE-ah**) and means that one is "broad and full of intelligence; full of the knowledge of very diverse matters."

It is lamentable that often in the church, these important qualities are overlooked, and people are chosen to serve for all sorts of reasons, other than those given here in Acts 6.

5 And the saying pleased the whole multitude: and they chose Stephen, a man full of faith and of the Holy Ghost, and Philip, and Prochorus, and Nicanor, and Timon, and Parmenas, and Nicolas a proselyte of Antioch:

The apostles' decision was embraced by the community. They agreed with the decision and began to select men who fit the requirements that the disciples had set forth. The first was Stephen, whom the text tells us was full of faith and the Holy Spirit. He would demonstrate that soon with his speech before the Sanhedrin. Nicolas, another one chosen to serve, was a proselyte. "*Proselyte*" in the Greek is *proselutos* (**pros-AY-loo-tos**) and means a newcomer, a stranger, alien, one who has come over from a Gentile religion to Judaism.

All of these men were likely Hellenists. The community decided that this was the best way to avoid further conflict. Thus they chose men who fit the requirements from among the group who had felt slighted. In so doing, they demonstrated their love for each other and avoided Satan's attempt to divide the community.

6:8 And Stephen, full of faith and power, did great wonders and miracles among the people.

Stephen, who was described in verse 5 as "full of faith and the Holy Ghost," is further described here as full of faith and power—attributes that flowed from the Holy Spirit within him. In the Greek, "power" is *dunamis* (**DOO-nam-is**) and means "mighty work, strength, miracles, virtue, ability, and inherent power." All these attributes enabled Stephen to minister effectively. Thus the text tells us that Stephen performed great signs and wonders among the people. We are not told what signs and wonders he performed, but we can assume that these signs and wonders included acts of healing.

9 Then there arose certain of the synagogue, which is called the synagogue of the Libertines, and Cyrenians, and Alexandrians, and of them of Cilicia and of Asia, disputing with Stephen. 10 And they were not able to resist the wisdom and the spirit by which he spake.

Stephen's ability was not limited, however, to the performing of signs and wonders but included the ability to expound the Scriptures in light of the truth of the Gospel. This brought him into conflict with the members of what appear to be either three different synagogues or a synagogue that included worshipers from Cyrene, Alexandria, Cilicia, and Asia (the Greek text here is unclear). The latter seems more likely since the dispute arose over Stephen's teaching, which would more likely have taken place in the context of the synagogue.

Synagogues were meeting places where Jews and Jewish converts met for worship and the exposition of the Scriptures. In the early life of the church, before the days of intense persecution, Christians did not avoid the temple courts or the synagogue. The members of this particular synagogue debated with Stephen but were unable to overcome his teaching because of his great wisdom and spirit. They found themselves on the losing end of this debate.

11 Then they suborned men, which said, We have heard him speak blasphemous words against Moses, and against God.

These men, frustrated because they couldn't silence Stephen, decided to call false witnesses against Stephen. In the Greek, the word for "suborned" is *hupoballo* (**hoop-ob-AL-lo**) and means "to suggest to the mind, to instruct privately, instigate, to bribe or induce (someone) unlawfully or secretly to perform some misdeed or commit a crime, or to induce (a person, especially a witness) to give false testimony." In other words, they found men who were willing to lie about Stephen—to say that he had spoken against Moses and God. They knew that such a claim would incite the anger of the Jewish leaders, and if they couldn't defeat Stephen with their arguments, they would do it with their deceit.

12 And they stirred up the people, and the elders, and the scribes, and came upon him, and caught him, and brought him to the council, 13 And set up false witnesses, which said, This man ceaseth not to speak blasphemous words against this holy place, and the law: 14 For we have heard him say, that this Jesus of Nazareth shall destroy this place, and shall change the customs which Moses delivered us.

So they stirred up the entire Jewish community and arrested Stephen and brought him before the Sanhedrin. And when they produced their false witnesses they added a charge against Stephen claiming that he had spoken blasphemous words. In Greek, "blasphemous" is *blasphemos* (**BLAS-fay-mos**) and means "speaking evil, slanderous, reproachful, railing, abusive things." They accused him of speaking out against the temple and the law. They claimed that Stephen taught that Jesus would destroy the temple and change the customs of Moses. The truth is that Jesus had indeed prophesied an end to the temple order. He taught that He, Himself, was the fulfillment of all that the temple promised. Stephen, thus, had taught what Jesus Himself had taught and was facing the same kind of persecution that his Lord had endured.

15 And all that sat in the council, looking stedfastly on him, saw his face as it had been the face of an angel.

It is not surprising that a man who was described as full of faith, the Holy Spirit, grace, and power should radiate on the exterior what was true on the interior. He was radiating the glory of God. The fact that the people saw this glory and ignored it is an indictment of their hardened hearts. Even gazing at God's glory, they were not deterred from their evil intentions.

Daily Bible Readings

M: No Other Name
Acts 4:1–12
T: What We Have Seen and Heard
Acts 4:13–22
W: Speaking the Word Boldly
Acts 4:23–31
T: Breaking Community Trust
Acts 5:1–11
F: Obeying God
Acts 5:27–39
S: Scattered but Proclaiming
Acts 8:1–8
S: Full of the Spirit and Wisdom
Acts 6:1–15

NOTES

TEACHING TIPS

October 19

Bible Study Guide 7

1. Words You Should Know

A. Damascus (Acts 9:2) *damaskos* (Gk.)—One of the most ancient and most important cities of Syria, lying in almost lovely and fertile plain at the eastern base of the Antilibanus.

B. Synagogues (v. 2) *sunagoge* (Gk.)—A Jewish institution for reading and teaching the Scriptures; places where these activities took place; by analogy, a Christian church.

C. Persecutest (v. 4) *dioko* (Gk.)—To make to run or flee; put to flight; drive away.

2. Teacher Preparation

Unifying Principle—New Vision. The "new community," the church, is to be tuned into God's vision, His plan for His kingdom, where He will reign forever and ever. We tune in by studying and meditating on His Holy Word and getting involved in the Great Commission—helping to win lost souls to Christ.

A. Prayerfully read Acts 9 in the King James Version (KJV) and at least one other translation.

B. Read some of the cross-references to make sure you have a clear understanding of the text.

C. Prayerfully read Bible Study Guide 7.

D. Think about different vices people have. Then consider how certain vices might harm our Christian testimony.

E. Complete lesson 7 in the *Precepts For Living*® *Personal Study Guide.*

3. Starting the Lesson

A. Pray with your students.

B. Ask volunteers to read the Focal Verses.

C. Briefly emphasize portions of key verses to spark the students' interest.

4. Getting into the Lesson

A. Ask a volunteer to read the In Focus section.

B. Invite the students to share similar stories of transformation in their lives.

C. Ask a student to read The People, Places, and Times and Background sections.

D. Allow the students a few minutes to complete the Search the Scriptures questions. Discuss.

5. Relating the Lesson to Life

A. Allow the students a few minutes to complete the Discuss the Meaning questions. Discuss.

B. Have a volunteer read the Lesson in Our Society section. Discuss.

6. Arousing Action

A. Have a volunteer read the Make It Happen section.

B. Encourage the students to review the Focal Verses and key sections of the lesson throughout the week.

C. Encourage the students to write down any questions they might have.

D. End the class in prayer for one another.

Worship Guide

For the Superintendent or Teacher
Theme: Transformed to Witness to the Community
Theme Song: "Make Me A Blessing"
Devotional Reading: Galatians 1:11–24
Prayer

TRANSFORMED TO WITNESS TO THE COMMUNITY

Bible Background • ACTS 9:1–31
Printed Text • ACTS 9:1–11, 16–19 Devotional Reading • GALATIANS 1:11–24

AIM for Change

By the end of the lesson, we will:
REVIEW the story of Saul's dramatic conversion experience;
REFLECT on how Christ's confrontation with Saul enabled Saul to become a witness in the community; and
DEVELOP a strategy for witnessing to others about Christ.

Keep in Mind

"The Lord, even Jesus, that appeared unto thee in the way as thou camest, hath sent me, that thou mightest receive thy sight, and be filled with the Holy Ghost" (from Acts 9:17).

Focal Verses

KJV **Acts 9:1** And Saul, yet breathing out threatenings and slaughter against the disciples of the Lord, went unto the high priest,

2 And desired of him letters to Damascus to the synagogues, that if he found any of this way, whether they were men or women, he might bring them bound unto Jerusalem.

3 And as he journeyed, he came near Damascus: and suddenly there shined round about him a light from heaven:

4 And he fell to the earth, and heard a voice saying unto him, Saul, Saul, why persecutest thou me?

5 And he said, Who art thou, Lord? And the Lord said, I am Jesus whom thou persecutest: it is hard for thee to kick against the pricks.

6 And he trembling and astonished said, Lord, what wilt thou have me to do? And the Lord said unto him, Arise, and go into the city, and it shall be told thee what thou must do.

7 And the men which journeyed with him stood speechless, hearing a voice, but seeing no man.

8 And Saul arose from the earth; and when his eyes were opened, he saw no man: but they led him by the hand, and brought him into Damascus.

9 And he was three days without sight, and neither did eat nor drink.

10 And there was a certain disciple at Damascus, named Ananias; and to him said the Lord in a vision, Ananias. And he said, Behold, I am here, Lord.

11 And the Lord said unto him, Arise, and go into the street which is called Straight, and enquire

NLT **Acts 9:1** Meanwhile, Saul was uttering threats with every breath and was eager to kill the Lord's followers. So he went to the high priest.

2 He requested letters addressed to the synagogues in Damascus, asking for their cooperation in the arrest of any followers of the Way he found there. He wanted to bring them—both men and women—back to Jerusalem in chains.

OCT 19th

3 As he was approaching Damascus on this mission, a light from heaven suddenly shone down around him.

4 He fell to the ground and heard a voice saying to him, "Saul! Saul! Why are you persecuting me?"

5 "Who are you, lord?" Saul asked. And the voice replied, "I am Jesus, the one you are persecuting!

6 Now get up and go into the city, and you will be told what you must do."

7 The men with Saul stood speechless, for they heard the sound of someone's voice but saw no one!

8 Saul picked himself up off the ground, but when he opened his eyes he was blind. So his companions led him by the hand to Damascus.

9 He remained there blind for three days and did not eat or drink.

10 Now there was a believer in Damascus named Ananias. The Lord spoke to him in a vision, calling, "Ananias!" "Yes, Lord!" he replied.

11 The Lord said, "Go over to Straight Street, to the house of Judas. When you get there, ask for a man from Tarsus named Saul. He is praying to me right now.

in the house of Judas for one called Saul, of Tarsus: for, behold, he prayeth,

9:16 For I will shew him how great things he must suffer for my name's sake.

17 And Ananias went his way, and entered into the house; and putting his hands on him said, Brother Saul, the Lord, even Jesus, that appeared unto thee in the way as thou camest, hath sent me, that thou mightest receive thy sight, and be filled with the Holy Ghost.

18 And immediately there fell from his eyes as it had been scales: and he received sight forthwith, and arose, and was baptized.

19 And when he had received meat, he was strengthened. Then was Saul certain days with the disciples which were at Damascus.

9:16 And I will show him how much he must suffer for my name's sake."

17 So Ananias went and found Saul. He laid his hands on him and said, "Brother Saul, the Lord Jesus, who appeared to you on the road, has sent me so that you might regain your sight and be filled with the Holy Spirit."

18 Instantly something like scales fell from Saul's eyes, and he regained his sight. Then he got up and was baptized.

19 Afterward he ate some food and regained his strength. Saul stayed with the believers in Damascus for a few days.

In Focus 

I don't know what the big deal is, Dan thought to himself. *A lot of Christians smoke. Some even enjoy their beer. I'm not hurting anybody; besides, everybody needs a vice,* Dan reasoned.

Dan had been a Christian for 10 years, but he never saw any reason to quit smoking. Dan and his brother Rob, who was a pastor, had gotten into a bit of a disagreement. Rob had led Dan to the Lord, and since then, Rob had been after his brother to quit smoking. Dan was sick and tired of hearing it. He knew his brother was concerned for his health, but Dan figured that when his time was up, it was up, and his smoking wouldn't make a difference. Their dad had smoked from the time he was a teenager, and he lived to the ripe old age of 88.

Smoking probably wasn't very good for his Christian testimony, and Dan did feel a little guilty about that from time to time. Rob had told him once that if the world doesn't see any difference between a Christian's life and their own, then they don't see any need to become a Christian. Maybe Rob was right as far as that was concerned, but Dan still didn't feel like he needed to quit.

One morning when Dan was driving to work he was stopped at a red light. There were three or four bumper stickers on the car in front of him, but one really stuck out. It said, "I don't need a vice. I have Christ." Dan couldn't get the words out of his head. When he got home from work, Dan called his brother and told him about the bumper sticker. Dan apologized to Rob for being so stubborn and thanked him for caring about him.

Dan did quit smoking, but it was the hardest thing he'd ever done. One Sunday, he gave his testimony in church and explained how God gave him victory over smoking. At the end of the service, a man came forward to accept Christ. His name was Joe. He was dying from terminal lung cancer. Dan's testimony had touched his heart and made him see his need for Christ.

Is there a destructive behavior in your life that you need to change? Like Dan and Saul in today's lesson, God can transform you to be a positive witness for Him, and then you can be all that He is calling you to be.

The People, Places, and Times

Tarsus. Saul was from Tarsus, the capital of Cilicia. It was ruled by the Roman empire and was declared free by Antony, under the authority of Augustus in 42 B.C. Tarsus was located on a fertile plain, and the Cydnus River flowed through the city. The city flowed to a harbor called Rhegma, which was located about 10 miles from Tarsus and thereby well-known for its commerce. It was considered a great hub of learning for its Greek culture, philosophy, and literature.

Damascus. Damascus was the capital city of Syria. The population was believed to be around 100,000

people. Damascus was a fertile land in the midst of a plain. It was lush with cypress and palm trees. Although it was 50 miles from the sea, two rivers and several streams ran through the city. The two rivers, the Amara and Abara, met at a place called the "meeting of the waters," which was located five miles outside the city.

Sources:

Barnes, Albert. *Barnes' Notes on the New Testament.* Grand Rapids, Mich.: Kregel Classics, 1962.

Clark, Adam. *Adam Clark's Commentary on the New Testament.* Nashville, Tenn.: Nelson Reference, 1997.

Jamieson, Robert, et. al., *Jamieson, Fausset, and Brown's Commentary on the Whole Bible (1871).* Grand Rapids, Mich.: Zondervan, 1999.

Background

Both of Saul's parents were native Jews, thus he referred to himself as a "Hebrew of the Hebrews." He belonged to the tribe of Benjamin. Saul was an educated man. In the schools of Tarsus, he studied Greek poetry and philosophy. He later studied divinity and Jewish law at the university in Jerusalem where his tutor was a Pharisee named Gamaliel. As was common in that day, Saul also learned a trade; in his case it was tentmaking. This was how he earned his living. He became a rabbi when he was 30 years old and was then probably in a position of power. It's possible that he was a member of the Sanhedrin at the time Stephen was stoned. Saul hated Christians with a passion. He was active in persecuting Christians and he also played an important role in Stephen's martyrdom.

Sources:

Barnes, Albert. *Barnes' Notes on the New Testament.* Grand Rapids, Mich.: Kregel Classics, 1962.

Clark, Adam. *Adam Clark's Commentary on the New Testament.* Nashville, Tenn.: Nelson Reference, 1997.

At-A-Glance

1. Saul Embarks on a Mission to Damascus (Acts 9:1–2)
2. Saul Encounters Christ (vv. 3–7)
3. Saul Obeys Christ (vv. 8–9)
4. Saul Meets Ananias (vv. 10–11, 16)
5. Saul Receives the Holy Spirit (v. 17)
6. Saul Receives His Sight and Is Baptized (vv. 18–19)

In Depth

1. Saul Embarks on a Mission to Damascus (Acts 9:1–2)

Damascus seemed a likely place to find a gathering of Christians. Many Christians had fled to that location after Stephen's death. The Christians in Damascus were said to feel safe there, but Saul knew that they brought with them the Gospel of Jesus Christ, and that made him seethe with anger. Because Saul was an educated and moral Jewish man committed to his religion and customs, he hated Christians and took full advantage of every opportunity to persecute them—both emotionally and physically.

The Sanhedrin maintained religious influence over the Jews in every country. Saul was able to stir up the high priest and the Sanhedrin against the Christians. He asked them to provide letters to the synagogues in Damascus, requesting that they be accommodating in the arrest of believers there. The Sanhedrin's support of Saul motivated him even more to execute this mission of vengeance.

People are often driven by emotions. This was the case with Saul. The righteous anger that boiled within him propelled him to action. He had no desire to contain it because he felt that he was doing what was right—getting rid of believers in Christ. People overcome by strong emotions have the ability to inspire the same in others. Simply put, emotions are contagious and so was Saul's anger.

2. Saul Encounters Christ (vv. 3–7)

God, the master of all things, is also the master of getting people's attention. Saul was traveling to Damascus, when suddenly an extremely bright flash of light encircled him. It likely startled and frightened him. Whatever Saul's emotions were at the moment, he was so overpowered by the light that he fell to the ground. Paul (Saul) himself says in Romans 10:17, "faith cometh by hearing" and that day on the Damascus road, Saul heard the voice of Christ. His fellow travelers heard a voice, but there was no indication that they understood what was being said (v. 7). Saul, on the other hand, heard Jesus speaking to him quite distinctly. Jesus asked Saul why he was persecuting Him and when Saul asked who He was, Jesus told him, "I am Jesus...."

Jesus doesn't usually reveal Himself to us in such dramatic ways today. However, perhaps some of us wish He would. It would certainly make it easier for us to know His bidding, if He just appeared and told us. That's one of the reasons it's so important to walk in the Spirit. The better we know Him, the easier it will be for us to recognize Him when He speaks to us. Have you ever thought you were really doing what God wanted you to do and it turned out you were wrong? Sometimes our own logic and reasoning can fool us into thinking we're doing what God wants, when in fact it's not. The more we study God's Word, the more we learn what pleases God.

Saul had no doubts in his mind. God succeeded in getting Saul's undivided attention and there was no mistaking it.

3. Saul Obeys Christ (vv. 8–9)

Physically spent from the supernatural ordeal, Saul picked himself up off the ground. When he opened his eyes, he discovered that he was blind. Temporary blindness, due to exposure to an extreme light, is not uncommon. However, one could rightly assume that there was a more significant purpose for Saul's blindness. Let's consider. First, Jesus wanted to leave a lasting impression on Saul. Many times when we are under the gun, we are inclined to make life-changing decisions and promises. We often react to fear impulsively and when the fear subsides, we quickly return to our old selves. Whatever promises or deals we made with God don't stick because we weren't sincere. We were merely reacting to our fear, rather than admitting that we were wrong or in need of some changes in our lives.

Saul was so infected with anger and hate toward Christians that perhaps without his blindness his encounter with Christ might not have had a lasting effect. Sightless, Saul had nothing to distract him. He was able to reflect on his life, admit his sin, and fully accept Jesus Christ. It's true that he immediately responded by asking Jesus what he wanted to do. The question is, would Saul have followed through and would he have truly been converted if he had not been stricken with blindness? Another possibility is that Saul needed to be completely humbled before he could be an effective minister of the Gospel. In order to fully appreciate the gift of salvation, he needed to realize the depth of his sin, he needed to experience guilt, and he needed to realize the extent of his unworthiness.

Saul was so overcome that he didn't eat or drink for the three days he was blind. It's as though he was experiencing a total cleansing of spirit, mind, and body.

4. Saul Meets Ananias (vv. 10–11, 16)

A devout follower of Christ named Ananias lived in the city of Damascus. The Jews, who lived there, thought very highly of him. In a vision, God spoke to Ananias and instructed him to go to the house of Judas on Straight Street and ask for Saul of Tarsus. When God instructed Ananias to go to Saul, He said, "for, behold, he prayeth." Indeed, Saul was praying, and although we don't know exactly what his prayer was, we know that Ananias was the answer.

Have you ever needed someone to care for you? Saul had just been through a traumatic experience that had affected every part of his being. He needed someone to care for him, while he gained his strength and composure. When a baby is born, he needs someone to take care of him and see that his needs are met while he grows. If the baby is neglected, he won't grow and thrive. Saul, in a spiritual sense, had experienced rebirth. He was a brand-new babe in Christ, and he needed to be nurtured. Saul needed the guidance of someone mature in the faith. Ananias was that person, and he obeyed God. God was preparing the man, who breathed hate for Christians, for great service. Saul, who caused so much suffering for followers of Christ, would now himself suffer for the cause of Christ.

5. Saul Receives the Holy Spirit (v. 17)

When Ananias arrived at Saul's house, he touched him and called him "Brother Saul." What a loving way to greet someone! Reaching out to touch someone, whether in the form of a handshake, a hug, or a gentle pat on the back, is such a warm and welcoming gesture.

Years ago, our church started something that has turned into a tradition. Every Sunday morning before the preaching begins, we sing the chorus of "Heavenly Sunshine." Then, while the pianist plays it through at least once—but usually two or three times—the congregation walks around the church and greets everyone with a hello, a handshake, or sometimes a hug. We started this tradition as a way to welcome visitors, but it's something we've continued whether we have visitors or not. After all, church family is just an extension of real family. The only difference is that it's Christ's blood that binds us together. "Brother Saul" was an indicator that

Ananias had already accepted Saul into the family of God. He treated him with the same warmth that he would extend to any of his family members.

Jesus had sent Ananias so that Saul could regain his sight and be filled with the Holy Spirit. God could have easily healed Saul, without any help from Ananias; but He chose not to do it that way. It would make sense that Ananias was there to welcome Saul into the family of God and to be his friend.

6. Saul Receives His Sight and Is Baptized (vv. 18–19)

Immediately and miraculously, Saul was healed and regained his sight. His corneas may have been severely damaged when he saw the bright flash of light. After Ananias greeted Saul and laid his hand upon him, he could see again, and much more clearly! His vision was no longer distorted by anger and hate. He looked through the eyes of a gentle man, a man who had been redeemed.

Then Saul was baptized. Probably Ananias performed the baptism. Baptism is public expression of our faith in Jesus Christ and an indicator that one desires to identify with Jesus. Saul didn't hesitate. He didn't say, "Now wait a minute, God. This is going a little too fast for me." He was sincere. Saul was a changed man, and he wanted everyone to know it.

At this point, Saul was probably running on divine adrenaline. He had not had food or water in three days, and his physical body was very low on energy. Saul needed to be fueled so that he could be about his business of serving Christ. So he ate and his body was strengthened.

Sources:

Barnes, Albert. *Barnes' Notes on the New Testament.* Grand Rapids, Mich.: Kregel Classics, 1962.

Clark, Adam. *Adam Clark's Commentary on the New Testament.* Nashville, Tenn.: Nelson Reference, 1997.

Search the Scriptures

1. What did Saul request from the high priest (Acts 9:2)?

2. How did Saul react when he saw the sudden light on the road to Damascus (v. 4)?

3. In the vision Ananias had, what did the Lord instruct him to do (v. 11)?

4. What two reasons did Ananias give Saul for God sending him (v. 17)?

5. What did Saul do to profess his newfound faith (v. 18)?

Discuss the Meaning

1. Why do you think Saul hated Christians so much (Acts 9:1)?

2. What do you think was the significance of the Lord addressing Saul by using his name twice (v. 4)?

3. Knowing how Saul felt about Christians, do you think Ananias was fearful when he obeyed the Lord's instruction to go to Saul (v. 11)?

4. In today's In Focus story, Dan finally realized that smoking was hurting his Christian testimony. Is there anything questionable in your life that affects your testimony? If you're not sure, imagine seeing another Christian doing the same thing. Do you feel that it would it change your opinion of that person? Why?

Lesson in Our Society

America may well be the greatest country in the world. Known as the "land of opportunity," people from all over the globe long to live here. Americans are blessed with freedoms that citizens from many other countries can only dream about. Unfortunately, our freedoms often lead to ill-advised and even immoral choices. American Christians must not allow their freedoms to become a license for apathy or indifference to God's holy standard of living. There are so many lost souls that need Christ. Who is going to tell them about our loving Saviour if we don't? As believers, we must live out our transformed lives so that others can see Jesus in us and come to know Him as their Lord and Saviour.

Make It Happen

How is your Christian testimony? Is there anything in your life—a bad habit, a bad attitude, or bad behavior—that you need to give to the Lord? If you ask Him, Jesus Christ will give you victory. Jesus came to transform lives so that we can be a witness for Him.

Follow the Spirit

What God wants me to do:

____

____

Remember Your Thoughts

Special insights I have learned:

____

____

More Light on the Text

Acts 9:1–11, 16–19

1 And Saul, yet breathing out threatenings and slaughter against the disciples of the Lord, went unto the high priest, 2 And desired of him letters to Damascus to the synagogues, that if he found any of this way, whether they were men or women, he might bring them bound unto Jerusalem.

Saul, who was a Pharisee and a zealous one at that, was consumed by hatred for the Christian community. The text expresses this zeal by using the Greek word *empneo* (**emp-NEH-o**), which means "breathing out." Threats of murder flowed out of Saul. His whole life became consumed with the destruction of the Christian faith. He saw Christianity as a heretical movement that needed to be rooted out wherever it was found. Thus, he set out to get authority from the high priest to root out Christianity in Damascus, where there was a large Jewish population. The Christians in Damascus were most likely refugees dispersed by the growing persecution in Jerusalem.

Christians are referred to several times in Acts as followers of "the Way," which was a designation used early on to describe Christians as followers of the way of life and salvation taught to them by the Lord Jesus Christ. Paul wanted to bring the followers of "the Way" in Damascus back to Jerusalem in chains.

3 And as he journeyed, he came near Damascus: and suddenly there shined round about him a light from heaven: 4 And he fell to the earth, and heard a voice saying unto him, Saul, Saul, why persecutest thou me? 5 And he said, Who art thou, Lord? And the Lord said, I am Jesus whom thou persecutest: it is hard for thee to kick against the pricks. 6 And he trembling and astonished said, Lord, what wilt thou have me to do? And the Lord said unto him, Arise, and go into the city, and it shall be told thee what thou must do.

Saul was unaware of his upcoming confrontation with the Lord. While he was on his way to carry out his plan against the Christian community, he was suddenly stopped in his tracks by a light flashing all around him. In the original Greek, the word *periastrapto* (**per-ee-as-TRAP-to**) conveys the idea of lightning flashing, though in this case there was no storm. However, we are not left in the dark about the light's origin. The text tells us that it was from heaven. The light was so startling that it caused Paul to fall to the ground.

He then heard a voice speaking to him in Hebrew, "Saul! Saul! Why are you persecuting me?" It is worth noting that Jesus did not ask Saul why he was persecuting His church, but why he (Saul) was persecuting Him. What an amazing thought—that our relationship with Jesus is such that to persecute us is to persecute Him!

Of course, Saul wanted to know the origin of the voice, so he asked. "I am Jesus whom you are persecuting." The one with whom Saul was speaking, whose glory had knocked him to the ground, was none other than the risen and glorified Lord. Saul was in the presence of the risen Lord. No wonder he was never able to get that vision out of his mind. The book of Acts contains several examples of Paul recounting the story.

After being confronted with the Lord's glory, Saul was commanded by the Lord to go into the city where he would be told what to do. Thus, the man who had been on his way to persecute Christians in Damascus, was instead on his way to becoming a Christian.

7 And the men which journeyed with him stood speechless, hearing a voice, but seeing no man.

In Acts 26:14, Paul said that they all had fallen to the ground, while here it says they stood speechless. There is no contradiction. The likely explanation is that these men were able to rise to their feet after falling to the ground, while Saul remained on the ground. In Acts 22:9, Paul said that the men who were with him did not hear the voice of the one who spoke to him. The explanation is similar to what happened at another time (John 12:29). The men heard the sound but could not distinguish what was being said.

8 And Saul arose from the earth; and when his eyes were opened, he saw no man: but they led him by the hand, and brought him into Damascus. 9 And he was three days without sight, and neither did eat nor drink.

Paul's experience with the Lord left him blind. He had to be led into the city by his companions. For three days, he would see nothing; and he was in such a state of shock that he didn't eat for three days, either. What a reversal! Saul had headed toward Damascus with authority from the high priest and a zeal for hunting down Christians. Instead, he had to be led helplessly into the city and would soon be aided by a member of the very community he had come to destroy. God must really have a love of irony.

10 And there was a certain disciple at Damascus, named Ananias; and to him said the Lord in a vision, Ananias. And he said, Behold, I am here, Lord. 11 And the Lord said unto him, Arise, and go into the street which is called Straight, and enquire in the house of Judas for one called Saul, of Tarsus: for, behold, he prayeth,

God spoke to one of His servants, Ananias, in Damascus, telling him in a dream Saul's exact location. The Lord told Ananias that Saul was praying. He went on to tell him that Saul had seen Ananias in a vision, lay hands on him, and restored his sight. Of course, God intended for the ensuing events to be another means of helping Saul understand who Jesus is.

9:16 For I will shew him how great things he must suffer for my name's sake.

Ananias had protested the Lord's decision regarding Saul. Ananias had not experienced Saul's attacks directly, but he knew of Saul's acts. He knew the extent to which Saul was persecuting Jesus' followers. He could not understand why the Lord would send him to a man who had dedicated his life to opposing Him. Perhaps he was also afraid because of Saul's reputation. Yet the Lord had a higher purpose for Saul and, therefore, overruled Ananias' protest. Saul had kingdom business to perform. Indeed, Jesus had plans for Saul that included much suffering for His name.

17 And Ananias went his way, and entered into the house; and putting his hands on him said, Brother Saul, the Lord, even Jesus, that appeared unto thee in the way as thou camest, hath sent me, that thou mightest receive thy sight, and be filled with the Holy Ghost. 18 And immediately there fell from his eyes as it had been scales: and he received sight forthwith, and arose, and was baptized. 19 And when he had received meat, he was strengthened. Then was Saul certain days with the disciples which were at Damascus.

Ananias obeyed his Lord and went to the location given to him. There he fulfilled his commission. As soon as he entered the house, he spoke to the one he had previously counted as an enemy, calling him brother. He made Saul aware that what he was about to do was not by his own authority but by the authority of the One he had seen on the road to Damascus. He told Saul that he had come to give him his sight and something even more amazing than that—the Holy Spirit. He had come to restore Saul's physical sight and give him new vision through the indwelling power of the Holy Spirit.

After laying his hands on Saul, something like flakes or scales (Gk. *lepis*, **lep-IS**) fell from Saul's eyes and he received his sight. He was then able to eat and began to regain his energy. He stayed in Damascus for several days. The one who had persecuted the church was now a member of the community of believers.

Daily Bible Readings

M: A Revelation of Jesus Christ
Galatians 1:11–17
T: Persecutor Now Proclaimer
Galatians 1:18–24
W: The Surpassing Value of Christ
Philippians 3:2–11
T: Befriended by Barnabas
Acts 9:22–31
F: Content in All Circumstances
Philippians 4:10–20
S: A Light from Heaven
Acts 9:1–9
S: God's Chosen Instrument
Acts 9:10–21

NOTES

TEACHING TIPS

October 26

Bible Study Guide 8

1. Words You Should Know

A. Ministered (Acts 13:2) *leitourgeo* (Gk.)—To serve.

B. Sorcerer (v. 6) *magos* (Gk.)—The name given by the Babylonians (Chaldeans), Medes, Persians, and others to wise men, teachers, priests, physicians, astrologers, seers, interpreters of dreams, augers, and soothsayers.

C. Pervert (v. 10) *diastrepho* (Gk.)—Divert, mislead, or lead astray.

D. Doctrine (v. 12) *didache* (Gk.)—Teaching; learning.

2. Teacher Preparation

Unifying Principle—Set Apart to Work. In the "new community"—the church—God has called us to be set apart to do His work. In addition, the Holy Spirit and the church work together to set apart some Christians for leadership, not only in reaching out through missions but also within God's body.

A. Prayerfully read Acts 13:1–12 in the King James Version (KJV) and at least one other translation.

B. Read some of the cross-references to make sure you have a clear understanding of the text.

C. Prayerfully read Bible Study Guide 8.

D. Make a list of different examples of missionary work in your community.

E. Complete lesson 8 in the *Precepts For Living® Personal Study Guide.*

3. Starting the Lesson

A. Pray with your students.

B. Ask volunteers to read the Focal Verses.

C. Briefly emphasize portions of key verses.

D. Review the Words You Should Know.

4. Getting into the Lesson

A. Ask a volunteer to read the In Focus section.

B. Invite the students to share their areas of interest in the mission field.

C. Ask a volunteer to share The People, Places, and Times information.

D. Ask another volunteer to read the Background section.

E. Allow the students a few minutes to complete the Search the Scriptures questions. Discuss.

5. Relating the Lesson to Life

A. Allow the students a few minutes to complete the Discuss the Meaning questions. Discuss.

B. Have another volunteer read the Lesson in Our Society section. Discuss.

6. Arousing Action

A. Discuss the Make It Happen section.

B. Ask the students to discuss the pros and cons of missionary work in the United States and missionary work in foreign countries.

C. Encourage the students to review the Focal Verses and key sections of the lesson throughout the week.

D. End the class in prayer.

Worship Guide

For the Superintendent or Teacher
Theme: Commissioned by the Community
Theme Song: "Rescue the Perishing"
Devotional Reading: Matthew 28:16–20
Prayer

COMMISSIONED BY THE COMMUNITY

Bible Background • ACTS 13
Printed Text • ACTS 13:1–12 Devotional Reading • MATTHEW 28:16–20

AIM for Change

By the end of the lesson, we will:
SUMMARIZE the church's commissioning of Saul and Barnabas;
CONSIDER the challenges and rewards of being sent out by the community on a mission for God; and
SHARE our own stories of being called to a task or ministry in the church.

Keep in Mind

"And when they had fasted and prayed, and laid their hands on them, they sent them away" (Acts 13:3).

Focal Verses

KJV **Acts 13:1** Now there were in the church that was at Antioch certain prophets and teachers; as Barnabas, and Simeon that was called Niger, and Lucius of Cyrene, and Manaen, which had been brought up with Herod the tetrarch, and Saul.

2 As they ministered to the Lord, and fasted, the Holy Ghost said, Separate me Barnabas and Saul for the work whereunto I have called them.

3 And when they had fasted and prayed, and laid their hands on them, they sent them away.

4 So they, being sent forth by the Holy Ghost, departed unto Seleucia; and from thence they sailed to Cyprus.

5 And when they were at Salamis, they preached the word of God in the synagogues of the Jews: and they had also John to their minister.

6 And when they had gone through the isle unto Paphos, they found a certain sorcerer, a false prophet, a Jew, whose name was Barjesus.

7 Which was with the deputy of the country, Sergius Paulus, a prudent man; who called for Barnabas and Saul, and desired to hear the word of God.

8 But Elymas the sorcerer (for so is his name by interpretation) withstood them, seeking to turn away the deputy from the faith.

9 Then Saul, (who also is called Paul,) filled with the Holy Ghost, set his eyes on him.

10 And said, O full of all subtilty and all mischief, thou child of the devil, thou enemy of all righteousness, wilt thou not cease to pervert the right ways of the Lord?

NLT **Acts 13:1** Among the prophets and teachers of the church at Antioch of Syria were Barnabas, Simeon (called "the black man"), Lucius (from Cyrene), Manaen (the childhood companion of King Herod Antipas), and Saul.

2 One day as these men were worshiping the Lord and fasting, the Holy Spirit said, "Dedicate Barnabas and Saul for the special work to which I have called them."

3 So after more fasting and prayer, the men laid their hands on them and sent them on their way.

4 So Barnabas and Saul were sent out by the Holy Spirit. They went down to the seaport of Seleucia and then sailed for the island of Cyprus.

5 There, in the town of Salamis, they went to the Jewish synagogues and preached the word of God. John Mark went with them as their assistant.

6 Afterward they traveled from town to town across the entire island until finally they reached Paphos, where they met a Jewish sorcerer, a false prophet named Bar-Jesus.

7 He had attached himself to the governor, Sergius Paulus, who was an intelligent man. The governor invited Barnabas and Saul to visit him, for he wanted to hear the word of God.

8 But Elymas, the sorcerer (as his name means in Greek), interfered and urged the governor to pay no attention to what Barnabas and Saul said. He was trying to keep the governor from believing.

9 Saul, also known as Paul, was filled with the Holy Spirit, and he looked the sorcerer in the eye.

11 And now, behold, the hand of the Lord is upon thee, and thou shalt be blind, not seeing the sun for a season. And immediately there fell on him a mist and a darkness; and he went about seeking some to lead him by the hand.

12 Then the deputy, when he saw what was done, believed, being astonished at the doctrine of the Lord.

10 Then he said, "You son of the devil, full of every sort of deceit and fraud, and enemy of all that is good! Will you never stop perverting the true ways of the Lord?

11 Watch now, for the Lord has laid his hand of punishment upon you, and you will be struck blind. You will not see the sunlight for some time." Instantly mist and darkness came over the man's eyes, and he began groping around begging for someone to take his hand and lead him.

12 When the governor saw what had happened, he became a believer, for he was astonished at the teaching about the Lord.

In Focus

Bill and Karen were overcome with disappointment. Five years ago they were called to the mission field in Afghanistan. After a missionary to that country had visited their church, the couple were deeply burdened for the Afghan people. Subsequently, after months of prayer, they both heard the Lord calling them. They started preparing for the mission trip.

They were due to leave in two weeks when they were notified that that they didn't have enough financial support to make the trip. Bill and Karen made a last-minute attempt to raise the needed funds. Now it was two weeks later, and they weren't going anyplace. They couldn't understand why "God would change His mind now." It just didn't make sense to them.

Together, they prayed that God would give them some answers. Two months passed, and Bill and Karen continued to pray. One Sunday afternoon, the phone rang and Bill answered. Karen was listening intently, and she'd heard enough to know something exciting was happening. The man who had called Roger was from one of the churches they had visited while raising their support. He provided temporary housing for immigrants. Five families from Afghanistan were in his facility. Roger wanted Bill and Karen to move into the group home where these families were housed. Their job would be to minister to the needs of these families and prepare them to make their transition to life in America.

When Bill and Karen didn't have the funding to go to Afghanistan, they found that God had brought the mission field to them. We don't need to travel to another country to be missionaries. Some are called to serve in their own country and in their own communities.

The People, Places, and Times

Saul and Barnabas visited these cities on their missionary journey:

Seleucia. Seleucia was built in 300 B.C. by Seleucus I Nicator, ruler over Syria. It was located near the mouth of the Orontes River. Pompey made this great city a free city.

Cyprus. Cyprus was the native home of Barnabas. It was a large Mediterranean island, about 148 miles long. They produced fine quality corn, wine, and oil and were well-known for their business of commerce.

Salamis. Salamis was located on the southeast coast of Cyprus. It served as the most important seaport for Cyprus. Later the city was called Constantia. Today, the city is known as Famagusta.

Paphos. Paphos was the capital of Cyprus and was located on the west coast.

Sources:

Barnes, Albert. *Barnes' Notes on the New Testament.* Grand Rapids, Mich.: Kregel Classics, 1962.

Clark, Adam. *Adam Clark's Commentary on the New Testament.* Nashville, Tenn.: Nelson Reference, 1997.

Background

Many Christians lived in Antioch. So many, in fact, that they needed an abundance of prophets and teachers to minister at the different gathering places.

Simeon was also called Niger or the Black Prince. Some believe he was also Simon of Cyrene, who carried Jesus' Cross. Little is known about him.

Lucius of Cyrene was an educated man believed to have first heard the Gospel in a Cyrenian synagogue in Jerusalem.

Manaen was a foster brother to Herod Antipas. Some Jewish writers contend that Manaen had the gift of prophesying and foretold that Herod would be a king. It is ironic that the two raised together would turn out so different. Herod was, for the most part, a persecutor of God's prophets. Manaen was a devout Christian and prophet of the church in Antioch. These were the prophets and teachers mentioned besides Barnabas and Saul.

Sources:

Barnes, Albert. *Barnes' Notes on the New Testament.* Grand Rapids, Mich.: Kregel Classics, 1962.

Clark, Adam. *Adam Clark's Commentary on the New Testament.* Nashville, Tenn.: Nelson Reference, 1997.

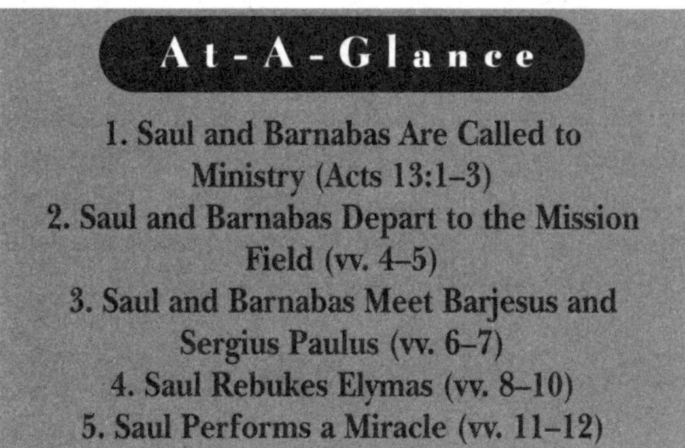
At-A-Glance

1. Saul and Barnabas Are Called to Ministry (Acts 13:1–3)
2. Saul and Barnabas Depart to the Mission Field (vv. 4–5)
3. Saul and Barnabas Meet Barjesus and Sergius Paulus (vv. 6–7)
4. Saul Rebukes Elymas (vv. 8–10)
5. Saul Performs a Miracle (vv. 11–12)

In Depth

1. Saul and Barnabas Are Called to Ministry (Acts 13:1–3)

The church in Antioch abounded with teachers and prophets. Many are mentioned by name. There was Simeon, who was also called Niger. Niger means "black" in Latin; it's assumed that he acquired that name due to either his complexion or hair color. There was also Lucius. He came from Cyrene in Africa and therefore was referred to as Lucius of Cyrene. Also mentioned was Manaen, who was raised with Herod Antipas. Antipas was tetrarch of Galilee. He was the Herod responsible for beheading John the Baptist and also the one who instigated the mocking of Jesus. Since Manaen was associated with the royal family, it's likely that he was educated and a man of high position. The Gospel was not solely directed toward the poor, as Manaen's conversion shows. The wealthy are in need of salvation, too.

Then there were Saul and Barnabas. Saul, the apostle, and Barnabas were to be set apart in the ministry. The Lord had a special mission for them. One day, while the teachers and prophets fasted and prayed, the Holy Spirit spoke to them and called Saul and Barnabas into service. Their mission was to preach the Gospel to the Gentiles, and it was of vast importance. It would also be a very dangerous mission and one wrought with adversity.

Missionaries today must also face dangerous situations and all kinds of hardships. In July 2007, two Christian missionaries in Uttarakhand, India, were forced to hide in a sugar cane field to avoid some threatening anti-Christian extremists. The extremists then threatened the life of their pastor. On June 8, 2007, in India, Pastor Laxmi Narayan Gowda was assaulted and made to parade naked through the streets by Hindu extremists. In March 2004, four Baptist missionaries were killed in Mosul, Iraq, in a drive-by shooting. Missionaries know the risks, but they are still devoted to spreading the Gospel of Jesus Christ at all costs.

Saul and Barnabas would face danger as well, and they knew it. When the prayer and fasting were done, the leaders laid hands on Saul and Barnabas and sent them into the mission field with the church's blessings.

2. Saul and Barnabas Depart to the Mission Field (vv. 4–5)

The Holy Spirit sent Barnabas and Saul on their mission and was present with them in their ministry. This had to be a great encouragement to them. Regardless of whatever dangers they might face, they knew they didn't have to face them alone. With their hearts and minds at peace, they could be about the business of their mission.

Did you ever experience "the peace of God, which passeth all understanding" (Philippians 4:7)? One day, I was struck by panic over my son Jacob. He was in a different state, and I hadn't been able to contact him. Moms and dads sometimes get this feeling in their gut when their child is in danger. Immediately, I bowed my head and started praying. I called my mom and our pastor's wife and asked them if they would please pray for him, too. When I checked my e-mail, someone had sent me an e-mail card. I almost deleted it without looking, but then I changed my mind. When I opened the card it said, "Peace I leave with you, my peace I give unto you:

not as the world giveth, give I unto you. Let not your heart be troubled, neither let it be afraid" (John 14:27). Immediately, peace washed over me. What an amazing experience that was! Saul and Barnabas carried that same peace with them on every moment of their journey. The two missionaries traveled through Seleucia, Cyprus, and Salamis, where John Mark joined them. Everything seemed to be going smoothly until they arrived at Paphos.

3. Saul and Barnabas Meet Barjesus and Sergius Paulus (vv. 6–7)

Upon their arrival in Paphos, Saul and Barnabas met a sorcerer named Barjesus. They also met Sergius Paulus, the governor of that country under Roman rule. Sergius Paulus was a circumspect man, who ruled by his sensibilities. He was also an educated and thoughtful man, much like Saul and Barnabas. The governor asked to see the two missionaries so he could hear the Word of God.

Saul and Barnabas must have been bursting with excitement—not just because Sergius Paulus was a man of position, but he had called for them so he could be ministered to regarding God's Word. Perhaps they thought if the governor was interested in hearing about God, maybe the people he governed would be interested as well. Paphos was truly ripe for the harvest.

4. Saul Rebukes Elymas (vv. 8–10)

Elymas (the other name of the sorcerer Barjesus) was a Jew. He was also a false prophet with a wicked heart, who was given to deceitfulness and trickery. This sorcerer masqueraded as a prophet of God when in fact he was not. Elymas sought to turn the governor away from hearing God's Word and was determined to do so by any means necessary. He knew that if Sergius heard and accepted the Word of God, many of those he governed would follow suit.

Elymas was nothing more than a servant of Satan himself. Saul (Paul) knew exactly what he was up to. Elymas proved to be no match for Paul, who was full of the Holy Spirit. Paul set his eyes firm upon Elymas for the showdown. He did so with a confidence and boldness given him by the Holy Spirit.

We all know the importance of eye contact. It signifies that we mean business and we mean what we say. Parents tend to have "the look" that all kids dread. It is a look of authority. Paul rebuked Elymas, calling him "thou child of the devil." In being so, he was against all that was righteous, good, and true. He was an enemy of God.

5. Saul Performs a Miracle (vv. 11–12)

Empowered by the Holy Spirit and the wrath of the Lord, Paul declared blindness upon Elymas. He indicated that this wouldn't be a permanent blindness by adding that Elymas would not see the sun for a season. The blindness was immediate and Elymas was left searching for someone to lead him about.

Although we are more accustomed, especially in the New Testament, to miracles in the form of healing, casting out demons, and other such things, in this case the miracle was Elymas losing his sight. Can you imagine the fear that must have struck his heart?

This miracle served two purposes: First, it was God's punishment upon Elymas. Second, it was proof that the Gospel of Jesus Christ was the truth. It was proof enough for the sensible governor of Paphos. Sergius Paulus became a believer in Jesus Christ and in the truth of God's Word. This was a wondrous victory for the Lord, and Paul and Barnabas took part in it.

Sources:

Barnes, Albert. *Barnes' Notes on the New Testament.* Grand Rapids, Mich.: Kregel Classics, 1962.

Clark, Adam. *Adam Clark's Commentary on the New Testament.* Nashville, Tenn.: Nelson Reference, 1997.

Search the Scriptures

1. Name the six prophets and teachers from the church at Antioch (Acts 13:1).

2. What three things were done before Barnabas and Saul were sent on their mission (v. 3)?

3. Who was Elymas (vv. 6–8)?

4. What miracle did the deputy witness that made him a believer (v. 11)?

Discuss the Meaning

1. What do you think was the purpose for fasting, prayer, and the laying on of hands before Saul and Barnabas were sent on their mission (Acts 13:3)?

2. How do you think Saul and Barnabas felt when the deputy of the country requested to hear about God's Word (v. 7)?

3. What do you think was the purpose for Saul asking Elymas, "wilt thou not cease to pervert the right ways of the Lord" (v. 10)?

4. In today's In Focus story, Bill and Karen were disappointed because they couldn't make their mission trip to Afghanistan. Still, they continued to pray. Do you think the outcome would have been the same had they just given up altogether? Why or why not?

Lesson in Our Society

Many people think of missionaries as those who minister in foreign countries, and many of them do. However, not all missionaries are called to far-off places. Mission work in our own communities is vastly important. If all missionaries left our country, then who would share the Gospel with Americans in need of the salvation that Jesus Christ offers?

Imagine the growth of an apple tree. It starts with a seed and then it starts to root itself in the soil. Strong roots are the key to healthy growth. When the roots are healthy, the branches and then the leaves grow; then it blossoms. Eventually the tree will flourish and bear fruit. If the tree's roots are weak, then growth is slow and it will eventually stop growing. It won't bear much fruit. If left untended, what has grown will wither and die.

Our individual local churches are the seeds that are planted. From those seeds, roots begin to grow. The roots represent our communities. If we tend to our tree, it will branch out. The branches represent missionaries in other countries. Eventually, the tree will flourish and bear fruit. The fruit represents those who accept Christ on foreign soil. Then we are back to the seed and repeat the process.

We must also nurture or minister to those in our own communities. In doing so, our roots will be strengthened. Then we can start branching out and bearing the fruit of saved souls in other countries.

Make It Happen

Has God burdened your heart for missionary work either in your community, another city, or in another country? Most missionaries minister to mental and physical needs as well as spiritual needs. Have you been called to minister to a specific need?

Follow the Spirit

What God wants me to do:

____

____

Remember Your Thoughts

Special insights I have learned:

____

____

More Light on the Text

Acts 13:1–12

1 Now there were in the church that was at Antioch certain prophets and teachers; as Barnabas, and Simeon that was called Niger, and Lucius of Cyrene, and Manaen, which had been brought up with Herod the tetrarch, and Saul.

The diversity of the leadership in the early church is of note. Barnabas was introduced to us earlier in the book of Acts, beginning in chapter 4. He was a Levite from the island of Cyprus. It was Barnabas, whose name means "son of encouragement," who convinced the disciples to accept Paul's conversion as genuine.

The word "prophets" in the Greek is *prophetes* (**prof-AY-tace**), which means "one who, moved by the Spirit of God and hence His organ or spokesman, solemnly declares to men what he has received by inspiration, including future events, and in particular such as relate to the cause and kingdom of God and to human salvation." In other words, these men were spokespersons for God, Himself. They were to represent Him and do as He instructed them to do.

Two of the men here are likely from Africa, though we do not know much else about them. Simeon was called Niger, which means "black," alluding to his dark complexion. About Lucius, we know only that he was from the city of Cyrene in North Africa.

Manaen is Greek for the Hebrew name Menahem. The name means "comforter." In the Greek the word for "brought up" is *suntrophos* (**SOON-trof-os**) and can be translated as "foster brother." This was the title given to boys around the same age as the prince who were raised with him in the royal court.

2 As they ministered to the Lord, and fasted, the Holy Ghost said, Separate me Barnabas and Saul for the work whereunto I have called them.

In the Greek, "they ministered" is *leitourgeo* (**li-toorg-EH-o**) and means "Christians serving Christ, whether by prayer, or by instructing others concerning the way of salvation, or in some other way." The

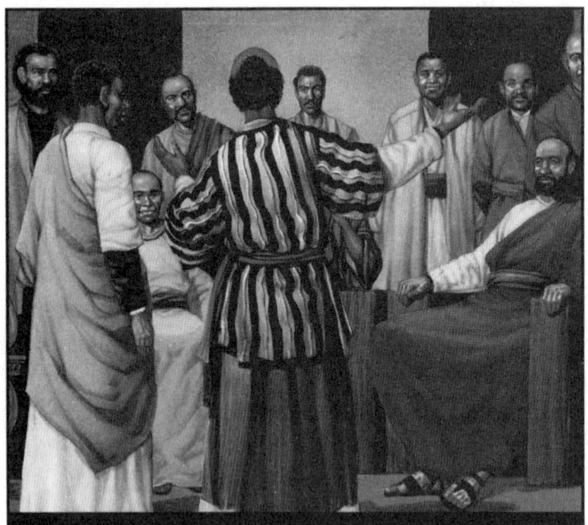
"And when they had fasted and prayed, and laid their hands on them, they sent them away" (Acts 13:3).

word "fasted" in the Greek is *nesteuo* (**nace-TYOO-o**) and means "to abstain, as a religious exercise, from food and drink"—either entirely, if the fast lasted but a single day, or from customary and choice nourishment, if it continued several days. Therefore, they were found fasting and praying, which made them sensitive to the leading of the Holy Spirit. In the midst of carrying out their leadership and ministry responsibilities, these men were instructed by the Holy Spirit to appoint Paul and Barnabas to the work to which God had called them. It is worth noting that these men were ministering to the Lord. They understood to whom their service was to be directed. Subsequently, they ministered to God's people as to the Lord.

3 And when they had fasted and prayed, and laid their hands on them, they sent them away.

Having been instructed by the Spirit to appoint Barnabas and Saul to their work, the leaders at Antioch laid their hands on their brothers and sent them away with their blessing. It should be noted that the leaders sent them off as representatives of the entire body. Thus, through its leaders, the church at Antioch gave its blessings to these two missionaries and sent them to the work.

4 So they, being sent forth by the Holy Ghost, departed unto Seleucia; and from thence they sailed to Cyprus. 5 And when they were at Salamis, they preached the word of God in the synagogues of the Jews: and they had also John to their minister.

In the Greek, "being sent forth" is *ekpempo* (**ek-PEM-po**) and means "to send away, send forth." Luke, the writer of Acts, tells us here that it was the Holy Spirit who sent Barnabas and Paul forth on their missionary journey. The emphasis, of course, is on the calling of the Spirit to the work of ministry. It is ultimately the Lord who calls people into the work of ministry. The church is to discern if the call is valid and then to commission for service those whose calling is from the Lord.

Having been commissioned, Paul and Barnabas set out for the island of Cyprus. Cyprus is about 60 miles off the coast of Syria. It is the third largest island in the Mediterranean. Barnabas and Paul most likely chose it as the starting point for their missionary journey because it was close to Antioch, had a large Jewish population, and was familiar territory, being the hometown of Barnabas. They preached the Word first in the city of Salamis, which was on the east coast of the island. They began in the synagogue, not because their ministry was to be exclusively to Jews but because this was a good bridge to the Gentile community, since it was here that they would encounter Gentiles who were already God-fearing.

John Mark was the cousin of Barnabas. He traveled with the two men as an attendant early in the first missionary journey. He would later be the cause of a split between Paul and Barnabas (Acts 15:36–41). Afterward, he would be reconciled to Paul (2 Timothy 4:11).

6 And when they had gone through the isle unto Paphos, they found a certain sorcerer, a false prophet, a Jew, whose name was Barjesus: 7 Which was with the deputy of the country, Sergius Paulus, a prudent man; who called for Barnabas and Saul, and desired to hear the word of God. 8 But Elymas the sorcerer (for so is his name by interpretation) withstood them, seeking to turn away the deputy from the faith.

Advancing the purposes of God is not without its challenges. From Salamis, Paul and Barnabas traveled to the west coast of the island, spreading the Gospel. In the city of Paphos they encountered the false prophet Barjesus, also called "Elymas." Interestingly enough, the name Barjesus means "son of salvation," something this Barjesus was not. He was a magician who falsely claimed to be a medium of divine revelation. He had somehow attached himself to the governor at that time, Sergius Paulus. The text tells us that Sergius Paulus was a prudent man (v. 7). "Prudent" in the Greek is *sunetos* (**soon-ET-os**) and means "intelligent, having understanding, wise, learned." He had heard either about Paul and Barnabas' teaching or had heard them preach the Gospel himself and so summoned them in order to hear some further explanation of the Gospel. Elymas, no doubt afraid of losing the governor's favor, opposed Paul and Barnabas and tried to keep Sergius from believing the Gospel.

9 Then Saul, (who also is called Paul,) filled with the Holy Ghost, set his eyes on him. 10 And said, O full of all subtilty and all mischief, thou child of the devil, thou enemy of all righteousness, wilt thou not cease to pervert the right ways of the Lord? 11 And now, behold, the hand of the Lord is upon thee, and thou shalt be blind, not seeing the sun for a season. And immediately there fell on him a mist and a darkness; and he went about seeking some to lead him by the hand.

Paul "set his eyes" on Elymas (v. 9). In the Greek, this phrase is *atenizo* (**at-en-ID-zo**) and means "look steadfastly, fasten (one's) eyes, look earnestly on." Paul then said, "O full of all subtilty and all mischief" (v. 10). "Subtilty," in the Greek, is *dolos* (**DO-los**) and means "guile, deceit, craft." Then Paul severely rebuked Elymas for trying to hinder the governor from coming to faith in Christ. We are told that Paul's rebuke was the result of his being filled with the Holy Spirit, as Stephen was when he spoke before the Sanhedrin. Indeed throughout the book of Acts, we hear of the filling of the Spirit, as the people of God accomplish the work of ministry.

Paul began with a rebuke centered on the wickedness of Elymas' character. He had shown by his attempts to sway the governor from the truth that he was, in fact, not a medium of divine revelation but a son of the Devil whose heart was filled with deceit and who never ceased in confusing the way of salvation. He was an enemy of the Gospel of Christ. Thus, because he had attempted to blind the governor to the truth of the Gospel, he would suffer the Lord's judgment of physical blindness for some time. We are not told how long nor does it seem that Elymas was told either. That this judgment was from the Lord was evidenced by the results. Elymas was immediately struck blind and began to fumble about, looking for someone to guide him. What a warning this text is to those who would oppose the Gospel! God does not look lightly on attempts to hinder the spread of His truth. He will respond to those who seek to destroy the work of the Gospel in the lives of those whom He is calling to Himself.

12 Then the deputy, when he saw what was done, believed, being astonished at the doctrine of the Lord.

Elymas tried to deter the governor from the faith, but the Lord used His judgment on Elymas to bring the governor to faith. The governor was so amazed by what he saw that he believed the teaching of the Lord. Notice that the text does not say that he believed Paul's teaching, because God was using Paul to teach the Word of the Lord. Sergius Paulus believed that what he had been told by Elymas was indeed false, and the message that he heard from the mouths of Barnabas and Paul was true. Glory to God for the truth and power of the Gospel of Jesus Christ!

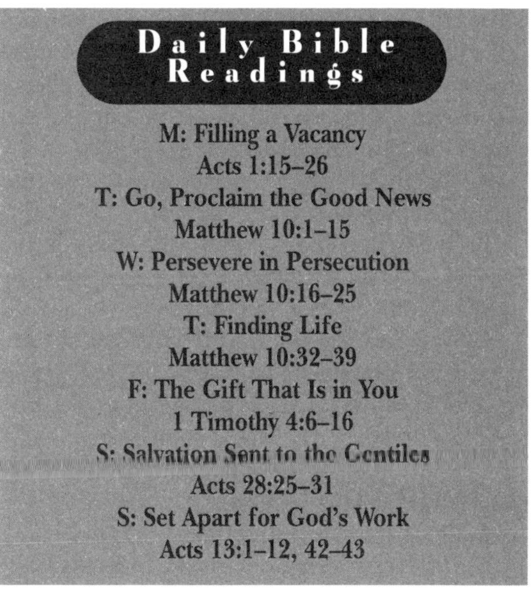

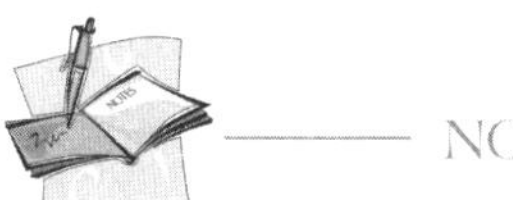

NOTES

TEACHING TIPS

November 2
Bible Study Guide 9

1. Words You Should Know

A. Apostles (Ephesians 4:11) *apostolos* (Gk.)—One sent forth.

B. Prophets (v. 11) *prophetes* (Gk.)—One who speaks forth; proclaimer of a divine message.

C. Evangelists (v. 11) *euaggelistes* (Gk.)—A messenger of good; preacher of the Gospel.

D. Pastors (v. 11) *poimen* (Gk.)—One who guides and tends a flock (of people).

E. Teachers (v. 11) *didaskalos* (Gk.)—One who teaches truth in the churches.

2. Teacher Preparation

Unifying Principle—Embracing Diversity. Diversity is a reality in every human community. In what ways is diversity important to the unity of the church? Paul's letter to the church at Ephesus challenges us to use our diverse identities and gifts to build up the Christian community.

A. Begin with prayer, and then read the Devotional Reading.

B. Read the Focal Verses, and consult the *Precepts For Living®* CD-ROM for additional commentary and background history.

C. After reading the AIM for Change section, write down on paper the diverse gifts you see in operation in your local congregation. Be prepared to discuss.

3. Starting the Lesson

A. Open the class with prayer.

B. Have a volunteer discuss the In Focus story.

C. Ask the students to think about what gifts God has given them. Ask them to jot down, on a small slip of paper, what they perceive their gifts to be. Tell them not to put their names on them. Then take the slips of paper, and list the gifts written on them on a large piece of paper or chalkboard.

4. Getting into the Lesson

A. Ask the students to read the Background and The People, Places, and Times sections. Discuss.

B. Ask them to review the Words You Should Know section.

C. Read the In Depth section and let the students answer the Search the Scriptures questions. Discuss.

5. Relating the Lesson to Life

A. Call the students' attention to the list of gifts on the paper in front of the class. Discuss.

B. After reading the Discuss the Meaning section, let the class reflect on how to apply the seven-part formula of unity.

6. Arousing Action

A. Direct the students' attention to the Lesson in Our Society and Make It Happen sections. Discuss.

B. Close the class with prayer.

Worship Guide

For the Superintendent or Teacher
Theme: Fitting into the Community
Theme Song: "What a Fellowship, What a Joy Divine"
Devotional Reading: 1 Corinthians 12:4–20
Prayer

FITTING INTO THE COMMUNITY

Bible Background • 1 CORINTHIANS 12:3–21; EPHESIANS 4:1–16
Printed Text • EPHESIANS 4:1–16 Devotional Reading • 1 CORINTHIANS 12:4–20

AIM for Change

By the end of the lesson, we will:
DISCUSS the issues on which the apostle Paul and the church at Ephesus differed;
CONSIDER how the gifts in our community contribute to building up Christian unity; and
IDENTIFY our personal gifts, which are vital to the life of the community of faith, and USE them more effectively.

Keep in Mind

"Every one of us is given grace according to the measure of the gift of Christ" (from Ephesians 4:7).

Focal Verses

KJV **Ephesians 4:1** I therefore, the prisoner of the Lord, beseech you that ye walk worthy of the vocation wherewith ye are called,

2 With all lowliness and meekness, with longsuffering, forbearing one another in love;

3 Endeavoring to keep the unity of the Spirit in the bond of peace.

4 There is one body, and one Spirit, even as ye are called in one hope of your calling;

5 One Lord, one faith, one baptism,

6 One God and Father of all, who is above all, and through all, and in you all.

7 But unto every one of us is given grace according to the measure of the gift of Christ.

8 Wherefore he saith, When he ascended up on high, he led captivity captive, and gave gifts unto men.

9 (Now that he ascended, what is it but that he also descended first into the lower parts of the earth?

10 He that descended is the same also that ascended up far above all heavens, that he might fill all things.)

11 And he gave some, apostles; and some, prophets; and some, evangelists; and some, pastors and teachers;

12 For the perfecting of the saints, for the work of the ministry, for the edifying of the body of Christ:

13 Till we all come in the unity of the faith, and of the knowledge of the Son of God, unto a perfect man, unto the measure of the stature of the fulness of Christ:

NLT **Ephesians 4:1** Therefore I, a prisoner for serving the Lord, beg you to lead a life worthy of your calling, for you have been called by God.

2 Always be humble and gentle. Be patient with each other, making allowance for each other's faults because of your love.

3 Make every effort to keep yourselves united in the Spirit, binding yourselves together with peace.

4 For there is one body and one Spirit, just as you have been called to one glorious hope for the future.

5 There is one Lord, one faith, one baptism,

6 and one God and Father, who is over all and in all and living through all.

NOV 2nd

7 However, he has given each one of us a special gift through the generosity of Christ.

8 That is why the Scriptures say, "When he ascended to the heights, he led a crowd of captives and gave gifts to his people."

9 Notice that it says "he ascended." This clearly means that Christ also descended to our lowly world.

10 And the same one who descended is the one who ascended higher than all the heavens, so that he might fill the entire universe with himself.

11 Now these are the gifts Christ gave to the church: the apostles, the prophets, the evangelists, and the pastors and teachers.

12 Their responsibility is to equip God's people to do his work and build up the church, the body of Christ.

13 This will continue until we all come to such unity in our faith and knowledge of God's Son that

14 That we henceforth be no more children, tossed to and fro, and carried about with every wind of doctrine, by the sleight of men, and cunning craftiness, whereby they lie in wait to deceive;

15 But speaking the truth in love, may grow up into him in all things, which is the head, even Christ:

16 From whom the whole body fitly joined together and compacted by that which every joint supplieth, according to the effectual working in the measure of every part, maketh increase of the body unto the edifying of itself in love.

we will be mature in the Lord, measuring up to the full and complete standard of Christ.

14 Then we will no longer be immature like children. We won't be tossed and blown about by every wind of new teaching. We will not be influenced when people try to trick us with lies so clever they sound like the truth.

15 Instead, we will speak the truth in love, growing in every way more and more like Christ, who is the head of his body, the church.

16 He makes the whole body fit together perfectly. As each part does its own special work, it helps the other parts grow, so that the whole body is healthy and growing and full of love.

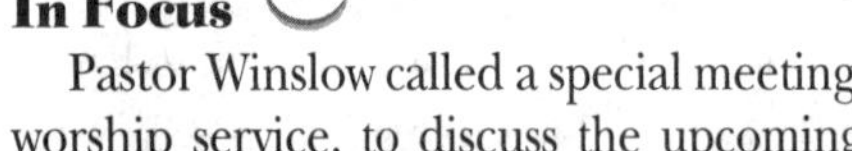

In Focus

Pastor Winslow called a special meeting, after the worship service, to discuss the upcoming community outreach program.

"Thank you all for staying after worship to assist with coordinating the community outreach program. Next Saturday, we will be helping remodel the library and bathrooms for the grade school around the corner. I attended a community meeting last week and discovered that the vast majority of the students who attend the school are physically handicapped. The library and bathrooms must be updated to meet their needs. The school is in desperate need of our help. Some of you have already signed up to volunteer; however, we are still short on volunteers. Who else can volunteer to help out next weekend?"

"Pastor, I can help. I'm a plumber," Brian responded.

"I'm not a plumber," said Rhonda, "but I want to help."

"You don't need to be a plumber, sister. They need help in all capacities. Aren't you a professional decorator?"

"Yes, I am," she replied.

"Well, the library and bathrooms will need to be repainted once the plumbing and electrical work is completed. Can you help do that?"

"You bet."

"What about me? How can I help?" asked Brother Carey.

"I am sure they could use your culinary skills to help prepare lunch for all the volunteers," Pastor Winslow said.

God has uniquely gifted each of us in the body of believers. Even though the gifts are diverse, we are to use them to help others and build unity.

The People, Places, and Times

Tychicus. He was a leader in the Ephesian church who accompanied Paul to Jerusalem with a collection from his church (Acts 20:4). He was the apostle Paul's personal representative as a bearer of the letters to the Colossians (Colossians 4:7–9) and Ephesians (Ephesians 6:21–22), as well as to other Asian churches. Paul sent him to Ephesus when Timothy was needed elsewhere (2 Timothy 4:12). He was a faithful leader whom Paul trusted as a minister to the people.

Ephesus. It was the most important city in the Roman province of Asia, a commercial, political, and religious center for all of Asia Minor. Ephesus' religious importance was central because of the three temples erected for their emperor cult, including the Greek goddess Artemis.

There was a large colony of Jews at Ephesus who enjoyed a privileged position under Roman rule. The church at Ephesus was established about A.D. 52, when Paul made a short visit and left Aquila and Priscilla there as he made his way to Jerusalem (Acts 18:18–21). He returned a year later on his third missionary journey and stayed there three years teaching and preaching (Acts 19:1–20). On another visit, he met with the Ephesian elders, and prior to his departure he left Timothy to serve as their leader (1 Timothy 1:3).

Paul (Saul). Born in Tarsus of the tribe of Benjamin, Saul was a Roman citizen and a zealous member of the Pharisee party. Saul was educated by Gamaliel and was a teacher of the Law. He knew the Jewish Scriptures and believed that the Christian movement was dangerous to Judaism. As a member of the Sanhedrin council, Saul was given official authority to direct the persecution of Christians.

After his conversion experience, he became a preacher for Christ (Acts 9). Saul used a new name: Paul (Acts 13:9). On three missionary journeys, he spread the Gospel throughout the Roman Empire. Paul wrote letters to the churches, which now compose most of the New Testament. He is considered the apostle to the Gentiles.

Sources:

Life Application Study Bible (New Revised Standard Version). Wheaton, Ill.: Tyndale House Publishers, 1989.

Unger, Merrill. *The New Unger's Bible Handbook.* Chicago, Ill.: Moody Press, 1984.

Background

Paul was sent as a prisoner to Rome in about A.D. 59 or 60. In Rome, messengers, including Tychicus of Ephesus, visited him from various churches. Paul wrote this letter to the Ephesian church and sent it with Tychicus. It was not written to confront any heresy or problem in the churches. The purpose was to strengthen and encourage the churches in the area, and all believers everywhere. Paul was very close to the Christians in Ephesus. He described the nature and appearance of the church, and he challenged believers to function as the living body of Christ on Earth.

After a warm greeting, Paul affirmed the nature of the church and praised God for all the spiritual blessings that come to men in Christ (Ephesians 1:1–14). He expressed thanksgiving for the believers' faith and prayed for their experience of the wisdom and power of God (vv. 15–23). Paul said God's purpose is to raise men from spiritual death to new life in Christ (2:1–10). God wants to not only reconcile men to Himself, but to one another—in particular to bring Jews and Gentiles together into the one people of God. As part of God's house, we stand with the prophets, apostles, Jews, Gentiles, and Christ Himself (2:11–3:11). Paul challenged them to live close to Christ and then praised God for all He has done (3:12–21).

In today's Scripture, because we are one body in Christ, Paul expresses the need for unity in the church. This requires believers to work together in building up the body.

Sources:

Life Application Study Bible (New Revised Standard Version). Wheaton, Ill.: Tyndale House Publishers, 1989.

Unger, Merrill, *The New Unger's Bible Handbook.* Chicago, Ill.: Moody Press, 1984.

At-A-Glance

1. Walk Worthy (Ephesians 4:1–3)
2. Walk in Unity (vv. 4–7)
3. Walk in Your Gift (vv. 8–16)

In Depth

1. Walk Worthy (Ephesians 4:1–3)

Paul was a prisoner at Rome and in the Lord. He counted it an honor to suffer for the sake of the Gospel. Based on what Christ has done, Paul asks believers to live worthy of our calling as Christians. As representatives of Jesus, we are to be humble, gentle, patient, and understanding. Our witness to the world is how we live every day.

Unity in the body of believers comes when we exhibit love toward others. "God is love" (1 John 4:8). No one is perfect so we must strive to accept and love others, in spite of their faults. Love is manifested in "lowliness and meekness, with longsuffering, forbearing one another in love" (Ephesians 4:2). We should be humble and not seek after our own selfish desires. Neither should we seek revenge for wrongdoing on the part of others toward us but patiently endure suffering on behalf of Christ as His witness. Bearing with the weaknesses of others is also a principle of love. We have to forgive other Christians, even as God forgives us. Without humility, patience, forgiveness, and love, there can be no unity.

Many churches are divided and in chaos because the members are not living out the principles of Christ contained in the Word. The slightest difference or offense can cause a major split in the church. Instead of working through our problems, it often seems easier to lash out, slander someone's name, or seek revenge. Thus we damage the unity of the church. Paul is challenging all believers to walk a life worthy of being called a Christian. This means emulating the life of Christ, who is humble, forgiving, loving, and patient.

Unity begins as the Holy Spirit moves upon the very heart and soul of a person. The Spirit will impart peace to the believer, which unites persons and makes them live in harmony with one another. When we endeavor to keep the peace, the body is strengthened (Ephesians 4:3). Moreover, discord and quarrelling cease to divide us.

2. Walk in Unity (vv. 4–7)

Paul gives a seven-part formula of unity that embodies the oneness of all believers. We often focus on the doctrinal differences we have, instead of the areas of commonalities. Christians can only walk in unity when we embrace others and appreciate the unique qualities God has given each of us.

"There is one body, and one Spirit" (Ephesians 4:4). This reminds us that we all belong to the same body, which is made up of many members (1 Corinthians 12:12). Once a person accepts Jesus as Lord and Saviour, that person becomes a part of the family of God. Since we are all a part of the same body, the Holy Spirit at work within our lives is the common denominator that unifies the fellowship of believers. Moreover, the Holy Spirit has given each of us gifts and graces to use in building up that body.

"Even as ye are called in one hope of your calling" (Ephesians 4:4) reveals that all believers have hope in eternal life. Christians know Earth is not our home. We have a new home awaiting us in heaven, where Jesus has prepared a place for us to spend eternity with Him (John 14:1–4). And since all believers will be spending eternity together, we need to begin to unite in fellowship here on Earth. Now is the time that we have an opportunity to reflect the kingdom of God on Earth.

There is "one Lord, one faith, one baptism" (Ephesians 4:5). Christ, the head of the church and to whom we all belong, is Lord. When we accept Him by faith as our Lord and Saviour, we are subject to His rule. Faith in Christ is the only way a person is saved. All Christians are saved by grace through faith (Ephesians 2:8). Once saved, baptism is a public confession of an inner change. It signifies that the person is now a member of the fellowship of believers. Professing our faith and being baptized are what unite us (1 Corinthians 12:13).

We have "one God and Father of all" (Ephesians 4:6), who claims us all as His children and members of the church. We are His creation and are being kept secure by Him for eternal purposes. By His very nature, He is above all—exercising dominion over all creatures, including the church. He is active in the lives of all believers, through the Holy Spirit that dwells in us.

Since we are all part of one body, we should make it our mission to be in harmony with one another. Paul gives us a blueprint for promoting unity. It takes work, but each believer has been given special abilities, from God, that can strengthen the body.

God gives each Christian a measure of grace and gifts (v. 7). He has bestowed gifts upon every believer. These gifts differ but come from the same Lord (1 Corinthians 12:4, 5). However, they are to be used for the mutual help of one another. Because God has given each according to what he knows we can handle, we need not be envious of others. If we use our gifts and work together, the body will be strengthened.

3. Walk in Your Gift (vv. 8–16)

Before Paul discusses some of the gifts God has bestowed upon us, he quotes from Psalm 68:18. "When he ascended up on high, he led captivity captive, and gave gifts unto men" (Ephesians 4:8). This is referring to the ministry of the ascended Christ. It celebrates His victory over evil. It assures all of us, who believe in Christ, that by trusting Him we can overcome evil. He also enriched His disciples with the gift of the Holy Spirit.

Paul notes that Jesus "descended first into the lower parts of the earth" (v. 9). Our Lord humbled himself first, and then he was exalted. This was to "fill all things" (v. 10). The gift of ministry is the fruit of Christ's ascension. He gave all the members of his church gifts and graces suitable to their diverse conditions and positions. God knows why He gave each of us specific gifts. We have to be grateful for His blessings and use them wisely.

"He gave some, apostles; and some, prophets; and some, evangelists; and some, pastors and teachers" (v. 11). This is not an exhaustive list of gifts but an emphasis on gifted people who help equip the body of Christ. God has given His people many other gifts. However, He determines providentially or directly through the Holy Spirit the places of their service. If we are completely submitted to His will, we do not determine where or how God uses our gifts. The gifts are for the building up of the body, advancing His kingdom and interests in the world (v. 12). Together, as members of His body, we can make disciples in every nation (Matthew 28:18–20).

We have to examine how we are making use of the gifts God has given us. If you know what your gifts are, use them to help others. When you serve and minister to others, the more unified the body becomes. Our individuality is not being inhibited; we are just operating in the diversity of gifts with which Christ has empowered us. We are to serve until all true believers meet together in heaven. The body of believers will then be unified for eternity with the Son of God (v. 13). From experiencing the fullness of Christ's presence, every person will have fully matured in gifts and graces, thus eliminating the childish tendency to be seduced and deceived by false doctrines.

Today, because ungodly people prey on their weaknesses, many have turned from the truth of God's Word (v. 14). In order to avoid the traps of the enemy, we have to carefully study and teach the Word of God. When the truth is "spoken in love" to fellow Christians, the Holy Spirit is able to convict them of sin and move them to repentance. The person is then reconciled with God and within the body of believers. God wants us to promote love, peace, and unity among the body. This is the only way, as members of the same body, we can be helpful to one another. Spiritual maturity happens in the body through Christ, the Head, which provides nourishment to every member and is the embodiment of love.

Source:

Henry, Matthew. *Commentary on the Whole Bible, Complete and Unabridged.* Peabody, Mass.: Hendrickson Publishers, 1991.

Search the Scriptures

1. Walking worthy as a Christian means we should exhibit godly behavior. List the qualities mentioned (Ephesians 4:2–3).

2. What is the seven-part formula of unity that Paul offered (vv. 4–6)?

3. Why did God give each of us gifts (v. 12)?

Discuss the Meaning

Divisions between individuals and various groups of people have been constant since the Fall, described in Genesis 3. Conflicts such as those in Northern Ireland between the Catholics and Protestants, in the former Yugoslavia between Serbians and Bosnians, or in the United States between races, create long-standing challenges to true life in community. The church, which is composed of people from all nations, should be an example of the unity that comes from the transforming power of the Gospel, yet Christians do not have a great history in this area. The church, in the African American community, in particular, is hindered by divisions rooted in class, denominationalism, and generational differences. What could change this? How would the apostle Paul's seven-part formula for unity make life different in our modern churches and communities?

Lesson in Our Society

In today's communities, we often find multiple churches within a few blocks of each other, and many of them even share the same beliefs and values. Yet, in some instances, the church leaders have never even met face-to-face; they are complete strangers. There is no unity. Our witness to the world is affected by how well we get along with each other (John 17:20–23). If we are all believers in Christ, we should appreciate others' gifts and work together for the glory of God.

Make It Happen

This week, pray and ask God to reveal how you can use your gifts more effectively. Wherever He leads you to go, He will empower you through the Holy Spirit to accomplish His work.

Follow the Spirit

What God wants me to do:

____

____

Remember Your Thoughts

Special insights I have learned:

____

____

More Light on the Text

Ephesians 4:1–16

1 I therefore, the prisoner of the Lord, beseech you that ye walk worthy of the vocation wherewith ye are called,

The last section, Ephesians 3, ends with Paul's prayer for the members of the new community, that God—through Christ—might dwell richly in their hearts, and that they will be able to entirely realize the magnitude of God's love for them in Christ Jesus. He then turns, in chapter four, to an appeal asking the people to lead a Christ-filled life, in this new community.

Paul used an emphatic first person pronoun "I" (Gk. *ego*, **eg-O**) to reintroduce himself as he did in 3:1 as the prisoner of the Lord. With this, Paul appeared to assert his apostolic authority. Both his authority, as an apostle of Christ Jesus, and his conviction, as one under arrest, seem to motivate his appeal to the people. His entreaty, as we shall discover shortly, is a call for unity and love in God's new community.

Paul writes, "I...beseech you that ye walk worthy of the vocation wherewith ye are called." The word "walk" is an idiomatic expression often used in Scriptures, indicating behavior, conduct, or demeanor (see 2:2). Here, Paul urged them to conduct or lead their lives in a manner that is fitting to their calling, to their commitment to Christ and the new community.

The Christian life is a response to God's calling in one's life; one then has to conduct oneself in a way that shows that commitment. The nature and characteristics of this calling are also expressed in different ways in the letter. First, they are called into one single family—into "one new man" (2:15). This speaks of unity, which occupies Paul's thought in chapters 1–3 and this passage under review (4:1–16).

Second, they are called into a holy family, separate from and distinct from the world. This speaks of the purity of God's new community—the church (4:17–5:21). John 17 and this passage are two classic moments in Scripture that show how important the unity of the church is in the mind of Christ and the first-century apostles. The death of Christ is the vehicle through which those "afar off and ... them that were nigh" had been united into one household of God (2:17). The unity of the church has long been the "child cry" of the church of Jesus Christ through the centuries, and it continues to elude it.

2 With all lowliness and meekness, with longsuffering, forbearing one another in love;

Paul listed five characteristics of the life worthy of our calling: lowliness, meekness, patience (longsuffering), mutual forbearance, and love. Maintaining unity in the new community begins with the individual commitment, including the keeping of moral qualities.

The first of the virtues needed for maintaining unity in the church is "lowliness." This word comes from the Greek *tapeinophrosune* (**tap-i-nof-ros-OO-nay**), which means "humility or modesty." Humility was a debasing virtue in their society, especially in the Greek world. The word is better translated "lowliness of mind," a state of mind that recognizes the worth and value of others.

The same mind was in Christ, and He emptied Himself and took the form of a servant, even unto death on the Cross (Philippians 2:3–8). In his epistle to the Philippians, Paul urged the church to imitate this virtue. Whereas in the present passage, he states that humility is essential in maintaining unity in the church.

The second virtue Paul advocated that would help unify the church is "meekness," or in the Greek *prautes* (**prah-OO-tace**) meaning "gentleness." Meekness is a demonstration of power under control. It has the idea of the character of one who, although he or she has the right to authority, decides to lay no claim on it before God and others. Both virtues are found in Christ Jesus (Matthew 11:29). Paul directed Timothy to teach others with gentleness and meekness of mind (2 Timothy 2:24–25).

The next two characteristics that will foster unity in the church seem to go together: "longsuffering," *makrothumia* in Greek (**mak-roth-oo-MEE-ah**), meaning "patience," and "forbearing" or *anechomai* (**an-EKH-om-ahee**), which has the idea of "to put up with or endure." It speaks of being tolerant toward people and having a mutual understanding between and among people.

Without these first four characteristics, unity will continue to elude the church. But the final characteristic—love—is the one in which all the others must be grounded. Love, in this instance, can mean the consideration of others' welfare and the readiness to act for their good rather than one's own.

3 Endeavouring to keep the unity of the Spirit in the bond of peace.

Verse 3 identifies the nature of the unity Paul had been advocating as "the unity of the Spirit." Paul called on the church at Ephesus to "endeavor" (Gk. *spoudazo*, **spoo-DAD-zo**) to keep the unity of the Spirit in the bond of peace. To "endeavor" here

"Every one of us is given grace according to the measure of the gift of Christ" (from Ephesians 4:7).

means to be diligent (see Titus 3:12; 2 Peter 3:14; 2 Timothy 4:9), to spare no effort or, as idiomatically expressed, "leave no stones unturned" to keep (preserve) the unity of the Spirit. In other words, Paul called on the church to do their utmost to preserve the unity.

By unity of the Spirit, Paul meant the union that the Holy Spirit creates or gives. This unity begins within the heart of the individual believer, but also depends on the attitudes of all members of the body of Christ. These heart attitudes are manifested through the above listed traits (v. 2), which include the fruit of the Spirit listed in Galatians 5:22–23.

This unity created by the Spirit is the unification of Jews and Gentiles into one community of believers—God's new community—which is explained in the first three chapters of the epistle. The phrase "in the bond of peace" indicates that peace, which is a fruit of the Spirit, is an essential element in the preservation of unity in the church. The absence of peace in any family, group, or organization, whether it is secular or religious, leads to disintegration and dysfunction.

4 There is one body, and one Spirit, even as ye are called in one hope of your calling; 5 One Lord, one faith, one baptism, 6 One God and Father of all, who is above all, and through all, and in you all.

In these three verses, Paul declared that the unity of the church arises from the unity of the Godhead, making deliberate allusion to the Trinity. First, the church is "one body" because there is "one Spirit" that created it. In Romans 12:5, Paul called the church the body of Christ, which encompasses both Jews and Gentiles. The unity of the body is made possible as a result of the work of the Holy Spirit, who also indwells it.

The human body is made up of many parts, with many functions: the feet, the hands, the eyes, the mouth, and all other parts are joined to the head. They function as one body. In the same way the church, which is made of many members, is joined to the Head, Christ Jesus, by the Holy Spirit to function as one body. The church is called to "one hope," which refers to the present reality and the future benefit of life everlasting. Paul referred to the Holy Spirit in Ephesians 1:13 as our seal, which guarantees us of the fullness of the everlasting life—life beyond the grave. It is also the Holy Spirit that sustains that hope in the Christian's present earthly life.

Second, the reality of the Christian calling and hope is established on Jesus Christ, who alone is the object of our faith. "One faith" refers both to the Gospel, which embodies the doctrine of the Christian faith and the gift of faith by which we are saved (see 2:8–10). "One baptism" is the liturgical act through which we publicly profess our belief in the atoning death and resurrection of Christ for the forgiveness of our sin. By being baptized in the name of the Father, Son, and the Holy Spirit, we declare our union with the one Lord and Saviour, Jesus Christ.

Third, Paul described the church as one family in which every believer belongs and has equal rights and privileges. The one God who is the "Father of all, who is above all, and through all, and in you all" heads this family. The God whom the Jews acclaim as "One," as opposed to the Gentiles' many gods, is now the God and Father of all, both Jewish and Gentile believers.

7 But unto every one of us is given grace according to the measure of the gift of Christ. 8 Wherefore he saith, When he ascended up on high, he led captivity captive, and gave gifts unto men.

Following his clarification of the unity, or oneness, of the church and its importance, Paul turned his attention to diversity and its importance in the functionality in the body of Christ. Notice the change from the use of "all" meaning "us all" (v. 6) to "every one" of us (v. 7). Paul emphasized that unity does not constitute uniformity. The apostle began this section with the conjunction "but," which suggests that in spite of the unity (oneness in the body), there is room for the individuality of each member as well. This is evident in the gifts He gives to each individual member of the church. Paul wrote that each one of us "is given grace according to the measure of the gift of Christ."

The word "grace" (Gk. *charis*, **KHAR-ece**), used here, is not the same we encounter in 2:5 and 8, by which sinners receive forgiveness. It is *charismata* **(khar-IS-mah-tah)** or "gifts" that equip God's people for service. This *charismata*, Paul wrote, is given according to the measure of the gift of Christ. The word "measure" tends to imply generosity (see Romans 12:3; Luke 6:38; John 3:34). Paul identified the source of the gifts as Christ.

The word "measure" also implies that the gift is granted to all Christians, and every individual has enough to enable him or her to function with the body of Christ and to live as he or she ought to live. All this comes from Christ and through Him, and it is given according to His own plan and purpose. There is, therefore, no room for complaints or boasting, division, or disunity in the body of Christ, since we have been given diverse gifts for the benefits of all.

To confirm the importance of this gift from Christ Jesus, Paul appealed to an Old Testament passage (Psalm 68:18), which says, referring to Christ "Thou hast ascended on high, thou hast led captivity captive: thou hast received gifts for men; yea, for the rebellious also, that the LORD God might dwell among them." There is debate in the appropriate use of language in the two versions (here and in Psalms). However, the statement "When he ascended up on high, he led captivity captive, and gave gifts unto men" refers to Christ's ascension to the right hand of the Father as conqueror over death, sin, and Satan and his cohorts. Christ liberated those who were bound by Satan and took them like captives into heaven. From there, He equipped and gave gifts to the church, which probably also refers to the imparting of gifts of the Holy Spirit on the day of Pentecost.

9 (Now that he ascended, what is it but that he also descended first into the lower parts of the earth? 10 He that descended is the same also that ascended up far above all heavens, that he might fill all things.)

In verses 9 and 10 Paul, applying the principles of apologetics, elaborated and defended the death, resurrection, and ascension of Jesus Christ. He argued that for Christ to ascend into heaven, He must have descended. Paul had earlier alluded to this idea in Ephesians 1:20–22, where he stated that God "set him at his own right hand in the heavenly (places), far above all principality, and power, and might, and dominion, and every name that is named, not only in this world, but also in that which is to come."

Emphasizing the same theme, Paul insisted (Ephesians 4:10) that the One, who descended, is the same One that ascended far above everything else, that He might fill all things. The phrase "fill all things" (Gk. *pleroo*, **play-RO-o**) means "to accomplish" or "fulfill." The purpose of His ascension into heaven, then, is to free Him to accomplish fully the mission for which He descended on Earth.

11 And he gave some, apostles; and some, prophets; and some, evangelists; and some, pastors and teachers; 12 For the perfecting of the saints, for the work of the ministry, for the edifying of the body of Christ:

The gift the ascended Christ gave to the church is the Holy Spirit, whom He promised to send to His disciples, after He was glorified (John 7:39). The Holy Spirit, then, equipped the church with special abilities, bestowed on individual members for the benefit of all. We recall the variety of gifts Paul recorded in Romans 12 and 1 Corinthians 12, where a more extensive list of gifts for the building of the church is given. In this section, Paul listed five administrative offices that Christ gave to the church: apostles, prophets, evangelists, pastors, and teachers.

The first in the list is "apostles," from the Greek word *apostolos* (**ap-OS-tol-os**). There are three possible ways in which the word *apostolos* is used in the New Testament. First, it is used to mean the "sent ones" (John 13:16). In this sense, it applies to every Christian, for we are all called and sent as Christ's ambassadors. Second, there were the apostles of the church (2 Corinthians 8:23) sent out by the church as messengers and missionaries. Third, there was the small group with the special title of "apostle." The group comprised the original Twelve (including Matthias), Paul, James (the brother of Jesus), and a few others. They were eyewitnesses to the risen Lord, chosen and authorized by Christ (Acts 1:21–22; 10:40–41). This probably is the sense in which Paul uses the term here.

The next gift given to the church is "prophets" (Gk. *prophetes*, **prof-AY-tace**) with special abilities from God to give guidance to the Christian community and to declare the will of God. Next is "evangelists" (Gk. *euaggelistes,* **yoo-ang-ghel-is-TACE**), preachers, or those who proclaim the Gospel. The next group of gifts is "pastors" (Gk. *poimen,* **poy-MANE**), or shepherds, who are also teachers. Some argue that pastors and teachers are two names for the same office or ministry. But most agree that they are two different offices with different functions, since we can have Christian teachers who are not pastors. Nevertheless, all five gifts relate to one form of teaching or another, and they are set in the church to fulfill certain purposes and functions.

The King James Version (KJV) suggests three functions: (1) perfecting of the saints, (2) doing the work of ministry, and (3) edifying of the body. Some other translations reflect the view that the functions are cumulative—that is, perfecting the saints prepares them for works of ministry; that, in turn, results in the edification of the body of Christ. The word "perfecting" is from the Greek *katartismos* (**kat-ar-tis-MOS**), which means "to equip, to prepare, or to make ready." Therefore, the apostles, prophets, evangelists, pastors, and teachers' function is to prepare God's people for the work of ministry or for service.

The second function of the people endowed with the special gifts is to edify or build up the body of Christ, the church. The word used here by the KJV is "edifying," in Greek *oikodome* (**oy-kod-om-AY**), with an architectural undertone. It has the idea of building a house. However, the church here should not be mistaken to mean the physical church edifice; rather it means building up people. We are called to the task of building one another up in the Lord, in love.

13 Till we all come in the unity of the faith, and of the knowledge of the Son of God, unto a perfect man, unto the measure of the stature of the fulness of Christ: 14 That we henceforth be no more children, tossed to and fro, and carried about with every wind of doctrine, by the sleight of men, and cunning craftiness, whereby they lie in wait to deceive;

While the major function and purpose of the gifts are to equip God's people for the work of the ministry and to build up the body of Christ, the ultimate objective is fourfold. The church is to be built up until it attains complete unity of faith. Paul was speaking to the Jews and Gentiles about being knit together in faith, in the belief of the Gospel of Christ. The ministry of God's people will help the church to grow in the knowledge of the Son of God, Christ Jesus.

Paul had already mentioned our knowledge of God in 1:17, and next he focused on the knowledge of Christ. Here the word "unity" modifies both faith and knowledge. Therefore, the ambition of every Christian should be to attain this unity, which is based on the united understanding and knowledge of who Christ is.

The full unity and knowledge of the Son of God leads to maturity—unto a perfect man. The word "perfect" (Gk. *teleios,* **TEL-i-os**) here refers to that which has reached the age of maturity or adulthood, rather than moral perfection. The proof of this maturity is the unity the church attains on the basis of its knowledge of Christ. Although it can be interpreted as an individual maturity in Christ, which is also a New Testament concept, this maturity refers to the whole body of Christ. When we reach it, we will not be deceived or led astray by false doctrine or teaching.

We know that children have the tendency of being easily swayed by new things. But when they grow into adulthood, that tendency diminishes. Spiritually immature people easily fall prey to the sleight and cunning craftiness of men who lie in wait to deceive. The word for "sleight" (Gk. *kubeia,* **koo-BI-ah**) literally means "dice playing," "gambling," or "fraud" and is used metaphorically here to describe the trickery and manipulation of unscrupulous men who take advantage of people's ignorance and vulnerability. Paul was plainly speaking about what happens in our own time. In today's church scene, we have witnessed more than a few preachers and cult leaders who deceive people to enrich themselves.

Maturity in the knowledge of Christ protects the Christian from being easily manipulated. That is why Paul insisted that both individual and corporate maturity are necessary in the church.

15 But speaking the truth in love, may grow up into him in all things, which is the head, even Christ:

The apostle Paul shifted his attention from the mark of immaturity, which is doctrinal instability, to the qualities of mature (perfect) Christianity, which will promote unity and peace in the church. These qualities are the seemingly rare combination of truth and love. These two traits are essential in the life of the body of Christ. They lead to growth in the church. It is imperative for the Christian to hold firmly and be loyal to the truth of the Gospel on one hand and to have a loving concern for others' welfare on the other. Many Christians seem to hold so firmly to the truth that we become intolerant and unfriendly in our treatment of those who seem to violate it.

There is nothing more prone to dividing the church of Christ than being so dogmatic in one's belief that it offends others. Such an attitude causes hatred. The issue Paul identified here is communication. How can one communicate the truth so that unity can be maintained? Paul answered, "Speak the truth in love." This carries the idea of being genuine and truthful to one another as opposed to the dishonesty of those described in the previous verse (v. 14), whose goal is to deceive others for their own selfish benefit.

16 From whom the whole body fitly joined together and compacted by that which every joint supplieth, according to the effectual working in the measure of every part, maketh increase of the body unto the edifying of itself in love.

Using biological metaphors, the apostle Paul illustrated the relationship between church and Christ. The human body, with its many parts, is joined together by different ligaments to the head, and each part works corporately with other parts for its growth. This is a picture of the church, which is composed of many members with diverse gifts and functions, joined together by the Holy Spirit, with Christ Jesus as its Head.

When every member does his or her part working together as one entity and each one contributes his or her own share, the body will maintain unity and grow in maturity and love. Conversely, if there is lack of coordinated effort on the part of any member or if one decides to function on his or her own, the body will become dysfunctional and stagnant. Therefore, for the body of Christ to grow, function properly, and fully mature in Christ, there must be harmony and obedience to the Head, through which the whole body derives its life.

Just as He begins this section with a call to "walk worthy of the vocation wherewith ye are called...in love" (vv. 1–2), Paul also concluded by calling and reminding us to function in love so as to build up one another. In a community filled with such diversity as the body of Christ, the only thing that will help its functionality and growth is love. Jesus says that love should be the trademark of His followers (John 13:35) and unity is His great prayer for the church (17:20–23).

Daily Bible Readings

M: Drawn by God's Power
Acts 8:12–25
T: Drawn from a Distant Land
Acts 8:26–38
W: Drawn from Other Nations
Acts 22:3–16
T: Drawn to Be Christians
Acts 11:19–26
F: Seekers Among All People
Acts 17:22–28
S: A Worthy Calling
Ephesians 4:1–6
S: Joined and Knit Together
Ephesians 4:7–16

NOTES

TEACHING TIPS

November 9

Bible Study Guide 10

1. Words You Should Know

A. Dissimulation (Galatians 2:13) *sunupokrinomai* (Gk.)—To join in acting the hypocrite, in pretending to act from one motive whereas another motive really inspires the act.

B. Justified (v. 16) *dikaioo* (Gk.)—The legal and formal acquittal from guilt by God as Judge; the pronouncement as righteous of the sinner who believes on the Lord Jesus Christ.

C. Transgressor (v. 18) *hamartolos* (Gk.)—A sinner.

D. Crucified (v. 20) *sustauroo* (Gk.)—Spiritual identification with Christ in His death.

2. Teacher Preparation

Unifying Principle—Confronting Opposition. When we are afraid of what others might think about us, we sometimes behave in ways inconsistent with our beliefs. How can we live so that our lives witness to our beliefs? Through writing and example, Paul admonishes believers that our acceptance before God comes not by following the rules but through living faithfully to Christ.

A. Begin with prayer and then study the Devotional Reading.

B. Study the Focal Verses and AIM for Change.

C. Consult the *Precepts For Living*® CD-ROM for additional commentary and background history.

3. Starting the Lesson

A. Open the class with prayer.

B. Ask for a volunteer to read the In Focus story. Next ask the class to think of a time in their lives when they compromised what they believed as a Christian just to please others. Allow two or three volunteers to share their stories with the class.

4. Getting into the Lesson

A. Have volunteers read the Background and The People, Places, and Times sections. Then discuss with the class Paul's life and how he was qualified to confront false teachers (refer to Acts 8 and 9).

B. Review the Words You Should Know section. Ask the students to explain how they understand being "justified" by God versus being "justified" by a judge in court.

C. After discussing the In Depth section, have the students answer the questions in the Search the Scriptures section, and discuss their answers.

5. Relating the Lesson to Life

According to the Word, we must have faith in Christ alone to be saved. Discuss with the class the differences in what we believe versus other religions, such as Islam or Buddhism. (You may have to do research in the library or on the Internet prior to class.)

6. Arousing Action

A. Direct the students' attention to the Lesson In Our Society and Make It Happen sections.

B. Have the class report next week what changes they are making to remain faithful to Christ.

C. Close the class with prayer.

Worship Guide NOV 9th

For the Superintendent or Teacher
Theme: Conflict in the Community
Theme Song: "Yield Not to Temptation"
Devotional Reading: Romans 10:5–17
Prayer

CONFLICT IN THE COMMUNITY

Bible Background • GALATIANS 2:11–3:29
Printed Text • GALATIANS 2:11–21 Devotional Reading • ROMANS 10:5–17

AIM for Change

By the end of the lesson, we will:
DISCUSS what caused conflict between the Jewish and Gentile Christians;
IDENTIFY situations in which we compromised our own principles; and
STRATEGIZE ways to remain faithful to our beliefs in Christ's demands.

Keep in Mind

"There is neither Jew nor Greek, there is neither bond nor free, there is neither male nor female: for ye are all one in Christ Jesus" (Galatians 3:28).

Focal Verses

KJV **Galatians 2:11** But when Peter was come to Antioch, I withstood him to the face, because he was to be blamed.

12 For before that certain came from James, he did eat with the Gentiles: but when they were come, he withdrew and separated himself, fearing them which were of the circumcision.

13 And the other Jews dissembled likewise with him; insomuch that Barnabas also was carried away with their dissimulation.

14 But when I saw that they walked not uprightly according to the truth of the gospel, I said unto Peter before them all, If thou, being a Jew, livest after the manner of Gentiles, and not as do the Jews, why compellest thou the Gentiles to live as do the Jews?

15 We who are Jews by nature, and not sinners of the Gentiles,

16 Knowing that a man is not justified by the works of the law, but by the faith of Jesus Christ, even we have believed in Jesus Christ, that we might be justified by the faith of Christ, and not by the works of the law: for by the works of the law shall no flesh be justified.

17 But if, while we seek to be justified by Christ, we ourselves also are found sinners, is therefore Christ the minister of sin? God forbid.

18 For if I build again the things which I destroyed, I make myself a transgressor.

19 For I through the law am dead to the law, that I might live unto God.

20 I am crucified with Christ: nevertheless I live; yet not I, but Christ liveth in me: and the life which

NLT **Galatians 2:11** But when Peter came to Antioch, I had to oppose him to his face, for what he did was very wrong.

12 When he first arrived, he ate with the Gentile Christians, who were not circumcised. But afterward, when some friends of James came, Peter wouldn't eat with the Gentiles anymore. He was afraid of criticism from these people who insisted on the necessity of circumcision.

13 As a result, other Jewish Christians followed Peter's hypocrisy, and even Barnabas was led astray by their hypocrisy.

14 When I saw that they were not following the truth of the gospel message, I said to Peter in front of all the others, "Since you, a Jew by birth, have discarded the Jewish laws and are living like a Gentile, why are you now trying to make these Gentiles follow the Jewish traditions?

15 "You and I are Jews by birth, not 'sinners' like the Gentiles.

16 Yet we know that a person is made right with God by faith in Jesus Christ, not by obeying the law. And we have believed in Christ Jesus, so that we might be made right with God because of our faith in Christ, not because we have obeyed the law. For no one will ever be made right with God by obeying the law."

17 But suppose we seek to be made right with God through faith in Christ and then we are found guilty because we have abandoned the law. Would that mean Christ has led us into sin? Absolutely not!

18 Rather, I am a sinner if I rebuild the old system of law I already tore down.

I now live in the flesh I live by the faith of the Son of God, who loved me, and gave himself for me.

21 I do not frustrate the grace of God: for if righteousness come by the law, then Christ is dead in vain.

19 For when I tried to keep the law, it condemned me. So I died to the law—I stopped trying to meet all its requirements—so that I might live for God.

20 My old self has been crucified with Christ. It is no longer I who live, but Christ lives in me. So I live in this earthly body by trusting in the Son of God, who loved me and gave himself for me.

21 I do not treat the grace of God as meaningless. For if keeping the law could make us right with God, then there was no need for Christ to die.

In Focus

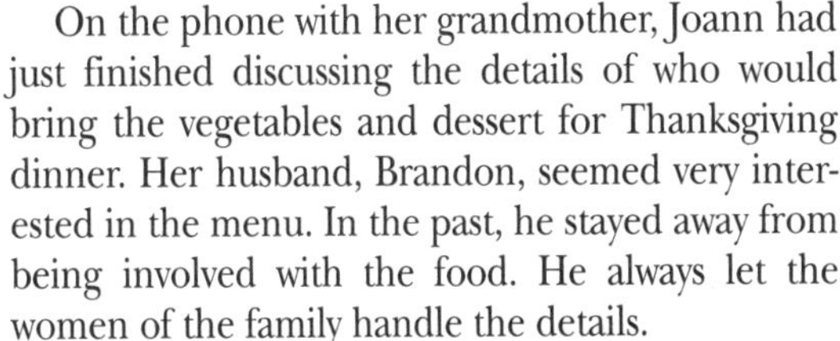

On the phone with her grandmother, Joann had just finished discussing the details of who would bring the vegetables and dessert for Thanksgiving dinner. Her husband, Brandon, seemed very interested in the menu. In the past, he stayed away from being involved with the food. He always let the women of the family handle the details.

"Brandon, you seem very interested in the menu this year. You know the menu has not changed. We will be eating all of your favorite foods plus much more. Do you want to add something different this year?" She handed him the menu to review.

"I was just concerned about the meats being served."

"You know we are having the same meats we've served for the last 12 years: turkey, roast beef, ham, and chicken." She looked at him, puzzled.

"I think we should eliminate ham from the menu."

"Brandon, what is wrong with you? We do not eat ham except on special holidays. I rarely buy bacon because you are trying to lose weight. Please tell me what caused this sudden change."

"Most of my coworkers are Muslim. They believe that pork is unclean and should not be eaten. They won't eat anything that has even a little pork in it. They have made some comments about my eating habits. So I thought it is time we make a change."

"Brandon, we are not Muslims. We believe whatever God has given us is clean. Once we pray and thank God for the food, it is OK to eat. No, we should not be gluttons who constantly eat food that is fattening. Or if a person has health problems, they should not eat pork if it will make them sick. Otherwise, it's OK. Don't change because it is easier to fit in with your coworkers. You just live by example, and they will see Christ in you."

"You're right, Joann. It is so easy to compromise what I believe sometimes. They seem to be real religious, praying five times a day and eating special meals. But I know only through faith in Jesus Christ can anyone be saved. Maybe I need to witness to them about what I believe."

In today's In Focus story, Brandon thought he had to compromise His beliefs in order to show his Muslim coworkers that he is truly saved. In the Scripture text, we find Gentile Christians being persuaded to believe they must follow the laws of Moses to truly be saved. It is OK for Brandon to give up eating pork around his Muslim coworkers if it offends them and in order to win them to Christ, but giving it up will not save them. Remember that our works do not save us; only faith in Christ will save us. We are saved by grace and not by the law.

The People, Places, and Times

Judaizers. These were Jewish Christians who wanted to turn Gentile Christians into Jews. They believed Old Testament Jewish laws and traditions, such as circumcision and dietary restrictions, should be required of all believers. They denied that salvation is by faith in Jesus alone. Paul called them "false teachers."

Antioch. This is the capital of the Roman province of Syria. It was a major trade center in the ancient world. It was heavily populated by Greeks, but eventually it became a strong Christian center. It became the headquarters for the Gentile church.

During the persecution that followed the death of Stephen, some of the disciples went to Antioch and preached to the Jews (Acts 11:19). The Jerusalem church sent Barnabas there when numerous conversions occurred. After assessing the situation, Barnabas left and brought Paul back with him. They stayed in Antioch a year, teaching the people. Antioch was the base from which Paul often started and/or ended his missionary journeys. The disciples were first called Christians there (Acts 11:26).

Galatia. It is a Roman province located in the center of Asia Minor (present-day Turkey). It was a large, fertile plateau that had favorable land for agriculture, so the population increased steadily. The Galatian Christians were mainly Greek, unfamiliar with Jewish laws and customs.

Sources:

Life Application Study Bible (New Revised Standard Version). Wheaton, Ill.: Tyndale House Publishers, 1989.

Unger, Merrill. *The New Unger's Bible Handbook.* Chicago, Ill.: Moody Press, 1984.

Background

Paul wrote this letter about A.D. 49 to the churches in Galatia, founded on his first missionary journey (Acts 13:2–14:28). After his return to Antioch, the Judaizers accused him of not preaching the true Gospel. They wanted the Gentile converts to adhere to Jewish laws, specifically circumcision and food restrictions. Some had followed Paul to the Galatian cities and urged new converts to follow the laws of Moses in order to be saved. The Jerusalem Council settled this dispute (Acts 15). Moreover, Paul's apostolic status was being questioned by some of the people in Galatia.

His purpose for writing this urgent letter was to refute the Judaizers' teaching of mixing grace and law as the means for salvation. Paul called the believers to remember salvation is by God's grace, through faith in Jesus Christ. He wanted them to hold fast to their faith and not be bound by the law.

Source:

Life Application Study Bible (New Revised Standard Version). Wheaton, Ill.: Tyndale House Publishers, 1989.

At-A-Glance

1. Paul Confronts Peter (Galatians 2:11–14)
2. Paul Confronts Legalism (vv. 15–19)
3. Paul Calls for Commitment (vv. 20–21)

In Depth

1. Paul Confronts Peter (Galatians 2:11–14)

Paul related to the Galatians the details of another journey he took to Jerusalem and how he behaved at that time (vv. 1–10). When the Judaizers wanted Titus to be circumcised, he had argued that Gentile converts should not adhere to this law as a means for salvation. James, Peter, and John accepted his apostleship as genuine and acknowledged he was called to witness to the Gentiles.

Then Paul revealed he had a confrontation with Peter in Antioch. Peter, Paul, the Judaizers, and some Gentile Christians had all gathered together for a meal. Peter was a leader of the church, but he was acting like a hypocrite. While in the Gentile churches, he ate with them, even though they were not circumcised. He had been told in a vision to call nothing common or unclean (Acts 10). But after Jewish Christians from Jerusalem came to visit, to appease the Jews, Peter began to separate himself from the Gentile Christians. He did not want to offend them. Then other Jews, including Barnabas, an apostle who helped plant the Gentile churches, did the same. It sometimes appears easier to follow the crowd than to obey the commands of God. However, when we disobey God there are consequences.

Paul felt it was necessary to personally confront him to stop the behavior from damaging the Christian church. If a brother or sister in Christ sins, we are to speak with them about their actions so corrections can be made. If the sin goes unchallenged, it can polarize and damage a church. It only takes one person to destroy a church. Paul did not want Peter's actions to nullify the Gospel message that had been shared with the new converts.

Since Peter had publicly offended the Gentile Christians, Paul publicly confronted him about his behavior, which had diverted from the truth of the Gospel. He asked a question, "If thou, being a Jew, livest after the manner of Gentiles, and not as do the Jews, why compellest thou the Gentiles to live as do the Jews?" Peter's conduct was contradicting what he was telling the Gentiles. He did not obediently adhere to the ceremonial laws, so why was he trying to compel the Gentiles to observe them? He knew Christians were no longer under the law but were instead under the covenant of grace. Peter just wanted to expect that Gentiles had to comply with the Jews or risk not being accepted into Christian fellowship. How disheartening is it for people to feel they have to conform to a cultural set of rules to be accepted into the body of believers! Some have turned back to the world where they are accepted without prequalifications.

2. Paul Confronts Legalism (vv. 15–19)

Paul appealed to Peter by saying, "We who are Jews by nature and not sinners of the Gentiles" to imply that those who have been born and trained in the Jewish religion are not considered impure Gentiles. They both knew that obedience to the law does not save us, but only through faith in Jesus Christ, who pronounces us righteous. In rebuttal to the Judaizers, "Justification by faith, in Christ" is the core message Paul gives the Galatians. It would be foolish for Jewish Christians to digress into believing works, ceremonial sacrifices, and rituals can justify a person. In doing so, Jesus' sacrifice would be declared ineffective and hope for redemption from sin would be lost. Paul did not want Christians' witness to be considered false.

When someone challenges our witness, by implying works are required to be saved we can witness that Jesus redeemed us with His own blood (Hebrews 9:12). That was the only act required to save us from sin. No matter how much we put in the offering plate, how many positions we hold in the church, or how much service we give to others, only Jesus can save us. Yes, the laws have a place in our spiritual lives—to give us standards of behavior to follow as well as convict us of sin. However, because we cannot always consistently obey the Ten Commandments we must trust Jesus to forgive us of our sins.

Paul stated, "For I through the law am dead to the law, that I might live unto God" (v. 19). The coming of Christ superseded the law. There was no further need for sacrifices and purification ceremonies. These aspects of following the law had ended with the coming of Christ. So there was no need for believers to continue under its obligations. Though dead to the law, he now was more spiritually alive and united with God through Christ (Romans 7:4). He felt freedom from bondage. "But now we are delivered from the law, that being dead wherein we were held; that we should serve in the newness of spirit, and not in the oldness of the letter" (Romans 7:6).

3. Paul Calls for Commitment (vv. 20–21)

Paul said he was being "crucified with Christ," which means the old sinful man died with Christ (Romans 6:6). Yet, he was alive in Christ, through His resurrection. But on a daily basis, we must crucify the desires of the flesh that draw us away from following Christ. That means dying to self. If we resist the temptation to follow the flesh, the Spirit will direct us in godly living.

"I live; yet not I, but Christ liveth in me" refers to living by grace, which comes from God. We are dependent on God to bestow His favor and blessings upon us. Therefore, no one can boast of works being the means of salvation. It is only by grace we are not destroyed by sin. God graciously forgives us.

Paul proclaims, "the life which I now live in the flesh I live by the faith of the Son of God, who loved me, and gave himself for me." He lives his everyday life like others do, but he totally depends on his faith in Christ to live in a way that honors God. "The just shall live by faith" (Romans 1:17). Without believing in God's love for us, we have no basis for our faith.

The love God has for us cannot be denied. "God showed his great love for us by sending Christ to die for us while we were still sinners" (Romans 5:8, NLT). We are to commit our lives to showing love to others, even when they oppose us. Paul corrected Peter and the Judaizers, in love. He wanted them to commit to sharing the true Gospel so that others would be saved. We, too, must help others come to know Christ, through the truth of the Word. The best way is to be a living testimony before others. As we commit to being faithful to God, others will be drawn to Him. We cannot compromise our faith to satisfy others. Paul reminds us that justification does not come from laws but from faith in Christ. Otherwise, Jesus' death would be meaningless.

Once a person puts their trust in Christ, they become a part of the family of God. In the family of God, there is no distinction based on nationality, position in society, or sex (Galatians 3:28). God views us as one body of believers. Paul was calling the people to break down the old ways of distinguishing groups. We all are different in some ways, but our faith in Christ unites us as one. In remembering this fact, we can stop many of the conflicts in the Christian community. Why do we allow our church denominations and unique traditions to cause division among the community of believers?

One is not more favored by God than the other. If we accept Jesus as Lord and Saviour, we are all part of the body.

Source:

Henry, Matthew. *Commentary on the Whole Bible, Complete and Unabridged.* Peabody, Mass.: Hendrickson Publishers, 1991.

Search the Scriptures

1. Why did Paul confront Peter (Galatians 2:12)?
2. According to Paul, how is a person justified (v. 16)?
3. What was the core message Paul gave the Galatians in rebuttal to the Judaizers (vv. 15–19)?
4. What was Paul's relationship to the law (v. 19)?
5. Who did Paul say lives in Him (v. 20)?

Discuss the Meaning

1. As Christians, we are saved through the sacrifice Jesus made on the Cross. Have you ever encountered people like the Judaizers? How did you respond to them?
2. According to Romans 10:14–5, 17, how can we help others come to know the truth of the Gospel?

Lesson in Our Society

In today's society, many religious people have false ideas about what is required to inherit eternal life. A study conducted a few years ago revealed some interesting theological beliefs of Americans. Almost half of those surveyed believed the Bible, Koran, and Book of Mormon are all different expressions of the same spiritual truths. The same percentage believed that when Jesus lived on Earth He sinned like other people. These false beliefs and others often creep into the church and can cause conflict.

We have to constantly watch what message is being proclaimed. When that message causes believers to turn away from the truth of the Gospel, we have to take corrective action and teach the plan of salvation (Romans 10:9). We cannot compromise on the precepts of the Word. Teaching and witnessing to the world also means exposing ourselves to possible persecution and ridicule. However, what we may suffer is nothing in comparison to the sacrifice Jesus paid on our behalf.

Make It Happen

During the week, evaluate any areas where you may have compromised your principles. Think about why you have chosen to behave in ways inconsistent with your faith. Repent and ask God to forgive you. Subsequently, search the Bible for answers that apply to your specific issues. Then seek out additional help from spiritual leaders to receive guidance in living faithful to Christ. Finally, pray and ask God for strength to take a stand for Christ in every situation.

Follow the Spirit

What God wants me to do:

____

____

Remember Your Thoughts

Special insights I have learned:

____

____

More Light on the Text

Galatians 2:11–21

In his letter to the Galatians, Paul wrote in defense of the Gospel of justification by faith—in opposition to the teachings of the Judaizers. The Judaizers insisted that observance of the ceremonial law is an essential component in the plan of salvation. In today's passage, we learn how Paul confronted Peter in this matter; he condemned Christian double standards and stated that we should be able to stand firm and sincere on our beliefs and never be afraid of what people might say or think of us.

11 But when Peter was come to Antioch, I withstood him to the face, because he was to be blamed.
12 For before that certain came from James, he did eat with the Gentiles: but when they were come, he withdrew and separated himself, fearing them which were of the circumcision.

Paul had just narrated his encounter with the leadership of the Church at Jerusalem, who validated his message of justification by faith and never insisted that the Gentile Christians keep the law of circumcision. This encounter is recorded in Acts of the Apostles (15:1–11), where the apostle Peter also endorsed that teaching (Acts 15:6–11) by recalling his earlier revelation from the Lord, as recorded in Acts 10:9–22. Using the conjunction "but" or the Greek *de* (**deh**), Paul introduces another significant part of his narrative—his confrontation with the apostle Peter.

Paul stated that when Peter came to Antioch, probably to visit the brethren, he "withstood him to the face." The phrase "withstood him to the face" comes from the Greek *prosoopon auto antesten*, (**PROS-o-pon ow-TO an-TES-tayn**), which can be interpreted as "I opposed him in his face" or "I challenged him face-to-face." The word *antesten* means to "oppose, stand against or resist," and *prósoopon* means "face, presence, or front." The idea here is that "because he [Peter] was to be blamed," Paul was able to boldly and publicly confront him. The word used here—*kataginosko* (**kat-ag-in-O-sko**)—may mean that he brought the blame upon himself or he deserved blame. However, the idea here is that Paul reproved Peter because what he did or was doing was wrong. There is no indication of the time when Peter took this journey to Antioch or when this event happened. However, it appears that it was after Paul's visit to Jerusalem and his encounter with the apostles in Jerusalem, usually referred to as the "Jerusalem Council," when the leadership, including Peter, endorsed his message of justification by faith. What was it that Peter did wrong that prompted such a rebuke from Paul?

Paul answered that question in verse 12. Apparently, Peter had gone to Antioch, as has been indicated above, to visit the churches and encourage them. It appears that a group "from James" (meaning from Jerusalem—see Acts 15:12ff) also came later to Antioch. We learn that James presided over that Jerusalem Council. So he was a prominent member of the Jerusalem church. James probably either sent this group officially or they came on their own. However, this group was made of Jews who were now Christian converts. It is apparent that the Jewish rites were still observed in Jerusalem by these Jewish converts long after they converted to Christianity. It appears that when they came to Antioch, they observed the ceremonial rites and insisted that the Gentiles do the same. We are not informed what the mission of the group to Antioch was. The important thing is that Peter was already in Antioch before they came. Having known the truth, he was socializing with the Gentile converts, eating and drinking with them. However, when this group arrived from Jerusalem, Peter "withdrew and separated himself" from the Gentile Christians. Because he was afraid of those who were "of the circumcision"—the Jewish converts—he stopped fellowshipping with them.

There are a number of speculative suggestions why Peter was afraid of these people. He probably was afraid of what they would think about him; he was afraid of their reproach or opposition against him; or he was afraid that they might report him to the Jerusalem church. Whatever the reason, it reminds one of Peter's character traits of inconsistency and cowardice. This is the same Peter who boldly stepped on the water walking toward his Master but trembled and began to sink in the waves. This is also the same Peter who confessed the Lord and promised to die with Him but then vehemently denied Him. He was a bold, zealous, ardent, and forward man and at the same time a timid, fearful, and irresolute one. Here again, he exhibited the same traits of not standing up for what he believed. Such behavior oftentimes influences other people, especially when one is in a leadership position as Peter was.

13 And the other Jews dissembled likewise with him; insomuch that Barnabas also was carried away with their dissimulation.

The consequence of Peter's action is made evident, for Paul wrote, "the other Jews dissembled likewise with him." The phrase "and the other Jews" definitely refers to other Jewish Christian converts, who probably traveled with Peter to Antioch or who were living in the city. The word translated "dissembled" here is the Greek *sunupokrinomai* (**soon-oo-pok-RIN-om-ahee**), which means "to act hypocritically in concert with." These converts, like Peter, probably had been associating with the Gentiles, eating and drinking freely with them; but when the group from James arrived, they tried to conceal their true belief. They withdrew from the Gentile converts. Because they would logically look upon him as their leader, they likely were influenced by Peter's example.

Peter's actions did not affect only the other Jewish Christians; Barnabas also was affected, for he was carried away with their hypocrisy. The word "dissimulation" is a translation of the Greek noun *hupokrisis* (**hoop-OK-ree-sis**), from which we have the English "hypocrisy." It means "to act on pretense or with a purpose to deceive." This means that these people, together with Peter, believed one way and behaved in another. So influential were their actions that Barnabas, an ardent believer, an apostle, and a companion with Paul to the Gentiles, who had been influential in planting churches of the Gentiles, also succumbed to their deception. This appeared to infuriate Paul the more and made it more imperative that he challenge and reprove Peter's conduct and behavior publicly. This he did in order to preserve the truth of the Gospel and the welfare of the church.

14 But when I saw that they walked not uprightly according to the truth of the gospel, I said unto Peter before them all, If thou, being a Jew, livest after the manner of Gentiles, and not as do the Jews, why compellest thou the Gentiles to live as do the Jews?

Paul stated that when he realized their hypocrisy,"that they walked not uprightly according to the truth of the gospel" he talked to Peter. The word "walk," as used in the Scripture, expresses behavior, conduct, or demeanor. So the phrase "they walked not uprightly" literally means they did not walk uprightly or straightly. It also indicates that they behaved in a dishonest way. As such, their conduct and actions contradicted the truth of the Gospel, which requires honesty and integrity and therefore needed to be corrected instantly. Paul confronted Peter before everyone present. The congregation probably included the Jewish Christians from the Jerusalem church, the Jewish converts living in Antioch, and also the Gentile Christians who assembled. We can only guess how the issue came about or where and on what occasion the issue was raised. Whatever the occasion or circumstance, since it affected the whole church, Paul thought it essential to deal with it publicly rather than privately.

In order to achieve this mission Paul posed a rhetorical question to Peter, in front of the crowd. The question served both as a rebuke and an argument to state his case against Peter's hypocritical conduct. Paul asked that if Peter, being a Jew by birth, had done away with the Jewish laws and was living like the Gentiles and believed that salvation was only by faith and not by the law then why was he trying to compel the Gentiles to live like Jews, by obeying or keeping the Jewish laws and ritual he himself has discarded? The word "compellest" in Greek is *anagkazo* (**an-ang-KAD-zo**), which means "to constrain, induce, or to persuade."

The idea was that Peter's hypocritical behavior here led the Gentile brethren to believe that in addition to receiving Christ by faith, it was necessary for them to be circumcised in order to be saved. Of course, Peter did not seem to have an answer to Paul's charge against him. The attitude of Peter and the other brethren toward the Gentile Christians was not only hypocritical, but through their conduct, they were also propagating a false doctrine. Paul then expounded the truth of the Gospel in the rest of the passage (vv. 15–21).

15 We who are Jews by nature, and not sinners of the Gentiles, 16 Knowing that a man is not justified by the works of the law, but by the faith of Jesus Christ, even we have believed in Jesus Christ, that we might be justified by the faith of Christ, and not by the works of the law: for by the works of the law shall no flesh be justified.

After challenging Peter and the rest of the Jewish converts, including Barnabas, for their hypocrisy, Paul spoke on the subject of justification by faith. By the phrase "we who are Jews by nature," Paul referred to those of the Jewish converts, who are descendants of the Jewish nation and of Jewish parents, who have been brought up with the knowledge of God and the law. By the phrase "not sinners of the Gentiles," Paul meant that he and the rest of the Jewish converts were not like the Gentile converts, who didn't have the privilege of being raised with the knowledge of God and of the law. Here Paul was not saying that the Jews were not sinners. His stand on this issue was clear (Romans 2; 3) for he placed everyone under the same category before God—sinners. The difference is that the Jewish people have the knowledge of the true God, and they thought the law was necessary in order to be right with God; but the Gentile nations never had such knowledge, and so they were without God.

Paul then argued in verse 16 that they (the Jewish Christians) knew becoming right with (justified before) God was not because of keeping the law but because of faith in Christ. Therefore, Paul said they "believed in Jesus Christ" so that they might be acceptable to God, through their faith in Christ. This is not achievable by obeying or keeping the law. Paul went on to emphasize that justification is by faith in Christ alone and that no one will be justified or acceptable to God because he or she observes the law (Romans 3:30). Rather salvation is totally by grace, through faith in Christ, and not by works (Ephesians 2:8–9; 1 John 1:9). On this basis, everyone is equal before the Lord, whether Jew or

Gentile. Everyone is saved under the same condition—by the grace of God, through faith without the law, for by keeping the law, no one is justified.

Paul's objective was to establish the fact that since they have believed in Christ and accordingly have been justified, obedience to the Law of Moses is, therefore, no more a requirement for the purpose of being justified before God.

17 But if, while we seek to be justified by Christ, we ourselves also are found sinners, is therefore Christ the minister of sin? God forbid. 18 For if I build again the things which I destroyed, I make myself a transgressor.

Verse 17 poses a question some find difficult to understand. Aware that his teaching on justification by faith may be misconstrued to mean that one does not have to observe the moral law, Paul tried to set things straight. The basic idea here is that we are saved by faith only, but this is not a license to break the law or do whatever we like. In other words, the fact that one is saved by grace, through faith in Christ, does not release one from the responsibility of the law. That would be contradictory to the teachings of Christ. So Paul's argument, posed as a rhetorical question, states, "But suppose we seek to be made right with God, through faith in Christ, and then we are found guilty because we have abandoned the law. Would that mean Christ has led us into sin?" (NLT). Paul answers emphatically with a resounding negation: *Me genoito*! (Gk. **may GHEN-oy-to**). This means "God forbid" or "may it never be." Such an attitude of sin cannot be traced to Jesus and His teaching, and such is not what justification by faith implies—living a lawless life.

Paul continued his argument in defense of the truth of the Gospel and the true meaning of justification by faith. Using the first person singular pronoun but intended as a general principle, Paul argued, "If I build again the things which I destroyed, I make myself a transgressor." The idea here is that if somebody having discarded or abolished that which was wrong or evil reintroduces or reestablishes it then he or she is a wrongdoer and a transgressor of the Law of God. The particular application here tends to refer to the question of circumcision and the other Jewish rites of the Mosaic Law. The coming of Christ, with the doctrine of justification by faith, has in effect abolished these ritualistic laws and rites. Peter and the other Jewish Christians were quite aware of this (see Peter's argument in Acts 15:7–10). Yet, by compelling the Gentiles to keep the rites and by their actions and influence, they seem to reestablish that which has been abolished and rebuild that which has been torn down (Ephesians 2:14–15; Colossians 2:14–17). To do such a thing is sin and rejection of the work of grace, which Christ wrought through His crucifixion on the Cross.

19 For I through the law am dead to the law, that I might live unto God.

Paul then turned to personal application of the effect of the law in his life. Paul stated, "I through the law am dead to the law." He probably referred to the Law of Moses and its requirements. By this, Paul appeared to say that after considering the true nature and design of the Law of Moses and the degree of its demands, because he fell short in keeping it, he had laid aside all prospects of being justified by it. By his upbringing, before he met the Lord on the road to Damascus, Paul anticipated the Law as a means of being justified or saved. He, therefore, made every effort to obey it. The main object of his life was to comply with the demands of the Law so that he would be saved. After his encounter on the Damascus Road with the Lord, he became aware of the spiritual implications of the Law. His expectation to be saved by the Law died. He, therefore, became dead to the law so that he "might live unto God."

20 I am crucified with Christ: nevertheless I live; yet not I, but Christ liveth in me: and the life which I now live in the flesh I live by the faith of the Son of God, who loved me, and gave himself for me.

Not only is he dead to the Law, but Paul said that he was crucified with Christ. It should be pointed out here that this statement does not imply that Paul was crucified literally as Christ. Rather he says that his faith in, acceptance of, and relationship with Christ, who was crucified for our sin, is tantamount to being crucified with Him. In other words he is no longer living on his own power of keeping the law; but by accepting the work of Christ on the Cross, he is crucified with Christ. Consequently, he is no more being influenced by the law or things of this world. Just as, through His death on the Cross, Christ became insensitive to the things of this world, in like manner, Paul had become insensitive to worldly things, and they did not affect him anymore. Being crucified with Christ is a spiritual experience rather than a physical one. Paul expressed the same idea in Philippians, where he said, "That I may know him, and the power of his resurrection, and the fellowship of his sufferings, being made conformable unto his death; if by any means I might attain unto the resurrection of the dead" (3:10–11).

Writing to the Romans, Paul expressed this idea thus:

> Knowing this, that our old man is crucified with him, that the body of sin might be destroyed, that henceforth we should not serve sin. For he that is dead is freed from sin. Now if we be dead with Christ, we believe that we shall also live with him: Knowing that Christ being raised from the dead dieth no more; death hath no more dominion over him. For in that he died, he died unto sin once: but in that he liveth, he liveth unto God. Likewise reckon ye also yourselves to be dead indeed unto sin, but alive unto God through Jesus Christ our Lord (Romans 6:6–12).

Although spiritually he was crucified with Christ and dead to sin and the rudiments of the law, Paul affirmed that physically he was alive and living. He then described his physical life as not living on his own but Christ was living in and through him. Having committed his life totally to Christ, Paul's life reflected the life of Christ; it was no more Paul living his own life, doing whatever pleased him, rather Christ was now living through him. Christ was now directing him. Paul stated that the life he now lived was a life of faith in Christ Jesus, and it was He who made it possible through His love, which He demonstrated by dying on the Cross for Paul and all humanity's redemption. This is done only through the grace of God, which He bestows to everyone.

21 I do not frustrate the grace of God: for if righteousness come by the law, then Christ is dead in vain.

Paul concluded his argument. He stated that he did not "frustrate the grace of God." The word "frustrate," used here, is the Greek verb *atheteo* (**ath-et-EH-o**). It means "to set aside, to disesteem, neutralize or to disregard." Here Paul said that he did not annul or disregard the grace of God. The phrase "grace of God" refers to God's favor to mankind manifested in the plan of salvation. It is through the grace of God (God's favor) that a person receives forgiveness and, thus, is justified or is declared righteous before God.

The most popular definition of "grace" or its Greek equivalent, *charis* (**KHAR-ece**), is "unmerited favor" or a free gift. That means salvation is a gift from God to an unmeriting and sinful world; no one can take credit for it. It is all God! In other words, Paul was saying that he did not, in any way, discount the grace of God. This is another way Paul was emphasizing the centrality and essentiality of God's grace in the plan of salvation.

Paul argued, "For if righteousness come by the law, then Christ is dead in vain." Recalling Peter and the Jewish Christians' attitude, Paul said that if one is justified, meaning they earn salvation, or if observance of the law makes them righteous; then Christ's death is in vain.

Source:

Unaegbu, Alajemba R. *Attitude For Living: Commentary On Paul's Epistle To The Philippians: An African Perspective.* Baltimore, Md.: Publish America, 2006.

Daily Bible Readings

M: Dissension and Debate
Acts 15:1–5
T: Evidence of God's Work
Acts 15:6–11
W: The Basis for Unity
Acts 15:12–21
T: The Confession That Saves
Romans 10:5–9
F: Everyone May Be Saved
Romans 10:10–17
S: Not Running in Vain
Galatians 2:1–10
S: Living by Law or Faith
Galatians 2:11–21

NOTES

TEACHING TIPS

November 16
Bible Study Guide 11

1. Words You Should Know

A. Rejoice (Philippians 4:4) *chairo* (Gk.)—To feel joy or great delight.

B. Supplication (v. 6) *deesis* (Gk.)—To express a need or want.

C. Peace (vv. 7, 9) *eirene* (Gk.)—An inward quietness; well-being.

2. Teacher Preparation

Unifying Principle—Mutual Support. During difficult times, people in community support one another and find reasons to give thanks. How do people in community come together in the midst of struggle? Paul exhorted the Philippians to follow examples of those who worked together for the common good and to rejoice together.

A. After spending time in prayer, study the Focal Verses. Think about a time you needed support during a time of personal struggle. Who helped you? How? Jot some notes down on paper.

B. Tape a large piece of paper up in front of the class. At the top write the words "Community Support." Later, you will have the students offer ideas that can build community support. Look up in the dictionary the words "community" and "support."

C. Read the AIM for Change and The People, Places, and Times sections.

3. Starting the Lesson

A. After opening with prayer, read the definition of "peace" from the Words You Should Know section. Ask the students what gives them peace when they are dealing with personal struggles. Have a volunteer read the Keep in Mind verse.

B. Take a few minutes to read the Devotional Reading Scripture and discuss how it relates to the Keep in Mind verse.

4. Getting into the Lesson

A. Briefly summarize the Background and The People, Places, and Times sections.

B. Remind the students that in last week's lesson, Paul had to address conflict in the community between Jewish and Gentile Christians. In today's lesson, Paul encourages the believers to focus on the return of Christ, and to support one another during struggles. This enhances unity in the body. Read the In Depth sections and discuss Paul's writing concerning mutual support.

5. Relating the Lesson to Life

A. Ask the class to answer the questions in the Search the Scriptures and Discuss the Meaning sections.

B. Ask the students to give examples of how they were supported during a personal time of struggle. Then ask, "How can the community of believers offer support for those in the midst of struggles?" Write their responses on the sheet of paper in front of the class.

6. Arousing Action

A. Remind the students that in spite of our diversity, we have to focus on Jesus Christ's return. Our relationship with God and others is necessary in working together as a community.

B. Using the responses from the class, help them to strategize in developing a stronger mutual support system (refer to the Make It Happen section).

Worship Guide NOV 16th

For the Superintendent or Teacher
Theme: Communion with God in the Midst of Struggle
Theme Song: "Lead Me, Guide Me"
Devotional Reading: Psalm 46
Prayer

COMMUNION WITH GOD IN THE MIDST OF STRUGGLE

Bible Background • PHILIPPIANS 3:3–4:9
Printed Text • PHILIPPIANS 3:17–4:9 Devotional Reading • PSALM 46

AIM for Change

By the end of the lesson, we will:
REVIEW Paul's writing;
GRASP the importance of building community and the personal support we receive from that community; and
DEMONSTRATE how God's people can live together.

Keep in Mind

"And the peace of God, which passeth all understanding, shall keep your hearts and minds through Christ Jesus" (Philippians 4:7).

Focal Verses

KJV **Philippians 3:17** Brethren, be followers together of me, and mark them which walk so as ye have us for an ensample.

18 (For many walk, of whom I have told you often, and now tell you even weeping, that they are the enemies of the cross of Christ:

19 Whose end is destruction, whose God is their belly, and whose glory is in their shame, who mind earthly things.)

20 For our conversation is in heaven; from whence also we look for the Saviour, the Lord Jesus Christ:

21 Who shall change our vile body, that it may be fashioned like unto his glorious body, according to the working whereby he is able even to subdue all things unto himself.

4:1 Therefore, my brethren dearly beloved and longed for, my joy and crown, so stand fast in the Lord, my dearly beloved.

2 I beseech Euodias, and beseech Syntyche, that they be of the same mind in the Lord.

3 And I intreat thee also, true yokefellow, help those women which laboured with me in the gospel, with Clement also, and with other my fellow labourers, whose names are in the book of life.

4 Rejoice in the Lord always: and again I say, Rejoice.

5 Let your moderation be known unto all men. The Lord is at hand.

6 Be careful for nothing; but in every thing by prayer and supplication with thanksgiving let your requests be made known unto God.

NLT **Philippians 3:17** Dear brothers and sisters, pattern your lives after mine, and learn from those who follow our example.

18 For I have told you often before, and I say it again with tears in my eyes, that there are many whose conduct shows they are really enemies of the cross of Christ.

19 They are headed for destruction. Their god is their appetite, they brag about shameful things, and they think only about this life here on earth.

20 But we are citizens of heaven, where the Lord Jesus Christ lives. And we are eagerly waiting for him to return as our Savior.

21 He will take our weak mortal bodies and change them into glorious bodies like his own, using the same power with which he will bring everything under his control.

4:1 Therefore, my dear brothers and sisters, stay true to the Lord. I love you and long to see you, dear friends, for you are my joy and the crown I receive for my work.

2 Now I appeal to Euodia and Syntyche. Please, because you belong to the Lord, settle your disagreement.

3 And I ask you, my true partner, to help these two women, for they worked hard with me in telling others the Good News. They worked along with Clement and the rest of my co-workers, whose names are written in the Book of Life.

4 Always be full of joy in the Lord. I say it again—rejoice!

5 Let everyone see that you are considerate in all you do. Remember, the Lord is coming soon.

7 And the peace of God, which passeth all understanding, shall keep your hearts and minds through Christ Jesus.

8 Finally, brethren, whatsoever things are true, whatsoever things are honest, whatsoever things are just, whatsoever things are pure, whatsoever things are lovely, whatsoever things are of good report; if there be any virtue, and if there be any praise, think on these things.

9 Those things, which ye have both learned, and received, and heard, and seen in me, do: and the God of peace shall be with you.

6 Don't worry about anything; instead, pray about everything. Tell God what you need, and thank him for all he has done.

7 Then you will experience God's peace, which exceeds anything we can understand. His peace will guard your hearts and minds as you live in Christ Jesus.

8 And now, dear brothers and sisters, one final thing. Fix your thoughts on what is true, and honorable, and right, and pure, and lovely, and admirable. Think about things that are excellent and worthy of praise.

9 Keep putting into practice all you learned and received from me—everything you heard from me and saw me doing. Then the God of peace will be with you.

In Focus

A hurricane hit a small town in Mississippi and destroyed most of the homes, businesses, and churches. The mayor held a meeting to discuss what steps the community would take to rebuild.

"I'm happy you all were able to meet tonight to discuss this terrible disaster," said Mayor Whittle. "First, I thank God no one died during this storm. Based on our survey of the town, it is a miracle we all survived. Buildings can be replaced, but not lives." Many in the crowd nodded their heads in agreement.

"Contact your insurance companies to file claims," he continued. "The Red Cross and Salvation Army are located outside the mobile police station to provide assistance. Our children will be bused to the neighboring schools for classes until ours can be rebuilt. I do not have any ideas what to do about the houses of worship. I want everyone to have a place to worship again. However, most of them were either partially or totally destroyed, except for the Interdenominational Worship Center."

"Mayor Whittle, may I say a word?" Pastor Calley was a very familiar voice to the mayor. He attended every town council meeting and always spoke out against any injustices. Mayor Whittle begrudgingly allowed Pastor Calley to take the podium.

"I know we all have suffered losses during this hurricane," the pastor began. "I would like to propose that we put our resources together and help each other. We at the Interdenominational Worship Center are willing to allow the community churches as well as anyone else to join us for worship beginning this Sunday. We may be different denominations, but there is now one commonality—we need each other. Let's take this opportunity to unite and give thanks to God for His goodness. God is so good and worthy to be praised!" Pastor Calley was going to start preaching. He had to be quieted before he got carried away.

"Pastor Calley, I'll bring some of the Bibles and hymnals we got out of the rubble of our church." Because he did not care for Pastor Calley's style of leadership nor did any of the other church leaders, Pastor Robinson had never worshiped with this congregation. But due to the circumstances, it was the best thing to do. Other church leaders agreed to bring chairs, food, and other resources to share.

The service was Spirit-filled. The support felt, during worship, created a greater sense of unity among the people. As a result, the church leaders agreed to assist each other in rebuilding the churches and to fellowship together more often.

In today's lesson, we will learn how to work together and offer mutual support to the community.

The People, Places, and Times

Philippi. A Roman colony located in northern Greece, it was called Macedonia in Paul's day. Philip II of Macedon (the father of Alexander the Great) took the town from ancient Thrace in about 357 B.C. He enlarged and strengthened it against attacks. Philip II renamed the city after himself. It was a thriving commercial center that sat at the crossroads between Europe and Asia.

Paul visited Macedonia after he had a vision of a Macedonian man bidding him, "Come over to Macedonia, and help us" (Acts 16:9). Paul recognized it as a summons from God. So around A.D. 50, Paul, Silas, Timothy, and Luke crossed the Aegean Sea from Asia Minor and landed at Philippi (second missionary journey, Acts 16:11–40). The church consisted mostly of Gentile believers. It was the first church established on the European continent.

Source:

Life Application Study Bible (New Revised Standard Version). Wheaton, Ill.: Tyndale House Publishers, 1989.

Background

Paul wrote this letter to all Christians at Philippi and believers everywhere. It was written about A.D. 61 from a Roman prison. He wanted to thank the Philippian church for the gift they had sent with Epaphroditus (Philippians 4:18) and encourage them in their faith.

Paul deeply loved the Philippian church. They gave him great joy. He emphasized in this letter that the source of real joy in a Christian's life is God's love at work in us. The joy of faith helps us, through suffering, so Paul did not fear dying (1:21–24).

Philippi was a cosmopolitan city, with a great diversity of people. This diversity was also evident in the church and sometimes caused divisions. Paul encouraged believers to unite and oppose the enemy, who seeks to divide the body. He wanted them to keep the faith in the midst of suffering, even as he had done (1:27–28). He considered it a privilege to suffer for Christ (v. 29).

Being a humble servant, like Christ, further strengthens the unity in the community. Paul said, "Let each esteem others better than themselves" (2:1–4). When attitudes of pride and jealousy, mumbling and complaining cease, unity can be maintained. There is joy in serving God and others. For Paul, all other things in life he had attained were considered a loss in comparison to knowing Christ Jesus as Lord (3:7–9). His goal was to deepen his relationship with Christ and emulate Him. So Paul said, "forgetting those things which are behind, and reaching forth unto those things which are before, I press toward the mark for the prize of the high calling of God in Christ Jesus" (3:13–14). If we as believers do the same, we can mature spiritually. Thus, the body will be built up and strengthened.

Source:

Life Application Study Bible (New Revised Standard Version). Ill.: Tyndale House Publishers, 1989.

At-A-Glance

1. Living in Unity Without Compromise (Philippians 3:17–19)
2. Focusing on Christ (vv. 20–21; 4:1–3)
3. Rejoicing Through Anxiety (vv. 4–9)

In Depth

1. Living in Unity Without Compromise (Philippians 3:17–19)

Paul encouraged the Philippians to imitate his example in living like Christ. Not that he was perfect (3:12), but he strived to be like Christ. Paul was faithful and lived righteously. Therefore, he was a person the believers could imitate. We have to not only be hearers of the Word but doers as well (James 1:22). When we seek to humble ourselves and serve others in the spirit of love, the Christ in us will shine brightly. However, not every person professing to be a Christian is living for Christ.

Paul warned the people about those who are seducers and false teachers, just as he did about the Judaizers (3:2–3). He was so grieved by their actions that he was moved to tears. Paul's passion was for all to come to know Jesus and the power of His resurrection. For "the enemies of the cross" were not concerned with faithful commitment and service to God, they were consumed with satisfying their own desires. "Their god is the belly" means they were gluttons and drunkards, who only cared for fulfilling their sensual desires. Instead of being focused on seeking first the kingdom of God, they focused on all that is in the world—"the lust of the flesh, and the lust of the eyes, and the pride of life" (1 John 2:16). They even boasted of their sin. Because "you shall know them by their fruit," it is easy to discern those who are enemies of the Cross.

Because their "end is destruction," Paul wanted believers to think about the foolishness of following such leaders. If believers are tempted to unite with them, we shall experience the same end—death and hell. We cannot yield to such evil living, but should imitate Christ and leaders such as Paul. A church focused on God and service to others will have the fortitude to resist such teachers and seek to support each other in times of need. We have to take a stand for Christ and not compromise the truth of the Word.

2. Focusing on Christ (vv. 20–21; 4:1–3)

The Philippian church was composed of a diverse group of believers, and this sometimes caused conflict. Paul warned against allowing the enemy to slip in and divide the community. Because our citizenship is in heaven, we have to set our "affection on things above, not on things on the earth" (Colossians 3:2). If believers focus our conversations and fellowship on heavenly principles, we can work through any difficulties. Why? We are all looking forward to the coming of the Saviour, the Lord Jesus Christ. When Jesus appears, we shall be transformed and given a new glorified body. Our new bodies shall be free from pain, physical limitations, or disabilities. We all shall have glorified bodies, even as Jesus' body was transformed at His resurrection. His power to subdue all things will result in our new bodies and lives. This united hope and focus build community.

Preoccupation with living like the world can cause believers to lose focus. How easy it is to skip church to go to a sporting event, or catch a weekend sale at the mall, or not attend Bible study because we want to watch our favorite television show. We can even allow theological differences, race, or socioeconomic status to pull us away from Christ. The smallest thing is often used by the enemy to distract us. These distractions increase over time until a person is completely off-track with the kingdom of God and the body. Communion with God and fellowship with believers are the means by which support is found, not in the pursuit of selfish desires.

The Philippians gave Paul great joy. The evidence of their sincere faith and obedience caused him to rejoice. Paul affectionately urged the brethren "to stand fast in the Lord." The believers' hope and prospect of eternal life should engage us to be steady, even, and consistent in our Christian walk. We have to keep our eyes fixed on Jesus and remember the world is not our home. It is the only way to keep unity amongst the believers. Paul had deep concerns about relationships within the church.

Euodia and Syntyche, workers in the church, seemed to be at odds with either one another or with the church—either upon a civil account (it may be they were engaged in a lawsuit) or upon a religious account (it may be they were of different opinions and sentiments). Whatever the problem, Paul urged them to be "of the same mind in the Lord." The conflict was affecting others in the church who had come to know Christ through their efforts. When "one member suffers, all the members suffer with it" (1 Corinthians 12:26). Paul knew the fellowship of the believers had to be preserved. We have to keep the peace and live together in love for the sake of the community.

The identity of the "true yoke-fellow" Paul mentions is a mystery. It could be Epaphroditus, who was supposedly one of the pastors of the church of the Philippians and bearer of this letter. Whoever it was, Paul wanted this person to support these women in resolving their dispute. Along with others, the women had labored with Paul in the Gospel. Now Paul wanted the believers to offer assistance to them. No matter the difficulties, those who labor in the Gospel and are faithful to the interests of Christ have their names in the Book of Life (Revelation 20:11–15). Mutual support is important in the community.

3. Rejoicing Through Anxiety (vv. 4–9)

Paul calls for the church to "rejoice in the Lord always." Rejoice means "to feel joy or great delight." He had an inner joy because of his relationship with Christ and confidence he was not alone, even while in prison. The Philippians needed to rejoice in the midst of struggles and suffering. The joy of suffering like Christ was not a dishonor but an honor. It binds us with Christ, who suffered the humiliation of the crucifixion. There is no need for God's people to constantly remain discouraged about unpleasant circumstances. It is a part of living in a place that is inhabited by sinful people. But we are only pilgrims traveling toward our heavenly home. We have hope for eternal life, which in itself is a reason to rejoice, and our perspective should be based on God's ongoing faithfulness to us in all circumstances.

Christ dwelling within us should mean that we exhibit gentleness toward everyone—believers and nonbelievers alike. This includes being patient, bearing afflictions, being reasonable, fair-minded and charitable. "The Lord is at hand." The consideration of the Lord's second coming and our final account should keep us from retaliating against our fellow-servants, support us under present sufferings, and moderate our affections to outward good.

"Do not be anxious about anything" (v. 6, NIV) means to avoid anxious care, worry, and distracting thought in the wants and difficulties of life. It is the duty of Christians to live without undue care. Yes, we may have circumstances that cause concern, but we have to cast our cares upon Him because He cares for us (1 Peter 5:7). Anxiety about life issues can weaken our faith and trust in Christ. Being in communion with God on a consistent basis and fellowshiping with others strengthens us in the midst of personal struggles. Paul proceeds to tell believers that one of the keys is to turn your cares into prayers. "By prayer and petition, with thanksgiving, present your requests to God" (Philippians 4:6).

Praying is important when dealing with difficulties. It is through prayer that we release all our cares, express our needs, and thank God for answering our requests. Because we have complete confidence in His power to do the impossible, we can give thanks to God in advance of the answer. Not only is personal prayer vital, but corporate prayer is as well. In the midst of corporate prayer time, in the community of believers, God speaks to His people. There can be miracles of healing, reconciliation, and deliverance, as the Holy Spirit moves upon the hearts and minds of those gathered. Prayer builds community.

As a result of prayer, the peace of God (John 14:27) comes. The peace comes because we know He is in control, and no matter what is presently happening, heaven is our home. We have the victory over sin. His peace guards our hearts and minds so we do not have to resort to sinning to achieve victory over our enemies or circumstances.

The peace of God guards our hearts and minds, but we have to be careful what thoughts are permitted to enter. Paul's final exhortation to the believers is to meditate on thoughts that are "true, noble, right, pure, lovely, admirable, excellent and praiseworthy" (v. 8). Whatever we allow to penetrate our minds through books, the Internet, television, conversations, and music can possibly be harmful. We have to remove thoughts of destructive care and injustice and replace them with positive, life-giving thoughts. The primary source for believers is the Bible coupled with prayer. All the support we need to transform our thinking is contained within the Word. We can help other believers by sharing the Word when they encounter struggles as well.

Once again, Paul offers his life as an example as one who embodies the characteristics of a godly leader and can be emulated by others. He demonstrates with his life how to face difficulties, but not compromise the principles of the Word. When dealing with problems, we do not have to resort to acting like the world. If our focus is on Christ and we trust Him, His love and peace will sustain us; we can live together in harmony with everyone.

Sources:

Henry, Matthew. *Commentary on the Whole Bible, Complete and Unabridged.* Peabody, Mass.: Hendrickson Publishers, 1991.

Wesley, John. *Commentary on the Bible, Philippians.* Grand Rapids, Mich.: Zondervan, 1990.

Search the Scriptures

1. Who are the "enemies of the cross of Christ"? What will their end be (Philippians 3:19)?

2. What did Paul want Euodia and Syntyche to do (4:2)?

3. How are anxiety and worry to be dealt with (v. 6)?

Discuss the Meaning

1. In building up the community and supporting one another, why is prayer important?

2. Our thoughts often determine our behavior. What thoughts or ideas contribute to conflict and struggles in the church today?

3. What changes can believers make to improve support in the community?

Lesson in Our Society

The In Focus story shows how the community had to come together in the aftermath of a hurricane. The church leaders had to put aside their personal difficulties and support one another. In doing so, they were able to pray and worship together, drawing strength from each other and God. It was a time of rejoicing and giving thanks to God for sparing the lives of the people. Instead of permitting difficulties to divide members of the body of Christ, we have to be of the same mind and work together. While serving Christ, everyone faces some type of crisis or difficulty. How we respond is the key. In the fellowship of believers, there are brothers and sisters who have endured trials and suffering, too. We can learn from their faithful examples and get support. Because we know Christ has given us the victory, we can rejoice and give thanks. His peace will sustain us through any circumstance.

Make It Happen

Look at the list the class created on community support, and identify the top three things needed in your church. Discuss how you and the other students can develop a mutual support system, which will build a stronger community inside and outside the church.

Follow the Spirit

What God wants me to do:

____

____

Remember Your Thoughts

Special insights I have learned:

____

____

More Light on the Text

Philippians 3:17–4:9

17 Brethren, be followers together of me, and mark them which walk so as ye have us for an example.

In this joyful letter, Paul gloried in the Philippians' partnership with him in the Gospel, speaking to them with great fondness and giving thanks for the good report of their faithfulness before the Lord. Particularly in contrast to other churches, Paul was able to say without regret or hesitation: "I thank my God upon every remembrance of you" (Philippians 1:3). In the passage we consider in this lesson, Paul urged the Philippians to even greater zeal for God, who had won them at the Cross. Despising hypocrisy as he gave them this glorious call, in chapter 3, verses 1–14, he laid before them his own passion for the ways of Christ. There, after recounting the reasons he might have to boast in his identity according to the flesh, he dramatically cast such things aside and declared that following after the glorious suffering of Christ was the only thing that captivated his heart. It is this, his grace-inspired faithfulness to his apostolic call, which enabled him to set up his own example as worthy of imitation.

How can Paul be so bold as to demand that his flock follow after his way of life? Several features of this verse help us understand this high calling. First, his address to them as "brethren" shows that he was not lording it over them in this call to imitation but rather regarded them as equal sharers in the Gospel of Christ. He was, in essence, standing like a general amidst the battle, saying "Follow me!" as he was the first to charge the front lines. Second, he used the Greek word *summimetes* (**soom-mim-ay-TACE**) to show that the following was not a matter of each one imitating him by themselves, but rather that they followed "together." This communal understanding of discipleship will deeply influence this passage. The cooperative aspect of following an example gives much life and power to the task, as opposed to a lonely, solitary walk. Third, Paul did not egomaniacally call them to simply imitate him but rather urged them to follow the pattern of all who walk in the same way—showing that what is ultimate is the pattern, not the individual disciple.

This leads us to the final, and most important, aspect of this call to follow: Paul called the Philippians to imitate him *in order that* they might be imitating Christ. The earlier parts of chapter 3 make clear that Paul did not have in mind mindless obedience to him in the way that a mirror mimics the exact motions of its object but rather a similar disposition of heart and way of life set upon Christ. With the weight of not only his apostolic authority but also his exemplary pattern of life, Paul called his hearers to unremitting faithfulness to their Lord.

18 (For many walk, of whom I have told you often, and now tell you even weeping, that they are the enemies of the cross of Christ:

The King James Version rightly puts the next two verses in parentheses, for Paul here interrupted his train of thought to set up a vivid contrast. He reminded them of the way many "walk" (Gk. *peripateo,* **per-ee-pat-EH-o**); for Paul, "walking" concerned one's normal, everyday pattern of life—the beliefs, thoughts, and actions that repeatedly demonstrate one's character (see Galatians 5:16 and Ephesians 5:15 for helpful cross-references). To Paul's great grief, there are many who, not simply in occasional backsliding or moral slipups but in the dominant pattern of their lives, show themselves to be "enemies of the cross of Christ." What does Paul have in mind in using this phrase? We need only think of what the Cross represents. As it shows us the glory of the dying Lord, no doubt it means at least these things: (1) Ultimate obedience, without regard to the cost thereof, (2) a mind fixed on eternal realities and not on temporary pain or pleasure, and (3) sacrificial love and mercy prevailing over

"And the peace of God, which passeth all understanding, shall keep your hearts and minds through Christ Jesus" (Philippians 4:7).

personal comfort. We can infer, then, that those who "walked" in this way despised obedience to God, scorned the heavenly in favor of lustfully pursuing earthly pleasures, and lacked a true heart of love and mercy for one another. But, in fact, we have further help in understanding what this enmity meant, for the next verse brings these people's condition to light.

19 Whose end is destruction, whose God is their belly, and whose glory is in their shame, who mind earthly things.)

Paul no doubt intended this awful description to motivate the Philippians to the opposite course. The Greek word translated "end" is *telos* **(TEL-os)**, which Paul occasionally used to refer to one's "goal" (1 Timothy 1:5) but more often employed to refer to the ultimate outcome of a way of life (see Romans 6:21–22). This is obviously the meaning here; it is not the unbeliever's goal to be destroyed, but it is the ultimate outcome of his faithless way of life. That life is governed by the earthly appetite, as suggested by the phrase "whose God is their belly."

Given the rest of the verse, Paul in no way meant to limit this phrase to mere gluttony, but expanded it to any sort of pervasive lust that overtakes a person. This kind of life brings forth a great irony: that the things in which they happily put their confidence ("glory") are actually to their utter and undying shame. Their spiritual vision is so impaired that they are unaware of this fact. Finally, in contrast to the believer in the following verse, these wayward ones are preoccupied night and day with "earthly things," a probable reference to the objects of their lustful desires and the idols in which they put their confidence and find their glory.

20 For our conversation is in heaven; from whence also we look for the Saviour, the Lord Jesus Christ:

Since verses 18–19 present a bit of a detour in Paul's thinking, the "for" beginning verse 20 should be understood as connected not only to them, but also to verse 17. This verse shows why Paul issued the command to imitate his pattern of life in verse 17 and also contrasts the heaven-bound believer with those described in verses 18–19. For the Christian, one's "conversation" is in heaven. The unusual use of the Greek word "conversation" to translate *politeuma* (**pol-IT-yoo-mah**) can be misleading, given our modern understanding of the word. The word means a "place of citizenship" or "realm of belonging." This phrase gives us a powerful contrast to the way of life described in verse 19; it reveals that the Christian life has both a different ultimate outcome (life in heaven, rather than destruction) and a different ultimate focus (matters of God who is in heaven, rather than matters of this decaying world).

The reason that heaven preoccupies the Christian's interest, said Paul, is found in the words "from whence" in the next phrase. Notice that the apostle did not simply say that heaven is merely "where Christ is" but also "from whence" He will come. This is an explicit reference to Jesus' Second Coming as Lord and Judge; the anticipation of this coming provides the Christian motivation to live distinctly from those described in verses 18–19. The command is similar to Christ's command to "lay up for yourselves treasures in heaven" (Matthew 6:20) and to Paul's word in Colossians 3:1–4: "If ye then be risen with Christ, seek those things which are above, where Christ sitteth on the right hand of God. Set your affection on things above, not on things on the earth. For ye are dead, and your life is hid with Christ in God. When Christ, who is our life, shall appear, then shall ye also appear with him in glory." The logic is clear: Focus on the place where your life truly is and not on where it is not!

21 Who shall change our vile body, that it may be fashioned like unto his glorious body, according to the working whereby he is able even to subdue all things unto himself.

Paul shows here how absurd it would be to focus on the "earthly" matters of the "belly," since in fact our current bodies are not yet in their truly glorious form. He revealed exactly what Christ will do when He comes again: transform our bodies after the fashion of His own glorious, resurrected body. In 1 Corinthians 15:35–57, Paul gave more details on the nature of this transformation; we see there that the King James Version's "vile" is a poor translation of the Greek word *tapeinosis* (**tap-I-no-sis**), which merely means "humble" or "lowly." We must be careful to avoid the heresy of Gnosticism, rejected by the New Testament that the body is purely bad while the spirit is purely good. Paul did not tell us here that our earthly bodies are evil but rather that they are passing away in their present form and not as glorious as they one day will be.

We see the grand scope of God's purpose in the final coming of Christ—in His great power He will not only transform us but also the whole creation ("all things"), putting them all under Christ the Lord to His own glory. In order to avoid a self-centered view of God's redemptive work, where we become the center of the universe and of God's purpose, it is important for the Christian not to lose sight of this overarching purpose. Rather, for His own glory, God is bringing together all things under the headship of Christ. In this process, we are transformed into the glorious likeness of Christ, body and soul.

4:1 Therefore, my brethren dearly beloved and longed for, my joy and crown, so stand fast in the Lord, my dearly beloved.

Paul's tender love for his Philippian flock comes out vividly in this verse. Calling them "dearly beloved" twice in the span of 12 (Greek) words, the apostle demonstrates how personally he longed for the Philippians to live out his Christ-centered vision for their lives. The Philippians were (the source of) his "joy" and also his "crown." The people being Paul's "joy" calls to mind 2 Corinthians 3:2: "Ye are our epistle written in our hearts, known and read of all men." In a similar way, the "crown," in the New Testament, often designates "the eternal reward of the faithful." We see Paul's tenderness in the fact that he considers the reward of his faithfulness to be the people themselves, dear friends and disciples set apart in the love of Christ.

This loving exhortation arises from (therefore) his tearful grief over those who walk as Christ's enemies and from the great expectation of Christ's appearing. The central command, which in many ways could be considered the theme of the entire letter to the Philippians, is this: "Stand fast in the Lord." The horrifying alternative is that the Philippians will become like those described in 3:18–19, over whom Paul wept. If they are to avoid this fate, they are to stand firm "so" or "in this way"—the way given to those whose citizenship is in heaven.

2 I beseech Euodias, and beseech Syntyche, that they be of the same mind in the Lord.

While it seems Paul began a totally new thought here, we can be sure that in his letters one thought is never totally unrelated to the previous one. Clearly such is the case here: He makes very clear in other places (see 1 Corinthians 1–3, for example), disunity is, in Paul's mind, the very opposite of what it means to "stand firm in Christ." We do not know who these women are, but their division must have been a serious threat to the Philippians' ability to remain faithful to the Gospel. Their "same mind" is the mind of Christ, as described in 2:5 and the mind set upon heaven, as in 3:20.

3 And I intreat thee also, true yokefellow, help those women which laboured with me in the gospel, with Clement also, and with other my fellow labourers, whose names are in the book of life.

We cannot certainly identify the "yokefellow" described here; suggestions in the history of the church have included Timothy or Epaphroditus (both mentioned in chapter 2), Silas or Luke (both known to have spent time in Philippi), or even the proper name Syzygos, which also means "yokefellow" (though no one in the ancient world is known to have had that name). We can be content to conclude that the Philippians knew the one to whom Paul was referring. Their task was clear: to bring about unity between these two feuding women. Notice that Paul does not only plead with the women but also with another Christian to bring about unity. Maintaining unity and seeking reconciliation are the jobs of all Christians. One of the reasons to strive for unity is that all of these believers' names are "in the book of life"; the unity of believers, in heaven, makes disunity on Earth tragic and absurd.

Paul noted that these women had "laboured with me in the gospel" (along with Clement, who may have been the same Clement who was bishop in Rome just after Paul's death); they were therefore among many women with whom Paul labored. The New Testament is striking for how many women accompanied and labored with both Jesus and the apostles. This was due to the radical nature of the Gospel, according to which "there is neither Jew nor Greek, there is neither bond nor free, there is neither male nor female: for ye are all one in Christ Jesus" (Galatians 3:28). This fact does not resolve all questions about the role of women in church ministry, but it certainly suggests that women should be empowered to serve according to the dignity given to them by the Gospel.

4 Rejoice in the Lord always: and again I say, Rejoice.

It appears that the mention of the "book of life"—that sweet guarantee of a home with the Lord—causes Paul's heart to well up once again with joy and delight. Joy pops up its refreshing head many places in Philippians (see 1:25, 2:18, 28–29; 3:1). For Paul, it is a by-product of the Gospel, but that hardly means that the believer must passively wait for it. On the contrary, here twice, as in 3:1, Paul *commanded* that joy be sought and experienced. This can only be because of the glorious promises of Christ's good news, which were and are available to the believer at all times. After all, those promises point to the Lord, Himself, joyful and giving joy.

The command to rejoice "in the Lord" can mean either that Christians rejoice *because* of the Lord or with the Lord in one's spiritual vision as she or he rejoices. Most likely both ideas are here! For a life characterized by joy "always," in contrast to the pattern of "walking" described in 3:18, will give ample opportunity to enjoy the many facets of the Lord's redemption. And so Paul said, literally, "again I *will* say, Rejoice"—showing resolve to repeat this command as long as necessary for the growth and joy of his flock.

5 Let your moderation be known unto all men. The Lord is at hand.

The Greek word *epieikes* (**ep-ee-i-KACE**), here translated "moderation," is a rich word meaning "a balanced, intelligent, decent outlook in contrast to licentiousness." It was often used in the context of persecution, describing the sort of reaction that would forgo revenge and justice-seeking in favor of patience and mercy. To let such an attitude "be known unto all men" would not, of course, mean to flaunt this attitude and boast about it but rather to practice this "mind of Christ" (see 2:1–5), especially before the harshness of people in their unjust acts. Christ's imminent appearing would have been, and still is, a powerful motivation, as it allows believers to await his perfect justice, rather than seeking revenge themselves. See also Romans 12:19–21.

6 Be careful for nothing; but in every thing by prayer and supplication with thanksgiving let your requests be made known unto God.

Many readers will be more familiar with the phrase "be anxious for nothing" than with the King James Version's (KJV) use of "careful." Indeed, "anxious" is a much better translation of *merimnao* (Gk. **mer-im-NAH-o**), which can mean a positive sort of concern (see Timothy's concern in 2:20) but which, in this context, means an unreasonable, excessive concern. The way out of this anxiety is made clear. Paul set "prayer," "supplication," and "making known one's requests" against anxiety in such a way as to show that the two cannot really coexist. The mind must be occupied with one or the other; as it has been well said, "The way to be anxious about nothing is to be prayerful about everything."

Yet there is another kind of prayer that buttresses the Christian's battle against anxiety: thanksgiving. What explains the inclusion of "thanksgiving" in a command to those dealing with anxiety? It can only be the certainty of God's goodness and deliverance, for believers are not called to thank God for pain or suffering but rather for the promise of God to be faithful within them and to bring us out of them. And so this command to pray brings anxiety out of the realm of helplessness and into the realm of the believer's thoughts, which can be turned to prayer and thanksgiving through the power of the Holy Spirit.

7 And the peace of God, which passeth all understanding, shall keep your hearts and minds through Christ Jesus.

In a passage, verses 4–7, where all other sentences exist unconnected, standing alone, Paul painted the beautiful picture of transcendent peace with the connecting "and." This difference is significant, as the apostle clearly wants to connect the peace he will describe with the prayer he has commanded. Prayer begets peace! Yet, because its coming is mysterious, this peace "passeth all understanding." It cannot be summoned up magically, simply by mouthing a few words. In addition, Paul probably meant to indicate that it—the understanding it surpasses—is the mental activity of the worrying mind. That mind will not gain peace; on the other hand, both "mind" and "heart" (here probably pointing together to the whole person, both the realm of the thoughts and the realm of the emotions) will find the peace of Christ, when prayerful thanksgiving becomes the Christian's watchword.

The Greek word *phroureo* (**froo-REH-o**) was used of a guard in military contexts and therefore should probably be translated as something stronger than the King James Version's (KJV) "keep." At the time of Paul's writing, he himself was under secure guard in a jail (probably in Rome), and the city of Philippi, a royal city, would have been surrounded and protected by a Roman garrison. So the Philippians would have been easily able to grasp this metaphor! So the "peace of God" is an indestructible, protective peace, coming forth from the God who brings peace between God and man. This reconciliation, accomplished by grace and joyfully announced in the Gospel, is the foundation for what Hebrew Scriptures call *shalom*—a complete wholeness and well-being under the loving protection of God.

8 Finally, brethren, whatsoever things are true, whatsoever things are honest, whatsoever things are just, whatsoever things are pure, whatsoever things are lovely, whatsoever things are of good report; if there be any virtue, and if there be any praise, think on these things.

Having commanded a prayerful mind that will bear the fruit of peace (4:6–7), Paul commanded a virtuous mind that will bear the fruit of peace (vv. 8–9). Summing up many of his teachings "finally," he brings forth a list of virtues upon which the Christian should set his mind. Such lists of virtues were common in non-Christian writings among the Greeks and Romans. Paul took these ideas, as he often did, and recast them in light of the Gospel.

The first two virtues have to do with truth, both in words "true" and in one's overall demeanor: "honest." Because of the Gospel, the truth about God is not to be feared but can be freely adored. In fact, God's truth renews the mind, transforms the soul, and motivates the will (see Romans 12:1–2).

Similarly, the next two virtues—justice and purity—bring together complementary ideas. Justice is goodness and righteousness toward others, whereas purity is goodness and righteousness at work with us. God commands both an internal and external fruit of the Gospel and brings it forth through the Holy Spirit.

Things that are "lovely" are those things which inspire us to praise their beauty; thus, can we see how something "of good report" complements this idea, urging believers to contemplate the good in what they can see and what they cannot see, but only know of through hearing. Finally, Paul sums up these ideas by speaking about "virtue" (Gk. *arete,* pronounced **ar-ET-ay**, meaning "moral excellence") and "praise," by which he means not the act of praise but things which are worthy of praise. The overall picture is a mind set on things holy and good, beautiful and true, with no limits in the midst of God's good creation to what those things might be.

9 Those things, which ye have both learned, and received, and heard, and seen in me, do: and the God of peace shall be with you.

We have now come full circle, as Paul here urged his hearers to imitate him with their whole lives, just as he did in 3:17. Beginning with the phrase "those things," he brings to mind the virtuous and good things discussed in verse 8, implying that the Philippians have not only heard him talk about such things, but also seen his life to be redolent of such things. In using the word "received" to describe his teaching and life before the Philippians, Paul pointed up an idea often used of how the Gospel was passed down from teacher to learner. No doubt this is no accident, as Paul's message centered on the Gospel in every way, and one can only understand the "laws" he sets forth in light of the glorious coming of Christ for our salvation and purification. The result of a life of imitation of Paul, and therefore ultimately Christ, is once again "peace." Whereas verse 7 promised the "peace of God," verse 9 promises the "God of peace," showing that none of the benefits of God can be separated from the very presence of God, Himself, by the Holy Spirit. We see that following after the glorious example of Christ and those who lay that example before us on Earth produce profound inward peace and joy, which in turn motivate further obedience, through the Spirit and according to Christ's Good News.

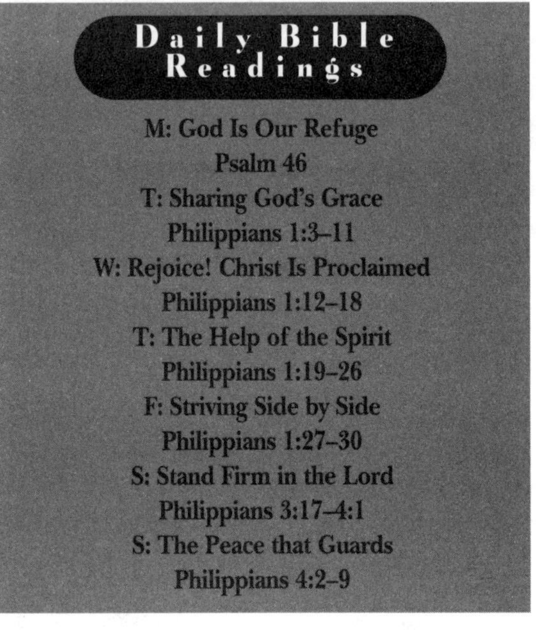
Daily Bible Readings

M: God Is Our Refuge
Psalm 46

T: Sharing God's Grace
Philippians 1:3–11

W: Rejoice! Christ Is Proclaimed
Philippians 1:12–18

T: The Help of the Spirit
Philippians 1:19–26

F: Striving Side by Side
Philippians 1:27–30

S: Stand Firm in the Lord
Philippians 3:17–4:1

S: The Peace that Guards
Philippians 4:2–9

NOTES

TEACHING TIPS

November 23
Bible Study Guide 12

1. Words You Should Know

A. Endure (2 Timothy 2:3) *hupomeno* (Gk.)—To hold up courageously under suffering.

B. Hardness (v. 3) *kakopatheo* (Gk.)—To suffer a hardship.

C. Preach (4:2) *euaggelizo* (Gk.)—To proclaim the good news of the Gospel.

D. Rebuke (v. 2) *elegcho* (Gk.)—To convict or reprove.

E. Exhort (v. 2) *parakaleo* (Gk.)—An appeal.

2. Teacher Preparation

Unifying Principle—A Good Example. Through constructive living, people have a positive influence on and set a good example for others in their community. What characterizes a good example? Paul wrote that living as Jesus did was a strong witness for others to follow in good times and bad and that this message should be shared with all who would listen.

A. Read the Focal Verses and Background.

B. Look up the word "witness" in the dictionary.

C. Read Acts 4:13–20.

D. On the Internet or at the library, do research on persecuted Christians around the world.

3. Starting the Lesson

A. Begin the class with prayer. Focus on the AIM for Change and the need for strong witnesses for Christ.

B. Have volunteers read the Keep in Mind verse.

C. Role-play the In Focus story with two students taking the parts of Caleb and Mr. Ellis.

4. Getting into the Lesson

A. Review the definitions of "endure" and "hardness," found in the Words You Should Know section.

B. Summarize the content of the Focal Verses.

C. Have a volunteer read Acts 4:13–20. Then discuss how Peter, John, and Paul were strong witnesses for others.

5. Relating the Lesson to Life

A. Share with the class the hardship Christians are enduring around the world for their faith. Yet the Gospel is spreading at a rapid pace because others see their faith in the midst of suffering.

B. Ask the students to discuss how they react when difficulties arise in their lives. Is their faith and actions lining up with the Word?

6. Arousing Action

A. Have the class answer and discuss the Search the Scriptures and Discuss the Meaning questions.

B. Encourage the students to proclaim the Word and live as faithful witnesses.

C. Close the class with prayer, asking God to empower the students to be good examples for others in their community.

Worship Guide

For the Superintendent or Teacher
Theme: Witness of the Community
Theme Song: "Come We that Love the Lord"
Devotional Reading: Acts 4:13–20
Prayer

WITNESS OF THE COMMUNITY

Bible Background • 2 TIMOTHY 2:1–3; 4:1–5
Printed Text • 2 TIMOTHY 2:1–3; 4:1–5 Devotional Reading • ACTS 4:13–20

AIM for Change

By the end of the lesson, we will:
EXAMINE Paul's writings about the need for a strong Christian witness;
UNDERSTAND the necessity of telling others about our Christian life and faith; and
DEDICATE ourselves to proclaiming and living our Christian witness.

Keep in Mind

"And the things that thou hast heard of me among many witnesses, the same commit thou to faithful men, who shall be able to teach others also" (2 Timothy 2:2).

Focal Verses

KJV **2 Timothy 2:1** Thou therefore, my son, be strong in the grace that is in Christ Jesus.

2 And the things that thou hast heard of me among many witnesses, the same commit thou to faithful men, who shall be able to teach others also.

3 Thou therefore endure hardness, as a good soldier of Jesus Christ.

4:1 I charge thee therefore before God, and the Lord Jesus Christ, who shall judge the quick and the dead at his appearing and his kingdom;

2 Preach the word; be instant in season, out of season; reprove, rebuke, exhort with all longsuffering and doctrine.

3 For the time will come when they will not endure sound doctrine; but after their own lusts shall they heap to themselves teachers, having itching ears;

4 And they shall turn away their ears from the truth, and shall be turned unto fables.

5 But watch thou in all things, endure afflictions, do the work of an evangelist, make full proof of thy ministry.

NLT **2 Timothy 2:1** Timothy, my dear son, be strong through the grace that God gives you in Christ Jesus.

2 You have heard me teach things that have been confirmed by many reliable witnesses. Now teach these truths to other trustworthy people who will be able to pass them on to others.

3 Endure suffering along with me, as a good soldier of Christ Jesus.

4:1 I solemnly urge you in the presence of God and Christ Jesus, who will someday judge the living and the dead when he appears to set up his Kingdom:

2 Preach the word of God. Be prepared, whether the time is favorable or not. Patiently correct, rebuke, and encourage your people with good teaching.

3 For a time is coming when people will no longer listen to sound and wholesome teaching. They will follow their own desires and will look for teachers who will tell them whatever their itching ears want to hear.

4 They will reject the truth and chase after myths.

5 But you should keep a clear mind in every situation. Don't be afraid of suffering for the Lord. Work at telling others the Good News, and fully carry out the ministry God has given you.

In Focus

After a hurricane hit a small Mississippi town, basic necessities and resources were limited. Many residents began to get upset and loot the stores that were damaged by the storm.

Mr. and Mrs. Ellis noticed their neighbors coming back with trucks filled with looted items. They did not believe this was the proper way to react. One morning, Mr. Ellis confronted his neighbor's son, Caleb.

"Caleb, can I talk to you?" Mr. Ellis said.

"Wait one minute until we unload this stuff from my truck." Caleb had a generator, freezer, and washer. About 15 minutes later, Caleb and his brother finished moving the items into the house. He was out of breath and sweaty; yet he greeted Mr. Ellis with a hug. Since his own father had died two years ago, Mr. Ellis was like a second father to him.

"Caleb, my wife and I have watched how you and the other neighbors have been bringing looted items home from stores. We all are suffering because of this storm, but it does not give us a right to take someone else's property."

"Mr. Ellis, there's no disrespect intended, but I have to look out for my mom and little brother. You know because of her heart condition, she needs her oxygen machine. Plus, we need food. Since we can't rely on anyone to help us, I just have to do what is needed."

Mr. Ellis was gritting his teeth, and Caleb could see he was upset. "That is no excuse to steal!" he said firmly. "My wife needs her insulin, but we did not steal from a pharmacy. We prayed for help. God sent a mobile health clinic van to the neighborhood. The doctors told us to go to the hospital in the next town for free insulin. Before driving home, we stopped at the town's community building and asked about additional help. The city worker said he had been given resources to distribute to those affected by the storm, but very few people had taken advantage of it. We were able to rent a generator and get fresh food and new clothing."

"How am I to know what's going on in another town? Remember, there is no electricity! We need help now, Mr. Ellis!" Caleb flopped down on the curb in front of his house in utter frustration.

Mr. Ellis sat next to him and placed his hand on his shoulder. "Caleb, I understand your predicament. Remember that I'm suffering, too. How about we drive to the community center tomorrow morning?"

"I appreciate that, Mr. Ellis. Maybe I can get some clean clothes for Mom. I'll be ready in the morning."

In today's lesson, we learn that Christians, in both good and bad times, have to set a good example for others. We must be living witnesses for Christ.

The People, Places, and Times

Timothy. The son of a mixed marriage, Timothy's mother was a Jewess and his father a Greek (Acts 16:1; 2 Timothy. 1:5). He was a native of Lystra and was highly regarded by the Christian brethren. Timothy had an in-depth knowledge of the Scriptures. His grandmother, Lois, was a Christian and may have had an influence on his early upbringing as well. Timothy was converted during Paul's first missionary journey, which included Lystra on its itinerary. His mother Eunice became a Christian prior to Paul's second missionary journey.

Paul had a sincere fondness for the younger Timothy. He added Timothy as his traveling companion maybe to replace John Mark, whom Paul refused to take (Acts 15:36). Timothy was set apart for the work (1 Timothy 1:18). He received a special endowment for his mission, by the laying of hands of the elders and Paul (1 Timothy 4:14; 2 Timothy 1:6). He joined Paul on his second and third missionary journeys. Since Paul wanted to prevent any disputes with the local Jews, he circumcised Timothy.

He was commissioned to go to Thessalonica to encourage the persecuted Christians. Timothy was present with Paul during his work at Corinth (2 Corinthians 1:19). He was sent to Corinth on a mission (1 Corinthians 4:17), but because Timothy was timid, he was not successful. He did go back to Corinth with Paul on his second visit as a fellow worker.

Source:
Unger, Merrill. *The New Unger's Bible Handbook.* Chicago, Ill.: Moody Press, 1984.

Background

Timothy went with Paul on his journey to Jerusalem with the collection for the impoverished believers (Acts 20:4–5; 2 Corinthians 8:1ff). Paul eventually left Timothy at Ephesus (1 Timothy 1:3, 4) and commissioned him to deal with false teachers, supervise public worship, and appoint church officials.

Paul wrote two letters to Timothy—one written to him while Timothy was in Ephesus. This second letter was written about A.D. 66 or 67 from a Roman prison. Luke visited Paul, but he requested visits from other friends. Most of them had abandoned him. He wanted them to also bring his books, including biblical manuscripts. Before his death, this was Paul's final opportunity to encourage Timothy.

Timothy was affectionate but very fearful, needing personal admonitions from his father in the ministry. In this passionate letter, Paul revealed to Timothy how to be an effective leader. Paul warned him not to yield to youthful lusts (2 Timothy 2:22) and not be ashamed of the Gospel (2 Timothy 1:8).

Timothy had insecurities and weaknesses, but he was loyal to Christ and the calling.

Source:

Life Application Study Bible (New Revised Standard Version). Wheaton, Ill.: Tyndale House Publishers, 1989.

At-A-Glance

1. Witness in the Midst of Suffering (2 Timothy 2:1–3)

2. Proclaim the Word Faithfully (4:1–5)

In Depth

1. Witness in the Midst of Suffering (2 Timothy 2:1–3)

Paul wanted to encourage Timothy before he died. Timothy was a young preacher who needed to hold to the truth of the Word and prepare others for discipleship. Paul tells him to be "strong in the grace that is in Christ Jesus." Grace is undeserved favor with God. We are saved by grace (Ephesians 2:8–9) and should live by grace (Colossians 2:6–7). Reliance on Christ and His power is necessary in doing His work. We cannot rely on our own strength. Timothy was in need of strength from God to lead the church in Ephesus.

As Timothy grew in grace, he would be able to witness and teach others what he had learned. He had been taught the Word by Paul, his mother, and grandmother. Their witness empowered Timothy to live for Christ. Now he had to do the same for others. "Faith cometh by hearing and hearing by the word of God" (Romans 10:17). If we do not teach others about Christ, how will they come to know Him? We have to become living witnesses for the faith we claim to believe. Paul was a living witness for God. He served God faithfully and suffered so the Gospel could be spread. Many people came to know Christ as Paul traveled on three missionary journeys. He had to endure much to fulfill the will of God. But as a result of his faithfulness, churches were birthed.

As he ministered, Timothy would also have to endure suffering. Like soldiers in the military, we have to let go of our desires and endure discipline. Because people will be won for Christ and one day Jesus shall reward us in eternity, we cannot give up in the bad times. It is in the difficult times that our witness is greatest. Paul, while in prison waiting to be executed, took the time to write a letter to encourage Timothy. He was a living witness for others.

During times of sickness, financial problems, marital conflict, or unexpected tragedies, we can still be witnesses for Christ. Instead of focusing on our problems, we can pray, knowing God is in control, and continue to share the love of God with others. We can offer a kind word, send a card, offer a ride, or bake a cake. By sowing into another's life, in the midst of our struggles, we become witnesses for Christ, who while he suffered on the Cross, thought about others and not Himself.

2. Proclaim the Word Faithfully (4:1–5)

In his last instructions to Timothy, Paul commands him to preach the Gospel. Paul knew the key to Christianity—the Gospel—was spread through the preached Word. He understood one day Jesus was coming back to claim his people. Only those who believed, by faith in the Son of God, would inherit eternal life. Because they have not accepted Christ, many people in the world would be doomed for eternity. In wanting all to be born again, Paul had a missionary's heart. So we can understand the urgency in his voice as he wrote these words to Timothy.

Do we have an urgency to tell others about Christ, or are we afraid of their response to our witness? Jesus is coming back unexpectedly! How many of the people we see every day have never heard the Gospel? When the opportunity presents itself, we can offer them a choice. Yes, it may cost us some personal suffering, but we have to be diligent at all times and places, whether convenient or inconvenient. It is the most important responsibility believers have been given. If we continue in what we have been taught, souls will be saved through our witness.

Allow the Scriptures to speak to the hearts of people. The Holy Spirit will convict people of their sins. Appeal to them continually to correct their behavior and be transformed into new creations in Christ. Only through faith in Christ can anyone be saved.

Even as Paul predicted, many people do not want to hear the truth of the Word. "Sound doctrine" has given way to people only seeking teachers who will affirm their lifestyles and worldly preoccupations. People do not like being exposed to the truth. It makes them confront their sins. It's easier to find teachers who only preach "feel-good" sermons without appealing for change. Some people move from church to church seeking a preacher who will not confront the sin in their lives. The Word is watered down to placate the "itching ears" of the people. Paul did not want Timothy to be such a leader. Timothy knew "all scripture is given by inspiration of God, and is profitable for doctrine, for reproof, for correction, and for instruction in righteousness" (3:16).

As a leader, Timothy is warned to exercise caution, not to be influenced by people or circumstances that may cause him to behave inappropriately. It is difficult dealing with a diverse group in a leadership position. There can be many conflicts and problems that make you lose patience. However, we have to endure afflictions and continue serving God. In living out our faith, in spite of the difficulties, the world experiences the love of God in action. If Timothy followed the good example shown to him by Paul, he would be an effective witness for Christ in the community and so will we.

Source:
Wesley, John. *Commentary on the Bible, 2 Timothy*. Grand Rapids, Mich.: Zondervan, 1990.

Search the Scriptures

1. And the things that thou hast heard of me among many _______, the same commit thou to _______ men, who shall be able to _____ others also (2 Timothy 2:2).

2. _________ the word; be instant in season, out of season; reprove, ___________, exhort with all _____________ and doctrine (4:2).

3. But watch thou in all things, endure ___________, do the work of an evangelist, make full proof of thy ___________(4:5).

Discuss the Meaning

1. What did Paul mean when he told Timothy to be "strong in grace"?
2. How is enduring hardship a witness to others?
3. How can the preached word transform lives?

Lesson in Our Society

John Wesley, Richard Allen, Harriet Tubman, and Martin Luther King Jr. were all strong witnesses of faith. Their courageous acts and faithful service impacted the world. Yes, they suffered for being faithful to God's call. But because they endured and continued serving God, the world was forever changed.

We cannot allow the sufferings of this world to hinder us from being a witness for Christ. We all know "all that will live godly in Christ Jesus shall suffer persecution" (2 Timothy 3:12). We have the victory, through Christ, who has "all power in heaven and on earth." Our witness to others, as we have trials, positively impacts their lives for Christ.

Make It Happen

What names come to mind when you think of faithful servants of God? How do they demonstrate their faith on a daily basis? Pray and ask God to empower you to become a witness in your community and a godly example for others. This week, share your faith with someone and show the love of Christ in action.

Follow the Spirit

What God wants me to do:

____

____

Remember Your Thoughts

Special insights I have learned:

____

____

More Light on the Text

2 Timothy 2:1–3; 4:1–5

1 Thou therefore, my son, be strong in the grace that is in Christ Jesus.

From a rotting dungeon, Paul exulted in the glories of Christ's Gospel, as displayed for us in chapter 1 of this his second letter to his protégé, Timothy. He spoke of a living power, which must be "stirred up" (1:6), a living Lord who "abolished death, and hath brought life and immortality to light" (v. 10) and a living Holy Spirit "which dwelleth in us" (v. 14). His grief, at desertion by his fellow Christian laborers, has impressed upon him the need to cling ferociously to the Gospel (v. 15). In addition, his refreshment, at the hands of a friend and brother, has encouraged him that God has been preserving a faithful remnant that would do just that (vv. 16–18).

With these things in mind, the apostle charged Timothy, the young pastor of the flock at Ephesus, to nurture a community that would produce and send heralds of Jesus' good news to the rest of the city, and the rest of the world. The apostle obviously considered Timothy to be his spiritual offspring, calling him "my son" (elsewhere Paul says that

"And the things that thou hast heard of me among many witnesses, the same commit thou to faithful men, who shall be able to teach others also" (2 Timothy 2:2).

"though ye have ten thousand instructers in Christ, yet have ye not many fathers: for in Christ Jesus I have begotten you through the Gospel," 1 Corinthians 4:15). Though 1:5 suggests that Timothy became a Christian through the influence of his own family, Timothy would at the very least be like an adopted son to Paul. After all, the apostle, awaiting his imminent death, revealed in this letter his deep concern that Christ's good news flourish beyond the age of the apostles, and he viewed his protégé Timothy as one of the vital carriers of that message.

As the "therefore" at the front of the verse suggests in the first chapter of his letter, Paul grounded his solemn commands to Timothy. From that chapter come the truths concerning both the preciousness and fragility of the Gospel—preciousness because of the infinite value of the Christ it lifts up but fragility because of the fallible human carrier who carry its glorious message (compare 2 Corinthians 4:7). Because of Timothy's own fragility, being well-known (implied in 1:6–7 and in 1 Timothy 4:12), Paul called him to look outside of himself for strength to persevere in Christ. More precisely, Paul urged Timothy to find his strength "in the grace that is in Christ Jesus." As 1:9–10 show us, this grace is the overflowing favor of God that causes him, through Christ's death and resurrection, to rescue a people for his own possession out of death and sin. The King James Version retains the rich ambiguity implied in the phrase "in the grace"

(Gk. *en te chariti*, **en tay KHAR-ee-tee**). The Greek phrase could mean that Timothy should be strengthened *in the midst or sphere* of that saving grace, or directly *by* such powerful grace. It is probably best to see both ideas operating here, retaining the luxurious fullness of the Greek. In other words, Timothy was to be strengthened both *by* and *in* grace: both by the knowledge of God's unshakeable love for him and by remaining in that knowledge rather than falling back into the ever-present danger of seeking salvation and well-being through obedience to the law. If Timothy was to follow the treasured example of Onesiphorus (1:16–18), he was to fight with weapons not his own but rather with power from God in the Gospel (see Romans 1:16–17).

2 And the things that thou hast heard of me among many witnesses, the same commit thou to faithful men, who shall be able to teach others also.

Paul expounded more deeply what it would look like for Timothy to keep "that good thing which was committed" to him (1:14). Keeping the message, entrusted to him by Paul, would be more than simply a matter of steadfastly believing it himself (1:1). The good news of Christ, like the church, always a generation away from extinction, must be passed on from one faithful generation to another. Paul's overwhelming concern here was clearly not his own legacy, but the presentation of the pure Gospel, until the return of Christ. Note that four generations of Gospel carriers are mentioned here: (1) Paul himself; (2) Timothy, who has received the message from Paul ("among many witnesses"; see below); (3) those whom Timothy will commit the good deposit of the Gospel; and (4) the "others also" who will be taught by Timothy's disciples. Notice also that Paul had two requirements for those who would receive this leadership development within the church: first, that they be faithful and second, that they be able to teach. Note the similarity between these qualifications and the more expansive list given for elders in 1 Timothy 3:1–7.

Three details from the Greek are worth mentioning here. First, the word translated "among" here is the word *dia* (Gk. **dee-AH**), which more commonly means "through." If the phrase here then is "through many witnesses," then the idea is that not only Paul but also many others have proclaimed the Word of Christ—which is no doubt true. If we follow the King James Version's (KJV) "among many witnesses," then the focus is not on the many who have proclaimed the Gospel but on the many who have heard it—also unquestionably true. The overall sense is not greatly affected either way.

Second, one should note that the Greek word *anthropois* (**an-THROW-poice**), here translated "men," could also refer to a mixed company of men and women. Whatever one's views on gender roles in ministry, it seems likely that Paul intended both men and women to be carriers and teachers of the Gospel. Finally, the verb translated "commit" here is related to a noun, which in the New Testament is often translated "tradition." Though *tradition* can be a negative term, when it is considered a rival to the authority of the Scriptures, we do well to understand that the apostles considered their message of good news to be a "tradition," in the simple sense that it was to be faithfully handed down from one generation to the next. In this sense, all churches that faithfully proclaim Christ's Gospel are heirs and successors to the apostles.

3 Thou therefore endure hardness, as a good soldier of Jesus Christ.

At first glance, it might seem hard to see the connection between this verse and the one preceding it. Verse 2:2 concerns those who would follow Paul and Timothy in the faith, while verse 2:3 returns to the subject of Timothy's own faithfulness to his calling. What ties the two together is Paul's overriding passion that the Gospel grow and bear fruit after his death. This explains the "therefore" of verse 3; Paul knew that the health of the church in Ephesus—and the flourishing of the Gospel for generation after generation of believers—depended in large part on this young pastor's faithfulness. That faithfulness, in turn, was endangered by intense persecution, which had turned many (including, presumably, Phygellus and Hermogenes, 1:15) away from the "hardness" (to use the KJV's word) that it entailed. (See also Paul's lament over Demas in 4:10, where he is described as "having loved this present world," which is more or less the opposite of the perseverance commanded here.)

The key Greek term in this verse is *sugkakopatheo* (**soong-kak-op-ath-EH-o**), which the KJV translates as "endure hardness." The prefix *sun*, when connected to a verb, either serves to intensify the meaning of the verb or to add the idea of "with." In this case it seems to be the latter. Paul used the same term in 1:8, where the King James Version translates the phrase, "be thou partaker of the afflictions of the gospel." To be a "partaker" means to participate in something, and that idea is present here as well. In fact, though the Greek word "me" is not present in either 1:8 or 2:3, most translations correctly include the phrase "with me" in both verses. In other words, the best rendering of the verse is "endure hardness *with me* as a good soldier of Jesus Christ." The phrase "good soldier" may imply that Timothy had specific antagonists in his quest to be faithful to the Gospel (almost certainly true, in light of persecution of Christians at this time). However, it probably has a broader meaning than that to cover all sorts of suffering. The meaning is clear: Faithfulness to the Gospel will involve suffering of various kinds, and Timothy must be prepared for this reality and in the midst of it "be strong in the grace that is in Christ Jesus."

4:1 I charge thee therefore before God, and the Lord Jesus Christ, who shall judge the quick and the dead at his appearing and his kingdom;

Since this passage is disconnected from the one paired with it in this lesson, it is helpful to consider what themes intervene between the two. Clearly Paul's abiding concern, in this letter, was Timothy's endurance for the Gospel's sake in the face of great difficulty. On this theme, he continues to preach to his protégé in chapter 2, setting that exhortation in the light of the destructive and rotting false teaching of those who have strayed from the truth (2:16–18). Paul referred to this teaching as a "canker," or, in other translations, like "gangrene," which rots away the body. In chapter 3, we can see why Paul would be so dramatic in his condemnation of false teaching. There Paul decribed more fully the hopeless and heartless condition of these heretics, showing that false teaching leads inevitably to corrupt and polluted lives. Timothy's mentor called him to a life that reflected the opposite of each of these dimensions. Where false teaching gives birth to foul living, Timothy was to cling to the powerful truth of God's Word (3:14–17), which will forge in him a refined and godly character (2:22–26).

Having laid out these two ways to live, Paul returned to the charge he left off with at the beginning of chapter 2. In order to show how solemn and urgent his charge, he unfolded a formula common in the Scriptures and in Paul's letters (see 1 Timothy 5:21; 2 Timothy 2:14). Paul reminded Timothy, quite simply, of the backdrop of all life that the church would later refer to as *coram Deo*, "before the face of God." Grounding the weighty commands that would follow in the reality of God's omnipresent gaze, Paul did not remain content with that abstract idea. He went on to connect his God-inspired charge to the imminence and significance of Christ's return. The message is this: Christ will come again to judge all the world and this should deeply motivate you, Timothy, to walk in the ways I charge you and not in the ways of those around you!

The peculiar phrasing of Paul's charge might make us wonder: Is he implying that "Jesus Christ, who shall judge," is less than God, whom he mentions first? What is the relationship between the two? We have at least three clues to answer. The first is Paul's use of "Lord" to refer to Jesus. This New Testament word is the same word used in the Septuagint, the Greek translation of the Old Testament for "Yahweh," the holy covenant of the one true God. In other words, in calling Jesus, "Lord," Paul was saying a mouthful! That reference alone is enough to show how the New Testament writers viewed Jesus as divine. Second, Paul's reference to Christ as the one who "shall judge the quick and the dead" leaves little doubt as to Christ's deity. Throughout the Bible, the inspired writers viewed God alone as the one who would enact this all-encompassing judgment. Finally, we have other references to Jesus in this group of letters (1 and 2 Timothy and Titus) often called the "pastoral epistles"—references like Titus 2:13, where Paul spoke of "the glory of the great God and Saviour Jesus Christ." Calling Jesus not only "Saviour," but also "God" Paul made clear that he viewed Jesus as nothing less than God, Himself, distinct from God the Father (as the verse we consider here shows) but equal with him in every way. This teaching of Christ's equality with the Father would later be confessed by the church in the Nicene Creed, where Jesus is described as being of "one substance with the Father."

2 Preach the word; be instant in season, out of season; reprove, rebuke, exhort with all longsuffering and doctrine.

This verse begins with Paul's famous exhortation

to the young pastor Timothy: "preach the word." Gordon Fee notes that this command puts flesh on the repeated exhortation to guard "that good thing which was committed unto thee" (2 Timothy 1:14; see also 1 Timothy 6:20). We see here the strangely glorious nature of God's truth: The church "guards" the Gospel by letting it go—by preaching it far and wide! Like seed that only accomplishes its purpose when scattered on the ground, the good news of Christ bears its fruit only when generously proclaimed. And the Gospel is indeed the "word" talked about here, as shown in several other places in the Pastoral Epistles (see 1 Timothy 5:17; 2 Timothy 2:15, 19; 4:2; Titus 1:3; 2:5).

The King James Version's translation of the next phrase is famous: "Be instant in season, out of season." The Greek verb used in the command—*ephistemi* **(ef-IS-tay-mee)**—has many meanings in the New Testament, all related to the idea of "standing," "placing," or "putting." Probably the closest we can come in English to the sense of the word is the common phrase "stand by," meaning "be at the ready." One can see how that idea fits here and why most translations render this command as "be prepared." Similarly challenging is the phrase "in season, out of season"; the idea seems to be "when it is convenient and when it is not"—though it is not clear whether that means convenient for the preacher or convenient for the hearers. Thankfully, though some of the terms in this command are vague, the overall meaning is not: Timothy was to persevere in his task of preaching the Gospel—whatever the response, whatever the cost. And this command fits perfectly with the overall theme of preserving the Gospel.

The three commands here translated "reprove, rebuke, exhort" have a lot of overlapping meaning. Each one contains a very real sense of urgency, which fits with Paul's urgency over the continuation of the Gospel ministry after his death. Though "rebuke" is the most direct of the terms, all three points to rousing people out of complacency and/or disobedience, which can lead to the abandonment of the Gospel task. These tasks are to be carried out with "longsuffering" in light of a world that provides an inhospitable climate to the Gospel. Finally, Timothy's call was to carry out this charge with "all doctrine," or, as we might better understand in modern English, "with all (sorts of) teaching." In other words, Timothy must hold forth the full range and breadth of the glorious Gospel of grace that all might be captivated by it and brought in obedience to it.

3 For the time will come when they will not endure sound doctrine; but after their own lusts shall they heap to themselves teachers, having itching ears;

Paul now resumed his role as a kind of prophet, predicting that those who hear the Gospel would ultimately scorn and despise it to their own destruction. Paul's own account of his rejection by those he loved, and of many abandoning the truth (referred to earlier in this lesson), gave him every reason to anticipate further denial of the Gospel's truth by people led astray by their sin. The actual situation is left vague. Paul simply said that "the time will come" and referred to the unfaithful simply as "they." Paul used the word here translated "endure" (Gk. *anechomai*, **an-EKH-om-ahee**) nine other times in his letters, all of which refer either to enduring suffering and persecution or to enduring other people, with the idea of being patient with them. Clearly, then, we can see how Paul here described people to whom sound (or "healthy") teaching first becomes a burden that they must endure, then a burden that they will not endure. The change in their desire for and attitude toward truth is apparent.

In very graphic terms, then, Paul showed what would be the result of turning from sound teaching. As the Bible consistently teaches, a person cannot be truly neutral; he or she will always give allegiance to something or someone. In this vein, Paul showed here turning from healthy doctrine did not result in harmless neutrality but in fact in an eager and lustful quest to find different teaching, pleasing to the ravenous heart. So such people will "heap to themselves," as the KJV beautifully puts it, a different teaching to replace the sound teaching, from which they have turned. Paul's colorful phrase, "having itching ears," showed the insatiable curiosity with which they will pursue any sort of teaching that will gratify or excite them. One is reminded of the philosophers of Athens engaged in debate by Paul: "For all the Athenians and strangers which were there spent their time in nothing else, but either to tell, or to hear some new thing" (Acts 17:21).

4 And they shall turn away their ears from the truth, and shall be turned unto fables.

Paul repeated a similar idea here, once again

describing the "ears" of those who will turn away from the truth. His repeated use of the Greek word *akoe* (**ak-o-AY**) shows the importance the Bible places on the human faculty of hearing, though, of course, when the Bible writers refer to "hearing," it does not simply mean the hearing of the ears, but the understanding and acceptance of the mind and heart. So Paul elsewhere could affirm, "So then faith cometh by hearing, and hearing by the word of God" (Romans 10:17).

The tragic irony of those described here is that their turning mirrors exactly the biblical picture of repentance but in the opposite direction. For examples of repentance being correlated with turning from one thing to another, see Jeremiah 4:28, Ezekiel 14:6, Jonah 3:9, and Acts 26:20. In each of these examples, we see that repentance involves forsaking the path of sin and unbelief and turning to God and His righteousness. It is a decisive two-stage process—a turning of the whole being. Sadly, we see the same sort of process going on in these verses. The people lamented here by Paul first forsake true and healthy teaching, very intentionally, before they turn hungrily to fascinating myths and fables. The sober reality surrounding Timothy's task, and those of anyone who would proclaim the Gospel, could not be clearer.

5 But watch thou in all things, endure afflictions, do the work of an evangelist, make full proof of thy ministry.

In contrast to the reckless lust of those who want to satisfy their curious cravings, Timothy's charge (notice the solemn charge to be different: "but … thou") was to "watch," that is, to be sober and self-controlled. Even while those all around him are being taken in by attractive myths, he must stand by "the old, old story." In light of the suffering he will no doubt encounter (mentioned repeatedly above), he is to "endure afflictions." Interestingly, Paul used almost exactly the same word he used in 2:3, except that in this case the prefix *sun* (**soon**) is absent, so the idea of "suffering *with* someone" is not present here. Paul intended a wider meaning here, including whatever suffering may come, even if Timothy would suffer it alone.

Paul's command to "do the work of an evangelist" pointed back to the urgent summons of 4:2: "preach the word." It appears that Timothy, in addition to being pastor of the flock at Ephesus, also possessed the gift of evangelism described in Ephesians 4:11. However, we should not overemphasize this point, remembering that the word "evangelist" comes from the same root as the noun "Gospel" and the verb "to preach the Gospel." Paul was probably not speaking here of a gift, specifically given and narrowly exercised, as much as the duty of any and all pastors and indeed any who would pass on the word of truth faithfully.

Finally, Paul called on Timothy to "make full proof of thy ministry." The verb translated "make full proof of" carries the idea of remaining set on something doggedly until the task is complete. The *New International Version*'s (NIV) translation helps us get the idea: "Discharge all the duties of your ministry." We understand the power and urgency of this command when we remember that Paul knew himself to be close to his execution, himself having "fought a good fight" of faith (4:7). We see once again the apostle's weighty charge to Timothy, inspired by his own intense longing for the Gospel to flourish well beyond his own death.

Daily Bible Readings

M: Power, Love, Self-Discipline
2 Timothy 1:3–7
T: I Am Not Ashamed
2 Timothy 1:8–14
W: The Power of the Gospel
Romans 1:8–17
T: The Unchained Word of God
2 Timothy 2:8–13
F: An Approved Worker
2 Timothy 2:14–19
S: Continue in What You Learned
2 Timothy 3:14–17
S: Proclaim the Message!
2 Timothy 2:1–3; 4:1–5

NOTES

TEACHING TIPS

November 30
Bible Study Guide 13

1. Words You Should Know

A. Perils (2 Corinthians 11:26) *kindunos* (Gk.)—Danger.

B. Weak (v. 29; 12:10) *asthenes* (Gk.)—Infirm; feeble.

C. Glory (v. 30; 12:9) *kauchaomai* (Gk.)—To boast.

D. Grace (12:9) *charis* (Gk.)—Undeserved favor of God.

E. Reproaches (v. 10) *hubris* (Gk.)—Injury.

2. Teacher Preparation

Unifying Principle—Grace in Times of Trouble. People will face many trials in life, from friend and foe and from expected and unexpected sources. How can one overcome such hardships? Paul says that through his weaknesses, he finds strength in the grace of God.

A. Pray for the class.

B. Using the *Precepts For Living*® CD-ROM, research the Corinthian church as well as the meaning of grace.

C. Read 1 Corinthians 1:18–25.

D. Review the AIM for Change, Keep in Mind, and Focal Verses sections.

3. Starting the Lesson

A. Ask a volunteer to open the class with prayer.

B. Have the class read the Keep in Mind verse together. Read the AIM for Change section and expound on it.

C. Ask a volunteer to read the In Focus story. How did Makia handle her circumstances? Discuss how Makia's presentation may have impacted Jared.

4. Getting into the Lesson

A. Review the early struggles of the Christian community, discussed in the previous lessons, during this month.

B. After reviewing the Background and The People, Places, and Times sections, ask if they know of any individuals or groups who are being persecuted as a result of their faith. Ask them to share with the class.

C. Summarize the Focal Verses and discuss how Paul viewed weakness.

5. Relating the Lesson to Life

A. Allow the students to work on the Search the Scriptures section.

B. Review the Discuss the Meaning section.

6. Arousing Action

A. Read the Lesson in Our Society and Make It Happen sections.

B. Have each student identify one person they can partner with for support during difficult times. Discuss how they can offer support to each other.

Worship Guide

For the Superintendent or Teacher
Theme: Persecution within the Community
Theme Song: "When Peace Like A River"
Devotional Reading: 1 Corinthians 1:18–25
Prayer

PERSECUTION WITHIN THE COMMUNITY

Bible Background • 2 CORINTHIANS 11:16–12:10
Printed Text • 2 CORINTHIANS 11:17, 21–30; 12:9–10 Devotional Reading • 1 CORINTHIANS 1:18–25

AIM for Change

By the end of the lesson, we will:
REVIEW Paul's writing about the inevitability of facing difficulties in the Christian life and the reliability of God's grace;
ACCEPT that being a Christian will not keep us from facing persecution; and
SUPPORT one another as we witness to our faith.

Keep in Mind

"Therefore I take pleasure in infirmities, in reproaches, in necessities, in persecutions, in distresses for Christ's sake: for when I am weak, then am I strong" (2 Corinthians 12:10).

Focal Verses

KJV **2 Corinthians 11:17** That which I speak, I speak it not after the Lord, but as it were foolishly, in this confidence of boasting.

11:21 I speak as concerning reproach, as though we had been weak. Howbeit whereinsoever any is bold, (I speak foolishly,) I am bold also.

22 Are they Hebrews? so am I. Are they Israelites? so am I. Are they the seed of Abraham? so am I.

23 Are they ministers of Christ? (I speak as a fool) I am more; in labours more abundant, in stripes above measure, in prisons more frequent, in deaths oft.

24 Of the Jews five times received I forty stripes save one.

25 Thrice was I beaten with rods, once was I stoned, thrice I suffered shipwreck, a night and a day I have been in the deep;

26 In journeyings often, in perils of waters, in perils of robbers, in perils by mine own countrymen, in perils by the heathen, in perils in the city, in perils in the wilderness, in perils in the sea, in perils among false brethren;

27 In weariness and painfulness, in watchings often, in hunger and thirst, in fastings often, in cold and nakedness.

28 Beside those things that are without, that which cometh upon me daily, the care of all the churches.

29 Who is weak, and I am not weak? who is offended, and I burn not?

30 If I must needs glory, I will glory of the things which concern mine infirmities.

NLT **2 Corinthians 11:17** Such boasting is not from the Lord, but I am acting like a fool.

11:21 I'm ashamed to say that we've been too "weak" to do that! But whatever they dare to boast about—I'm talking like a fool again—I dare to boast about it, too.

22 Are they Hebrews? So am I. Are they Israelites? So am I. Are they descendants of Abraham? So am I.

23 Are they servants of Christ? I know I sound like a madman, but I have served him far more! I have worked harder, been put in prison more often, been whipped times without number, and faced death again and again.

24 Five different times the Jewish leaders gave me thirty-nine lashes.

25 Three times I was beaten with rods. Once I was stoned. Three times I was shipwrecked. Once I spent a whole night and a day adrift at sea.

26 I have traveled on many long journeys. I have faced danger from rivers and from robbers. I have faced danger from my own people, the Jews, as well as from the Gentiles. I have faced danger in the cities, in the deserts, and on the seas. And I have faced danger from men who claim to be believers but are not.

27 I have worked hard and long, enduring many sleepless nights. I have been hungry and thirsty and have often gone without food. I have shivered in the cold, without enough clothing to keep me warm.

12:9 And he said unto me, My grace is sufficient for thee: for my strength is made perfect in weakness. Most gladly therefore will I rather glory in my infirmities, that the power of Christ may rest upon me.

10 Therefore I take pleasure in infirmities, in reproaches, in necessities, in persecutions, in distresses for Christ's sake: for when I am weak, then am I strong.

28 Then, besides all this, I have the daily burden of my concern for all the churches.

29 Who is weak without my feeling that weakness? Who is led astray, and I do not burn with anger?

30 If I must boast, I would rather boast about the things that show how weak I am.

12:9 Each time he said, "My grace is all you need. My power works best in weakness." So now I am glad to boast about my weaknesses, so that the power of Christ can work through me.

10 That's why I take pleasure in my weaknesses, and in the insults, hardships, persecutions, and troubles that I suffer for Christ. For when I am weak, then I am strong.

In Focus

Jared was a good student at school. He made friends as soon as his family moved to the neighborhood. Jared was always invited to parties. His friends did not know he lived in a homeless shelter with his parents. He did not allow anyone to visit where he lived. Jared constantly complained to his parents about his situation. Even on Thanksgiving Day, he grumbled about not having a home. One day the shelter manager asked Jared's parents if Jared could go to hear a presentation at the library. They agreed.

Jared arrived a few minutes early at the library on a bitterly cold Saturday morning. He noticed a lot of the people in attendance were high school students. He wondered why the shelter manager urged him to come. The manager had to stay at the shelter due to an emergency. Signs on the podium mentioned Darfur. Jared knew some bad stuff had happened to the people there.

After a brief introduction, a young woman approached the microphone. She was about 19 years old, five-feet-nine inches tall, with a slender build.

"Good morning. My name is Makia," the woman said. "I am a Darfur refugee. I have come here to share my story. I was born in Darfur, a region in the Sudan, and lived there all my life. My family owned a farm and made a living selling dairy products. One day a militia army came into my town and burned all the houses down. Five of my ten siblings were burned alive because they could not escape the flames. My parents suffered severe burns trying to save them. Then the soldiers took a machete and cut my parents' limbs off right in front of us. My sisters and I watched in horror as they bled to death.

"We were taken as slaves to serve the army. We were gang-raped every day and starved. After many months of praying, two of us escaped and walked for a month through barren land to get to a refugee camp. A group of Christians came to the camp and helped some of us move to the United States. I have been here one year and live with a foster family who is my sponsor. I urge all of you to be grateful for the life you have here in the USA. Every night I thank God for giving me a chance to be in such a wonderful place. Thank you!"

Everyone stood to their feet and applauded. There was not a dry eye in the auditorium.

In today's lesson, we learn that all Christians will face difficulties in life. But we have to rely on God's grace to sustain us through the tough times.

The People, Places, and Times

Corinth. Corinth's great temple, on its ancient acropolis, was dedicated to the goddess Aphrodite. According to most sources, there were more than one thousand temple prostitutes employed at the Temple of Aphrodite.

Following a siege in 146 B.C., the Romans destroyed Corinth. Before the city was torched, all the men died by the sword, and the women and children were sold into slavery. Julius Caesar refound the city in 44 B.C., shortly before his assassination. The new settlers were drawn from freedmen of Rome. Under the Romans, it became the seat of government for Southern Greece or Achaia (see Acts 18:12–16).

Corinth was noted for its wealth and for the luxurious, immoral, and vicious habits of the people. It had a large mixed population of Romans, Greeks, and Jews.

When the apostle Paul first visited the city (A.D. 51 or 52), Gallio, the brother of Seneca, was proconsul. Paul resided here for 18 months (see Acts 18:1–18). Here he first became acquainted with Aquila and Priscilla, and soon after his departure, Apollos came from Ephesus. According to Acts 20:3, although Paul, before he visited Macedonia, intended to pass through Corinth the second time, circumstances were such that he went from Troas to Macedonia. He then likely passed into Corinth for a "second benefit" (see 2 Corinthians 1:15) and remained for three months. During this second visit in the spring of 58, it is likely Paul wrote the epistle to the Romans.

Paul also wrote two of his epistles to the Christian community at Corinth—the first epistle to the Corinthians and the second epistle to the Corinthians. The first epistle reflects the difficulties of maintaining a Christian community in such a cosmopolitan city.

Source:

Unger, Merrill. *The New Unger's Bible Handbook.* Chicago, Ill.: Moody Press, 1984.

Background

In about A.D. 58, within a year of the first letter, Paul wrote this epistle to the Corinthians from Macedonia. In addition to dealing with the unspiritual and immoral condition of the Corinth church, his authority was being questioned. He wanted to affirm his ministry, defend his authority as an apostle, and refute the false teachers.

He began by reminding the Corinthians that he had always been honest and straightforward with them. He was planning on visiting them again. Paul dealt with false teachers, so to demonstrate the validity of his message and urge the people not to turn away from the truth, he reviewed his ministry.

Paul also defended the collection for the poor Christians in Jerusalem. He told them how others have given, and he urged them to show their love in a tangible way as well. In chapter 11, in opposition to the false apostles, Paul went on with his discourse. They had been very industrious to lessen his reputation among the Corinthians and had prevailed. He apologized for having to commend himself (or toot his own horn), and gave the reasons for what he did (vv. 1–4). He mentioned, in his own necessary vindication, his equality with the other apostles and in particular with the false apostles, of preaching the Gospel to the Corinthians freely, without wages (vv. 5–15). He made another preface to what his mission was and went on further to justify his actions (vv. 16–21). He gave a large account of his qualifications, labors, and sufferings, in which he exceeded the false apostles (v. 22 to the end).

Source:

Life Application Study Bible (New Revised Standard Version). Chicago, Ill.: Tyndale House Publishers, 1989.

At-A-Glance

1. Paul Boasts About His Qualifications (2 Corinthians 11:17, 21–23)

2. Paul Boasts About Suffering for Christ's Sake (vv. 24–30)

3. Paul Boasts About Grace (12:9–10)

In Depth

1. Paul Boasts About His Qualifications (2 Corinthians 11:17, 21–23)

Paul let his readers know that boasting is not of the Lord. The Lord requires His people to be humble. But in some circumstances, we may have to defend our calling and confidence in Christ. Many false apostles were boldly boasting of their credentials and sufferings. Because he had more valid reasons to boast than the false apostles, Paul entreated the Corinthians to bear with him.

Here the apostle gave a large account of his own qualifications, labors, and sufferings (not out of pride or vainglory, but to the honor of God, who had enabled him to do and suffer so much for the cause of Christ). Therein, he excelled the false apostles, who would lessen his character and usefulness among the Corinthians. He presented his credentials to counteract the charges that the false teachers were making against him. His heritage and credentials were valid evidence of his authority.

Paul mentioned the privileges of his birth, which were equal to or surpassing any of the false apostles. He was a Hebrew of the Hebrews (Philippians 3:5) of a family among the Jews that never intermarried with the Gentiles. He was an Israelite and could boast of his being descended from the beloved Jacob and was also of the seed of Abraham and not of the proselytes. It would seem from this that the false apostles were of the Jewish race and were hassling the Gentile converts. Sometimes, by degrading others, people try to make themselves feel more important. God does not show partiality.

Paul was a minister of Christ, whose apostleship was validated by the Jerusalem Council (Acts 15:2–29). They gave him their approval to teach and preach the Gospel. Therefore, he had the credentials to minister, whereas the false apostles could not make such a claim. He even had suffered as a servant of Christ. He chiefly insisted upon this, that he had been an extraordinary sufferer for Christ; this was what he gloried in or rather he gloried in the grace of God that had enabled him to endure very great labors and sufferings. The apostle proved himself to be an extraordinary minister, and included the fact that he had been an extraordinary sufferer. Paul was the apostle to the Gentiles, and for that reason, he was hated of the Jews. They did all they could against him, and among the Gentiles also he met with hardship. Bonds and imprisonments were familiar to him, but Paul knew it was for righteousness' sake. The jail, the whippings, and all the other hardships of those who are accounted the worst of men were what Paul was accustomed to.

2. Paul Boasts About Suffering for Christ's Sake (vv. 24–30)

Paul recounted some of his trials and sufferings. He knew false teachers would never sacrifice as he had for the sake of Christ. Paul had experienced great trials such as: five times given 39 lashes by the Jews (Deuteronomy 25:2–3), three times beaten with rods (Acts 16:22–24), stoned (Acts 14:19), three times shipwrecked (Acts 27), and encountered danger wherever he went. And this was not the end of his suffering.

Paul was exposed to perils of all sorts. If he journeyed by land or voyaged by sea, he was in danger of robbers or enemies of some sort. The Jews, his own countrymen, sought to kill him or do him a mischief; the Gentiles, to whom he was sent, were not more kind to him—for among them he was in danger. If he was in the city or in the wilderness, still he was in danger. He was in danger not only among enemies but among those also who called themselves brothers and sisters—but were false brethren.

We often think our friends, family members, and fellow Christians would never be the cause of our suffering and trials. Often the ones who are the closest to us create the most hardship. David shared a similar experience (Psalm 41:9). This betrayal seems worse than having an enemy persecute us. Because the world hates Christ and we represent Him, all these things can be expected.

Besides all this, Paul had great weariness and painfulness in his ministerial labors. After His experience on the Damascus Road, Paul was a stranger to wealth and plenty, power and pleasure. He only knew hardship, hunger, thirst, and nakedness. Jesus never promised we would have it easy being one of His disciples. We just have to keep serving and trusting Him. In some circumstances, it is very hard to do.

Paul was the overseer of many young churches. He was very concerned about their spiritual well-being. There were false teachers trying to infiltrate the churches. The babes in Christ were being persuaded to follow false doctrines and not the true Gospel. Personal conflicts were threatening to destroy the unity and fellowship within the church. This caused him a great deal of stress, in addition to all the other trials he faced. Trouble can come from any source, even the church. In the midst of it all, we have to "know whom I have believed, and am persuaded that he is able to keep that which I have committed unto him against that day" (2 Timothy 1:12).

He sympathized with all who suffered some weakness or trial. Why? He had endured the same in order to save souls (1 Corinthians 9:22). He had experienced severe testing and trials, which gave credence to his testimony. Our sufferings are for God's glory and to strengthen our faith. Paul boasts of his weakness as it honored God and gave Him glory. His witness is not like the false teachers but authentic in every aspect. That is why Paul could be a strong witness to others.

3. Paul Boasts About Grace (12:9–10)

Paul had a "thorn in his flesh" (12:7–9). It may have hindered him from ministering on some occasions. He appealed to the Lord three times in prayer to heal him, but it did not happen. Sometimes God does not answer our prayers for deliverance from illness, persecution, or other trials. Paul was humbled, and others benefited as they saw the power of God at work in his life.

God's only response to Paul's request was "My grace is sufficient for thee" (v. 9). God does not always remove our troubles and temptations, yet if

He gives us grace sufficient for us, we have no reason to complain. It can be a great comfort to us, whatever thorns in the flesh cause us pain, that God's grace is sufficient for us. Grace signifies two things: (1) the goodwill of God toward us—and this is sufficient to strengthen and comfort us, to support our souls and cheer up our spirits, in all afflictions and distresses; (2) the good work of God in us—the grace we receive from the fullness that is in Christ—our Head—and from Him, there shall be communicated that which is sufficient for us. Christ Jesus understands our case, knows our need, and will proportion the remedy to our malady. He will not only strengthen us, but glorify Himself as well.

Verse 9 says, "For my strength is made perfect in weakness." The fact that God's power shows up in weak people is encouragement for all who recognize their need for help. Whenever we are experiencing difficulties, God can use us to witness to others how to endure through relying on His strength. Paul was a servant of Christ who suffered, but he witnessed of God's grace to encourage others and win souls. We cannot let trouble hinder our witness for God. Others are encouraged when they see us suffering but still worshiping and serving Christ. That is why Paul said, "I take pleasure in infirmities, in reproaches, in necessities, in persecutions, in distresses" (v. 10) so that the power of Christ may rest upon him. He took a form of pleasure in his afflictions and persecutions because they enabled him to witness more powerfully for God.

And the reason of his glory and joy on account of these things was this—they were fair opportunities for Christ to manifest the power and sufficiency of his grace resting upon him. Through this suffering, he had so much experience of the strength of divine grace that he could say, "for when I am weak, then am I strong" (v. 10). This is a Christian paradox: When we are weak in ourselves, then we are strong in the grace of our Lord Jesus Christ. When we see ourselves as weak, then we go out of ourselves to Christ and are qualified to receive strength from Him and experience more of the supplies of divine strength and grace.

Source:

Henry, Matthew. *Commentary on the Whole Bible, Complete and Unabridged.* Peabody, Mass.: Hendrickson Publishers, 1991.

Search the Scriptures

1. If I must needs ______, I will glory of the things which concern mine __________ (2 Corinthians 11:30).

2. My ________ is sufficient for thee: for my __________ is made perfect in weakness (12:9).

3. Therefore I take pleasure in ___________, in __________, in necessities, in persecutions, in ___________ for Christ's sake: for when I am weak, then am I _________ (v. 10).

Discuss the Meaning

Persecution happens to anyone who is a follower of Christ. It is not unusual to suffer. If we look at the lives of the disciples, we can understand the intense sacrifice they made for Christ. For example: Philip was scourged, thrown into prison, and afterwards crucified. James, at the age of 94, was beaten and stoned by the Jews and finally had his brains dashed out with a fuller's club. Matthias was stoned at Jerusalem and then beheaded. Andrew was taken and crucified on a cross, the two ends of which were fixed transversely (crosswise, diagonally) in the ground. Mark died by being dragged to pieces by the people of Alexandria. Peter was crucified upside down, with his feet extended upward. He asked to be executed this way because he felt unworthy to be crucified after the same form and manner of his Lord.

How did the disciples' lives glorify God? Do you think the spread of the Gospel was impeded or advanced as a result of their deaths?

Lesson in Our Society

Many of the early Christian communities faced struggles. The church in Ephesus had to deal with the diversity of identities and gifts in the community. They had to embrace diversity to build up the community of faith. The Galatian church had to confront opposition from Judaizers, who wanted Gentile converts to adhere to the law as a means of salvation, not relying on grace alone.

Paul encouraged the Philippians to rejoice in the midst of struggles, even as he did while imprisoned. Paul set an excellent example for others in the community as he lived as a strong witness in good and bad times. He wanted Timothy and other Christians to do the same. So when persecution and trials come, we do not have to be alarmed. We can rely on the grace of God to sustain us. As a community, we have to support one another and witness of God's faithfulness.

Make It Happen

As you think about personal struggles you have experienced, thank God for how He sustained you. Seek out opportunities to share your faith with others who are struggling. Pray with them, listen, and offer as much support as possible.

Follow the Spirit

What God wants me to do:

____

____

Remember Your Thoughts

Special insights I have learned:

____

____

More Light on the Text

2 Corinthians 11:17, 21–30; 12:9–10

17 That which I speak, I speak it not after the Lord, but as it were foolishly, in this confidence of boasting.

This perplexing verse introduces well the unusual tone with which Paul wrote the Scriptures that are the subject of this lesson. Paul's strange demeanor throughout this passage, and in this verse in particular, shows the danger of "prooftexting," or taking verses out of their context and quoting them in isolation to support a particular argument. Based on this verse alone, we might conclude that God calls Christians (1) to speak however they choose and not how God would have them speak; (2) to follow after foolishness wherever they can find it, and (3) to brag and boast with ultimate self-confidence! Needless to say, understanding Paul, inside the broader framework of his second letter to the Corinthians, will produce a different interpretation.

This chapter begins with words that will govern all Paul has to say throughout the verses considered in this lesson: "Would to God ye could bear with me a little in my folly: and indeed bear with me. For I am jealous over you with godly jealousy: for I have espoused you to one husband, that I may present you as a chaste virgin to Christ. But I fear, lest by any means, as the serpent beguiled Eve through his subtilty, so your minds should be corrupted from the simplicity that is in Christ" (2 Corinthians 11:1–3). These heartfelt and pastoral words could be considered a summary of Paul's attitude in the last part of this letter, which begins at 10:1 and proceeds to the end of the epistle. They show the deep emotion with which Paul wrote in 2 Corinthians—probably the most personal and passionate of his letters—and also the scorn and insult he had experienced from members of the church in Corinth.

We see this contempt in what Paul quotes the Corinthians as saying in 10:10: "For his letters, say they, are weighty and powerful; but his bodily presence is weak, and his speech contemptible." As Paul Barnett attests, the Corinthians had probably been deeply attracted to the teaching of Peter (who would have appealed to Jewish Christians in particular) or Apollos (who would have appealed to those who styled themselves as intellectual and sophisticated)—both of whom had visited Corinth more recently than Paul. Besides this, the Corinthians would have no doubt been tempted to ignore Paul in favor of other teachers, since Paul had rebuked them deeply and painfully in both 1 Corinthians 3:1, 5:1–2, 6:5, 11:22 and in a letter (many believe is now lost to us) written between 1 Corinthians and 2 Corinthians (see 2 Corinthians 2:3–4; 7:8–12). Why not listen to other teachers, who would likely be easier on the Corinthians than was Paul, who confronted them with "tough love"? So instead they maligned Paul as weak, hypocritical, and cowardly (as shown in chapters 10–11 in particular). Out of deep personal hurt, but also profound pastoral concern, Paul spoke to these accusations. His way of doing so, as the "folly" of 11:1 shows, is to ironically adopt their characterization of him as "weak" and "foolish," but to turn those descriptions into badges of honor, summing up his thoughts in 12:10 with the declaration that concludes this lesson: "For when I am weak, then I am strong." This sort of talk serves Paul's purpose of once again seeking to "espouse" the Corinthians "to one husband," to present them "as a chaste virgin to Christ" (11:2).

Thus can we understand both Paul's goal (to counteract Satan's deceptive wiles and restore the Corinthians to the simple beauty of Christ) and his method (to adopt the language of "weakness" and "folly" to defend his own apostleship and the glory of Jesus as well). We can now see why Paul wrote in the way he did in 11:17. It is difficult to understand what he meant with the phrase "that which I speak, I speak it not after the Lord." Given the way Paul turned everything upside down in this passage (boasting in weakness and foolishness), what he is likely saying is that he would be boasting in a way that appeared at first to be ungodly. But there is of

"Therefore I take pleasure in infirmities, in reproaches, in necessities, in persecutions, in distresses for Christ's sake; for when I am weak, then am I strong" (2 Corinthians 12:10).

course an irony even in this boasting, as shown by the single Greek word translated by the King James Version as "as it were." The boasting Paul pursued was not boasting in glorious victories, as did the pagan Roman rulers. He was boasting in lowliness, defeat, and shame—after the pattern of the suffering Christ, Himself. In fact, later in this very passage, Paul included a seemingly out-of-place note about his narrow escape from persecutors in Damascus, by being lowered down through a hole in the wall (11:32–33; compare Acts 9:23–25). Paul Barnett shows the significance of this incident and why Paul would mention it here: "One of the Roman soldier's most glorious achievements in battle, the *corona muralis,* was awarded for being the first over the wall of the city under siege. As Christ's fool, Paul boasts of being lowered *down* a wall as a fugitive." This was Paul's glory, Paul's reason for boasting, and Paul's folly. With such talk, he intended to shame the Corinthians into repentance of their own boasting—something that, in fact, was truly foolish before God.

11:21 I speak as concerning reproach, as though we had been weak. Howbeit whereinsoever any is bold, (I speak foolishly,) I am bold also.

Paul began to lay out exactly what he would boast about before those who accused and maligned him. When he said, "I speak as concerning reproach," it was not immediately clear whose "reproach" (or, as we would say it, "shame") he had in mind. In other words, he was either saying, "I say this to *your* shame" or "I say this to *my* shame" (the actual pronoun is not present). The first is possible, since he meant to shame the Corinthians into repentance, but the second is more likely, as he was focusing on his own shame, about which he would boast since it made him like his suffering Lord. In contrast to those who would boast in their own spirituality or in other apostles (true apostles or false ones), he would also brag with great audacity, but in the opposite thing: shame and weakness. The side note about "speaking foolishly" shows that Paul wanted to make it absolutely clear that he was turning his hearers' words upside-down; whereas they would exalt themselves, he would exalt Christ through the lowering of himself in "reproach."

22 Are they Hebrews? so am I. Are they Israelites? so am I. Are they the seed of Abraham? so am I.

This verse is fairly straightforward. Paul's overall point is clear: I am as Jewish as anybody! Why would it be so important to defend his Jewishness? Second Corinthians was likely written around A.D. 56, about 25 years after Christ's death, resurrection, and the founding of the new covenant church at Pentecost. In these very early years of Christianity, having ties to the Judaism, out of which Christianity had sprung, was especially important. Claiming to speak for Yahweh, the God of the Old Testament was almost unthinkable if one was not Jewish. All of the apostles were Jewish—the original Twelve, plus Matthias, Paul, and James, the brother of Jesus. We often neglect the essential Jewishness of Christianity; Christians are justified in claiming an Old Testament heritage, for their Saviour is the fulfillment of all the Old Testament promised.

Paul repeats essentially the same claim in three different ways. A "Hebrew" was an ethnic member of the Jewish nation; sometimes the term was used to describe a Jew who not only had Jewish heritage but who also spoke Hebrew and Aramaic (as opposed to Greek-speaking Jews). An "Israelite" was a member of the people of God, called out by God through Abraham and his descendants. Being the "seed of Abraham" meant he was not only naturally but also spiritually descended from Abraham—the children of God by faith, as Galatians 3:16–19 shows. But since Paul was focusing on his ethnic Jewishness here, he no doubt meant to point to the fact that he was not only a Christian, but also a *Jewish* Christian.

23 Are they ministers of Christ? (I speak as a fool) I am more; in labours more abundant, in stripes above measure, in prisons more frequent, in deaths oft.

The word translated "ministers" (*diakonos*, **dee-AK-on-os**) more closely means "servants," which shows what Paul has in mind: showing himself to be a more comprehensive servant of Christ. Again, Paul acknowledged that this would normally be a non-Christian way of speaking, but he was "speaking as a fool" to show that his shame and weakness, ironically, confirm him as a true apostle. The other three phrases show what he meant by calling himself "more…a minister of Christ": hard work in Christian service ("labours"; compare 1 Thessalonians 2:9), physical pain ("stripes"), imprisonment, and "deaths," by which Paul meant all sorts of suffering, probably in which one is in danger of death, for Christ's sake (see also Romans 8:36).

24 Of the Jews five times received I forty stripes save one.

The "forty stripes save one" was a common practice in the first century; Deuteronomy speaks about a "wicked man worthy to be beaten" by saying, "Forty stripes he may give him, and not exceed: lest, if he should exceed, and beat him above these with many stripes, then thy brother should seem vile unto thee" (Deuteronomy 25:2–3). In this way, God established a punishment that would serve justice, without being unduly harsh. We cannot know for what crimes Paul was punished in this way (the book of Acts does not record any of these lashings), but since this persecution was "of the Jews" it was likely for something against Jewish law, like associating with Gentiles or eating unclean food.

Wisdom and mercy require that we be careful in dealing with the phrase, "of the Jews." Without question, Jewish people (including Paul, before his Damascus Road experience [Acts 9:4–5]) were responsible for much early persecution, both of Christ and of his followers. Paul, a Jew who would have been considered a traitor and a blasphemer for converting to Christianity, would have been a particular target for persecution by non-Christian Jews. Paul used the shorthand phrase "the Jews" to refer not of course to all Jews (for all the Christian apostles and many other Christians were also Jews), but to those Jews who set themselves against the kingdom of God inaugurated by Jesus. (The gospel of John also uses the phrase "the Jews" in this way; see John 1:19; 2:18, 20; 5:10, 15–16; 7:15; 8:22; 10:24; 18:12.) This phrase no more refers to all Jews than derogatory references to "Gentiles" (such as

Ephesians 4:17) refer to all Gentiles. When used negatively, both terms—"the Jews" and "the Gentiles"—refer to the number among those ethnic groups who oppose the rule of God.

Jews, throughout history, have experienced many horrors at the hands of Christians, supposedly as revenge for crucifying Christ and persecuting Christians. This is an unspeakable sin. We would do well to remember the words of Acts 4:27–28: "For of a truth against thy holy child Jesus, whom thou hast anointed, both Herod, and Pontius Pilate, with the Gentiles, and the people of Israel, were gathered together, for to do whatsoever thy hand and thy counsel determined before to be done." We learn from these verses first of all that many groups (Jews, Gentiles, Roman rulers, etc.) were responsible for Christ's crucifixion, not just one. But even more importantly, we see that all this was *planned beforehand by God* to bring about His glorious redemptive purposes through the Cross.

25 Thrice was I beaten with rods, once was I stoned, thrice I suffered shipwreck, a night and a day I have been in the deep;

Beating with rods was a Roman punishment; though Paul, as a Roman citizen, should not have been subjected to such torment (see Acts 16:22, 37–38). It appears that in these cases, either those responsible did not know he was a Roman citizen or else they did not strictly follow Roman law. The stoning mentioned here is probably the one found in Acts 14:19, which Paul survived by God's mercy alone. As for the shipwreck, Paul had taken many voyages by the time he wrote 2 Corinthians, though he had not yet endured the shipwreck described in Acts 27. However, he had already taken countless journeys by sea during his journeys to Asia Minor (modern-day Turkey) and Greece. On one of these occasions, according to this verse, he even remained in the sea for an entire night and day, waiting for rescue.

26 In journeyings often, in perils of waters, in perils of robbers, in perils by mine own countrymen, in perils by the heathen, in perils in the city, in perils in the wilderness, in perils in the sea, in perils among false brethren;

Paul continued to recount the massive persecution he had endured through this list of "perils." The opening phrase "in journeyings often" gives the backdrop for where these perils occurred. The first peril, "waters," is a specific reference to rivers, which would have often been unpredictable and difficult to cross. One need look no further than the parable of the good Samaritan (Luke 10:30–37) to see the danger of robbers to those who traveled. The next two perils show the comprehensive danger for an early Christian, provided by both Jew and Gentile (see discussion on verse 26). Though Acts records more persecution by Jews than by the Romans or other Gentiles, Paul showed that both groups were enemies of the way of God in Christ and presented much danger.

The following two perils, in the same way, show danger everywhere—both in the city and in the wilderness. In the cities there were perils that accompanied the presence of many people at once, including mob violence (see Acts 19:28–41). The wilderness, on the other hand, was almost always a dangerous setting in the Scriptures; the Israelites' long wandering in the wilderness and Jesus' parallel 40-day temptation in the desert would be two examples of this theme. Finally, after mentioning again the danger of the sea, Paul brought these "perils" to a climax by referring to the danger of "false brethren." Why mention this danger last? Probably because these "false brethren" were the very people Paul was confronting in 2 Corinthians; in fact, throughout the New Testament false teachers or false brothers are considered most dangerous to the church of God (see, as one of many examples, Galatians 1:8–9). By finishing his list of "perils" with his own enemies—those who would corrupt and lead astray the Corinthians—Paul powerfully shows how great the danger is of a false Gospel: worse even than the danger of death

27 In weariness and painfulness, in watchings often, in hunger and thirst, in fastings often, in cold and nakedness.

In contrast to the "perils" listed in verse 26, which generally pointed to the danger of death, Paul here focused on the (often extreme) discomfort he experienced as a result of his calling. Paul used the combination of words here translated "weariness and painfulness" also in 1 Thessalonians 2:9 and 2 Thessalonians 3:8, in both cases to emphasize how he went through this "weariness and painfulness" in order to sacrificially serve his flock, even to the point of asking nothing from them in return. In the same way, the "watchings" and "fastings" mentioned here were no doubt provoked by constant, unremitting concern over those to whom he brought the Gospel (see the next two verses for greater detail on this pastoral burden). Even caring for the flock, entrusted to him by God, entailed "hunger and thirst...cold and nakedness." However, Paul persevered. And we must remind ourselves once again of his overall purpose in laying forth this awful catalogue of his sufferings: not to provoke anyone's pity; but rather to accomplish this ironic task of "boasting" in all sorts of weakness and shame, that he might win his hearers again to the way of Christ—confirming his own apostleship in the process.

28 Beside those things that are without, that which cometh upon me daily, the care of all the churches.

If Paul had stopped his list of pressures and sufferings at verse 27, he could have been crowned a great martyr, a sort of Hercules-like hero, able to endure great physical and emotional torment. But these next two verses add a new dimension to our picture of Paul. They reveal him to be not a one-dimensional superman but rather a flesh-and-blood pastor—enduring pain and weakness not for their own sake but for a greater good: the progress of his churches in the faith. Paul, here, presented his deep concern for the churches as the greatest of his burdens, for "beside those things that are without" it was the thing that "cometh upon me daily." The apostle served as the spiritual father of many churches, with his Gospel preaching being the foundation for many churches in Asia Minor and Greece. We understand from this verse that the call of apostle includes not only laying the foundation for churches (see Ephesians 2:20), but laboring tirelessly and with tears (see Acts 20:31 and also Philippians 3:18) for their growth in the Lord.

29 Who is weak, and I am not weak? who is offended, and I burn not?

Paul showed the Corinthians here what it means to have the "care of all the churches." As he made clear in 1 Corinthians 9:19–23, his ministry was truly incarnational. Like Christ, who shared flesh with his people, Paul sought to become "all things" so as to share in the experience of his beloved flock, in order to "win them" for Christ. The "weak" in this verse could be those who have no physical strength or social stature—the "meek and lowly" of the world—or perhaps the weak in faith, as described in 1 Corinthians 8 and Romans 14. Probably both dimensions are present, but Paul may have had the second kind of weakness especially in mind, since he went on to talk about those who are "offended," which is how the weak brother is described in 1 Corinthians 8:13 and Romans 14:21. Biblical "offense" is not the kind we speak of today, in which individuals or groups might take umbrage at someone else's words and actions. Rather, the Greek word *skandalizo* (**skan-dal-ID-zo**), which the KJV translates as "offend," refers to the act of doing something that makes a brother or sister in Christ succumb to his or her weakness and fall in to sin. This is why Paul said he "burns" when someone is offended—not because they are upset emotionally, but because they are led to fall into sin. In this sense the brother or sister is "destroyed" (see Romans 14:15), and the apostle, in turn, is burned with anger and grief. In this, he stood like his master, the Lord Jesus, who said, "And whosoever shall offend one of these little ones that believe in me, it is better for him that a millstone were hanged about his neck, and he were cast into the sea" (Mark 9:42).

30 If I must needs glory, I will glory of the things which concern mine infirmities.

Having shown the extent of his weakness and shame, Paul returned to the theme with which he began: upside-down boasting. As he made clear, he would show himself to be the opposite of worldly rulers who boast in their glorious achievements, and more importantly the opposite of the so-called "super-apostles," who oppose him and deceive the brethren. To the end, he will make his boast on the weakness with which he shows himself identified with the suffering Christ.

Interestingly, the word which the KJV translated "boast" in verse 17 (Gk. *kauchaomai*, **kow-KHAH-om-ahee**), is here rendered "to glory," another way of conveying the idea of "put one's confidence in." We will see in the next two verses why Paul would show this strange and unexpected confidence.

12:9 And he said unto me, My grace is sufficient for thee: for my strength is made perfect in weakness. Most gladly therefore will I rather glory in my infirmities, that the power of Christ may rest upon me.

The "he" in this passage is of course God, who

spoke to Paul after both greatly exalting and greatly humbling him. In verses 1–8, Paul gives us the account of his grandiose vision of heaven, where he "heard unspeakable words, which it is not lawful for a man to utter" (12:4). But after the glory of this vision, he was given a "thorn in the flesh"—some sort of persistent pain or temptation—to prevent him from being overcome by pride at his privileged status. Presumably, he told the story both to demonstrate his authority as an apostle—for he has been transported in a vision to heaven itself—but also to explain once again the nature and purpose of his weakness. And the purpose is this, as C. K. Barrett says: "A scene of human weakness is the best possible stage for the display of divine power."

The Greek verb *teleo* **(tel-EH-o)**, here translated "made perfect," refers to something brought to its intended goal or ultimate end. Often in the Scripture the word is translated "fulfilled," as in "the Scripture was fulfilled...." In other words, that which the Scripture looked forward to has now come to pass. Similarly, Jesus used the same word when uttering the famous words from the Cross: "It is finished" (John 19:30). Using the same word here, Paul brought forth the profound and surprising biblical truth that in human weakness, God's strength finds its greatest use, and God's glory is magnified to the greatest possible degree. For earlier in this same letter, Paul proclaimed that "we have this treasure in earthen vessels, that the excellency of the power may be of God, and not of us" (2 Corinthians 4:7).

10 Therefore I take pleasure in infirmities, in reproaches, in necessities, in persecutions, in distresses for Christ's sake: for when I am weak, then am I strong.

Paul beautifully summed up the themes brought forth in this passage, declaring that whatever "infirmities" (see 11:27), whatever "reproaches" (vv. 24–25), whatever "necessities" (v. 27), whatever "persecutions" (vv. 24–26), whatever "distresses" (vv. 27–29) he experienced, he was able to "take pleasure" in them. It cannot be said enough that Paul was not a masochist, who delights in pain for pain's sake. He delighted in such awful circumstances only because of their grand purpose in God's design and the glorious end that they bring about: strength for the sufferer, growth for the church, and glory to God. In these results, all believers, not just the church's apostles, can find something to boast about.

Source:

Barrett, C. K. *Second Epistle to the Corinthians.* New York, N.Y.: HarperCollins, 1974.

Daily Bible Readings

M: Persecution in the World
John 16:25–33
T: Suffering in Similar Ways
1 Thessalonians 2:13–16
W: Present Suffering, Future Glory
Romans 8:18–25
T: Through Many Persecutions
Acts 14:21–23
F: Sharing Christ's Sufferings
1 Peter 4:12–19
S: Come to Our Help!
Psalm 44:17–26
S: Made Perfect in Weakness
2 Corinthians 11:16–18, 21–30; 12:9–10

NOTES

December 2008 Quarter At-A-Glance

Human Commitment

The study this quarter focuses on humankind's response to Almighty God's call. Therefore, commitment of a specific person or persons is examined in each of the 12 lessons.

UNIT 1 • COMMITMENT TO THE MESSIAH

Drawing from passages in Luke, this unit looks at the commitment of Mary, the mother of Jesus; Elizabeth and her commitment as mother of John the Baptist; the shepherds who glorify God at the birth of Jesus; and the commitment of John the Baptist to prepare the way for the Messiah.

Lesson 1: December 7, 2008
Mary's Commitment
Luke 1:46–55

The young virgin, Mary, receives a visit from the angel Gabriel, who announces that she will be the vessel through whom the Messiah will come. The desire of every woman in Israel was to be that vessel. Mary receives the angel's message and pours out her heart in thanksgiving in her personal song that has been called the "Magnificat." She praises God for the honor and privilege of being the instrument that God will use. Subsequently, Mary recognizes the glory of God and makes her total commitment to Him.

Lesson 2: December 14, 2008
Elisabeth's Commitment
Luke 1:39–45

Elisabeth is visited by her younger cousin, Mary, who is pregnant with the Messiah. The older woman plays a supporting role, as the son she is carrying will, in confirming the divine nature of Mary's pregnancy and is happy to do so. Elisabeth remembers God's promise to her and to Zechariah, her husband; recognizes the fulfillment of God's promise to Mary; and commits herself to the Messiah.

Lesson 3: December 21, 2008
Shepherds Glorify God
Luke 2:8–20

The Messiah has been born as prophesied and the angelic announcement was made to the shepherds. After paying Him a visit, the shepherds glorified and praised God for the gift of the long-awaited Messiah and told others the Good News.

Lesson 4: December 28, 2008
John the Baptist Proclaims God's Message
Luke 3:7–18

John the Baptist walked in his calling and prepared the people for the Messiah's coming. He confronted them with their need for repentance. Thus, when John told the Good News, he challenged them to make a response.

UNIT 2 • OLD TESTAMENT PEOPLE OF COMMITMENT

This unit examines several Old Testament personalities and provides various examples of their commitments to God. We should learn much from their examples.

Lesson 5: January 4, 2009
Midwives Serve God
Exodus 1:8–21

God honors obedience in the face of possible persecution or death. Shiphrah and Puah were two midwives who feared God more than they feared the Pharaoh. They remained faithful to God and His people, while denying Pharaoh's edict to kill all of the male Hebrew babies. Because of their faithfulness, God blessed these midwives and gave them families of their own.

Lesson 6: January 11, 2009
Rahab Helps Israel
Joshua 2:1–4, 12–14; 6:22–25

Joshua sent spies to check out Jericho in preparation for war against the city.

A woman named Rahab lived inside the city wall. She made a deal with the spies to save her family when the time came. When the attack occurred, in exchange for her help to the spies, Joshua promised to save her and her household. In essence, Rahab willingly faced great personal danger in order to save her family.

Lesson 7: January 18, 2009
Joshua Leads Israel
Joshua 3:1–13

As they prepared to cross the Jordan into the Promised Land, Joshua instructed the people concerning the Ark of the Covenant, which represented the very presence of Almighty God. He committed himself to becoming a leader of the Israelites and received power from God to meet the challenge.

Lesson 8: January 25, 2009
Samson's Mother Prepares for His Birth
Judges 13:1–7, 8–13, 24

The Israelites had turned their backs on the Lord and, once again, God used their enemies to discipline them. When they cried out to God, He sent a judge to help fight their battles and deliver them. This time the judge would come through a childless couple, who would have to sacrifice to live the Nazirite lifestyle and raise their son in the same standard. Therefore, an all-knowing, all-powerful God sent an angel to prepare Samson's mother for Samson's coming birth.

Lesson 9: February 1, 2009
A Shunammite Woman Helps
2 Kings 4:8–17

The Shunammite woman was very generous in her commitment to the man of God, Elisha. She simply wanted to be hospitable to him and expected nothing in return. At first, it appears she really didn't need anything. However, God knew the secret desires of her heart; the woman had no child. Elisha rewarded her commitment by prophesying that she would have her desire, and just as the prophet said, the Shunammite woman later gave birth to a son. In essence, she was glad to serve Elisha without remuneration or payment; but God rewarded her with His great favor.

Lesson 10: February 8, 2009
Nathan Challenges David
2 Samuel 12:1–7, 13–15

The prophet Nathan helped David see his own sin by telling him a story he could relate to. David then realized that the story was really about him. He was repentant for taking Uriah's wife, Bathsheba, and having Uriah killed. Subsequently, he accepted his punishment. Thus, Nathan's commitment to God led him to confront King David and helped David to recommit and reconcile to a holy God.

Lesson 11: February 15, 2009
Esther Risks Her Life
Esther 4:1–3, 9–17

Esther had been married for five years to Xerxes, the king, when she discovered an edict had gone out against her people, the Jews. She decided to act, but before she approached the king, she called for all in the city of Susa to fast three days. Then, going in to see the king unannounced, she risked her life to save her people. In this light, Queen Esther willingly sacrificed her life for the people of God and was rewarded for her efforts.

Lesson 12: February 22, 2009
Isaiah Answers God's Call
Isaiah 6:1–8

In this passage, Isaiah recalled the death of King Uzziah, as a result of Uzziah's violating the law of God. In the presence of the Lord, Isaiah became fully and painfully aware of how far he, too, fell from the glory of God. Before accepting God's call upon his life, Isaiah needed a reminder of God's omnipotence. "Woe is me," he cried. "I am a man of unclean lips." What did he mean? Simply that there was nothing his mouth could utter that would be appropriate worship for the great, almighty God! Subsequently, Isaiah answered God's call to commitment by giving up everything and obeying God.

"I Do, Lord! I Will!" (God Calls His Bride!)

by Evangeline Carey

Wow! It was a splendid day for a wedding! Nature smiled on us with exceptional weather, and the church, which was arrayed in rich burgundy and white flowers adorning each pew, communicated elegance. A huge arch covered with matching flowers had been strategically situated at the front of the church. All attendees were seated, anxiously waiting for the commencing of the blessed event—this time of celebration of love and commitment. After the appropriate songs and prayer, the wedding party entered. Subsequently the musician played, "Here Comes the Bride," the minister asked the congregants to stand, and the bride joined her groom before the clergy.

She wore a white, flowing gown that complemented her beauty in every way. Following tradition, her face was hidden beneath her white veil. As the minister read the list of promises (the covenant agreement), both answered "I do! I will!" The bride and groom voiced their marriage commitment loudly and clearly before God and humanity. They pledged to be loyal to each other both in sickness and in health. They pledged never to violate their marriage vows.

The church—the new community—means "a called-out group." The term may refer to a local church (1 Thessalonians 1:1) or the universal church, all (across the world) who have believed on the Lord Jesus Christ as their Lord and Saviour (John 3:16). Also, the Old Testament believers, including Abraham, Samuel, Moses, Elijah, etc., are also a part of God's universal church. Genesis 15:12 says, "And he (Abraham) believed in the LORD;

and he counted it to him for righteousness." Therefore, they are still a part of the triumphant church. Revelation 14:13 says: "And I heard a voice from heaven saying unto me, Write, Blessed are the dead which die in the Lord from henceforth. Yea, saith the Spirit, that they may rest from their labours; and their works do follow them."

The universal church is also called Christ's Body (Ephesians 1:22–23) (Enns 1989). God's Word metaphorically describes the church as "the bride" of Christ. Revelation 21:2 declares, "And I John saw the holy city, new Jerusalem, coming down from God out of heaven, prepared as a bride adorned for her husband." The New Jerusalem is where a holy God lives among His people, who have been made holy by the shed blood of the Lamb, Jesus Christ. The apostle John saw in the vision that God gave him while he was exiled on the Island of Patmos off the coast of Asia *the bride (the church—the new community) and her husband, the Lamb (Jesus Christ).*

When believers accept Jesus Christ as Lord and Saviour, they are saved (John 3:16). They become a part of the church community. Symbolically, they are included with the "bride" and are invited (called) to the "wedding of the Lamb" (Revelation 19:6–9). Here Christ refers to the coming of His kingdom as a wedding. Jesus Christ (the husband) did much to secure His bride's salvation—to bridge her broken, shattered relationship with God. In fact, He gave His all; He gave His life to pay her sin-penalty in full. When believers accept Him as Lord and Saviour, He expects total commitment from His bride to Him and His cause—building His kingdom. Believers, then, must declare their faithfulness and commitment to a holy (set apart from sin) God by choosing daily to let Him be their God—their only God. They must also answer His call upon their lives to be witnesses for Him.

As a husband and wife should expect faithfulness in their marriage, Jesus Christ expects no less from believers. Therefore, God's church—His bride—is called to be faithful! In fact, Exodus 20:1–3, the beginning of the Ten Commandments, gives us this edict: "And God spake all these words, saying, I am the LORD thy God, which have brought thee out of the land of Egypt, out of the house of bondage. Thou shalt have no other gods before me." It is the Lord our God who has brought us out of our Egypt of sin and bondage. He brought us out of sin by covering our sins with His own precious blood.

The Israelites

After choosing Israel to be His chosen people, God entered into a covenant relationship or commitment with them—a marriage (Genesis 12:1–25:18). He would be their God, and they were called to be His people. They were called to worship only Him as their God and not serve other, lesser gods. God was faithful to this marriage or covenant; however, the Israelites broke their vows again and again. They committed spiritual adultery. They were a hardheaded, stiff-necked, rebellious people.

The book of Hosea depicts Israel's willful whoring after other gods and her unfaithfulness to the one true God. Hosea represents God and Gomer, his wandering, wayward, whorish wife, represents Israel. God told the prophet Hosea to marry Gomer (Hosea 1:2). In other words, a holy God commanded His prophet, Hosea, to marry a woman who would be unfaithful to him to illustrate the Israelites' unfaithfulness in their commitment to God. As Gomer broke her marriage vows to Hosea time and time again, Israel did the same to a faithful, loving, and merciful God.

Being obedient to God's instructions—being obedient to God's call—Hosea constantly went after his unfaithful wife. God also constantly went after unfaithful Israel, who compounded their sin by worshiping both Baal and God. He called judges, prophets, and priests to warn His chosen people of their breach of the marriage contract. Of course with God it is either/or. He will share His glory and His position in our lives with no one or nothing else.

The Rolls of the Faithful (Those Who Answered God's Call)

The Bible tells us that Mary, Joseph, Elisabeth, and Zechariah answered God's call upon their lives. They committed themselves to the Messiah, Jesus Christ. They kept their marriage covenant to a holy God. In fact, they took God at His Word, believed His promises, and saw them come to fruition when John the Baptist (the one who came to prepare the way for Jesus' coming) and Jesus Himself were born. The long-awaited Messiah indeed came to fulfill God's promise of a Saviour to save humanity from their sins (Romans 5:15, 17; 1 Corinthians 15:21). He was one-hundred percent God and one-hundred percent man—the God/man, who was without sin. Yet, He took on the sins of humanity and paid our death penalty in full.

Because of Jesus Christ, we can join the rolls of sold-out believers to God, those who obeyed God's call upon their lives. These rolls include the midwives, Shiphrah and Puah, who were so devoted to God that when Pharaoh decreed that all the Hebrew boy babies should be killed at birth, they saved baby Moses (Exodus 1:15–21). Moses grew up and later led God's people, the Israelites, out of Egypt—after more than 400 years of slavery.

Add to these rolls the prostitute, Rahab, who was committed to helping God's people spy out Jericho before they went to war and took the land. Because of her dedication—because she faithfully answered God's call—she saved herself and her household and became a part of the Messiah's lineage (Joshua 2:1–4, 12–14; 6:22–25).

We can also join the rolls with Joshua, who obeyed God's call upon His life, and after the death of Moses led God's chosen people to the Promised Land, Canaan (Joshua 3:1–13). Then there was Samson's mother, who prepared for Samson's birth. Of course, Samson was one of the great judges that God used to deliver His people out of bondage—the hands of the Philistines, after the Israelites had sinned against the living God yet again (Judges 13:1–13, 24).

We can join the rolls of the faithful with the barren Shunammite woman, who faithfully helped the man of God, Elisha, by preparing a room for him whenever he was in town. Even though she expected nothing in return for her services, Elisha prophesied that she would have the child she so desperately wanted (2 Kings 4:8–17).

We can join with the prophet Nathan, who answered God's call upon his life and did not recoil from confronting King David about King David's adulterous affair with Bathsheba. Nathan helped David to see his sin in taking Uriah's wife, impregnating her, and having her husband killed (2 Samuel 12:1–7, 13–15).

We can also join with Queen Esther, who faced an edict designed to destroy her people. The letter decreed that all Jews, young and old, including women and children, must be killed, slaughtered, annihilated on a single day (Esther 3:13). Even though she could have been killed, she committed to go before King Xerxes with her plea for them. Because of her commitment—because she faithfully answered God's call—her people were saved from extermination (Esther 8:5–7).

Finally, we can join the rolls of the faithful with the prophet Isaiah, who had an active ministry for 60 long years. He answered God's call to be a spokesman for Him, warning, condemning, and encouraging God's disobedient children to recommit to God (Isaiah 6:1–8). Even though the Israelites would not hear His message, Isaiah still obeyed God's call upon his life. Even though he suffered much in carrying out his ministry, he was still faithful to God.

Our Call to Commitment

Today, God wants our complete loyalty. He wants us, too, to answer His call to faithfulness and sincerity, to be His bride, to be a part of His church. He wants us to acknowledge Him for who He is—the living God—Creator of all that is. He wants us to love Him with all our heart, soul, and strength (Deuteronomy 6:5). He wants us to avoid hypocrisy, apathy, and careless living—to avoid having lesser gods in our lives. Sometimes we make bank accounts, cars, education, family, power, pleasure, and other things our gods.

Be reminded that upon accepting Jesus Christ as our personal Saviour, we enter into a covenant commitment (a marriage) with God. In essence, we are standing before Him and promising to be faithful and loyal. We are saying, "I do! I will! I pledge to keep my vows to love, honor, respect, and fear You because of who You are—Almighty God. You will be my only God!"

God wants us to honor our covenant commitment to Him and His call upon our lives. He wants us to set or reset our spiritual compasses to obey and follow Him. He is true to His vows to you. Are you true to your vows to Him?

Sources:

Enns, Paul. *The Moody Handbook of Theology.* Chicago, Ill.: Moody Press, 1989.

Life Application Study Bible (New Living Translation). Wheaton, Ill.: Tyndale House Publishers, 1996.

***Evangeline Carey** is a staff writer and the developmental editor of* Precepts For Living® *for UMI. Evangeline has also been an adult Sunday School teacher for more than 25 years.*

Suffering and the South

by Carl F. Ellis Jr.

"For there our captors asked us for songs, our tormentors demanded songs of joy; they said, 'Sing us one of the songs of Zion!' How can we sing the songs of the LORD while in a foreign land?" (Psalm 137:3–4, NIV).

Christianity vs. "Christianity-ism"

When the Gospel is applied in a particular cultural context, the result is Christianity. There are many expressions of Christianity because there are many different cultures. Because of our cultural differences, it is not wrong to have a Black Christianity or a White Christianity. Christianity is cross-cultural. However, these cultural expressions of Christianity should never contradict each other if they are true to God's Word. In fact, they will have a complementary relationship as they focus on God's redeeming grace through Jesus Christ. It is this shared foundation of biblical truth that anchors these cultural applications of the Gospel.

In contrast, there is what I call "Christianity-ism." This is a negative form of religion that avoids the truth of God and the true application of His Word. Instead, it seeks to impose its own agenda and carries it out through human effort. Christianity-ism tries to squeeze God into a man-made mold or reduce Him to a system that can be manipulated. It is an attempt to hold the Gospel hostage in an anti-God framework. Although it is preached in the language of Christianity, under Christianity-ism, biblical truth is diluted, polluted, and erased by the paganisms of culture.

The System of Slavery

The dehumanization experienced by the enslaved Africans brought to this country is difficult to imagine. They had been captured, branded, and herded into foreign ships. They survived the long journey of the Middle Passage under horrific conditions that included extreme overcrowding, rampant disease, frequent rape, and fatal beatings. Upon arrival in America, they were stripped of all dignity and power and divorced from their native language and culture. With physical characteristics that made their identification unmistakable, they were forced to work under a system that seemed impossible to escape.

In *Free At Last? The Gospel in the African-American Experience,* I expose the mind-set behind the cruel actions of the early White slave masters as follows:

The whole basis of this dehumanizing practice was an illegitimate view of humanity—a view in which skin color determined not only a person's status but indeed the presence or lack of the image of God. It became a time-honored belief among many adherents of White Christianity-ism that the uprooted African had no soul. Black people were therefore classified as nonhuman—in later history as three-fifths human. So raping a female slave was not a crime, nor was it considered fornication or adultery (43).

The use of Christianity-ism to justify slavery is not unique to America. During the days of apartheid, the Dutch Reformed Church of South Africa was also guilty of this. In fact, all who would identify God with only one race of people are guilty of distorting biblical truth (see Acts 10:28, 34; Romans 1:6; 10:13).

Suffering and Salvation

Since African culture always presupposed the existence of God, African American slave culture became fertile ground for the Gospel. From various sources, many slaves began to pick up bits and pieces of biblical truth. By God's grace, they were able to put these fragments of the Gospel together and derive some interesting ideas. These early Black preachers began to stir the hearts of their fellow slaves as they shared their insights. Thus, slaves began to get the notion that they were created in the image of God. This confirmed their sense of human worth and reaffirmed their awareness that being a slave was a contradiction to their dignity as human beings.

As the fires of revival began to spread among the slaves, freedom from slavery came to symbolize human dignity, the outworking of salvation in this life. The slave masters attempted to suppress the slave revival, but it proved to be futile. So they tried instead to preempt it as they attempted to force on the slaves their own "more appropriate" Christianity-ism.

Slave master Christianity-ism was rejected by most Christian slaves, but, under its cover, they began to develop an indigenous theological outlook and practice. As the slaves interacted with biblical themes in their life situation, they developed a theology of suffering.

In the South during the antebellum period prior to the American Civil War (1861–1865), the institution of slavery was king. While volumes have been written about the antebellum period, we cannot find a set of volumes written by southern antebellum African American theologians. For this, we simply have to listen to the oral tradition of that time. In the themes of the Negro spirituals, we hear lyrics like "I've been 'buked and I've been scorned and I've been talked about sure as you're born." Or "Sometimes I feel like a motherless child a long way from home." Or "Soon I will be done with the troubles of the world; goin' home to be with God."

These themes of suffering are prevalent throughout the music that emerged from the experience of slavery in the South. Although many had become Christians, African American slaves never would have come up with a triumphant perspective like "Onward Christian soldiers marching as to war with the cross of Jesus going on before." Why? Because the main theme in their lives was suffering. Thus, they developed a theology of suffering. And it is interesting to note that when we listen to more recent expressions of oral tradition, we still hear many of these same themes.

The southern theology of suffering addresses several core issues that are related to the concept of salvation. The church was seen as a place where slaves did not have to deal with the suffering that so dominated their lives. That is why salvation in the African American church in those days was seen more in collective terms. This view is very similar to the way the Israelites looked at salvation in the Old Testament (see Exodus 14:13).

The theology of suffering was presented in the paradigm of the Exodus. We've heard these themes of deliverance from slavery and oppression many times: "Deep river. I want to cross over Jordan. Deep river. I want to cross over to campground." Or the classic, "Go down Moses, way down in Egypt land. Tell ol' Pharaoh to let my people go." Now we know that they weren't singing about some Egyptian across the water. Everybody knew who "Pharaoh" was. So it was that slaves couched the theology of suffering in the Exodus paradigm.

While the southern theology of suffering also encompasses personal and social issues, for our purposes I want to focus on three cultural core issues: survival, refuge, and resistance to oppression.

Survival and Refuge

The first cultural core issue addressed by the theology of suffering was survival. Obviously, the slaves found themselves in a perilous situation. As a result, survival was a critical issue for them. Refuge was the second important issue. The church was seen as the place where they could escape, to some extent, the domination of the White slave masters.

While it is not always stated, the slave masters did not want their slaves to be exposed to Christianity because of its dangerous ideas. The Bible teaches us that we were created in the image of God (Genesis 1:27), that God has called us to freedom (Isaiah 61:1; Galatians 5:1, 13), and other truths like these. So the slave masters initially resisted the conversion of slaves to Christianity until they managed to develop what I call White Christianity-ism. Then certain teachings, like slaves are to be obedient to their masters, were emphasized and the other basic truths of the Bible were excluded. Of course, these slave masters paid no attention to the fact that the form of slavery that Paul was talking about in Ephesians 6:5 had no resemblance to American slavery.

With this system in place, the masters thought that slaves were pacified by being allowed to have church. But the slaves outsmarted their masters by developing a way of worshiping and communicating through double entendre. In other words, they made it appear that they were going along with the false Christianity-ism, but, in fact, they weren't.

Today I am often asked, "Why do African American church services last so much longer than White services?" My response to them, "Well, I think the answer is obvious. It is a tradition that began during slavery. What would you do as a slave if you knew that as soon as church was over you'd have to go out and pick cotton? Would you have a 45 minute service, or would it last for five hours?"

Even in later forms of oral tradition, some of the prayers uttered by the saints include lines like, "Lord, make a place for me in your kingdom where every day will be Sunday." This indicates that the church is still considered a place of refuge.

Songs of Resistance

The third cultural core issue addressed by the theology of suffering was resistance to oppression. The institution of slavery was so overwhelming that it was virtually impossible to resist it completely. However, many of the slaves began to resist it physically by having church all day Sunday and verbally through the oral tradition. For example, if their masters were present and claimed to be Christians, slaves would sing songs with lyrics like, "Heaven, heaven. Everybody talking about heaven ain't going to heaven." These subtle comments empowered their resistance.

Negro spirituals were the first expression of African American theology. This form of oral tradition and its double meaning was an important form of communication. These old spiritual songs contained both a theological meaning and a message of freedom; they still reveal much to us today.

The Theology of Suffering in the Struggle for Civil Rights

The southern theology of suffering can also be seen in the African American struggle for civil rights. By 1900, most African Americans who lived in the rural South were sharecroppers. Under the thumb of White supremacy, the African American church continued to function on the theology of suffering. This theology was intuitive and ethical. It was a means of survival and a method of coping with the harsh realities of economic deprivation, racism, and social injustice.

Much later in the twentieth century, the theology of suffering continued to carry the southern church. In 1955, Dr. Martin Luther King Jr. transformed this theology from a method of coping with injustice into a powerful spiritual weapon against injustice and segregation. This happened at the beginning of the Montgomery bus boycott.

On December 1, 1955, Rosa Parks boarded a Montgomery, Alabama, city bus after work. She entered the front door, paid her fare, exited the front door, reentered through the back door, and took a seat in the first row in the "Colored" section. This demeaning procedure was dictated by the Jim Crow Law and customs of the day. After a few stops, the seats in the White section in the front of the bus became full, and the bus driver moved the sign that designated the beginning of the Colored section back a few rows. Since Mrs. Parks was now in the White section, the bus driver ordered her to move further back (where there was standing room only) and let a White man have her seat. She refused, the driver called the police, and she was arrested.

In response to her arrest, community leaders organized a one-day bus boycott scheduled for December 5. On that cold and cloudy morning, onlookers watched as the buses drove by with no Black passengers on board. The boycott was a success.

That afternoon, the leaders met and formed the Montgomery Improvement Association, and they chose Dr. Martin Luther King Jr. as their spokesperson. Dr. King then was scheduled to speak at a rally that evening at Holt Street Baptist Church. This rally was held to determine whether to continue the boycott. After only a few hours of preparation and without referring to his notes, Dr. King spoke about human dignity, Christian love, and nonviolence. His powerful message set the tone for the Montgomery Bus Boycott, which lasted 381 days.

In this pivotal speech, Dr. King demonstrated that the theology African American people held all along could be a very powerful weapon to bring justice into their situation. Thus, the southern theology of suffering was used to begin to level the playing field and bring about racial desegregation on public buses and in society.

The Good News of the Gospel is that God has provided salvation for His people. This salvation includes freedom and deliverance from oppression. And this biblical truth continues to be good news for all who seek Him today.

Source:

Ellis Jr., Carl F. *Free At Last? The Gospel in the African-American Experience.* Downers Grove, Ill.: InterVarsity Press, 1996.

Carl F. Ellis Jr., Ph.D., *is the author of the book* Going Global (Beyond the Boundaries). *"Suffering and the South" is an excerpt from his book.*

December 2008

Heritage Profile

Oseola McCarty

(1908–1999)

Philanthropist

Oseola McCarty was born March 7, 1908, in Wayne County, Mississippi. As a young girl at Eureka Elementary School, she ironed for her neighbors to make money to take care of her grandmother. What she didn't use, she saved.

When Oseola was in middle school, her aunt was admitted to the hospital. Since her aunt had no children of her own, Oseola decided to take on the responsibility of being her caretaker. In the sixth grade, she stopped going to school in order to look after her paralyzed aunt. She continued to wash and iron clothes for her neighbors. She also continued to save money.

After her grandmother, mother, and aunt died, she added the little money they left her to her savings account. As she grew older, she realized that she was accumulating a sizable amount of money.

Oseola didn't travel much, so she never needed a car. In fact, she walked wherever she went. She lived a very frugal life and saved most of her money. Toward the end of her life, she began to ponder what she would do with her savings. She wanted to help somebody.

Actually, she voiced that she wanted to "help somebody's child go to college." She desired to help someone who not only appreciated it but would also learn. In fact, this is what this generous woman did.

As she thought about how she never received a formal education, she decided to leave her life savings to a college so young people who needed help getting to college could go and be educated.

From working for over 75 years as a domestic—washing, ironing, and folding clothes for other people—Oseola McCarty had saved over $250,000! In 1995, she decided to leave 60% of her life's savings ($150,000) to the University of Southern Mississippi. She was 87 years old.

According to Southern Mississippi's president, Aubrey Lucas, "Miss McCarty's gift has shown great unselfishness and sensitivity in making possible for others the education she never had."

Her philanthropic act received much media attention. She was honored by former President Bill Clinton with the Presidential Citizens Medal, Harvard University with an honorary doctoral degree, the National Urban League with the Community Heroes Award, and *Essence Magazine* with the 1996 Essence Award. She was even chosen to carry the Olympic torch in the 1996 Olympic Games.

Oseola McCarty read her Bible daily and lived a life of service to others. She died at the age of 91. She will always be remembered for her selfless generosity. "It wasn't hard," Sharon Wertz quotes her as saying. "The Lord helped me, and He'll help you, too.... It's an honor to be blessed like that."

Sources:
http://www.usm.edu/pr/oola1.htm
http://www.usm.edu/pr/oolayear.htm

TEACHING TIPS

December 7
Bible Study Guide 1

1. Words You Should Know

A. Magnify (Luke 1:47) *megaluno* (Gk.)—To magnify, extol, or praise. Mary's song of praise on learning she would give birth to the Davidic Messiah is called the Magnificat (Luke 1:46–55). The Latin names come from the phrase that begins the hymn, "Magnificat anima mea Dominum." In English it reads, "My soul doth magnify the Lord." These words have been used in worship by the church for centuries.

B. Mercy (vv. 50, 54) *eleos* (Gk.)—Compassion extended to relieve misery.

2. Teacher Preparation

Unifying Principle—Making Total Commitment. Many people encounter someone or something so charismatic and powerful that it demands their complete commitment. Who or what is able to command such a commitment? Mary recognized the glory of God and made her total commitment to Him.

A. Begin your preparation with prayer, asking God to prepare you for this teaching experience. Ask God to help you teach well.

B. Read and study the Daily Bible Readings and Focal Verses for today's lesson. Be sure to study the *Precepts For Living® Personal Study Guide* for further insights.

3. Starting the Lesson

A. Open the class with prayer.

B. Review the AIM for Change with the class.

C. Read the Words You Should Know definitions aloud. Discuss.

D. Summarize the information provided in The People, Places, and Times and Background sections.

4. Getting into the Lesson

A. Ask for one or more volunteers to read the Focal Verses.

B. Summarize the In Depth Section. Ask for individual responses to the questions found in Search the Scriptures.

5. Relating the Lesson to Life

A. Select a volunteer to read In Focus and/or Lesson in Our Society. Ask the participants to comment on how the context relates to today's lesson.

B. To answer questions in the Discuss the Meaning section, divide the class into groups. Assign one or two questions to each group, depending on class size. Have them report their responses to the rest of the class.

6. Arousing Action

A. Read the Lesson in Our Society section and ask for volunteers to share.

B. Challenge your students to commit to the Make It Happen exercise.

C. Remind the class to read the Daily Bible Readings in preparation for next week's lesson. Also suggest that they complete lesson 1 in the *Precepts For Living® Personal Study Guide.*

Worship Guide

For the Superintendent or Teacher
Theme: Mary's Commitment
Theme Song: "I Surrender All"
Devotional Reading: 1 Samuel 2:1–10
Prayer

MARY'S COMMITMENT

Bible Background • LUKE 1:26–38, 46–55
Printed Text • LUKE 1:46–55 Devotional Reading • 1 SAMUEL 2:1–10

AIM for Change

By the end of the lesson, we will:
REVIEW Mary's hymn of commitment to God;
CONSIDER the characteristics in others that may lead them to commitment; and
REMEMBER commitments to others and to God and strategize ways to be faithful in these commitments.

Keep in Mind

"And Mary said, My soul doth magnify the Lord, And my spirit hath rejoiced in God my Saviour" (Luke 1:46–47).

Focal Verses

KJV **Luke 1:46** And Mary said, My soul doth magnify the Lord,

47 And my spirit hath rejoiced in God my Saviour.

48 For he hath regarded the low estate of his handmaiden: for, behold, from henceforth all generations shall call me blessed.

49 For he that is mighty hath done to me great things; and holy is his name.

50 And his mercy is on them that fear him from generation to generation.

51 He hath shewed strength with his arm; he hath scattered the proud in the imagination of their hearts.

52 He hath put down the mighty from their seats, and exalted them of low degree.

53 He hath filled the hungry with good things; and the rich he hath sent empty away.

54 He hath helped his servant Israel, in remembrance of his mercy;

55 As he spake to our fathers, to Abraham, and to his seed for ever.

NLT **Luke 1:46** Mary responded, "Oh, how my soul praises the Lord.

47 How my spirit rejoices in God my Savior!

48 For he took notice of his lowly servant girl, and from now on all generations will call me blessed.

49 For the Mighty One is holy, and he has done great things for me.

50 He shows mercy from generation to generation to all who fear him.

51 His mighty arm has done tremendous things! He has scattered the proud and haughty ones.

52 He has brought down princes from their thrones and exalted the humble.

53 He has filled the hungry with good things and sent the rich away with empty hands.

54 He has helped his servant Israel and remembered to be merciful.

55 For he made this promise to our ancestors, to Abraham and his children forever."

In Focus

Tyrone was an account executive for one of the biggest accounting firms in the country. He praised God for his great success and his climb up the corporate ladder. What separated him from other account executives was his integrity. His reputation added value to his company. Now the company wished to use Tyrone's name to cheat their vendors out of excess revenues. They offered Tyrone a substantial salary increase, more perks, and a spot in the Who's Who in his business sector. He wrestled with the decision. Although there were no legal ramifications to be considered, he knew that what the company had in mind was unethical.

Refusing to go along with the company's plan would likely damage his career and cost him financially. As a young newlywed with a child on the way, what should he do? Could Tyrone stay committed to his Christian convictions with his social status and such great material rewards at stake?

After fasting and praying with his wife for three days, Tyrone returned to his company with his response. Although he was committed to excelling in his career and providing for his family, he understood that devotion to God could not be compartmentalized from the rest of his life. Nor could it be compromised by the dreams and plans we have for our future. Therefore, he respectfully declined their offer. Instead, he presented an alternative plan to the senior partners, one designed to increase the company's revenue. The proposal was adopted and eventually successfully implemented.

Many people encounter someone or something so charismatic and powerful that it demands their complete commitment. Who or what is able to command such a commitment of you? Tyrone was committed to his company and totally committed to his God. Mary, mother of Jesus, also recognized the glory of God and made her total commitment to Him as well.

The People, Places, and Times

Abraham. The father of the Jewish nation and an ancestor of Christ. His name was changed from Abram ("the father is exalted") to Abraham ("father of multitudes") (Genesis 11–26; Matthew 1:1–2).

Mary. Greek form of Miriam, meaning "strong." Mary is the mother of Jesus, James, Joseph, Judas, Simon, and some daughters. She gave birth to Jesus in Bethlehem and is the wife of Joseph.

Judea. Means "the praise of the Lord" and was first mentioned as a Persian province in Ezra 5:8. It became a Roman province (Matthew 2:1). It is bounded by Joppa on the north, Gaza (through Beersheba) on the southwest, and the Dead Sea on the east and south.

Caesar Augustus (also called Augustus Caesar). Caesar is the name of a branch of the aristocratic family of the Julii, which gained control of the Roman government. It became a formal title of the Roman emperors. In the time period presented in the gospel of Luke, Palestine was under foreign occupation by Romans. Caesar Augustus, the first Roman Emperor, was in charge. He ordered the census that required Mary and Joseph to leave Nazareth and travel approximately 70 miles to Bethlehem, where Jesus was born (Luke 2:1).

Sources:

Life Application Study Bible (New International Version). Wheaton, Ill.: Tyndale House Publishers, 1991.

Packer, J. I., Merrill C. Tenney, and William White. *Nelson's Illustrated Encyclopedia of Bible Facts.* Nashville: Thomas Nelson Publishers, 1995.

Background

Luke, called the beloved physician by his friend the apostle Paul, is traditionally believed to be the author of this book. Where he wrote it is widely debated—Greece, Caesarea, Alexandria, and Rome have been proposed. Luke was a Greek Christian, believed to be a native of Antioch, and the only known Gentile author of a New Testament book. The gospel of Luke is the longest book in the New Testament and a companion to the book of Acts.

It is widely accepted that Luke's audience was Gentile Christians in general and Theophilus, a civic leader of some type, in particular. Luke wrote the book around A.D. 60. He desired to present an accurate account of the life of Christ (Luke 1:3), perhaps to thwart the religious persecution of believers arising from the false accusations of Jewish leaders. Given his audience, it makes sense that Luke, who wrote with the detail of a historian, related the events he recorded to politics of the day.

Luke 1:5–4:15 belongs to the genre of accounts of the pre-public life of a hero often found in ancient biographies. Mary and her story is important to Luke's account to determine Jesus' family background, highlight His humanity, and prepare the audience for His ministry as the Saviour.

Though Luke drew heavily from the gospel of Mark and eyewitness accounts, his book has the distinction of describing some events that the other Gospels do not. For example, Luke's gospel gives the most detailed account of Jesus' birth, youth, and ministry. According to John Drury, he also structured his work after the classic prophetic message. Characteristic of the prophetic message is a pattern of reversal of fortunes, in which God's acts of judgment and mercy shape human history. Accordingly, Luke's gospel emphasizes that the Messiah's purpose is, in essence, redemptive and not political and involves all humanity including those traditionally marginalized by the established order—sinners, poor people, and women.

Sources:

Drury, John. *Tradition and Design in Luke's Gospel.* Atlanta, Ga.: John Knox Press, 1976.

Illustrated Dictionary of Bible Life & Times. Pleasantville, N.Y.: *Reader's Digest,* 1997.

Life Application Study Bible (New International Version). Wheaton, Ill.: Tyndale House Publishers, 1991.

Packer, J. I., Merrill C. Tenney, and William White. *Nelson's Illustrated Encyclopedia of Bible Facts.* Nashville: Thomas Nelson Publishers, 1995.

At-A-Glance

1. Mary Praises God's Work in Her Life (Luke 1:46–49)
2. Mary Praises God's Work in the World (vv. 50–53)
3. Mary Praises God's Work in Salvation History (vv. 54–55)

In Depth

1. Mary Praises God's Work in Her Life (Luke 1:46–49)

Mary's song of praise, the Magnificat, is understood to be largely based on Hannah's song in 1 Samuel 2:1–10. As in Hannah's doxology and typical of most psalms, Mary begins with individual concern and personal testimony. Mary's hymn praises God for His treatment of her. She rejoices in the grace that has come into her heart and her life and places emphasis on the greatness of God's magnificence and the particularity of God's care. While she does this in an individualistic way, Mary is also aware of her mission to all humanity as indicated by verse 48. She has a unique place as the mother of the Messiah, and she recognizes the great historical importance of her obedient response to God's vocation for her. Mary responds to her calling with thanksgiving and gratitude. Are we likewise thankful when we reflect on God's great work in our lives?

2. Mary Praises God's Work in the World (vv. 50–53)

In classic prophetic tradition, and similar to 1 Samuel 2:3–10 and Psalm 113, this section of Mary's hymn describes a pattern of reversal of fortunes in which God's acts of judgment and mercy shape human history. God's justice, or righteousness, is founded in His essential nature. But, just as with man, it is seen in His relation to the world, where what is right is established or maintained. This part of Mary's hymn indicates that God's justice can be retributive, meaning it is retaliation for or correction of a wrongdoing. Mary indicates that God is not indifferent toward evil and suffering (Habakkuk 1:13). In God's judgment, the achievements of disobedient human pride are destroyed. The dominant perspective and present social order are dismantled.

The Scriptures most often conceive God's justice, or righteousness, as the action of His mercy. God's justice means the relief of the oppressed and needy, so justice and mercy are constantly joined together. "God's mercy," from the Greek word *eleos,* refers to compassion extended to relieve misery.

God will raise up some and tear down others. This is already confirmed by God's actions in Elisabeth's and Mary's lives. Elisabeth goes from barren to pregnant and Mary from humiliation to one regarded as fortunate by generations to come.

3. Mary Praises God's Work in Salvation History (vv. 54–55)

The mercy Mary speaks of encourages Israel to live with anticipation of the newness that God has promised and will faithfully deliver. God's mercy, here, inspires hope in the promise of another person, time, and situation toward which the community of faith is moving. Mary connects God's work in her life with the promise God made to Abraham to bring forth kings from his lineage that will secure the Promised Land for his descendants (commonly understood in the first century A.D. as a political leader to deliver Israel from foreign occupation—see Genesis 17; Matthew 1:1–17; Luke 3:23–38). She had faith that she would birth this long-awaited "anointed one" from the lineage of David (Luke 1:28–33).

Sources:

Brueggemann, Walter. *The Prophetic Imagination.* Philadelphia, Pa.: Fortress Press, 1978.

Drury, John. *Tradition and Design in Luke's Gospel.* Atlanta, Ga.: John Knox Press, 1976.

Orr, James, ed. "Definition for 'JUSTICE.'" *International Standard Bible Encyclopedia.* Accessed 29 June 2007. http://www.bible-history.com/isbe/J/JUSTICE/

———. "Definition for 'MERCY; MERCIFUL.'" *International Standard Bible Encyclopedia.* Accessed 29 June 2007. http://www.bible-history.com/isbe/M/MERCY%3B+MERCIFUL/

Search the Scriptures

1. For what reasons does Mary's soul rejoice in the Lord (Luke 1:48–49)?

2. How does God exercise justice and mercy and toward whom (vv. 50–53)?

3. God's mercy toward Israel reveals what about God's character (vv. 54–55)?

Discuss the Meaning

1. Why do you think this song has been one of the most celebrated in Christian history?

2. Based on what you know of other characters in the Bible, what is unique about the way Mary responded to God's calling on her life?

Lesson in Our Society

Today, many Christians are concerned with acquiring massive wealth, attaining mega-ministries, and having great names among nations. The Bible consists of an abundance of stories that highlight the lives of ordinary people used in extraordinary ways by God. Paul, expressing sentiment as the Magnificat, says:

> ...think of what you were when you were called. Not many of you were wise by human standards; not many were influential; not many were of noble birth. But God chose the foolish things of the world to shame the wise; God chose the weak things of the world to shame the strong. He chose the lowly things of this world and the despised things—and the things that are not—to nullify the things that are, so that no one may boast before him (1 Corinthians 1:26–29, NIV).

Remember the beginnings of Moses, David, Mary, many of the disciples, and Jesus. This paradox allows us to transform how we calculate worth and importance and reevaluate who can be used by God. This lesson serves as a wake-up call for those of us who believe God is impressed with our greatness or that God only uses people like us. It also serves as encouragement for those of us who, like Moses, believe we are too inadequate to serve God purposefully in the world.

Make It Happen

This week ask the Lord to reveal to you how you can be used for God's purposes in the world, if you aren't already aware. Write a list of barriers that prohibit you and a separate list of supports required for you to act on your understanding. Finally, create a companion timeline and action steps to guide you in the process of totally committing yourself to the Lord and purposeful ministry.

Follow the Spirit

What God wants me to do:

____

____

Remember Your Thoughts

Special insights I have learned:

____

____

More Light on the Text

Luke 1:46–55

The song of Mary is often called the Magnificat, a name taken from the Latin Bible, the Vulgate. It is an expression of praise dominated by the patterns of Hebrew writing. It resembles Hannah's song, found in 1 Samuel 2:1–10. It shows Mary's joyful gratitude for her personal blessing (Luke 1:46–49), God's graciousness to all who worship Him (v. 50), His special love for the lowly (vv. 51–53) and for Israel (vv. 54–55). The entire song is a psalm of praise to God, in recognition of His redemptive purpose, as it had worked itself out in history and was still working itself out in Mary's experience.

46 And Mary said, My soul doth magnify the Lord,
47 And my spirit hath rejoiced in God my Saviour.

Here, there is no difference in this context between "soul" (Gk. *psuche,* **psoo-KHAY**) and "spirit" (Gk. *pneuma,* **PNYOO-mah**). It is used synonymously as a requirement of the Hebrew poetic parallelism. They serve to describe Mary in her intrinsic existence, her real person. She magnified God from the depths of her inner being. She glorified Him wholeheartedly. The parallelism is carried forward by the two verbs "magnify" (present tense) and "rejoice" (aorist tense). "Magnify" (Gk. *megaluno,* **meg-al-OO-no**) literally means "to make great." It denotes a habitual act. She kept magnifying the Lord. Her soul dwelled on the greatness of the Lord and on what He was doing to His people.

"Rejoice" (Gk. *agalliao,* **ag-al-lee-AH-o,** meaning "to be glad exceedingly," "to exult") expresses Mary's inner state of joyful well-being as she contemplated what was going to happen to her. It points to a special act of rejoicing, probably when the angel brought the news about what was going to happen to her. Rejoice is a strong word. The Greek word used here can also be rendered as "exulted."

The words "Lord" (Gk. *kurios,* **KOO-ree-os**) and "God my Saviour" (Gk. *theos,* **THEH-os** and *soter,* **so-TARE**) are parallel. Here there is no categorical distinction between the two names. The redeeming God of Israel and the Lord of Mary's life is the object of her joyful praise. God is known as Saviour in the Old Testament, the deliverer of Israel (see Habakkuk 3:18; Psalm 106:21). "God my Saviour" shows that Mary recognized her need of redemption, just like other people.

48 For he hath regarded the low estate of his handmaiden: for, behold, from henceforth all generations shall call me blessed.

Verses 48 and 49 point out the particular work that God had accomplished in Mary. She gives the reason for her rejoicing: God had "regarded" (Gk. *epiblepo*, **ep-ee-BLEP-o**, in the aorist; "to regard with favor") her "low estate," a woman of poor condition (see 1 Samuel 1:11 to read how Hannah expresses the same thought in a vow). She recognized her humble condition. She felt richly favored by God. From henceforth she would always be called blessed.

"Low estate" (*tapeinosis*, **tap-I-no-sis**, meaning "humble state") is an expression of humility. Here it is not in a moral sense. It designates her humble state, the humbleness of Mary as a simple young woman of Nazareth. From now on or in time to come, all generations will call Mary "one happy or blessed" (see Genesis 30:13 for Leah's similar expression).

49 For he that is mighty hath done to me great things; and holy is his name.

Mary turned to the contemplation of God Himself. She sang of the glorious deeds of redemption of God. His mighty acts of old were certainly in Mary's mind. She was also referring to a new mighty act of God, the messianic deliverance, whose meaning surpassed her comprehension. Mary was thankful for what God had done for her, by choosing her as the mother of His incarnate Son.

She pointed out three attributes of God: He is all-powerful, omnipotent, and "mighty" (v. 49); He is "holy" (v. 49); and He is merciful (v. 50). "Holy" (Gk. *hagios*, **HAG-ee-os**) is used here not in a moral sense, but in the sense of God's being. His holiness talks about who He is. The name in the Bible stands for the whole person. It reveals the person. His name is His very nature. God's name must be used reverently. His name will be recognized as holy, completely set apart, and awesome.

50 And his mercy is on them that fear him from generation to generation.

Verses 50 to 55 point out the work God had accomplished in Israel, the people of His redemptive purpose, and His work in the affairs of men. God is a merciful God. His "mercy" (Gk. *eleos*, **EL-eh-os**, meaning "pity"), in every generation, is certain for those who fear Him.

The word "fear" (Gk. *phobeo*, **fob-EH-o**) is used with the meaning of "awe, reverence." It is not just to be afraid. The fear of God is a description of piety. It means to honor God lovingly, by avoiding what is contrary to His will, and by striving after what pleases Him.

51 He hath shewed strength with his arm; he hath scattered the proud in the imagination of their hearts.

The structure of verses 51–53 is that of dramatic contrast through parallelism: The proud, the mighty, and the rich are put in contrast to those of low degree—the humble, the lowly, and the hungry. The series of six aorist tenses (forms of verbs that express past action) (vv. 51–53), in the Greek, used in these verses, can be interpreted in three ways:

1. They mean that Mary may have been looking back to specific occasions in the past when God had done the things she enumerated. The past tenses, thus, speak of God's past deeds in the history of Israel from Abraham to Mary. The more prominent part of that history is the exodus and its subsequent events.

2. They may be referring to acts still to come in the future, but which have begun to be realized. The future acts of God are often viewed as already accomplished, in the Old Testament. The aorist tenses should be taken in their ingressive force, meaning that God had already begun the reversal of things described here and will continue it. Mary was, thus, looking forward, in a spirit of prophecy, to what God will do. She was so certain that it was spoken of as accomplished. The promise of God has the efficacy of the act itself (Genesis 17:5). His word is a word of power.

3. Mary may be referring to what God does habitually. The habitual action of God is known to His servants. Mary may have seen God's choice of her as just one example of what God always does, has done, and will do. What was happening to her is an activity of God as Redeemer. He scatters the proud, puts down rulers, and sends the rich away empty but exalts the lowly and feeds the hungry.

Mary used a prophetic language to describe her own experience. This has been the experience of many who experienced God's salvation (see 1 Corinthians 1:18–31).

The word "strength" (Gk. *kratos,* **KRAT-os,** meaning "power," "might") denotes an irresistible force to which all must bow. The term "scattered" (Gk. *diaskorpizo,* **dee-as-kor-PID-zo**) refers to a fight in which the enemy is driven apart and scattered. The acts of God are described in an anthropomorphic manner (see Exodus 15:6; Psalm 98:1; Isaiah 51:9).

Huperephanos (**hoop-er-AY-fan-os**), the Greek word for "proud," means literally "to show oneself preeminent." Here it is used with a pejorative sense, meaning arrogant. "Heart" (Gk. *kardia,* **kar-DEE-ah**), in the Bible, includes human thoughts, desires, and emotions. It denotes human life in its fullest extent. The Hebrews see it as the seat of the intellect and will.

52 He hath put down the mighty from their seats, and exalted them of low degree. 53 He hath filled the hungry with good things; and the rich he hath sent empty away.

The song of Mary describes a complete turnaround of the human way of thinking. Through the Messiah, God was about to bring changes. In His choices of Mary and Elisabeth, He had begun the turnaround of things. He is not bound by what people do. He turns attitudes and orders of society upside down. He will reverse the status of many in the coming age. In sovereign purpose, He puts down and exalts. He manifests thereby both His justice and His great mercy.

"The mighty" (Gk. *dunastes,* **doo-NAS-tace,** meaning "the ruler," "authority") refers to those ruling, not simply of powerful people. By pursuing their own purposes, they were world rulers who were opposed to the purposes of God. The oppressors, who tyrannized over the poor and lowly, were deprived of their power and high standing.

Those who are truly humble are exalted to great things. The Greek word *tapeinos* (**tap-i-NOS**) means "humble, either as possessing humility or as of humble origin or position." The hungry are those who realize their own need and long for spiritual food. The rich are those who are self-satisfied and proud (Cf. Luke 6:6:20–21, 24–25).

54 He hath helped his servant Israel, in remembrance of his mercy;

The Greek verb *antilambanomai* (**an-tee-lam-BAN-om-ahee**) has the meaning of "to assume the care of" or "to take in hand." Mary talked of God's care for His people. She was probably speaking of the help that would come through the Messiah. She put another, larger, context to what had happened to her. What was happening to her was happening to her as part of her nation. It was happening not because she was special but because of God's faithfulness to Abraham and his seed (see Genesis 12:2–3).

55 As he spake to our fathers, to Abraham, and to his seed for ever.

God's mercy was a continuation of His promise to Abraham and the forefathers (see Genesis 17:8; Acts 3:13, 25; Galatians 3:16, 29). God is true to His promises of salvation through a coming Redeemer, the Messiah. "His seed for ever" does not refer to all descendants according to the flesh, but His true seed, first Christ, and then all who belong to Him (John 8:39, 44, 56; Romans 9:7–8; Galatians 3:16).

Sources:

Life Application Study Bible (New International Version). Wheaton, Ill.: Tyndale House Publishers, 1991.

Packer, J. I., Merrill C. Tenney, and William White. *Nelson's Illustrated Encyclopedia of Bible Facts.* Nashville: Thomas Nelson Publishers, 1995.

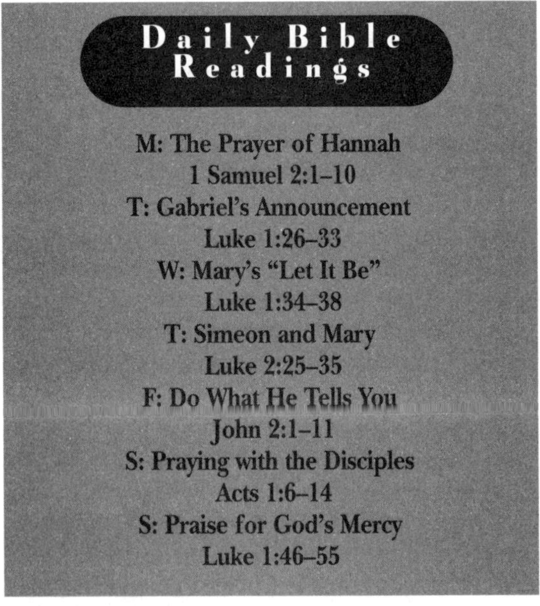
Daily Bible Readings

M: The Prayer of Hannah
1 Samuel 2:1–10
T: Gabriel's Announcement
Luke 1:26–33
W: Mary's "Let It Be"
Luke 1:34–38
T: Simeon and Mary
Luke 2:25–35
F: Do What He Tells You
John 2:1–11
S: Praying with the Disciples
Acts 1:6–14
S: Praise for God's Mercy
Luke 1:46–55

NOTES

TEACHING TIPS

December 14
Bible Study Guide 2

1. Words You Should Know

A. Haste (Luke 1:39) *spoude* (Gk.)—Earnestness, diligence.

B. Blessed (v. 42) *eulogeo* (Gk.), (v. 45) *makarios* (Gk.)—Blessed, happy.

2. Teacher Preparation

Unifying Principle—Coping with Multiple Commitments. Sometimes a commitment varies in its degree of complexity. How can a person make multiple commitments? Elisabeth remembered God's promise to her and to Zacharias, recognized the fulfillment of God's promise to Mary, and committed herself to the Messiah.

A. Begin your preparation with prayer. Ask God to teach through you.

B. Read and study the Daily Bible Readings and Focal Verses for today's lesson. Be sure to study the *Precepts For Living® Personal Study Guide* for further insights.

C. Look up the word "commitment" in a dictionary, on your computer, etc., and be ready to discuss its meaning.

3. Starting the Lesson

A. Open the class with prayer.

B. Review the AIM for Change with the class, and share your definitions of the word "commitment."

C. Read the Words You Should Know definitions aloud. Discuss.

D. Summarize the context information provided in The People, Places, and Times and Background sections.

4. Getting into the Lesson

A. Ask for one or more volunteers to read the Focal Verses.

B. Summarize the In Depth Section. Ask for individual responses to the questions found in Search the Scriptures.

5. Relating the Lesson to Life

A. Select a volunteer to read In Focus and/or Lesson in Our Society. Ask the students to comment on how the context relates to today's lesson.

B. To answer questions in the Discuss the Meaning section, divide the class into groups. Assign one or two questions to each group, depending on class size, and then allow them to share their responses with the rest of the class.

6. Arousing Action

A. Discuss the Lesson in Our Society section, allowing students to insert their testimonies.

B. Challenge the students to commit to the Make It Happen exercise.

C. Remind the class to read the Daily Bible Readings in preparation for next week's lesson. Also suggest that they complete lesson 3 in the *Precepts For Living® Personal Study Guide* as well.

Worship Guide

For the Superintendent or Teacher
Theme: Elisabeth's Commitment
Theme Song: "Precious Jesus"
Devotional Reading: Isaiah 7:10–14
Prayer

ELISABETH'S COMMITMENT

Bible Background • LUKE 1:5–24, 39–45
Printed Text • LUKE 1:39–45 Devotional Reading • ISAIAH 7:10–14

AIM for Change

By the end of the lesson, we will:
REVIEW Elisabeth's response to God's action in Mary's life;
EVALUATE the complexities of one's own commitments; and
RECOGNIZE God's actions in our lives and respond by making a commitment to God.

Keep in Mind

"Elisabeth was filled with the Holy Ghost: And she spake out with a loud voice, and said, Blessed art thou among women, and blessed is the fruit of thy womb" (from Luke 1:41–42).

Focal Verses

KJV **Luke 1:39** And Mary arose in those days, and went into the hill country with haste, into a city of Juda;

40 And entered into the house of Zacharias, and saluted Elisabeth.

41 And it came to pass, that, when Elisabeth heard the salutation of Mary, the babe leaped in her womb; and Elisabeth was filled with the Holy Ghost:

42 And she spake out with a loud voice, and said, Blessed art thou among women, and blessed is the fruit of thy womb.

43 And whence is this to me, that the mother of my Lord should come to me?

44 For, lo, as soon as the voice of thy salutation sounded in mine ears, the babe leaped in my womb for joy.

45 And blessed is she that believed: for there shall be a performance of those things which were told her from the Lord.

NLT **Luke 1:39** A few days later Mary hurried to the hill country of Judea, to the town

40 where Zechariah lived. She entered the house and greeted Elizabeth.

41 At the sound of Mary's greeting, Elizabeth's child leaped within her, and Elizabeth was filled with the Holy Spirit.

42 Elizabeth gave a glad cry and exclaimed to Mary, "God has blessed you above all women, and your child is blessed.

43 Why am I so honored, that the mother of my Lord should visit me?

44 When I heard your greeting, the baby in my womb jumped for joy.

45 You are blessed because you believed that the Lord would do what he said."

In Focus

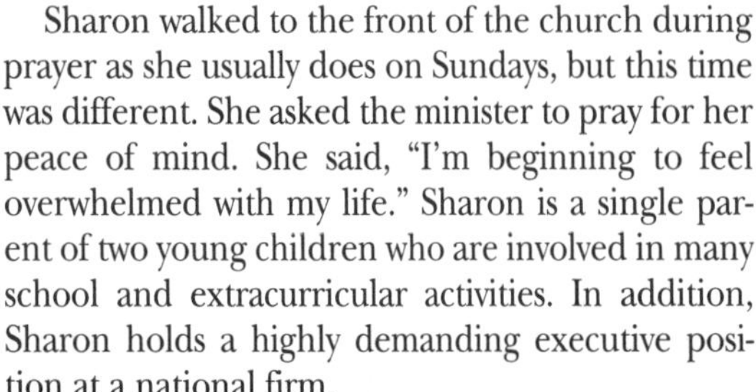

Sharon walked to the front of the church during prayer as she usually does on Sundays, but this time was different. She asked the minister to pray for her peace of mind. She said, "I'm beginning to feel overwhelmed with my life." Sharon is a single parent of two young children who are involved in many school and extracurricular activities. In addition, Sharon holds a highly demanding executive position at a national firm.

She never, ever seems to have enough time! She tries, to no avail, to successfully juggle all of her responsibilities. To complicate matters, though she already feels pulled in too many directions, Sharon regularly experiences guilt over not serving in any ministries at church. She exclaims, "How is it possible that I feel so tremendously blessed and stressed at the same time?" She continued, "When your life seems to be running you instead of you being in charge of it, what do you do?"

Sharon received prayer, decided to also address her concerns in pastoral counseling, and took advantage of a spiritual retreat her church was sponsoring. At the retreat, Sharon realized there were many Christians like herself. They, too, find themselves with plenty of time to receive God's blessings and too little time to pass them on to others. At the retreat, she created a schedule that would allow her to more effectively balance the time she devotes to pursuing her purpose, priorities, and play.

Sometimes we are so overcommitted by our secular lives that we find little time to do what God has called us to do for Him. As Elisabeth and Zacharias did in today's lesson, we must make time to commit to the Messiah. He must be first in our lives.

The People, Places, and Times

Judah or Juda. Means "the praise of the Lord." It was the territory of one of the original 12 tribes. Judah, along with Benjamin, formed the southern kingdom after Solomon's death. The uncertain border between Israel to the north and Judah ran between Bethel in Israel and Ramah in Judah. Jerusalem was its capital (2 Chronicles 13:18; 15:8).

Zacharias. Means "memory of the Lord." He was Elisabeth's husband and father of John the Baptist. Zacharias was a priest. Both he and his wife came from priestly families. An angel appeared to him about the birth of his son, but he responded with doubt.

Elisabeth. It means "oath of God." Elisabeth's kinship ties included being the wife of Zacharias, the cousin of Mary, and the mother of John the Baptist. Before the birth of Jesus, she spent months with Mary.

Source:

Packer, J. I., Merrill C. Tenney, and William White. *Nelson's Illustrated Encyclopedia of Bible Facts*. Nashville: Thomas Nelson Publishers, 1995.

Background

Mary and Elisabeth were related, perhaps cousins (Luke 1:36). Elisabeth's home city is not named, but it was in the hill country of Judah (v. 39). Theologians believe that Mary, as she considered her God-given favored state of giving birth to the long-awaited Messiah, probably uttered her thoughts over and over again until they took the beautiful poetic form in which we call "Mary's Song of Thanksgiving"—"the Magnificat."

The young teenage girl, Mary, felt the need to then share her blessing with another woman—an older relative. So Mary went to Elisabeth, who was of the tribe of Levi (1:5). Elisabeth, a woman of "unusual piety, faith, and spiritual gifts" (Zondervan Compact Bible Dictionary 1965) encouraged her. Mary was with Elisabeth until John the Baptist's birth (v. 36), for three months (v. 56). Afterward, she returned to Nazareth.

Sources:

Halley's Bible Handbook. Grand Rapids, Mich.: Zondervan, 1965.

Zondervan Compact Bible Dictionary. Grand Rapids, Mich.: Zondervan, 1965.

At-A-Glance

1. Elisabeth Receives a Blessing (Luke 1:39–41)
2. Elisabeth Blesses Mary (vv. 42–45)

In Depth

1. Elisabeth Receives a Blessing (Luke 1:39–41)

After hearing the news of God's faithfulness in keeping His promise to her people to send the Messiah, Mary did not keep the news to herself. Luke tells us that she arose. Here Luke uses the word to show that Mary did not get the news and just sit but took the news elsewhere—just as we are to take the Good News we receive about the Gospel of Christ. Mary left from Nazareth, a city in the northern region of Galilee, to travel down to the southern region of Judah. She went into the hill country where her cousin Elisabeth lived, in order to tell her the news.

Upon entering the home of Zacharias, Mary greeted Elisabeth. Luke says "saluted." This word connotes not just a casual greeting, but a welcome with gestures that included embracing and kissing. While the greeting was taking place, the Holy Spirit was already at work. Luke records that when Elisabeth heard the salutation, the babe in Elisabeth's womb leaped, and Elisabeth was filled with the Holy Spirit. Elisabeth received a blessing because of Mary's desire to share the Good News with her of what God had done in her and for her.

2. Elisabeth Blesses Mary (vv. 42–45)

Elisabeth knew that Mary was pregnant. The Holy Spirit bore witness to that fact by the babe's response, in her womb, during the greeting. The moment was filled with tremendous excitement and joy. She realized that not only had God blessed her in her old age but that Mary was also blessed.

Elisabeth's pregnancy was the result of God blessing the procreative activity of Zacharias and herself, but Mary's pregnancy was the result of God's direct creative intervention. The way the Messiah was conceived would model the means to salvation: human submission to divine will or initiative. Mary was blessed because she had been chosen for special service, and having received an amazing promise, she believed that there would be a fulfillment of what the Lord had told her. Elisabeth recognized this and spoke favorably of God's work in Mary's life.

Knowing Mary was carrying the Messiah, Elisabeth was amazed and honored at the visit from her cousin but wondered why she would be privileged to have Mary come to her (v. 43). Though she had responded positively to God's plan for her, Mary would still need a little encouragement. The visit to Elisabeth's home served as confirmation of the angel's message to her (Luke 1:36).

Sources:

Caird, G. B. *The Gospel of Luke.* Baltimore, Md.: Penguin Books, 1963.

Robertson, A. T. Edited by James A. Swanson. *Word Pictures in the New Testament.* Nashville: B & H Publishing, 2000.

Search the Scriptures

1. Name two important events that resulted from Mary greeting Elisabeth (Luke 1:41).
2. What was Elisabeth filled with (v. 41).
3. Elisabeth recognized that Mary is the Mother of whom (v. 43)?
4. Explain why Mary is blessed (v. 45).

Discuss the Meaning

1. How does Mary's response to her call for service differ from the responses of other biblical personalities?
2. Based on Elisabeth's response, in what ways is Mary a role model for believers today?

Lesson in Our Society

Elisabeth did not simply receive a blessing; she gave one as well. We should emulate her. Sometimes the testimony of what God is doing in our lives serves as a witness to encourage someone about God's faithfulness concerning His promises. Who have you blessed this past week, past month, or even this past year? Who have you blessed by sharing your testimony? As we focus on giving and responsibly handling multiple commitments this season, remember that not all gifts can be bought in a store.

Make It Happen

Check your commitment to blessing other believers. This week, identify someone to speak favorably of (or speak favor into their lives) and another person to share the testimony of God's work in your life.

Follow the Spirit

What God wants me to do:

____

____

Remember Your Thoughts

Special insights I have learned:

____

____

More Light on the Text

Luke 1:39–45

39 And Mary arose in those days, and went into the hill country with haste, into a city of Juda;

To obtain a confirmation of her faith, Mary lost no time paying a visit to her relative, Elisabeth. She reacted at once when she learned from the angel that God had also blessed Elisabeth (Luke 1:36). Mary was an ordinary human girl of flesh and blood who had been chosen for a gigantic and unique task; her faith needed strengthening. Her visit to Elisabeth was to someone who had also been miraculously blessed. She was able to find encouragement and understanding.

In Elisabeth's sixth month (v. 36), the angel Gabriel spoke to Mary. Her visit with Elisabeth lasted for approximately three months, just before the birth of John (vv. 56–57). Therefore, Mary must have left her home to go to visit Elisabeth almost immediately after the angel's visit. The phrase "Mary arose. . .went. . .with haste" ("arose," Gk. *anistemi,* **an-IS-tay-mee**, meaning "to rise, stand up"; "went," *poreuomai,* **por-YOO-om-ahee**, meaning "to journey, to depart"; and "haste," *spoude,* **spoo-DAY**, meaning "haste, to hasten") points to the fact that Mary almost immediately left to go to visit Elisabeth.

The expression "the hill country...into a city of Juda" does not locate the home of Elisabeth with any precision, but it shows that she was living in a rural area. Attempts to identify it have not been successful. Like many priests, Zacharias lived outside Jerusalem.

40 And entered into the house of Zacharias, and saluted Elisabeth. 41 And it came to pass, that, when

"Elisabeth was filled with the Holy Ghost: And she spake out with a loud voice, and said, Blessed art thou among women, and blessed is the fruit of thy womb" (Luke 1:41–42).

Elisabeth heard the salutation of Mary, the babe leaped in her womb; and Elisabeth was filled with the Holy Ghost:

When Mary arrived at Elisabeth's, not only did she find that Elisabeth was miraculously pregnant as the angel had said but that Elisabeth knew, by the inspiration of the Holy Spirit, that Mary was going to be the mother of the Messiah (vv. 41–44). At the moment that Mary "saluted" (Gk. *aspazomai,* **a-spa-zo-MAY**) Elisabeth, the baby moved in her mother's womb. It is a natural phenomenon for an unborn child frequently to make movements. The movement made by Elisabeth's unborn child was extraordinary. Elisabeth was filled with the Holy Spirit and interpreted the movement of her baby as an expression of joy ("leaped," *skirtao,* **skeer-TAH-o,** meaning "to leap" or "jump for joy"; see also v. 44).

42 And she spake out with a loud voice, and said, Blessed art thou among women, and blessed is the fruit of thy womb.

The Greek verb *anaphoneo* (**an-af-o-NEH-o**) means "to raise the voice" or "to call out." Elisabeth raised her voice with a cry. The loud cry shows her excitement. She greeted Mary as "blessed among women." The Greek word *eulogeo* (**yoo-log-EH-o**) literally means "to speak well of." The expression reflects a Hebrew construction meaning the most blessed of women: Of all women most blessed are you. Mary stands forth alone as the recipient of a unique blessing.

"Fruit of thy womb" primarily refers to the baby inside of Mary but also indicates the full humanity of Jesus, although begotten by the Holy Spirit. We confess that Jesus is fully divine and fully human, and this text reminds us that Christ truly came into the world in a way that completely identifies with us.

43 And whence is this to me, that the mother of my Lord should come to me?

The use of the title "my Lord" shows that Elisabeth recognized, through the Holy Spirit, that Mary's child would be the Messiah (see 2:25–30; Psalm 110:1). She acknowledged that a much greater honor had been granted to Mary than to her. In humility of heart, she expressed her amazement and her privilege of being visited by the mother of her Lord.

Elisabeth accepted, in grateful worship, God's gift to her. When she met Mary, to whom a still greater gift had been given, she did not become jealous. She humbled herself and gave honor to Mary. It is important to point out here that honoring Mary is not something problematic. Many Protestants might regard honoring Mary as indicative of worshiping Mary as if she was divine; but this is not the case. Elisabeth set before us an example of honoring Mary because of her unique status—without elevating her to an object of worship. Elisabeth's humility was also instructive. Jealousy would have darkened her life. Her humble attitude opened for her the gates to true joy. He who elevates himself is constantly engaged in ruining his own life. But he who humbles himself finds richness of life (see Proverbs 3:34; James 4:6).

44 For, lo, as soon as the voice of thy salutation sounded in mine ears, the babe leaped in my womb for joy.

The Greek word *idou* (**id-OO**) announces an unexpected and extraordinary event. Elisabeth explained to Mary that, at her greeting, her own baby exulted for joy in her womb. It was the exultation of her baby that was the sign from the Holy Spirit that enabled her to recognize Mary for who she was.

45 And blessed is she that believed: for there shall be a performance of those things which were told her from the Lord.

Elisabeth further blessed (Gk. *makarios,* **mak-AR-ee-os**, meaning "blessed," "happy") Mary. She told Mary that the Lord had blessed her because she believed that He would keep His promise. The Greek word for the word "for" is *hoti* (**HOT-ee**) and can be understood:

1. As "**that**." In that case it is an object of "believed" and is to be translated as: "Blessed is she that believed" that there will be an accomplishment of those things, which were told her from the Lord. This makes the phrase "there shall be a performance of those things which were told her from the Lord" an indication of the content of the faith of Mary.

2. Or as "**because**." In that case it is to be translated as: "You are blessed because you believed that there would be a performance of those things, which were told her from the Lord." Thus, the phrase "there shall be a performance of those things which were told her from the Lord" is an explanation of the happiness of Mary.

Elisabeth affirmed that the fulfillment would certainly happen. Mary believed and went on believing the message from the Lord. She bore the immense honor and the immeasurable burden without losing faith. She remained humble and committed to the Lord. True faith gives happiness, and there is no true happiness without faith.

Source:

Packer, J. I., Merrill C. Tenney, and William White. *Nelson's Illustrated Encyclopedia of Bible Facts.* Nashville: Thomas Nelson Publishers, 1995.

Daily Bible Readings

M: Do Not Pass by Your Servant
Genesis 18:1–8
T: Hope for the Barren
Genesis 18:9–14
W: Righteous and Blameless
Luke 1:5–11
T: The Promise of a Son
Luke 1:12–20
F: The Lord's Favor
Luke 1:21–25
S: Faith in God's Promises
Luke 1:39–45
S: He Is to be Called John
Luke 1:57–63

TEACHING TIPS

December 21

Bible Study Guide 3

DEC 21st

1. Words You Should Know

A. Shepherds (Luke 2:8, 15, 18, 20) *poimen* (Gk.)—Those responsible for or hired to keep watch over sheep.

B. Glorifying (v. 20) *doxazo* (Gk.)—To honor or speak well of by offering praise or worship.

2. Teacher Preparation

Unifying Principle—The Gift of Kept Promises. People yearn to hear the good news of the fulfillment of promises. What results from our appreciation for promises that are kept? The shepherds glorified and praised God for the gift of the long-awaited Messiah and told others the good news.

A. Read the AIM for Change section and the Keep in Mind verse.

B. Then study the Focal Verses in two different translations.

C. Complete lesson 3 in the *Precepts For Living® Personal Study Guide.*

D. Come prepared to discuss how one feels when a promise is kept.

3. Starting the Lesson

A. Open the class with prayer.

B. Review the AIM for Change with the class.

C. Read the Words You Should Know definitions aloud.

D. Summarize the information provided in The People, Places, and Times and Background sections.

4. Getting into the Lesson

A. Ask for one or more volunteers to read the Focal Verses.

B. Summarize the In Depth section. Ask for individual responses to the questions found in Search the Scriptures.

5. Relating the Lesson to Life

A. Select a volunteer to read In Focus and/or Lesson in Our Society. Ask the students to comment on how the context relates to today's lesson.

B. To answer questions in the Discuss the Meaning section, divide the class into groups. Assign one or two questions to each group, depending on the class size and their responses to the rest of the class.

6. Arousing Action

A. Challenge the students to commit to spreading the Good News of Jesus Christ.

B. Ask a volunteer to read Matthew 28:18–20.

C. Ask another volunteer to explain what Matthew 28:18–20 means.

D. Finally, ask the question, "Why is carrying out the Great Commission not just intended for the pastor or other ministers?" (Remember that we should spread the Good News as the Shepherds did.)

Worship Guide

For the Superintendent or Teacher
Theme: Shepherds Glorify God
Theme Song: "Go Tell It on the Mountain"
Devotional Reading: Psalm 107:1–15
Prayer

SHEPHERDS GLORIFY GOD

Bible Background • LUKE 2:1–20
Printed Text • LUKE 2:8–20 Devotional Reading • PSALM 107:1–15

AIM for Change

By the end of the lesson, we will:
RECOUNT the angel's announcements to the shepherds and the shepherds' responses;
EXPLORE issues of proclamations, promises, and commitment; and
DEMONSTRATE our commitment to God in acts of praise.

Keep in Mind

"The shepherds returned, glorifying and praising God for all the things that they had heard and seen, as it was told unto them" (Luke 2:20).

Focal Verses

KJV **Luke 2:8** And there were in the same country shepherds abiding in the field, keeping watch over their flock by night.

9 And, lo, the angel of the Lord came upon them, and the glory of the Lord shone round about them: and they were sore afraid.

10 And the angel said unto them, Fear not: for, behold, I bring you good tidings of great joy, which shall be to all people.

11 For unto you is born this day in the city of David a Saviour, which is Christ the Lord.

12 And this shall be a sign unto you; Ye shall find the babe wrapped in swaddling clothes, lying in a manger.

13 And suddenly there was with the angel a multitude of the heavenly host praising God, and saying,

14 Glory to God in the highest, and on earth peace, good will toward men.

15 And it came to pass, as the angels were gone away from them into heaven, the shepherds said one to another, Let us now go even unto Bethlehem, and see this thing which is come to pass, which the Lord hath made known unto us.

16 And they came with haste, and found Mary, and Joseph, and the babe lying in a manger.

17 And when they had seen it, they made known abroad the saying which was told them concerning this child.

18 And all they that heard it wondered at those things which were told them by the shepherds.

19 But Mary kept all these things, and pondered them in her heart.

NLT **Luke 2:8** That night there were shepherds staying in the fields nearby, guarding their flocks of sheep.

9 Suddenly, an angel of the Lord appeared among them, and the radiance of the Lord's glory surrounded them. They were terrified,

10 but the angel reassured them. "Don't be afraid!" he said. "I bring you good news that will bring great joy to all people.

11 The Savior—yes, the Messiah, the Lord—has been born today in Bethlehem, the city of David!

12 And you will recognize him by this sign: You will find a baby wrapped snugly in strips of cloth, lying in a manger."

13 Suddenly, the angel was joined by a vast host of others—the armies of heaven—praising God and saying,

14 "Glory to God in highest heaven, and peace on earth to those with whom God is pleased."

15 When the angels had returned to heaven, the shepherds said to each other, "Let's go to Bethlehem! Let's see this thing that has happened, which the Lord has told us about."

16 They hurried to the village and found Mary and Joseph. And there was the baby, lying in the manger.

17 After seeing him, the shepherds told everyone what had happened and what the angel had said to them about this child.

18 All who heard the shepherds' story were astonished,

19 but Mary kept all these things in her heart and thought about them often.

20 And the shepherds returned, glorifying and praising God for all the things that they had heard and seen, as it was told unto them.

20 The shepherds went back to their flocks, glorifying and praising God for all they had heard and seen. It was just as the angel had told them.

In Focus 

My family has played a gift exchange game every Christmas for the past 10 years. We believe it helps us spend more time focusing on fellowship, devotion, and thanksgiving and less time shopping. Every person buys one gift with a $50 maximum and places it near the fireplace in the family room of my grandparents' home. To determine the order for choosing a gift, everyone pulls a number from a hat. Two things always happen. First, my grandfather always goes for the biggest, most handsomely wrapped package. Second, my grandmother always breaks the spending limit rule.

My grandfather loves to open gifts. Although he has everything a person could ever need in a lifetime, he sure does get excited about receiving wrapped gifts. The bigger and prettier the package, the more anticipation he builds. So we place items in boxes more than two times their size and have them wrapped in colorful paper with fancy scripted words. We hire specialists to elaborately tie velvet or satin bows, perfectly fold the ends, and then seal them with invisible tape for a seamless finish. Gift wrapping is big business because of people like my grandfather. He attacks the gift in a way that exposes the item only seconds later, with pieces of shredded packaging materials remaining around him. He examines the gift for a moment. Suddenly, all the excitement disappears. He looks up and responds, "Oh, thank you." How courteous, but we all know that he is generally more excited about opening the gift than using what may be inside.

Grandmother, on the other hand, gets excited about giving great gifts. She never goes shopping or gives much detail to packaging. She is, however, notorious for putting $100 bills under recycled gifts in old, plain boxes (disregarding two rules).

According to Christine Fleming Heffner in *Parables for the Present*, when it comes to presenting gifts, God behaves in ways similar to my grandmother. Most of God's gifts seem to come in modest packages—a brown paper bag even—but turn out to be extremely valuable. Let's compare the nativity stories of John's and Jesus' births in the gospel of Luke (1:57–66; 2:1–8). Elisabeth shared the joy of John's birth with a host of family and neighbors at home, while the shepherds found Mary and Joseph in isolation and Baby Jesus in the filth and discomfort of a manger.

Most of us are like my grandfather. We overlook the modestly wrapped presents in favor of the shiny ones. Sometimes in life, the pretty packages we encounter have penny candy inside—it's sweet for a moment but has no lasting value. Don't be in such a hurry to always open shiny packages that disappoint you by promising so much and offering so little.

God delights in giving great gifts. The greatest of these came in the promise fulfilled when God's only begotten son entered the world in the person of Jesus Christ. People yearn to hear the good news of the fulfillment of promises. What results from our appreciation for promises that are kept? The shepherds glorified and praised God for the gift of the long-awaited Messiah and told others the good news.

Source:

Heffner, Christine Fleming. *Parables for the Present.* New York: Hawthorn Books, 1974.

The People, Places, and Times

Mary. Greek form of Miriam meaning "bitter" or "rebellion" (though some suggest meanings such as "beloved" based on other language derivations). Mary is the mother of Jesus, James, Joseph, Judas, Simon, and some daughters. She gave birth to Jesus in Bethlehem and is the wife of Joseph.

Joseph. Greek name meaning "increaser." Joseph is Mary's betrothed husband and is from the lineage of David.

Bethlehem (City of David). Means "house of bread." This is where Mary gave birth to Jesus. It is a town about six miles south of Jerusalem. It was originally called Ephratah (Genesis 35:16; Ruth 4:11).

Cyrenius. The governor of Syria, who carried out the orders of Caesar Augustus to implement a census of the Roman world. Mary and Joseph were traveling to Bethlehem to register for the census when Jesus was born (Luke 2:1–6).

Source:
Packer, J. I., Merrill C. Tenney, and William White. *Nelson's Illustrated Encyclopedia of Bible Facts.* Nashville: Thomas Nelson Publishers, 1995.

Background

Even though the Jews did not have to serve in the Roman army, they still had to pay taxes to the Roman government. Therefore, a census (registration) was taken to aid in the collection process. But a Sovereign God, who controls history, was and always is in control of His universe. This omnipotent (all-powerful) God had a plan to bring His one and only Son into the world to serve as: (1) Prophet, (2) the Suffering Priest, and (3) King of kings and Lord of lords. Therefore, the decree from the Roman ruler, Augustus, went out to all the Jews in God's perfect timing. God used this announcement to work His plan to get Joseph and Mary to the place where Jesus was to be born. Thus, Emperor Augustus's decree fulfilled prophecy that Jesus was to be born in Bethlehem (Micah 5:2).

It was also in God's sovereign plan that He would continue to reveal His Son. God chose to first reveal Him to lowly shepherds working in the fields. Bible scholars tell us that these shepherds may have supplied the sacrificial lambs for the temple. These lambs were used to pay the Jews' sin penalty and grant them forgiveness of sin. However, now on the scene would be the Lamb without spot or blemish, Jesus Christ, the Son of the Living God. He would die on a cruel Cross, rise from the dead in three days, and win victory over sin and death (eternal separation from a Holy God). He would pay all believers' sin-penalty in full.

Another Old Testament prophecy was also fulfilled. In fact, the Old Testament declared that the Messiah (Jesus Christ) would be born in King David's royal line (Isaiah 11:1; Jeremiah 33:15; Ezekiel 37:24; Hosea 3:5). Whereas the Jews were looking for a Messiah to deliver them from Roman rule, God sent His Son to save them from their sins. God was and is building His own kingdom, which will consist of everyone who believes on the Lord Jesus Christ as Lord and Saviour (John 3:16). As we study today's lesson, be challenged to see the hand of God in the birth of His Son and the salvation of humanity.

Sources:
Drury, John. *Tradition and Design in Luke's Gospel.* Atlanta, Ga.: John Knox Press, 1976.

Illustrated Dictionary of Bible Life & Times. Pleasantville, N.Y.: *Reader's Digest*, 1997.

Life Application Study Bible (New International Version). Wheaton, Ill.: Tyndale House Publishers, 1991.

Packer, J. I., Merrill C. Tenney, and William White. *Nelson's Illustrated Encyclopedia of Bible Facts.* Nashville: Thomas Nelson Publishers, 1995.

At-A-Glance

1. Signs Will Guide Shepherds to the Messiah (Luke 2:8–12)
2. Heaven and Earth Rejoice Over the Messiah's Birth (vv. 13–20)

In Depth

1. Signs Will Guide Shepherds to the Messiah (Luke 2:8–12)

An angel is, by definition, a divine messenger. Throughout the biblical text, angel appearances, in which they communicate with people, have served as indicators that something important is about to happen in salvation history. God continued to reveal plans for delivering the promised Messiah, although not to those whom it may be expected. In Luke's account, an angel announced Jesus' birth to shepherds while they were keeping watch over sheep in the field (Luke 2:8–9).

The shepherds were terrified, but their fear turned to joy as the angel announced the Messiah's birth (Luke 2:9–12). Although the Jews had long awaited a messianic ruler to bring security and peace (see Micah 5), according to the divine messenger, the glorious news was for all people. Here is a parallel theme with Luke 1:26–38, which tells of the angel's announcement of Jesus' conception and birth to Mary. However, the angels make no promise to the shepherds; they simply proclaim that the promise has been fulfilled.

The child, Jesus, is revealed to the shepherds as the greatly anticipated King and Saviour of the Jews (Luke 2:11). The sign provided to the shepherds would be the rare sight of a swaddled baby lying in a manger. This sign served to guide them in their search and validation of the truth of God's words.

2. Heaven and Earth Rejoice Over the Messiah's Birth (vv. 13–20)

Another function of an angel is to praise God (Luke 2:13; also see Revelation 5). "Glory to God the highest," they sing, acknowledging God's holiness and greatness over all other created beings. They applaud God for all the goodness and joy that the fulfillment of the messianic promise will bring into the world (v. 14).

The shepherds patterned their behavior after the angels. First, they were obedient to the mission God set before them. They hurried off to Bethlehem to see what God had revealed to them (Luke 2:15–16) and found Mary, Joseph, and the infant Messiah in the humble setting of a stable. Then, by sharing and spreading the Good News, they became God's earthly messengers (vv. 17–18). Finally, once they completed their assignment, they, too, responded with praise and worship (v. 20). Verse 19 shows us how Mary responded to this wondrous, cosmos-changing event. She quietly reflected upon and treasured the rejoicing and celebration of her child's birth.

Sources:

Drury, John. *The Gospel of Luke. The J.B. Phillips' New Testament Commentaries.* New York: MacMillan, 1973.

Life Application Study Bible (New International Version). Wheaton, Ill.: Tyndale House Publishers, 1991.

Thompson, G. H. P. *The Gospel According to Luke.* New York: Oxford University Press, 1972.

Search the Scriptures

1. How did the shepherds respond to the angel's presence (Luke 2:9)?
2. What message did the angel provide (vv. 10–11)?
3. What sign were the shepherds to look for (v. 12)?
4. What did the shepherds have in common with the heavenly host (vv. 13–14, 20)?
5. After the angels returned to heaven, what did the shepherds do (vv. 15–16)?
6. Compare Mary's response to that of others who heard the shepherds' story (vv. 18–19).

Discuss the Meaning

1. Discuss the relationship, if any, between praise and obedience.
2. What responsibility do believers have in spreading the Good News? Discuss practical ways each person can share in carrying out the Great Commission.

Lesson in Our Society

Always celebrate God's faithfulness and generosity! Today, there are many who fail to recognize Gods' gifts to us because they are too busy complaining about things not going according to their plans. Instead of letting our frustrations blind us, we should respond like the shepherds when God provides gifts like love, faith, peace, hope, joy, or a promise fulfilled. Embrace the 4 *P*s:

1. **P**ractice obedience to God's leading and direction.
2. **P**lan for change or be prompt in your actions when possible.
3. **P**roclaim the Good News by sharing it with others.
4. **P**raise and worship God for everything.

Make It Happen

Identify where, if anywhere, in your life that you can apply the 4 *P*s. Then do so. Also evaluate whether you skipped implementing one or more of the *P*s in a process you are currently in or have completed.

Follow the Spirit

What God wants me to do:

____

____

Remember Your Thoughts

Special insights I have learned:

____

____

More Light on the Text

Luke 2:8–20

8 And there were in the same country shepherds abiding in the field, keeping watch over their flock by night.

A small group of shepherds were keeping watch over their flock somewhere in the fields not far from Bethlehem. The words "keeping watch" (from two Greek words *phulasso,* **foo-LAS-so,** meaning "to keep" and *phulake,* **foo-lak-AY,** meaning "to watch") indicate that the shepherds were guarding vigilantly in order to protect against dangers. The shepherds were guarding their sheep "by night." The night darkness must have made the brilliance of the angelic appearance all the more vivid.

"Abiding in the field" (Gk. *agrauleo,* **ag-row-LEH-o**) indicates that the field was the habitual residence of the shepherd. It comes from two Greek words: *agros* (**ag-ROS**) meaning "field" and *aule* (**ow-LAY**) meaning "residence."

The shepherds came from a despised class. They were considered robbers, deemed unreliable, and were not allowed to give testimony in the courts of law. But God chose to send to this assembled group

"Suddenly, an angel of the Lord appeared among them, and the radiance of the Lord's glory surrounded them. They were terrified," (Luke 2:9).

of simple shepherds His angel with the good news of the birth of the Messiah.

9 And, lo, the angel of the Lord came upon them, and the glory of the Lord shone round about them: and they were sore afraid.

The angel of the Lord suddenly "appeared" (*ephistemi,* **ef-IS-tay-mee,** meaning "to come upon and stand by") to the shepherds. This glorious appearing relates to appearances of the *shekinah,* or God's shining presence, elsewhere in the Bible (Exodus 3:1–10; Luke 9:28–36). The angel's appearance struck terror into the shepherds as the brightness of the Lord's glory shone around them (Gk. *perilampo,* **per-ee-LAM-po,** meaning "to shine around"). "The glory" (Gk. *doxa,* **DOX-ah**) was the radiating, brilliant splendor or majesty of God.

10 And the angel said unto them, Fear not: for, behold, I bring you good tidings of great joy, which shall be to all people.

The angel first reassured the shepherds, urging them to "stop being afraid" (see Luke 1:13, 30). The Greek word *me* (**may**), with a present imperative, indicates forbidding continuation. Here the shepherds are forbidden to remain fearful, for there is no basis for fear.

The angel then explained to the shepherds that he had come with "good and joyful news" (Gk. *euaggelizo,* **yoo-ang-ghel-ID-zo**). The good news is not for the shepherds alone, but for everyone. "People" (Gk. *laos* **lah-OS**, meaning "people" or "nation") refers to the people of Israel, not to people in general. The news of the Saviour would mean much to people in every land, but it came in the first instance to Israel.

11 For unto you is born this day in the city of David a Saviour, which is Christ the Lord.

The good and joyous news is that in Bethlehem, the city of David, the promised Messiah was born. He is the Saviour, the One who gives blessedness in the fullest sense of the word.

The Greek word *semeron* (**SAY-mer-on**) means "this day" or "today." The day for the Jews starts at sunset. This implication is that Jesus was born at night and the angel appeared to the shepherds that same night.

"A saviour" (Gk. *soter,* **so-TARE**) means a deliverer. The Saviour is called Christ the Lord (Gk. *christos kurios,* **khris-TOS KOO-ree-os**), meaning literally "the anointed king" (see Acts 2:36; 2 Corinthians 4:5; Philippians 2:11), a startling title giving a description of the child in the highest possible terms.

The term Christ (Gk. *christos,* **khris-TOS**) means the "anointed one." Anointing was for special service like that of a priest, a prophet, or a king. The Jews expected that one day God would send a very special Saviour. He would not be simply an anointed king, but the Anointed, Christ, the Messiah, the fulfiller of the promises of God. He would be the perfect prophet, priest, and king. It is He whom the angel announced.

The word "Lord" (Gk. *kurios,* **KOO-ree-os**), means "ruler" or "king." It has a definite messianic connotation here. Thus, the angel declared that a Deliverer (Saviour) from the line of King David was the Anointed and the Lord and not simply the anointed Lord.

12 And this shall be a sign unto you; Ye shall find the babe wrapped in swaddling clothes, lying in a manger.

The angel completed his message by giving the shepherds a sign to help them find the "child" (Gk. *brephos,* **BREF-os,** also meaning "a fetus" as well as "a newborn baby"). The "sign" (Gk. *semeion,* **say-MI-on,** meaning "a sign" or "a miracle") would attest to the shepherds the truth of the angel's words.

They would find Him not surrounded by outward glory but as a baby wrapped in swaddling clothes and lying on a bed of hay. No other baby in Bethlehem would be lying in a manger like this. "Lying in a manger" will distinguish the child from any other. The verb "lying" (Gk. *keimai,* **KI-mahee**) can also be translated by "have been placed."

The child Saviour, Christ, and Lord will be recognized by His humble estate, just as His disciples would be (see Philippians 2:1–11; Luke 22:24–27; John 13:14–17; Matthew 20:26–28).

13 And suddenly there was with the angel a multitude of the heavenly host praising God, and saying,

At the end of the angel's message, a multitude of other angels praising God suddenly appeared. They are called "a host." The word "host" (Gk. *stratia,* **strat-EE-ah**) refers to an "army" or a "troop." It indicates a group of angels who are part of the celestial army (Joshua 5:13–15). An army of angels would probably praise God through song, but the word translated "praising" (Gk. *aineo* **ahee-NEH-o**) carries no indication either of singing or not singing.

14 Glory to God in the highest, and on earth peace, good will toward men.

They are an army that announces peace. They sing the glory of God. The glory of God is the first step to real peace on Earth. The expression "good will toward men" is replaced in some manuscripts by "to men on whom his favor rests" and is parallel to "people" (Gk. *laos*) in verse 10. It refers to people upon whom God's redemptive mercy has been bestowed and with whom He is well pleased. God will bring peace for people on whom His favor rests. The emphasis is on God, not man. The peace, which the angels announce, is not the external and temporary Roman peace. It is peace between God and humanity. It is the peace that heals the rupture between sinful men and a holy God (see Isaiah 9:6; Romans 2:10).

15 And it came to pass, as the angels were gone away from them into heaven, the shepherds said one to another, Let us now go even unto Bethlehem, and see this thing which is come to pass, which the Lord hath made known unto us.

The word "and" (Gk. *kai,* **kahee**) indicates the correlation between the departure of the angels and the action of the shepherds, who were about to act on what the angels had told them. The angels had appeared unexpectedly and suddenly, but they departed gradually as the shepherds saw them ascending to heaven. They knew that the event had actually taken place, and they realized it was the Lord who had sent them the good news through His angels. The shepherds were silent during the angelic apparition. Afterward, they started talking to each other and said: "Let us now go…and see…." Many people, when the Good News is proclaimed to them, do not have the same good sense as the shepherds (John 1:46; 4:42). But those who do have good sense, as the shepherds did, receive true joy.

16 And they came with haste, and found Mary, and Joseph, and the babe lying in a manger.

The shepherds hurried to Bethlehem to see for themselves the amazing child. The expression "they came with haste" is composed of two Greek verbs (*erchomai,* **ER-khom-ahee,** meaning "to come," and speudo, **SPYOO-do**, meaning "to haste"). They "found" (Gk. *aneurisko,* **an-yoo-RIS-ko**) all, as the angel had said, with the baby lying in a manger.

17 And when they had seen it, they made known abroad the saying which was told them concerning this child.

The verb "had seen" (Gk. *eido,* **I-do**) has no object. It is the action of seeing confirming the word of the angel. The shepherds became the first to proclaim the birth of the Messiah to others. It is implied that between verses 16 and 17 that the shepherds left after their visit and started "making known" (Gk. *diagnorizo,* **dee-ag-no-RID-zo**, meaning "to publish" or "to make known thoroughly") the news concerning the child.

18 And all they that heard it wondered at those things which were told them by the shepherds.

People who heard the witness of the shepherds were "surprised" (Gk. *thaumazo,* **thou-MAD-zo**), which means "as though traumatized, disturbed or marveled." They are not identified.

19 But Mary kept all these things, and pondered them in her heart.

Mary "kept" (Gk. *suntereo,* **soon-tay-REH-o**, meaning "to keep safe" or "to preserve") all these things, meditating on them in her heart (see Genesis 37:11). She "pondered" (Gk. *sumballo,* **soom-BAL-lo,** literally meaning "to put together," "reflect on") all this and retained it in her heart.

20 And the shepherds returned, glorifying and praising God for all the things that they had heard and seen, as it was told unto them.

The story concluded with the shepherds returning to where they came from, full of praise to God (Gk. *aineo,* **ahee-NEH-o,** meaning "acknowledging the glory of God"), for they had confirmation of the news they had heard.

Sources:

Drury, John. *The Gospel of Luke. The J.B. Phillips' New Testament Commentaries.* New York: MacMillan, 1973.

Life Application Study Bible (New International Version). Wheaton, Ill.: Tyndale House Publishers, 1991.

Packer, J. I., Merrill C. Tenney, and William White. *Nelson's Illustrated Encyclopedia of Bible Facts.* Nashville: Thomas Nelson Publishers, 1995.

Daily Bible Readings

M: God's Plan Fulfilled
Isaiah 46:8–13
T: The King of Glory
Psalm 24
W: Who Is Like the Lord?
Psalm 113
T: Praise the Lord
Psalm 148
F: Glory Forever
Romans 16:25–27
S: Mary's First Baby
Luke 2:1–7
S: Glory to God!
Luke 2:8–20

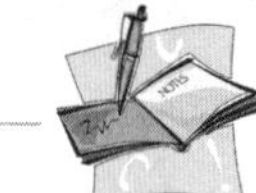

NOTES

TEACHING TIPS

December 28

Bible Study Guide 4

1. Words You Should Know

A. Baptized/Baptize (Luke 3:7, 12, 16) *baptizo* (Gk.)—To immerse in water, to wash. Some believe that baptism can be applied through pouring or sprinkling.

B. Repentance (v. 8) *metanoia* (Gk.)—To turn from one's sins, to change one's ways, a change of heart.

C. Publicans (v. 12) *telones* (Gk.)—Tax collectors. The biblical text implies that because they extorted money from their own people, the Jewish community despised them (Luke 3:12–13; 5:30).

2. Teacher Preparation

Unifying Principle—Acting on One's Commitment. Making a commitment requires action to accompany verbal assent. What actions may be required to fulfill a commitment? When John took the message to the people about the coming of the Messiah, he challenged them to make a response.

A. Using different versions of the Bible, study the Focal Verses.

B. As part of your daily devotions, study the Daily Bible Readings. Then meditate on these verses.

C. Complete lesson 4 from the *Precepts For Living® Personal Study Guide.*

D. Finally, review The People, Places, and Times; Background; and In Depth sections of this guide to enhance your insight of the lesson.

3. Starting the Lesson

A. Open the class with prayer.

B. Review the AIM for Change with the class.

C. Read the Words You Should Know definitions aloud.

D. Summarize the context information provided in The People, Places, and Times and Background sections.

4. Getting into the Lesson

A. Ask for one or more volunteers to read the Focal Verses.

B. Summarize the In Depth section. Ask for individual responses to the questions found in Search the Scriptures.

5. Relating the Lesson to Life

A. Select a volunteer to read In Focus and/or Lesson in Our Society. Ask the students to comment on how the context relates to today's lesson.

B. To answer questions in the Discuss the Meaning section, divide the class into groups. Assign one or two questions to each group depending on the class size. Then have each group leader give their responses to the rest of the class.

6. Arousing Action

A. Review the Make It Happen section. Conduct an in depth discussion of how to implement the ideas presented there. Encourage your class to make a personal commitment in the suggested areas, found in this section.

B. Remind the class to do their Daily Bible Readings so that they can grow in wisdom and knowledge of God's Word.

Worship Guide

For the Superintendent or Teacher
Theme: John the Baptist Proclaims God's Message
Theme Song: "Believe and Obey"
Devotional Reading: Psalm 51:10–19
Prayer

JOHN THE BAPTIST PROCLAIMS GOD'S MESSAGE

Bible Background • LUKE 3:1–20
Printed Text • LUKE 3:7–18 Devotional Reading • PSALM 51:10–19

AIM for Change

By the end of the lesson, we will:
EXAMINE John's commitment to call people to repentance;
EXPLORE the range of possible actions that are required by commitment; and
EVALUATE actions you have taken because of your commitment to God.

Keep in Mind

"Bring forth therefore fruits worthy of repentance" (from Luke 3:8).

Focal Verses

KJV **Luke 3:7** Then said he to the multitude that came forth to be baptized of him, O generation of vipers, who hath warned you to flee from the wrath to come?

8 Bring forth therefore fruits worthy of repentance, and begin not to say within yourselves, We have Abraham to our father: for I say unto you, That God is able of these stones to raise up children unto Abraham.

9 And now also the axe is laid unto the root of the trees: every tree therefore which bringeth not forth good fruit is hewn down, and cast into the fire.

10 And the people asked him, saying, What shall we do then?

11 He answereth and saith unto them, He that hath two coats, let him impart to him that hath none; and he that hath meat, let him do likewise.

12 Then came also publicans to be baptized, and said unto him, Master, what shall we do?

13 And he said unto them, Exact no more than that which is appointed you.

14 And the soldiers likewise demanded of him, saying, And what shall we do? And he said unto them, Do violence to no man, neither accuse any falsely; and be content with your wages.

15 And as the people were in expectation, and all men mused in their hearts of John, whether he were the Christ, or not;

16 John answered, saying unto them all, I indeed baptize you with water; but one mightier than I cometh, the latchet of whose shoes I am not worthy to unloose: he shall baptize you with the Holy Ghost and with fire:

NLT **Luke 3:7** When the crowds came to John for baptism, he said, "You brood of snakes! Who warned you to flee God's coming wrath?

8 Prove by the way you live that you have repented of your sins and turned to God. Don't just say to each other, 'We're safe, for we are descendants of Abraham.' That means nothing, for I tell you, God can create children of Abraham from these very stones.

9 Even now the ax of God's judgment is poised, ready to sever the roots of the trees. Yes, every tree that does not produce good fruit will be chopped down and thrown into the fire."

10 The crowds asked, "What should we do?"

11 John replied, "If you have two shirts, give one to the poor. If you have food, share it with those who are hungry."

12 Even corrupt tax collectors came to be baptized and asked, "Teacher, what should we do?"

13 He replied, "Collect no more taxes than the government requires."

14 "What should we do?" asked some soldiers. John replied, "Don't extort money or make false accusations. And be content with your pay."

15 Everyone was expecting the Messiah to come soon, and they were eager to know whether John might be the Messiah.

16 John answered their questions by saying, "I baptize you with water; but someone is coming soon who is greater than I am—so much greater that I'm not even worthy to be his slave and untie the straps

17 Whose fan is in his hand, and he will thoroughly purge his floor, and will gather the wheat into his garner; but the chaff he will burn with fire unquenchable.

18 And many other things in his exhortation preached he unto the people.

of his sandals. He will baptize you with the Holy Spirit and with fire.

17 He is ready to separate the chaff from the wheat with his winnowing fork. Then he will clean up the threshing area, gathering the wheat into his barn but burning the chaff with never-ending fire."

18 John used many such warnings as he announced the Good News to the people.

In Focus 

A young woman accepted a new position working for a national youth development agency. Having been involved in youth ministry for nearly 10 years, she didn't think she would be facing much of a learning curve. She was in for quite the awakening! Due to a staff shortage, she found herself intimately involved in program delivery. This wouldn't usually be a problem, but it was springtime and urban gardening was the program focus of the season. Like most Americans, she knew absolutely nothing about the process of producing food and getting it to the table. She just cooked and ate and was perfectly fine with that being the extent of her knowledge.

Despite the shock of being plunged into the new task, she found she liked working in the community gardens so much that she decided to start one at her home. She purchased the soil, plants, and wood chips within a week. She also pulled up weeds and prepared beds.

It is sad to say but she still doesn't have a garden in her backyard; other, more urgent, tasks have consumed her time. The soil remains in bags in the garage. The plants are still in the pots they came in. Most of the wood chips sit in a pile alongside her house.

The Bible is filled with stories or parables that use farming metaphors. What lesson can be learned from this story? Simply, the difference between interest and commitment is action! Making a commitment requires action to accompany verbal assent. What actions may be required to fulfill a commitment? When John took the message to the people about the coming of the Messiah, he challenged them to make a response.

The People, Places, and Times

John. It is a contraction of the name Jehohanan, meaning "gift of God." He is known as John the Baptist. Because Elisabeth and Zacharias were his parents, John and Jesus were cousins. He was a prophet who openly proclaimed a divine message to prepare people for the coming Messiah. John was beheaded by Herod (Luke 1:13–17; 3:16; 9:7–9).

Herod Antipas. He was the son of Herod the Great. He ruled the region of Galilee and Perea as tetrarch. He was the murderer of John the Baptist (Matthew 14:1–11; Luke 13:31–32).

Source:

Packer, J. I., Merrill C. Tenney, and William White Jr., eds. *Nelson's Illustrated Encyclopedia of Bible Facts.* Nashville: Thomas Nelson Publishers, 1995.

Background

Because he serves as one of the omens to predict Jesus' greatness, John the Baptist is important to Luke's account. John's preaching and prophetic ministry help Luke's audience anticipate the greatness of Jesus' destiny.

John's activity fits nicely into the structure of Luke, which, according to biblical scholar John Drury, is modeled after the classic prophetic message. In the classic prophetic message, there is a pattern of reversal of fortunes, in which God's acts of judgment and mercy shape human history.

Sources:

Drury, John. *Tradition and Design in Luke's Gospel.* Atlanta, Ga.: John Knox Press, 1976.

Illustrated Dictionary of Bible Life & Times. Pleasantville, N.Y.: *Reader's Digest,* 1997.

Life Application Study Bible (New International Version). Wheaton, Ill.: Tyndale House Publishers, 1991.

Packer, J. I., Merrill C. Tenney, and William White Jr., eds. *Nelson's Illustrated Encyclopedia of Bible Facts.* Nashville: Thomas Nelson Publishers, 1995.

At-A-Glance

1. John Calls People to Repent (Luke 3:7–14)
2. John Prepares People for the Messiah (vv. 15–18)

In Depth

1. John Calls People to Repent (Luke 3:7–14)

In the classic prophetic tradition, John openly proclaimed divine warnings. The first task of prophetic ministry is dismantling the dominant consciousness. This is done by rejecting and rendering the present social order illegitimate. John did this by delivering a shocking message to the Jewish nation and their religious leaders. He insisted, contrary to traditional notions, that their religious and national status would not protect them in the new era (Luke 3:8). It was widely believed the Promised Messiah would come to deliver the Jewish people from oppression and foreign occupation. John, however, was upsetting this notion with his interpretations of a God and messianic mission that are not confined to these distinctions.

John asserted that God would raise up some and tear down others (Luke 3:8–9). Luke shows John the Baptist addressing the "crowds" and those traditionally marginalized by the established religious order: tax collectors, gentiles, etc. (vv. 10–14). These sinners, as dishonest instruments of foreign oppression and occupation, could repent and be baptized as well. In the tradition of Old Testament prophets, he directed them to live in right relationship with others (e.g., share what you have with the poor, do your job well and fairly). They are the biological descendants of Abraham, but if their hearts and behavior do not turn back toward God, they may be cut off from the promised covenant relationship.

2. John Prepares People for the Messiah (vv. 15–18)

In prophetic ministry, rebuilding always follows destruction. This is apparent in the way—after he warns them—that John the Baptist energized his audience. He inspired hope in the promise of another person, time, and situation toward which his audience might move. He encouraged them to live in fervent anticipation of the newness that God had promised and would surely give.

Some people mistook John the Baptist for the Messiah. He pointed away from himself and promised another—one who would deliver more than he. John had a very clear sense of his message and his purpose. He was fully committed to God and obedient in proclaiming a message of repentance, while announcing the advent of the Messiah. His unique role required him to pronounce words of peril and promise that ultimately put him at risk. Are we ready to follow his example?

Sources:

Brueggemann, Walter. *The Prophetic Imagination.* Philadelphia: Fortress Press, 1978.

Drury, John. *Tradition and Design in Luke's Gospel.* Atlanta, Ga.: John Knox Press, 1976.

Search the Scriptures

1. What warnings did John the Baptist provide to the crowd he was addressing (Luke 3:8–9)?
2. Compare and contrast John the Baptist's instructions for the crowds, the tax collectors, and the soldiers (vv. 10–14).
3. Describe how John the Baptist responded to those who thought he might be the Messiah (vv. 15–17).

Discuss the Meaning

1. In what ways, if any, is a prophetic ministry like John's serving to reform and energize today's church?
2. What does it mean to baptize one with the Holy Spirit and fire? Identify where in Scripture, if any, this promise has been fulfilled.

Lesson in Our Society

There are many people in our society who claim to be committed Christians, but they are simply interested in learning about Jesus or applying a few Christian principles to their lives. Their Christianity is more like an aspect of their culture than the central commitment in their lives. However, we should all ask ourselves, "Where will I spend eternity and what does God require for eternal life?"

Make It Happen

Create a chart with three columns. In the first column provide a heading titled "Priorities." The second column should be titled "Actions." The third heading should read "Frequency." In the rows, write your top five priorities, the actions that accompany them, and how frequently you perform them. Based on the information you provided, determine whether each priority is an interest or commitment. Then evaluate what changes, if any, you would like to make. Finally, share your testimony about what you've learned this week and any insights you gained about the difference between interest and commitment with someone you believe may benefit.

Follow the Spirit

What God wants me to do:

____

____

Remember Your Thoughts

Special insights I have learned:

____

____

More Light on the Text

Luke 3:7–18

7 Then said he to the multitude that came forth to be baptized of him, O generation of vipers, who hath warned you to flee from the wrath to come?

The "multitudes" (Gk. *ochlos*, **OKH-los,** meaning "crowd" or "people") came to hear John's preaching. Matthew 3:7 gives the additional information that many in the crowd were Pharisees and Sadducees. John addressed the people in fearless and harsh terms, drawing their attention to their sins and calling them to true repentance. He did not hesitate to call some of his hearers "vipers", trying to flee the wrath to come.

The Greek word *hupodeiknumi* (**hoop-od-IKE-noo-mee**) means "to point out," "to suggest," or "to counsel," in the sense of talking to the ear of someone to persuade him. John asked the people, "Who has suggested to you to escape the wrath to come?"

The people, hurrying to baptism, reminded John of a bunch of snakes moving ahead of a brush fire. The brush fire here was the approaching judgment of God, which would be part of the Messiah's confrontation of man with God (Malachi 4:1). They wanted to escape the flames but had little intention of having their evil natures changed. They behaved as though to escape the coming wrath, all they needed to do was to submit to the mere outward rite of baptism, without giving any practical evidence of genuine repentance.

John drew the attention of the multitudes to their tortuous behavior. They lived in self-satisfaction and sin. They now desired participation in the baptism to protect themselves against the coming judgment, without true repentance.

8 Bring forth therefore fruits worthy of repentance, and begin not to say within yourselves, We have Abraham to our father: for I say unto you, That God is able of these stones to raise up children unto Abraham.

John invited the people to wholehearted repentance, after which they must have themselves been baptized as an outward sign of their acknowledgment of their spiritual impurity (Matthew 3:6). For those who repented, baptism was to be a sign and a seal of the forgiveness granted by God.

The wrath of God would come upon the people unless their repentance was demonstrated with appropriate fruits. John gives examples of genuineness in verses 10–14. He warned them against relying on the fact that they were Abraham's physical descendants. Because of Abraham's merits, many Jews believed that God would ultimately be kind to them. John stressed that everybody stands before God as individuals. Physical relation to Abraham is no substitute for repentance and no defense against the coming wrath. It does not necessarily produce spiritual sons of Abraham (see John 8:33–47; Romans 4; Galatians 3:6–29). John said with sarcasm that God could turn the stones into better children of Abraham.

There is a play on words between "stones" (Aramaic: *abnayya*) and "children" (Aramaic: *benayya*) in the original Aramaic language spoken by John and the Jews at the time of Jesus.

9 And now also the axe is laid unto the root of the trees: every tree therefore which bringeth not forth good fruit is hewn down, and cast into the fire.

A tree is not judged by its botanical label but by whether its fruit is good or bad. People are judged the same way. If their lives are found to have produced bad fruit, they will be cut down and sent to the fire, no matter whose children they are. Only repentance and the production of practical evidence, to show genuine repentance, could save from the coming wrath.

The axe, lying by the root of the trees, was a clear warning. It was a symbol of judgment. The coming of the Messiah meant both salvation and judgment. Therefore, there must be no postponement of repentance. The trees are not yet cut down. The judgment is on people who stay unrepentant.

10 And the people asked him, saying, What shall we do then?

Alarmed at John's urgent invitation, three groups of people inquired of John what would be an acceptable evidence of sincerity deserving baptism: What are we to do? They each wanted to know what was expected of them—what repentance meant in their case. They asked what they should do, thinking probably that they must do something special.

11 He answereth and saith unto them, He that hath two coats, let him impart to him that hath none; and he that hath meat, let him do likewise.

John gave them a very practical answer (see Isaiah 1:16–19): They should share what they had with those who had nothing. They should carry out the well-known demand of God to love their neighbor.

Normally a "coat" (Gk. *chiton,* **khee-TONE,** meaning "a tunic") was worn under the outer garment, but someone might wear more than one for extra warmth or have an extra tunic he was not wearing. God required them to have an attitude of compassion toward others.

Similarly if they had food, they should share it with someone who was hungry.

12 Then came also publicans to be baptized, and said unto him, Master, what shall we do?

The tax collectors (Gk. *telones,* **tel-O-nace**, or "custom officers," "publicans") came to John. They were actually Jews who paid the Romans for the right to collect taxes. They were hated by other Jews who thought of them as traitors to their nation and to their religion. They worked for the Roman colonizers and overtaxed people. John's preaching had convinced some of them that what they were doing was wrong. They came to him wanting to express their repentance in baptism. They asked him what they should do to escape the wrath to come.

The Greek word *didaskalos* (**did-AS-kal-os**) can be translated as "a master" (in the sense of doctor or professor) or "a teacher."

13 And he said unto them, Exact no more than that which is appointed you.

John did not ask them to give up their jobs. He requested them to show the genuineness of their repentance by never again abusing their position and by never extorting excessive taxes for their own enrichment. They should not collect from people more than what was appointed to them. In other terms, they were required to be honest in carrying out their business transactions.

14 And the soldiers likewise demanded of him, saying, And what shall we do? And he said unto them, Do violence to no man, neither accuse any falsely; and be content with your wages.

We do not know whether the soldiers were Jewish or Roman. They usually assisted the tax collectors in collecting taxes. They were in a privileged position. To "do violence to" (Gk. *diaseio,* **dee-as-I-o**) means "to rob with violence." "Accuse falsely" (Gk. *sukophanteo,* **soo-kof-an-TEH-o**) indicates "to rob through false accusations or intimidation." John did not ask them to leave their jobs. He told them not to force people to pay money in order to be left alone. They were to be content with the wages agreed upon for their service. They should rob no one by violence or by false accusation. They were challenged to act uprightly, using integrity in their office and honesty in dealings with their fellow man.

15 And as the people were in expectation, and all men mused in their hearts of John, whether he were the Christ, or not;

People were waiting for the revelation of the Messiah. John's prophetic authority and unique preaching raised in their mind the question of whether he was the Messiah (see John 1:20, 25). The Greek word *dialogizomai* (**dee-al-og-ID-zom-ahee**) implies "a debate." There was a debate going on in their hearts as to whether or not John was the Messiah.

16 John answered, saying unto them all, I indeed baptize you with water; but one mightier than I cometh, the latchet of whose shoes I am not worthy to unloose: he shall baptize you with the Holy Ghost and with fire:

John clearly rejected the idea that he was the Messiah. He stated that the Messiah would be mightier than he. He made two points: (1) He was inferior to the Messiah, who was yet to come. He saw himself as unfit to untie the thong of the Messiah's sandals. To carry and to take off the master's sandals were characteristic services of a slave. John was saying that he was unworthy even to be the Messiah's slave. (2) His baptism was inferior to the work of the Messiah. He had come to administer the outward baptism.

The Messiah would bring about the inward purification and renewal. He would give the true baptism with the Holy Spirit and with fire.

Spirit and fire are governed by one word in the Greek, the preposition *en* (**en**, indicating the means or the instrument used by the agent). The same people are baptized with the Holy Spirit as with fire. Those who accept him will be purified as by fire and strengthened by the Holy Spirit (see Malachi 3:1–4). Fire refers to purification (see 1 Corinthians 3:13; 1 Peter 1:7). The verb "cometh" (Gk. *erchomai*, **ER-khom-ahee**) indicates the fact that he was already coming.

17 Whose fan is in his hand, and he will thoroughly purge his floor, and will gather the wheat into his garner; but the chaff he will burn with fire unquenchable.

The coming of the Messiah would not mean salvation for all. He would sift and separate people like a farmer at harvest time separated the grain from the chaff. Winnowing was the process by which the grain, having been loosened from the husks, was thrown into the air against the wind. The wind carried the chaff away, but the grain fell straight down. The winnowing fork was the shovel by which the grain was tossed into the air. The threshing-floor was cleared by this means. The wheat was brought into the barn, but the chaff was burned with unquenchable fire.

This strong expression emphasizes the certainty and completeness of the judgment. Those receiving baptism must see that their repentance was genuine. Judgment would overtake all who were not prepared for His coming through a true change of heart. Judgment was an integral part of the good news. In the end evil would be decisively overthrown.

18 And many other things in his exhortation preached he unto the people.

John preached many such things. He was "exhorting" (Gk. *parakaleo*, **par-ak-al-EH-o**, meaning "to call over") and bringing the "good news" (Gk. *euaggelizo*, **yoo-ang-ghel-ID-zo**) to the people. John was challenging the people to come and accept the Good News.

Sources:

Drury, John. *Tradition and Design in Luke's Gospel.* Atlanta, Ga.: John Knox Press, 1976.

Packer, J. I., Merrill C. Tenney, and William White Jr., eds. *Nelson's Illustrated Encyclopedia of Bible Facts.* Nashville: Thomas Nelson Publishers, 1995.

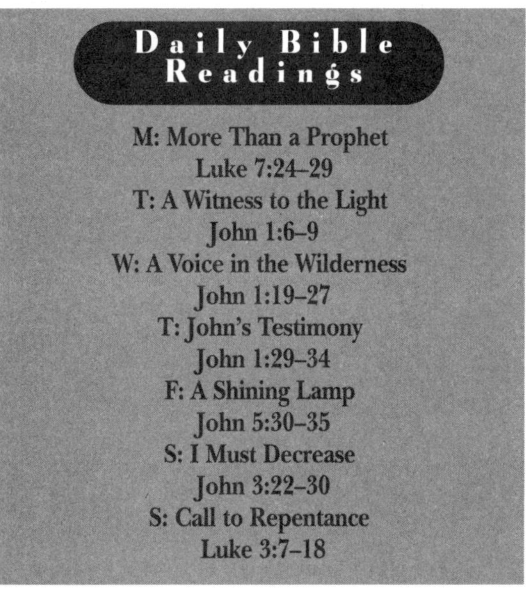

Daily Bible Readings

M: More Than a Prophet
Luke 7:24–29

T: A Witness to the Light
John 1:6–9

W: A Voice in the Wilderness
John 1:19–27

T: John's Testimony
John 1:29–34

F: A Shining Lamp
John 5:30–35

S: I Must Decrease
John 3:22–30

S: Call to Repentance
Luke 3:7–18

NOTES

TEACHING TIPS

January 4
Bible Study Guide 5

1. Words You Should Know

A. Taskmasters (Exodus 1:11) *sar* (Heb.)—A ruler, governor, or keeper.

B. Afflict (v. 11) *'anah* (Heb.)—Implies dealing with forcefully or harshly.

C. Treasure cities (v. 11) *miqnah* (Heb.)—Implies cities used for storage.

D. With rigour (vv. 13, 14) *perek* (Heb.)—With severity and cruelty.

E. Upon the stools (v. 16) *'oben* (Heb.)—A birthstool that allowed the pregnant woman to deliver the baby while they were in a crouching position.

2. Teacher Preparation

Unifying Principle—Choosing Among Commitments. There are often competing demands for our commitment. How does one evaluate these competing claims and choose an appropriate course of action? The midwives knew they belonged to God's people and remained faithful to God while denying Pharaoh's edict.

A. Look up a definition of the word "commitment," and be prepared to discuss it with your students.

B. Prepare a list of pressing commitments that your students may deal with in their everyday lives.

C. Study the Background Scriptures and Focal Verses in two different versions of the Bible.

3. Starting the Lesson

A. Start the class session with prayer. Be sure to include your church leaders in the prayer.

B. Ask the students to share accounts of when someone in authority asked them to do something they knew to be wrong.

C. Discuss their responses to those requests or orders.

4. Getting into the Lesson

A. Read and discuss the Keep in Mind verse.

B. Have volunteers read the Focal Verses.

C. Ask a volunteer to read the In Focus section.

D. Lead the class in a discussion of the In Focus story.

5. Relating the Lesson to Life

A. Divide the class into two or three groups. Assign each group one of the Discuss the Meaning questions, and ask them to answer it. Reconvene the class, and share the groups' answers.

B. As a group, discuss the Lesson in Our Society section.

6. Arousing Action

A. Encourage the class to reflect on the Make It Happen section.

B. Remind class members to complete the Daily Bible Readings, Remember Your Thoughts, and Follow the Spirit sections.

C. Ask a volunteer to close the class with prayer.

Worship Guide

For the Superintendent or Teacher
Theme: Midwives Serve God
Theme Song: "I Have Decided to Follow Jesus"
Devotional Reading: Proverbs 16:1–7
Prayer

MIDWIVES SERVE GOD

Bible Background • EXODUS 1:8–21
Printed Text • EXODUS 1:8–21 Devotional Reading • PROVERBS 16:1–7

AIM for Change

By the end of the lesson, we will:
EXAMINE how the midwives obeyed God, rather than Pharaoh;
CONSIDER the compelling demands people face in making appropriate commitments; and
PRIORITIZE those commitments around our primary loyalty to God and to the community of faith.

Keep in Mind

"But the midwives feared God, and did not as the king of Egypt commanded them, but saved the men children alive" (Exodus 1:17).

Focal Verses

KJV **Exodus 1:8** Now there arose up a new king over Egypt, which knew not Joseph.

9 And he said unto his people, Behold, the people of the children of Israel *are* more and mightier than we:

10 Come on, let us deal wisely with them; lest they multiply, and it come to pass, that, when there falleth out any war, they join also unto our enemies, and fight against us, and *so* get them up out of the land.

11 Therefore they did set over them taskmasters to afflict them with their burdens. And they built for Pharaoh treasure cities, Pithom and Raamses.

12 But the more they afflicted them, the more they multiplied and grew. And they were grieved because of the children of Israel.

13 And the Egyptians made the children of Israel to serve with rigour:

14 And they made their lives bitter with hard bondage, in morter, and in brick, and in all manner of service in the field: all their service, wherein they made them serve, *was* with rigour.

15 And the king of Egypt spake to the Hebrew midwives, of which the name of the one *was* Shiphrah, and the name of the other Puah:

16 And he said, When ye do the office of a midwife to the Hebrew women, and see *them* upon the stools; if it *be* a son, then ye shall kill him: but if it *be* a daughter, then she shall live.

17 But the midwives feared God, and did not as the king of Egypt commanded them, but saved the men children alive.

NLT **Exodus 1:8** Eventually, a new king came to power in Egypt who knew nothing about Joseph or what he had done.

9 He said to his people, "Look, the people of Israel now outnumber us and are stronger than we are.

10 We must make a plan to keep them from growing even more. If we don't, and if war breaks out, they will join our enemies and fight against us. Then they will escape from the country."

11 So the Egyptians made the Israelites their slaves. They appointed brutal slave drivers over them, hoping to wear them down with crushing labor. They forced them to build the cities of Pithom and Rameses as supply centers for the king.

12 But the more the Egyptians oppressed them, the more the Israelites multiplied and spread, and the more alarmed the Egyptians became.

13 So the Egyptians worked the people of Israel without mercy.

14 They made their lives bitter, forcing them to mix mortar and make bricks and do all the work in the fields. They were ruthless in all their demands.

15 Then Pharaoh, the king of Egypt, gave this order to the Hebrew midwives, Shiphrah and Puah:

16 "When you help the Hebrew women as they give birth, watch as they deliver. If the baby is a boy, kill him; if it is a girl, let her live."

17 But because the midwives feared God, they refused to obey the king's orders. They allowed the boys to live, too.

18 So the king of Egypt called for the midwives. "Why have you done this?" he demanded. "Why have you allowed the boys to live?"

18 And the king of Egypt called for the midwives, and said unto them, Why have ye done this thing, and have saved the men children alive?

19 And the midwives said unto Pharaoh, Because the Hebrew women *are* not as the Egyptian women; for they *are* lively, and are delivered ere the midwives come in unto them.

20 Therefore God dealt well with the midwives: and the people multiplied, and waxed very mighty.

21 And it came to pass, because the midwives feared God, that he made them houses.

19 "The Hebrew women are not like the Egyptian women," the midwives replied. "They are more vigorous and have their babies so quickly that we cannot get there in time."

20 So God was good to the midwives, and the Israelites continued to multiply, growing more and more powerful.

21 And because the midwives feared God, he gave them families of their own.

In Focus

Roger stormed out of the bedroom, slamming the door behind him. Lauren sat on the edge of the bed, trying hard not to cry. This was the third time they had fought this week, always with the same results. Ten months ago, Roger had been laid off by his employer. Gone was the comfortable salary he had earned and also most of the luxuries they had enjoyed in the five years they had been married. Roger had been certain that his company would call him back to work, so he had not looked for another job. They had depleted their savings in a few months. The bank had foreclosed on their large, beautiful home, and now they lived in a shabby studio apartment. Lauren had to leave school and worked as a cosmetics salesperson in a department store. Her salary was barely enough to pay the rent and put some food on the table.

Last week Roger's brother had told him about a new real estate opportunity. Lauren had read the paperwork and done some research on her own. The "opportunity" involved them buying up the notes of people whose homes were being foreclosed. Lauren had told Roger how much it had hurt to lose their home and how she just did not feel comfortable taking advantage of people who were undergoing financial difficulties.

Roger had insisted that it was just "business" and was a way for them to recover financially and live well again. No matter how she tried to reason with him, Roger just grew angrier. He accused her of not wanting him to be successful again. Roger would not listen to her when she tried to tell him she thought the venture was unscrupulous. "What's the matter?" Roger had demanded. "Everything we would be doing is legal!"

Sometimes we may be called on to do things that we know will hurt others and, thus, displease the Lord. These things may be popular, and they may even be legal, but if they are ungodly, we must fear God and be willing to honor our commitment to Him. The Hebrew midwives, in this lesson, were forced to choose between their fear of the powerful Pharaoh and their fear of and love for the one true God.

The People, Places, and Times

Midwives. In biblical times, the role of the midwife was multiple: (1) to assist a pregnant woman during her labor by advising and encouraging her through the process; (2) to announce to the mother that the child was alive and healthy, cut the umbilical cord, bathe the newborn child, rub the baby with salt and oil, and wrap the baby in cloth bands or clean rags; and (3) to present the newborn to the father (see Ezekiel 16:4). Although the midwife was often a female relative or neighbor who had given birth, midwifery required special skills and knowledge. Births were sometimes difficult, as in the case of Rachel's delivery of Benjamin (Genesis 35:18-19). In the case of twins, the midwife was responsible for reporting which child was born first, as in the case of Tamar's delivery of the twins, Pharez and Zarah (Genesis 38:28). As a result, it was a full-time and honored professional occupation for some women.

Source:

Packer, J. I., Merrill C. Tenney, and William White Jr., eds. *Illustrated Manners and Customs of the Bible.* Nashville: Thomas Nelson Publishers, 2003.

Background

Exodus begins with the recounting of the children of Jacob, the grandson of Abraham. Although the number of Jacob's immediate family members was relatively small, we can see that God had fulfilled

His promise to Abraham and blessed his seed to greatly multiply. We learn that Jacob's beloved son, Joseph, had been sold into slavery by his jealous brothers. Joseph, although originally a slave, had risen to be a man of great prominence in Egypt. Joseph's God-given ability to interpret dreams had saved Egypt from a horrific famine. During Joseph's lifetime, his brothers came to Egypt to escape the famine that was afflicting Canaan.

According to Scripture, when Joseph initially brought his family to be with him in Egypt, the reigning pharaoh was gracious. He ordered that Jacob and his sons be permitted to dwell "in the best of the land" (Genesis 47:6), and he also ordered Joseph to make his brothers "rulers" over the pharaoh's cattle. After Joseph's death, the arrangement was forgotten. A new pharaoh came to power, and the Hebrew people began to be seen as a threat. This led to the fulfillment of God's Word to Abraham: "Know of a surety that thy seed shall be a stranger in a land that is not theirs, and shall serve them; and they shall afflict them four hundred years" (Genesis 15:13). The book of Exodus opens with the Hebrews having been enslaved for those 400 years.

At-A-Glance

1. Pharaoh's Fear of God's People (Exodus 1:8–10)
2. Pharaoh's Plan to Afflict God's People (vv. 11–14)
3. Pharaoh's Plan to Destroy God's People (vv. 15–16)
4. God's Plan to Preserve His People (vv. 17–19)
5. God's Reward for Faithful Service (vv. 20–21)

In Depth

FEAR

1. Pharaoh's Fear of God's People (Exodus 1:8–10)

During Joseph's lifetime, his father and his brothers had enjoyed the hospitality and patronage of the ruling pharaoh. They had been allowed to live in fertile land located in Goshen, a city close to the border of Egypt and Canaan. Their descendants had multiplied for hundreds of years. While it appears that initially the Egyptians tolerated the descendants of Jacob, they were, nonetheless, resident aliens or strangers in a foreign land. Their culture was different; more importantly, unlike the Egyptians, the Hebrews recognized and worshiped the one true God. Their status had changed, and they no longer enjoyed the privileges given them under the pharaoh Joseph served. As the book of Exodus opens, we find that the number of the Hebrews has grown tremendously: "And the land was filled with them" (Exodus 1:7). In spite of their situation, we can see that God continued to honor the covenant promise He had made to Jacob: "And thy seed shall be as the dust of the earth, and thou shalt spread abroad to the west, and to the east, and to the north, and to the south" (from Genesis 28:14).

This tremendous increase in the Hebrew population was problematic to the new pharaoh. It would seem that the esteem the old pharaoh held for Joseph had been forgotten. This new pharaoh's concerns appear to have been twofold: (1) Goshen, the area occupied by Jacob's descendants, bordered an area of Canaan occupied by tribes that were hostile toward Egypt. This pharaoh feared that the Hebrews would align themselves with enemies of Egypt and become a security threat to Egypt; (2) He worried that the Hebrews might leave Egypt, deprive Egypt of a huge resident labor force, and negatively impact Egypt's economy. Both concerns were legitimate. During this period in Egypt's history, the nation was not only at the pinnacle of its military might but it was also undertaking a number of tremendous building projects, including the construction of great storage cities.

Both of the Egyptian pharaoh's concerns were driven by fear. Not only did this pharaoh not know Joseph but he did not know the one true God, and so he was unaware that the situation was totally under the design and control of God. Present-day Christians should find comfort in this confidence. We can live our lives and operate under faith and not fear. The only fear that should control our actions is the fear of God. We are cautioned: "Fear God, and keep His commandments: for this is the whole duty of man. For God shall bring every work into judgment, with every secret thing, whether it be good, or whether it be evil" (Ecclesiastes 12:13–14).

Duty of Man

2. Pharaoh's Plan to Afflict God's People (vv. 11–14)

Motivated by a fear of losing his power and perhaps even his kingdom to the numerical strength of the Hebrews, Pharaoh reasoned that the solution to his worry was to decrease the size of the Hebrew population. This, he thought, would keep them from becoming allied with Egypt's enemies and from leaving Egypt and depriving Egypt of a resident labor force. Pharaoh ordered that the Hebrews be placed into forced labor, or slavery. Let us recall that the original Hebrews (Jacob and his sons) had voluntarily come to Egypt and were, for a time, guests. Some 360 years had passed, and the descendants of Jacob and his sons had no doubt intermarried, had children, and begun to assimilate into the Egyptian culture. It is quite possible that the generation of Hebrews we encounter in the first chapter of Exodus had forgotten God's promise to Abraham and his descendants—that He would make them a great nation and provide them with a land of their own. If indeed these Hebrews now identified with Egypt, they were in for a rude awakening.

While all forms of slavery are repugnant, the slavery imposed by Pharaoh was marked by particular cruelty. The Children of Israel were not merely to be worked; many of them were worked to death. This "affliction" of the Hebrews was, no doubt, used by Pharaoh to intimidate and demoralize them, hence making them less threatening. While he enslaved and worked the Hebrews to exhaustion to keep them from leaving, he also benefited by using them as a labor resource.

The enslaved Hebrews were used by the Egyptians to construct public buildings. Verse 11 tells us that Hebrew slave labor was used to build Pithom and Raamses. These "treasure cities" were actually huge storage cities. That the Hebrews were made to "serve with rigour" (v. 13) implies that harsh measures were used on the Hebrews. This harshness was a sign of Pharaoh's fear.

Fear is a powerful and sometimes dangerous motivator. Here we see it at its worst. Fear drove Pharaoh to evil. It presents the same danger to us! Left unchecked, fear can drive us to wickedness. Through the blood of Jesus, each believer has been freed from the curse of fear. The choice is ours: a life of fear or freedom to fellowship with God through His Son, Christ Jesus.

Pharaoh probably thought his plan to enslave and oppress the Hebrews would be successful. He failed, however, to understand to whom the Hebrews belonged. His plan of destruction was in direct opposition to God's promise to His chosen people. Rather than the population of Israel being curtailed by Pharaoh's ruthlessness, the people of God reproduced rapidly and experienced phenomenal growth. Miraculously, "the more they afflicted them, the more they multiplied" (v. 12). How do we act and react during times of adversity? During these periods of emotional darkness, we must cling more closely to our faith in God to see us through. While He may not deliver us from our turmoil, He most certainly will remain with us and provide the necessary strength to endure any situation. Through Christ, adversity can make us stronger.

3. Pharaoh's Plan to Destroy God's People (vv. 15–16)

A considerable amount of time had gone by since Pharaoh had initiated the first stage of oppression. Frustrated by his utter failure to curtail the rapid growth of the Children of Israel, Pharaoh's concern escalated to near panic as he watched the Hebrew birth rate increase dramatically. Pharaoh now turned to the Hebrew midwives, two of whom are specifically mentioned here. That Shiphrah and Puah alone are mentioned may mean that they were the only two women directly addressed by Pharaoh. More likely, these two women were leaders of the Hebrew midwives.

Pharaoh's plan to use midwives points to the depth of his desperation. A midwife is someone who facilitates birth, who recognizes the signs of new life, and provides support and encouragement to women through the pain and struggle of giving birth. Shiphrah and Puah had, no doubt, been trained to reverence, facilitate, and celebrate life. Yet Pharaoh tried to use them as instruments of death. Shiphrah and Puah represent the privilege and the challenge that all Christians share. We are responsible to recognize and encourage the unique gift of life present in each person.

Pharaoh's demands to Shiphrah and Puah were appalling. His request that they kill the male babies as they delivered them is a horrific act of violence against the innocent. Pharaoh was seeking to have the midwives solve what he viewed as a national security risk: the continually rising Hebrew birth rate. The plan was monstrous to say the least!

4. God's Plan to Preserve His People (vv. 17–19)

In spite of Pharaoh's desperation, God was still in

control of the situation. We are told, "the midwives feared God, and did not as the king of Egypt commanded them" (Exodus 1:17). Because they feared God and understood the value of life, Shiphrah and Puah did not obey Pharaoh's edict that they murder the male newborns. What a remarkable act of courage! Certainly commands from Pharaoh were rarely questioned. These women were taking their lives in their hands by defying this powerful man. Their courage highlights the stark contrast between a person who fears God and one who fears other people. People who do not know God, regardless of their position in life, are understandably weak and filled with fear. Without the knowledge of God, people do not have the wisdom to see the blessings of doing what is right and are rarely able to see beyond their own selfish needs and desires. On the other hand, a man or woman who fears God should seek to do what is right. The most accurate measurement of our fear of the Lord is the consistency of our trust in God.

Shiphrah and Puah defied Pharaoh. They continued to deliver the Hebrew babies and allowed the male children to live. When an enraged Pharaoh questioned them about their disobedience, the women lied and told him that the Hebrew women were in such excellent physical condition that their babies were delivered before the midwives even arrived in their homes. This must have been especially galling to Pharaoh, who had gone to great lengths to physically tax or "afflict" the Hebrews through brutal treatment.

5. God's Reward for Faithful Service (vv. 20–21)

The midwives, Shiphrah and Puah, prioritized their commitments and chose to fear God rather than obey Pharaoh. They were rewarded for their faithfulness to the one true God. First, through their courage, God blessed the Hebrews. "Therefore God dealt well with the midwives: and the people multiplied, and waxed very mighty" (Exodus 1:20). Here we see that God acknowledged and honored a personal commitment made by the midwives with a national blessing. Our choices affect others! Prioritizing God in our lives is not merely a personal matter. Whether we are aware of it or not, our choice to honor God affects the lives of others. Many present-day Christians can witness to the transformative effects of a godly parent or grandparent in their lives. Additionally, because the midwives feared God, He "made them houses." An acceptable translation of this would be that God gave them families of their own. Shiphrah and Puah were instruments of God's plan to bless His people. God thwarted Pharaoh's plan to use their vocation as midwives for his evil purposes. These midwives were godly women who feared the God who made the very human life they were entrusted with. Because of their faithfulness, God blessed, protected, and multiplied them.

Search the Scriptures

1. Now there arose up a new ____ over Egypt, which knew not Joseph (Exodus 1:8).

2. Therefore they did set over them ____ to afflict them with their burdens (v. 11).

3. And the king of Egypt spake to the Hebrew ____, of which the name of the one *was* Shiphrah, and the name of the other Puah (v. 15).

4. But the midwives ____ God, and did not as the king of Egypt commanded them, but saved the men children alive (v. 17).

5. Therefore God dealt well with the midwives: and the people ____, and waxed very mighty (v. 20).

Discuss the Meaning

1. Do you see any similarities between the plight of the enslaved Children of Israel and that of present-day migrant workers, day laborers, and other similarly marginalized and exploited groups in our society? What, if any, is the role of the church in their deliverance?

2. Jesus once said that in their interaction with the world, His followers should be "wise as serpents, and harmless as doves" (Matthew 10:16). How do we see this played out in the actions of the Hebrew midwives? How does their desire to advance God's plan for God's people and their deception of Pharaoh exhibit both wisdom and innocence?

3. This lesson raises the issue of lying. Shiphrah and Puah did actually lie to Pharaoh. However, their lie revealed the deeper truth that life is sacred to God. Can you find other instances in the Bible where a lie is told so that a greater "truth" can be revealed? How should these examples inform our lives and our behavior?

Lesson in Our Society

Twenty-first century Christians have many commitments (work, school, home, church, etc.). As a result, we are often faced with moral choices. At our jobs, in our classrooms, in our homes, and sometimes in our churches, we find ourselves having to choose between doing what is right and doing what is wrong. Like Shiphrah and Puah, we are faced with two fears: (1) Will we choose to fear man and do what is asked of us or what everyone around us is doing? (2) Or will we be strong enough to risk the dissatisfaction of man and choose to honor our commitment to our God, and do what is pleasing to Him? Concerning our commitment to God, we are taught: "Let him be your fear, and let him be your dread. And he shall be for a sanctuary" (Isaiah 8:13–14).

Make It Happen

The account of Shiphrah and Puah's defiance of Pharaoh provides us with clear representation of what it means to understand the world and its commitments, and, yet, to have an unshakable commitment to following God's ways. During a time of crisis, their lives were characterized by their fear of God. Indeed, they are models of faith lived out in a real world. We say that we love the Lord with our whole hearts, but are we committed to following His truths in the world in which we now live? How strong is our commitment to the ways and the will of Jesus Christ? We may never be challenged to the degree these women were. Yet challenges occur for us every day. At work, during a staff meeting, we may have to decide what is the right thing to do when a coworker tells a racist or ethnic joke. This week, ask the Lord to provide you with an opportunity to demonstrate your commitment to Him. Be sure to share this opportunity with your class members next week.

Follow the Spirit

What God wants me to do:

Be faithful, obedient, steadfast, committed
prayerful, hear His voice

Remember Your Thoughts

Special insights I have learned:

____

____

More Light on the Text

Exodus 1:8–21

8 Now there arose up a new king over Egypt, which knew not Joseph.

When the new king, or Pharaoh, came into power over Egypt (Heb. *mitsrayim*, **mits-RAH-yim,** meaning both "the country at the northeastern section of Africa, adjacent to Palestine" and "the inhabitants or natives of Egypt"), he was not aware that God had preserved the Egyptians for Joseph's sake. As a matter of fact, this king did not know (Heb. *yada'*, **yaw-DAH,** meaning "to know, to perceive, to discern, to distinguish") God nor the mighty acts God had done on behalf of the Israelites.

9 And he said unto his people, Behold, the people of the children of Israel are more and mightier than we: 10 Come on, let us deal wisely with them; lest they multiply, and it come to pass, that, when there falleth out any war, they join also unto our enemies, and fight against us, and so get them up out of the land.

The Pharaoh, anxious over the likelihood of being overthrown, spoke this pro-war propaganda to his people (Heb. *'am*, **am,** meaning "nation, kindred"). A definite indicator that Pharaoh did not know the God of Israel (Heb. *Yisra'el*, **yis-raw-ALE,** meaning "God prevails") is found in his strategizing against a nation whose name and nature assured victory. Threatened by the procreative vitality of the Hebrews, Pharaoh sought to reduce their population by an evil and diabolical plot. This plan, in his reasoning, would prevent the Israelites from "joining" (Heb. *rab*, **rab,** meaning "more numerous, strong") the Canaanite army and turning against the Egyptians.

11 Therefore they did set over them taskmasters to afflict them with their burdens. And they built for Pharaoh treasure cities, Pithom and Raamses.

Because of God's favor upon the Israelites, even while in captivity the Egyptians' envy compelled them to make Israel their "slave" (Heb. *mac*, **mas,** meaning "forced service"). In addition to taking this entire race and nation of people into slavery, the Egyptians sought to break their spirits by being particularly brutal in their treatment of Israel. The work to which many of these new slaves, under this new king, was assigned was backbreaking labor to build "coffers" (Heb. *mickenah*, **mis-ken-AW**, mean-

"But the midwives feared God, and did not as the king of Egypt commanded them, but saved the men children alive" (Exodus 1:17). Pictured is Baby Moses' basket among the reeds.

ing "storage house") for the king in the two cities of Raamses and Pithom.

12 But the more they afflicted them, the more they multiplied and grew. And they were grieved because of the children of Israel. 13 And the Egyptians made the children of Israel to serve with rigour: 14 And they made their lives bitter with hard bondage, in morter, and in brick, and in all manner of service in the field: all their service, wherein they made them serve, was with rigour.

In spite of the severity of the Egyptians' oppression of the Israelites, they "grew" (Heb. *parats*, **paw-RATS**, meaning "to break through"). Instead of succumbing to the oppression, they broke through the census numbers, broke through production numbers, and broke through expected human limitations under such dire circumstances. This phenomenal show of God's favor and power "worried" (Heb. *quwts*, **koots**, meaning "to be grieved" or "to feel a sickening dread") the Egyptians. Their response was to magnify the grueling conditions under which the Israelites labored more severely (Heb. *perek*, **PEH-rek,** meaning "harshness, cruelty") as they made "brick[s]" (Heb. *lebenah*, **leb-ay-NAW,** meaning "tile" or "brick") and "morter" (Heb. *chomer*, **KHO-mer**, meaning "cement" or "clay").

15 And the king of Egypt spake to the Hebrew midwives, of which the name of the one was Shiphrah, and the name of the other Puah:

Fearing the seemingly unlimited strength of the Israelites to prosper and multiply physically in spite of extreme abuse, Pharaoh sought the assistance of the ones closest to the birth and delivery of Israelite children. Pharaoh called for two of the main "midwives" (Heb. *yalad*, **yaw-LAD,** meaning "to bear, bring forth, travail") to assist him with his plot to annihilate his perceived enemies, the Israelites. These two midwives were named Shiphrah (Heb. *Shiphrah*, **shif-RAW,** meaning "fair") and Puah (Heb. *Puw'ah*, **poo-AW,** meaning "splendid"). True to their

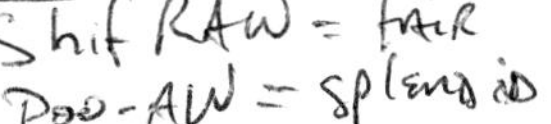

names, their qualities would soon be clearly demonstrated in their act of civil disobedience to Pharaoh and acts of committed obedience to God.

16 And he said, When ye do the office of a midwife to the Hebrew women, and see them upon the stools; if it be a son, then ye shall kill him: but if it be a daughter, then she shall live.

Pharaoh commanded the midwives that at the point of helping the Hebrew women give birth (Heb. *'oben,* **O-ben,** meaning "child-bearing stool" or "potter's wheel") they should kill all of the boys (Heb. *ben,* **bane,** meaning "son, male child") while allowing the girls (Heb. *bath,* **bath,** meaning "daughter, female child") to live. This act could have been committed with little fanfare had the midwives desired to commit genocide. They could have suffocated the babies as they emerged from the birth canal or drowned them in the river or basin of water into which newborns were immediately immersed upon delivery.

17 But the midwives feared God, and did not as the king of Egypt commanded them, but saved the men children alive.

Although such a notion would be abhorrent to anyone, the midwives were even more compelled to disobey Pharaoh because they feared (Heb. *yare',* **yaw-RAY,** meaning "to revere, to honor, to respect") God (Heb. *'elohiym,* **el-o-HEEM,** meaning "the true God")! This new Pharaoh might not have known God, but these midwives surely did! They made no attempt to carry out Pharaoh's plan. It is likely that this well-executed act of civil disobedience was accomplished in various ways, including training others and lay midwives to deliver the babies or having the midwives delay arriving until after the births were complete. Regardless of the strategy, this is an ideal example of pacifist resistance to social injustice.

18 And the king of Egypt called for the midwives, and said unto them, Why have ye done this thing, and have saved the men children alive? 19 And the midwives said unto Pharaoh, Because the Hebrew women are not as the Egyptian women; for they are lively, and are delivered ere the midwives come in unto them.

Infuriated, Pharaoh called for the midwives to come to him. Certain that the midwives acted against his orders—but lacking proof—Pharaoh accurately accused them of disobeying his order to kill all Hebrew newborn sons. For their defense, the midwives replied that the Hebrew women demonstrated unusual "strength" (Heb. *chayeh,* **khaw-YEH,** meaning "vigorous, lively") in childbirth and that the babies were already born by the time the midwives arrived.

20 Therefore God dealt well with the midwives: and the people multiplied, and waxed very mighty. 21 And it came to pass, because the midwives feared God, that he made them houses.

The midwives' actions continue to create a theological quandary for some who cannot reconcile their obedience to God and with their action of lying to Pharaoh. However, this quandary is resolved at the end of the story. The midwives' choice to honor God at the risk of being executed themselves brought forth God's blessings (Heb. *yatab,* **yaw-TAB,** meaning "to be good, pleasing, glad") upon them! Not only did the Israelites continue to prosper and multiply (Heb. *'atsam,* **aw-TSAM,** meaning "to be vast, be numerous, be mighty") in numbers in spite of their oppressive predicament but God specifically blessed the midwives with families (Heb. *bayith,* **BAH-yith,** meaning "house, family of descendants") of their own.

Source:

Packer, J. I., Merrill C. Tenney, and William White Jr., eds. *Illustrated Manners and Customs of the Bible.* Nashville: Thomas Nelson Publishers, 2003.

Daily Bible Readings

M: Honor Those Who Fear God
Psalm 15

T: Whom Shall I Fear?
Psalm 27:1–6

W: Fear No Evil
Psalm 23

T: Delivered from Fear
Psalm 34:4–14

F: The Friendship of the Lord
Psalm 25:12–21

S: Let All Fear the Lord
Psalm 33:8–18

S: Courage in the Face of Threat
Exodus 1:8–21

TEACHING TIPS

January 11
Bible Study Guide 6

1. Words You Should Know

A. Harlot (Joshua 2:1) *'ishshah zanah* (Heb.)—Denotes a prostitute.

B. Search out the Country (v. 2) *chaphar* (Heb.)—Implies covert surveillance or spying.

2. Teacher Preparation

Unifying Principle—Risking One's Life for Good. Commitments may create conflicting priorities, require risks, and exact a cost. How does one balance the value of the different sides of a commitment? Rahab willingly faced great personal danger in order to save her family.

A. Begin your preparation with prayer, asking God to prepare you for this teaching experience and help you to teach well.

B. Read and study the Daily Bible Readings and Focal Verses for today's lesson. Be sure to study your *Precepts For Living® Personal Study Guide* for further insights.

3. Starting the Lesson

A. Using a modern language Bible translation, read Joshua 1–2. Write questions as they come to you as a result of your reading.

B. Read the Scriptures for the Devotional Reading and the In Depth sections of this Bible Study Guide.

C. Answer the Discuss the Meaning questions so you will be prepared to engage your students during the class session.

D. For further insights and discussion, read the More Light on the Text section.

4. Getting into the Lesson

A. Ask a student to begin the class with a prayer.

B. Read the AIM for Change.

C. Have the class read the Keep in Mind verse in unison.

D. Write "Commitments" and "Priorities" on a chalkboard or dry erase board. Then ask the students to give you a list of the various commitments and the numerous priorities they face each day. Encourage them to point out situations when the commitments and the priorities are in conflict. Allow the discussion to continue for about 10 minutes.

E. Ask volunteers to read the Focal Verses.

5. Relating the Lesson to Life

A. Ask a volunteer to read the Lesson in Our Society section. Discuss.

B. Divide the class into groups, and assign a Discuss the Meaning question to each group.

C. Allow time for each group to share their answers with the entire class.

JAN 11th

6. Arousing Action

A. Discuss the Lesson in Our Society section, allowing the students to insert their testimonies.

B. Challenge the students to commit to the Make It Happen exercise.

C. Remind the class to read the Daily Bible Readings in preparation for next week's lesson. Also suggest that they complete lesson 6 in the *Precepts For Living® Personal Study Guide* as well.

Worship Guide

For the Superintendent or Teacher
Theme: Rahab Helps Israel
Theme Song: "If You Can Use Me, Lord"
Devotional Reading: Hebrews 11:23–31
Prayer

RAHAB HELPS ISRAEL

Bible Background • JOSHUA 2; 6:22–25
Printed Text • JOSHUA 2:1–4, 12–14; 6:22–25 Devotional Reading • HEBREWS 11:23–31

AIM for Change

By the end of the lesson, we will:
TELL about Rahab's commitment to saving her family;
CONSIDER the possible risks and costs of making a commitment; and
WEIGH thoughtfully the demands of our own commitments and the need to make appropriate changes.

Keep in Mind

"The LORD your God, he is God in heaven above, and in earth beneath. Now therefore, I pray you, swear unto me by the LORD, since I have shewed you kindness, that ye will also shew kindness unto my father's house" (from Joshua 2:11–12).

Focal Verses

KJV **Joshua 2:1** And Joshua the son of Nun sent out of Shittim two men to spy secretly, saying, Go view the land, even Jericho. And they went, and came into an harlot's house, named Rahab, and lodged there.

2 And it was told the king of Jericho, saying, Behold, there came men in hither to night of the children of Israel to search out the country.

3 And the king of Jericho sent unto Rahab, saying, Bring forth the men that are come to thee, which are entered into thine house: for they be come to search out all the country.

4 And the woman took the two men, and hid them, and said thus, There came men unto me, but I wist not whence they were:

2:12 Now therefore, I pray you, swear unto me by the LORD, since I have shewed you kindness, that ye will also shew kindness unto my father's house, and give me a true token:

13 And that ye will save alive my father, and my mother, and my brethren, and my sisters, and all that they have, and deliver our lives from death.

14 And the men answered her, Our life for yours, if ye utter not this our business. And it shall be, when the LORD hath given us the land, that we will deal kindly and truly with thee.

6:22 But Joshua had said unto the two men that had spied out the country, Go into the harlot's house, and bring out thence the woman, and all that she hath, as ye sware unto her.

23 And the young men that were spies went in, and brought out Rahab, and her father, and her mother, and her brethren, and all that she had; and

NLT **Joshua 2:1** Then Joshua secretly sent out two spies from the Israelite camp at Acacia Grove. He instructed them, "Scout out the land on the other side of the Jordan River, especially around Jericho." So the two men set out and came to the house of a prostitute named Rahab and stayed there that night.

2 But someone told the king of Jericho, "Some Israelites have come here tonight to spy out the land."

3 So the king of Jericho sent orders to Rahab: "Bring out the men who have come into your house, for they have come here to spy out the whole land."

4 Rahab had hidden the two men, but she replied, "Yes, the men were here earlier, but I didn't know where they were from.

2:12 "Now swear to me by the LORD that you will be kind to me and my family since I have helped you. Give me some guarantee that

13 when Jericho is conquered, you will let me live, along with my father and mother, my brothers and sisters, and all their families."

14 "We offer our own lives as a guarantee for your safety," the men agreed. "If you don't betray us, we will keep our promise and be kind to you when the LORD gives us the land."

6:22 Meanwhile, Joshua said to the two spies, "Keep your promise. Go to the prostitute's house and bring her out, along with all her family."

23 The men who had been spies went in and brought out Rahab, her father, mother, brothers, and all the other relatives who were with her. They moved her whole family to a safe place near the camp of Israel.

they brought out all her kindred, and left them without the camp of Israel.

24 And they burnt the city with fire, and all that was therein: only the silver, and the gold, and the vessels of brass and of iron, they put into the treasury of the house of the LORD.

25 And Joshua saved Rahab the harlot alive, and her father's household, and all that she had; and she dwelleth in Israel even unto this day; because she hid the messengers, which Joshua sent to spy out Jericho.

24 Then the Israelites burned the town and everything in it. Only the things made from silver, gold, bronze, or iron were kept for the treasury of the LORD's house.

25 So Joshua spared Rahab the prostitute and her relatives who were with her in the house, because she had hidden the spies Joshua sent to Jericho. And she lives among the Israelites to this day.

In Focus

Kim looked at her family members seated around the table. Kristine, her oldest child, was scowling and biting her fingernails. Bereana, Kim's other daughter, sat next to Joseph, Kim's husband. Her head was bent over, and she was doodling on a tablet of paper. Joseph cleared his throat and began talking. Joseph explained that his company was experiencing some serious financial setbacks. They were downsizing, and a number of his coworkers had been laid off. Joseph told them that his hours had been cut and that he was now on a part-time schedule. Bereana looked up and asked Joseph if this meant they were going to be homeless. He put his arms around his young daughter and hugged her.

"No," he told them. "Mommy's salary can cover the mortgage but not much more than that. We're going to have to do some serious budgeting, and there may be some things we can't do for a while."

Kristine looked at her dad and asked, "Does this mean I won't be able to start college in the fall?"

Joseph opened his mouth to answer. Then he just as quickly closed it and looked down. Kim could see that her husband was struggling. They had discussed this most of last night. There was no way that they would be able to pay Kristine's tuition with the amount of money they had to work with now.

Kim spoke up. "Daddy and I have talked about this, and I might have a solution. I spoke with my manager last night, and they need a store manager in the new Glenview Mall store. It just opened last month, and they've had some serious turnover, so my experience would be helpful to them." She hesitated and looked at Joseph. "The only problem is that I'd have to work on Sundays until I manage to get that store profitable.

Kim is facing a serious commitment challenge. As a wife and a mother, she wants to do what she thinks is best for her family by providing for them as best she can. She also has commitments to her church and a commitment to honor the Word of God, so she wants to do what is right. In this lesson, a Canaanite woman is faced with a similar challenge and must make a decision to do what is best for her and her family. Rahab's challenge means the difference between life and death. We must remember that the choices we make today, tomorrow, next week, and next year impact our future as well.

The People, Places, and Times

Jericho. The name means the "City of Palms." Jericho is located west of the Jordan River, north of the Dead Sea, and lies about 800 feet below sea level. After 40 years of wandering through the desert, Moses climbed to the top of Mount Nebo and viewed the Promised Land of Canaan, including the city of Jericho. Jericho was the first Canaanite city to be conquered by the Children of Israel. Under the leadership of Joshua, the city was sacked and burned. During the division of lands between the tribes of Israel, Jericho was allocated to the tribe of Benjamin. The city remained in ruins for about 500 years, until the reign of King Ahab. Then the town was rebuilt. When the Lord took the prophet Elijah away in a windstorm, the prophet Elisha remained in Jericho and healed the city's water supply. In the New Testament, Jericho continued to be featured. When Jesus told the parable of the Good Samaritan, he referred to the road between Jerusalem and Jericho. It was the site of the restoration of blind Bartimaeus' sight and Zacchaeus' conversion.

Source:

Alexander, David and Pat Alexander, eds. *Eerdmans' Handbook to the Bible.* Grand Rapids, Mich.: Wm. B. Eerdmans Publishing Company, 1973.

Background

The book of Joshua is action-packed. Whereas Exodus provides us with a narrative of the Children of Israel being redeemed *out* of Egyptian slavery, the book of Joshua presents their redemption *into* the land promised to them by God. The book opens with God, Himself, appointing a successor to Moses. His personal choice is Joshua, son of Nun.

Joshua was born in Egypt and was a descendant of Joseph. Joshua's original name was Hosea, which means "salvation." Moses changed his name to Joshua, which means "the Lord is salvation." The name change is fitting when we remember that it is not Moses or Joshua but only the Lord who can and does save His people.

When the Children of Israel left Egypt, Joshua was about 40 years old. At that time, he was a personal aide to Moses. His service to Moses included service in the army. Shortly after God provided for Israel's miraculous delivery at the Red Sea, the army of the Amalekites attacked the Israelites. Here we read that Moses appointed Joshua to lead the Israelite army, and we read "And Joshua discomfited Amalek and his people with the edge of the sword" (Exodus 17:13).

Moses' confidence in Joshua was confirmed when he selected representatives or "rulers" of each of the 12 tribes to cross over the Jordan and go into Canaan to see if the Promised Land was habitable. Ten of the twelve spies were disheartened and brought back reports that Israel could not conquer the powerful inhabitants of the land. Only Joshua, representing the tribe of Ephraim, and Caleb, representing the tribe of Judah, brought Moses reports that expressed their unwavering confidence in God's promise that Israel could indeed occupy Canaan. It is interesting to note that Joshua and Caleb's faithfulness was rewarded. These two men would be the only two Egyptian-born Israelites allowed to move into Canaan.

We pick up the story some 40 years later. Joshua was about 80 years old. He and the Children of Israel were camped in the hills of Moab, just across the river from Canaan. God commanded him to "go

over this Jordan, thou, and all this people, unto the land which I do give to them, even to the children of Israel" (Joshua 1:2). Here we see God reaffirming His promise to His chosen people to provide them with a land of their own. Although God was giving the land to Israel, the book of Joshua makes it clear that Israel had to take possession of the land, which is already occupied. Joshua and the Children of Israel had witnessed God delivering them from Egyptian bondage. It was up to them to trust Him to lead them into the land He had promised them.

The key to Israel gaining possession of the Promised Land lay in God's continual encouragement to their new leader, Joshua, to "Be strong and of a good courage; be not afraid, neither be thou dismayed: for the LORD thy God is with thee whithersoever thou goest" (Joshua 1:9). Present-day Christians should take great comfort in these words. God's promise to Joshua is ours. We, too, can be strong because we have blessed assurance that whatever battles we face, God is with us, and through faith in Him, we can take possession of the spiritual blessings He has promised to us.

Source:

Life Application Study Bible (New Living Translation). Wheaton, Ill.: Tyndale House Publishers, Inc., 1996.

At-A-Glance

1. Rahab Encounters the Israelite Spies (Joshua 2:1)
2. Rahab Defies the King of Jericho (vv. 2–4)
3. Rahab Covenants with the Israelite Spies (2:12–14)
4. Rahab Is Saved by the Israelite Spies (6:22–25)

In Depth

1. Rahab Encounters the Israelite Spies (Joshua 2:1)

Joshua had become the God-selected leader of the Children of Israel. Moses, the man God used to bring them out of Egypt, was dead. Joshua and the Israelites were encamped in the hills of Moab and were looking across the Jordan River and into the land that God had promised to His people. Before they could occupy the land, they had to deal with the inhabitants of the city. Jericho, 8.25 acres in size, is strategically located in the fertile plains of the Jordan valley. This Canaanite city was the strongest of the fortified cities in Canaan. In spite of the daunting task that lay before him, Joshua's mission was clear. The Canaanite inhabitants of Jericho were among the people that God had ordered Moses to "utterly destroy" (Deuteronomy 20:17). The city and all of its inhabitants had to be destroyed.

The text tells us that Joshua sent two spies into Jericho. It is interesting to note that Joshua did not seek the counsel of anyone in the Israelite camp; he did this secretly. Joshua's reason for keeping this reconnaissance mission a secret is not disclosed by the text; however, Joshua's own past may offer us a clue. We should remember that years earlier, Moses had sent 12 spies into Egypt to see if the land was habitable. Only two of the twelve spies brought back favorable reports; Joshua had been one of these two spies. Perhaps Joshua did not ask for advice because he did not want to risk the people becoming disheartened by hearing unfavorable reports. To Joshua, there could be no turning back. God had promised them this land, and he knew that they must take possession of it, regardless of how bad the situation appeared. More importantly, God had promised Joshua that "there shall not any man be able to stand before thee all the days of thy life: as I was with Moses, so I will be with thee: I will not fail thee, nor forsake thee" (Joshua 1:5). What a joy to know that this same promise is extended to all believers—the Lord will never fail us!

Often we are faced with the tension that arises when we try to decide how to prioritize our commitments in our home and work lives with our church ministries. We must balance them, and the only way we can accomplish this is to seek the Lord's guidance. He has promised He will be with us.

The two spies probably blended with the busy pedestrians outside the city walls during the day to avoid detection. They could not help but be impressed by the fortifications of Jericho. The city's 20-foot-high mud walls must have seemed daunting. Additionally, from inside the city, the spies could also see that Jericho was actually surrounded by two walls with a wide gap between them. If an enemy succeeded in scaling the first wall, they would be trapped and become an easy target for the Jericho defenders. It must have been clear to the two spies that they would indeed need divine intervention to breach these fortifications. Still, the spies' primary job was to take mental notes of the city's layout and fortifications. Instantly they realized that these impressive man-made barriers would never be breached or destroyed unless God miraculously intervened for the Israelites.

At various intervals around the walls of the city, houses were built over the gaps between the two sets of walls. One of these houses was an inn and the home of Rahab, a prostitute, living in the city. It is in this inn that the spies decide to "lodge," or spend the night.

2. Rahab Defies the King of Jericho (vv. 2–4)

The spies' decision to lodge or stay at the inn of a prostitute, while initially puzzling, was actually a smart choice for men trying to blend in and remain anonymous in a strange city. Because of her occupation, their presence would draw minimal attention, as it would not have been unusual to see men entering and leaving her establishment. Additionally, an inn would have an array of guests at any given time. Within the walls of the inn, the spies could listen closely and possibly attain useful information from the conversations of the other guests. The presence of the two spies did not, however, go unnoticed. We are told that word of their presence at the home of Rahab got back to the king of Jericho, and he dispatched solders to her inn. The king of Jericho had identified the two men as spies, and his soldiers demanded that Rahab turn them over for arrest.

Rahab was faced with a momentous choice. She was being asked to honor her commitment as a citizen of Jericho and to obey the local authority (the king). What tremendous pressure she must have felt! The city of Jericho was on a wartime alert. Joshua and his people, including an army, were poised on the opposite banks of the Jordan River. Most certainly, their movements were known to the king of Jericho. The patriotic thing for Rahab to do was to comply with the orders of the king. The two Israelite men in her inn had been identified as enemies. Rahab chose to disobey the king. In fact, she hid the two spies and then lied to the soldiers and sent them on a wild goose chase.

God often places us in positions where we have to make decisions that call upon us to prioritize our commitments. Sometimes, like Rahab, we may be called on to make these choices quickly or under pressure. We must always remember that while God demands that we make judgments, He does not demand that our judgments be perfect in every situation. What God wants from us is not our perfection but our complete trust in Him. Our choices should be guided not by fear but by our faith in Him and in His Word.

After the soldiers left her inn, Rahab went up on

the roof, where she had hidden the spies under some drying flax. It is here we learn the reason she risked her life. Rahab told the spies that she had heard about the power of their God. She referred to the Red Sea miracle—an event that occurred more than 40 years before—as evidence of her faith in their God. Additionally, Rahab went on to tell the men that she knew about Israel's more recent military defeat of the Amorite armies of the kings: Sihon and Og. From these two events, Rahab acknowledged that "the LORD your God, he is God in heaven above, and in earth beneath" (Joshua 2:11). This confession of faith in the one true God is all the more remarkable when we remember that it was coming from a Canaanite prostitute. Rahab not only identified God by name but she provided the two spies with a critical piece of information when she told them "all the inhabitants of the land faint because of you" (Joshua 2:9). When the gates of the city were locked, Rahab's assessment of the fears of the inhabitants of Jericho was confirmed by the reaction of the king.

Here we see Rahab's commitment as a citizen of Jericho, as a Canaanite, being abandoned in the face of her understanding that the true God is on the side of these Israelites. Because she had heard of what God did for the Israelites, she came to believe that He was the one true God. It is not enough that we know that Jesus Christ is the Son of God. It is not even enough that we know about Jesus dying on the Cross for our sins. Our salvation lies in our acknowledgment, our committed belief in Him as our personal Saviour. As mature Christians, we must trust God to meet our needs, while serving others. Certainly, we want our spouses, our children, and our parents to know they are vitally important to us and that we love them. But they are not the center of our universe; that position is reserved for God alone! God requires that we be committed to Him first.

3. Rahab Covenants with the Israelite Spies (2:12–14)

Rahab had heard of the mighty deeds of God and was willing to leave her Canaanite home in Jericho, abandon pagan worship, and take all of her relatives with her. Thus far, she had treated the spies honorably, and she asked that Israel treat her honorably by saving her and her family from the destruction that she was certain was coming on the city of Jericho, under the hand of Almighty God and the fighting men of Israel.

It is telling that Rahab asked that the spies "swear unto me by the LORD" God of Israel and not by the gods she had served all her life (Joshua 2:12). Her desperation is obvious, and we are reminded of Jacob's desperation when he wrestled with the stranger and insisted that he would not let the stranger go until he blessed him (Genesis 32:24–26). Like Jacob, Rahab would not let the two spies go unless they blessed her and her entire family. Her commitments were undergoing a radical change. Her salvation, she understood, did not lie in the power of the king of Jericho, not in the strength of the walls of the city, and not even in the might of the army of Jericho. Rahab's commitment to and her confidence was now in the God she had heard could dry up the Red Sea. Only He could save her and her family.

Rahab insisted that the soldiers give her a "true token." This indicated the strength of her belief that the Lord God of Israel could be trusted to do whatever He promised to do.

4. Rahab Is Saved by the Israelite Spies (6:22–25)

Rahab's inn was one of the dwellings built in the city wall, so during the night, she was able to lower the spies down out of her window, using a dyed red rope. The spies told her to leave the scarlet cord dangling from the window. This would allow the Israelite army to clearly identify this particular house and to spare the lives of this household. The use of the red cord mirrors the red blood of the Passover lamb, which was smeared on the doorposts of the Israelite homes, on the night the Israelites left the bondage of Egypt. During the tenth plague, the angel of death, upon seeing the red blood, passed over and spared the lives of the people dwelling inside those crimson-marked homes (Exodus 12:7–13).

After the two spies escaped, they returned and informed Joshua what they had found out. They told Joshua, "Truly the LORD hath delivered into our hands all the land; for even all the inhabitants of the country do faint because of us" (Joshua 2:24). It is clear that the spies had been moved by the confession of the Canaanite harlot, Rahab. Her confidence in their God seemed to bolster their confidence in His promise that they could destroy this heavily fortified city.

Following the instructions of the Lord, the walls of Jericho did indeed fall on the seventh day. The two spies honored their oath, and the lives of Rahab and her entire family were spared. The entire city was destroyed; everyone except Rahab and her family was killed. Rahab, because of her commitment to the Lord God of Israel, found favor in His eyes. Paul reminds us in Hebrews that "By faith the harlot Rahab perished not with them that believed not, when she had received the spies with peace" (Hebrews 11:31).

God's Word provides us with the necessary guidelines to mentally equip us to make the choices that are pleasing to Him. Our utter trust and dependence on Jesus will feed all areas of our lives and help us maintain the balance needed to honor our commitments to God, our family, work, and church ministries.

In addition to saving her family, God blessed Rahab by allowing for her complete adoption into the nation of Israel, including the right to marry an Israelite. This placed her in the genealogical line that led to the birth of Israel's greatest king, David, and—more importantly—to the birth of Jesus, the Christ.

Search the Scriptures

1. "And Joshua the son of ________ sent out of Shittim two men to spy secretly" (Joshua 2:1).

2. "And it was told the king of ________, saying, Behold, there came men in hither to night of the children of Israel to search out the country" (v. 2).

3. "And the woman took the ________ men, and hid them, and said thus, There came men unto me, but I wist not whence they were" (v. 4).

4. "Now therefore, I pray you, ________ unto me by the LORD, since I have shewed you kindness, that ye will also shew kindness unto my father's house, and give me a true token" (v. 12).

Discuss the Meaning

1. At first glance it might appear that the use of a prostitute to aid Israel seems like a strange choice. How important is Rahab's occupation to our understanding of this biblical narrative? Does the fact that she is a prostitute make the account more or less remarkable? Why do you think this?

2. In last week's lesson, the Hebrew midwives were an integral part of the salvation plan for Israel. Again this week, a woman, Rahab, is featured. What does this tell us about the role of women in God's plan?

3. When she first encountered the Israelite spies, Rahab told them that she had heard about how the Lord had been on Israel's side. Although Rahab was a Canaanite, she was familiar with the Lord's role in Israel's journey to the Promised Land. Compare this to people of today who "know" about the Lord, yet are not saved. What are the similarities? What are the differences? What is the role of the Christian in the lives of those who "know" Jesus but have not come to accept Him as their personal Saviour? How might we best witness to them?

Lesson in Our Society

Each of us has multiple commitments in our lives. We have commitments to people (spouses, children, friends, and parents), our jobs, our churches, and social and civic organizations. Our commitments are usually made on the basis of our beliefs about ourselves, about our community, our family, and about the world in which we live. Many of the commitment choices we have made in our past have brought us to where we are today. Many of us struggle in marriages because we chose a partner based on impulse, rather than seeking God's guidance. Our decision to become "friends" with our children, rather than parent and nurture them, often results in tormented days and sleepless nights. Our youthful decisions to drift through school, instead of studying and applying ourselves, may have resulted in low-paying jobs as adults. The choices we make today, tomorrow, next week, or next year impact our future. Some of those choices will be split-second decisions. They will come out of our commitments about who we believe we are and what we believe about ourselves and our God. These decisions will determine the actions we take. The strength of our commitment to God impacts the decisions we may be called to make. The only way we can properly make the decisions that will be pleasing to our God is to be armed with the truth from God's own Word.

Make It Happen

1. What are the various commitments in your life? Don't place them in order; just list them.

2. Prioritize those commitments. Place the most important commitment at the top and the least important at the bottom.

3. Set aside five minutes each night to pray and ask God about the wisdom of the commitments you have listed.

4. Come to class on Sunday prepared to share whether or not you were directed to make changes to those commitments.

Follow the Spirit

What God wants me to do:

Remember Your Thoughts

Special insights I have learned:

More Light on the Text

Joshua 2:1–4, 12–14; 6:22–25

1 And Joshua the son of Nun sent out of Shittim two men to spy secretly, saying, Go view the land, even Jericho. And they went, and came into an harlot's house, named Rahab, and lodged there.

After Moses' death, "Joshua" (Heb. *Yehowshuwa'* **yeh-ho-SHOO-ah,** meaning "Jehovah is salvation") received instruction from God to cross the Jordan River and to possess the land of Jericho. Instead of gathering up the people and moving posthaste, Joshua sent two men to spy on the land and its inhabitants. Not willing to proceed only on the Word of God, Joshua sent the spies to "view" (Heb. *ra'ah,* **raw-AW,** meaning "to see, perceive, consider") what awaited them in Jericho. After working the day, the two men sought accommodations at the house of "Rahab" (Heb. *Rachab,* **raw-KHAWB,** meaning "wide"), a woman whose reputation was that of one known to be a "harlot" (Heb. *zanah,* **zaw-NAW,** meaning "to commit fornication, to commit adultery"). Some biblical scholars conclude that it is least likely that Rahab herself was a prostitute. Rather, since she was in a position to make decisions about the fate of her family, she was thought to be a brothel madam, an entrepreneur, and head of her household.

2 And it was told the king of Jericho, saying, Behold, there came men in hither to night of the children of Israel to search out the country. 3 And the king of Jericho sent unto Rahab, saying, Bring forth the men that are come to thee, which are entered into thine house: for they be come to search out all the country.

There must have been obvious cultural clues that the two spies were not local fellows. Word got back to the king of Jericho that they had come to "spy" (Heb. *chaphar,* **khaw-FAR,** meaning "to search out, explore") on the land. With that knowledge and fearing the spies were for military purpose, the king commanded that Rahab turn the men—last seen going into her home—over to him.

4 And the woman took the two men, and hid them, and said thus, There came men unto me, but I wist not whence they were:

Wisdom, and perhaps some good old-fashioned gut feeling, led Rahab to become the men's ally. Refusing to turn them in, she "hid" (Heb. *tsaphan,* **tsaw-faN,** meaning "to hide from discovery") the two spies and feigned that she did not know, or "wist" (Heb. *yada',* **yaw-DAH,** meaning "to recognize, confess"), where they were from.

2:12 Now therefore, I pray you, swear unto me by the LORD, since I have shewed you kindness, that ye will also shew kindness unto my father's house, and give me a true token: 13 And that ye will save alive my father, and my mother, and my brethren, and my sisters, and all that they have, and deliver our lives from death.

When the imminent threat of danger passed, Rahab, being a businesswoman and also being aware of what the one true God had done in vanquishing the enemies of Israel, negotiated an oath ("swear," Heb. *shaba',* **shaw-BAH,** meaning "to swear") upon the reputation of God with the two men. She asked that they would help her and her family, since she had helped them. Believing the spies that Jericho would indeed be conquered, she compelled them to show "kindness" (Heb. *checed,* **KHEH-sed,** meaning "goodness, kindness") enough to remember her kindness and to leave her with some guarantee, or "token" (Heb. *'owth,* **oth,** meaning "distinguishing mark"), that she and her family would be saved. Rahab spread her request for salvation broadly to her father, her mother, her brothers, her sisters, and all relatives. With this act, Rahab demonstrated that she was indeed the head of the household and acting matriarch of the family.

14 And the men answered her, Our life for yours, if ye utter not this our business. And it shall be, when the LORD hath given us the land, that we will deal kindly and truly with thee.

The two spies sealed the deal with their very own

lives ("life," Heb. *nephesh,* **NEH-fesh,** meaning "soul, self, life"). Holding Rahab fast to her commitment not to betray them, they vowed to keep their promise to save her and her household.

6:22 But Joshua had said unto the two men that had spied out the country, Go into the harlot's house, and bring out thence the woman, and all that she hath, as ye sware unto her. 23 And the young men that were spies went in, and brought out Rahab, and her father, and her mother, and her brethren, and all that she had; and they brought out all her kindred, and left them without the camp of Israel.

When the Iraelites won Jericho—as God had promised—Joshua commanded that the two spies keep their promise to Rahab to deliver ("brought out," Heb. *yatsa',* **yaw-TSAW,** meaning "to bring out, to lead out") her and her family to safety. Although Rahab and her family were saved from the destruction of Jericho, they were still kept outside of full fellowship with the Israelites. They were established near Israel's camp instead of within Israel's boundaries. According to Jewish laws, all strangers had to be purged before fully assimilating.

24 And they burnt the city with fire, and all that was therein: only the silver, and the gold, and the vessels of brass and of iron, they put into the treasury of the house of the LORD.

Conquest of Jericho included burning ("burnt," Heb. *saraph,* **saw-RAF,** meaning "to burn") every structure and item in it. The only things of value that were spared were items of value to be set apart for use in the Lord's "treasury" (Heb. *'owtsar,* **o-TSAW,** meaning "treasure, storehouse"). These items were: silver coins, gold, copper, and ironworks.

25 And Joshua saved Rahab the harlot alive, and her father's household, and all that she had; and she dwelleth in Israel even unto this day; because she hid the messengers, which Joshua sent to spy out Jericho.

Because Rahab believed the power and promises of God through the spies, even though she was not a Jew, she was saved, lived among the Israelites, and lived on in the lineage of Jewish royalty as part of the genealogy of the Messiah. One should note here that the words "saved" and "alive" are the same word (Heb. *chayah,* **khaw-YAW,** meaning "to live, remain alive, live prosperously"), thereby meaning that God just doesn't simply save our lives but that God saves us that we might live out that salvation with prosperity, good success, and peace.

Sources:

Life Application Study Bible (New International Version). Wheaton: Tyndale House Publishers, 1991.

Packer, J. I., Merrill C. Tenney, and William White. *Nelson's Illustrated Encyclopedia of Bible Facts.* Nashville: Thomas Nelson Publishers, 1995.

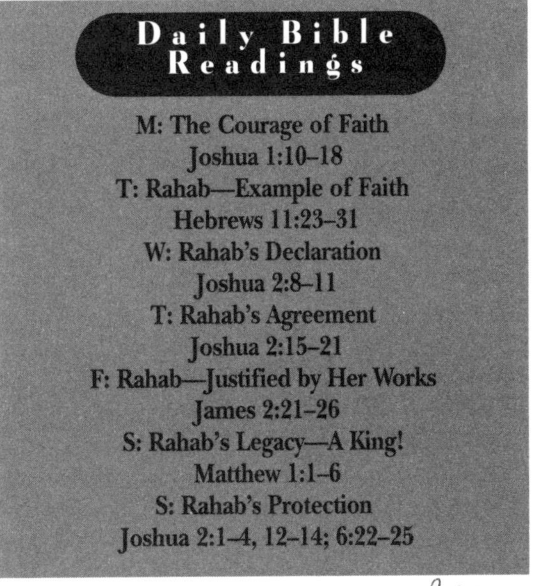

Daily Bible Readings

M: The Courage of Faith
Joshua 1:10–18
T: Rahab—Example of Faith
Hebrews 11:23–31
W: Rahab's Declaration
Joshua 2:8–11
T: Rahab's Agreement
Joshua 2:15–21
F: Rahab—Justified by Her Works
James 2:21–26
S: Rahab's Legacy—A King!
Matthew 1:1–6
S: Rahab's Protection
Joshua 2:1–4, 12–14; 6:22–25

NOTES

TEACHING TIPS

January 18
Bible Study Guide 7

1. Words You Should Know

A. Passed over (Joshua 3:1) *'abar* (Heb.)—Means to traverse, march over, or to go across.

B. Host (v. 2) *machaneh* (Heb.)—An army encampment.

C. Cubits (v. 4) *'ammah* (Heb.)—A unit of measurement 18 inches.

2. Teacher Preparation

Unifying Principle—Leadership Requires Resources. Sometimes people make commitments without assurance that resources to fulfill them are available. From where do the resources come for fulfilling commitments? Joshua committed himself to becoming a leader of the Israelites and received power from God to meet this commitment.

A. Pray for the students in your class.

B. Review the Bible Study Guide to prepare for this lesson. Use the information contained on the *Precepts For Living® Personal Study Guide* and CD-ROM.

C. Using a flip chart or dry erase board, prepare a chart with the heading "Qualifications for Godly Leadership."

3. Starting the Lesson

A. Ask a volunteer to lead the class in prayer.

B. Read the AIM for Change.

C. Have volunteers read the Focal Verses.

D. Ask a volunteer to read the In Focus story.

E. Using the chart you prepared earlier, ask the students to list the various qualifications they think are necessary for Christian leaders. Allow them time to discuss the list and to make changes to it if necessary.

4. Getting into the Lesson

A. Have the students review the Words You Should Know.

B. Ask for a volunteer to read The People, Places, and Times section.

C. Follow the At-A-Glance outline and the Search the Scriptures questions to discuss the Focal Verses.

5. Relating the Lesson to Life

A. Ask the students to talk about how they think the situation in the In Focus story can best be resolved in a way that honors God and provides for the needs of the church.

B. Ask for a volunteer to read the Lesson in Our Society section.

6. Arousing Action

A. Encourage the students to complete the Make It Happen section.

B. Ask for a volunteer to pray for your church's leaders.

C. Ask for a volunteer to pray for our nation's leaders.

Worship Guide

For the Superintendent or Teacher
Theme: Joshua Leads Israel
Theme Song: "I'll Go with Him All the Way"
Devotional Reading: Psalm 142
Prayer

JOSHUA LEADS ISRAEL

Bible Background • JOSHUA 3
Printed Text • JOSHUA 3:1–13 Devotional Reading • PSALM 142

AIM for Change

By the end of the lesson, we will:
REVIEW Joshua's commitment to God;
IDENTIFY areas of responsibility and the resources necessary for making and keeping commitments; and
UTILIZE those resources for making and fulfilling our commitments to God and others.

Keep in Mind

"And the LORD said unto Joshua, This day will I begin to magnify thee in the sight of all Israel, that they may know that, as I was with Moses, so I will be with thee" (Joshua 3:7).

Focal Verses

KJV **Joshua 3:1** And Joshua rose early in the morning; and they removed from Shittim, and came to Jordan, he and all the children of Israel, and lodged there before they passed over.

2 And it came to pass after three days, that the officers went through the host;

3 And they commanded the people, saying, When ye see the ark of the covenant of the LORD your God, and the priests the Levites bearing it, then ye shall remove from your place, and go after it.

4 Yet there shall be a space between you and it, about two thousand cubits by measure: come not near unto it, that ye may know the way by which ye must go: for ye have not passed this way heretofore.

5 And Joshua said unto the people, Sanctify yourselves: for tomorrow the LORD will do wonders among you.

6 And Joshua spake unto the priests, saying, Take up the ark of the covenant, and pass over before the people. And they took up the ark of the covenant, and went before the people.

7 And the LORD said unto Joshua, This day will I begin to magnify thee in the sight of all Israel, that they may know that, as I was with Moses, so I will be with thee.

8 And thou shalt command the priests that bear the ark of the covenant, saying, When ye are come to the brink of the water of Jordan, ye shall stand still in Jordan.

9 And Joshua said unto the children of Israel, Come hither, and hear the words of the LORD your God.

10 And Joshua said, Hereby ye shall know that

NLT **Joshua 3:1** Early the next morning Joshua and all the Israelites left Acacia Grove and arrived at the banks of the Jordan River, where they camped before crossing.

2 Three days later the Israelite officers went through the camp,

3 giving these instructions to the people: "When you see the Levitical priests carrying the Ark of the Covenant of the LORD your God, move out from your positions and follow them.

4 Since you have never traveled this way before, they will guide you. Stay about a half mile behind them, keeping a clear distance between you and the Ark. Make sure you don't come any closer."

5 Then Joshua told the people, "Purify yourselves, for tomorrow the LORD will do great wonders among you."

6 In the morning Joshua said to the priests, "Lift up the Ark of the Covenant and lead the people across the river." And so they started out and went ahead of the people.

7 The LORD told Joshua, "Today I will begin to make you a great leader in the eyes of all the Israelites. They will know that I am with you, just as I was with Moses.

8 Give this command to the priests who carry the Ark of the Covenant: 'When you reach the banks of the Jordan River, take a few steps into the river and stop there.'"

9 So Joshua told the Israelites, "Come and listen to what the LORD your God says.

10 Today you will know that the living God is among you. He will surely drive out the Canaanites, the living God is among you, and that he will without fail drive out from before you the Canaanites, and the Hittites, and the Hivites, and the Perizzites, and the Girgashites, and the Amorites, and the Jebusites.

11 Behold, the ark of the covenant of the LORD of all the earth passeth over before you into Jordan.

12 Now therefore take you twelve men out of the tribes of Israel, out of every tribe a man.

13 And it shall come to pass, as soon as the soles of the feet of the priests that bear the ark of the LORD, the LORD of all the earth, shall rest in the waters of Jordan, that the waters of Jordan shall be cut off from the waters that come down from above; and they shall stand upon an heap.

Hittites, Hivites, Perizzites, Girgashites, Amorites, and Jebusites ahead of you.

11 Look, the Ark of the Covenant, which belongs to the Lord of the whole earth, will lead you across the Jordan River!

12 Now choose twelve men from the tribes of Israel, one from each tribe.

13 The priests will carry the Ark of the LORD, the Lord of all the earth. As soon as their feet touch the water, the flow of water will be cut off upstream, and the river will stand up like a wall."

In Focus

Minister Valerie had just put away her purse when she heard the soft knocking at her office door. Before she said "Come in," she already knew who was on the other side of the door. Pastor Bryan, the church's senior pastor, had asked her to handle this matter because she was the Christian education minister. Valerie had prayed about this situation all night, but she still wished that someone else on the church's staff had been assigned to handle this meeting. Pastor Bryan had asked her to replace June as chairperson of the church's singles ministry. June was a lovely young woman. She was outgoing, friendly, and she was very popular with church members.

Under her direction, the singles ministry attendance had skyrocketed. Instead of 11 or 12 people at each meeting, there were now between 40 and 50 singles at each meeting. She had been a member of the church for three years but did not attend Sunday School or any of the church Bible studies or training sessions.

After Pastor Bryan had expressed some concerns about June's leadership, Valerie had begun attending the singles meetings. She had been surprised to find that, in their discussion periods, the group rarely referred to the Scriptures. At one meeting Minister Valerie had attended, the group had spent an hour discussing the issue of celibacy. June, the discussion leader, frequently referred to the opinions of television talk show hosts and other celebrities. At one point during the meeting, Valerie had tried to steer the discussion on what the Bible had to say about celibacy. June's response was that while she understood what the Bible had to say, it was her belief that times have changed, and she was certain that God understood that people today have to "keep it real."

Christian leaders are often called upon to make difficult decisions. Unlike secular leaders, the primary responsibility of a Christian leader is to uphold the integrity of God's Word. Rather than rely on their own understanding, Christian leaders must follow the lead of godly leaders like Joshua and trust in the Lord in all things.

The People, Places, and Times

Jordan River. The Jordan River valley area is one of the most famous places in the Bible, and the river itself is the main body of water in the Promised Land. The Jordan River is mentioned about 175 times in the Old Testament, and it is referenced about 15 times in the New Testament. The Hebrew name for the river is *Yarden* (**yar-DANE**), meaning "descender." This is appropriate since the highest point of the river is near Mt. Hermon and it descends to the Dead Sea, a declension of about 2,380 feet. The Jordan is about 200 miles long. The river forms a natural border between most of east and west Palestine. Flowing through numerous valleys, basins, and gorges, the Jordan empties into the Sea of Galilee, at its southernmost point, and into the Dead Sea. The waters of the Jordan are relatively shallow, between three to ten feet deep; however, it contains numerous rapids, whirlpools, and swift currents. During the spring, melting snow from Mt. Hermon floods the Jordan, and wading is virtually impossible.

The earliest biblical mention of the Jordan River is during the parting of Abraham from his nephew Lot and Lot's selection of the Jordan Valley for his family (Genesis 13:10–11). Jacob wrestled with the stranger and was renamed Israel at the Jabbok River, a tributary of the Jordan (Genesis 32:22–28). Naaman was cured of leprosy at the Jordan (2 Kings 5:10–14). The Jordan River was headquarters to John the Baptist for most of his ministry, and it was there, in the Jordan, that John baptized Jesus.

Source:
Alexander, David and Pat Alexander, eds. *Eerdmans' Handbook to the Bible.* Grand Rapids, Mich.: Wm. B. Eerdmans Publishing Company, 1973.

Background

The book of Joshua opens with God commissioning Joshua, a close aide of Moses, to succeed Moses and lead the Children of Israel. "Moses my servant is dead; now therefore arise, go over this Jordan, thou, and all this people, unto the land which I do give to them" (Joshua 1:2). Canaan, a rich and fertile land, had been promised to the Children of Israel; they simply needed to be obedient, follow God's direction, and take possession of it.

In chapter 2, we read that Joshua sent two spies into the city of Jericho to determine the best way to defeat the heavily fortressed city. Inside the city gates, the spies encountered a prostitute named Rahab. When these spies came into her inn, she bravely hid them, even though she was under orders from the king of Jericho to surrender the spies to his soldiers. Rahab lied to the soldiers and sent them on a wild goose chase.

While the soldiers were following her false directions, Rahab made a remarkable testimony to the Israelite spies. She told them that she and the people of Jericho knew "that the Lord hath given you the land, and that your terror is fallen upon us, and that all the inhabitants of the land faint because of you. For we have heard how the LORD dried up the water of the Red Sea for you, when ye came out of Egypt" (Joshua 2:9–10). What a surprise it was to the spies to learn that the people of Jericho were living in fear of Israel and of the God of Israel! In today's text, we find Joshua leading the Israelites into the Promised Land. The fulfillment of the promise has arrived.

God has made promises to today's Christians. He only asks that we trust and obey Him and follow His directions. What a blessed assurance to know that the battle is not ours; it's the Lord's!

At-A-Glance

1. Joshua Prepares the People for the Crossing (Joshua 3:1–4)
2. Joshua Calls for Sanctification of the People (vv. 5–6)
3. Joshua Receives Affirmation from God (vv. 7–8)
4. Joshua Directs the People to Follow God's Instructions (vv. 9–13)

In Depth

1. Joshua Prepares the People for the Crossing (Joshua 3:1–4)

As the chapter opens, Joshua and more than two million of his people and their vast herds of cattle are poised on the eastern banks of the Jordan River. Directly across the river lies the land of Canaan, a narrow strip of land between the Jordan River and the Mediterranean Sea. This is the land that God had promised to His people. Not only was the land promised but it contained all the provisions the people would need. The land God had prepared for His people was fertile and abundant, a land described as "flowing with milk and honey" (Exodus 3:8). After 40 years of wandering through the Sinai Wilderness, the former slaves would now be free to thrive in a land of their own.

Just as God provided for the Children of Israel, our life in Jesus Christ is given to us without any effort on our part. We didn't earn it, and we don't deserve it. We are sinners saved by His marvelous grace. Our salvation is a gift freely given by God, who loves us. We, like the Children of Israel, need only take possession of God's gift.

Just across the river and within their sight was the heavily fortified city of Jericho and her army. Because of the three-day reconnaissance efforts of his two spies, Joshua knew that the inhabitants of Jericho were terrified. Between Joshua's encampment and Jericho was the swollen Jordan River. There was no bridge. There were no boats. It was springtime, and snows from Mount Hermon had melted. The Jordan's current was swift, and its normally shallow waters were deeper. It was one thing for two spies to make their way across the river; it would be quite another for a nation of millions, their livestock, and their possessions to make it.

Certainly many of the Israelites standing on the banks looking at the raging waters before them must have felt utterly helpless.

We can, however, assume that their leader, Joshua, remained confident. For 40 years, he served under Moses in the wilderness. While Moses was talking face-to-face with God "as a man speaketh unto his friend," Joshua was there, too. While the other people remained in their tents, "Joshua the son of Nun, a young man, departed not out of the tabernacle" (Exodus 33:11). Even in his youth, we can see Joshua's determination to remain connected to God. Present-day saints who seek to be effective church leaders must have a deep devotion, reverence, and awe of God.

Joshua was no longer a young man, but his determination to trust God was stronger than ever. Joshua was confident that just as God had opened a way through the Red Sea, He would open a way through the Jordan River.

Joshua's eagerness to be obedient to God was indicated in his getting started "early in the morning." God had already told the people of Israel to wait three days at the shores of the Jordan River (Joshua 1:11). The people were commanded to cross the Jordan River. The Ark of the Covenant was to be brought ahead, about three thousand feet in front of the people. It is important to note that the ark symbolized the meeting place between God and Israel. Here we see that the people were to follow the ark and move when the ark moved. So it should be with us, too. We must be prepared to move when God moves.

The priests would carry the ark and would stand on the edge of the Jordan River. God required that they keep some 1,000 yards behind the ark—to keep the people respectful of the holiness of the Ark of the Covenant. More importantly, the distance would allow everyone a clear view of the ark. Joshua understood that only by keeping their eyes on God's presence and following His presence would Israel be able to accomplish the daunting task ahead.

2. Joshua Calls for Sanctification of the People (vv. 5–6)

Joshua also understood that the battle ahead would be a spiritual battle. He required that the people have a spiritual preparation. When Joshua instructed the people to "sanctify" themselves, he meant that they were to separate themselves from common things to focus solely on the Lord. Specifically, to show they were cleansed from the world and prepared to stand in the presence of God, they were expected to take part in ceremonial washings to purify themselves. When people were "consecrated," it was understood they belonged to God and were expected to live according to His will and to live in His service. Israel was instructed that "Ye shall be holy: for I the LORD your God am holy" (Leviticus 19:2). Their designation as a people special to God was reiterated: "Ye shall be unto me a kingdom of priests, and an holy nation" (Exodus 19:6). Joshua certainly would have understood the need for Israel's consecration. Moses had obeyed God's instructions to "Take thee Joshua the son of Nun, a man in whom is the spirit, and lay thine hand upon him" (Numbers 27:18). God recognized that He could use Joshua to complete His plan for His people, and He had Moses "lay hands" to consecrate Joshua for service to God.

While all Christians are called toward "sanctified," or holy, living (1 Corinthians 1:2; 3:17), this charge is essential in Christian leaders. A major responsibility of leadership in the church is to set examples of godly, righteous living. Effective Christian leaders must model spiritual maturity and responsiveness to the will of God to the unbelievers and to the body of Christ. This can only be achieved when leaders are "set apart" from their worldly past and lay claim to their future in Christ Jesus and to His service.

3. Joshua Receives Affirmation from God (vv. 7–8)

Joshua had the Children of Israel in position to cross the Jordan. He had taken the next step and commanded that they be sanctified. Up until this point, Joshua had been operating on faith. God had provided for him in the past, and Joshua had faith that God would continue to do all that He had promised. Now, God rewarded Joshua's faithful service with affirmation. He told Joshua, "Today I will begin to exalt you in the eyes of all Israel" (Joshua 3:7, NIV). This promise is critical to Joshua's success as the leader of the Children of Israel.

For 40 years, the people had followed Moses. They had witnessed God's hand in Moses' leadership. They had seen the Red Sea parted, been fed bread from heaven, been led by a pillar of fire at night, and witnessed the defeat of larger and more powerful armies. There was no doubt in their minds that God was with Moses. Not only did the people have confidence in Moses but they loved him, too.

After his death, the Children of Israel wept in the plains of Moab for 30 days. It was difficult for them to imagine life without their great leader.

Joshua was their new leader, and God was going to aid in the transition. God promised Joshua that the same way He guided Moses to bring Israel out of Egypt He would guide Joshua to bring Israel into the Promised Land. God rewarded Moses' obedience. He was now about to reward Joshua's obedience.

Until this point, the people had been following Joshua because they saw him appointed by Moses. Now, God was going to show the people that *He* appointed Joshua. God had already told this to Joshua. Now He demonstrated His love for and His commitment to Joshua in view of all the people. We must remember that God always knows the needs of His people, and He is faithful to meet those needs. Like Joshua, if their ministries are to be successful, today's Christian leaders will need obedience, confidence, and faithfulness from the people they lead. Our education and our skills are not enough. In order for us to facilitate leading lost souls to Christ and building up the body of believers, we must have the approval of God. That approval can only be gained by our steadfast devotion and faithfulness to Him and His Word.

4. Joshua Directs the People to Follows God's Instructions (vv. 9–13)

Joshua reassured the people that God was with them and would help them overcome the inhabitants of Jericho. The multitude of men, women, and children must have been astonished as they watched the priests carry the Ark of the Covenant into the swollen Jordan River. The Ark of the Covenant, which was ordinarily hidden from sight in the Holy of Holies, was now exposed for all the people to see. Joshua also reassured the Israelites that God would be with them and that He would help them overcome all of their enemies in the land of Canaan.

God assured Joshua that he would make him a leader, like Moses, in the eyes of the people. God would accomplish this by using Joshua to miraculously lead the people across an impossible body of water. God had given Joshua specific instructions for the priests carrying the ark: "When you reach the edge of the Jordan's waters, go and stand in the river" (v. 8, NIV). With complete confidence in God, Joshua encouraged the people to believe that a miracle was about to take place. He told them, "This is how you will know that the living God is among you" (v. 10, NIV). Here we see Joshua express his understanding that God's plan to move on Israel's behalf now was a promise that God would bless them in the future. The seemingly impossible situation that the Children of Israel saw before them—an impassable river—was an opportunity for them to witness their God working on their behalf.

Joshua assured the people that the waters of the Jordan "will be cut off and stand up in a heap" (v. 13, NIV). His communication of God's promise to Israel was full of confidence and assurance. Joshua was calling for the people to step out on faith. This is a wonderful model for today's Christian leaders. It is imperative that our communication echoes our confidence and faith in Jesus Christ.

He reminds them that the Ark of the Covenant would be just ahead of them. This is a reminder to Israel that they were not simply following Joshua's orders; rather, a living God was among them. They would be following the very presence of God. It is the responsibility of Christians to reassure others that Jesus' death on the Cross has cleared the way for our victory over all obstacles. "Having disarmed the powers and authorities, he made a public spectacle of them, triumphing over them by the cross" (Colossians 2:15, NIV).

Search the Scriptures

1. "And ______ rose early in the morning; and they removed from Shittim, and came to ___________, he and all the children of Israel, and lodged there before they passed over" (Joshua 3:1).

2. "And it came to pass after _________days, that the officers went through the host" (v. 2).

3. "And they commanded the people, saying, When ye see the __________ of the ____________ of the LORD your God, and the priests the Levites bearing it, then ye shall remove from your place, and go after it" (v. 3).

4. "Yet there shall be a space between you and it, about ____ thousand cubits by measure: come not near unto it, that ye may know the way by which ye must go: for ye have not passed this way heretofore" (v. 4).

5. "And Joshua spake unto the ____________, saying, Take up the ark of the covenant, and pass over before the people. And they took up the ark of the covenant, and went before the people" (v. 6).

6. "Now therefore take you ________ men out of the tribes of Israel, out of every tribe a man" (v. 12).

Discuss the Meaning

1. In Joshua 3:1, we read, "And Joshua rose early in the morning." Read Ephesians 6:12. Do these Scriptures support the importance of praying and studying God's Word at the start of each day? Why or why not?

2. Before Joshua was chosen as Israel's leader, he served Moses for 40 years. Discuss how our willingness to serve and our faithfulness in service can help develop our leadership skills.

Lesson in Our Society

Christian leadership is an awesome responsibility. Christian leaders are called to show the same trust in God that Joshua showed. Sometimes God will place us in situations that seem impossible. We cannot attempt to overcome these trials on our own. We must remember that the battle is not ours; it's the Lord's. This means we must seek His will. This seeking may require that we spend hours on knees. Our power to achieve the seemingly impossible comes through the Holy Spirit, who dwells in us (1 Corinthians 3:16; 6:19). Before we can experience a miraculous spiritual victory in our lives, we must be willing to trust God completely. In order to live by faith in His victory, which of God's promises do you need to reaffirm today?

Make It Happen

Prayerfully consider the leadership commitments you have in your church. Honestly assess your performance over the past year. Is the work of your ministry introducing unsaved people to Christ? Are your ministry efforts in line with the vision of the church? Ask God to renew your passion for these areas. Pray for the people under your leadership. Ask God's guidance in moving forward with your ministry efforts.

Follow the Spirit

What God wants me to do:

____

____

Remember Your Thoughts

Special insights I have learned:

____

____

More Light on the Text

Joshua 3:1–13

1 And Joshua rose early in the morning; and they removed from Shittim, and came to Jordan, he and all the children of Israel, and lodged there before they passed over.

The first clause appears to indicate that one day following the return of the spies with the good news of victory, Joshua woke up early in the morning. If we assume this to be correct, then it appears that Joshua was so excited and committed that he did not want to wait a day longer to carry out God's command. Here Joshua demonstrated the spirit of leadership, taking the initiative, working with the people, and trusting the Lord. He woke first and gathered the people to start the journey. They set out from Shittim and came to the bank of the Jordan. They lodged there. It is estimated that the distance between Shittim and the Jordan is between six and eight miles.

2 And it came to pass after three days, that the officers went through the host; 3 And they commanded the people, saying, When ye see the ark of the covenant of the LORD your God, and the priests the Levites bearing it, then ye shall remove from your place, and go after it. 4 Yet there shall be a space between you and it, about two thousand cubits by measure: come not near unto it, that ye may know the way by which ye must go: for ye have not passed this way heretofore.

Joshua and the people arrived at the bank of the Jordan River and camped there. The phrase "after three days" probably refers to the end of three days, after Joshua took over the command of the army and following the return of the spies with the good report (1:11). It also shows that before they passed over, they camped by the Jordan for three days (3:1). However, on the third day, as they had been directed by Joshua, the officers went to the people and instructed them on how the journey would commence. First they were to watch for the sign. When they saw the Ark of the Covenant being carried by the priests and the Levites, they were to follow and begin to move toward Canaan.

Verse 4 gives a more detailed requirement for their movement. They were not to move from their positions or camps until the priests and Levites bearing the ark went to a distance of 2,000 cubits. This distance translates to about 4/5 of a mile. There were two reasons for this specific instruction. One was implicit and the other explicit. The first was to keep a distance from the ark out of reverence to the Lord, because the ark represented the presence of the Lord. However, the second reason given here is that the ark, which symbolized the presence of the Lord, would pilot the way, since the people had not traveled that road before. Therefore the Ark of the Covenant needed to be seen by all the people, so it could guide the way. If the people were to crowd the ark, many of the people would not be able to see it. They needed to be able to see the ark. It is symbolic of the way we look to the Lord to be our leader and guide. In addition to this reason, the ark needed to go ahead of the people to make a way through the Jordan, as we shall see later (v. 14ff).

5 And Joshua said unto the people, Sanctify yourselves: for to morrow the LORD will do wonders among you. 6 And Joshua spake unto the priests, saying, Take up the ark of the covenant, and pass over before the people. And they took up the ark of the covenant, and went before the people.

As the people waited for the moving of the ark, Joshua addressed the people and ordered them to "sanctify" (Heb. *qadash*, **kaw-DASH**) themselves in preparation for the journey and for the miracle God was about to perform. *Qadash* means "to be set apart, to make oneself clean (ceremonially or morally), consecrate, or to wash oneself." Here Joshua appeared to order the people to sanctify themselves by washing themselves, their bodies and clothes, in preparation for the miracle that was about to take place the next day—the holding back of the waters of the Jordan and the drying of the sea floor for the period of their passage through the river. This is comparable to God's order to Moses: "Go down and prepare the people for my arrival. Consecrate them today and tomorrow, and have them wash their clothing" (Exodus 19:10, NLT). Although the command tends to point to the spiritual, ceremonial, and moral cleansing, it also probably includes physical hygiene—the cleaning of their bodies and washing of their clothes in preparation to their journey.

Following his instruction to the whole congregation to purify themselves in anticipation for the wonders the Lord will perform among them the next day, Joshua directed the priests to take up the Ark of the Covenant and move ahead of the people. Taking up the ark here is equivalent to Yahweh getting up and starting the journey ahead of them, as in Numbers 10:33–35. The priests obeyed. They picked up the Ark of the Covenant and moved before the people toward the Jordan. These acts of obedience on the part of Joshua, the people, and the priests began the days of wonders and miracles the Lord promised to show the whole of Israel.

7 And the LORD said unto Joshua, This day will I begin to magnify thee in the sight of all Israel, that they may know that, as I was with Moses, so I will be with thee. 8 And thou shalt command the priests that bear the ark of the covenant, saying, When ye are come to the brink of the water of Jordan, ye shall stand still in Jordan

In obedience, as the priests carrying the ark moved ahead of the people, the Lord spoke to Joshua and reaffirmed him as His chosen leader before the people. The Lord promised Joshua that, on that very day, He would begin to "magnify" (Heb. *gadal*, **gaw-DAL**) him before the people. The word *gadal* here means "to honour, to make great, to become or to make important." It also means to exalt someone. As indicated earlier, the immediate obstacle that appeared to inhibit Joshua from conquering Jericho was the Jordan River. Although the dividing and crossing of the Jordan was the immediate event through which the Lord was about to exalt Joshua and authenticate his leadership, the Lord would magnify him through other future wonders and miracles. These include the conquering of the nations and the occupying of the lands by Israel. These wonders would assure the people that, just as Yahweh was with Moses, He was also with Joshua. They would acknowledge, respect, and have confidence in Joshua as they did in Moses at the parting of the Red Sea: "When the people of Israel saw the mighty power that the LORD had unleashed against the Egyptians, they were filled with awe before him. They put their faith in the LORD and in his servant Moses" (Exodus 14:31, NLT).

Following this promise, the Lord directed Joshua to give the priests bearing the ark a specific instruction. The instruction was that when they reached the bank of the river, they should stand still. This direction was necessary since the priests were 2,000 cubits ahead of the people and leading the way. The reason for the instruction can only be assumed here—probably so that the people would come closer in order to see the wonders that were about to happen. The narrator leaves off whether or not Joshua gave the instruction. The omission of this part of the narrative is not unique to this story but consistent with the Old Testament narrative, which generally presumes that God's commands are passed on as directed (see Exodus 14:15; Deuteronomy 31:28).

It is noteworthy that, while in the case of the miracle of the Red Sea, Moses was directly involved in parting the sea by raising his shepherd's rod over the waters (Exodus 14:16, 21); Joshua, on the other hand, was only to give orders to the priests. As already indicated, the Ark of the Covenant symbolized the presence of the Lord and played a role in the time of Joshua, especially in the crossing of the Jordan. However, the ark was not yet established at the time Moses and the people crossed the Red Sea. Therefore Moses used the rod. In either case, it was the Lord at work, because He was present with His servants and He accomplished His purposes through various means. In 2 Kings 2:8–15, we find a record of the parting of the Jordan by both Elijah and Elisha on two separate occasions. The people watching Elisha perform this miracle prostrated before him, which served the same purpose meant here—to magnify or make him great. As the Lord exalts and authenticates His servants' calling through His miracles, in the process He honors and magnifies Himself.

9 And Joshua said unto the children of Israel, Come hither, and hear the words of the LORD your God. 10 And Joshua said, Hereby ye shall know that the living God is among you, and that he will without fail drive out from before you the Canaanites, and the Hittites, and the Hivites, and the Perizzites, and the Girgashites, and the Amorites, and the Jebusites.

After hearing from the Lord and being reassured of God's presence and affirmation of leadership, Joshua summoned the people together for an important announcement. To get the attention of such a large crowd must have proved to be difficult, since they did not have sophisticated public address systems such as we have today. Nonetheless, Israel was famous for the use of ram's horns for their public announcement or warning in emergencies (see Joshua 6:4–5). The use of the ram's horn to call the attention of the people or as warning in emergencies reminds one of the same methods used by most African villages.

The Igbos of Nigeria use town criers, armed with the *ekwe* (a wooden gong) around the village to make announcements from the village head or the village council. When there is an emergency or an urgent issue to discuss that requires the immediate presence or attention of every person, they use the *ikoro* (a much larger *ekwe* carved from a big tree trunk with hollow inside). This instrument makes a big sound to summon the people to the village arena. The Yoruba people, another Nigerian tribal group, use the metal gong for the same purposes.

Joshua assembled the people and told them to listen to what the Lord their God had to say to them. He announced that their Lord was about to do something very miraculous; therefore, they needed to pay attention. Joshua was so committed to and so convinced of the power and source from which it originated that he confidently declared to the people, "Hereby ye shall know that the living God is among you...." The Hebrew word "know" (***YADA*, yaw-DAH**) is not merely rational knowledge but also experiential. It means to "acknowledge, recognize, or to discover" the presence of the Lord among them; they would know for sure that the Lord was really with them. This immediate miracle was a taste of other miracles that would follow and an emblem of God's faithfulness.

We notice Joshua called his God "living," as opposed to gods of other nations. Here he uses the Hebrew word *chay* (**KHAH-ee**), which can be translated as "alive, quick, or strong." In contrast to the gods of the nations that are lifeless, dormant, and inactive (Psalm 96:5; 115:3–7), Israel's God, Yahweh, is very alive and active. He is lively, powerful, and strong to deliver His people. He reveals Himself in wonders, miracles, and signs.

Having the knowledge of the ever-living presence, the Lord God among His people evoked absolute trust and worship. The immediate act or miracle that God was about to do would further confirm His power and authority and serve as a prelude for future acts in the process of achieving the goal of possessing the Promised Land. Joshua said that Yahweh "will without fail drive out from before you" the nations along the way.

The phrase "without fail drive out" is the doubled Hebrew *yarash* (**yaw-RASH**), which gives emphasis and the certainty of God's commitment to His promise. The use of this double infinitive usually referred as "infinitive absolute" can be translated as "unquestionably" or "without a doubt." This unflinching assurance of God's future activity was intended to give the people the confidence to trust and obey the Lord their God and to listen to Joshua their leader. With this confidence, they could march forward toward achieving their set goal. Joshua then precisely named the nations that God was about to deliver into their hands, namely: Canaanites, the Hittites, the Hivites, the Perizzites, the Girgashites, the Amorites, and the Jebusites. These nations were situated along the way to the Promised Land and were potential obstacles to achieving what the Israelites had set out to accomplish.

11 Behold, the ark of the covenant of the LORD of all the earth passeth over before you into Jordan. 12 Now therefore take you twelve men out of the tribes of Israel, out of every tribe a man.

Having assured the people of God's presence and the miracles that He was about to perform, Joshua called their attention to the Ark of the Covenant. At this point, the priests bearing the ark must have started moving toward the Jordan banks. Joshua pointed to them and said to the people that the Ark of the Covenant of the Lord of all the earth was crossing over ahead of them into the Jordan. We have already established that the ark represents the presence of the Lord and the people were quite familiar with this knowledge. This statement reaffirmed that belief; it reminded them that God, who had gone before them, is "the Lord (Heb. *'Adonay*, **ad-o-NOY**) of all the earth," the creator and sustainer of all things, the omnipotent God, the one who has authority over nature. With such a supreme being ahead of the journey, they had the confidence and trust to march on to claim the land promised them by God.

The tone of Joshua's instruction in these verses 11 and 12 appears to suggest urgency. This urgency is further heightened by the use of the Hebrew word *'attah* (**at-TAW**) or "now therefore," also translated "straightway, now then." It seems that Joshua is saying, since the Lord has gone ahead toward the Jordan, now select 12 men, one from each tribe, to represent the entire nation. The function of these 12 is not explained until the next chapter (4:2–5).

13 And it shall come to pass, as soon as the soles of the feet of the priests that bear the ark of the LORD, the Lord of all the earth, shall rest in the waters of Jordan, that the waters of Jordan shall be cut off from the waters that come down from above; and they shall stand upon an heap.

Verse 13 is the climax of this narrative. Joshua picked up the instruction to his people from where he stopped in verse 11. The peak of the story is the dividing of the Jordan River. Joshua gave precise detail of how this river was going to be parted. With confidence, Joshua told the people that as soon as the priests carrying the Ark of the Covenant stepped into the river the waters would be parted.

Skeptics and critics of all generations have attempted to use natural causes to explain the phenomenon that was about to take place on the Jordan. Some call it coincidence. Could not God have been able to cause the water to freeze or congeal before the people arrived at the bank and walked across the bed of the river? Yes! He could have. But that would validate the critics' claim of natural phenomenon. During winter or cold seasons, we have frozen lakes and rivers in certain parts of the world. However, the fact that Joshua announced what was going to happen, ahead of time, substantiates the miracle. Joshua's confidence and commitment to leading the people came from his commitment to and trust in the living God, "the Lord of all the earth," who 40 years earlier had performed a very similar miracle of dividing the Red Sea under the leadership of his predecessor, Moses. Joshua was a witness of that and was reminded of the prophecy and promise that followed that miracle (Exodus 15:15–17).

Joshua used the same phrase, "the Lord of all the earth," twice (vv. 11, 13) to describe Yahweh as the one who is in control of His creation and for the purpose of instilling in the people confidence and trust in the omnipotence of their God. It is interesting to note that certain things were required to achieve the desired outcome—faith and obedience. The priests had to obey the instructions by carrying the ark and stepping into the water, and then God did His part by stopping the natural flow of the Jordan. Partial obedience to God's direction will only result in failure. Here we see that God uses and involves humans to achieve His purpose.

Joshua described, in detail, what would happen when God's direction was followed. He said that as soon as the priests stepped into the shores of the river, the waters flowing from upstream "shall be cut off" (Heb. *karath*, **kaw-RATH**) and would stop flowing; they would pile up as a heap and form a solid wall. Logically, the waters downstream would flow off and drain into the Dead Sea. Consequently, a path would be created in the middle of the river for the people to pass through. This was the work of a supreme and sovereign God, who is in charge and in control of His creation. All creation obeys Him—even the wind and storms (Matthew 8:26–27; Luke 8:24–25). Reminiscing on the greatness and awesomeness of "the Lord of the whole earth," the psalmist declares, "He divided the sea, and caused them to pass through; and he made the waters to stand as an heap" (Psalm 78:13). The next few verses describe the historical fulfillment of Joshua's instruction and announcement to the people.

Throughout this passage, Joshua, as the leader, showed commitment and confidence in leading the people to their destination. This commitment and confidence was built on his faith in the Lord of the whole Earth, a faith based on his experience of the past workings and faithfulness of the real leader of the people: the Lord God of Israel. Based on this experience and his encounter with this God, who assured him of His unfailing presence (1:9), Joshua was able to commit himself under the leadership of the unchanging God of Israel to lead his people to the Promised Land. To carry out our responsibility and commitments to God and others, we need to commit ourselves to the lordship and leadership of the Lord of all the earth through whose power, presence, and faithfulness we can meet our commitment.

Source:

Packer, J. I., Merrill C. Tenney, and William White Jr., eds. *Nelson's Illustrated Encyclopedia of Bible Facts.* Nashville: Thomas Nelson Publishers, 1995.

Daily Bible Readings

M: Military Leader
Exodus 17:8–16
T: Optimistic Spy
Numbers 14:6–10
W: Moses' Successor
Numbers 27:12–23
T: Moses' Charge to Joshua
Deuteronomy 31:1–8
F: The Spirit of Wisdom
Deuteronomy 34:1–9
S: The Lord Is with You
Joshua 1:1–9
S: Joshua's Leadership Affirmed
Joshua 3:1–13

NOTES

TEACHING TIPS

January 25
Bible Study Guide 8

1. Words You Should Know

A. The angel of the LORD (Judges 13:3) *mal'ak* (Heb.)—Messenger, ambassador, representative.

B. Unclean thing (v. 4) *tame'* (Heb.)—Denotes something that is ritually, ethically, or religiously impure.

C. Terrible (v. 6) *yare'* (Heb.)—To inspire reverence or godly fear or awe.

D. Intreated (v. 8) *'athar* (Heb.)—To plead, make supplication, or pray for.

2. Teacher Preparation

Unifying Principle—Preparing for Commitment. Promise and commitment may arise out of great disappointment. How are people challenged to make new commitments? God sent an angel to prepare Samson's mother for his coming birth.

A. Pray for your students.

B. Read Judges 13:1–13, 24 in at least two different versions.

C. Review the AIM for Change and the Keep in Mind verses.

D. Read the Devotional Reading: Psalm 91.

E. Study the In Depth and the More Light on the Text sections.

3. Starting the Lesson

A. Open the class with a prayer, keeping today's AIM for Change in mind.

B. Have the class read the Keep in Mind verse in unison.

C. Have volunteers take turns reading the Focal Verses aloud.

4. Getting into the Lesson

A. Ask a volunteer to read The People, Places, and Times section. Discuss.

B. Ask another volunteer to read the Background section aloud. Discuss.

C. Discuss the Focal Verses.

D. Allow time for the students to complete the Search the Scriptures section.

5. Relating the Lesson to Life

A. Have the students divide into small groups, and assign each of the small groups one of the Discuss the Meaning questions.

B. Ask a volunteer to read the In Focus story and Lesson in Our Society sections. If time permits, allow the students to discuss the implications of each.

6. Arousing Action

A. Give the reading assignment for the week, and encourage the students to use the Daily Bible Readings for their personal devotions.

B. Read the Keep in Mind verse, and give your students your final thoughts on it.

C. Before closing the class, ask for prayer requests and praise reports.

D. Ask a volunteer to close the class with prayer.

Worship Guide

JAN 25th

For the Superintendent or Teacher
Theme: Samson's Mother Prepares for His Birth
Theme Song: "Search Me, Lord"
Devotional Reading: Psalm 91
Prayer

SAMSON'S MOTHER PREPARES FOR HIS BIRTH

Bible Background • JUDGES 13

Printed Text • JUDGES 13:1–13, 24 Devotional Reading • PSALM 91

AIM for Change

By the end of the lesson, we will:
EXAMINE the circumstances surrounding Samson's birth;
SENSE God's promise amid disappointments; and
ACCEPT new challenges and begin to act on them.

Keep in Mind

"Thou shalt conceive, and bear a son; and no razor shall come on his head: for the child shall be a Nazarite unto God from the womb: and he shall begin to deliver Israel out of the hand of the Philistines" (from Judges 13:5).

Focal Verses

KJV **Judges 13:1** And the children of Israel did evil again in the sight of the LORD; and the LORD delivered them into the hand of the Philistines forty years.

2 And there was a certain man of Zorah, of the family of the Danites, whose name was Manoah; and his wife was barren, and bare not.

3 And the angel of the LORD appeared unto the woman, and said unto her, Behold now, thou art barren, and bearest not: but thou shalt conceive, and bear a son.

4 Now therefore beware, I pray thee, and drink not wine nor strong drink, and eat not any unclean thing:

5 For, lo, thou shalt conceive, and bear a son; and no razor shall come on his head: for the child shall be a Nazarite unto God from the womb: and he shall begin to deliver Israel out of the hand of the Philistines.

6 Then the woman came and told her husband, saying, A man of God came unto me, and his countenance was like the countenance of an angel of God, very terrible: but I asked him not whence he was, neither told he me his name:

7 But he said unto me, Behold, thou shalt conceive, and bear a son;

8 Then Manoah intreated the LORD, and said, O my Lord, let the man of God which thou didst send come again unto us, and teach us what we shall do unto the child that shall be born.

9 And God hearkened to the voice of Manoah; and the angel of God came again unto the woman as she sat in the field: but Manoah her husband was not with her.

NLT **Judges 13:1** Again the Israelites did evil in the LORD's sight, so the LORD handed them over to the Philistines, who oppressed them for forty years.

2 In those days a man named Manoah from the tribe of Dan lived in the town of Zorah. His wife was unable to become pregnant, and they had no children.

3 The angel of the LORD appeared to Manoah's wife and said, "Even though you have been unable to have children, you will soon become pregnant and give birth to a son.

4 So be careful; you must not drink wine or any other alcoholic drink nor eat any forbidden food.

5 You will become pregnant and give birth to a son, and his hair must never be cut. For he will be dedicated to God as a Nazirite from birth. He will begin to rescue Israel from the Philistines."

6 The woman ran and told her husband, "A man of God appeared to me! He looked like one of God's angels, terrifying to see. I didn't ask where he was from, and he didn't tell me his name.

7 But he told me, 'You will become pregnant and give birth to a son.'"

8 Then Manoah prayed to the LORD, saying, "Lord, please let the man of God come back to us again and give us more instructions about this son who is to be born."

9 God answered Manoah's prayer, and the angel of God appeared once again to his wife as she was sitting in the field. But her husband, Manoah, was not with her.

10 And the woman made haste, and ran, and shewed her husband, and said unto him, Behold, the man hath appeared unto me, that came unto me the other day.

11 And Manoah arose, and went after his wife, and came to the man, and said unto him, Art thou the man that spakest unto the woman? And he said, I am.

12 And Manoah said, Now let thy words come to pass. How shall we order the child, and how shall we do unto him?

13 And the angel of the LORD said unto Manoah, Of all that I said unto the woman let her beware.

13:24 And the woman bare a son, and called his name Samson: and the child grew, and the LORD blessed him.

10 So she quickly ran and told her husband, "The man who appeared to me the other day is here again!"

11 Manoah ran back with his wife and asked, "Are you the man who spoke to my wife the other day?" "Yes," he replied, "I am."

12 So Manoah asked him, "When your words come true, what kind of rules should govern the boy's life and work?"

13 The angel of the LORD replied, "Be sure your wife follows the instructions I gave her.

13:24 When her son was born, she named him Samson. And the LORD blessed him as he grew up.

In Focus 

Gayle and Elsworth sat across from each other at the kitchen table. Gayle picked at her breakfast. Her husband, Elsworth, glared at his coffee cup. The discussion had gotten heated, and they had both agreed to cool off for a few minutes before continuing. Gayle and Elsworth had moved into their new home two months ago. The house was everything they had dreamed it would be. It was large and was located in a lovely part of town. Their new home had a huge backyard, and it was only two blocks from the elementary school their twin daughters attended. Their dream of owning a home had finally come true. Since the day they married, Gayle and Elsworth had prayed each night asking God to allow them to buy a home. The twins were born three years after they married, and for five years they had to live in a cramped apartment. They had both worked second jobs for the last two years, and they had finally saved enough money to make a down payment on the house.

Last week, Gayle's sister had called from Georgia. Her job was transferring her out of the country, and she had told Gayle that she would no longer be able to care for their mother. Gayle's mother was 88 and had recently been diagnosed with Alzheimer's disease. According to Gayle's sister, their mother was becoming more disoriented every day, and there was simply no way she could live alone.

Gayle had talked it over with Elsworth, who quickly told her that her mother was welcome to come and live with them. Elsworth had pointed out that their new home had an extra bedroom, and there would be plenty of room for Gayle's mother. Instead of being happy, Gayle was very upset. She loved her mother, but she finally had her own home; she wanted to enjoy it with her husband and their children. Gayle was also worried that caring for her mother would be more than she could handle. She just didn't want the extra stress in her life. Instead of understanding her concerns, Gayle felt that Elsworth was disappointed that she didn't jump at the opportunity to have her mother with them. Elsworth had accused Gayle of being selfish. Why couldn't he understand? Was it so wrong for her to want to enjoy her new home, without the burden of having to care for her ailing mother?

What is our response to answered prayer? Do we view it as a gift from God? If so, are we prepared to thank Him with our willingness to use His gifts in the service of others? In today's lesson, we will see a godly response to the fulfillment of God's promise.

The People, Places, and Times

Nazarites/The Vow of the Nazarites. There were two types of Nazarites referenced in the Bible: those who were appointed by God, such as Samson, and those who volunteered to serve as a Nazarite for a certain period of time. The voluntary vow, as given by God to Moses, was "When either man or woman shall separate themselves to vow a vow of Nazarite, to separate themselves unto the Lord….All the days of his separation he is holy unto the Lord" (Numbers 6:2, 8). Although women were allowed to take the vow of a Nazarite, if a woman's father or husband did not approve, he could cancel the vow (see Numbers 30:3–8).

Regulations governing those who volunteered can be found in Numbers 6. The three primary restrictions were: (1) They could not eat any fruit of the vine—ripe, unripe, or dried—nor could they drink any intoxicating beverage; (2) Nazarites could not cut the hair on their heads; and (3) Nazarites were prohibited from touching a dead body, including that of a close family member. The requirement to "let the locks of the hair of his head grow" served to make the Nazarites easily recognizable. The prohibitions against drinking intoxicating beverages and against touching any dead body were also required of Israel's high priests. This indicates the serious responsibility assigned to the Nazarites.

Violation of the Nazarite vows, whether intentional or accidental, rendered the Nazarite "unclean" for seven days and required a ritual purification, including the shaving of the head and presenting a gift offering. Additionally, the stipulated period had to start all over again. At the end of their time, the men and women were expected to go to the priests and present a number of offerings, including a young ram as a burnt offering, a female lamb for a sin offering, and a ram for a communion sacrifice. The long hair of the Nazarite was cut off and offered as a part of the peace offering (see Numbers 6:13–21).

Those Nazarites, who were appointed by God, were expected to honor their vows for the rest of their lives. The commandments for them differed somewhat from those who took a voluntary vow. In the case of Samuel, his mother, Hannah, made the vow to set aside her yet unborn child for God's service as a Nazarite (1 Samuel 1:11). In the New Testament, John the Baptist is set apart as a Nazarite even prior to his conception (Luke 1:11–15).

Source:

Packer, J. I., Merrill C. Tenney, and William White Jr., eds. *Illustrated Manners and Customs of the Bible.* Nashville: Thomas Nelson Publishers, 2003.

Background

The book of Judges covers the 300-year period in Israel's history from Joshua's death until Samuel. The book's name comes from the title of the 12 men and one woman who served as judges. Unlike Moses and Joshua, who preceded them, and unlike the kings who would come after them, the judges had no national leadership. Rather, their sphere of influence seems limited to a specific geographic area. Following their entry into the land of Canaan, Israel was faithful to God and served Him as long as Joshua and the older people who lived after Joshua lived.

The generation that followed them didn't know God and were unaware of "the works of the LORD, that he had done for Israel" (Joshua 24:31). This new generation quickly began a pattern of disobedience. God had instructed Israel to drive out and destroy all of the pagan inhabitants they encountered, but Israel disobeyed. In the opening chapter of Judges, we read how the various tribes began to live among the various Canaanites, "And it came to pass, when Israel was strong, that they put the Canaanites to tribute, and did not utterly drive them out" (Judges 1:28).

Contrary to the commandments of God, the Children of Israel began to mingle and intermarry with the Canaanites, Hittites, Amorites, Perizzites, Hivites, and Jebusites. All these tribes were descendants of Ham. They even began to adopt the godless ways of their Canaanite neighbors and began to worship the pagan god and goddess of the Canaanites, Baal and Astharoth. The idolatrous worship included sacrificing children. Because Israel refused to obey God's instruction that they "make no league with the inhabitants of this land" (Judges 2:2), the Lord's anger waxed hot against His chosen people. The people God had loved and cherished were now turning their backs on Him. As He had warned them, because of their disobedience, God now allowed the various inhabitants of Canaan to afflict Israel and to become "as thorns in your sides" (Judges 2:3).

Their behavior began a cycle of behavior that is the theme of the book of Judges. When they began to suffer at the hands of the Canaanites, Israel repented and called on God for deliverance. In His mercy, God raised up judges who would deliver Israel. Israel, however, would never remain faithful. Instead, when the judge died, the people would backslide and begin the cycle of idolatrous sinning again. Time and time again, God delivered Israel. Time and time again, "the children of Israel again did evil in the sight of the Lord." The judges, however, were committed to bringing them back to a Holy God.

At-A-Glance

1. The Philistines Oppress Israel (Judges 13:1–2)
2. The Angel Promises a Son (vv. 3–5)
3. Manoah Asks for a Confirmation (vv. 6–12)
4. The Promise Is Kept (vv. 13, 24)

In Depth

1. The Philistines Oppress Israel (Judges 13:1–2)

God allowed the Philistines to test Israel's faithfulness to Him. Because of their disobedience and idolatry, we read "and the children of Israel did evil again in the sight of the LORD; and the LORD delivered them into the hands of the Philistines" (Judges 13:1). God allowed the Philistines to occupy the southwest coast of Canaan and exercise a harsh and oppressive rule over Israel that lasted almost 40 years. What is remarkable is that, under the oppression of Philistines, there is no mention of the people of Israel turning to God or crying out to God. Not only was Israel rebellious, but Israel had forsaken God and become morally apathetic.

During this dark period of national degeneration, we are introduced to a family from the tribe of Dan. Manoah and his wife lived in Zorah, a town about 15 miles west of Jerusalem located in the area that had been allotted to the tribe of Dan. Manoah's wife is not named and is only referred to as "the woman." We are told that she is barren. However, the text does not indicate that she is beyond childbearing age. In biblical times, the worst fate that could befall someone was to be "cut off" from one's people. This could happen by being exiled for certain crimes, by public execution, or by dying without leaving any children. Having many children was viewed as a sign of God's favor. Conversely, as a woman's worth was linked to her ability to provide

her husband with children, female barrenness was considered a curse. The moral darkness that is encompassing Israel is mirrored in the psychological darkness taking place in Manoah's home.

2. The Angel Promises a Son (vv. 3–5)

Manoah's wife is the fourth biblical woman we encounter who suffers from barrenness. She is preceded by Abraham's wife, Sarah; Isaac's wife, Rebekah; and Jacob's favorite wife, Rachel. Through the experiences of these three women, we already know that angelic appearances announce the birth of someone significant. More importantly, through them, we learn that when God closes or opens a woman's womb, there is always a reason for doing so.

In verse 3, we read that an "angel of the LORD" appeared to Manoah's wife and announced that she would have a son. While angels rarely appear to women in the Old Testament, this is reminiscent of an earlier other Old Testament occurrence. An angel appeared to Hagar, the Egyptian servant of Abraham and Sarah, two times. On his first appearance, "the angel of the LORD said unto her, Behold, thou art with child, and shalt bear a son, and shalt call his name Ishmael; because the LORD hath heard thy affliction" (Genesis 16:11). The angel went on to command Hagar not to leave Abraham. This angelic visitation ensured that Ishmael would remain under his father's watchful guidance during his formative years and, more importantly, that Ishmael's descendants, to this present day, would identify themselves as children of Abraham. Note that the angel's promise is followed by a commitment on the part of Hagar to return to her mistress.

When God promised that His people would inhabit Canaan, the promise required a commitment on Israel's part. They would be faithful to God and obey His word. A divine promise and a commitment were now given to Manoah's wife. The angel told Manoah's wife that she would have a son, but this son will not be an ordinary child. The angel told the woman that from his conception, her son would be a Nazarite.

Nazarites were men and women who were dedicated "to separate themselves unto the LORD" (Numbers 6:2). The Nazarites were to live holy lives and were bound by three restrictions. First, the Nazarite was forbidden to drink wine or grape juice or eat anything that came from the vine. This prohibition is significant because throughout the Old Testament, we see that the fruit of the vine depicts joy. For the Nazarites to forsake this worldly joy indicates their separation from sensual pleasures to dedicate themselves to the service of God.

The second prohibition was that during the time of separation the Nazarite could not cut his hair. If his vow was for an extended period of time, his position as a Nazarite would be indicated by his long hair. In biblical times, it was considered shameful for a man to have long hair: "Doth not even nature itself teach you, that, if a man have long hair, it is a shame unto him?" (1 Corinthians 11:14).

The third prohibition was against touching any dead body. This included even a close family member—mother, father, sister, or brother. This represented the Nazarite's total separation from death.

It is significant that all three of these prohibitions are symbolic of the life required of a true believer. In order for present-day saints to serve the Lord, we must separate ourselves from the things of this world, we must be willing to suffer shame for His name's sake, and we must forego the attractions of the world and recognize it as "dead." Paul teaches, "God forbid that I should glory, save in the cross of our Lord Jesus Christ, by whom the world is crucified unto me, and I unto the world" (Galatians 6:14). Our response to the fulfillment of God's promises should be a continued or renewed commitment to follow Him.

While the angel of the Lord has made a promise to Manoah's wife, the promise requires a commitment. Notice that the Nazarite prohibitions are placed on both mother and child. During her pregnancy, the woman was instructed to abstain from the same foods and drinks forbidden to Nazarites. After the angel told Manoah's wife about the Nazarite prohibitions, he went on to describe the significance her son would have on Israel. Her son would be no ordinary child. He would be the one sent to "begin to deliver Israel out of the hand of the Philistines" (Judges 13:5). Here we see that although Israel had broken its covenant and lapsed into idolatry, God had not turned His back on them. God was continuing to act on their behalf; He was continuing to act on His commitment.

3. Manoah Asks for a Confirmation (vv. 6–12)

God, through His grace, was promising to accomplish what Manoah and his wife had been unable to accomplish in their flesh. Not only was God preparing to bless the household of Manoah and his wife, but through them He would bless all of Israel. The son that was promised would help deliver Israel from Philistine oppression. This oppression, we must remember, was caused when the Israelites disobeyed God and turned their backs on Him. The hearts of God's people had hardened to the extent that they slipped into a state of moral degeneration. Israel's apathy and rebellion led them into this dark period in their history, which finds them living within the Promised Land but under the subjection of a heathen nation. The Philistines were a warlike people who traced their origin back to Crete and the land of Egypt. They had migrated from Egypt and invaded Canaan just prior to Israel's entrance into the Promised Land. The Philistines settled along the Mediterranean coast and remained bitter enemies of Israel.

Undoubtedly, Manoah's wife was full of expectant hope when she sought out her husband and began to relate what she had been told. Just imagine! If what the angel told her was true, she would hold a child of her own in her arms at last. Her husband's name would live on through their child. At last, she was going to be relieved of the shame of her barrenness. God often relieves us of barrenness by giving us a new home or a new job. We must be careful to recognize these as gifts from God that should be dedicated to Him and sanctified, or set apart, for His good purpose.

Judging by how she recollected the visitation to her husband, we can assume Manoah's wife was a thoughtful woman. The man's "countenance," or appearance, seemed to her like an "angel." While she may not have been certain of this, she was certain he was no ordinary man. She repeated what the angel had told her: She would have a son, and he would be a lifelong Nazarite from birth.

After hearing this amazing account from his wife, Manoah prayed and asked God to "let the man of God which thou didst send come again unto us, and teach us what we shall do unto the child that shall be born" (Judges 13:8). Notice that Manoah did not express any disbelief in what his wife had told him. Manoah's response to God's answered promise was his readiness and willingness to commit to dedicating the child to God's use. Manoah's child was being ordained as a Nazarite from his birth, which was highly unusual. Ordinarily, a person would take the Nazarite vow later on in life. Manoah did not question this. Instead, his prayer request to be taught how to teach the child indicates Manoah's commitment to ensuring that his son would honor his commitment as a Nazarite. Manoah's concern about the future of his child is especially pertinent when we remember that he was living in the time when many of the Children of Israel were doing evil in the sight of the Lord. The child had not even been born yet, and already Manoah was committed to "train up a child in the way he should go" (Proverbs 22:6).

God answered Manoah's prayer, and when the angel appeared to his wife the second time, she ran and brought her husband to the angel. Again, Manoah wanted instruction on how he should rear the child: "How shall we order the child, and how shall we do unto him" (Judges 13:12)? Christians should appreciate Manoah's concern. The need for the right ordering both for ourselves and for our children allows us to live in ways that glorify God. While the angel responded to Manoah, notice that he did not give him instructions on how to raise the child. Instead, the angel told him, "Of all that I said unto the woman let her beware" (v. 13). In other words, "just do what I told your wife." What a wonderful lesson for present-day saints. All we need to do is what God has told us to do. The first step in our commitment to God is to obey God. There is no better way for us to demonstrate the presence of the Lord in our lives than to trust and obey Him.

4. The Promise Is Kept (vv. 13, 24)

The text, in describing the birth of Manoah's son, informs us that "the child grew and the LORD blessed him" (Judges 13:24). The child was named Samson. God answered the prayers of this couple. They now had a son, whose birth most certainly brought sunshine into their lives. We must remember that God never fails to keep His promises. "While we were yet sinners, Christ died for us" (Romans 5:8). Our salvation was purchased by the grace of God, who kept His promise to give us a Saviour. Through the blood of His Son, Jesus, we are saved from the oppression of sin and free to live in the promises of God, rather than the condemnation of the world. In return, He asks only that we commit to Him and submit our lives to His will.

Search the Scriptures

1. How long were the Children of Israel delivered into the hands of the Philistines (Judges 13:1)?

2. To which of the 12 tribes did Manoah belong (v. 2)?

3. During her pregnancy, what two prohibitions did the angel place on Manoah's wife (v. 4)?

4. After the first time the angel appeared to Manoah's wife, what did Manoah request of the Lord (v. 8)?

5. What was the name given to the child (v. 24)?

Discuss the Meaning

1. Why do you think the angel appeared to Manoah's wife and not to her husband? His second appearance was due to Manoah's prayer, so why do you think the angel didn't just go to Manoah?

2. As we see in today's lesson, the child is to become a Nazarite. People who took the Nazarite vow were easily visible because of their long, flowing hair. Their diet also made them easily identifiable. What connection does our lifestyle have to our inner commitment? Do you think that the Christian lifestyle should be in all respects identical for all believers?

3. Do you think that Christians today take seriously enough our responsibility to safeguard, before they are born, the physical, moral, and spiritual well-being of our children?

Lesson in Our Society

Today's Christians, like Samson, have been given God's calling to be "sanctified" or set apart for His purposes. One of God's primary purposes for our lives is to bring about reconciliation. God's reconciling us to Him is to enable us to be people who will love Him and love others the way God loves us. Just as the Nazarites stood out in their day, we, too, are to stand out in this world. We are special. We are unique. Paul tells us, "Therefore, if anyone is in Christ, he is a new creation; the old has gone, the new has come" (2 Corinthians 5:17, NIV). God fulfilled His promise to reconcile humanity to Himself when He sent His only beloved Son, Jesus Christ, to die in our place for our sins. Jesus sacrificed his life to pay for the penalties of our sins that is death. By His Son's death, God removed the sin barrier and reconciled us back to Him.

Make It Happen

1. What promises has God answered in your life?

2. Set aside time this week to pray and ask God for direction on how to use His promises to glorify Him and bless someone else.

3. Ask God to direct you in renewing your commitment to Him.

Follow the Spirit

What God wants me to do:

Remember Your Thoughts

Special insights I have learned:

____

____

More Light on the Text

Judges 13:1–13, 24

1 And the children of Israel did evil again in the sight of the LORD; and the LORD delivered them into the hand of the Philistines forty years.

The author of the book begins this section of the narrative with the same formula he has used repeatedly all over the book, which has now become very familiar (see Judges 2:11; 3:7, 12; 4:1; 6:1; 10:6). Verse 1 summarizes the first two parts of the pattern: provocation and punishment. The people sinned against God, and God sent them into servitude and used the Philistines to punish them.

This chapter begins with the Hebrew word *yacaph* (**yaw-SAF**), which means "and again," a conjunction connecting us to the previous chapter and a transition introducing us to the next section or scene of the story. The writer states, "the children of Israel did evil again in the sight of the LORD." The word "did" is from the Hebrew *'asah* (**aw-SAW**), meaning "to commit." Although the verb is translated in the past tense here, the idea portrayed is a habitual type of behavior. The English word "again" is from the Hebrew *yacaph* (**yaw-SAF**), which has the idea "to continue to do a thing, to add or augment." Apart from the fact that the people reverted to their old life of doing evil in the sight of the Lord after each period of deliverance, they habitually continued to do evil in the sight of the Lord. Hence the sentence can be rephrased, "Again and again (over and over again), the children of Israel did evil in the sight of the LORD."

The word "evil" comes from the Hebrew noun *ra'* (**rah**), which means "bad, displeasing, hurtful or wrong." The Children of Israel, the writer states, did something bad or hurtful in "in the sight of the Lord." The phrase "in the sight of the Lord," along with other possible interpretations, simply means that they did something, which according to God's opinion, judgment, or standards is evil and wicked.

It is noticeable that the writer does not reveal to us the evil that Israel committed. He leaves the readers to assume it. However, from the writer's previous accounts (Judges 2:11–13; 3:7; 10:6), we know Israel had committed the sin of idolatry, rebellion, and the rejection of the Lord their God. Rather than worship the living God, the Lord of all the earth, the new generation of Israel abandoned their God and worshiped the gods of the other nations. This statement, "And the children of Israel did evil again in the sight of the LORD, and served Baalim, and Ashtaroth, and the gods of Syria, and the gods of Zidon, and the gods of Moab, and the gods of the children of Ammon, and the gods of the Philistines, and forsook the LORD, and served not him" (10:6), fully describes the evil. That means breaking the first three of the Ten Commandments the Lord gave Israel to guide them in life. This act was so hurtful and provocative that "the LORD delivered them into the hand of the Philistines forty years."

2 And there was a certain man of Zorah, of the family of the Danites, whose name was Manoah; and his wife was barren, and bare not. 3 And the angel of the LORD appeared unto the woman, and said unto her, Behold now, thou art barren, and bearest not: but thou shalt conceive, and bear a son.

As already noted, verse one is a summary of Israel's provocative action against the Lord and the Lord's reaction and punishment. It also introduces us to the next main scene of the story: God's plan of salvation or act of pardon in the spiral cycle of events as noted above. That is the prophecy of the birth and preparation of another deliverer—Samson, the last of the judges of Israel.

The author begins this major scene by introducing us to the family of this would-be deliverer: his parental and ancestral background. From verse 2, he hints how God, through His providential plan, uses ordinary and not very popular people to carry out His purposes. Here we learn that God uses not the famous but the faithful people, who are willing and committed to Him to carry out His mission. Here, as in other instances, such as Isaac, Joseph, Samuel, and John the Baptist, God employs the services of men whose parents have been kept childless for a while to bring about His plan.

This new deliverer's parents were from Zorah, a city of the tribe of Dan, which was between Eshtaol and Zorah (v. 25; 16:31; 18:2–11). His father's name was Manoah. The name means "rest." He and his wife were barren. The Lord visited Manoah's wife, through an angel, and brought her good news. The good news is that she would conceive and would bear a son, even though she had been barren. She was one of six barren women mentioned in the Bible and the only one whose name is not given. The others are Sarah (Genesis 11:30), Rebekah (Genesis 25:21), Rachel (29:31), Hannah (1 Samuel 1:5), and Michal (2 Samuel 6:23). Why Samson's mother remained nameless is open to speculation. However, this is the woman God chose to bear the next deliverer for Israel. We are not informed how long she and her husband had been waiting to have their own children. However, this woman was promised that she would indeed bear a son. The certainty of this promise is contained in the words of the angel, "Behold now, thou art barren" Judges 13:3). The Hebrew for the word "behold" is *hinneh* (**hin-NAY**) and can be interpreted as "indeed, certainly, or without a doubt." The angel seems to say to the woman, "It is evident that you are barren; there is no doubt about it. But that is about to change! You are surely going to bear a son." This promise is echoed in verse 5, which goes further to strengthen the announcement and its fulfillment.

4 Now therefore beware, I pray thee, and drink not wine nor strong drink, and eat not any unclean thing: 5 For, lo, thou shalt conceive, and bear a son; and no razor shall come on his head: for the child shall be a Nazarite unto God from the womb: and he shall begin to deliver Israel out of the hand of the Philistines.

The announcement of the good news is followed with some conditions that require strict obedience and commitment. The seriousness of the conditions is evident through the first two opening phrases of verse 4: a command followed by an appeal or plea. The first phrase, "Now therefore beware," is derived from two Hebrew words *'attah* (**at-TAW**) and *shamar* (**shaw-MAR**), which means "to be careful or be diligent." The second phrase, "I pray thee," or the Hebrew *na'* (**naw**), is a plea. Here the angel pleadingly instructed the woman to be very diligent and meticulous in keeping the instruction that followed because of its grave importance to the events that were to follow. The accomplishment of the task ahead, the delivery of Israel from the hands of the Philistines, appears to be dependent upon her keeping of the instructions. One can sense the urgency of the instruction.

The angel prescribed two sets of instructions. The first set concerned the parents of the forthcoming deliverer, and the second set concerned the deliverer. The woman was asked to abstain from drinking "wine or strong drinks" and from eating "any unclean thing." That means, therefore, that the mother must be subject (be committed) to the regulation of the Nazarites and shall drink no wine or strong drink so long as this child was being nourished through her, either in her pregnancy or at birth by breastfeeding. This commitment is strict, for she must deny herself of certain food for the sake and preparation of the one who was to lead God's people. That means that this deliverer must be holy and devoted to the Lord in the strictest way, right from his mother's womb.

The next set of instructions was specifically for the child–deliverer to be born. His hair should remain unshaven (Numbers 6:5). The angel instructed the woman that the child should be a Nazarite to the Lord. The word "Nazarite" comes from the Hebrew *naziyr* (**naw-ZEER**), which means "to be separate, consecrated." He was to be set aside for God and, by implication, to be used of Him. Therefore the conditions and rites of a Nazarite needed to be fully observed.

Although the first set of instructions was directed to the mother of this child, it was implicitly meant for the child. God was preparing him for the task ahead even before he was conceived. The task was to deliver the Children of Israel from the hands of their enemies, the Philistines. The Lord said to Jeremiah, "Before I formed thee in the belly I knew thee; and before thou camest forth out of the womb I sanctified thee, and I ordained thee a prophet unto the nations" (Jeremiah 1:5). In the same way, the Lord knew and sanctified this child for His purpose.

Following the instruction, the angel foretold the type of child the woman was going to bear, his task, and service for his country. He was going to be a leader "and he shall begin to deliver Israel out of the hand of the Philistines." This phrase "and he shall begin to deliver" signifies two things. First, the deliverance of Israel from the hands of the Philistines would not commence until this child had grown to the age when he would be able to lead Israel. Second, it meant that this unborn child would begin the task of deliverance but not complete it. That task would be a prolonged one.

6 Then the woman came and told her husband, saying, A man of God came unto me, and his coun-

tenance was like the countenance of an angel of God, very terrible: but I asked him not whence he was, neither told he me his name: 7 But he said unto me, Behold, thou shalt conceive, and bear a son;

Overwhelmed by this strange encounter and probably excited, the woman ran and reported the good news to her husband. Notice how she described the angel. She said that he was "a man of God" with a countenance like "an angel of God, very terrible." The word "countenance" used here is the Hebrew *mar'eh* (**mar-EH**), and it simply means "appearance." There is something special about this man of God that shows he is more than an ordinary man—an angel of the Lord, something "very terrible," meaning his appearance was "very spectacular or glorious" to look at. Awed and overwhelmed with such splendor and amazed with such a joyous pronouncement, the woman failed to ask the man who he was, where he was from, or his name. She rushed to her husband to proclaim the good news. She not only announced the message, she reported in detail the instructions and precepts that she needed to follow (v. 7), perhaps for accountability.

8 Then Manoah intreated the LORD, and said, O my Lord, let the man of God which thou didst send come again unto us, and teach us what we shall do unto the child that shall be born.

After hearing the good news from his wife, Manoah prayed for a further revelation of God. He asked God to send the messenger to confirm the news again. It is important to note the purpose of the prayer. Manoah was not asking for the angel to confirm the good news of the birth of the child. He appears to have instantly believed his wife's story. Rather, as we read from the passage, Manoah was more concerned about the special instructions that needed to be followed. Thus, he asked God to send the messenger the second time in order to teach them what they "shall do unto the child that shall be born."

He also probably wanted to make sure that his wife, in her excitement, had not forgotten any detail of the instructions. There is nothing in this text to indicate that Manoah doubted his wife or that he was jealous of her, as some may suppose. The contrary is the case. Manoah believed his wife's story. However, he wanted to be certain that no part of the instruction regarding this miraculous child was lost or missed. He was committed to carrying out—to the smallest detail—any instructions regarding this child, who was going to deliver his people from the Philistines. As he prayed to God, one can clearly hear the ring of faith and commitment in Manoah's voice. It is an honest and selfless prayer; the prayer of one who sincerely desires to obey and do the will of God. Such a committed prayer never goes without being answered.

9 And God hearkened to the voice of Manoah; and the angel of God came again unto the woman as she sat in the field: but Manoah her husband was not with her. 10 And the woman made haste, and ran, and shewed her husband, and said unto him, Behold, the man hath appeared unto me, that came unto me the other day.

God granted Manoah's prayer and sent the angel a second time. As she was alone in the field, again the angel appeared to the woman. Some contend that she was in the field tending the flock or working on the farm. There is nothing in the passage to verify these assumptions. Rather it appears that she was sitting in their courtyard when the angel appeared to her. As soon as the angel showed up, the woman recognized him and quickly ran to her husband and announced his arrival. The phrase "shewed her husband" could be misinterpreted as if the angel and the woman went together to meet her husband and she introduced (showed him) the angel. Rather the word "shewed" comes from the Hebrew *nagad* (**naw-GAD**), which means "to declare, to announce, to report or to rehearse." This is substantiated by the next verse, which states, "And Manoah arose, and went after his wife and came to the man."

11 And Manoah arose, and went after his wife, and came to the man, and said unto him, Art thou the man that spakest unto the woman? And he said, I am. 12 And Manoah said, Now let thy words come to pass. How shall we order the child, and how shall we do unto him?

Immediately after the wife announced the arrival of the man of God, Manoah instantly went with his wife to meet him. He then inquired from the man whether he was the same person who appeared to his wife previously. The man answered in the affirmative. Satisfied that it was the same man, Manoah declared, "Now let thy words come to pass," somewhat like the Virgin Mary (Luke 1:38). He believed and accepted the promise. He never doubted or required a sign like Zacharias (Luke 1:18–20).

Instead, he asked the man of God to repeat the instructions that he gave his wife previously on how to raise the child. The purpose of repeating the instruction is apparent: to familiarize themselves with the precise requirements.

13 And the angel of the LORD said unto Manoah, Of all that I said unto the woman let her beware.

It is important to note the angel's answer to Manoah's request, "Of all that I said unto the woman let her beware." That means that he should have made sure that his wife strictly kept all the instructions that had been given to her. The angel repeated the instructions in verse 14. The angel again used the same word "beware" or *shamar* (**shaw-MAR**) as in verse 4, which serves as a warning and stresses the importance of the instruction. Commitment and obedience to the instructions are of paramount importance to the fulfilling of God's promise to them. Consequently, the woman must be diligent in obeying it to the fullest, and the man is to support her so that she may not falter in keeping them. Perhaps because she was the direct instrument through whom the deliverer would be prepared, the angel appeared only to the woman the two times and required only her to keep the instructions.

13:24 And the woman bare a son, and called his name Samson: and the child grew, and the LORD blessed him.

By telling us of the birth of this child, verse 24 concludes the story. Here we come to assume that the woman kept all the instructions. Because we know that He is a covenant–keeper, we know that God kept His own part of the pledge. The saga of verse 15–23 took place the same day after the dialogue between the angel and Manoah. The narrator did not think it necessary to tell us what happened in between that day and the day of the birth of the child. The important thing is that the promised child was born according to God's promise to the woman, who was barren. The child is named Samson or in Hebrew *Shimshown* (**shim-SHONE**), meaning "sunlight." We can only speculate why he is called Sunlight, as it is not made clear here. All we know is that God made a commitment to a woman who was termed barren, to give her a son who would deliver Israel from their enemies, the Philistines. The Lord gave the woman specific instructions to be obeyed in preparation for this would-be deliverer. The woman and her husband committed themselves to obeying the instructions in preparation for this child; the result is the birth of the deliverer. God foreknew that the child would be born, and "the child grew, and the Lord blessed him." The rest of Samson's story is contained in chapters 14–16 of Judges.

Sources:

Life Application Study Bible (New International Version). Wheaton, Ill.: Tyndale House Publishers, 1991.

Packer, J. I., Merrill C. Tenney, and William White Jr., eds. *Illustrated Manners and Customs of the Bible.* Nashville: Thomas Nelson Publishers, 2003.

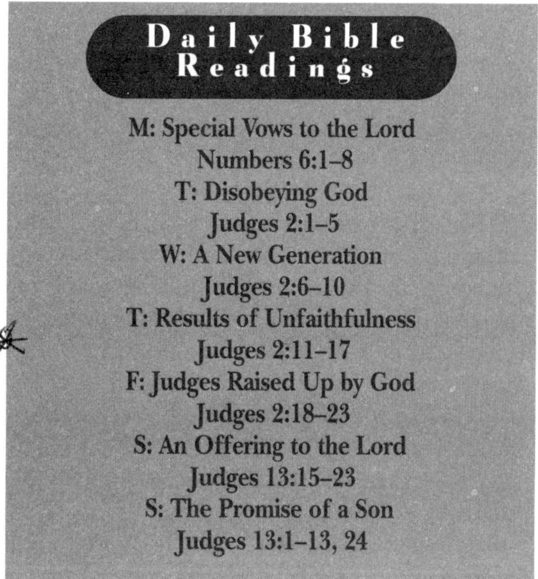

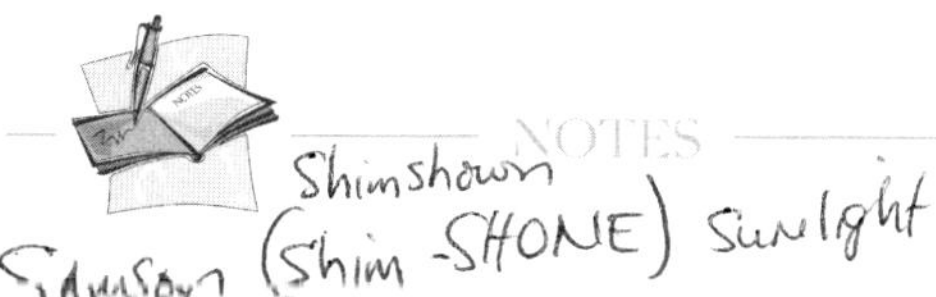

TEACHING TIPS

February 1

Bible Study Guide 9

1. Words You Should Know

A. Constrained (2 Kings 4:8) *chazaq* (Heb.)—To encourage strongly.

B. On the wall (v. 10) *qiyr* (Heb.)—Indicates a partition built into the wall.

C. Captain of the host (v. 13) *sar (*Heb.)—Indicates a lord or a master or an officer with authority.

D. Time of life (v. 16) *'eth* (Heb.)—Indicates a given time for such an event.

2. Teacher Preparation

Unifying Principle—Commitment Without Reward. Oftentimes people make commitments that do not seem to benefit them. What kind of person would commit freely without requiring anything in return? The Shunammite woman was glad to serve Elisha without reward, but she received one anyway.

A. Study the Bible Background section and the Daily Bible Readings.

B. Study the Focal Verses in at least two different versions.

C. Study the More Light on the Text section to gain further insights into today's lesson.

3. Starting the Lesson

A. Begin your class with prayer.

B. Reflect on the AIM for Change and the Keep in Mind verse.

4. Getting into the Lesson

A. Ask for volunteers to read the Focal Verses.

B. Provide your students with some historical background for the setting of this lesson. Remind them that the nation of Israel had been divided and that Elisha was ministering in the northern kingdom of Israel.

C. Do the Search the Scriptures section. Discuss.

5. Relating the Lesson to Life

A. Ask for a volunteer to read the In Focus story. Discuss.

B. Allow 10–15 minutes for students to answer and discuss the Discuss the Meaning questions. You might have them form groups, and select a group leader who will share the answers with the rest of the class.

C. Read Lesson in Our Society section and discuss.

6. Arousing Action

A. Review the Make It Happen section. Conduct an in-depth discussion of how to implement the ideas presented there. Encourage your class to make a personal commitment in the suggested areas found in this section.

B. Remind the class to do their Daily Bible Readings so that they can grow in wisdom and knowledge of God's Word and share it with others.

Worship Guide

For the Superintendent or Teacher
Theme: A Shunammite Woman Helps
Theme Song: "Hold to God's Unchanging Hand"
Devotional Reading: Luke 6:32–36
Prayer

A SHUNAMMITE WOMAN HELPS

Bible Background • 2 KINGS 4:8–17
Printed Text • 2 KINGS 4:8–17 Devotional Reading • LUKE 6:32–36

AIM for Change

By the end of the lesson, we will:
STUDY the relationship between Elisha and the Shunammite woman;
EXPLORE the possibility of commitment without apparent benefits (rewards); and
MAKE commitments without thought of personal gain.

Keep in Mind

"Behold now, I perceive that this is an holy man of God, which passeth by us continually. Let us make a little chamber. . .and it shall be, when he cometh to us, that he shall turn in thither" (from 2 Kings 4:9–10).

Focal Verses

KJV **2 Kings 4:8** And it fell on a day, that Elisha passed to Shunem, where was a great woman; and she constrained him to eat bread. And so it was, that as oft as he passed by, he turned in thither to eat bread.

9 And she said unto her husband, Behold now, I perceive that this is an holy man of God, which passeth by us continually.

10 Let us make a little chamber, I pray thee, on the wall; and let us set for him there a bed, and a table, and a stool, and a candlestick: and it shall be, when he cometh to us, that he shall turn in thither.

11 And it fell on a day, that he came thither, and he turned into the chamber, and lay there.

12 And he said to Gehazi his servant, Call this Shunammite. And when he had called her, she stood before him.

13 And he said unto him, Say now unto her, Behold, thou hast been careful for us with all this care; what is to be done for thee? wouldest thou be spoken for to the king, or to the captain of the host? And she answered, I dwell among mine own people.

14 And he said, What then is to be done for her? And Gehazi answered, Verily she hath no child, and her husband is old.

15 And he said, Call her. And when he had called her, she stood in the door.

16 And he said, About this season, according to the time of life, thou shalt embrace a son. And she said, Nay, my lord, thou man of God, do not lie unto thine handmaid.

17 And the woman conceived, and bare a son at

NLT **2 Kings 4:8** One day Elisha went to the town of Shunem. A wealthy woman lived there, and she urged him to come to her home for a meal. After that, whenever he passed that way, he would stop there for something to eat.

9 She said to her husband, "I am sure this man who stops in from time to time is a holy man of God.

10 Let's build a small room for him on the roof and furnish it with a bed, a table, a chair, and a lamp. Then he will have a place to stay whenever he comes by."

11 One day Elisha returned to Shunem, and he went up to this upper room to rest.

12 He said to his servant Gehazi, "Tell the woman from Shunem I want to speak to her." When she appeared,

FEB 1st

13 Elisha said to Gehazi, "Tell her, 'We appreciate the kind concern you have shown us. What can we do for you? Can we put in a good word for you to the king or to the commander of the army?'" "No," she replied, "my family takes good care of me."

14 Later Elisha asked Gehazi, "What can we do for her?"

15 Gehazi replied, "She doesn't have a son, and her husband is an old man." "Call her back again," Elisha told him. When the woman returned, Elisha said to her as she stood in the doorway,

16 "Next year at this time you will be holding a son in your arms!" "No, my lord!" she cried. "O man of God, don't deceive me and get my hopes up like that."

17 But sure enough, the woman soon became

that season that Elisha had said unto her, according to the time of life.

pregnant. And at that time the following year she had a son, just as Elisha had said.

In Focus

The 10:00 a.m. worship service had just ended, and Priscilla was standing near the door of the sanctuary shaking hands and speaking with other church members. When Ralph walked over to shake her hand, Priscilla looked around and asked him where his mother was. Priscilla had been a member of the church for a little more than a year and had always noticed Ralph escorting the elderly woman.

Ralph looked puzzled for a second and then told Priscilla that Mother Thomas was not his real mother. Ralph went on to share that he had met Mother Thomas's husband on the golf course some 15 years ago. The two men had taken an instant liking to one another, and in no time at all, they were golfing together every Saturday morning. Mr. Thomas had passed away eight years ago. The Thomases never had any children, and Ralph had taken care of Mother Thomas ever since.

In addition to taking her to church, Priscilla found out that Ralph took her to her doctor's appointments, took her grocery shopping, and arranged for a housekeeper to come to her house to clean it twice a month. Mother Thomas had dinner with Ralph and his family every Sunday afternoon and had gone on several vacations with Ralph's family. Ralph's small children called Mother Thomas their "Nana." As Ralph continued to talk, Priscilla recalled how lovingly Ralph handled the elderly woman. Priscilla had just assumed that they were mother and son. Priscilla could not help but be amazed that this young man had undertaken the commitment to love and care for this older woman. Not only did Ralph embrace Mother Thomas, but he had made sure that his family did, too.

In today's lesson, we will meet a woman who showed remarkable kindness and attended to the needs of a man of God with no expectation of repayment, just as Ralph did. Her motivation was purely selfless.

The People, Places, and Times

Shunem. Shunem was a city about three miles north of Jezreel near Mt. Gilboa. When the Promised Land was divided during the days of Joshua, this city was part of the land that was allocated to the tribe of Issachar. The Philistines encamped in this city and during a battle, King Saul was killed (1 Samuel 28:4). Abishag, the woman who nursed the aging King David and was referred to as the Shunammite, came from this city.

The Prophet Elisha. Elisha, whose name means "God is salvation," was plowing in his father's fields when he was appointed to become a disciple of the prophet Elijah (1 Kings 19:19). He served Elijah for about six years, before Elijah ascended to heaven in a windstorm, and Elisha received divine confirmation as Elijah's successor (2 Kings 2:9–15). Elisha's ministry lasted about 50 years. During that period, he prophesied in the northern kingdom of Israel, during the reigns of kings Ahab, Ahaziah, Jehoram, Jehu, and Jehoash.

Elisha's ministry centered on trying to get Israel to turn from idol worship and apostasy and return to serving the one true God. His ministry efforts encompassed the personal and the political. Unlike his predecessor, Elijah, who lived in caves, Elisha lived in the city and was easily accessible to the people. His miracles often affected the lives of common people. These miracles include the purification of the spring (2 Kings 2:19–22), multiplication of the poor widow's oil supply (4:1–7), providing an antidote for a poisonous stew (4:38–41), and the healing of Namaan's leprosy (5:1–14). Elisha was also involved in the national affairs of the kingdom. His ministry efforts in this area include: providing water to the Israelite army (2 Kings 3:4–20), warning Israel's king of the plans of the enemies (6:8–12), helping to avoid disaster at the hands of the Syrians (6:13–7:16), and prophesying on his deathbed Joash's defeat of the Syrians (13:14–19).

Source:

Packer, J. I., Merrill C. Tenney, and William White Jr., eds. *Illustrated Manners and Customs of the Bible.* Nashville: Thomas Nelson Publishers, 2003.

Background

When the prophet Elijah summoned Elisha from plowing in his father's fields, the young man immediately obeyed. From that point on, he was Elijah's unfailing companion. Before Elijah was taken away into heaven, Elisha asked his teacher to give him a double portion of his wondrous spirit. His request was granted. During his lifetime, the Lord enabled Elisha to perform double the number of miracles that Elijah had performed.

Elisha's appointment, like Elijah's, was to minister the northern kingdom of Israel. His home base was at Mt. Carmel and in Samaria, the capital city of Israel. In spite of the tension between the kings of Israel and God's prophets, we see Elisha interacting with all levels of society. He was tenderhearted, and we see him sympathetically minister to the poor and the oppressed. Similarly, he was a fierce and outspoken man of God, and he boldly faced leaders who abused their power. Elisha also interacted with the religious community. During his lifetime, he was the recognized head of the prophets' schools located in Gilgal, Jericho, and Bethel.

The primary goal of Elisha's ministry was to restore respect for God's Word. While the prophet revealed God's punishment for sin, especially that of disobedience, Elisha, through his miracles, revealed God's blessings for those who obeyed the Word of God.

At-A-Glance

1. Elisha Meets A Hospitable Woman (2 Kings 4:8–11)
2. Elisha Recognizes the Kindness of the Woman (vv. 12–14)
3. Elisha Promises the Shunammite Woman a Child (vv. 15–17)

In Depth

1. Elisha Meets A Hospitable Woman (2 Kings 4:8–11)

In verse 8, we read that Elisha, the successor to Elijah, was going about his ministry and he "passed over to Shunem." Like Samuel before him (1 Samuel 7:15–16), the prophet Elisha apparently traveled a regular circuit within the northern kingdom of Israel. Perhaps from seeing him on a regular basis, Elisha drew the attention of a "great" woman of that city. Her designation as "great" implies she may have been a wealthy woman or one having social influence. While her wealth was not specified, what was immediately clear is that she had tremendous spiritual perception. She "constrains," or strongly urged, the prophet to eat at her home. We want to remember that in ancient biblical times, travelers depended on the kindness and hospitality of others. This woman graciously opened her home to the man of God and offered him rest and sustenance.

What is especially significant is that the Shunammite woman's invitation was not solicited. Elisha did not ask to be a guest. Rather, the woman graciously made the offer to be of assistance to the prophet. Her kindness was both sincere and genuine. Present-day Christians should take note and ask themselves: (1) When I see the need, can I be counted on to offer hospitality? (2) Have I opened my home for Bible study or other ministry activity? (3) Do I offer to visit with sick or homebound church members, or do I assume that responsibility belongs to someone else? The world says "it's all about me"; however, Christians must operate under a more godly value system. Paul reminds us that we "have been called unto liberty; only use not liberty for an occasion to the flesh, but by love serve one another" (Galatians 5:13).

The second indication we get about the woman's spiritual perception is when the woman went to her husband and asked his permission to lodge the prophet. What a wonderful lesson we see demonstrated here! By bringing the matter to him and asking for his agreement, this woman acknowledged her husband's authority. What a lovely demonstration of the godly influence a wife can have on her husband! Her husband had probably seen the prophet but, unlike his wife, had not discerned the needs of the prophet. In this case, the Shunammite wife exhibited a benevolent concern for the prophet that her husband had not recognized. We see no resentment expressed by her husband. He, no doubt, appreciated this ability in his wife and acquiesced to her request to make a special space in their home for Elisha.

2. Elisha Recognizes the Kindness of the Woman (vv. 12–14)

Notice that the Shunammite woman was able to see the degree of Elisha's need. She was not content to just feed him and give him a bed for the night. She wanted to provide the prophet with a space that would allow him privacy to pray and to meditate. She perceived that Elisha needed a private place to be alone with the Lord. She, with her husband's approval, provided her home as a haven to the prophet.

Here she illustrated Peter's exhortation that "As every man hath received the gift, even so minister the same one to another, as good stewards of the manifold grace of God" (1 Peter 4:10). She and her husband apparently had enough space, and her thoughtfulness dictated that she bless the prophet by sharing God's blessings to her. While she may not have been aware of it, the Shunammite woman, by her actions, was actually promoting Elisha's mission. Again, we want to call attention to the fact that she was doing all of this without having been asked. What a marvelous testimony for us—to have the means available to us and to set about using it for the glory of God. It is a good thing to recognize the work done by local missionaries. It is also a marvelous thing to share our homes or our finances with these same missionaries, to enable them to better perform their ministry works.

We need never worry that our acts of kindness go unnoticed. In these verses, we read that Elisha recognized and was grateful for the hospitality the Shunammite woman had shown toward him. He sent for his servant, Gehazi, and instructed him to go to the woman to find out if there was anything she needed. In particular, Elisha offered to speak a word on her behalf to the king or to the commander of the army. Her reply to this offer was brief and, at first glance, sounds strange: "I dwell among my own people." The *New Contemporary English* translation renders her response a bit more clearly for us: "With my relatives nearby, I have everything I need." Let us keep in mind that this woman knows who Elisha is. The prophet is no stranger to this area. We can believe that she had heard of the miracles he had performed. No doubt, she also knew that whatever Elisha asked of God on her behalf would be granted. Yet, we see her decline Elisha's generous offer of the protection of the king and the commander of the army.

The Shunammite woman, unlike so many of us, was content with what God had given her. She was satisfied with her home, her position, her friends, and her ministry. We can safely assume that she believed she was exactly where God wanted her to be and doing what God wanted her to do. This is the godly contentment all Christians should aspire to. It is the type of contentment Paul speaks of when he writes, "For we brought nothing into this world, and it is certain we can carry nothing out. And having food and raiment let us be therewith content" (1 Timothy 6:7–8).

By her declaration that she didn't need anything, it becomes clear to us that the Shunammite woman was gracious to Elisha because it was her nature to be gracious and not because she expected to be repaid. What motivates our acts of charity and kindness toward others? Do we show love because God is love and we want to reflect Him?

3. Elisha Promises the Shunammite Woman a Child (vv. 15–17)

The Shunammite woman had declined Elisha's offer to speak to the king or to the officer of the army on her behalf. In short, he had offered her the protection of the government and the military. Yet the Shunammite woman believed perhaps because she had her family and community, there was absolutely nothing else that she wanted or needed.

Elisha was not content to leave matters like this. Surely she had some need that he might be able to meet. Elisha left it to his servant, Gehazi, to find out what that need might be. Gehazi immediately recognized what he believed to be the Shunammite woman's greatest unmet need—her desire to have a son. A barren woman, no matter how materially wealthy she may have been, was viewed negatively in many ancient cultures. One problem was that her husband was elderly. Elisha summoned the woman and prophesied that in a year's time she would be holding an infant son in her arms. At first glance, it appears her response was one of disbelief: "And she said, Nay, my lord, thou man of God, do not lie unto thine handmaid" (v. 16). It is probably more accurate to surmise that the woman was merely hesitant, probably because this was more than she could have ever hoped for.

This encounter is reminiscent of the announcement made to Abraham's barren wife, Sarah. Like Sarah, the Shunammite woman received the news of her impending pregnancy while standing in a doorway. The phrase "at this time next year" and the woman's protest all hearken to Sarah's disbelief that her barrenness would be removed (Genesis 18).

The deepest desire of both women, Sarah and the Shunammite woman, could only be fulfilled through divine intervention. In spite of her reservations, her womb was opened, and, as promised, within a year the Shunammite woman gave birth to a son. This woman, who had demonstrated loving kindness with no expectation of repayment, was rewarded with divine favor.

Search the Scriptures

1. "And it fell on a day, that Elisha passed to __________, where was a great woman; and she constrained him to eat bread" (2 Kings 4:8).

2. "Let us make a little __________, I pray thee, on the wall; and let us set for him there a bed, and a table, and a stool, and a candlestick" (v. 10).

3. "And he said to __________ his servant, Call this Shunammite. And when he had called her, she stood before him" (v. 12).

4. "Verily she hath no __________, and her husband is old" (v. 14).

5. "And he said, Call her. And when he had called her, she stood in the __________" (v. 15).

6. "And he said, About this __________, according to the time of life, thou shalt embrace a son" (v. 16).

Discuss the Meaning

1. Why do you think the Shunammite woman's husband did not offer to house the prophet? Is it possible he did not notice the needs of Elisha the way his wife did? What does this say to us about the special insight and perception of women?

2. Read 1 Timothy 6:6. Determine how that Scripture enhances your view of the Shunammite's response in 2 Kings 4:13.

3. In ancient biblical cultures, barren women were looked upon in an extremely negative light. In view of the social pressures she must have been facing, how do you understand the Shunammite woman's response to Elisha that she didn't need anything?

Lesson in Our Society

"What's in it for me?" This question is asked with alarming regularity. It is especially troublesome when the questioner is a person who professes to be a Christian. True Christianity means that the motivation for all our actions is Christ-informed and Christ-centered. What we do for others should be motivated by our love for them and by our genuine concern for their well-being. "Christ" is the root word in Christian. It is not enough that we profess being followers of Jesus Christ. Our lives must mirror His as closely as possible. Our Saviour's very existence was a supreme act of love: "For God so loved the world that he gave his only begotten Son" (John 3:16). While what we achieve in this world may matter in the realm of earthly matters, it is only what we do for our Christ that will matter in eternity.

Make It Happen

Make a commitment to find out the names and addresses of some missionaries serving in your area. Locate these missionaries and find out from them what their needs are. They may need supplies or funds. Many of them may just need a periodic telephone call or letters to ensure them that other believers care about them and are praying for them. Assist them in whatever way you can. Your help will enable them to further carry the Word of God.

Follow the Spirit

What God wants me to do:

____

____

Remember Your Thoughts

Special insights I have learned:

____

____

More Light on the Text

2 Kings 4:8–17

8 And it fell on a day, that Elisha passed to Shunem, where was a great woman; and she constrained him to eat bread. And so it was, that as oft as he passed by, he turned in thither to eat bread.

In his usual and customary travels, the prophet Elisha (Heb. *'Eliysha'*, **el-ee-SHAW**, meaning "God is salvation") often traveled through the town of Shunem (Heb. *Shuwnem*, **shoo-NAME**, meaning "double resting place"). One "great" (Heb. *gadowl*, **gaw-DOLE**, meaning "older in age, important") woman took particular notice of Elisha's presence, pattern, and purpose while there. She insisted (Heb. *chazaq*, **khaw-ZAK**, meaning "be resolute, prevail upon") that Elisha find a hot meal and hospitality in her home whenever he was in town.

"But the midwives feared God, and did not as the king of Egypt commanded them, but saved the men children alive" (Exodus 1:17). Pictured is Baby Moses' basket among the reeds.

9 And she said unto her husband, Behold now, I perceive that this is an holy man of God, which passeth by us continually.

This woman elicited support of her hospitable heart from her husband because she discerned (Heb. *yada'*, **yaw-DAH**, meaning "to know, recognize, acknowledge") that there was something especially holy about this man, a prophet who came through town from time to time.

10 Let us make a little chamber, I pray thee, on the wall; and let us set for him there a bed, and a table, and a stool, and a candlestick: and it shall be, when he cometh to us, that he shall turn in thither.

The woman was inspired to make an add-on room on her roof (Heb. *'aliyah*, **al-ee-YAW**, meaning "roof-room") for Elisha's exclusive use for study and prayer. The position of the room would afford him privacy to rest and to prepare to do the work of the prophet. Although the items she placed there seemed scant, modest, and meager; they were sufficient for this holy man doing God's work. These items were: a bed (Heb. *mittah*, **mit-TAW**, meaning "couch, bed"), a table (Heb. *shulchan*, **shool-KHAWN**, meaning "table for private, sacred use"), a chair (Heb. *kicce'*, **kis-SAY**, meaning "seat of honor, stool"), and a candlestick (Heb. *menowrah*, **men-o-RAW**, meaning "lampstand"). When humble items are offered to God's servants, they become holy instruments for God's purpose. Transformed objects

11 And it fell on a day, that he came thither, and he turned into the chamber, and lay there. 12 And he said to Gehazi his servant, Call this Shunammite. And when he had called her, she stood before him. 13 And he said unto him, Say now unto her, Behold, thou hast been careful for us with all this care; what is to be done for thee? wouldest thou be spoken for to the king, or to the captain of the host? And she answered, I dwell among mine own people.

On a typical day of passing through Shunem, Elisha went into his upper room to rest (Heb.

shakab, **shaw-KAB**, meaning "to lie down"). While there, he asked of his servant–companion, Gehazi, to ask the woman how best he could show his appreciation for her hospitality (Heb. *charad,* **khaw-RAD**, meaning "to take anxious care"). When the woman ascended the stairs of her home and came (Heb. *'amad,* **aw-MAD**, meaning "to present oneself as a servant of") into Elisha's private quarters, he offered to speak favorably of her to the king or to the army commander (Heb. *sar,* **sar**, meaning "official under the king"). If she accepted these offers, the woman would find favor, recognition, and protection from some important people. Gracefully and humbly the woman denied need or desire of either, as she did not offer hospitality to the man of God with strings attached. The woman gave to the prophet simply because she wanted to be a blessing to him.

14 And he said, What then is to be done for her? And Gehazi answered, Verily she hath no child, and her husband is old. 15 And he said, Call her. And when he had called her, she stood in the door.

Elisha depended on his assistant's service to determine the best token of appreciation for this woman's hospitality. Gehazi observed that the woman lived in the constant cultural shame of being barren and having no son (Heb. *ben,* **bane**, meaning "son, male child, children"). He further pointed out the unlikelihood that she ever would, by noting that the woman's husband was too old (Heb. *zaqen,* **zaw-KANE**, meaning "to be old, show age") to make her pregnant. What seemed impossible for man, God was preparing to show forth as possible!

16 And he said, About this season, according to the time of life, thou shalt embrace a son. And she said, Nay, my lord, thou man of God, do not lie unto thine handmaid.

Emphatically, excitedly, Elisha got a word from God and told the woman that by this time, (Heb. *mow'ed,* **mo-ADE**, meaning "appointed time") next year (Heb. *'eth,* **ayth**, meaning "usual time"), as would indicate the time of a normal pregnancy, the woman would be holding (Heb. *chabaq,* **khaw-BAK**, meaning "embrace") her very own son! Overwhelmed by the reality of her barrenness and her husband's age, the woman insisted that the prophet, whom she addressed as lord, would not be so cruel as to lie (Heb. *kazab,* **kaw-ZAB**, meaning "to deceive, disappoint, and fail") to her! Imagine having her hope stirred up when she had resigned herself to a hopeless situation!

17 And the woman conceived, and bare a son at that season that Elisha had said unto her, according to the time of life.

But God! Just as the prophet had spoken, the woman became pregnant (Heb. *harah,* **haw-RAW**, meaning "conceived") soon after his prophecy. After the normal time of gestation, the woman gave birth to her son! God, again, was faithful over God's word to perform it in the lives of those who obey, even when they can't believe!

Source:

Packer, J. I., Merrill C. Tenney, and William White Jr., eds. *Illustrated Manners and Customs of the Bible.* Nashville: Thomas Nelson Publishers, 2003.

Daily Bible Readings

M: The Call of Elisha
1 Kings 19:15–21
T: The Prophet's Mantle
2 Kings 2:9–15
W: Elisha's Prayer for a Child
2 Kings 4:27–37
T: The Death of Elisha
2 Kings 13:14–20
F: Jesus Speaks of Elisha
Luke 4:23–30
S: Welcoming a Prophet
Luke 6:27–36
S: Blessed By Blessing
2 Kings 4:8–17

NOTES

TEACHING TIPS

February 8
Bible Study Guide 10

1. Words You Should Know

A. Ewe lamb (2 Samuel 12:3) *kibsah* (Heb.)—A young female sheep.

B. To dress (v. 4) *'asah* (Heb.)—Implies sacrificing or killing to serve as part of a meal.

2. Teacher Preparation

Unifying Principle—Challenging Leadership. Some commitments we make involve people who have no part in agreeing to the decision. Do we consider how our commitments affect everyone involved? Nathan's commitment to God led him to confront King David.

A. To familiarize yourself with the background of the account, read 2 Samuel 11–12.

B. Use at least two different translations to study 2 Samuel 11–12.

C. Study the More Light on the Text section.

D. For information about prophets and their roles, read The People, Places, and Times.

3. Starting the Lesson

A. Ask a volunteer to open the class with a prayer.

B. Read the Keep in Mind verse in unison.

C. Review the transition from judges to a monarchy. Provide your students with information about David and his selection as king of Israel.

4. Getting into the Lesson

A. Review the Words You Should Know section.

B. Ask for a volunteer to read the Background section. Then, discuss.

C. Have volunteers read the Focal Verses.

D. Discuss the In Depth section with your class.

5. Relating the Lesson to Life

A. Review the Discuss the Meaning section with the class.

B. Ask a volunteer to read the In Focus story, and have the class discuss how it relates to today's lesson.

6. Arousing Action

A. Encourage the students to read the Daily Bible Readings.

B. Direct the students to the Make It Happen suggestions and discuss.

C. Ask if there are any prayer requests and end the class with a prayer, addressing these requests.

Worship Guide

For the Superintendent or Teacher
Theme: Nathan Challenges David
Theme Song: "Search Me Lord"
Devotional Reading: Psalm 51:1–9
Prayer

NATHAN CHALLENGES DAVID

Bible Background • 2 SAMUEL 12:1–15
Printed Text • 2 SAMUEL 12:1–7, 13–15 Devotional Reading • PSALM 51:1–9

AIM for Change

By the end of the lesson, we will:
REVIEW Nathan's commitment to God that resulted in a confrontation with King David;
DISCOVER how our commitments affect (influence) others; and
APPROACH commitments with awareness of effects (outcome) to other people.

Keep in Mind

"The thing that David had done displeased the LORD. And the LORD sent Nathan unto David. And he came unto him, and said unto him, There were two men in one city; the one rich, and the other poor" (from 2 Samuel 11:27–12:1).

Focal Verses

KJV **2 Samuel 12:1** And the LORD sent Nathan unto David. And he came unto him, and said unto him, There were two men in one city; the one rich, and the other poor.

2 The rich man had exceeding many flocks and herds:

3 But the poor man had nothing, save one little ewe lamb, which he had bought and nourished up: and it grew up together with him, and with his children; it did eat of his own meat, and drank of his own cup, and lay in his bosom, and was unto him as a daughter.

4 And there came a traveller unto the rich man, and he spared to take of his own flock and of his own herd, to dress for the wayfaring man that was come unto him; but took the poor man's lamb, and dressed it for the man that was come to him.

5 And David's anger was greatly kindled against the man; and he said to Nathan, As the LORD liveth, the man that hath done this thing shall surely die:

6 And he shall restore the lamb fourfold, because he did this thing, and because he had no pity.

7 And Nathan said to David, Thou art the man.

12:13 And David said unto Nathan, I have sinned against the LORD. And Nathan said unto David, The LORD also hath put away thy sin; thou shalt not die.

14 Howbeit, because by this deed thou hast given great occasion to the enemies of the LORD to blaspheme, the child also that is born unto thee shall surely die.

15 And Nathan departed unto his house. And

NLT **2 Samuel 12:1** So the LORD sent Nathan the prophet to tell David this story: "There were two men in a certain town. One was rich, and one was poor.

2 The rich man owned a great many sheep and cattle.

3 The poor man owned nothing but one little lamb he had bought. He raised that little lamb, and it grew up with his children. It ate from the man's own plate and drank from his cup. He cuddled it in his arms like a baby daughter.

4 One day a guest arrived at the home of the rich man. But instead of killing an animal from his own flock or herd, he took the poor man's lamb and killed it and prepared it for his guest."

5 David was furious. "As surely as the LORD lives," he vowed, "any man who would do such a thing deserves to die!

6 He must repay four lambs to the poor man for the one he stole and for having no pity."

7 Then Nathan said to David, "You are that man!"

12:13 Then David confessed to Nathan, "I have sinned against the LORD."

Nathan replied, "Yes, but the LORD has forgiven you, and you won't die for this sin.

14 Nevertheless, because you have shown utter contempt for the LORD by doing this, your child will die."

15 After Nathan returned to his home, the LORD sent a deadly illness to the child of David and Uriah's wife.

the LORD struck the child that Uriah's wife bare unto David, and it was very sick.

In Focus 

In 1964, the story of a single crime galvanized the attention of the entire nation. A 28-year-old woman was returning to her home at 3:20 in the morning. After parking her car, she began walking toward her apartment building in a middle-class area of Queens, New York. A man ran behind her, grabbed her, and stabbed her. The woman began screaming. Her neighbors heard her, and lights immediately went on in her 10-unit apartment building.

The woman screamed, "Oh my God, he stabbed me! Please, help me!

One neighbor leaned out of the window and yelled, "Let that girl alone."

The attacker ran away. The bleeding woman struggled to her feet. Lights in the apartments went back off. The attacker came back and stabbed the woman again. Again, she cried out, "Help me! I'm dying! I'm dying!" Again, the apartment lights of her neighbors went on. This time the attacker got into his car and drove away.

A city bus went past the woman as she staggered, bleeding. It was now 3:35 a.m. The woman made it into the lobby of her apartment building. The attacker found her at the foot of the stairwell and stabbed her again. The police received the first call at 3:50 a.m. They responded within two minutes and found the young woman dead.

Only one of her many neighbors had bothered to pick up the telephone and call the police; the call wasn't received until after the woman was dead. When asked why he didn't call when he first saw the woman attacked, the man replied, "I didn't want to get involved." For more than 30 minutes, 38 law-abiding citizens watched a man stalk and stab a woman three separate times, yet no one called. After more than 44 years, the brutal murder of Catherine "Kitty" Genovese still begs the question, "The neighbors knew what they were seeing, so why didn't anyone call for help?"

In this lesson, we will see that King David has committed a horrible crime, and everyone in the court has kept quiet. No one has the boldness to confront the king—until Nathan, the prophet, does what no one else will. Nathan's commitment to God leads him to speak up and speak out against unrighteousness.

Source:
http://www.crimelibrary.com/serial_killers/predators/kitty_genovese/1.html

The People, Places, and Times

Prophets. The Hebrew word for prophet is *nabiy'* (**naw-BEE**) and has come to be understood as one through whom God's will and purpose is revealed. Employing various methods, including direct verbal communication and communication through angels, visions, and dreams, God sent His message through the prophets. In the Bible, prophets were men and women who served as human spokespersons for God. To the prophets, God revealed His intimate matters. In Scripture, the word *nabiy'* is first applied to Abraham. When he left his homeland of Ur to seek the promise of God, Abraham acted as a prophet. The role of the prophet is clearer with Moses. With Moses, we see a very intimate and sometimes two-way communication with God.

During the period of the judges, the word *nabiy'* is only used with two persons: an unnamed man in Judges 6:8 and Deborah. Samuel served as a prophet from childhood. The fulfillment of the messages Samuel delivered from God caused "all of Israel from Dan even to Beersheba" to accept Samuel as "a prophet of the Lord" (1 Samuel 3:20). The mention of the "sons of prophets" in 2 Kings 2:3 probably refers to a school of instruction for young men called to prophetic service. These groups were located in Bethel, Jericho, Ramah, and Gilgal. The Bible infers that Samuel and Elisha were recognized as leaders of these schools (1 Samuel 19:20; 2 Kings 4:38).

During the time of Israel's monarchy, there was a continuous line of prophets, most notably Gad and Nathan, who prophesied during King David's reign. Both men often served as royal advisors. In the time of the divided kingdom, prophets were active in both the northern (Israel) and southern (Judah) kingdoms. The prophets encouraged the people to turn away from idolatry and maintain their faithfulness to the one true God. They often chastised ungodly kings and declared God's impending judgment against wickedness (1 Kings 14:1–16). During the exile and postexilic periods, Daniel, Haggai, Zechariah, and Malachi rendered prophetic service.

The Bible records female prophets as well. The most notable is Huldah, whose ministry is recorded in 2 Kings 22:11–20. This prophetess lived during the reign of King Josiah. When the lost books of the Law were found in the temple, the religious leaders were so confident that God had spoken through her that they asked her for advice on what the nation should do. Other women performed the ministry of the prophets. They include Moses' sister, Miriam (Exodus 15:20); Deborah (Judges 4:4); and the wife of Isaiah (Isaiah 8:3). In the New Testament, Anna and the daughters of Philip are identified as prophetesses.

True prophets were hand-selected by God. Some of them were Levites: Samuel, Zechariah, Jeremiah, and Ezekiel. The ministry of the prophets was not easy and was often dangerous. The boldness and honesty of the prophets in delivering messages from God frequently made them targets for mockery and sometimes violent retribution (2 Chronicles 36:16).

Source:

Packer, J. I., Merrill C. Tenney, and William White Jr., eds. *Illustrated Manners and Customs of the Bible.* Nashville: Thomas Nelson Publishers, 2003.

Background

The Bible lists some 37 "mighty men" who were responsible for guarding and fighting alongside David during his many battles against Saul, the Philistines, and other enemy nations. Included in this list of elite fighting men, we find the names of Uriah the Hittite and Eliam, the son of Ahithophel the Gilonite (2 Samuel 23:34, 39). Ahithophel is David's counselor or prime minister. These men were the husband, the father, and the grandfather of Bathsheba. So we see that when David committed adultery with Bathsheba, he was betraying the very men who fought side by side with him and risked their lives for him.

The fact that David could see Bathsheba bathing from the rooftop of his palace implies that the house occupied by Uriah and his wife was in close proximity to the palace. We can reasonably assume this closeness was a reward to Uriah for his years of loyal service to King David. Rather than repay the loyalty of Uriah and Eliam honorably, David, by sinning with the wife of his comrade, dishonored these men and the entire nation. David's sins were numerous: betrayal, adultery, and murder. More importantly, David's multiple sins provided an opportunity for other nations to blaspheme God. What an important lesson this is for present-day saints! There is no such thing as a private sin—all sin has consequences. It is the work of the enemy to trick us into believing that we can turn our backs on God, do as we please, and think it affects no one. When we commit sin, it is easier for us to minimize it and think of our sins as inconsequential ("a little white lie"), affecting no one except ourselves. God, on the other hand, sees the past, present, and future effects of our sin. He knows that our sins have consequences that can and will destroy our bodies, our families, and our friendships for many years to come. Thus, God is calling for true believers to confront sin and hold each other accountable.

When chapter 11 closes, we see that a child has been born to Bathsheba. We can safely assume that about a year has gone by. After all of this time, David probably thought that no one knew what he had done, but God was watching and God knew. Through his sin with Bathsheba, David had turned his back on God, but God had not turned His back on David. Because of sin, David was incapable of discerning spiritual things. Because of God's love and concern for David, God moved on his behalf. We read: "And the Lord sent Nathan unto David." God provided assistance to David in the form of Nathan, the prophet. In order to reach David, God used a man who was totally committed to Him and to His will.

At A-Glance

1. Nathan Reveals David's Sin Using a Parable (2 Samuel 12:1–4)
2. David Responds in Anger (vv. 5–6)
3. Nathan Announces God's Judgment (vv. 7, 13–15)

In Depth

1. Nathan Reveals David's Sin Using a Parable (2 Samuel 12:1–4)

Chapter 11 closes ominously: "But the thing that David had done displeased the Lord." King David had committed a terrible sin. First, David committed adultery with the wife of Uriah, one of his trusted generals. He then compounded that sin by dispatching Uriah into the heat of a battle and ordering the troops to withdraw from him, ensuring that Uriah was killed. What David had not done was to confess and acknowledge his sin. Instead, he attempted to hide his sin. He needed someone to confront him and tell him that God was not pleased with his actions. David needed someone to help him come to repentance. That someone was a committed prophet: Nathan.

This is often the case with us, too. We continually sin and, in time, we become comfortable in our sinning. The sinning becomes easier to us. The apostle Paul, in Ephesians 4:27, warns us not to allow Satan to gain a foothold in our lives. Left unchecked, our sins multiply; slowly but surely, we will find ourselves being separated from God. It is doubtful that when David became involved with Bathsheba, he intended to murder her husband. The murder was a result of his trying to cover the sin he had committed.

Bathsheba's advanced pregnancy could not have gone unnoticed. David, however, was the king, and although many people must have been aware of his sin, no one dared to confront the king. Still, however, God saw, God knew, and God wanted the sin confronted.

It is important to note that God selected a prophet to handle such a sensitive matter. God's selection of Nathan is telling. First, it shows that although David had strayed far from God, the heart of God was still with David. God could have destroyed David for his sins, but God wanted to honor the covenant promise He had made with David to establish David's kingdom forever. God always honors His promises to us, and He often goes to extraordinary lengths to recover us when we fall from grace. We must recognize that God's decision to dispatch Nathan to confront David was an act of mercy. When His beloved falls into sin, God will not allow us to remain there.

Nathan was not only a prophet but also a counselor to the king. Earlier in David's reign, he had wanted to build a house for the Lord, and God sent Nathan to counsel David. Through Nathan, the Lord decreed to David to make the preparations for the building of the original temple (2 Samuel 7:4–17). As a prophet in the king's court, it fell to Nathan to share the will of the Lord to the king. In this instance, God used Nathan to deliver a message of promise to David. Now, years later, Nathan was tasked with confronting the king with the truth of the crimes he had committed against the nation, Uriah, Bathsheba, himself, and God. Although he served at the pleasure of the king, Nathan's true authority was as a messenger of God. Pleasing the king was secondary to pleasing God. Our decision to speak out, when we witness wrongdoing, should be motivated by our desire to please God. The greater our desire to please Him, the more willing we will be to confront evil.

Nathan's decision to confront the king was not only uncomfortable but dangerous. As king, David could have had Nathan killed. David's propensity to violence had already been demonstrated by his cold-blooded decision to dispatch Bathsheba's husband into the heat of the battle, thus ensuring his death. We must remember that although Nathan was a subject of the king, his first loyalty was to the Lord and to the nation. If Nathan had chosen not to do as God commanded him, he would be faced with the awful consequences of disobeying God.

Rather than confront David directly and accuse him of adultery and murder, Nathan wisely revealed the king's sin to him in the form of a complaint. Nathan told David the story of two men. One was poor and only owned one lamb. The other man was wealthy and owned many sheep and cattle. The poor man had worked hard to purchase the single lamb and he "nourished" it. The poor man raised the lamb along with his children. So great was his affection toward the lamb that not only was it allowed to eat from his plate, but we also read in verse 3 that the man cuddled the lamb and allowed it to "lay in his bosom, and was unto him as a daughter." One day a visitor came to the rich man's house. Instead of killing one of the many lambs in his own flock, the wealthy man killed the beloved lamb owned by the poor man. The use of this particular story revealed Nathan's skillfulness and keen understanding of David's sense of justice.

Present-day Christians should witness in everyday matters like prophets who are called to bring God's truth to light. Effective ministry to believers and nonbelievers requires that we become the audible voice of God. In order to do that, we must know His Word. This can only be accomplished if we are listening to the Lord. We do this through our daily Bible readings and devotionals, placing His Word in our hearts and praying to Him so that we might feel His promptings.

2. David Responds in Anger (vv. 5–6)

While it appeared that Nathan was telling the account of two unknown men, if we look closely, we will see that David's actual sins were revealed in the story. David, like the rich man in the story, had many wives and concubines. The poor man, like Uriah the Hittite, had only one wife. Instead of choosing from the many women available to him, David first coveted and then took the wife of another. It is likely that David believed the story Nathan related to him was an actual case. It is also possible that Nathan used the story of the poor man's stolen ewe lamb because he knew that David used to be a shepherd and would be able to empathize with the plight of the poor man who loved the ewe lamb. In either case, what is important is that Nathan's confrontation was not accusatory. Instead, the indirect approach Nathan took leads us to believe that the prophet was more concerned about creating a sense of awareness and remorse in David. Not accusatory

Note that the confrontation between the two men did not even take place until after Nathan heard from God. Like Nathan, we will only be able to bring God's truth to someone after we have asked the Lord to guide us in the matter. Many of us have heard someone boast that they are "brutally honest." This is an oxymoron for Christians. Honesty, when motivated by genuine love and concern for our brothers and sisters, is never brutal. When we confront someone with the truth, our motivation must be to reveal God's truth to them in a way that affirms His love for them.

David's reaction to the story of the mistreatment of the poor man was immediate and strong. He was infuriated. "As the LORD liveth," he vowed, "the man that hath done this thing shall surely die! And he shall restore the lamb fourfold, because he did this thing, and because he had no pity." It is interesting that when he heard the account of the rich man's mistreatment of the poor man, David reacted so emotionally. Yet up until this point, he had behaved so cruelly in his treatment of Uriah.

This should make us question the indifference we show toward the injustice we witness around us. How easy is it for us to turn a deaf ear to the homeless people we encounter on our city streets? Why then are we so moved when we watch televised accounts of children starving in Third World countries? Despite his sins, adultery, and murder, David's conscience had been awakened.

3. Nathan Announces God's Judgment (vv. 7, 13–15)

By using the vague representation of the rich and poor man, Nathan was able to encourage David to pronounce a sentence upon a supposed offender (the rich man) for crimes far less malignant than the ones he had committed. Then Nathan, with boldness, declared, "You are the man" (v. 7). It is at this point that, through Nathan, God announced His judgment of David. God decreed that David's kingdom would suffer publicly for the very injuries that he inflicted on Uriah in secret. David, in turn, showed his greatness by immediately admitting his guilt and confessing, "I have sinned against the LORD" (v. 13). Nathan told David that God had forgiven him and that he would not die for his sins, but the unnamed son of David and Bathsheba bore the punishment for David's sin, and he died. Innocent impacted

Here we see that God did not allow David to enjoy the fruit of his sin. David's willingness to humble himself and accept God's judgment enabled God to show him grace and continue to work with him.

It would have been understandable for Nathan to balk when God commissioned him to confront David. Nathan knew that rebuking the king was not going to be easy, but Nathan understood that the integrity of the nation of Israel was in jeopardy. Concern for his personal safety was less important to Nathan than his desire to please God. Similarly, the tasks that God will assign to each of us will not always be easy, but we must remain faithful to our calling as ambassadors of our Lord, Jesus Christ. We must pray, as Paul did, "that utterance may be given unto me, that I may open my mouth *boldly*" (Ephesians 6:19).

Search the Scriptures

1. Who does the Lord send to King David to confront him about his sin (2 Samuel 12:1)? Nathan
2. What single animal does the poor man own (v. 3)? Ewe lamb
3. When the traveler comes to the rich man, what offensive act does the rich man commit (v. 4)?
4. Upon hearing the story, what is King David's reaction (v. 5)? infuriated
5. When Nathan reveals that King David is the rich man in the story, what confession does David make (v. 13)? that he sinned vs- God

Discuss the Meaning

1. How do you think David might have reacted if Nathan had been accusatory? If Nathan had just

pointed out that David was an adulterer and a murderer and the law says that he should be put to death, how might the outcome changed?

2. Discuss how we handle confrontation at home. Do we bring the truth in love? Are we more direct in our approach and simply present the facts? Which approach do you believe is better? Discuss why.

Lesson in Our Society

As Christians, we have been called to follow Christ. This calling means we are committed to His will and His ways. It also means that we are committed to calling to notice what others choose to ignore or cannot see. Our commitment requires us to speak up and confront, even if no one else will. The decision to confront someone will oftentimes be difficult. This decision brings consequences. If we confront a friend about something, it may cause a rift in the friendship. If we confront an employer, it may cost us a future promotion. If we confront a spouse, it may result in receiving the silent treatment for a few days. Our decision about whether or not to confront someone with the truth must be based on what is right and not on what is convenient for us. The perpetrator's right-standing with God is more important than our selfish needs and desires. Nathan intervened because God wanted him to save David and Israel. Our decision to step in and confront someone with the truth must be motivated by our commitment to follow the Word of God.

Make It Happen

This week, ask God to speak to you about your personal style or the approach you use when you confront someone. Do you put people off with a confrontational or "too direct" approach? Are you "wishy-washy," or are you perhaps more concerned with having people like you than telling them the truth? Determine to listen even more, and pray even more for a word from God—not just about what you say, but how you say it.

Follow the Spirit

What God wants me to do:

Remember Your Thoughts

Special insights I have learned:

More Light on the Text

2 Samuel 12:1–7, 13–15

It has been suggested that the truest measure of a man's character is the degree to which he honors his commitments. David, as king, made a commitment to God to rule over God's people. As God's ruler, David was to be the embodiment of justice, mercy, love, and righteousness before the people. But in his willful sin with Bathsheba and then in orchestrating the death of her husband, Uriah, David abused and dishonored God's trust and the commitment he made as king. For this, he would need to be punished. Still, David was king and in many of the societies around him, the king was viewed as deity, and deity can do no wrong.

The Jewish nation differed from other nations around them in that they did not view their king as deity. The king, like the common man, had committed himself to obedience to the laws of the only living God. David had violated at least three of those laws and tried to cover it up. His sin was known, however, by God and by His prophet, Nathan, and it would become Nathan's responsibility to confront the king with his sin.

1 And the LORD sent Nathan unto David. And he came unto him, and said unto him, There were two men in one city; the one rich, and the other poor.

Because of the king's commitment to lead God's people, it is not surprising that King David would agree to an audience with Nathan, whom he knew to be God's messenger and prophet. Nathan, because of his commitment to be obedient to God's call upon his life and because of his responsibility before the people to be God's voice, responded positively when God instructed him to go and confront David. Having committed himself to being God's prophet, Nathan held a very special kind of influence with God's people and its leadership. Nathan would be able to place before David his failure as God's anointed, but even Nathan had to be careful how he carried out the task. The king held the power of life and death, even the life or death of a prophet seeking only to be obedient to the God he obligated himself to serve.

Nathan began his audience with King David by telling him a parable that appeared on the surface

"The thing that David had done displeased the LORD. And the LORD sent Nathan unto David. And he came unto him, and said unto him, There were two men in the city; the one rich, and the other poor" (2 Samuel 11:27–12:1).

to be an innocent story. His purpose in shaping the story the way that he did was to appeal to the king's sense of justice and fair play. The prophet understood that, as king, David had committed himself to being the arbiter of justice for the people. So Nathan began by setting up a conflict where the king could easily identify any hint of injustice. The parable begins by presenting two characters, a "rich" (Heb. *'ashiyr*, **aw-SHEER**) man and one who is "poor" (Heb. *ruwsh*, **roosh**) or destitute. David, who came from a background of poverty (1 Samuel 18:23) and is now wealthy, should be able to identify with both men.

2 The rich man had exceeding many flocks and herds: 3 But the poor man had nothing, save one little ewe lamb, which he had bought and nourished up: and it grew up together with him, and with his children; it did eat of his own meat, and drank of his own cup, and lay in his bosom, and was unto him as a daughter.

Nathan started his story by establishing the great distance between the rich man and the poor man. The rich man's wealth increased simply by the increase of his "flocks" (Heb. *tso'n*, **tsone**) and "herds" (Heb. *baqar*, **baw-KAWR**), but the poor man has only the one little "ewe lamb" (Heb. *kibsah*, **kib-SAW**) he somehow was able to purchase. After establishing the wealth of the one and the poverty of the other, Nathan then focused the king's attention on the poor man with only one prized possession. A good king, like David tried to be, was committed to caring for the poor and was empowered by the nation to insure that the poor received fair treatment. Nathan proceeded to paint a picture for David of the love and compassion that the poor man developed for the little lamb. In time, the two of them became so close that the lamb became like a daughter to the man. It became his companion and family. In the parable, David is like the rich man. The flocks and herds symbolize David's wives and concubines, while the poor man and his lamb symbolize Uriah and his wife.

4 And there came a traveller unto the rich man, and he spared to take of his own flock and of his own herd, to dress for the wayfaring man that was come unto him; but took the poor man's lamb, and dressed it for the man that was come to him.

The king must have perked up with eager attentiveness as Nathan shifted the story to the rich man and a visiting guest. The display of hospitality to travelers is always a welcomed occurrence in David's kingdom, but this was different. The rich man "spared" (Heb. *chamal,* **khaw-MAL**) using one of his own animals. He had pity on his own animals, but complete disregard for the poor man's single lamb. The rich man exploited the poor man, and this would not be tolerated. As King David had obligated himself to be both judge and protector, he was committed to this role and was determined that his administration as king would be marked by an overwhelming preference toward the poor. David would see that justice was served.

5 And David's anger was greatly kindled against the man; and he said to Nathan, As the LORD liveth, the man that hath done this thing shall surely die:

King David had become completely caught up in Nathan's story. In a righteous anger, David invoked God's name in a solemn oath as he pronounced a sentence of death upon the rich man. His outrage, however, was out of proportion with the man's offense. Usually a judgment was proportional to a person's crime. When he was not guilty of taking human life, David would not pronounce a death penalty upon a man. There is, within his outrage, the hint that David was subconsciously using this opportunity to elevate himself above his own human failings. The fire in his voice probably reminded the prophet of the proud, God-fearing leader who could dance before the Ark of the Covenant in joyous abandonment. But Nathan stood silent and still before the king and permitted David his indignation.

6 And he shall restore the lamb fourfold, because he did this thing, and because he had no pity.

Justice demanded restitution, and David would have the rich man recompense the poor man "fourfold" (Heb. *'arba'tayim,* **ar-bah-TAH-yim**) for his loss. David pronounced a sentence that corresponds in its exaggeration to the poor man's attachment to his lamb. He meant to see that the evildoer suffered for his misdeed. The essence of David's heart was revealed as he sought to punish the rich man because he had no pity on his poorer neighbor. Unaware that the parable was referring to him, David did not recognize that he was being trapped by his own judicial sentence.

7 And Nathan said to David, Thou art the man.

Suddenly David's eyes were opened to the truth that his sin with Bathsheba and her late husband was known. In the power of Nathan's story and David's condemnation of the rich man, David confronted his own guilt. Just as the man in the parable had no pity on the poor man, David acted likewise in taking Bathsheba from her husband and then orchestrating his death in battle to cover his own sin. David has acted like a wealthy oppressor, but Nathan had confronted him with his selfishness and injustice. David was not merely wealthy but also one who had misused his authority. In informing King David that the story was about him, Nathan stood in the full power of his commitment to serve God as His voice. The amount of courage it took for Nathan to utter those words to the king, we can only guess. But Nathan's commitment to his role as God's voice to the nation would permit him to do nothing less. Nathan's Commitment

12:13 And David said unto Nathan, I have sinned against the LORD. And Nathan said unto David, The LORD also hath put away thy sin; thou shalt not die.

David's commitment to God was genuine. He knew that he had held a favored position with God, and in honor of the relationship they had shared together, David confessed that he had sinned. Further, David acknowledged that his sin was not just against man, Bathsheba, Uriah, or the nation of Israel; rather he had "sinned" (Heb. *chata',* **khaw-TAW**) against God. God had a decision to make. Would he allow the judgment that David had pronounced from his own lips, to be David's own fate? No, God would not visit death upon His anointed king. God had made a commitment to David, and while his sin must be punished, David's life would be spared.

14 Howbeit, because by this deed thou hast given great occasion to the enemies of the LORD to blaspheme, the child also that is born unto thee shall surely die.

No such commitment existed between God and the fruit of David's sin, however, and Nathan informed the now-humbled king that the child he had fathered with Bathsheba would die. With the public knowledge of David's sin comes the opportunity for God's enemies to "blaspheme" (Heb. *na'ats*, **naw-ATS**, "to hold in contempt, spurn"), and God will not allow His reputation to be tarnished by this public sin. The child would die. The importance of this act cannot be overstated. David knew that God had promised that the King of kings would come through his lineage. Have his actions ended God's favor toward him? No. God's plans would come to fruition.

Nathan had just completed one of the most difficult tasks of his life. He told a king that he had sinned against God and that the fruit of that sin will die. In so doing, Nathan had indicated that his commitment to doing God's will was more important than even his own life.

15 And Nathan departed unto his house. And the LORD struck the child that Uriah's wife bare unto David, and it was very sick.

Nathan left the king and began the long trek home. When one has confronted a king like that, there is no place within the realm where one can feel safe. Nathan had to rely on the belief that God walked with him and that he has been faithful to the commitment he made as a prophet.

Little is known about the first child that Bathsheba bore to David. Neither the sex of the child nor its age when it died is revealed in the passage. Probably some time lapsed between Nathan's confrontation with the king and the birth of the baby. Sometime after the birth of the child, God's judgment against David was actualized. The Lord "struck" (Heb. *nagaph*, **naw-GAF**, "to smite, plague") the child with a fatal disease, and the death that God withheld from His anointed servant was visited upon the fruit of his sin. Still, we must remember that Nathan was more committed to God than he was to King David.

He knew that he had to answer to Almighty God, the God of Abraham, Isaac, and Jacob—the God who had called him to be His spokesman.

Source:
Packer, J. I., Merrill C. Tenney, and William White Jr., eds. *Illustrated Manners and Customs of the Bible.* Nashville: Thomas Nelson Publishers, 2003.

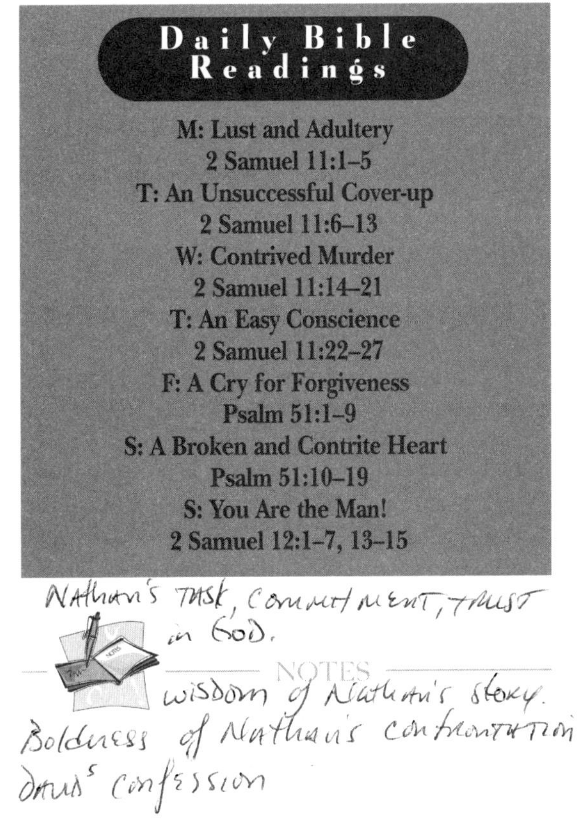

TEACHING TIPS

February 15

Bible Study Guide 11

1. Words You Should Know

A. Perceived (Esther 4:1) *yada‘* (Heb.)—Means recognizing or coming to understand or know.

B. Rent (v. 1) *qara‘* (Heb.)—Tear or rip into pieces.

C. Gave him commandment (v. 10) *tsavah* (Heb.)—Ordered or commanded.

2. Teacher Preparation

Unifying Principle—Risky Commitments. Some people are willing to make commitments that break rules at the risk of their own safety. Even at personal risk, for what people, cause, circumstance, or situation are you willing to commit to? Queen Esther was willing to sacrifice her life for the people of God.

A. Esther is a relatively short book, so read the book of Esther in its entirety. Use the King James Version and a modern translation such as the *New International Version* to enhance your study.

B. Study The People, Places, and Times and the More Light on the Text sections.

C. Pray and ask God to enable you to teach this lesson with passion and insight.

3. Starting the Lesson

A. Ask a volunteer to open the class with prayer.

B. Read the AIM for Change and Keep in Mind sections in unison.

C. Ask a volunteer to read the Background section, and then discuss the salient points.

D. Ask volunteers to take turns reading the Focal Verses, or have someone (who has already read and studied the verses) tell what the Focal Verses are about.

4. Getting into the Lesson

A. Share the In Depth section with the students, and then invite discussion.

B. Spend about 15 minutes discussing the Discuss the Meaning questions.

5. Relating the Lesson to Life

A. Ask a volunteer to read the In Focus story.

B. Allow time for the students to respond to the story.

6. Arousing Action

A. Encourage the students to follow through on the Make It Happen section.

B. Remind the students to do their Daily Bible Readings and meditate on each Scripture.

C. Close the class in prayer, asking God to provide opportunities for you and your students to demonstrate your commitment to our Lord, Jesus Christ.

Worship Guide

For the Superintendent or Teacher
Theme: Esther Risks Her Life
Theme Song: "In Times Like These"
Devotional Reading: Philippians 1:20–30
Prayer

ESTHER RISKS HER LIFE

Bible Background • ESTHER 4–5
Printed Text • ESTHER 4:1–3, 9–17 Devotional Reading • PHILIPPIANS 1:20–30

AIM for Change

By the end of the lesson we will:
IDENTIFY Esther's and Mordecai's commitments;
CONSIDER the implications of making commitments without respect to potential personal harm; and
MAKE commitments in spite of personal risk.

Keep in Mind

"Go, gather together all the Jews that are present in Shushan, and fast ye for me, and neither eat nor drink three days, night or day: I also and my maidens will fast likewise; and so will I go in unto the king, which is not according to the law: and if I perish, I perish" (Esther 4:16).

Focal Verses

KJV **Esther 4:1** When Mordecai perceived all that was done, Mordecai rent his clothes, and put on sackcloth with ashes, and went out into the midst of the city, and cried with a loud and a bitter cry;

2 And came even before the king's gate: for none might enter into the king's gate clothed with sackcloth.

3 And in every province, whithersoever the king's commandment and his decree came, there was great mourning among the Jews, and fasting, and weeping, and wailing; and many lay in sackcloth and ashes.

4:9 And Hatach came and told Esther the words of Mordecai.

10 Again Esther spake unto Hatach, and gave him commandment unto Mordecai;

11 All the king's servants, and the people of the king's provinces, do know, that whosoever, whether man or woman, shall come unto the king into the inner court, who is not called, there is one law of his to put him to death, except such to whom the king shall hold out the golden sceptre, that he may live: but I have not been called to come in unto the king these thirty days.

12 And they told to Mordecai Esther's words.

13 Then Mordecai commanded to answer Esther, Think not with thyself that thou shalt escape in the king's house, more than all the Jews.

14 For if thou altogether holdest thy peace at this time, then shall there enlargement and deliverance arise to the Jews from another place; but thou and

NLT **Esther 4:1** When Mordecai learned about all that had been done, he tore his clothes, put on burlap and ashes, and went out into the city, crying with a loud and bitter wail.

2 He went as far as the gate of the palace, for no one was allowed to enter the palace gate while wearing clothes of mourning.

3 And as news of the king's decree reached all the provinces, there was great mourning among the Jews. They fasted, wept, and wailed, and many people lay in burlap and ashes.

4:9 So Hathach returned to Esther with Mordecai's message.

10 Then Esther told Hathach to go back and relay this message to Mordecai:

11 "All the king's officials and even the people in the provinces know that anyone who appears before the king in his inner court without being invited is doomed to die unless the king holds out his gold scepter. And the king has not called for me to come to him for thirty days."

12 So Hathach gave Esther's message to Mordecai.

13 Mordecai sent this reply to Esther: "Don't think for a moment that because you're in the palace you will escape when all other Jews are killed.

14 If you keep quiet at a time like this, deliverance and relief for the Jews will arise from some other place, but you and your relatives will die. Who knows if perhaps you were made queen for just such a time as this?"

15 Then Esther sent this reply to Mordecai:

thy father's house shall be destroyed: and who knoweth whether thou art come to the kingdom for such a time as this?

15 Then Esther bade them return Mordecai this answer,

16 Go, gather together all the Jews that are present in Shushan, and fast ye for me, and neither eat nor drink three days, night or day: I also and my maidens will fast likewise; and so will I go in unto the king, which is not according to the law: and if I perish, I perish.

17 So Mordecai went his way, and did according to all that Esther had commanded him.

16 "Go and gather together all the Jews of Susa and fast for me. Do not eat or drink for three days, night or day. My maids and I will do the same. And then, though it is against the law, I will go in to see the king. If I must die, I must die."

17 So Mordecai went away and did everything as Esther had ordered him.

In Focus

Dolores had just sat down in the cafeteria when several of the women from the firm's accounting department sat down at the table next to her and began to chat. Dolores took a sip of her juice, opened the quarterly report, and began reading in preparation for a departmental meeting scheduled for the afternoon. The women at the table next to her were talking so loudly that it was difficult for her to concentrate on the numbers in front of her. One of the women said, "I know it's wrong, but I can't stand those people!"

Dolores looked up. She recognized the speaker as Celeste, a young woman who attended the 8:00 a.m. services at her church. Dolores was shocked by the vehemence she heard in Celeste's voice. "They don't believe in God, just in that Muhammad or whatever. All I know is that all of them are going straight to hell! They own every gas station in town, and now this company is hiring them, too. It's just wrong!"

One of the other women joined in. "If I see one more woman with a veil on, I don't know what I'll do. They come over here to America, but they want to keep their own ways, like they think they're better than us. If this country is good enough to come to, then they ought to dress like us."

Another woman, June, sucked her teeth and chimed in, "You know the company had the nerve to assign three of them to my section. If this company thinks I'm actually going to train them while American soldiers have died over there, they must be crazy! They had better figure it out on their own, because I'm not going to teach them anything!"

Dolores continued to listen as the three women complained about the Arab women who had recently been hired by the firm. The women, all African American, criticized the religion and modest dress of the Arab women and expressed their outrage that although the Arab women spoke English, their accents made them difficult to understand at times. There were continued references to 9/11. One of the women had said that she wouldn't be surprised if the new workers were terrorists.

Dolores was shocked by the hatred she heard. Many of the things the women were saying were not true. Dolores was assistant director of personnel, and she had been involved in the hiring of all three of the Arab women. She knew that two of them were Christian Arabs; in fact, one of them was the wife of a missionary. All three of the women were well educated, and although they did have accents, she had found them articulate and had no problem understanding them.

Dolores was especially concerned about June's declaration that she was not going to train the woman assigned to her unit. From the conversation she had overheard, Dolores knew the Arab women in Celeste's unit would not receive proper training and would probably be dismissed at the end of their probation periods. Dolores also knew that June was a department manager; she had been with the company for 29 years and was scheduled to retire at the end of the year. If Dolores reported what she knew, it could possibly threaten June's pension. If that happened, she knew many of the people at the firm would hold her responsible. Celeste and the other women at the table were not the only ones who held strong anti-Arab sentiments. Dolores' own manager had refused to sit on the interview panels of all three of the Arab women.

In today's lesson, like Delores, Esther is called to make a commitment. However, if Esther decides to stand up and take action, her position and her life are in jeopardy.

The People, Places, and Times

Jewish Exile in Persia. The people known in the Bible as the Persians are actually a combination of two groups—the Medes and the Persians. These two groups were descendants of ancient Indo-Iranian tribes. Persians were a nomadic group, primarily concerned with agriculture and raising livestock. The Persians controlled the southwestern portion of the Iranian plateau. The Median Empire came under the control of the Persians during the rule of Cyrus the Great; however, the two groups continued to exhibit a dual nature in the kingdom. In 539 B.C., Cyrus led a combined army of Persians, Medes, and Elamites to conquer Babylon. The Persian Empire was thus expanded west to the Aegean Sea, and, more importantly, the land of Judah came into the Persian domain. Babylon served as the religious and commercial capital of the Medo-Persian Empire. Shushan was the site of the royal palace and the administrative center of the empire. Darius was tolerant of the Jews, who were busy trying to complete the construction the temple in Jerusalem and reestablish their lives in Palestine. The relations between Darius and the Jews were relatively peaceful and free from strife.

The reign of Xerxes I (Ahasuerus in the book of Esther), the son of Darius the Great, began in 495 B.C. At this time, his empire extended from India to Ethiopia. Serious errors in judgment marked Xerxes' reign, including angering the Egyptian priests by looting their temples, enraging the Greeks by burning Athens, destroying the temples of Babylon, and forbidding the Jews to complete the building of the walls of Jerusalem. It was apparently during the third year of his reign that Xerxes hosted an elaborate banquet for his princes, governors, and high-ranking army personnel. This feast and subsequent actions of Xerxes are recorded in the Book of Esther.

Source:

Packer, J. I., Merrill C. Tenney, and William White Jr., eds. *Illustrated Manners and Customs of the Bible.* Nashville: Thomas Nelson Publishers, 2003.

Background

The book of Esther is among those books of the Old Testament known as "the Writings." The account is set during the time following the Persian conquest of Babylon, about 486–465 B.C. It recounts the story of Hadassah, or Esther, a Jewish orphan of the tribe of Benjamin. Esther's guardian was Mordecai, the nephew of Esther's father (Esther 2:15). Mordecai was a servant in the palace of King Xerxes I, or Ahasuerus. During the third year of his reign, Ahasuerus hosted a royal banquet. As a grand finale, the king summoned Vashti, the queen, to appear in her regal attire to display her beauty and enhance the king's glory. Vashti refused, and a humiliated Ahasuerus deposed her for this act of disobedience. In the seventh year of his reign, Ahasuerus selected Esther, from all of the beautiful virgins in his kingdom, to replace Vashti as his queen. Esther followed the counsel of Mordecai and did not reveal to the king that she was a Jew.

When Mordecai uncovered a plot to kill the king, he told Esther, who in turn told her husband the king. He had the would-be assassins executed. The book of Esther presents a prosperous and well-integrated Jewish community living in Persia. The books of Ezra and Nehemiah describe the events that followed the conquest of Babylon by the Persian King Cyrus. After this conquest, Cyrus issued a declaration permitting all the conquered nations in exile in Babylon to return to their homelands. As Babylon declined and the kingdom of Persia rose, 70 years of exile came to an end. The Jews had finally been allowed to return to their homeland. Surprisingly, only a few participated in the return. Many of the Jews had become comfortable, and they had elected to remain in the land of their captivity. Mordecai was among this large population of Jews who, although free to return to Israel, chose to remain.

In chapter 3, we are introduced to Haman, "the son of Hammedatha the Agagite," a prime minister in the royal court. The king admired Haman so much that he "set his seat above all the princes that were with him" (Esther 3:1). Mordecai alone refused to bow and reverence Haman in recognition of his advancement by the king. When asked why he would not bow before Haman, Mordecai revealed for the first time that he was a Jew.

Haman was enraged and would not allow this slight to go unpunished. He approached the king and told him of an alleged act of treason. Haman told the king that "There is a certain people scattered abroad and dispersed among the people in all the provinces of thy kingdom; and their laws are diverse from all people; neither keep they the king's laws: therefore it is not for the king's profit to suffer them" (Esther 3:8). Haman pointed to the religious differences of the Jews and purported to the king that these differences posed a threat to national security. While it was true that the Jews were dispersed throughout the kingdom, he was lying when he told the king the Jews were not lawful.

Haman was outraged at Mordecai's refusal to bow before him. Here we see him attempt to exact his revenge on the entire Jewish population. Haman pressed further and offered a very large sum of money to Ahasuerus to proclaim a certain day as the time when anyone in the kingdom could kill every living Jew he encountered and then confiscate their property. Unknown to Ahasuerus, Haman had a personal agenda, and he was using the king to annihilate all the Jews in the empire. Ahasuerus, perhaps still bitter about Vashti's refusal to be submissive to his rule, authorized Haman's plan and issued a decree to carry out Haman's plan. The king was unaware of the ethnic identity of his wife, Esther, and so when he authorized the decree, Ahasuerus was unaware the he was signing her death warrant.

At-A-Glance

1. Mordecai Mourns for His People (Esther 4:1–3)
2. Mordecai Challenges Esther (v. 9)
3. Esther Reluctantly Responds (vv. 10–12)
4. Mordecai Expresses Confidence in God's Plan (vv. 13–14)
5. Esther Commits to Confrontation (vv. 15–17)

In Depth

1. Mordecai Mourns for His People (Esther 4:1–3)

When chapter 4 begins, Haman, enraged that Mordecai would not bow down before him, gave false information to King Ahasuerus. He suggested that certain unnamed groups within the kingdom posed a national security threat. Haman talked the king into allowing him to issue a royal decree. The decree was that on a specific day—"the thirteenth day of the twelfth month, which is the month Adar" (Esther 3:13)—permission would be given for all people of the empire to rise up and put to death every Jew (every man, woman and child) and that they could do this without fear of prosecution. They could kill them all and confiscate their lands and their possessions.

When Haman took his plan to the king for the king's signature on the decree, Ahasuerus had only a few minor questions. Haman cleverly replied to whatever questions the king asked, suggesting that the unnamed people were unruly and that they did not follow the laws of the king. Haman appealed to the greed of the king by offering ten thousand talents of silver to be deposited into the coffers of the king.

With the authority—if not complete understanding of the king—Haman proceeded to try to eradicate the Jews. The first step in his evil plan was notification of the proclamation. The Persian Empire was vast and so "letters were sent by posts into all the king's provinces, to destroy, to kill, and to cause to perish, all Jews, both young and old, little children and women, in one day" (Esther 3:13). While Mordecai's refusal to bow down before Haman seems to be the catalyst for Haman's maniacal plot to destroy millions of Jews, Haman's hatred of the Jews may have deeper and farther-reaching implications. Biblical scholars have surmised that Haman was a descendant of King Agag of the nation of Amalek. The Amalekites were ancient enemies of the Jews. Israel's first king, Saul, had fought a war with the Amalekites and had been instructed by God to wipe out the entire nation. However, Saul had disobeyed, and instead of killing King Agag, Saul had taken him captive. These scholars argue that Agag managed to father a child during his imprisonment and it was from this child that Haman descended.

When Mordecai learned of the decree, he was immediately overcome with sorrow and grief. He tore his clothes and put on sackcloth and ashes. This was the attire worn by the ancient prophets to indicate they were in mourning. Mordecai's mourning was not done in private. He went into the center of the city and began to cry and wail loudly. This further demonstrates the sincerity of Mordecai's grief. We can reasonably assume that a part of Mordecai's sorrow lay in the fact that his refusal to bow down to Haman had caused the catastrophe that now threatened the life of every Jew in the kingdom. Like Mordecai, the hearts of present-day Christians should break when they perceive or understand that their actions have caused pain or suffering to others.

Mordecai was not alone in grieving for the fate of his people. As the written decree arrived, Jews in every province shared Mordecai's grief. Their mourning, fasting, weeping, and wailing are evidence that they recognized the terrible danger they now faced. Like Mordecai, they put on sackcloth and ashes.

2. Mordecai Challenges Esther (v. 9)

Mordecai cried and wailed right in front of the "king's gate (4:2). When Esther heard that her guardian, Mordecai, was standing in the middle of the city weeping and wearing sackcloth and ashes, she immediately sent him clothes. Initially, Esther did nothing to find out why Mordecai was distressed. Instead, she sought to silence his mourning by offering him clothes. Sadly, too often this is the response of modern-day people. We readily respond to the misery and suffering of others with a check. Money is not the only answer, nor is it an indication of our commitment to love our neighbor. True Christian commitment is our compassion and concern for their welfare.

It is possible Esther was embarrassed that Mordecai should behave so unseemly in public. Another possibility for the clothing offer is that Esther knew Mordecai was prohibited from entering the palace while wearing sackcloth. She probably wanted him to have the new clothing so that he could come to her and speak with her face-to-face. It is also likely that Esther was genuinely concerned about Mordecai's distress, and her offer of clothing was made to comfort him. In either case, Mordecai refused the clothing Esther offered, and he continued mourning. It is only when he refused the clothing that Esther tried to find out why Mordecai was so grief-stricken. She sent her servant, Hatach, to Mordecai. Mordecai told Hatach about the decree and explained that it would mean the slaughter of Jews. Mordecai went on to report exactly who was responsible and even how much money Haman had offered to pay into the king's treasury to bring about the Jews' destruction.

To help Esther see for herself just how grave the situation was, Mordecai even sent her a copy of the decree itself. He then gave instruction to Esther to go herself to talk to the king and appeal to him on behalf of her people.

Here we see that Mordecai did more than just grieve over the problem—he had a plan for dealing with it. Mordecai believed that Esther was in a position to influence the king, so he asked her to use her influence as a means to benefit her people. When we face difficult circumstances in our lives, we must trust God for deliverance, but we should also consider what we can do about the problem and use our opportunities to resolve it. The urgency felt by Mordecai is revealed in the fact that by sending this message through the servant, he was risking the secret that the queen is a Jew.

3. Esther Reluctantly Responds (vv. 10–12)

When Hatach delivered the message to Esther, her initial response was avoidance. Esther could only look at the difficulties of the situation and make excuses why she could not help.

In the message she sent back to Mordecai, Esther reminded him that Persian law forbade anyone to enter the king's inner court unless the king first summoned them. Unless the king held out his golden scepter to an uninvited guest, the person would be killed. Esther went on to explain that she had not been called to an audience with the king in the previous 30 days. This would indicate that she foresaw no opportunity to speak to the king.

4. Mordecai Expresses Confidence in God's Plan (vv. 13–14)

Mordecai did not accept any of Esther's excuses. We should not take this to mean that he did not believe the danger to Esther was real. However, Mordecai did not allow his personal attachment to his cousin to sway his judgment about what she needed to do. He had raised Esther. He had shown his love for her repeatedly. Yet, now, he wanted Esther to act, despite the danger.

When making a decision to stand up to something that is wrong, something that could bring hardship into our lives, in many ways we face similar situations. Like Esther, we have a choice. Our natural tendency will be to avoid confrontation and to seek comfort and safety. Our commitment to the Lord dictates that we overcome those tendencies and act in ways that God's will requires. This does not mean that we ignore the possibility of facing hardship. Our call is to act despite those hardships.

While our commitment to please the Lord may result in our displeasing men, we must do as Mordecai and remember that we face a far worse danger if we disobey God.

Because of the threat to her position as queen and the possible threat to her very life, Esther made excuses. Mordecai responded to her excuses by offering her encouragement to do right. Perhaps believing that Esther was not aware of exactly what was at stake, Mordecai pressed on. He told her, "Think not with thyself that thou shalt escape in the king's house, more than all the Jews" (v. 13). Here Mordecai was direct with Esther and warned her that she could not hide behind the crown. He insisted that she, too, would suffer if she did not use her position to benefit God's people. Mordecai said she and her father's house would perish. His next statement was outstanding. He told Esther that even if she did fail to act, he was confident that God would find some other means to save His people. While the name of God is not mentioned in the text, it is clearly divine intervention to which Mordecai refers.

The law of the king was universal and final at that time. Mordecai expressed belief that only God can override a royal decree, and only the will of God can supersede the will of the king. It is important to note that Mordecai's statement is one of supreme confidence. He knew the Jews were God's chosen people, and he would also have known that the promises of God to Abraham required that his descendants must continue, not be destroyed. Mordecai was letting Esther know that somehow God would spare His people and honor His covenant promise that the Jews—His people—would be a blessing on all nations. Although this would mean that many Jews would suffer and perhaps be killed, God's chosen nation would survive to fulfill God's purposes.

Mordecai also proposed that Esther may have come to power as queen for the very purpose of being useful to God's purpose as this very time: "who knoweth whether thou art come to the kingdom for such a time as this?" (v. 14). Here we are reminded of how God used his servant Joseph. Joseph rose from the position of Egyptian slave to prime minister at the exact time he was needed to save the Israelites. In the case of Esther and Joseph, it is important that we recognize that God does not violate the free will of any individual. Esther, like Joseph, had the ability to choose whether or not she would respond to the call of God. This right is extended to present-day Christians. God will not force us to act; the decision to commit is ours. How wonderful it is to know that God delights in using men and women for His purposes, even though He does not *need* them. God has many resources available to Him.

5. Esther Commits to Confrontation (vv. 15–17)

After she considered Mordecai's appeal, Esther sent her answer. She decided that she would go before the king. Her determination is expressed in her simple declaration, "If I perish, I perish!" Esther's statement is not one of resignation, nor should we view it as fatalistic. Rather, Esther's remark is a statement of faith. She was willing to serve God, according to His will, regardless of the price she may have needed to pay. Regardless of the potential difficulties or dangers that lie ahead, Esther was committed to proceeding. When Esther says, "I go in unto the king, which is not according to the law," we should recognize that Esther's approaching the king uninvited would be against the law, only if the king did not choose to recognize her. Even so, Esther was demonstrating great courage in her decision to obey God rather than men. Is our commitment deep enough that we will be able to demonstrate Esther's courage and to violate human law when necessary to obey God?

Notice that now Esther's understanding of the task before her is much deeper. While she had the resolve to face the king, she also knew that she must prepare. Before making her request of the king, she realized the need for her and her servants to fast. Esther called on all the Jews in Shushan to join her in this fast. Again, we note that God was not mentioned; however, examples in Ezra and Nehemiah make it clear that Esther's purpose for fasting was to make an appeal to God before she made her request to her husband, the king. This, too, should be our attitude. When we are about to undertake the work of the Lord, we want to ask Him for His blessings on our work. The time may come when our work for God involves some dangers. What a blessed assurance it is to know that we can cast our burdens on Him in prayer!

After he heard of Esther's decision to confront the king, Mordecai demonstrated his support of Esther by urging the Jews to fast on her behalf.

Search the Scriptures

1. "When Mordecai perceived all that was done, Mordecai ________ his clothes, and put on sackcloth with ashes" (Esther 4:1).

2. "And came even before the king's gate: for none might enter into the king's gate clothed with ________" (v. 2).

3. "And in every province, whithersoever the king's commandment and his decree came, there was great ________ among the Jews, and fasting, and weeping, and wailing; and many lay in sackcloth and ashes" (v. 3).

4. "For if thou altogether holdest thy ________ at this time, then shall there enlargement and deliverance arise to the Jews from another place" (v. 14).

5. "Then Esther bade them return Mordecai this ________" (v. 15).

6. "Go, gather together all the Jews that are present in ________ and fast ye for me, and neither eat nor drink three days, night or day" (v. 16).

Discuss the Meaning

1. What actual power did Esther have or not have in the Persian court? Discuss how this influences your view of her actions.

2. Consider times in your own life when you might have been challenged to use what you have been given for the benefit of others who were being oppressed. How did you respond?

3. No affirmation of personal faith is made in the book of Esther, nor are any clear references to prayer or repentance made by either Esther or Mordecai. Does this make it more difficult for you to view this account as an example of Esther making a commitment to God? Why or why not?

Lesson in Our Society

In this lesson Esther, a Jew, found herself in a position of power and influence as queen in the court of the Persian emperor. When the Jewish people were threatened, her cousin challenged her to consider if God had raised her to a position of power "for such a time as this." We should consider times in our own lives when we might have been challenged to use our influence for the benefit of others, who were being oppressed. How did we respond? Let us consider our commitment to God. He is calling on us to use what He has given us "for such a time as this!"

Make It Happen

If your commitment to Jesus Christ is sincere, ask God to give you more insight so that you can recognize and address injustices that are occurring around you every day. First, it would be best for you to enter into a period of fasting, praying, and targeted Bible study.

Follow the Spirit

What God wants me to do:

____

____

Remember Your Thoughts

Special insights I have learned:

____

____

More Light on the Text

Esther 4:1–3, 9–17

1 When Mordecai perceived all that was done, Mordecai rent his clothes, and put on sackcloth with ashes, and went out into the midst of the city, and cried with a loud and a bitter cry; 2 And came even before the king's gate: for none might enter into the king's gate clothed with sackcloth.

When Mordecai, Esther's cousin and adoptive father, learned of the diabolical decree to annihilate the Jews, he "rent" (Heb. *qara'*, **kaw-RAH**, meaning "to tear in pieces") his good clothes and royal robes and put on "sackcloth" (Heb. *saq*, **sak**, meaning "sackcloth worn in mourning or humiliation"), clothes worn as a sign of suffering, lamentation, and desperation. He adorned his face with "ashes" (Heb. *'epher*, **AY-fer**, meaning "ashes," figuratively means "worthlessness"). Leaving the sanctuary of the palace, Mordecai stood out in the open streets and "cried" (Heb. *za'aq*, **ZAH-ak**, meaning "to call out for help") with a loud voice. He was careful to not dishonor the palace with his lament; however, Mordecai protested the fate of the Jews openly and loudly!

3 And in every province, whithersoever the king's commandment and his decree came, there was great mourning among the Jews, and fasting, and weeping, and wailing; and many lay in sackcloth and ashes.

As news of the king's "decree" (Heb. *dath*, **dawth**, meaning "law, edict")—acquired through Haman's trickery—spread abroad to all in the land, the Jews

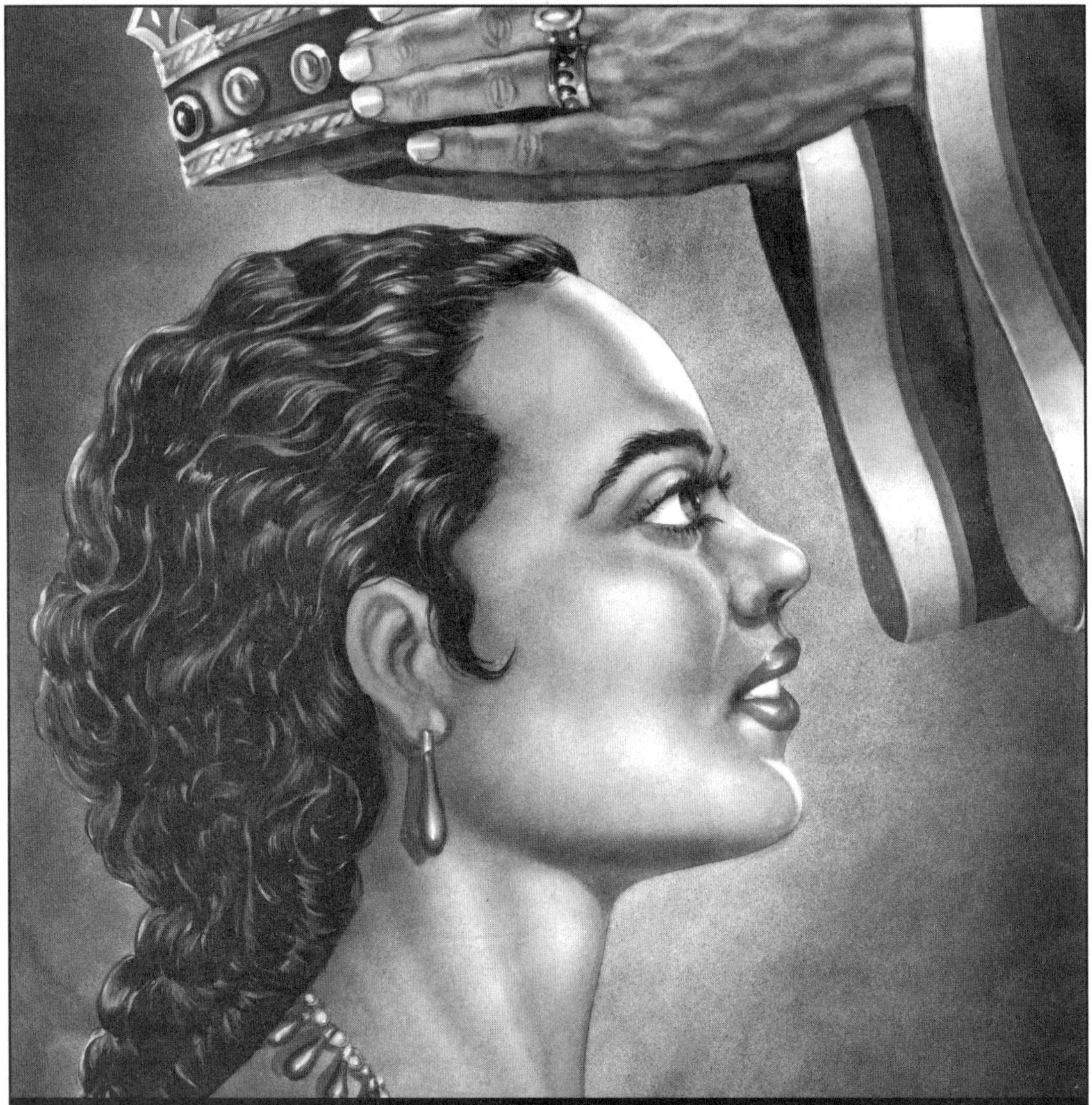

"Go, gather together all the Jews that are present in Shushan, and fast ye for me, and neither eat nor drink three days, night or day: I also and my maidens will fast likewise; and so will I go in unto the king, which is not accorkding to the law: and if I perish, I perish" (Esther 4:16). Pictured here is Esther being crowned.

were overcome with grief and were "mourning" (Heb. *'ebel,* **AY-bel**). In response to Mordecai's example and as was customary for the Jews when facing a formidable foe, they began "fasting" (Heb. *tsowm,* **tsome**), "weeping" (Heb. *bekiy,* **bek-EE**), and "wailing" (Heb. *micped,* **mis-PADE**).

4:9 And Hatach came and told Esther the words of Mordecai. 10 Again Esther spake unto Hatach, and gave him commandment unto Mordecai; 11 All the king's servants, and the people of the king's provinces, do know, that whosoever, whether man or woman, shall come unto the king into the inner court, who is not called, there is one law of his to put him to death, except such to whom the king shall hold out the golden sceptre, that he may live: but I have not been called to come in unto the king these thirty days.

As Mordecai initiated a plan of salvation for the Jews, it was Mordecai's former colleague in the king's court, Hathach, a eunuch who served in Ahasuerus' court, who became the messenger between Mordecai and "Esther" (Heb. *'Ecter,* **es-TARE**, meaning "star, happiness" and whose Jewish birth name is *Hadassah*, **had-as-SAW**). Esther replied to his message with an excuse of a certain "death" (Heb. *muwth*, **mooth**, meaning "to have one executed"), unless the king called for her presence or was so moved to hold out his scepter of protection and acceptance should she arrive without him calling for her.

12 And they told to Mordecai Esther's words. 13 Then Mordecai commanded to answer Esther, Think not with thyself that thou shalt escape in the king's house, more than all the Jews.

Fearing that Esther had forgotten her roots, Mordecai cut to the chase and challenged her fears with the reality that once she was found out to be a Jew, even her life ("thyself," Heb. *nephesh*, **NEH-fesh**, meaning "soul, life") would not be spared ("escape," Heb. *malat*, **maw-LAT**, meaning "to be delivered, saved").

14 For if thou altogether holdest thy peace at this time, then shall there enlargement and deliverance arise to the Jews from another place; but thou and thy father's house shall be destroyed: and who knoweth whether thou art come to the kingdom for such a time as this?

Mordecai further challenged Esther that if she remained undercover, comfortable, and silent, certainly "deliverance" (Heb. *hatstsalah*, **hats-tsaw-LAW**) for the Jews would surely come. However, Esther, Mordecai, and their relatives would be killed or "destroyed" (Heb. *'abad*, **aw-BAD**, meaning "be exterminated, perish, vanish"). Mordecai exhorted Esther to consider whether she had been set in the queenly position ("kingdom," Heb. *malkuwth*, **mal-KOOTH**, meaning "royalty, royal power, sovereign power") so that she might be in position to speak up in this crisis.

15 Then Esther bade them return Mordecai this answer, 16 Go, gather together all the Jews that are present in Shushan, and fast ye for me, and neither eat nor drink three days, night or day: I also and my maidens will fast likewise; and so will I go in unto the king, which is not according to the law: and if I perish, I perish. 17 So Mordecai went his way, and did according to all that Esther had commanded him.

Upon Mordecai's urgent insistence, Esther finally got the message and the courage to respond based on her position as queen. She sent a message beyond the palace walls to Mordecai to have all of the Jews in the region of "Shushan" (Heb. *Shuwshan*, **shoo-SHAN**, meaning "lily" also named "Susa") to sanctify a fast on her behalf. Esther then called into prayerful agreement the "maidens" (Heb. *na'arah*, **nah-ar-AW**, meaning "female servants") assigned to serve her to also fast and pray. Esther, being covered on the outside and on the inside, found courage to reconcile her willingness to die, or "perish" (Heb. *'abad*, **aw-BAD**, meaning "to perish, be destroyed"), with the stark realization that she was to serve her people in this time of national crisis and attempted ethnic cleansing. Risking her very life, Esther chose this path of cultural dishonor and civil disobedience to effect Jewish national salvation.

Source:

Packer, J. I., Merrill C. Tenney, and William White Jr., eds. *Illustrated Manners and Customs of the Bible.* Nashville: Thomas Nelson Publishers, 2003.

Daily Bible Readings

M: The Search for a Queen
Esther 2:1–11
T: A New Queen
Esther 2:15–18
W: A Plot Thwarted
Esther 2:19–23
T: An Evil Edict
Esther 3:7–13
F: The Evil Intent Revealed
Esther 7:1–10
S: The People Rescued
Esther 8:3–8
S: If I Perish, I Perish
Esther 4:1–3, 9–17

NOTES

TEACHING TIPS

February 22

Bible Study Guide 12

1. Words You Should Know

A. Train (Isaiah 6:1) *shuwl* (Heb.)—The skirt or the hem of a robe.

B. The seraphims (v. 2) *saraph* (Heb.)—Majestic beings with six wings, human hands, or voices in attendance upon God.

C. Twain (v. 2) *shenayim* (Heb.)—Two, both, double, twice.

D. Of hosts (v. 3) *tsaba'* (Heb.)—That which goes forth; army, war, warfare, host.

2. Teacher Preparation

Unifying Principle—A Commitment to Change. Some people may be required to give up a way of life in order to fulfill their commitments. How much are we willing to sacrifice for a commitment? Isaiah answered God's call to commitment by giving up everything and moving on. He did what God had called Him to do.

A. Pray for the students in your class and ask God how to navigate them through the lesson to enhance their takeaway value.

B. Study and meditate on the lesson.

C. To enhance you and your students' learning experience, also study the More Light on the Text in detail. Then see what spiritual principles you can draw from the lesson.

D. Bring some 3 x 5" index cards to class.

3. Starting the Lesson

A. Pray for the students in your class, asking God to open their hearts to today's lesson.

B. Review the Focal Verses; Bible Background; The People, Places, and Times; and the In Depth sections.

C. Review AIM for Change, and reflect on how this lesson relates to your own life.

4. Getting into the Lesson

A. Ask for a volunteer to lead the class in prayer.

B. Have the students read the Keep in Mind verse in unison.

C. Have volunteers read the Focal Verses. Stimulate discussion.

5. Relating the Lesson to Life

A. Ask for a volunteer to read the In Focus story.

B. Allow time for the students to discuss the story.

6. Arousing Action

A. Read the Lesson in Our Society and Make It Happen sections aloud.

B. Pass out 3 x 5" index cards, and ask the students to make a list of things that God has asked them to do, but they have not committed to doing them.

C. Encourage your students to take out the cards during the week and make the items on the card a matter of prayer.

Worship Guide

For the Superintendent or Teacher
Theme: Isaiah Answers God's Call
Theme Song: "Here Am I, Lord Send Me"
Devotional Reading: Revelation 4
Prayer

ISAIAH ANSWERS GOD'S CALL

Bible Background • ISAIAH 6
Printed Text • ISAIAH 6:1–8 Devotional Reading • REVELATION 4

AIM for Change

By the end of the lesson, we will:
DISCOVER the motivation for Isaiah's commitment;
EXPLORE the limits of our commitment and identify circumstances in which we might be willing to go beyond those limits; and
MOVE beyond our present limits to expand our commitments to God.

Keep in Mind

"Also I heard the voice of the Lord, saying, Whom shall I send, and who will go for us? Then said I, Here am I; send me" (Isaiah 6:8).

Focal Verses

KJV **Isaiah 6:1** In the year that king Uzziah died I saw also the LORD sitting upon a throne, high and lifted up, and his train filled the temple.

2 Above it stood the seraphims: each one had six wings; with twain he covered his face, and with twain he covered his feet, and with twain he did fly.

3 And one cried unto another, and said, Holy, holy, holy, is the LORD of hosts: the whole earth is full of his glory.

4 And the posts of the door moved at the voice of him that cried, and the house was filled with smoke.

5 Then said I, Woe is me! for I am undone; because I am a man of unclean lips, and I dwell in the midst of a people of unclean lips: for mine eyes have seen the King, the LORD of hosts.

6 Then flew one of the seraphims unto me, having a live coal in his hand, which he had taken with the tongs from off the altar:

7 And he laid it upon my mouth, and said, Lo, this hath touched thy lips; and thine iniquity is taken away, and thy sin purged.

8 Also I heard the voice of the Lord, saying, Whom shall I send, and who will go for us? Then said I, Here am I; send me.

NLT **Isaiah 6:1** It was in the year King Uzziah died that I saw the Lord. He was sitting on a lofty throne, and the train of his robe filled the Temple.

2 Attending him were mighty seraphim, each having six wings. With two wings they covered their faces, with two they covered their feet, and with two they flew.

3 They were calling out to each other, "Holy, holy, holy is the LORD of Heaven's Armies! The whole earth is filled with his glory!"

4 Their voices shook the Temple to its foundations, and the entire building was filled with smoke.

5 Then I said, "It's all over! I am doomed, for I am a sinful man. I have filthy lips, and I live among a people with filthy lips. Yet I have seen the King, the LORD of Heaven's Armies."

6 Then one of the seraphim flew to me with a burning coal he had taken from the altar with a pair of tongs.

7 He touched my lips with it and said, "See, this coal has touched your lips. Now your guilt is removed, and your sins are forgiven."

8 Then I heard the Lord asking, "Whom should I send as a messenger to this people? Who will go for us?" I said, "Here I am. Send me."

In Focus

Gina splashed some cold water on her face and dried it. She hesitated before leaving the bathroom and returning to her bedroom. She and her husband, Jerome, had been arguing all evening. Last week, Jerome had told Gina that he believed they ought to cut off their relationship with another couple, Bill and Kathy. She and Jerome had known Bill and Kathy for more than 20 years. Jerome and Bill had retired from the same company six years ago, and they fished together regularly. Gina and Kathy shopped together and were members of the same book club. The couples had taken numerous vacations together, and they went out to dinner on the last Friday of every month. Now, Jerome wanted to end all of that. He had explained that he had been in prayer about the situation for months. He was concerned that the lifestyle and beliefs of Bill and Kathy were not pleasing to God, and he thought it was hypocritical for Gina and him to continue such a close relationship.

Gina knew that neither Bill nor Kathy was saved. Over the years, she had attempted to witness to both of them, but Bill would just throw up his hands and leave the room. Kathy always turned it into a joke. She would laugh and accuse Gina of being a "religious fanatic." Bill and Kathy were both heavy drinkers. Gina and Jerome would always insist on driving. When they were drinking, Kathy would often curse and swear, and Bill would tell off-color jokes. Because the couples had known each other for so long, Gina had overlooked all of this. She disliked their behavior, but she loved both of them dearly. How in the world was she going to convince her husband to just turn a deaf ear and just continue to look the other way?

Gina's husband, Jerome, believes God is leading him to break off the relationship with his friend. Do you agree that he should? In today's lesson, we will study the prophet Isaiah's call and see that a revelation of the holiness of God will result in a corresponding change in the heart.

The People, Places, and Times

Isaiah. He was the son of Amoz and a prophet of the southern kingdom of Judah who lived in the eighth century B.C. Isaiah lived and ministered in Jerusalem for 58 years. He prophesied during the reigns of kings Uzziah, Jotham, Ahaz, and Hezekiah. Although the Bible does not record the tribe from which Isaiah is descended, Jewish tradition suggests that Isaiah may have been related to Judah's royal family. This would explain why Isaiah enjoyed relatively easy access to the kings of Judah.

Isaiah was married, and his wife is referred to as a prophetess (Isaiah 8:3). It is unclear whether this means that she was married to a prophet or if she acted in the office of a prophet. Isaiah was the father of at least two children, both of whom were given symbolic names. One was named Shear-Jashub, which means, "a remnant shall return." The name of the other was Maher-shalal-hash-baz.

According to the Scriptures, Isaiah had disciples (Isaiah 8:16). These disciples acted as scribes and may have assisted Isaiah in his ministry work. This relationship with his disciples appears to have been similar to that which Samuel and Elisha had with the "sons of the prophets" or that Jeremiah had with Baruch.

Isaiah is believed to have been the author of the biographies of King Uzziah (2 Chronicles 26:22) and King Hezekiah (2 Chronicles 32:32). At God's direction, Isaiah humbled himself and he went about for three years "naked" and barefoot (Isaiah 20). No other prophet predicted the birth of the Messiah, Christ Jesus, to the extent Isaiah did. He also prophesied extensively about the ministry and the sufferings of the Messiah for the sins of humanity. While it is not certain exactly how Isaiah died, a pseudepigraphical work called "The Ascension of Isaiah," states that he was sawn in two with a wooden saw during the reign of Manasseh. It is possible that the writer of Hebrews is referring to this event when he wrote: "They were stoned, they were sawn asunder" (Hebrews 11:37).

Source:

Packer, J. I., Merrill C. Tenney, and William White Jr., eds. *Illustrated Manners and Customs of the Bible.* Nashville: Thomas Nelson Publishers, 2003.

Background

The eighth century B.C. was a tumultuous time for the northern and southern kingdoms of Israel and Judah. This period saw the rise of four major prophets: Amos and Hosea in Israel and Isaiah and Micah in Judah. According to Isaiah 6:1, Isaiah received his call in about 642 B.C.: "the year King Uzziah died." King Uzziah, also known as Azariah, began his long reign in 783 B.C. In about 750 B.C. Jotham, his son, was made co-regent. After the death of his father, Jotham reigned another seven years. When Isaiah began his ministry, Menahem was king of Israel. Menahem was the fourth king in less than one year. Jeroboam II's death in 746, after 40 years on the throne, was followed by six kings, leading to the fall of Samaria in 721 B.C. to the Assyrians. In the southern kingdom, Jotham was succeeded by Ahaz and then by Hezekiah. This age was marked by the rise of Assyria to become the dominant power in the Near East. Tiglath-Pileser III ascended the throne in 745 B.C. and ruled until 727

B.C. In his second year in power, shortly before Isaiah began his ministry, he marched his army westward and occupied Israel.

As a vassal state, Israel was expected to make regular payments to the Assyrians. After a reign of 10 years, King Menahem was succeeded by his son, Pekahiah. The following year, the Assyrian king, Tigleth-Pileser, sent his army into Palestine. Syria and Israel invaded Judah in 733 B.C. This was called the Syro-Ephramite war. Although many were killed, including the son of the king, these armies were unable to invade the capital city of Jerusalem. Rather than rely on God, King Ahaz foolishly sent tribute of gold and silver to Tiglath-Pileser III and asked for his assistance. The Assyrians defeated the Syrian and Northern armies, but very quickly Judah became a vassal state of Assyria. The combination of exile and resettlement of foreign peoples in Israel and Judah led to the creation of the people known as the Samaritans of the New Testament.

Source:

Packer, J. I., Merrill C. Tenney, and William White Jr., eds. *Illustrated Manners and Customs of the Bible.* Nashville: Thomas Nelson Publishers, 2003.

At-A-Glance

1. Isaiah Recognizes God's Holiness (Isaiah 6:1–4)
2. Isaiah Acknowledges His Sinfulness (v. 5)
3. Isaiah Receives God's Grace (vv. 6–7)
4. Isaiah Accepts His Call (v. 8)

In Depth

1. Isaiah Recognizes God's Holiness (Isaiah 6:1–4)

As Isaiah began the narrative of his ministerial calling, he set the date as "in the year that King Uzziah died." Uzziah was one of Judah's greatest kings. His reign lasted for more than 50 years. According to 2 Chronicles 26:4, "he did that which was right in the sight of the LORD." The sin of pride seems to have overcome Uzziah, and he usurped his authority by going into the temple to burn incense on the "altar of incense" (2 Chronicles 26:16). This was a task to be performed only by priests who were consecrated to burn incense. Azariah the priest and 80 other priests confronted Uzziah, yet the king disregarded them. God punished Uzziah by striking him with leprosy in his forehead, and he was thrown out from the temple. For his sin, King Uzziah was a leper until the day of his death. Because of the leprosy, he was cut off from the house of the LORD, and he had to live in a separate dwelling. Isaiah would have been familiar with Uzziah, as he had been an official in the king's court.

Since there is no biblical record otherwise, we can safely assume that during Uzziah's reign, Isaiah's life had been relatively comfortable. The death of Uzziah may have left the young man unsure of his future. It is perhaps this uncertainty that led him to seek the presence of the Lord, something it appears he had not done before. In this, Isaiah is like many modern-day saints. When things are going well in our lives, we don't seek the presence of the Lord. It is not until we are struck with problems or illnesses that we seek God. At those times, when all of our hopes have failed—when we have exhausted our dear brothers and sisters—we seek God's help in our lives. Like Isaiah, when we are prosperous and successful, we rarely, if ever, seek the presence of the Lord. But when we face problems or when we are struck with diseases, all our hopes fail, and we have exhausted all human remedies; then finally we seek the presence of Almighty God. Christian maturity requires that we continually seek God's presence and not wait until things are going wrong. The purpose of our daily prayers and devotionals is to keep us in constant communication with the God of the universe.

According to Isaiah, although his body was inside the temple, his soul was taken up to heaven, and there he saw a magnificent vision of God and the heavenly hosts. Isaiah recounts seeing the Lord, Himself, seated upon a throne. Here we see God's throne as the representation of God's supreme authority and power. Isaiah describes God's position as "high and lifted up." We should understand this to mean that God has no equal. He alone is the Supreme Being. Notice that the God Isaiah is viewing is neither remote nor obscure. Because Isaiah sees beyond the realm of the visible, he is able to view a God who is both majestic and wonderful. If God is to occupy the center of our lives, we, too, must not view Him as distant or mysterious. God is concerned in the affairs of mankind, especially those of His chosen people.

Isaiah continued his description of God's majesty by reporting that the robes of the Lord are so massive that the "train" or the hem of His robe filled the entire temple. This majesty of God is shown in the behavior of the heavenly hosts. These six-winged creatures are seraphs or seraphim. Using two of their six wings, the seraphs cover their faces in reverence for God, recognizing that they are unworthy to look upon Him directly. Hiding one's face from God in reverence and in fear was also shown in the actions of Abraham, who fell on his face before the Lord (Genesis 17:3); in Moses, who hid his face from God (Exodus 3:6); and also with the prophet Elijah, who wrapped his face with his mantle (1 Kings 19:13). When Peter realized that Jesus was the Messiah, he fell to the ground and asked Jesus to go away and not look on his unworthiness (Luke 5:8).

The seraphim use another pair of their wings to cover their feet as they bow down in honor before Him. This action symbolizes that their authority is a derived authority; it does not spring from them, but from the God they worship. The seraphim use two wings to fly, showing that they are in constant service to God. The holiness the angels recognize, in the presence of God, is reflected in their continuous praise: "Holy, holy, holy is the Lord." The use of the word "holy" three times signifies their recognition of the plurality of God: the Father, the Son, and the Holy Spirit.

Isaiah further reported on the effectiveness of God. As the seraphs cried "holy," the doorposts of the temple shook and the temple became filled with the glory of God. As creatures created for the glory of God, how much more ought we to recognize His majesty and strive to serve Him in reverence and humility?

2. Isaiah Acknowledges His Sinfulness (v. 5)

Everywhere we turn, we see evidence of just how awesome our God is. The dawning of each new day, the setting of the sun, the birth of a child, the blooming of flowers in the spring all provide evidence of just how incredible the Lord is. Unfortunately, as we view these wonders, we, like Isaiah, are quickly reminded of just how unholy we are. God's majesty and splendor serves to point out mankind's helplessness and unworthiness. It is this realization that prompted Isaiah's response when he witnessed the tremendous heavenly scene: "Then said I, Woe is me! for I am undone; because I am a man of unclean lips, and I dwell in the midst of a people of unclean lips: for mine eyes have seen the King, the LORD of hosts." We have to admire Isaiah's honesty. He recognized his sinfulness and openly confessed it to God. Notice that as Isaiah viewed the majesty of God, his immediate reaction was to view himself in a new light.

The symbolic use of the "lips" or mouth to reveal what is in our hearts is used frequently in Scripture. Proverbs tells us, "Out of the fullness of the heart the mouth speaks." Isaiah's reference to "unclean lips" may mean that his sense of unworthiness stemmed from something he may have said or perhaps something he should have said. He also refers to living among "people of unclean lips." We want to remember that Isaiah already had a ministry when this event occurred. His first message to the people of Judah is recorded in chapter 1. At this point, he had already prophesied for some years during the reign of King Uzziah. After Uzziah's death, trouble began in the kingdom as the young prince Jotham came to the throne. It is possible that Isaiah's ministry had not been effective in combating the unrighteous acts that he had witnessed, and now he was asking God to empower him.

3. Isaiah Receives God's Grace (vv. 6–7)

After seeing the majesty, the glory, and the effectiveness of God, Isaiah was filled with a burning desire to be used of God. God's response to Isaiah's confession was immediate. God dispatched one of the seraphim to take a burning hot coal and touch Isaiah's lips. Note that the hot coal was removed from the brazen altar where the sacrifices were offered. This symbolizes redemption, or the price paid to obtain forgiveness. The seraph told Isaiah "Lo, this hath touched thy lips; and thy iniquity is taken away, and thy sin purged." This action is symbolic of God's cleansing and His forgiveness. We should note that God did not chastise Isaiah. Rather, God, in response to Isaiah's humility, immediately responded to Isaiah's need. God cleansed, forgave, and equipped Isaiah. We should be reminded how deeply God loves us and wants to be reconciled to us, His most beloved creation.

We should ask ourselves if there are areas in our lives that need God's cleansing. If so, we must be willing to allow Him. Many times these areas are secret. Our family and friends may be unaware that we struggle in these areas. Only God is able to reach in and cleanse us from all unrighteousness that we have hid from others.

The live coal placed in Isaiah's mouth must have

been excruciatingly painful. This reminds us that God's cleansing may entail discomfort or pain. What areas of your life need His cleansing? Are you willing to let Him go there? Are you willing to allow Him into those places that really need His touch—those places that you would rather no one know about? Are you willing to let Him take that burning coal and touch your lips with it? There is no getting around the fact that the cleansing God wants to do in our lives is hard—really hard at times—and the process can be painful. Despite how much it may hurt, our usefulness to God is dependent on our willingness to allow Him to cleanse and forgive us. Our call or commission from God follows His cleansing and forgiveness.

4. Isaiah Accepts His Call (v. 8)

The pattern of forgiving, cleansing, and commissioning is one we see Jesus adopt throughout the Gospels. Again and again, we see Jesus forgiving the sinners He meets, then cleansing and finally commissioning them. In Isaiah's case, we have seen Him recognize and acknowledge God's glory. We then see Isaiah confess his unrighteousness and we see God's loving response of purification. Now Isaiah reports his call to service: "Also I heard the voice of the Lord, saying, Whom shall I send, and who will go for us? Then said I, Here am I; send me." God had been seeking to reach the sinful and stubborn Jews of Judah. This was Isaiah's commission to try to awaken the people who had turned their backs on God.

Isaiah was being commissioned to be an instrument of God's mercy, grace, and God's prophetic words. Isaiah's response was swift and certain: "Here am I. Send me!" He told the Lord that he was ready to go wherever God wanted him to go, and he was prepared to do whatever God wants him to do. Isaiah made this commitment without even knowing what God would ask him to do. Isaiah's commitment to serve God was so sincere that he was willing to go before he knew where he would have to go!

This should make us examine our response to God's call. How often are we quick to respond "Use me"? Or are we fearful and reluctant? Saying "Send me" to God means giving up control of our lives. Our wishes and desires will no longer be the priority. His will and His Word will be all that matters. This loss of control is frightening, only if we forget that the benefits are God's blessings.

Search the Scriptures

1. "In the year that ________ died I saw also the LORD sitting upon a throne, high and lifted up, and his train filled the temple" (Isaiah 6:1).

2. "Above it stood the ________: each one had six wings; with twain he covered his face, and with twain he covered his feet, and with twain he did fly" (v. 2).

3. "Then said I, Woe is me! for I am undone; because I am a man of ________ lips, and I dwell in the midst of a people of ________ lips: for mine eyes have seen the King, the LORD of hosts" (v. 5).

4. "Then flew one of the seraphims unto me, having a live ________ in his hand, which he had taken with the tongs from off the altar" (v. 6).

5. "Also I heard the voice of the Lord, saying, Whom shall I send, and who will go for us? Then said I, ________ ________ ________; send me" (v. 8).

Discuss the Meaning

1. Read Revelation 1:17. How does John's encounter with God on the Isle of Patmos compare with Isaiah's? How are the two encounters similar? In what ways do they differ?

2. The angels Isaiah saw were crying, "Holy, holy, holy." Many of today's Christians are reluctant to be referred to as "holy." Why do you think this is? Discuss what view this lesson encourages you to take on being referred to as "holy."

3. Think about the biblical accounts of Moses, Peter, the soldiers who arrested Jesus, and Isaiah. They all immediately realized their helplessness when they saw God. Have you or anyone you know had such a life-changing encounter with God?

Lesson in Our Society

It is only when we have a proper vision of the majesty of God and His holiness that we will come to understand just how sinful and unworthy we are. Without a clear recognition of the awesomeness of God, we may wrongly believe that we have something to boast about. It is only after we truly encounter God that we will know the full measure of our unrighteousness. He and He alone can cleanse and forgive us and prepare us for service that honors Him and our fellow man.

Make It Happen

Remember that God wants to use every one of us and that each one of us has this higher calling of the Lord. For further insight, read 1 Peter 2:9 where we are told that we are a royal priesthood. Contemplate on what it means to be "a royal priesthood." Pray that you will be able to hear God calling to you and that you will be able to say, "Here I am, Lord. Send me!"

Follow the Spirit

What God wants me to do:

___

___

Remember Your Thoughts

Special insights I have learned:

___

___

More Light on the Text

Isaiah 6:1–8

1 In the year that king Uzziah died I saw also the LORD sitting upon a throne, high and lifted up, and his train filled the temple.

Do you remember a time when you did something wrong and, after you were caught, you were sent to your room to wait until your father or mother got home so you could be punished? All day long you probably anticipated his/her arrival and the punishment he/she would give you. Finally your father or mother came home. Your worst fears were about to be realized. This is the scene with which Isaiah greets us. He had been like a disobedient child. This is made clear in the first chapters of the book. As a nation, Israel turned its back on God and His requirements for His chosen people. The king, having finally been struck by God with leprosy, was now dead after living in a continuous state of alienation from the people and from God. The people so enjoyed their sin that even the nation's prophets had been unsuccessful in guiding them from their headlong plunge into a darkness devoid of God's light. Isaiah must have felt like a failure, fearfully standing alone in the highest heaven awaiting the punishment from his Holy Father that he was sure was to come.

For years Israel had traveled a path of its own choosing and now existed in a state of spiritual and moral darkness. The nation's leadership had aided in its departure from God and now that leadership was dead. A righteous God would be justified in pronouncing the same judgment of death upon the rebellious nation and all of its inhabitants as well. This was Isaiah's state of mind as he stood observing God upon His "throne" (Heb. *kicce'*, **kis-SAY**), "high" (Heb. *ruwm*, **room**) and "lifted up" (Heb. *nasa'*, **naw-SAW**).

2 Above it stood the seraphims: each one had six wings; with twain he covered his face, and with twain he covered his feet, and with twain he did fly.

The scene is all the more frightening to Isaiah as he witnessed the "seraphims" (plural of Heb. *saraph*, **saw-RAWF**) standing in God's presence worshiping and serving Him. The Hebrew word used here for God's messengers places an emphasis on the fact that God is utterly holy and the seraphim (burning ones) must appear to Isaiah like living fire, standing above the throne waiting to serve God. With one pair of wings, the seraphim covered their eyes lest they peer into the divine, and with a pair of their wings, they covered their feet in humble acknowledgment that they stand upon holy ground. Isaiah now saw himself all the more clearly as an unclean creature, dwelling in the midst of unclean and rebellious creatures.

3 And one cried unto another, and said, Holy, holy, holy, is the LORD of hosts: the whole earth is full of his glory. 4 And the posts of the door moved at the voice of him that cried, and the house was filled with smoke.

Every utterance of the seraphs confirmed for Isaiah that God is "holy" (Heb. *qadowsh*, **kaw-DOSHE**). God is utterly transcendent; He is so far above and distinct from His created beings that none is truly worthy to be in His presence. God's holiness is central to His identity, and some scholars argue that it is His primary attribute that permeates all of the others (such as love, sovereignty, omnipotence, etc.). While He is utterly distinct and transcendent from the creation, God's "glory" (Heb. *kabowd*, **kaw-BODE**) fills the whole earth, so it is impossible to escape His presence. The scene is one that must have been overwhelming and frightening, as not only were the seraphs proclaiming God's holiness and glory, but the temple itself shook. Then there was "smoke" (Heb. *'ashan*, **aw-SHAWN**), which may be analogous to the shekinah cloud that represented God's presence with the Israelites in the

"Also I heard the voice of the Lord, saying, Whom shall I send, and who will go for us? Then said I, Here am I; send me" (Isaiah 6:8).

desert. What a predicament for Isaiah, who by this time must have felt that his death was imminent. No explanation was necessary as to why he should die. Isaiah's presence, in the midst of such holiness, was sufficient for him to convict himself. As if to confirm Isaiah's suspicions, smoke filled the chamber and once more concealed God from Isaiah's sight.

5 Then said I, Woe is me! for I am undone; because I am a man of unclean lips, and I dwell in the midst of a people of unclean lips: for mine eyes have seen the King, the LORD of hosts.

Finally, Isaiah gave voice to what he was feeling. The word "woe" in Hebrew is *'owy* **(O-ee)** and stands for a passionate cry of grief or despair. Seeing all that was transpiring around him, he declared himself and his people guilty before God and prepared for his death. He was "undone" (Heb. *damah*, **daw-MAW**), or on the verge of perishing in the face of this revelation of God. Faced with the unfiltered experience of God's holiness, Isaiah recognized his own sinfulness with equal clarity. A seraph was headed in his direction, and Isaiah was certain that it was about to carry out God's judgment against him. Isaiah still had not realized the depth of God's commitment to His chosen people, Israel. The nation had broken faith with the only living God, but God did not break faith with them.

6 Then flew one of the seraphims unto me, having a live coal in his hand, which he had taken with the tongs from off the altar: 7 And he laid it upon my mouth, and said, Lo, this hath touched thy lips; and thine iniquity is taken away, and thy sin purged.

From within the midst of the cloud-filled chamber, Isaiah was only able to see a seraph use a pair of tongs and remove a burning coal from the altar. The living being then proceeded toward Isaiah with the coal. Isaiah must have thought death was approaching, until the coal was pressed against his mouth. Then, for the first time, Isaiah realized what it felt like to be fully cleansed of all sin and shame. The text here refers not only to "sin" (Heb. *chatta'ah*, **khat-taw-AW**) but also "iniquity" (Heb. *'avon*, **aw-VONE**), which refers to "depravity, perversity and the guilt from sin." Rather than the expected punishment, God had pardoned Isaiah. Rather than the deserved death (eternal separation from the living God), Isaiah was given life and began to experience God's love in a way he had never understood before. He was truly and completely loved. With the sin and shame now removed, Isaiah was now able for the first time, to hear God speak.

8 Also I heard the voice of the Lord, saying, Whom shall I send, and who will go for us? Then said I, Here am I; send me.

Isaiah heard God inquire who would be God's servant to go and carry out the mission and message He had for His covenant people. Then Isaiah answered the call. In accepting God's call to be a prophet to the nation, Isaiah understood that he was committing to represent God's holy authority and love on Earth. His task would be to guide the people and their leaders into right relationship with God. Isaiah's experience with God and the burning coal from the altar had helped the prophet understand that God was not interested in exacting punishment on His rebellious people. Rather, God wanted to purge the nation of that which separated the two of them. The proclamation of this message was the task to which Isaiah was committing himself. Isaiah would spend the rest of his life in this missionary enterprise.

In embracing this call from God, Isaiah would live the rest of his life separated from the people he was to serve. The price for accepting God's assignment was loneliness and isolation. From this point on, everything in the prophet's life took a subordinate position to God's mission. Because he had glimpsed God's glory, Isaiah willingly paid this price.

Source:

Packer, J. I., Merrill C. Tenney, and William White Jr., eds. *Illustrated Manners and Customs of the Bible.* Nashville: Thomas Nelson Publishers, 2003.

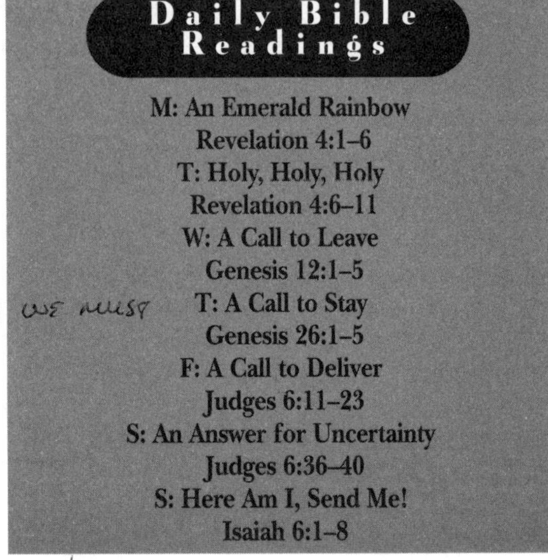

Daily Bible Readings

M: An Emerald Rainbow
Revelation 4:1–6
T: Holy, Holy, Holy
Revelation 4:6–11
W: A Call to Leave
Genesis 12:1–5
T: A Call to Stay
Genesis 26:1–5
F: A Call to Deliver
Judges 6:11–23
S: An Answer for Uncertainty
Judges 6:36–40
S: Here Am I, Send Me!
Isaiah 6:1–8

NOTES

March 2009
Quarter At-A-Glance

New Creation in Christ

This quarter explores the creative nature of Christ, as it affects human life and the implications of His life for the world in which we live. It is a study in the books of Ezekiel, Luke, Acts, Ephesians, and 1 John.

UNIT 1 • THE PROMISE OF NEW LIFE

Lessons 1–5 are derived from the book of Ezekiel.

Lesson 1: March 1, 2009
A New Spirit
Ezekiel 11:14–21

Holding on to the promises of God, in challenging situations, can save us from the turmoil we experience when we feel hopeless. In this text, Ezekiel prophesied to the exiled Jews, who were in captivity in Babylon. He promised that God was with them as their sanctuary, in this strange and distant land, and that God would restore them to their homeland.

Lesson 2: March 8, 2009
New Leadership
Ezekiel 34:23–31

God calls us "the sheep of His pasture." To depict our relationship with Him, He utilizes the characteristics of the human shepherd. As finite beings, the role of servant-leader can sometimes seem futile. In lieu of the fact that the most powerful leaders can sometimes be self-serving or manipulative, what remedy can be found when such a person is in a leadership position? Ezekiel tells us that God will provide new servant-leaders who care tenderly for their flock, just as God the "Good Shepherd" does.

Lesson 3: March 15, 2009
God's People Restored Again
Ezekiel 36:22–32

Israel's decadence and defeat led the nations of the world to see God as powerless. This passage shows that God would use the restoration of the house of Israel and their return to the land to enhance the way other nations viewed the power of God. According to Ezekiel, God's promise to restore Israel was not motivated by Israel itself but was for the sake of God's holiness.

Lesson 4: March 22, 2009
Prophesying New Life
Ezekiel 37:1–14

Ezekiel has a powerful vision in which the Lord demonstrated God's ability to bring new life to that which was dead. Sometimes situations seem so overwhelming that we fall into despair. Where can we find hope? Ezekiel's prophecy of the valley of dry bones vividly illustrates how God enlivens people and fills them with the breath of life and hope.

Lesson 5: March 29, 2009
Envisioning New Life
Ezekiel 47:1–12

In a vision, Ezekiel observed a sacred, life-giving river that flowed freely from God's throne. This river was bordered by trees and produced fruit that was nourishing food and had leaves that could be used for healing. What impact do bodies of water have on humanity and all creation? We know that humankind depends on the water that covers the vast areas of Earth's landscape for survival. Humankind also depend on the Creator of that water, a loving, merciful God for healing, survival, and eternal life.

UNIT 2 • THE PATH TO NEW LIFE

Lessons 6-9 are developed from three passages in Luke and one in Acts. Lessons 6 and 7 examine the suffering and death of Jesus and His triumph over death on the first Easter Sunday. Lesson 8 continues with the last resurrection appearance of Jesus in Luke. Lesson 9 finds Peter in Lydda and Joppa bringing new life to others in the name and power of Christ.

Lesson 6: April 5, 2009 (Palm Sunday)
Suffering unto Death
Luke 23:32–46

This passage depicts Jesus' final moments on the Cross and His prayer to the Father.

Luke's account of the last week in the life of Jesus reveals that His trust in God sustained Him in suffering and led Jesus to victory.

Lesson 7: April 12, 2009 (Easter)
Resurrected unto New Life
Luke 24:1–12

In essence, this passage is the core of the "Gospel Message." The writer reminds the disciples that Jesus told them He would be handed over to sinners and crucified, and on the third day, He would rise again. Death seems final, totally defeating, and irreversible. Luke's record of Easter morning assures us that because Jesus rose from the dead, new-resurrected life is possible.

Lesson 8: April 19, 2009
Witnesses to New Life
Luke 24:44–53

Jesus appeared to His disciples and explained to them, through the Old Testament Scriptures, that He was the Messiah (Christ), the One sent by God the Father to save the people from their sins. The Scriptures affirm that Jesus is the Messiah, and according to Luke's gospel, Jesus appeared to His disciples and commissioned them to witness to the new life they have in Him.

Lesson 9: April 26, 2009
Bringing New Life to Those in Need
Acts 9:32–43

Various sources of physical and spiritual assistance clamor for the world's attention. The above passage tells us that, through the power of Christ, Peter was able to heal Aeneas and raise Tabitha from the dead.

UNIT 3 • THE WAY OF NEW LIFE

These lessons explore Ephesians through four concepts: the church as family, life, revelation, home life, and equipping ourselves for Christian living.

Lesson 10: May 3, 2009
New Family in Christ
Ephesians 1:3–14

Through the Holy Spirit, we can receive the inheritance of eternal life, which is also sealed by the Holy Spirit. Family life offers opportunities for rewards and challenges, for close ties, and for estranged relationships. In letters to first-century churches, Paul and John celebrated and gave thanks for those whom God had adopted into a new family in Christ.

Lesson 11: May 10, 2009
New Life in Christ
Ephesians 2:1–10

By grace, Christians are saved, through faith, empowered to do good works in Christ, and receive the gift of eternal life with God. Before we invest our time, our money, or ourselves, we often want to be certain that our outlay will repay us well. Both Paul and John claim that when we, by faith, invest our lives in Christ, we receive new life, the unparalleled benefit of God's love.

Lesson 12: May 17, 2009
New Revelation in Christ
Ephesians 3:1–13

Paul had been chosen by God to reveal God's mystery of salvation, Jesus, to the Gentiles (non-Jews). Mysteries pique interest because most people want to uncover "the rest of the story." As highlighted in this study, New Testament apostles believed that the revelation of Jesus unlocks mysteries concerning God's eternal and all-inclusive plan of salvation.

Lesson 13: May 24, 2009
New Life in the Home
Ephesians 5:21–6:4

Family life is often disrupted by internal conflict. How can families learn to live together in harmony? In Ephesians, Paul called all Christians to be subject to one another in reverence to Christ. He urges believers to serve one another, in the home and in the name and Spirit of Christ.

Lesson 14: May 31, 2009
Equipped for New Life
Ephesians 6:10–18

Life is challenging because there are numerous forces pulling us in different directions. In this study, Paul calls all Christians to be subject to one another in reverence to Christ. He also teaches that God arms us to fight spiritual battles that are sure to come against God's family.

Engaging the Theme

The New Life in Christ

by Dr. Louis H. Wilson

Paul's Mars Hill sermon to the Athenians (Acts 17:22–31) is a concise outline of many of the creative works of Christ that we will feast upon this quarter.

- He made the world and everything in it and is Lord of heaven and earth.
- He gives life, breath, and all things.
- From one man, He made all "nations" (a more accurate rendering is "ethnicities") and determined their times and places to live, for the totality of our existence is through Him.
- He did this (the above) so men would seek and find Him.
- He is judge of the world and commands repentance, and He has proven His testimony by being raised from the dead.

It is these truths, precepts, and principles, with application to daily living, that we will address this quarter.

The first unit of our study leads us into a biblical exploration into the creative power of Christ, which enables us to transcend the bonds of sin. By His power (His Holy Spirit), Christ gives us a new spirit. Lesson 2 will show us that an extension of the Spirit's work will be godly leaders that model Christian maturity and service to God. The testimony of time, however, in the lives of many, is that the shackles of sin and disobedience have wrought a gulf between humanity and God that cannot be overcome. Again, Christ makes the difference; we will learn in lessons 3 and 4 that restoration is not only possible but it is a promise God gives His people to offer hope and encouragement during difficult times. Lesson 5 will show us it is Christ, Himself, who perpetually feeds us in this life and beyond and supplies us with all we need to enjoy our relationship with Him.

Our lessons in Unit I come from the book of Ezekiel. Ezekiel was born in the eighteenth year of King Josiah's reign (625 B.C.). He received his calling in approximately 595 B.C. It is altogether possible to assume revivals, influenced by the prophetic ministries of Jeremiah, Zephaniah, and Habakkuk a few years before, had led many to feel secure that Judah was about to experience restoration in its immediate future. God confirmed, through the prophet Ezekiel, that He was after more than religious conformity. He would rather change negative behavior, and that changed behavior would emanate from a changed heart. In lesson 1, Ezekiel speaks to how that change will come.

The number of religious television programs, books, and the resurgence in gospel music can be deceptive. Weighted against today's violent crime, the number of fatherless, and, yes, motherless households, and the age in which our youth engage in physical intimacy, we would do well to ask whether we are really making any substantive changes. God told Ezekiel to let the leaders around him know all was not well on the home front. They needed to repent from misleading the people for their own gain because judgment was coming (Ezekiel 11:1–13).

As in this postmodern era, God's words of judgment paint a bleak picture for a believing and faithful remnant and even a less-hopeful one for those who have been playing the harlot (no gender is meant by this term). Words of judgment, however, are not meant to drive us away but to draw us near to our Lord. God says, through the prophet Ezekiel to the Israelites, that He will draw them near to Himself because He will change them in the inside (the inner man—the heart).

What Adam and Eve could not do, what the patriarchs could not do, what the judges and kings could not do, nor what the Levites or priests could do, God would do; He would create a clean heart in them. It is God, the Lord God Jehovah, who would give them and us a thirst and an ability to obey His statutes. All believers will no longer battle with inconsistent hearts, vacillating between good and evil. He will give them a new spirit devoted to Him (Ezekiel 11:19).

A reality of life is, however, that when those we trust for spiritual leadership are themselves corrupt, living for God is difficult. Corrupt leaders seemingly make a mockery of those who are dedicated and ignore many of who truly need God's help (Ezekiel 34:1–6). Reminiscent of the Lord's announcement found in Luke 4:18–19 and His charge to the apostle Peter found in John 21:15–17, God declares that a new day is coming when He will raise up a Shepherd and shepherds that rescue His people (Ezekiel 34:11–31).

Increasingly in the news lately, polluted waters are cited as carriers of disease and harmful bacteria. Fresh water is a sought after commodity. Actually, it always has been. Using a metaphor, Ezekiel likens pure life-giving water as that which comes from the temple of God. We will discover the real essence of this water's power comes from the throne of God. The similarities between Ezekiel 47:1–12 and Revelation 22:1–5 are undeniable. The river changes all life as we know it, the river sustains, maintains, and all nourished by it are perpetually and eternally pure.

In Unit II, we will continue our study of the source of life by refocusing our attention on our Lord. We saw in the last unit that a new spirit of restoration costs us nothing; God does all the work. We must never forget, however, the sin that bound us and the price, which we could not pay, that the Lord paid in full, by dying on the Cross for our sins and being resurrected from the dead.

The resurrected Christ took the time to open the Scriptures to those who had walked with Him (Luke 24:44–45). Should we do any less with new converts? All He asks of us is that we, empowered by the Holy Spirit, testify of Him by life, word, and deed. In other words, if we understand just how good the news is, we will share it. Clearly that means we have a job to do.

Unit III begins by telling us heaven's "storehouse of blessings" are poured out on the saints of God. For all the dysfunctions in our world we read about, there is a functional remedy we can access. That remedy may be within the heart of the person in the pew sitting next to us.

Time and again we read about the writers of the New Testament thanking and praising God for the saints and God's work among them (1 Corinthians 1:4; Philemon 1:4). It is within this body of believers that we can feel voids left by broken relationships and see the healed scars of emotional trauma. All that we need have been purchased by His blood, guaranteed by His Spirit (Ephesians 1:3–13), and gifts have been distributed accordingly and shared among His people (Ephesians 4:11–16).

What God has done for us is because of His goodness, not ours. He is working it out. We are living epistles (letters) and are living out today some of the prophecies we read in Unit I. We will discover in this unit that diversities and cultural, social/economic, and even gender differences do not mean that the Spirit of God cannot unite us around the throne of grace. An argument could be made that it is not our differences that divide us but it is our lack of understanding of the work of Christ and the Holy Spirit.

The mystery concealed in the Old Testament is the mystery revealed in the New Testament. Sin was the problem then, and sin is the problem today. Still, only the blood of Jesus gives anyone the right to approach a Holy God. This was the mystery and God tells us to "come one and come all." There is one Lord, one faith, one baptism, one way in, and praise to God—no way out!

Jesus said, "My sheep hear my voice, and I know them, and they follow me: And I give unto them eternal life; and they shall never perish, neither shall any man pluck them out of my hand" (John 10:27–8).

It does not matter how much we discuss the problems we face "out there." Come evening time, we know most of the stuff that plagues us is within and with those closest to us—family members. As we journey through lesson 13, God reveals another blessing—a family unit who models the church is a family who experiences the blessings of the church.

Finally, Unit III closes with lesson 14. Get ready for battle. Yes, the battle is the Lord's. The lessons in this unit will take us into a deeper understanding of all that God has graciously done on our behalf. Appropriately, the last lesson concludes by letting us know to receive His blessings and ward off the enemy. Such victorious living, by His power, does require one little small thing from us; we have to go into His closet and put on His armor. Read on, you will discover there is a suit just your size!

***Dr. Louis H. Wilson** holds a doctorate in leadership and organizational development from the University of Phoenix and has been involved in church leadership and development for the past 25 years.*

Christ and Creation

Focusing on the Bigger Picture of God's Salvation Plan

by Evangeline Carey

This quarter, as we study and meditate on Christ and Creation, using the books of Ezekiel, Luke, Acts, and Ephesians, it is imperative that we help those under our tutelage to see the bigger picture of God's salvation plan. Believers as well as nonbelievers need to know that God is creating and building His church and building His kingdom. Consequently, we need to reflect on the three main roles that Jesus Christ walked in when He stepped out on the sands of time and entered Earth. He came as: (1) Prophet (to reveal who God, the Creator and Sustainer of Life, truly is and why He should be worshiped in Spirit and in truth); (2) the Sacrificial Priest (who would die and pay the sin-penalty of humanity); and (3) the King of kings (who is building His kingdom, where Jesus will reign as King of kings and Lord of lords for all eternity—forever and ever).

Sometimes, as we cover so many Scriptures throughout the different quarters, we may fail to see that there is a common thread running through the whole Bible. That common thread is "salvation." From Genesis to Revelation, we find the story of a holy and loving God revealing His character and His salvation plan to sinful humanity. From Genesis to Revelation, God is creating and interacting with a people who will reign with Him forever in the New Jerusalem (Revelation 21). "Whosoever believe on Him will be saved" (John 3:16) and share in this new community that He is creating for His glory. Therefore, we must see this bigger picture ourselves and teach it as we carry out the "Great Commission" (Matthew 28:19–20).

The Bible is God's inerrant Word and every believer's blueprint for successful Christian living. However, we must be able to recognize and appreciate what God is doing throughout the 66 books. The role of the Christian educator is to help students recognize and appreciate.

The four books that we will examine this quarter also have a common link. As we study, we should readily see that connection and draw principles that will help us in our daily walk with our Lord and Saviour, Jesus Christ. We cannot walk and obey what we do not know. Therefore, we must help students to *know* so that they can put their faith into action.

Ezekiel

In continuing the salvation narrative, the book of Ezekiel reveals that God has already chosen the Israelites, who were a rebellious, stiff-necked populace, as His chosen people. They were to be a model to a lost and dying world of how to walk with a Holy (set apart from sin) God. Even though the Israelites continuously broke their covenant relationship with God, it is through these chosen people that the Messiah–seed will come. Therefore, Christian educators need to emphasize the fact that God's salvation plan is not dependent on the Israelites' actions. Because it is His desire to do so, our sovereign God will bring His plan to fruition, despite our lack of obedience.

In the book of Ezekiel, the new generation of Israelites has already gone over into the Promised Land, Canaan, and is in Babylonian captivity—due to their own sins of rebelling against God. Almighty God uses the prophet Ezekiel to announce God's judgment, not only on Israel, but other nations. Ezekiel also foretells the coming salvation of God's people (all believers). Therefore, in the book of Ezekiel, God is still creating a new community, consisting of people who are not only called by His name, but will obey His commands.

Luke's Gospel

The thread continues to stretch across the annals of time, and the physician Luke tells us that the long-awaited Messiah—the Suffering or Sacrificial Priest—has come. The Saviour of humanity has come, even though He did not enter Earth wrapped in the package that the Israelites expected. Instead, He came as a Baby in a lowly manger. They hoped that He would come as an earthly king and rescue them from slavery. However, He came as a suffering servant—the perfect Lamb of God, without "blemish or spot" (1 Peter 1:19). The book of Luke spells out, in detail, Jesus' birth, ministry, death, burial, and resurrection.

Remember that without Jesus' death and resurrection, there would be no Christianity; there would be no salvation, where humanity's relationship with a Holy God is restored (1 Corinthians 15:1–28). This is another facet of the bigger picture that we should stress to those we teach or share the Gospel message.

Acts

The thread stretches even farther, and we come to the book of Acts. This book is a continuation of Luke's gospel. Acts, or the Acts of the Apostles, begins with Jesus' ascension and His subsequent sending of the Holy Spirit to indwell all believers. After Jesus ascends, He goes to heaven, to sit at the right hand of the Father, a place of distinction and power—a place that is symbolic of the authority and the active rule of Christ.

In fact, the book of Acts could also be called "the Acts of the Holy Spirit" because it vividly shows the Holy Spirit at work in the new community—the church. He is at work not only in building her, but teaching, guiding, and protecting her. Thus, we should be able to see why the Lord poured out His Spirit and then the church He created, grew from 11 disciples to 12, then 120 in the Upper Room, from 3,000 to 5,000, and kept going. God was growing the church He created, not man. According to Jesus' plan, His Gospel was to go from Jerusalem (community), to Judea (the surrounding community), to Samaria (the nation), and to the ends of the earth (the whole world [Acts 1:8]).

An omniscient God knew that the church would need His Holy Spirit not only for spiritual and numerical growth, but because she would continuously be under persecution for Christ's sake. This is another tenet of the salvation narrative that Christian educators need to stress. Without the Holy Spirit, the new community—God's church—can do nothing.

Ephesians

As the thread stretches across time again, we pull from one of the many epistles, or letters, that a concerned apostle Paul wrote to various infant churches that He helped to establish on three separate missionary journeys. Paul was one of the vessels that God used. He wrote his letter to the church at Ephesus for three purposes: (1) to encourage them; (2) to strengthen these new believers in the new community that God is creating; and (3) to explain the nature and purpose of the church, the body of Christ, to aid in their spiritual growth. Here, again, is a component that Christian educators need to underscore. Even today, the nature and purpose of the church needs to be taught to infant believers as well as mature believers so that we will always know and appreciate that Christ is the Creator, Builder, and Head of His church.

This new community that God is creating must always remember—and Christian educators must help students of the Word to understand—that another part of the bigger picture is Christ's return. Jesus Christ is coming back again for His church—His bride. We are presently in the Church Age, and we are looking forward to this Second Coming, where we will reign with Jesus in His Kingdom for all eternity.

See and teach the bigger picture! Jesus Christ is a Prophet, the Sacrificial Priest, and King of kings; we should worship Him with our whole being for who He is.

Sources:

Alexander, T. Desmond, Brian S. Rosner, D.A. Carson, Graeme Goldsworthy, eds. *New Dictionary of Bible Theology*. Downers Grove, Ill.: InterVarsity Press, 2000.

Ryrie, Charles C. *Basic Theology*. Chicago, Ill.: Moody Press, 1999.

Evangeline Carey *is a staff writer and the developmental editor of* Precepts *for UMI, and has been an adult Sunday School teacher for more than 25 years.*

Perspective

Missions in the Motherland

"Princes shall come out of Egypt; Ethiopia shall soon stretch out her hands unto God" (Psalm 68:31).

by Carl F. Ellis Jr., Ph.D.

African Presence in the Bible

While it is seldom mentioned, African Americans have a rich African heritage in the Bible. When the Bible mentions Ethiopians, it means black-skinned, kinky-haired people who looked very much like those who were forced into slavery and brought to America. When Jesus stumbled under the weight of the Cross, Simon, a Black man from Cyrene, Africa, was forced to carry it the rest of the way (Luke 23:26). On the Day of Pentecost, people from Africa were among those who heard the Gospel and were converted (Acts 2:5–12). The New Testament church had many African members, including Simeon, who was called the Black man, and Lucius the Cyrenian (Acts 13:1).

Early Christian scholars like Augustine, Tertullian, Athanasius, and Origen were Africans. Because they were brown-skinned North Africans and not Black sub-Saharan Africans, these theologians were classified as Caucasian by some. However, if these same men were brought to America, they would have been identified as Black.

Goals of African American Missions

Throughout the 1800s, there was a considerable African American missions presence in Africa. During this time there was also a developing European colonial presence in sub-Saharan Africa, whose interest was primarily commercial. Therefore, they did not pay much attention to the efforts of African American missionaries.

Black missionaries in Africa during this time operated under the banner of what has been called the three C's: Christianity, commerce, and civilization.

Their first purpose was to spread the Gospel of Jesus Christ. A major strategy they employed was to establish Christian communities in the target mission fields. Paul Cuffey, for example, was the first African American to lead such a missionary effort in Africa. He was a wealthy Quaker sea captain and a strong Christian from Boston, Massachusetts. In 1815, Cuffey organized, led, and personally financed the emigration of 38 African American Christians to Sierra Leone, West Africa.

They were soon followed by hundreds of others including Lott Carey and Colin Teague, both Baptist ministers. Later, Carey moved to Liberia where he became a key leader in the Christian community. He was the organizing pastor of the first Baptist church in Liberia, the Providence Baptist Church in Monrovia. The Lott Carey Foreign Mission Convention, a strong supporter of Christian missions worldwide, was founded 60 years after his death in 1828.

The second purpose of African American missions in Africa was connected with commerce. These missionaries brought with them an empowerment approach of community development. A major spokesman of this movement was Reverend Alexander Crummell. For him, economic development in Africa was an essential part of missions. He believed the prosperity of Africa could be assured if its natural resources and wealth were properly developed and controlled by its people. Of course, the Colonialists wanted all the resources of Africa for their own countries.

The third purpose of African American missions was to promote civilization. This is where I believe these missionaries fell short. In those days, of course, civilization was defined as American civilization. This caused tension between some missionaries and the African people. However, it must be said that African American missionaries did an outstanding job of promoting economic development and preaching the Gospel in Africa.

***Carl F. Ellis Jr., Ph.D.**, is the author of the book* Going Global (Beyond the Boundaries). *"Suffering and the South" is an excerpt from his book.*

March 2009
Heritage Profile

Howard O. Jones

(1921–)

Evangelist

As a young man, Howard Jones dreamed of becoming a jazz musician. Jones, who played clarinet and alto saxophone, "wanted to become the next big name in jazz music," he said.

Jones gave up that dream to pursue a life in ministry, and God used Jones' surrendered life to draw countless others to Him. Jones became a youth minister, a broadcaster, a pastor, and an evangelist. Along the way, Jones became the first Black preacher to join evangelist Billy Graham's crusade team. He's often called "the Jackie Robinson of evangelism."

Jones and his wife, Wanda, pastored their first congregation, Harlem's Bethany Alliance Church, when he was 22. During his eight years there, he started Soldiers for Christ, an evangelistic ministry to teens.

In 1952, Jones and Wanda returned to Cleveland, Jones' hometown, to lead Smoot Memorial Alliance Church. During that time, he learned about a Liberian radio station that was interested in receiving recordings of Negro spirituals performed by Black churches. Jones and his church began sending tapes featuring songs and a message.

Jones was overwhelmed by the number of positive letters he received from Africans who had learned about Christ through the prime-time broadcasts. "They said it was the first time they had ever heard the voice of an American Black man," Jones told his biographer.

The response was so positive that the radio ministry invited Jones and Wanda to come to Africa to preach. They spent three months holding evangelistic rallies in Liberia, Ghana, and Nigeria. The couple was welcomed as family.

In 1957, Jones received a letter from evangelist Billy Graham, who had learned about his work. After the Supreme Court's 1954 ruling in *Brown* v. *Board of Education of Topeka*, Graham had decided not to hold any more segregated crusades. But few people of color came to his crusades.

Just a few years after Jackie Robinson broke the color barrier in baseball, Jones served a similar function—and suffered similar loneliness—during that crusade. Ministers in New York threatened not to support the crusade if Graham had minorities on his ministry team. Jones was often slighted and mistreated by other pastors and altar call counselors. "There were nights when I went back to my hotel room and literally wept before God and told him, 'Lord, I can't take this pressure,'" he says. "But . . . God gave me the strength to endure." Jones eventually joined the staff of the Billy Graham Evangelistic Association and served for more than 35 years.

Jones used his position not only to share the Gospel verbally throughout the world but also to initiate humanitarian programs in Africa. He helped expand the organization's idea of evangelism to include meeting physical as well as spiritual needs. He also served as the first president of the National Black Evangelical Association, and is the first African American to be inducted into the National Religious Broadcasters' Hall of Fame. Now retired, Jones' passion is to see African American churches apply the transformative power of the Gospel to issues in their communities.

Photo of Howard O. Jones at the 1957 NYC Crusade. Photo Credit: ©BGEA (Billy Graham Evangelistic Association).

Sources:

Gilbreath, Edward. "The 'Jackie Robinson' of Evangelism." *Christianity Today* magazine, February 9, 1998.

Jones, Howard O., with Edward Gilbreath. "The New York Experiment." *Today's Christian* magazine, May/June 2004.

TEACHING TIPS

MAR 1st

March 1

Bible Study Guide 1

1. Words You Should Know

A. Sanctuary (Ezekiel 11:16) *miqdash* (Heb.)—Sacred place, holy place, the tabernacle of the Most High.

B. Heart (vv. 19, 21) *leb* (Heb.)—Mind, inclination, will, mind-set, temper.

C. Spirit (v. 19) *ruwach* (Heb.)—Wind, breath, mind.

2. Teacher Preparation

Unifying Principle—A New Spirit of Hope. Many times life's frustrations, especially those of our own making, may cause us to give up hope for change. Is everything truly lost because we must reap the rewards of our own mistakes? No. Holding on to the promises of God in challenging situations can save us from the turmoil we experience when we feel hopeless.

A. Pray and ask God to reveal to you where you need to rely on His promises.

B. Read and study the Daily Bible Readings, and then read the entire lesson.

C. As you navigate this lesson, draw salient points from each section that you might share with the class.

D. In addition to reading the *Precepts For Living®* Bible Study Guide for this lesson, read other commentaries.

E. Make notes of your thoughts from the Scriptures you've read, the Bible Study Guide, and other commentaries.

F. Practice with a student doing the In Focus story as a dramatic reading.

3. Starting the Lesson

A. With a volunteer, present a dramatic reading of the In Focus story.

B. Engage your students in a discussion of the following questions: "Do you know anyone like the main character of the story?" Also ask, "Can you relate with the main character; if so, in what ways can you relate?"

4. Getting into the Lesson

A. Present the information from The People, Places, and Times and Background sections. Discuss.

B. Have volunteers read the Focal Verses aloud.

C. Discuss how the text fits into God's overall plan of salvation.

5. Relating the Lesson to Life

A. Have volunteers share their answers from the Starting the Lesson section.

B. Create a chart on the board with one column entitled "Shirley," the main character from the story. The other column should be entitled the "Exiles." Have the students compile a list of comparisons of the two.

C. Add another column entitled "Us" and use the questions in the Discuss the Meaning section to fill in this column.

6. Arousing Action

A. Read the Lesson in Our Society and Make It Happen sections.

B. Ask the students to take a few moments to write down how God helped them cope while they were waiting on His promises.

C. Instruct the students to keep what they have written and refer to those words when they need encouragement or want to encourage others.

Worship Guide

For the Superintendent or Teacher
Theme: A New Spirit
Theme Song: "I Will Do a New Thing in You"
Devotional Reading: 2 Corinthians 3:1–11
Prayer

A NEW SPIRIT

Bible Background • EZEKIEL 11:14–21
Printed Text • EZEKIEL 11:14–21 Devotional Reading • 2 CORINTHIANS 3:1–11

AIM for Change

By the end of the lesson, we will:
EXPLORE the promises God made to His people living in exile;
ACCEPT the fact that God is a promise maker and promise keeper; and
RELY on God's promises when faced with challenging situations.

Keep in Mind

"I will give them one heart, and I will put a new spirit within you" (from Ezekiel 11:19).

Focal Verses

KJV

Ezekiel 11:14 Again the word of the LORD came unto me, saying,

15 Son of man, thy brethren, even thy brethren, the men of thy kindred, and all the house of Israel wholly, are they unto whom the inhabitants of Jerusalem have said, Get you far from the LORD: unto us is this land given in possession.

16 Therefore say, Thus saith the Lord GOD; Although I have cast them far off among the heathen, and although I have scattered them among the countries, yet will I be to them as a little sanctuary in the countries where they shall come.

17 Therefore say, Thus saith the Lord GOD; I will even gather you from the people, and assemble you out of the countries where ye have been scattered, and I will give you the land of Israel.

18 And they shall come thither, and they shall take away all the detestable things thereof and all the abominations thereof from thence.

19 And I will give them one heart, and I will put a new spirit within you; and I will take the stony heart out of their flesh, and will give them an heart of flesh:

20 That they may walk in my statutes, and keep mine ordinances, and do them: and they shall be my people, and I will be their God.

21 But as for them whose heart walketh after the heart of their detestable things and their abominations, I will recompense their way upon their own heads, saith the Lord GOD.

NLT

Ezekiel 11:14 Then this message came to me from the LORD:

15 "Son of man, the people still left in Jerusalem are talking about you and your relatives and all the people of Israel who are in exile. They are saying, 'Those people are far away from the LORD, so now he has given their land to us!'

16 "Therefore, tell the exiles, 'This is what the Sovereign LORD says: Although I have scattered you in the countries of the world, I will be a sanctuary to you during your time in exile.

17 I, the Sovereign LORD, will gather you back from the nations where you have been scattered, and I will give you the land of Israel once again.'

18 "When the people return to their homeland, they will remove every trace of their vile images and detestable idols.

19 And I will give them singleness of heart and put a new spirit within them. I will take away their stony, stubborn heart and give them a tender, responsive heart,

20 so they will obey my decrees and regulations. Then they will truly be my people, and I will be their God.

21 But as for those who long for vile images and detestable idols, I will repay them fully for their sins. I, the Sovereign LORD, have spoken!"

In Focus

What am I going to do? thought Shirley as she stood among the charred remains of her home. *I have nowhere to go. Why would God let this happen to me?*

Shirley had been saved for most of her adult life. She faithfully went to church every Sunday. She served on several auxiliaries. God had used her many times to spread the Word to the lost. One could see the number of people who had come to Christ through Shirley's witnessing. If anyone's faith could not be shaken, it was Shirley's—right? Yet, as the firefighters set at her feet water-damaged family albums, broken Christmas decorations, and soot-covered dolls from her childhood, she was on the edge of collapsing.

Shirley had no children. She had never married. Both of her parents had gone to be with the Lord years ago.

Although it would have been wise to do so, I never saved money. I didn't think I could afford to put it away. As soon as I made it, I spent it—especially on things for the house. My parents left me this place. I thought that as long as I had it, I would be safe, she thought.

That night, Shirley sobbed uncontrollably as she lay across the bed at the homeless shelter. By morning, she had wept until her eyes were almost swollen shut. Each night that week was a sleepless one for Shirley as she wrestled with the question, "How am I going to make it?" By dawn of her seventh day of homelessness, her body riddled with exhaustion, Shirley finally prayed.

"Lord, I don't know what's going to happen tomorrow, but I'm going to trust You. You promised to never leave me and that You would always take care of me, and I've never known You to go back on Your Word."

Like Shirley, the Children of Israel needed hope. Ezekiel prophesied to the exiled Jews in captivity in Babylon. Ezekiel promised that God was with them as their sanctuary in this strange and distant land and that God would restore them to their homeland.

The People, Places, and Times

Ezekiel. He was the son of the priest named Buzi (Ezekiel 1:3). In addition to being a prophet of God, he was a priest like his father. His name means "God will strengthen," which is what he did for the Jewish exiles. Ezekiel was taken into captivity during the second wave of the Babylonian exile around 597 B.C. along with King Jehoiachin and his officials (2 Kings 24:12–15). Following the command of God for all Jews in exile (Jeremiah 29:5–7), Ezekiel settled into Babylonian life, living along the Chebar River in his home (Ezekiel 8:1). He even took a wife, who later died (24:18). His ministry began the fifth year of Jehoiachin's captivity (592 B.C.). Ezekiel was highly regarded among the exiles in his area and was even counsel for the Jewish elders (8:1; 11:25; 14:1; 20:1).

Source:

Unger, Merrill F. *The New Unger's Bible Dictionary*. Edited by R.K. Harrison. Chicago: Moody Press, 1988.

Background

The Babylonian captivity happened in three waves. The passage in today's lesson occurred some time between the second (597 B.C.) and third (586 B.C.) waves. Ezekiel's initial audience would have been the Jews who had been living in exile at least five years and had settled along the Chebar River in Babylon.

The Jews were in captivity because of their own sinfulness. Although they had committed all sorts of abominations, one sin that was most prevalent was idolatry. They loved to worship false gods (Isaiah 57:5). This, of course, was in violation of God's covenant in which He said He would punish to the "third and fourth generation of those who hate Him" (Deuteronomy 5:7–10).

Despite the many warnings against idol worship, the people continued their evil practices. This led to the destruction of Jerusalem and the temple (Jeremiah 32:28–35). However, even though they had sinned against Him, prophets like Ezekiel were sent to comfort the Jews in exile. God's purpose was to preserve a remnant of the people, one that He would allow to return to their land (Jeremiah 23:3).

Source:

Unger, Merrill F. *The New Unger's Bible Dictionary*. Edited by R.K. Harrison. Chicago: Moody Press, 1988.

At-A-Glance

1. Words of the Wicked (Ezekiel 11:14–15)
2. God's Promise to Keep and Restore (vv. 16–17)
3. God's Promise of a New Spirit (vv. 18–20)
4. Fate of the Wicked (v. 21)

In Depth

1. Words of the Wicked (Ezekiel 11:14–15)

This week's passage begins with "The word of the LORD." This revealed to the prophet Ezekiel's audience, his brethren, blood relatives, and others of the house of Israel that he was sharing with them an authentic word. Because what he was about to say would have been hard for the Jewish exiles to hear, it was important to authenticate his words. The people of Jerusalem, those who had yet to be taken into captivity, had disowned the exiles. Furthermore, they insisted that God had forsaken and forgotten them. According to those left in Jerusalem, even the land the exiles held so dear had been taken from them and their possessions given to those not in captivity. The words of the wicked would have dealt a deathblow to the already despondent exiles. If these claims were true, it would have realized their worst fears: God, indeed, did not love them anymore, and they would never see their beloved homeland again.

Unfortunately, in the midst of our afflictions, we sometimes encounter people who like to "rub it in." They have little knowledge of the ways of God and equate His allowance of trials and tribulations, in the lives of His people, with disinheritance. "You must have done something wrong to be punished like this," they say. "You don't have enough faith and that's why you are in this situation." Job, for example, certainly could relate to such statements, as they are similar to the words of his friends (Job 8:4, NLT; 11:6). However, even in instances unlike Job's, when we are the source of our own affliction, "the LORD will not cast off for ever" (Lamentations 3:31), for He knows "the thoughts that I think toward you, saith the LORD, thoughts of peace, and not of evil, to give you an expected end" (Jeremiah 29:11).

2. God's Promise to Keep and Restore (vv. 16–17)

"Therefore say, Thus saith the Lord GOD" begins both verses 16 and 17. Here and in other places where this phrase and variations of it are used, it ushers in God's correction of a past action (Ezekiel 12:21–23, 26–28; 13:6–8, etc.). Those in Jerusalem said God had forsaken the exiles and given away their land, but God's words say the exact opposite. It's interesting to note that before instructing Ezekiel to relay these words, God told Ezekiel to refer to Him as Lord GOD. In the NIV, this is translated the "Sovereign LORD." Consequently, before the exiles heard what God had to say, they were reminded that He is sovereign. This was important for the exiles to know, because what Ezekiel was going to momentarily share with them would seem improbable, and only through a sovereign God would it be possible.

God stated that He would be a sanctuary to them. By this time, the Jewish exiles would have begun to accept that it was their own sinfulness that put them in their current predicament (Lamentations 3:37–42). They had been warned by the prophets numerous times and had perhaps begun to see that God had been justified in punishing them and, from their perspective, leaving them alone. They believed their identity was lost. The one thing that distinguished the Jews from the pagan people around them was the temple at Jerusalem or rather what it represented. The temple was where the Lord dwelled (1 Kings 6:11–13; 8:10–12). As long as the Jews had the temple, they knew God was with them. In their belief system, without the temple, they had no foundation, no place to worship, no place to be in relationship with God. Therefore, the exiles believed they would forever be lost among the heathen. So when God says, "I will be your sanctuary in the countries where I have scattered you," this is foreign to the exiles' beliefs. You can almost hear them say, "How can this be? We are not in Jerusalem." God is saying your sanctuary, or sacred place of worship, is not tied to a geographical location. This is a precursor of sorts to John 4:21, 23, in which Jesus told the woman at the well "the hour cometh, when ye shall neither in this mountain, nor yet at Jerusalem, worship the Father…the hour cometh, and now is, when the true worshippers shall worship the Father in spirit and in truth: for the Father seeketh such to worship him."

Unlike the Jews in today's lesson, we believers know that we do not have to wait to get to a certain place to communicate with God. We know that wherever we are, in whatever spiritual state, we are assured that God is with us and keeping us. We also know that because His promises are true, upon them, we can build the foundation of our lives.

3. God's Promise of a New Spirit (vv. 18–20)

The time the Jews spent in captivity would have changed them. God used the exile to rid the house of Israel of those who wanted to rebel against Him (Ezekiel 20:38). For this reason, when finally restored to their land, the remnant—the faithful ones—would not have the desire to worship other gods as had the Jews of generations past. They would rid the land of their idols. It is one thing to have the idols destroyed by natural disasters like a hurricane or earthquake, but for those who were once devotees to these images, to destroy them is quite another story. If we were to think of worshiping idols as an addiction, to voluntarily destroy them would be comparable to an addict voluntarily deciding to put down his/her addiction. Only when the addict is able to do this has true changed happened; he/she is ready to be restored. For the Jews to willingly rid their land of idols was monumental. The exile experience would have taught them: (1) to rely on God and trust His promises; (2) that God's mercy is great because by His mercy they would return to their land; and (3) to not only stop doing evil, but to start doing good.

In verse 19, God's promise to the exiles is threefold. First, after having learned well, God promised to give them one heart. Their desire, their will, would be fixed on God, not wavering. Second, God promised to give them a new spirit, a new temperament, different inclinations. Sinful things they once found enjoyable would become distasteful for them. Third, God promised to take out their stony hearts and replace them with ones of flesh. Before the exile, the Jews had become so hardened by sin that they were desensitized to the leading of God. After completing the purging of the exiles, the Jews would have softened hearts—ones malleable enough to cause them to bend to the will of God and walk in His ways. The result of a new spirit and changed hearts would be a restored relationship between the Jews and God. The Lord had already established the requirement for being His people. One simply had to follow His ways (Deuteronomy 28:9). The Jews had to experience the exile in order to learn that following God's ways was best for them.

4. Fate of the Wicked (v. 21)

After having spent great detail in laying out His promise through Ezekiel, God added a simple reminder for the Jews. He made it clear that if the people chose to continue down the evil path of idol worship, they could only blame themselves for the punishment they received. To be sure, God did not have to give them this warning. He had given it so many times before. This, however, illustrates His great love. God does not want anyone to perish, and therefore, reminds us of what not to do.

Sources:

Gower, Ralph. *The New Manners and Customs of Bible Times.* Chicago: Moody Press, 1987.

Henry, Matthew. *Commentary on the Whole Bible: Genesis to Revelation,* Vol. IV, *Isaiah to Malachi.* Public Domain. http://www.ccel.org/ccel/henry/mhc4.html.

Strong, James. *The New Strong's Exhaustive Concordance of the Bible.* Nashville: Thomas Nelson Publishers, 1990.

Search the Scriptures

1. How did those in Jerusalem view the situation of those in exile (Ezekiel 11:14–15)?

2. How did God promise to restore and keep the Jews in exile (vv. 16–17)?

3. Once they removed the idols, what did God promise the exiles He would give them (vv. 18–19)?

4. Why would God call the exiles His people (v. 20)?

5. What was the fate of those who continued in sin (v. 21)?

Discuss the Meaning

1. How do the promises of God differ from the promises people make?

2. In the past, what was your initial reaction to challenging situations?

3. Think about the trials God has brought you through. How did those experiences change you?

4. What did those experiences teach you about God?

Lesson in Our Society

Sometimes we want our lives to be easy. We don't want the challenging times, but they still come because of no fault of our own, or unwise decisions, or because of sin we have willfully committed. When these problems come, we want to know immediately every detail of how God is going to get us through them. More often than not, God does not share every detail, but He does ask that we trust in Him and in the promises He has made.

Make It Happen

When facing life's trials, some days are great. Because everything went according to our plans, there are times when we believe the trials are over. Other days are bad. Those are the times when nothing goes right and we feel alone and rejected. It's easy enough to rely on God at the high points, but it's challenging to do so at the low points. At these moments, reflect upon the ways God helped you cope in the past. Jot down those experiences and periodically read them as a source of encouragement to you. You can also share them with someone else who may need encouragement.

Follow the Spirit

What God wants me to do:

____

____

Remember Your Thoughts

Special insights I have learned:

____

____

More Light on the Text

Ezekiel 11:14–21

In contrast to the preceding section, Ezekiel 11:11–13, that is filled with a concern for the corruption of Jerusalem and its consequent judgment, verses 14–21 focus on the well-being of the exiles, and its message is that of hope. Whereas verses 11–13 announced the judgment of God against those wicked persons who remained in Jerusalem and made a mockery of the types and predictions of the prophets (1–13), God promised to favor those who had gone into captivity, and intimated their restoration from the Babylonian yoke (14–21). When reading Ezekiel, it is evident that one of the primary motivations for Yahweh's activity at this point in the lives of His chosen people was a concern for self-vindication. It appears that because of this self-vindication, the people of Israel are to receive an astounding gift. This gift is one that they have never been able to muster for themselves, namely, the ability to respond to and obey Yahweh's will. This gift is that of a "new heart" and a "new spirit." The latter is the subject of consideration in this lesson.

14 Again the word of the LORD came unto me, saying, 15 Son of man, thy brethren, even thy brethren, the men of thy kindred, and all the house of Israel wholly, are they unto whom the inhabitants of Jerusalem have said, Get you far from the LORD: unto us is this land given in possession.

The oracle opened in a customary manner with Ezekiel addressed as "son of man" (Heb. *ben 'adam*, **bane aw-DAWM**), which literally means "human." Then God identified the central concern of the oracle—the exiles. Ezekiel's great concern for the remnant of Judah was noticed by the Lord (Ezekiel 11:14). First of all, the prophet had interceded for the inhabitants of Jerusalem (Ezekiel 9:8) and then for the rulers of the nation. He asked God whether He would entirely destroy the remnant of Israel. God replied with three expressions that brought the case home to the prophet. First is "thy brethren, even thy brethren." Its duplication shows its emphatic nature. Second is "the men of thy kindred" (Heb. *'iysh ge'ullah*, **eesh gheh-ool-LAW**), literally meaning "men of your redemption." This probably referred to the circle of relatives, the extended family, on whom Ezekiel would have depended for help in time of trouble. The point was that Ezekiel's entire clan had been dragged into exile. With the third expression "and all the house of Israel wholly" (Heb. *kol bayith yisra'el*, **kole bah'-yith yis-raw-ALE**), the scope of God's concern was broadened. In this last phrase, God's sympathy for the exiles was shown. It was the exiles rather than those in Jerusalem who were worthy of the name Israel. To those in Jerusalem, the exile of Ezekiel and his kinsfolk was clear proof that God had rejected them. The inhabitants of Jerusalem had looked on the exiles as the unclean and sinful part of the nation. They thought God must have been judging them by their deportation. Because God had given the land to those still in Judah, not to the sinful exiles, they encouraged the exiles to get as far away from the land of Israel as possible. This was opportunistic profiteering at its worst—a situation where people cashed in on the troubles of others.

God told Ezekiel that his brethren, in whom he was to interest himself, were not those inhabitants of Jerusalem and those rulers of the nation, but the Israelites carried into exile who were regarded by these inhabitants at Jerusalem as cut off from the people of God. God encouraged Ezekiel, in this message, that he and a remnant—his kindred—were purposely being kept by God through the captivity. The exiles were not lost to history or to the future.

16 Therefore say, Thus saith the Lord GOD; Although I have cast them far off among the heathen, and although I have scattered them among the

countries, yet will I be to them as a little sanctuary in the countries where they shall come.

God showed that even though He had deported the remnant, He still cared for them; and He showed His care by promising to gather the exiles back to their land. Though exiled from their own land, God had not forgotten them. This is the first mention in Ezekiel of a future restoration. The prophets held out restoration as a continual hope to the righteous.

The pronouncement "I will be to them as a little sanctuary" (Heb. *miqdash*, **mik-DAWSH**), literally "a place consecrated," is rather revolutionary. It is a statement without parallel in the Old Testament. The word was previously used in 8:6 and 9:6 where an explicit distinction is made between Yahweh and His sanctuary. But here God personalized the place of worship. God promised to be for the exiles what the temple up to that point had been to them in Jerusalem. They had, indeed, lost the outward temple (at Jerusalem), but the Lord Himself had become their temple. What made the temple into a sanctuary was the presence of Jehovah, the covenant God. Thus, the exiles would enjoy God's presence in their captivity, and in this, they would possess a substitute for the outward temple. Thus, God changed the locus of worship, promising to be with the exiles in their land of captivity.

God was to have a relationship with the people apart from the temple. Moreover, it was a "little sanctuary," which could also suggest its limited duration. For a little while they were to be satisfied with God's special presence in a foreign land, but they were to look forward to a renewal of His presence in the restored temple of Jerusalem. "Sanctuary" means here strictly "the holy place," the tabernacle of the Most High." Yahweh would Himself be to the exiles in the place of the local sanctuary, in which the Jews of Jerusalem so much prided themselves.

17 Therefore say, Thus saith the Lord GOD; I will even gather you from the people, and assemble you out of the countries where ye have been scattered, and I will give you the land of Israel. 18 And they shall come thither, and they shall take away all the detestable things thereof and all the abominations thereof from thence.

Ezekiel rebutted the claim of those who remained in Jerusalem. It was not the current inhabitants to whom Yahweh had given the land for possession. God promised that when He had finished disciplining the remnant of Israel, He would bring them back to the land and restore them to the land of Israel. And because the others denied that they had any share in the possession of the land, the Lord would gather them together again and give them the land of Israel (v. 17). God not only set up His covenant but also provided all the qualifications for living under the covenant. So, in verse 18, God demanded that upon their return, they would remove all detestable things and abominations in their midst. As such, the land would become a new land. Like the territory that the Israelites had originally wrested from the Canaanites, the land to which the exiles would return had become a polluted land, defiled by centuries of "detestable" (Heb. *shiqquwts*, **shik-KOOTS**) and "abominable" (Hebrew, *tow'ebah*, **to-ay-BAW**) conduct by the Israelites themselves. Although God would deliver His people Himself, the responsibility for ridding the land of its contaminants was left with the people.

19 And I will give them one heart, and I will put a new spirit within you; and I will take the stony heart out of their flesh, and will give them an heart of flesh:

The verse recapitulates Jeremiah 31:31–34. The new covenant promised in Jeremiah 31:31–34 provided for a change of heart and a new spirit. The new heart and spirit would replace Israel's old heart of stone (Zechariah 7:12), which had become hardened against the Lord and His ways. The "new heart" and "new spirit" both refer primarily to the gift of a renewed capacity to respond to God in obedience.

The promise in verse 19 has for its basis the prediction in Deuteronomy 30:6. The circumcision of the heart is there, namely, the removal of all uncleanliness. Outward circumcision was both the type and pledge and is represented here as the giving of a heart of flesh instead of one of stone. The heart of stone has no susceptibility to the impressions of the word of God and the drawing of divine grace. In the natural condition, the human heart is as hard as stone. This new spirit would be the outpouring of the Spirit promised by the prophets (Deuteronomy 30:6; Jeremiah 31:33; Joel 2:28–29), further developed in Ezekiel 36:26–27 and initially instituted in Acts 2. This can only be effected by His giving a "new spirit," taking away the stony heart and giving a heart of flesh instead. The old spirit fosters nothing but egotism and discord. The people would be empowered by God's Spirit to live in the godly manner set forth in the stipulations of the Mosaic covenant (v. 20). They would truly reflect the Mosaic covenant formula—they would be God's people, and He would be their God. Through His death for our sins, once and for all, Christ, the Mediator of the new covenant (Hebrews 8:6), made it possible for all believers to receive the Spirit's divine enablement. This enablement gives them the power to live according to God's righteous standards revealed in the Mosaic covenant. This is available to all today who place their faith in the resurrected Messiah, Jesus Christ.

20 That they may walk in my statutes, and keep mine ordinances, and do them: and they shall be my people, and I will be their God.

If the previous verse represents the removal of Israel's unreceptive and unresponsive hearts, the first part of verse 20 corrects the disobedience that God deplored in 5:5–7. Whereas in 11:20 the purpose of the gift is defined as being "that they may walk in my statutes and keep my commandments and obey them," in 36:27, it says, "I will cause you to walk in my statutes and be careful to observe my commandments." These are synonymous expressions, each conveying the two aspects of the promised renewal—the pure guiding of the conscience and the steadfast power of the will to act as appropriate. The holiness of the lives of the returned exiles would demonstrate the work of God upon their hearts. In addition, their holy conduct would show that they were God's people. The fruit of this renewal of heart is walking in the commandments of the Lord; the consequence of the latter is the perfect realization of the covenant relation, true fellowship with the Lord God.

21 But as for them whose heart walketh after the heart of their detestable things and their abominations, I will recompense their way upon their own heads, saith the Lord GOD.

But judgment goes side by side with the renewal God promised. The happy future belonged only to those who trusted and obeyed the Lord. It was no comfort to those already in Jerusalem, worshiping their images and mistreating their neighbors. Ezekiel quickly returned to the prospect of judgment, for this is the primary theme of his vision and of these prophecies. God warned those who did not repent and follow Him that they would be held accountable and judged. It cannot be overemphasized that as it was then, so it is now. Anyone who blatantly rejects God's claims upon their lives will experience His judgment. Salvation is the reward of His true people.

Sources:

Henry, Matthew. *Commentary on the Whole Bible: Genesis to Revelation*, Vol. IV, *Isaiah to Malachi*. Public Domain. http://www.ccel.org/ccel/henry/mhc4.html.

Unger, Merrill F. *The New Unger's Bible Dictionary*. Edited by R.K. Harrison. Chicago: Moody Press, 1988.

Vine, W.E. *Vines Complete Expository Dictionary of Old and New Testament Words*. Edited by Merrill F. Unger and William White Jr. Nashville: Thomas Nelson Publishers, 1996.

Daily Bible Readings

M: Evil Hearts
Genesis 6:1–8
T: Willing Hearts
Exodus 25:1–9
W: Defiant Hearts
Deuteronomy 2:26–30
T: Obedient Hearts
Deuteronomy 5:28–33
F: Proud Hearts
Deuteronomy 8:11–19
S: Loving Hearts
Deuteronomy 10:12–21
S: One Heart, a New Spirit
Ezekiel 11:14–21

NOTES

TEACHING TIPS

March 8

Bible Study Guide 2

MAR 8th

1. Words You Should Know

A. Shepherd (Ezekiel 34:23) *ra'ah* (Heb.)—To pasture, tend, graze, feed, or ruler, teacher, of people as flock.

B. Covenant (v. 25) *beriyth* (Heb.)—Alliance, pledge between men, between God and man.

2. Teacher Preparation

Unifying Principle—The Importance of Servant–Leaders. As finite beings, the role of servant–leader can sometimes seem futile. In view of the fact that the most powerful leaders can sometimes be self-serving or manipulative, what remedy can be found when such a person is in a leadership position? Ezekiel tells us that God will provide new servant–leaders who care tenderly for their flock, just as God, the Good Shepherd, does.

A. Pray and ask God to make you a better servant–leader.

B. Read the entire chapter surrounding the printed text, using several translations. Then read the printed text alone.

C. In addition to reading the *Precepts For Living*® Bible Study Guide for this lesson, read other commentaries and make notes.

D. Look for pictures of people from all walks of life and create a handout with them entitled "Who's the Best Leader?"

3. Starting the Lesson

A. Pass out the handout you created, and ask each group to take a few minutes to pick the picture depicting the best leader.

B. The groups should consider: Why would this person be the best leader? What kind of work does this person do? How does this person treat his or her constituents?

C. Ask a volunteer to read the In Focus story aloud.

4. Getting into the Lesson

A. Ask a spokesperson from each group to present the list the group prepared outside of class.

B. Write on a board the most common points and expound on them.

C. Read and discuss the Focal Verses.

D. Tie your discussion in with God's overall plan of salvation and His kingdom-building initiative.

5. Relating the Lesson to Life

A. The groups should make a chart comparing the characteristics of the main character, the pastor in the story, and the servant–shepherd from the Scripture.

B. Ask the students how their choices for leaders compare to the main character, pastor, and the servant–shepherd.

C. Lead a discussion of the Discuss the Meaning section.

6. Arousing Action

A. Have the students take a moment to silently read the Lesson in Our Society and Make It Happen sections.

B. Ask each student to compile a list of three servant–leaders.

C. Ask the students to share their lists, and then you make a list of the top three people.

D. The class should decide and implement a way that they can encourage each leader.

Worship Guide

For the Superintendent or Teacher
Theme: New Leadership
Theme Song: "Lead Me, Guide Me"
Devotional Reading: John 10:11–18
Prayer

NEW LEADERSHIP

Bible Background • EZEKIEL 34
Printed Text • EZEKIEL 34:23–31 Devotional Reading • JOHN 10:11–18

AIM for Change

By the end of the lesson, we will:
KNOW the importance of servant–leadership;
APPRECIATE God-appointed leaders; and
CELEBRATE God as our Great Shepherd and encourage our leaders to be God-like in caring for us as sheep.

Keep in Mind

"And ye my flock, the flock of my pasture, are men, and I am your God, saith the Lord GOD" (Ezekiel 34:31).

Focal Verses

KJV **Ezekiel 34:23** And I will set up one
shepherd over them, and he shall feed
them, even my servant David; he shall feed them,
and he shall be their shepherd.
24 And I the LORD will be their God, and my servant David a prince among them; I the LORD have
spoken it.
25 And I will make with them a covenant of
peace, and will cause the evil beasts to cease out of
the land: and they shall dwell safely in the wilderness, and sleep in the woods.
26 And I will make them and the places round
about my hill a blessing; and I will cause the shower
to come down in his season; there shall be showers
of blessing.
27 And the tree of the field shall yield her fruit,
and the earth shall yield her increase, and they shall
be safe in their land, and shall know that I am the
LORD, when I have broken the bands of their yoke,
and delivered them out of the hand of those that
served themselves of them.
28 And they shall no more be a prey to the heathen, neither shall the beast of the land devour
them; but they shall dwell safely, and none shall
make them afraid.
29 And I will raise up for them a plant of renown,
and they shall be no more consumed with hunger in
the land, neither bear the shame of the heathen any
more.
30 Thus shall they know that I the LORD their
God am with them, and that they, even the house of
Israel, are my people, saith the Lord GOD.
31 And ye my flock, the flock of my pasture, are
men, and I am your God, saith the Lord GOD.

NLT **Ezekiel 34:23** And I will set over them
one shepherd, my servant David. He
will feed them and be a shepherd to them.
24 And I, the LORD, will be their God, and my
servant David will be a prince among my people. I,
the LORD, have spoken!
25 "I will make a covenant of peace with my people and drive away the dangerous animals from the
land. Then they will be able to camp safely in the
wildest places and sleep in the woods without fear.
26 I will bless my people and their homes
around my holy hill. And in the proper season I will
send the showers they need. There will be showers
of blessing.
27 The orchards and fields of my people will
yield bumper crops, and everyone will live in safety.
When I have broken their chains of slavery and rescued them from those who enslaved them, then
they will know that I am the LORD.
28 They will no longer be prey for other nations,
and wild animals will no longer devour them. They
will live in safety, and no one will frighten them.
29 "And I will make their land famous for its
crops, so my people will never again suffer from
famines or the insults of foreign nations.
30 In this way, they will know that I, the LORD
their God, am with them. And they will know that
they, the people of Israel, are my people, says the
Sovereign LORD.
31 You are my flock, the sheep of my pasture.
You are my people, and I am your God. I, the
Sovereign LORD, have spoken!"

In Focus

As he stood outside of the building with his briefcase in one hand and a mocha latte in the other, Kevin thought he was pretty lucky to be assigned to this church. From the moment he stepped onto the seminary campus, his fellow classmates talked about how they each hoped to get assigned there for their service requirement. The church was certainly up and coming.

"They've got 1,000-plus members, and they're still growing," said one of his classmates.

"They do a lot of community outreach. You can see the changes in the surrounding neighborhood," said another.

At 1,000, the church's membership had already surpassed that of any church to which Kevin had ever belonged, and that was fine with him.

He thought *I'm so tired of little churches. I need to go somewhere I can make a name for myself.*

All Kevin had wanted since he believed he had received the call to ministry was to pastor a large church. He asked God once, "You wouldn't want me to pastor in some little backwoods town for some poor congregation, would You? Wouldn't my talents be better suited for a big church?"

As Kevin walked up the steps of the church, he noticed the janitor standing outside talking to a homeless woman. He thought, *Once I have the pastor's ear, we'll have to do something about the help standing idle and bums hanging around the facilities. Yes, I'll get a lot of stuff done here.* Kevin was on top of the world.

Once inside, he barely noticed the nice marble floors someone had polished until they looked like fine glass. He was feeling so pleased with himself that he thought surely he could make three points from where he stood to the trash can across the foyer. So he put down his briefcase, drank the last of his mocha latte, posed like Jordan, and swoosh—all net.

"Yes!" Kevin said and proceeded to the pastor's office.

"Excuse me, brother, you spilled something."

Kevin whirled around to see the janitor pointing down to the long coffee trail from the door to the trash can.

"Oh, you can get that." Kevin dismissed the janitor and continued on his way.

In the pastor's office he sat on an old wooden chair in front of an equally old wooden desk. He looked around at the decor and saw there wasn't much to it. He saw a lopsided rusty metal bookcase, a yellow wool upholstered couch, and a tattered leather Bible on the desk. Kevin thought, *Once I have the pastor's ear, this will be the first room we get remodeled. A big mahogany desk, fine leather chairs, and glass bookshelves ought to do nicely. After all, this will eventually be my office.*

Just then, a man entered the office and proceeded to shake Kevin's hand. "You must be Kevin. We've been expecting you," he said.

His suit is nice enough, Kevin thought. *Not like mine though. But we can work on that, too.* Kevin stood up and said, "It's nice to meet you, sir."

"Please, sit, sit," said the man.

Kevin didn't even hear the man say it would be a minute's wait because he immediately began to share all the great ideas he had for the church. When he was in mid-description of the new Investors' Club Ministry, in walked the janitor and the homeless woman.

"Could you show Sister Lisa here to the list of houses that are available?" the janitor asked the man to whom Kevin had been speaking. "Oh, and I almost forgot—give her some tracts she can take down to the shelter. Sister Lisa is starting a homeless ministry."

"Right away, pastor," said the man as he led Lisa out.

"Kevin, I see you've already met my assistant," said the pastor as he offered him his hand.

Kevin sank down into his chair when he realized the man he thought was the janitor was the pastor.

The pastor in our story was indeed a servant–leader as God calls for His leaders to be. He also calls us "the sheep of His pasture." God utilizes the characteristics of the human shepherd to depict our relationship with Him. He was willing to be a servant–leader. Are we willing to walk in His footsteps?

The People, Places, and Times

The Bedouin Shepherd. The Bedouin shepherd of the East could either be a nomad or a town-dweller. Nomadic shepherds traveled around looking for the appropriate pastures and sources of water. A shepherd who lived in a town would take the sheep to nearby meadows. The town shepherd did not own the sheep under his charge, but would have been hired to tend several flocks in the town. He would be the chief shepherd (Genesis 47:6) and would hire help. In poor families, the youngest son was the shepherd. Because sheep could easily wander off, the shepherd had to keep a close watch on each one. Most of his day was spent out to pasture alone with the animals. In those long hours, he got to know each sheep and would give each one a name. They learned his voice.

Sheep were a valuable commodity. For this reason the shepherd, who had to answer to the owner, would search high and low for one lost sheep. He would even risk his life protecting the flock from robbers or wild animals (Genesis 31:39; John 10:11). The hired help did not have as much invested; therefore, if his own life was in danger, he would flee, leaving the flock unprotected (John 10:12–13). At night, the shepherd would guide each flock into its sheepfold. This was a partially enclosed cave or a section of land encircled with layers of stone, with no door. The shepherd would sleep at the entrance, using his body to hold the flock inside and to shield it from the dangers outside.

Sources:

Gower, Ralph. *The New Manners and Customs of Bible Times.* Chicago: Moody Press, 1987.

Unger, Merrill F. *The New Unger's Bible Dictionary.* Edited by R.K. Harrison. Chicago: Moody Press, 1988.

Background

From the history of the kingdom of Judah, we know that it had many sinful kings. For instance, King Manasseh, known as the most sinful king of Judah, adamantly sought after idolatry. He launched a fierce attack upon the prophets of God (2 Kings 21:2–16; 24:3–4). The judges were also corrupt. When they dealt with people at the gate to the city, the place where court cases were heard, they would bend the law for those who could afford to pay them a bribe. They systematically deprived the poor of justice and would take what little the poor had to line their own pockets (Amos 5:10–13). The sin and corruption were not relegated to the government officials. The priests and so-called prophets were no better. In addition to maintaining the temple sacrifices to God, the priests practiced idolatry (Isaiah 1:11, 14–15). The so-called prophets, those not appointed by God, gave false messages to the people to suit their own purposes. Prevalent in the upper echelon of society, this blatant disregard for God eventually filtered down into the rest of the community. In a nutshell, the leaders were self-serving, abusive, power-hungry, and destructive.

Source:

Unger, Merrill F. *The New Unger's Bible Dictionary.* Edited by R.K. Harrison. Chicago: Moody Press, 1988.

At-A-Glance

1. The Lord's Appointed Shepherd (Ezekiel 34:23–24)
2. The Lord's Promises to the Flock (vv. 25–29)
3. The Lord's Flock (vv. 30–31)

In Depth

1. The Lord's Appointed Shepherd (Ezekiel 34:23–24)

When God, through Ezekiel, said He would set up one shepherd, He was ushering in a new system in which the servant–shepherd would be a leader who was self-sacrificing, tender, humble, and encouraging. A shepherd takes great care to provide good pasture for his master's sheep. Good pasture has lush green grass, fresh water nearby, and is located far from animals that would devour the flock. The shepherd God would choose would take care of His people with the same diligence. He would feed the people. This feeding is not literal, although this shepherd would be capable of meeting the physical needs of God's people. This feeding deals more with their spiritual welfare.

Whereas Israel's other leaders led them astray, this God-appointed shepherd would lead them "in the paths of righteousness" (Psalm 23:3). This servant–shepherd would be of the house of David, who in the eyes of the Jewish exiles in Babylon was Israel's greatest king. He was known for his abiding love for and enduring faith in God. The Lord held David in high regard, saying of him, "I have found David the son of Jesse, a man after mine own heart, which shall fulfill all my will" (Acts 13:22). However, as great as David was, he was only a type of servant–shepherd. A type would be the "rough draft," a form of the real thing, the predecessor of the Great One still to come. The image of the perfect servant–leader is the Messiah. Ezekiel told the Jewish exiles that the coming Messiah would be able to fulfill their every need. The Lord would hold Him in the highest regard. "Behold my servant, whom I uphold; mine elect, in whom my soul delighteth; I have put my spirit upon him: he shall bring forth judgment to the Gentiles" (Isaiah 42:1).

Imagine how much comfort the exiles must have found in these words. A Messiah would come, who would take care of their physical needs and who would not rule over them with a cruel hand but would offer true justice. Perhaps the exiles would have been overjoyed that despite their current circumstances, their nation would not die out but would continue because the Lord would be with them. Certainly, they did not comprehend the full ramifications of having the perfect servant–leader, but we, today, understand. Jesus Christ performed the ultimate service so all nations would have the opportunity to be in right relationship with God. He is our example of what a servant–leader should be.

2. The Lord's Promises to the Flock (vv. 25–29)

The better system would be a covenant of peace between God and His people. A covenant was a pact normally made between two equal parties and sealed with an oath. This oath was only valid if the parties involved swore by someone greater than themselves. When God made a covenant with man, since no one was greater than Himself, He swore by Himself (Hebrews 6:13–18). This fact makes His covenant more than a mere promise but a certainty. For the Jewish exiles, this covenant meant returning to Israel without fear of the turmoil they would have left behind as they were dragged into captivity. They would be able to live safely wherever in the land.

Before they were exiled, it seemed all the blessings of God had dried up. There was a great drought (Jeremiah 14:1–6). The famine had been so severe that the women had taken to eating their own children (Lamentations 2:20). However, when the remnant would return, there would be showers of blessings—no more droughts and no more famine—because God would have abundantly blessed the land. They would be able to till the land, and crops would begin to grow again. The land would become renowned for its plentiful harvest.

Before the exile, the poor in Jerusalem suffered extreme cruelty at the hands of their leaders. They had been stripped of their most basic human rights to have homes, to work their land and eat of its harvest, and to live with dignity. Imagine their joy when hearing the yoke of poverty and injustice forced upon them would be broken. They would no longer be prey to the wicked.

Ezekiel's words were for the future of the exiles, but they were also for the distant future, one yet to occur. In this regard, because the Messiah will have already come, the covenant will reflect a more profound peace. Isaiah prophesied of this same distant future (Isaiah 11:6–11). In this world without war, not only will the remnant of Israel be restored but all believers from every nation will be restored and brought together in the kingdom of Jesus Christ. Whether in the near future of the exiles or in the distant future for us today, this covenant would never have been possible had it not been for the sacrifice of the Good Shepherd. This Good Shepherd, Jesus Christ, "made himself of no reputation, and took upon him the form of a servant, and was made in the likeness of men: And being found in fashion as a man, he humbled himself, and became obedient unto death, even the death of the cross" (Philippians 2:7–8).

3. The Lord's Flock of God (vv. 30–31)

When the sovereign Lord said He would be with the Jews, it was a fact, not a possibility. He promised they would be the "flock of His pasture," and He would be their God. Because they knew to what extent shepherds cared for sheep in their charge, comparison to a shepherd's flock spoke volumes to the Jews in exile. The comparison served to reiterate all that God, through Ezekiel, promised His people. It is significant that He not only called them "my flock" but that they were of "His" pasture. This would mean His flock would have a definite place of rest, not having to wander about, uncertain of their fate.

Christians today also have this promise of a definite rest through the Good Shepherd. He has never left us, abused us, or led us astray. He has cared for us so well; how can we not desire to serve Him?

Sources:

Gower, Ralph. *The New Manners and Customs of Bible Times.* Chicago: Moody Press, 1987.

Halley, Henry H. *Halley's Bible Handbook.* Grand Rapids, Mich.: Zondervan, 1965.

Henry, Matthew. *Commentary on the Whole Bible: Genesis to Revelation, Vol. IV, Isaiah to Malachi.* Public Domain. http://www.ccel.org/ccel/henry/mhc4.html.

Search the Scriptures

1. Who would be the one shepherd of God's choosing (Ezekiel 34:23–24)?

2. Make a list of all the promises encompassed in the covenant of peace (vv. 25–29).

3. To whom does the word "flock" refer (vv. 30–31)?

Discuss the Meaning

1. Think of an experience you have had with a self-serving leader and a servant–leader.

2. How do those experiences differ?

3. How did the constituents respond to their self-serving leader and their servant–leader?

4. Why is it necessary that leaders in the church be servants?

Lesson in Our Society

In the world, those usually considered the best leaders are people who are smart and have charismatic personalities. They can also be ruthless, egocentric, power-hungry scoundrels who will stop at nothing to get to the top. Many times, they are heralded for their misdeeds even though they destroy people's lives along the way. Their actions are excused by phrases like "It's just business," or "It's a dog-eat-dog world." Christians must be careful not to accept these characteristics in our leadership. Many ministries have been ripped to shreds because of self-serving leaders. God set up the example for our leaders to follow in the person of Jesus Christ. Jesus, the Good Shepherd, spared nothing—not even His life—in service to the Father for the benefit of His people.

Make It Happen

We have all dealt with self-serving leaders before, perhaps even in the church. Hopefully, that experience has not caused you to think there are no servant–leaders left. Ask God to lay on your heart at least three servant–leaders who are diligently serving God and people. Think of what you can do to encourage them in their ministries and do those things.

Follow the Spirit

What God wants me to do:

Remember Your Thoughts

Special insights I have learned:

More Light on the Text

Ezekiel 34:23–31

In Ezekiel 34, the prophet employed the shepherd motif both to show the failure of Israel's past leadership as well as to focus on God's provision of new leadership for Israel in the future. He preceded his promise of good leadership with a searing attack on the greed and selfishness of the leaders of the past. The former shepherds were self-serving and ruthless. They had failed to care for the poor, the weak, and the sick. In the oracle, Ezekiel stated that God would weed out the abusive leaders. Not only would the flock be purified but also the bad leaders would be removed. The shepherds would be punished and the sheep, scattered by exile, would be rescued and returned to their own pastures and cared for by their Good Shepherd, God. So, in the final climactic section of his vision, Ezekiel concluded the shepherd and flock motif (vv. 23, 31) around a portrayal of the new age, which shows that blessings would accompany God's act of renewal of His people and His covenant with them. In contrast to these abusive leaders, Ezekiel preached a message of Gospel compassion and grace to his people. The language Ezekiel employed was most gentle and comforting.

23 And I will set up one shepherd over them, and he shall feed them, even my servant David; he shall feed them, and he shall be their shepherd.

The Lord would deliver Israel from all distress, whether from poor leadership or from the predatory nations (vv. 22, 28–29). In place of the many unworthy and irresponsible shepherds who have fattened themselves by spoiling the flock of Israel, God would now give His people one good shepherd, reviving the royal line of David. God would appoint one true and responsible shepherd for His people: the Messiah. Verses 23–24 take further the shepherding theme of verses 2–16 and the covenantal concept of Yahweh's flock shared by verses 2–16 and 17–22. In verse 23, the personal pronoun "he" (Heb. *huw'*, **hoo**) emphasizes that the Messiah will be the shepherd. "I will set up" (Heb. *quwm*, **koom**) points back to the Davidic covenant in 2 Samuel 7:12–16, where the Lord promised to establish David's line on the throne of the everlasting kingdom.

It is significant to note that Ezekiel highlights the fact that God will set up *one shepherd*, something that indicates the future unity of God's people (John 10:16). The mention of this one shepherd in both Ezekiel and John points to a time of unity, reconciliation, and peace among all the peoples of the world. Originally, Ezekiel's audience likely thought and believed that this referred to their immediate or near-future situation, wherein God would unite all of the divided and scattered Israelites from all corners of the then-known world. He would bring them together, to be reconciled with each other and live in peace.

24 And I the LORD will be their God, and my servant David a prince among them; I the LORD have spoken it.

This is a verse with great theological implications. It begins with the covenant formula, "And I the LORD will be their God." It then goes on to speak of the servant. The term "servant" (Heb. *'ebed*, **EH-bed**) is a term used to describe the expected character of Israel's kings. A king was to be a servant who always obeyed his master (Yahweh), sought first his master's desire, and lived by faith in his master's every provision for him. Moreover, it is a term of honor that was conferred on historical David. However, the ultimate fulfillment of this verse is in Jesus, the Messiah, who was the perfect servant to his Heavenly Father. The true shepherd of God's people is the Lord Himself. Contrary to human leaders, who jockey for positions of power and privilege for personal gain, He has the interests of His people at heart. But the servant is also a "prince." The title "prince" (Heb. *nasiy'*, **naw-SEE**) shows that the Messiah, David's descendant, would become the "leader" ("prince") over Israel, in contrast to the past leaders. It is synonymous with the word "king" in this context.

25 And I will make with them a covenant of peace, and will cause the evil beasts to cease out of the land: and they shall dwell safely in the wilderness, and sleep in the woods.

The promises in this verse and verses 26–28 are similar to those in Leviticus 26:4–6. The Lord would establish a "covenant of peace" with Israel (vv. 25–31; cf. 37:26–28; 38:11–13; 39:25–29). This covenant was not the new covenant. This covenant would usher in the new age—a paradise-like age that guarantees the ultimate removal of all evil beasts from Israel's land so that she might live securely, ensuring safety, fertility, and productivity for all those who dwell in it (v. 25; cf. vv. 13–15; 35:1–36:15; 38–39). This vision transcends the nation Israel. Instead, it merges the prospect of the restoration of justice and order under the Davidic ruler into a cosmic vision of a world that will be free of oppression and enslavement—a world in which, above all things, fear has been abolished. Here is a description of an environment so secure the people will be able to sleep out in the open anywhere they please: "they shall dwell safely in the wilderness, and sleep in the woods."

26 And I will make them and the places round about my hill a blessing; and I will cause the shower to come down in his season; there shall be showers of blessing.

God promised to restore His people to the mountains of Israel. "My hills" most likely refers to Mount Zion, the place of the temple and of the Lord's special meeting with His people, Israel. An important aspect of God's covenant with His people of God was "showers of blessing," that is, abundant and sufficient rainfall (cf. Leviticus 26:4), without which there would be famine. God would bless Israel and her land with showers of blessings. The result would be full satisfaction from the land's abundant produce (vv. 26–27a, 29a; cf. 36:16–38). Never again would she experience famine. Here then is a reversal of one of the fundamental elements in the covenant curses in Leviticus 26:19–20 and Deuteronomy 28:23–24 (NASB): "The heaven which is over your head shall be bronze, and the earth which is under you, iron. The Lord will make the rain of your land powder and dust; from heaven it shall come down on you until you are destroyed."

27 And the tree of the field shall yield her fruit, and the earth shall yield her increase, and they shall be safe in their land, and shall know that I am the LORD, when I have broken the bands of their yoke, and delivered them out of the hand of those that served themselves of them.

The showers (v. 25) have an invigorating effect on the vegetation, causing the "tree of the field" (Heb. *'ets hassadeh*, **ates has-saw-DEH**, literally "wild trees") and the earth to "yield her increase," that is, produce an abundance of fruit (Heb. *peri*). It is significant to note that the promises, "And the tree of the field shall yield her fruit, and the earth shall yield her increase," are the exact words of Leviticus 26:4b. God was starting a renewed covenant relationship between His people and Himself. As a result of this relationship, God's people would dwell safely in their land. To dwell safely is surely the mark of the coming age in all its aspects, that is, freedom from fear (v. 25), freedom from hunger (vv. 26–27), and freedom from slavery (v. 27). Ezekiel declared that God would break "the bands of the yoke" of Israel and rescue them from the hands of those who enslaved them. Thus, Ezekiel described the restoration of Israel in a manner that is reminiscent of their previous deliverance from Egyptian bondage. When God delivered Israel from all her captors and restored her safely to her land, then she would have realized that He truly is the Lord her God. God will be finally vindicated.

28 And they shall no more be a prey to the heathen, neither shall the beast of the land devour them; but they shall dwell safely, and none shall make them afraid. 29 And I will raise up for them a plant of renown, and they shall be no more consumed with hunger in the land, neither bear the shame of the heathen any more.

Verse 28 recapitulates what has been previously said in verses 25–26. God's people will no longer be prey to the heathen, subject to their manipulation, whims, and caprices. God guaranteed His people victory over their enemies. But it is not just victories over human enemies. They would also be safe from animal predators. They would also dwell securely and be free from fear. A time of safety was coming: "but they shall dwell safely, and none shall make them afraid." It is important to notice the reiterated, double *no more* in vv. 28–29. It underlines the security that God would provide for His people. In reversal of 16:52, 54, the taunts of the nations would be completely stopped. The emphasis on freedom from fear is significant.

30 Thus shall they know that I the LORD their God am with them, and that they, even the house of Israel, are my people, saith the Lord GOD. 31 And ye my flock, the flock of my pasture, are men, and I am your God, saith the Lord GOD.

Although the external demonstrations of the gift of peace are welcome and encouraging, more important is Ezekiel's depiction of the new day, which is brought to a climax with his announcement of the new covenant. He declares the goal of God's salvific activity: "thus shall they know that I the LORD their God am with them." Israel would realize the presence of God with them and the reestablishment of the covenant relationship between them and their God. What a blessing—the tragedy of the captivity is finally reversed.

The Mosaic formula of relationship between Israel and the Lord would become a reality. The Lord would truly become their God and they would finally be His people—following His ways at every turn (vv. 30–31; cf. Exodus 6:7; Deuteronomy 29:12–15). According to Jeremiah, this relationship will be entered when Israel accepts the new covenant (Jeremiah 31:31–34) instituted by the mediator of that covenant, the Messiah (Hebrews 8:6).

Sources:

Henry, Matthew. *Commentary on the Whole Bible: Genesis to Revelation*, Vol. IV, *Isaiah to Malachi*. Public Domain. http://www.ccel.org/ccel/henry/mhc4.html.

Unger, Merrill F. *The New Unger's Bible Dictionary*. Edited by R.K. Harrison. Chicago: Moody Press, 1988.

Vine, W.E. *Vines Complete Expository Dictionary of Old and New Testament Words*. Edited by Merrill F. Unger and William White Jr. Nashville: Thomas Nelson Publishers, 1996.

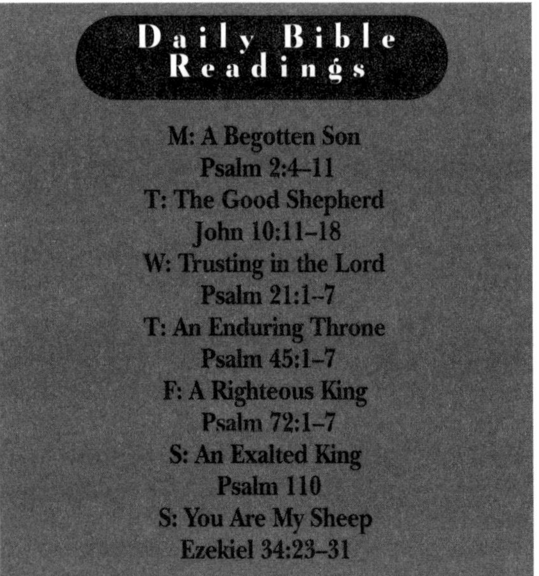

NOTES

TEACHING TIPS

March 15

Bible Study Guide 3

MAR 15th

1. Words You Should Know

A. Name (Ezekiel 36:22–23) *shem* (Heb.)—Reputation, fame, glory.

B. Sanctify (v. 23) *qadash* (Heb.)—To consecrate, prepare, dedicate, to cause Himself to be hallowed (of God).

2. Teacher Preparation

Unifying Principle—Restoring Human Lives. The fruits of certain actions are often visible. But the reasons for an action, taken in a particular time and at a certain place, are more difficult to discern. What motivates actions? According to Ezekiel, God's promise to restore Israel is not motivated by Israel itself, but rather for the sake of God's holiness.

A. Pray, and ask God to guide you through the lesson.

B. Read the entire chapter surrounding the Printed Text using several translations and then read the Printed Text.

C. Read the *Precepts For Living*® Bible Study Guide for this lesson and make notes of the salient points.

D. Collect six strips of cloth and create excavation sites with six little boxes of sand. On each box write "The Ruins."

E. Bury one of the following artifacts in each box along with other miscellaneous things: a picture of a house (Shirley's new home), a house key (new homes), a picture of a briefcase (new jobs), a small light bulb (salvation), a picture of the sun (glory of God), and a picture of a heart (inward change).

3. Starting the Lesson

A. Announce that God promises to restore what seems to be ruined.

B. Break the students into six groups, giving each group a box of sand and a strip of cloth.

C. Instruct the groups to dig in the sand for artifacts and to place anything they find on the cloth.

D. Announce that some of the artifacts found are related to the In Focus story, and ask volunteers to read the story to the class.

E. Ask the students to take notes on the story, keeping in mind the question, "Who benefited from the restoration of the main character?" Afterward, have the students put their artifacts aside.

F. If your class is too small to divide into groups, simply display some artifacts and discuss them, tying them into the In Focus story.

4. Getting into the Lesson

A. Ask two volunteers to read The People, Places, and Times and Background sections.

B. As they read, write down the main points and then discuss.

C. Have each group take two verses of the lesson Scripture and read them aloud.

D. Do an exposition of the Focal Verses.

5. Relating the Lesson to Life

A. Ask the students again, "Who benefited from the restoration of the main character?"

B. Each group should choose one of their artifacts that reflects an answer to the above question, and explain what the artifact represents.

C. Lead a discussion of the Discuss the Meaning section.

6. Arousing Action

A. Have the students read the Make It Happen section.

B. Ask the students to start a "list of artifacts" for their life as a reminder that God is restoring them.

Worship Guide

For the Superintendent or Teacher
Theme: God's People Restored Again
Theme Song: "Redeemed"
Devotional Reading: Psalm 25:11–22
Prayer

GOD'S PEOPLE RESTORED AGAIN

Bible Background • EZEKIEL 36:22–32
Printed Text • EZEKIEL 36:22–32 Devotional Reading • PSALM 25:11–22

AIM for Change

By the end of the lesson, we will:
UNDERSTAND God's ability to rescue and restore;
GRASP the concept that God is all powerful; and
PRAY that God's great power will be manifested in our lives and the lives of those who do not believe.

Keep in Mind

"The heathen shall know that I am the LORD, saith the Lord GOD, when I shall be sanctified in you before their eyes" (from Ezekiel 36:23).

Focal Verses

KJV **Ezekiel 36:22** Therefore say unto the house of Israel, thus saith the Lord GOD; I do not this for your sakes, O house of Israel, but for mine holy name's sake, which ye have profaned among the heathen, whither ye went.

23 And I will sanctify my great name, which was profaned among the heathen, which ye have profaned in the midst of them; and the heathen shall know that I am the LORD, saith the Lord GOD, when I shall be sanctified in you before their eyes.

24 For I will take you from among the heathen, and gather you out of all countries, and will bring you into your own land.

25 Then will I sprinkle clean water upon you, and ye shall be clean: from all your filthiness, and from all your idols, will I cleanse you.

26 A new heart also will I give you, and a new spirit will I put within you: and I will take away the stony heart out of your flesh, and I will give you an heart of flesh.

27 And I will put my spirit within you, and cause you to walk in my statutes, and ye shall keep my judgments, and do them.

28 And ye shall dwell in the land that I gave to your fathers; and ye shall be my people, and I will be your God.

29 I will also save you from all your uncleannesses: and I will call for the corn, and will increase it, and lay no famine upon you.

30 And I will multiply the fruit of the tree, and the increase of the field, that ye shall receive no more reproach of famine among the heathen.

31 Then shall ye remember your own evil ways,

NLT **Ezekiel 36:22** "Therefore, give the people of Israel this message from the Sovereign LORD: I am bringing you back, but not because you deserve it. I am doing it to protect my holy name, on which you brought shame while you were scattered among the nations.

23 I will show how holy my great name is—the name on which you brought shame among the nations. And when I reveal my holiness through you before their very eyes, says the Sovereign LORD, then the nations will know that I am the LORD.

24 For I will gather you up from all the nations and bring you home again to your land.

25 "Then I will sprinkle clean water on you, and you will be clean. Your filth will be washed away, and you will no longer worship idols.

26 And I will give you a new heart, and I will put a new spirit in you. I will take out your stony, stubborn heart and give you a tender, responsive heart.

27 And I will put my Spirit in you so that you will follow my decrees and be careful to obey my regulations.

28 "And you will live in Israel, the land I gave your ancestors long ago. You will be my people, and I will be your God.

29 I will cleanse you of your filthy behavior. I will give you good crops of grain, and I will send no more famines on the land.

30 I will give you great harvests from your fruit trees and fields, and never again will the surrounding nations be able to scoff at your land for its famines.

31 Then you will remember your past sins and

and your doings that were not good, and shall lothe yourselves in your own sight for your iniquities and for your abominations.

32 Not for your sakes do I this, saith the Lord GOD, be it known unto you: be ashamed and confounded for your own ways, O house of Israel.

despise yourselves for all the detestable things you did.

32 But remember, says the Sovereign LORD, I am not doing this because you deserve it. O my people of Israel, you should be utterly ashamed of all you have done!

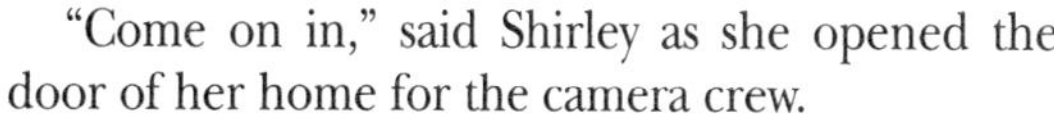

In Focus

"Come on in," said Shirley as she opened the door of her home for the camera crew.

In no time, there were cable cords making snake patterns all over the floor. Big, bright lamps were strategically placed for the best lighting. There were probably slightly over a dozen men and women bustling about rearranging the furniture to create the appropriate atmosphere for the camera shots. The reporter, pad in hand, jotted down notes as she spoke to a few of the residents.

Shirley didn't like all of this fuss, so when the local news station approached her about doing a human interest story on her Home for the Homeless organization, she initially said no. But her pastor encouraged her to reconsider. He said, "People need to see the work God is doing in this ministry. Who knows, there might be somebody out there watching who needs a decent place to stay. Somebody else might see God's goodness here and come to Christ because of it."

So Shirley reconsidered.

The countdown to air began. Five, four, three, two….

"Good evening. I'm Sue Jackson and this is 'Heroes in the City,'" the reporter said. "Tonight's heroine is Sister Shirley, as she is known in the community. Sister Shirley has made her home into a not-so-typical shelter called 'Home for the Homeless,' where she takes in people who have been homeless for more than 10 years. Is that correct?"

"Yes," Shirley timidly answered. "They come here and we help them to desire to be vital members of society again. We help them find a stable job and a home."

"How did you come up with this concept?"

"The Lord gave it to me when I found myself at a shelter."

"Yes, that's right, Sister Shirley, you were homeless yourself once. What was that experience like for you?"

"Initially I was scared. I had always had a home until the day my house burned down and everything I owned with it. I loved my home. I thought I was safe as long as I had it. When it was gone, I was devastated. And then the way people treat you when you're homeless, the way they dismiss you, made me depressed. I cried, asking the Lord why He did this to me. Then I finally stopped crying and said, 'Lord, I trust You.' I was homeless for four years. Sometimes I was up and sometimes I was down, but I kept saying 'Lord, I trust You.' He used the homelessness to help me see that I had been trusting in things and not Him. When I learned how to truly trust Him, He restored me. He gave me this 10-bedroom house. And He didn't do it just for me. He restored me so I could be a blessing to others. He restored me so others will give Him the glory."

Sister Shirley's story and mission showed Sue and millions of others the power of God to restore again. In the past, Israel's decadence and defeat led the nations of the world to see God as powerless. However, today's Scripture passage shows that God would use the restoration of the house of Israel and their return to the land to enhance the way other nations viewed the power of God.

The People, Places, and Times

The Names of God. The names of God reflect different aspects of His character. His names show relationship with His people. He called Himself Jehovah-Jireh because Abraham needed a sacrifice and God provided a ram in the bush (Genesis 22:13–14). The name El Shaddai, Almighty God, illustrates His power and His ability to do what He said He would do (Genesis 35:11–12). Adon or Adonay, Sovereign Ruler, shows His authority to reward or punish (Hosea 12:14).

Sources:

Unger, Merrill F. *The New Unger's Bible Dictionary.* Edited by R.K. Harrison. Chicago: Moody Press, 1988.

Vine, W.E. *Vines Complete Expository Dictionary of Old and New Testament Words.* Edited by Merrill F. Unger and William White Jr. Nashville: Thomas Nelson Publishers, 1996.

Background

For the exiles, life in Babylon had many negative aspects. If they worshiped God, they were ridiculed

(Psalm 137:3–5). If they did not worship the gods of Babylon, some could be sent to the furnace to be burned alive (Daniel 3:8–11). The exiles had to pay extremely high taxes to live in Babylon. They were not allowed to observe their holy days. The Babylonians did not recognize the governmental or religious ranking within the Jewish community and therefore treated Jewish officials with disrespect.

There were also positive aspects to the Babylonian life. Jews could hold political office and actually move up to high-ranking positions (Daniel 2:48). Many exiles settled down and had homes, bore children, and worked the land (Jeremiah 29:5–6). Their numbers increased and some of them had become wealthy. To remedy the fact that they had no temple, the exiles started the practice of having synagogues in every city and many became well versed in their laws.

Source:
Unger, Merrill F. *The New Unger's Bible Dictionary*. Edited by R.K. Harrison. Chicago: Moody Press, 1988.

At-A-Glance

1. God Will Sanctify His Name (Ezekiel 36:22–23)
2. God Will Restore (vv. 24–30)
3. His People Will Repent (vv. 31–32)

In Depth

1. God Will Sanctify His Name (Ezekiel 36:22–23)

Ezekiel 36:22 is a response to the sinful actions of the Jews. For hundreds of years, while in the land of Israel, they had defiled the name of the Lord with their idol worship. For their continued sin, the Lord scattered them among the nations. Even in those nations, the Jews brought dishonor to God's name. Imagine what those pagan people must have thought of the God of Israel, whose people, at the time, did not even have a place to call home. They would have heard of the power of God from all the stories passed down about those peculiar people, the Jews. These were the people whose God parted the Red Sea. Perhaps they heard tales of how these people, with the power of their God, knocked down the walls of Jericho with a shout. Surely they heard about the great King David, who under the guidance of his God conquered their very ancestors. Who could forget Solomon and the wisdom and riches his God gave him? Looking at the current state of the exiles, the pagans would have thought this God of the Jews was not so powerful after all. They said, "These are the people of the LORD, but he couldn't keep them safe in his own land!" (Ezekiel 36:20, NLT).

In response to this dishonoring of His name, God announced, through Ezekiel, that what He was about to do was not for the sake of Israel but for His name's sake. They had not nor could not do anything to deserve the blessings He was going to bestow. God wanted to sanctify His name. The names God uses to reveal Himself are a reflection of who He is and what He does. The "name," in this regard, can be akin to character and reputation. Through the actions of His people, God's character and reputation were called into question. However, through His own actions, He would proclaim His power and holiness. God would choose to restore Israel so that unbelievers would know He is the all-powerful, holy, sovereign God. To be sure, God was not moved to bless Israel so the pagan nations would accept Him but so He would be glorified.

2. God Will Restore (vv. 24–30)

In these verses, God directed Ezekiel to give, in detail, the extent of His plan of restoration for Israel. After the appointed time of their captivity was over, the Jewish exiles would be allowed to come back to their land. They would be able to settle down, build homes (Isaiah 65:22), and work the land. Initially, they would have been overjoyed to hear this news, but then perhaps memories of the condition of the land, before they were captured, would flood their minds.

God had allowed a severe drought and famine. The ground ceased to yield any crops. The exiles may have thought the land would be in an even worse state after it had lain desolate all the years of their captivity. However, when God made the promise to restore them to the land, He made the preparations for that promise. Before His people would return, God would prepare the land for them to inhabit it again (Ezekiel 36:8–9). He has the power to speak to the ground and it must give its increase. Because God would have blessed the land, causing it to yield its crops, tilling the soil would no longer be in vain. In addition to a restoration of the land, God promised a restoration of the heart.

God said, with the sprinkling of water, He would cleanse the exiles of their filthiness. This refers to a ceremonial cleansing in which the ashes of a heifer would be mixed with water and sprinkled over the unclean person or object (Numbers 19:9–18). In the Jewish belief system, this would cleanse their flesh. As this cleansing is used here, it is symbolic of a cleansing to occur within the heart and spirit of the people. It was not enough to plant them back in Israel with only a physical restoration. The desires, inclinations, and motives of the people had to be changed. Otherwise, the Jews would quickly go back to their old wicked ways. In Ezekiel 11, God made almost exactly the same promise of a new heart and a new spirit, but in today's Scripture text, we see He had refined His promise. He added that He would put His spirit within the people. Only then would they truly be able to follow His decrees. We know that for a time when the remnant returned to Judah, they were a changed people, though the indwelling of the Spirit did not occur until Pentecost. The temporary change was only a precursor to an even greater change to come. At the return from Babylon, the partial reformation was representative of the full renewal hereafter under the Messiah. A complete reformation could only be realized through Jesus Christ.

3. His People Will Repent (vv. 31–32)

In the presence of the mercy of God, His people would be moved to remember their evil ways and loathe themselves for the sins they had committed. The exiles had experienced God's mercy before and had, in the past, turned away from their sins for a time, especially when under the rule of a righteous king (2 Kings 18). In spite of this, they would always return to their wicked ways and would not loathe themselves. However, this time would be different, because of the extent to which God would go to show His mercy. After allowing the destruction and 70-year desolation of His beloved city and temple—His dwelling place—in His mercy, God would also allow the people responsible for the destruction to return. This great display of God's goodness, seen through the eyes of those to whom He would have given a new heart and a new spirit, would cause the exiles to loathe their sins. Yet, as great as this display would be, an even greater one would come through the Messiah. The full extent of God's power and mercy encompasses the sacrifice of His "only begotten Son, that whosoever believeth in him should not perish, but have everlasting life" (John 3:16). With the Holy Spirit in our hearts, at the thought of this act of mercy, we more than loathe our sins. We repent of them. When God restores, sinners repent!

Sources:

Gower, Ralph. *The New Manners and Customs of Bible Times.* Chicago: Moody Press, 1987.

Henry, Matthew. *Commentary on the Whole Bible: Genesis to Revelation*, Vol. IV, *Isaiah to Malachi.* Public Domain. http://www.ccel.org/ccel/henry/mhc4.html.

Jamieson, Robert, A. R. Fausset, and David Brown. *Commentary, Critical and Explanatory on the Bible.* Public Domain, 1871. http://www.biblestudytools.net/Commentaries/Jamieson Fausset Brown/

Search the Scriptures

1. Why did God want to sanctify His name (Ezekiel 36:22–23)?

2. How did God plan to restore His people (vv. 24–30)?

3. What would the people remember (vv. 31–32)?

Discuss the Meaning

1. Recall a time when God restored something in your life or in the life of someone you know.

2. How did this restoration benefit yourself and others?

3. Why do you think that when God restores, He not only blesses one person but many others?

Lesson in Our Society

We talk about the power of God all the time, but do we understand what that power encompasses? In a society where many hear messages about God's power to give them all of their dreams, we may need to adjust our perspectives. It's true that God has enough power to do anything. He is able to keep the earth spinning on its axis while it simultaneously journeys around the sun and still manages to catch us when we stumble. God is so great and powerful that He does whatever He pleases. He could use His power to respond to all our selfish desires, or He could use His power to give us, the great sinners that we are, what we deserve. Yet, because of His love and compassion, when He displays His power, He often uses it to restore the saved and rescue the lost.

Make It Happen

Every second the clock ticks, someone faces some kind of trial. That someone could be you. When you woke up this morning, you thought about your circumstances and became discouraged. You thought, *I've been going through this so long, it seems like nothing will ever change.* The first thing you must do is remember that God is powerful enough to restore what seems to be ruined. To encourage yourself as you wait on God, take a small memo pad, journal, or notebook, and create a list of artifacts. These are "thank you(s)" that you dig out of your day to remind yourself that God is keeping you as He is preparing to restore you.

Follow the Spirit

What God wants me to do:

____

____

Remember Your Thoughts

Special insights I have learned:

____

____

More Light on the Text

Ezekiel 36:22–32

Ezekiel focuses on the restoration of Israel as well as God's covenant faithfulness to His people. However, his main emphasis, in this section of the book, is on Yahweh's concern for Himself. Without doubt, the restoration will happen, but its purpose is to be directed by two primary and important considerations: (1) the holiness of Yahweh's own name, that is, a restoration of the reputation of God's name, and (2) the knowledge of God among the nations. God must be known for who He truly is, and He must be known universally. God's ultimate purpose is to be glorified among the nations, among whom Israel has profaned His name.

22 Therefore say unto the house of Israel, thus saith the Lord GOD; I do not this for your sakes, O house of Israel, but for mine holy name's sake, which ye have profaned among the heathen, whither ye went. 23 And I will sanctify my great name, which was profaned among the heathen, which ye have profaned in the midst of them; and the heathen shall know that I am the LORD, saith the Lord GOD, when I shall be sanctified in you before their eyes.

This passage is linked to the preceding one by the word "therefore." In Old Testament times one's name and person were equivalent; a name represented the person. For example, Jacob means "supplanter," Joshua means "Jehovah saves," etc. "Name" (Heb. *shem,* **shame**), especially when referring to Yahweh, is inextricably bound up with His being, conveying the whole person of God in His holiness. So important is God's name to Him that, in the Ten Commandments, He forbids its being taken in vain. As a result of Israel's rebellion against God, the people had profaned God's name and thereby defamed God's person. Therefore, not only would His covenant faithfulness be displayed when He restored Israel to her land but He would also bring honor and sanctity to His name and person throughout the nations, through His supernatural regathering of Israel. Then the nations would know that the righteous and loving God of Israel was the only true God.

24 For I will take you from among the heathen, and gather you out of all countries, and will bring you into your own land.

In a manner reminiscent of Israel's exodus from Egypt, God once again promised to "take [Israel] from among the heathen," "gather" them, and "bring [them] into [their] own land." God was going to do it one more time. God would accomplish a new exodus and a new deliverance from bondage. One must not fail to notice the recurrence of "*I will*" in this verse and the following. It is emphatic. Israel's restoration is to be effected by God's divine power. It will be an act of grace (unmerited favor).

25 Then will I sprinkle clean water upon you, and ye shall be clean: from all your filthiness, and from all your idols, will I cleanse you.

Israel was defiled and filthy (v. 17). But God promised a cleansing from all their filthiness and idols. God would "sprinkle clean water" upon His people and cleanse them from all those things that have rendered them unworthy. Sprinkling with clean water symbolized cleansing through divine forgiveness (cf. Psalm 51:7; 1 Corinthians 6:11). The lesson in this verse is of utmost importance: sin defiles. And for ceremonial cleansing to be more than a ritual, it was essential that the people repent and acknowledge their past iniquity, about which God would remind them. In the present context, God promised cleansing for His people corporately. But it is to be recognized that in the Old and New

Testaments, people who have a longing to fellowship with God always had an intense desire to be clean.

26 A new heart also will I give you, and a new spirit will I put within you: and I will take away the stony heart out of your flesh, and I will give you an heart of flesh.

These words are very striking, and very similar words occur in Ezekiel 11:19–20. The word "heart" (Heb. *leb,* **labe**) is used in a variety of ways. It is used of the physical organ that beats in the breast (Jeremiah 4:19). It is also used, as in the common metaphorical use of "heart" in English, of the emotions (for example, 1 Samuel 2:1: "My heart rejoiceth in the Lord"). It is used to mean rational faculty (1 Kings 3:9; Exodus 36:1; Ezekiel 3:10). However, in this passage, the word denotes the locus of the moral will (1 Samuel 24:5) as well as the symbol of inner reality as opposed to mere outward appearance. God promised to give Israel a new heart—a heart that was responsive to God. The problem of Israel was not in her behavior but its source. As such, their whole inner world would be transformed. God would change the whole of their infected nature and give them new appetites, new passions. He would remove the heart that was hard, impenetrable, and cold. He would change the affections and passions that were unyielding and frozen into good desires. He would change the heart that was slow to credit the words of God and replace it with one that could feel, enjoy, feel love for God and all men, and be a proper habitation for the living God.

27 And I will put my spirit within you, and cause you to walk in my statutes, and ye shall keep my judgments, and do them.

The purpose of the transformation to be effected was wholehearted obedience. However, that required further action of God upon Israel. "I will put my spirit (Heb. *ruwach,* **roo-ahk**) within you." The remarkable infusion of God's Spirit upon Israel would lead Israel to obey God's law and walk in it. God, Himself, by the gift of His Spirit, would see to it that His renewed and restored people would fulfill the covenant conditions that He has set. In the new covenant, the people would also receive a new spirit, God's Holy Spirit (vv. 26–27; cf. 11:19–20; 18:31; 37:14; 39:29; Joel 2:28–29; Acts 2:17–18; 2 Corinthians 3:6–18), who would enable them to live God's way, strengthening them to follow the Mosaic covenant's commandments (v. 27; cf. Romans 7:7–8:9; Hebrews 8:6–10:39). The law would be written on the heart of those living under the new covenant (Jeremiah 31:33). The new covenant provided forgiveness of sin once and for all and the indwelling of the Holy Spirit.

28 And ye shall dwell in the land that I gave to your fathers; and ye shall be my people, and I will be your God.

Ezekiel continued his recital of God's restorative activity with the announcement of the fulfillment of God's initial design: a transformed people living in their homeland and related to the Lord by covenant. A cleansed Israel would return permanently to a productive and plentiful land and would be able to live in harmonious relationship with God and in the midst of the blessing and abundance of the land. The heart of God's covenant with Israel was that that they should be His people. This would be realized and is now trenchantly expressed: "and ye shall be my people, and I will be your God."

29 I will also save you from all your uncleannesses: and I will call for the corn, and will increase it, and lay no famine upon you. 30 And I will multiply the fruit of the tree, and the increase of the field, that ye shall receive no more reproach of famine among the heathen.

These verses give further details of the restoration of God's people, particularly its more physical aspects, and underline the fact that it is "in spite of" rather than "because of" Israel's behavior that all this is to happen. God's reputation is not rehabilitated simply through Israel's inhabiting their homeland; it depends also on the quality of their life on the land. Ezekiel shows that the productivity of the land is contingent upon the cleansing of the nation, here described as salvation from all "uncleannesses." It is interesting to note that the word "save" (Heb. root, *yasha',* **yaw-SHAH**) occurs only in the book three times (34:22; 37:23). Ordinarily, it means to rescue from trouble, especially deliverance from a person by whom one has been held captive or under whose authority one is oppressed. However, in this passage, the Israelites were held in captivity, not by human enemies, but by their own uncleanness. Salvation is by the removal of uncleannesses, since defilement and pollution involve separation from the holy God.

God's involvement in the people's prosperity was underlined with three pronouncements. First, He would "call" (Heb. *qara'*, **kaw-RAW**), that is literally "summon," for the corn. The word is very striking as it evokes an image of a general summoning of troops to battle. Second, God would increase or multiply productivity both of corn and of the tree of the field. Third, He would "lay no famine" (Heb. *ra'ab*, **raw-AWB**), His instrument of judgment and agent of death, upon them.

God expanded on the importance of their productivity in verse 30. The nation would no longer experience the reproach or shame of infertility and famine among the nations. Instead, they would realize that the curse had been lifted and that God had once again visited them. The mouths of the mockers would be shut.

31 Then shall ye remember your own evil ways, and your doings that were not good, and shall lothe yourselves in your own sight for your iniquities and for your abominations.

The focus shifted from God's restoring activity to Israel's response. The return would not be based on what the people deserved; God acted in spite of them. The emphasis here is that when God begins to act favorably toward His people, it has nothing to do with their initiative or merit. It is all grace. They had turned away from God, had gone after idols, and had sunk into detestable moral corruption; as a result, they were removed into captivity. However, God promised restoration to His people. Although one would expect that there would be rejoicing and triumphant shouting when they were restored to the Promised Land (Canaan) and full privilege of being God's children, the context shows that the return was not an occasion for jubilation but rather for shame and humiliation. Confronted with God's gracious love and mercy, the first and truest emotion called forth would be remembrance of past transgressions and therefore self-loathing. An experience of divine grace should produce disgust over one's perverted ways. The sight of God's mercy enduring forever, the sight of the overflowing of the cup of love from His hand, calls forth this intense sorrow, this bitter loathing. For those who have experienced divine grace, the memory of our guilt, deserving of judgment, should not be suppressed.

32 Not for your sakes do I this, saith the Lord GOD, be it known unto you: be ashamed and confounded for your own ways, O house of Israel.

The verse repeats and emphasizes the thought of verse 22—that the true ground of God's gracious dealing with Israel and their deliverance should be found not in their merit, but in His grace. So far as their behavior and ways were concerned, there was cause only for judgment on God's part and humiliation on their part. And, as if to heighten the shame, the text explicitly states that the promised restoration was to take place in spite of Israel's unworthiness.

Sources:

Unger, Merrill F. *The New Unger's Bible Dictionary*. Edited by R.K. Harrison. Chicago: Moody Press, 1988.

Vine, W.E. *Vines Complete Expository Dictionary of Old and New Testament Words*. Edited by Merrill F. Unger and William White Jr. Nashville: Thomas Nelson Publishers, 1996.

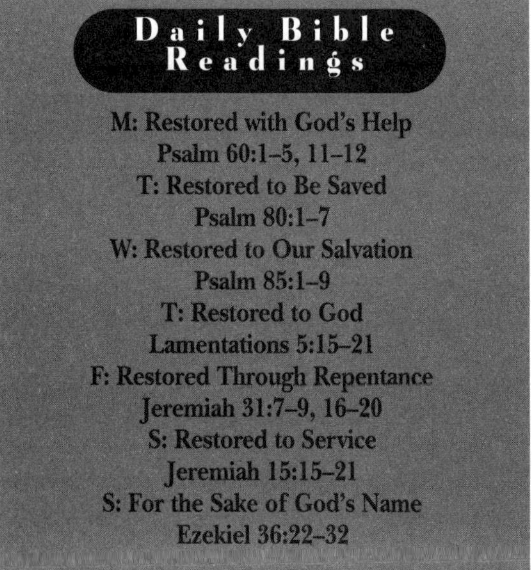

Daily Bible Readings

M: Restored with God's Help
Psalm 60:1–5, 11–12
T: Restored to Be Saved
Psalm 80:1–7
W: Restored to Our Salvation
Psalm 85:1–9
T: Restored to God
Lamentations 5:15–21
F: Restored Through Repentance
Jeremiah 31:7–9, 16–20
S: Restored to Service
Jeremiah 15:15–21
S: For the Sake of God's Name
Ezekiel 36:22–32

NOTES

TEACHING TIPS

March 22

Bible Study Guide 4

1. Words You Should Know

A. Prophesy (Ezekiel 37:4, 7, 9, 12) *naba'* (Heb.)—To predict under the influence of the divine spirit.

B. Live (vv. 3, 5, 6, 9, 10, 14) *chayah* (Heb.)—To have life, remain alive, sustain life, live prosperously, live for ever, be quickened, be alive, be restored to life or health.

2. Teacher Preparation

Unifying Principle—Renewal of Life. Sometimes situations seem so overwhelming that we fall into despair. Where can we find hope? Ezekiel's prophecy of the valley of dry bones vividly illustrates how God enlivens people and fills them with the breath of life and hope.

A. Read the Focal Verses in several different translations. Ask God to give you insight into what you have read.

B. Pray for your students by name, praying especially for those who are going through difficult situations.

C. Read through the In Depth and More Light on the Text sections, taking time to familiarize yourself with any words or concepts you might not know.

3. Starting the Lesson

A. Before the students arrive, write the word "Hope" on the board.

B. Begin the class with prayer, using the AIM for Change as a guideline.

C. Ask the students to call out the first thing that pops into their mind when they hear the word "hope." Write the responses on the board.

4. Getting into the Lesson

A. Lead a brief discussion of what hope is (refer to the student responses) and why hope is important.

B. Ask for a volunteer to read The People, Places, and Times and Background sections. Discuss the plight of the Israelites at that time of history, and why they needed hope.

C. Ask for a volunteer to read the Focal Verses out loud. Then, using the In Depth and More Light on The Text sections, discuss the Focal Verses. Tie in The People, Places, and Times and Background sections with the Focal Verses.

5. Relating the Lesson to Life

A. Ask for a volunteer to share a time in their life when God brought hope in a hopeless situation.

B. Divide the class into pairs or small groups, giving each group one of the questions from the Discuss the Meaning section.

C. After a few minutes, call the class back together. Read the Discuss the Meaning questions one at a time, having each group give their response to the question they discussed. Give time for questions or for class members to share their thoughts.

6. Arousing Action

A. Allow a time of silence for the students to complete the Follow the Spirit and/or Remember Your Thoughts sections. Ask for a volunteer to share their answer.

B. Read the Make It Happen section out loud. Challenge your students to take the steps listed in this section. Ask them to be ready to give a report about it next week.

C. Close the class in prayer, thanking God that He can breathe life and hope into any situation.

Worship Guide

For the Superintendent or Teacher
Theme: Prophesying New Life
Theme Song: "Revive Us Again"
Devotional Reading: Romans 6:1–14
Prayer

PROPHESYING NEW LIFE

Bible Background • EZEKIEL 37
Printed Text • EZEKIEL 37:1–14 Devotional Reading • ROMANS 6:1–14

AIM for Change

By the end of the lesson, we will:
ANALYZE Ezekiel's prophecy of dry bones as it relates to the captives in Babylon;
LEARN to place our hope and trust in God in times of despair; and
IDENTIFY opportunities for God to move in overwhelming situations.

Keep in Mind

"I will lay. . .put breath in you, and ye shall live; and ye shall know that I am the LORD" (from Ezekiel 37:6).

Focal Verses

KJV

Ezekiel 37:1 The hand of the LORD was upon me, and carried me out in the spirit of the LORD, and set me down in the midst of the valley which was full of bones,

2 And caused me to pass by them round about: and, behold, there were very many in the open valley; and, lo, they were very dry.

3 And he said unto me, Son of man, can these bones live? And I answered, O Lord GOD, thou knowest.

4 Again he said unto me, Prophesy upon these bones, and say unto them, O ye dry bones, hear the word of the LORD.

5 Thus saith the Lord GOD unto these bones; Behold, I will cause breath to enter into you, and ye shall live:

6 And I will lay sinews upon you, and will bring up flesh upon you, and cover you with skin, and put breath in you, and ye shall live; and ye shall know that I am the LORD.

7 So I prophesied as I was commanded: and as I prophesied, there was a noise, and behold a shaking, and the bones came together, bone to his bone.

8 And when I beheld, lo, the sinews and the flesh came up upon them, and the skin covered them above: but there was no breath in them.

9 Then said he unto me, Prophesy unto the wind, prophesy, son of man, and say to the wind, Thus saith the Lord GOD; Come from the four winds, O breath, and breathe upon these slain, that they may live.

10 So I prophesied as he commanded me, and the breath came into them, and they lived, and stood up upon their feet, an exceeding great army.

NLT

Ezekiel 37:1 The LORD took hold of me, and I was carried away by the Spirit of the LORD to a valley filled with bones.

2 He led me all around among the bones that covered the valley floor. They were scattered everywhere across the ground and were completely dried out.

3 Then he asked me, "Son of man, can these bones become living people again?" "O Sovereign LORD," I replied, "you alone know the answer to that."

4 Then he said to me, "Speak a prophetic message to these bones and say, 'Dry bones, listen to the word of the LORD!

5 This is what the Sovereign LORD says: Look! I am going to put breath into you and make you live again!

6 I will put flesh and muscles on you and cover you with skin. I will put breath into you, and you will come to life. Then you will know that I am the LORD.'"

7 So I spoke this message, just as he told me. Suddenly as I spoke, there was a rattling noise all across the valley. The bones of each body came together and attached themselves as complete skeletons.

8 Then as I watched, muscles and flesh formed over the bones. Then skin formed to cover their bodies, but they still had no breath in them.

9 Then he said to me, "Speak a prophetic message to the winds, son of man. Speak a prophetic message and say, 'This is what the Sovereign LORD says: Come, O breath, from the four winds! Breathe into these dead bodies so they may live again.'"

11 Then he said unto me, Son of man, these bones are the whole house of Israel: behold, they say, Our bones are dried, and our hope is lost: we are cut off for our parts.

12 Therefore prophesy and say unto them, Thus saith the Lord GOD; Behold, O my people, I will open your graves, and cause you to come up out of your graves, and bring you into the land of Israel.

13 And ye shall know that I am the LORD, when I have opened your graves, O my people, and brought you up out of your graves,

14 And shall put my spirit in you, and ye shall live, and I shall place you in your own land: then shall ye know that I the LORD have spoken it, and performed it, saith the LORD.

10 So I spoke the message as he commanded me, and breath came into their bodies. They all came to life and stood up on their feet—a great army.

11 Then he said to me, "Son of man, these bones represent the people of Israel. They are saying, 'We have become old, dry bones—all hope is gone. Our nation is finished.'

12 Therefore, prophesy to them and say, 'This is what the Sovereign LORD says: O my people, I will open your graves of exile and cause you to rise again. Then I will bring you back to the land of Israel.

13 When this happens, O my people, you will know that I am the LORD.

14 I will put my Spirit in you, and you will live again and return home to your own land. Then you will know that I, the LORD, have spoken, and I have done what I said. Yes, the LORD has spoken!'"

In Focus

Shaun sighed as he sank down into the chair at his favorite coffee shop. He sipped his coffee, letting his mind wander through the last few months. His business was failing, his relationship with his girlfriend was falling apart, and his kids were pushing the limits every time he turned around. When would it all end? Would his heart ever stop aching?

"Mind if I join you?"

Shaun glanced up at the guy, recognizing him as another coffee shop regular. "Suit yourself."

"I'm Aaron," the man said. "Looks like you're having a rough day."

Shaun grimaced. "A rough year is more like it."

"What's going on, man?" Aaron asked.

Shaun began to pour out his heart as Aaron quietly listened. Afterward, Aaron began to tell Shaun of the new life and hope that is found in Jesus Christ.

A few weeks later, Shaun chose to give his life to Christ. Shaun's life did not instantly become perfect. His relationship with his girlfriend ended painfully, and he's still learning how to deal with his kids and run his business. But for the first time in Shaun's life, he has hope.

Sometimes life becomes so difficult that we can't see any way out. In today's lesson, we will learn that God can bring life into lifeless, hopeless situations.

The People, Places, and Times

Visions. The book of Ezekiel records four major visions that Ezekiel received from God. The third vision is of a valley of dry bones, representing the plight of the Jewish exiles. We will examine this vision in today's lesson.

Prophecy. A dictionary definition of prophecy is "the inspired declaration of divine will and purpose." As we will learn in today's lesson, God's Word is creative, powerful, living, and active. When we, by faith, speak God's Word into our situations, hope blossoms.

Sources:

Bruce, F. F., ed. *The International Bible Commentary*. Grand Rapids, Mich.: Zondervan, 1986.

The NIV Study Bible, 10th Anniversary Edition. Grand Rapids, Mich.: Zondervan, 1995.

Background

Ezekiel's prophecy of the valley of dry bones was one of his major visions. There is no date given, but it must have occurred after 586 B.C. Until this vision, Ezekiel had received only divine messages of judgment. Israel had sinned, defiling God's temple and the whole land of His holy city, Jerusalem. God's judgment upon His people was national destruction. Their nation and their personal lives lay in ruin. Those who remained in Israel eked out a living amidst the rubble, while the exiled mourned in far-off Babylon.

Then, in Ezekiel 37, God gave Ezekiel a vision of consolation and redemption. The nation of Israel, hopeless and in exile, was given a promise of restoration. In today's lesson, we'll examine how the symbolism of Ezekiel's vision is still meaningful to believers today.

Source:
The NIV Study Bible, 10th Anniversary Edition. Grand Rapids, Mich.: Zondervan, 1995.

At-A-Glance

1. The Vision (Ezekiel 37:1–10)
2. The Vision Interpreted (vv. 11–14)

In Depth

1. The Vision (Ezekiel 37:1–10)

Ezekiel was a prophet, ordained by God to be His spokesman to the Children of Israel. As such, Ezekiel was given messages to preach to his fellow exiles. In today's passage, Ezekiel is given a vision "in the Spirit of the Lord" (Ezekiel 37:1). In this vision, Ezekiel was "carried" by God and set down in the midst of a valley full of dry bones. The image here is not a valley full of many graves but of scattered and exposed bones—disjointed and strewn across the valley.

Verse 2 emphasizes the condition of the bones: They were very dry, that is, there was no possibility of life in them. The nation of Israel was in the same condition. For all practical purposes, their nation was dismembered, disjointed, and thoroughly dead.

God then spoke to Ezekiel, asking, "Can these bones live?" Ezekiel, mindful of God's sovereignty, answered, "O Lord God, thou knowest" (Ezekiel 37:3). Ezekiel knew it was not probable or possible that dead bones would come to life, but he had seen God do too many "impossible" acts to doubt his maker.

God instructed Ezekiel to "prophesy" the word of the Lord to the dead bones (Ezekiel 37:4). God told Ezekiel to preach, so Ezekiel preached. As he spoke the creative word of God to the bones, the bones came together and were covered with skin, but they were still dead. By divine command and authority, Ezekiel then spoke to the "breath" (v. 9). God's breath (the Holy Spirit) came and the dead rose to life.

Ezekiel was not an uninvolved spectator of this event. Even though the situation seemed hopeless, Ezekiel was faithful and obedient to speak the word of God as God instructed him. He then watched in amazement as the dry bones were resurrected and filled with life.

We all have times in our lives when we feel hopeless and powerless to change our situation. It is precisely in these times that we need to remember the power of God's Word. We don't have to be mere spectators, taking whatever life dishes out to us. We can take action and turn to God and His Word! By His Spirit, God breathes life into us. That which we thought was lifeless can come back to life by the power of God. Even the most difficult situation is not hopeless for a God who can raise the dead to life!

2. The Vision Interpreted (vv. 11–14)

When trouble continues for a long time, hope fades and we begin to find ourselves swallowed up in despair. Proverbs 13:12 (NIV) says, "Hope deferred makes the heart sick, but a longing fulfilled is a tree of life." The house of Israel found itself in a hopeless situation. They had long ago lost hope and had given themselves up for dead (Ezekiel 37:11). But God had a plan. He told Ezekiel to tell the exiles that He would raise them from the "grave" of destruction and bring them home to their own land, Israel (v. 12). When this restoration came, God promised that He would also put His Spirit within them, that they would know that it was God who delivered them (v. 14).

God wants to do the same for His people today. He wants us to trust in Him alone for our deliverance, even in the midst of a seemingly hopeless situation. He wants to give us His wonderful Holy Spirit to empower and teach us and to remind us that we belong to God. Nothing is impossible with God on our side!

we don't know what's problem: possible

Sources:
Buttrick, George Arthur, ed. *The Interpreter's Bible*, Vol. 6. Nashville: Abingdon Press, 1956.

Henry, Matthew. *Matthew Henry's Complete Commentary on the Bible*. http://eword.gospelcom.net/comments/ezekiel/mh/ezekiel37.htm. Accessed February 20, 2008.

Search the Scriptures

1. What did God cause Ezekiel to see in the first part of his vision (Ezekiel 37:1)?

2. What question did God ask of Ezekiel (v. 3)?

3. What did God specifically instruct Ezekiel to do (v. 4)?

4. What did God do after Ezekiel was obedient and prophesied to the bones (vv. 7–10)?

5. What did this vision symbolize (v. 11)?

Discuss the Meaning

1. What did Ezekiel mean when he said that the hand of the Lord "carried me out in the Spirit of the LORD" (Ezekiel 37:1)? Can today's believers be directly led by the Holy Spirit as Ezekiel was?

2. God instructed Ezekiel to "prophecy," or speak God's Word to the dry bones. What happened when Ezekiel did so? Why is it important to speak God's Word into our negative situations?

3. In this interaction with Ezekiel, God showed how He can bring the dead back to life. What does verses 11–14 show us that God desires to do for those He brought back to life? What comfort can we take from this passage? What actions should we take?

Lesson in Our Society

We don't make it very far in life without hope. Yet we live in a world that is increasingly hopeless. We are bombarded with depressing and fearful images, dire predictions, and difficult personal situations. Many people turn in desperation to violence, drugs, pornography, or alcohol to try to relieve the feelings of futility and hopelessness.

Sometimes even those in the body of Christ face situations that seem hopeless. We are tempted to despair. Yet, God has provided for revival. As we choose to keep our focus on God, He will breathe new life and hope into our hearts. Those situations that seem hopeless are no match for a sovereign God.

This message needs to be shared with anyone in the world who feels hopeless; including ourselves. What can you do this week to share God's message of new life?

Make It Happen

It is difficult to apply God's Word to your situation if you don't know what His Word says! This week, examine your attitude and commitment toward the Bible. Do you read God's Word every day? How often do you memorize Scripture? Have you ever meditated on God's Word? Ask God to make His Word come alive to you; then make a commitment to spend more time in it.

Follow the Spirit

What God wants me to do:

Remember Your Thoughts

Special insights I have learned:

More Light on the Text

Ezekiel 37:1–14

In 586 B.C., Jerusalem was totally ruined by Nebuchadnezzar and his great Babylonian army. Solomon's temple, which was the pride and glory of Israel for almost 400 years, was reduced to ashes. Most of the inhabitants of Jerusalem had been taken to Babylon in captivity, including Mattaniah, last king of Judah, who was blinded and taken in chains to Babylon. Although they had been warned repeatedly by God, through His prophets, including Ezekiel, they had turned a deaf ear! Now they were spiritually dead. They had come to complete despair in their captivity. Ezekiel's vision of the open valley that is strewed with very dry bones depicts the hopeless state of the Jews who were saying, "Our bones are dried up and our hope is gone; we are cut off." They thought that God would never take them back. Since they had no hope, they also had completely lost their faith in God. But God, contrary to every human probability, restored those bones to life, thereby prefiguring the restoration of that people from the Babylonian captivity, and their resettlement in the land of their forefathers.

1 The hand of the LORD was upon me, and carried me out in the spirit of the LORD, and set me down in the midst of the valley which was full of bones, 2 And caused me to pass by them round about: and, behold, there were very many in the open valley; and, lo, they were very dry.

What a sad view this must have been for Ezekiel! He was led back and forth among them and saw a great many bones on the floor of the valley, bones that were very dry. These were not bodies that had recently passed away that could be revived with CPR. Rather, these were completely dead and rotted bodies without an ounce of life in them, which needed nothing short of a miracle and a demonstration of God's supernatural power to live again.

3 And he said unto me, Son of man, can these bones live? And I answered, O Lord GOD, thou knowest.

Ezekiel's answer was so wise: "O Lord God, thou knowest." He neither doubted nor presumed God's power. He seemed to say, "Lord, it doesn't seem possible, but You know if they can live." There is no faith in "death valley." Those who once knew God, but whose souls have dried up, were among the most hopeless. They were cut off. Their whole life was a discouragement. That's because life wasn't meant to be lived without the Lord. How could they achieve the impossible? Would they ever see their homeland again? When will it all end? Why has God forsaken us? Can these bones live again? Ezekiel could only fall back on the sovereignty of God, who knows and can do all things.

4 Again he said unto me, Prophesy upon these bones, and say unto them, O ye dry bones, hear the word of the LORD.

God spoke directly to Ezekiel, telling him to do something. What a lesson for us to learn! First, we've got to be actively involved. We must realize that we are not spectators of life. We are to be actively involved in it, but we are not alone. Second, what God told Ezekiel to do was prophesy. He was to speak the Word of the Lord. Through his words, the bones began to come together. But they weren't just Ezekiel's words; they were God's words spoken through him. It wasn't Ezekiel who brought the bones together and put flesh upon them and covered them with skin. It was God's Word, in Ezekiel, that made it happen.

5 Thus saith the Lord GOD unto these bones; Behold, I will cause breath to enter into you, and ye shall live: 6 And I will lay sinews upon you, and will bring up flesh upon you, and cover you with skin, and put breath in you, and ye shall live; and ye shall know that I am the LORD.

The Lord promised to breathe life into the bones (v. 5). The word "breath" or "spirit" (Heb. *ruwach*, **ROO-akh**) is also found in verses 6, 8, 9, 10, and 14. It can be translated as breath, wind, or spirit, the latter signifying the spirit of God, as in verse 14. It has all three meanings in this passage. When translated as breath as it is in this verse, it signifies life. Ezekiel's proclamation would bring life to the dry bones. As better explained in the New Testament, God's words are "spirit" and "life" (John 6:63). Not only would God breathe life into the bones but also put flesh on the skeletons. They arose and evidenced a complete restoration to life and began to perform their functions (v. 10).

7 So I prophesied as I was commanded: and as I prophesied, there was a noise, and behold a shaking, and the bones came together, bone to his bone. 8 And when I beheld, lo, the sinews and the flesh came up upon them, and the skin covered them above: but there was no breath in them.

Ezekiel did exactly as the Lord commanded and proclaimed the Lord's words to the dead, dry bones. While he was speaking, all the bones came together and took on themselves tendons, flesh, and skin. But no breath was found in them. The vision could be used to depict the spiritual state of several types of people in the twenty-first century church. There are those who have: (1) theological knowledge, without personal relationship with Christ; (2) knowledge without service and faith without love; and (3) there are those who are full of words, but devoid of spiritual works—displaying a form of godliness, yet denying the power thereof. Their religion is superficial and empty.

9 Then said he unto me, Prophesy unto the wind, prophesy, son of man, and say to the wind, Thus saith the Lord GOD; Come from the four winds, O breath, and breathe upon these slain, that they may live.

Ezekiel was then to prophesy to the wind and command it to enter into these well-organized bodies that they may live. Here *ruwach* has both of its most general meanings: wind or breath. Verse 9 gives us the lesson in coping with the impossible. Ezekiel and his people understood that breath was that part of humanity that gave life. If you took away the breath, living things died.

10 So I prophesied as he commanded me, and the breath came into them, and they lived, and stood up upon their feet, an exceeding great army.

Again, Ezekiel did as he was commanded. He then witnessed a remarkable sight. The breath entered the bodies, and they came to life and stood up on their feet. It is an experience that not only is analogous to that of Ezekiel, himself (2:1–2; 3:24), but also is reminiscent of 2 Kings 13:21, according to which contact with the bones of Elisha causes a dead man to revive and stand up. This is not just merely a resuscitation story. This is God bringing life where there was no life. What was the power that brought the life from God? It wasn't a bolt of lightning or a cosmic defibrillator. It was God's spirit.

11 Then he said unto me, Son of man, these bones are the whole house of Israel: behold, they say, Our bones are dried, and our hope is lost: we are cut off for our parts.

As one examines the vision and its divine interpretation, several factors are noteworthy. The bones are identified as the whole house of Israel, the slain ones of verse 9. The bones (or entire house of Israel in that day) would declare four things about themselves. First, they were dry, an obvious condition of bones from people who have been dead for a very long time. Second, the bones declared that their hope had perished. The people of Israel, having been deceased as a nation for so long, had lost all hope of becoming a nation again or of seeing God's covenants fulfilled. Third, the bones said that they were separated from one another, "cut off from their parts"—that is, the people would be separated and dispersed from one another immediately before their restoration. The phrase "we are cut off" (Heb. *nigzarnu lanu*, **nig-ZAHR-noo LA-noo**) conveys the idea of the division of God's people into parts. In this verse the emphasis is on the division of the plural subject, Israel, into many parts. That was their current condition. Fourth, it is without question as God spoke to "the whole house of Israel" and addressed the promise of new life to "my people" (Heb. *omi*) that this passage refers not to individual resurrection, but to corporate renewal. This corporate understanding does not deny that particular individuals are involved in the renewal of the nation.

12 Therefore prophesy and say unto them, Thus saith the Lord GOD; Behold, O my people, I will open your graves, and cause you to come up out of your graves, and bring you into the land of Israel.

God aroused the attention of the people by the word "behold," (Heb. *hinneh*, **hin-NAY**). It is then followed by three promises. First, God announced that He would open their graves. The second promise goes further. God would not only open the graves, but also raise them up. Third, God would bring them back to their homeland. Israel, who had been nonexistent as a people on their own land and scattered throughout the nations, would be brought back to life physically as a nation in their own land.

13 And ye shall know that I am the LORD, when I have opened your graves, O my people, and brought you up out of your graves,

God does the impossible—brings life out of death. God's goal in the restoration of His people is made plain: the acknowledgment of His person and His claims on His restored people. Because of their presence in the land, Israel had presumed upon their relationship with God for too long. Israel's coming back to life would be accompanied by a spiritual revival. God's restoration of Israel was beyond their hope; they had deemed it impossible. Therefore, it should have reminded them that indeed He is God.

14 And shall put my spirit in you, and ye shall live, and I shall place you in your own land: then shall ye know that I the LORD have spoken it, and performed it, saith the LORD.

Although they had breath and were living, God promised to put His spirit within His people. So when Ezekiel conveyed this vision to the Israelites, who were living under captivity, it gave them hope! Israel's only hope rested in her God.

Source:

Bruce, F. F., ed. *The International Bible Commentary*. Grand Rapids, Mich.: Zondervan, 1986.

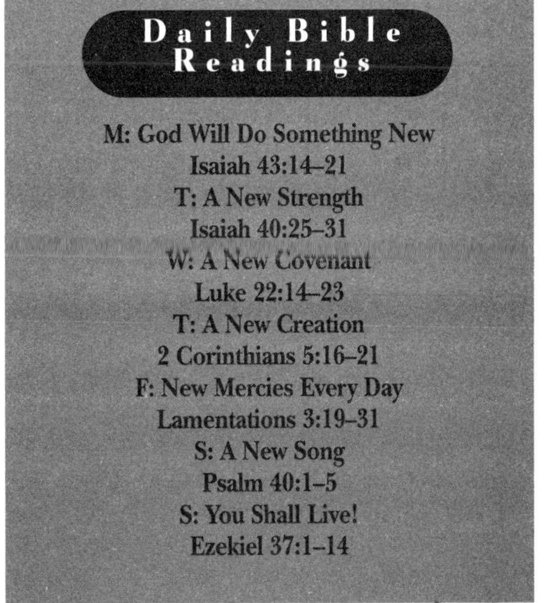

TEACHING TIPS

March 29

Bible Study Guide 5

1. Words You Should Know

A. House (Ezekiel 47:1) *bayith* (Heb.)—Temple.

B. Miry Places (v. 11) *bitstsah* (Heb.)—Swamps or marshes.

2. Teacher Preparation

Unifying Principle—Spiritual Fruitfulness and Healing. Humankind depends on the water that covers the vast areas of the earth's landscape. What impact do these bodies of water have on humanity and all creation? In a vision, Ezekiel saw a sacred river that flowed freely from God's throne, sustaining life, bringing spiritual fruitfulness and healing.

A. Read the Focal Verses in a different translation. Pray that God will give you understanding and insight into His Word.

B. Complete lesson 5 in the *Precepts For Living® Personal Study Guide.*

C. Study The People, Places, and Times; In Depth; and More Light on the Text sections.

3. Starting the Lesson

A. Open the class with prayer, thanking God for His refreshing and healing grace.

B. Ask for one or two volunteers to share the results of last week's Make It Happen section.

C. Ask a volunteer to read the Focal Verses, then ask the class, "What do you think is the spiritual significance of the river in these verses?" Discuss briefly.

4. Getting into the Lesson

A. Have the class silently read The People, Places, and Times and Background sections. Discuss.

B. Use this information to help the students understand what was going on during the time Ezekiel, the son of Buzi, a Zadokite priest, wrote the book bearing his name. Encourage the students to ask questions.

5. Relating the Lesson to Life

A. Read the Lesson in Our Society section.

B. Ask the students to share any insights they may have received from today's lesson.

6. Arousing Action

A. Call the students' attention to the Make It Happen suggestion and encourage them to carry out its mandates this week.

B. Challenge the students to faithfully read the Daily Bible Readings, emphasizing how these readings will give them the background they need to understand the lessons.

C. Ask if there are any prayer concerns and end the session with prayer.

Worship Guide

For the Superintendent or Teacher
Theme: Envisioning New Life
Theme Song: "River of God"
Devotional Reading: John 4:7–15
Prayer

ENVISIONING NEW LIFE

Bible Background • EZEKIEL 47:1–12
Printed Text • EZEKIEL 47:1–12 Devotional Reading • John 4:7–15

AIM for Change

By the end of the lesson, we will:
ANALYZE the references to water in Ezekiel's vision;
REFLECT on God's ability to refresh and to heal; and
CELEBRATE the influence of God on all creation (humankind and nature).

Keep in Mind

"Every thing shall live whither the river cometh" (Ezekiel 47:9).

Focal Verses

KJV **Ezekiel 47:1** Afterward he brought me again unto the door of the house; and, behold, waters issued out from under the threshold of the house eastward: for the forefront of the house stood toward the east, and the waters came down from under from the right side of the house, at the south side of the altar.

2 Then brought he me out of the way of the gate northward, and led me about the way without unto the utter gate by the way that looketh eastward; and, behold, there ran out waters on the right side.

3 And when the man that had the line in his hand went forth eastward, he measured a thousand cubits, and he brought me through the waters; the waters were to the ankles.

4 Again he measured a thousand, and brought me through the waters; the waters were to the knees. Again he measured a thousand, and brought me through; the waters were to the loins.

5 Afterward he measured a thousand; and it was a river that I could not pass over: for the waters were risen, waters to swim in, a river that could not be passed over.

6 And he said unto me, Son of man, hast thou seen this? Then he brought me, and caused me to return to the brink of the river.

7 Now when I had returned, behold, at the bank of the river were very many trees on the one side and on the other.

8 Then said he unto me, These waters issue out toward the east country, and go down into the desert, and go into the sea: which being brought forth into the sea, the waters shall be healed.

9 And it shall come to pass, that every thing that liveth, which moveth, whithersoever the rivers shall

NLT **Ezekiel 47:1** In my vision, the man brought me back to the entrance of the Temple. There I saw a stream flowing east from beneath the door of the Temple and passing to the right of the altar on its south side.

2 The man brought me outside the wall through the north gateway and led me around to the eastern entrance. There I could see the water flowing out through the south side of the east gateway.

3 Measuring as he went, he took me along the stream for 1,750 feet and then led me across. The water was up to my ankles.

4 He measured off another 1,750 feet and led me across again. This time the water was up to my knees. After another 1,750 feet, it was up to my waist.

5 Then he measured another 1,750 feet, and the river was too deep to walk across. It was deep enough to swim in, but too deep to walk through.

6 He asked me, "Have you been watching, son of man?" Then he led me back along the riverbank.

7 When I returned, I was surprised by the sight of many trees growing on both sides of the river.

8 Then he said to me, "This river flows east through the desert into the valley of the Dead Sea. The waters of this stream will make the salty waters of the Dead Sea fresh and pure.

9 There will be swarms of living things wherever the water of this river flows. Fish will abound in the Dead Sea, for its waters will become fresh. Life will flourish wherever this water flows.

10 Fishermen will stand along the shores of the Dead Sea. All the way from En-gedi to En-eglaim, the shores will be covered with nets drying in the sun. Fish of every kind will fill the Dead Sea, just as they fill the Mediterranean.

come, shall live: and there shall be a very great multitude of fish, because these waters shall come thither: for they shall be healed; and every thing shall live whither the river cometh.

10 And it shall come to pass, that the fishers shall stand upon it from Engedi even unto Eneglaim; they shall be a place to spread forth nets; their fish shall be according to their kinds, as the fish of the great sea, exceeding many.

11 But the miry places thereof and the marishes thereof shall not be healed; they shall be given to salt.

12 And by the river upon the bank thereof, on this side and on that side, shall grow all trees for meat, whose leaf shall not fade, neither shall the fruit thereof be consumed: it shall bring forth new fruit according to his months, because their waters they issued out of the sanctuary: and the fruit thereof shall be for meat, and the leaf thereof for medicine.

11 But the marshes and swamps will not be purified; they will still be salty.

12 Fruit trees of all kinds will grow along both sides of the river. The leaves of these trees will never turn brown and fall, and there will always be fruit on their branches. There will be a new crop every month, for they are watered by the river flowing from the Temple. The fruit will be for food and the leaves for healing."

In Focus

Over a long hot summer, Brock and Ella watched as the brook behind their home slowly dried up. Where there had once been lush green overgrowth, there were now a few plants struggling to survive. The water that had gurgled over the rocks was now just the tiniest trickle. The fishing hole was one big stagnant mud hole, flies buzzing endlessly over the tepid muck. What little water was left was green with algae.

The birds no longer splashed in the shallow edge. The deer no longer came to drink. There were no fish. Even the tadpoles had found a better place to inhabit. It was a drought.

Summer passed into fall and fall into winter. Winter brought heavy snows, covering the dead streambed. Spring came, and with it came the rain.

One glorious spring morning, Brock and Ella awoke to the sound of rushing water. The brook was alive again! Over the next few weeks, new life seemed to burst forth. Wildflowers sprouted and bloomed. The birds sang joyfully from the green underbrush. Frogs croaked, and fish jumped. Ella laughed with joy when she saw the first deer peer through the trees.

Water sustains life. God's Living Water brings refreshment, healing, and life to all who will receive it.

The People, Places, and Times

Ezekiel's Vision. Ezekiel's vision of the river is the third major vision in the book of Ezekiel. In this vision, Ezekiel observes a life-giving river. The river is bordered by trees that produce fruit. This fruit is nourishing food, and the leaves can be used for healing. Because the temple was the place around which the life of Israel revolved, it is significant that this river originated from under the temple. The altar of God, where God met with consecrated people, was the centerpiece of the temple. The waters came from the side of the altar, therefore signifying that God is the source and fountainhead of the "river" that brings life and healing to all who receive it.

Sources:

Buttrick, George Arthur, ed. *The Interpreter's Bible*, Vol. 6. Nashville: Abingdon Press, 1956.

Henry, Matthew. *Matthew Henry's Complete Commentary on the Bible.* http://eword.gospelcom.net/comments/ezekiel/mh/ezekiel47.htm. Accessed February 20, 2008.

Background

God's sovereignty is a major theme of Ezekiel. But the Sovereign God is also a God who wants to be known by His people. In Ezekiel, alone, there are 65 occurrences of the clause (or variations): "Then they will know that I am the Lord." Chapters 1–24 reveal God in the fall of Jerusalem and the ensuing national destruction. Chapters 25–32 teach God's revelation of Himself through His judgments upon the nations, and chapters 33–48 emphasize God's character through the restoration and renewal of Israel—both literally and spiritually.

It is in the context of this last section that Ezekiel receives a multipart vision of the new temple of God that is to come. In today's lesson, we will examine the last part of Ezekiel's "temple tour" where Ezekiel was standing just inside the gate of the temple and saw the river flowing from under the temple.

Source:

The NIV Study Bible, 10th Anniversary Edition. Grand Rapids, Mich.: Zondervan, 1995.

At-A-Glance

1. The Rise of the River (Ezekiel 47:1–6)
2. The Result of the River (vv. 7–12)

In Depth

1. The Rise of the River (Ezekiel 47:1–6)

Ezekiel's third vision begins with him standing in the inner court of the new temple in Jerusalem. He saw water coming out from under the temple, flowing from the side of the altar. In Revelation 22:1 (NIV), we also see "the river of the water of life, as clear as crystal, flowing from the throne of God and of the Lamb." It is significant that this river proceeds from where God dwells. He is the Source. This river flows directly from the very presence of Almighty God, Himself. Therefore, the river is able to give life and sustenance. The flow of God's Spirit, through Jesus, then, brings energizing life and healing to those who will accept it.

As the river flowed from the temple and over the mountains, instead of eventually waning to a trickle, it gained in depth and strength. Ezekiel, in his vision, waded into the river. It was ankle-deep (v. 3). A little further downstream, the river was knee-deep (v. 4). One final check revealed that the river was so deep that "no one could cross" (v. 5, NIV).

And so it is with our spiritual life. When we first begin our relationship with God, we wade out ankle-deep. We learn the first things about God. As we begin to mature, we search out the deeper things of God that require some "knee-deep" wading into the river. And then there are some things that we will never fully understand, and we must be content to say with the apostle Paul, "Oh, the depth of the riches of the wisdom and knowledge of God! How unsearchable his judgments, and his paths beyond tracing out!" (Romans 11:33, NIV).

2. The Result of the River (vv. 7–12)

The waters that proceed from God have a healing, restorative effect. Even the lowest, saltiest body of water in the world, the Dead Sea, will be made fresh by the healing river of God (v. 8). In the very end, when God finally establishes His kingdom in fullness, life will truly exist in abundance. In place of this "dead" water, where no life can be sustained, there will be "swarms of living creatures" (v. 9, NIV). This signifies great provision for humankind—fishermen will stand along the shore, from one end of the country to the other, to fill their nets with the abundance of fish (v. 10). Fruit trees of all kinds will bear bountiful crops—a different kind of fruit every month, because "the water from the sanctuary flows to them. Their fruit will serve for food and their leaves for healing" (v. 12, NIV).

The water of the sanctuary…oh, that it would flow over us! Today, God desires to give us a foretaste of the fullness of life to come. We constantly need the healing, reviving presence of God in our lives. How we need His grace, His healing, His forgiveness in our lives to wash away the stagnant, dead waters of our lives. Only when we bask in His presence and soak up the living water of His words will we become bountifully fruitful servants of God.

Sources:

Buttrick, George Arthur, ed. *The Interpreter's Bible*, Vol. 6. Nashville: Abingdon Press, 1956.

Henry, Matthew. *Matthew Henry's Complete Commentary on the Bible.* http://eword.gospelcom.net/comments/ezekiel/mh/ezekiel47.htm. Accessed February 20, 2008.

Search the Scriptures

1. Where did Ezekiel's vision of the river begin (Ezekiel 47:1)?
2. Who was "the man" (vv. 1–8)?
3. What was growing on both sides of the river (v. 12)?

Discuss the Meaning

1. Why is it significant that the wellspring of the river was at the temple? How can we liken this river to our lives?
2. What happened when the river flowed into the Dead Sea? What happens when God's Spirit is allowed to flow unhindered in our lives?

3. Describe the trees that grew along the banks of God's river. What kind of spiritual principles can we learn from these trees?

Lesson in Our Society

According to scientists, 97 percent of all water on Earth is salty. Another two percent of Earth's water is ice, leaving about one percent of all water on Earth for human use. Water conservation and pollution are major concerns in our world today; yet we have approximately the same quantity of water that has cycled continuously for centuries. King Solomon took note of this when he wrote, "All streams flow into the sea, yet the sea is never full. To the place the streams come from, there they return again" (Ecclesiastes 1:7, NIV). God has blessed all of humanity—both saved and sinner—with the life-giving gift of water.

We've all seen the pleas for help from Third World countries. Their people are dying for lack of pure water. God's people should not be hardened to the plight of these nations, but we should do what we can to help. God calls believers to hold out a cup of cold water to those who are thirsty—both literally and spiritually.

God's Living Water is available to quench the thirsty souls of those around us. God's well will never run dry; His river will never be dammed up. But it's up to us to lead the lost and dying to the water's Source—God.

Make It Happen

What is happening in your life spiritually? Is your stream of spiritual life getting stronger and deeper over time, or is it drying up and growing stagnant? This week, examine your life. Compare your life today to where you were spiritually a year ago. Are you in "ankle-deep" or "knee-deep"? Ask God for a desire to go deeper into His river.

Follow the Spirit

What God wants me to do:

Remember Your Thoughts

Special insights I have learned:

More Light on the Text

Ezekiel 47:1–12

Ezekiel is a book of visions. This passage is a fitting climax to the book and to Ezekiel's entire experience. Where the vision of the dry bones had announced the removal of the curse of death, the vision in this passage proclaimed the renewal of all aspects of life. It is a visionary experience that depicts and portrays the temple as a source of blessing for the land. Ezekiel sees the river, which would heal the land, issuing out of the temple—an emblem of the power of God's grace under the Gospel. The temple has been measured; then the glory of God returned through the east gate, which is permanently closed since God will remain with His people. It is important to note that Ezekiel's vision of a life-giving, healing river comes immediately before his account of the boundaries and divisions of the land. Before it could be inhabited again, the land must be healed and cleansed of all defilement. There are several elements of the Christian life seen in these 12 verses.

1 Afterward he brought me again unto the door of the house; and, behold, waters issued out from under the threshold of the house eastward: for the forefront of the house stood toward the east, and the waters came down from under from the right side of the house, at the south side of the altar.

After Ezekiel's guided tour of the temple (Heb. *bayith*, **BAH-yith**), he was brought back to the entrance of the temple building to the inside of the inner court. Upon reaching the gate of the temple, he saw waters that had their spring under the threshold of that gate. These waters, which looked toward the east and passed to the south of the altar of burnt offerings on the right of the temple, ran from the west to the east. The most important fact about the river is its Source. The river issues directly from the presence of God, Himself. This is the reason why it is able to give life and sustenance, for they are both gifts of the living God. The river had its spring out of sight—the fountainhead was invisible—but it proceeded out of the sanctuary of God. We need to remember that all renewal in the church and the world flow by God's wonderful grace from His presence and is not something that could be generated or controlled by humans.

2 Then brought he me out of the way of the gate northward, and led me about the way without unto the utter gate by the way that looketh eastward; and, behold, there ran out waters on the right side.

The waters seemed to have dropped out in small quantity at the beginning. The words "ran out" (Heb. *pakah,* **paw-KAW**) suggest that they were at first so small that they came in trickles—drop by drop. It was no larger than the flow of water from the mouth of a small vessel or liquid gurgling out of a flask or bottle.

3 And when the man that had the line in his hand went forth eastward, he measured a thousand cubits, and he brought me through the waters; the waters were to the ankles. 4 Again he measured a thousand, and brought me through the waters; the waters were to the knees. Again he measured a thousand, and brought me through; the waters were to the loins. 5 Afterward he measured a thousand; and it was a river that I could not pass over: for the waters were risen, waters to swim in, a river that could not be passed over.

The divine messenger took Ezekiel to explore the extent of this stream. A measuring line was used to mark off four one-thousand cubit intervals, approximately one-third of a mile each. At each interval, Ezekiel was taken out into the stream to examine its depth. The waters increased so that they became a river in which one could swim. What an amazing transformation that a river so tiny at its source could become a mighty river within just over a mile! The depth increased at each interval from ankle-deep to knee-deep to waist-deep and finally to a depth in which one must swim. At the four-thousand cubit mark, the stream had become a river of such magnitude that it could not be crossed. The river appeared so torrential and/or so wide that it was not possible to swim across it. A miracle was, no doubt at work, something like the unspent jar of meal and unfailing cruse of oil in 1 Kings 17:12–16 or like the growth of the kingdom of God from mustard seed to a spreading tree (Mark 4:31–32).

We all have plenty of room for improvement! With each step of obedience, Ezekiel found himself going deeper into dependence upon the grace of God. With each venture of forward progress, more of Ezekiel was submerged in the river with less of Ezekiel being visible. The Christian life is progressive in nature. Both measurable and discernible, God does not make us grow. We must choose to walk on into greater maturity.

Ezekiel had gone so far from the shore that he could no longer walk back. Wherever the river flowed, that was where Ezekiel was going. The current was so strong and the volume of water was so great that Ezekiel was in over his head. Still God was carrying him and there was no danger of the prophet drowning. God was still in control of the water and the life of the prophet.

6 And he said unto me, Son of man, hast thou seen this? Then he brought me, and caused me to return to the brink of the river. 7 Now when I had returned, behold, at the bank of the river were very many trees on the one side and on the other.

Ezekiel must have been left in such utter amazement that he continued to stare at the scene. Ezekiel was brought right back to the brink—back to the starting point. But there was more to see. Ezekiel saw a new sight that he had not noticed before. Both sides of the river were lined with trees. The purpose of the river was becoming clearer. Its basic purpose was to bring life. Many trees lined its sides. Every kind of fruit tree grew on both sides. There was an oasis of trees growing in the wilderness of Judah, between Jerusalem and the Dead Sea. What a sight, and what a miracle!

8 Then said he unto me, These waters issue out toward the east country, and go down into the desert, and go into the sea: which being brought forth into the sea, the waters shall be healed.

The guide did not leave the prophet in doubt concerning the interpretation of what he had just seen. Ezekiel learned that the river, which he had just seen, eventually flowed into the sea. "The sea" is a term commonly applied to the Dead Sea. Compare Deuteronomy 3:17, "the sea of the plain [Arabah], even the salt sea." The waters were miraculously healed. The word "healed" (Heb. *rapha,'* **raw-FAW**) normally referred to the healing of a diseased body. However in this case, the miracle involved the neutralizing of the corrupting chemicals in the water so it became fresh and life was no longer suppressed.

9 And it shall come to pass, that every thing that liveth, which moveth, whithersoever the rivers shall come, shall live: and there shall be a very great mul-

titude of fish, because these waters shall come thither: for they shall be healed; and every thing shall live whither the river cometh.

The thoroughness of the healing is evident in the phrase "withersoever the rivers shall come." Everywhere else, the river brought its life-giving power. Every living thing would abound in the "healed" waters. The absence of living creatures in the Dead Sea has been remarked by ancient and modern writers. In the same way the Living Water that Jesus would give would bring life to the dead in trespasses and sins. Compare John 4:14 and Revelation 22:2–3. This river is similar to the rivers in the Garden of Eden and the eternal state.

10 And it shall come to pass, that the fishers shall stand upon it from Engedi even unto Eneglaim; they shall be a place to spread forth nets; their fish shall be according to their kinds, as the fish of the great sea, exceeding many.

Ordinarily, the salt and minerals of the Dead Sea permitted no life in it of any kind, but in the ideal (coming) age, it will miraculously teem with life. The entire Dead Sea and the Arabah plain were healed by these waters, causing the Dead Sea to swarm with marine life to the extent that fishermen fished its entire length from Engedi to Eneglaim, catching a great variety of fish.

11 But the miry places thereof and the marishes thereof shall not be healed; they shall be given to salt.

The guide informed Ezekiel that there would be exceptions to the remarkable picture of life that he had just seen. The Arabah bloomed (cf. Isaiah 35:1–2, 6–7; Joel 3:18); only the swamps and marshes were not healed. They were left to provide salt for the people. The exception, which reserves for sterility—places to which the living water does not reach—probably indicates that life and health are solely due to the stream, which proceeds from beneath the throne of God.

12 And by the river upon the bank thereof, on this side and on that side, shall grow all trees for meat, whose leaf shall not fade, neither shall the fruit thereof be consumed: it shall bring forth new fruit according to his months, because their waters they issued out of the sanctuary: and the fruit thereof shall be for meat, and the leaf thereof for medicine.

The vision comes to a conclusion with a focus on the abundance of the growth of the trees and their benefits for human use. Both banks are filled with "all" (Heb. *kol*, **kole**), literally "every" tree, possibly to suggest profusion and variety. Their fruit provided food and their leaves provided healing (v. 12). The source of the land's redemption and healing came from God and His throne. He would heal the land in the time of the consummation of the kingdom. Ultimately, the river of life in Ezekiel, as in Revelation, anticipates the new creation. In this new creation, God will have lifted the curse from the earth forever and will dwell in life-giving abundance with His redeemed people gathered from all nations.

Source:

Henry, Matthew. *Matthew Henry's Complete Commentary on the Bible.* http://eword.gospelcom.net/comments/ezekiel/mh/ezekiel47.htm. Accessed February 20, 2008.

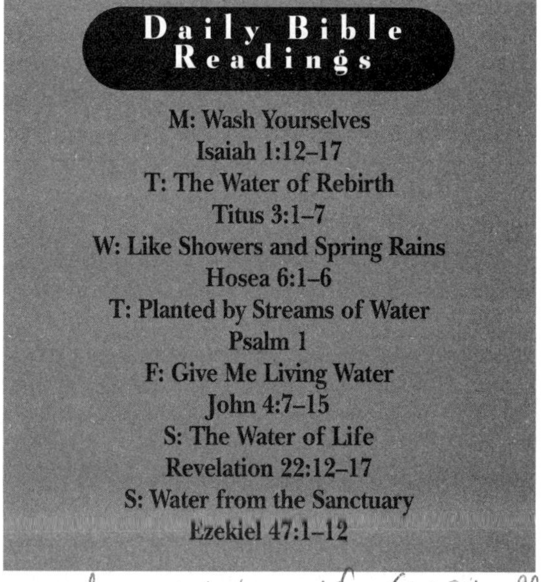

Daily Bible Readings

M: Wash Yourselves
Isaiah 1:12–17
T: The Water of Rebirth
Titus 3:1–7
W: Like Showers and Spring Rains
Hosea 6:1–6
T: Planted by Streams of Water
Psalm 1
F: Give Me Living Water
John 4:7–15
S: The Water of Life
Revelation 22:12–17
S: Water from the Sanctuary
Ezekiel 47:1–12

NOTES

TEACHING TIPS

April 5

Bible Study Guide 6

1. Words You Should Know

A. Malefactors (Luke 23:32) *kakourgos* (Gk.)—Literally meaning evil workers (*kakos* "evil" and *ergon* "work").

B. Paradise (v. 43) *paradeisos* (Gk.)—A garden, pleasure ground, grove, or park. Used in the New Testament to describe the upper region of heaven or the presence of God.

2. Teacher Preparation

Unifying Principle—Facing Death. The death event can cause a mixture of emotions, from suffering to joy. How then can we face death? Luke's account of the last week in the life of Jesus reveals that His trust in God led Jesus through triumph and sustained Him in suffering.

A. Using your *Precepts For Living® Commentary* and your *Precepts For Living® Personal Study Guide*, study the lesson in detail.

B. To enhance your teaching, make sure that you can answer all the questions in the *Precepts For Living® Personal Study Guide* for this lesson.

C. Research on the Internet or in your library on the topic of preparation for death and grief. Be prepared to share your research with your class.

3. Starting the Lesson

A. Ask a volunteer to lead the class in prayer, focusing on the AIM for Change.

B. Have a few students share their experiences from last week's Make It Happen suggestion.

C. Present your information on preparation for death and grief, and then tie in Jesus' agony as discussed in today's lesson.

D. Glean information from the In Focus section, and discuss the importance of preparing for our physical death with written directives for a will. Link that to preparing for eternal life.

E. Ask two volunteers to read the Focal Verses for today's lesson according to the At-A-Glance outline. After each section stop and ask: "What are the key points in the verses?"

F. Ask volunteers to share their answers from the Search the Scriptures section. Discuss.

4. Getting into the Lesson

A. Have a volunteer read the Background information. Discuss.

B. Have another volunteer read The People, Places, and Times section.

5. Relating the Lesson to Life

A. Break the class into two groups, and assign each group a question from the Discuss the Meaning section. After the groups talk over the questions, have each group present their conclusions to the rest of the class.

APR 5th

B. The Lesson in Our Society can help the students see how the lesson parallels with many present-day situations. Using today's lesson, ask the students if it is possible that they have let something in their lives become more important than serving God.

6. Arousing Action

The Make It Happen section contains a suggestion of what may be done to implement principles learned. Since it is a suggestion, you will want to tailor the implementations to your own specific needs.

Worship Guide

For the Superintendent or Teacher
Theme: Suffering Unto Death
Theme Song: "At the Cross"
Devotional Reading: 1 Corinthians 15:1–11
Prayer

SUFFERING UNTO DEATH

Bible Background • LUKE 23:32–46
Printed Text • LUKE 23:32–46 Devotional Reading • 1 CORINTHIANS 15:1–11

AIM for Change

By the end of the lesson, we will:
KNOW Christ's commitment to us as revealed by His suffering;
FEEL the confidence in God the Father that Jesus must have felt when He endured suffering; and
TRUST God in all things and commit our spirit to Him.

Keep in Mind

"Father, into thy hands I commend my spirit: and having said thus, he gave up the ghost" (from Luke 23:46).

Focal Verses

KJV **Luke 23:32** And there were also two other, malefactors, led with him to be put to death.

33 And when they were come to the place, which is called Calvary, there they crucified him, and the malefactors, one on the right hand, and the other on the left.

34 Then said Jesus, Father, forgive them; for they know not what they do. And they parted his raiment, and cast lots.

35 And the people stood beholding. And the rulers also with them derided him, saying, He saved others; let him save himself, if he be Christ, the chosen of God.

36 And the soldiers also mocked him, coming to him, and offering him vinegar,

37 And saying, If thou be the king of the Jews, save thyself.

38 And a superscription also was written over him in letters of Greek, and Latin, and Hebrew, THIS IS THE KING OF THE JEWS.

39 And one of the malefactors which were hanged railed on him, saying, If thou be Christ, save thyself and us.

40 But the other answering rebuked him, saying, Dost not thou fear God, seeing thou art in the same condemnation?

41 And we indeed justly; for we receive the due reward of our deeds: but this man hath done nothing amiss.

42 And he said unto Jesus, Lord, remember me when thou comest into thy kingdom.

43 And Jesus said unto him, Verily I say unto thee, Today shalt thou be with me in paradise.

44 And it was about the sixth hour, and there was a darkness over all the earth until the ninth hour.

NLT **Luke 23:32** Two others, both criminals, were led out to be executed with him.

33 When they came to a place called The Skull, they nailed him to the cross. And the criminals were also crucified—one on his right and one on his left.

34 Jesus said, "Father, forgive them, for they don't know what they are doing." And the soldiers gambled for his clothes by throwing dice.

35 The crowd watched and the leaders scoffed. "He saved others," they said, "let him save himself if he is really God's Messiah, the Chosen One."

36 The soldiers mocked him, too, by offering him a drink of sour wine.

37 They called out to him, "If you are the King of the Jews, save yourself!"

38 A sign was fastened above him with these words: "This is the King of the Jews."

39 One of the criminals hanging beside him scoffed, "So you're the Messiah, are you? Prove it by saving yourself—and us, too, while you're at it!"

40 But the other criminal protested, "Don't you fear God even when you have been sentenced to die?

41 We deserve to die for our crimes, but this man hasn't done anything wrong."

42 Then he said, "Jesus, remember me when you come into your Kingdom."

43 And Jesus replied, "I assure you, today you will be with me in paradise."

44 By this time it was about noon, and darkness fell across the whole land until three o'clock.

45 The light from the sun was gone. And suddenly, the curtain in the sanctuary of the Temple was torn down the middle.

46 Then Jesus shouted, "Father, I entrust my

45 And the sun was darkened, and the veil of the temple was rent in the midst.

46 And when Jesus had cried with a loud voice, he said, Father, into thy hands I commend my spirit: and having said thus, he gave up the ghost.

spirit into your hands!" And with those words he breathed his last.

In Focus 

An unfortunate fact of life is that many people fail to realize that living life to its fullest involves preparing for death. Knowing that loved ones will be taken care of after your death provides a sense of peace and security for those facing death and their families. That's why it is so vitally important to keep insurance policies and wills up to date.

Many of the same people who plan so carefully for their family's financial well being are lax in planning for their own medical care in cases where death is preceded by a period of incapacity. Advance directives are legal documents that establish personal control over medical care when a person becomes incapacitated. They are called "advance directives" because they direct, in advance, decisions about aspects of medical care to be carried out when a person can no longer effectively communicate those decisions. There are two types of legal documents that extend personal control over medical care when a person becomes incapacitated: "a living will" and "a durable power of attorney" for health care.

Advance directives become effective only after incapacity has been determined. If no advance directive has been prepared, someone must be appointed to take control of medical care decisions. In such cases, doctors and hospitals usually turn to the next of kin. In the rare event that the issue is referred to a court, control is usually given to a family member. If no appropriate family member can be found, the court appoints a guardian or conservator, who may be a friend or a stranger, to oversee care. An advance directive eliminates almost any need for the courts to get involved and helps ensure that the person's health care decisions will be respected.

As important as it is to prepare for the end of our physical existence, it is much more important, when we leave this world, to prepare for our eternal existence. There is a spiritual advance directive that we put into effect by a single decision we make while alive and competent. This vitally important decision determines whether or not our name is written in the book of life, which determines where we will spend eternity.

In today's lesson two criminals are crucified along with Christ, and the decisions they make during the final hours of their lives will determine the final home of their immortal souls. The question should be asked, "Are they prepared for life after death?"

The People, Places, and Times

Satan Judged. The prince of this world, Satan, is an angel who rebelled against the Living God. Not only is he real (not symbolic), but he is constantly working against God and believers (those who believe on the Lord Jesus Christ as their personal Saviour and obey God). Even though Satan has great power, God is omnipotent. He has all power. Satan has a reign of spiritual darkness, but people can be delivered from his power because of Christ's victory on the cross at Calvary (John 12:30–32). Jesus' resurrection, then, shattered Satan's deathly power (Colossians 1:13, 14), and Satan is thereby judged and defeated.

Source:

Life Application Study Bible (New Living Translation). Wheaton, Ill.: Tyndale House Publishers, 1996.

Background

After sharing the Passover meal, Jesus and the 11 disciples (Judas had left earlier to carry out his infamous deed) left the Upper Room and took the 15-minute walk to the Mount of Olives. They may have arrived at the Garden of Gethsemane sometime between 10 and 11 p.m. When they arrived in the garden, Jesus (before His upcoming passion) withdrew from the group to pray. Separated from His friends, He passionately called out to His Father: "Father, if you are willing, take this cup from me; yet not my will, but yours be done" (Luke 22:42, NIV). When He completed His prayers, He went back to the disciples; while He was speaking to them about their sluggishness, Judas arrived followed by the temple guard. He identified Jesus by affectionately kissing Him on the cheek.

After a brief scuffle, the soldiers seized Jesus and led Him away to the house of the High Priest. When they arrived, Jesus was blindfolded and the soldiers denigrated Him. They beat and ridiculed Him for hours. At daybreak the full Sanhedrin Council met and questioned Jesus. They asked him, "Are you then the Son of God?" He replied, "You are right in saying I am" (v. 70, NIV). This was all they needed to convict Jesus of being a subversive revolutionary. Under Roman law, the religious leaders did not have the power to decree the death sentence so the entire assembly and their soldiers made their way to Pilate, the Roman governor of Judea. They accused Him of subverting the nation, opposing the payment of taxes to Caesar, and claiming to be a king.

Pilate apparently saw their claims as being religious in nature and found no basis for the charges they had brought. The priests insisted that Jesus was stirring up the people in Galilee to revolt. When Pilate heard that Jesus was Galilean and therefore under the jurisdiction of Herod Antipas, he ordered Jesus to be taken to the Jewish king.

Herod is the same king who ordered the beheading of John the Baptist. He was excited for the opportunity to finally meet Jesus, whom he had heard so much about. He questioned Jesus and tried to get Him to perform a miracle. When Jesus refused to answer his questions or perform for him, Herod became enraged and began mocking the so-called King of the Jews. He had Jesus dressed in a royal robe and then sent Him back to Pilate.

Since Herod could not find any crime to convict this apparently hapless man, Pilate was inclined to have Jesus whipped and released. The Jewish leaders were incensed; they wanted blood! "With one voice they cried out, 'Away with this man!' they kept shouting, 'Crucify him! Crucify him!'" (Luke 23:18–21, NIV). Finally Pilate gave in to their demands and ordered Jesus crucified. The soldiers took Jesus away to be beaten before His execution, and afterward they made their way through the city to the place of execution.

At-A-Glance

1. The Crowd (Luke 23:32–38)
2. The Criminals (vv. 39–43)
3. The Cross (vv. 44–46)

In Depth

1. The Crowd (Luke 23:32–38)

It is a truism of life that you will never get out of it alive. Until Jesus returns, everyone who is born will surely die. However, physical death is not the end but a transition. We transition from the temporal to the eternal and from the physical to the spiritual. Since death is not the end, the most crucial question in life is where we will spend eternity, and the answer to that question depends on the choices we make in life.

Jesus would spend the final hours of His earthly existence in the company of two men. Luke describes them as malefactors or robbers. Under Roman law, robbery was not punished by crucifixion. The word Luke uses to describe the men refers to hoodlums or thugs. Some believe these men were members of the gang headed by Barabbas, the murderer whom the Jewish leaders had demanded be released instead of Jesus.

When they reached the top of the hill called Calvary, meaning "the skull," the three men were placed on the three crosses, which were lying on the ground. Then six-inch nails were hammered through their wrists. The executioners next moved down to the feet, which were placed together with the knees slightly bent. Again, nails were driven through their ankles into the rugged wood beneath. Finally, the crosses were stood upright, and the three completely naked men would spend the final hours of their lives exposed to the insects, the elements, and the scorn of the watchers as their lives slowly ebbed away.

The crowd gathered in front of Jesus and ignored the criminals to His right and left. Their fury was reserved for the man in the middle—Jesus, the Son of God. He had upset their lives by bringing the light of truth into the darkness of their existence. They hated the light, so they hated the light bringer. They would have their revenge!

As the suffering Saviour hung from the Cross, His agony was apparent to all who saw Him; but this did not deter the bloodthirsty crowd. They wanted to compound His agony. Using the only weapons left to them, the vengeful crowd hurled insults and taunts at the dying man. "He saved others; let him save himself" (Luke 23:35, NIV). Even the highly trained Roman soldiers got caught up in the hysteria, "If you are the king of the Jews, save yourself" they shouted as they rolled the dice to see who would claim His clothing (v. 37, NIV).

The rulers, the people, and the Roman soldiers were correct in their assumption that as King of the Jews Jesus could have come down from the Cross. He could have called down legions of angels to exact His revenge on His tormentors and executioners. Instead He chose, for their sakes, to stay on the Cross. Not only did He choose to suffer and die for His tormentors and us, He prayed for them and us: "Father, forgive them, for they do not know what they are doing" (v. 34, NIV).

The last two choices of Jesus' life were to sacrifice and forgive. Noble decisions made while living affect those we leave behind and oftentimes lead them into eternity.

2. The Criminals (vv. 39–43)

One of the most perplexing things about Calvary is the attitude of the two criminals. These men had been sentenced by the same Roman court as Jesus and condemned to the same fate. Yet as they hung in agony on their individual crosses, they somehow found the energy and hatred to join the crowd in mocking and insulting Jesus (Mark 15:32). As the torturous day wore on, both men saw how Jesus responded to what was happening. He did not plead for mercy, or curse His executioners, or even proclaim His innocence. Instead, He quietly prayed for His tormentors. One of the criminals looked at the evidence and hardened his heart. In spite of his own shame and pain, he continued to mock the Lord: "Aren't you the Christ? Save yourself and us," he screamed at the seemingly helpless man hanging next to him (Luke 23:39, NIV). In his mocking was also a plea: "save me and I'll believe." In spite of all he had witnessed, he refused to let the light of life into his heart.

The same selfishness that brought him to the end of his physical life would now keep him from experiencing eternal life. If Jesus had saved the poor wretch from his much-deserved fate, chances are he would have become a follower of Jesus—at least for a while. Many of us are just like that criminal. In times of trouble and stress, we cry out, "Lord, if you'll just get me out of this mess, I promise to turn my life around!" By demanding proof before we believe, we mock Jesus. He requires us, before we see the proof, to believe. On the cross, next to the dying man, was the one man who was willing to pay the cost of his crimes. All he had to do was to admit his sins and accept the sacrifice; instead, he lashed out and lost out.

The second criminal somehow came to his senses. The light of God's truth entered his heart, and he recognized Jesus for who He is.

3. The Cross (vv. 44–46)

None of the Gospel writers imply that the day grew darker. Instead all of the writers seem to imply that the darkness was sudden (Luke 23:44–45, cf. Matthew 27:45; Mark 15:33). For three solid hours, darkness covered the land from noon to 3:00 p.m. The phrase "over all the earth" probably refers to all of Israel or maybe the city of Jerusalem. Luke did not explain the cause of the darkness, but the suddenness of the event clearly ruled out an eclipse.

Many believe that God used the darkness to veil the judgment endured by Christ on our behalf. Others believe the darkness was sin itself—every person's past, present, and future coming sins together at one time, at one place, on one person (see 2 Corinthians 5:21). Christ paid the heavy price for every dark thought and every dark deed ever committed or yet to be committed through all generations.

The veil, or curtain, that separated the Holy of Holies from the rest of the temple (Exodus 26:36; Hebrews 9:3) was miraculously split in half from top to bottom. The tearing of the veil symbolized that the sin debt had been paid. There was a new and living way available to enter the presence of God.

Normally a person in the late stages of crucifixion would not have the strength to speak above a moan, but Luke tells us that Jesus cried out in a loud voice, "Father, into your hands I commit my spirit" (v. 46, NIV). This cry, taken from Psalm 31:5, was used by Jews as the prayer to end the day. It is appropriate that the Lord Jesus began His ministry on Earth alone in the desert quoting Scripture and ended His ministry on a Cross quoting Scripture.

Search the Scriptures

1. When Jesus, the crowd, and His executioners arrived at the place called the skull, they nailed him to the Cross. How many other men were crucified with Jesus at that time (Luke 23:32)?

2. How did Jesus respond to the cruelty and humiliation heaped on Him by Jewish leaders, spectators, and even soldiers (v. 34)?

3. There was a notice nailed above Jesus' head declaring His crime. What did the message say (v. 38)?

4. One of the criminals who was crucified along-

side Jesus scorned and mocked Him; the other finally realized who Jesus was. What request did the second condemned man make to Jesus (v. 42)?

Discuss the Meaning

1. When Jesus asked for forgiveness for His tormentors, He explained that they did not realize what they were doing. How many people do you know who really don't understand that their lifestyles are offensive to God and that He stands ready to forgive them, if they would only ask? How are these people ever going to come to the true realization of their situations and God's readiness to forgive?

2. Before Jesus breathed His last breath, He committed His spirit to the hands of God. When a person dies, the person's spirit departs the body and goes somewhere. How can anyone be confident of the final destination of his or her spirit? How can believers help nonbelievers to become sure of the destination of their spirits?

Lesson in Our Society

As much as modern medicine has advanced, it has not progressed to the point of being able to conquer death. Hebrews 9:27 informs us that it is appointed to man once to die and then the judgment. Everyone who lives will die and then face the judgment of God. The Bible makes it clear that every person who dies separated from God will suffer eternal damnation. How many people in your immediate circle of friends and relatives are in danger of eternal damnation?

Make It Happen

This week, ask at least three people what they think will happen after they die. When the opportunity presents itself, share with them the Good News of Christ's sacrifice on their behalf. Be prepared to share your experiences with the class next week.

Follow the Spirit

What God wants me to do:

Remember Your Thoughts

Special insights I have learned:

More Light on the Text

Luke 23:32–46

32 And there were also two other, malefactors, led with him to be put to death.

The events leading up to our passage will be familiar to many. Commonly referred to as Jesus' "passion" (Gk. *pascho,* **PAS-kho**, meaning "to suffer"), the narrative common to all the Gospel writers includes Jesus' betrayal by Judas, Jesus' arrest, Peter's denial of his Saviour, the mocking and beating of the Lord by Roman soldiers, Jesus' appearance before the high priest and the Jewish council, His appearance before the Roman governor of Judea (Pontius Pilate), Pilate delivering Jesus over to be crucified at the insistence of the crowds (spurred on by Jewish religious leaders), and the crucifixion itself. Luke's account of Christ's passion includes one other element not found in the other three Gospels: Jesus being brought before Herod, the Roman governor of Galilee. Luke probably included this historical account because of his concern to show Jesus' connection to Galilee, the land of His upbringing. Luke often focused on the humble nature of Jesus' upbringing and how it connected Him with outsiders rather than the insiders in Jerusalem.

In Luke's account, Jesus appeared before Pilate (23:1–5), then before Herod (23:6–12); both governors found Him to have done nothing worthy of death. But the crowds, in 23:13–25, overcame Pilate's finding of innocence. They demanded that the murderer and insurrectionist Barabbas, instead of Jesus, be handed over to them and cleared from guilt. Mark 15:6 makes clear that Pilate had established a tradition of releasing one prisoner to the Jews at the Passover feast. The crowd, in their frenzy, prevailed over Pilate. The governor turned Jesus over for Him to be crucified. We then have another detail given to us only by Luke: the account of the people—especially women—who followed Jesus, weeping as He was led to be crucified. This detail fits another of Luke's unique themes: the prominent role of women among those who followed, supported, and ministered to Jesus. Luke records Jesus' compassionate response to these faithful women: that they should weep not for Him but for the evil of the human race in general—as shown by their wicked judgment of Jesus the Lord—and for the judgment that will fall upon humanity and Israel, in particular, because of this great evil (see Luke 21:20–24).

"Father, into thy hands I commend my spirit: and having said thus, he gave up the ghost" (from Luke 23:46).

This background brings us to our passage, which covers the event of the crucifixion itself, along with the response of others present at the crucifixion, including two criminals crucified with Jesus and the soldiers who were executing the terrible deed. This short opening verse establishes one brief, but important, point: Jesus was crucified with criminals.

33 And when they were come to the place, which is called Calvary, there they crucified him, and the malefactors, one on the right hand, and the other on the left.

The King James Version translates the Greek word *kranion* (**kran-EE-on**), meaning "skull," as "Calvary," which comes from the Latin word for skull (*calvaria*). The place was called "the Skull" because of the shape of the rock jutting out from the land there. One can imagine why the Romans would have chosen a place with this name for public executions! The point of these executions, after all, was to serve as a warning to other criminals.

Luke continued to mention the other criminals to hammer home the tragic irony of Jesus sharing the fate of "malefactors," as the KJV memorably puts it. One can picture the scene: Jesus was surrounded and hemmed in on both sides by those society considered so guilty as to be unworthy of continuing to live. No one watching could have avoided the implication intended by both Jews and Romans: Jesus was utterly defeated, discredited, and unfit to live.

34 Then said Jesus, Father, forgive them; for they know not what they do. And they parted his raiment, and cast lots.

If Jesus was not guilty, like those surrounding him, as Luke made clear throughout his account, then his crucifixion was a horrible evil, due not to Jesus' guilt, but to others' misunderstanding of God's work in the world. Jesus addressed the guilt of His accusers and all those watching by demonstrating radical love and mercy, even during His own dying hours: "Father, forgive them, for they know not what they do." Jesus' wording prompts us to ask: Is Jesus asking forgiveness only for those who were mistaken but not malicious? Though it might seem so at first, we would search the Gospel accounts in vain to find anyone involved in Jesus' crucifixion who was innocent and simply caught in ignorance. No, both Jew and Gentile are wickedly culpable for Jesus' crucifixion. Acts 4:27–28 makes it clear: "For of a truth against thy holy child Jesus, whom thou hast anointed, both Herod, and Pontius Pilate, with the Gentiles, and the people of Israel, were gathered together, For to do whatsoever thy hand and thy counsel determined before to be done." Every sort of person was involved in the most wicked (yet most blessed) event in history! It seems wiser to say that Jesus was asking for pardons for guilty sinners, who "know not what they do," in the sense that they had not recognized Him as the Saviour of the world—due to their own sinful and willful blindness.

The casting of lots for Jesus' clothing recalls the words of Psalm 22:18: "They part my garments among them, and cast lots upon my vesture." The suffering one who narrated this psalm anticipated the ultimate suffering One, who cried out as did the psalmist, "My God, my God, why hast thou forsaken me?" (Psalm 22:1; compare Matthew 27:46). The ugly sight of Roman soldiers playing games while Jesus suffered and died adds to the horror of the situation and the greatness of Jesus' mercy to those who reviled Him.

35 And the people stood beholding. And the rulers also with them derided him, saying, He saved others; let him save himself, if he be Christ, the chosen of God.

One of the events that helps us understand the gospel of Luke occurs in chapter 2, where we read of the righteous Simeon beholding the Baby Jesus in the temple. Filled with the Holy Spirit, Simeon tells the baby's mother, "Behold, this child is set for the fall and rising again of many in Israel; and for a sign which shall be spoken against; (Yea, a sword shall pierce through thy own soul also,) that the thoughts of many hearts may be revealed" (Luke 2:34–35). Later, Jesus Himself spoke of the divisive nature of His mission by saying, "The father shall be divided against the son, and the son against the father; the mother against the daughter, and the daughter against the mother; the mother in law against her daughter in law, and the daughter in law against her mother in law" (12:53).

The crucifixion account shows us this separation of people in response to Jesus. In Luke 23:27, many women are shown to be faithful to Jesus, but the rulers in this verse have the opposite reaction.

36 And the soldiers also mocked him, coming to him, and offering him vinegar,

Once again, Acts 4:27 is shown to be true: No type of person was exempt from culpability in the death of Jesus. While verse 35 pictures the Jewish leaders, this verse shows the Romans eagerly joining in the mocking. The "vinegar" (Gk. *oxos,* **OCK-sos**) they offered Him was probably a type of sour wine common among the poor. They intended it for mocking reasons and not to satisfy Jesus' thirst in any sense. Their actions, like so many details in history that work toward God's purposes, reveal a greater meaning yet. In giving Jesus wine used by the poor, they were pointing to His own love for and solidarity with the poor. So this account shows Jesus dying like a wicked man and like a poor man—though in His nature, He was righteous and gloriously rich beyond all telling!

37 And saying, If thou be the king of the Jews, save thyself.

Like children on a playground, the soldiers followed the lead of others in heaping mockery upon the outcast. Whereas the synagogue rulers focused on Jesus' claim to be "Messiah" and "chosen one," the Romans were more interested in His claim to be King. As a King, this set Him up as a rival to Caesar. This probably explains why Pilate asked, "Are you the King of the Jews?" (Luke 23:3, NLT) and put a sign saying, "This is the King of the Jews" over Jesus' Cross (v. 28). To the Romans, someone claiming to be king was the ultimate fool for challenging Caesar (though Jesus did not challenge Caesar's earthly rule, as Luke 20:25 shows). Jesus, to them, was getting just what a traitor deserved.

38 And a superscription also was written over him in letters of Greek, and Latin, and Hebrew, THIS IS THE KING OF THE JEWS.

The superscription referred to here was called an *epigraphe* **(ep-ig-raf-AY)** in Greek and a *titulus* in Latin. It was a sign placed over a condemned criminal, usually with the criminal's name and the charge for which he was being executed. This inscription, in God's perfect providence, once again showed the identity of Jesus, though neither Jewish nor Roman leaders believed it. Jesus' claims of kingship, as already mentioned, were the focus of the Romans' interest in putting up the sign. But their understanding of Jesus' identity as a Jew and His claim to religious and spiritual kingship shows, in fact, that they include the words "of the Jews." The rightful king over the whole earth and the head over the elect people of God (first Israel, then the church) was acknowledged as neither—except sarcastically. The sickening irony goes deeper and deeper.

39 And one of the malefactors which were hanged railed on him, saying, If thou be Christ, save thyself and us.

The ridicule heaped upon the Lord was not even limited to those watching the crucifixion. Even one of the dying men added his mocking voice to the chorus. His scornful words were a pathetic mix of unbelief and selfishness. On the one hand, he clearly did not believe that Jesus was "the Christ." But just in case Jesus surprised him and was indeed "the Christ," he dared Jesus to save not only Himself but also "us"—that is, both of the criminals hanging on either side of Jesus. This picture of a man justly condemned and dying for a crime, yet so unrepentant as to revile the Lord, adds an even deeper sense of tragedy to the picture of the crucifixion. Given this man's hardness of heart, it's no wonder that the Greek word here translated "railed on" is *blasphemeo* **(blas-fay-MEH-o)**, which often translated "blasphemed." The man is blaspheming indeed, denying both the power of God and the righteousness of His Son.

40 But the other answering rebuked him, saying, Dost not thou fear God, seeing thou art in the same condemnation?

The second criminal rebuked the first and in doing so became the only person in this whole account who sided with Jesus. By asking, "Dost not thou fear God?" the second criminal showed his understanding that God was indeed present in the situation. He did not approve of Jesus' condemnation, as the Jewish leaders thought. He recognized, in Jesus, God's messenger. Therefore, he rebuked the other criminal for his blindness. The repentant criminal pointed out what was so ugly about the mocking criminal's insults: He (the criminal) also stood condemned yet he failed to show remorse for his sin or mercy for a fellow sufferer. And so Luke introduces a hopeful note of faith and understanding concerning the identity of Jesus, as continued in the next verse.

41 And we indeed justly; for we receive the due reward of our deeds: but this man hath done nothing amiss.

The thief on the cross continued to testify to Jesus' identity as Messiah, showing yet deeper understanding of who Jesus was. He contrasted what he and his counterpart experienced "justly" (Gk. *dikaios*, **dik-AH-yoce**) with the horrible injustice that Jesus, the righteous one, was experiencing (the noun form of *dikaios* can also mean "righteous"). He showed the depth of his own repentance by speaking of "the due reward of our deeds" but also recognized (somehow, by faith) the innocence of the man hanging next to him. And so he sought salvation by faith in Jesus. Indeed, the key to salvation, at the cross, is recognizing just how different we are from Jesus!

42 And he said unto Jesus, Lord, remember me when thou comest into thy kingdom.

The repentant criminal turned to Jesus with a faith we cannot help but find striking in contrast to the vicious unbelief of the others portrayed in this scene. The irony of the Gospel shows profoundly, in that the person who would have been considered least likely to follow God's way—a condemned criminal—demonstrated faith in Jesus. He did this despite his wretched condition. He knew that Jesus would one day return in great power. This is no doubt the meaning of "when thou comest into thy kingdom." Jews at the time did not have a concept of immediately passing into heaven upon death but rather emphasized the end times coming of God to vindicate, embrace His people, and defeat their enemies. This is what the criminal looked for as he addressed Jesus. By calling Him "Lord," he showed that he recognized Jesus' divine power and expected Him to be the one who returned to rescue Israel. In the face of so many who saw Jesus' dramatic miracles and yet did not believe, we should marvel at the God-given faith of one who saw Jesus dying and despised yet believed in His powerful return!

43 And Jesus said unto him, Verily I say unto thee, Today shalt thou be with me in paradise.

Was this man a fool for making such a request of another man condemned to die on a cross? No! Jesus' gracious and comforting response confirmed to the repentant criminal that he had seen the true state of things, despite all appearances. In response to this act of faith, Jesus gave more than He was asked for: He went beyond granting the criminal's prayer concerning the end and insisted that the man would accompany Jesus in paradise "today." This is one example of the way the New Testament clarifies the hazy and mysterious Old Testament picture of life after death. Jesus established here the doctrine of the soul's immediate communion with God after death. By saying "today," Jesus guaranteed the criminal's immediate bliss in paradise with God, even as his body awaited the resurrection. And we need not question this promise in light of the fact that Jesus' body rested in its grave until the third day. Here we can confess the profound Christian mysteries of the Trinity and of Jesus' God-and-human identity. We can have confidence that Jesus made sure what He promised was granted.

44 And it was about the sixth hour, and there was a darkness over all the earth until the ninth hour.

To this point, the "darkness" that Luke referred to was the darkness of the human heart in alliance with the powers of the Devil, as shown especially in 11:35 and 22:53. It also refers to a broader darkness that surrounds those who face "the shadow of death" with little hope of deliverance, as shown in the prophecy of Zechariah, the father of John the Baptist (1:79). In light of these references to darkness, the heavens' "comment," by bringing literal darkness, seems to be that the darkness of men's hearts has here found its ultimate consummation, and the evil of this deed has brought the darkness of the shadow of death into the life of the Chosen One. God the Father made the ultimate testimony to Jesus' greatness and the blasphemous tragedy of His death by sending darkness over the whole land.

45 And the sun was darkened, and the veil of the temple was rent in the midst.

This verse, along with the last one, calls to mind the repeated Old Testament theme of the Day of the Lord. The reference to the sun being darkened is a fulfillment of Joel 2:28–32, of which verses 30–31 are of special interest to us. These verses say, "And I will shew wonders in the heavens and in the earth, blood, and fire, and pillars of smoke. The sun shall be turned into darkness, and the moon into blood, before the great and the terrible day of the LORD come." According to the Old Testament, the Day of the Lord would be the worst of all days for the enemies of God. But on this day, the enemies of God seem to triumph, and Jesus, the spotless Lamb of God, becomes the enemy of God for our sakes. This is the mystery of the Gospel: that on the Day of the Lord, it is not God's enemies who are crushed, but rather God, Himself. And so comes the hope for all those who cry out to God by faith, as Joel goes on to say in 2:32: "And it shall come to pass, that whosoever shall call on the name of the LORD shall be delivered: for in mount Zion and in Jerusalem shall be deliverance, as the LORD hath said, and in the remnant whom the LORD shall call."

46 And when Jesus had cried with a loud voice, he said, Father, into thy hands I commend my spirit: and having said thus, he gave up the ghost.

The humanness of Jesus could hardly be more vividly evoked than in this verse, which describes Jesus' heartrending death cry and tender plea to His Father in heaven. Once again, Jesus showed Himself to be the embodiment of Israel's hopes by quoting the Psalms (31:5, in this case). In doing so, He also expressed His own trust in the Father to raise Him from the dead. We might be puzzled that Jesus, the divine Son of God, would need to show this sort of dependence and trust; but in that puzzlement, we forget about the full humanity of Jesus. Being human, He relied on God for His very life and for the fulfillment of His destiny.

Sources:

Henry, Matthew. *Matthew Henry's Complete Commentary on the Bible.* http://eword.gospelcom.net/comments/ezekiel/mh/ezekiel47.htm. Accessed February 20, 2008.

Vine, W.E. *Vines Complete Expository Dictionary of Old and New Testament Words.* Edited by Merrill F. Unger and William White Jr. Nashville: Thomas Nelson Publishers, 1996.

Daily Bible Readings

M: The Message of the Cross
1 Corinthians 1:18–25

T: The Suffering Servant
Isaiah 53:1–9

W: A Ransom for Many
Mark 10:32–44

T: A Sacrifice of Atonement
Romans 3:21–26

F: A Single Sacrifice for Sin
Hebrews 10:10–18

S: Bought With a Price
1 Corinthians 6:12–20

S: The Death of Jesus
Luke 23:32–46

TEACHING TIPS

April 12

Bible Study Guide 7

1. Words You Should Know

A. Shining (Luke 24:4) *astrapto* (Gk.)—A participle from the noun *astrape,* meaning lightning, in this case referring to garments said to gleam like lightning.

B. Idle Tales (v. 11) *leros* (Gk.)—Silly talk or nonsense.

2. Teacher Preparation

Unifying Principle—Implication of New Life. Death seems final, totally defeating, and irreversible. Are these widely held assumptions really true? No! Luke's record of Easter (Resurrection) morning assures us that because Jesus rose from the dead, new resurrected life is possible.

A. Using a Bible commentary, look up the words "Easter," "sin," "forgiveness of sin," "resurrection," "atonement," "substitutionary death," "propitiation," and "eternal life."

B. Be prepared to write the words on a board, discuss their meaning, and tie them in to today's theme.

C. Read through Bible Study Guide 7, and decide which major ideas you would like to discuss.

D. Then complete the lesson from the *Precepts For Living® Personal Study Guide* to round out your lesson plan.

3. Starting the Lesson

A. Ask a volunteer to open the class in prayer, focusing on the AIM for Change.

B. Ask volunteers to share their experiences from last week's Make It Happen suggestion.

C. Put the words "Easter," "sin," "forgiveness of sin," "resurrection," "atonement," "substitutionary death," "propitiation," and "eternal life" on the board. Discuss.

D. Ask volunteers to read this week's Focal Verses. Discuss.

E. Review the Search the Scriptures questions. Discuss.

4. Getting into the Lesson

A. Discuss The People, Places, and Times and Background information.

B. To provide context to the In Depth section, share the Background information and At-A-Glance outline.

5. Relating the Lesson to Life

A. Next have the same groups tackle the Discuss the Meaning section.

B. Discuss the Lesson in Our Society section.

6. Arousing Action

A. The Make It Happen section contains a suggestion of what may be done to implement principles learned. Since it is a suggestion, you will want to tailor the implementations to your own specific needs.

APR 12th

B. Challenge the students to read the Daily Bible Readings for the week. This will help build their faith and biblical knowledge so that when they go out to share with other believers they will be well versed in Scripture.

C. Encourage the students to study next week's lesson, and come to class prepared to share what they have learned in their studies.

D. Close the class with prayer.

Worship Guide

For the Superintendent or Teacher
Theme: Resurrected Unto New Life
Theme Song: "I Know My Saviour Lives"
Devotional Reading: 1 Corinthians 15:12–26
Prayer

RESURRECTED UNTO NEW LIFE

Bible Background • LUKE 24:1–12
Printed Text • LUKE 24:1–12 Devotional Reading • 1 CORINTHIANS 15:12–26

AIM for Change

By the end of the lesson, we will:
KNOW what Christ's victory over death means for believers;
BE CONVINCED that the resurrected living is possible in Jesus Christ; and
LIVE and reflect the value of a victorious life, through a resurrected Christ.

Keep in Mind

"Why seek ye the living among the dead? He is not here, but is risen" (from Luke 24:5–6).

Focal Verses

KJV **Luke 24:1** Now upon the first day of the week, very early in the morning, they came unto the sepulchre, bringing the spices which they had prepared, and certain others with them.

2 And they found the stone rolled away from the sepulchre.

3 And they entered in, and found not the body of the Lord Jesus.

4 And it came to pass, as they were much perplexed thereabout, behold, two men stood by them in shining garments:

5 And as they were afraid, and bowed down their faces to the earth, they said unto them, Why seek ye the living among the dead?

6 He is not here, but is risen: remember how he spake unto you when he was yet in Galilee,

7 Saying, The Son of man must be delivered into the hands of sinful men, and be crucified, and the third day rise again.

8 And they remembered his words,

9 And returned from the sepulchre, and told all these things unto the eleven, and to all the rest.

10 It was Mary Magdalene and Joanna, and Mary the mother of James, and other women that were with them, which told these things unto the apostles.

11 And their words seemed to them as idle tales, and they believed them not.

12 Then arose Peter, and ran unto the sepulchre; and stooping down, he beheld the linen clothes laid by themselves, and departed, wondering in himself at that which was come to pass.

NLT **Luke 24:1** But very early on Sunday morning the women went to the tomb, taking the spices they had prepared.

2 They found that the stone had been rolled away from the entrance.

3 So they went in, but they didn't find the body of the Lord Jesus.

4 As they stood there puzzled, two men suddenly appeared to them, clothed in dazzling robes.

5 The women were terrified and bowed with their faces to the ground. Then the men asked, "Why are you looking among the dead for someone who is alive?

6 He isn't here! He is risen from the dead! Remember what he told you back in Galilee,

7 that the Son of Man must be betrayed into the hands of sinful men and be crucified, and that he would rise again on the third day."

8 Then they remembered that he had said this.

9 So they rushed back from the tomb to tell his eleven disciples—and everyone else—what had happened.

10 It was Mary Magdalene, Joanna, Mary the mother of James, and several other women who told the apostles what had happened.

11 But the story sounded like nonsense to the men, so they didn't believe it.

12 However, Peter jumped up and ran to the tomb to look. Stooping, he peered in and saw the empty linen wrappings; then he went home again, wondering what had happened.

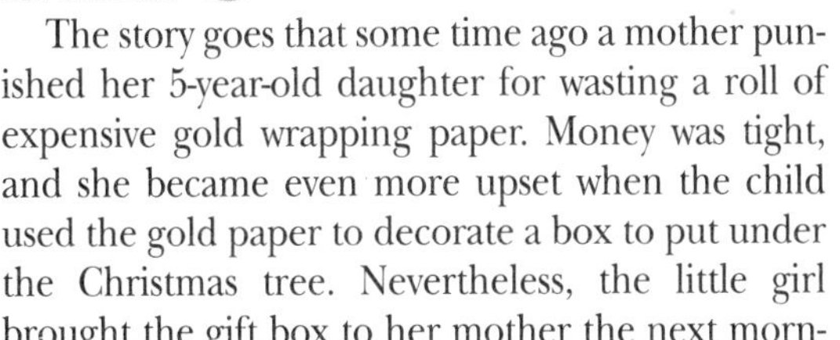

In Focus

The story goes that some time ago a mother punished her 5-year-old daughter for wasting a roll of expensive gold wrapping paper. Money was tight, and she became even more upset when the child used the gold paper to decorate a box to put under the Christmas tree. Nevertheless, the little girl brought the gift box to her mother the next morning and then said, "This is for you, Mama."

The mother was embarrassed by her earlier overreaction, but her anger flared again when she opened the box and found it was empty. She spoke to her daughter in a harsh manner. "Don't you know, young lady, that when you give someone a present there's supposed to be something inside the package?"

She had tears in her eyes and said, "Oh, Mama, it's not empty! I blew kisses into it until it was full."

The mother was crushed. She fell on her knees and put her arms around her little girl, and then she begged forgiveness for her thoughtless anger.

A short time later an accident took the life of the woman's child, and it is told that the mother kept that gold box by her bed for the remaining years of her life. Whenever she was discouraged or faced difficult problems, she would open the box and take out an imaginary kiss and remember the love of the child who had put it there.

God has given each of us the gift of an apparent empty tomb. In a very real sense, even though the body of Jesus was missing from the tomb, it was filled with hope for the future, faith in the resurrected Christ, and assurance of new life. Whenever we are discouraged or face difficult problems, we should remember what was left when the body was removed.

The People, Places, and Times

The Historical Evidence of the Resurrection of Jesus. Even though Christian belief in the resurrection of Christ is rooted in faith, there is ample historical evidence to support our belief. In fact, few historical facts have such a preponderance of evidence as the resurrection of the Lord Jesus. Though its authenticity is questioned by the same crowd who questions the accuracy of the Gospels, there is actually more evidence in support of the resurrection than there is for most ancient historical figures and events. First, let's consider what Jewish historian, Flavius Josephus (A.D. 37–A.D. 103), wrote in his *Antiquities of the Jews*:

They could recall another occasion when, after healing a boy possessed by demons, Jesus told them, "Listen to me and remember what I say. The Son of Man is going to be betrayed into the hands of his enemies" (Luke 9:44, NLT). Finally, the women remembered that right before their final trip up to Jerusalem, Jesus told them, "Listen, we're going up to Jerusalem where all the predictions of the prophets concerning the Son of Man will come true. He will be handed over to the Romans, and he will be mocked, treated shamefully, and spit upon. They will flog him with a whip and kill him, but on the third day he will rise again" (18:31–33, NLT).

3. The Mocking of Truth (vv. 9–12)

Anytime a loved one dies, believers can look to the Scriptures for comfort, for the Bible alone contains the message of hope. However, the message must be accepted by faith. Scripture asks us to believe that a dead man got up from the dead, never to die again. Jesus had ascended to the Father, so we cannot present any physical proof of our claim. No one else has ever been resurrected, so there is no precedent for our claim. That's why it is so easy for skeptics to dismiss our claim. And, surprisingly enough, the very first skeptics were the followers of Christ!

Mary Magdalene and her companions: Joanna, Mary, the mother of James, and the others left the tomb and found the apostles. They reported to them all they had both seen and heard. "But the story sounded like nonsense to the men, so they didn't believe it" (Luke 24:11, NLT). The first unbelievers of the resurrection were the apostles themselves! They responded like you or I probably would have if we had been in their shoes. "Nonsense! If the tomb is really empty then there must be a logical explanation for it. Perhaps the body was transferred to another tomb, or maybe the women went to the wrong tomb. Anything is possible—anything except the resurrection!" Unbelief is a common response today. Not even everyone in church today really believes it actually happened. "Impossible," they say. "The dead don't come back to life!"

Peter got up and ran to the tomb. When he reached the opening, he bent over and looked inside. Sure enough the body was gone. All he saw was the undisturbed shroud Jesus had been wrapped in. The bewildered apostle had no explanation for the empty tomb. Jesus' body was gone, but surely the women were mistaken. But wait a minute, didn't Jesus bring Lazarus back to life? Didn't He speak to the wind and quiet the sea? Is it possible? He went away wondering. Peter didn't get it!

Do you get it? What is your reaction to the empty tomb? The bodily resurrection of Christ is the cornerstone of Christian faith and your eternal destiny rests on your answer to this question.

Search the Scriptures

1. What is the first thing the women noticed when they arrived at the burial site? What did they find after they entered the tomb (Luke 24:2)?

2. As the women were pondering the missing body, what suddenly happened, and how did the women react (v. 4)?

3. The angels seemed a bit surprised that the women were expecting Jesus to be in the tomb. What question did one of them ask the women (v. 5)?

4. When the women reported to the disciples what they had experienced, how did most of the men react to their story? How did Peter react (vv. 11–12)?

5. When Peter arrived at the tomb and found it empty, how did he react (v. 12)?

Discuss the Meaning

The angels told the women that Jesus' body was not in the tomb because "He is risen." Then they told them to remember what Jesus had told them about His betrayal, death, and resurrection. Why is it so important, during times of doubt, stress, or confusion, for all believers to recall and meditate on Scripture?

Lesson in Our Society

Many people in our society can accept the story of Jesus up to the point of His resurrection from the dead. They have invented several theories to explain away the resurrection and the fact that so many people saw the risen Saviour. There's the "vision theory," which suggests that the disciples wanted to see Jesus so badly they just imagined they saw Him. Another theory is the "swoon theory," which says that Jesus didn't really die on the Cross but had just fainted; then He woke up in the cool air of the tomb. An even more outlandish theory is the "telegraph theory," which says that Jesus somehow telegraphed a picture of Himself in bodily form back from heaven to His followers. Then, there was the theory that claimed everyone who had seen Him was lying. Why is the resurrection of Jesus the central point of Christianity? Why is the resurrection a source of hope for all believers?

Make It Happen

Last week, you asked different people their views on the sacrificial death of Christ. This week, ask a different set of at least three people their thoughts on the resurrection of Christ and what it means to them. Read 1 Thessalonians 4:13–18, and be prepared to share this text about the final resurrection of Christians with them. Share your experiences with the class next week

Follow the Spirit

What God wants me to do:

____

____

Remember Your Thoughts

Special insights I have learned:

____

____

More Light on the Text

Luke 24:1–12

1 Now upon the first day of the week, very early in the morning, they came unto the sepulchre, bringing the spices which they had prepared, and certain others with them.

Our last lesson ended at the low point of human history. Thanks be to God, Luke's account (and the other Gospel stories) does not end with those unthinkable words about the Son of God: that He "gave up the ghost." Instead, Luke immediately began to offer notes of hope and faithfulness that prepare us for the glorious resurrection story we cover today. First, Luke tells us about a Roman centurion who, unlike his mocking counterparts whom we encountered in the last lesson, saw the death of Jesus with the eyes of faith. He said, "Certainly this was a righteous man." Luke also shows us how many, who were witnessing the crucifixion, were pierced with horror and regret and "smote their breasts" at what they had just seen. Another faithful light, shining in the darkness of Luke 23, is Joseph of Arimathea, a member of the council who had condemned Jesus but who had not agreed to the condemnation. Luke tells us that Joseph asked Pilate for Jesus' body and sought to bury Him with the honor

He deserved. Finally, Luke once again focuses on the faithful women followers of Christ, telling us first that these women had followed Him from Galilee (23:49), and they followed Joseph to the tomb, prepared spices to lovingly anoint Jesus' body, and then further showed their obedience to God by resting on the Sabbath. This brings us to the "Resurrection Story" as Luke begins it here.

2 And they found the stone rolled away from the sepulchre.

Luke is a master storyteller. Having shown us that the women prepared spices to bring to the tomb, he sets up only one possible expectation for them: to find a dead body inside when they return! Only if we truly strive to put ourselves within the story—instead of yawning because we know how the story ends—will we begin to experience even a shadow of the wonder, fear, confusion, and excitement of the women at the tomb.

3 And they entered in, and found not the body of the Lord Jesus.

The situation described here would have brought the women to a state modern psychologists call "cognitive dissonance." It happens when one's certainty about things being a certain way is confronted by indisputable facts that show things are not, in fact, that way. Of course, anyone familiar with the story of Christianity knows exactly what has taken place, but we must remember that the women would have had no explanation for what they were witnessing. Despite Jesus' words to them, during His life—that He would die and then rise on the third day—the rest of this passage shows that they had not understood what He meant. Instead, they were dealing with total confusion about what their eyes were seeing.

Luke inserts here a little detail with enormous significance. Rather than simply talking about the "body of Jesus," he refers to Him as "the Lord Jesus." Such an appellation probably does not surprise us, but it would have been a very strange way to speak about a man who had just suffered the shameful death of a criminal. The Greek word *kurios* (**KOO-ree-os**) connects directly to the Hebrew word *Yahweh*, God's personal covenant name in the Old Testament. So when the New Testament writers refer to Jesus, they were not simply calling Him Master, they were calling Him God! But how could God suffer the despicable death of crucifixion and reside in a tomb? Luke, the all-knowing narrator who understood the end of the story, gives us a shining hint as to its outcome by using the word "Lord."

4 And it came to pass, as they were much perplexed thereabout, behold, two men stood by them in shining garments:

This scene reveals much about the grace of God and the way in which He enables His disciples to interpret their experiences. Though the women had been told that this would take place (see verses 6–8) and therefore should need no further word, God sent His word to them in their confusion. In this case it comes through divine messengers, angels (though this verse says "two men," verse 23 makes clear this was a "vision of angels") bringing God's merciful message to His people. The Greek word meaning "behold" (*idou*, **id-OO**) draws attention to something happening suddenly and often surprisingly. While these women still had their minds on earthly explanations of Jesus' disappeared body, the angels represented a shocking and glorious appearance from heaven. Their "shining garments" added a further source of fear for the women, as their reaction in the next verse makes clear. Their message, however, ultimately would not bring fear and trepidation but joy and relief.

5 And as they were afraid, and bowed down their faces to the earth, they said unto them, Why seek ye the living among the dead?

This terrified reaction to an angelic appearance seems universal in the Bible, as Luke, himself, shows by the reactions of Zechariah (Luke 1:12) and Mary (v. 29). The Scriptures reveal angels to be awesome and fear-inspiring heavenly beings—not the cute, cuddly-looking cherubs that often appear in devotional art and on the covers of personal journals. And while the angels' message was ultimately joyous and merciful, their initial question matched their fearsome demeanor in its sternness: "Why seek ye the living among the dead?" This mild rebuke calls to mind what Jesus had to say to the Sadducees (who disbelieved in the resurrection) in 20:38: "For He is not a God of the dead, but of the living." Indeed, despite the fact that most Jews at the time (Sadducees aside) believed in the resurrection in theory, not even Jesus' most faithful disciples believed Him.

6 He is not here, but is risen: remember how he spake unto you when he was yet in Galilee,

The angels announced the joyful news that began the spread of the Gospel throughout the whole world. Indeed, Luke's story ends in chapter 24 with the fulfillment of the promise given to Mary by the angel, Gabriel, in Luke 1:32–33: "He shall be great, and shall be called the Son of the Highest: and the Lord God shall give unto him the throne of his father David: And he shall reign over the house of Jacob for ever; and of his kingdom there shall be no end." By announcing the simple words, "He is not here," the angels confirmed that Jesus was not a heinous criminal suffering justly for His sins (as to many, He appeared to be) but rather the King of the Nations, the Son of David. They also introduced the problem that has troubled, and will always trouble, those who deny the truth of the bodily resurrection. Where, after all, did the body go? Did the Romans take it? Did the Jewish leaders? Neither group would have wanted to have anyone believe that Jesus had risen from the dead, so they simply would have produced the body! Obviously they did not possess it—nor did anyone else. These faithful women were about to be reminded by the angels about a truth that the church continues to proclaim every Easter: "He is not here; He is risen!"

7 Saying, The Son of man must be delivered into the hands of sinful men, and be crucified, and the third day rise again.

The angelic reminder calls to mind two warnings that Jesus gave to His disciples (including these women, it appears). In 9:22, just after Peter confessed Jesus' true identity, the Saviour says: "The Son of man must suffer many things, and be rejected of the elders and chief priests and scribes, and be slain, and be raised the third day." Later, just before the disciples' argument about who was the greatest, Luke again reports Jesus' prediction of His suffering, though this time without the specific resurrection promise: "Let these sayings sink down into your ears: for the Son of man shall be delivered into the hands of men" (v. 44). From this passage, it is clear enough that none of the disciples had ears of faith, such that Jesus' promise about His great work of death and resurrection could "sink down into their ears." Yet, the Lord is merciful to repeat the message through the mouths of these angels.

8 And they remembered his words,

This short verse is set on fire by the significance of one word: "remembered" (Gk. *mnaomai*, **MNAH-om-ahee**). This rich word means so much more than simply recalling facts or associations. From mankind's perspective, it speaks of a faithful and loyal focus on the words of God. Perhaps the best known occurrence of this concept in the Old Testament comes in Exodus 20:8: "Remember the Sabbath day, to keep it holy." Clearly this command does not refer simply to a momentary acknowledgement that the Sabbath day exists. Instead, Yahweh here commanded a deep, abiding, covenantal obedience to God that remembers Him first and foremost, throughout the observance of the Sabbath. But this word also describes God's remembrance of His creation and His covenant people—again, not a mere acknowledgement but a loving loyalty and abiding care.

9 And returned from the sepulchre, and told all these things unto the eleven, and to all the rest.

The scriptural pattern is that those transformed by the Word and work of Christ go forth and tell others of His kindness and glory. These women fell squarely in line with that glorious tradition. Their first act was to go to the rest of the disciples and share the news. Those who receive the women's message were first of all "the eleven." Eight times Luke has referred to the core of the disciples (soon to be apostles) as "the twelve," but only here in chapter 24 does Luke speak of the "eleven." This is due to the fact that Judas Iscariot had already gone astray and betrayed the Lord Jesus. To these 11 remaining, despite their cowardly desertion of Jesus in His time of greatest need (Mark 14:50), God mercifully brought the message of Jesus' resurrection. Also the women spoke to "the rest," a reference to the many other disciples who followed Jesus, including, no doubt, many other women as well as men. These disciples were numbered at 120 in Acts 1:15, though the number was probably less than that at this point—before the glorious news of Jesus' resurrection had spread and been fully believed.

10 It was Mary Magdalene and Joanna, and Mary the mother of James, and other women that were with them, which told these things unto the apostles.

Luke now identifies the women who had gone to the tomb and beheld the angelic vision and the absence of Jesus from the tomb. We might wonder, why mention their names now and not earlier in chapter 24 or in chapter 23, when they were first spoken of as preparing spices to anoint the dead body of Jesus? The answer probably has to do with the importance of eyewitness testimony in the Bible. For one thing, the Bible consistently shows that an account of the truth must be established and verified on the testimony of "two or three witnesses" (Deuteronomy 17:6; Matthew 18:16); so Luke brings forth three witnesses here. Further, it would have been important that these witnesses were trustworthy, for what they were reporting would have been astonishing, even to the point of being unbelievable. To this end, Luke mentions two women whom he commended for their ministry to and support of Jesus in 8:1–3 (Mary Magdalene and Joanna). By adding "Mary the mother of James," Luke not only introduces a third witness but also brings forth a relative of one of the apostles, who would have been trusted because of her relationship to James.

11 And their words seemed to them as idle tales, and they believed them not.

However, the apostles (Luke focuses in on the 11 remaining apostles by naming them at the end of verse 10) would have none of what they believe to be foolishness. The KJV translates the Greek word *leros* (**LAY-ros**) as "idle tales." Simply put, the apostles thought these women were crazy. Why did they fail to receive the message? For one thing, throughout the book of Luke, these men had consistently shown a failure to understand Jesus' mission. They simply could not grasp the picture of a Messiah and heavenly king who would suffer and die for His people. Even the fact that the women claimed angels had confirmed Jesus' message did not change the apostles' minds. They probably assumed the women were hallucinating in their great grief over Jesus' death. But another factor probably weighed in as well: distrust in this culture for the testimony of women. No doubt these apostles were deeply tainted by cultural prejudice as they evaluated the women's eyewitness testimony.

12 Then arose Peter, and ran unto the sepulchre; and stooping down, he beheld the linen clothes laid by themselves, and departed, wondering in himself at that which was come to pass.

And yet there was one among the apostles who at least lent some credence to the women's amazing story. Peter, always the first to jump in headlong, went to verify the story for himself. Given the unbelieving response of the apostles in general, Luke certainly means to approve of Peter, for he at least made the effort to see what the women had seen, even if (perhaps) he went to the tomb with doubt about their story. Like the women, he entered all the way into the tomb. Luke makes it clear that no one who witnessed the empty tomb could have possibly been mistaken about Jesus' absence. Jesus, unmistakably, was not there! Peter's reaction was not quite the same as the women's. He left "wondering in himself at that which was come to pass," a description that leaves some doubt about how much Peter really believed in the resurrection at those moments. Further, unlike the women, Peter did not tell anyone else about what he had seen. He did not appear to have yet fully understood what had taken place, in spite of Jesus' earlier promise. So the resurrection is filled with hope, longing, the graciousness of God, and also with hesitation and unbelief on the part of those who follow Christ.

Sources:

Henry, Matthew. *Matthew Henry's Complete Commentary on the Bible.* http://eword.gospelcom.net/comments/ezekiel/mh/ezekiel47.htm. Accessed February 20, 2008.

Vine, W.E. *Vines Complete Expository Dictionary of Old and New Testament Words.* Edited by Merrill F. Unger and William White Jr. Nashville: Thomas Nelson Publishers, 1996.

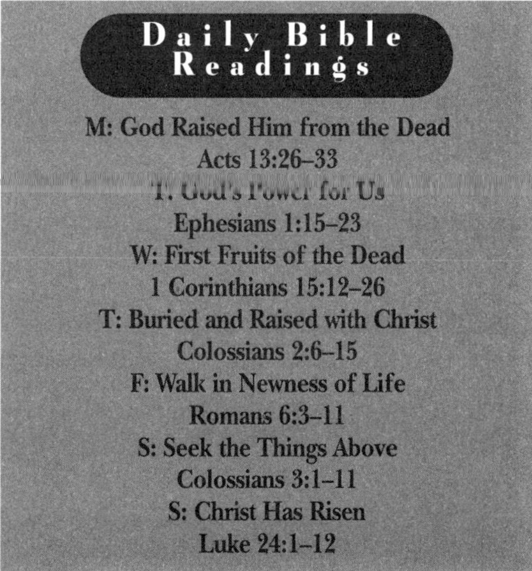

TEACHING TIPS

April 19

Bible Study Guide 8

1. Words You Should Know

A. Fulfilled (Luke 24:44) *pleroo* (Gk.)—To accomplish, perform, or fully satisfy what was foretold or prefigured in the Old Testament.

B. Preached (v. 47) *kerusso* (Gk.)—To preach, herald, or proclaim; generally to announce or proclaim publicly.

2. Teacher Preparation

Unifying Principle—Good News Is for Sharing. People are often willing to give testimonials on behalf of products or services they believe in. What or who are we willing to endorse? According to Luke's gospel, Jesus appeared to His disciples and commissioned them to witness to the new life they had in Him, for the Scriptures affirmed that He is the Messiah.

A. Prepare to share the Good News with your class.

B. Read Matthew 28:18–20, and prepare to share the Great Commission.

C. Be prepared to give some pointers on how to share the Good News and when it should be shared.

3. Starting the Lesson

A. Ask a volunteer to lead the class in prayer, focusing on the AIM for Change as well as thanking God for the opportunity of studying His Word this week.

B. Review the highlights of last week's lesson. Then ask volunteers to share how the lesson affected them.

C. Share the Good News with your class.Then, ask a student to read the In Focus section. Discuss.

D. After reading Matthew 28:18–20, discuss the Great Commission, giving pointers on how and when to share the Good News.

4. Getting into the Lesson

A. Ask the students to share their experiences from last week's Make It Happen suggestion.

B. Ask them to share any insights from their Daily Bible Readings.

C. Have the students silently read the Focal Verses. Afterward, have them share some of the key points and relate them to where we are today?

D. Review the Search the Scriptures questions. Ask the students to attempt to answer the questions without opening their Bibles. Then, open the Bible to the verse and review.

5. Relating the Lesson to Life

A. Break the class into four groups, and assign each group a question from the Discuss the Meaning section. After they discuss, then have each group present their conclusions to the rest of the class.

B. The Lesson in Our Society section can help the students see how the lesson parallels with many present-day situations. Using today's lesson, ask the students what they plan to do to find individuals who are discouraged with life and encourage them.

6. Arousing Action

A. The Make It Happen section contains a suggestion of what may be done to implement learned principles. Tailor the implementations to your own specific needs.

B. So they can become well versed in the Scriptures, challenge the students to read the Daily Bible Readings for the week.

C. Encourage your students to study next week's lesson and prepare for the next class.

Worship Guide

For the Superintendent or Teacher
Theme: Witnesses to New Life
Theme Song: "I Love to Tell the Story"
Devotional Reading: Acts 2:22–32
Prayer

WITNESSES TO NEW LIFE

Bible Background • LUKE 24:36–53
Printed Text • LUKE 24:44–53 Devotional Reading • ACTS 2:22–32

AIM for Change

By the end of the lesson, we will:
EXPLORE what Jesus revealed about His identity as Messiah and the significance of the Messiah's suffering;
REALIZE that Jesus' explanation and commission to the disciples apply to us today; and
PARTICIPATE in fulfilling the mission Jesus gave His disciples.

Keep in Mind

"Ye are witnesses of these things. And, behold, I send the promise of my Father upon you" (from Luke 24:48–49).

Focal Verses

KJV **Luke 24:44** And he said unto them,
These are the words which I spake
unto you, while I was yet with you, that all things
must be fulfilled, which were written in the law of
Moses, and in the prophets, and in the psalms, concerning me.
45 Then opened he their understanding, that
they might understand the scriptures,
46 And said unto them, Thus it is written, and
thus it behooved Christ to suffer, and to rise from
the dead the third day:
47 And that repentance and remission of sins
should be preached in his name among all nations,
beginning at Jerusalem.
48 And ye are witnesses of these things.
49 And, behold, I send the promise of my Father
upon you: but tarry ye in the city of Jerusalem, until
ye be endued with power from on high.
50 And he led them out as far as to Bethany, and
he lifted up his hands, and blessed them.
51 And it came to pass, while he blessed them, he
was parted from them, and carried up into heaven.
52 And they worshipped him, and returned to
Jerusalem with great joy:
53 And were continually in the temple, praising
and blessing God. Amen.

NLT **Luke 24:44** Then he said, "When I
was with you before, I told you that
everything written about me in the law of Moses and
the prophets and in the Psalms must be fulfilled."
45 Then he opened their minds to understand
the Scriptures.
46 And he said, "Yes, it was written long ago that
the Messiah would suffer and die and rise from the
dead on the third day.
47 It was also written that this message
would be proclaimed in the authority of his
name to all the nations, beginning in Jerusalem:
'There is forgiveness of sins for all who repent.'
48 You are witnesses of all these things.
49 "And now I will send the Holy Spirit, just as
my Father promised. But stay here in the city until
the Holy Spirit comes and fills you with power from
heaven."
50 Then Jesus led them to Bethany, and lifting
his hands to heaven, he blessed them.
51 While he was blessing them, he left them and
was taken up to heaven.
52 So they worshiped him and then returned to
Jerusalem filled with great joy.
53 And they spent all of their time in the
Temple, praising God.

In Focus

One of the greatest effects of Christ's resurrection can be seen in two stories. The first story is of well-known agnostic intellectual Dr. Robert Ingersoll (d. 1899)—lawyer, military officer, attorney general of the state of Illinois). He traveled across the country and overseas lecturing against the Christian faith and promoting his agnostic beliefs. He was known as the "Great Agnostic." He would sway large audiences by standing on a stage and shouting, "If there is a God, let him strike me dead! I'll give you 10 minutes." And God graciously let it pass. One day, Ingersoll became fatally ill. These were his final words: "Life is now a narrow vale between two cold and barren peaks of two eternities. I strive in vain to look beyond the heights. I cry aloud. And the only answer is the echo of my wailing cry." And then he died in a state of hopeless despair.

Our second story involves a boy named Clifford. One day, he was on a fishing trip out in the Atlantic Ocean with his father and brothers. The wind picked up in the afternoon, and the boat was capsized by a giant wave. Everyone began to swim toward shore, but six-foot waves and a strong current made swimming almost impossible. Clifford swam as long as he could, but he was the first to perish. Before he drowned he called out to his father these final words: "I'd rather be with Jesus than to go on fighting." He died that day with hope and peace, anticipating seeing the risen Lord.

These were two deaths but two very different perspectives about death! The intellectual met death with hopelessness and despair. The young child welcomed death with peace and hope.

Why the difference? Faith in the risen Christ!

Today's lesson examines the final resurrection appearance of Christ and His ascension into heaven. It is His resurrection that gives us hope for eternal life. His ascension assures us that He is making intercession for us, preparing a place for us, and has sent His Holy Spirit to lead, guide, and indwell us.

The People, Places, and Times

Accounts of People Raised from the Dead

1. Elijah raised the son of the Zarephath widow from the dead (1 Kings 17:17–22).

2. Elisha raised the son of the Shunammite woman from the dead (2 Kings 4:32–35).

3. A man was raised from the dead when his body touched Elisha's bones (2 Kings 13:20–21).

4. Many saints rose from the dead at the resurrection of Jesus (Matthew 27:50–53).

5. Jesus rose from the dead (Matthew 28:5–8; Mark 16:6; Luke 24:5–6).

6. Jesus raised the son of the widow of Nain from the dead (Luke 7:11–15).

7. Jesus raised the daughter of Jairus from the dead (Luke 8:41–42, 49–55).

8. Jesus raised Lazarus from the dead (John 11:1–44).

9. Peter raised Dorcas from the dead (Acts 9:36–41).

10. Paul raised Eutychus from the dead (Acts 20:9–10).

Sources:

Elwell, Walter A., ed. *The Shaw Pocket Bible Handbook.* Wheaton, Ill.: Harold Shaw Publishers, 1984.

Meredith, J. L. *Meredith's Big Book of Bible Lists.* New York: Inspirational Press, 1980.

Background

After His appearance to the women at the tomb, Jesus made another appearance on the same day to two men on their way to a village called Emmaus, about seven miles from Jerusalem. As the two men were walking and talking to each other about the execution of Christ, Jesus came up and started to walk along with the men. It was not at all unusual for Him to join up with a small company who were making their way home after the Passover pilgrimage to Jerusalem. Jesus did not allow Himself to be recognized by the men.

As they walked, Jesus asked, "What are you discussing so intently as you walk along?" (Luke 24:17, NLT). The men stopped in their tracks, completely surprised by the man's ignorance of the happenings in Jerusalem of the past few days. One of the men named Cleopas answered in disbelief, "You must be the only person in Jerusalem who hasn't heard about all the things that have happened there the last few days" (v. 18, NLT). And Jesus, still pretending ignorance, asked, "What things?" (v. 19, NLT).

The men began explaining to the stranger all the things that happened in Jerusalem over the past week. They told Him of Jesus, who was a powerful prophet of God, and how they hoped that He had been the one who was going to redeem Israel. They explained how the Pharisees and chiefs of priests had conspired against Him and handed Him over to the Roman governor to be crucified.

They told Him about some of the women from their group who had gone out to the tomb earlier that morning only to find the body missing. These women were claiming that angels had appeared to them and told them that Jesus was alive. Then some of the disciples went to the tomb and confirmed that the body was indeed gone, but they did not report seeing any angels. Jesus interrupted their discourse to remind them of what the Old Testament prophets had prophesied about the Christ, how He had to suffer these things and then enter into His glory. Beginning with Moses, He taught them what all the prophets had said about His coming and suffering.

As the sun was starting to go down, Cleopas and his companion stopped to make camp for the night, but Jesus acted as if He would continue ahead. Ancient rules of hospitality demanded that the men ask the stranger to join them for a meal and some rest until morning. As they sat down to eat, Jesus took the bread, blessed it, and broke and passed it out to the men. As they received the bread, suddenly their eyes were opened and they recognized who had been sharing their journey. However, the minute they realized who Jesus was, He disappeared from their sight.

The two men immediately turned around and headed back to Jerusalem to share the good news. They found the 11 and other disciples who were with them, but before they could speak some men shouted to them, "The Lord has really risen! He appeared to Peter" (v. 34, NLT). After hearing the miraculous news, Cleopas and his companion then shared their experience on the road to Emmaus. As the disciples were discussing the events, Jesus suddenly appeared in their midst and confirmed His resurrection to them all.

At-A-Glance

1. The Fulfillment (Luke 24:44–45)
2. The Witness (vv. 46–49)
3. The Ascension (vv. 50–53)

In Depth

1. The Fulfillment (Luke 24:44–45)

While Jesus was with the disciples and before He ascended into heaven, He proceeded to give them final instructions. He explained to them how everything He had told them as well as everything that had been written about Him in the Law of Moses, the prophets, and the Psalms, had to be fulfilled.

On several previous occasions, the Lord had explained to His followers all that would happen to Him and about His resurrection from the dead (cf. Luke 9:21–22, 45, 18; 31–33). Although the disciples understood the words, the full impact of their meaning was hidden from them "and they were afraid to ask him about it" (9:45, NLT). Along with the teachings of Jesus, the disciples had the Old Testament Scriptures that spoke of Him. Isaiah 53:5 speaks of His being wounded, and Moses describes His role as prophet in Deuteronomy 18:15–18. The prophet Isaiah also speaks of His carrying our sins and weaknesses to the Cross (Isaiah 53:4–6), while David encouraged us with predictions of Christ's resurrection (Psalm 16:10–11).

It may seem strange that with the Old Testament Scriptures and the words of Jesus, Himself, the disciples failed to comprehend the truth. However, Luke explains the situation with the words "Then he opened their minds to understand the scriptures" (Luke 24:45, NLT). Through their own efforts, no one is capable of truly understanding Scripture.

2. The Witness (vv. 46–49)

Once their minds were opened, Jesus began explaining to the disciples the things that were written of Him. He told them about His suffering. In this case suffering implies the experience of affliction on behalf of someone else. As the prophet Isaiah wrote: He was pierced for our rebellion, crushed for our sins. "He was beaten so we could be whole. He was whipped so we could be healed" (Isaiah 53:5, NLT). He took onto Himself the suffering we deserved. This suffering was both physical and spiritual. His physical suffering reflected the evil inflicted on Him at the hands of sinful men. His spiritual suffering occurred when He took on the sins of sinful humanity so that we could be declared righteous in the sight of God (see 2 Corinthians 5:21). This is called "imputation"; our sins were laid on Christ at His crucifixion, and His righteousness is laid on us at conversion.

It would be wonderful if the story ended there, but three days after His suffering and death, Christ came back from the dead, never to die again. His resurrection is our guarantee that we, too, will one day be resurrected to spend an eternity with the Lord (cf. 1 Corinthians 15:20–23).

The Scriptures not only declare the death and resurrection of our Lord but decree that the message of redemption, through repentance and the forgiveness of sins, will be preached to all nations. "Repentance" is a reorientation of a person's moral compass. The person acknowledges the error of his ways, appreciates that his lifestyle has been offensive to God, and turns toward the divinely approved way of life and truth. This reorientation takes place in the person's mind and will, and then, over time, the person's actions begin to line up with his new beliefs and desires. True repentance brings about the remission of sins (Luke 24:47). Remission is much more than a simple pardon from the penalty of sin; it dismisses the sin itself. It's just as if the sin had never occurred.

The Lord concluded His post-resurrection teaching with a declaration and a promise. He declared that His disciples were to be His witnesses, and He promised to clothe or cover them with power from on high. This is the promise of the Holy Spirit who would empower the disciples to boldly share what they had witnessed with others.

3. The Ascension (vv. 50–53)

When Jesus finished His teaching and gave His final instructions, He led the disciples out of Jerusalem to a place near the village of Bethany. There He lifted up His hands and blessed them (Luke 24:50). While blessing His disciples, Jesus was close to them. We can imagine that they saw the holes—the marks of the nails in Jesus' hands. If the disciples saw Jesus' pierced hands, they could have realized that the blessing they were receiving had been bought by Jesus' sacrifice on the Cross. His crucifixion bought continuous blessing for all redeemed.

At the opening of Luke's book, the priest, Zechariah, was rendered mute so he was unable to pronounce the priestly blessing on the people after leaving the temple (Luke 1:22). Luke closed the book with Jesus ascending to "that greater, more perfect Tabernacle in heaven, which was not made by human hands" (Hebrews 9:11, NLT) pronouncing a blessing on the disciples. Luke's intent is clearly to highlight Christ's role as our great High Priest. Because Christ is in the heavenly temple, our redemption is secured.

Search the Scriptures

1. When explaining the fulfillment of Scripture to the disciples, what three parts of Old Testament Scripture did Jesus mention (Luke 24:44)?

2. What did Jesus do to the disciples so they would be able to truly understand the Scriptures and His teachings (v. 45)?

3. What are the two things that Jesus wanted preached in His name and to whom would it be preached (v. 47)?

4. What did Jesus promise to send to the disciples (v. 49)?

5. How did the disciples react after Jesus had blessed them and ascended to heaven (v. 52)?

Discuss the Meaning

1. The disciples were told, too, that repentance and the forgiveness of sins would be preached in Jesus' name. Why is "true repentance" necessary before forgiveness of sin can occur? How would you define "true repentance"?

2. Christ described His disciples as witnesses. What were they witnesses of, and what does this mean for modern-day disciples, in general, and you, in particular?

Lesson in Our Society

What is your response to the truth of the resurrection of Jesus? The resurrection of Jesus is essential to the validity of the Gospel message. Paul wrote: "And if Christ has not been raised, then your faith is useless and you are still guilty of your sins" (1 Corinthians 15:17, NLT). If you deny the truth of the resurrection of Jesus, you are denying that He is the Messiah and you will die in your sins and face eternal damnation. Consider this: "For since we believe that Jesus died and was raised to life again, we also believe that when Jesus returns, God will bring back with him the believers who have died" (1 Thessalonians 4:14, NLT).

If you recognize the truth of the resurrection of Jesus, this becomes a powerful reason for you to put your trust in Him and share the Good News with others.

Make It Happen

This week, seek to worship God more fully by grasping the deep reality of Jesus' resurrection and ascension. Consider how the resurrection and ascension make a difference to the way you regard and practice your faith.

Follow the Spirit

What God wants me to do:

____

____

Remember Your Thoughts

Special insights I have learned:

____

____

More Light on the Text

Luke 24:44–53

44 And he said unto them, These are the words which I spake unto you, while I was yet with you, that all things must be fulfilled, which were written in the law of Moses, and in the prophets, and in the psalms, concerning me.

Joel Green, in his book *The Gospel of Luke,* helps us see how this passage brings together the whole book of Luke and even the whole Bible: "If one were to think of the stories of Israel, Jesus, and the early church as in some sense distinct, in these verses one would find the seam wherein they are sown together in one cloth." By explaining to the disciples how His resurrection fit together with both the past and the future, Jesus prepared them for the mission that lay before them. He begins in this verse by reminding them, as the angels had reminded the women at the tomb, of the global and glorious purpose for His life on Earth. Again, He refers to His warnings (found in Luke 9:22, 44, among other places) that things would play out exactly as they have: with His horrible, but redemptive, suffering, followed by His resurrection to life. In a very important statement for Christians, Jesus declared that His suffering and glory are all for the fulfillment of the Scriptures.

The word "fulfill" (Gk. *pleroo,* **play-RO-o**) plays an important role in the Gospels, as the Gospel writers make clear that Jesus' life and ministry are of one piece with the Hebrew Scriptures. Matthew uses the word the most, but Luke finds it important as well. Luke is the only one to tell of Jesus' reading the scroll of Isaiah 61 in the temple and saying, "This day is this Scripture fulfilled in your ears." Evidently, both the Bible writers and Jesus, Himself, believe firmly that the Old Testament points unmistakably to Him. Without doubt, as we read the Bible in our day, we should follow their lead!

45 Then opened he their understanding, that they might understand the scriptures,

We have here a beautiful picture of the two-stage fashion in which God gets His truth into believers' lives. In the previous verse, Jesus reminded the disciples how He preached to them repeatedly of how the Scriptures pointed to Him as their goal and focus (and what wonderful sermons those must have been)! But as we have already seen, their minds, like ours, were spiritually sluggish and even rebellious and, thus, they were slow to understand. And so Jesus, in great mercy, did not leave them in their ignorance and blindness. He came to them in His person. Not only so, but He worked His divine power in them, such that their eyes were opened to see the truth of the Scriptures—the Scriptures that pointed to Him. As the Bible makes clear elsewhere (see 1 Corinthians 2:12–15), the human problem is not one of information, but of *mal*formation, in need of *trans*formation. Jesus knew well that, then as now, people would not see Him merely through receiving correct information about Him. The Jewish leaders and Roman rulers proved that well enough, so no more was needed. However, spiritual transformation in their minds and hearts—that they might see Him clearly and believe—was definitely needed.

46 And said unto them, Thus it is written, and thus it behooved Christ to suffer, and to rise from the dead the third day:

Michael Wilcock, in his book *The Message of Luke,* gives us a helpful breakdown of Jesus' pronouncements and commission to the disciples in the next four verses. He says, "Four guiding lights show them (the disciples) the direction in which they are expected to go. They are given a biblical theology (24:46), an evangelistic program (24:47), an apostolic authority (24:48), and a spiritual dynamic (24:49)." We will follow this breakdown over the course of these verses. First, there is a *biblical theology.* This phrase might be intimidating, but it need not be. If we remember that the word "biblical" refers to the redemptive story that points always to Jesus and that the word "theology" just means "talk about God and His work in the world," we can stay on a straight and profitable course. As He commonly does, Jesus introduces His biblical theology with the single Greek word *gegraptai* (**GEH-grahp-tahee**), meaning "it is written." It is this word that Jesus used repeatedly to counter the Devil's temptations in the wilderness (see Luke 4:1–13), foiling Satan with the power of God's Word.

Again, Jesus does not necessarily point to a specific Scripture that announces His suffering and glory; rather, He speaks of the whole of Scripture pointing to this central event in history: His death and resurrection. And so the biblical theology that Jesus gives to the disciples revolves around these

"Ye are witnesses of these things. And, behold, I send the promise of my Father upon you" (from Luke 24:48–49).

transforming, world-altering events, as any good biblical theology must always do.

47 And that repentance and remission of sins should be preached in his name among all nations, beginning at Jerusalem.

Jesus now gives the disciples an *evangelistic program.* That program has several important features. First, it will involve *preaching.* The rest of the New Testament records the history and significance of preaching in the church and in the world; as Paul will later say, "Faith cometh by hearing, and hearing by the word of God" (Romans 10:17). Luke, a companion of Paul during several of his missionary journeys, no doubt understands the vital necessity of preaching for the growth and well-being of the church.

But what sort of preaching shall it be? Jesus speaks of two themes in particular that the disciples must preach: *repentance* and *remission (forgiveness) of sins.* Of repentance, Joel Green gives us a helpful definition: "'Repentance' will be a key term describing the appropriate response to the offer of salvation in Acts and connotes the (re)alignment of one's life—that is, dispositions and behaviors—toward God's purpose." It is important to see the importance of repentance in the book of Acts, since Luke wrote this biblical book as well as a sort of second volume for his Gospel (see Luke 1:1–4; Acts 1:1). Acts 11:18 uses the Greek word *metanoia* (**met-AN-oy-ah**); this word for "repentance" has the idea of turning around with the whole self: "When they heard these things, they held their peace, and glorified God, saying, Then hath God also to the Gentiles granted repentance unto life." (Notice that repentance is not only something worked up by man, but rather granted by God.)

The announcement of *remission of sins* is related, of course, to repentance. When one responds to the preaching of the Gospel with repentance—turning away from sin and unto God in Christ—those sins are forgiven through the merits of Christ's blood. Many Bible texts mention the forgiveness of sins; of special note are the ones that pair it with repentance, like this one. These texts all have to do with John the Baptist's preaching, which makes sense because he prepared the way for the preaching and the sacrificial ministry of Christ. So Luke 3:3 says, "And he came into all the country about Jordan, preaching the baptism of repentance for the remission of sins." Luke's baptism anticipates Jesus' baptism of His people, not with water, but with the Holy Spirit, the Spirit who will bring to the people all the benefits of Christ's death.

The last feature we need to see about this evangelistic program is its *scope*: in other words, the fact that the preaching of the Gospel will "begin at Jerusalem" and go "among all the nations." This is one of the radically new elements of the new covenant: what we might call the "direction" of God's good news of salvation.

48 And ye are witnesses of these things.

We now we come to the *apostolic authority* Jesus gives to those He commissions. One of the qualifications for apostleship was having seen the risen Lord Jesus. There was enormous foundational importance to being "witnesses" of Jesus' resurrection. As Michael Wilcock puts it, "No doubt later generations of the church have produced many a bigger brain and many a sharper wit than Peter's or John's; but these men had the unsurpassed advantage of being able to say, 'It was so; so I heard and saw' and of having been divinely commissioned to speak in this way."

This authority was *foundational,* as Ephesians 2:20 shows. One of the purposes of the 12 apostles was overseeing the writing of the New Testament, so that the latter part of our Bibles comes to us from Jesus, through the apostles (see John 16:12–15). This also helps us to understand how God primarily speaks to us in our day. He does so, not mainly through private revelations but through the Scriptures. These Scriptures reveal all we need to know about our faith and practice, following after the Jesus to whom the Scriptures testify.

49 And, behold, I send the promise of my Father upon you: but tarry ye in the city of Jerusalem, until ye be endued with power from on high.

Finally, we have the *spiritual dynamic* Jesus gives to His disciples. The word "spiritual" is another word that may produce much confusion and differing understandings of its meaning. However here by saying "spiritual," we only mean the plainest biblical understanding of the word: that which is of the Holy Spirit. This is the "promise of the Father" that Jesus refers to here. Acts 1:8 and the story of Pentecost in chapter 2 make clear that Jesus' departure from them will result in the giving of the Holy Spirit, even the baptism of the Holy Spirit as John the Baptist promised. By means of the Holy Spirit, sent by the risen and ascended Christ, the disciples will be transformed from a quivering, questioning remnant to a powerful, confident witness to all the world of Christ's transforming power. For Jesus will keep His promise, and the disciples will be "endued with power from on high."

Jesus repeats this promise in a different way in Acts 1:8, where He says, "But ye shall receive power, after that the Holy Ghost is come upon you: and ye shall be witnesses unto me both in Jerusalem (community), and in all Judaea (surrounding communities), and in Samaria (the nation), and unto the uttermost part of the earth (the world)." This glorious promise is fulfilled for these disciples with the coming of the Holy Spirit at Pentecost (Acts 2). The book of Acts, then, shows how the Spirit comes on all believers at the time of belief, as it reaches Samaritans in chapter 8, Gentiles in chapter 10, and disciples of John the Baptist, who did not know of Jesus, in chapter 19. All Christians are heirs of these various groups, receiving the glorious power of the Holy Spirit when they believe, just as Jesus promised.

50 And he led them out as far as to Bethany, and he lifted up his hands, and blessed them.

Now, at the very close of Luke, the Spirit-inspired writer tells us of a final encounter with Jesus at Bethany. This town, the location of Jesus' triumphal entry into Jerusalem (Luke 19:29–40), serves as a fitting location for Jesus to once again be triumphant, in keeping with His glory and His destiny. Here Jesus lifted His hands, a common pose of blessing in the ancient world, and gave the disciples the ultimate benediction. This blessing would be part of the many ways He had blessed them since the resurrection: by reminding them of His words, by appearing to them in person, by opening their minds to the glorious truth of the Gospel, and by promising the Holy Spirit.

John records in his gospel that Jesus, at this point, breathed on them and said, "Receive ye the Holy Ghost" (John 20:22). Probably Jesus' blessing here was the continuation of His promise to give them the Holy Spirit and a final word of comfort that they would, in fact, receive the Spirit with great joy, even as they grieved the departure of their Lord from them.

51 And it came to pass, while he blessed them, he was parted from them, and carried up into heaven.

Luke tells us that Jesus departed while giving a blessing to His people. Luke then tells us that He was "carried up into heaven." In the Bible, "up" is always the way toward God, whether it is the mountain (Mount Sinai, the Mount of Transfiguration, etc.) or heaven itself. Though heaven, in a real sense, is probably not "up," Luke's point is that Jesus was returning to God and going back to the glory from which He departed, in order to work salvation in the world. Also, there is a correlation between Jesus' "going up" and the Holy Spirit's "coming down"; the "Comforter" promised in John 14–16 would only come upon Jesus' departure. And because the Holy Spirit and Christ are both persons of one Holy Trinity, Jesus can truly say, "I will not leave you comfortless; I will come to you" (John 14:18). He does not go up from His disciples saying "You're on your own." He goes saying, "I will be with you wherever you go."

52 And they worshipped him, and returned to Jerusalem with great joy:

After all their times of consternation (fear) and unbelief, the disciples finally got it. There is great significance in the fact that "they worshipped him." As Joel Green says, "In Luke and Acts, worship is denied images, the Devil, and mere mortals, and allowed only in the case of God." There can be no doubt: The disciples understood Jesus to be God in the flesh! As a result of their spiritual understanding, they now possess great joy—a joy that replaces their earlier fear when Jesus would do a work of awesome power. It is no doubt an abiding biblical principle that worship in faith—"worship in Spirit and in truth," as Jesus calls it elsewhere (John 4:24)—brings joy to the believer. At the recognition of Jesus as Lord and Saviour, billions since the day of Christ have also experienced the joy of that "aha!" moment when, through the Holy Spirit, their eyes are opened to the true identity of Christ.

53 And were continually in the temple, praising and blessing God. Amen.

The disciples return to the temple, showing their piety and devotion in light of Jesus being revealed to them. This does not mean that the Christian church should confine itself to the Jewish temple; rather, the disciples are obedient to Jesus' words that their mission is to happen "beginning at Jerusalem." Here they await the promised Holy Spirit, which they receive quite soon, as the book of Acts demonstrates. Until then, they express themselves as the faithful Jews they are, worshiping their risen Messiah until He comes to them again.

The closing word of the King James Version of Luke—"Amen"—is curious, since that word is absent from most early manuscripts. However, that word is certainly an appropriate response for the reader of Luke to make! Most likely, a scribe recording the book of Luke added his own worshipful "amen" as he completed this glorious story. He can hardly be blamed for doing so. But Luke gives us no such "amen"—perhaps with the intention that our lives become the "amen" to the wonderful, liberating, saving work of Christ.

Sources:

Green, Joel. *The Gospel of Luke.* Grand Rapids, Mich.: Wm. B. Eerdmans Publishing Company, 1997.

Wilcock, Michael. *The Message of Luke* (*The Bible Speaks Today* Series). Downers Grove, Ill.: InterVarsity Press, 1979.

Daily Bible Readings

M: Women at the Tomb
Matthew 28:6–10
T: Mary Magdalene
John 20:11–18
W: On the Road to Emmaus
Luke 24:13–23, 28–31
T: Thomas
John 20:24–29
F: Seven Disciples
John 21:1–14
S: Witnesses of the Resurrection
1 Corinthians 15:1–8
S: You Are Witnesses
Luke 24:44–53

NOTES

TEACHING TIPS

April 26

Bible Study Guide 9

1. Words You Should Know

A. Disciple (Acts 9:36) *mathetria* (Gk.)—Feminine form of *mathetes,* meaning "a learner." From *manthano,* meaning "to learn," only here in the New Testament.

B. Tabitha (v. 36) *Tabitha* (Gk.)—Aramaic form of the Hebrew *Tsebi* and, like the Greek word "Dorcas" (*Dorkas*), means "gazelle."

2. Teacher Preparation

Unifying Principle—Seeking Help in Times of Need. Various sources of physical and spiritual assistance clamor for the world's attention. Where do we turn for help in times of physical illness and death? Through the power of Christ, Peter was able to heal Aeneas and raise Tabitha from the dead.

A. Be prepared to share a miraculous healing in your own life or the life of a friend or loved one. (God could have even used doctors to bring about the healing.)

B. Research some of the miraculous healings that Jesus did in His ministry.

C. Be prepared to share your findings with the class.

D. Thoroughly study lesson 9 in both the *Precepts For Living® Commentary* and the *Precepts For Living® Personal Study Guide.*

E. Jot down any salient points that you would like to make during your classroom discussion.

3. Starting the Lesson

A. Ask a volunteer to lead the class in prayer, focusing on the AIM for Change and thanking God for the opportunity of studying His Word.

B. Review the highlights of last week's lesson. Then ask volunteers to share how the lesson affected them.

C. Ask the students to share their experiences from last week's Make It Happen suggestion and any insights from their Daily Bible Readings.

D. Share your miraculous healing experience or that of a friend or loved one.

E. Tie in the experience with today's lesson.

4. Getting into the Lesson

A. Review the Search the Scriptures questions.

B. Divide the class into groups, and have them read the Background information and then explain the responsibilities of the nearest relative and how this might pertain to Jesus.

C. Discuss The People, Places, and Times information.

5. Relating the Lesson to Life

A. Break the class into four groups, and assign each group a question from the Discuss the Meaning section. Afterward, have them discuss with the rest of the class.

B. Discuss the Lesson in Our Society section. Challenge the students to follow this week's suggestion and share their experiences with the class next week.

6. Arousing Action

A. Challenge the students to read the Daily Bible Readings for the week.

B. Encourage the students to study next week's lesson and prepare to share what they have learned.

Worship Guide

For the Superintendent or Teacher
Theme: Bringing New Life to Those in Need
Theme Song: "Healing at the Fountain"
Devotional Reading: John 14:8–14
Prayer

BRINGING NEW LIFE TO THOSE IN NEED

Bible Background • ACTS 9:32–43
Printed Text • ACTS 9:32–43 Devotional Reading • JOHN 14:8–14

AIM for Change

By the end of the lesson, we will:
STUDY how Peter used his gifts to bring healing and life to people in need;
FEEL the satisfaction Peter must have felt helping others; and
UTILIZE our God-given talents and abilities to assist someone.

Keep in Mind

"And forasmuch as Lydda was nigh to Joppa, and the disciples had heard that Peter was there, they sent unto him two men, desiring him that he would not delay to come to them" (Acts 9:38).

Focal Verses

KJV **Acts 9:32** And it came to pass, as Peter passed throughout all quarters, he came down also to the saints which dwelt at Lydda.

33 And there he found a certain man named Aeneas, which had kept his bed eight years, and was sick of the palsy.

34 And Peter said unto him, Aeneas, Jesus Christ maketh thee whole: arise, and make thy bed. And he arose immediately.

35 And all that dwelt at Lydda and Saron saw him, and turned to the Lord.

36 Now there was at Joppa a certain disciple named Tabitha, which by interpretation is called Dorcas: this woman was full of good works and almsdeeds which she did.

37 And it came to pass in those days, that she was sick, and died: whom when they had washed, they laid her in an upper chamber.

38 And forasmuch as Lydda was nigh to Joppa, and the disciples had heard that Peter was there, they sent unto him two men, desiring him that he would not delay to come to them.

39 Then Peter arose and went with them. When he was come, they brought him into the upper chamber: and all the widows stood by him weeping, and shewing the coats and garments which Dorcas made, while she was with them.

40 But Peter put them all forth, and kneeled down, and prayed; and turning him to the body said, Tabitha, arise. And she opened her eyes: and when she saw Peter, she sat up.

41 And he gave her his hand, and lifted her up, and when he had called the saints and widows, presented her alive.

NLT **Acts 9:32** Meanwhile, Peter traveled from place to place, and he came down to visitthe believers in the town of Lydda.

33 There he met a man named Aeneas, who had been paralyzed and bedridden for eight years.

34 Peter said to him, "Aeneas, Jesus Christ heals you! Get up, and roll up your sleepingmat!" And he was healed instantly.

35 Then the whole population of Lydda and Sharon saw Aeneas walking around, and they turned to the Lord.

36 There was a believer in Joppa named Tabitha (which in Greek is Dorcas). She was always doing kind things for others and helping the poor.

37 About this time she became ill and died. Her body was washed for burial and laid in an upstairs room.

38 But the believers had heard that Peter was nearby at Lydda, so they sent two men to beg him, "Please come as soon as possible!"

39 So Peter returned with them; and as soon as he arrived, they took him to the upstairs room. The room was filled with widows who were weeping and showing him the coats and other clothes Dorcas had made for them.

40 But Peter asked them all to leave the room; then he knelt and prayed. Turning to the body he said, "Get up, Tabitha." And she opened her eyes! When she saw Peter, she sat up!

41 He gave her his hand and helped her up. Then he called in the widows and all the believers, and he presented her to them alive.

42 The news spread through the whole town, and many believed in the Lord.

43 And Peter stayed a long time in Joppa, living with Simon, a tanner of hides.

42 And it was known throughout all Joppa; and many believed in the Lord.

43 And it came to pass, that he tarried many days in Joppa with one Simon a tanner.

In Focus 

Linda was looking forward to celebrating her 50th birthday. She had taught in the Chicago Public School system for 15 years. Linda had never been married but her magnetic and outgoing personality had won her many friends. She was well loved by many, including her students.

Days before Linda's birthday, she was told she needed gallbladder surgery. The doctor told her this was a fairly routine, simple surgery, and he expected no complications. Linda arranged to take off from work for a couple weeks to recuperate. The Board of Education gives teachers 10 paid sick days each year. Shortly after the surgery, Linda suddenly came down with a blood disorder. The doctors were puzzled; it was a rare disease and not often seen. Things were not going according to schedule. Two weeks was her allotted time to be off work with the surgery; however, she ended up spending two months in intensive care.

Linda's mother, known in church as Mother Allie B., was a prayer warrior and ardent witness for the Lord. She stayed by Linda's side, witnessing to and praying for every doctor, nurse, visitor, and patient she came in contact with. And, of course, she was in constant prayer for her daughter.

One day Linda's niece, LeMise, felt the Lord was leading her to go to the hospital to pray and lay hands on her aunt, and He would heal her. LeMise thought Linda's mom would be much better suited for the job, but God thought differently. So LeMise obediently went to the hospital. She prayed for her aunt, laying hands on her just as God had instructed.

God did just what He said. Linda was healed. Her prognosis had not been positive, and the doctors and nurses were amazed. Soon Linda was able to leave the hospital, go home, and take care of herself. Throughout the ordeal, Linda's mother had continually shared her faith with all who would listen and led a few people to Christ. Now, before their eyes, there was physical evidence of the power of Jesus Christ.

In today's lesson, the apostle Peter travels around the country preaching the Good News of salvation, and God confirms his preaching with miraculous healings.

The People, Places, and Times

Joppa. The city of Joppa sits "125 feet above sea level overlooking the Mediterranean Sea" and was an important and old, profitable port city on the coast of Palestine. It was under Jewish control for about 40 years until it came under direct Roman authority in A.D. 6. Today, it is on the southern section of Tel Aviv-Jaffa.

Scriptures tell us that, after Joshua's conquest, in the division of the land, Joppa was assigned to the tribe of Dan (one of the 12 tribes of Israel [Joshua 19:46]). However, the tribe of Dan had trouble taking possession of their land, so they fought against the town of Laish, captured it, slaughtered its people, and settled there (v. 47).

Sources:

Pfeiffer, Charles F., Howard F. Vos, John Rea, eds. *Wycliffe Bible Dictionary.* Peabody, Mass.: Hendrickson Publishers, Inc., 1998.

Life Application Study Bible (New Living Translation). Wheaton, Ill.: Tyndale House Publishers, 1996.

Background

A now Holy Spirit-filled Peter was busy with his ministry. He had become the recognized leader among Jesus' disciples and he was one of the inner group of three (Peter, James, and John). Even though he was not a perfect person and knew what it was to fail God, he went on to do great things for the One who had forgiven him of so much. In fact, Peter was the first great minister of the Gospel, not only during Pentecost but afterward as well. In today's text, he traveled from place to place to visit the believers, and one of these places was the ancient crossroads town of Lydda (the capital of one of the Judean districts that included non-Jews). It was in Lydda and Joppa that God continued to do miracles through Peter. God used him to heal crippled Aeneas. Then, after Tabitha (Dorcas) died, the people in Joppa sent for him.

Because corpses had to be buried immediately (before sundown), it is important to mention that Lydda was near Joppa. Therefore, since the distance between Lydda and Joppa was approximately 10 miles, biblical historians estimate that it would have taken three or four hours both ways for the messengers to reach Peter and for Peter to return to Joppa.

Sources:

Keener, Craig S. *The IVP Bible Background Commentary (New Testament).* Downers Grove, Ill.: InterVarsity Press, 1993.

Life Application Study Bible (New Living Translation). Wheaton, Ill.: Tyndale House Publishers, 1996.

At-A-Glance

1. The Healing of Aeneas (Acts 9:32–35)
2. The Healing of Dorcas (vv. 36–43)

In Depth

1. The Healing of Aeneas (Acts 9:32–35)

After the conversion of Saul, the church experienced a period of peace (Acts 9:31) and used the time to visit and strengthen the infant churches in Israel. Peter traveled throughout Israel and eventually wound up in the city of Lydda, about 32 miles west of Jerusalem. There he met a man named Aeneas, who had been paralyzed and bedridden for eight years. This was a long time to be sick and not able to do for one's self. Undoubtedly he had tried other remedies but to no avail. Eight years of sickness had probably made him very skeptical.

Peter just told him, "Aeneas, Jesus Christ maketh thee whole: arise, and make thy bed" (Acts 9:34). Peter had experienced the power of Jesus Christ firsthand. He had been with Christ when a paralyzed man was brought to Jesus on a mat. Jesus told the man to take heart. He also told Him his sins had been forgiven. The scribes and other religious leaders thought he had blasphemed. Jesus said He would prove He is the Son of Man and has the authority on Earth to forgive sins. So Jesus turned to the paralyzed man and said, "Arise, take up thy bed, and go into thine house" (Matthew 9:6). Jesus just spoke the Word because He is the Word.

Peter just spoke the word to Aeneas. He didn't have him go through any process or question him about his faith. He spoke with authority—"Jesus Christ has healed you." Peter had experienced and was confident with who Jesus was. He didn't doubt for a second that Aeneas would be healed. Peter was certain to make sure that all glory went to Christ for the healing. He recognized the source of his power and strength. Jesus Christ heals you—not anyone else. Jesus Christ is due all the credit.

Peter instructed Aeneas to get up and make his bed. He didn't doubt or question whether Jesus had really done the healing. Instead, he instructed him to act upon it as if it were an accomplished fact. In obedience, Aeneas got up and made his bed and was healed instantly. We know that faith without works is dead. Aeneas got up and made his bed. He didn't wait; immediately he was healed. It is important to take God at His Word and not doubt Him. Hearing, trusting, and obeying show true faith in action.

When the population of Lydda and Sharon saw Aeneas walking, they turned to the Lord. They didn't turn to Peter, who had no power without Christ. They turned to the Lord. They recognized the power of Jesus, working through Peter, and turned to the Lord.

This is the primary reason for the miracles: to reveal God's power and confirm His Word so that people might turn to the Lord.

2. The Healing of Dorcas (vv. 36–43)

Near Lydda, in the city of Joppa, lived a woman named Tabitha, which translated into Greek is Dorcas. Dorcas was a disciple of Christ, who was dedicated to acts of kindness and helping the poor. She demonstrated her faith by doing good deeds; she was truly a doer and not just a hearer of the Word. Luke describes her as "full of good works and almsdeeds which she did" (Acts 9:36). Her kindness had become a way of life. This was who she was. She reminds us of the virtuous woman spoken about in Proverbs 31, who sewed for the poor and generously helped those in need.

During the time when Peter was in Lydda, Dorcas fell ill and died. Dorcas' friends prepared her body and took her to the upstairs room. The upstairs room made the environment more private. Her friends were very sad, but they had heard the story of Aeneas' miraculous healing. Since Joppa was only about six miles away, they immediately sent two men to beg for Peter to come to Joppa. The friends knew Dorcas was dead, and it was too late to send for a doctor, but it was not too late to send for Peter.

As soon as Peter got there, they took him upstairs where Dorcas was lying. When he entered the room, he saw the widows mourning and wailing. They showed him all the coats and garments Dorcas had made for them. It was customary for mourners to wail loudly for the dead. These poor widows were grieving for someone they would truly miss. So, Peter asked all the widows to leave the room. After they left, Peter got down on his knees and prayed.

When he finished praying, he turned to Dorcas and said, "Tabitha, arise" (v. 40), and immediately she opened her eyes. When she saw Peter, Dorcas sat up, and Peter extended his hand to help her. Then he called the believers and widows back in the room. Next, Peter presented Dorcas to them. The faith of the believers was confirmed. Dorcas had been raised from the dead by a miracle from the power of God.

Search the Scriptures

1. As Peter traveled about the country whom did he go to visit in Lydda (Acts 9:32)?
2. What did Peter say to Aeneas, the paralytic, who had been bedridden for eight years (v. 34)?
3. After he sent the widows out of the room, what did Peter do (v. 40)?
4. After Peter told her to get up, what was the first thing Dorcas did (v. 40)?
5. After the news traveled in Joppa, what happened (v. 42)?

Discuss the Meaning

1. The end result of the healings of Aeneas and Dorcus was that people believed and turned to the Lord (see Acts 9:35, 42). What are other reasons God might have for healing people?
2. In these healings, Peter was the instrument God used to demonstrate His power. Do you think it is possible for God to use you as an instrument of His power? How should we prepare ourselves to be God's instruments?

Lesson in Our Society

We live in a society where most people claim to believe in God. We see bumper stickers, T-shirts, baseball caps, slogans on personal checks. We hear church clichés, all indicating a belief in God. However, when we listen to the news and see society falling apart spiritually, it calls for a question of which ones are really God's disciples. When a person has a near-death experience and is in the hospital, he/she usually send for the chaplain to pray with and for the family. As a society, we practice good religious rituals all the time. We know the right things to wear, we know the right things to say, and it even appears we know the right things to do. A true relationship with Christ exemplifies true Christlike characteristics. To say we believe in God and live contrary to His obedience is sin. When so-called Christians continue to live like the world in sin, we hinder people from coming to Christ.

Make It Happen

Tabitha is described as a "woman who was full of good works and almsdeeds which she did." She impacted her community by her acts of kindness and generosity. God draws people to Him by the words we speak and also by the lives we live. All of us have something we can offer to others. This week commit to doing at least one act of kindness for someone each day. Be prepared to share your experiences with the class next week.

Follow the Spirit

What God wants me to do:

____

____

Remember Your Thoughts

Special insights I have learned:

____

____

More Light on the Text

Acts 9:32–43

As we delve into these two accounts of miracles done by the Holy Spirit in Jesus' name, through Peter, we need to understand where these pictures fit into the larger picture of the book of Acts. As mentioned in the last lesson, Acts is a sequel to or continuation of the book of Luke, written by the same author and addressed to the same person, Theophilus. Whereas the gospel of Luke tells the story of Jesus' life, ministry, death, and resurrection, Acts is the story of the birth and growth of the New Testament church, under the banner of Jesus' name. The outline of the book of Acts can be understood in light of Jesus' promise in Acts 1:8: "But ye shall receive power, after that the Holy Ghost is come upon you: and ye shall be witnesses unto me both in Jerusalem, and in all Judaea, and in Samaria, and unto the uttermost part of the earth."

Before the book moves toward an emphasis on the Gentile mission, we have the miracle accounts considered in this lesson. On the whole, they demonstrate the power of the Holy Spirit and confirm Peter in his role as one of the chief apostles in the church. Going forth from the spiritual victory of these healings, he will be made ready to accept the Gentiles—the "ends of the earth" of Acts 1:8—into the church.

32 And it came to pass, as Peter passed throughout all quarters, he came down also to the saints which dwelt at Lydda.

As the account begins, Peter was "passing through all quarters," presumably preaching in various locations along the west coast of Palestine, along the Mediterranean Sea. Peter's acquaintance with many areas of the church is later shown in his letters, especially 1 Peter, which addresses churches throughout Asia Minor (modern-day Turkey). He came to Lydda, a town about 25 miles from Jerusalem on the way to the coast.

The King James Version's phrase "it came to pass" could make it sound as if the comings and goings of the apostles and missionaries in Acts were often accidental. Indeed, the Greek word translated "it came to pass" (*ginomai*, **GHIN-om-ahee**) appears four times in this passage and very commonly elsewhere in the New Testament, serving to move the action along. But if we merely translated the word something like "and then ..." we would fail to catch the richness of its appearance in Acts. The reader of Acts can hardly avoid an overwhelming sense of God's sovereignty as He moves events along for His purposes. Without a doubt, it did not just "happen" that Peter showed up in Lydda. There was a need there that God was determined to meet, and so He would through His servant, the apostle Peter.

33 And there he found a certain man named Aeneas, which had kept his bed eight years, and was sick of the palsy.

In the book of Acts, the scope and breadth of the power of God seems to be matched only by the profound and aching neediness of mankind. Everywhere the apostles went, bringing the Good News of salvation in Jesus Christ, they were confronted with pressing, immediate needs. The way they responded to these challenges would reveal a lot about the nature of this new movement of God, inaugurated by Jesus of Nazareth. Would the apostles ignore or trivialize earthly needs in favor of preaching a heavenly Gospel? Such a response would show God to be concerned about the things of the next world in opposition to the things of this world. But on the contrary, we see a very different response from Peter in the passage: He addressed the physical needs of those God brought into his path. Responding to need, just like his master Jesus did, he demonstrated that Christianity is about healing the whole person and that the Gospel brings hope, not just for the next life but for this one as well.

Aeneas, though he possessed a Greek name (made famous by the Roman author Virgil in the *Aeneid*), was probably a Jew, as this part of Acts is still focusing largely on Jews, and probably already a believer in Christ, since Peter did not confront him with the Good News but rather seemed to assume his knowledge of it. This Aeneas had suffered from paralysis for eight years ("since the age of eight" is also a possible but much less likely, translation). It is this very real and physical need that first confronted Peter upon his entry to Lydda. The King James Version translated the Greek word *paraluo* (**par-al-OO-o**) as "sick of the palsy"; though he was no doubt "sick of the palsy" (in the sense of being very tired of it!), a more modern translation would be "sick with the palsy" or simply "paralyzed."

34 And Peter said unto him, Aeneas, Jesus Christ maketh thee whole: arise, and make thy bed. And he arose immediately.

Luke recounts the healing with powerful brevity. We should note several things here. First, Peter leaves no question about the origin of the power for healing. Whereas elsewhere people are healed "in the name of Jesus Christ" (Acts 3:6), here Peter states things even more directly: "Jesus Christ maketh thee whole." In the Greek, the word *iaomai* (**ee-AH-om-ahee**), meaning "heals," has the same opening sound as the word *Iesous* (**ee-ay-SOOCE**), adding to the power of the phrase. The phrase translated "make thy bed" did not, in that context, likely mean to arrange the sheets after sleeping, as we would understand the sense of "make your bed." More likely it meant making ready a couch to sit at a table so that one could make a meal. Either way, Luke makes obvious the miracle: this man, wretchedly bound to a bed for eight years, was now performing normal tasks (compare Mark 1:31). In the Bible, being restored to wholeness means being restored to work, as mankind fulfills the creation mandate of Genesis 1:26–28. Aeneas had regained his dignity through the power of God, and his rising "immediately" showed the power and completeness of the restoration.

35 And all that dwelt at Lydda and Saron saw him, and turned to the Lord.

The miracles of the book of Acts are never the ultimate goal in themselves but always a means to an end. Not only do they demonstrate, to the person healed, the power of God and the purpose of the Gospel but they also, in many cases, result in repentance and salvation on the part of many others who witness the power of God at work. Here, the turning of the people to God would have been especially significant because this region contained many Gentiles, so the fact of the whole region turning to God suggests that the expansion of the Gospel "to the end of the earth" (Acts 1:8) is continuing. Saron (or Sharon) was the plain that stretched northward from Lydda; clearly the glorious witness of Aeneas' healed body accompanied with his own testimony had a tremendous effect. As a result, many "turned" (Gk. *epistrepho*, **ep-ee-STREF-o**) to God. Although this word is not the same as that translated "repentance" in Acts (Gk. *metanoia*, **met-AN-oy-ah**), it has a great similarity to that word. In both Old and New Testaments, the picture of someone converting to true worship of God involves a profound sense of "turning," showing that conversion is not simply a matter of getting new information but rather a profound transformation of the orientation of one's life. These dwellers of Lydda and Saron forsook a life oriented away from God and turned toward the one true God, in response to the power of God in Aeneas' life.

36 Now there was at Joppa a certain disciple named Tabitha, which by interpretation is called Dorcas: this woman was full of good works and almsdeeds which she did.

The story moves to the second episode, in which the power of Christ was demonstrated through the apostle Peter. Joppa was not far from Lydda, about 12 miles away on the Mediterranean coast. Luke introduces to us at great length this woman Tabitha, or Dorcas (the Aramaic and Greek words, respectively, for "gazelle"). In referring to Tabitha's "good works" and "almsdeeds," Luke is drawing on a rich Jewish tradition in which a life characterized by these virtues was highly valued. Christianity, being a Jewish religion at heart, does not disown this value but keeps it, provided that such works and almsdeeds are not seen as gaining salvation for the person who performs them. In the New Testament, this sort of person has typically demonstrated by his or her good works how much he or she is waiting for the kingdom of God to come (see the description of Cornelius in Acts 10:2 and also the powerful picture of salvation to the Gentiles shown in the "good Gentile" centurion in Matthew 8:1–13). Luke's point is not to show that Tabitha somehow *deserved* to be raised from the dead because of her good life; rather, he is showing that wherever the kingdom of God spreads, it brings not only power for miracles but also power for a changed life. We can assume that Tabitha had already been favored by God, as demonstrated by her life of works done in worship of Him. In the miraculous account to come, God will show how He treats those whom He favors.

37 And it came to pass in those days, that she was sick, and died: whom when they had washed, they laid her in an upper chamber.

As already mentioned, the words "it came to pass" do not suggest randomness. Tabitha's death came at just the time God intended—that He might display His power through it. We are told that "they" (probably Tabitha's family and friends) washed her body, but rather than burying it, they laid it in the upper chamber. By mentioning this, Luke intends his readers to recall the Old Testament accounts in which the dead were placed in upper rooms, with the specific hope of their being healed by the prophet Elijah or Elisha (1 Kings 17:19; 2 Kings 4:10, 21). As the book of Acts makes clear, Jesus is the great Prophet of all prophets (see Acts 7:52); in His name, great things will be done—things accompanying salvation. I. Howard Marshall, in his commentary on Acts, points out another reason why Tabitha may have been laid in an upper room: "the hope of the resurrection coming soon." Either way, these disciples were full of hope, even in the midst of their mourning. In the arrival of the apostle Peter, in Jesus' name, their hope will find joyful realization.

38 And forasmuch as Lydda was nigh to Joppa, and the disciples had heard that Peter was there,

they sent unto him two men, desiring him that he would not delay to come to them.

No doubt the disciples had heard of the miracle done, not far away, in the life of Aeneas. Such an event would have rippled throughout the surrounding country. At this time in salvation history, the word of Jesus was spreading rapidly, but it depended heavily on the apostles. The people had generally not yet formed churches, and the apostles were recognized as those commissioned by Jesus to carry His truth and exercise His power. This delegation of disciples did not seek out Peter because he was some kind of unique faith healer but because he was an apostle—an eyewitness to the majesty of Christ. We see here the distinction between "disciples" and "apostles." Disciples were true believers in the power of Christ. However, in the early days of the church, it was not always understood how to avail oneself of that power, and so the apostles were heavily relied upon. As the church would grow and solidify, under the apostles' teaching, Christians would begin to understand the power available to all of them, through Christ and the Holy Spirit. As the apostles died away, the church would continue in the power of the Word.

39 Then Peter arose and went with them. When he was come, they brought him into the upper chamber: and all the widows stood by him weeping, and shewing the coats and garments which Dorcas made, while she was with them.

Peter's quick response showed the faithfulness and rightness of the disciples in seeking him out. Here the story begins to resemble the account given to us in Mark 5:35–43, in which Jesus was called upon to heal a sick girl, who died while he was on the way. This similarity is no accident. Once again, Luke is showing that Jesus had given His authority to the apostles to carry out His mission. Where the apostles are, there the power of Jesus is.

Although we cannot be sure, it seems likely that the widows, who were present at Tabitha's side, were actually *wearing* the coats and garments they showed Peter. The point would be to show that Tabitha had followed the Jewish tradition of kindness to widows (a Christian tradition as well; see James 1:27). Whether they were wearing the garments or not, the presence of these widows and their great grief at Tabitha's death show us for certain how kind the women had been to those in need.

40 But Peter put them all forth, and kneeled down, and prayed; and turning him to the body said, Tabitha, arise. And she opened her eyes: and when she saw Peter, she sat up.

Like his Master, Jesus, in Mark 5:40, Peter told all the people to leave the room. He then accessed the two sources of power that Jesus had given to His apostles and to His church: prayer and the word of Jesus. Peter's prayer would have been an expression of absolute dependence upon Jesus for any power. Again, he did not possess it in his own strength or by some sort of magic. But why would we say that Peter is using the word of Christ here? Once again, it is because of the way this story mirrors the healing account in Mark 5. Speakers of Aramaic would have recognized that Peter's words to Tabitha—*Tabitha, cumi*—were almost identical to the words Jesus spoke in Mark 5:41: *Talitha, cumi* ("little girl, arise"). Luke shows us, by means of this similarity, that the word of Jesus brings power to His disciples, even as that Word will be understood more deeply in the word of the apostles. As a result of prayer and Jesus' Word, the disciples' great hopes are realized, the power of God is once again shown forth, and the identity of Peter—as a vessel of Christ's glory—is confirmed anew.

41 And he gave her his hand, and lifted her up, and when he had called the saints and widows, presented her alive.

The main new piece of information given to us in this verse is the detail of Peter presenting Tabitha alive to the saints and widows. Once again, Peter reflected Jesus in the way he carried out this miracle. Like Jesus, when He raised the widow's son in Luke 7:15, Peter gave attention to those grieving, not just to the one raised from the dead. Like Jesus, Peter presented the dead-and-now-living person to those who loved her. By this, Luke shows us again that the purpose of miracles extends well beyond those immediately healed or raised. The disciples had been faithful in seeking the true Source of power and grace in their grief, and their faithfulness was honored by God.

42 And it was known throughout all Joppa; and many believed in the Lord.

Just like in the case of Aeneas in Lydda, this miracle brought about the conversion of many in the surrounding area. Thus, the miracle had once again reached its fullest purpose: producing faith. Unlike the religious leaders and others who resisted Jesus, even despite seeing His miracles (John 12:37), those favored by God see His miracles and believe. Whereas the last account focused on many people "turning" in repentance to God, this verse focuses on their faith, which was an equally important part of conversion. We see in this pairing the biblical truth that faith and repentance are two sides of the same coin. When the Holy Spirit enlightens a person to see the glory of God in Christ, that person turns *from* sin and believing *to* Christ, trusting in His person and work for salvation.

43 And it came to pass, that he tarried many days in Joppa with one Simon a tanner.

The apostles were not just itinerant miracle workers; they were pastors at heart. Like Paul, who stayed and suffered long with those to whom he ministered, Peter now stayed in the region in which the healings had taken place in order to ground these disciples—both new and old—in the realities of the Gospel of Christ. We can take an important lesson from the apostles' focus on doing more than simply healing and evangelism; true discipleship involves deep relationship, even for those so powerful in Word and deed as were Peter, Paul, and the other apostles.

Finally, Luke adds a seemingly insignificant but ultimately powerful detail: that Peter stayed with "a tanner." Since tanning was ceremonially defiling because dead animals were regarded as unclean, in the Jewish mind-set, a "tanner" was an unclean occupation. How could a good Jew like Peter stay in the house of a ceremonially unclean man? Luke is setting the stage for the vision that Peter is about to experience in chapter 10—a vision that will show him beyond a doubt that God intends for the Gentiles to be included in the body of Christ. Peter's lodging with a tanner foreshadowed this world-changing event and the coming of the Gentiles full-force into the church. So in these accounts Luke has shown that (1) Peter is indeed an apostle blessed with the power of Christ, and that (2) Jesus calls Gentiles and Jews alike to Himself. In the beautiful profundity of the Bible, we see both Jesus' power for those in need and the broader, more historical purposes that God works out under His sovereign hand.

Sources:

Marshall, I. Howard. *Acts. Tyndale New Testament Commentaries.* Grand Rapids, Mich.: InterVarsity Press, 1980.

Vine, W.E. *Vines Complete Expository Dictionary of Old and New Testament Words.* Edited by Merrill F. Unger and William White Jr. Nashville: Thomas Nelson Publishers, 1996.

Daily Bible Readings

M: Father Is Glorified
John 14:8–14
T: The Promise of Healing
Isaiah 57:14–21
W: O Lord, Heal Me
Psalm 6
T: Heal My Sin
Psalm 41
F: Return and Be Healed
Jeremiah 3:19–23
S: Joy Comes With the Morning
Psalm 30:1–5
S: God Healing Through Peter
Acts 9:32–43

NOTES

TEACHING TIPS

May 3
Bible Study Guide 10

1. Words You Should Know

A. Predestinated (Ephesians 1:5) *proorizo* (Gk.)—To decide beforehand.

B. Redemption (v. 7) *apolutrosis* (Gk.)—To set free for a ransom; is used of prisoners of war, slaves, and criminals condemned to death.

2. Teacher Preparation

Unifying Principle—The Spiritual Family. Family life offers opportunities for rewards and challenges, for close ties and for estranged relationships. How do we see ourselves within the context of our families? In letters to first-century churches, Paul and John celebrated and gave thanks for those whom God had adopted into a new family in Christ—His spiritual family.

A. Study the Focal Verses in several versions of the Bible.

B. Read The People, Places, and Times and Background sections to familiarize yourself with the context of Ephesians.

C. Make use of helpful information found on the CD-ROM that came with your *Precepts For Living®* teaching materials.

D. Read through the In Depth section, and glean salient points for discussion.

E. Pray that God will help you teach the lesson in such a way that your students' lives will be changed.

3. Starting the Lesson

A. Ask a volunteer to open the class with prayer.

B. Have a volunteer read the In Focus story, and then ask the students to discuss the similarities and differences between an earthly adoption and spiritual adoption into the family of God.

4. Getting into the Lesson

A. Ask for a few volunteers to read the Focal Verses out loud.

B. Present The People, Places, and Times and Background sections. Discuss.

C. Ask for volunteers to define "predestinated" and "redemption" from today's Words You Should Know. Write the students' definitions on the board; then read and discuss the definitions given above.

D. Present the In Depth section. Discuss.

5. Relating the Lesson to Life

A. Divide the class into pairs or small groups. Instruct them to complete the Search the Scriptures section together, and discuss it among themselves.

B. Bring the class back together. Read the Lesson in Our Society section. Discuss ways that believers can enter into relationships with unbelievers, with the intention of lovingly inviting them into the family of God.

6. Arousing Action

A. Read the Make It Happen section.

B. Ask the students to list hindrances to sharing the story of redemption.

C. Have the students pray with a partner in regard to these areas.

D. Instruct the students to read the Daily Bible Readings in preparation for the lesson next week.

Worship Guide

For the Superintendent or Teacher
Theme: New Family in Christ
Theme Song: "The Family of God"
Devotional Reading: Exodus 19:1–8
Prayer

NEW FAMILY IN CHIRST

Bible Background • EPHESIANS 1:3–14
Printed Text • EPHESIANS 1:3–14 Devotional Reading • EXODUS 19:1–8

AIM for Change

By the end of the lesson, we will:
LEARN the benefits of being adopted into God's family;
SENSE the joy of being accepted into God's family; and
DECIDE to become a part of God's family or invite someone to become a member.

Keep in Mind

"Having predestinated us unto the adoption of children by Jesus Christ to himself, according to the good pleasure of his will" (Ephesians 1:5).

Focal Verses

KJV **Ephesians 1:3** Blessed be the God and Father of our Lord Jesus Christ, who hath blessed us with all spiritual blessings in heavenly places in Christ:

4 According as he hath chosen us in him before the foundation of the world, that we should be holy and without blame before him in love:

5 Having predestinated us unto the adoption of children by Jesus Christ to himself, according to the good pleasure of his will,

6 To the praise of the glory of his grace, wherein he hath made us accepted in the beloved.

7 In whom we have redemption through his blood, the forgiveness of sins, according to the riches of his grace;

8 Wherein he hath abounded toward us in all wisdom and prudence;

9 Having made known unto us the mystery of his will, according to his good pleasure which he hath purposed in himself:

10 That in the dispensation of the fulness of times he might gather together in one all things in Christ, both which are in heaven, and which are on earth; even in him:

11 In whom also we have obtained an inheritance, being predestinated according to the purpose of him who worketh all things after the counsel of his own will:

12 That we should be to the praise of his glory, who first trusted in Christ.

13 In whom ye also trusted, after that ye heard the word of truth, the gospel of your salvation: in whom also after that ye believed, ye were sealed with that holy Spirit of promise,

14 Which is the earnest of our inheritance until the redemption of the purchased possession, unto the praise of his glory.

NLT **Ephesians 1:3** All praise to God, the Father of our Lord Jesus Christ, who has blessed us with every spiritual blessing in the heavenly realms because we are united with Christ.

4 Even before he made the world, God loved us and chose us in Christ to be holy and without fault in his eyes.

5 God decided in advance to adopt us into his own family by bringing us to himself through Jesus Christ. This is what he wanted to do, and it gave him great pleasure.

6 So we praise God for the glorious grace he has poured out on us who belong to his dear Son.

7 He is so rich in kindness and grace that he purchased our freedom with the blood of his Son and forgave our sins.

8 He has showered his kindness on us, along with all wisdom and understanding.

9 God has now revealed to us his mysterious plan regarding Christ, a plan to fulfill his own good pleasure.

10 And this is the plan: At the right time he will bring everything together under the authority of Christ—everything in heaven and on earth.

11 Furthermore, because we are united with Christ, we have received an inheritance from God, for he chose us in advance, and he makes everything work out according to his plan.

12 God's purpose was that we Jews who were the first to trust in Christ would bring praise and glory to God.

13 And now you Gentiles have also heard the truth, the Good News that God saves you. And when you believed in Christ, he identified you as his own by giving you the Holy Spirit, whom he promised long ago.

14 The Spirit is God's guarantee that he will give

us the inheritance he promised and that he has purchased us to be his own people. He did this so we would praise and glorify him.

In Focus

Shelly and Curtis longed for a child of their own. Married for six years, they still had not been able to conceive. They decided to start the adoption process, praying that God would give them a child who needed them.

Shortly after meeting with the adoption agency, Shelly began having dreams. Every night for months, she dreamed of a small, dark-haired child. In her dreams, the child was crying. Shelly would run to the child, reaching out her arms, but the child would push her away.

Night after night, Shelly dreamed the same thing. She was deeply troubled about the dream and shared it with Curtis.

"Honey, I think God has a child for us," Curtis said. "Maybe it's just not the right time."

Shelly and Curtis kept praying. One night, Shelly dreamed about the child again. This time, when she ran to the child, the child reached out to her and smiled. When Shelly woke, she knew that God was answering her many prayers.

Over the next few months, everything fell into place. Finally, Shelly and Curtis signed the adoption papers. It was official! They welcomed 4-year-old Shayla into their family as their daughter. It didn't matter that Shayla had been abused by her stepfather. It didn't matter that she was too thin or her hearing would never be "normal." Shayla was their daughter, and they would see that she was loved and cared for, for the rest of her life. They would feed her, clothe her, educate her, and—most of all—love her. She was part of the family.

God loves every person individually and longs to adopt them into His family. This week, we will see how He provided a way for this to happen—redemption through His Son, Jesus Christ.

The People, Places, and Times

The Book of Ephesians. The book of Ephesians was written by the apostle Paul while he was imprisoned (see Ephesians 3:1; 4:1; 6:20), perhaps from Rome. Most scholars agree that Ephesians was written for a wider readership than just the church at Ephesus and was probably circulated to many churches in the Roman province of Asia, where Ephesus was located.

Paul wrote Ephesians to strengthen the faith and spiritual foundations of his recipients. He shared with them the vast scope of God's plan of redemption through Christ. He assured them of God's plan for them as the church but also as individuals of God's family.

Source:

Arrington, French L., and Roger Stronstad, eds. *Life in the Spirit New Testament Commentary.* Grand Rapids, Mich.: Zondervan, 1999.

Background

In the original Greek text, the 12 verses of Ephesians 1:3–14 were a single sentence. This is one of the most joyful and profound passages in the Bible. Like an anthem of praise, it celebrates God's eternal and glorious plan of redemption. It is broken up into three stanzas, each beginning or ending with the phrase "to the praise of his glorious grace" (Ephesians 1:6, NIV) or "for" or "to the praise of his glory" (1:12, 14, NIV).

This passage examines the plan of redemption from a triune perspective: the first stanza (1:3–6) praises the Father for choosing to redeem us from our sin; the second stanza highlights Jesus as the Redeemer (1:7–12); and the third stanza (1:13–14) reveals the Holy Spirit as the living, divine presence to the church and the world.

In these 12 short verses, the vast plan of redemption is revealed from eternity before creation, to the time of its future completeness at the time of Christ's Second Advent. The focus of redemption is always Christ, and the phrase "in Christ" or "in him" occurs repeatedly throughout this passage. In fact, this phrase is the key phrase of this entire epistle.

According to verse 5, it is God's great pleasure and will, by virtue of Christ's redemption, to adopt us into the family of God.

Source:

Arrington, French L., and Roger Stronstad, eds. *Life in the Spirit New Testament Commentary.* Grand Rapids, Mich.: Zondervan, 1999.

At-A-Glance

1. We Are Blessed by God (Ephesians 1:3–6)
2. We Are Redeemed by Jesus Christ (vv. 7–12)
3. We Are Sealed by the Holy Spirit (vv. 13–14)

In Depth

1. We Are Blessed by God (Ephesians 1:3–6)

Paul begins this passage with joyful praise. He praises God the Father for His plan of redemption. He blesses God, because God has blessed us through Christ Jesus. Because of Christ's redemptive work, believers are beneficiaries of all the spiritual blessings of the "heavenly realms" (v. 3, NIV). These spiritual blessings come from living and abiding "in Christ."

Verse 4 tells us of the first blessing: We are chosen to be holy and blameless. God did not choose us because we *are* holy and blameless, but He chose us that we might *become* holy and blameless. What a concept! The blessing of being chosen by God is awesome enough. But think of the implications—when we accept Christ as our Saviour and Redeemer, we are accepting God's offer to make us holy and blameless. He is promising to take us, unworthy sinners, and make us into His very own children. And we are not only joining the family, but we are joining the family and gaining all rights and privileges that come with the position.

If it were not enough to be chosen to become holy and blameless, we were predestined to become God's children and freely given the gift of God's glorious grace. This means that God chose "in Christ" a people for Himself and decided beforehand His plan for those who were chosen. He chose beforehand what He planned for His chosen to become or do. Some of these plans are listed in this passage of Scripture. He chose His people to be holy and blameless (v. 4), adopted as His sons (v. 5), redeemed (v. 7), for the praise of His glory (vv. 11–12), recipients of the Holy Spirit (v. 13), and recipients of an inheritance (v. 14).

Verse 6 says God has freely given us all these blessings by His grace and through Christ Jesus. It's up to us to accept them.

2. We Are Redeemed by Jesus Christ (vv. 7–12)

This second "stanza" of Paul's hymn highlights the wonder of God's grace, revealed in the life and death of Jesus Christ. In verse 7, we see that our redemption comes through Christ's blood. God forgives our sins when we choose to accept Jesus Christ through faith. God takes sin very seriously, and it is only because of Christ's sacrifice on our behalf that we can be forgiven. But God does not forgive grudgingly. Rather, He forgives us "according to the riches of God's grace" (v. 7, NIV). God "lavished on us" his grace and forgiveness (v. 8, NIV). Just as parents love their children, God loves us. He not only adopts us into His family but He does so in generosity and abundance.

God also promises that one day His plan for humankind will be fully accomplished. Verse 9 tells us that God has made known the "mystery" of His will by revealing the plan of redemption in Jesus. And when it is the right time, the culmination of God's plan will come to pass, and all will be brought together under the Lordship of Jesus Christ (v. 10). In these confusing and fearful times, it is comforting to know that there will come a time when everything will come into right relationship under the leadership of Jesus.

Verse 11 begins with "in him," reminding us once again that it is only within the bounds of a relationship with Jesus Christ that there is meaning in life. In Him, we as individuals and the church, as a whole, were chosen and predestined to fulfill God's will. We were adopted as children "for the praise of his glory" (v. 12, NIV). What a joyful thought! God accepted us into His family, and He enjoys us! We give Him praise by living our lives according to His will for us.

3. We Are Sealed by the Holy Spirit (vv. 13–14)

In ancient times, a "seal" denoted ownership. In this last "stanza" of Paul's theological hymn, he speaks of the Holy Spirit's role in our redemption. God planned our redemption. Jesus paid for our redemption. The Holy Spirit "seals" the deal. When earthly parents are adopting a child, they have to sign legal papers in order to claim the child as their own. When God adopts us into His family, He gives us the Holy Spirit as evidence that we are truly His sons and daughters (Romans 8:9). We are full members of the family, with all rights and responsibilities.

The Holy Spirit is also a promise of greater things to come—when God's entire plan is accomplished and our full redemption is realized. On that great day, when all is fulfilled, the family of God will truly be "to the praise of his glory" (v. 14).

Sources:

Arrington, French L., and Roger Stronstad, eds. *Life in the Spirit New Testament Commentary*. Grand Rapids, Mich.: Zondervan, 1999.

The NIV Study Bible, 10th Anniversary Edition. Grand Rapids, Mich.: Zondervan, 1995.

Search the Scriptures

1. When and why did God choose us to become part of His family (Ephesians 1:4)?

2. How do we obtain redemption (v. 7)?

3. What role does the Holy Spirit fulfill in the redemption plan for believers (vv. 13–14)?

Discuss the Meaning

1. How do you view yourself in the context of your own earthly family? As a believer, how do you view yourself in the context of God's family?

2. How should believers respond to new members of God's family?

3. What are some of the benefits of being a part of God's family?

4. How do we know we are part of God's family?

Lesson in Our Society

In our impersonal and hurried world, people are longing for connection—a place to belong. Some search for relationships at work, at the gym, or even online. Others hope for a sense of belonging within their own family. Still others move from relationship to relationship, never really feeling loved or accepted anywhere.

As believers, we can offer others the blessing of meaningful relationships within the body of Christ. In fact, it is usually through relationships that we are able to lovingly invite others to join us in the family of God.

Make It Happen

Many people don't have a clear understanding of sin. If people do not have a clear understanding of sin, then they don't know that they need repentance and redemption. As believers, so that others may join us in the family of God, we must clearly point the way to the Cross. God's grand plan for redemption is good news! God loves every person in the world and wants them to join His family. Let's give them an invitation!

Write down how you would lead a nonbeliever to Christ. What would you say? What Scriptures would you use? Memorize those Scriptures. Ask the Holy Spirit to guide you. Ask Him to lead nonbelievers to you, that you may invite them into the great family of God.

Follow the Spirit

What God wants me to do:

____

____

Remember Your Thoughts

Special insights I have learned:

____

____

More Light on the Text

Ephesians 1:3–14

3 Blessed be the God and Father of our Lord Jesus Christ, who hath blessed us with all spiritual blessings in heavenly places in Christ:

Paul begins his letter to the Ephesians with an extended section of praise to God for the blessing of salvation in Christ Jesus. Verses 3–14 are actually one long sentence in the Greek.

The adjective "blessed" (Gk. *eulogetos*, **yoo-log-ay-TOS**) literally means "praised, well-spoken of" or "in a place of favor and benefit." Many scholars debate which meaning applies to the first word of this verse, largely because the verb "be" is implied, not stated, in the text. Therefore, Paul's intended meaning could be either "God is to be praised" or "God is characterized by blessedness." The first is preferred.

The reason that Paul directs blessing to God is the favor that God has poured out on His people. The blessings in question here are "spiritual" (Gk. *pneumatikos*, **pnyoo-mat-ik-OS**)—that is to say they relate to our spiritual welfare—rather than material or physical. The spiritual blessings we have received are also comprehensive; the list to follow in verses 4–14 will show us what he means by "all."

The blessings are further described as "in heavenly places" and "in Christ." "Heavenly places" (Gk. *epouranios*, **ep-oo-RAN-ee-os**) could literally be translated "heavenlies." The heavenlies are mentioned in Ephesians 1:20 as the place where Christ sat down after ascending to heaven. Then, 2:6 tells us that we are now seated in the heavenlies with Christ. The "heavenlies" are, therefore, the realm where God lives.

The spiritual blessings of God are only available through our spiritual union with Christ. The phrase "in Christ" and a number of equivalents ("in the beloved," for example, in v. 6) appear frequently in this passage and throughout Ephesians and other Pauline writings. This is Paul's way of expressing what Jesus, Himself, taught: The Christian's spiritual life and blessing is actually Jesus' life and blessing, which He shares with us by virtue of the fact that we are in Him and He is in us (cf. John 14:20).

4 According as he hath chosen us in him before the foundation of the world, that we should be holy and without blame before him in love:

Paul goes on to say that God has blessed His people "according as" (or "just as/in the same way as") He has chosen us. This passage and others that speak of God's electing work have been the subject of much intense debate in the Christian community for many years, as Christians have struggled to understand the relationship of God's sovereign will and the free moral agency of human beings. Some passages, like this one, emphasize God's will in His choice of His people; other passages emphasize human responsibility for faith in Christ.

The word "chosen" (Gk. *eklegomai*, **ek-LEG-om-ahee**) simply means "to pick out" or "to select." It is the same word used to describe Jesus' selection of His disciples (Luke 6:13; John 15:16), of the Jerusalem counsel's selection of men to accompany Paul and Barnabas (Acts 15:22, 25). A similar word is used of God's selection of Jesus for the work of redeeming mankind from sin (Luke 23:35). The Scriptures teach that God chose the people of Israel to play a leading role in the redemption of mankind (Deuteronomy 7:6; Isaiah 45:4).

Since the Scriptures are clear that God has chosen His people, the issue that Christians debate is the basis on which He has chosen them. Christians who follow in the steps of Augustine and the reformers argue that God's choice is solely based on His sovereign will. Their position is based on the perspective that sin has so thoroughly corrupted man that no one is able to choose Christ unless God first regenerates his heart (John 5:21; Ephesians 2:1). Christians who follow in the footsteps of Arminius, Finney, and Wesley believe that God's choice of individuals is based on His perfect foreknowledge (prescience) of what those individuals would do if they were left to their own free will. They hold that the "prevenient" grace of God is sufficient for anyone to choose to believe in Christ apart from a special work of God. This perspective is based on the Scripture's free offer of salvation to the entire world (John 3:16) and argues that God would not offer mankind something (salvation) that we are not able to accept on our own.

God's election of sinners to receive grace happened "in him," that is, "in Christ." God the Father is the architect of the plan of redemption. But the application of Christ's redeeming work is what saves.

The Father's work in the redemption of His people began before the foundation of the world.

Being chosen by God is a high privilege, but it also involves accountability. The word "holy" (Gk. *hagios*, **HAG-ee-os**) means "consecrated, set apart, morally perfect." It is sometimes used in the New Testament as a noun to mean "saint." "Without blame" (Gk. *amomos*, **AM-o-mos**) is a word used ceremonially to describe a sacrifice as "without blemish" (cf. 1 Peter 1:19). In this context, it describes a state of moral faultlessness (cf. Philippians 2:15; Revelation 14:5).

5 Having predestinated us unto the adoption of children by Jesus Christ to himself, according to the good pleasure of his will,

The word translated "predestinated" (Gk. *proorizo*, **pro-or-ID-zo**) means "to decide upon beforehand; to predetermine, to foreordain." When the authors of the New Testament use this word to describe God's action in the redemption of mankind, they intend for us to understand that God did more than simply plan our redemption. He caused it to happen.

Our salvation is also described as "adoption of children" (Gk. *huiothesia*, **hwee-oth-es-EE-ah**). Adoption as sons was part of God's promise to Abraham and his descendants (Exodus 4:22; Deuteronomy 14:1; Romans 9:4), but now in Christ every Christian is extended the blessings and privileges of sonship, including peace and assurance of God's love through the "Spirit of sonship" and the hope of a divine inheritance (Romans 8:14–17).

The predestination to adoption is based on the good pleasure (Gk. *eudokia*, **yoo-dok-EE-ah**) of God's will. *Eudokia* is used in the New Testament to mean "satisfaction, good pleasure, favor, approval." It is the word used in Luke 2:14 for "good will" toward men. It is also the word used by Jesus in Luke 10:21 to describe the Father's pleasure in hiding things from many and revealing them only to His children. *Eudokia* is also used in verse 9 of this passage to describe God's pleasure in revealing His will to His people. The message of the Scriptures is clear: God purposed, planned, and accomplished our redemption, not because of any obligation or compulsion but because He is merciful and compassionate.

6 To the praise of the glory of his grace, wherein he hath made us accepted in the beloved.

"Praise" (Gk. *epainos*, **EP-ahee-nos**) is used here and in verses 12 and 14 to refer to the words of recognition that are due God for His work to save His people. The Lord will receive praise, thanksgiving, and honor from the redeemed for all eternity (Revelation 7:10).

"Glory" (Gk. *doxa*, **DOX-ah**) can refer to brightness, splendor, and majesty or to fame, renown, and honor. Here the emphasis seems to be on the fame and renown of God's incredible grace (Gk. *charis*, **KHAR-ece**). *Charis* here refers to the favor that God has shown to His people by selecting them and orchestrating their salvation, in spite of their sin.

"Wherein he hath made us accepted" is translated, "which he has bestowed on us" or "with which he has blessed us" by other English translations. The Greek verb *charitoo* (**khar-ee-TO-o**) means "to bestow favor on, favor highly, bless." Our experience of God's grace and favor is wholly by virtue of our union with Christ, the One beloved by the Father.

7 In whom we have redemption through his blood, the forgiveness of sins, according to the riches of his grace;

Paul now switches his focus from the orchestrating work of the Father to the role of the Son, who accomplished the salvation of God's people. All of the blessings of salvation are experienced "in Christ" (see comments on v. 3).

"Redemption" (Gk. *apolutrosis*, **ap-ol-OO-tro-sis**) is a release from slavery or captivity brought about by the payment of a ransom—a "buying back." God's work to redeem His people from spiritual bondage and oppression was prefigured by His redemptive acts such as the Exodus (Exodus 15:13; Deuteronomy 7:8), release from exile (Nehemiah 1:10), and deliverance from personal peril (2 Samuel 4:9).

"Forgiveness" (Gk. *aphesis*, **AF-es-is**) is the cancellation of an obligation—namely the obligation of payment for our sin. Christ's work means that God promises to erase our sin from our record (Isaiah 43:25), to not count our sin against us (Romans 4:8), to not remember our sins any more (Hebrews 10:17), and to cleanse our conscience so that we may walk in newness of life (Hebrews 9:14; 10:22).

We experience redemption and forgiveness through the "riches" (Gk. *ploutos*, **PLOO-tos**) of God's grace. *Ploutos* can mean a literal abundance of wealth; here the emphasis is on the fullness of the blessing experienced by believers in Christ.

8 Wherein he hath abounded toward us in all wisdom and prudence;

God has "abounded" or "lavished" (Gk. *perisseuo*, **per-is-SYOO-o**) the blessings of salvation upon us. In this context, *perisseuo* means "to make extremely rich." His generosity is so great that it might cause us to question the soundness of His judgment. However, Paul uses two overlapping terms to clarify that the lavishing is deliberate and based on sound judgment. "Wisdom" (Gk. *sophia*, **sof-EE-ah**) is "the capacity to understand and function accordingly." "Prudence" (Gk. *phronesis*, **FRON-ay-sis**) is "intelligence" or "the ability to understand."

9 Having made known unto us the mystery of his will, according to his good pleasure which he hath purposed in himself:

The verb "having made known" (Gk. *gnorizo*, **gno-RID-zo**) means "to reveal" and may indicate either the time or means of God's lavishing in verse 8. Alternate translations include: "when he revealed to us" or "by revealing to us." What God revealed was the "mystery" (Gk. *musterion*, **moos-TAY-ree-on**) of His will. A biblical mystery is a secret that God has not previously disclosed. According to Ephesians 3:3–6, the mystery of the Gospel is that the Gentiles are now fellow heirs of the Gospel. However, Paul elsewhere uses the term "mystery" to refer to other aspects of the Gospel message that were somewhat hidden until Christ revealed them, such as the crucifixion of the incarnate Son of God (1 Corinthians 2:7). The exact nature of the mystery, however, is not necessarily the point of this passage. The point is that God has entrusted the message of His plan for the redemption of mankind with the church. We are responsible to steward that message by faithfully preserving it, guarding it from corruption, and sharing it with those who need to hear it.

The revelation of the mystery of God's will happened according to His good pleasure. The Greek word for "good pleasure" (*eudokia*, **yoo-dok-EE-ah**) was also used in verse 5 to describe the way God adopted us as His children. The word "purposed" (Gk. *protithemai*, **prot-ITH-em-ahee**) means "to set before oneself, propose to oneself." The word is used figuratively here to mean "plan, purpose, or intend." Again we see that God's lavish blessing of His people in Christ, although motivated by passionate love, is deliberate and carefully planned.

10 That in the dispensation of the fulness of times he might gather together in one all things in Christ, both which are in heaven, and which are on earth; even in him:

God's plan, rooted in love and guided by wisdom, concerns more than the redemption of mankind. His goal is to change or renew the order of the entire created universe by manifesting the Lordship of Christ in a powerful and dramatic way.

The first word of this verse is the Greek participle *eis* (**ice**), which means "into, toward, to." The King James Version translates *eis* as "that." Other versions use "as," "unto," or "with a view toward." Regardless of the English word used to translate it, *eis* conveys a sense of purpose or destination. All of the events of history have been moving to a predetermined conclusion—one in which Christ is glorified as Lord and all things are subjected to Him.

"Dispensation" (Gk. *oikonomia*, **oy-kon-om-EE-ah**) means "management of a household; administration; arrangement." Here it refers to God's plan of salvation, which He is bringing to pass in the "fulness of times." As sovereign king of the universe, God did not simply set the events of history in motion, step back, and watch to see how things would play out. He is actively involved in bringing about His intended purpose for the world He created.

"Gather together in one" (Gk. *anakephalaiomai*, **an-ak-ef-al-AH-ee-om-ahee**) could also be translated "unite" or "sum up." It would be hard to understand the precise meaning of this word if not for the phrase "all things in Christ." God's purpose is for Christ to be revealed and exalted as Redeemer and Lord of the entire universe (Ephesians 1:22; Philippians 2:9–10; Revelation 5:9). "All things" includes all people, as well as everything that Christ created when He formed the universe (John 1:3; Colossians 1:16–17).

11 In whom also we have obtained an inheritance, being predestinated according to the purpose of him who worketh all things after the counsel of his own will:

"In whom" refers to Christ and continues the thought of verse 10 into verse 11. There is debate among scholars about how to translate the verb "have obtained an inheritance," (Gk. *kleroo*, **klay-RO-o**). The main question is whether the people of God have received an inheritance from God (cf. Colossians 1:12) or whether we have become God's possession or inheritance (cf. Deuteronomy 4:20; 9:29). Both ideas are consistent with the message of this passage and the rest of Scripture, although the first option fits most naturally with the flow of thought and mirrors Paul's use of a related word in Colossians 1:12. Another option is that Paul intentionally chose this word as a double entendre—a skillful transition to a focus on the glory that God will receive as a result of His work to redeem us.

The benefits of our status as God's heirs (or inheritance) are not the product of chance. Paul emphasizes the determining influence of God's sovereignty with a flourish of words that repeat themes from earlier in the passage and overlap in meaning. The word "predestinated" (Gk. *proorizo*, **pro-or-ID-zo**) is the same word used in verse 5 to describe God's loving act of foreordaining our adoption. "Purpose" (Gk. *prothesis*, **PROTH-es-is**) here refers to a plan or something that has been resolved. "Counsel" (Gk. *boule*, **boo-LAY**) means "plan, purpose, resolution, or decision." "Will" (Gk. *thelema*, **THEL-ay-mah**) has already been used in verses 5 and 9.

12 That we should be to the praise of his glory, who first trusted in Christ.

The "we" of this verse is complemented by the "you" of verse 13—both of which groups are clearly composed of believers in Jesus. The "praise of his glory" is, of course, the appropriate response to God's saving grace (cf. v. 6). The question, then, is which believers are the "we"? There are really only two options: They are Jews who looked forward in faith to the coming of the Messiah, or they are Paul, the other apostles, and their associates. The first option is helped by the word "first trusted" (Gk. *proelpizo*, **pro-el-PID-zo**), which has the possible meaning of "hoped beforehand." In the context of the previous three verses, this kind of comment makes sense. God chose and called the people of Israel to believe in the coming Messiah, but revealed the salvation that He would bring through signs and symbols, such as the temple worship and the Levitical priesthood. His purpose was not to restrict salvation to the Jewish people, but to make them a light for the nations of the world so that many would experience His salvation (Isaiah 49:6).

13 In whom ye also trusted, after that ye heard the word of truth, the gospel of your salvation: in whom also after that ye believed, ye were sealed with that holy Spirit of promise,

The verb translated "trusted" and "believed" (Gk. *pisteuo,* **pist-YOO-o**) actually only appears once in the verse. "Trusted" is supplied by the translators to make the thought of the verse clearer.

At this point in the passage, Paul continues to point out the priceless benefits of the Gospel but with special emphasis on the fact that Jews (the "we" of v. 12) and Gentiles ("ye") have shared equally in those benefits. Experience of salvation comes from hearing the word of truth not from being born or being circumcised as a Jew.

The phrase "the gospel of your salvation" brings to mind Romans 1:16, which states that the Gospel is the power of God, which saves everyone who believes—both Jews and Gentiles. The Gentiles, having believed, also experienced the baptism of the Holy Spirit. "Holy Spirit of promise" is best understood as "the promised Holy Spirit." Elsewhere in the New Testament, Paul and the apostles refer to the baptism of the Spirit as the fulfillment of both Old Testament prophecy (Joel 2:28) and the promise of Jesus (Luke 24:49). The fact that Gentiles experienced the same baptism as Jews did on the Day of Pentecost was something that many Jewish Christians found extraordinary. It served as incontrovertible evidence that Gentiles could be saved by faith in Jesus, without first becoming Jews (Acts 10:44–46; 11:15–18).

"Sealed" (Gk. *sphragizo,* **sfrag-ID-zo**) means "to mark for the purpose of identification or indicating ownership." Sealing also carries with it a sense of certification—a guarantee of authenticity. The experience of Spirit baptism is, therefore, not a "second blessing" that believers must seek after their conversion but, as suggested by 1 Corinthians 12:13, is a confirmation that Christ has indeed saved us through faith, and a "down payment" toward the full benefits Christ has purchased for us.

14 Which is the earnest of our inheritance until the redemption of the purchased possession, unto the praise of his glory.

An "earnest" (Gk. *arrhabon,* **ar-hrab-OHN**) is a "first installment, deposit or down payment." "Our" now refers again to all of God's people—Jews and Gentiles. We normally think of an "inheritance" (Gk. *kleronomia,* **klay-ron-om-EE-ah**) as property that changes hands at death. Even though God cannot die, the New Testament frequently uses this word to refer to the possessions promised by God to His children for their rightful enjoyment. The emphasis, therefore, is on God's incredible love for His children—that He longs to lavish everything He owns on them.

"Redemption" is the same word used in verse 5 to describe salvation as an act in which God buys people back from sin and death. The "purchased possession," therefore, is the people of God. While the modern reader might be offended by the notion of being bought, and thought of as a mere possession, the authors of Scripture considered this a high privilege. The people of Israel were God's "peculiar treasure" or "treasured possession" (Exodus 19:5). To be God's special possession is to be "a kingdom of priests, a holy nation"—endowed with special privileges and responsibilities.

Sources:

Marshall, I. Howard. *Acts. Tyndale New Testament Commentaries.* Grand Rapids, Mich.: InterVarsity Press, 1980.

Vine, W.E. *Vines Complete Expository Dictionary of Old and New Testament Words.* Edited by Merrill F. Unger and William White Jr. Nashville: Thomas Nelson Publishers, 1996.

Daily Bible Readings

M: A Priestly Kingdom
Exodus 19:1–8
T: An Inheritance Promised
Galatians 3:15–18
W: Children of God Through Faith
Galatians 3:23–29
T: Adoption as God's Children
Galatians 4:1–7
F: Inheriting Eternal Life
Matthew 19:23–30
S: Guided by the Spirit
Galatians 5:16–25
S: God's Own People
Ephesians 1:3–14

TEACHING TIPS

May 10

Bible Study Guide 11

1. Words You Should Know

A. Flesh (Ephesians 2:3) *sarx* (Gk.)—Denotes human nature that has been universally corrupted by sin.

B. Saved (vv. 5, 8) *sozo* (Gk.)—To deliver.

C. Workmanship (v. 10) *poiema* (Gk.)—God's "work of art" or "masterpiece."

2. Teacher Preparation

Unifying Principle—Receiving Benefits. Before we invest our time, our money, or ourselves, we want to be certain that our outlay will repay us well. How do we know that a potential investment will yield a good return? Both Paul and John claim that when we, by faith, invest our lives in Christ, we receive new life—the unparalleled benefit of God's love.

A. Pray for your students.

B. Be prepared to share your own testimony of salvation.

C. Study the Focal Verses in another translation.

D. Complete lesson 11 in the *Precepts For Living® Personal Study Guide.*

3. Starting the Lesson

A. Start the class with prayer.

B. Write the AIM for Change on the board, and ask the class to read it aloud with you.

C. Share your own testimony of salvation and how it brought you new life in Christ.

4. Getting into the Lesson

A. Ask for a volunteer to summarize the Focal Verses.

B. Read The People, Places, and Times section. Discuss briefly.

C. Summarize the In Depth section.

5. Relating the Lesson to Life

A. Ask for a volunteer to read the In Focus and/or Lesson in Our Society. Invite discussion.

B. If possible, divide the class into small groups. Assign each group one question from the Discuss the Meaning section. Provide a few minutes for the groups to discuss their question, and then ask one person from each group to summarize the question and answer to the rest of the class.

6. Arousing Action

A. Provide a few minutes of silence for the students to complete the Follow the Spirit section. Ask for volunteers to share their answers.

B. Close in prayer, using the content of the Make It Happen section as the basis for your prayer.

Worship Guide

For the Superintendent or Teacher
Theme: New Life in Christ
Theme Song: "Redeemed"
Devotional Reading: Psalm 86:1–13
Prayer

NEW LIFE IN CHRIST

Bible Background • EPHESIANS 2:1–10
Printed Text • EPHESIANS 2:1–10 Devotional Reading • PSALM 86:1–13

AIM for Change

By the end of the lesson, we will:
EXPLORE what it means to be saved by God's grace;
REFLECT on how we should respond to salvation by grace; and
COMMIT to living a life of good works that reflects appreciation for God's free salvation.

Keep in Mind

"For by grace are ye saved through faith; and that not of yourselves: it is the gift of God" (Ephesians 2:8).

Focal Verses

KJV

Ephesians 2:1 And you hath he quickened, who were dead in trespasses and sins;

2 Wherein in time past ye walked according to the course of this world, according to the prince of the power of the air, the spirit that now worketh in the children of disobedience:

3 Among whom also we all had our conversation in times past in the lusts of our flesh, fulfilling the desires of the flesh and of the mind; and were by nature the children of wrath, even as others.

4 But God, who is rich in mercy, for his great love wherewith he loved us,

5 Even when we were dead in sins, hath quickened us together with Christ, (by grace ye are saved;)

6 And hath raised us up together, and made us sit together in heavenly places in Christ Jesus:

7 That in the ages to come he might shew the exceeding riches of his grace in his kindness toward us through Christ Jesus.

8 For by grace are ye saved through faith; and that not of yourselves: it is the gift of God:

9 Not of works, lest any man should boast.

10 For we are his workmanship, created in Christ Jesus unto good works, which God hath before ordained that we should walk in them.

NLT

Ephesians 2:1 Once you were dead because of your disobedience and your many sins.

2 You used to live in sin, just like the rest of the world, obeying the devil—the commander of the powers in the unseen world. He is the spirit at work in the hearts of those who refuse to obey God.

3 All of us used to live that way, following the passionate desires and inclinations of our sinful nature. By our very nature we were subject to God's anger, just like everyone else.

4 But God is so rich in mercy, and he loved us so much,

5 that even though we were dead because of our sins, he gave us life when he raised Christ from the dead. (It is only by God's grace that you have been saved!)

6 For he raised us from the dead along with Christ and seated us with him in the heavenly realms because we are united with Christ Jesus.

7 So God can point to us in all future ages as examples of the incredible wealth of his grace and kindness toward us, as shown in all he has done for us who are united with Christ Jesus.

8 God saved you by his grace when you believed. And you can't take credit for this; it is a gift from God.

9 Salvation is not a reward for the good things we have done, so none of us can boast about it.

10 For we are God's masterpiece. He has created us anew in Christ Jesus, so we can do the good things he planned for us long ago.

In Focus

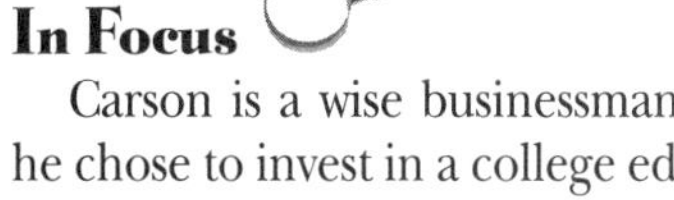

Carson is a wise businessman. As a young man, he chose to invest in a college education when most of his friends were partying. As an adult, he grew his business from the ground up. He is cautious about making new investments, considering every possible angle, then making his decisions carefully.

Recently, Carson's neighbor Rick presented Carson with the idea of investing his life in the kingdom of God. Becoming a Christian was not a new idea to Carson, but the idea of "investing" his life had not crossed his mind. Carson knew that commitment to Christ would be a costly, lifelong commitment. Was it worth it? What could he expect to gain in return? Was the Christian life really all it was cracked up to be? For days, he weighed the options.

Finally, Carson turned to the Bible that Rick had given him. Carson opened it and read God's plan for his life. God's plan offered so much more than Carson had been able to provide for himself. His excitement grew as he realized that faith in Jesus Christ is rewarded by salvation, eternal life, peace, and hope. Carson's decision was made.

When we invest our lives in Christ, we are making the decision of a lifetime. We choose to invest ourselves in God's kingdom, and, in return, we receive a brand-new life. What a deal!

The People, Places, and Times

Transgressions and Sins. "Transgressions and sins" (Ephesians 2:1, NIV) are the lot of the nonbeliever. The word "transgressions" (Gk. *paraptoma*, **par-AP-to-mah**) carries with it the connotation of stumbling into sin. All people, as descendants of Adam, are prone to sinful behavior.

On the other hand, in the context of Ephesians, "sin" means "sin as a habit" or "sin as a power." This word therefore refers more to the sinful thoughts, desires, and purposes of the human heart than to just the natural inclination to sin.

Source:

Arrington, French L., and Roger Stronstad, eds. *Life in the Spirit New Testament Commentary.* Grand Rapids, Mich.: Zondervan, 1999.

Background

In Ephesians 1, Paul praised God for His glorious plan of redemption. He explained that, through God's son, we can receive the inheritance of eternal life sealed by God the Holy Spirit. Then at the end of chapter 1, Paul prays for believers that they would want to know God more and that their spiritual eyes would be open to understanding more fully the plan of salvation and their relationship with God and His family, the church.

Now in Ephesians 2, Paul expounds further on the results of redemption and adoption into God's family. He shows us that when we, by faith, invest our lives in Christ, we receive new life—the unparalleled benefit of God's love.

Source:

Arrington, French L., and Roger Stronstad, eds. *Life in the Spirit New Testament Commentary.* Grand Rapids, Mich.: Zondervan, 1999.

At-A-Glance

1. Dead in Sin (Ephesians 2:1–3)
2. Alive in Christ (vv. 4–7)
3. Created by God (vv. 8–10)

In Depth

1. Dead in Sin (Ephesians 2:1–3)

The apostle Paul begins this chapter by describing the terrible plight of sinners. First, Paul says, we need to understand that without Christ we are spiritually dead in our sinful lifestyle, hopeless, and desperate. To be "spiritually dead" means to be separated from God by our sin.

Secondly, when we are without Christ, we follow "the ways of this world" (v. 2, NIV). To "follow the ways of the world" means to live our lives in accordance with the sinful world around us, instead of following God's ways.

Thirdly, those who do not accept salvation are under the influence of the "prince of the power of the air, the spirit that now worketh in the children of disobedience" (v. 2). This, of course, refers to Satan. Though Satan's power is limited, those who choose not to become God's children are influenced by Satan for evil purposes.

Fourthly, humans have a bent toward selfishness and fulfilling their own desires (v. 3). Without God's saving grace, our human nature is constantly tainted by sin. This sinful human nature will inevitably indulge in sinful acts to fulfill its own desires and lusts.

Lastly, before we come to Christ, we are "by nature the children of wrath" (v. 3). Does this mean that God was angry with us from the moment we were born? No. It means that because every human has a sin nature, we have all sinned (Romans 5:12). God cannot tolerate sin and must pass judgment.

Without Christ, there is no hope for sinful humanity. We are doomed and desperate. We need a Redeemer.

2. Alive in Christ (vv. 4–7)

In these next verses, the redeeming power of God is in strong contrast to the miserable plight of sinful humanity in verses 1–3. In verses 4–7, Paul describes in detail the process and results of redemption. Why would God provide such a wonderful salvation for us? Paul tells us it's because of God's mercy and love (v. 4), His grace (vv. 5, 8), and His kindness (v. 7).

Verse 4 tells us that even while we were still in sin, God loved us. Our redemption is solely His doing. There is no room for us to exalt ourselves or to speak with pride because we have no power or ability to change our plight from death to life. Neither do we deserve to be saved from our sin.

Thank God that He is "rich" in mercy. The awesome, omnipotent God of the universe is full of undeserved mercy toward us—even before we know or acknowledge Him. Then by His grace, He saves us! This grace is a gift from God. Every believer is a sinner and we have all been saved by grace. "Grace" is undeserved favor, which God pours out on us when we come to Him by faith.

When we are saved by grace, we are born again spiritually. We come alive in Christ Jesus, and our life is then lived in Him by the power of the Holy Spirit. We are raised up with Christ Jesus and seated with Him in the "heavenly places" (v. 6). In other words, our focus is no longer on things of this world, but on things of God. We are not taken out of this world, but we now have a new perspective. This verse also tells us of our position in Christ. We are "seated" with Him, meaning that we now have the rights, privileges, and authority that come with being a child of God.

Ultimately, everything about our salvation brings glory to God. Verse 7 tells us that because of God's kindness to us, through Jesus, people throughout the ages will see and know of God's grace, goodness, and salvation to those who will accept His offer.

3. Created by God (vv. 8–10)

Verses 8–10 are the core of the message of grace. Verse 8 sums up the plan of salvation: God saves us, by His grace, when we exercise our faith. This salvation is nothing we can accomplish on our own, but it is a gift from God.

When we are saved, we are God's new creation—His "workmanship," verse 10 says. "Workmanship" means "work of art" or "masterpiece." Isn't it an amazing thought that God transforms us into a new work of art, so to speak? He changes us into the image of His beloved Son, Jesus Christ, who suffered that we might receive this great gift.

Although we can never do enough good deeds to obtain salvation on our own, God did design us for good works. Just as we were predestined to be adopted into the family of God (Ephesians 1:4), we are predestined to do good works and should "walk in them" (v. 10). When we become a new creature in Christ, we start on the journey of walking out our faith. We don't just believe that we are saved; we learn how to live our new life as God's child. We are empowered by the Holy Spirit to do good works for the glory of God.

These good works should flow out of our relationship with Christ Jesus as a testimony of our new life in Him. Living a life of good works also reflects appreciation for God's free gift of salvation and should be a hallmark of every believer.

Sources:

Arrington, French L., and Roger Stronstad, eds. *Life in the Spirit New Testament Commentary*. Grand Rapids, Mich.: Zondervan, 1999.

Henry, Matthew. *Matthew Henry's Commentary in One Volume*. Grand Rapids, Mich.: Zondervan, 1961.

Search the Scriptures

1. Before coming to Christ, we were dead in what (Ephesians 2:1)?

2. What are some characteristics of a life apart from Christ (vv. 2–3)?

3. Why did God "raise us up" from the dead (vv. 6–7)?

4. In verse 8, how is salvation described (v. 8)?

Discuss the Meaning

1. What does it mean to be spiritually dead? List some of the consequences or difficulties of living life apart from God.

2. What is redemption? Why did God choose to offer redemption to us?

3. How do we become "alive in Christ"? Contrast being "alive in Christ" with being "dead in sin."

4. What role do good deeds play in our salvation and our life as a "new creature" in Christ Jesus? What should be our motivation for good deeds?

5. When we, by faith, invest our lives in Christ, what do we receive in return? What are some immediate benefits of becoming part of God's family?

Lesson in Our Society

"I'm a good person. God wouldn't send me to hell." This reasoning is prevalent in our world today. Unfortunately, this reasoning is wrong. No matter how many good works a person does, their sin will always separate them from God. No matter how hard they try, they will always be trapped. Without God, there is no hope of escape from the death sentence of sin.

Fortunately, God has a plan to take care of sin. He offers to save us from our sin. Salvation means much more than just forgiveness. Salvation means deliverance—deliverance from our own destructive ways, deliverance from the ways of the world, the oppression of Satan, and the wrath of God.

Salvation is the whole of our new life in Christ Jesus. Salvation encompasses the past: forgiveness of sin, bought by the blood of Jesus. Salvation encompasses the present: our life of faith in and relationship to Christ Jesus. Salvation encompasses the future: the promise of eternal life through Christ Jesus. It is both our obligation and joy to share this message with others. New life is the benefit of accepting God's love.

Make It Happen

This week, ask God to renew your wonder, excitement, and appreciation for His great gift of salvation and eternal life. Ask Him to show you how you can effectively communicate this good news to unbelievers by living out a life of good works.

Follow the Spirit

What God wants me to do:

____

____

Remember Your Thoughts

Special insights I have learned:

____

____

More Light on the Text

Ephesians 2:1–10

1 And you hath he quickened, who were dead in trespasses and sins;

Verse one begins a three-verse sentence and lacks a predicate verb in the Greek. The verb "hath he quickened" is supplied by the translators of the King James Version (it occurs in the Greek in verse five) to make the sentence easier to understand.

"And you being dead" is a literal rendering of the first four Greek words. The participle "being" is in a tense that communicates an ongoing condition. Spiritual death is the condition in which we are alienated from God, the source of all life (Ephesians 4:18). It is also the condition in which we are destined for eternal death and condemnation (Romans 6:21).

By using an extreme word like "dead," the author emphasizes the helpless condition of nonbelievers. A dead man can do nothing for himself. He needs a miracle—divine intervention—in order to live again. And that is what God has done for us.

"Trespasses" (Gk. *paraptoma*, **par-AP-to-mah**) are lapses or deviations from what has been revealed as the right way of living. "Sins" (Gk. *hamartia*, **ham-ar-TEE-ah**) are acts in which we "miss the mark"—as an archer sometimes misses the target for which he aims. These terms overlap and reinforce each other, not to expand our understanding of the technical distinction between different kinds of wrongdoing but to show us the magnitude of the problem of sin. Sin is a poison that is 100 percent fatal to the human soul. Every descendant of Adam is born infected. Thus, every unsaved person alive today is a "dead man walking."

2 Wherein in time past ye walked according to the course of this world, according to the prince of the power of the air, the spirit that now worketh in the children of disobedience:

"Wherein" is translated "in which" by modern translations. Grammatically, it refers only to the "sins" from verse 1. However, according to the logic of the passage, it also refers to the "trespasses."

Paul now uses an imagery that is familiar to the student of the Scriptures: Life is a journey. Every person must travel in one of two directions. Either we walk the broad, easy path that leads to destruction or the difficult, narrow path that leads to life (Matthew 7:13–14). In the Greek, the "course of this world" is literally "the age of this world." "Age" (Gk. *aion*, **ahee-OHN**) normally refers to a period of time, and it retains that meaning here. Before our conversion, we lived—not for eternity, but for temporary pleasure—the same way everyone else lives their life. We were corrupted by the false beliefs and debased values that permeate this world.

"The prince of the power of the air" is a clear reference to Satan, whom the Bible teaches is real, powerful, and actively trying to subvert God's purposes in this world. The ancients thought of the "air" as the space between the earth and the moon; the Greeks used this term (*aer,* **ah-AYR**) to refer to the lower, impure air where spirits live. Paul, while not endorsing this pagan view of the spirit world, uses the terminology of the day to make the point that Satan wrongly claims the right to exercise his will in the physical universe. Paul later refers to Satan and his spiritual allies as "the rulers...the authorities...the powers of this dark world...the spiritual forces of evil in the heavenly realms" (Ephesians 6:12, NIV). During his ministry on Earth, Jesus referred to Satan as "the prince of this world" (John 12:31; 14:30; 16:11). This does not mean that there is anything evil about the created world or any part of it—such as the air—but that the physical universe is the domain in which Satan's efforts are focused.

Satan's goal is to mislead and dominate people by keeping them from believing the truth of the Gospel. His tactics are the same today as they were in the Garden of Eden—by disobeying his Creator, he tempts humanity to be a god unto himself (Genesis 3:4–5). The children of God are characterized by obedience to God's will (1 Peter 1:14). Those who disobey, however, reveal themselves to be children of the Devil (Matthew 13:38; 1 John 3:10); thus, they are called "children of disobedience."

3 Among whom also we all had our conversation in times past in the lusts of our flesh, fulfilling the desires of the flesh and of the mind; and were by nature the children of wrath, even as others.

In Greek, the phrase "among whom" is nearly identical to the phrase "in which" from verse two, which draws our attention to the way the two verses complement each other. Verse two describes our former life characterized by sinful actions; verse three points out our former alliance with sinful people.

Paul is describing a situation in which we were not only surrounded by sinful people, but we were influenced by them and did the same things. "Had our conversation" (Gk. *anastrepho,* **an-as-TREF-o**) is a verb used metaphorically to mean "conduct or behave oneself." "Lusts" (Gk. *epithumia,* **ep-ee-thoo-MEE-ah**) simply means "desires." The desires that dominated us were "of the flesh." The "flesh" (Gk. *sarx,* **sarx**), in Pauline writings, is the sinful nature that continues to think, speak, and act out of depravity (cf. Galatians 5:19–21). Christians are called to put this nature within them to death by living in the power of the Holy Spirit (Romans 8:13).

"Fulfilling the desires of the flesh and of the mind" intensifies the thought of the previous clause. A more literal translation of the Greek would read "doing the will of the flesh and of the mind." Apart from Christ, sin not only influenced us, but it dominated our entire being. The picture Paul paints is not one in which we chose to repeatedly sin out of a free will, but one in which we were bound involuntarily to sin and driven compulsively by it.

A tragic destiny awaits those whose lives are held captive by sinful desire. "Children of wrath" speaks to an eternal destiny full of God's just punishment for our rebellion. "Wrath" (Gk. *orge,* **or-GAY**) is anger or indignation. In the Bible, it is used to mean "judgment" or "punishment."

4 But God, who is rich in mercy, for his great love wherewith he loved us,

The conjunction "but" introduces a stark contrast. Out of the picture of gloom and despair comes hope and light. God has seen the plight of His people and purposed to do something to deliver them. "Rich" (Gk. *plousios,* **PLOO-see-os**) tells us that He has an abundant supply of what we need. "Mercy" (Gk. *eleos,* **EL-eh-os**) is God's compassion and pity for us in our helpless condition.

"For" is translated "because of" in other English versions and helps the modern reader to see Paul's line of reasoning a little bit more clearly. The reason God gives us, for His merciful act of deliverance, is His love (affection) for His people. The author intensifies the description of this love with repetition by saying, in essence, that God "loved us with love."

5 Even when we were dead in sins, hath quickened us together with Christ, (by grace ye are saved;)

God's love is magnified when we understand that, after we were already dead in sin, He had mercy on us. The phrase "dead in sins" uses the exact same Greek words as verse one. We might ask how this could be, since God sent Christ to die for our sins long before our lifetimes—and probably before the lifetimes of many of the Ephesians, who originally read this letter. Plus, chapter one talks about the blessings of salvation as having been arranged "before the foundation of the world" (Ephesians 1:4). Before we or our first parents had even taken their first breath, how could we have been "dead in sin"? The only possible explanation is that God, being sovereign over all the affairs of man, knew that Adam and Eve would sin and planned to create them with the purpose of redeeming them. Titus 1:2 confirms that "before the world began," God promised eternal life. The way that God saved us was by uniting us spiritually to Christ. "Quickened together with" (Gk. *suzoopoieo*, **sood-zo-op-oy-EH-o**) is a phrase formed by adding the preposition "with" to the verb "made alive." It is the first of three consecutive "together with" verbs. Since the next verb speaks to our resurrection, this word seems to refer mainly to the new condition of spiritual life—the opposite of the spiritual death described earlier in the passage—we currently experience in Christ. Since Christ was born and lived without sin, we have this spiritual life when we share in Christ's life. He is our source of spiritual vitality.

Paul interjects a parenthetical comment in the midst of his comments about what we gain through our union with Christ, to remind us that salvation is a miraculous, generous work of God. Everything we have in Christ is through grace. In this context, we see that God's grace overcomes our inability to save ourselves. Dead in sin, we need a rescuer—and God has come to our aid.

Although grace is normally used in the New Testament in reference to God's good gifts to undeserving sinners, "grace" and "mercy" overlap in their meaning (cf. 2:4). On the other hand, mercy is used more generally in reference to God's kindness.

"Ye are saved" (Gk. *sozo*, **SODE-zo**) is in the perfect tense, which denotes a past action with continuing consequences—"Ye have been saved" would be a more literal translation. We experience our salvation in the present, but it is rooted in God's real-life intervention in time and eternity past. *Sozo* has a range of possible meanings, all of which illuminate our understanding of what God has done for us in Christ: rescue, liberate, keep from harm, heal, preserve.

6 And hath raised us up together, and made us sit together in heavenly places in Christ Jesus:

This verse strongly echoes 1:20, which uses nearly the exact same words to tell us that God raised Jesus from the dead and set Him at His right hand in the heavenly places. The similarity of both theme and vocabulary is a powerful reinforcement of the "in Christ" motif. What God did for all His children, He did first in Christ. We experience our salvation, through faith, by becoming partakers in Christ's experience.

Specifically, those who are in Christ are promised that, if we die before Jesus returns, we will rise from the grave to eternal life and perfect blessedness (John 5:28–29; 6:39–40; Romans 8:11). "Raised up together" (*sunegeiro*, **soon-eg-I-ro**) is a compound word made out of the verb "to raise" and the preposition "with." Other New Testament passages speak of the resurrection of the dead with the verb "to raise." By using "raised with," Paul is emphasizing the fact that our resurrection is a sharing with Christ in His resurrection. Paul even goes so far as to say in 1 Corinthians 15:14, that "if Christ has not been raised, our preaching is vain, and your faith is also vain." If Jesus had remained in the grave, we would have no hope of life after death. This is why Paul speaks of our resurrection, even though it is future, as a past event. Because we can look back in history at the foundational event, we have the assurance that our resurrection is a certainty. Christ is the "firstfruits" from the grave (1 Corinthians 15:20, 23).

The promises of life and resurrection are not all that we receive in our union with Christ. We also receive the promise of great privilege and responsibility. "Made us sit together with" (Gk. *sugkathizo*, **soong-kath-ID-zo**) is the final "together with" verb of the sentence. A compound of "with" and "sit down," the verb, can mean "to sit down with" or "to cause to sit down with." Since the subject of the sentence is God and we are the objects of His action, the latter is the obvious meaning here.

The "sitting down" together with Christ is a direct reference to Jesus' promise. He promised that His true followers will be seated with Him on thrones as rulers in the eternal kingdom of God (Luke 22:29–30; Revelation 3:20–21). "Heavenly places" (Gk. *epouranios*, **ep-oo-RAN-ee-os**) is the same phrase used in 1:3, 1:20, and 3:10 to designate the spiritual realm in which God has blessed His children, in which Christ is currently seated, and in which we encounter Satan and other spiritual opponents of God's plan of redemption.

Since "with Christ," in verse five, already made it perfectly clear who we are joined "together with" in these different aspects of our salvation, "in Christ" is repetitive and emphatic. Paul is consumed by his enthusiasm for what Jesus has done for us—so enthusiastic that he is willing to express himself in a way that comes across as less sophisticated in both Greek and English.

7 That in the ages to come he might shew the exceeding riches of his grace in his kindness toward us through Christ Jesus.

Now we come to see the reason for God's merciful acts described in verses five and six: for all of eternity, God wants to lavish His kindness on His children. An "age" (Gk. *aion*, **ahee-OHN**) is an era, duration, or period of time in God's plan of redemption. Paul is not here instructing us on the precise number or order of the "ages". This is evident when we consider that in 1:21, he speaks of the present "age" and one (singular) "age to come." Rather, the author is speaking of eternity as the endless future era, which will begin when Christ returns.

The "riches of his grace" describes the means by which God could afford to do all that He has done for His people. The fact that He plans to continue to show us His riches, for all of eternity, reminds us that God is infinitely wealthy—not just in terms of material wealth and spiritual power. The love He shows to His people is also never-ending (Psalm 103:17).

8 For by grace are ye saved through faith; and that not of yourselves: it is the gift of God: 9 Not of works, lest any man should boast.

Having focused on how our salvation ends in grace, Paul reminds us of the point he made in his verse five interjection: Our salvation also begins and continues in grace. In verse five, the exact same statement helped us to see that grace miraculously accomplishes our salvation, in spite of our spiritually dead condition. Here we see that grace generously gives us what we do not deserve.

The words "through faith" do not appear in verse five. "Faith" (Gk. *pistis*, **PIS-tis**) is belief or conviction. True saving faith is that which trusts or relies on what God has done for our salvation. Paul uses the term "works" (Gk. *ergon*, **ER-gon**) to mean "obedience to God's law." Salvation, through works, then, is the opposite of salvation through faith. Faith relies on Christ's perfect obedience to the law of God. Faith trusts that Christ's sacrifice completely paid for our sin and that His perfect righteousness is fully credited to our account. But those who rely on their own works hope that their obedience earns them God's favor.

This is why salvation is a gift. If it were something that we could earn or demand, it would be a right—a "wage" or a "debt" in the terms of Romans 4:4–5. Moreover, salvation is a gift in the fullest sense—unrequested, unexpected, and undeserved. The only way in which the recipient of a gift is involved in the giving process is in his receipt or rejection of the gift and his expression of either gratitude or contempt toward the giver.

Another aspect of this gift becomes clear when we consider the demonstrative pronoun "that." In the English it seems to refer most naturally to "faith," which means faith would be the gift of God. However, in the Greek this is highly unlikely because "faith" is a feminine noun and "that" appears in the neuter. "Grace" is even more unlikely to be the referent because it is also a feminine noun and the logic of the passage makes it clear that God is the source of grace. The verb construction "are ye saved" is proposed as a referent by some commentators, but this would require a masculine pronoun "that," not a neuter. The best understanding of the passage is to see "that" as referring to the entire preceding passage from verses four through eight, but with special emphasis on the first part of verse eight: "by grace are ye saved through faith." The gift of God, therefore, includes the work of Christ on our behalf as well as the faith necessary to receive that work. God, not man, is the source of everything that is necessary for salvation to be accomplished (1 Corinthians 1:30).

Taken seriously, this knowledge challenges our understanding of what it means to be free moral agents. It contradicts the widespread assumption that each of us has the ability to do whatever we want—including the ability to choose to receive Christ as Savior. However, if we redefine the concept of "free will" as "the ability to choose to serve God" we realize the Scriptures explicitly teach that, since the fall of man in Genesis 3, human will is not free. To summarize Romans 6:17–22, apart from Christ, we are slaves to sin and able to bear only fruit that leads to death. But God has set us free from sin so that, in Christ, we are slaves to righteousness—free to bear fruit that leads to eternal life.

More than challenging our understanding, this passage challenges our pride. We would like to think that even if we can't take credit for earning our salvation, at least we can take credit for trusting in Christ to save us. When we understand the Gospel, though, we see that there are no grounds for anyone to boast. To "boast" (Gk. *kauchaomai*, **kow-KHAH-om-ahee**) means "to glory in or on account of something." Many Jews of Paul's day boasted that their faithful obedience to the law of the Old Testament would earn them righteous standing before God. In fact, you can read Paul's list of the things he formerly boasted about in Philippians 3:4–6.

The problem with boasting is that it comes from thinking that we are the source of our own salvation. Such claims attempt to take glory away from God. The Scriptures clearly teach that God saves sinners for His own glory (Isaiah 42:6–8). The people of God are not to glory in themselves but in the One who has saved them (1 Corinthians 1:31; Galatians 6:14; Philippians 3:3).

10 For we are his workmanship, created in Christ Jesus unto good works, which God hath before ordained that we should walk in them.

This passage ends with a touch of irony. We are not saved by our works, but our salvation means that we are God's workmanship. "Workmanship" (Gk. *poiema*, **POY-ay-mah**) means "what is made, creation." Elsewhere in Scripture, God uses the metaphor of pottery to help us understand this concept. He is the master potter; we are the clay (Isaiah 64:8; Jeremiah 18:6). The only purpose for a potter to put a lump of clay on his wheel is to make something useful. In Genesis, God created man in His image in order to fill the earth with the reflection of His glory. The entry of sin into our world corrupted God's original creation but did not destroy it. In Christ, God is re-creating mankind. His purpose for saving us is to use each and every one of us for "good works"—the kind that we are unable to do without the empowering presence of the Holy Spirit.

Good works are not optional for Christians. The Scriptures teach us they are not just a calling but also an identifying mark of true faith. James 2:14–18 warns us that "faith, if it hath not works, is dead" The commands and laws of the Old and New Testaments can't save us, but they help us to tell good works from evil. Good works are those that flow from love for God and love for our fellow man (Matthew 22:37–40; Romans 13:8).

Good works are such an integral part of our new identity in Christ that God has "before ordained" them (Gk. *proetoimazo*, **pro-et-oy-MAD-zo**), meaning He has "prepared (them) beforehand." All that remains for us, then, is to "walk in them"—to follow the path He has laid out for us. The preparation of our good works includes such blessings as the perfect example of Christ, who we are called to imitate (Ephesians 5:2), the power of the Holy Spirit to live a holy life (2 Peter 1:3), the understanding of what God's will is for our life (Romans 12:2), the pouring out of God's own love into our hearts (Romans 5:5), and spiritual gifts that enable us to build up the body of Christ in unique and meaningful ways (1 Corinthians 12:7). Paul was so consumed with living the life the Lord had ordained for him that he said, "It is no longer I who live, but Christ lives in me" (Galatians 2:20).

Sources:

Henry, Matthew. *Matthew Henry's Complete Commentary on the Bible.* http://eword.gospelcom.net/comments/ezekiel/mh/ezekiel47.htm. Accessed February 20, 2008.

Vine, W.E. *Vines Complete Expository Dictionary of Old and New Testament Words.* Edited by Merrill F. Unger and William White Jr. Nashville: Thomas Nelson Publishers, 1996.

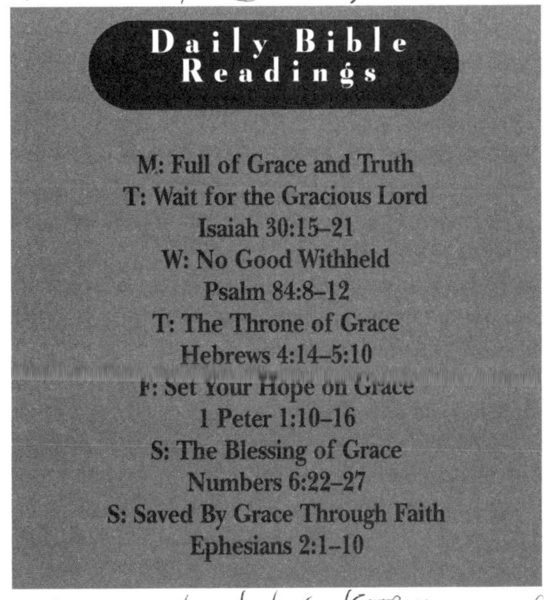

TEACHING TIPS

May 17
Bible Study Guide 12

1. Words You Should Know

A. Mystery (Ephesians 3:3) *musterion* (Gk.)—Hidden thing, secret, mystery.

B. Fellowheirs (v. 6) *sugkleronomos* (Gk.)—In Messianic usage, those who receive his allotted possession by right of sonship.

C. Boldness (v. 12) *parrhesia* (Gk.)—Freedom in speaking, unreservedness in speech, free and fearless confidence, cheerful courage, boldness, assurance.

2. Teacher Preparation

Unifying Principle—Come One and All. Mysteries pique interest because most people want to uncover "the rest of the story." What mysteries would you like to have uncovered? New Testament apostles believed that the revelation of Jesus unlocks mysteries concerning God's eternal and all-inclusive plan for salvation.

A. Review God's plan of salvation.

B. Study lesson 12 in its entirety in the *Precepts For Living® Commentary.*

C. Complete lesson 12 in the *Precepts For Living® Personal Study Guide.*

D. Pray and ask the Lord for insight while preparing to teach the lesson.

E. Ask God to renew your joy and wonder at the mystery of salvation, that you may communicate this attitude to your students.

3. Starting the Lesson

A. Begin the class with prayer, using the AIM for Change as a guide.

B. Ask for two volunteers—one to read the In Focus story and the other to read the Focal Verses from the *New Living Translation.*

C. Ask for several volunteers to share their Good News of salvation with the class.

4. Getting into the Lesson

A. Allow time for class to silently read the Focal Verses, Background section, and The People, Places, and Times. Provide an opportunity for questions.

B. Divide the class into two groups. Assign each group an In Depth section. Instruct the groups to read and discuss their section. Ask one individual from each group to summarize.

C. Bring the class back together, and ask for individual responses to the Discuss the Meaning section.

5. Relating the Lesson to Life

A. Read the Lesson in Our Society.

B. Ask the class to discuss specific ways to share the Good News of God's grace with others, both as a class and on an individual basis. Discuss.

6. Arousing Action

A. Challenge your students to choose one of the suggestions from the Relating the Lesson to Life activity, and put it into action this week.

B. Remind the students to read the Daily Bible Reading for next week.

C. Close in prayer, asking God to use the people in your class/church to share the joy of their salvation with others.

Worship Guide

For the Superintendent or Teacher
Theme: New Revelation in Christ
Theme Song: "Thank You, Lord (for saving my soul)"
Devotional Reading: Isaiah 40:1–11
Prayer

NEW REVELATION IN CHRIST

Bible Background • EPHESIANS 3:1–13

Printed Text • EPHESIANS 3:1–13 Devotional Reading • ISAIAH 40:1–11

AIM for Change

By the end of the lesson, we will:

REALIZE that salvation is for everyone;

REFLECT God's love for all people; and

SHARE the Good News of God's grace with the people around us.

Keep in Mind

"Unto me, who am less than the least of all saints, is this grace given, that I should preach among the Gentiles the unsearchable riches of Christ; And to make all men see what is the fellowship of the mystery, which from the beginning of the world hath been hid in God, who created all things" (Ephesians 3:8–9).

Focal Verses

KJV

Ephesians 3:1 For this cause I Paul, the prisoner of Jesus Christ for you Gentiles,

2 If ye have heard of the dispensation of the grace of God which is given me to you-ward:

3 How that by revelation he made known unto me the mystery; (as I wrote afore in few words,

4 Whereby, when ye read, ye may understand my knowledge in the mystery of Christ)

5 Which in other ages was not made known unto the sons of men, as it is now revealed unto his holy apostles and prophets by the Spirit;

6 That the Gentiles should be fellowheirs, and of the same body, and partakers of his promise in Christ by the gospel:

7 Whereof I was made a minister, according to the gift of the grace of God given unto me by the effectual working of his power.

8 Unto me, who am less than the least of all saints, is this grace given, that I should preach among the Gentiles the unsearchable riches of Christ;

9 And to make all men see what is the fellowship of the mystery, which from the beginning of the world hath been hid in God, who created all things by Jesus Christ:

10 To the intent that now unto the principalities and powers in heavenly places might be known by the church the manifold wisdom of God,

11 According to the eternal purpose which he purposed in Christ Jesus our Lord:

12 In whom we have boldness and access with confidence by the faith of him.

NLT

Ephesians 3:1 When I think of all this, I, Paul, a prisoner of Christ Jesus for the benefit of you Gentiles . . .

2 assuming, by the way, that you know God gave me the special responsibility of extending his grace to you Gentiles.

3 As I briefly wrote earlier, God himself revealed his mysterious plan to me.

4 As you read what I have written, you will understand my insight into this plan regarding Christ.

5 God did not reveal it to previous generations, but now by his Spirit he has revealed it to his holy apostles and prophets.

6 And this is God's plan: Both Gentiles and Jews who believe the Good News share equally in the riches inherited by God's children. Both are part of the same body, and both enjoy the promise of blessings because they belong to Christ Jesus.

7 By God's grace and mighty power, I have been given the privilege of serving him by spreading this Good News.

8 Though I am the least deserving of all God's people, he graciously gave me the privilege of telling the Gentiles about the endless treasures available to them in Christ.

9 I was chosen to explain to everyone this mysterious plan that God, the Creator of all things, had kept secret from the beginning.

10 God's purpose in all this was to use the church to display his wisdom in its rich variety to all the unseen rulers and authorities in the heavenly places.

13 Wherefore I desire that ye faint not at my tribulations for you, which is your glory.

11 This was his eternal plan, which he carried out through Christ Jesus our Lord.

12 Because of Christ and our faith in him, we can now come boldly and confidently into God's presence.

13 So please don't lose heart because of my trials here. I am suffering for you, so you should feel honored.

In Focus 

The phone rang. Clarissa stared at it, her mouth going dry. Was it the news she had been dreading ever since her biopsy last week?

She made herself pick up the receiver. "Hello?"

"Clarissa, it's Dr. Thompson."

He paused, and Clarissa's heart pounded wildly.

"I have good news," he said. "Your tests were fine—the cancer has not come back."

Clarissa started to laugh and cry at the same time. She thanked the doctor, then she danced out the door of her office. She ran up to the first person she saw in the hallway. "I don't have cancer!" she exclaimed. She ran further down the hall to find her boss. "I'm OK! The cancer has not come back!" she cried. She could not keep the good news to herself—she had to share it with someone else.

Believers have received the best news of all—God's grace. It is our mandate to share this glorious news of salvation with everyone around us. Don't hold it in!

The People, Places, and Times

Saul. Saul (known as Paul after his conversion to Christ) was a Jew—and not just an ordinary Jew. Saul was educated under Gamaliel, one of the foremost rabbis of the first century. Saul was a "Jew of Jews," meaning that he was highly educated in Jewish law and very devout. He followed Jewish law zealously and vigorously persecuted the followers of Christ (see Acts 22:1–4).

After Saul's dramatic conversion (and subsequent name change to Paul), God called him to minister specifically to the Gentiles (see Acts 22:14, 21). In that day, it was against Jewish law for a Jew to associate with a Gentile in any way (Acts 10:28). The Jews of that day were highly offended by Paul's association with Gentiles, especially since Paul taught that circumcision and other Jewish laws were not binding on the Gentiles. Paul's experience with a crowd of hostile Jews in Jerusalem nearly cost him his life and resulted in a four-year imprisonment at Caesarea and Rome. This imprisonment was a direct result of his ministry to the Gentiles. It is for this reason that Paul reminds the Gentiles, with no rancor, that he is a prisoner for their sake (Ephesians 3:1).

Sources:

Arrington, French L., and Roger Stronstad, eds. *Life in the Spirit New Testament Commentary.* Grand Rapids, Mich.: Zondervan, 1999.

Gill, John. *John Gill's Exposition of the Bible.* "Commentary on Ephesians 3:1." <http://bible.crosswalk.com/Commentaries/GillsExpositionoftheBible/gil.cgi?book=eph&chapter=003&verse=001>. 1999.

Background

A church consisting of both Jews and Gentiles united in their faith was a part of the new revelation given by God to the apostle Paul. It was also a difficult concept for the Jews to understand. According to Jewish law, a male Gentile desiring to become a member of God's chosen people must be circumcised. Both men and women wishing to become a part of the so-called "people of the covenant" were required to perform certain purification rituals. But Jesus Christ changed all the rules. Now, anyone and everyone could come to God through faith in Jesus. All people were on equal footing before God. This, Paul explains, is part of the "mystery"—salvation is for everyone.

Source:

Keener, Craig S. *The IVP Bible Background Commentary: New Testament.* Downers Grove, Ill.: InterVarsity Press, 1993.

At-A-Glance

1. The Mystery Revealed (Ephesians 3:1–6)
2. The Mystery Explained (vv. 7–13)

In Depth

1. The Mystery Revealed (Ephesians 3:1–6)

Paul begins Ephesians 3 by directly addressing the Gentiles. He reminds them of his imprisonment, and does not shy away from reminding them of their part in his situation. It is because of his ministry to them that he finds himself in prison. He goes on to remind them that God has given him special "grace" for the Gentiles. This means that Paul was charged by God to deliver the message of the Gospel to the Gentiles. Part of this commission was to reveal to them the "mystery" of God's plan. This mystery, outlined in verse 6, is that because of grace, Gentiles are full members of the body of Christ and "fellow heirs" with the Jews.

This mystery was the plan of God, revealed by God to Paul. Paul did not make up this doctrine on his own but received it directly as new revelation. Not only did Paul receive this new revelation but he was charged by God to make it known to others.

The core of the mystery is the "mystery of Christ" (v. 4), meaning that it is both because of Christ and through Christ that both Jews and Gentiles receive salvation. In Colossians 2:2, Christ himself is called the "mystery of God." It is through Christ that God's plan is revealed to mankind.

2. The Mystery Explained (vv. 7–13)

Because of God's commission upon his life, Paul became a minister of the Gospel of Jesus Christ (v. 7). Paul did not choose to become an apostle. God chose Paul and worked through him to accomplish His will. Paul goes on to explain that it wasn't because of special talent or any other personal merit that God chose him. In fact, Paul says, he was "less than the least" of all the saints. Paul, who had persecuted the followers of God, was now ministering God's grace to them.

God calls every believer to active service for Him. No matter our successes or failures, God has a job for every one of us. It doesn't matter to God what happened in the past. What matters is that we are obedient to His will today, just as Paul was obedient to the task God called him to.

God had given Paul the specific job of revealing and explaining the mystery that up until now had been kept as a secret from mankind. This mystery, Paul says, had been God's plan all along (v. 9), but was only now being revealed and explained. Now that it was the right time, God was pleased to show the wisdom of His age-old plan. How did God plan to accomplish this display of wisdom? The church was the perfect venue. When God united the Jews and Gentiles spiritually, His wisdom was made known to all, including the "principalities and powers in heavenly places" (v. 10)

Just as Paul served as the messenger of revelation to the Gentiles, the church serves as the messenger of revelation to the world at large, including the spirit world. Most evangelical scholars believe that the "principalities and powers" in verse 10 refer to both God's angels as well as Satan's demonic forces. It is a sobering thought that the church is "watched" by these spiritual entities, and that our unity (or lack thereof) is somehow involved in displaying God's omniscient wisdom.

When Jesus was still on Earth, He prayed that the church would be "brought to complete unity" (John 17:23, NIV) in love so that all would know that Jesus was sent by God, because of His great love. When believers live in self-sacrificing unity with each other, God's will is being accomplished. This is in accord with God's "eternal purpose" (Ephesians 3:11)—that Jesus will one day assume lordship over the entire universe (Ephesians 1:10). Because of our unity with each other and with Jesus Christ, the church has a prominent place in this eternal purpose.

When we became believers, we became participants in God's eternal purpose. We also received the right, through faith in Jesus, to approach God freely and "with confidence" (v. 12). The mystery has been revealed through Jesus Christ, and because of God's merciful love, the gift of salvation is offered to all.

Sources:

The NIV Study Bible, 10th Anniversary Edition. Grand Rapids, Mich.: Zondervan, 1995.

Arrington, French L., and Roger Stronstad, eds. *Life in the Spirit New Testament Commentary.* Grand Rapids, Mich.: Zondervan, 1999.

Search the Scriptures

1. What was given to Paul for the Gentiles (Ephesians 3:2)?

2. What is the "mystery" that Paul speaks of in Ephesians (v. 6)?

3. How does Paul describe himself (v. 8)?

4. What is God's intent for the church (v. 10)?

5. As believers, how should we approach God (v. 12)?

Discuss the Meaning

1. In verse 1, why did Paul describe himself as a

prisoner of Christ? Why did he also add that he was imprisoned "for the sake of the Gentiles"?

2. The title of today's lesson is "New Revelation in Christ." What is the new revelation? How does this new revelation apply to the church? How does it apply to you personally?

3. Paul remarked that he was "less than the least" of all God's people, yet God had given him a great task. What can we learn from Paul's attitude in this passage? What can we learn about God's attitude toward Paul? Toward us?

4. How does the church display the wisdom of God to others outside of the faith? Why is unity in the body of Christ so important?

5. As believers, we are to share the good news of salvation with others. How does our unity and love for others in the church impact our witness for Christ?

Lesson in Our Society

The Bible says that God is the "revealer of mysteries" (Daniel 2:29, NIV). Many people in our world today need someone to help unravel the mysteries of life. Heartache, hopelessness, sickness, and sin run rampant in our society. Life will never make sense apart from God. As we saw in today's lesson, God's eternal plan is salvation for all mankind. From the beginning of time, it has been God's loving desire to provide an answer to the problems of sin.

As believers, we have already heard and understood the mystery of redemption, through faith in Jesus. And just like Paul, it is now given to us to reveal this mystery to others.

Make It Happen

This week, remember to thank God for your salvation. Ask Him to reveal to you how you can share the mystery of salvation with someone else. Pray for God to lead you to a specific person who needs to hear the good news of God's grace.

Follow the Spirit

What God wants me to do:

____

____

Remember Your Thoughts

Special insights I have learned:

____

____

More Light on the Text

Ephesians 3:1–13

1 For this cause I Paul, the prisoner of Jesus Christ for you Gentiles,

"For this cause" refers to Ephesians 2:11–22, which describes how, at one time, Gentiles were excluded from the people of God, but have been made one with the Jewish people through the work of Christ, who "hath broken down the middle wall of partition between us" (v. 14). God eliminated the barrier that the Old Testament ceremonial law created between the two peoples (v. 15). He reconciled both Jews and Gentiles to God (v. 16) so that now there is no ground for hostility or alienation. Now, together, we are a "holy temple in the Lord…for an habitation of God through the Spirit" (vv. 21–22).

Most commentators see Ephesians 3:1 as an introductory comment, followed by an extended interjection that continues through verse 13. One main reason for this interpretation is that "for this cause" (Gk. *toutou charin*, **TOO-too KHAR-in**) is an extremely unusual expression—used only three times in the entire New Testament, and it is used both here and in verse 14. In essence, it serves as a bookmark in the flow of Paul's thought. Indeed, verse 14, when read in this light, appears to resume the thought started in verse 1 and carried over from chapter 2.

Paul describes himself as a "prisoner" (*desmios*, **DES-mee-os**), meaning "a captive." Ephesians is one of Paul's four "prison epistles"—the others being Philippians, Colossians, and Philemon. The time in which he wrote these letters is probably during the two-year house imprisonment in Rome, documented in Acts 28, when he lived in a rented house guarded by a Roman soldier. While not free to move about, he was permitted to receive visitors and correspond freely, both of which he seems to have done quite frequently.

By describing himself as a prisoner "of Jesus Christ," Paul expresses both the cause of his literal imprisonment (his fearless proclamation of the Gospel) and Christ's ownership of his life. "For you Gentiles" expresses not resentment for what his ministry to the Gentiles has done to him, but Paul's sense of divine calling and purpose. Paul was specifically called to be an apostle to the Gentiles—not that he excluded Jews from his ministry but that bringing the Gospel to Gentiles was a primary focus of his ministry (Acts 9:15; Romans 11:13).

2 If ye have heard of the dispensation of the grace of God which is given me to you-ward:

Paul now begins his explanation of how and why he has come to fill this particular role in God's kingdom. He has received a "dispensation" (Gk. *oikonomia*, **oy-kon-om-EE-ah**), which could also be translated "stewardship" or "administration." This word was used to describe the management or oversight of another person's affairs by a household manager. By using *oikonomia*, Paul is expressing a deep sense of privilege and accountability. God has, quite literally, given him significant responsibility for making sure that a large number of people come to experience His grace.

"Grace" (Gk. *charis*, **KHAR-ece**) is the biblical word for "God's favor." Since we only experience God's favor through faith in Jesus Christ, Paul is using the term "grace" as shorthand for the Gospel. The phrase, "To you-ward," is translated "for you" by modern English translations. Paul was given the message for the express purpose of delivering it to those who needed it. "You" here are the same Gentile recipients addressed in verse one.

One of the most fascinating aspects of the Gospel message is that, although God has acted in sovereign power and grace to redeem us from sin, He has chosen to use people as the messengers through whom the Gospel is distributed. The preaching of the Gospel—not miraculous acts of divine self-revelation—are the ordinary means by which people come to faith in Christ (Romans 10:14–15).

3 How that by revelation he made known unto me the mystery; (as I wrote afore in few words,

Paul claims to have received knowledge from God by "revelation" (Gk. *apokalupsis*, **ap-ok-AL-oop-sis**), which means "uncovering" or "disclosure." What Paul means by this is not entirely clear, but Galatians 1:12 provides additional insight: "For I neither received it [the Gospel] of man, neither was I taught it, but by the revelation of Jesus Christ." It certainly seems as though Paul is claiming to have had a supernatural experience in which the content of the Gospel message was revealed to him. It is possible that the revelatory experience was his "Damascus Road" conversion experience; however, none of the accounts of his conversion mention any extended teaching about what he would preach. The important point to realize is that Paul's message is not of human origin, which means it is authoritative and trustworthy.

What was revealed to Paul was the "mystery" (Gk. *musterion*, **moos-TAY-ree-on**). A biblical mystery is simply something that God has kept hidden. Verses four and five make this clearer: The mystery of Christ was not revealed to mankind in previous times but has now been made known.

4 Whereby, when ye read, ye may understand my knowledge in the mystery of Christ) 5 Which in other ages was not made known unto the sons of men, as it is now revealed unto his holy apostles and prophets by the Spirit;

"Whereby" refers to what was written earlier. The word "understand" (Gk. *noeo*, **no-EH-o**) means "to perceive with the mind" or "gain insight into." This is not to say that human mental power alone is sufficient to comprehend the Gospel. Paul assumes that his readers are aided in their quest for understanding by the Holy Spirit. Because it is "spiritually discerned," he writes elsewhere that his understanding of the "mystery of Christ" is not based on human understanding. To the perishing, the truth of God seems like foolishness (1 Corinthians 2:12–14).

The work of Christ was predicted, hinted at, and prefigured by previous revelation (the Old Testament). However, enough information was withheld from the people of God to keep them from understanding precisely what God was going to do in Christ. "Other ages" could also be translated "other generations." The word "ages" (Gk *genea*, **ghen-eh-AH**) literally means "clan, race, kind, generation." In view of the phrase "sons of men," it seems likely that Paul has specific groups of people in mind. Peter indicates that the ancient prophets actually inquired of God as to when the Christ would come and who He would be. Their inquiries were apparently only answered with the assurance that the Christ would come, after their lifetimes, and that future generations would witness His suffering and glory (1 Peter 1:10–12).

Certain individuals were entrusted with the truth that God chose to reveal. An "apostle" (Gk. *apostolos*, **ap-OS-tol-os**) is a "delegate, envoy or messenger." The apostles were a very special group—those who received the words of Jesus and passed them on to the church through their preaching and writing. Jesus designated twelve of His disciples to be apostles (Luke 6:13) and specially appointed Paul at a later time (1 Timothy 2:7). The New Testament only uses the term "apostle" to refer to members of the original twelve, Paul, and a few select other associates of the apostles, such as James, the brother of Jesus, Barnabas, and Andronicus. All of the books of the New Testament were either written by an apostle or a close associate of an apostle.

A "prophet" (Gk. *prophetes*, **prof-AY-tace**) is someone who declares what God has revealed. A prophet's words are considered to be the very words of God.

Although the New Testament indicates there was some genuine prophetic activity in the early church, the prophets to whom Paul refers seem most likely to be the prophets of the Old Testament—men like Isaiah, Jeremiah, and Micah who looked forward to the coming Messiah and called the people of Israel to be steadfast in their faith. Their words are like the bones of a skeleton in that they formed the foundational framework of the mystery of Christ. The revelation of Christ and the apostles built on that foundation, allowing us to fully understand the message of the prophets, which was partially veiled by God's design.

6 That the Gentiles should be fellowheirs, and of the same body, and partakers of his promise in Christ by the gospel:

Because of what Christ has done, Gentiles and Jews share equally in the blessings of salvation. (Prior to Christ, Gentiles could experience the blessing of salvation, but it required that they become Jewish. In Christ, the cultural and ethnic distinctions between Jew and Gentile are rendered meaningless). Paul describes this mutual benefit with three compound words that are formed by combining "with" and another word. "Fellowheirs" (Gk. *sugkleronomos*, **soong-klay-ron-OM-os**) is used in Hebrews 11:9 to refer to Abraham, who shared the promise of God with his descendants Isaac and Jacob and in 1 Peter 3:7 to refer to Christian wives, who share the grace of life along with their believing husbands. The best parallel passage is Galatians 3:26–29, which emphasizes that everyone who believes in Jesus, without regard to race, gender, or socioeconomic status, is a son of God and an heir of God's promise to Abraham. "Of the same body" (Gk. *sussomos*, **SOOS-so-mos**) does not appear anywhere else in the New Testament or in literature of the time, so it may have been a word that Paul himself coined. It is based on the word *soma* ("body"). "Partakers" (Gk. *summetochos*, **soom-MET-okh-os**) literally means "joint partaker."

The "promise" in which we share is not explicitly specified, but the promises God made to Abraham are clearly in view. God made three specific promises to Abraham: that his descendants would inhabit the Promised Land, that his descendants would be innumerable, and that he would be a blessing to all the peoples of the earth. In Galatians 3:14–16, Paul explains that, in Christ, the blessings of Abraham have come to the Gentiles. His rationale for this conclusion is that God made His original promise to "Abraham and his seed"—not Abraham and his *seeds*. The singular "seed" is Christ, so all who have faith in Christ are "Abraham's seed and heirs according to the promise" (Galatians 3:29). Paul seems to allude to this principle when, in 2 Corinthians 1:20 he says, "For all the promises of God in him are yea, and in him Amen…."

The "gospel" (Gk. *euaggelion*, **yoo-ang-GHEL-ee-on**) is the "good news" of what God has done for His people, in Jesus Christ. The word "by" (Gk *dia*, **dee-AH**) communicates agency: "by means of." We experience the blessing of salvation only through believing the message.

7 Whereof I was made a minister, according to the gift of the grace of God given unto me by the effectual working of his power.

Paul now begins to explain his role in the unfolding plan of God. The verb "was made" (Gk. *ginomai*, **GHIN-om-ahee**) means "become" but appears in the passive voice to make it clear that God was the actor and Paul had nothing to do with his new job. "Minister" (Gk. *diakonos*, **dee-AK-on-os**) is the word translated "deacon" elsewhere in the New Testament. It literally means "servant" or "helper" but is sometimes translated "minister" when it refers to one engaged in service to the people of God on God's behalf (Colossians 1:25).

Paul's calling as a minister is the result of God's gift of grace—a fact that Paul explains more fully in the next verse. This gift became his, through God's work. "Power" (Gk. *dunamis*, **DOO-nam-is**) means "potential for functioning in some way." It is a word used in 1:19–20 to describe the strength God exhibited in raising Jesus from the dead—the same power available for "us who believe" for the carrying out of God's work.

8 Unto me, who am less than the least of all saints, is this grace given, that I should preach among the Gentiles the unsearchable riches of Christ;

Paul felt a large debt of gratitude for his call to

Paul was willing to endure anything for the sake of those who needed to hear the message of Jesus. In fact, the two-year Roman imprisonment, at the time Paul wrote this letter, was the culmination of a chain of events in which he was nearly killed by a Jerusalem mob, falsely accused of blasphemy (a capital offense) by the Jewish authorities, narrowly escaped a plot on his life, and put in a Caesarean jail for two years, while the Roman governor waited for a bribe. When he was eventually transferred to Rome for the hearing of his appeal, his ship was wrecked during the voyage.

The suffering and hardship involved in doing his job may cause us to think his call was undesirable, but Paul saw it as an honor to play such a key role in advancing God's purposes. Moreover, his suffering has made it possible for the readers to share in something almost too good for words. He asks the reader to not "faint" (Gk *ekkakeo*, **ek-kak-EH-o**), which means "to lose motivation; to be afraid in the face of a great difficulty." His "tribulations" (Gk. *thlipsis*, **THLIP-sis**)—"trouble that inflicts distress"—are their glory.

"Glory" (Gk. *doxa*, **DOX-ah**) describes the brightness and splendor, as well as the honor and renown, of God. Although God is clear on the fact that He does not allow mere men to steal His glory (Isaiah 48:11), at times the Bible speaks of glory being ascribed to God's people. In John 17:22, Jesus says that He has given the glory the Father gave Him to His followers. And in 1 Peter 5:1, the author describes himself as a "partaker in the glory that shall be revealed"—a clear reference to the full glory of Christ.

Sources:

Keener, Craig S. *The IVP Bible Background Commentary: New Testament.* Downers Grove, Ill.: InterVarsity Press, 1993.

The NIV Study Bible, 10th Anniversary Edition. Grand Rapids, Mich.: Zondervan, 1995.

ING TIPS

lay 24

udy Guide 13

5. Relating the Lesson to Life

A. Divide the students into pairs. Instruct each pair to complete the Search the Scriptures section. Allow time for discussion.

B. Call the class back together, and ask for a volunteer to give a testimony of how following God's principles has made a difference in their family.

C. Read and answer the Discuss the Meaning questions, encouraging students to relate the questions to their own lives.

6. Arousing Action

A. Allow a few minutes of silence for students to read the Make It Happen section and to complete the Follow the Spirit section.

B. Ask for volunteers to share their thoughts or responses to today's lesson.

C. Ask for prayer requests and end the session with prayer, thanking God for creating families.

Worship Guide

For the Superintendent or Teacher
Theme: New Life in the Home
Theme Song: "A Christian Home"
Devotional Reading: 1 Corinthians 1:4–17
Prayer

NEW LIFE IN THE HOME

Bible Background • EPHESIANS 5:1–6:4
Printed Text • EPHESIANS 5:21–6:4 Devotional Reading • 1 CORINTHIANS 1:4–17

AIM for Change

By the end of the lesson, we will:
EXPLORE the biblical basis for building strong families;
VALUE the fact that families are important to God: and
LIVE in harmony with our loved ones.

Keep in Mind

"Submitting yourselves one to another in the fear of God" (Ephesians 5:21).

Focal Verses

KJV **Ephesians 5:21** Submitting yourselves one to another in the fear of God.

22 Wives, submit yourselves unto your own husbands, as unto the Lord.

23 For the husband is the head of the wife, even as Christ is the head of the church: and he is the saviour of the body.

24 Therefore as the church is subject unto Christ, so let the wives be to their own husbands in every thing.

25 Husbands, love your wives, even as Christ also loved the church, and gave himself for it;

26 That he might sanctify and cleanse it with the washing of water by the word,

27 That he might present it to himself a glorious church, not having spot, or wrinkle, or any such thing; but that it should be holy and without blemish.

28 So ought men to love their wives as their own bodies. He that loveth his wife loveth himself.

29 For no man ever yet hated his own flesh; but nourisheth and cherisheth it, even as the Lord the church:

30 For we are members of his body, of his flesh, and of his bones.

31 For this cause shall a man leave his father and mother, and shall be joined unto his wife, and they two shall be one flesh.

32 This is a great mystery: but I speak concerning Christ and the church.

33 Nevertheless let every one of you in particular so love his wife even as himself; and the wife see that she reverence her husband.

6:1 Children, obey your parents in the Lord: for this is right.

2 Honour thy father and mother; which is the first commandment with promise;

NLT **Ephesians 5:21** And further, submit to one another out of reverence for Christ.

22 For wives, this means submit to your husbands as to the Lord.

23 For a husband is the head of his wife as Christ is the head of the church. He is the Savior of his body, the church.

24 As the church submits to Christ, so you wives should submit to your husbands in everything.

25 For husbands, this means love your wives, just as Christ loved the church. He gave up his life for her

26 to make her holy and clean, washed by the cleansing of God's word.

27 He did this to present her to himself as a glorious church without a spot or wrinkle or any other blemish. Instead, she will be holy and without fault.

28 In the same way, husbands ought to love their wives as they love their own bodies. For a man who loves his wife actually shows love for himself.

29 No one hates his own body but feeds and cares for it, just as Christ cares for the church.

30 And we are members of his body.

31 As the Scriptures say, "A man leaves his father and mother and is joined to his wife, and the two are united into one."

32 This is a great mystery, but it is an illustration of the way Christ and the church are one.

33 So again I say, each man must love his wife as he loves himself, and the wife must respect her husband.

6:1 Children, obey your parents because you belong to the Lord, for this is the right thing to do.

2 "Honor your father and mother." This is the first commandment with a promise:

3 If you honor your father and mother, "things will go well for you, and you will have a long life on the earth."

3 That it may be well with thee, and thou mayest
live long on the earth.
4 And, ye fathers, provoke not your children to
wrath: but bring them up in the nurture and admonition of the Lord.

4 Fathers, do not provoke your children to anger
by the way you treat them. Rather, bring them up
with the discipline and instruction that comes from
the Lord.

In Focus

Sharinda read through her students' papers, her heart breaking. A fifth-grade teacher, Sharinda had assigned her students a paper that began, "I wish…" The students were instructed to write at least two sentences on the topic.

Sharinda expected to read things like "I wish we could go on vacation to Hawaii," or "I wish I could have a new computer." Instead, 15 out of 20 students wrote about their families:

"I wish my dad would come back."

"I wish my parents didn't fight all the time."

"I wish I could get good grades so my parents would love me."

"I wish my brother wasn't so mean."

"I wish my mom's boyfriend didn't live with us."

"I wish we could have Christmas all together for once."

Sharinda bowed her head over the papers and wept. Her students needed the love of Christ to permeate their lives and transform their families.

Strong families are built upon the principles of God's Word. In this lesson, we will see how serving one another, in love, creates an atmosphere where families can grow and thrive.

The People, Places, and Times

A Household Code. The verses found in Ephesians 5:21–6:4 comprise what is called a "household code." At the time Paul wrote Ephesians, many Romans were concerned that religions such as Judaism and Christianity would negatively influence traditional Roman family values. To allay these fears and show their support for these values, Christians, Jews, and other religious groups would often employ a standard form of statements.

These statements were developed by the philosophers of the day and delineated a group's belief on how the head of a household should lead his family. Also known as "household codes," the statements were often broken down into discussions of husband and wife, father and children, and master-slave relationships.

In Ephesians 5 and 6 Paul employs this form of discussion, knowing his readers will be familiar with the format. According to the codes of the day, it was customary for wives, children, and slaves to have to submit in various ways. The male head of the household was considered to be the absolute authority.

In Ephesians 5, Paul changes the premise for the code. God's plan called for Christ to be the head of the household and for all members of the household to mutually respect and submit to each other. It was a new and shocking concept.

Source:
Keener, Craig S. *The IVP Bible Background Commentary: New Testament.* Downers Grove, Ill.: InterVarsity Press, 1993. 551.

Background

The first four chapters in Ephesians deal with the great mystery of Christ's redeeming power. At first, the focus is on personal transformation from sinner to new creation in Christ. The focus then shifts to the behavior of a believer in relation to others in the body of Christ.

Now in Ephesians 5, Paul calls on believers to live out a life of holiness in relation to the world around them. He challenges them to live wisely, being led by the Spirit. A spirit-led life will produce a believer who is becoming more like Christ every day. As we become more like Christ, we will learn to respect and submit to others in love and humility.

Source:
Arrington, French L., and Roger Stronstad, eds. *Life in the Spirit New Testament Commentary.* Grand Rapids, Mich.: Zondervan, 1999.

At-A-Glance

1. Instructions for Wives (Ephesians 5:21–24)
2. Instructions for Husbands (vv. 25–33)
3. Instructions for Children and Parents (Ephesians 6:1–4)

In Depth

1. Instructions for Wives (Ephesians 5:21–24)

Ephesians 5:21 is a general instruction to all believers to submit to one another in love. This principle is directly associated with verse 18, where Paul instructs believers to "be filled" with the Spirit. The following verses list some results of being filled with the Spirit (v. 18): speaking (v. 19), singing (v. 19), making music (v. 19), giving thanks (v. 20), and submitting (v. 21).

When we are living a Spirit-led life, God gives us the grace to live in an attitude of humility and submission to others. In the next verses, we will see how having such an attitude is beneficial in all family relationships.

Paul addresses the wives first. He instructs wives to submit to their husbands "as unto the Lord" (v. 22). The word "submit" in this verse means to yield one's rights or to cooperate. This word does not imply slavish obedience or being silent in the home. Though the "household codes" of ancient days often required a wife to obey her husband, Paul does not make this a requirement. Rather, he appeals to a wife's dedication to God as a basis for submission to her husband. In other words, when a wife honors and respects her husband, she is submitting to God and His plan for the family.

In verse 23, Paul explains why a wife is to submit to her husband: because he is the "head" of the wife and family, just as Christ is the "head" of the church. Christ was appointed by God to be the head of the church. On the basis of this authority, the church is to submit to Him.

Some people might conclude from these verses that there is an inequality between male and female. But Paul makes clear that in Christ, all are equal (see also 1 Corinthians 11:8–12, Galatians 3:28). Within this equality, however, order and respect for authority should exist. Just as there is to be order in the church, there is also an order in the husband-wife relationship. Paul explains, "But I would have you know, that the head of every man is Christ; and the head of the woman is the man; and the head of Christ is God" (1 Corinthians 11:3).

The husband's headship is therefore not based on cultural norms nor sexist premises but on God's purposes and order of His creation. Jesus is not inferior to God yet God is Christ's "head." A wife who follows Jesus' example of submission is following God's plan for marriage and the family.

2. Instructions for Husbands (vv. 25–33)

Paul now turns his attention to the husbands. Interestingly, he does not stress the husband's authority or headship over the wife. Instead, Paul charges the husband to love his wife. And not only is the husband supposed to love the wife, he is to love her "even as Christ also loved the church, and gave himself for it" (v. 25).

A husband's love for his wife is to follow the pattern of Christ's love for the church. Christ's love for the church was self-sacrificing. A self-sacrificing love is unselfish love. A husband with a self-sacrificing love will demonstrate his love by seeking the best for his wife. This kind of love is committed and faithful, even through rough times. This kind of love does not depend on emotions or circumstances but will hold the marriage together forever.

A loving, Christlike husband will also provide for his wife. Just as the church is the body of Christ, a wife is a part of her husband. God says that a husband should love his wife just like he loves himself. As a husband nourishes, protects and provides for his wife, he "loves himself" (v. 28).

Christ's love for the church is a secure love. The love of a husband for his wife should be the same (v. 31). When a couple are married, they become "one flesh." Paul explains this as part of the "mystery" of marriage. Within the security of this relationship, a wife can submit to her husband. The husband, who loves his wife with a godly—self-sacrificing love, allows his wife to blossom into the beautiful woman God created her to be. This is marriage as God intended it to be.

3. Instructions for Children and Parents (Ephesians 6:1–4)

After discussing the husband-wife relationship, Paul now gives specific instructions to children. Children are exhorted to obey their parents "in the Lord," that is, in the spirit of obedience as if they were obeying God. Paul also instructs children to obey their parents because it is the right thing to do. In Colossians 3:20, we read that obedience to parents "is well-pleasing to the Lord."

Obedience to parents is also a commandment of God (Exodus 20:12; Deuteronomy 5:16). And according to Ephesians 6:2–3, when a child honors, respects, and obey his parents, that child is blessed.

Just as children have a responsibility to obey their parents, parents also have responsibilities to their children. In verse 4, Paul speaks specifically to fathers as the head of the family. He first gives the fathers a negative instruction—"do not exasperate your children" (v. 4, NIV). A father's role in his child's life ultimately impacts the child's concept of God the Father. Fathers, therefore, need to be watchful and consider how their behavior is influencing their child's behavior. Unreasonable expectations, harsh or unfair punishment, or playing favorites will dishearten a child and can lead to disillusionment or rebellion.

Instead of these behaviors, fathers are encouraged positively to "bring them up in the nurture and admonition of the Lord" (v. 4). It is the father's responsibility to see that his children are being raised according to God's principles. Fathers are to "nurture" their children, which means to care for them tenderly—to lead them gently into God's ways. The word "admonition" is related to training and instructing. Therefore, parents are to give correction and instruction with the goal of developing their child's character and pointing the child toward righteousness. We give our children a great gift when we teach them early how to obey God and His Word.

Sources:

Arrington, French L., and Roger Stronstad, eds. *Life in the Spirit New Testament Commentary.* Grand Rapids, Mich.: Zondervan, 1999.

The NIV Study Bible, 10th Anniversary Edition. Grand Rapids, Mich.: Zondervan, 1995.

Search the Scriptures

1. Why are believers commanded to submit to one another (Ephesians 5:21)?

2. How are wives to submit to their husbands (v. 22)?

3. How are husbands to love their wives (v. 25)?

4. What specific instructions does Paul give to fathers (Ephesians 6:4)?

Discuss the Meaning

1. What does Paul mean when he says that wives should submit to their husbands just like the church submits to Christ (Ephesians 5:24)?

2. How can a husband love his wife "as his own body" (v. 28)? Why is this important?

3. What does it mean to bring up your children in the ways of the Lord? What are some tangible ways you can teach your children God's principles?

Lesson in Our Society

We often witness the breakdown of the family unit. Marriages are disintegrating. Children are disobedient and disrespectful to parents and others in authority. Single-parent homes are becoming the norm.

Families are important to God. He created them! He also laid out specific principles for a loving, harmonious family life. When we live according to these principles, a godly family is the result. And a godly, harmonious family is a living testimony to the truth of God's Word.

Make It Happen

How can we serve one another in the home, in the name and Spirit of Christ? Think about your relationship with each family member. Are you following God's principles for family life? Pray that God would show you areas that need improvement, and then be willing to change and grow. Pray for your family members that they, too, would be willing to follow God's plan for your family. If possible, pray together as a family, committing to grow together in God's ways.

Follow the Spirit

What God wants me to do:

____

____

Remember Your Thoughts

Special insights I have learned:

____

____

More Light on the Text

Ephesians 5:21–6:4

These verses espouse and present a unifying principle of building strong family ties. These strong family ties are built in order to help families live together, in the home, as believers serving one another in the name and Spirit of Jesus Christ. Family life was originated and ordained by God in the Garden of Eden. He set the first man, Adam, in a family situation of his marriage to Eve and bearing of children (Genesis 1:26–28; 4:1–25). God encouraged and tutored His people, in both the Old and New Testaments, to value strong family networks and live in harmony and peace with all loved ones. However, as believers, this idea of a healthy family life cannot be achieved without being in subjection to one another and in reverence to Christ.

"Submitting yourselves one to another in the fear of God" (Ephesians 5:21).

21 Submitting yourselves one to another in the fear of God. 22 Wives, submit yourselves unto your own husbands, as unto the Lord. 23 For the husband is the head of the wife, even as Christ is the head of the church: and he is the savior of the body. 24 Therefore as the church is subject unto Christ, so let the wives be to their own husbands in every thing.

Some scholars have argued that the phrase "submitting yourselves one to another in the fear of God" seems to be unexpected. They comment on how it probably does not fit into this context, since it grammatically belongs to a discourse on worship. It is, however, not illogical. The key word in the text is "submission" (Gk. *hupotasso,* **hoop-ot-AS-so**), and it lays a framework for a discussion on how to discharge Christian duties in dynamic relationships of mutuality, in an act of true Christian spirituality. This idea, put forth in the text, suggests the potential danger that individualism poses against a true community life or fellowship. It becomes very serious when individualism is expressed without an intentional desire to willingly bear one another's burdens for the sake of Christ. Whenever there is a true submission for the sake of the Lord, it leads to a frame of heart and an attitude that is penetrated with a deep sense of obligation. True submission seeks not to repudiate or dominate others in a relationship.

It is within this context of understanding that the word "submission" sets an agenda for reverence to God and His divine principles. This is done as a means to cultivate a submissive spirit, which values and seeks to unselfishly support, love, and respect others for the sake of Christ. Thus, Paul laid this framework for his teaching regarding the marriage relationship and true harmony in the home. Paul underscored how a husband and a wife, through devotion for the sake of Christ, must dutifully exercise love and respect for each other in a marriage relationship. The quality of the nature of relationship that should exist between husbands and wives was primarily illustrated by Paul, when He drew on the analogy of Jesus Christ and the church. The key verb "submit," from the Greek, connotes an understanding of voluntarily placing under, or ordering oneself under, a leader or an authority source. The church, out of love, gratitude, and reverence, subjects itself to the Lord Jesus Christ as its head. It does this in compliance with God's authority. In the same vein, wives are instructed to submit, in the marriage relationship, to the husband. They should do so in acknowledgment of the fact that God ordained the husband as the leader of the household. This divine arrangement is for the sake of producing ordered household conditions, which are necessary to bring glory to God's name and also bring peace and productivity in family life. This is God's pattern of true governance or leadership.

The contextual meaning of the word "head" (Gk. *kephale,* **kef-al-AY**), in this passage, in reference to a husband's relationship with his wife, has generated different interpretations among scholars. While some claim that the word "head" denotes an idea of a source, others choose to explain it as portraying leadership. The former "source" carries an understanding of delegated authority from a higher being or power, which must be exercised with great responsibility and knowledge. In other words, it does not imply that the wife should act like a slave and be a mindless person in the relationship.

The latter, leadership, which seems to be the most probable interpretation of the word "head," in this context, has its foundation on ability to provide good leadership. This is accomplished by loving others, who are followers. We love them by listening and respecting them. We also love them by carrying out given responsibilities in a manner that takes into consideration the feelings of others. We assess their strengths and weaknesses. Thus a wife, out of love and humility, submits to the husband. In conjunction, the husband must seek the holistic welfare of his wife and the entire household. He does this out of reverence for God and the position God has given him.

25 Husbands, love your wives, even as Christ also loved the church, and gave himself for it; 26 That he might sanctify and cleanse it with the washing of water by the word, 27 That he might present it to himself a glorious church, not having spot, or wrinkle, or any such thing; but that it should be holy and without blemish. 28 So ought men to love their wives as their own bodies. He that loveth his wife loveth himself.

The Greek word *agapao* (**ag-ap-AH-o**), used in verse 25 for "love," is rooted in an understanding of a person who has unconditionally subordinated his or her own desires, inclinations, and personality for the benefit of others in a relationship context. It expresses an idea of an intention and activities that are based on virtues that encourage people to act by saving, building, and restoring others in love.

Jesus Christ expressed this kind of love to the church when He vicariously laid down His life so that the church could be born, developed, and expanded. In Paul's epistle to the Philippians, he states that Christ restrained Himself unselfishly from engaging in a lifestyle that would put personal glory over and above God's purpose. Christ, out of love and devotion, had to make "himself of no reputation" (Philippians 2:7), so that He could fully serve God's purpose for the church. The key motivation for His life was to fulfill God's purpose, by serving the ultimate needs of God's people, through a shameful death on the cross. In the same way, husbands are admonished to follow the example of Christ to unconditionally and sacrificially serve the holistic—spiritual, physical, psychological/emotional, economic/material—needs of their wives. This analogy or concept of how to sacrificially express love for the sake of others should not be misunderstood, in the marriage relationship, as a requirement for wives to overdepend on their husbands for everything. This is because although Christ loves the church, gave himself for it, and still serves consistently its needs, God has also given to the church spiritual and moral responsibilities. These must be carried out with great maturity and decorum. After all, the Scriptures teaches that as a result of the grace of Christ's redemptive work of love believers must act as "workers together with Him" (2 Corinthians 6:1).

In principle, the church must see itself as forming/building a *team* with Christ and having as an aim the fulfilling of God's purpose on Earth. In the same vein, wives must not be overreliant on their husbands for everything in life, since both the former and latter must work as a team to fulfill the needs of a healthy home. This means that wives must learn to complement responsibly the efforts of their husbands. This is done through their God-given gifts and graces, in order to mutually establish a home or household that is full of peace, progress, and order.

In verses 26–27, the love that Christ expressed in order to fulfill God's divine purpose on earth is presented as being motivated by the "sanctifying and cleansing" of the church. Sanctification and cleansing of the church of Christ lead to its glorification and splendor in the midst of a world system that is characterized by sin and darkness. This implies that in a marriage context, it is important to work toward values of purity and true spirituality of thoughts and actions, just as Christ purposed for the church.

In verse 28, the apostle Paul reemphasizes the basic foundations that God put in place for Adam and Eve (Genesis 2:23–25). This imagery of the marriage relationship, in which Adam declared Eve as the "bone of my bones, and flesh of my flesh," proclaims forcefully a unique kind of spiritual and bodily union. It also declares an identification in which Adam's heart was prepared to love his wife despite her weaknesses and failures.

29 For no man ever yet hated his own flesh; but nourisheth and cherisheth it, even as the Lord the church: 30 For we are members of his body, of his flesh, and of his bones.

The two key words in these verses are "nourisheth" (Gk. *ektrepho*, **ek-TREF-o**) and "cherisheth" (Gk. *thalpo*, **THAL-po**). It is known that some people who present themselves as eccentrics have engaged in self-mutilation of different forms. Others, for example the ascetics, have often been involved in activities that make their own bodies uncomfortable. However, there are still others who have generally acted in a way to specially feed and care for their lives. This is what the Scripture passage means by "nourisheth." The word "nourisheth" can be defined, in a generic sense, as providing sustenance and attending carefully to the others' necessities of life. It means that the husband has been endowed with the godly responsibility of participating in the personal life of his wife. He is to meet her holistic needs in a manner that brings about progress in the marriage relationship, as ordained by God. However, this idea does not mean that the wife is socially, psychologically, or economically inferior to the husband. The author is simply emphasizing the husband's responsibility to play his role as a God-ordained leader of the family or household.

Second, by the use of the word "cherisheth" the writer is referring to a husband's promise to his wife to nurture, protect, and shelter her emotionally, physically, psychologically, and spiritually in all situations.

31 For this cause shall a man leave his father and mother, and shall be joined unto his wife, and they two shall be one flesh. 32 This is a great mystery: but I speak concerning Christ and the church.

Verse 31 seems to be the central and organizing phrase in the periscope of verses 22–33. These verses focus on marriage life and building authentic relationship in a family context based on true love. The key phrases "shall a man leave," "joined unto his wife" and "shall be one flesh" are grounded on Genesis 2:24. Marriage has been presented as the fundamental relationship between a man and woman. It requires characteristics of devotion that inspires transactions of self-sacrifice, deep-affection, and total commitment. The new bond and obligation that marriage involves transcend any attachment or commitment to other forms of relationships that are outside the marriage context. There must be a "leaving" of anything (except worshiping God) that stands between the love relationship between husbands and wives. The "joining," in this context, is a work of God's grace.

Finally, the writer connected the marriage relationship with the "great mystery" of God's plan of salvation. This plan was concealed, but was later unfolded through the redemptive work of Christ and the ministry of His apostles. The Greek word used for "mystery" was *musterion* **(moos-TAY-ree-on)**. Its use in this context denotes some particular deep truth about Christ's great love and concern for the church which cannot be fully grasped by the power of the mind, without the help of the Holy Spirit.

33 Nevertheless let every one of you in particular so love his wife even as himself; and the wife see that she reverence her husband.

The apostle Paul summarizes the quality of marriage relationship necessary for building a healthy Christian home by, once again, admonishing the husband to "love his wife" and the wife to "see that she reverence her husband." Some commentators have wondered why the teachings in this passage did not specifically mention that wives should "love their husbands" and that husbands should "reverence their wives." Perspectives on this issue sometimes present different views. However, it is important to state that this line of reasoning is sensible and that there is a need for a human response to another's love. But since biblical presentation made a connection between Christ's mysterious love for the church and a husband's love for his wife, the emphasis was put on the husband to love his wife. This is the model that Christ laid down in the Scriptures.

6:1 Children, obey your parents in the Lord: for this is right. 2 Honour thy father and mother; which is the first commandment with promise; 3 That it may be well with thee, and thou mayest live long on earth.

This new chapter opens with a shift from husband–wife relationship to a relationship between fathers (parents) and children. In this context, Paul now lays out reciprocal duties and responsibilities between parents and children. First, children were instructed to "obey" their parents, like the preceding exhortation that was given to wives to "submit" to their husbands. This pattern of instruction seems to follow the divine structure and order that must exist within the framework of God's idea of delegated authority and leadership. This delegated authority and leadership has been structured on the heavenly framework of "ordered relationships." Children have been instructed to "honour thy father and mother" through an appeal to Old Testament Scriptures. This appeal is to reinforce the divine and ordered spiritual authority that has been structured from God's perspective (Exodus 20:12; Deuteronomy 5:16).

There are two basic elements that easily catch the attention of the reader. First, a reason was given that it is "right" for children to obey their parents, in the Lord. Second, the writer reminded children that the Old Testament commandment that was quoted in this passage was the only one that had a promise attached to it. On one hand, the word "right," used in this discourse, was probably because it was traditionally or conventionally accepted and proper behavior in that society for children to obey their parents. On the other hand, the word "promise" seems to bring encouragement to children that their obedience to parents has both personal and community implications. Personally, because children listened to their parents' corrections, leadership, and teachings, they are prepared to live morally and spiritually decent lives. Effectively, this line of action will prevent the children from falling prey to temptations and "life-systems" that may be destructive to their future progress or well-being. In terms of community life, children's disobedience to parents may lead to a breakdown of family bonds. These bonds foster generational continuity. The result of such a breakdown would be the decadence of a community and an eventual destruction of a community's continuity—"mayest not live long on earth."

4 And, ye fathers, provoke not your children to wrath: but bring them up in the nurture and admonition of the Lord.

Parents have been instructed not to "provoke" (Gk. *parorgizo,* **par-org-ID-zo**) their children to anger. The etymology of the word "provoke" from the original Greek connotes an idea of a capricious, domineering, and overstretched exercise of authority by parents on their children. Parents were instructed not to put unreasonably harsh demands or expectations on their children, to refrain from always being negative and condemning, and to treat their children fairly and not humiliate them. But parents should be intentional in training, educating, nurturing, and loving their children, by the Lord's assistance, in ways that will help the children be prepared to be successful in both secular and Christian communities. Parents should realize that their children are God's gift and given to them as a heritage. Therefore, they are responsible to love, discipline, teach, and care for the children in a way that brings glory to God.

Source:

Vine, W.E. *Vines Complete Expository Dictionary of Old and New Testament Words.* Edited by Merrill F. Unger and William White Jr. Nashville: Thomas Nelson Publishers, 1996.

Daily Bible Readings

M: Trained by God's Grace
Titus 2:1–13

T: Partnership in Marriage
Genesis 2:18–25

W: Interpreting Traditions
Exodus 12:21–28

T: Parental Advice
Proverbs 4:1–9

F: Spiritual Guidance for Families
Colossians 3:12–24

S: Providing for Family Members
1 Timothy 5:1–8

S: Christian Family Relationships
Ephesians 5:21–6:4

TEACHING TIPS

May 31

Bible Study Guide 14

1. Words You Should Know

A. Power (Ephesians 6:10) *kratos* (Gk.)—Force, strength.

B. Take (v. 13) *analambano* (Gk.)—To take up in resolute fashion.

C. Stand (vv. 13–14) *histemi* (Gk.)—To make firm, fix, establish.

2. Teacher Preparation

Unifying Principle—Armed for Battle. Because there are numerous forces pulling us in different directions, life is challenging. How can we stand firm in the face of opposition to what we believe? Paul teaches that God arms us to fight spiritual battles.

A. Pray that God would give you a thorough understanding of the importance of wearing the armor of God.

B. Review the lesson, then study the More Light on the Text section for deeper understanding.

C. Complete lesson 14 in the *Precepts For Living® Personal Study Guide.*

3. Starting the Lesson

A. Before your students arrive, prepare a slip of paper for each student. Write "God is…" on half of the papers. Write "Satan is…" on the other half.

B. As students arrive, hand them one slip of paper and instruct them to write as many descriptive words as they can think of to complete the sentences that begin with "God is…" and "Satan is…".

4. Getting into the Lesson

A. On one side of the board, write "God is…" and "Satan is…" on the other side. Ask students to call out the descriptions they wrote on their papers. Write their responses on the board.

B. Have a brief discussion about the opposing characteristics of God and Satan. Ask: "Is Satan's power equal to God's power?" Discuss.

C. Read the AIM for Change in unison, and then discuss The People, Places, and Times and Background sections.

D. Summarize the In Depth material, pausing occasionally to ask if there are any questions.

5. Relating the Lesson to Life

A. Ask for a volunteer to share a spiritual battle they are experiencing in their life.

B. Ask if anyone else has faced a similar battle in their life and see if they would like to share as well.

C. Ask, "What are some specific ways we can encourage fellow believers in the midst of the battle?"

D. Write the responses on the board, then challenge them to put into practice what they just suggested.

6. Arousing Action

A. Discuss the Lesson in Our Society.

B. Ask your students for a specific plan to implement Make it Happen. Ask for commitments to report next week.

C. Close the class with prayer, thanking God for His provision of spiritual armor.

Worship Guide

For the Superintendent or Teacher
Theme: Equipped for New Life
Theme Song: "I Will Serve Thee"
Devotional Reading: Luke 11:14–23
Prayer

EQUIPPED FOR NEW LIFE

Bible Background • EPHESIANS 6:10–18
Printed Text • EPHESIANS 6:10–18 Devotional Reading • LUKE 11:14–23

AIM for Change

By the end of the lesson, we will:
INVESTIGATE what it means to put on the armor of God;
TRUST that God's armor is the only means for defeating the unseen powers of the devil;
USE God's armor for our spiritual warfare, and CHOOSE to stand firm in the face of opposition.

Keep in Mind

"Wherefore take unto you the whole armour of God, that ye may be able to withstand in the evil day, and having done all, to stand" (Ephesians 6:13).

Focal Verses

KJV **Ephesians 6:10** Finally, my brethren, be strong in the Lord, and in the power of his might.

11 Put on the whole armour of God, that ye may be able to stand against the wiles of the devil.

12 For we wrestle not against flesh and blood, but against principalities, against powers, against the rulers of the darkness of this world, against spiritual wickedness in high places.

13 Wherefore take unto you the whole armour of God, that ye may be able to withstand in the evil day, and having done all, to stand.

14 Stand therefore, having your loins girt about with truth, and having on the breastplate of righteousness;

15 And your feet shod with the preparation of the gospel of peace;

16 Above all, taking the shield of faith, wherewith ye shall be able to quench all the fiery darts of the wicked.

17 And take the helmet of salvation, and the sword of the Spirit, which is the word of God:

18 Praying always with all prayer and supplication in the Spirit, and watching thereunto with all perseverance and supplication for all saints;

NLT **Ephesians 6:10** A final word: Be strong in the Lord and in his mighty power.

11 Put on all of God's armor so that you will be able to stand firm against all strategies of the devil.

12 For we are not fighting against flesh-and-blood enemies, but against evil rulers and authorities of the unseen world, against mighty powers in this dark world, and against evil spirits in the heavenly places.

13 Therefore, put on every piece of God's armor so you will be able to resist the enemy in the time of evil. Then after the battle you will still be standing firm

14 Stand your ground, putting on the belt of truth and the body armor of God's righteousness.

15 For shoes, put on the peace that comes from the Good News so that you will be fully prepared.

16 In addition to all of these, hold up the shield of faith to stop the fiery arrows of the devil.

17 Put on salvation as your helmet, and take the sword of the Spirit, which is the word of God.

18 Pray in the Spirit at all times and on every occasion. Stay alert and be persistent in your prayers for all believers everywhere.

In Focus

Sonny decided that he was going to quit smoking. It wasn't good for his body, and he felt that God wanted him to quit. Sonny had tried to quit many times in the past, but he never seemed to be able to get past a few days without a cigarette. But lately, Sonny had been learning how to use God's Word.

Monday was the big day. Sonny flushed his remaining cigarettes down the toilet and declared, "I'm free in the name of Jesus!" He went to work rejoicing that he had made the right decision. But around mid-morning, Sonny started to feel that old, familiar craving. He felt in his pocket for his cigarettes, but then realized what he was doing. In the past when this would happen, Sonny would immediately start beating himself up for being weak. Now, he had a new weapon in his arsenal.

To replace his usual pack of cigarettes in his pocket, Sonny had put an index card on which he had written some personalized, encouraging Scriptures. Instead of giving in to the temptation to borrow a cigarette, or beat himself up for thinking about it, Sonny turned to the Word of God. Every time he felt that craving, Sonny would say out loud, "Thank you, God, that Jesus gave Himself for my sins to rescue me from this evil world. Greater is He that is in me, than He that is in the world."

The battle was fierce, but Sonny was purposeful about renewing his mind and using the sword of the Spirit, which is God's Word. In time, Sonny won his fight against addiction because he chose to stand firm in the battle.

God gives us His armor that we may live a victorious Christian life. It is our choice to use what God has given us.

The People, Places, and Times

The Armor of God. Most of the Ephesian readers were familiar with the sight of Roman soldiers. Thus they could readily relate Paul's description of a warrior to their own spiritual warfare against demonic forces. The "armor of God" described in Ephesians does not include every piece of equipment typically used by the Romans, but provides for a solid analogy of the spiritual battle gear God has provided for His followers.

Source:

Keener, Craig S. *The IVP Bible Background Commentary: New Testament.* Downers Grove, Ill.: Intervarsity Press, 1993.

Background

At the Cross, Jesus secured the believer's ultimate victory. He "disarmed the [evil] powers and authorities [and] made a public spectacle of them" (Colossians 2:15, NIV). Our victory through Christ

is assured, but it is not yet complete.

The complete victory will come when Christ returns. Until then, believers are charged to stand strong in the "evil day" (Ephesians 6:13). In Paul's day, the Roman soldiers were trained to stand or hold their ground and not retreat in the face of the enemy's attack. They did not chase the enemy but stood together side by side in vast, virtually impenetrable ranks.

This study will help us to understand the offensive and defensive weapons God has given us. We will examine the various parts of the armor of God and how we can use them to live godly, victorious lives.

Source:

Keener, Craig S. *The IVP Bible Background Commentary: New Testament.* Downers Grove, Ill.: InterVarsity Press, 1993.

At-A-Glance

1. We Are Fighting a Battle (Ephesians 6:10–13)

2. God's Armor Helps Us Win the Battle (vv. 14–18)

In Depth

1. We Are Fighting a Battle (Ephesians 6:10–13)

Living the Christian life is a daily challenge. In Ephesians 6, Paul exhorts Christians to be strong in the Lord, and aware of satanic opposition. God and Satan are not equals—only God is infinite and omnipresent. But we must not underestimate or discount our spiritual enemy. Paul points out that the devil schemes against us (v. 11). Temptation, divisions, deception, and fear are just some of his tactics. In 2 Corinthians 2:11, Paul admonishes believers not to be ignorant of the schemes of Satan, lest he get the advantage over them. We cannot afford to close our eyes to the reality of spiritual warfare!

Satan and his demonic forces take advantage of any weakness, waging war on all who belong to God. As Paul points out, we do not fight or war against other humans (Ephesians 6:12). Instead, this war is fought in the spirit realm. We will be able to combat these spiritual attacks against us only when we utilize the spiritual armor God has given us and remember that it is only through Him that we will win the victory.

The victory is not won by trying to outmaneuver the enemy. Rather, our victory is won when we stand in the strength of the Lord. Verse 13 tells us to stand our ground—to stand firm in the face of opposition.

2. God's Armor Helps Us Win the Battle (vv. 14–18)

In order to stand firm against evil, we need to put on the armor God has given us. When we take up the pieces of armor and prepare ourselves for battle, we will be able to stand our ground even in the fiercest fight.

In verses 14–17, Paul lists the different pieces of armor and then makes spiritual application for all of them. The first pieces introduced are "truth" and "righteousness." Truth is likened to the belt that soldiers wore to keep their sword in place. Righteousness is like the breastplate the soldiers wore to protect their upper body. God's soldiers must be hallmarked by honesty and integrity. Our righteous and moral behavior will help to protect us from our enemy.

Verse 15 (NIV) says that our feet are "fitted with the readiness that comes from the gospel of peace." In other words, when we trust that Christ is working in us to win the battle, our hearts are at peace and we are able to stand our ground without fear.

The next piece of armor mentioned is the shield (v. 16). In ancient days, shields were often soaked in water, so that when the flaming darts of the enemy hit the shield, the fiery arrows were immediately quenched. In spiritual warfare, our faith is the shield that protects us. When Satan throws his fiery darts of temptation, fear, etc., we should counter those with our faith.

The last two pieces of armor listed are the "helmet" and "sword" (v. 17). The helmet, of course, is intended to protect the head. This is significant for believers, because the mind is a major battlefield in spiritual warfare. If we are to successfully stand our ground, our thought life must be constantly brought under the control of the Holy Spirit.

The sword is defined as "the sword of the Spirit, which is the word of God" (v. 17). The Holy Spirit gives power to the Word of God as we believe and confess it. The sword is also the only piece of armor that is not solely for defensive purposes. Because He has given us His Word to use as a weapon against the enemy of our souls, in battle, we are on the offense when we use God's Word. Jesus, who is our example in all things, used the Word of God to repel Satan (Matthew 4:4, 7, 10). Revelation 12:11 says, "They overcame him [Satan] by the blood of the Lamb and by the word of their testimony." When we use God's Word and the testimony of our mouths, we are using the sword to refute all attacks of Satan and his forces of evil.

Paul ends this passage by exhorting all Christians to be prayer warriors. Some scholars have even suggested that Paul meant for prayer to be the seventh weapon in spiritual warfare. But prayer is essential to every facet of a believer's life. If we don't pray, we are surrendering to the enemy without a fight. We are to pray and keep on praying. We are to pray about everything and for all other believers, being alert and watching for any attacks. We are also to pray in the Spirit, meaning that we are directed and empowered by Him as we pray.

God has given us mighty weapons, that we will be victorious in Him and have power to spread the Gospel. We are entrusted with the work of the kingdom—let's stand firm!

Source:

Arrington, French L., and Roger Stronstad, eds. *Life in the Spirit New Testament Commentary.* Grand Rapids, Mich.: Zondervan, 1999.

Search the Scriptures

1. Why are we to put on the full armor of God (Ephesians 6:11)?

2. Who are the "principalities," "powers," and "rulers of the darkness" (v. 12)?

3. What is the function of the "shield of faith" (v. 16)?

4. What is the "sword of the Spirit" (v. 17)?

Discuss the Meaning

1. What would happen if we attempted to combat Satan in our own strength?

2. What does it mean to "stand"? How do we do this?

3. How do we put on the armor of God?

4. In verse 18, what are two specific instructions for believers?

Lesson in Our Society

Satan and his demons are active in our society today. The rise in road rage, domestic violence, and terrorism are evidence of the spiritual warfare going on around us. Many people live their lives in fear of what tomorrow may hold. Others are tormented by anger, lust, or addictions, and the enemy seizes upon such weaknesses.

God created humans to have a spiritual relationship with Him. Those who don't know Him are grasping for spiritual truths—searching for something to fill the vacuum inside. The media today, by dispensing spiritual advice and philosophies from New Age mysticism to ancient mythology and everything in between, try to fill that void.

How can we help others see the truth of the spiritual battle—that there is a God, He is infinitely more powerful than the Devil, and He desires to deliver them from Satan's clutches into the kingdom of light?

Make It Happen

God calls every believer to enter the battle. This week, make it a habit to consciously "put on" the armor of God every day. Ask God to give you discernment concerning the Devil's schemes against you. Decide to use your sword (God's Word) to combat the enemy in your life.

Follow the Spirit

What God wants me to do:

Remember Your Thoughts

Special insights I have learned:

More Light on the Text

Ephesians 6:10–18

Life is challenging because there are numerous spiritual and physical forces pulling us in different directions. There are evil or demonic forces that are constantly waging war against people, especially Christians, to sway them from living a faithful life in worship of God. These negative powers are also bent on stopping people from fulfilling their life purpose and to prevent them from expressing fully their God-given potentials, abilities, and gifts. The primary purpose of Satan and His cohorts is to kill, steal and destroy (John 10:10). Believers need to have and put on the full armor of God to help them to stand firm as they face different oppositions that the enemy brings their way. Paul, therefore, teaches that God has given Christians spiritual armor to equip them to fight their daily spiritual battles, which are taking place in the unseen world.

10 Finally, my brethren, be strong in the Lord, and in the power of his might.

There are many issues that Christians contend with on a daily basis, and they have multiple dimensions. Sometimes the challenges are spiritual, moral, material, economical, or political in nature. There is a tendency, given the secularized doctrines and postmodern ideas of today, to either rule out or trivialize biblical teachings on spiritual warfare in the unseen world. Although the Scripture teaches that God created both the material and non-material world to serve His divine purpose and that humankind should work with/through both realms to live successfully to please Him, the origin of God's created order can be traced to the realm of the unseen (Genesis 1:1–3; Colossians 1:16–17). God is a Spirit and we were created in His own image (Genesis 1:26–28).

The Christian life, first and foremost, is a life of walking/living in the Spirit and engaging in spiritual warfare against the powers of the kingdom of darkness. In Ephesians 4:1, 17; 5:2, 8, 15; the key verb for the word "walk/live" (Gk. *peripateo*, **per-ee-pat-EH-o**) has been often used to focus on the Spirit-filled life of the believer, which empowers him or her to please God and overcome the enemy. And to overcome the powers of darkness, the author instructed believers to be "strong in the Lord" and "power of his might." Being strong or strengthened in the Lord has a number of Old Testament precedents. Yahweh was believed to be the source of all powers, especially when the Israelites were engaged in all kinds of warfare with their enemies (Joshua 1:6; 1 Samuel 30:6; Zachariah 10:12). The believer must completely depend on the Lord's resources before he or she can win any spiritual battle. This is because behind the human, moral, physical, natural, and spiritual problems and attacks in life, there is the presence of supernatural or unseen powers that work to accomplish Satan's purpose of destroying the "good and perfect" plans of God for His people.

11 Put on the full armor of God, that ye may be able to stand against the wiles of the devil.

The spiritual resources that God has given to us to wage war against the unseen powers of darkness has been described as "the full armor of God." This "armor" (Gk. *panoplia*, **pan-op-LEE-ah**) has been used as allegory in relation to certain essential qualities and characteristics that are very important in the believer's life. Paul, drawing heavily from the imagery of how soldiers dressed in the Greco-Roman world to illustrate the import of his teaching, built relevant and strong connections between natural warfare and spiritual warfare. He proceeded to list all the different parts or elements that make

"Wherefore take unto you the whole armour of God, that ye may be able to withstand in the evil day, and having done all, to stand" (Ephesians 6:13).

up the "full" amour of God in the verses following (vv. 12–18).

Although the pieces of the believer's armor listed in the following verses do not account for all the armor used by Roman soldiers in history, nevertheless, the essential parts of the armor are needed to prevail successfully in battle were mentioned. We must be aware that the enemy operates in different forms and shapes as he seeks to kill, steal, and destroy the blessings of believers. It is not enough to put on only parts or pieces of the armor. The cunning nature of the opposition makes it absolutely necessary to put on the whole armor. This is because the enemy seeks to work out schemes and strategies to hit through any loophole allowed by God's people. The spiritual battle calls for spiritual discipline on the part of believers to fully commit their time and energy to refrain from all forms of complacency as we live/walk in the spirit and engage in daily spiritual warfare. We must be conscious, intentional, and purposeful in making use of all the spiritual resources that God has given to us; that is the sure path to standing "against the wiles of the devil" in spiritual warfare.

12 For we wrestle not against flesh and blood, but against principalities, against powers, against the rulers of darkness of this world, against spiritual wickedness in high places.

The apostle Paul indicated that the spiritual warfare he was describing in this text does not apply selectively to some Christians. The use of the word "we" emphasizes the all-inclusive nature of spiritual warfare, and the author clearly identified himself with the ongoing battle. Every Christian is inevitably involved in the fight against satanic forces. Pastors, elders, deacons, leaders, new Christians, and rich or poor believers are all part and parcel of the battle. The term used by the apostle Paul to describe how the believer "wrestle(s)" (Gk. *pale,* **PAL-ay**) with the powers in the unseen world, has its etymology from the sport of wrestling in Asia Minor, especially parts of Ephesus, Pergamum, and Olympia. However, it is important to note that believers, unlike wrestlers, are not engaged in a human struggle that requires use of physical/material weaponry but with spirit beings that do not have "flesh and blood." It is a spiritual power encounter. Beyond and above what we see, touch, feel, hear, and taste through our five senses, there are spiritual entities and superhuman opponents who are operating under the control of Satan—the fallen angel from heaven—to disrupt the purposes of God in our lives (2 Corinthians 10:3–4).

We have been given categories in this text of spiritual powers that we wrestle against in our Christian lives. They are: "principalities and powers," "rulers of darkness," and "spiritual wickedness in high places." First, the "principalities" and "powers" (Gk. *arche*, **ar-KHAY**; *exousia*, **ex-oo-SEE-ah**) are a host of hostile powers and beings in the heavenly realms that rule and have dominion in the spiritual world. Their powers and influences extend to the realm of an unseen world, and they can cause things to move against the will of God for the Christian. But it is important to know that Jesus Christ has authority and power over them; they are all subordinate to Him.

Second, "rulers" (Gk. *kosmokrator*, **kos-mok-RAT-ore**) is a compound term used by ancient Greeks to represent "world system" (Gk. *kosmos*) and "rule" (Gk. *krateo*) to stand for a number of mystery cults and pagan deities or gods. Third, "spiritual wickedness in high places" refers to influential evil forces that operate by the direction of Satan and his agents to work in the world to inflict and sustain evil among men. They are dispatched to various posts and points to cause havoc and destroy whatever is light.

In different societies, communities, cultures, and generations, these unseen forces of darkness work together under the command of Satan to fight against the kingdom of God, mislead people, destroy whatever is good, make people disbelieve the Word of God, and hamper spiritual activities of God's people. The categories or plurality of the unseen satanic powers described above are sometimes given names and descriptions in different cultures and religions of the world. This is done to match up these categories of unseen satanic powers to the worldview of the people living in those contexts. The believer must learn to discern what kinds of spirits are operating and what forms they have assumed in an attempt to deceive God's people. To overcome them in spiritual warfare, the believers must depend completely on the power of the Lord and must be wholly equipped by putting on the whole armor of God.

13 Wherefore take unto you the whole armour of God, that ye may be able to withstand in the evil day, and having done all, to stand.

After giving all the descriptions of the satanic forces in the preceding verses, the apostle concluded that the only way to stand and prevail against these forces is to put on the "whole armor of God." Although the phrase "in the evil day" has been interpreted to mean future-eschatological (End Times) conflicts brought upon humankind by the antichrist, it is important to note that Satan attempts to bring evil upon people at all times. There are, however, times in people's lives when the enemy brings a deluge of sustained destructive activities to dislodge the soul, spirit, and body of the believer. In the midst of all these situations, those who have been well-prepared spiritually through the divine equipment they have received from God, will be able to stand and overcome the works of the enemy. The Greek word *histïmi* (**HIS-tay-mee**), which means to be "ready," suggests that anyone who is seriously engaged in spiritual warfare with the unseen world should stand his/her ground, with all the might and grace received from the Lord, without giving up. It also implies that the enemy will bring all kinds of pressures on the believer who is engaged in spiritual warfare to create discouragement, fear, or panic, and fatigue. It is, therefore, important that the Christian warrior hold on to the Word and power of the Lord to the very end. God is near and is able to give victory to anyone who stands fast to the end.

14 Stand therefore, having your loins girt about with truth, and having on the breastplate of righteousness;

In the world culture in which the author was living, most people had to tie garments around their waist in a manner that made them battle-ready. In case of a skirmish, the individual might quickly have to jump into action to defend either himself or the society. With the Roman soldier, either a "leather apron" or "sword belt" seems to be the direct reference here, and it is worn in a way that makes the warrior ready to fight anytime the battle-cry sounds. The Christian, who is involved in spiritual warfare, has been instructed to gird his/her waist or loins with "truth" and to have on the "breastplate of righteousness." The word "truth" in this context, according to most commentators, has two frames of reference. The Gospel of Christ or the Word of God has been referred to in the Scriptures as truth (John 17:17; Colossians 1:5).

The Christian must also walk in integrity, honesty, and faithfulness in the body of Christ (2 Corinthians 6:7). This means the believer must apply to his/her life every word of the values of the Gospel in every situation in life in order to be prepared to overcome the enemy. The word "righteousness," in the Scriptures, has been generally used to mean "justification" (Gk. *dikaiosune*, **dik-ah-yos-OO-nay**), which represents sinners being "declared righteous" as a result of the redemptive work of Christ. The other word is "godliness" (Gk. *dikaios*, **DIK-ah-yos**), which represents the character and moral quality of a redeemed person in Christ. Both concepts are relevant in this passage concerning spiritual warfare. It important for the believer, who is standing in the forefront of spiritual battle, to live in holiness by separating him/herself from all forms of sin, deceptive or misleading activities, and waywardness that creates gaps for darkness to infiltrate the Christian's life and service. Sin creates darkness and Satan operates in darkness.

15 And your feet shod with the preparation of the gospel of peace;

In spiritual warfare, the Gospel is the power, instrument, and weapon that God has given to Christians to face Satan and his cohorts directly. It brings lost people, who are living in a fallen world system, back to God and His purpose. The Gospel is also God's "dynamite" to destroy evil forces, ungodly ideas and concepts, and demonic-inspired secular and spiritual structures and systems, which are contrary to the wisdom and values of the kingdom of God. As believers, because we live/walk by faith and not by sight, and because faith "cometh by hearing, and hearing by the word of God" (Romans 10:17), it is crucial that our feet be shod (bind on) with the Gospel of peace and power. However, as we proceed with our faith walk and as we wear the Gospel on our feet, there is an important element. The word "preparation" (Gk. *hetoimasia*, **het-oy-mas-EE-ah**) connotes an idea of battle-readiness, and an ambassadorial posture in which one is psychologically, intellectually, and physically ready to "speak for" and defend the country from which the person was sent. The believer must learn to be always prepared to fight in spiritual warfare.

16 Above all, taking the shield of faith, wherewith ye shall be able to quench all the fiery darts of the wicked.

In spiritual warfare, the believer has been admonished to carry his/her "shield of faith" in every given situation, in addition to the other pieces of the weapons earlier mentioned. Why the shield of faith? Because there is what the writer described as the "fiery darts" (Gk. *ta bele ta pepuromena*, tah BEL-ay tah **peh-pur-o-MEN-ah**), or burning arrows, that the enemy can release against the people of God. These are projected missiles from Satan's camp aim at penetrating the soul, spirit, and body of the Christian warrior and cause fatal damage. The attack can take different forms and shapes, depending on what the enemy strategically wants to accomplish. Practically, these attacks can be presented in the form of words that bring discouragement, doubt, and fear to the believer. They can also be in the form of events and situations that are carefully designed to thwart the believer's onward march to victory. They may come in shapes of human beings that are sent into your life to trouble you, books that have been written to lead you away from knowing and living in the truth, or spiritual forces or entities that are assigned to torture, depress, and inflict your life with things that are destructive to the growth of your faith life.

The weapon to use to quench these burning arrows is what the Scripture calls the "shield of faith." The word used by the author in reference to "shield" describes a protective war device wielded by individuals in battle to protect them from the rain of fiery arrows that are shot by the enemy. Although the shield described in this text suggests that it has wooden components, it is also known to have fireproof metal lining to stop the fiery points of the arrows.

In the Old Testament, God has oftentimes presented Himself to the Israelites as their shield. Specifically, He said to Abraham, the father of faith, "I am thy shield" (Genesis 15:1). God is the source or origin of any faith that we can ever possess. In the New Testament, we are exposed to different kinds of faith: saving faith (Ephesians 2:8), faith as a fruit of the Spirit (Galatians 5:22), faith as a spiritual gift (1 Corinthians 12–13), etc. In spiritual warfare, the "shield of faith"—referenced in this text for spiritual warfare against the unseen satanic forces—can be used for both defensive and offensive maneuvers.

Wearing this piece of weapon, through complete dependence on the power of the Holy Spirit, equips the believer to prevail successfully over all forms and shapes of the spiritual attacks described in the preceding paragraph. The victory comes from the Almighty God, as the believer stays strong in faith against every kind of spiritual arrow that the enemy will throw against him/her.

17 And take the helmet of salvation, and the sword of the Spirit, which is the word of God.

The last two pieces of armor to be received by believers are "helmet of salvation" and "the sword of the Spirit." First, the "helmet" (Gk. *perikephalaia*, **per-ee-kef-al-AH-yah**) is a protective headgear required to be worn when one is engaged in battle. Naturally speaking, the head of an individual is the center for all intellectual activities and the thinking processes. When a person is brainwashed, misinformed, and miseducated, that individual can be misdirected into a wrong life purpose. In like manner, the believer—who is involved in spiritual warfare—needs to protect his/her head from being damaged or misinformed by the deceptive activities and lies from Satan's camp.

The believer's salvation is the foundation for his/her ability to think about what to do about the misleading paths the enemy will offer. Our salvation is primarily grounded in the Word of God and the work of the Holy Spirit in our lives. The Bible teaches that God's plan for our salvation is an already-accomplished work. It has been sealed through Christ, before the foundations of the world. In John 10:27–30, Jesus said, "My sheep hear my voice, and I know them, and they follow me: And I give unto them eternal life, and they shall never perish, neither shall any man pluck them out of my hand. My Father, which gave them me, is greater than all; and no man is able to pluck them out of my Father's hand. I and my Father are one." Therefore, even though Satan may cause the believer to suffer, he cannot harm the believer's soul or take away his/her eternal life with Christ Jesus.

The "sword of the Spirit" represents God's Word. The literal interpretation can be rendered "the sword which the Spirit provides" (Gk. *ten machairan tou pneumatos*, **tayn MAH-khahee-ran too PNOO-ma-tos**). This implies that the Holy Spirit gives the Word the power and potency it needs to be creative and powerful. After all, the Bible teaches that the "letter killeth, but the spirit giveth life" (2 Corinthians 3:6); and the Word of God is "sharper than any twoedged sword" (Hebrews 4:12).

18 Praying always with all prayer and supplication in the Spirit, and watching thereunto with all perseverance and supplication for all saints.

The apostle Paul concludes the discussion on spiritual warfare by stressing the prominence and importance of consistent prayer and supplications in all our engagements. As some people put it, "A praying Christian is a powerful Christian." The power to live and succeed in our walk with God depends how we receive empowerment from the presence of the Almighty God. We must have a devoted prayer life. The phrase "watching thereunto" in prayer means that the believer should always be spiritually alert—ready and "sold out"—to engage in the different forms of prayer that the Bible teaches. Also, the word "all" has been used three times in the text. It suggests an all-inclusive approach to prayer life, to being alert, and intercession for every believer. In spiritual warfare, we must know what kind of prayer we must use to minister to specific needs in every situation, as the Holy Spirit leads us. There are prayers of commitment, dedication, intercession, supplication, protection, thanksgiving, and guidance that we can pray in spiritual warfare for all the saints.

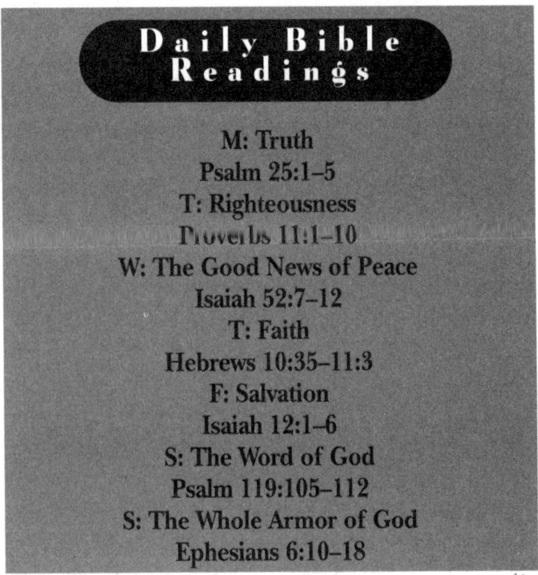

Daily Bible Readings

M: Truth
Psalm 25:1–5
T: Righteousness
Proverbs 11:1–10
W: The Good News of Peace
Isaiah 52:7–12
T: Faith
Hebrews 10:35–11:3
F: Salvation
Isaiah 12:1–6
S: The Word of God
Psalm 119:105–112
S: The Whole Armor of God
Ephesians 6:10–18

June 2009 Quarter At-A-Glance

Call Sealed with a Promise

The study this quarter begins with the theme of God's call of a covenant community as reflected in the Old Testament books of the law, specifically Exodus, Leviticus, Numbers, and Deuteronomy. The call of God to live in covenant community today is emphasized through these lessons.

UNIT 1 • CALLED OUT OF EGYPT

This unit covers four lessons. It is concerned with God's call to Moses, the response of Moses and Aaron, Pharaoh's refusal of God's call, and God's call to the people to leave Egypt.

Lesson 1: June 7, 2009
God Calls Moses
Exodus 3:1–12

Sometimes a special person is called to help another person or a people to overcome difficulties and to survive in times of hardship. Who has the power and position to help us? In this passage of Scripture, God spoke to Moses in the burning bush and called Moses to be the deliverer of the Israelites, who were oppressed and suffering in Egypt. God chose Moses to save God's people and promised to give him all the help he needed.

Lesson 2: June 14, 2009
Moses and Aaron Respond
Exodus 4:10–16, 27–31

Some persons believe they are not adequate to complete a task, so they are fearful of and resistant to accept it. How can people, who are afraid, be encouraged to do the work assigned them? In today's Scripture passage, because of his lack of eloquence, Moses expressed reluctance to God's call. To aid him, God provided Moses' brother, Aaron, to speak on his behalf. Subsequently, they went to the elders of Israel and told them what God had revealed to Moses.

Lesson 3: June 21, 2009
Pharaoh Ignores God's Call
Exodus 5:1–9, 22–6:1

Some people fail to recognize true authority and power, erroneously believing that the authority and power rest within themselves. What brings us to recognize a higher authority? Moses went to Pharaoh and told him God commands that His people be set free. Pharaoh responded by refusing and making life harder for the Israelites. Afterward, Moses went to God in distress and God promised, because of who God is—His mighty hand—that Pharaoh would indeed set the Israelites free.

Lesson 4: June 28, 2009
God Calls the People Out of Egypt
Exodus 14:15–25, 30

Many people have "protectors" to help them through difficult, even perilous, times. Where do we look for protection in difficult times? By parting the Red Sea so that they can pass to the other coast, God delivered the Israelites from the Pharaoh and the Egyptians. Therefore, He led them out of slavery, in Egypt, and destroyed the Egyptians, the Israelites' enemies.

UNIT 2 • CALLED TO BE GOD'S PEOPLE

This unit has four lessons. It shows how God's call led to the establishment of a new covenant and focuses on the people's response to that call in celebration and worship, in commitment to special service, and in establishing the ideal of Jubilee.

Lesson 5: July 5, 2009
God Calls People to Covenant
Deuteronomy 5:1–9, 11–13, 16–21

People make agreements to give structure and rules for their life together. What regulations are necessary to enjoy mutually beneficial lives? In this Scripture passage, God set forth 10 rules of conduct governing behavior, property, relationships, and worship. Moses announced to Israel God's Ten Commandments.

Lesson 6: July 12, 2009
God Calls People to Remember
Deuteronomy 16:1–8

Individual persons and communities regularly remember and celebrate great occasions with thanksgiving. How do we commemorate significant events in our lives? God commanded the Israelites to annually remember the Passover and to celebrate it for seven days. The Passover celebrated not only human freedom but the right to own land and flocks and to plant crops. It also helped the Israelites to recall the events of their deliverance from slavery and forced labor, while they were in Egypt.

Lesson 7: July 19, 2009
God Calls People to Special Service
Leviticus 8:1–13

Some individuals in a community are set aside for special service to that community. How do we discern, acknowledge, and affirm those people chosen for special service? In this text, God called Aaron and his sons to be priests for the Israelites. He commanded that they be recognized by consecrating them with water and holy garments.

Lesson 8: July 26, 2009
God Calls People to Jubilee
Leviticus 25:8–21, 23–24

The accumulation of property, in the hands of very few people, means that some are wealthy while others have no chance to escape poverty. How can communities care for the poor in just ways? God gave laws for the just redistribution of wealth to provide for the poor and thereby to honor God, who provides all. God instituted the year of Jubilee and gave laws for just transactions of land and crops.

UNIT 3 • CALLED TO CHOOSE LIFE

This unit reflects on God's ongoing call to obedience and defines what actions demonstrate faithfulness and rebelliousness. Five Old Testament lessons illustrate that God remains faithful to God's promise whether or not we choose to obey.

Lesson 9: August 2, 2009
People Grumble
Numbers 11:1–6, 10–15

When people experience difficulties, they often forget their blessings. During times of trouble, what happens when we forget our blessings? When God brought the people out of slavery in Egypt and provided for them in the desert, Moses and the people complained repeatedly, loudly, and often about their hardships. Truly, the Israelites had forgotten what a merciful, loving God had done for them—He delivered them from slavery in Egypt.

Lesson 10: August 9, 2009
People Rebel
Numbers 14:1–12

When dissatisfaction grows great, people may rebel against their leaders and benefactors. What leads people to rebel against leadership and authority? After the 12 spies returned from Canaan, the people rebelled against God's command to take possession of the land, complained against Moses and Aaron, and spoke about getting another leader and returning to Egypt.

Lesson 11: August 16, 2009
Moses Disobeys
Numbers 20:1–13

Even great leaders may fail to heed higher authority. Why do people disregard authority? As the Israelites arrived at Kadesh, there was no water and the people grumbled. An all-knowing God told Moses to speak to the rock before them and water would come out for them to drink. In his anger with and tiredness of the people, Moses disobeyed God's command and hit the rock. Because he did not trust God to provide for the people, Moses disobeyed God. God was displeased and Moses suffered a great consequence; he did not get to go over into the Promised Land (Canaan).

Lesson 12: August 23, 2009
God Calls for Obedience
Deuteronomy 6:1–9, 20–24

When people obey laws, they expect that life will be good. Why do people care at all about laws and try to follow them? Deuteronomy states that God gives laws for our benefit.

Lesson 13: August 30, 2009
God Calls for Decision
Deuteronomy 30:1–10

People want to experience a satisfying life to attain joy and prosperity. How do we get what we want out of life? This lesson in Deuteronomy tells us how.

Engaging the Theme

The Callings of God

by Dr. Louis H. Wilson

The two most commonly used words for "call" and its various forms in the Bible are *kaleo* (**kal-eh-o**) in the New Testament Greek, including Greek Septuagint and *qara'* (**kaw-raw**) in Old Testament Hebrew. According to "Strong's Concordance of the Bible," these two words and a few others are used 844 times in the King James Version. Of all the many nuances in meaning, a summary definition might read like this, "to identify, summon, request, or command." This summer quarter will cover these basic definitions and their implications to those called children of God.

Units I, II, and III will touch on: (1) God's calling us into and to be a covenant community; (2) God's calling us into service; (3) God's calling us to obedience; and (4) God's calling to and for us to respond.

Many of us have placed a telephone call only to discover the line was busy. Before answering machines, voice mail, and the like, there were only a few ways to make contact if it was an important call: call back later, send a telegram, write a letter, or make a personal visit. Of course, given the location of the person we were trying to contact, any of these methods may or may not work. After all, they could have moved. Even today, communicating with someone is based upon two circumstantial variables: (1) the forms of communication we and other persons have access to and (2) our and their location.

The limitations that constrain us from communicating with one another do not bind an omnipotent (all-powerful), omniscient (all-knowing), omnipresent (all-present) God. He is free to contact us when He wants, how He wants, and for reasons of His own choosing. We will answer His call according to His purposes. This is the core message of this quarter.

In our study this quarter, we will discover God calling a community of people to be in relationship with Him. The callings that we will explore affirm the covenants made with the patriarchs and emphasize the relationship between God's calling and their obedience (Genesis 12:1–3; 49:10). We will also discover that a call from God is universal in its implications.

Whether implicitly or explicitly, when God calls, all are required to respond. Pharaoh made the mistake of assuming he could

ignore the call (command) of God (Exodus 5:2). The price he paid for not heeding God's call was the ultimate decimation of his army. However, as obedience was not arbitrary for Pharaoh, we will learn neither is obedience arbitrary for God's people.

God's covenantal calling is unconditional; the called will come, and no one can snatch those who are His out of His hand (John 10:28). This truth, however, does not negate a responsibility to obey God nor free us from the consequences of disobedience. Experiencing the blessings of the covenant was conditional. The Scriptures, in this series, will show us God made promises—promises of blessing and promises of cursing (Deuteronomy 30:1–10). When we receive and subject ourselves to God's authority, it is an indication that we believe the covenantal promises. When we persistently disobey, it is an indication we have rejected the covenant and thereby God.

We will see in the lives of a few of the biblical characters in this study, including Moses, Aaron, and the people of God, that perfection is not God's expectation—desired yes but wisely and knowingly not expected. He prepares for imperfections, even among His servants. Moses hesitates in responding to his call and disobeys God, doubting His provision (Exodus 4; Numbers 20), and the people grumble and refuse to trust the Lord at His word (Numbers 11; 14). Nevertheless, even with this knowledge, before the foundation of the world, God does not hesitate to deliver, sustain, use, and provide for His people.

It took God 80 years to get Moses ready for God's use, but He used Moses. God had to leave and allow the passing away of every person over 20 in the wilderness, to fulfill His promise to *deliver* His people to the Promised Land; but He does get them there. Moses, Aaron, and the other chosen people of God, to lesser and greater degrees, demonstrated behavior inconsistent with God's call; still none of God's promises were not and will not be fulfilled.

By examining God's calling of individuals, even entire families to service, we will see that God is a God of organism, organization, and relationship. When rightly applied, Christian service and leadership are principled activities and benefit the one called, the community, and the kingdom of God, thereby making us effective ambassadors for Jesus Christ. All have a calling and a charge to keep.

What we will find is that God will use, from a human standpoint, the most unimpressive people, who faced impossible odds and difficulties, to affirm and accomplish all that He desires. Then, He alone gets the glory (see 1 Corinthians 1:26-31). In other words, over the next Unit, we will see testimonies that God is able, documented by the assurance of what He has done and promised to do. It is to that end God calls people to worship and consciously recall the wonders He has performed (Deuteronomy 16:1–8).

Contemporarily, we think of worship and praise as what happens in church, specifically during Sunday services. It is important to sing and rejoice in the Lord's goodness. Psalm 150 ends on this note: "Let everything that has breath praise the Lord. Praise ye the Lord" (v. 6). An argument could be made that would be supported by lessons 5 and 6 is that true worship, in the *house,* is an extension of what our commitments are outside of the house.

The old quote of record repeated by many, "Those who cannot remember the past are condemned to repeat" applies to God's people. Compelled through discussion and exposition, we will see just how far God brought the people of Israel and prayerfully incite us to consider and give Him worship and praise for how far He has brought us and how we can be used to bring others along.

God commanded the Israelites to be mindful of others by how they managed their resources. The "Year of Jubilee" was instituted so no one was left out in the cold—perpetually deprived the Israelites from having the ability to transfer goods and resources only to the rich and powerful among the covenant people. The idea of separating the spiritual and the practical in the life of the community are concepts foreign to Scripture. This lesson will challenge us to be biblically relevant and creative and politically active.

The bottom line, as the unit ends, is that we have a decision to make. Which path will we take? We can hear, listen, and obey the callings of God or close our ears, ignore, and disobey. Standing in the middle is not an option.

Dr. Louis H. Wilson *holds a doctorate in leadership and organizational development from the University of Phoenix and has been involved in church leadership and development for the past 25 years.*

Called and Sealed with a Promise

by Luvell Anderson

We are called to a covenant community. It is made evident in the Pentateuch (the first five books of the Bible or the books of the Law—Genesis, Exodus, Leviticus, Numbers, Deuteronomy) that God desires a covenant community that will display His glory to a watching world. Moses, while speaking to the Israelites, informed them of their special status: "for you are a people holy to the LORD your God. Out of all the peoples on the face of the earth, the LORD has chosen you to be his treasured possession" (Deuteronomy 14:2, NIV). While there is tremendous benefit in being a member of God's covenant community, membership should also be recognized as a tremendous privilege. God's choice of a people is based purely on His grace alone. No one can boast that it was because he or she was so great that God had to let that person into His community. Speaking through Moses, God explicitly made His gracious choice clear: "The LORD did not set his affection on you and choose you because you were more numerous than other peoples, for you were the fewest of all peoples" (Deuteronomy 7:7, NIV). Having awareness of the basis of God's choice ought to humble us and compel us to express gratitude for His grace.

The theme for this quarter's study is designed to teach us how we are to live as members of God's covenant community. In the last four books of the Pentateuch, Moses set forth God's instructions and decreed for the newly emancipated Israelites, who were being brought into "a land flowing with milk and honey" (see Exodus 3:8, Leviticus 20:24, Deuteronomy 6:3). In the Hebrew, the phrase "with milk" is *chalab* (**khaw-lawb)** and means "abundance of land." Therefore, as a nation, they would be blessed with abundance in land and possessions.

God didn't just call the Israelites to be a people for His own possession but He also provided instruction for living life the way He intended it to be lived. After all, it is in Him that we "live and move and have our being" (Acts 17:28, NIV). Consequently, an omniscient (all-knowing) God would know what is best for our lives.

The lessons in this quarter are centered on three main themes: (1) how God called Israel out of Egypt; (2) how God called Israel to be His people; and (3) how God called Israel to choose life. These three themes cover the initiation into the covenant community, identity as a member of the community, and finally, the responsibilities that come with being a member of the community.

Initiation

As we have already seen, God's choice to make Israel His covenant community was based on His grace alone. We begin to see the extent of His grace in the way He initiates them into the community. As is often noted in Old Testament passages, Egypt is commonly understood to be a symbol of oppression and suffering. The people of Israel, after initially enjoying several years of peace and prosperity, found themselves slaves in the land. Moses explains that their lives were made "bitter with hard service" (Exodus 1:14, ESV). Yet, even in the face of cruel slavery, signs of God's favor upon them were still evident: "But the more they were oppressed, the more they multiplied and the more they spread abroad" (Exodus 1:12, ESV). As a result of their ever-increasing numbers, Pharaoh ordered the euthanizing of every male Hebrew child (Exodus 1:22). Of course, this action only compounded the amount of sorrow and suffering endured by the Israelites. Yet, it is in the midst of this suffering that God makes His power known. Through the plagues brought upon Egypt to the parting of the Red Sea, God made it clear that He desired to rescue Israel from their bondage.

God's call to Israel, to come out of Egypt, was also

a command. They were not just being emancipated from their slavery but they were also being called to leave behind their former way of life. Having spent more than 400 years in an idolatrous land such as Egypt, it is reasonable to expect that the Israelites would have been influenced by the Egyptian culture, especially its idolatrous practices. We also see at one point Israel desiring to return to Egypt (see Numbers 14:1–4). So, God's call was a call to embrace freedom as well as for them to leave behind their former life of bondage.

Called to be God's People

In addition to the call to come out of Egypt, God called Israel to be his people. As a result, He placed a distinctive mark on Israel. They had been brought out of Egypt by miraculous acts. God displayed His choice of them as "His representatives" in a very visible way. Now God was calling them to assume a unique identity as the people of God.

It is through this people that God chose to make Himself known. We see that in the incident where Moses and Aaron went to Pharaoh to tell him of God's command for Pharaoh to free God's people. Of course, Pharaoh did not respond favorably: "Pharaoh said, 'Who is the LORD, that I should obey him and let Israel go? I do not know the LORD and I will not let Israel go'" (Exodus 5:2, NIV). By the end of the plagues, it is clear that Pharaoh came to know who the Living God truly is (Exodus 12:31). He was the God of Israel, His chosen people.

God's call to Israel to be His people also included a call to exclusive worship. The first commandment, tells of God's desire to be the sole object of their affection. God instructed, "You shall have no other gods before me" (Exodus 20:2, ESV). Therefore, to be God's people meant to worship Him alone. Unfortunately, Israel found this a bit difficult to internalize. Not long after God emancipated them from Egyptian slavery—while Moses was still receiving the Law from God Himself on Mount Sinai—the people decided to erect a golden calf to worship (Exodus 32). As a result, there were serious repercussions (vv. 27–29). So we see that the call to be God's people also has ramifications for worship.

A Call to Choose Life

The third and final theme of this quarter has to do with God's call to choose life. After rehearsing God's laws and decrees, telling them what is expected of them, Moses told the Israelites, "This day I call heaven and earth as witnesses against you that I have set before you life and death, blessings and curses. Now choose life, so that you and your children may live" (Deuteronomy 30:19, NIV). It seems obvious that with the choices of life and death before you, choosing life would be a no-brainer. But, if you recall, there were several moments when the Israelites desired to go back to the death they once were enslaved (see, for example, Exodus 16:3; 17:3; Numbers 14). Even though the life God designed for Israel was clearly better, the familiarity of their past experience still had a strong hold on the Israelites. Consequently, in order for Israel to enjoy the fullness of salvation, it was not enough to just have the shackles loosened; Israel also had to intentionally embrace freedom by making a deliberate choice. As we will see, choosing life meant obeying God's Law (Deuteronomy 4:1). Israel had been in slavery for more than 400 years, so its perspective on life was distorted. God is the only one who has the perfect vantage point—He has a perspective that is situated above all distortions. Obviously, He can tell us what truly constitutes life. That is why Moses urges the people to obey God's statutes and rules, so they can truly live (Deuteronomy 4:1).

God's call is deep and all encompassing. Its effects have ramifications for every part of our lives. Even though there is great benefit; there is also great responsibility. However, let us take comfort in the promise Paul expounded in his letter to the Romans: "And those he predestined, he also called; those he called, he also justified; those he justified, he also glorified" (Romans 8:30, NIV).

***Luvell Anderson** obtained his bachelor's degree in philosophy from the University of Missouri at St. Louis.*

Devastating Developments in Africa and America

by Carl F. Ellis Jr., Ph.D.

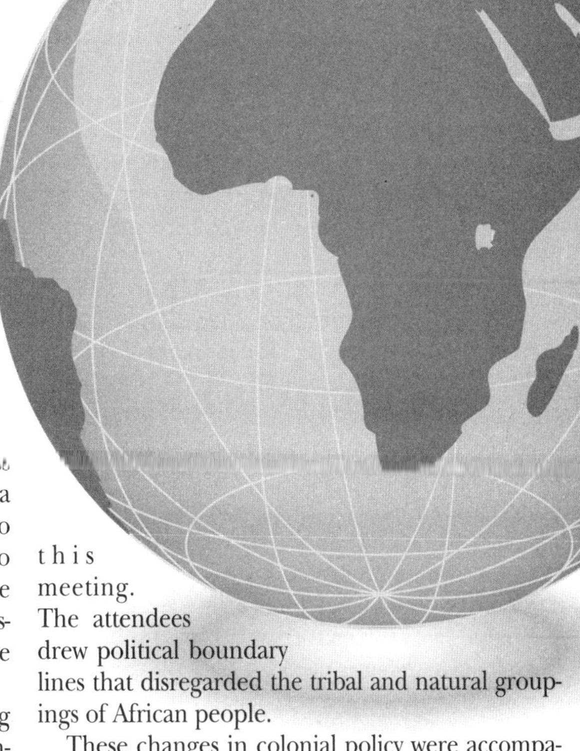

The mid-1800s witnessed three developments that profoundly affected the African situation. They were: (1) the industrial revolution in Europe, (2) the development of the oceangoing steam ship, and (3) the opening of the Suez Canal (in 1869). With the increased need for raw materials and greater access to them, European colonial activity in sub-Sahara intensified. As a result, the colonialists began to fight among themselves over territory and rights to the vast resources of the African continent. The British were disputing with the Dutch, who were disputing with the French, who were disputing with the Belgians, and on and on.

Eventually, the colonialists got tired of fighting each other. Portugal proposed an international conference to resolve these and other issues. In response, German Chancellor Otto von Bismarck convened the Berlin Conference in 1884 and 1885. At this meeting, the colonial powers carved up sub-Saharan Africa. Sadly, not one African was present at this meeting. The attendees drew political boundary lines that disregarded the tribal and natural groupings of African people.

These changes in colonial policy were accompanied by radical changes in attitude toward the peoples of Africa. As a result, the aims of the African American missionaries were in conflict with the aims of the colonialists. The anti-colonial stance of these missionaries was seen as an obstacle to the commercial interests of the colonial powers. Therefore, these missionaries were marginalized. Some came under persecution, some were jailed, and others were expelled from the colonies. To make matters worse, the colonial administrations denied entry to new African American missionaries.

Within a few years, the entire African American missions movement in colonial Africa was devastated. This also had several negative effects: (1) the church associated missions with trauma, (2) the church suffered missions' amnesia as people stopped sharing our missionary history, and (3) by the early twentieth century, the church gave up on missionary efforts outside of this country. As a result, our missions history was lost inside of a generation and the missions consciousness of the African American church was practically obliterated.

During these years, the status of Blacks in America also began to deteriorate with the appalling rise in bigotry and inhumane treatment. For example, in the South in 1870, if I demanded respect from a White person, I'd get it. However, in 1890, in that same situation, I would probably be swinging from a tree within about two hours, a victim of lynching.

After the post-Civil War Reconstruction period ended, White supremacy was reestablished in the South by various means, including terrorism. Many believed the former slaves had made too much progress too fast. Thus, the southern states created a racial caste system through segregation by way of creating Black codes in 1865 (state laws that enforced racism). After gaining freedom and the right to vote, African Americans were stripped of their civil and voting rights through devices such as literacy tests, the poll tax, the grandfather clause, and terrorist attacks by the Ku Klux Klan. Even the federal government participated in injustice. The U.S. Supreme Court declared the Civil Rights Act of 1875 unconstitutional. In 1896, the high court ruling in the *Plessy* v. *Ferguson* case affirmed the principle of "separate but equal."

Current African American Missionary Efforts

The late 1960s saw the rise of the Black Consciousness Movement. With it came a renewed interest in our Black history and tracing our African roots. Though it did not catch on immediately in most church circles, by the 1980s, African identity was embraced by most African American Christians. Church choirs began to adorn their robes with Kente cloth. Others began to take a keen interest in the Black presence in the Bible.

The advent of the jumbo jet made travel abroad more affordable and more accessible. Thus, the increased interest in Africa was accompanied by an increased frequency of African Americans traveling to the motherland and other overseas destinations. All these factors and more contributed to a reawakening of interest in global missions in general and African missions in particular.

Today African American Christians are participating in short-term missions in greater numbers than ever before. Black churches across the country are developing partnerships with churches in Africa. Many of us are discovering that the church around the world is anxious to hear our story—"how God has brought us from a mighty long way."

Could we be on the verge of a great missions movement emerging from the African American church? If these are indeed the "last days," could God be calling us to play a key role in preaching the Gospel of the kingdom "in the whole world as a testimony to all nations" (Matthew 24:14)?

It is not enough for us just to celebrate these possibilities. We must act wisely on them. We must learn from wisdom of our forefathers and be willing to learn from those God sends us to. "For this is what the Lord has commanded us: '"I have made you a light for the [nations], that you may bring salvation to the ends of the earth"'" (Acts 13:47, NIV).

Carl F. Ellis Jr., Ph.D., *is the author of the book* Going Global (Beyond the Boundaries). *"Suffering and the South" is an excerpt from his book.*

Rev. James W. C. Pennington

(1809–1870)

Minister, Teacher, Orator, Abolitionist

It was 1855, even before the Civil War began, but already African American ministers in the north were protesting injustice in some of the same ways that we associate with the Civil Rights era of the last century. Rev. James W. C. Pennington was kicked off the street car in New York City for refusing to sit in the area designated for Blacks. When he complained to the police, they briefly jailed him. After this, he along with a doctor from Scotland and Rev. Henry Highland Garnet, formed the Legal Rights Association to fight for an end to segregation in public accommodations.

The first 21 years of Pennington's life he was a slave in the state of Maryland. Although he was trained to be an excellent blacksmith, he was not taught to read or write and had no religious education. He did not even know of Jesus Christ. But when he escaped north to freedom, he was shielded the first six months by Quakers who began educating him. He had a voracious appetite for education, especially loving astronomy and logic, learning German, French, Greek, and Latin. He sat in on classes at Yale but was not allowed to enroll formally. He traveled to Paris, Brussels, and London. The University of Heidelberg in Germany conferred on him the degree of doctor of divinity.

But before all this, while he was still in his first year of freedom, he became aware that he was in a different kind of slavery—slavery to sin. He did not forget his brothers and sisters still in slavery but he felt that he could not petition God to end slavery since his own heart was not yet right with God. He continued in deep turmoil for several weeks, until he came into a saving relationship with God through Jesus Christ.

Reverend Pennington used his education as a teacher, advocating independently run and controlled schools and seminaries until desegregation could be achieved in the North. He was also a minister in Congregational, Presbyterian, and African Methodist Episcopal churches. As a minister, he conducted the wedding of a 21-year-old escaped slave named Frederick Douglass.

Because of the Fugitive Slave Act, even slaves who escaped to freedom in the north were in danger, so Reverend Pennington hid his enslaved past, even from his wife. But while he was in Britain speaking, he revealed his past and a wealthy benefactor paid for his freedom so that he could continue in the fight for the abolition of slavery. At this time, he began writing his autobiography, *The Fugitive Blacksmith.* The complete text is available online and from his own words, the awfulness of the institution of slavery is revealed. He also wrote *A Text Book of the Origin and History of the Colored People*, in which he argued for African origins of western European civilization and against European claims to superiority. He also founded the Union Missionary Society, which was created to evangelize Africa, Jamaica, and other parts of the world.

Sources:

Durham, Dr. Joseph, and Dr. C. D. Coleman. *Civil Rights.* Elgin, Ill.: David C. Cook Publishing Co., 1972.

Pennington, James W. C. *The Reluctant Blacksmith or, Events in the History of James W. C. Pennington.* http://www.cwo.com/~lucumi/pennington.html. Accessed April 3, 2008.

TEACHING TIPS

June 7
Bible Study Guide 1

1. Words You Should Know

A. Bush (Exodus 3:2–4) *cenah* (Heb.)—Thorn bush, probably the acacia, a small variety of the shittim tree found in the Sinai region.

B. Consumed (v. 2) *'akal* (Heb.)—Absorbed or engrossed.

C. Oppression (v. 9) *lachats* (Heb.)—The unjustly harsh exercise of authority or power.

D. Token (v. 12) *'owth* (Heb.)—Something meant to represent an act, event, or feeling; a memento or keepsake.

2. Teacher Preparation

Unifying Principle—Hearing Requires Listening! Sometimes a special person is called to help another person or a people to overcome difficulties and to survive in times of hardship. Who has the power and position to help us? God chose Moses to save God's people and promised to give Moses all the help he needed.

A. Prepare by reading the Bible Study Guide for lesson 1 and making notes to share with your class.

B. Study and meditate on the Focal Verses.

C. Pray for your students, asking God to open their hearts to today's lesson.

3. Starting the Lesson

A. Read the AIM for Change aloud and include it in the opening prayer.

B. Begin the lesson by asking the students to get quiet. When they are silent, ask them to identify what they hear. Ask them to identify what they had to do to be able to hear. Then, tell them that Moses had to do some of the same things to be able to hear God, including listening.

C. Read the In Focus section. Ask the students how they can relate to the story. Spend no more than five minutes in discussion.

4. Getting into the Lesson

A. Ask the students when we are most likely to listen for and hear from God—in times of trouble or when things are well? Have them explain their answers.

B. Tell the students that the Israelites were oppressed and suffering in Egypt when God called Moses to deliver them. Solicit volunteers to read Focal Verses.

C. Ask three students to role-play the text; choose a narrator, a Moses, and God.

D. Select other volunteers to read the Background; The People, Places, and Times; and In Depth sections.

5. Relating the Lesson to Life

A. Divide the students into two groups and have one group answer the Search the Scriptures questions and the other group answer the Discuss The Meaning questions.

B. Have the students compare and contrast how God spoke to Moses and how He speaks to us today.

C. Ask if there are any volunteers who are willing to share how God called them to a specific task.

6. Arousing Action

A. Review the Make It Happen section. Ask your students to give their suggestions. Then challenge them to put them into practice.

B. Assign the Daily Bible Readings as homework for next week. Emphasize that these readings will enhance their learning of God's Word and give them context for the lessons.

C. Before the closing prayer, ask the students if they have any prayer requests they would like to share with the class.

Worship Guide

For the Superintendent or Teacher
Theme: God Calls Moses
Theme Song: "Speak To My Heart, Lord"
Devotional Reading: Exodus 2:23–3:12
Prayer

JUN 7th

GOD CALLS MOSES

Bible Background • EXODUS 2:23–3:12
Printed Text • EXODUS 3:1–12 Devotional Reading • HEBREWS 3:1–13

AIM for Change

By the end of the lesson, we will:
LEARN that when there is a proper response to God's call, His work gets done;
KNOW that He calls us today; and
OBEY what He tells us to do.

Keep in Mind

"Come now therefore, and I will send thee unto Pharaoh, that thou mayest bring forth my people the children of Israel out of Egypt" (Exodus 3:10).

Focal Verses

KJV **Exodus 3:1** Now Moses kept the flock of Jethro his father in law, the priest of Midian: and he led the flock to the backside of the desert, and came to the mountain of God, even to Horeb.

2 And the angel of the LORD appeared unto him in a flame of fire out of the midst of a bush: and he looked, and, behold, the bush burned with fire, and the bush was not consumed.

3 And Moses said, I will now turn aside, and see this great sight, why the bush is not burnt.

4 And when the LORD saw that he turned aside to see, God called unto him out of the midst of the bush, and said, Moses, Moses. And he said, Here am I.

5 And he said, Draw not nigh hither: put off thy shoes from off thy feet, for the place whereon thou standest is holy ground.

6 Moreover he said, I am the God of thy father, the God of Abraham, the God of Isaac, and the God of Jacob. And Moses hid his face; for he was afraid to look upon God.

7 And the LORD said, I have surely seen the affliction of my people which are in Egypt, and have heard their cry by reason of their taskmasters; for I know their sorrows;

8 And I am come down to deliver them out of the hand of the Egyptians, and to bring them up out of that land unto a good land and a large, unto a land flowing with milk and honey; unto the place of the Canaanites, and the Hittites, and the Amorites, and the Perizzites, and the Hivites, and the Jebusites.

9 Now therefore, behold, the cry of the children

NLT **Exodus 3:1** One day Moses was tending the flock of his father-in-law, Jethro, the priest of Midian. He led the flock far into the wilderness and came to Sinai, the mountain of God.

2 There the angel of the LORD appeared to him in a blazing fire from the middle of a bush. Moses stared in amazement. Though the bush was engulfed in flames, it didn't burn up.

3 "This is amazing," Moses said to himself. "Why isn't that bush burning up? I must go see it."

4 When the LORD saw Moses coming to take a closer look, God called to him from the middle of the bush, "Moses! Moses!" "Here I am!" Moses replied.

5 "Do not come any closer," the LORD warned. "Take off your sandals, for you are standing on holy ground.

6 I am the God of your father—the God of Abraham, the God of Isaac, and the God of Jacob." When Moses heard this, he covered his face because he was afraid to look at God.

7 Then the LORD told him, "I have certainly seen the oppression of my people in Egypt. I have heard their cries of distress because of their harsh slave drivers. Yes, I am aware of their suffering.

8 So I have come down to rescue them from the power of the Egyptians and lead them out of Egypt into their own fertile and spacious land. It is a land flowing with milk and honey—the land where the Canaanites, Hittites, Amorites, Perizzites, Hivites, and Jebusites now live.

of Israel is come unto me: and I have also seen the oppression wherewith the Egyptians oppress them.

10 Come now therefore, and I will send thee unto Pharaoh, that thou mayest bring forth my people the children of Israel out of Egypt.

11 And Moses said unto God, Who am I, that I should go unto Pharaoh, and that I should bring forth the children of Israel out of Egypt?

12 And he said, Certainly I will be with thee; and this shall be a token unto thee, that I have sent thee: When thou hast brought forth the people out of Egypt, ye shall serve God upon this mountain.

9 Look! The cry of the people of Israel has reached me, and I have seen how harshly the Egyptians abuse them.

10 Now go, for I am sending you to Pharaoh. You must lead my people Israel out of Egypt."

11 But Moses protested to God, "Who am I to appear before Pharaoh? Who am I to lead the people of Israel out of Egypt?"

12 God answered, "I will be with you. And this is your sign that I am the one who has sent you: When you have brought the people out of Egypt, you will worship God at this very mountain."

In Focus

Teresa was already running behind, so she sped to her infant daughter's daycare. If only she could run inside, evade a conversation with the staff, and drop her baby off, then she might make it to work on time.

She threw both diaper bags across her shoulder and positioned the baby in her arms. She was getting ready to close the car door when she noticed her purse in the passenger seat. It took her all of a minute to decide what to do. The daycare was not situated in the best neighborhood. Leaving her purse in the open wasn't the smartest decision to make, but her arms were too full to grab it.

As soon as she closed the door and took a few steps, she noticed a suspicious-looking man walking across the lawn toward her. She thought to go back and lock her car door or get her purse but it would only slow her down. It wasn't an audible voice, but clearly she heard, *Get your purse.* She stopped in her tracks and looked at the man. She thought that if she went back and got her purse, it would look like she judged the man to be a thief. So she prayed for God's protection and went inside the daycare.

In less than a minute, she returned to her car, looked for her purse, and found it missing. She looked under the seat and in the backseat, trying to remember if she hid it like she had considered. Next thing she knew she burst into tears. She was angry with herself for not listening to God when He told her to go back and get her purse.

When God speaks to us (and often it is in a still, small voice), we must learn to listen and obey.

The People, Places, and Times

Jethro. Jethro's name means "his excellence." He was Moses' father-in-law. Moses married his daughter, Zipporah. Jethro was the priest of Midian.

Source:
Smith's Bible Dictionary. Peabody, Mass.: Hendrickson Publishers, Inc., 2000.

Background

Before he was even born, Moses had been marked for death. At the time of his conception, an Egyptian edict had been issued: All Hebrew boys were to be killed. It was a perilous time to be born. His people were oppressed and burdened by Pharaoh. While Moses' peers were being thrown into the Nile, his mother hid him for three months, gently placed him into the river in a basket, and trusted God with the outcome.

Of course, God had marked Moses, too. The Lord strategically placed the baby into the hands of an Egyptian woman—not any woman but Pharaoh's daughter. The woman, whose father killed Hebrew boys, raised one herself. God saw to it that Moses received the best of everything, even to being the prince of Egypt.

Witnessing the harsh treatment of the Hebrews caused Moses to have compassion on them, so much so that when an Egyptian taskmaster used excessive force with a Hebrew slave, Moses killed him. Shortly afterward, he tried to end a quarrel between two Hebrews, and one of the men threatened him: "Will you kill us like you did the Egyptian?" Upon hearing this, Moses ran. He fled to Midian, an Arab place, probably in the Sinai Peninsula. This turned out to be another divine placement for Moses, as he was readily accepted by Jethro, the priest of Midian, who later became his father-in-law.

Meanwhile, back in Egypt, the Israelites cried out to God for deliverance. God heard them, and in His compassion for them, He called Moses to deliver His people.

At-A-Glance

1. Moses Looks (Exodus 3:1–3)
2. Moses Hears (vv. 4–10)
3. Moses Responds (vv. 11–12)

In Depth

1. Moses Looks (Exodus 3:1–3)

Moses was at work when God called him. Contrary to what many people assume about the kind of people God chooses, Moses was not in a glorious occupation at the time; he tended to sheep all day. While other shepherds were probably complaining about their mundane, thankless, and low-paying jobs, Moses apparently didn't say a word. Even after living, eating, and having the finest things in Egypt, we have no record that Moses lodged a complaint about being underemployed in hot, arid, smelly Midian. To him, it was better than what he felt he really deserved—death, for taking the life of the Egyptian.

The day began like any other, with Moses leading his sheep to the backside of the mountain of Horeb to graze. As this was mostly a mindless job, Moses could have used the time to think and reflect. He could have looked over his life and wondered how in the world he ended up in such a lonely place. He probably asked himself a lot of questions. Why would God allow him to be born at a time when his peers were being killed? Why would his mother save him and then let him go? How could he go from being raised in Pharaoh's house to running from the man? Where was the God of Israel?

With questions turning over in his head, he could have felt like he was about to lose his mind. So, to him, a burning bush would be a confirmation of his insanity.

Considering how hot and arid it was in Midian, a bush on fire may have been a common sight. But a bush not consumed by the fire was another thing. It definitely got Moses' attention; he drew closer to have a look.

2. Moses Hears (vv. 4–10)

We don't know how many times God had called Moses by name, but the man could have felt so overcome with guilt, worthlessness, and anxiety. This day when Moses herded his sheep, did he feel alone, lonely, and think that he had gone too far to be used by God? It would take a miracle to get his attention. And that's what God provided when the bush caught fire and did not burn up.

"Moses, Moses!" God called.

How wonderful it is to hear God call one's name, to have one's personage and existence acknowledged. Just when Moses thought he was alone, the Lord Almighty was with him.

Though God had initiated an invitation for Moses to come closer, there were boundaries he could not cross. While God had made Himself known to Moses, the man still had to respect and reverence who and what God was. So God told Moses to take off his sandals. Taking off one's sandals was a sign of respect and submission, as taking off one's hat when entering a public place is today. God's presence deemed the place sacred.

Not that God needed an introduction, but He identified Himself to Moses, "I am the God of thy Father." As bad and long as the Israelite's oppression and suffering were in Egypt, Moses probably questioned what he had heard from his forefathers about God. If God had done all of that for his forefathers, where was He now? How could He allow this cruelty? Was He even real? But when God identified Himself, Moses hid his face with shame for questioning His existence.

Moses listened as God validated him and his concerns. God let him know that he was very well aware of the Israelites' situation, He had heard their cries, and that He was going to do something about it. Moses listened and heard God's promises and His plan to deliver His people from their troubles. The thing that caught Moses by surprise was that he was a part of the promise and the plan. He had to decide how to respond.

3. Moses Responds (vv. 11–12)

Obviously Moses had not heard the rules of religion that plague some of us today. Many of us believe that we cannot question God, answer Him, or reason with Him. Moses responds by doing all of the above. "Who am I that I should go to Pharaoh? And that I should bring the Israelites out of Egypt?"

Considering his own anxieties, insecurities, and inabilities, Moses believed that God was making a big mistake by calling Him for the task at hand. Moses probably had a slew of other questions: "Don't you know I'm on the run? Do you know how bad I messed up in Egypt?"

What Moses saw as disqualifiers, God disregarded because of the purpose He had for Moses. When God promised Moses that He would be with him, assured him of his success, and told him that the Israelites would worship God in the place they were standing, Moses eventually responded with faith and accepted the challenge.

Search the Scriptures

1. What was Moses' job in Midian (Exodus 3:1)?
2. Who was Jethro (v. 1)?
3. What got Moses' attention (v. 3)?
4. Who called to Moses out of the bush (v. 4)?
5. What did God want Moses to do (v. 10)?
6. Did Moses readily accept the challenge (v. 11)?
7. Did God give up on Moses? (v. 12)

Discuss the Meaning

1. Why did Moses have to take off his shoes?
2. Why did Moses hide his face when God identified Himself?
3. Why would God give his people a land flowing with milk, honey, and enemies?

Lesson in Our Society

As we can see from the text, God responds to human suffering, but He calls us to do the work. Like Moses, many of us allow our inadequacies, lack of resources, and fears to keep us from intervening. How can we use the plan and promise that God gave to Moses to find courage to do God's work?

Make It Happen

Do you know what God has called you to do? If so, are you walking in your calling? If not, why not? This week, recommit yourself to the Lord and to fulfilling His purpose for your life. If you do not know your calling, set aside time this week to ask God. In your prayer time, consider your life, what He saved you from, and what burns you up inside. That particular area may be where you are called to intervene.

Follow the Spirit

What God wants me to do:

Remember Your Thoughts

Special insights I have learned:

More Light on the Text

Exodus 3:1–12

The study this quarter begins with the theme of God's call of a covenant community as reflected in the Old Testament books of the law, specifically Exodus, Leviticus, Numbers, and Deuteronomy. The call of God to live in covenant community today is emphasized through these lessons.

1 Now Moses kept the flock of Jethro his father in law, the priest of Midian: and he led the flock to the backside of the desert, and came to the mountain of God, even to Horeb.

The Hebrew text for this lesson begins by emphasizing that the subject of this short narrative is about God's call upon Moses to be the deliverer of His people. The word "now" is a common and often used Hebrew conjunction (**vahv,** representing the letter "w") that precedes Moses' name. In other words, because they are part of a much bigger story, the following events have immutable (unchanging) value. It is as though the writer wants readers to realize that Moses' birth, childhood, and time spent in Pharaoh's palace are irrevocably associated with God's remembering the covenant made with Abraham, Isaac, and Jacob (Exodus 2:24) and the ensuing call of Moses.

There is somewhat of a dispute among Bible scholars regarding whether God, in His sovereignty, sent Moses to Midian to further prepare him for service and ready him to receive the call. The text suggests Moses had some inkling as to the call of God on his life (see Exodus 2:14) and was willing to sacrifice temporal gratification for eternal gain (Hebrews 11:24–26). Maybe the combined 80-year experiences in Egypt and Midian were to teach Moses not only what he was to do but more importantly what he was to be. He was not to deliver God's people; rather his calling was to be a shepherd of the people God was delivering.

The King James Version translates the Hebrew word *ra'ah* **(raw-AW)** as "kept." *Ra'ah* is used 173

"Come now therefore, and I will send thee unto Pharaoh, that thou mayest bring forth my people the children of Israel out of Egypt" (Exodus 3:10).

times in the Old Testament; it is translated as "feed" 75 times and "shepherd" 65 times. In its simplest verbal form, *ra'ah* means "to shepherd." The King James text correctly emphasizes the responsibilities of the shepherd, keeping the flock.

The text is clear. These sheep did not belong to Moses, but were Jethro's sheep. Moses had taken a 40-year course on what it meant to keep, tend to, protect, and care for someone else's flock. While Moses was performing his shepherding duties, God revealed Himself to Moses.

Although the exact location of Mount Horeb is debated, there is biblical evidence that suggests Mount Horeb and Mount Sinai are one and the same (cf. Exodus 19:11; Deuteronomy 4:10–11; 1 Kings 8:9). Among shepherds, the lower foothills of Mount Horeb were known as a seasonal place to pasture and water flocks. From this time forth, Mount Horeb becomes a place where God calls, commands, and enters into covenant with His people.

2 And the angel of the LORD appeared unto him in a flame of fire out of the midst of a bush: and he looked, and, behold, the bush burned with fire, and the bush was not consumed.

The text does not suggest otherwise, therefore, one can assume Moses had made the trip to Horeb before. This day, however, would be different; an angel of the Lord appeared to him in a flame of fire that was not consuming a burning bush.

The phrase, "angel of the Lord," is used some 69 times in the Bible. Many Bible commentators believe it is a reference to the Son of God before He took on human flesh. In speaking to Abraham on Mount Moriah, the angel of the Lord referred to himself as "Lord" (Genesis 22:16). It was this angel, God incarnate, that appeared to Moses at the burning bush (Exodus 3:2).

The word "appeared" (Heb. *ra'ah,* **raw-AW**) means "to cause or to see." This word in Hebrew sounds like the word for "kept" in verse one, but in Hebrew the vowel in the middle is different. Moses, by his own volition, could not physically *see* God. Nevertheless, Moses' call was a revelation initiated by God. At the time, God did not cause Moses to see all that was to come in this initial revelation. For Moses was awestruck, not by the Lord in the midst of the flame but rather by a burning bush that was not consumed by fire. Moses could not have possibly known everything that God had in store for him or for the Hebrew children.

Moses assumed the fire should consume the bush. The Hebrew word used for "bush" (*cenah,* **sen-EH**) does not give us a clue as to what kind of bush it was. However, given the region, one can speculate that it was a thorny shrub of some kind. Moses' first response to this unnatural phenomenon was to examine it through his human senses. Translated "he looked," here the Hebrew word *ra'ah* (**raw-AW**) means "to see with the eyes." Nevertheless, the miracle got Moses' attention so he decided to investigate, seemingly unaware that God was behind this miracle.

3 And Moses said, I will now turn aside, and see this great sight, why the bush is not burnt.

The Hebrew word for "said" (*'amar,* **aw-MAR**), can mean "to say in one's heart." Taken in context, then, this verse could mean much the same as if one were to ask a person, "Can you explain to me what I am seeing?" In this example, the emphasis is not on what is seen but the reason behind it.

Moses turned to "see" (Heb. *ra'ah,* **raw-AW**) why the bush was not burning. Is it possible that God was teaching Moses to look beyond what was discernible through human logic and inquiry? Is it possible that those called of God begin to search Him out before they can clearly hear His voice? The text suggests, at least for Moses that this was true.

4 And when the LORD saw that he turned aside to see, God called unto him out of the midst of the bush, and said, Moses, Moses. And he said, Here am I. 5 And he said, Draw not nigh hither: put off thy shoes from off thy feet, for the place whereon thou standest is holy ground.

Moses had moved beyond a mere desire to observe the mystery of this phenomenon to having an internal need to understand it. Again, the word "see" is the same Hebrew word, *ra'ah* translated previously. In this instance, the "see" is used as an infinitive or verbal noun that expresses the attitude behind the action.

Once Moses demonstrated a heartfelt desire to understand this phenomenon, the Lord called his name twice—"Moses, Moses." Moses responded, "Here I am." However, before extending a formal call to service, the Lord needed Moses' undivided attention, and He needed Moses to understand who it was that was calling him.

"Moses, don't come any closer. Take your shoes off; the place you are standing is holy ground" (v. 5, paraphrased) was God's response to Moses. Translated "ground" (Heb. *'adamah*, **ad-aw-MAW**), the place where Moses stood literally means "earth." The only other like instance in Scripture where this command is given is when the commander of the Lord's army confronted Joshua near the walls of Jericho (Joshua 5:13–15).

It was a universal concept, even in Egypt, to take one's shoes off in the presence of a superior or when entering a home. There was also a social expectation when one entered a place of religious significance that they would take off their shoes. These were customary signs of respect and honor.

God implicitly warned and instructed Moses, as a precursor to his call, that approaching and serving the Lord has conditions (cf. Exodus 19:12), and any place God chooses to manifest Himself becomes holy ground. Undeniably, it is the presence of the Lord that makes a place—any place—holy.

6 Moreover he said, I am the God of thy father, the God of Abraham, the God of Isaac, and the God of Jacob. And Moses hid his face; for he was afraid to look upon God.

Following "moreover he said," the text reads, "I am." The Hebrew personal pronoun *'anokiy* (**aw-no-KEE**), translated "I," is used to refer directly to the one who is doing the speaking. Moses, as the writer (see discussion below), was emphasizing that God identified Himself as the God of promise.

The phrase "the God of Abraham, Isaac, and Jacob" was a familiar expression to Hebrews that God and they used to speak of the promise-keeping covenantal Lord, God—Jehovah. It is also a phrase that signifies "the" God of the living, as attested by our Lord (see Matthew 22:23). There is little doubt that Moses knew he was in the presence of God. As a result, he hid his face so that he might not look upon God.

Some Old Testament scholars conclude that Moses wrote Exodus and the book was later compiled by Joshua or Eleazar. Concurring that Moses wrote the book, we can paraphrase verse 6 by saying "Moses (I) did not feel myself worthy to look God in the face." This is a fitting—and we might argue, necessary—attitude for anyone to hear and respond to the call of God. Even so, arguably responding to the call of God is a passionate undertaking, an undertaking that must emerge from God's heart and purposes.

7 And the LORD said, I have surely seen the affliction of my people which are in Egypt, and have heard their cry by reason of their taskmasters; for I know their sorrows; 8 And I am come down to deliver them out of the hand of the Egyptians, and to bring them up out of that land unto a good land and a large, unto a land flowing with milk and honey; unto the place of the Canaanites, and the Hittites, and the Amorites, and the Perizzites, and the Hivites, and the Jebusites.

God let Moses know, before extending a specific call, that what He was about to ask Moses to do came out of His compassion and desire to deliver His people from their oppressive conditions. Using a powerful Hebrew word to convey that He was about to intercede on behalf of His people, God said He "saw their afflictions." This time the Hebrew word for see, *ra'ah* (**raw-AW**), is in its root form (*qal*) and has the idea that the one doing the seeing has a right to make judgments concerning what he sees.

His judgments, however, were not arbitrary; they were based on the facts. God had an accurate account of his people's sufferings. He heard (Heb. *shama'*, **shaw-MAH**) His people—that is He had a deep interest in them and understood their cry (Heb. *tsa'aqah,* **tsah-ak-AW**) as a despairing of the soul. But that's not all. God understood both the symptoms and causes of His children's afflictions, suggesting that His plan of deliverance was holistic.

The word "affliction" (Heb. *'oniy,* **on-EE**) conveyed the notion that the speaker was focusing on the experiences endured by that suffering, hardship, and trouble. *Nagas* (Heb. **naw-GAS**), translated as "taskmasters," literally means "to exploit, oppress or cause hardships," especially in the context of forced labor. By using these words, God was telling Moses, "I am aware of the mental and physical anguish that is at the root of My peoples' despair and hopelessness." The writer of the book of Hebrews says this about Christ (4:15), and the apostle Paul also says that identifying with the "burdens" of others is an attitude that should mark the life of every believer (Romans 15:1).

However brief these two verses may seem, they offer a clear picture of the mercy and grace of God specifically toward those whom He is calling us to witness and serve. The next verse, verse 8, contains a phrase that ultimately finds its fulfillment in the incarnation of the Lord Jesus Christ: "I am come down to deliver." The idea of coming down has the notion of descending from a loftier place. Prefixed by the Hebrew preposition *l* (the letter *lamed*), "to, towards" and a powerful verbal form (*hifil*) of the word "delivers" (Heb. *natsal,* **naw-TSAL**), which can mean "to retake/plunder the context," suggest God's plan of deliverance was twofold: to free His people from servitude and give them a place to enjoy His blessings.

Palestine, with its varied climates, argued Rabbi Meir, was truly plentiful. Verse 8 is the first of many references to milk and honey and has direct reference to being the land of promise and blessing (Deuteronomy 27:3; Ezekiel 20:6). Identifying this land of milk and honey as the land of the Canaanites, and the Hittites, and the Amorites, and the Perizzites, and the Hivites, and the Jebusites may have been God's affirmation that He was responding not just to the conditions of His people but also to an existing covenant made to Abraham (Genesis 15:18–21). It was because of God's promises that Moses was called into service.

9 Now therefore, behold, the cry of the children of Israel is come unto me: and I have also seen the oppression wherewith the Egyptians oppress them. 10 Come now therefore, and I will send thee unto Pharaoh, that thou mayest bring forth my people the children of Israel out of Egypt.

The normal word order in Hebrew is verb, subject, object; a difference in word order "marks" the initial clause for emphasis. Literally, the first few words in verse 9, before the verb "come," are "the cry of the children of Israel." Seemingly, this is redundant. Apparently, when Moses wrote or dictated this narrative, he understood that "responding to the call" was more than a matter of personal, compassionate sympathies and allegiances. Answering the call of God begins and ends with His purposes. Moses was ready for his commission.

"Come now . . . I am sending you to deliver My people out of Egypt." Again, the literal translation leaves nothing to the imagination. "Send" means "to move" but has the idea of moving toward something specific or because of a specific mission (see Isaiah 6:8; Jeremiah 1:7). God was telling Moses to go to a specific place to do a specific thing.

It is often overlooked that God did not call Moses to deliver the people of God. He called Moses to bring forth the people God was delivering. In the second of this two-part command, He told Moses to bring out (Heb. *yatsa',* **yaw-TSAW**). To summarize the last three verses, we could say, "Moses, you go get (v. 10) those I am delivering (v. 8a), and then bring them out (v. 10) to the place I have chosen (v. 8b)." Responding to God's call required Moses to go to Pharaoh and lead the people out. God would, by a mighty hand, do the rest. In fact, later (Exodus 32:11) Moses attributed all that he did to God.

11 And Moses said unto God, Who am I, that I should go unto Pharaoh, and that I should bring forth the children of Israel out of Egypt?

Nevertheless, for Moses at the time of his call, confronting Pharaoh, the son of Ramses the Great, was a tall order. He had tried once, during the prime of life when he was most able, and barely escaped with His life. We may judge Moses as making excuses. But when we add to this the rejection of his Hebrew brethren (see Acts 7:25), the following verse is understandable.

At one time, Moses assumed what God could do through him; now, in contrast, he questioned his abilities. Nevertheless, this interchange may well reveal that Moses' focus was still on himself. Forty years ago, Moses' focus was on what he thought he could do; now his focus was on what he thought he could not do. Is it possible that Moses had to be brought to this point—questioning both personal sufficiency and insufficiency? Second Corinthians 3:5 suggested that Moses' sufficiency was "Godward" (v. 4).

Notice also that Moses questioned both parts of God's command: to go and to bring forth. God did not directly answer Moses' question. What God did was to make Moses a promise. In other words, He told Moses that the confirmation Moses was looking for demanded a walk of faith.

12 And he said, Certainly I will be with thee; and this shall be a token unto thee, that I have sent thee: When thou hast brought forth the people out of Egypt, ye shall serve God upon this mountain.

First, Moses must be confident of the Lord's presence. God would be with him. Second, Moses was to accept his calling and walk in faith. The word "token" (translated "sign" in other versions and in many other contexts) is used 94 times in the Old Testament. With the exception of 13 instances in the Historical Books, the word "token" or "signs," as cited in the Pentateuch (the first five books of the Bible) and the books of the Prophets, almost always refers to miracles, events, or words God uses to evidence His person, plans, purposes, promises, and precepts (Exodus 31:13; Deuteronomy 28:45, 46; Psalm 105:27; Ezekiel 4:3).

God told Moses, "when I have used you to bring the people out of Egypt and I am served in this mountain, that will be the token/sign of your calling." "Serve" (Heb. *'abad*, **aw-BAD**) appears to be word choice of significance. There are 12 other words in Hebrew translated "serve." Here the writer chooses to use a word that accentuates service rendered on behalf of someone else. God was not calling Moses to lead His children to independence but rather to a God-centered dependence.

It's no wonder that in Hebrews 11, Moses receives commendation in the "Hall of Fame of Faith." Yes, there are a few more questions, as we shall see in the next lesson. Ultimately, the fact that Moses did exactly what God told him to do, the way God told him to do it, was assured only by God's word. Hebrews 11:27 says, "By faith he forsook Egypt, not fearing the wrath of the king: for he endured, as seeing him who is invisible." Responding to God's call demands little of us, yet all of us. We hear, we obey, and we believe. The rest is up to Him.

Sources:

Unger, Merrill F. *The New Unger's Bible Dictionary.* Edited by R.K. Harrison. Chicago: Moody Press, 1988.

Vine, W.E. *Vines Complete Expository Dictionary of Old and New Testament Words.* Edited by Merrill F. Unger and William White Jr. Nashville: Thomas Nelson Publishers, 1996.

Daily Bible Readings

M: Moses' Birth
Exodus 2:1–10
T: Moses Flees
Exodus 2:11–22
W: Moses' Purpose Misunderstood
Acts 7:23–29
T: Moses' Call
Acts 7:30–34
F: Moses' Death Foretold
Deuteronomy 32:48–52
S: Moses' Uniqueness
Deuteronomy 34
S: Come, I Will Send You
Exodus 3:1–12

NOTES

TEACHING TIPS

June 14
Bible Study Guide 2

1. Words You Should Know

A. Eloquent (Exodus 4:10) *dabar* (Heb.)—Speech or writing that is vivid, forceful, fluent, graceful and persuasive.

B. Affliction (v. 31) *'oniy* (Heb.)—Anything causing pain or distress.

2. Teacher Preparation

Unifying Principle—Accepting Responsibility. Because some people believe they are not adequate to a task, they are fearful and resistant to accepting it. How can people, who are afraid, be encouraged to do the work assigned them? Moses resisted God's call, but then, according to God's command, he accepted aid from his brother Aaron.

A. Pray for the students in your class, asking for open hearts to process this lesson and make its principles a part of their lives.

B. Read Exodus 4 in its entirety.

C. Think about what it really means to be a responsible person.

D. Think of a situation when you chose to accept responsibility, even though you felt incapable of completing the task. What were the results, once the task was completed? Consider sharing this situation with the class.

3. Starting the Lesson

A. Open the class in prayer using the AIM for Change.

B. Read the In Focus story. Discuss.

C. Make a list on the chalkboard of some possible consequences the class could have faced if fear had kept them from fulfilling their responsibilities. Discuss some of the consequences and the alternative outcomes.

D. Have a volunteer read the Focal Verses. Discuss.

4. Getting into the Lesson

A. Read and discuss the Background section.

B. Discuss the In Depth section, and answer the Search the Scripture questions.

5. Relating the Lesson to Life

A. Divide the class into two groups, and give each group a different question from the Discuss the Meaning section. Solicit a volunteer in each group to write the responses, and then ask another volunteer to present the responses to the class.

B. Ask the class how they can apply today's lesson to their lives so that everyone around them will be positively affected.

6. Arousing Action

A. Read the Make It Happen section, and encourage all the students to apply it to their lives in the upcoming week.

B. Challenge the students to take on a small task that can be completed in a short length of time (an hour, day, or week), wherein they will confront fears or feelings of inadequacy. Ask them to keep a journal or write down how they felt starting the project and how they felt once it was completed. You may even suggest they write down the obstacles they had to overcome to complete the task.

Worship Guide

For the Superintendent or Teacher
Theme: Moses and Aaron Respond
Theme Song: "I Surrender All"
Devotional Reading: Proverbs 1:20–33
Prayer

MOSES AND AARON RESPOND

Bible Background • EXODUS 4:10–16, 27–31
Printed Text • EXODUS 4:10–16, 27–31 Devotional Reading • PROVERBS 1:20–33

AIM for Change

By the end of the lesson, we will:
STUDY the account of Moses' resistance to God's commands and Aaron's acceptance of his role in leading the people;
EXPLORE our own feelings of inadequacy for God's call on our lives; and
BELIEVE what God says about us, and take responsibility for the tasks to which God has called us.

Keep in Mind

"And Aaron spake all the words which the LORD had spoken unto Moses, and did the signs in the sight of the people" (Exodus 4:30).

Focal Verses

KJV **Exodus 4:10** And Moses said unto the LORD, O my LORD, I am not eloquent, neither heretofore, nor since thou hast spoken unto thy servant: but I am slow of speech, and of a slow tongue.

11 And the LORD said unto him, Who hath made man's mouth? or who maketh the dumb, or deaf, or the seeing, or the blind? have not I the LORD?

12 Now therefore go, and I will be with thy mouth, and teach thee what thou shalt say.

13 And he said, O my Lord, send, I pray thee, by the hand of him whom thou wilt send.

14 And the anger of the LORD was kindled against Moses, and he said, Is not Aaron the Levite thy brother? I know that he can speak well. And also, behold, he cometh forth to meet thee: and when he seeth thee, he will be glad in his heart.

15 And thou shalt speak unto him, and put words in his mouth: and I will be with thy mouth, and with his mouth, and will teach you what ye shall do.

16 And he shall be thy spokesman unto the people: and he shall be, even he shall be to thee instead of a mouth, and thou shalt be to him instead of God.

4:27 And the LORD said to Aaron, Go into the wilderness to meet Moses. And he went, and met him in the mount of God, and kissed him.

28 And Moses told Aaron all the words of the LORD who had sent him, and all the signs which he had commanded him.

29 And Moses and Aaron went and gathered together all the elders of the children of Israel:

NLT **Exodus 4:10** But Moses pleaded with the LORD, "O Lord, I'm not very good with words. I never have been, and I'm not now, even though you have spoken to me. I get tongue-tied, and my words get tangled."

11 Then the LORD asked Moses, "Who makes a person's mouth? Who decides whether people speak or do not speak, hear or do not hear, see or do not see? Is it not I, the LORD?

12 Now go! I will be with you as you speak, and I will instruct you in what to say."

13 But Moses again pleaded, "Lord, please! Send anyone else."

14 Then the LORD became angry with Moses. "All right," he said. "What about your brother, Aaron the Levite? I know he speaks well. And look! He is on his way to meet you now. He will be delighted to see you.

15 Talk to him, and put the words in his mouth. I will be with both of you as you speak, and I will instruct you both in what to do.

16 Aaron will be your spokesman to the people. He will be your mouthpiece, and you will stand in the place of God for him, telling him what to say.

4:27 Now the LORD had said to Aaron, "Go out into the wilderness to meet Moses." So Aaron went and met Moses at the mountain of God, and he embraced him.

28 Moses then told Aaron everything the LORD had commanded him to say. And he told him about the miraculous signs the LORD had commanded him to perform.

30 And Aaron spake all the words which the LORD had spoken unto Moses, and did the signs in the sight of the people.

31 And the people believed: and when they heard that the LORD had visited the children of Israel, and that he had looked upon their affliction, then they bowed their heads and worshipped.

29 Then Moses and Aaron returned to Egypt and called all the elders of Israel together.

30 Aaron told them everything the LORD had told Moses, and Moses performed the miraculous signs as they watched.

31 Then the people of Israel were convinced that the LORD had sent Moses and Aaron. When they heard that the LORD was concerned about them and had seen their misery, they bowed down and worshiped.

In Focus

Cynthia was in the second week of her summer internship with a local advertising agency when the project manager of the company's largest client called her into her office and handed her a packet of information. Cynthia was told to review the information in preparation for a lunch meeting later that afternoon, where she would do a presentation. Feeling a bit overwhelmed, Cynthia hesitantly accepted the packet and returned to her desk.

All kind of thoughts went through Cynthia's mind. "I need more time. I can't do this. I know I'll mess up. This isn't fair." She was too consumed with fear to even comprehend the information she read. When she finally told herself that she had no choice but to do what she had been asked, she looked at the packet and realized that she already knew the information. She had researched and written a report on it earlier last week.

Oftentimes we give God excuses as to why He can't or shouldn't use us. But just as God sent Aaron to aid Moses, He will equip us with what we need to fulfill the tasks He assigns to us.

The People, Places, and Times

Moses. He was the man who led the Israelites out of Egypt, during a time of oppression, and into the Promised Land. As a baby, his mother and sister saved his life by putting him in a basket and placing the basket in the Nile River, where Pharaoh's daughter found him and took him to be her own son. After He killed an Egyptian, he fled to Midian, where he was called by God to deliver the Israelites.

Aaron. He was Israel's first high priest and Moses' brother. He was an eloquent speaker—so much so that when he went to talk to Pharaoh, God used him as a spokesman for Moses. He was also the one who made a golden calf for the freed Israelites to worship, while Moses was up on the mountain praying.

Background

After expressing concern about whether he could complete the assignment given to him, Moses then questioned God about how he should answer the Israelites. "What if they ask me your name? What shall I say to them?" God called Himself by name, "Tell them that 'I am who I am.'" This explained His name Jehovah, and it signified that He is self-existent, self-sufficient, eternal, and unchangeable.

Since they had thrust him away 40 years ago, Moses was concerned that Israel would not listen to him. But God assured Moses that Israel would listen to him this time. Still, Moses asked God for the ability to show them signs and wonders. God equipped him to work three miracles, two of which he performed immediately. When he threw down the rod, it became a snake. When he picked it up, it became a rod again. Unlike magicians, Moses had no need for spells, charms, or incantations; he was empowered by God. The other miracle included the use of his hand. He put his hand in his bosom, and when he took it out, it was leprous. Then he put it back, took it out again, and it was well. For the third miracle, Moses would turn water into blood.

At-A-Glance

1. Moses Runs Out of Excuses (Exodus 4:10–13)
2. God Equips Moses to Do His Will (vv. 14–16)
3. Aaron Receives His Assignment (4:27–31)

In Depth

1. Moses Runs Out of Excuses (Exodus 4:10–13)

Moses ran out of excuses to get God to change His mind. His hesitance to accept the assignment could no longer be imputed to humility or modesty but to fear and unbelief. To counterbalance Moses' weaknesses, God reminded him of His strengths. "Who gave man his mouth? Who makes the blind see, or the deaf to hear?" Then God assured Him of His presence, "I will be with you. I will teach you what to say." How often do we let our inadequacies and fears stand in the way of obeying God or moving forward? God wants us to recognize and believe that He is sufficient to supply us with what we need to accomplish His purposes. What are your excuses, and what keeps you from moving toward God's will and purpose for your life?

2. God Equips Moses to Do His Will (vv. 14–16)

God grew tired of Moses' excuses and became angry (Exodus 4:14). Though He was angry, God still reasoned with Moses. No amount of pouting, doubt, or excuses would change the Lord's faith in those He chooses. In His mercy, He jointly commissioned Aaron to help his younger brother, Moses. Together, they would make a good team. God would use Aaron's mouth and Moses' head and heart to deliver God's people out of Egypt.

Moses and Aaron had not seen each other in years. But at an opportune time, God sent Aaron to meet his brother and filled his heart with joy. Aaron would be the spokesperson, and Moses would be the performer of miracles. The rod that Moses had carried as a shepherd had become a staff of authority. God will give us what we need to accomplish His purposes! Have you even begun to look for God's provision?

3. Aaron Receives His Assignment (4:27–31)

God told Aaron exactly where to find his brother—in the wilderness, near Midian, at the mountain of God. The place where God had met Moses was the place where his brother met him. God's providence is beautiful and complete. He never calls one for a task without providing what he needs to carry it out. He does it so fully that even the provision is happy to find its rightful owner. The text records that when Aaron saw his brother, they embraced.

Who could not be in agreement with the brothers? When the Israelites heard them speak, saw them in agreement, and witnessed their faith and joy, how could they not believe God? It was just as God foretold: The Israelites believed and they worshiped God.

Search the Scriptures

1. What excuse did Moses give God for not being able to do what God had called him to do (Exodus 4:10)?

2. How did God respond (v. 14)?

3. How did the people receive Moses and Aaron (v. 31)?

Discuss the Meaning

1. Why was Moses so reluctant to accept his calling?

2. Besides being eloquent, what other godly characteristics did Aaron seem to have?

3. When faced with unfamiliar tasks, what things can be done to prepare us for the job?

Lesson in Our Society

Parenting is just as much of a calling as ministry. Many have allowed their feelings of inadequacy and perceived inabilities to keep them from raising their children. There are hundreds of thousands of single parent-led households in America.

How can we use today's lesson to urge parents to accept responsibility for and trust God to help them raise their children?

Make It Happen

Even though they may not be aware exactly of what it is, God has given each person a purpose and destiny. For example, Moses was a great leader and did not know it until he accepted the responsibility of leadership. What are some ways believers can find out what God is calling them to do? How will accepting this responsibility change your family, church, and community?

Follow the Spirit

What God wants me to do:

Remember Your Thoughts

Special insights I have learned:

More Light on the Text

Exodus 4:10–16, 27–31

Before a strong request that God send or call someone else to go to Pharaoh (Exodus 4:13), Moses attempted to enlighten God as to why he was not the man for the job. God already answered three of Moses' objections: Who was he that he should go to Pharaoh, how would the people know God sent him, and by what signs would the people and Pharaoh know God had sent Moses, respectively (Exodus 3:11–14; 4:1–9)?

Moses was to tell the people he was sent from God—that the God of promise had seen their plight and had come to deliver them. Furthermore, the Lord told Moses the leaders of the community would listen to him, and he would have a successful mission (Exodus 3:15–21). Again, Moses had questions. One was, "What if the leaders do not believe him?" God told him not to worry because a plan was in place. God would enable him to perform signs and wonders, and the people would believe, and they would listen (Exodus 4:1–9) to the message and God's messenger, Moses.

Although chosen, Moses was still not convinced that he was the man for the job. The Scriptures say God knows what we need, even before we ask (Matthew 6:8). Heavenly preparations for Moses not willingly accepting his call were already in the works. After another short dialogue, God assured Moses the help he needed was on the way.

10 And Moses said unto the LORD, O my Lord, I am not eloquent, neither heretofore, nor since thou hast spoken unto thy servant: but I am slow of speech, and of a slow tongue.

Lord, or any title of social or religious significance, when combined with the Hebrew word *biy* (**bee**), translated "O," has a history of being used to convey a sense of supplication (Genesis 43:20; 44:18). Qualified by an adverb that means "not," the context supports the Hebrew word *dabar* (**daw-BAWR**), which literally means "to speak," being translated as "eloquent." Moses was begging God to consider that he (Moses) lacked the necessary skills to communicate effectively.

Moses used the same word twice, "slow" (Heb. *kabed,* **kaw-BADE**), to stress his inabilities: "I am of slow speech and tongue." In a broad sense, to be slow means to find difficulty or be weighted down by something. Both meanings may be in view here. Referring to his mouth and his tongue, Moses may have been trying to persuade God that he lacked both the physical and mental ability to communicate persuasively. Literally, the Hebraic understanding of the "tongue," *lashown* (**law-SHONE**), included not just the organ but also its use in communication. What Moses said of himself, however, was in stark contrast to what the Scriptures say of him in the seventh chapter of Acts.

Again as referenced in the last lesson, Acts 7, in particularly verse 22, informs us Moses was trained in all the wisdom of Egypt and was "mighty in words and deeds." Had Moses forgotten his training or just had been boldly lying to the Lord? There is an alternative view.

For Moses to consider himself as inept and unprepared for such a task as the Lord was calling him to would not be a stretch. Notice, Moses specifically notes he could speak "neither heretofore" (Heb. *temowl,* **tem-OLE**), literally in days gone by, nor even now; nothing has changed. Bad timing and a premature act of deliverance changed the last 40 years of his life. Now God was asking that he confront a powerful Egyptian ruler and assert leadership among people whose rejection was part of his reason for being in the wilderness. If Moses was using past experience as a key to measure his abilities, it is understandable why he might believe he lacked the necessary skills to accept God's call. We will always find reasons to run from the call, until we have the right perception of the One who calls. Anyone who has been on the battlefield for the Lord knows God must constantly remind us to trust the One who calls and not our qualifications.

Our confidence must not rest in human abilities (see Philippians 3:3). This is a lesson that it seems Moses needed to learn. Nevertheless, as the Lord reminded Moses, it is presumptuous to think that the God who calls us is not preparing us.

11 And the LORD said unto him, Who hath made man's mouth? or who maketh the dumb, or deaf, or the seeing, or the blind? have not I the LORD? 12 Now therefore go, and I will be with thy mouth, and teach thee what thou shalt say.

The Hebrew word translated "made" and "maketh," in this verse, is the same word: *suwm* (**soom**). The one important distinction is the tense. "Made" is a perfect tense and "maketh" is an imperfect tense. In other words, very literally and graphically, God asked Moses, "Who gave humanity their senses and enables their effective use?" Of course, the answer should be obvious, but not leaving anything to doubt, the Lord says to Moses, "Is it not I, the Lord!" (paraphrased).

Verse 12 begins by saying "now therefore." This phrase is actually one word in Hebrew. It is constructed to emphasize that what follows is to be closely associated with the preceding context. Because I have already given you what you need to do, God says to Moses, "Go with the understanding I will use what I have provided you; and I will teach you anything else you need to know" (paraphrased).

What a statement of enablement and provision. "The mouth I gave you I will use; any understanding you lack I will provide." *Yarah* (**yaw-RAW**), a poignant Hebrew word for "teach," means to "cast, throw (such as arrows in a battle), or teach." The verb form in this verse for "teach" is the Hebrew word *hifil*. The idea is "purposeful and deliberate instruction." God was saying more than "I am going to give you some knowledge."

God was unequivocally telling Moses, "Know that I will give you what you need to know at the right time to meet the specific need." This same Lord (remember this is the Angel of the Lord speaking) told His disciples, "Don't worry when the Holy Spirit comes; He 'shall teach you in the same hour what ye ought to say'" (see Luke 12:11, 12). Reservations answered, excuses faltering, and fears allayed, Moses still made one last plea: "Send someone else!"

13 And he said, O my Lord, send, I pray thee, by the hand of him whom thou wilt send.

An exact rendering of the Hebrew is difficult in this verse. There are only seven Hebrew words used, and their linguistic emphasis is difficult to discern. Moses, by saying "by your hand," was recognizing the sovereignty, blessing, and provision of the Lord (Ezra 7:6; Isaiah 25:10). As we should be, the translators of the King James Version were, however, mindful of the context. By the Lord's response, it appears He understood Moses was acknowledging His power and His right to commission but not trusting in the Sovereignty of His calling.

14 And the anger of the LORD was kindled against Moses, and he said, Is not Aaron the Levite thy brother? I know that he can speak well. And also, behold, he cometh forth to meet thee: and when he seeth thee, he will be glad in his heart. 15 And thou shalt speak unto him, and put words in his mouth: and I will be with thy mouth, and with his mouth, and will teach you what ye shall do. 16 And he shall be thy spokesman unto the people: and he shall be, even he shall be to thee instead of a mouth, and thou shalt be to him instead of God.

Yes, humility has its place, but one must also "*think* soberly: according as God hath dealt to every man the measure of faith" (Romans 12:3). Moses was denying God's provision, his call, and therefore not walking by faith. This angered God. There are four primary words used in Hebrew translated "anger." The word in verse 14 is one that is often used; it means to become angry, to have a strong feeling of resentment toward a person or situation.

Moses had ruffled God's feathers. The text goes on to say, "God's anger was kindled against Moses." With a particular focus on the action that follows, "kindled" also means "to be angry." When we resist God's call, He will take action. God is omnipotent and gracious. He knew the reservations Moses would have and, therefore, had already had a support system in the works.

Some commentators have suggested God would have given Moses the gift to speak had he not resisted God's call. Speculation aside, one thing is for sure, God had a complete plan, reflecting His awareness of Moses' inadequacy as an orator. The Lord told Moses that his brother, Aaron—a Levite—was coming to meet him, and he had the ability to speak well. What God has said was simply a statement of facts.

If it were not for the last phrase of verse 14, there would be nothing out of the ordinary in God's reply to Moses. God's response was justifiable. Aaron was a Levite, a possibly prophetic reference to his future role as high priest, and he was Moses' older brother. Verse 14 can be divided into parts a, b, and c: God's response to Moses, a statement concerning Aaron, and last, a significant reference to Aaron's abilities and his coming to meet Moses. While Moses, whether real or by psychological impediment, could not speak, God said, "I know Aaron can" (paraphrased).

Using a perfect tense of the Hebrew word *yada'* (**yaw-DAH**), to "know," God (who is omniscient) told Moses, even before this conversation began, He "knew" Aaron had the wherewithal to take up the slack—that is to speak. "Know" means "to perceive" or "experience." Yes, Aaron was especially gifted by God (Exodus 4:15) and Aaron had been cultivating an ability that God would use.

What Moses said of his inability as a speaker, "not eloquent" that is, God says Aaron can speak eloquently (see v. 10). Both "eloquent" and "speak" (v. 14) are the same Hebrew word. Even though Moses' excuses have run out, he discovered God would use him in spite of himself and do so in a way that was comforting and reassuring. Aaron was coming to meet Moses, and when they met, Aaron would see their meeting as a happy occasion.

The text offers no explanation why Moses needed to be told of and would later experience Aaron's affection (Exodus 4:27). The paragraph above implies some assumptions expanded in the following paragraphs and specifically when discussing verse 27. Right now, let's turn our attention to verses 15 and 16. Moses had the information and Aaron would do the communication.

I think it is safe to say, even though Moses was to remain the man-on-point, God knew that going it alone is tough. The idea of partnership and teamwork to accomplish God's kingdom business is more the norm in Scripture than the unusual: David and Jonathan, Paul and Barnabas, not to mention many other commissioned colaborers of the Lord's work prove this point. Christ sent His disciples out in twos. Few of us, whatever the call, are adequate to work alone.

By God's decree, the people would still be given a message of deliverance. The content remained the same, what had changed was that Aaron would now be the voice they heard.

'Asah (**aw-saw**) is the Hebrew word translated "do." Need it be said, it takes some attentive listening to hear when God speaks and appropriately respond and do what He says. Moses and Aaron had one coordinated call—to present an uncompromising message in an uncompromising way.

Verse 16, in particular, seems to emphasize the above point. Aaron was to speak to the people for Moses. Moses was to speak to Aaron for God—one unified message, individuals with distinctive but unified calls but just one Source of authoritative inspiration—the Word of the Lord. I dare say nothing has changed from that day until this!

**4:27 And the LORD said to Aaron, Go into the
wilderness to meet Moses. And he went, and met
him in the mount of God, and kissed him. 28 And
Moses told Aaron all the words of the LORD who
had sent him, and all the signs which he had commanded him.**

Verse 27 resumes the focus of our lesson by telling us about Aaron's call. Unlike Moses, Aaron did not demonstrate any reservations to following God's call. God told him to go and meet Moses in the wilderness, and he went. (Although the text does not say, we can be sure God provided directions that are more specific. The Sinai desert is approximately 22,000-plus square miles.)

The Lord did not give Aaron a mission plan. The text simply states that he obeyed God and went to meet his brother, a brother that we may assume he had only had limited contact with and probably had not seen in recent years. As a side note, it may not be prudent to make too much of the differences in Moses and Aaron's initial responses to God's call. Their experiences had been different and heeding God's call occurs under different situations for different people.

It seems that what God did was to give Moses someone to run the race with. Aaron felt an emotional attachment to Moses, and as it says in verse 27, so demonstrated his affection. He kissed his brother. Yes, Moses needed a mouthpiece. I think Moses also needed to know he was not forgotten and that someone still cared.

Moses "told" (Heb. *nagad*, **naw-GAD**) Aaron "all" (Heb. *kol*, **kole**) the Lord had said. Moses did not give Aaron information for information's sake. The word "told" refers to "purposeful information," and by the way, Moses left nothing out. He told him all. Colaborers need to know the whole story. Moses not only told Aaron what God said but also by what signs He would display His power and affirmation of Moses' call (Exodus 4:1–8). Now, seemingly convinced of God's calling and directives, the brothers undertook what was probably a two-week journey from Mount Horeb to the land of Goshen (Genesis 47:27), where the Israelites lived.

**29 And Moses and Aaron went and gathered
together all the elders of the children of Israel: 30
And Aaron spake all the words which the LORD had
spoken unto Moses, and did the signs in the sight of
the people. 31 And the people believed: and when
they heard that the LORD had visited the children**

of Israel, and that he had looked upon their affliction, then they bowed their heads and worshipped.

Moses and Aaron "gathered" (Heb. *'acaph*, **aw-SAF**) the leaders to tell them what God had said, and to perform the signs as instructed. The word here translated "gather" means "to collect in one place." This was not a time for mixed messages, which often happens when not all the leaders among the people are present.

A literal translation of the Hebrew word for "elders," *zaqen* (**zaw-KANE**), would be "aged or old." However, elder was a common term to identify those chosen among the people as their representatives (Deuteronomy 5:23; Joshua 24:1; Lamentations 2:10; Matthew 21:23; Mark 15:1). Nonetheless, maturity that comes with age was probably a qualifier. Whether there was a time of introductions, we do not know. Verse 30 says Aaron got straight to the matter at hand. Here's what God said, and these signs are evidence that He said it. It was the leaders' responsibility to believe.

The profundity of simple obedience can be amazing. God had told Moses that Aaron would be glad to see him; He was. God told Moses the people would believe him; they did. The word "believe" (Heb. *'aman*, **aw-MAN**) carries the notion of trustworthiness and reliability. The response of the elders suggests what they have heard—they did not doubt. However before closing out this lesson, let us not overlook these last words in verse 31; they affirm the one called and the calling.

The promise made to Moses was that the people would accept the message and, implicitly, the messenger. The text tells us that when the people believed and heard the Lord had visited them and was aware of their afflictions, they bowed and worshipped. Although not yet back at Mount Horeb, where God told Moses the people serving Him would be a token of his calling (Exodus 3:12), this initial worshipful response may be seen as a forerunner to that event.

All God said to Moses had come to pass. Moses learned, as we all must, that God is our supplier. It is not our duty to convince others or ourselves that we can get the job done. Accepting God's call is a matter of faith and obedience. Whatever allegiances we need, He will take care of them; whatever proof of our ministry is needed, He will supply. The proof of our call is both now and in the future, when people bow and worship the living God.

Sources:

Bruce, F. F., ed. *The International Bible Commentary.* Grand Rapids, Mich.: Zondervan, 1986.

The NIV Study Bible, 10th Anniversary Edition. Grand Rapids, Mich.: Zondervan, 1995.

Daily Bible Readings

M: The God Who Calls
Exodus 3:13–18a
T: The God Who Equips
Exodus 4:1–9
W: The God Who Sends Back
Exodus 4:18–23
T: Do Not Be Afraid
Zechariah 8:11–17
F: God Will Help You
Isaiah 41:8–13
S: Refusing God's Call
Proverbs 1:20–33
S: A Team of Two
Exodus 4:10–16, 27–31

NOTES

TEACHING TIPS

June 21
Bible Study Guide 3

JUN 21st

1. Words You Should Know

A. Pharaoh (Exodus 5:1, 2, 5, 6, 23; 6:1) *Par'oh* (Heb.)—The common title of native kings of ancient Egypt. In this text, it is the pharaoh of the exodus—distinguished from the pharaoh of the oppression (Exodus 1:8)—who with his army, pursued the Israelites and was overwhelmed in the Red Sea.

B. Pestilence (v. 3) *deber* (Heb.)—Any virulent or fatal contagious or infectious disease sent as special judgment, and was supernaturally rapid in its effects.

2. Teacher Preparation

Unifying Principle—Recognizing True Authority. Some people fail to recognize true authority and power, erroneously believing that the authority and power rest within themselves. What brings us to recognize a higher authority? When Pharaoh refused to obey God's command to release the Israelites from slavery in Egypt, God promised to force obedience with a mighty hand.

A. Pray that all the students will have receptive hearts.

B. Read and study the Focal Verses intensely. You want to feel as if you were right there with Moses, when he went to Pharaoh to ask for the release of God's people. You want to fully understand Moses' faith, discouragement, and obedience.

C. Answering the Search the Scriptures and Discuss the Meaning questions will help you prepare for the class discussion.

3. Starting the Lesson

A. Begin the class with prayer, asking God to open the students' spiritual eyes so that they can recognize God as the true and final authority. Include the AIM for Change in the prayer.

B. Read and discuss the In Focus story.

C. Ask the class to name people who are in authority over them, and talk about their roles as authority figures.

4. Getting into the Lesson

A. Ask for volunteers to read the Background and The People, Places, and Times sections.

B. Write the Words You Should Know on the board and discuss their meanings.

C. Solicit a volunteer to read the Focal Verses. Discuss.

5. Relating the Lesson to Life

A. Have a volunteer to read the Lesson in Our Society and lead a brief class discussion.

B. Ask the students if they can relate to Moses.

C. Ask: Have you ever followed God's instructions and felt like it backfired on you? Encourage them to share.

D. Choose volunteers to answer the Discuss the Meaning questions. Discuss.

6. Arousing Action

A. Encourage the students to read the Daily Bible Readings and be prepared to share their experiences during class next week.

B. Read the Make It Happen section, and challenge the students to do the activity in the upcoming week.

C. Close with prayer, thanking God for humbling every student's spirit, enabling them to submit to people in authority over them.

Worship Guide

For the Superintendent or Teacher
Theme: Pharaoh Ignores God's Call
Theme Song: "What a Mighty God We Serve"
Devotional Reading: Psalm 10:1–14
Prayer

PHARAOH IGNORES GOD'S CALL

Bible Background • EXODUS 5:1–6:1
Printed Text • EXODUS 5:1–9, 22–6:1 Devotional Reading • PSALM 10:1–14

AIM for Change

By the end of the lesson, we will:
RECOUNT Pharaoh's refusal to obey God;
EXPLORE issues of authority and obedience in our lives; and
RECOGNIZE and respect God's authority.

Keep in Mind

"Thus saith the LORD God of Israel, Let my people go, that they may hold a feast unto me in the wilderness" (from Exodus 5:1).

Focal Verses

KJV **Exodus 5:1** And afterward Moses and Aaron went in, and told Pharaoh, Thus saith the LORD God of Israel, Let my people go, that they may hold a feast unto me in the wilderness.

2 And Pharaoh said, Who is the LORD, that I should obey his voice to let Israel go? I know not the LORD, neither will I let Israel go.

3 And they said, The God of the Hebrews hath met with us: let us go, we pray thee, three days' journey into the desert, and sacrifice unto the LORD our God; lest he fall upon us with pestilence, or with the sword.

4 And the king of Egypt said unto them, Wherefore do ye, Moses and Aaron, let the people from their works? get you unto your burdens.

5 And Pharaoh said, Behold, the people of the land now are many, and ye make them rest from their burdens.

6 And Pharaoh commanded the same day the taskmasters of the people, and their officers, saying,

7 Ye shall no more give the people straw to make brick, as heretofore: let them go and gather straw for themselves.

8 And the tale of the bricks, which they did make heretofore, ye shall lay upon them; ye shall not diminish ought thereof: for they be idle; therefore they cry, saying, Let us go and sacrifice to our God.

9 Let there more work be laid upon the men, that they may labour therein; and let them not regard vain words.

5:22 And Moses returned unto the LORD, and said, Lord, wherefore hast thou so evil entreated this people? why is it that thou hast sent me?

NLT **Exodus 5:1** After this presentation to Israel's leaders, Moses and Aaron went and spoke to Pharaoh. They told him, "This is what the LORD, the God of Israel, says: Let my people go so they may hold a festival in my honor in the wilderness."

2 "Is that so?" retorted Pharaoh. "And who is the LORD? Why should I listen to him and let Israel go? I don't know the LORD, and I will not let Israel go."

3 But Aaron and Moses persisted. "The God of the Hebrews has met with us," they declared. "So let us take a three-day journey into the wilderness so we can offer sacrifices to the LORD our God. If we don't, he will kill us with a plague or with the sword."

4 Pharaoh replied, "Moses and Aaron, why are you distracting the people from their tasks? Get back to work!

5 Look, there are many of your people in the land, and you are stopping them from their work."

6 That same day Pharaoh sent this order to the Egyptian slave drivers and the Israelite foremen:

7 "Do not supply any more straw for making bricks. Make the people get it themselves!

8 But still require them to make the same number of bricks as before. Don't reduce the quota. They are lazy. That's why they are crying out, 'Let us go and offer sacrifices to our God.'

9 Load them down with more work. Make them sweat! That will teach them to listen to lies!"

5:22 Then Moses went back to the LORD and protested, "Why have you brought all this trouble on your own people, Lord? Why did you send me?

23 For since I came to Pharaoh to speak in thy name, he hath done evil to this people; neither hast thou delivered thy people at all.

6:1 Then the LORD said unto Moses, Now shalt thou see what I will do to Pharaoh: for with a strong hand shall he let them go, and with a strong hand shall he drive them out of his land.

23 Ever since I came to Pharaoh as your spokesman, he has been even more brutal to your people. And you have done nothing to rescue them!"

6:1 Then the LORD told Moses, "Now you will see what I will do to Pharaoh. When he feels the force of my strong hand, he will let the people go. In fact, he will force them to leave his land!"

In Focus

Jermaine was so happy to get home that he could have kissed his driveway. After a full day at his office, all he wanted to do was go inside and go to bed. As soon as he stepped out of his car, he spotted a business card attached to his door. He shrugged his shoulders, confident that it was just another solicitation or a note from a friend who'd stopped by.

When he retreived the card from the door and learned that his car was scheduled for repossession, he didn't wait to get inside and call the number on the card; he used his cell phone. The person on the other end didn't care that Jermaine was waiting on his tax return check and was having financial problems. All he cared about was doing his job and picking up the car.

Jermaine went inside his house and cried. He couldn't believe that he'd allowed things to get so bad for himself. He had been so confident that God would give him favor with the IRS: that they would change their minds about auditing his tax return. What was supposed to be an eight-week process had gone into the twenty-fourth week. Now, he was about to lose his car, and it seemed like God was doing nothing to help.

In today's lesson, Moses felt the same as Jermaine did. Both had trusted God to meet a need and found that while they were in the battle God had not come through as they had envisioned. God's timing was not their timing. Still, God is the true authority and should be looked to and depended on in our times of trouble.

The People, Places, and Times

Egypt. This land lies in Northeast Africa. It was extremely fertile. The Nile River is its chief blessing, fertilizing and sustaining the country. The atmosphere is remarkably dry, except on the seacoast, which accounts for the perfect preservation of monuments with their writings and pictures. The heat is extreme during a large part of the year, and the winters are mild, from 50 to 60 degrees.

Source:

Smith, William. *Smith's Bible Dictionary*. Peabody, Mass.: Hendrickson Publishers, Inc. 2000.

Background

Imagine how encouraged Moses and Aaron must have felt. The people back home were overjoyed at the promise of being delivered. They sent the two off with an abundance of well-wishes and high expectations. God had finally heard their prayers. Moses and Aaron were excited, eager to meet this Pharaoh who had held onto the Lord's people for far too long. How honored the two must have felt, being used by God to perform such a mighty act. What they didn't know was that the Pharaoh was not going to be pleased to see them.

At-A-Glance

1. Request Denied (Exodus 5:1–3)
2. Workload Increased (vv. 4–9)
3. Complaint Filed (vv. 22–23; 6:1)

In Depth

1. Request Denied (Exodus 5:1–3)

With faith and much boldness, Moses and Aaron requested that Pharaoh let the Israelites go, in the name of the God of Israel. Heretofore, God was called the God of our fathers, but when speaking to Pharaoh, Moses called Him the God of Israel. He formed them into a people by calling God their God, and it was in His great name that they boldly requested that His people be let go.

But Pharaoh denied the request just as boldly, declaring that he did not know the Lord and did not care to know Him, and he refused to let the people go.

Seeing that Pharaoh had no care for the Lord, they tested him to see whether he had any compassion for the people. They made a humble and modest request for a short vacation, three days' journey into the wilderness to offer sacrifices unto God. Pharaoh denied that request, too, suggesting that Moses was wasting his time. As far as Pharaoh was concerned, the people did not need a vacation; they were lazy as it was. He had a plan to take care of that.

2. Workload Increased (vv. 4–9)

Pharaoh's plan was unreasonable and cruel. Instead of granting a vacation, he doubled the Israelites' workload. In his mind, anybody who had time to whine and complain was not busy enough. He demanded that they produce the same number of bricks, without the help of their taskmasters. The straw that their taskmasters used to supply for them they now had to gather themselves. This response revealed that Moses and Aaron had a tougher task than they might have anticipated. Though Moses and Aaron were called by God to deliver the people, they were not exempt from the work Pharaoh prescribed. They had to share in the common slavery of their nation. What better motivation to get freed from Pharaoh's oppression?

3. Complaint Filed (vv. 22–23; 6:1)

The Israelite foremen complained to Pharaoh, the people complained to Moses, and Moses complained to the Lord. Things went from bad to worse. Pharaoh looked upon the Israelites as whining babies. He taunted them. The people cursed Moses, "May the Lord look upon you and judge." In what appeared to be a lack of fairness, Moses must have felt confused, embarrassed, and like he was at the end of his rope. He turned to the Lord and asked, "Why aren't you doing anything to deliver your people? Why have you sent me?"

A closer look at Moses' question reveals something interesting. On the surface, his question looked like a complaint. But could Moses have been challenging the Lord? Could he have been saying, "Lord, I know this is not why you have sent me, to have your children in even more bondage than they were before we came! What else should I do to get your people freed?" Looking at Moses' statement in this way makes way for God's response. "Now you will see what I will do to Pharaoh." God took the work into His own hand.

Source:

Henry, Matthew. *The NIV Matthew Henry Commentary.* Grand Rapids, Mich.: Zondervan, 1992.

Search the Scriptures

1. What did Moses and Aaron tell Pharaoh they were going to do if he set the Israelites free (Exodus 5:3)?
2. What did Pharaoh instruct the taskmasters to do (v. 7)?
3. Why did Pharaoh tell the taskmasters to add to the Israelites' burdens (v. 8)?
4. What did Moses go back and tell God about Pharaoh's response to his request (v. 22)?

Discuss the Meaning

1. Why was Pharaoh so hard-hearted and mean toward the Israelites?
2. What would make Pharaoh think the enslaved Israelites were lazy and didn't want to work?
3. Why didn't Pharaoh know the Lord?

Lesson in Our Society

Oftentimes, Christians suffer persecution and rejection when on assignment for God or for being obedient to His Word. When God is no longer the focal point, it is just as easy to get sidetracked and distracted by life's obstacles. If Moses and Aaron had allowed Pharaoh's hard-heartedness to be a deterrent to completing their assignment, the Israelites may not have been freed. Even when on assignment from God, there will be some disappointments and restrictions; but those situations must not be used to keep us from doing what God said to do in the way He said to do it.

Make It Happen

Think about how Moses and Aaron must have felt, after they were obedient to God to have Pharaoh deny their request. Now consider what you would have done in a similar situation. Would you have continued to do as God instructed or give up in defeat?

In your personal prayer time this week, ask God to show you if you are truly being submissive to the people who are in authority over you. If you are not, ask that He change your heart to be receptive to them and their position of authority.

Follow the Spirit

What God wants me to do:

Remember Your Thoughts

Special insights I have learned:

More Light on the Text

Exodus 5:1–9, 22–6:1

1 And afterward Moses and Aaron went in, and told Pharaoh, Thus saith the LORD God of Israel, Let my people go, that they may hold a feast unto me in the wilderness.

The amount of time that passed between Moses and Aaron's visit with the people and their confrontation of Pharaoh is unclear. The Hebrew word translated "afterward" (Heb. *'achar,* **akh-AR**) can refer to a shorter or longer time. A good supposition would be that an audience with the Pharaoh was normally not immediate. Then again, Moses' prior status may have, and certainly God's sovereignty could have, afforded Aaron and Moses' quick access.

The request was clear, the Lord God of Israel said, "Let the Hebrews go that they may go and pay homage to their God." Recognizing even a conquered people's right to pay homage—celebrate the god or gods of their choosing—was a common practice in ancient cultures. "Festival" (Heb. *chagag,* **khaw-GAG**) means "to celebrate, keep a solemn feast or make a pilgrimage to a holy place in order to make sacrifices." This was an appropriate request and one the most insensitive of rulers would honor.

Of course, Moses was making more than a request. Instructed by God, he was giving Pharaoh a command from heaven. Using the imperative form, a command, the Hebrew phrase "let go" (Heb. *shalach,* **shaw-LAKH**) means "to release or send, send away, or cast off." The biblical record does not reveal that, prior to this meeting, God gave Moses instructions to command Pharaoh to let the people have a feast in the wilderness. Nevertheless, Moses did say, "thus saith the Lord God of Israel." Obedience to this command may have been a pathway for God to open Pharaoh's heart. Pharaoh had a choice and an opportunity to stand with God or against God; he chose the latter.

2 And Pharaoh said, Who is the LORD, that I should obey his voice to let Israel go? I know not the LORD, neither will I let Israel go.

Boldly, Pharaoh questioned the very essence or character of God. The adverb "who" (Heb. *miy,* **me**) is a primitive interrogative participle. In context, Pharaoh was asking what it was about Yahweh that he should do as He said, "Yes, Pharaoh even used the name of the Lord."

In referencing the Lord, Pharaoh clearly understood for whom Moses was speaking. However, as is often the case when we decide to ignore God, a command becomes a simple statement to be followed or not. "Obey" (Heb. *shama'*, **shaw-MAH**), literally is most often translated "hear or hearken" 785, 196 times respectively; 81 times it is translated "obey." The connotation seems to be listening perceptively with some action to follow. In the Hebrew text, "obey" is a *qal* imperfect. It can refer to static or active states of being that express the condition of the subject. Pharaoh is the subject in the phrase. In other words, "Why would I *ever* obey/listen to God?" Furthermore, he was using the same word as Moses for "let go." Pharaoh's position was clear. I have no basis for listening to what your God says or conceding to His commands. As with all of us, however, outward actions reflect inward realities. Let's look closely at the last phrase of the verse.

Evident thus far, the verbal forms in these verses are telling. Pharaoh declared he did not know the Lord. The Hebrew word translated "know" is *yada'* (**yaw-DAH**). It means not only "to have knowledge of," but also in the *qal* form it includes "the processes involved with knowing." Pharaoh was saying much more than he did not know God; he was unconditionally affirming he did not intend to involve himself in knowing the Lord. He refused to obey God when he said to Moses and Aaron, "I will not let the people go."

3 And they said, The God of the Hebrews hath met with us: let us go, we pray thee, three days' journey into the desert, and sacrifice unto the LORD our God; lest he fall upon us with pestilence, or with the sword.

Moses and Aaron asserted in unequivocally familiar terms to Pharaoh to let the people go into the desert to sacrifice to God or face consequences. As stated in the commentary on verse 1, Pharaoh understood this was a social, cultural, and religious request. The God of Israel was commonly and historically known as the God of the Hebrews (Exodus 1:15, 19). In addition, Pharaoh, unless vehemently atheistic, would have understood that gods reveal themselves and demand sacrifices.

Regardless of how Pharaoh felt, the consultation of priests in his own court would have been to let the Hebrews worship their God. Moses and Aaron tried to directly appeal to Pharaoh's sensibilities of the times in which he lived. They essentially begged him. "We pray thee" is a translation of one Hebrew word, *Na'* (**naw**); this is a formal address and focuses on the desire of the speaker literally, "I beg you! Let us go on a three day journey and sacrifice."

Using the word *zabach* (**zaw-BAKH**), which specifically meant to "sacrifice" rather than festival (v. 1), leaves no room for confusion. If the Children of Israel could not make sacrifices to their God, suffering would be the result. "To strike" means "to incur physical contact that inflicts harm or death." The word for "pestilence" is *deber* (**DEH-ber**) and is often used in reference to some kind of plague or sickness that is widespread and happens because of judgment. Could these words be prophetic? For we know God did not strike Israel, but He did, however, strike the Egyptians. Was God vindictive? I think not. Pharaoh had many opportunities to repent and acknowledge God. To deny this request was to suggest, no—to affirm—the Hebrew God was not even "a" god! Worship denied is rebellion implied!

4 And the king of Egypt said unto them, Wherefore do ye, Moses and Aaron, let the people from their works? get you unto your burdens. 5 And Pharaoh said, Behold, the people of the land now are many, and ye make them rest from their burdens.

At this point Pharaoh probably knew his back was against the wall. Is it any less different today? Instead, he purposely challenged Moses and Aaron's request and stated that their real goal was to take the people away from their assigned responsibilities.

Translated "let," the Hebrew word in this instance is *para'* (**paw-RAH**), which is an interesting word choice. In this *hifil* form, it literally means "to cause disorder or promote wickedness"; however, in its root form *(qal)*, it means a lack of restraint. Both nuances may be in view. Pharaoh accused Moses and Aaron of having a desire to disrupt the status quo, that is to take the Hebrews from their work for illegitimate reasons. Pharaoh also, however, instructed Moses and Aaron to get back to their burdens; burdens commonly refer to "forced and difficult labor."

Furthermore, in verse 5, Pharaoh made the comment that the people of the land, referring to the Hebrews, were many. The phrase "people of the land" was often used to distinguish between ruling and lower classes (Ezekiel 7:27)—in this case, the slave-labor class of Egypt. Pharaoh once again made an insidious claim; Moses and Aaron's goal was to get those who were slaves by culture, ethnicity, and birth to cease from their work. "Rest" is the translated Hebrew word *shabath* (**shaw-BATH**). Here it means "to cause to cease." The words of Scripture ring so true. What is in a man comes out of a man (Mark 7:20). The deceptive premeditation Pharaoh saw in others was a reflection of his own heart. Pharaoh was accusing Moses and Aaron of attempting to give the Hebrew people reasons not to work when he was searching for reasons to disobey God.

Nevertheless, notwithstanding his unfounded changes, his own words help us to see he was consumed by his own thirst for control and power. Pharaoh must have felt that a large number of well-rested slaves would be a threat. Therefore from his vantage point, allowing them to make sacrifices would be undesirable, empowering rebellion—a risk Pharaoh was not willing to take.

6 And Pharaoh commanded the same day the taskmasters of the people, and their officers, saying, 7 Ye shall no more give the people straw to make brick, as heretofore: let them go and gather straw for themselves. 8 And the tale of the bricks, which they did make heretofore, ye shall lay upon them; ye shall not diminish ought thereof: for they be idle; therefore they cry, saying, Let us go and sacrifice to our God. 9 Let there more work be laid upon the men, that they may labour therein; and let them not regard vain words.

It is noteworthy that verses 6–9 contain no imperatives—that is, there are no commands. It was as if the writer of Exodus was now making the distinction. The only ultimate authority over God's people is God—a lesson Pharaoh would learn and a lesson all God's children must persistently remind themselves.

Pharaoh's commands were perpetual from his perspective. Using a series of imperfect tense verbs,

Pharaoh declared provisions, if they can be called that, would no longer be made for the Hebrews to make bricks. He commands the taskmasters of the people and their supervisors not to supply the necessary straw to make bricks.

The Hebrew word *shoter* (**sho-TARE**) is translated "officers." *Shoter* is used a number of times to refer to those in authority in Israel (Deuteronomy 20:9; Joshua 1:10; 2 Chronicles 19:11). The taskmasters were Israelites also; they worked more closely with the people. This is the oldest trick in the book—use one's own to oppress one's own, divide and conquer! For the Hebrew word *nagas* (**naw-GAS**), translated "taskmasters," has reference not only to the title, but the actions performed, that is to oppress. The people were getting it from every direction: from Pharaoh, their own leaders—where support and guidance was expected—and the neighbor next door. Their only consolation was to stay focused on the promises of God.

In any case, Pharaoh made this declaration in verse 7; "give them no more straw and let them gather the straw necessary to make their quota of bricks." Clay was the primary material used to make Egyptian bricks. Adding straw made the bricks more durable during inclement weather.

An appropriate rendering in the 1600s, when the King James Version was written, the first phrase of verse 8 begins by including a word that may be confusing: "*tale*." A literal contemporary translation for this word, "tale" (Heb. *mathkoneth*, **math-KO-neth**), translated is "quota, tally, or fixed measure." The context supports this understanding. For Pharaoh qualifies his initial statement, the tale/quota of bricks that were made before shall remain the same and will not change.

It is possible that Pharaoh was thinking about a specific point in time when production levels were at the highest. I propose an alternate view. Verse 8 contains three Hebrew words translated "which they did make heretofore." Two of these words, *temowl* (**tem-OLE**) and *shilshowm* (**shil-SHOME**), combine and are translated "heretofore." Respectively, the first word points to a time that is near or recent past time; the second word, however, usually refers to the day before. Assuming there was a short time frame between Moses and Aaron's meeting with the people and Pharaoh, it may be that Pharaoh was directly and explicitly rebelling against the Word of the Lord. To paraphrase, "you may have received a Word from your God, but it is my word that will stand. Nothing changes; in fact, things will get worse! Even though you are now to gather straw for making bricks, there is no reduction in the required quota."

Continuing to feed his disdain for the Lord, Pharaoh did not acknowledge that the people of Israel could have a genuine desire to worship their God. Rather, he relentlessly focused on his own interests, suggesting that to allow the Hebrews to make sacrifices would promote their becoming unproductive workers. The Hebrew word translated "idle" is *raphah* (**raw-FAW**). This particular *nifal* verbal form carries the connotation of "a lack of desire to be diligent in one's work endeavors."

Pharaoh's comments thus far in verse 8 may be the ancient precursor to the modern-day saying, "Religion is a waste of time." In essence, it appears Pharaoh does suggest this; for he follows his previous comments by saying their cries to go sacrifice are a result of idleness. We can assume the Hebrews came together to worship, even if in a limited way. If this assumption is correct, Pharaoh was implying the only reason the Hebrews wanted to go and make sacrifices to their God was because they didn't understand the significance of their existence was in what they did for him, the Pharaoh and not what they did for God. To this, in essence Pharaoh says "I will not have it."

One thing Pharaoh did seem to understand was that targeting the men disrupts the social system of any culture. He made another declaration: "let there be more work laid upon the men." Literally, the text reads "heavy work." The goal was nothing less than to deplete the Hebrew men of all mental and physical energies for anything other than accomplishing their assigned responsibilities to Pharaoh: no time for wife, no time for children, and certainly no time for God.

Again, translated "that they may labour therein" is really only two Hebrew words, one means "to do," the other means "in." We cannot overlook the power of this short and succinct phrase. It would be as if someone said, "you may do only this." Emphasizing the commentary above, we can already see the beginning of the end—a hardened heart (Exodus 7:13; 11:10). Pharaoh already declared (see v. 2) that he had no concerns for God and was only driving his own goals. He also wanted the Hebrews to be driven by his goals.

Notice Pharaoh's final comment, in verse 9, "lets them not regard vain words." The word for "regard" is the Hebrew word *sha'ah* (**shaw-AW**), which means to have a favorable opinion about something. "Vain" is a translation of the word *sheqer* (**SHEH-ker**). In this context, the idea is communication based on falsehoods. Let's just say it as Pharaoh would have: "Moses, Aaron, and their God are liars." That was Pharaoh's final assessment. Whether or not this comment was directly or indirectly a condemnation of Moses, Aaron, God, or all three is inconsequential. The men were only messengers; God was the authority behind the words.

Because the people were facing unbearable conditions and could not turn to God and His chosen servants but had to turn to Pharaoh, Pharaoh would have a short-lived victory and Moses would face a brief period of dependency. Moses and Aaron were, as the saying goes, caught between a rock and a hard place. Moses promised one thing and Pharaoh demanded another; and it looked like Pharaoh was winning the battle. At these times, the leader must have the wisdom to go to the one that has the plan and the power. He or she must not retaliate against the people or get in God's way. This is a lesson that Moses needed to learn.

5:22 And Moses returned unto the LORD, and said, LORD, wherefore hast thou so evil entreated this people? why is it that thou hast sent me? 23 For since I came to Pharaoh to speak in thy name, he hath done evil to this people; neither hast thou delivered thy people at all.

A powerful statement begins this verse! Moses returned to the Lord. "Returned" is a translation of the Hebrew word *shuwb* (**shoob**). It means "to go back to a place previously departed." Moses knew where to turn and to whom. Notice that he mentioned nothing of how the people had treated him—only how they had been treated by Pharaoh. Denied by Pharaoh and now after an initial jubilant welcoming, rejected by the people, Moses questioned again God's purpose and His call. I don't think the emphasis here, in verse 22, is on God doing evil to the people. Rather, as evidenced in many of the Psalms (Psalm 74:1; 89:46–9), it is a cry of desperation, a cry that says, "How can a good God allow bad things to happen to good people?" It is a cry we know that spans the boundaries of human existence.

The word for "evil" is *ra'a'* (**raw-AH**). It is in the perfect tense and *hifil* verbal form. It means "to bring trouble, disaster, or cause hardship." The context helps explain the tense. Rhetorically, Moses asked a question and makes a statement. "Lord, since I, Moses, have followed Your directives and proclaimed Your Name, the only thing Pharaoh has done is make matters worse." The Hebrew wording is enlightening. Moses literally said, "From the time I came to Pharaoh and spoke Your Name, there's been trouble." You know, "since I became a Christian . . . ?"

The English rendering in the King James Version of the last half and last words of verse 23 emphasizes Moses' despair: "at all." The Hebrew word for "deliver" is *natsal* (**naw-TSAL**). It is used twice in the original text. In the first instance, it is an infinite absolute and second it is a verb. Infinite absolutes are often used to intensify the meaning of the verb. The verbal form of deliver is the same as used in Exodus 3:8. Moses was calling on God to respond to His Word and His faithfulness. This is a proper and fitting request. James 4:4, paraphrased, says "We have not because we ask not"; yes, even though before we ask He knows what we have need of (Matthew 6:8). God knew what He was going to do. His objective, as it is in all things, was to make sure everyone else knew it was Him bringing about His people's deliverance and that His people depended on Him alone.

6:1 Then the LORD said unto Moses, Now shalt thou see what I will do to Pharaoh: for with a strong hand shall he let them go, and with a strong hand shall he drive them out of his land.

The Lord inspired the writer of Exodus to use a coordinating conjunction to connect verses 5:23 and 6:1. I believe the connection is linking more than Moses' cry to the Lord but is also linking to what previously happened in Pharaoh's court. Chapters 7–11 tell us that through signs and wonders, using Moses and Aaron as instruments, God delivered His people.

Nevertheless, first things first, "Moses, you will see what I will do." Exact dating is unknown but a good guess is that it was a few months at the most between these words of God and the deliverance of His people. The point is, "Moses, you will come to have a greater understanding of who I am as you watch Me do My thing." *Ra'ah* (**raw-AW**) is the Hebrew word translated "see." It means seeing in a way that one can make an assessment based on what one sees. Moses was not going to be a bystander or passive instrument. We are called not just to serve Him but to know Him and the power of His resurrection (Philippians 3:10). It is not enough that we shout that deliverance has come; we shout because the Deliverer has come!

Read too quickly, it could be assumed by the construction of verse 6:1 that the strong hand was Pharaoh's. This is not the case! "Mighty or strong hand" never refers to any other person but the Lord God, Jehovah. In case there are any questions, listen to the words of the prophet Jeremiah, "And hast brought forth thy people Israel out of the land of Egypt with signs, and with wonders, and with a strong hand, and with a stretched out arm, and with great terror" (Jeremiah 32:21). God is the potter; we are the clay. Some are molded into vessels of righteousness, some unrighteousness, but all are to ultimately fulfill His sovereign purposes (Jeremiah 18:1; Romans 9:1).

Remember the command Moses gave Pharaoh from God in verse one—God said to let His people go. Well, Pharaoh did not know it yet but his destiny was wrapped up in that command. He would let the people go. Ignoring God or pretending we have not heard God changes nothing of what He says. It will change us, however. Pharaoh sure changed. The phrase "drive out" means to expel; it is derived from an ancient Aramaic term that means "divorce."

When I think of a divorce, I think of two people who, for some reason or another, no longer value one another. In a convoluted kind of way, Pharaoh would get to the point where trying to hold on was just too costly. Anything that we value more than God is subject to being stripped from us. Moses had to learn this, the people would learn this, and Pharaoh would learn this.

Sources:

Bruce, F. F., ed. *The International Bible Commentary*. Grand Rapids, Mich.: Zondervan, 1986.

Henry, Matthew. *The NIV Matthew Henry Commentary*. Grand Rapids, Mich.: Zondervan, 1992.

The NIV Study Bible, 10th Anniversary Edition. Grand Rapids, Mich.: Zondervan, 1995.

Daily Bible Readings

M: Making Bricks Without Straw
Exodus 5:10–21

T: The Voice of the Lord
Psalm 29

W: Return to God and Heed Him
Deuteronomy 4:25–31

T: God's Plan to Strengthen
Zechariah 10:6–12

F: The Lord's Deliverance
Psalm 18:13–19

S: All Nations Shall Worship God
Zechariah 14:12–19

S: Moses' Complaint
Exodus 5:1–9, 22–6:1

NOTES

TEACHING TIPS

June 28
Bible Study Guide 4

1. Words You Should Know

A. Rod (Exodus 14:16) *matteh* (Heb.)—Any straight or almost straight stick, shaft, bar, staff of wood, metal, or other material.

B. Chariots (vv. 17, 18, 23, 25) *rekeb* (Heb.)—Horse-drawn two-wheeled carts used in ancient times for war. One could seat two to three people.

C. Pillar (vv. 19, 24) *'ammuwd* (Heb.)—A figurative use of the word "pillar" in reference to the cloud and fire accompanying the Israelites. It is derived from the notion of an isolated column not supporting a roof.

2. Teacher Preparation

Unifying Principle—Finding and Giving Protection. Many people have protectors to help them through difficult, even perilous, times. Where do we look for protection in difficult times? God protected the Israelites by parting the waters, leading them out of slavery in Egypt, and destroying their enemies.

A. Study the entire lesson, taking notes that you would like to emphasize with your class.

B. Pray for the class that they may have receptive hearts and ears to hear the Word of the Lord.

C. Read, meditate, and include in your prayer the AIM for Change.

3. Starting the Lesson

A. Open the class in prayer, including the AIM for Change in the prayer.

B. Briefly review last week's lesson and tie it in with this week's focus.

C. The Background and The People, Places, and Times sections will set the stage for today's lesson. Have the students read them and discuss salient points.

D. Solicit a volunteer to read the Focal Verses.

E. Discuss the In Depth and More Light on the Text sections, highlighting how God cares for His people even in their times of troubles.

F. Read and discuss the In Focus story. Also tie it in with today's discussion.

4. Getting into the Lesson

A. Divide the class into three groups and give each group one question from Search the Scriptures and Discuss the Meaning sections.

B. Have the groups answer and discuss the questions.

C. Have a member from each group present the answers to the class.

D. Read the Keep in Mind verse, and discuss its significance to the lesson.

5. Relating the Lesson to Life

A. Have a volunteer read the Make It Happen section and spearhead a discussion on what is to be gained from volunteering at a shelter.

B. Ask a volunteer to read the Lesson in Our Society section. Discuss.

C. Have one or two volunteers talk about a difficult situation they had to face and how they overcame the obstacles.

6. Arousing Action

A. Challenge the students to follow through with the Make It Happen assignment.

B. Sum up the lesson with the Keep in Mind verse. Have the students read it in unison, while contemplating how they can apply it to their lives this week.

C. Close in prayer.

Worship Guide

For the Superintendent or Teacher
Theme: God Calls the People out of Egypt
Theme Song: "He's an On Time God"
Devotional Reading: Exodus 15:1–13
Prayer

GOD CALLS THE PEOPLE OUT OF EGYPT

Bible Background • EXODUS 13:17–14:30
Printed Text • EXODUS 14:15–25, 30 Devotional Reading • EXODUS 15:1–13

AIM for Change

By the end of the lesson, we will:
LEARN about the Israelites' miraculous escape from the Egyptians;
BELIEVE that God provides safety for God's people; and
TRUST God for help and seek to help others in times of trouble.

Keep in Mind

"Thus the LORD saved Israel that day out of the hand of the Egyptians" (from Exodus 14:30).

JUN 28th

Focal Verses

KJV **Exodus 14:15** And the LORD said unto Moses, Wherefore criest thou unto me? speak unto the children of Israel, that they go forward:

16 But lift thou up thy rod, and stretch out thine hand over the sea, and divide it: and the children of Israel shall go on dry ground through the midst of the sea.

17 And I, behold, I will harden the hearts of the Egyptians, and they shall follow them: and I will get me honour upon Pharaoh, and upon all his host, upon his chariots, and upon his horsemen.

18 And the Egyptians shall know that I am the LORD, when I have gotten me honour upon Pharaoh, upon his chariots, and upon his horsemen.

19 And the angel of God, which went before the camp of Israel, removed and went behind them; and the pillar of the cloud went from before their face, and stood behind them:

20 And it came between the camp of the Egyptians and the camp of Israel; and it was a cloud and darkness to them, but it gave light by night to these: so that the one came not near the other all the night.

21 And Moses stretched out his hand over the sea; and the LORD caused the sea to go back by a strong east wind all the night, and made the sea dry land, and the waters were divided.

22 And the children of Israel went into the midst of the sea upon the dry ground: and the waters were a wall unto them on their right hand, and on their left.

NLT **Exodus 14:15** Then the LORD said to Moses, "Why are you crying out to me? Tell the people to get moving!

16 Pick up your staff and raise your hand over the sea. Divide the water so the Israelites can walk through the middle of the sea on dry ground.

17 And I will harden the hearts of the Egyptians, and they will charge in after the Israelites. My great glory will be displayed through Pharaoh and his troops, his chariots, and his charioteers.

18 When my glory is displayed through them, all Egypt will see my glory and know that I am the LORD!"

19 Then the angel of God, who had been leading the people of Israel, moved to the rear of the camp. The pillar of cloud also moved from the front and stood behind them.

20 The cloud settled between the Egyptian and Israelite camps. As darkness fell, the cloud turned to fire, lighting up the night. But the Egyptians and Israelites did not approach each other all night.

21 Then Moses raised his hand over the sea, and the LORD opened up a path through the water with a strong east wind. The wind blew all that night, turning the seabed into dry land.

22 So the people of Israel walked through the middle of the sea on dry ground, with walls of water on each side!

23 Then the Egyptians—all of Pharaoh's horses, chariots, and charioteers—chased them into the middle of the sea.

24 But just before dawn the LORD looked down on the Egyptian army from the pillar of fire and

23 And the Egyptians pursued, and went in after them to the midst of the sea, even all Pharaoh's horses, his chariots, and his horsemen.

24 And it came to pass, that in the morning watch the LORD looked unto the host of the Egyptians through the pillar of fire and of the cloud, and troubled the host of the Egyptians,

25 And took off their chariot wheels, that they drave them heavily: so that the Egyptians said, Let us flee from the face of Israel; for the LORD fighteth for them against the Egyptians.

14:30 Thus the LORD saved Israel that day out of the hand of the Egyptians; and Israel saw the Egyptians dead upon the sea shore.

cloud, and he threw their forces into total confusion.

25 He twisted their chariot wheels, making their chariots difficult to drive. "Let's get out of here—away from these Israelites!" the Egyptians shouted. "The LORD is fighting for them against Egypt!"

14:30 That is how the LORD rescued Israel from the hand of the Egyptians that day. And the Israelites saw the bodies of the Egyptians washed up on the seashore.

In Focus

When Victoria realized that her husband's hands were around her throat, she vowed that if she made it out of the house alive, she would never come back. She'd only been married for 13 months, but the trouble had just recently started. She dated her husband for three years before marriage, and he had been one of the gentlest men she knew. But since he'd lost his job, he'd become angry and depressed. A month ago, she noticed that he was verbally aggressive toward her, but she ignored his putdowns. Then one day he cut off the hot water because he said that she was wasting electricity taking long showers. There was one time when he shoved her, but he quickly apologized. But the one thing Victoria knew was that if a man choked a woman he was not far from killing her.

When her husband loosened his grip, Victoria gasped until she caught her breath. Her husband apologized, with much sobbing, and promised to get help. When he excused himself to get a cool rag and a glass of water for Victoria to drink, boldness superseded her fears, and she grabbed her car keys, ran out the door, and got into her car, where she drove to the police station to file a restraining order. She knew that it was only God that made a way of escape for her.

Just as Victoria found out in this story, and the Children of Israel in today's lesson, sometimes when the enemy is in hot pursuit, we have to trust God for help and receive the protection that only He can give. He can work things out and help to get us out of Egypt (our place of suffering) or use our Egypt to build character in us.

The People, Places, and Times

Red Sea. It is the body of water that divides Egypt and Arabia. The water was not red, but a blue-green color. It was called red either because of its red banks or because of the Erythreans, who were called the red people.

The text records that a path was made through the Red Sea, and that the waters were a "wall" on both sides. The word "wall" probably means a barrier, rather than implying that the sea stood up like a cliff. Some modern Bible translations now believe Israel crossed the "Sea of Reeds" or "Reed Sea."

Source:

Smith, William. *Smith's Bible Dictionary*. Peabody, Mass.: Hendrickson Publishers, 2000.

Background

God hardened Pharaoh's heart so that the Egyptians would know that God is the LORD. God did so until Pharaoh was so stiff-necked that it took 10 plagues to get him to release the Israelites (Exodus 7:3–4). Pharaoh was not impressed when God turned water into blood or plagued the land with frogs, gnats, and flies. When Pharaoh remained obstinate during the plague on cattle, the people were plagued with boils and sores, and then there was a plague of hail. The plague of locusts got Pharaoh to confess his sins but not wholly; he endured it and the plague of darkness. Though all the plagues were great, none were as magnificent and terrible as the plague of death of all the first-born of Egypt. It was this plague that caused Pharaoh to command the Israelites to leave. But before the Israelites could think that their problems were over, they learned that Pharaoh and his army were close on their trail.

At-A-Glance

1. God Instructs Moses (Exodus 14:15–18)
2. God Protects the Israelites (vv. 19–22)
3. God Defeats the Enemies (vv. 23–25, 30)

In Depth

1. God Instructs Moses (Exodus 14:15–18)

Imagine the Israelites' distress. They went from praising the Lord and expressing joy one minute to being paralyzed by fear and crying out to the Lord in the next. When they learned that their enemies were in hot pursuit of them, they cried out to the Lord. Their fears caused them to murmur against Moses. But Moses held on to his faith. He encouraged the people not to be afraid.

The Lord spoke to him. On the surface God's question would seem funny: "Why are you crying out to me?" Who else would Moses cry out to? But on a closer look, we learn that God asked Moses why he continued to cry out to Him when his prayer had already been answered. God had already given Moses what was necessary, but in the moment of great crisis, he did not have a clear perspective. Moses had told the Israelites to stand still to be able to receive a word from the Lord, but the Lord told Moses to tell the Israelites to move on.

Where would they go? It's not like there were a fleet of ships and boats on the coast to carry them away.

2. God Protects the Israelites (vv. 19–22)

Had God made a mistake? Walk into the Red Sea? It was nighttime; how would they see? Of course, God thought of everything. He sent an angel. This angel's ministry was to make use of the pillar of fire and cloud, to be a guard between God's children and God's enemies. Then God divided the sea. According to *Matthew Henry's Commentary*, "It was by a gulf or arm of the sea, two or three leagues over, which was divided." The Israelites walked across the water on dry ground to the other shore. God performed a miracle and demonstrated His power for all to see, and He also validated the leadership of Moses.

3. God Defeats the Enemies (vv. 23–25, 30)

After the Israelites began to cross the sea, the Egyptians began to pursue them. The closer the Egyptians got to the Israelites, the angrier they became. They probably breathed threats, remembering the trouble they'd been through with the 10 plagues. They were confident that they would outrun the Israelites and overtake them. While the Israelites were on foot, the Egyptians were well-equipped with horse-driven chariots. Their confidence was short-lived when the Lord threw them into confusion. They got far enough onto the dry path of the Red Sea to be overcome with water. The Egyptians and their horses drowned in the water. The Israelites had all made it to the other shore.

Source:

Henry, Matthew. *The NIV Matthew Henry Commentary.* Grand Rapids, Mich.: Zondervan, 1992.

Search the Scriptures

1. What did God instruct Moses to do when the Israelites cried out to Him (Exodus 14:15)?
2. What did the Egyptians say they were going to do when the wheels fell off of their chariots (v. 25)?
3. Why did the Egyptians want to flee (v. 25)?

Discuss the Meaning

1. Why were the Israelites crying out to God?
2. Why did the pillar of the cloud appear dark to the Egyptians and light to the Israelites?
3. What does the parting of the Red Sea say about God's love for Israel and His disappointment with Egypt?

Lesson in Our Society

Sometimes when we are faced with a difficult or an unfamiliar job situation, we have a tendency to stop or want to back up and do what is familiar. But when God is the one who has made the assignment, we must keep in mind that He is the one to make the provisions so that the job can be completed and that He can get the glory out of it.

We can learn a great deal from the ordeal the Israelites faced. When adversities are in front of us, the only thing left to do is to call on God and allow Him to work the situation out on our behalf and to His glorification.

Make It Happen

From what "pharaohs" has God delivered you?

Make a list of them, and keep them in a place where you can be reminded of God's faithfulness. Be reminded that when things get tough for you, you can easily remember this: if God protected and delivered you then, He's brought you too far to not do it again. Each day, this week, take time and thank God for what He has done in your life. For a class summer project, try volunteering at the local women's crisis or homeless shelter.

Follow the Spirit

What God wants me to do:

____

____

Remember Your Thoughts

Special insights I have learned:

____

____

More Light on the Text

Exodus 14:15–25, 30

Pharaoh's persistent attempts to stop God's people from leaving Egypt caused a dreadful fear to fall upon the Israelites (Exodus 14:10). In Exodus 14:1–10, with a hardened heart, Pharaoh and his officials planned their last attempts to defy the living God, leaving the people of God in a state of dreadful fear. It is a decision the Egyptians would come to regret. Positively, it is also a decision that consequentially allows God to demonstrate the lengths He will go to protect His people.

Nevertheless, before the final victory, with Pharaoh at their heels, the people grumbled, "It would have been better for us to remain in Egypt than die in the wilderness" (Exodus 14:12, paraphrased). Psychologists do not tell us why people remain in abusive situations and relationships. Sometimes, as depicted here, a known abhorrent past seems better than obstacles never faced before. Moses assured the people this was the last go round and that the Lord, Himself, would fight their battles (vv. 13–14).

15 And the LORD said unto Moses, Wherefore criest thou unto me? speak unto the children of Israel, that they go forward:

The Lord directly addressed Moses, and questioned him, "Why do you cry out to Me?" Initially, it seemed like an unjust rebuke. Did not Moses say God would deliver and fight for the people? Assuming Moses prayed and expressed a need for God's help, to "cry" in this basic *qal* form means "to call out for help." What more could he, a man, have done? It may have been something as simple as expressing a more confident charge to the people or confidence in God, while he cried out to God. This was no time for passivity from the people or doubts by Moses.

God was about to do the impossible and unthinkable, and all hands needed to be on deck. God instructed Moses to speak to the people to move forward. Is there any reason to doubt that the Children of Israel were thinking, "Move where? The Egyptians are all around us and nothing but water is in front of us." It does not matter: When God says move, move. These newly freed people had to learn that their confidence must remain not in the security of the situation or assessments of potential outcomes but in trust and obedience to God.

Translated "forward," the actually Hebrew word *naca'* (**naw-SAH**), carries the notion of "pulling up stakes with a specific destination in mind," such as the stakes of a tent. Translators emphasized the apparent destination. We would be remiss not to also emphasize they were setting out on a no-return trip, for as Moses has said, on this day they would see the Egyptians no more. Moses' instructions from the Lord are a little different.

16 But lift thou up thy rod, and stretch out thine hand over the sea, and divide it: and the children of Israel shall go on dry ground through the midst of the sea.

The first word in this verse "but," if literal, would read "and you," which is the Hebrew combined conjunction *waw* and the pronoun for you. Contemporarily, we might say, "as for you." The command is specific: "You, Moses, lift up your rod." "Lift up" is the English translation of the Hebrew word *ruwm* (**room**). The command conveyed in the meaning was not just to lift the rod up but to lift it high. Moses was to lift the rod, stretch out his hand over the sea, and divide it. "To divide" means to be split into two parts with great power (Heb. *baqa'*, **baw-KAH**). Once this was done, the Children of Israel would march out on dry land into the sea.

Steps of faith in verses 13, 15, and 16 include: fear not, go forward, lift up, and stretch out your hand. I cannot adequately explain it. The relationship

"Thus the LORD saved Israel that day out of the hand of the Egyptians" (from Exodus 14:30).

between God's covenant promises and our faith are irrevocable. Nevertheless, faith applied does not mean we live free of trials and attacks from the enemy. The Bible says the enemy roams about like a roaring lion seeking whomever he may devour (1 Peter 5:8). In our story, the enemy is Pharaoh, and he will not give up.

17 And I, behold, I will harden the hearts of the Egyptians, and they shall follow them: and I will get me honour upon Pharaoh, and upon all his host, upon his chariots, and upon his horsemen. 18 And the Egyptians shall know that I am the LORD, when I have gotten me honour upon Pharaoh, upon his chariots, and upon his horsemen.

It is only here in verse 17 that the text says God hardened the hearts of the Egyptians. The Hebrew word for "harden" is *chazaq* (**khaw-ZAK**). The basic meaning of *chazaq* is "to strengthen," and a nuance of that form is "to harden." It seems the whole of this definition is contextually and theological appropriate. God strengthened Pharaoh's and the Egyptian's hearts to continue steadfastly on paths they had chosen for themselves. It is only by God's grace that any of us have hearts malleable to the Gospel.

Yes, God said that he would harden Pharaoh's heart (Exodus 4:21). The first seven plagues tell us that Pharaoh and his Egyptian subjects hardened their hearts (Exodus 9:34, 35). It is not until the plague of locusts, the eighth plague, that we read God hardened Pharaoh's heart. In conclusion, as we see here, they chose to follow the Hebrews and continued their disobedience, in deference to God's command to let the people go. Verses 17 and 18 give us the reason God had permissively chosen to allow Pharaoh and the Egyptians to persist in their disobedience. They were unknowingly a part of a divine plan that gave glory to God.

God said to Moses, in this portion of Scripture, that there were two things that would happen as a result of Pharaoh's hardened heart: "I will get glory (vv. 17b, 18) and "the Egyptians will know that I am Yahweh" (v. 18). Yahweh is the Hebrew name for God, which highlights His self-existence and His being the God of promise. The God who Pharaoh denied and denounced (Exodus 5:2) would be the same one through whom judgment would come and God's glory be revealed.

This conversation God had with Moses was permeated with prior promises from God and confrontations with Pharaoh. We know these Egyptians do finally acknowledge God (v. 25). Who knows what tales were told that influenced other Egyptians in the years ahead? We can decisively conclude that this conversation was to be a record for the Children of Israel and all God's people—God would be glorified.

The verb "honour" (Heb. *kabad*, **kaw-BAD**) is the most common word used in the Old Testament for "glory." Two different verbal forms of the word "glory" are used in these verses. In 17b, it is a passive cohorative (the cohorative is likened to an imperative; that is a command). In 18, it is an infinitive absolute. As a passive cohorative, God was saying, unconditionally, "Pharaoh will give Me glory." As an infinitive absolute, it intensifies the relationship between knowing (a verb) who the Lord is and the honor (glory) He receives as a result.

Notice the sequence. God did not say in verse 17 that the Egyptians will give Him glory (that would be a third person rendering of the first use of glory); He just states the facts. "I will get glory. Then, as I the Lord take direct and deliberate actions against the Egyptian army to protect my people, they will know I am the Lord and I used Pharaoh to My glory."

19 And the angel of God, which went before the camp of Israel, removed and went behind them; and the pillar of the cloud went from before their face, and stood behind them:

It goes without saying that this Hebrew mass of people about to cross the sea could not outrun Egyptian chariots. They needed some breathing room to gather their belongings and time to march, (carts to carry people and riding animals would have been few), and cross over a rocky sea bed, even if dry. The Israelites got what they needed and the Egyptians got what they could not comprehend.

The angel of the Lord, which had been leading the Hebrews by day in a cloud and by pillar of fire by night (Exodus 13:21), took another position. This time, he was behind the camp of Israel and in front of the Egyptian camp. This is a wonderful description of God protecting His people.

Often when we think of the Lord's intervention, they are thoughts of His passive presence of reassurance, and sometimes that is all we need. I think, however, God is much more active than we know. We were told in verse 7 that the Egyptian force was 600 of the best chariots along with other chariots, officers over them all, plus an army. A normal chariot was a two-man operation, one driver and one designated fighting warrior. During significant engagements, an officer who managed the battle plan also rode in the chariot, a formidable force indeed. Presence is good, but the Israelites needed a display of His power. What is amazing is that God did a simple thing that was more than sufficient to create an insurmountable impasse between His people and Pharaoh's forces. It became very, very dark.

20 And it came between the camp of the Egyptians and the camp of Israel; and it was a cloud and darkness to them, but it gave light by night to these: so that the one came not near the other all the night.

The cloud that was between the Israelites and the Egyptians was magnificently peculiar. On the Egyptian side, it was dark. On the Israelite side, it was light. One camp was blinded by darkness; one camp was given light to see. The Hebrew word *choshek* **(kho-SHEK)** is translated "darkness," an enveloping darkness (a place where light cannot penetrate) that is terrifying. "Gave light" is the Hebrew word *'owr* (**ore**). Its meaning is translated as "to cause to brighten."

Whereas God guided the Hebrews by giving them light, He created an abiding habitation of intrinsic darkness for the Egyptians. Such conditions would have negated any marching advantages the Egyptians had. At best, they could only proceed by what amounted to a slow walk, while the Hebrews could advance toward a safe destination on the other side on a well-lit path. The reason for the peculiarities of this cloud is explicit: so the two groups would not come near one another all night long. God's protection is not partial. It is exhaustive!

21 And Moses stretched out his hand over the sea; and the LORD caused the sea to go back by a strong east wind all that night, and made the sea dry land, and the waters were divided. 22 And the children of Israel went into the midst of the sea upon the dry ground: and the waters were a wall unto them on their right hand, and on their left.

Our narrative now returns to the specifics of what happened when Moses stretched out his hand over the sea. In verse 15, we were told that Moses was to divide the waters, and now we are told how that division occurred. Using the elements of nature, God directed the east wind to dry the sea and part the waters so that His people might cross.

Biblical archaeologists do not all agree exactly where the crossing took place. Some suggest it was one of the directly northern bodies of waters, the Gulf of Suez or the Gulf of Aqaba. Others remain steadfast that it was the Red Sea cited in the King James Version—Exodus 15:22. The normal Hebrew word used for "Red Sea" is *cuwph* (**soof**). Verse 22 uses this word in reference to the Red Sea being the place of crossing. The basic meaning of *cuwph* is a large body of water, such as a lake or sea. In extra biblical texts of antiquity, *cuwph* refers to the waters mentioned thus far and other large bodies of waters. It is the only word used in reference to the Red Sea. The word "sea" in this verse and verse 9 is *yam* (**yawm**). Although not translated as such here, it, too, is often used to refer to the Red Sea. Nevertheless it is also used to refer to other bodies of water or none in particular.

While the debate may still continue, let us resist any temptations to believe the crossing had to occur in shallow waters, where the ebb of water's flow was reduced to a trickle—that this was not a miracle, but a natural phenomenon. Shallow waters could not have engulfed the Egyptian army and washed dead bodies to the shore (v. 30). Given the contextual evidence, the Red Sea appears to be a good option for the crossing. Therefore, Israel, trusting God, went into the midst of the sea, a wall of water one side, and a wall of water on the other (v. 22).

What Pharaoh's commanders were thinking, we do not know. We can assume, however, although engulfed in darkness, the dry ground may have been an incentive to continue their mission. Giving up was not an option yet.

23 And the Egyptians pursued, and went in after them to the midst of the sea, even all Pharaoh's horses, his chariots, and his horsemen. 24a And it came to pass, that in the morning watch the LORD looked unto the host of the Egyptians through the pillar of fire and of the cloud,

The taste of victory and the smell of defeat might have been on the minds of Pharaoh and the Hebrews respectively, in verse 23. I can only imagine the terror of marching between two walls of water and hearing the thunderous roar of the chariots of Egypt. The Egyptian commanders would have every reason to think that when daylight came, victory was theirs.

If we are mindful and discerning, we can learn a lesson from Pharaoh. Persistence has a payoff. The Hebrew word for "pursued" is *radaph* (**raw-DAF**), and it means "to follow with intense effort and focus." Pharaoh threw all he had militarily into pursuing the Hebrews. Of course, negatively, as we shall see, the lesson we learn is the consequences associated with persistent disobedience. Pharaoh has had many opportunities to repent, 10 to be exact, and even in this we can learn a lesson. God has been gracious and merciful to Pharaoh. Therefore, how much more will He be toward those called by His name who persistently love, obey, and depend on Him (Romans 8:28). Nevertheless, as far as Pharaoh is concerned, God says, "Enough is enough!

God is a right-on-time God. Just as Pharaoh's men may have felt victory was in their grasp, the Lord made His move. A few hours had gone by and it was the morning watch. The morning watch most likely was between 2 a.m. and sunrise. In Egypt, during the month of April, the sun rose at about 5:45 a.m. There is little reason not to think the advantage would soon be with the Egyptian army. The advantage, however, is with God, for He had other plans.

While Pharaoh's commanders were contemplating a forward move of conquest, God was looking and about to enact His own judgment on the Egyptian army. "Look" is a translation of the Hebrew word *shaqaph* (**shaw-KAF**). Basically, it means "to look down." It has a nuance that is instructive. It refers to more than what the eyes see; it also refers to the *point* of view.

The text says He looked to the Egyptians through the pillar of fire. The enemies of God may devise schemes of wickedness in darkness. That darkness, however, cannot block the light of the Lord from looking into their midst and taking the necessary steps to protect His people.

24b and troubled the host of the Egyptians, 25 And took off their chariot wheels, that they drave them heavily: so that the Egyptians said, Let us flee from the face of Israel; for the LORD fighteth for them against the Egyptians.

Verse 24 says, "the Lord troubled the Egyptians." This was not a random effort to confuse the enemy. *Hamam* (**haw-MAM**) is the Hebrew word translated "troubled"; literally it is a word used that is associated with the control exercised over carts or wagons pulled by animals. Verse 25 (paraphrased) says, "the Lord took the wheels off their chariots." Often our adversaries use our weaknesses and their strengths to our disadvantage. When God intervenes, He targets the specific thing that strips the enemy of advantages they have.

Can you imagine chariots without wheels attached to powerful horses trained to run with abandon? With their chariots bouncing around controllably, drivers, officers, and warriors would have spent their energies just trying to hold on. What they thought was going to be an easy victory has become a fight for their own survival.

"Drave" is the Hebrew word *nahag* (**naw-HAG**). The meaning, in this context, is associated with "the control drivers had to direct their horses." The Hebrew word *kebeduth* (**keb-ay-DOOTH**) is translated "heavily." In its root form, it means "to quench," like the light of a fire. The Egyptian chariots, and thus, their men were out of control. What a contrast! Pharaoh had tried to control the movements of the Hebrews. Now, his army, at the hand of God, was out of control.

Finally, the Egyptians got the point. They had been fighting a battle they could not win. Literally translated, "flee" (Heb. *nuwc*, **noos**) means "escape to a safe place." As Moses had declared to the Children of Israel (Exodus 14:14), the Egyptians now declared, "the Lord fighteth for them." This is a lesson that echoes through time and a lesson so often forgotten. God fights our battles—our enemies are His enemies, our struggles are His struggles, and His victories are our victories. We must add that He protects us for His name's sake—that is, His glory. Sadly for the Egyptians, their realization was too little, too late.

14:30 Thus the LORD saved Israel that day out of the hand of the Egyptians; and Israel saw the Egyptians dead upon the sea shore.

This Hebrew word for "saved," *yasha'* (**yaw-SHAH**), according to *Strong's Concordance,* is used 215 times. From the root form of *yasha'*, we get such concepts as "salvation, deliver/deliverance, help, and preserve."

God brought (delivered, saved, gave the Israelites an escape) His people to a place where they were free to worship. Notice, however, the verse specifically notes Israel was saved from the hand of the Egyptians. I paraphrase this as, "saved from the shackles of Egyptian slavery, and they and those things that would destroy the Israelites were dead and lying at their feet." The journey of salvation and sanctification is horizontal and vertical. We are moving ever closer to Him. He is nevertheless actively involved with protecting us along the way.

Sources:

Life Application Study Bible (New International Version). Wheaton, Ill.: Tyndale House Publishers, 1991.

Packer, J. I., Merrill C. Tenney, and William White. *Nelson's Illustrated Encyclopedia of Bible Facts.* Nashville: Thomas Nelson Publishers, 1995.

Daily Bible Readings

M: Led to Freedom by God
Exodus 13:17–22
T: Pursued by the Enemy
Exodus 14:1–9
W: Overtaken by Fear
Exodus 14:10–14
T: God is Our Refuge
Psalm 46
F: Trust in the Lord
Proverbs 3:3–10
S: Celebrating Deliverance
Exodus 15:1–13
S: Saved from the Enemy
Exodus 14:15–25, 30

TEACHING TIPS

July 5

Bible Study Guide 5

1. Words You Should Know

A. Statutes (Deuteronomy 5:1) *choq* (Heb.)—Something prescribed; enactments, decrees, ordinances either divine or human. From the root *haqaq* (Heb.), meaning to cut in or on, upon, engrave, inscribe upon a rock.

B. Judgments (v. 1) *mishpat* (Heb.)—Ordinances.

C. Covet (v. 21) *'avah* (Heb.)—Incline, desire. It refers to one's attitude. It concerns not only the deed, but also the motive.

2. Teacher Preparation

Unifying Principle—Accepting Rules for Living. People make agreements to bring structure and order to their lives. What regulations are necessary to enjoy mutually beneficial lives? God set forth 10 rules of conduct (the Ten Commandments) governing behavior, property, relationships, and worship.

A. Read Exodus 20:1–17 and Deuteronomy 4:44–5:22.

B. Write down any questions that you may have and review, for guidance, the commentary on the *Precepts For Living*® CD-ROM.

C. Read the Unifying Principle, and write down some responses to the question, "What regulations are necessary to enjoy mutually beneficial lives?"

3. Starting the Lesson

A. Open the lesson with prayer, incorporating the theme in your prayer.

B. Explain that today's lesson is about God calling people to covenant. Read the AIM for Change aloud and discuss it with the students.

C. Ask a volunteer to read the In Focus story. Discuss how agreements work and whether a prenuptial agreement would have made certain aspects of Charles and Marlene's life together easier or more difficult.

D. Discuss how agreements can make situations easier. Does it make any difference if the agreement is verbal or written?

4. Getting into the Lesson

A. Ask for volunteers to read The People, Places, and Times.

B. Ask the class if they have ever had to play the role of a mediator.

C. Read the Focal Verses, and summarize the In Depth section, stressing salient points.

D. Discuss the importance of Moses rereading the covenant.

E. Read and answer the Search the Scriptures questions together.

5. Relating the Lesson to Life

A. Use the Discuss the Meaning section to help the students relate the lesson to their daily lives.

B. Read the Lesson in Our Society section, and explain how rules make belonging to a family or community easier.

6. Arousing Action

A. Read the Keep in Mind verse. Reiterate to the students the importance of remembering that they have a responsibility to learn God's principles so that they will not stumble.

B. Remind the students to complete the Make It Happen section and bring it with them to next week's class.

Worship Guide

For the Superintendent or Teacher
Theme: God Calls People to Covenant
Theme Song: "The Family of God"
Devotional Reading: Matthew 22:34–40
Prayer

GOD CALLS PEOPLE TO COVENANT

Bible Background • DEUTERONOMY 5:1–27
Printed Text • DEUTERONOMY 5:1–9, 11–13, 16–21 Devotional Reading • MATTHEW 22:34–40

AIM for Change

By the end of the lesson, we will:
RECOUNT how God gave the Ten Commandments to the people;
UNDERSTAND how covenants work; and
MAKE better agreements with people in our lives.

Keep in Mind

"Hear, O Israel, the statutes and judgments which I speak in your ears this day, that ye may learn them, and keep, and do them" (from Deuteronomy 5:1).

Focal Verses

KJV **Deuteronomy 5:1** And Moses called all Israel, and said unto them, Hear, O Israel, the statutes and judgments which I speak in your ears this day, that ye may learn them, and keep, and do them.

2 The LORD our God made a covenant with us in Horeb.

3 The LORD made not this covenant with our fathers, but with us, even us, who are all of us here alive this day.

4 The LORD talked with you face to face in the mount out of the midst of the fire,

5 (I stood between the LORD and you at that time, to shew you the word of the LORD: for ye were afraid by reason of the fire, and went not up into the mount;) saying,

6 I am the LORD thy God, which brought thee out of the land of Egypt, from the house of bondage.

7 Thou shalt have none other gods before me.

8 Thou shalt not make thee any graven image, or any likeness of any thing that is in heaven above, or that is in the earth beneath, or that is in the waters beneath the earth:

9 Thou shalt not bow down thyself unto them, nor serve them.

5:11 Thou shalt not take the name of the LORD thy God in vain: for the LORD will not hold him guiltless that taketh his name in vain.

12 Keep the sabbath day to sanctify it, as the LORD thy God hath commanded thee.

13 Six days thou shalt labour, and do all thy work:

5:16 Honour thy father and thy mother, as the

NLT **Deuteronomy 5:1** Moses called all the people of Israel together and said, "Listen carefully, Israel. Hear the decrees and regulations I am giving you today, so you may learn them and obey them!

2 "The LORD our God made a covenant with us at Mount Sinai.

3 The LORD did not make this covenant with our ancestors, but with all of us who are alive today.

4 At the mountain the LORD spoke to you face to face from the heart of the fire.

5 I stood as an intermediary between you and the LORD, for you were afraid of the fire and did not want to approach the mountain. He spoke to me, and I passed his words on to you. This is what he said:

6 "I am the LORD your God, who rescued you from the land of Egypt, the place of your slavery.

7 "You must not have any other god but me.

8 "You must not make for yourself an idol of any kind, or an image of anything in the heavens or on the earth or in the sea.

9 You must not bow down to them or worship them, for I, the LORD your God, am a jealous God who will not tolerate your affection for any other gods. I lay the sins of the parents upon their children; the entire family is affected—even children in the third and fourth generations of those who reject me.

5:11 "You must not misuse the name of the LORD your God. The LORD will not let you go unpunished if you misuse his name.

12 "Observe the Sabbath day by keeping it holy, as the LORD your God has commanded you.

LORD thy God hath commanded thee; that thy days may be prolonged, and that it may go well with thee, in the land which the LORD thy God giveth thee.

17 Thou shalt not kill.

18 Neither shalt thou commit adultery.

19 Neither shalt thou steal.

20 Neither shalt thou bear false witness against thy neighbour.

21 Neither shalt thou desire thy neighbour's wife, neither shalt thou covet thy neighbour's house, his field, or his manservant, or his maidservant, his ox, or his ass, or any thing that is thy neighbour's.

13 You have six days each week for your ordinary work,

5:16 "Honor your father and mother, as the LORD your God commanded you. Then you will live a long, full life in the land the LORD your God is giving you.

17 "You must not murder.

18 "You must not commit adultery.

19 "You must not steal.

20 "You must not testify falsely against your neighbor.

21 "You must not covet your neighbor's wife. You must not covet your neighbor's house or land, male or female servant, ox or donkey, or anything else that belongs to your neighbor.

In Focus

Charles and Marlene had been friends since they were in grade school. They had attended a school built with funds raised by Blacks in the community and a grant from a foundation established to help fund schools for Black children. The local school board closed the school and bused the students to a White school across town, after the Supreme Court decision outlawing racial segregation in America's schools. Charles and Marlene, members of the last graduating class at their old school, went separate ways after graduation.

Charles and Marlene's paths crossed again at a reunion 20 years later for the Black alumni of their former school. Charles was married with two children by then. Marlene had immersed herself in an education career. Nearly another 20 years would pass before they would meet again. This time, Charles was a retired widower. After months of becoming reacquainted with each other, Charles proposed marriage to Marlene.

Charles and Marlene were discussing financial matters when Marlene brought up the subject of a premarital agreement to provide for Charles's children from his previous marriage.

"The thought crossed my mind, but I didn't want you to think that I did not trust you or believed that you were marrying me for my money," commented Charles, sheepishly.

"Charles, I know most people are uncomfortable talking about love and money together, but a prenuptial agreement, contrary to popular belief, is not just for rich people and will not doom our marriage to failure," said Marlene.

"A prenuptial agreement allows you to leave to your children what you would like them to inherit, rather than the state making that decision in the event something happens to you. Sometimes such agreements can make life together easier," Marlene explained.

Charles decided that the agreement was worth looking into.

Entering into agreements (covenants) helps give structure to our lives and maintain a rule of law, whether the agreement is with communities, citizens, or couples. In today's lesson, God calls His people to covenant as well, so that they can maintain an intimate, unbroken relationship with Him. God always kept His covenant agreement with them. However, they broke theirs with Him time and time again.

The People, Places, and Times

Moses, the Mediator. God called Moses to be God's intermediary between Pharaoh and the Israelites, to bring deliverance to the people (Exodus 3:10). God used Moses to part the Red Sea so that the Israelites could see God's glory and power (14:13–18; 30–31). God used Moses throughout his life to intercede between God and the people. However, Moses also acted on behalf of the people. It was Moses whom the Israelites asked to receive the law in their behalf from God, because they feared God's presence on the mountain (Deuteronomy 5:5, 22). When the people complained about the lack of food and water in the wilderness, Moses appealed to God and God provided fresh water (Exodus 15:23–25), bread (16:4–5), and quail (16:13; Numbers 11:31–33). When the people refused to enter the Promised Land the first time, as God had instructed, because they dreaded the inhabitants God threatened to strike them with pestilence and disinherit them. But Moses interceded for the people and God forgave them (Numbers 14:1–25).

Of all of Moses' acts of mediation, it is his role as intermediary that the book of Deuteronomy lifts up as Moses' greatest legacy. It was in this role that God established God's covenant with the Israelites. Moses was the one whom God entrusted to deliver God's commands, ordinances, and statutes.

Mount Horeb. Mount Horeb is an alternative name for Mount Sinai, the hill or mountain in the wilderness of Sinai, where God was believed to live (Deuteronomy 33:2; Judges 5:5; Psalm 68:9). Mount Sinai is located on the southern tip of the Sinai Peninsula, a triangular-shaped piece of land located in Egypt. Sinai lies between the Mediterranean Sea to the north and the Red Sea (or Reed Sea) to the south. It is also the territory the Israelites had to traverse to enter Canaan.

Mount Horeb is mentioned in Deuteronomy 5:2 (cf. Exodus 19) as the place where the Israelites entered into a covenant with God after God delivered them from bondage in Egypt and where Moses received laws and instructions for the people as to how they were to live as the covenanted people of God.

Mount Horeb is also significant in the story of Moses' call and leadership in the wilderness. Moses first encountered God in a burning bush at Mount Horeb (Exodus 3:1), struck a rock causing water to pour forth after having been instructed by God to do so at Mount Horeb (17:6), and Mount Horeb is the place where Moses interceded on behalf of the Israelites, when God threatened to destroy them because they made a golden calf to worship while Moses was on the mountain (32; 33:6).

Source:

McBride Jr., S. Dean. "Deuteronomy." In *The Harper Collins Study Bible.* New York: HarperCollins Publishers, 1989.

Background

When the events in the book of Deuteronomy occur, the Israelites are in the plains of Moab, preparing to cross the Jordan River and enter the land promised to their ancestors. This is a new generation of Israelites. Their ancestors' disobedience stirred God's anger against them, and God promised that they would not enter the land (Deuteronomy 1:19–45; cf. Numbers 13–14). The consequences that befell the first generation in the wilderness are almost a foretelling of the circumstances in which the Israelites will find themselves during King Josiah's reign.

Before entering the land, Moses gave the law to this generation as he had done in the presence of their ancestors nearly 40 years previously. Deuteronomy is the Greek title for the book, meaning "second law" (*deuteros* "second" and *nomos* "law"), a Septuagint mistranslation of the Hebrew *mishneh hattorah hazzoth* "a copy of this law" (Deuteronomy 17:18). Nevertheless, the "second law" or second giving of the law by Moses to the new generation reiterates that the covenant made between God and the Israelites on Mount Horeb included those present.

Source:

McBride Jr., S. Dean. "Deuteronomy." In *The Harper Collins Study Bible.* New York: HarperCollins Publishers, 1989.

At-A-Glance

1. The Covenant at Mount Horeb (Deuteronomy 5:1–5)

2. The Ten Commandments (vv. 6–9, 11–13, 16–21)

In Depth

1. The Covenant at Mount Horeb (Deuteronomy 5:1–5)

The Hebrew name for the fifth book of the Bible and the last attributed to Moses is *'elleh haddevarim* ("these are the words"), the opening words of the book. The title is shortened to *devarim* ("words") in the Hebrew Bible. The narrator introduces the book of Deuteronomy, in the preface, as "the words of Moses to the Israelites on the fortieth anniversary of their departure from Egypt and the evening before their march across the Jordan River into the Promised Land." Moses had gathered all the people to deliver the law. As Moses prepared this generation of Israelites to receive the covenantal law, as God had commanded him, Moses recounted the reason why God did not allow their ancestors to enter the land and instructed them that if they wanted to remain in the land, they must learn God's law, which consists of decrees, statutes, and ordinances (613 in all) and obey them at all times.

The covenant made at Mount Horeb was the agreement that established the Israelites as the people of God and the terms of that relationship. Moses reaffirmed that God is faithful to this generation as God was to their ancestors, even though their ancestors rebelled against God. Moses understood the importance of the law being given once again, before they entered Canaan, because he knew that they could forget the law and become rebellious like their ancestors. Keeping God's law was a matter of life and death for this fledgling nation:

"See, I have set before you today life and prosperity, death and adversity. If you obey the commandments of the Lord your God that I am commanding you today, by loving the Lord your God, walking in his ways, and observing his commandments, decrees, and ordinances, then you shall live and become numerous, and the Lord your God will bless you in the land that you are entering to possess" (Deuteronomy 30:15–16)

The Akan people of Ghana, West Africa, have a saying, "Go back and fetch it," which expresses the sentiment that one must look back in order to move forward. The symbol of the Sankofa is depicted as a bird flying forward while looking backward and carrying an egg, which represents the future, in its beak. The symbol also serves as a warning for what can happen when people forget or abandon their past. Moses cautioned the Israelites, as they were preparing to enter the land God promised to them, that they should live according to God's commandments in the land and not rebel against God as their ancestors had. The Israelites would need constant reminding that they were God's covenanted people, whom God had brought out of bondage in Egypt, and that they were to worship God only.

2. The Ten Commandments (vv. 6–9, 11–13, 16–21)

The covenant was an agreement enacted between God and the Israelites, made under an oath that established the rule of God in the lives of the Israelites. The agreement resembled the covenants of their ancient near Eastern neighbors. Such agreements usually contained an identification of the covenant giver, the historical prologue for the agreement, stipulations as to the rules and regulations, and blessings and curses. God states that the purpose for establishing the covenant was because God had delivered them from servitude out of Egypt, the land of their bondage. The biblical writers remind the Israelites many times that God had brought them out of the land of Egypt, often as a way to get the people to turn from their sins and turn back to God (1 Samuel 12:6; Psalm 81:10; Daniel 9:15).

The Ten Commandments or Decalogue (Greek for 10 "words" or 10 "utterances") are repeated, with some variation, as they were first read to the people in Exodus 20 (cf. Deuteronomy 5:12; 14–16).

The first four stipulations of the covenant concern the relationship between God and the people. The Israelites were commanded not to have other gods besides God, or make any idols or worship them. The golden calf incident at Mount Horeb, mentioned above, might have come to mind when the Israelites heard this commandment. They were also commanded not to use God's name when making oaths with people the speaker knows to be false or deceitful, or to work on the Sabbath day. However, the fourth commandment is expressed differently in the rereading (cf. Exodus 20:8–11). In Exodus the command is to "remember" the Sabbath day as a time of rest in honor of God, the Creator. In Deuteronomy, the Sabbath day links worship intrinsically with God's justice. The Israelites are commanded to "observe" the Sabbath in remembrance of God's deliverance of the people from slavery in Egypt.

The last six commandments govern the life of the Israelite community. By establishing the covenant with Israel, God insured that the rights, interests, and the needs of everyone were addressed. The covenant was integrally linked to the existence of Israel as a nation. The Israelites would thrive if they kept all the commandments; they would perish if they did not.

Source:

Mendenhall, George E., and Gary A. Herion. "Covenant." In the *Anchor Bible Dictionary*. Vol. 1. New York: Doubleday, 1992.

Search the Scriptures

1. Moses convened the Israelites to hear the law that God had given them, through Moses, so that they could __________ them, and __________, and __________ them (Deuteronomy 5:1).

2. What does God say will happen to anyone who takes God's name in vain (v. 11)?

3. Why do you think God commanded the people to, "Honor thy father and thy mother" as part of the covenant (v. 16)?

Discuss the Meaning

1. Share an example from your life when you broke a rule and suffered the consequences.

2. Charles was reluctant to bring up the subject of a premarital agreement. Are premarital agreements ever appropriate for Christian couples in a covenant marriage? What are the advantages and disadvantages?

3. Many Christian couples today are entering into "covenant marriages," a movement begun in 1999 to help reduce the divorce rate among Christian couples by "uplifting God's ideal of marriage." Couples vow to God, one another, their families, and communities to remain married. What are the similarities and differences between the principles of a covenant marriage and the covenant between God and the Israelites?

Lesson in Our Society

1. Children have a strong sense of fairness. They understand that being part of a family or community means that everyone is supposed to adhere to a specific set of rules and behave in a certain way. For children this means sharing, putting away their toys, listening, and being listened to. They learn the rules by following the examples set by adults in their life, being taught them, and practicing them. What are some of the most important rules you learned as a child, and who taught them to you?

2. God entered into a covenantal relationship with the Israelites, because God loved them and had made a promise to their ancestors (Deuteronomy 7:7–8). As people of God, they had certain responsibilities. Failure to adhere to them brought consequences. As members of God's family, God has expectations of us. What do you think are some of those expectations?

3. The Ten Commandments teach us how to be in relationship with God, our families, and our neighbors. Obedience to God's instructions leads to a better spiritual life, stronger families, and stronger communities. How do the Ten Commandments help guide our lives?

Make It Happen

Make a list of some of the relationships in which you are involved. How are the rules different for relationships with your family, your friends, business acquaintances, or church members? Think of ways that rules, agreements, etc. help your relationships to function better. What can you do to strengthen the rules that help make your relationships stronger?

Follow the Spirit

What God wants me to do:

____

____

Remember Your Thoughts

Special insights I have learned:

____

____

More Light on the Text

Deuteronomy 5:1–9, 11–13, 16–21

1 And Moses called all Israel, and said unto them, Hear, O Israel, the statutes and judgments which I speak in your ears this day, that ye may learn them, and keep, and do them.

By divine calling, Moses was renowned as Israel's great leader. He was used by God as her deliverer, prophet, and lawgiver. Endowed with such greatness, power, and authority, he acted as a mediator between God and the people of Israel. When the Israelites entered Egypt, they entered as a family; but Moses led them out as a nation. His leadership brought about their deliverance from the bondage of Egypt, under which the Israelites had suffered over a period of 430 years. His encounter with God at Mount Horeb, in a burning bush, marked the beginning to his call to such great status. There God communicated with him, appointing him to be Israel's leader and deliverer. There he also started receiving messages from God, which he proclaimed to Pharaoh and the Israelite people, thus functioning as God's prophet. He communicated to the Israelites God's will and plan and also His requirements for them concerning their service to Him and their socioeconomic life. He upgraded the practices and customs performed by Abraham and their patriarchs to the status of a religion, thus modifying them and becoming the founder of the Jewish religion. As is typical of any religious, social, and economic life of any people, practices, customs, and usages are naturally stipulated by laws. The quintessential part of the divine revelation Moses commu-

"Hear, O Israel, the statutes and judgments which I speak in your ears this day, that ye may learn them, and keep, and do them" (from Deuteronomy 5:1).

nicated to the Israelites was a body of laws, by which they would live as God's own people and serve Him in the ways acceptable to Him. Here, Moses announced to them the Ten Commandments, otherwise known as the Decalogue.

Moses called on all Israel to receive from him God's statutes and judgments. The Hebrew word translated "statutes" is *choq* (**khoke**); it means "prescription, enactment, regulation, rule or law." *Hoq* is a noun derived from the verb *haqaq* (**haw-KAK**), which means "to cut in, determine, or to decree." The Israelites, by inheritance, had become God's own people. They had become subject to His influence; God's sovereignty was to be exercised over them. Because they were God's people, the Lord, Himself, by giving them His statutes, "cut in" on them to determine the flow of their lives. By His statutes, he prescribed a direction for them on how they should live.

The Hebrew word for "judgments" is *mishpat* (**mish-PAWT**). This word is used in two senses: one refers to "the act of presiding over a case as a judge and rendering a proper verdict"; the other refers to "the rights and privileges of someone, the instance in which things are in proper relationship to one's claim and an established ordinance." This second sense applies in the text. Moses' call on the Israelites to hear the judgments of God is to make them know the grounds on which they have certain rights and privileges, which God has established as an ordinance. When they know these judgments, they are to learn, keep, and do them. And so with the Decalogue, God set forth 10 rules of conduct to govern their behavior, properties, relationships, and their worship. The Decalogue is set of decrees to order their lives in these areas.

2 The LORD our God made a covenant with us in Horeb.

Moses speaks of God's initiative in the establishment of a covenant with the people of Israel on Mount Horeb. Israel was a nation through which God made Himself known to the world, a nation through which He manifested His power, might, awesome presence, ways, divine government, and glory. Israel was God's inheritance (Deuteronomy 4:20). It was appropriate, by God's own standard, to establish a covenant between Him and His people to make them not only acknowledge Him as their God but to provoke their response, obedience, and commitment to Him. The Hebrew word translated "covenant" is *beriyth* (**ber-EETH**), which means "confederacy, league." By making a covenant with His people, God entered into a confederacy with them—a confederacy in which they become united with Him, sharing His aims and purposes for their lives. In a covenant relationship with God, the people were bound to fulfill certain conditions (those stipulated by the Ten Commandments), for which they were to be subjects of His blessings, when they kept the covenant, or incurred upon themselves punishment for breaking the covenant.

3 The LORD made not this covenant with our fathers, but with us, even us, who are all of us here alive this day.

Moses emphasized the fact that the covenant God made was with them, the new generation of Israelites—a generation still alive to fulfill the covenant. This emphasis undoubtedly was to show that the covenant did not concern their fathers. The word translated "fathers" is *'ab* (**awb**), meaning "forefathers, ancestors."

The "fathers" specifically refer to the most prominent of their ancestors with whom God began to have dealings and with whom He had a covenant. This is talking about Abraham. The time of Abraham marked the period when God's purpose of begetting a nation out of the inhabitants of the earth began in earnest.

4 The LORD talked with you face to face in the mount out of the midst of the fire.

Divine communication was made directly with the people. God spoke to them face-to-face. The awesome manifestation of God on Mount Horeb, which was a combination of thunder, lightning, smoke, fire, and the quaking of the mountain, was a terrifying sight to the people of Israel. From the midst of the fire, the voice of God relayed His words to them. This was how He gave them the Ten Commandments. The word translated "face" is *paniym* (**paw-NEEM**); in its most basic meaning it refers to the frontal part of the human head. It means the part of something most exposed to view; it also means presence in a general sense. In this text, the phrase "face to face" is applied differently from when it would be applied in a situation concerning two humans. The first "face" in the phrase refers to God's presence and glory: the awesome manifestation of God at Mount Horeb to the people. The second "face" definitely refers to the frontal part of their heads with which they viewed the divine manifestation.

5 (I stood between the LORD and you at that time, to shew you the word of the LORD: for ye were afraid by reason of the fire, and went not up into the mount;) saying,

This is one of the prominent instances that exhibits the actual and practical function of Moses as a mediator between God and the Israelites, and he declares this himself. He stood between God and the people to shew them God's Word. The Hebrew word for "shew" is *nagad* (**naw-GAD**), meaning "to announce, to expose, and to explain." As one called to the privileged status of a mediator, Moses was used to the divine communication; he understood the revelations and the words of God to the letter. He had the ability to articulate the words of God so that the people would understand. This he did by announcing and explaining God's words to them.

The Hebrew word for "afraid" is *yare'* (**yaw-RAY**). It means "to stand in awe, to dread, to be frightened, to revere." The sight of the smoking and fiery mountain frightened them. It roused in them a psychological disposition of fear or dread that made them draw back. This fear also made them act in reverence to God, as they restrained themselves from moving up into the mountain. This restraint was in compliance with the command God gave to Moses in Exodus 19:12, "And thou shalt set bounds unto the people round about, saying, Take heed to yourselves, that ye go not up into the mount, or toucheth the border of it."

6 I am the LORD thy God, which brought thee out of the land of Egypt, from the house of bondage.

This verse contains two elements of the Sinai covenant: the preamble and the historical prologue. God declares Himself as the author of the covenant; He declares Himself as "the Lord"—this was the preamble that identified God as the author of the covenant. The Hebrew word translated "Lord" is *Yehovah* (**Yeh-ho-VAW**). This refers to the Tetragrammaton, YHWH, the name by which the Jews called God; it appeared without vowels. Other variant spellings of the name are Jehovah, Jahweh, and Yahweh, with vowels included to make it communicable. The Jews called God by this name because He chose it as His personal name by which He related to them, a name so significant, and should be supremely regarded within the context of a covenant relationship. In other words, outside a covenant relationship, He is just God to all the creatures of the earth.

God says in this verse, "I am the Lord." The definite article *the*, which qualifies the name, denotes God's status as the "one and only," which should be acknowledged by His people. He further says, "thy God"; with this He conveys upon them a possessive status, as a people who has Him as their God. He revealed to them that He was responsible for the greatest and most remarkable experience of their history—their deliverance from the bondage of Egypt. This was a historical prologue to refresh their memory.

7 Thou shall have none other gods before me.

Here Moses announced the first of the Ten Commandments. They are the special stipulations of the Sinai Covenant. The Lord gave them this first statute to restrict them from worshiping any other god. The Hebrew word for "gods" is *'elôhiym* (**el-o-**

HEEM); it is a plural form of the word *'elowahh* (**el-O-ah**), which signifies "deity."

The Lord, Himself, knows that man has the need for a god, and so He gave the Israelites this command to govern their worship, to direct their focus toward Him, the one and only true God.

8 Thou shalt not make thee any graven image, or any likeness of any thing that is in heaven above, or that is in the earth beneath, or that is in the waters beneath the earth. 9 Thou shalt not bow down thyself unto them, nor serve them:

Humans' need for a god provokes the passion to capture an image that can abstractly repose in the mind or be made to assume a physical form. This physical form is a graven image. This second statute is meant to nullify every inclination to idolatry in the minds of God's people, to replace their need for a god with the need for the Almighty God alone. The Hebrew word translated "graven image" is *pecel* (**PEH-sel**); it denotes "an image carved or sculpted from stone, wood, or metal—it is an idol." An idol or cult object was used to represent deities or gods, and by this was the god worshipped. The carved image usually was in the likeness of a creature, such as a beast, a tree, a fish or other aquatic animals; it could be in the form of a star, moon, or other celestial bodies, in angelic form, or even in human form.

This statute forbade the Israelites from making unto themselves idols that they would bow down to in allegiance and worship, as was the practice of other nations around them. They were to be distinguished from the heathen nations by worshiping God alone.

5:11 Thou shalt not take the name of the LORD thy God in vain: for the LORD will not hold him guiltless that taketh his name in vain.

God's name identifies Him alone; it invokes His presence and carries His power. Prior to the deliverance from the Egyptian bondage, all that the new generation of Israelites knew about God came from historical accounts of His dealings with their fathers. From then on, they came to know His name as the Lord, the God of Abraham, Isaac, and Jacob. When Moses came, he introduced God's name to them as "I am." Then God introduced Himself to them as "the Lord" in the opening of the Sinai Covenant (Deuteronomy 5:6). To His people, God's name had a covenantal significance.

The Israelites experienced God's mighty acts of judgment against the Egyptians and deliverance from bondage. They saw God's awesome manifestations at Mount Horeb. All these credibly depicted a great covenantal significance of God's name to them. It depicted God as the almighty, the deliverer, and the provider. Upon attaining this level of awareness, they were not to take the name of God in vain. The Hebrew word translated "take" is *nasa'* (**naw-SAW**), which means "to lay hold of, to handle, play with or manipulate." It conveys the idea of using or handling something inappropriately. The Hebrew word for "vain" is *shav'* (**shawv**), which means "desolation, uselessness, false." The Israelites were sternly warned not to handle or use the name of the Lord inappropriately in order not to bring desolation to it, render it useless, or bring falsity to it.

12 Keep the sabbath day to sanctify it, as the LORD thy God hath commanded thee. 13 Six days thou shalt labour, and do all thy work:

God designated one day of the week to be accorded special regard by the Israelites. This fourth commandment instructs them to attach a spiritual significance to this day and to keep it. The Hebrew word translated "keep" is *shamar* (**shaw-MAR**); it denotes "to tend, retain, and to observe." The Jews were required by this commandment to observe a day of the week as a Sabbath day. The original Hebrew word *Shabbath* (**shab-BAWTH**) slightly differs in spelling with the English rendering, with a transposition of the "h." Shabbat means "to cease or to desist"; it implies a day of rest. The Sabbath day is the seventh day of the week designated by God for the Jews to cease from their work, and observe that day as a day of rest and worship. The Sabbath takes its root from the time of creation; it was instituted by God, Himself, when He ceased from His work of creation on the seventh day and rested. From then, God established it as a pattern for humanity: that we should work for six days and rest on the seventh day.

The word translated "sanctify" is *qadash* (**kaw-DASH**), which means "be holy." This makes the Sabbath a holy day. To sanctify the Sabbath further means to "proclaim it, to consecrate it into the Lord, rid it of all labours." The observance of the Sabbath, therefore, achieves a dual purpose: to cease from work and keep it hallowed unto God, and to rest—this is favorable to man.

5:16 Honour thy father and thy mother, as the LORD thy God hath commanded thee; that thy days may be prolonged, and that it may go well with thee, in the land which the LORD thy God giveth thee.

One's parents stand as one's roots of biological origin. In order to maintain a culture that upholds high family values, offspring are instructed by this commandment to honor their parents. The family is a unitary form of the larger society. Wholesomeness within it can be achieved in a variety of ways, but one major way—as it involves children—is to have the offspring honor their parents. The Hebrew word translated "honour" is *kabad* (**kaw-BAD**); it means "to glorify, make to be in great quantity, make weighty, hold in good reputation, promote, make great." *Kabad* conveys the idea of rendering much or great obedience, respect, or esteem to one's parents; to consider them great or of a weightier status in one's eyes.

Our parents happen to be the immediate representatives of our ancestors before our eyes. As the terminal points of a long line of ancestors to us, they form our immediate roots or source of origin. To "honor" them, according to the original Hebrew meaning of the word, further conveys the idea of making them weightier than us, make them out to be of a great quantity, by reason of the fact that they are part of a great "multitude" of forefathers before our existence.

This commandment, no doubt, was meant to foster good relationships between parents and their children; to govern the behavior of children toward their parents. It was also meant to create a distinct, morally sound, obedient, and righteous generation of offspring among the Jews, as they proceeded to possess Canaan land, where the heathen children must have been living a contrary life.

17 Thou shalt not kill.

This commandment offers security for human life. It forbids the death of an individual, resultant of any form of violence generated by malice, murderous thoughts, anger, hatred, or vengeance. *Ratsach* (**raw-TSAKH**) is the Hebrew word translated "kill" in this verse. It denotes "to kill a human being, to murder, to put to death." This is a commandment that underscores the principle of the sanctity of life and serves to restrain every act of murder against anyone, particularly premeditated murder. It also serves to protect people from being deprived of their right to life. Life is a gift from God and man is made in His image. Murder of a human being destroys both the gift and the image that is of divine origin. This is a violation against the Creator.

18 Neither shalt thou commit adultery.

This commandment is a matrimonial law to restrain married couples from sexual intercourse outside their marriage. The Hebrew word translated "commit adultery" is *na'aph* (**naw-AF**); it implies "to break wedlock." Sexual intercourse, apart from one's spouse, assuredly breaks wedlock; it is a process in which both flesh—that of the man and the woman—are joined together. Marriage joins a man and a woman together legally, and the union is consummated in flesh through sexual intercourse. An earlier proclamation, by God, in Genesis 2:24 made provision for marriage and its consummation, "Therefore shall a man leave his father and his mother, and shall cleave unto his wife; and they shall be one flesh." Sex makes the two one flesh. Adultery breaks the marital law and vows.

19 Neither shalt thou steal.

Material possessions represent the quantifiable material life of the one who owns them. In other words, every person has one physical body, but the material effects that pertain to them abound in numbers. Through greed, lack, discontentment, envy, or sheer cruelty to dispossess another; one person assumes ownership of another's belongings. If the process by which such ownership assumed is illegal, it becomes stealing. The Hebrew word translated "steal" is *ganab* (**gaw-NAB**), which means to "carry away secretly, to get by stealth." It bears the intrinsic meaning "to deceive," obtaining by deception, which also includes the idea of "duping" and "defrauding" others.

Verse 13, which stipulates that a person should labor for six days, certainly acknowledges that a man may possess that which is the just reward of his labor, by implication approving the right to own property. This verse is a restraining commandment forbidding a man from stealing the property of another.

20 Neither shalt thou bear false witness against thy neighbour.

The words of a person's mouth bear certain significances or effects in various instances. God is concerned with the quality of words spoken by a man, as it relates to his neighbor. This commandment exhorts the Jews to honest speech; it deals specifically with testimony in court, but in a general sense, it prohibits all false testimony against another person. The Hebrew word translated "false" is *shav'* (**shawv**), meaning "evil, ruin, guile." While the word translated "witness" is *'ed* (**ayd**), which refers to a person, who is present when something happened and can testify to what he saw and heard. The word "witness," therefore, refers to both the individual and his testimony about a case. A "false witness" is someone with evil intent, who presents an evil testimony to a judge in a law court against his neighbor, in order to pervert justice and cause harm to his neighbor.

21 Neither shalt thou desire thy neighbour's wife, neither shalt thou covet thy neighbour's house, his field, or his manservant, or his maidservant, his ox, or his ass, or anything that is thy neighbour's.

While the previous nine commandments prohibit transgressions that have become fully matured as actions or deeds, this tenth and final commandment kind of nips it in the bud. It aims at stopping the transgression at the very incipient stage, where it originates—the mind. The Hebrew word for "desire," as used in this verse, is *chamad* (**khaw-MAD**), meaning "to delight in, to lust after, to covet." It is synonymous with the word "covet," translated from *'avah* (**aw-VAW**), which also means "to desire, to long for or to lust after." These words speak of sinfulness in one's desire for unlawful things. Desiring a neighbor's wife simply means "lusting after her." Such desire is sinful, as it is directed to the wrong object—a woman, who belongs to another, who has already set his desire on her and possessed her legally as his wife. Coveting a neighbor's belongings (house, field, servant, ox, or any of his possessions) is to wrongfully delight in his properties, to direct an evil desire to his possessions for the aim of appropriating them to one self. This is unlawful, as these possessions are already legally covered by the ownership of another. Covetousness is a sin that can be the root cause of murder (prohibited by the sixth commandment), adultery (prohibited by the seventh), and stealing (prohibited by the eighth).

In order to forestall such social vices and to protect the rights and interests of people within a community, rules and regulations are made. And only when people earnestly desire to live orderly lives will they accept rules for living. By mutual agreement, people make laws that structure their lives together, laws that forbid acts that are detrimental to their well-being, such as those forbidden by the Ten Commandments and many more.

Sources:

Life Application Study Bible (New International Version). Wheaton, Ill.: Tyndale HousePublishers, 1991.

Packer, J. I., Merrill C. Tenney, and William White. *Nelson's Illustrated Encyclopedia of Bible Facts.* Nashville: Thomas Nelson Publishers, 1995.

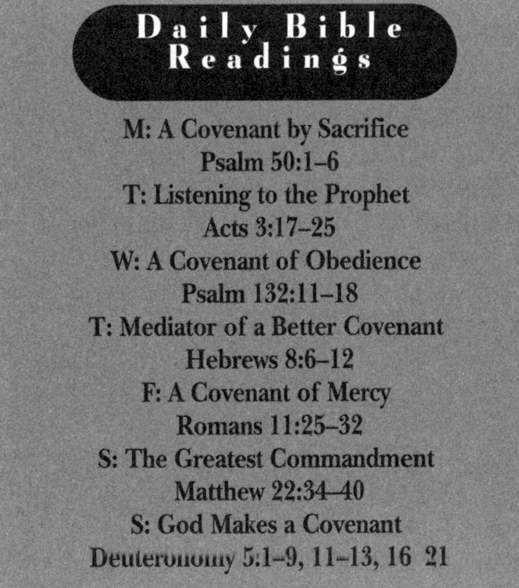

NOTES

TEACHING TIPS

July 12
Bible Study Guide 6

1. Words You Should Know

A. Month (Deuteronomy 16:1) *chodesh* (Heb.)—New moon; day, time of new moon, as religious festival.

B. Place (vv. 2, 6, 7) *shakan* (Heb.)—Establish; make to dwell.

2. Teacher Preparation

Unifying Principle—Remembering and Celebrating. Individuals and communities regularly remember and celebrate great occasions with thanksgiving. How do we commemorate significant events in our lives? God commanded the Israelites to remember their deprivation by eating only unleavened bread and simple meat at sundown.

A. Study the Daily Bible Readings and the Focal Verses.

B. Look up "Passover" in one of the dictionaries, using the *Precepts For Living*® CD-ROM for guidance.

C. Purchase some matzo bread (available in most general grocery stores in the kosher section) for display in a bowl or platter in the classroom. On the board, write the phrase "bread of affliction," scrambling the letters so that it will not be easily recognizable.

3. Starting the Lesson

A. Open the lesson with prayer.

B. Ask the students how their assignment from the previous week went. Explain that last week's lesson focused on God calling people to covenant. Today's lesson is about God calling people to remember. Read the AIM for Change section aloud to the students.

C. Ask for volunteers to read the In Focus section. Ask one student to be the narrator, one to be Alison, and one to be the reporter. Discuss the importance of commemorating events such as Juneteenth. Ask the students to name other celebrations that commemorate God's redemption and liberation in our lives.

4. Getting into the Lesson

A. Ask for volunteers to read The People, Places, and Times. Ask the class to discuss some of the reasons leaven or *chametz* might be prohibited. Hint: In the Jewish tradition, *chametz* symbolizes an oversized ego and idolatry.

B. Ask for two volunteers to unscramble the words on the board. Explain that they have 30 seconds to solve the puzzle. After they have unscrambled "bread of affliction," explain that unleavened bread, or matzo, is the primary symbol of Passover.

C. Have volunteers read the Background and Focal Verses sections. Stop along the way to discuss or make salient points.

D. Discuss the In Depth section.

E. Allow volunteers to answer the Discuss the Meaning questions.

F. Read the Search the Scriptures, and discuss.

5. Relating the Lesson to Life

A. Read the Lesson in Our Society section, and discuss the questions.

B. Allow volunteers to highlight this part of the lesson.

6. Arousing Action

A. Read the Make It Happen section.

B. Invite the students to read the Devotional Reading throughout the week, focusing on how the Scripture relates to the lesson.

C. Share the matzo bread with the students before concluding class.

Worship Guide

For the Superintendent or Teacher
Theme: God Calls People to Remember
Theme Song: "Let Us Break Bread Together"
Devotional Reading: 1 Corinthians 5:1–8
Prayer

GOD CALLS PEOPLE TO REMEMBER

Bible Background • DEUTERONOMY 16:1–8
Printed Text • DEUTERONOMY 16:1–8 Devotional Reading • 1 CORINTHIANS 5:1–8

AIM for Change

By the end of the lesson, we will:
LEARN about the first Passover celebration;
UNDERSTAND the significance of occasions that call for commemoration and praise; and
ENCOURAGE the celebration of significant events in the life of our faith community.

Keep in Mind

"Observe the month of Abib, and keep the passover unto the LORD thy God: for in the month of Abib the LORD thy God brought thee forth out of Egypt by night" (Deuteronomy 16:1).

Focal Verses

KJV **Deuteronomy 16:1** Observe the month of Abib, and keep the passover unto the LORD thy God: for in the month of Abib the LORD thy God brought thee forth out of Egypt by night.

2 Thou shalt therefore sacrifice the passover unto the LORD thy God, of the flock and the herd, in the place which the LORD shall choose to place his name there.

3 Thou shalt eat no leavened bread with it; seven days shalt thou eat unleavened bread therewith, even the bread of affliction; for thou camest forth out of the land of Egypt in haste: that thou mayest remember the day when thou camest forth out of the land of Egypt all the days of thy life.

4 And there shall be no leavened bread seen with thee in all thy coast seven days; neither shall there any thing of the flesh, which thou sacrificedst the first day at even, remain all night until the morning.

5 Thou mayest not sacrifice the passover within any of thy gates, which the LORD thy God giveth thee:

6 But at the place which the LORD thy God shall choose to place his name in, there thou shalt sacrifice the passover at even, at the going down of the sun, at the season that thou camest forth out of Egypt.

7 And thou shalt roast and eat it in the place which the LORD thy God shall choose: and thou shalt turn in the morning, and go unto thy tents.

8 Six days thou shalt eat unleavened bread: and on the seventh day shall be a solemn assembly to the LORD thy God: thou shalt do no work therein.

NLT **Deuteronomy 16:1** "In honor of the LORD your God, celebrate the Passover each year in the early spring, in the month of Abib, for that was the month in which the LORD your God brought you out of Egypt by night.

JULY 12th

2 Your Passover sacrifice may be from either the flock or the herd, and it must be sacrificed to the LORD your God at the designated place of worship—the place he chooses for his name to be honored.

3 Eat it with bread made without yeast. For seven days the bread you eat must be made without yeast, as when you escaped from Egypt in such a hurry. Eat this bread—the bread of suffering—so that as long as you live you will remember the day you departed from Egypt.

4 Let no yeast be found in any house throughout your land for those seven days. And when you sacrifice the Passover lamb on the evening of the first day, do not let any of the meat remain until the next morning.

5 "You may not sacrifice the Passover in just any of the towns that the LORD your God is giving you.

6 You must offer it only at the designated place of worship—the place the LORD your God chooses for his name to be honored. Sacrifice it there in the evening as the sun goes down on the anniversary of your exodus from Egypt.

7 Roast the lamb and eat it in the place the LORD your God chooses. Then you may go back to your tents the next morning.

8 For the next six days you may not eat any bread made with yeast. On the seventh day proclaim another holy day in honor of the LORD your God, and no work may be done on that day.

In Focus

Alison and her colleagues were excited to be riding in their local Juneteenth parade. The event's theme was, "Remembering Our Past and Celebrating Our Present," with a focus on education. Alison's team had made posters featuring milestones in African American education, such as the establishment of the United Negro College Fund by Frederick Douglass Patterson in 1944, the landmark *Brown* v. *Board of Education* decision in 1954, and the organizing in 1960 of the Black-led Student Nonviolent Coordinating Committee (SNCC).

As Alison's truck stopped for a drill-team performance ahead of them, a reporter walked up to the vehicle.

"What a great presentation you have here!" exclaimed the reporter.

Speaking into the camera she said, "Folks, take a look at these wonderful posters featuring black and white photographs of important events in African American education."

"Can you tell our viewing audience a little more about your display?" she asked Alison.

"Sure," Alison replied, "Juneteenth is a time of commemoration in the African American community of the arrival of the news in Galveston, Texas, in 1865 that the slaves were free," said Alison.

Alison continued, "This display is in keeping with the parade theme. We wanted to remember our deliverance as a people from slavery, as well as celebrate the people and events that have helped us to come as far as we have today, which we believe have been achieved largely through education."

"Wonderful. Ted, back to you in the studio," the reporter said before moving on.

To commemorate something or someone is to honor or keep the memory alive of that event or person by a ceremony. God commanded the Israelites to remember how God delivered them from death and destruction in Egypt by observing a Passover to God. In today's lesson we will learn that God expects us to commemorate the great things God has done in our lives.

The People, Places, and Times

Abib. Literally, in the Hebrew, it means "new ear of grain." Abib is the first month or "new moon" in the Jewish cultic (religious observance) calendar established at the beginning of the exodus period. God instituted this calendar, beginning with the month of Abib, in anticipation of the covenantal relationship between God and the Israelites. During the period when the Israelites were held captive in Babylon (Babylonian Exile), they adopted Nisan, the month in the Babylonian calendar which corresponds to the Hebrew Abib (Nehemiah 2:1; Esther 3:7).

Leaven. *Chametz* (**khaw-MATES**), in Hebrew, means "to be sour, to ferment, to be leavened." Any bread made from ground barley, wheat, rye, oat, or spelt and mixed with water and allowed to leaven (rise) or ferment is considered *chametz.* The prohibition against leavened bread takes effect the evening of Passover until the evening of the seventh day of Passover. God commanded the Israelites to remove all leaven from their homes (Exodus 12:15). Observant Jews today have a specific regimen for removing leavened products from their homes in preparation for Passover.

Passover or Festival of Unleavened Bread. The Hebrew term *pecach* (**PEH-sakh**) denotes both the Passover offering and the Passover feast and *hag hamatzot* (**hog ha-mats-SOT**) means "feast of unleavened bread." Exodus 12:3 relates that God instituted the Passover in the month of Abib. God commanded Moses and Aaron, while the Israelites were preparing to leave the land of Egypt, to instruct each family to set aside the tenth day of the month of Abib and to take an unblemished, year-old lamb and sacrifice it on the fourteenth day of the month (Exodus 23:15; 34:18). They were to take some of the lamb's blood and put it on the lintels and doorposts of their households. The same night they were to roast the lamb and eat it with unleavened bread and bitter herbs.

God instructed them that they should eat the meal hurriedly, while dressed and ready to leave at a moment's notice. God proclaimed this the "passover of the Lord," for God would pass through the land of Egypt that night and strike down every firstborn in the land, both human beings and animals, and defeat the Egyptian gods so that all would know that the God of the Israelites is Lord (Exodus 12:12:–13). Wherever there was blood on the lintels and doorposts, God would pass over and the inhabitants would be spared God's judgment.

God instructed the Israelites to remember the event and celebrate it as a festival to God forever (v. 14). The two names for the festival likely resulted from the combining of commemorations of two separate events: God's passing over the Israelites' homes with the blood smear, and eating of unleavened bread as the Israelites embarked hurriedly on their exodus from Egyptian bondage (Exodus 12:17; 23:14).

Background

Moses convened the Israelites in Deuteronomy 5:1 to read them the statutes and ordinances that God expected them to observe in the Promised Land, as part of their preparation to enter Canaan. Moses had already reviewed the Ten Commandments with them, along with the blessings they would receive if they kept God's decrees, statues, and ordinances, and the consequences of rebelling against God as the chosen people of God. Now he was reviewing the annual convocations the people were to observe. First among them was the Passover, or Festival of Unleavened Bread. Formerly a local celebration, God transformed the Passover into an annual communal pilgrimage in which the Passover sacrifice was offered at a central sanctuary, and where the unleavened bread was eaten with the sacrifice.

Source:

Bokser, Baruch M. "Unleavened Bread and Passover, Feasts of." In *The Anchor Bible Dictionary*, Vol. 6. New York: Doubleday, 1992.

At-A-Glance

1. The Passover Reviewed (Deuteronomy 16:1–2)
2. The Meaning of Unleavened Bread Reviewed (vv. 3–4)
3. The Prescribed Place of Worship Reviewed (vv. 5–8)

In Depth

1. The Passover Reviewed (Deuteronomy 16:1–2)

Moses reviewed with the Israelites God's directive to observe the first month in the religious calendar by keeping the Passover. Once again, the Israelites were reminded that they were where they were because of God's redemption and freedom. Moses recounted how their flight from Egypt occurred at night. Harriet Tubman, a former slave in America, reportedly guided more than 300 enslaved persons, including her parents and brothers, to freedom through the Underground Railroad. She led them through the night, with only the North Star as her guide, to northern free states and to Canada, where slavery was outlawed. Tubman credited God with her determination and courage. A symbol of freedom, she has been hailed as the "Moses of her people" for going down into "Egyptland" and bringing out as many slaves as she could.

Following the Passover sacrifice to the Lord, the Israelites ate the Passover meal the same night. The Passover feast had, until then, been a domestic ritual. Families initially gathered to eat the meal together in their homes (Exodus 12:3–4). However, God was about to do a new thing. God commanded the Israelites to celebrate the feast communally at the place that God would show them when they entered the Promised Land.

2. The Meaning of Unleavened Bread Reviewed (vv. 3–4)

The sacred meal consisted of roasted meat, vegetables (bitter herbs), and unleavened bread, constituting a complete meal. God instructed the Israelites to eat only bread without leaven so that they would remember that it was in great haste that they departed Egypt. The Egyptians were so outraged at the deaths of their firstborns that they insisted the Israelites leave quickly. There was no time for the bread to rise or ferment. They baked the bread before it leavened, on the outskirts of Egypt. Once again, Moses reiterated that they were to eat the unleavened bread to commemorate the exodus and to recall God's act of redemption and freedom all the days of their lives, forever linking the Passover and the exodus.

The Israelites were prohibited from possessing any leaven within their territory, including their homes, yards, or even in the town. Removing leaven might seem like a trivial thing. We might be tempted to be less than strict about following seemingly insignificant directives. However, it is making light of small things, such as removing leaven, that can lead to our downfall.

3. The Prescribed Place of Worship Reviewed (vv. 5–8)

God repeated the commandment to the Israelites to offer the Passover sacrifice only at the place that God would choose as a place where God's name would dwell. God stated two reasons for this injunction. As Moses read the statutes and the ordinances to the people, one of the statutes was the command to destroy all of the local sanctuaries, where the people of the land they were about to inhabit served their gods. This was to prevent the Israelites from doing as the indigenous people did. God also demanded that they bring their burnt offerings and sacrifices, tithes and donations to a central location (Deuteronomy 12:2–7, 11, 13). The centralization of the sanctuary effectively standardized their worship practices and promoted national unity around the worship of God among these disparate people and tribes, who had become the nation of Israel (Exodus 12:38).

The directive to observe the Passover sacrifice at a central location did not prevent the Israelites from worshiping God in their homes (v. 15). Moreover, God encouraged them to return to their homes to eat the unleavened bread for the remaining six days. However, on the seventh day they were to hold convocation in honor of God. Everyone was commanded to take the day off from work to participate in the festival.

Source:

Bokser, Baruch M. "Unleavened Bread and Passover, Feasts of." In *The Anchor Bible Dictionary*, Vol. 6. New York: Doubleday, 1992.

Search the Scriptures

1. How many days were the Israelites instructed to eat unleavened bread (Deuteronomy 16:3)?

2. Why did God instruct them to eat unleavened bread (v. 3)?

3. The Israelites were permitted to offer the Passover sacrifice to God anywhere they chose (vv. 5–6). True or False?

4. At the end of the seven days, the Israelites were instructed to hold a sacred assembly for the Lord (v. 8). True or False?

Discuss the Meaning

1. Alison shared the background of Juneteenth with the reporter and the viewing audience. Why is it importance to tell our stories, especially on a regular basis such as at annual commemorations?

2. God's power and might could have ensured the Israelites' safe passage out of Egypt during the daytime. What do you think is the significance of leading them out at night?

3. Identify some of the significant events in the life of your church, such as the church's anniversary, pastor's anniversary, baptisms, and weddings. Discuss how you celebrate them.

Lesson in Our Society

1. Following the Passover and the exodus, the Israelites were instructed to eat unleavened bread for seven days. In order to have enough unleavened bread to last the duration, they had to bake a large quantity. This meant that they had to have prepared enough dough in the first place. How prepared are you to respond to God's command at a moment's notice? Do you have your resume updated for when that job opportunity you have been praying for materializes? Do you have all your documents in order to meet with the bank, to qualify for the loan you applied for to start your own business?

2. We need to remember those occasions in our lives, personally and communally, past and present, when God has done great things for us. Have you ever sat down with the elders in your family?

Make It Happen

Chametz is the antithesis of *matzo*, the symbol of the Passover meal eaten to recall the hasty departure of the Israelites from Egypt. *Chametz* is puffed up, bubbling over, malleable. Characteristics of a *chametz* person are egotistical, easily angered, easily manipulated. Characteristics of a *matzo* person are humility, patience, steadfastness. Strive today to remove the *chametz* in your life and to add more *matzo*. Record your progress and celebrate the victories, big and small.

Follow the Spirit

What God wants me to do:

____

____

Remember Your Thoughts

Special insights I have learned:

____

____

More Light on the Text

Deuteronomy 16:1–8

1 Observe the month of Abib, and keep the passover unto the LORD thy God: for in the month of Abib the LORD thy God brought thee forth out of Egypt by night.

The Israelites' deliverance from the bondage of Egypt marked some significant beginnings, such as the beginning of their liberty, the beginning of their history as a nation, and the beginning of their cal-

"Observe the month of Abib, and keep the passover unto the LORD thy God: for in the month of Abib the LORD thy God brought thee forth out of Egypt by night" (Deuteronomy 16:1).

endar. On the Jewish calendar, there were dates considered to be of national importance that were based on divine ordinances, their experience, and the lunar cycle. On these dates they celebrated their appointed festivals. The month of Abib was the first month of the Jewish calendar. It was the month God brought them out of Egypt, and He commanded them to take it as their first month (Exodus 12:2). It was the month they had their first Passover, and God was saying to them here to observe this month. The Hebrew word translated "observe" is *shamar* (**shaw-MAR**), which means "to keep, to mark, and to regard." The Israelites were asked to regard the month of Abib, with particular reference to the Passover, as the "beginning of months," as earlier proclaimed by the Lord in Exodus 12:2.

Abib was a Canaanite name for "green ears of barley"—young, ripe, and soft, eaten either rubbed or roasted. The name was eventually used to name the month in which the barley ripened. The month of Abib was a witness in the Jewish sacred calendar of God's intervention in ending of the Israelites' slavery in Egypt, the gaining of the Israelites' independence, and God's part in the crisis experience of the exodus events. All these were ritually remembered in the Feast of Unleavened Bread and the Passover, in this same month.

After the exile in Babylon, the Jews later adopted Nisan, which was the Babylonian equivalent to Abib. Thus, the month was later referred to as Nisan. The period of the month of Abib corresponds with the period of March–April.

2 Thou shalt therefore sacrifice the Passover unto the LORD thy God, of the flock and the herd, in the place which the LORD shall choose to place his name there.

Apart from the fact that the month of Abib witnessed the birth of the Israelite nation and the gaining of her independence, one notable landmark in this month is mentioned in this verse: the Passover Feast. God commanded the Israelites to annually remember the Passover in the month of Abib. They were to celebrate it as a perpetual ordinance. The first day was the Passover and the following six days were the Feast of Unleavened Bread. From its first declaration and institution in Exodus 12, God had consistently repeated the keeping of the Passover in subsequent books: Leviticus and Numbers, right through to this last book of the Pentateuch (Deuteronomy), where it is repeated for the fourth time after its institution.

From Exodus to Deuteronomy, we see God's recurrent declarations of the Passover ordinance to the Israelites. Exodus 13 tells us that when God was giving them the ordinance concerning the consecration of every firstborn that opens the womb, the Passover was mentioned for the second time. In Exodus 34, which tells of God giving Moses an overview of His laws for the Israelites, He mentioned the Passover for the third time. In Leviticus 23, where the Lord was proclaiming to them sundry ordinances, which included their feasts—the Sabbath, the First Fruits, Feast of Weeks, Feast of Trumpets, Day of Atonement, and Feast of Tabernacles—the Passover was mentioned for the fourth time. Numbers 9 contains the fifth mention of Passover, when God reminded them to celebrate the feast in the first month of the second year, after they came out of Egypt. In Numbers 28, where the Lord was declaring to them the periodic sacrifices they were to perform—daily offerings, Sabbath offerings, and monthly offerings—the Passover was mentioned for the sixth time. Here in Deuteronomy 16, God was repeating the ordinances of the feast of weeks and of tabernacles, along with the judicial laws, and the Passover is mentioned again for the seventh time.

This means it was repeated six times after its institution, which makes it seven times it was mentioned in the Pentateuch.

The word *Passover* is used to refer to the feast, the meal (paschal supper) eaten during the feast, as well as the lamb that was sacrificed. Besides Exodus 12, where it was instituted for the first time, the other references mentioned above refer to the feast, save for Exodus 34:25, in which the sacrifice itself is implied as it is in this verse. The Hebrew word translated "sacrifice" is *zabach* (**zaw-BAKH**); it is a verb denoting "to slaughter an animal, to offer." The Passover as implied here refers to the lamb that is slaughtered as a sacrifice. This is denoted by the noun form, *zabach*, that is, *zebach* (**zeh-BAKH**), which refers to the animal that is slaughtered.

In this verse, God speaks of designating a place where the Passover lamb is to be slaughtered—a place He shall choose to place His name. The repeated mentioning of the Passover feast by the Lord gives it a growing significance in the religious life of the Jews. The fact that it is to be observed in a specially designated place of the Lord's choosing adds more strength and reverence to its significance.

3 Thou shalt eat no leavened bread with it; seven days shalt thou eat unleavened bread therewith, even the bread of affliction; for thou camest forth out of the land of Egypt in haste: that thou mayest remember the day when thou camest forth out of the land of Egypt all the days of thy life.

The original Passover regulation is hereby stated as a reiteration of God's previous words. Repeating the commandments served the aim of reminding the people. They were to keep the ordinances constantly fresh in their memory, pass them on to their descendants, and these ordinances were to provoke in them reverence and respect for the laws of God. The Passover Lamb (the sacrifice) was not to be eaten with leavened bread. The word translated "leavened" in the Hebrew is *chametz* (**khaw-MATES**); it refers to the sour taste or fermented state of dough used to make bread. Leavened bread, therefore, describes bread to which leaven has been added. When added to the dough, the leavening substance causes the bread to rise. The process of leavening the dough took time, and so it took a long time baking the bread. But when the bread or cake was to be baked within a short time, leaven was not added. Thus when the bread was required at short notice, it was baked unleavened. Unleavened bread, on the other hand, was not as palatable as leavened bread; it was tasteless and lacked the usual tasty bread flavor.

The 14th of Abib (Nisan) was the Passover, thereafter, from the 15th to the 21st was the Feast of Unleavened Bread. From the very first day (the 14th) through the seven days, the Israelites were required to eat unleavened bread. Since unleavened bread was the type that was hastily baked, the eating of unleavened bread was to remind the Israelites of the hastiness with which God brought them out of Egypt. The unleavened bread, lacking taste and flavor, also was to remind them of their afflictions in Egypt and so was called "the bread of affliction." This dual reminder was to produce a temperate attitude in them that would make them obey the laws of God. Remembering their afflictions in Egypt and God's intervention—which led to their deliverance—should make them not forget God and a historical slavery that was ended by His power. Remembering that should constantly remind them of their need for God.

4 And there shall be no leavened bread seen with thee in all thy coast seven days; neither shall there any thing of the flesh, which thou sacrificedst the first day at even, remain all night until the morning.

God strictly forbade not only the eating of leavened bread, but the very presence of it around their environment. The Hebrew word translated "coast" is *gebuwl* (**gheb-OOL**), and it constitutes "an enclosed territory or an area within boundary or limit." For the period of seven days, no leavened bread should be seen around their immediate area, territory, or premises, within the enclosure of the boundaries or limits of their homes. By extension, it may further imply that nothing should be baked or prepared with leaven—or no leaven should be found around their premises during this period. That they were forbidden to eat leavened bread was to remind them of their hasty departure from Egypt. But the regulation takes on an intense form with the restriction that forbids the presence of leavened bread even within their territory.

The Israelites were also forbidden from having any piece of flesh from the lamb they sacrificed the evening of the first day—the Passover. No flesh was to remain all night till the following morning.

5 Thou mayest not sacrifice the passover within any of thy gates, which the LORD thy God giveth thee:

This verse states a later modification to the sacrificing of the Passover Lamb, with regards to the place it was to be slain. The Hebrew word translated "gates" is *sha'ar* (**SHAH-ar**), meaning "an opening, a door in a wall, or barrier through which people pass into an enclosed area." The phrase, "within...thy gates" usually denotes within the area enclosed in general sense, referring to any one of the Israelite towns, but here it specifically means "Wherever you live." It speaks of their place of abode. This means the Israelites were not to sacrifice the Passover in their homes.

In the original Passover celebrated in Egypt, the lamb was slain in their homes. In this verse, God was commanding them not to slay the lamb in their homes anymore. This commandment is in view of the fact that the priesthood and the regulation of the service of the tabernacle had been established; the observance of the Passover was to assume a more official, standard, and religious form. The lamb was to be slain in the place that the Lord, Himself, would choose.

We commemorate significant events in our lives, such as those that signify major achievements, bring about certain new favorable beginnings, or terminate some prolonged adverse conditions in our lives. We commemorate some events by observing certain laid-down or generally accepted procedures, rules, or rituals. We observe them either by making elaborate preparations and celebrations or by maintaining a low profile. In the former case, more relatives and friends are usually involved, which is the result of an extensive publicity or invitation. But in the latter case, a few friends come together to be a part of the celebration.

6 But at the place which the LORD thy God shall choose to place his name in, there thou shalt sacrifice the Passover at even, at the going down of the sun, at the season that thou camest forth out of Egypt.

The new place for the sacrifice of the Passover lamb was to be devoid of domesticity—as was the case with the first Passover. The domestic setting wouldn't have made it look official; it would have made it look like a mere family practice, which eventually might be fraught with some defects that would mar its effect and significance. The Passover Feast was of great importance, as it commemorated the Exodus, particularly, signifying God "passing over" the Israelites, when He slew the firstborn of Egypt—the last of the 10 plagues that finally broke Pharaoh's hardened heart, and opened unto them the doors of freedom. With such great significance attached to the Passover, God gave them a new regulation as to its place of sacrifice. The Hebrew translated "the place" as *maqowm* (**maw-KOME**); it means "an abode, a dwelling or habitation." In this context, it refers specifically to "the abode of God (the tabernacle or temple) where God has put His name."

The Hebrew for the phrase, "to place" is *shakan* (**shaw-KAN**), which means "to put, to set, station or to fix." It speaks of God "fixing, putting or setting His name in the tabernacle."

After the establishment of the priesthood and the tabernacle, there came a fully developed ceremonial law that featured this new Passover regulation. At this developed level, the Passover lamb was to be slain in the tabernacle—the place that bears God's name—thus advancing it from a mere family practice to an official sanctuary regulation embedded in the religious life of the people.

This verse not only mentions the place, it also states the time. Here God is reminding the Israelites of the set time of the day to sacrifice the Passover Lamb. The "even" (evening) and "the going down of the sun" (twilight) point to the time preceding nighttime, and the Passover activities were to last through the night. Originally, the very night the Israelites were brought out of the land of Egypt was tagged "the night of the Lord" (Exodus 12:42) that the people of Israel were to observe in their generations to come; a night that was to occupy a place in the annals of their history. The season (the climactic division in which their Exodus took place) was also tagged "his season" (Exodus 13:10). The fact that the night and the season were designated as the Lord's seems to account for the reason why God, Himself, emphasized the time they were to perform the sacrifice. The season of the Exodus corresponded with their agricultural season when figs blossom and barley ripened for the harvest.

There is the question of where to celebrate significant events in our lives. It could be at home, the church, or in a public building. The venue plays a great role in creating an atmosphere of importance, awesomeness, or even reverence to God. The venue further adds some strength to the significance of the event we commemorate.

7 And thou shalt roast and eat it in the place which the LORD thy God shall choose: and thou shalt turn in the morning, and go unto thy tents.

During the first and original Passover celebrated in Egypt, the paschal lamb was eaten at home. Here God gave the Jews a new regulation as to where they were to prepare and eat the meal: the place He would choose. The place the Lord chose to put His name was the tabernacle that was situated in the center of the Israelites' camp. The sanctuary was the dwelling place of God; by it He dwelt among His people (Exodus 25:8). It was also called the "tabernacle of the congregation." As a place that bore the name of God, it was the central point of all their religious activities. They came to it for their religious services. In the later observation of the Passover, as stipulated by these new modifications, the paschal lamb was slain at the sanctuary, the blood sprinkled on the altar, and the meal eaten publicly by all the people at the sanctuary, after being roasted there.

The implication of God's proclamation concerning the place He would choose to put His name spans an extensive era in the history of the Israelites' religious life. In view of their journeying in the desert, where the tabernacle was mobile, camping at various places as they progressed toward the Promised Land, the designation "chosen place" applied primarily to the tabernacle alone. But when they entered the Promised Land, the tabernacle was lodged at different towns and cities, which by secondary implication of God's proclamation could be regarded as places where God had put His name, because of the presence of the tabernacle in those towns. And the people went to those towns to sacrifice and celebrate the Passover.

When the Israelites crossed the Jordan River, their first campsite was Gilgal (Joshua 4:19). This was where they observed their first Passover in the land of Canaan (Joshua 5:10). From there the tabernacle was moved to Shiloh. It was in Shiloh all through the period of the judges, which included the days of Eli and Samuel. Shiloh was evidently a place where God's name was stationed by the presence of the tabernacle there. The other tribes of Israel came to Shiloh to celebrate the Passover feast.

It was during the feast at Shiloh—the yearly sacrifice, as it was called in 1 Samuel 1:3, 21, that Hannah prayed for a child and eventually gave birth to Samuel. At Shiloh, the Philistines, in a war with the Israelites, captured the Ark of the Covenant. The ark was later restored to Israel and kept in the house of Abinadab at Kirjath-Jearim, a town in Judah. The tabernacle was later moved to Nob (1 Samuel 21:1, 19). From Nob, it moved to Gibeon (1 Chronicles 16:39). While at Gibeon, David made an imitation of it in Jerusalem, but his imitation lacked the original ark. The ark was later moved to Jerusalem. When Solomon finally built the temple in Jerusalem, the ark and the tabernacle were eventually kept in the temple.

The temple in Jerusalem became the final station and resting place of the ark and the tabernacle; and consequently a final and major "chosen place" for the name of the Lord. To Jerusalem, they all came to celebrate the Passover feast. The paschal lamb was slain, roasted, and eaten in Jerusalem, after which they all departed to their homes the following morning.

The Hebrew word translated "roast" is *bashal* (**baw-SHAL**), which means "to be made done in cooking by fire." When meat was roasted, the whole animal was placed directly on coals of fire. The roasting of the lamb, in the first and original Passover celebrated in Egypt, seemed to foreshadow the sanctuary regulation of burnt offerings, which were offered by fire. The various offerings made in the sanctuary, then, were roasted—in a sense—as they were made to have direct contact with the fire on the altar.

8 Six days thou shalt eat unleavened bread: and on the seventh day shall be a solemn assembly to the LORD thy God: thou shalt do no work therein.

To the Israelites, the Passover day was Independence Day—this is what it actually depicted to them, yearly. This same day was a Sabbath. Seven days followed the Passover Day, which were also elevated to significant status as days they ate unleavened bread, thus designated altogether as the Feast of Unleavened Bread. A meal of unleavened bread was a peculiar, unpalatable meal with great significance, eaten in reverence and honor to God, really touching their taste buds in an unusual way. It highlights the significance of the feast rather than the relish of the meal, and serves as a reminder of a period of transition from slavery to freedom.

The Feast of Unleavened Bread lasted a period of seven days, but for the sake of distinction and emphasis, a division is made in this verse. The first six days are distinguished from the last and seventh day. There is to be a solemn assembly unto the Lord on the seventh day. The Hebrew word translated "solemn assembly" is *'atsarah* (**ats-aw-RAW**); it denotes "a meeting, an assembly on a holiday." A synonymous phrase is "holy convocation," a summoned assembly held under particularly holy circumstances for the observance of sacred rites and occasions. The seventh day of the Feast of Unleavened Bread was a Sabbath. This was when they were to have the solemn assembly to observe the sacred rites of the feast in honor of the Lord. Being a Sabbath and a holy day, they were not required to do any servile work, except the necessary preparations of food.

Individuals, groups, or communities usually have special days on their calendars that they remember regularly, during which they celebrate great occasions with thanksgiving. There are events that change the course of people's lives, such as deliverance from any form of satanic activity, triumph in a legal tussle against an opponent, narrow escape from the claws of death in an accident, healing from a protracted illness, accomplishment of a project, a new phase of development at the workplace, or the dawn of a new era in an industry. Some calamitous events that involved death and destruction are sometimes remembered, but those that are positive, that bring some addition, enhancement, or promotion and are of great significance to us should be celebrated. Within our faith community, we should celebrate significant events that proclaim and promote the gospel of our Lord Jesus Christ and proclaim the wondrous works of God in our lives.

Daily Bible Readings

M: Remember and Rejoice
Ecclesiastes 11:7–12:1
T: Remember the Lord's Deeds
Psalm 77:3–15
W: Remember and Give Thanks
Psalm 105:1–11
T: Keeping the Covenant
2 Kings 23:1–3, 21–23
F: Preparing for the Passover
Luke 22:7–13
S: Christ, Our Paschal Lamb
1 Corinthians 5:1–8
S: The Passover Observance
Deuteronomy 16:1–8

NOTES

TEACHING TIPS

July 19
Bible Study Guide 7

1. Words You Should Know

A. Tabernacle (Leviticus 8:10) *mishkan* (Heb.)—Dwelling place; in the Hebrew refers to a portable worship place that God chose to dwell in.

B. Anointed (vv. 10–12) *mashach* (Heb.)—Smear; consecrate to religious service.

2. Teacher Preparation

Unifying Principle—Commissioning for Service. Some people in a community are set aside for special service to that community. How do we discern, acknowledge, and affirm those people chosen for special service? God commanded that Aaron and his sons be recognized by consecrating them with water and holy garments.

A. Study the information in The People, Places, and Times; Background; and In Depth sections.

C. Study the More Light on the Text section for further insight on the lesson.

D. Prior to the beginning of class, write the At-A-Glance outline on the board or on PowerPoint.

3. Starting the Lesson

A. Ask the students if any of them has ever witnessed a service of consecration or ordination. Discuss some of the details of the service, such as the person or persons involved in the ritual, the attire, the words of dedication, prayers, and so on.

B. Ask them if they understood the significance of all the elements involved. It might be helpful to research some of the differences of rituals of various communities, such as Episcopal, Baptist, and Pentecostal, starting with interviewing leaders from these communities if time permits.

C. Ask someone to read the In Focus story. Ask your students how aspects of Brenda's ordination were similar to or different from what they have witnessed.

4. Getting into the Lesson

A. Read the Background section and the Keep in Mind verse.

B. Ask a volunteer to read the AIM for Change goals. Discuss.

C. Allow some time for the students to read the Focal Verses silently and to answer the Search the Scriptures questions. Discuss.

5. Relating the Lesson to Life

A. Select two or three of the Discuss the Meaning questions to answer.

B. Have the students read the Lesson in Our Society section.

C. Lead them in discussing the various ministries that God has called individuals to serve.

6. Arousing Action

A. Read the Make it Happen section.

B. Ask the students to share how they can help those around them to discern God calling of them to ministry, acknowledge their call, and affirmation, once they have accepted the call to ministry.

C. Ask them to share ways that they can help each other discern the will of God in their lives. Write down the answers on the board.

Worship Guide

For the Superintendent or Teacher
Theme: God Calls People to Special Service
Theme Song: "Give Me a Clean Heart"
Devotional Reading: Romans 11:33–12:2
Prayer

GOD CALLS PEOPLE TO SPECIAL SERVICE

Bible Background • LEVITICUS 8:1–13
Printed Text • LEVITICUS 8:1–13 Devotional Reading • ROMANS 11:33–12:2

AIM for Change

By the end of the lesson, we will:
EXPLORE the details of the dedication of Aaron's family;
GRASP the principles of ordination and consecration for service; and
ACCEPT roles of special service and recognize other persons called for service.

Keep in Mind

"And he poured of the anointing oil upon Aaron's head, and anointed him, to sanctify him" (Leviticus 8:12).

Focal Verses

KJV **Leviticus 8:1** And the LORD spake unto Moses, saying,

2 Take Aaron and his sons with him, and the garments, and the anointing oil, and a bullock for the sin offering, and two rams, and a basket of unleavened bread;

3 And gather thou all the congregation together unto the door of the tabernacle of the congregation.

4 And Moses did as the LORD commanded him; and the assembly was gathered together unto the door of the tabernacle of the congregation.

5 And Moses said unto the congregation, This is the thing which the LORD commanded to be done.

6 And Moses brought Aaron and his sons, and washed them with water.

7 And he put upon him the coat, and girded him with the girdle, and clothed him with the robe, and put the ephod upon him, and he girded him with the curious girdle of the ephod, and bound it unto him therewith.

8 And he put the breastplate upon him: also he put in the breastplate the Urim and the Thummim.

9 And he put the mitre upon his head; also upon the mitre, even upon his forefront, did he put the golden plate, the holy crown; as the LORD commanded Moses.

10 And Moses took the anointing oil, and anointed the tabernacle and all that was therein, and sanctified them.

11 And he sprinkled thereof upon the altar seven times, and anointed the altar and all his vessels, both the laver and his foot, to sanctify them.

NLT **Leviticus 8:1** Then the LORD said to Moses,

2 "Bring Aaron and his sons, along with their sacred garments, the anointing oil, the bull for the sin offering, the two rams, and the basket of bread made without yeast,

3 and call the entire community of Israel together at the entrance of the Tabernacle."

4 So Moses followed the LORD's instructions, and the whole community assembled at the Tabernacle entrance.

5 Moses announced to them, "This is what the LORD has commanded us to do!"

6 Then he presented Aaron and his sons and washed them with water.

7 He put the official tunic on Aaron and tied the sash around his waist. He dressed him in the robe, placed the ephod on him, and attached the ephod securely with its decorative sash.

8 Then Moses placed the chestpiece on Aaron and put the Urim and the Thummim inside it.

9 He placed the turban on Aaron's head and attached the gold medallion—the badge of holiness—to the front of the turban, just as the LORD had commanded him.

10 Then Moses took the anointing oil and anointed the Tabernacle and everything in it, making them holy.

11 He sprinkled the oil on the altar seven times, anointing it and all its utensils, as well as the washbasin and its stand, making them holy.

12 Then he poured some of the anointing oil on

12 And he poured of the anointing oil upon Aaron's head, and anointed him, to sanctify him.

13 And Moses brought Aaron's sons, and put coats upon them, and girded them with girdles, and put bonnets upon them; as the LORD commanded Moses.

Aaron's head, anointing him and making him holy for his work.

13 Next Moses presented Aaron's sons. He clothed them in their tunics, tied their sashes around them, and put their special head coverings on them, just as the LORD had commanded him.

In Focus

Brenda could not believe that this day had finally come. She was being installed into the evangelistic ministry at her church. Earlier while she and her family waited in the narthex for the service to begin, she could barely hear the music playing in the sanctuary. She felt lightheaded. She took a couple of deep breaths and followed the ministers into the sanctuary.

Brenda reflected on her road to installation. The pastor of the church where Brenda attended had observed her kindness in caring for the youngest to the oldest members of the congregation. She served faithfully wherever she was sent to minister, including teaching Bible classes and leading devotions during Wednesday prayer meetings. One day, the pastor told Brenda that he recognized God calling her to evangelistic ministry and that he wanted to send her to seminary to receive training in the various skills she would need to better meet the needs of God's people. Now she was standing before her congregation as the pastor opened the service with prayer.

God has given each of us special gifts and talents to serve God and God's people. However, God sets apart certain persons for special service. Today's lesson focuses on the roles of special service and the rites as installation, or ordination, and consecration.

The People, Places, and Times

Aaron. The son of Amram and Jochebed, and brother of Moses and Miriam, Aaron was Israel's first high priest. Aaron's family was descended from the Levites. The Levites were Israel's first priests. Later they were subordinated to Aaron and his descendants. God commanded Moses to set apart Aaron and his sons from among the Israelites to serve God as priests by a perpetual ordinance. Moses ordained Aaron and his sons as God had instructed to make sacrifices, offerings, and atonement at the altar in the sanctuary. Prior to being consecrated as high priest, Aaron served as Moses' spokesman before Pharaoh in Egypt, when Moses protested that he was not able to speak directly to Pharaoh. One of Aaron's shortcomings was yielding to pressure from the Israelites to make a golden calf for worship at Mount Sinai (or Mount Horeb).

Tabernacle of the Congregation. Also referred to as the "tent of meeting" (*ohel mo'ed*) in Hebrew, the tabernacle of the congregation is the movable sanctuary where God's presence was made manifest. It was at the tabernacle that God communicated with the Israelites through Moses. Its construction was financed by the Israelites—an offering to God, as commanded by God (Exodus 25:1–8). God also instructed Moses on how the Israelites should construct the tabernacle, the sanctuary, its contents, and the vestments for the priests.

Background

The covenantal relationship between God and the Israelites had been ratified. However, the establishment of such a relationship between the people and the deity required a method for the Israelites to interact with God. This concern was resolved by the erection of a tabernacle that would allow communication between the two parties, through Moses. God gave Moses orders on how the tabernacle should be constructed and its contents. Then the construction of the tabernacle was complete, and all its contents were in place. The people had been instructed in the sacrificial laws and it was time to conduct the inaugural service. The only thing left to do was to ordain the priests and consecrate the sanctuary for use.

Source:

Hayes, John H. "Leviticus 8:1–10:20." In *The Harper's Bible Commentary*. San Francisco: Harper & Row, 1988.

At-A-Glance

1. The Presentation of Aaron and His Sons (Leviticus 8:1–5)
2. The Investiture of Aaron (vv. 6–9)
3. The Anointment of the Tabernacle and Aaron (vv. 10–12)
4. The Investiture of Aaron's Sons (v. 13)

In Depth

1. The Presentation of Aaron and His Sons (Leviticus 8:1–5)

Upon the completion of the tabernacle, Moses was assigned the task of conducting the inaugural service. Vestments, anointing oil, offerings, and unleavened bread in hand, Moses took Aaron and his four sons, Nadab, Abihu, Eleazar, and Ithamar to join the people at the entrance of the tabernacle for their ordination. Moses also assembled the Israelites, as instructed by God, at the entrance for the service. The tabernacle entrance was the place where the sanctuary rituals would occur from this point on.

The people were witnessing the inauguration of a new phase in their relationship with God. The sacrificial system at the tabernacle, as commanded by God, was a symbolic means of keeping the covenantal relationship between God and the Israelites intact. God had selected Aaron and his sons from among all the people to act as intermediaries on behalf of the people at the altar, and they were being presented before the people whom they would serve. Presentation of the ordained is a common practice during the rite of ordination. Moses reminded the Israelites that he was doing as God had ordered him.

2. The Investiture of Aaron (vv. 6–9)

Following their presentation to the people, Moses took Aaron and his sons and brought them forward to wash them with water. Washing them was an act of purification, but it was also intended to make clear that Aaron and his sons were the persons God had chosen to serve God as priests in perpetuity. Their initiation into the priesthood would change their status from lay (non-professional) to priestly (professional), from that of ordinary human beings to sanctified servants.

Once Moses completed the washing, he began adorning Aaron with the vestments of his new office. Moses placed the embroidered linen coat or tunic on Aaron, which he fastened with an embroidered sash (Exodus 28:39). A blue robe, with an opening for the head, was placed over the coat, but beneath the ephod made of gold, blue, purple and crimson yarns (vv. 6, 31). The hem of the robe was decorated with pomegranates of the same colors as the ephod yarn (v. 33). Moses then put the breastplate on Aaron, which was a pouch-like vest fastened to the ephod with chains. He placed the Urim and the Thummin over his heart. These were perhaps light and dark stones that Aaron wore in God's presence. They were used to give Aaron guidance from God concerning the people (v. 30). The mitre, a headdress or turban that Moses placed on Aaron's head, completed the investiture. The mitre was set with a golden ornament, the "holy crown," which designated Aaron as "holy to the Lord" (v. 36). Upon completion, Moses again announced that this was done according to God's commandment.

3. The Anointment of the Tabernacle and Aaron (vv. 10–12)

The act of anointing comes from the Hebrew word *mashach*, which means to smear or anoint with oil. It is usually performed to dedicate persons, such as a priest or king, or things, such as the temple vessels, for sanctuary use. Moses took the anointing oil that was in his possession and anointed the tabernacle and all its contents, dedicating them as holy or set apart for the service of God. Moses sprinkled the altar, its furnishings, and its base. He sprinkled the altar seven times, seven representing the number of completion. Next, Moses poured some of the oil over Aaron's head, anointing him as a sign of his official dedication to the office of high priest. Both the tabernacle and Aaron had now been transferred from the realm of the ordinary to the holy.

4. The Investiture of Aaron's Sons (v. 13)

Now it was Aaron's sons' turn to be outfitted in their robes of office. Moses put tunics upon them and fastened them with sashes. Then he tied headdresses on their heads, just as God had commanded. Aaron's vestments were distinguished from that of his sons because as high priest, Aaron's responsibilities were more specialized. Only the high priest, the one who had been anointed and consecrated, could enter the Holy of Holies in the tabernacle on the Day of Atonement. He was responsible for the other priests and was held to a higher standard (Leviticus 4:3; 21:10).

The period of ordination was completed at the end of seven days, at which time Aaron and his sons could begin their duties (Leviticus 8:33). As the priests, Aaron and his sons were responsible not only for the sacrifices and offerings but also for imparting to the people the distinctions between sacred and profane, between clean and unclean, to prevent them from sinning and defiling God's sanctuary.

Search the Scriptures

1. Where did the Lord command Moses to assemble the congregation (Leviticus 8:3)?

2. Moses brought Aaron and his sons to the tabernacle entrance and washed them with water. True or False (v. 6)?

3. What did Moses place upon Aaron (vv. 7–8)?

4. With what did Moses anoint the tabernacle and its contents (v. 10)?

5. Moses anointed the heads of Aaron's sons. True or False (v. 13)?

Discuss the Meaning

1. Why do you think God requires certain persons to be set aside to perform specific services on behalf of a community?

2. Why is it important that the congregation from which an individual has been called or will serve be present at the ordination of the individual?

3. What were some of Brenda's characteristics that set her apart, in her pastor's sight, from other members of the congregation?

4. What do you think is the significance of the act of investiture, of ceremonially clothing the person consecrated in special attire such as a robe?

Lesson in Our Society

1. God set aside Aaron and his sons to be priests for the Israelites for perpetuity. Hereditary priesthoods are a rarity these days, but God still calls individuals from among a community for special service to the community. We often think of an individual being set apart from among a church community for service to a particular congregation, usually as pastor, elder, or rector. However, God also sets apart individuals for special service in communities such as college campuses, hospitals, hospices, prisons, and the military as chaplains, in private practices as pastoral counselors, and as administrators. What are some other special services that you can identify that God has set aside individuals for in your community?

2. Do you know anyone who is ordained to the ministry? How was their call to ordained ministry discerned, acknowledged, and affirmed?

3. What is your church's position on the ordination of women? Why?

Make It Happen

Think of the people in your life that you believe God has called to ministry, whether they have been ordained or not. What are some of the attributes they display? What can you do to encourage, build up, and affirm their ministry? Not everyone has been set apart for special services but we all are to present ourselves as a living sacrifice to the service of God. Ask God's guidance for discerning the will of God in your life.

Follow the Spirit

What God wants me to do:

____

____

Remember Your Thoughts

Special insights I have learned:

____

____

More Light on the Text

Leviticus 8:1–13

1 And the LORD spake unto Moses, saying, 2 Take Aaron and his sons with him, and the garments, and the anointing oil, and a bullock for the sin offering, and two rams, and a basket of unleavened bread;

During the life and times of Levi, the third son of Jacob by his wife Leah, there was no indication of a priestly appointment on him, nor was there a consecrated character attributed to his descendants (the Levites) before the Exodus. Aaron emerged as the most prominent personality that was instrumental in the establishment of the priestly calling in the Levite tribe. The mantle of a great spiritual leader, placed by God upon Moses, proved to be of a diverse kind, in that it incorporated a broad range of ingredients, offices, and functions. In this spiritual leadership were: prophet, priest, legislator, nationalist, military commander, and guide. The priestly calling on Aaron seemed to be something that was divinely "shed" on him through Moses. From the onset, Moses felt the weight of the onerous task God was giving him; and because it was a task that involved a great deal of communication—proclaiming the words of God—his inability to speak eloquently caused him to initially resist the divine job. He disqualified himself on the basis of being slow of speech. This created an opportunity for Aaron, his elder brother, who was a good speaker and eloquent in speech. Moses' initial resistance to the divine job angered God, who made Aaron to fill in for Moses' shortcoming. Aaron became a spokesman to Moses.

We can identify three possible natural reasons that appeared to have encouraged and facilitated the emergence of the Aaronic priestly calling, which by extension established the Levitical priesthood order: (1) His relationship with Moses as his sibling (both of them were from the tribe of Levi); (2) His eloquence and oratory ability; and (3) His job as a spokesman and an assistant to Moses.

Three months after the Israelites left Egypt, God began to introduce His statutes and laws to them, which He prefaced with the Decalogue. He began to set for them moral structures to order their general conduct. As a developing nomadic nation, God established in her a great institution (the tabernacle, its regulation, and the priesthood) that became her divine heritage, and bestowed her with greatness among other nations. Naturally, Aaron fitted into this divine arrangement. As a spokesman and assistant to Moses, God used him to establish the priesthood. In these verses, Aaron is about to be ordained by Moses in compliance with God's commands. Before this time, the tabernacle in which they would minister had been constructed, the tabernacle furniture had been made, the sanctuary regulations have been spelled out, the priestly garments have been made for Aaron and his sons, and they have been consecrated as priests. Finally, they are to be ordained.

In verse 2, we read of God's requirements needed for the ordination: the garments with which Aaron and his sons would be dressed, the anointing oil that would be poured on them to set them apart for the service of the Lord, a bullock for the sin offering, and two rams and a basket of unleavened bread to be used for the ordination rites. The Hebrew word translated "sin offering" is *chatta'th* (**khat-TAWTH**), meaning "sin-purification." It conveys the idea of undergoing purification from one's habitual sinfulness—one's sinful state—but not referring to a particular sin that was committed. As imperfect people who lived natural lives of sin and were being made to move up to the higher priestly calling, it was appropriate for them to undergo such cleansing before the Lord to meet His requirements.

3 And gather thou all the congregation together unto the door of the tabernacle of the congregation.
4 And Moses did as the LORD commanded him; and the assembly was gathered together unto the door of the tabernacle of the congregation.

God demanded that a crowd of people witness Aaron's ordination, and so He asked Moses to gather the entire congregation. The Hebrew word translated "congregation" is *'edah* (**ay-DAW**); it means "a group or company of people assembled together." It refers to the multitude of people who make up the Israelite community. God requested that Moses gather this multitude of people to come before the "tabernacle of congregation." This is translated *mo'ed* (**mo-ADE**), meaning "appointed place of meeting." The Israelites' witnessing the ordination of Aaron and his sons achieved the following aims: (1) a national acknowledgment of the establishment of the priesthood—the essential officiating factor of the tabernacle and (2) the commitment of the priestly service to Aaron and his descendants in generations to come, which brings about the establishment of the priestly calling in the Levite tribe (Exodus 40:15).

At the door of the tabernacle of the congregation, as God instructed him, Moses gathered the assembly together. The door of the tabernacle was the entrance. This was where God's pillar of cloud descended; it stood at the door while He talked to Moses (Exodus 33:9).

5 And Moses said unto the congregation, This is the thing which the LORD commanded to be done.
6 And Moses brought Aaron and his sons, and washed them with water.

Moses made an introductory speech to the people as the ordination service was about to commence, by declaring to them what God commanded to be done. The priesthood was one of the major religious structures of the Jewish society. It constituted one of the dominant characteristics of the Old Testament religion and life. The sanctuary provided a human experience. This experience was derived from the effect of an earthly and physical thing bearing the mighty, awesome presence of God. This effect created a measure of revelation fitted for human understanding, which offered a level of interaction between God and man. The priesthood conveyed this level to the people. Thus, the priests were God's representatives. Due to the errant nature of humans, the priests were there to consistently bring the people into harmony with God by performing certain divinely-ordained sacred rites and making them conform to God's requirements. By doing so, it gave them a supremely supernatural view to life. It channeled their religious tendencies—typical to every human being—in the right direction, creating in them an awareness of a distinction between the holy and the common (Ezekiel 44:23).

Here Moses performed the first stage of the ordination process: washing. The Hebrew word translated "washed" is *rachats* (**raw-KHATS**), meaning "to bathe." This is a physical, ritual cleansing of Aaron and his sons to signify spiritual cleansing and separation unto service.

7 And he put upon him the coat, and girded him with the girdle, and clothed him with the robe, and put the ephod upon him, and he girded him with the curious girdle of the ephod, and bound it unto him therewith.

Moses began dressing Aaron with the priestly vestments. This garment with which Moses dressed Aaron for the priestly service was divided into nine parts. This verse lists five of the nine parts of the garment: coat, girdle, robe, ephod, and curious girdle. The "coat" (Heb. *kethoneth,* **keth-O-neth**), meaning "to cover," was first used to dress Aaron. It was an immediate shirt that covered his body directly. The "girdle" (Heb. *'abnet,* **ab-NATE**), meaning "a belt," was used to hold the shirt firmly to his body. These were a sort of inner garment, like our singlets or inner vests of today. Then the "robe" (Heb. *me'iyl,* **meh-EEL**), meaning "a covering, an upper and outer garment" was put on him as a main outer garment. The "ephod" (Heb. *'ephowd,* **ay-FODE**) refers to a sleeveless shoulder vestment that is a two part apron (front and back) was placed on top of the robe. Then the "curious girdle," which meant "skillfully woven band" was used to hold the aprons in place around the middle. Aaron's garments were different from those of other priests because he was a high priest. The garments of other priests were simpler in composition and lacked some of these parts.

8 And he put the breastplate upon him: also he put in the breastplate the Urim and the Thummim.

This verse mentions two other parts of Aaron's garments: the breastplate, and the Urim and Thummim. The word translated "breastplate" is *choshen* (**KHO-shen**), and it denotes "to contain" something like a pocket or a receptacle that contains gems. The breastplate was called a breastplate of judgment. With it Aaron was required to bear the names of the children of Israel and their judgments upon his heart before the Lord continually (Exodus 28:29, 30). The name of the 12 tribes of Israel on the breastplate was a constant memorial that reminded the Lord of His covenant with them. The word "Urim," from the Hebrew word *Uwriym* (**oo-REEM**), means "lights," while "Thummim," from the Hebrew word *Tummiym* (**toom-MEEM**), means "perfections." These were symbolic objects in the breastplate with which Aaron was dressed. It was only on the breastplate of the high priest, who was in the position to deliver God's judgment on the people, teach them the ways of the Lord, receive direct answers from God, or make any sort of proclamation or prophecy upon the people.

As symbols of light and perfection, they were supposed to influence the priest by way of reminding him or evoking divine reverence in him, when delivering God's judgment or making any proclamation on the people of God. Light and perfection are attributes of God. The presence of the Urim and Thummim in the breastplate of the high priest meant that he was supposed to speak the truth devoid of falsehood, partiality, or misconceptions, as is typical of the natural failings of humans. The Urim (light) symbolized truth, "for the fruit of the light consists in all goodness, righteousness and truth" (Ephesians 5:9, NIV). The Thummim (perfections) speaks of precision, exactness, and completeness in the priestly ministration or prescription to the people.

9 And he put the mitre upon his head; also upon the mitre, even upon his forefront, did he put the golden plate, the holy crown; as the LORD commanded Moses.

The dressing is concluded here with the last two parts of Aaron's garment: the mitre and the holy crown. The Hebrew word translated "mitre" is *mitsnepheth* (**mits-NEH-feth**); it refers to a turban. This was a large headgear worn by the priest. On the front of it was a golden plate on which was engraved, "Holiness to the Lord." This Scripture refers to this golden plate as the holy crown. This further attributes some royal status to Aaron's priestly calling.

The priests' clothes consecrated them; it invested them with a ceremonial purity that saved them from the death that other persons would incur from contact with the holy things of the tabernacle, and from engaging in its holy ministries. They were not required to come out to the people in their garments. They were supposed to leave their garments in the sacred rooms and put on other clothes when they left, so that they would not consecrate the people by means of their garments (Ezekiel 44:19)

The ordination service affirmed the calling of Aaron into the priesthood. God commanded Moses to make Aaron be recognized, by consecrating him with holy garments. With this, God used special apparel to distinguish between the priests and the people.

10 And Moses took the anointing oil, and anointed the tabernacle and all that was therein, and sanctified them. 11 And he sprinkled thereof upon the altar seven times, and anointed the altar and all his vessels, both the laver and his foot, to sanctify them.

After the dressing of Aaron, which set him up in preparation for his work and which marked the first phase in the ordination process, Moses gave attention to the station for priestly ministration—the tabernacle. The Hebrew word for "anointing" is *mishchah* (**meesh-KHAW**); it refers to the very act of applying the oil (unction). It is a present participle used as a verbal adjective to qualify oil, thereby designating a substance. Anointing oil, therefore, refers to the consecratory substance, the ointment or oil used for the act. It is a special oil made from ingredients prescribed by the Lord Himself (Exodus 30:23–26). The word translated "anointed" is *mashach* (**maw-SHAKH**); it means "to rub with the anointing oil, to consecrate." Moses took the anointing oil and anointed the tabernacle and all that was in it, to sanctify them as part of the ordination process.

The people had made the tabernacle and its furniture. After its construction, it obviously must have borne spiritual uncleanness from the hands of the people who made it. And so to meet God's requirements, it had to be sanctified with the anointing oil. The word translated "sanctified" is *qadash* (**kaw-DASH**), which means "to make clean, to purify." Since it was to be used for sacred purposes in service to God by the priests, the tabernacle had to be sanctified.

Because the number seven denotes perfection, the oil was sprinkled upon the altar seven times, probably to stipulate a perfect offering from the altar unto the Lord. Moses also anointed the altar, the vessels, and the laver. *Kiyowr* (**kee-YORE**) is translated "laver," which means a "washbowl." The laver was a large bronze basin that stood on a "foot"; that is, a stand. It held water for the priest's ablution.

The tabernacle, which was later developed fully into the temple, was the dwelling place of God. It is analogous to a New Testament worshiper who bears the presence of God. First Corinthians 3:16 queries us, "Know ye not that ye are the temple of God, and that the Spirit of God dwelleth in you?" The altar of the tabernacle can be likened to the heart. The Hebrew word for "altar" is *mizbeach* (**miz-BAY-akh**), meaning "a place of sacrifice." Animals were sacrificed from the altar as offerings unto the Lord. As the smoke of the burnt offerings ascended to God, so do our thoughts (motives, intent, purposes) and deeds ascend to God from our hearts. David said in Psalm 19:14, "Let the...meditation of my heart be acceptable in thy sight, O Lord." As Moses sprinkled the anointing oil on the altar seven times, to signify perfection on it, so the heart of a worshiper of God should aim at being perfect before Him.

12 And he poured of the anointing oil upon Aaron's head, and anointed him, to sanctify him.

Moses anointed Aaron. We can see an order in this whole ordination process. It began with the dressing of Aaron in the high priest's garments, then the anointing of the tabernacle, and finally the anointing of Aaron. Before now, the tabernacle had been constructed, made ready for use. Correspondingly, Aaron was dressed up, ready for service. He was only anointed after the tabernacle had been anointed. The tabernacle was God's abode, the place He was to put His name and that was to bear His presence. The presence of God was in the cloud, at the entrance to the tabernacle of congregation. It was also between the two cherubim, at the top of the Ark of the Covenant in the Holy of Holies. The tabernacle was made holy to enable the presence of God to descend on it. Aaron was made holy to enable him to enter into the holy chambers of the tabernacle, to perform sacred rites in the presence of a holy God. Consequently, after being sanctified, both the tabernacle and Aaron became clean. They were devoid of human uncleanness, fit for the Master's use.

The ordination and consecration of Aaron and his sons, for service unto God, reveal certain basic principles. It was mandatory that Aaron and his sons underwent a process of spiritual cleansing, signified by the washing of their bodies with water. The anointing oil, which was poured on them, sanctified them to set them apart for the service. The sanctification and ritual cleansing was to bring a transformation to their personalities. It was mandatory to affirm and authenticate Aaron's ordination publicly, before a crowd of witnesses in order for him to be recognized in the priestly office by all.

13 And Moses brought Aaron's sons, and put coats upon them, and girded them with girdles, and put bonnets upon them; as the LORD commanded Moses.

As descendants of Aaron, his sons also partook in the priestly service of their father. Here, Moses arrayed them in priestly garments, along with their father. Though their garments were not as elaborate as Aaron's, they consisted of coats, girdles, and bonnets. The Hebrew word translated "bonnets" is *migba'ah* (**mig-baw-AW**), which denotes "a cap." It was a linen cap differing from their father's headgear; it was a skullcap like an inverted bowl.

As Aaron was used to establish the Hebrew priesthood, his four sons (Nadab, Abihu, Eleazar, and Ithamar), were to follow the priestly calling that had been bestowed on the family. His first two sons, Nadab and Abihu, died because of their act of irreverence. They offered unauthorized fire before the Lord, contrary to His command, and so fire came out from the presence of the Lord and consumed them to death (Leviticus 10:1–2). Upon the death of Aaron, the succession went to Eleazar.

Service to God is the highest calling. It encompasses service to mankind beyond the limits of natural affinity. Aaron and his family were dedicated for special service to God and community; they were to serve the other tribes of Israel. The privileged status of Aaron was upon his sons, as God commanded that his sons be recognized by being consecrated with holy garments. Service to God and the community usually requires that the one called to service should offer his possessions in the process of serving: time, energy, resources, talent, and even relations (like Aaron and his sons). Joshua said, "But as for me and my house, we will serve the Lord" (Joshua 24:15).

It is a laudable thing to accept roles of special service. It creates opportunity for the optimum use of one's potential and also for learning. It requires serving different kinds of people with different needs and backgrounds. By this, one makes oneself a channel of blessing to others. Serving others is functioning in a leadership position where one is privileged to offer direction, purpose, guidance, and a vision to other people. The Israelites looked unto Moses and Aaron for these things.

In order to effect a healthy interactive system, it is appropriate to recognize others that are called to special service, to give them due honor and respect, and to work with them as the need arises to render service to the community.

Daily Bible Readings

M: We Are God's
Psalm 100
T: Sanctify the Congregation
Joel 2:12–16
W: The Ministry of Generosity
2 Corinthians 9:6–12
T: Doing the Father's Will
Matthew 21:28–32
F: Present Your Bodies
Romans 11:33–12:2
S: The Example Christ Left
Romans 15:1–6
S: Consecrated for Service
Leviticus 8:1–13

NOTES

TEACHING TIPS

July 26

Bible Study Guide 8

1. Words You Should Know

A. Trumpet (Leviticus 25:9) *showphar* (Heb.)—A curved horn, as of a cow or ram, mostly used in war; also used on religious occasions.

B. Jubile or Jubilee (vv. 10–13, 15) *yowbel* (Heb.)—Origin uncertain; possibly ram, ram's horn; designation of the fiftieth year, marked by blowing of ram's horns.

C. Liberty (v. 10) *derowr* (Heb.)—A flowing; free run, release from servitude or bondage.

D. Redemption (v. 24) *geullah* (Heb.)—Right (duty) of redemption; the purchase back of something that had been lost, by the payment of a ransom.

2. Teacher Preparation

Unifying Principle—Spreading the Wealth. The accumulation of property in the hands of a very few people means that some are wealthy while others have no chance to escape poverty. How can communities care for the poor in just ways? God gave laws for the just redistribution of wealth to provide for the poor, and thereby to honor God who provides all.

A. Read Leviticus 25 and the Devotional Reading in their entirety.

B. To prepare for the lesson, study the Background materials, In Depth, and More Light on the Text sections on the *Precepts For Living*® CD-ROM.

C. Before class begins, write the words "release," "return," "replenish," and "redemption" on the board or use PowerPoint.

3. Starting the Lesson

A. Ask the class to read the In Focus story. Ask them to discuss how forgiving developing countries of their unpayable debts could help the countries to improve their circumstances. Note: Unpayable debt is not the same as "odious" debt—debt incurred by the misuse of funds for personal gain by dictators. Following the discussion, read the AIM for Change.

B. To provide the students with additional information, read the Background section.

C. Ask for volunteers to read the Focal Verses, as outlined in the At-A-Glance section. Discuss.

4. Getting into the Lesson

A. Read the section related to "release" and ask the students to discuss the Discuss the Meaning question related to "release."

B. Read the section related to "return" and ask the students to discuss the second Discuss the Meaning question.

C. Read the section related to "replenishment" and ask the students to discuss the last Discuss the Meaning question.

D. Read the section related to "redemption" and discuss the meaning of "redemption," as used in Leviticus 25:24.

5. Relating the Lesson to Life

JULY 26th

A. Lead the class in a discussion of the Lesson in Our Society section.

B. Invite the class to share their personal experiences related to the questions.

6. Arousing Action

A. Provide the class with examples to help them get into the Make It Happen assignment, such as people who work to make payday loan charges less oppressive, support public school funding reform, advocate for fair living wages, and so on.

B. Remind the class that God expects us to deal justly with one another at all times.

Worship Guide

For the Superintendent or Teacher
Theme: God Calls People to Jubilee
Theme Song: "Glory, Glory, Hallelujah"
Devotional Reading: Matthew 18:21–35
Prayer

GOD CALLS PEOPLE TO JUBILEE

Bible Background • LEVITICUS 25:8–24
Printed Text • LEVITICUS 25:8–21, 23–24 Devotional Reading • MATTHEW 18:21–35

AIM for Change

By the end of the lesson, we will:
DISCOVER the issues addressed in God's commands to redistribute property and to deal justly with one another in Jubilee;
EMBRACE the biblical principles of economic justice and stewardship of God's creation; and
ENGAGE in an action that promotes economic justice and good stewardship.

Keep in Mind

"And ye shall hallow the fiftieth year, and proclaim liberty throughout all the land unto all the inhabitants thereof: it shall be a jubile unto you; and ye shall return every man unto his possession, and ye shall return every man unto his family" (Leviticus 25:10).

Focal Verses

KJV **Leviticus 25:8** And thou shalt number seven sabbaths of years unto thee, seven times seven years; and the space of the seven sabbaths of years shall be unto thee forty and nine years.

9 Then shalt thou cause the trumpet of the jubile to sound on the tenth day of the seventh month, in the day of atonement shall ye make the trumpet sound throughout all your land.

10 And ye shall hallow the fiftieth year, and proclaim liberty throughout all the land unto all the inhabitants thereof: it shall be a jubile unto you; and ye shall return every man unto his possession, and ye shall return every man unto his family.

11 A jubile shall that fiftieth year be unto you: ye shall not sow, neither reap that which groweth of itself in it, nor gather the grapes in it of thy vine undressed.

12 For it is the jubile; it shall be holy unto you: ye shall eat the increase thereof out of the field.

13 In the year of this jubile ye shall return every man unto his possession.

14 And if thou sell ought unto thy neighbour, or buyest ought of thy neighbour's hand, ye shall not oppress one another:

15 According to the number of years after the jubile thou shalt buy of thy neighbour, and according unto the number of years of the fruits he shall sell unto thee:

16 According to the multitude of years thou shalt increase the price thereof, and according to the fewness of years thou shalt diminish the price of it: for according to the number of the years of the fruits doth he sell unto thee.

NLT **Leviticus 25:8** "In addition, you must count off seven Sabbath years, seven sets of seven years, adding up to forty-nine years in all.

9 Then on the Day of Atonement in the fiftieth year, blow the ram's horn loud and long throughout the land.

10 Set this year apart as holy, a time to proclaim freedom throughout the land for all who live there. It will be a jubilee year for you, when each of you may return to the land that belonged to your ancestors and return to your own clan.

11 This fiftieth year will be a jubilee for you. During that year you must not plant your fields or store away any of the crops that grow on their own, and don't gather the grapes from your unpruned vines.

12 It will be a jubilee year for you, and you must keep it holy. But you may eat whatever the land produces on its own.

13 In the Year of Jubilee each of you may return to the land that belonged to your ancestors.

14 "When you make an agreement with your neighbor to buy or sell property, you must not take advantage of each other.

15 When you buy land from your neighbor, the price you pay must be based on the number of years since the last jubilee. The seller must set the price by taking into account the number of years remaining until the next Year of Jubilee.

16 The more years until the next jubilee, the higher the price; the fewer years, the lower the price. After all, the person selling the land is actually selling you a certain number of harvests.

17 Ye shall not therefore oppress one another; but thou shalt fear thy God: for I am the LORD your God.

18 Wherefore ye shall do my statutes, and keep my judgments, and do them; and ye shall dwell in the land in safety.

19 And the land shall yield her fruit, and ye shall eat your fill, and dwell therein in safety.

20 And if ye shall say, What shall we eat the seventh year? behold, we shall not sow, nor gather in our increase:

21 Then I will command my blessing upon you in the sixth year, and it shall bring forth fruit for three years.

25:23 The land shall not be sold for ever: for the land is mine; for ye are strangers and sojourners with me.

24 And in all the land of your possession ye shall grant a redemption for the land.

17 Show your fear of God by not taking advantage of each other. I am the LORD your God.

18 "If you want to live securely in the land, follow my decrees and obey my regulations.

19 Then the land will yield large crops, and you will eat your fill and live securely in it.

20 But you might ask, 'What will we eat during the seventh year, since we are not allowed to plant or harvest crops that year?'

21 Be assured that I will send my blessing for you in the sixth year, so the land will produce a crop large enough for three years.

25:23 "The land must never be sold on a permanent basis, for the land belongs to me. You are only foreigners and tenant farmers working for me.

24 "With every purchase of land you must grant the seller the right to buy it back.

In Focus

The year 2000 was, for many, greeted with both trepidation and jubilation. Although the calculation of the timing of the twenty-first century has been widely debated (January 1, 2001 vs. January 1, 2000), the year 2000 also marked the culmination of the Jubilee 2000 Afrika Campaign, a debt-relief program launched in Accra, Ghana in 1998. Jubilee 2000 was part of a worldwide movement advocating for the cancellation of debts incurred by developing countries.

The Jubilee 2000 Campaign was based on the Hebrew Bible (Old Testament) concept of jubilee. In the book of Leviticus, jubilee is described as a year-long celebration held every fifty years, and notable for its release of Israelites from debt slavery and restoration of land seized to cover their debts. The campaign sought to alleviate the exorbitant interest payments on loans by developing countries (unpayable debt), who produce less than they are able to repay.

Several African nations participated in the Jubilee 2000 Afrika Campaign. They did this to raise awareness about unpayable debt and to give their input into strategies that would help alleviate the debt, so that the funds being paid on the interest could be channeled into social programs for their people.

Jubilee 2000 was a short-lived, modern-day campaign. However, efforts to relieve the financial burdens of the poor go as far back as biblical times. In today's lesson, we learn how God's concern for economic justice and good stewardship of the earth was demonstrated by God's institution of the jubilee, a mandate for periodic relief from debts.

The People, Places, and Times

Kinship. Israel operated in its formative years within a kinship system, a classification of people related by birth or marriage. Israel's kinship system comprised the tribe, the clan, and the family household or *bet ab*, Hebrew for "father's house." Individual Israelites derived greatest social and economic benefits from the family unit. The family household consisted of immediate family members related by birth or marriage, and sometimes included servants. They were dependent on each other for security and protection.

The next level of social organization was the clan, or *mishpachah*. The clan consisted of a number of households and was identified by the names of Jacob's grandsons or other family members on the basis of patriarchal relationship. Each clan received land to distribute to households according to their needs. The clan also served to protect the land to assure that the land remained within the clan. The jubilee helped the clan in performing this responsibility.

The largest unit of social organization was the tribe, or *shebet*. The tribe represented a number of clans grouped together. The 12 tribes of Israel were named for the sons of Jacob and Joseph. The jubilee protected individual Israelites and the land from permanently being sold.

Background

The laws governing debt relief, release of debt slaves, and the return of the family property lost through economic hardship, form the basis of the jubilee year. In Canaan (the land inhabited by the Israelites), city-state kings and their nobles owned the land and distributed it as they saw fit. Individuals who fell on economic hard times could sell their land to settle their debts or they could enter indentured servitude agreements. The king had discretionary power to decree the release of citizens from slavery, military service, debts, and taxes.

When God delivered the Israelites from slavery in Egypt and established a covenant relationship with them, they understood themselves as belonging to God and the land as well. As long as they observed God's statutes and ordinances, they could remain in the land; if they failed God would expel them. The land was divided among the clans according to the needs of each family. Since the land was a gift from God, Israelites, who encountered economic hardship, could not sell their allotment of land to non-Israelites, who were outside the covenantal relationship. It had to be sold within the families belonging to their clan.

The jubilee ensured that Israelites who had lost their land to indebtedness or had sold themselves into slavery would not remain in this state permanently. It restored the confiscated land to its original owner and released him from all debt so he could return to his clan. The Jubilee also functioned to prevent the mass accumulation of an entire clan's property by a few wealthier families.

Source:

Wright, Christopher J. H. "Year of Jubilee." In *The Anchor Bible Dictionary*, Vol. 3. New York: Doubleday, 1992.

At-A-Glance

1. Jubilee: Release from Debts (Leviticus 25:8–12)
2. Return of Possessions (vv. 13–17)
3. Replenishment of Crops (vv. 18–21)
4. Redemption of Land (25:23–24)

In Depth

1. Jubilee: Release from Debts (Leviticus 25:8–12)

Every seven years marked a sabbatical year. Just as God demanded rest on the sabbath or seventh day, God also commanded that the seventh year would be a period of rest for the land. The Israelites were prohibited from planting crops or pruning the vineyards. Nor were they permitted to reap the harvest or gather grapes. Instead, everyone—free and slave—was required to live off the aftergrowth for one year. The year of Jubilee was to take effect following a series of seven sabbatical years. At the beginning of the fiftieth year, a trumpet was to sound throughout the land announcing the release of indentured slaves to return to their families (*bet ab*) and the return of their property seized to cover their debts. They also were to cancel all related debts. The Jubilee was to be an effective means of ensuring that the debtor and his family retained their standing within the Israelite community. The permanent loss of property would literally mean the loss of a family's inheritance from God, resulting in their loss of identity as a member of God's family.

Since the Jubilee year ran into a sabbatical year, the restrictions concerning the sowing or reaping of crops were still to be enforced. (Even though the people were supposed to do all of this, there is no record that they ever did it).

2. Return of Possessions (vv. 13–17)

The conditions of the law specified that anyone possessing the confiscated property of a fellow Israelite was required to return it to him in the year of Jubilee. The land itself had not been acquired but rather the use of the land, much like a lease rather than a sale. The ancient Israelites did not perform financial transactions in money, such as paper and coins. The sale price would have been determined by the number of potential harvests since the last Jubilee, and paid in measurements of sheep, goats, birds, grain, oil, or wine. The value of the land increased or decreased in relation to the Jubilee year.

The one forced to sell his property and the one taking possession of the land were required to deal fairly with one another. However, the one buying had an advantage that the one selling did not. Certainly the one making a purchase from someone forced to sell his land or himself into slavery because of debt had the upper hand. However, the debtor could tilt the balance (literally) in his favor by tampering with the weights on the scale used to determine the price, therefore cheating the buyer. Proverbs 11:1 comments on this, "A false balance is abomination to the Lord; but a just weight is his delight." Therefore both the seller and buyer are warned not to cheat one another.

3. Replenishment of Crops (vv. 18–21)

God understood the concern the people might have had about having enough food to last from the sabbath year until the end of the Jubilee year. Remember that the sabbath took effect the seventh year; the next year was Jubilee. This meant that the Israelites were not allowed to sow or reap the aftergrowth or prune the vineyards from the end of the sixth year until the harvest season of the ninth year. Therefore, God promised that if they were faithful and observed the Jubilee stipulations, they would live securely in the land. Moreover, God would bless the land to produce enough food to last until the harvest in the ninth year. If the Israelites would trust and obey God, they would not have to worry about where their next meal was coming from.

4. Redemption of Land (25:23–24)

Central to the theological understanding of the Jubilee was the Israelites' understanding that ultimately the land was God's and that they were merely guests or tenants on the land. God made it clear that the land cannot be sold in perpetuity (*tsemiythuth*), a term in Hebrew referring to real estate transactions in relation to land alienation. In real estate terminology, God's relationship to the Israelites was analogous to a landlord/owner, or lessor and tenant, or lessee in a leasehold estate agreement. The Israelites had rights of possession and use, but not ownership. They were permitted to use the land as long they observed the Mosaic covenant (tenancy at will). What God was saying was that the Israelites did not have the authority to permanently sell or transfer the use of the land because it did not belong to them (restraint on alienation). The land was theirs to use and could be passed down from generation to generation, but their heirs were bound to the same restriction.

In the event an Israelite lost the land to cover his debts, he had redemption (*geullah*) rights—the right to buy back the land, if funds could be obtained from a redeemer (*goel*) or next of kin. When Naomi's means of survival was lost upon the deaths of her husband and sons, Ruth approached Boaz, Naomi's kinsman, to redeem her husband's land. He told Ruth that there was a closer next-of-kin than he who might choose to fulfill the duty of redeeming the land; if not, then Boaz would gladly do so (Ruth 3:7–13). God made certain that there was a provision for redeeming the land, which was a gift to the Israelites from God.

Source:

Wright, Christopher J. H. "Year of Jubilee." In *The Anchor Bible Dictionary*, Vol. 3. New York: Doubleday, 1992.

Search the Scriptures

1. On what day did God command the Israelites to sound the trumpet announcing the Jubilee (v. 9)?

2. In the year of Jubilee, the people were required to sell all their possessions (v. 13). True or False?

3. According to God, to whom does the land belong (v. 23)?

Discuss the Meaning

1. "Liberation" is often understood in Western society as independence, or freedom, from some oppressive form of government rule. However, in Leviticus 25, the term *derowr* means "the emancipation from slavery or indentured servitude." How does this meaning impact your understanding of God's command to "proclaim liberty throughout all the land"?

2. Usually to gain the favor of the people affected, kings in the ancient Near East often enacted arbitrary liberty decrees. What is the significance of God establishing a regular, permanent ordinance for debt forgiveness and restoration of household property?

3. The Jubilee 2000 Campaign sought the cancellation of unpayable debt owed to developed countries by developing countries, whose income does not allow them to both provide social programs for their people and pay the debt. Why do you think these countries' debts should be forgiven?

Lesson in Our Society

1. Bible scholars have debated whether or not the Jubilee year was ever observed by the Israelites, although the prophet Jeremiah bemoaned the failure of the people to consistently observe the release of slaves in sabbath years (Jeremiah 34:6–16). Less important than the faithful observance of the Jubilee was the theological implication. What are the ramifications of a theology that states that per-

sons enslaved by debt should be freed and after a specified period, all their debts cancelled?

2. God promised the Israelites that if they observed God's statutes and kept God's judgments, God would provide for their needs. Do you trust God to provide for your needs, even when you are experiencing difficulties, especially financial worries?

3. Predatory lending and sub-prime mortgage loans are just two of the ways that homeowners can become vulnerable to losing their homes. How can we help prevent individuals, especially the elderly and poor, from being susceptible to such questionable lending practices?

Make It Happen

The Jubilee 2000 Campaign sought to embody the spirit behind the Jubilee, by promoting the biblical principles of economic justice for developing countries throughout the world. Identify at least one example of individuals or groups working to promote economic justice in your community and share it with the class next week.

Follow the Spirit

What God wants me to do:

____

____

Remember Your Thoughts

Special insights I have learned:

____

____

More Light on the Text

Leviticus 25:8–21, 23–24

8 And thou shalt number seven sabbaths of years unto thee, seven times seven years; and the space of the seven sabbaths of years shall be unto thee forty and nine years.

With the command to rest, God instituted the sabbath. The Jews were supposed to abstain from work and rest on the sabbath. But with a further instituting of the sabbatical year by God, the benevolence of rest was not only meant for humans, but also extended to the land of their inheritance. Before the Israelites entered the Promised Land, God commanded that the land itself must observe a sabbath unto Him. He said that for six years they were to sow their fields, prune their vineyards, and gather their crops; but on the seventh year, the land was to observe a sabbath of rest, during which they were not to sow anything in their fields, prune their vineyards, nor were they to reap what grew of itself or harvest the grapes of untended vines of the previous year. Whatever the land yielded during the sabbath year would be for food for them—themselves, their servants, hired workers, temporary residents who lived among them, their livestock, and the wild animals on their land. They were to eat whatever the land produced on its own that year, without having to sow on it.

A computation of a number of sabbath years by multiplication results in a given product. This is what we find in this verse. God was commanding the Israelites to number seven sabbath years unto themselves. The word translated "number" is *caphar*, (**saw-FAR**); it means "to count, enumerate or reckon." They were to count and reckon seven sabbath years, multiplying them by seven—"Seven times seven years." The Hebrew translated "space" is *yowm* (**yome**); this word means "year." In the context in which it is used, it denotes "the space or period of time defined by the number of years specified"; this number of years considered as a whole. This "space" (number of years) is the product arrived at when seven is multiplied by seven years, which is forty-nine years.

9 Then shalt thou cause the trumpet of the jubile to sound on the tenth day of the seventh month, in the day of atonement shall ye make the trumpet sound throughout all your land.

The sound of the trumpet was to rend the air on the tenth day of the seventh month of the forty-ninth year—the sound of the trumpet of Jubilee. The Hebrew word, *yowbel* (**yo-BALE**), originally meant "ram or ram's horn." Because the ram's horn was used as a trumpet that was blown to announce the arrival of the Jubilee year, it came to be used to mean "jubilee year." Thus *yowbel* represents "the trumpet of the jubilee." This was to be sounded on the tenth day of the seventh month, which happens to be the Day of Atonement. *Yom Kippur* (**yome kip-POOR**) is the Hebrew word translated "day of atonement." In order to receive forgiveness from the Lord, it was a day the Israelites were to observe for the cleansing of their sins. The Day of Atonement was observed once a year. Aaron was to use some specified number of animals (bull, rams, and goats) to make atonement for himself, his family, and the entire Israelite community. He was to make atonement also for the Most Holy Place, the tabernacle, and the altar, which were affected by their sins and uncleanness since the tabernacle and all in it dwelt among them. Consequently, the sounding of the trumpet of the Jubilee coincided with the great Day of Atonement.

10 And ye shall hallow the fiftieth year, and proclaim liberty throughout all the land unto all the inhabitants thereof: it shall be a jubile unto you; and ye shall return every man unto his possession, and ye shall return every man unto his family.

The Sabbath, that brought rest to the people, was stretched beyond the weekly cycle to a seven-year cycle, thus bringing rest to the land of their inheritance. The seventh year, after six years, was then known as the "Sabbath" year. The greatest stretch of the sabbath was further derived from the multiplication of the sabbath years by seven, thereby creating another cycle of forty-nine years to which one year was added to arrive at a sum total of 50 years. This addition resulted into the fiftieth year known as "the year of jubilee." God commanded the people of Israel to hallow this fiftieth year. The word translated "hallow" is *qadash* (**kaw-DASH**); it is a synonym to "sanctify." "Hallow" means "to consecrate, to observe as holy." In other words, the year of Jubilee was to be observed as a holy year.

The year of Jubilee was a year of liberty, restoration, and rest. The Israelites were to proclaim liberty throughout the entire land—freedom of bondservants. In the year of Jubilee, any Israelite who had subjected himself, as a means of livelihood, to slavery was to be set free and to return to his own family. Anyone who had been separated from his possession was to return to it. This year of Jubilee was to bring about an even distribution of wealth among the Israelites. The accumulation of property, in the hands of a very few people, means that some are wealthy while others have no chance to escape poverty. But the stipulations and provisions of the Jubilee were to effect the abolition of poverty among the Israelites. It allowed the unfortunate and less privileged ones to start all over again, with a measure of possession that would be restored to them in the year of Jubilee.

11 A jubile shall that fiftieth year be unto you: ye shall not sow, neither reap that which groweth of itself in it, nor gather the grapes in it of they vine undressed. 12 For it is the jubile; it shall be holy unto you: ye shall eat the increase thereof out of the field.

Abundance of rest and ease, lack of stress resulting from hard labor, and celebration of long holy days form a composite picture of the provisions of the year of Jubilee. The previous year, preceding the Jubilee (the forty-ninth) was a sabbath year, which already was a year of rest for the land. All that grew of itself in the fields, vineyards, and olive yards were not to be harvested, but left for the poor that they may eat. And what the poor left behind were to be eaten by beasts. This referred to some of the scanty crops that grew on their own from the previous sowing season of the previous year. They were not to be eaten in the sabbath year. At the end of every seven year, debts were to be cancelled—creditors were to cancel the debts of their fellow Israelites. Also in the sabbath year, the law was to be read for the instruction of the people at the Feast of Tabernacles. Poor Israelites, who bonded themselves to fellow Israelites as servants, were to be released.

The year of Jubilee offered nearly similar provisions. They were not to sow in their lands, neither reap that which grew of itself in their fields, nor gather the grapes of their undressed vine.

The word translated "undressed" is *naziyr* (**naw-ZEER**), which basically denotes "separate"—with particular reference to "a consecrated prince or Nazirite"—figuratively means "an unpruned vine." Pruning is the process of cutting off unwanted or dried leaves and branches from the vine plant as a way of dressing it and enabling it to grow well. Since the Israelites were forbidden by the law of the Jubilee year from working or tending their vineyards, their vines remained unpruned. They were not to gather grapes from unpruned vines. They were to observe the Jubilee year as a holy year. In other words, all the days of the year were to be observed as holy days before the Lord. They were only to eat the natural increase of their fields.

13 In the year of this jubile ye shall return every man unto his possession. 14 And if thou sell ought unto thy neighbour, or buyest ought of thy neighbour's hand, ye shall not oppress one another:

When the Israelites began to dwell in the Promised Land, these stipulations for the year of Jubilee were obviously to bring about a restoration of things to their original state. In the course of time, social classes among the people began to differ. Besides their natural inheritance (the land that fell to each of the tribes after the division of the land), their occupation and individual efforts determined their achievements in terms of acquisition of properties and other possessions. This certainly created different social classes among them—some became rich while others remained poor. Some, out of poverty, sold their possessions to others, while other poor folks made themselves bondservants to others.

The year of Jubilee was a year of restoration. In this year, every man was to return to his possession. The Hebrew word for "return" is *shuwb* (**SHOOB**), meaning "to come back home, to restore, to recover." Those who had sold their landed properties were to come back to them; their properties were to be restored to them for them to take possession again. God also commanded a fair and just transaction. If they sold or bought land from each other, they were not to oppress one another. The expression, "And if thou sell ought unto thy neighbour" is rendered in the *New International Version*, "And if you sell land to one of your country men." The idea conveyed in the phrase "sell ought" depicts a situation where one sells his property to another in needy circumstances; often one decides to sell out because of one's poor condition. God was commanding that the one buying shouldn't oppress the one selling out of need. The word translated "oppress" is *yanah* (**yaw-NAW**), which means "to be violent, to suppress, or to maltreat." The one buying shouldn't take advantage of the seller's needy condition to suppress or maltreat him in the course of the transaction, maybe by cheating or by some fraudulent acts.

God gave the Israelites the laws of the Jubilee to encourage the just redistribution of wealth, to provide for the poor, and thereby to honor God who provides for all. This was to discourage excessive, permanent accumulation of wealth and property, and the consequent deprivation of an Israelite of his inheritance in the land. The Israelites, as a people, were to comply with the divine laws of God to counter the natural order that causes uneven flow of material possessions amongst people, which designates some as poor and some as rich. God commanded that there was to be no poor person among them.

15 According to the number of years after the jubile thou shalt buy of thy neighbour, and according unto the number of years of the fruits he shall sell unto thee: 16 According to the multitude of years thou shalt increase the price thereof, and according to the fewness of years thou shalt diminish the price of it: for according to the number of the years of the fruits doth he sell unto thee.

The Lord stipulated that the Jubilee should become a determining factor in the pricing of landed properties. Anyone intending to buy land from his neighbor should take into consideration the number of years that have elapsed since the last Jubilee year. In other words, the price of the land was to be determined by the number of years after the year of Jubilee—and he should buy it on the basis of this. On the other hand, the one selling was to sell on the basis of the number of years of the fruits. The Hebrew word translated "fruits" is *tebuw'ah* (**teb-oo-AW**), meaning "produce, in increase"; it refers to the crops harvested. The seller was to sell his land according to the number of years left for harvesting crops. It then follows that the one selling was to base his pricing on the number of harvest seasons remaining between the time of the transaction and the next Jubilee year. These harvest seasons represent the actual value of the land to the one buying, since the land will be returned to its original owner in the next Jubilee year.

With the introduction of the years of Jubilee as determining factors in the pricing of landed properties, the number of years between a land business transaction and the next Jubilee becomes the criterion for fixing the price of a land. If the number of years is many, then the price of the land is to be increased because the number of harvest seasons in the years will definitely be many. But if the years are few, then the land is to be sold at a reduced price, since the seasons will be commensurately few.

17 Ye shall not therefore oppress one another; but thou shalt fear thy God: for I am the LORD your God.

The Lord repeats the command that restrains the Israelites from dealing violently with or maltreating one another. Social interactions among degenerate humans or among those who don't have the fear of God are mostly fraught with every form of vice ranging from physical violence, fraud, cheating, to extortion and the like. While this command was meant to discourage maltreatment among themselves, it serves to protect the rights and interest of every Israelite in any business transaction, regardless of social status. This command was also meant to uphold respect for the person of any Israelite, no matter his condition. By virtue of the fact that every Israelite had a covenant relationship with God, they were required to have the fear of God in their dealings with each other. *Yare'* (**yaw-RAY**) is the Hebrew word for "fear," which simply means "to show reverence." They were supposed to show reverence to God by dealing with one another uprightly, and not oppress each other.

The provisions of the Jubilee were to create a balanced society in which there was to be an even distribution of wealth. It was supposed to give new generations an opportunity to regain wealth lost in penury by their parents. Within a period of fifty years, a younger generation of descendants would have grown up to be able to take possession of restored properties. The Jubilee laws were to abolish perpetual poverty. Thus, the Jubilee was to bring a cycle of restoration to the people.

Communities can care for the poor by providing the basic amenities of life through the concerted contributory effort of the rich. Through encouragement, persuasion, or soliciting from the rich, communities can effect a distribution of resources to the poor in the society.

18 Wherefore ye shall do my statutes, and keep my judgments, and do them; and ye shall dwell in the land in safety.

The Lord charged the Israelites to obey His commandments. From the time of their deliverance from Egypt, God had been charging them to obey His commands. He had spoken His charge to them at various instances, using various expressions. After sweetening the bitter water of Marah for them to drink, He gave them His charge saying, "If thou wilt diligently hearken to the voice of the Lord...and wilt do that which is right in his sight" (Exodus 15:26). When He was about to give them His Ten Commandments, He also gave them a charge saying, "If ye will obey my voice...and keep my covenant" (Exodus 19:5). When He was specifying those offerings that would be acceptable to Him and denouncing those unacceptable, He also gave them a charge saying, "Therefore shall ye keep my commandments, and do them" (Leviticus 22:31). Now, in the process of giving them the commands that institute the year of Jubilee, He was charging them to do His statutes and keep His judgments.

The Hebrew word translated "do" is *'asah* (**aw-SAW**); it means "to fulfill, practice, maintain, or accomplish." The Hebrew word translated "to keep" is *shamar* (**shaw-MAR**), which means "to take heed to oneself, to observe." This was to condition their attitudes, to make them develop attitudes of willingness to practice and fulfill His laws, to maintain His statutes, to take heed to themselves of His judgments, to always be inclined to accomplish His laws in their lives.

Consequently, the land they were to possess by inheritance (the Promised Land) would offer the safety they require to dwell in it peacefully. The word translated "safety" is *betach* (**BEH-takh**); it means "a place of refuge." Safety was a benefit that made them free from any form of harassment or attack.

19 And the land shall yield her fruit, and ye shall eat your fill, and dwell therein in safety. 20 And if ye shall say, What shall we eat the seventh year? behold, we shall not sow, nor gather in our increase: 21 Then I will command my blessing upon you in the sixth year, and it shall bring forth fruit for three years.

God promised spontaneous increase from the land, without them having to sow. The land would be made to yield enough fruit for them to eat all they wanted. *Periy* (**per-EE**) is the Hebrew word translated "fruit"; it connotes "reward." The fruit of the land was its produce, increase of crops for their sustenance which was to come to them as their reward for obedience. In other words, the land would be made to respond to their obedience in obeying God's statutes. The fact that they would dwell in safety in the land is repeated here.

Their natural yearning for food to sustain, as depicted by the question, "what shall we eat the seventh year?" would be met by supernatural provision. Since they wouldn't be performing any agricultural activity that ensured harvest that year, God promised to command His blessing upon them in the sixth year that would bring forth fruit for three years. *Tebuw'ah* (**teb-oo-AW**) is the word translated "fruit." Here, it speaks of "income, produce, or increase." This meant the people would receive income and abundant produce for three years, without having to labor by sowing the land. These were the benefits of the year of Jubilee.

25:23 The land shall not be sold for ever: for the land is mine; for ye are strangers and sojourners

with me. 24 And in all the land of your possession ye shall grant a redemption for the land.

Canaan, the Promised Land, was also known as the Holy Land. It was a land chosen by God, which He promised Abraham that his descendants would possess. From the beginning, at creation, we see the carving out of a portion of the earth for a special divine ownership. The Garden of Eden was a special territory. It was a place God prepared uniquely for the habitation of our first parents—Adam and Eve. The presence of God was there. The Promised Land was also founded on a similar concept: it was a special territory carved out of the earth for divine ownership. It was a land where God had His dwelling among men, a land where God put His name in the presence of the tabernacle that later became a temple. It was a land where the presence of God abode, where natural forces and cycles were directly under His control. The Promised Land was God's own, which He gave to the Israelites, a people chosen out of the earth unto Himself—His inheritance.

God said that this land should not be sold out forever. This meant that the Israelites' possession of the land was temporary, and any sale of portions of the land was not permanent. The Lord, Himself, was the landowner. They were to consistently live with the awareness that God, with whom they had a covenant relationship, was the landlord and they were strangers and sojourners with Him. The word translated "strangers" is *ger* (**gare**), meaning "foreigner or alien." The word translated "sojourners" is *towshab* (**to-SHAWB**), meaning "a dweller in a foreign land, a resident alien." Both words are synonymous. They refer to one who is not an original inhabitant or a native citizen of a land; one who comes to dwell as a foreigner in another land. By this consciousness, the Israelites were supposed to use their service to God to pay tribute and a sort of tenancy rate to Him in addition to fulfilling His covenant.

The stipulations of the year of Jubilee were to be a constant reminder to the Israelites' status in the Promised Land. Though individuals could possess lands as subordinate landlords, they were to grant redemption to their lands in the year of Jubilee. The Hebrew word translated "redemption" is *geullah* (**gheh-ool-LAW**), meaning "to redeem, to deliver, a right." It speaks of original owners of lands redeeming their lands in the year of Jubilee from those to whom they sold them. Conversely, the buyer was the one to grant redemption to the land, by giving up the right ownership to its original owner.

The Israelites were made to understand that all the properties they possessed belonged to the Lord—as the land was His. This means they were stewards in charge of God's property. This is the case with anyone in possession of wealth. The economic life of communities and peoples is intrinsically the determining of sustenance and survival. Everyone— rich or poor—has a right to live—to sustain life. In order to promote economic justice and good stewardship, the wealth must be made to spread. This means those in possession of great wealth should consider themselves stewards and be willing to distribute to others in need.

Sources:

Unger, Merrill F. *The New Unger's Bible Dictionary.* Edited by R.K. Harrison. Chicago: Moody Press, 1988.

Vine, W.E. *Vines Complete Expository Dictionary of Old and New Testament Words.* Edited by Merrill F. Unger and William White Jr. Nashville: Thomas Nelson Publishers, 1996.

Daily Bible Readings

M: Jesus' Vision of Ministry
Luke 4:14–19
T: Forgiveness and Mercy
Matthew 18:21–35
W: Compassion and Mercy
Luke 10:25–37
T: Compassion for the Helpless
Matthew 9:35–38
F: Compassion for the Bereaved
Luke 7:11–17
S: Ministry to the Needy
Matthew 25:31–40
S: The Year of Jubilee
Leviticus 25:8–21, 23–24

NOTES

TEACHING TIPS

August 2
Bible Study Guide 9

1. Words You Should Know

A. Mixt (Mixed) Multitude (Numbers 11:4) *'acpecuph* (Heb.)—A collection or collected multitude—a mass or crowd.

B. Manna (v. 6) *man* (Heb.)—The bread from the sky that fed the Israelites, who wandered in the wilderness for 40 years.

2. Teacher Preparation

Unifying Principle—Complaints and Cravings. When people experience difficulties, they often forget their blessings. What happens when we forget our blessings during times of trouble? When God brought the people out of slavery in Egypt and provided for them in the desert, Moses and the people complained repeatedly.

A. Write down any words, concepts, or personal thoughts that will help reinforce this lesson on complaining.

B. Prepare for the lesson by reading today's Bible Study Guide in its entirety.

C. Take notes highlighting points within the lesson that specifically address the AIM for Change learning objectives and the Unifying Principle.

D. Materials needed: chalkboard and chalk or flip chart with markers, Bible, extra pens.

3. Starting the Lesson

A. Concentrate on the AIM for Change as you begin the lesson in prayer.

B. As an icebreaker, ask the class: What are some common things most people complain about? List the answers on the chalkboard or flip chart. Discuss.

C. Ask for a volunteer to briefly summarize (or read) today's In Focus story.

D. Based upon the In Focus story and the list of common complaints most people have, pose the question found in the Unifying Principle to the class.

4. Getting into the Lesson

A. Assess the student's knowledge of today's Scripture text by having the class answer the Search the Scriptures questions.

B. Provide the backdrop for today's lesson by giving an overview of The People, Places, and Times; Background; and Focal Verses sections.

C. Divide the class into two groups. Assign each group an In Depth section and two Discuss the Meaning questions to read, analyze, and answer. Allow each group 10 to 15 minutes of discussion time. Monitor each group's progress.

D. Reconvene the class.

5. Relating the Lesson to Life

A. Initiate an open discussion allowing class members to share their conclusions and/or thoughts drawn from the In Depth and Discuss the Meaning group discussions.

B. Highlight the three points from the Lesson in Our Society section designed to reinforce the Unifying Principle for today's lesson.

C. Review the list of common complaints given at the beginning of class.

6. Arousing Action

A. Ask the students to consider the questions in the Make It Happen section.

B. Instruct the students to partner with another member of the class. Have each student tell their partner one thing they constantly complain about. Have them join hands with their partner and begin to pray that their complaining be replaced with words of praise and encouragement.

C. Remind the students to read the Daily Bible Readings in preparation for next week's lesson.

Worship Guide

For the Superintendent or Teacher
Theme: People Grumble
Theme Song: "Speak Lord"
Devotional Reading: Psalm 142
Prayer

PEOPLE GRUMBLE

Bible Background • NUMBERS 11
Printed Text • NUMBERS 11:1–6, 10–15 Devotional Reading • PSALM 142

AIM for Change

By the end of the lesson, we will:
EXAMINE the Israelites' grumbling about life in the wilderness;
RECOGNIZE that grumbling reflects an ungrateful heart; and
GIVE THANKS for the blessings in our lives.

Keep in Mind

"And the mixt multitude that was among them fell a lusting: and the children of Israel also wept again, and said, Who shall give us flesh to eat? We remember the fish, which we did eat in Egypt freely; the cucumbers, and the melons, and the leeks, and the onions, and the garlick: But now our soul is dried away: there is nothing at all, beside this manna, before our eyes" (Numbers 11:4–6).

Focal Verses

KJV **Numbers 11:1** And when the people complained, it displeased the LORD: and the LORD heard it; and his anger was kindled; and the fire of the LORD burnt among them, and consumed them that were in the uttermost parts of the camp.

2 And the people cried unto Moses; and when Moses prayed unto the LORD, the fire was quenched.

3 And he called the name of the place Taberah: because the fire of the LORD burnt among them.

4 And the mixt multitude that was among them fell a lusting: and the children of Israel also wept again, and said, Who shall give us flesh to eat?

5 We remember the fish, which we did eat in Egypt freely; the cucumbers, and the melons, and the leeks, and the onions, and the garlick:

6 But now our soul is dried away: there is nothing at all, beside this manna, before our eyes.

11:10 Then Moses heard the people weep throughout their families, every man in the door of his tent: and the anger of the LORD was kindled greatly; Moses also was displeased.

11 And Moses said unto the LORD, Wherefore hast thou afflicted thy servant? and wherefore have I not found favour in thy sight, that thou layest the burden of all this people upon me?

12 Have I conceived all this people? have I begotten them, that thou shouldest say unto me, Carry them in thy bosom, as a nursing father beareth the sucking child, unto the land which thou swarest unto their fathers?

NLT **Numbers 11:1** Soon the people began to complain about their hardship, and the LORD heard everything they said. Then the LORD's anger blazed against them, and he sent a fire to rage among them, and he destroyed some of the people in the outskirts of the camp.

2 Then the people screamed to Moses for help, and when he prayed to the LORD, the fire stopped.

3 After that, the area was known as Taberah (which means "the place of burning"), because fire from the LORD had burned among them there.

4 Then the foreign rabble who were traveling with the Israelites began to crave the good things of Egypt. And the people of Israel also began to complain. "Oh, for some meat!" they exclaimed.

5 "We remember the fish we used to eat for free in Egypt. And we had all the cucumbers, melons, leeks, onions, and garlic we wanted.

6 But now our appetites are gone. All we ever see is this manna!"

11:10 Moses heard all the families standing in the doorways of their tents whining, and the LORD became extremely angry. Moses was also very aggravated.

11 And Moses said to the LORD, "Why are you treating me, your servant, so harshly? Have mercy on me! What did I do to deserve the burden of all these people?

12 Did I give birth to them? Did I bring them into the world? Why did you tell me to carry them in my arms like a mother carries a nursing baby? How can I carry them to the land you swore to give their ancestors?

13 Whence should I have flesh to give unto all this people? for they weep unto me, saying, Give us flesh, that we may eat.

14 I am not able to bear all this people alone, because it is too heavy for me.

15 And if thou deal thus with me, kill me, I pray thee, out of hand, if I have found favour in thy sight; and let me not see my wretchedness.

13 Where am I supposed to get meat for all these people? They keep whining to me, saying, 'Give us meat to eat!'

14 I can't carry all these people by myself! The load is far too heavy!

15 If this is how you intend to treat me, just go ahead and kill me. Do me a favor and spare me this misery!"

In Focus

Sandra was excited. After seven years on the job, she took a chance and interviewed for a management position in the international finance department, which paid several thousand dollars more per year than her current position. If offered the position, she would be making enough money to pay off her credit cards, her student loan, and finally get out of debt. Sandra prayed that she would get the position.

One afternoon, the vice president of finance called Sandra into his office. He told Sandra that hers was the most impressive interview of all the candidates who applied and the position was hers, if she wanted it. Overjoyed, Sandra thanked Mr. Santis and left his office with a huge smile on her face—her prayers were answered; now she could finally get out of debt.

After several months in her new position, Sandra sat in her office talking to Jalisa, a colleague from the marketing department, where she formerly worked.

"Girl, this job is working my last nerve. I hate it over here! My boss is overbearing and the people in this department work you like a slave. They expect you to make bricks with no straw! They expect me to work all this overtime and I don't even get paid time-and-a-half, because now I'm a *salaried* employee. All I do is go to work and come home. My social life is totally dead."

Tired of hearing her complain, Jalisa said, "What about the beautiful weather we've been having lately?"

"What?" Sandra responded. "What does the weather have to do with my drama at work?"

"Nothing! That's the point; I can't wrap my mind around the fact that you're complaining about your new position, not to mention the hefty increase in pay that came with it." Jalisa chuckled. "You know, you asked God to give you a way out of debt, and He did. My prayer is that you stop complaining about what's wrong with the job and realize that God has blessed you with a new job that allowed you to pay off your debt and purchase a new home and a new car. You'd better be careful, girl. God is not pleased."

When life doesn't proceed as we've planned, it is easy to become frustrated and start to grumble and complain. Today's lesson reminds us that often, we fail to appreciate the good things in our lives and realize just how much God has blessed us.

The People, Places, and Times

Moses. His name means "drawn out of the water." He was chosen by God to lead the Israelites out of Egypt, where they were enslaved and oppressed.

Taberah. A place near the wilderness of Paran, whose name means "burning." It is the place where God punished the Israelites for murmuring and complaining of only having manna to eat.

Cloud By Day and Pillar of Fire By Night. The cloud by day and pillar of fire by night were the manifestations of God's direction and His will. When the cloud by day lifted, the people were to follow it. When the cloud settled, it was God's will that the people stop and set up camp. The pillar of fire by night was a sign of God's protection during the darkness of night.

Source:
Life Application Study Bible. Wheaton, Ill.: Tyndale House Publishers, Inc. 1996.

Background

After their long enslavement, as they followed the cloud by day and the pillar of fire by night, the Children of Israel left Egypt and traveled from place to place. The book of Numbers chronicles the story of the 40 years during which the Children of Israel wandered in the desert before entering the Promised Land. After two years camped in the Sinai desert, God lifted the cloud and the Israelites left the wilderness of Sinai. They followed the cloud until it rested in the wilderness of Paran. Today's text finds the Israelites, only three days into their journey, mumbling and complaining about the hardships they have to endure while traveling in the desert.

At-A-Glance

1. The People Complain (Numbers 11:1–6)
2. Moses Complains (11:10–15)

In Depth

1. The People Complain (Numbers 11:1–6)

The Children of Israel began to complain only three days into their journey (10:32ff). Angered by their ungrateful attitude, God began to consume the Israelites' camp with fire, and many people were killed. The people looked to Moses and began to cry out for help. Moses prayed for the people, and when God heard his prayers, the fire stopped. Moses then named the place Taberah, which means "burning." The place served as a reminder of God's burning anger against the Israelites for their ungratefulness.

After the fire of judgment was quenched, the spirit of complaining returned, as the "mixed multitude" that followed the Israelites out of Egypt grew tired of eating manna. The Israelites quickly joined in and began complaining that they, too, were tired of eating manna every day. They longed for the days back in Egypt when they freely ate fish, cucumbers, and melons, etc. (v. 5).

Even though the smell of fire was still in their nostrils, the Israelites complained about their situation. How quickly they had forgotten their enslavement! They reminisced as though they had lived as princes and princesses in Egypt. When faced with hardships, they quickly forgot about God's provisions and began to grumble and complain yet again.

God is able to provide more than we can imagine. The daily provision (manna) from heaven simply exemplified the provisions and the compassion that God had for His people. If the Israelites had prayed to God instead of murmuring, what might the result have been?

When we complain, it's an indication that we do not trust God. Reflect on your personal experiences. During times of trials, do you forget God's blessings? Do you complain? Are you unhappy because God has not blessed you with more? Consider all that God has done for you. God gives you life, health, strength, family, employment, and many other blessings—too numerous to count. Because we are busy focusing on things we don't have, we appear ungrateful for God's blessings. After just two short years in the wilderness, the Israelites had forgotten that they were enslaved for more than four hundred years, when God delivered and saved them for a purpose.

Turn your complaints into praise. Consider praying instead of murmuring. Know that your wilderness experiences are moments to praise and thank God for everything He has provided in your life. By faith, ask God to provide for your needs and quietly wait for God's answer. When we take our concerns to God, He hears us and does something about it. Do not lose sight of God's hand in your life by focusing your attention on things that are not important. Allow God's blessings to lead your life, as you live each moment with a grateful heart.

2. Moses Complains (11:10–15)

God's servant, Moses, did his best for the good of the people. But when Moses heard the people complaining, he could not help but become agitated by their behavior. After all, God had blessed the nation by delivering them from slavery, directing them through the wilderness with a cloud by day and pillar of fire by night, and providing them with daily food from heaven. How could the people be so ungrateful? What more could they want?

Moses did the only thing he knew how to do; he took his concerns to God. Moses knew he was God's man and his divine commission obligated him to intercede on behalf of the Israelites. But he was so overwhelmed by the people's complaints that he, himself, began to grumble and complain so much so that he said he would rather God kill him than make him continue to deal with the ungrateful ramblings of the people (v. 15).

It's amazing how easy it is for someone else to make our life a living hell and cause us to forget God's divine providence. Moses was God's hand-picked servant and yet he would rather die than continue to intercede on behalf of an ungrateful people. During their time in desert, the Children of Israel had witnessed numerous miracles firsthand. Yet they readily joined the "mixt multitude" in complaining when things got a little rough. How about you?

Rebellion against God is a serious offense.

Because of their ungratefulness, the generation of Israelites that rebelled against God never got to see the Promised Land; they died in the wilderness. The Bible tells us that when we are saved, we are granted full access to all the valuable resources God has to offer. God lavishes His resources on us "according to the riches of his grace" (Ephesians. 1:7). As believers, it is our job to appreciate the good things God has provided and continually give Him praise for our many blessings.

Search the Scriptures

1. Why was God displeased with the Israelites (Numbers 11:1)?

2. How did God respond to the Israelites (v. 1)?

3. When God sent the fire, what did the people do (v. 2)?

4. Why did they name the place Taberah, and what does it mean (v. 3)?

5. Why was Moses displeased (v. 10)?

6. Who was this "mixt multitude" that following the Israelites out of Egypt (vv. 10–15)?

Discuss the Meaning

1. In the opening verses of Numbers 11, we read that the Israelites complained often. They forgot that God delivered them out of the hands of their oppressors. They had forgotten the numerous things God had done to provide for them and keep them during their wilderness journey. In many ways, we are no different from the Israelites. God blesses us each day, yet we complain about things we don't have or think we deserve to have. We become frustrated when life doesn't proceed as we have planned, and constantly grumble and complain. Discuss what it means to trust in God's provision, even when you feel like God has abandoned your cause.

2. The fact that the fire of God is sometimes harsh offers us insight into the severity with which God treats sin. Discuss a time in your life when you felt the fire of God. How did you react during this time of pressure? Did you gripe or complain or did you pray and wait on God's response?

3. The discontent of the "mixt multitude" (v. 4) greatly influenced the Israelites' attitude. Likewise, the Israelites' complaining affected Moses' attitude. What effect do other people's negative attitudes or complaining have on your behavior? Do you join in and start to complain as well? Or do you offer words of encouragement and gratitude?

Lesson in Our Society

Ours is a society of complainers. With very little effort, just about everyone can find something to complain about every day: the traffic is bad, the schools are horrible, gas prices are high, the crime rate is up. The list is endless. The Bible says that God is displeased when we grumble and complain.

First, because it reflects ingratitude, we must recognize that complaining is a sin.

Second, adopt a positive attitude. Things happen: the train made you late for work; your husband forgot to pay the light bill and now the lights are cut off; your son got into a fight at school and is suspended for three days. While these are frustrating things, our frustration is not final.

Finally, pray for change. Begin to pray that grumbling and complaining among your family, your church, your community, your neighborhood, and your workplace be replaced with words of encouragement and thanksgiving.

Make It Happen

The reality is that God does not change; He is faithful, omnipotent, omnipresent, and immutable. Do you find yourself complaining about situations instead of focusing on God? Do you need to recommit to following God faithfully? Ask God to forgive your complaining and negativity. Make a decision to focus on God, stop complaining, and begin to pray to God, who is able to answer your cries for help, according to His plans for your life.

Follow the Spirit

What God wants me to do:

____

____

Remember Your Thoughts

Special insights I have learned:

____

____

More Light on the Text

Numbers 11:1–6, 10–15

1 And when the people complained, it displeased the LORD: and the LORD heard it; and his anger was kindled; and the fire of the LORD burnt among them, and consumed them that were in the uttermost parts of the camp.

The Children of Israel were on the march. They left the Sinai and were moving steadily toward the Promised Land. There was a sense of unity and purpose as they progressed forward. Then after a short sojourn in the desert, they began to complain. The Hebrew word *'anan* (**aw-NAN**) refers to murmuring and complaining. It helps us see a consistent attitude of ingratitude on display. People complain when they are uncomfortable, and nothing makes people more uncomfortable than not having the basic needs of food, clothing, or shelter met. Up to this point in their journey, God had been sufficient to meet the needs of His chosen people. Now, however, and for the first time, the people complained that God was insufficient to meet their needs. So because they were uncomfortable, instead of glorifying God, they grumbled.

In response to the complaints of the multitude, God became angry. His anger was displayed by fire that burned only at the outer edges of the encampment. This display of holy anger was sufficient. The people got the message and sought out Moses, whom they asked to intercede with God on their behalf. Perhaps a little discomfort was better than death.

2 And the people cried unto Moses; and when Moses prayed unto the LORD, the fire was quenched. 3 And he called the name of the place Taberah: because the fire of the LORD burnt among them.

What Moses said to God is not reported. Perhaps he simply reminded God that the Children of Israel had been in captivity for a long time and were only now learning how to trust and follow the living God. Certainly, he appealed to God to be merciful to the people, especially because they were now terrified and fearful for their lives. God listened to what Moses had to say and stayed His anger. The fires were quenched, (Heb. *shaqa'*, **shaw-KAH,** which means "to sink down, subside") and the people were saved. As a result the place was named Taberah in remembrance of God's fiery response to ingratitude. The episode helped the emerging nation understand that Moses truly was God's anointed. His voice was heard when he prayed. The people also learned for the first time, if He deemed it necessary, God would punish them. Complaining was not the way to retain God's favor and blessing. But God responded favorably to the prayer of a righteous man.

4 And the mixt multitude that was among them fell a lusting: and the children of Israel also wept again, and said, Who shall give us flesh to eat? 5 We remember the fish, which we did eat in Egypt freely; the cucumbers, and the melons, and the leeks, and the onions, and the garlick:

The sun scorched the desert by day and its absence chilled the desert by night. It was not a hospitable environment. Water was in short supply and the food God had provided was boring. Manna was no longer a sweet, but rather a routine meal. Before long, some of the people, who were not descendents of Abraham, Isaac, or Jacob, but who had simply joined themselves to the Israelites as they left Egypt, began to want the pleasures and comforts of the life they had left behind. The "mixt multitude that was among them" was not quiet about their "lusting" (Heb. *ta'avah*, **TA-av-ah**) for the good life in Egypt. They now had a strong desire and intense longing for their old life. Their complaints soon infected the Children of Israel, who also began to want the more "pleasurable" conditions of Egypt. They wanted to eat meat or fish and anything other than manna. In their wanting, however, the Children of Israel distorted the memories of their reality in Egypt. Their description of their diet gives the impression that they were eating like those who were not slaves. In reality, in Egypt they were a captive people in bondage. In Egypt, they were slaves.

6 But now our soul is dried away: there is nothing at all, beside this manna, before our eyes.

For a year, God had been providing a miraculous substance for food for the multitude, but now they were tired of it. They refer to their souls (Heb. *nephesh*, **NEH-fesh**—in this context "soul" refers to life or to one's self), their very lives as dried away, (Heb. *yabesh*, **yaw-BASHE**). Day after day, God had provided nothing but the same dull substance to eat. The Children of Israel didn't even know what the substance was; they only knew that they were sick of it. There is something about human nature that craves variety.

11:10 Then Moses heard the people weep throughout their families, every man in the door of his tent: and the anger of the LORD was kindled greatly; Moses also was displeased.

The joy that the crowd had known during their trek out of Egypt was gone. No longer were the people remembering the strong hand with which God had delivered them from slavery. They had turned their focus inward and away from God. As a result, they stood at the door of their tents and tearfully lamented (Heb. *bakah,* **baw-kaw'**—"to cry, bewail, shed tears") their present state. Their ingratitude angered God once more and this time angered Moses as well. A crisis had arisen almost as quickly as the previous circumstance of ingratitude, and the tension was higher than before.

11 And Moses said unto the LORD, Wherefore
hast thou afflicted thy servant? and wherefore have
I not found favour in thy sight, that thou layest the
burden of all this people upon me? 12 Have I conceived
all this people? have I begotten them, that thou
shouldest say unto me, Carry them in thy bosom, as
a nursing father beareth the sucking child, unto the
land which thou swarest unto their fathers?

In his anger, Moses prayed. He wanted to know what he had done that would cause God to put the burden of millions of ungrateful, complaining people on him. Moses had learned to trust God to be sufficient to meet every need, but the people had gotten on his nerves and he had grown tired of them. Moses indicated that he felt afflicted (Heb. *ra'a',* **raw-AH**). In this context, it connotes the idea of being injured by having to contend with an ungrateful group of people. It is important to remember here that Moses was dealing with a nation on the move; this was not merely the grumbling of a few hundred people. He was dealing with thousands of people grumbling against him and God.

Moses did not ask God to give them more variety in their diet, something God probably would have done had He been asked. Rather, Moses began to follow the pattern of the people and complain about his situation. Moses' complaint was not one of ingratitude. His complaint was one of frustration. He had grown to love some of the men that he had seen standing in the door of their tents crying, and there was absolutely nothing that Moses could do to resolve their sadness. Moses' sense of affliction was tied to his helplessness as much as his frustration with the constant grumbling of the people.

13 Whence should I have flesh to give unto all
this people? for they weep unto me, saying, Give us
flesh, that we may eat. 14 I am not able to bear all
this people alone, because it is too heavy for me. 15
And if thou deal thus with me, kill me, I pray thee,
out of hand, if I have found favour in thy sight; and
let me not see my wretchedness.

Moses had been God's instrument for doing the miraculous to get Pharaoh to release the Children of Israel from their captivity. He had been used to work the miraculous to deliver them across the Red Sea, but now he was frustrated with the people and there was no thought of miracles. He had not asked God for anything at this point; he just wanted to complain. The lack of support and gratitude from the masses had caused Moses, the leader, to lament his position. Rather than interceding on behalf of the people, Moses looked inward and complained. His complaint was one that reflected a sense of tremendous inadequacy. He knew that he could provide nothing for the people, and the burden of their concerns made him focus more on venting his frustration than seeking after God's tremendous ability to provide.

Sources:

Packer, J. I., Merrill C. Tenney, and William White. *Nelson's Illustrated Encyclopedia of Bible Facts.* Nashville: Thomas Nelson Publishers, 1995.

Vine, W.E. *Vines Complete Expository Dictionary of Old and New Testament Words.* Edited by Merrill F. Unger and William White Jr. Nashville: Thomas Nelson Publishers, 1996.

Daily Bible Readings

M: Give Heed to My Cry
Psalm 142
T: A Test of Obedience
Exodus 16:1–12
W: Living Bread
John 6:41–51
T: Complaining and Turning Back
John 6:60–68
F: An Example to Instruct Us
1 Corinthians 10:1–11
S: Faith, Love, and Mercy
Jude 1:14–23
S: Complaining About Hardships
Numbers 11:1–6, 10–15

TEACHING TIPS

August 9

Bible Study Guide 10

1. Words You Should Know

A. Murmured (Numbers 14:2) *luwn* (Heb.)—To complain or to grumble.

B. Prey (v. 3) *baz* (Heb.)—Spoil or booty.

C. Congregation (v. 5) *'edah'* (Heb.)—A company, assembly, multitude of people.

D. Good (v. 7) *towb* (Heb.)—Best, precious, fine, wealth, prosperity, or excellence of its kind.

E. Rebel (v. 9) *marad* (Heb.)—To revolt or disobey authority.

2. Teacher Preparation

Unifying Principle—Dissatisfaction Leads to Rebellion. When dissatisfaction swells, people may rebel against their leaders and benefactors. What leads people to rebel against leadership and authority? The deprivation of the Israelites and the threats of destruction at the hands of others led the Israelites to seek new leadership and a return to Egypt, the place of their slavery.

A. Prepare for the lesson by studying and prayerfully meditating on the Devotional Readings and the Bible Background.

B. Next study the Focal Verses, paying special attention to the Keep in Mind verse.

C. Read the More Light on the Text, and complete lesson 10 in the *Precepts For Living*® *Personal Study Guide.*

3. Starting the Lesson

A. Begin the lesson in prayer, including the AIM for Change in your prayer.

B. Explain the word "rebel." Remind the class that the Israelites had a history of rejecting and not believing God's promises for their life.

4. Getting into the Lesson

A. Read the AIM for Change to the class, and have volunteers read the Focal Verses. Discuss.

B. Ask a volunteer to read the In Focus story. Then ask the class to consider the statement at the end.

C. Ask volunteers to comment on the Israelites' desire to return to Egypt.

5. Relating the Lesson to Life

A. Read The People, Places, and Times section.

B. Initiate an open discussion by posing the following questions: (1) How many times did you subtly complain today? (2) At this time of complaining, how many times did you encourage or pray for someone?

C. Read the Lesson in Our Society. Discuss.

6. Arousing Action

A. Review the Make It Happen section. Ask the class to share things they have created to inspire them as well as others. Encourage the class to create visual images that remind them of God's love, peace, and blessing. Give each class member a card with this paraphrase of Philippians 4:13— "We can do all things through Christ who strengthens us." Remind the class that, through Christ Jesus, we can remove the complaining from our life.

B. At the end of the lesson, encourage the class to read and meditate on the Daily Bible Readings. Remind the class that they will encourage and motivate them to continue to study the lesson throughout the week.

Worship Guide

For the Superintendent or Teacher
Theme: People Rebel
Theme Song: "Speak to Me"
Devotional Reading: Psalm 78:5–17
Prayer

PEOPLE REBEL

Bible Background • NUMBERS 14:1–25
Printed Text • NUMBERS 14:1–12 Devotional Reading • PSALM 78:5–17

AIM for Change

By the end of the lesson we will:
LEARN about the Israelites' rebellion against Moses and God in the wilderness;
IDENTIFY ways that complaining can lead to rebellion; and
CONFRONT our own anger and find ways to deal responsibly with it.

Keep in Mind

"And wherefore hath the LORD brought us unto this land, to fall by the sword, that our wives and our children should be a prey? were it not better for us to return into Egypt?" (Numbers 14:3).

Focal Verses

KJV **Numbers 14:1** And all the congregation lifted up their voice, and cried; and the people wept that night.

2 And all the children of Israel murmured against Moses and against Aaron: and the whole congregation said unto them, Would God that we had died in the land of Egypt! or would God we had died in this wilderness!

3 And wherefore hath the LORD brought us unto this land, to fall by the sword, that our wives and our children should be a prey? were it not better for us to return into Egypt?

4 And they said one to another, Let us make a captain, and let us return into Egypt.

5 Then Moses and Aaron fell on their faces before all the assembly of the congregation of the children of Israel.

6 And Joshua the son of Nun, and Caleb the son of Jephunneh, which were of them that searched the land, rent their clothes:

7 And they spake unto all the company of the children of Israel, saying, The land, which we passed through to search it, is an exceeding good land.

8 If the LORD delight in us, then he will bring us into this land, and give it us; a land which floweth with milk and honey.

9 Only rebel not ye against the LORD, neither fear ye the people of the land; for they are bread for us: their defence is departed from them, and the LORD is with us: fear them not.

10 But all the congregation bade stone them with stones. And the glory of the LORD appeared in the tabernacle of the congregation before all the children of Israel?

NLT **Numbers 14:1** Then the whole community began weeping aloud, and they cried all night.

2 Their voices rose in a great chorus of protest against Moses and Aaron. "If only we had died in Egypt, or even here in the wilderness!" they complained.

3 "Why is the LORD taking us to this country only to have us die in battle? Our wives and our little ones will be carried off as plunder! Wouldn't it be better for us to return to Egypt?"

4 Then they plotted among themselves, "Let's choose a new leader and go back to Egypt!"

5 Then Moses and Aaron fell face down on the ground before the whole community of Israel.

6 Two of the men who had explored the land, Joshua son of Nun and Caleb son of Jephunneh, tore their clothing.

7 They said to all the people of Israel, "The land we traveled through and explored is a wonderful land!

8 And if the LORD is pleased with us, he will bring us safely into that land and give it to us. It is a rich land flowing with milk and honey.

9 Do not rebel against the LORD, and don't be afraid of the people of the land. They are only helpless prey to us! They have no protection, but the LORD is with us! Don't be afraid of them!"

10 But the whole community began to talk about stoning Joshua and Caleb. Then the glorious presence of the LORD appeared to all the Israelites at the Tabernacle.

11 And the LORD said to Moses, "How long will these people treat me with contempt? Will they never believe me, even after all the miraculous signs

11 And the LORD said unto Moses, How long will this people provoke me? and how long will it be ere they believe me, for all the signs which I have shewed among them?

12 I will smite them with the pestilence, and disinherit them, and will make of thee a greater nation and mightier than they.

I have done among them?

12 I will disown them and destroy them with a plague. Then I will make you into a nation greater and mightier than they are!"

In Focus

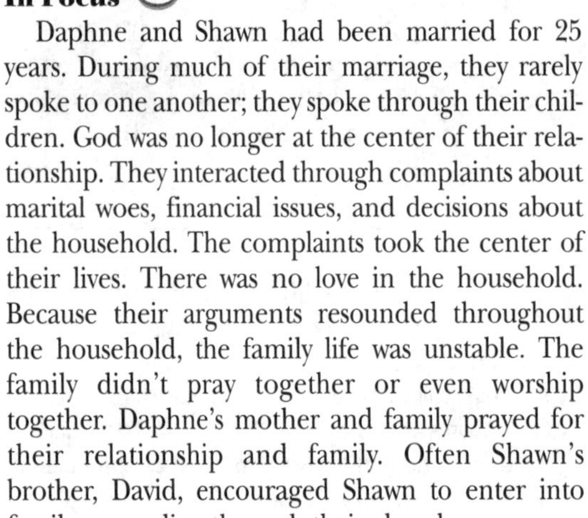

Daphne and Shawn had been married for 25 years. During much of their marriage, they rarely spoke to one another; they spoke through their children. God was no longer at the center of their relationship. They interacted through complaints about marital woes, financial issues, and decisions about the household. The complaints took the center of their lives. There was no love in the household. Because their arguments resounded throughout the household, the family life was unstable. The family didn't pray together or even worship together. Daphne's mother and family prayed for their relationship and family. Often Shawn's brother, David, encouraged Shawn to enter into family counseling through their church.

Shawn sadly responded, "When we married, I believed that Daphne was an answer to my prayers. Now I wish that I had never met her, even more that I had never married her. I'm miserable! Because everything has changed, counseling is not an option."

As he touched Shawn's hand and humbly kneeled to pray, David took another step to help Shawn.

When Shawn arrived home, Daphne was at the door with a notice of foreclosure on their home. Daphne threw the paper at Shawn as she said, "I'm leaving! I do not want to juggle bills anymore!"

As tears ran down his face, Shawn reached out to Daphne. He said, "Let's pray."

Daphne began to cry as she said, "I'm tired of struggling and arguing. We need spiritual counseling. We need help!"

Many times we become so angry that we cannot compromise or seek God's direction. Instead of taking responsibility for our current condition, as we humbly seek a resolution from God, we want to run away. However, today's lesson tells us that God does not want us to rebel or run away from our problems. He wants us to run to Him.

The People, Places, and Times

Date. The spies returned from investigating Canaan with a discouraging report. It was a magnificent land full of people, who were too strong for the Israelites to defeat without help from Almighty God. Two years earlier, the Israelites were slaves in Egypt This was their first approach to the Promised Land. Miriam and Aaron complained to Moses because he had married an Ethiopian woman, but the underlying issue was Moses' position. Because they were jealous of his position and influence, they complained about Moses' wife.

Joshua. He was one of the 12 spies sent to investigate Canaan. Joshua belonged to the tribe of Ephraim. He was the son of Nun and returned with a positive minority report about the land they would enter. His Christian badge of honor was that he was faithful to God; he was God's warrior and leader.

Caleb. He was one of the 12 spies sent to investigate Canaan. Caleb belonged to the tribe of Judah. He was the son of Jephunneh and returned with a positive minority report about the Promised Land.

Kadesh Barnea. When the people left Mount Sinai, they traveled directly to Kadesh Barnea, which was 150 miles north of Sinai and about 50 miles south of Beersheba. It was between the Wildeness of Zin and the Wilderness of Paran. Before entering the Promised Land, the Israelites remained at this location for about 38 years.

Source:

Walton, John H, Victor H. Matthews, and Mark W. Chavalas. *The IVP Bible Background Commentary: Old Testament.* Downers Grove, Ill.: InterVarsity Press, 2000.

Background

God directed Moses to send 12 men into the land of Canaan, which God had already promised to give them. They were in Kadesh Barnea, Moses' base camp, which was the southern gateway to Canaan.

Moses planned to take a straight path from Mount Sinai to Canaan. Earlier a census had been taken to determine the number of men able to fight. In addition, the people were set apart or sanctified for God. Moses' directions from God prepared the people physically and spiritually.

The scouts explored the land between the Jordan River and the Mediterranean, which was a 350-mile length. The scouts saw the Anakites, the descendants of Anak, who were considered giants. They were seven to nine feet tall. They saw a land that "floweth with milk and honey" (Numbers 13:27). The phrase evoked an image of wonderful pastoral lands. The abundant blessings of the land were overshadowed by the negative report that described giants, who were vast in numbers. This created fear among the Israelites, who complained about entering the Promised Land. Based upon the negative report, the Israelites wanted to rebel and return to Egypt.

Source:

Life Application Study Bible (King James Version). Wheaton, Ill.: Tyndale House Publishers, Inc., 1996.

Walton, John H, Victor H. Matthews, and Mark W. Chavalas. *The IVP Bible Background Commentary: Old Testament.* Downers Grove, Ill.: InterVarsity Press, 2000.

At-A-Glance

1. The People Speak Out in Rebellion (Numbers 14:1–4)
2. Joshua and Caleb Speak (vv. 5–10)
3. The Lord Speaks to Moses (vv. 11–12)

In Depth

1. The People Speak Out in Rebellion (Numbers 14:1–4)

After the 12 spies gave their reports about Canaan, the Israelites did not want to enter. The Israelites responded with mutiny and rebellion against God. Ten spies said they should not enter, while two spies encouraged them to receive God's blessings for their nation. The people listened to the 10 spies, who justified their desire to return to Egypt. Their response was a rebellion against God's instructions. The people complained and murmured against God and Moses. They "wept all night" (Numbers 11:1). Everyone complained, as their emotions had taken over. The negative report, given by the 10 spies, encouraged the complaints of the Israelites.

As they imagined their desperate condition, the people fretted, which gave credit to the spies instead of the Word of God. The people cried as though the enemy had already defeated them. They cried with no justification of the report or faith in their Provider.

When we do not trust God, our punishment is that we are constantly angered and irritated with ourselves and our situation. We are vexed due to distrust and lack of faith in God. As discontent spread through the entire unthinking, rebelling camp, the complaints grew like a fire. The previous months of pleasure and pleasant living, due to God's protection, were dismissed as the Israelites wished they had died in Egypt. Because they feared they would be dying soon, they wished they were already dead.

The Israelites looked forward with despair, without realizing that God did not save them from Pharaoh to die at the hands of the Canaanites. The Israelites responded to God's love with an audacity that God led them into a snare of death and destruction.

When we complain, we promote ill thoughts of God, because we promote belief that God does not desire the best for our life. However, God promotes "thoughts of peace and not of evil" (Jeremiah 29:11). When we complain, we lose any focus on God, and our complaining leads to rebellion. In our rebellion, because we live outside of God's direction and will, we enter into our own ruin.

The rebellion against Moses and God was a sin of disbelief, due to a lack of faith. Because God severely punishes our sins, rebellion against God is serious. As we subtly complain, our rebellion and sin begin and grow to an outward expression of rebellion and an attitude of anger. Are you subtly complaining through criticizing and grumbling? It is easy to find something to complain and grumble about, but make an effort to focus on the blessings of God in your life. Deal with your complaints and seek God's direction for your life. Make a choice to confront your anger and deal with it responsibly. We may subtly complain, but rebellion, which is sin, is a form of apostasy—it takes us away from the ways of God.

2. Joshua and Caleb Speak (vv. 5–10)

Through the clamorous cries of the Israelites, Moses and Aaron humbly prayed to God. The warning of God's servants was not heeded, so their blood was upon their own heads. The people murmured against Moses, who prayed to God on their behalf. As the people were throwing away their own mercies from God, Moses and Aaron prayed. As the complaints of the people continued to incite clamor and rebellion, Moses prayed that the people would not ruin themselves.

When we complain and rebel, we sin against God. The result is our own ruin, until we reconcile ourselves to God.

In response to the sins of the people and in dread of the wrath of God, which was ready to befall them, Joshua and Caleb "rent their clothes" (v. 6). As they assured the indignant Israelites of the blessings in the land they surveyed, they spoke with authority. The land would not engulf them, as the majority had reported, because Israel had the advantage. The Israelites did not confront their anger and fear of the land that awaited them. If the Israelites had confronted their fears, they would have realized that, through their own disbelief and sin, they had provoked God to leave them. The Israelites needed faith to enter the Promised Land. Joshua and Caleb saw the abundance of the land. It was a "good land" (v. 8) worth entering. They believed that they should take what God had promised them. Due to their lack of trust in God, the Israelites limited the abilities of God. Consider your relationship with God. Do you complain when something bad happens or do you pray to God? When we make a bad decision, we become angry and complain. When we seek God's direction for our life, as we give God control, we give up our control. When we are afraid of the future, we should pray to God for strength and direction. The Israelites expressed complaints and anger about their status and longed to return to Egypt. Due to their fears, they did not trust God and move forward into their blessing. As believers and as we seek God's direction, we must give all our concerns, fears, and anger to God.

Joshua and Caleb were distressed that the Israelites wanted to return to Egypt. The Israelites were not in danger from the Canaanites; but they were in danger from their own discontents, as they rebelled against God. Joshua and Caleb encouraged the Israelites to trust that God would bring them into the Promised Land. The Israelites responded in anger and distrust of God's leaders, who desired to give them good counsel. The complaints led to an enraged multitude that desired to stone God's servants. The Israelites were not reasonable and their anger was out of control.

Have you found yourself emotionally out of control? Did you turn to God for direction and counsel, or continue to be angry?

3. The Lord Speaks to Moses (vv. 10–12)

The glory of God appeared in response to the complaints that led to the sins of God's children. God passed His blessings to Israel, as well as His displeasure with Israel, through His servant Moses. Because they rejected God by their disbelief, when the Israelites complained, they provoked God. He kept an account of the amount of time that the Israelites, God's children, persisted in their provocations. Because the Israelites had experienced God's power and goodness, but rebelled against their provider, God was angry!

In anger, God desired to blot out the Israelites and disinherit them. Because God would preserve His covenant through the family of Moses, the blessings from God's covenant would not end with the blotted-out nation. Moses interceded on behalf of the Israelites. Prayer was Moses' response to the state of rebellion amongst the Israelites.

When we are unable to pray for ourselves, we are blessed with believers who intercede on our behalf. When we pray for wisdom and understanding, God will direct us if we are willing to hear from Him.

Moses, Aaron, Joshua, and Caleb, in response to God's mercy and promises, wept for the sins of the people. Moses prayed that the Israelites would reconcile to God and take responsibility for their rebellion. The glory of God appeared to save His faithful servants (Moses, Aaron, Joshua, and Caleb) from the Israelites, who wanted to stone them. The Israelites were outrageously angered; they would not hear nor believe the truth. Their unbelief provoked God. The glory of God is His majesty, beauty, and wonder. It is the ultimate display of who God is, it is His overwhelming presence. God told Moses that He would reject the entire nation of Israel. He would create a nation out of Moses. He would begin a new nation through Moses. God was angered that His children did not believe, after all the signs and promises, that He gave them.

Has God given a direction to your life that you do not believe? Because you depend on the physical versus the spiritual, have you dismissed His promises? If your disbelief has led to anger and rebellion, return to God and take responsibly for your actions. Ask God to forgive you and direct your life, as you humbly and obediently follow God. As believers, we must live by faith and our actions should reveal our faith. When we complain and our complaints reveal our wavering faith, we diminish our relationship with God. Our faith is diminished as a subtle complaint grows into anger, which does not reflect our trust and security that God is our provider. As believers, we must confront our disbelief and distrust and respond in love, not anger, because nothing is "impossible with God" (Luke 18:27).

Recognize that anger is a danger sign and we must deal with it responsibly. The Israelites' anger against the two faithful spies led to their desire to stone them. They were out of control. When we become angry, we must consider thought control, as we cease the thoughts that lead to our verbal complaints. With God we can control our attitude. We are accountable to God. God is pleased when we reflect an attitude of love. Would God be pleased with your attitude?

Source:

Life Application Study Bible (King James Version). Wheaton, IL: Tyndale House, 1996.

Search the Scriptures

1. Why did the Israelites cry (Numbers 14:1)?

2. What did the Israelites believe would happen to them in the unfamiliar land (v. 3)?

3. In their sense of despair and rebellion, what the Israelites conspire to do (v. 4)?

4. Why did Joshua and Caleb believe that they should enter the land (v. 8)?

Discuss the Meaning

1. Rebellion is a serious matter to God. When we rebel, we reject God's plan through His Word. The Israelites reacted emotionally to the report of the majority. They forgot that God had saved them from enslavement in Egypt, divided the Red Sea so they could pass, and provided food from heaven. God was faithful to the Israelites, who were not faithful to Him. Rebellion is a choice. Ask the class to describe the choices we can make that reveal God in our attitudes and actions.

2. Numbers 14:5 describes Moses and Aaron falling "on their faces"; they prayed for the rebellious people. When the Israelites disobeyed God, prayer was the response. They interceded on behalf of the Israelites, who did not realize that they needed to pray. Encourage the class to know that in the midst of anger, joy, death, and life, prayer is the correct response.

Lesson in Our Society

Consider volunteering at your local literacy organization. Volunteer to be a tutor and inspire your community by encouraging one life at a time. Allow God to help you make a difference in a person's future and family by teaching them to read. At the end of a tutoring session, read a simple Scripture and give that Scripture to the person on a postcard.

Make It Happen

Use a posterboard to make a visual display of God's blessings and promises for His children, or use postcards to inspire you to trust God's Word. Include God's response, when we complain and murmur. Refer to Philippians 2:12–18, which instructs believers to stay away from murmuring and complaining. Place the board and/or postcards in a place you see every day, to begin your day focused on God's blessings and promises.

Follow the Spirit

What God wants me to do:

____

____

Remember Your Thoughts

Special insights I have learned:

____

____

More Light on the Text

Numbers 14:1–12

1 And all the congregation lifted up their voice, and cried; and the people wept that night.

Nothing breaks a parent's heart like seeing a child cry, unless those tears are the fruit of selfish desires and ingratitude. The tears of the ungrateful often get an angry response. God had delivered the children of the promise to the edge of the Promised Land. Spies had been sent in and brought back a mixed report. The majority of the spies held that the inhabitants of the land were too formidable to be conquered and any attempt to do so would result in the destruction of the people and their children. Only two spies offered that God would be sufficient to deliver the land into the hands of the Children of Israel. The people believed the report from the majority of the spies and wept (Heb. *bakah*, **baw-KAW**). Their loud wailing was an expression of sadness and lament. They were wondering "Why does God continue to make it so hard?" Their perspective was based on the report of the spies, not on the promises of the one true God.

2 And all the children of Israel murmured against Moses and against Aaron: and the whole congregation said unto them, Would God that we had died in the land of Egypt! or would God we had died in this wilderness! 3 And wherefore hath the LORD brought us unto this land, to fall by the sword, that our wives and our children should be a prey? were it not better for us to return into Egypt?

All the hardships the people had endured for the previous two years piled on top of each other. The people embraced the report from the majority of the spies and turned on Moses and Aaron, God's appointed leaders. Nothing of the excitement and exuberance that had greeted the departure from Egypt remained, and now they just wanted to die. Now they feared that they would be prey (Heb. *baz*, **baz**). They envisioned themselves being carted off as the spoils of a losing war. They concluded that God had handed them a raw deal, by bringing them to the edge of the Promised Land only to ultimately be destroyed by the giants in the land.

Their earlier lust for the meat, fruit, and vegetables of Egypt had helped to dull the memories of the harsh conditions of the enslavement of the Children of Israel in that land. God had greeted their earlier complaints with fire and holy wrath, so the people now rebelled against God's appointed authority. If God wasn't going to make the task of occupying the Promised Land easy, then they would take matters into their own hands and go back to Egypt.

4 And they said one to another, Let us make a captain, and let us return into Egypt.

The rejection of the leadership of Moses and of God was complete. The Children of Israel no longer wanted anything to do with God's plan to deliver them to a Promised Land where they could be free. They decided among themselves to come up with an alternative plan. They appointed leaders to guide them back across the desert, and back into Egypt. The people were no longer complaining. They had a determined resolve to take their circumstances into their own hands and to do things their own way.

5 Then Moses and Aaron fell on their faces before all the assembly of the congregation of the children of Israel.

Both Moses and Aaron know that the actions of the people would not be pleasing to God. They fell on their faces in anticipation of what they felt God was about to do. Earlier complaining had resulted in fire and plague from God, and now in the face of outright rejection by the assembly, the prophets did not know how God would react. They only knew that it wouldn't be pleasant.

6 And Joshua the son of Nun, and Caleb the son of Jephunneh, which were of them that searched the land, rent their clothes: 7 And they spake unto all the company of the children of Israel, saying, The land, which we passed through to search it, is an exceeding good land.

As Moses and Aaron lay prostrate on the ground, Joshua and Caleb, the two spies who came back with a message of faithful anticipation that God would give the people the land, "rent" (Heb. *qara'*, **kaw-RAH,** which means "to tear into pieces") their clothes, stepped up, and addressed the people. Though they were the two spies who returned and gave the minority report concerning the Promised Land, Joshua's name was not mentioned until this time. This was probably because Joshua was second-in-command to Moses, and the company of people would have expected him to be in complete support of anything Moses communicated. Now he stood in support of Caleb and tried to help persuade the masses not to reject God and His appointed leaders. Though the journey had been difficult, they had not lost faith in God or His plan for Israel's future. They reminded the people that the land was truly a marvelous place.

8 If the LORD delight in us, then he will bring us into this land, and give it us; a land which floweth with milk and honey. 9 Only rebel not ye against the LORD, neither fear ye the people of the land; for they are bread for us: their defence is departed from them, and the LORD is with us: fear them not.

Clothes rent, Caleb and Joshua stood before the people and tried to make their case not to abandon God. Earlier, the people had seen a single branch of grapes, cut from a tree in the Promised Land, which required two men to carry back to the encampment. Caleb and Joshua did not refute the report of the other spies, but simply tried to remind the people that the God who had promised the land to them was sufficient to fulfill His word and deliver that land. They emphasized that if God delighted in His people, the land would be theirs. Thus they encouraged and warned the people not to rebel (Heb. *marad*, **maw-RAD,** which means "to be seditious") against God. They also indicated that, because God was with the people, the inhabitants of the land would be defenseless. It was almost as if Joshua and Caleb were reminding the people of the power of the same God who delivered them from Egypt. Yet the people to whom they spoke had already made up their minds not to listen.

10 But all the congregation bade stone them with stones. And the glory of the LORD appeared in the tabernacle of the congregation before all the children of Israel.

As Caleb and Joshua pleaded with the people to remember God, the crowd became more and more convinced that they wanted nothing to do with the things they were saying. As a response, they began to pick up stones in order to kill them. Stoning was a legitimate judicial punishment that an assembly had the authority to exact upon anyone they felt was guilty of a religious crime. The people did not believe that Caleb and Joshua were communicating the will of God to them. Rather, they felt they were false witnesses and worthy to be stoned. The congregation had allowed itself to become convinced that God was in favor of their desire to return to Egypt. The Children of Israel felt justified in their belief and actions until God's glory (Heb. *kabowd*, **kaw-BODE**) appeared before them and spoke to Moses.

11 And the LORD said unto Moses, How long will this people provoke me? and how long will it be ere they believe me, for all the signs which I have shewed among them? 12 I will smite them with the pestilence, and disinherit them, and will make of thee a greater nation and mightier than they.

God had had it. These people—the first generation out of Egypt—had been greedy, selfish, shortsighted, and ungrateful. In spite of all the promises God had made and the miracles He had performed on their behalf, they did not believe in Him. In fact, they believed themselves to be righteous and wanted to kill God's agents. They had provoked (Heb. *na'ats*, **naw-ATS**, which means "to spurn, despise, reject") God with unbelief and ingratitude. God determined that He was going to punish them severely and then disinherit them. God intended to destroy them, though Moses ultimately got God to relent. They would not go into the Promised Land. The Lord, then, helped Moses to understand that He had not forgotten His promise and would begin again with another group of people. This new group would share the faith of Moses, Aaron, Caleb, and Joshua and would be greater than the congregation standing before them.

Indeed, believers must learn to never provoke God with unbelief. He knows the way that we should take in life, and He is faithful, who promised to never leave or forsake us. He says, "When the poor and needy seek water, and there is none, and their tongue faileth for thirst, I the LORD will hear them, I the God of Israel will not forsake them. I will open rivers in high places, and fountains in the midst of the valleys: I will make the wilderness a pool of water, and the dry land springs of water" (Isaiah 41:17–18).

Sources:

Life Application Study Bible (New International Version). Wheaton, Ill.: Tyndale House Publishers, 1991.

Packer, J. I., Merrill C. Tenney, and William White. *Nelson's Illustrated Encyclopedia of Bible Facts*. Nashville: Thomas Nelson Publishers, 1995.

Unger, Merrill F. *The New Unger's Bible Dictionary*. Edited by R.K. Harrison. Chicago: Moody Press, 1988.

Daily Bible Readings

M: Rebelling Against God
Psalm 78:5–17

T: Reaping the Whirlwind
Hosea 8:1–10

W: An Offering for Transgression?
Micah 6:1–8

T: Mourning for Our Rebellion
Lamentations 1:16–21

F: Return to the Lord
Lamentations 3:39–50

S: A Compassionate God
Micah 7:14–20

S: Go Back to Egypt?
Numbers 14:1–12

TEACHING TIPS

August 16

Bible Study Guide 11

1. Words You Should Know

A. Chode (Numbers 20:3) *riyb* (Heb.)—To debate, plead, strive, to quarrel.

B. Smote (v. 11) *nakah* (Heb.)—To attack, beat, hit, strike.

C. Abundantly (v. 11) *rab* (Heb.)—Many, much, great, strong.

D. Sanctified (v. 13) *qadash* (Heb.)—To be set apart, consecrate, dedicate.

2. Teacher Preparation

Unifying Principle—Disregarding the Directive. Even great leaders may fail to heed higher authority. Why do people disregard authority? Moses disobeyed God because he did not trust God to provide for the people.

A. Pray for all the students in your class, asking God to open their eyes so they may see wondrous things from His law (Psalm 119:18).

B. Study and meditate on the Devotional Reading.

C. Get into the lesson by reading the Focal Verses, using at least three different translations of the passage.

D. Make notes that will help you give salient points to the class.

E. Carefully study the Lesson in Our Society and Make It Happen sections.

3. Starting the Lesson

A. Begin the lesson by asking one of your students to lead the class in prayer, remembering the AIM for Change.

B. Ask a volunteer to read the In Focus story aloud. Explain its relevance to today's AIM for Change.

C. Ask three volunteers to read the Focal Verses, according to the At-A-Glance outline. Discuss.

4. Getting into the Lesson

A. Read The People, Places, and Times as well as the Background section to help set the stage for today's lesson.

B. Have the students write down their thoughts in the Remember Your Thoughts section.

C. As you begin the discussion of the lesson, refer to the Search the Scriptures questions.

5. Relating the Lesson to Life

A. Toward the end of the lesson, spend time answering the questions in the Discuss the Meaning section.

B. Ask your students to share the seriousness of practicing holiness through obedience.

6. Arousing Action

A. Sum up the lesson with the Keep in Mind verse.

B. Ask the students to read it in unison, while contemplating how they can apply the verse to their everyday lives.

C. Challenge the students to follow through on the Make It Happen assignment.

D. Close the class with prayer.

Worship Guide

For the Superintendent or Teacher
Theme: Moses Disobeys
Theme Song: "Trust and Obey"
Devotional Reading: Psalm 95
Prayer

MOSES DISOBEYS

Bible Background • NUMBERS 20:1–13
Printed Text • NUMBERS 20:1–13 Devotional Reading • PSALM 95

AIM for Change

By the end of the lesson, we will:
EXAMINE the details of God's command and Moses' disobedience;
EXPLORE levels of authority and leadership and issues of obedience; and
COMMIT to support our church leaders in prayer.

Keep in Mind

"And the LORD spake unto Moses and Aaron, Because ye believed me not, to sanctify me in the eyes of the children of Israel, therefore ye shall not bring this congregation into the land which I have given them" (Numbers 20:12).

Focal Verses

KJV **Numbers 20:1** Then came the children of Israel, even the whole congregation, into the desert of Zin in the first month: and the people abode in Kadesh; and Miriam died there, and was buried there.

2 And there was no water for the congregation: and they gathered themselves together against Moses and against Aaron.

3 And the people chode with Moses, and spake, saying, Would God that we had died when our brethren died before the LORD!

4 And why have ye brought up the congregation of the LORD into this wilderness, that we and our cattle should die there?

5 And wherefore have ye made us to come up out of Egypt, to bring us in unto this evil place? it is no place of seed, or of figs, or of vines, or of pomegranates; neither is there any water to drink.

6 And Moses and Aaron went from the presence of the assembly unto the door of the tabernacle of the congregation, and they fell upon their faces: and the glory of the LORD appeared unto them.

7 And the LORD spake unto Moses, saying,

8 Take the rod, and gather thou the assembly together, thou, and Aaron thy brother, and speak ye unto the rock before their eyes; and it shall give forth his water, and thou shalt bring forth to them water out of the rock: so thou shalt give the congregation and their beasts drink.

9 And Moses took the rod from before the LORD, as he commanded him.

10 And Moses and Aaron gathered the congregation together before the rock, and he said unto

NLT **Numbers 20:1** In the first month of the year, the whole community of Israel arrived in the wilderness of Zin and camped at Kadesh. While they were there, Miriam died and was buried.

2 There was no water for the people to drink at that place, so they rebelled against Moses and Aaron.

3 The people blamed Moses and said, "If only we had died in the LORD's presence with our brothers!

4 Why have you brought the congregation of the LORD's people into this wilderness to die, along with all our livestock?

5 Why did you make us leave Egypt and bring us here to this terrible place? This land has no grain, no figs, no grapes, no pomegranates, and no water to drink!"

6 Moses and Aaron turned away from the people and went to the entrance of the Tabernacle, where they fell face down on the ground. Then the glorious presence of the LORD appeared to them,

7 and the LORD said to Moses,

8 "You and Aaron must take the staff and assemble the entire community. As the people watch, speak to the rock over there, and it will pour out its water. You will provide enough water from the rock to satisfy the whole community and their livestock."

9 So Moses did as he was told. He took the staff from the place where it was kept before the LORD.

10 Then he and Aaron summoned the people to come and gather at the rock. "Listen, you rebels!" he shouted. "Must we bring you water from this rock?"

them, Hear now, ye rebels; must we fetch you water out of this rock?

11 And Moses lifted up his hand, and with his rod he smote the rock twice: and the water came out abundantly, and the congregation drank, and their beasts also.

12 And the LORD spake unto Moses and Aaron, Because ye believed me not, to sanctify me in the eyes of the children of Israel, therefore ye shall not bring this congregation into the land which I have given them.

13 This is the water of Meribah; because the children of Israel strove with the LORD, and he was sanctified in them.

11 Then Moses raised his hand and struck the rock twice with the staff, and water gushed out. So the entire community and their livestock drank their fill.

12 But the LORD said to Moses and Aaron, "Because you did not trust me enough to demonstrate my holiness to the people of Israel, you will not lead them into the land I am giving them!"

13 This place was known as the waters of Meribah (which means "arguing") because there the people of Israel argued with the LORD, and there he demonstrated his holiness among them.

In Focus 

Bryant met Angie in New Progressive Church. They dated, married and had three beautiful children. Bryant accepted his calling in the ministry when his daughter, the youngest of the three, was 2 years old. He had become a husband, a father, and a minister.

Bryant, along with his wife, wanted to raise their children to reverence God. They realized that in order for their children to learn how to reverence God, first they had to be taught to respect them as parents. This was not an easy lesson to teach, and it is an ongoing lesson to learn for both the parents and the children.

One way the demonstration of this lesson was carried out was by the way the television is used in the home. Bryant Anthony, the oldest of the three children, Brandon Alphonso, and Bree Austrial were taught they couldn't watch just anything on television. It was easy to see to it that this rule was carried out when the children were younger. It became more difficult as the children grew older and were allowed to stay at home with no parental supervision.

The parents didn't always know whether or not the children would follow the rules in their absence. As with any parent and most situations, they hoped that the children would follow the rules and become trustworthy. Since children can't be watched at all times, there comes a time when you have to let them go and pray they will obey.

One day the children assumed they were home alone, because there was no evidence of a parent in sight. Dad had not made it home from work yet; however, Mom had come home early, before anyone else had arrived. The children came into the house, and as any other children probably would they went straight for the television. Mom listened quietly before announcing herself. Pleasingly, she was able to overhear them remind each other of what programs were prohibited by their parents.

God wants us to hear His laws and instructions. Then He wants us to obey them. It is not enough to just know to do right, but we have to go beyond that step and do what is right. God is holy and tells us to be holy; holiness is obedience.

In today's lesson, Moses was given specific instructions. He disobeyed God and was not allowed to enter the Promised Land (Canaan). Know that there are consequences to every action and that the wages of sin is death.

The People, Places, and Times

Miriam. She was the sister of Aaron and Moses, and the daughter of Amram and Jochebed. She is also one of the leaders sent by God to lead the Israelites. Moses married an Ethiopian woman and Miriam didn't like it, so she rebelled against Moses. She and Aaron spoke against Moses, and God heard them and rebuked them. God struck Miriam with leprosy. Moses prayed for her and she was quickly healed. She is not spoken of again until her death and burial at Kadesh.

Source:

Lockeyer Sr., Herbert, F.F. Bruce, and R.K. Harrison, eds. *The Illustrated Dictionary of the Bible.* Nashville: Thomas Nelson Publishers, 1986.

Background

Moses is one of the main characters in the book of Exodus as well as the book of Numbers. Numbers is actually a continuation of Exodus. In the book of Numbers, the Israelites are still encamped at Sinai. Throughout Numbers, we observe their wanderings through the wilderness of Sinai that continues for the next 40 years. Then they arrive at Moab, which is on the eastern side of the Jordan River. Despite all of the many challenges or obstacles the Children of Israel had to encounter, now they were ready to occupy the land—the land of Canaan, which God promised to them much earlier, through Abraham and his descendants.

Moses was leader to the Israelites, and just like with the older generation who died in the wilderness, the new generation pushed his patience to the limit with their murmuring and complaining. Finally his patience wore thin and he sinned. His hopes and dreams were shattered because of disobedience to a holy God. God told Moses that he would not lead the people into the Promised Land because of this disobedience. God had to punish Moses and the punishment was severe.

Source:

Lockeyer Sr., Herbert, F.F. Bruce, and R.K. Harrison, eds. *The Illustrated Dictionary of the Bible*. Nashville: Thomas Nelson Publishers, 1986.

At-A-Glance

1. The People Complain and Rebel (Numbers 20:1–5)
2. God Supplies Water (vv. 6–11)
3. God Announces Punishment (vv. 12–13)

In Depth

1. The People Complain and Rebel (Numbers 20: 1–5)

This text begins with the fortieth year after the exodus. Because of God's chosen people's disobedience, the desert journey had lasted for forty long years. Now, the new generation of Israelites was about ready to enter Canaan, the Promised Land. However, because of her rebellion against God, Miriam—Moses and Aaron's sister—would not enter. God punished Miriam for not believing Him and rebelling against Him and His servant, Moses. Consequently, because God deemed that she had to die for her transgression against Him, she could not reap the benefits of even seeing Canaan. The Bible teaches that the wages of sin is death. Therefore, she died and was buried in the sands of the desert wilderness.

How often does life cause us to want to complain? It is very easy to go back to what we know and are comfortable with. God is calling us to have faith in Him and not be satisfied with going back to what we feel brings us comfort. His Word cautions us about disbelief and rebellion against Him. This new generation of Israelites had taken on the true attributes of their parents. Their parents had complained and lacked trust in God knowing what was best for them. They walked right in their parents footsteps. They wanted to know where the food and water were. They let their desire or need for basic necessities, which God would provide, cause them to offend God.

God loved them and wanted what was best for them. They offended God and caused Him great pain, because He did love them. They did what their parents did and failed to realize that God would supply all their needs as they journeyed to the Promised Land.

The people rebelled against Moses and Aaron. Because there was no water to drink, they blamed Moses. They wished they had died with their brothers. They couldn't understand why Moses would bring them to this awful place. They could only focus on what they didn't have. They didn't have grain, nor figs, nor grapes, nor pomegranates, and especially no water to drink. Without water, they were assured they would die. "Why would Moses bring us all this way to die in the desert with animals?"

They argued with Moses and rebelled against him in the presence of God. They blamed Moses, because they felt this was all Moses' fault—he took them out of Egypt, where the land had so much. They felt they left a beautiful land, a land where there was no lack, a land where there was always enough, to come to a place that felt like death.

2. God Supplies Water (vv. 6–11)

Moses and Aaron heard the complaints of the people and turned away from them. They went to the entrance of the tabernacle and fell face-down on the ground. As God promised He would, He supplied their need. This was when the glorious presence of the Lord appeared to them. The Lord began to talk to Moses and Aaron. He began giving them specific directives. God had also heard the complaints of the people. He is a God who listens and answers prayer.

He told Moses that he and Aaron had to take the staff and gather the community together. He said as the people watch, *speak* to the rock and the rock will pour out its water. (There was a time when God instructed Moses to strike the rock, but this was not that time.) He told Moses that He would provide enough water from the rock to satisfy the whole community, and even enough water for the livestock. This was symbolic of Christ. Christ is our water; He is our living water. God promised there would be enough water to meet all their needs. Through Christ, God has met all of our needs.

At this point, Moses did as he was told. Moses took the staff from the place it had been kept, which was before the Lord. Then together, Aaron and Moses called for the people to come and gather at the rock.

Then Moses shouted to the people, seemingly in anger, "Must we bring you water from this rock?" He appeared to have been agitated by the rebellion of the people. He exploded. He sinned. He disobeyed God. Moses didn't honor God and show the people who God was. He didn't give God all the credit for what was being done for them. It seemed Moses had also forgotten that he was just an instrument in God's hands and not making all this happen himself. God will share His glory with no one. God is God and He alone is God.

Moses raised his hand with the staff in it and struck the rock twice. The water came gushing out. There was enough water for all the community to be satisfied and the animals, too. God had done His part, just as He promised.

God gave Moses and Aaron clear instructions as to how He wanted this directive to be carried out. However, by altering the instructions because of his anger, Moses put himself on the same level with God. He struck the rock instead of speaking to it.

He tried to share some of the credit for the water with God. He asked, "Must we bring water from this rock?" This was sin. He needed to let the people know that only God can supply the water that we need, which is living water. God supplies all of our needs and in this case, He supplied the water that was needed. God told Moses to speak to the rock. Remember that Jesus is referred to as the Rock, and this is all symbolic to point our eyes to Christ. Moses blew it; he had forgotten the real focus, which always should be on God. We can do nothing without Him. He is the one with all power to do all things, needing nothing or no one to assist Him in any way. God's work is all about Him.

3. God Announces Punishment (vv. 12–13)

God wanted His holiness to be known to the people. He was displeased with Moses and Aaron because they didn't trust Him enough to demonstrate His holiness to the people of Israel. The lack of trust is sin. The wages of sin is death. God was clear that, because they were disobedient, Moses and Aaron would not lead the people of Israel to the land He was giving them.

Moses had been with these people a long time. He was looking forward to seeing the Promised Land. However, because he lost his temper one time too many, he lost what he really wanted. It may seem to us that this was a harsh punishment for just losing his temper. We often make excuses for disobeying God. Some justify sin, by saying, "God knows my heart." The sad thing about that statement is the truth in it. God does know our heart. Genesis 6:5 says, "And God saw that the wickedness of man was great in the earth, and that every imagination of the thoughts of his heart was only evil continually."

The place where all this happened was known as Meribah, and it means "arguing." It was called Meribah, because this is where the people argued with the Lord. This is also where God demonstrated His holiness to the people.

Sources:

Lockeyer Sr., Herbert, F.F. Bruce, and R.K. Harrison, eds. *The Illustrated Dictionary of the Bible*. Nashville: Thomas Nelson Publishers, 1986.

Strong, James. Strong's Exhaustive Concordance of the Bible. Nashville: Thomas Nelson Publishers, Inc., 1990.

Search the Scriptures

1. Why did the people rebel against Moses and Aaron (Numbers 20:2)?

2. What did Moses and Aaron do before they went to the entrance of the tabernacle (v. 6)?

3. Why did the Lord say Moses and Aaron would not lead the people into the Promised Land (v. 12)?

Discuss the Meaning

1. What is our primary responsibility, now that we have come to the light of Christ?

2. As New Testament believers, what do we need to do to be holy in such a sinful world?

3. Share how Numbers 20:1–13 relates to our present situation, and the role church leaders play in the church's submission to God.

Lesson in Our Society

We live in a society where honoring God is not a priority. A lot of people go to church on a regular basis, religiously. Yet, if you look at our neighborhoods, attendance in church is not always noticeable. We have cameras to take pictures of the cars that disobey the stop lights and run red lights. We have to almost strip our clothes off as we try to board an airplane. As you leave the general store, there is usually someone to check your bags or some sort of metal detector to keep theft to a minimum. If honoring God was really a priority, would measures of enforcing the laws have to be carried out so aggressively?

God was and always is clear about His instructions. He unmistakably told Moses and Aaron "Because you did not trust me enough to demonstrate my holiness to the people of Israel, you will not lead them into the land I am giving them!" (Numbers 20:12). Could it be that we as a society do not honor God and passionately commit to obeying Him as we should? Could it be that we go to church (to the building), but we haven't become the church? Could it be that we do not realize the importance of obedience to a holy God? Even more sadly, could it be that we do not know our God?

Make It Happen

Moses was a leader to the Israelites; they depended on him to be a go-between for them and God. Moses listened and heard the instructions from God, but he only did part of what God said. Omission is just as much a sin as commission is. This week, be mindful of preparing your heart to hear God and obey Him fully. Remember, it is God who must be glorified. Be prepared to share your experiences next week.

Follow the Spirit

What God wants me to do:

____

____

Remember Your Thoughts

Special insights I have learned:

____

____

More Light on the Text

Numbers 20:1–13

1 Then came the children of Israel, even the whole congregation, into the desert of Zin in the first month: and the people abode in Kadesh; and Miriam died there, and was buried there.

The saga of God's chosen people, the Israelites, continues and we find that Moses' leading the new generation into the Promised Land has complications. Already, it had been 37 years since Israel's first spy mission into Canaan (Numbers 13–14). Now, 40 years after the Israelites left Egypt and 37 years of aimless wandering—after the old generation had died out in the Sinai wilderness (all but Aaron, Moses, Joshua, and Caleb)—it was time to go and possess the land. Today's lesson finds the whole congregation camped at Kadesh.

The Hebrew for the phrase "the whole congregation" is *'edah* (**ay-DAW**) and means "multitude, swam, gathering." Kadesh was the site of the first spy mission that was characterized by ten spies bringing back a bad report and two bringing back a good one. Of course, the people believed the negative report of the majority and proceeded to sin against God. The old generation rebelled and did not believe that the God who promises, is the God who will honor His own word. They do not believe that God will continue to be their provider. Therefore, their rebellion, which is sin, cost them their lives.

In today's lesson, the new wilderness generation is in the desert of Zin. This part of the desert is a tract of land between the Dead Sea and Arabah on the east, in which Kadesh Barnea was located. Since the old generation of murmurs and complainers was gone, Moses hoped that the new generation was ready to make a fresh start and obey their God. While they were there, Miriam (Moses and Aaron's sister) died and was buried.

2 And there was no water for the congregation: and they gathered themselves together against Moses and against Aaron.

Hoping for better days does not often bring better days or better behavior. Problems are known to bring out the best or worst in people. Because there was no water in this hot desert, this new congregation fell into murmuring and complaining as well. They voiced their complaints not to God, but to God's messengers, Moses and Aaron. In fact, the *New Living Translation* (NLT) tells us that "There was no water for the people to drink at that place, so they rebelled against Moses and Aaron." In other words, they blamed them for their plight.

3 And the people chode with Moses, and spake, saying, Would God that we had died when our brethren died before the LORD!

One would think that the new generation had learned something from their forefathers. However, they had not learned their lesson on God's intolerance of rebellion. Therefore, like their forefathers, they brought problems upon themselves. The text tells us that they "chode" with Moses. In Hebrew, "chode" is *riyb* (**reeb**), and it means, "to strive, to quarrel, to contend against." This new generation wanted to go over into the Promised Land, but they did not expect to go through anything or suffer before they got there. They wanted the land of "milk and honey" handed to them on a silver platter. Therefore, as their forefathers did in times of trouble, they demonstrated disobedience or lack of faith.

4 And why have ye brought up the congregation of the LORD into this wilderness, that we and our cattle should die there?

The congregation accused Moses of bringing them up into this wilderness to die. They did not see God's hand in their situation or remember His promises to their ancestors at all. Often when troubles come, people look for something or someone to blame. They do not look inward to their own shortcomings or sin. They look outward to see what or who they can attack; and given a chance, they seize the moment.

5 And wherefore have ye made us to come up out of Egypt, to bring us in unto this evil place? it is no place of seed, or of figs, or of vines, or of pomegranates; neither is there any water to drink.

Oftentimes in our lamenting or longing for the "good old days," we distort the true picture of what happened in those days. We magnify the good and forget the bad. We forget the suffering and problems. The new generation had forgotten the suffering that their forefathers had as slaves in Egypt. They forgot that their people had to make bricks without straw. Their focus was on what they did not have in the here and now. The phrase, "And wherefore have ye made us to come up" in the Hebrew is *'alah* (**aw-LAW**) and it translates, "to be led up, to be taken up into." In essence, the Israelites are asking Moses, "Why did you make us leave Egypt, where we had our basic needs met, and bring us here to this terrible place?" They noted that the wilderness where they are has no grain, figs, grapes, or pomegranates. Add to that, the place does not even have water for them and their cattle to drink.

6 And Moses and Aaron went from the presence of the assembly unto the door of the tabernacle of the congregation, and they fell upon their faces: and the glory of the LORD appeared unto them.

What do you do when all seems to go against you? What do you do when you are overwhelmed by life? Moses and Aaron knew that they needed Almighty God in this time of trouble. Therefore, when they saw and heard the discontentment of those thousands upon thousands of people, they went to their source; they went to God.

The phrase, "of the assembly" in Hebrew is *qahal* (**kaw-HAWL**) and means "congregation or organized body." To get their perspective and the help they needed, Moses and Aaron had to seek higher authority. Therefore, they turned away from the people, their problem, and turned to God—the problem solver. The phrase "and the glory" in the Hebrew is *kabowd* (**kaw-BODE**) and means "honor, dignity, reverence." In fact, they fell face-down on the ground. In other words, they reverenced God. They honored Him. Thus, before they asked God for anything, they first showed Him respect. They let God know that they recognized who He is. Subsequently, the Lord appeared unto them. They found themselves in the presence of an omnipotent (all-powerful), omniscient (all-knowing), and omnipresent (all-present) God.

7 And the LORD spake unto Moses, saying, 8 Take the rod, and gather thou the assembly together, thou, and Aaron thy brother, and speak ye unto the rock before their eyes; and it shall give forth his water, and thou shalt bring forth to them water out of the rock: so thou shalt give the congregation and their beasts drink.

When we go to an all-knowing God for help, He expects us to follow His directives—His edicts—His battle plan. If we have the strategies all figured out beforehand, why do we need Him? Why do we need to exercise our faith? Moses did not have a plan, but God did and He expected Moses to follow the blueprint. He told Moses to take the rod and speak to the rock. The word "rod" in Hebrew is *matteh* (**mat-TEH**) and it means "staff, branch (of vine)." The word, "speak" in Hebrew is *dabar* (**daw-BAR**) and means "talk, tell, commune, pronounce." It is obvious that God wanted to show the congregation God's power. He did not want to show them Moses' anger. He did not need Moses to hit anything. After all, in the beginning, the God we serve spoke things that were not into existence (Genesis 1–2). Since He made the water and the rock, they, too, are subject to His command. However, when Moses chose to disobey the living God, He disrespected God and God's authority. He took matters into His own hands. At that moment, He showed unbelief. He displayed gross disobedience.

9 And Moses took the rod from before the LORD, as he commanded him. 10 And Moses and Aaron gathered the congregation together before the rock, and he said unto them, Hear now, ye rebels; must we fetch you water out of this rock? 11 And Moses lifted up his hand, and with his rod he smote the rock twice: and the water came out abundantly, and the congregation drank, and their beasts also.

Notice that Moses followed God's directives to a point. (1) He did take the rod and (2) He did gather the congregation together before the rock. However, what comes next seals Moses' future and robs him of his blessing; he spoke to the people and vented his anger. When he said, "must we bring you water from this rock," he was taking credit for God's miracle. What "we" is Moses speaking of? There is no "we." There is only God doing what God does—working things to His glory. Moses, therefore, was usurping God's authority. Remember, Moses was God's chosen leader over the nation of Israel. The operative words are "chosen leader." He was not God, nor was he equal to God. The nation of Israel was still God's people and God was the supreme leader—the supreme head.

Sometimes leaders in the church can forget who the head of God's church really is. No man or woman is the head. The church belongs to God. I think if we could ask Moses, he would agree that it behooves leaders to always remember who is really in charge of God's salvation and kingdom-building program.

It is interesting that Moses called the people rebels (v. 10). The word "rebel" in Hebrew is *marah* (**maw-RAW**), and means "contentious, disobedient." Moses vividly saw the sins of his fellow human beings, but he could not see his own. He could see the mote in his brothers' eyes, but not the huge beam that was in his own eye (Matthew 7:3–4). He did not stop to think that he and Aaron were leaders. The word of God says, "For unto whomsoever much is given, of him shall be much required" (Luke 12:48). Consequently, Moses and Aaron did not have the luxury of laying godly character aside while they vented. God requires His leaders to lead by example. Therefore, by Moses' actions, thousands upon thousands of people saw what it was to disbelieve God. That was the message that Moses preached that day, in the desert of Zin.

Thus, Moses "smote" the rock. Yes, he got the intended outcome—the water did flow from the rock. However, instead of following God's guidelines, God's blueprint, Moses set himself up as God. The word "smote" in Hebrew is *nakah* (**naw-KAW**) and means "to strike, to smite, to beat." When all is said and done, Moses disobeyed God. God tells him to speak to the rock and instead, in his anger, he hit the rock. Sin is sin and disobedience is disobedience. Any way you cut it, Moses disobeyed the very God who had called him to lead God's people.

Therefore, as believers, we have to be careful that we do not act in the heat of emotions or in the heat of the moment. We need to take time to consider and collect ourselves. Acting in anger can cause us to get into serious trouble. You see, it is during our trials and tribulations that we can be a great witness for the Lord. Who cannot act like or be Christlike, when all is well? It is during those wilderness experiences—when the rubber meets the road—those agonizing, dry times that others want to see the Jesus in us. They need to see that we are still trusting in the God we say is more than enough in our times of trouble, when the trickles of rain in our lives have become a downpour—when our waiting on God goes from days, to weeks, to months, to years, and more years.

12 And the LORD spake unto Moses and Aaron, Because ye believed me not, to sanctify me in the eyes of the children of Israel, therefore ye shall not bring this congregation into the land which I have given them.

Moses had to pay a serious penalty for disobeying a holy God. Again, His actions showed disbelief and this is the message that God received as well as the congregation. The word "sanctify" in Hebrew is *qadash* (**kaw-DASH**) and means "to be set apart, be consecrated." Because Moses did not sanctify or reverence the Lord with His actions, his behavior brought death and the loss of his blessing. He did not get to go over into the Promised Land. Note that the text does not say, however, that Moses did not get to go to heaven.

Reflect on the fact that the person (Moses) from whom Yahweh wanted to make a nation (Exodus 32:10; cf. Numbers 14:12), who reminded Yahweh of His promise of descendants made to the patriarchs (Exodus 32:11–14), and who even requested that Yahweh "blot him out of the book" if he would not forgive the people (Exodus 32:32), was prohibited from entering Canaan. Instead, only the children of the wilderness generation (Numbers 14:21–23, 26–35) would enjoy the Promised Land

13 This is the water of Meribah; because the children of Israel strove with the LORD, and he was sanctified in them.

We have to be careful about striving with the Lord. We have to be careful about rebelling against the Lord. We have to be careful about disobeying the Lord. Meribah in Hebrew is *meriybah* (**mer-ee-BAW**) and "it is a fountain in the desert of Sin, at Rephidim; it is so called because the Israelites murmured against God." They "strove" with the Lord. Meribah, then, is a place where the Israelites argued with the LORD, and He showed them His holiness. Would you want to displease the Lord so much that He shows you who He really is; He shows you His holiness—His strength and might? Would you want a memorial built of the time you murmured and complained against God? This lesson cautions us to be careful how we use our mouths and be careful how we act in times of trouble. We must always remember: God sees! God knows! And God will judge and punish!

Sources:

Alexander, T. Desmond, et. al., eds. *New Dictionary of Biblical Theology*. Downers Grove, Ill.: InterVarsity Press, 2000.

The Life Application Study Bible (King James Version). Wheaton, Ill.: Tyndale House Publishers, Inc., 1996.

The Life Application Study Bible (New Living Translation). Wheaton, Ill.: Tyndale House Publishers, Inc., 1996.

Daily Bible Readings

M: Rebelled Against the Command
Numbers 20:22–29
T: Tested at Meribah
Psalm 81:1–10
W: Do Not Harden Your Hearts
Psalm 95
T: Trust in the Lord
Jeremiah 17:5–10
F: The Foundation of Faith
Matthew 16:13–18
S: Water for the Thirsty
Revelation 21:1–7
S: Because Moses Did Not Trust
Numbers 20:1–13

NOTES

TEACHING TIPS

August 23
Bible Study Guide 12

1. Words You Should Know

A. Heart (Deuteronomy 6:5) *lebab* (Heb.)—The seat of understanding, intellect, and intention.

B. Soul (v. 5) *nephesh* (Heb.)—A breathing creature, soul.

2. Teacher Preparation

Unifying Principle—Obeying the Commands. Believers know that God's Word cautions us to fear the Lord. The word "fear" means to reverence, respect, and trust the Lord. If we reverence, respect, and trust Him, we will also obey His commands and edicts. This is not optional. Disobedience can lead to a broken relationship with God and even death.

A. Prepare for this lesson by studying the Devotional Readings, the Focal Verses, and the More Light on the Text sections. Meditate on them as you study.

B. Answer the Search the Scriptures and Discuss the Meaning questions.

C. Pray that the Lord will guide you as you lead His people in the lesson.

3. Starting the Lesson

A. Pray that the Lord would use the class time to illuminate His Word in the hearts of His people.

B. Ask for a volunteer to read the In Focus section. Discuss, tying it in with the overall theme for today's lesson.

C. Ask for volunteers to read or summarize the Background section. Discuss.

4. Getting into the Lesson

A. Read Focal Verses aloud.

B. Ask for volunteers to share in the discussion of the In Depth section.

5. Relating the Lesson to Life

A. Answer the Search the Scriptures and Discuss the Meaning questions. Discuss.

B. Ask your students to share the seriousness of obeying God's commands.

6. Arousing Action

A. Read the Make It Happen section.

B. Encourage the class to give to God those areas of their life where they are failing to follow His commands.

C. Close the class with prayer.

Worship Guide

For the Superintendent or Teacher
Theme: God Calls for Obedience
Theme Song: "Lead Me, Guide Me"
Devotional Reading: Proverbs 2:1–11
Prayer

GOD CALLS FOR OBEDIENCE

Bible Background • DEUTERONOMY 6
Printed Text • DEUTERONOMY 6:1–9, 20–24 Devotional Reading • PROVERBS 2:1–11

AIM for Change

By the end of the lesson, we will:
EXPLORE the meaning of the "Great Commandment";
SENSE the importance of the Great Commandment to our lives; and
ACCEPT God's Great Commandment, to live accordingly, and teach it.

Keep in Mind

"Hear, O Israel: The LORD our God is one LORD: And thou shalt love the LORD thy God with all thine heart, and with all thy soul, and with all thy might. And these words, which I command thee this day, shall be in thine heart" (Deuteronomy 6:4–6).

Focal Verses

KJV **Deuteronomy 6:1** Now these are the commandments, the statutes, and the judgments, which the LORD your God commanded to teach you, that ye might do them in the land whither ye go to possess it:

2 That thou mightest fear the LORD thy God, to keep all his statutes and his commandments, which I command thee, thou, and thy son, and thy son's son, all the days of thy life; and that thy days may be prolonged.

3 Hear therefore, O Israel, and observe to do it; that it may be well with thee, and that ye may increase mightily, as the LORD God of thy fathers hath promised thee, in the land that floweth with milk and honey.

4 Hear, O Israel: The LORD our God is one LORD:

5 And thou shalt love the LORD thy God with all thine heart, and with all thy soul, and with all thy might.

6 And these words, which I command thee this day, shall be in thine heart:

7 And thou shalt teach them diligently unto thy children, and shalt talk of them when thou sittest in thine house, and when thou walkest by the way, and when thou liest down, and when thou risest up.

8 And thou shalt bind them for a sign upon thine hand, and they shall be as frontlets between thine eyes.

9 And thou shalt write them upon the posts of thy house, and on thy gates.

6:20 And when thy son asketh thee in time to come, saying, What mean the testimonies, and the

NLT **Deuteronomy 6:1** "These are the commands, decrees, and regulations that the LORD your God commanded me to teach you. You must obey them in the land you are about to enter and occupy,

2 and you and your children and grandchildren must fear the LORD your God as long as you live. If you obey all his decrees and commands, you will enjoy a long life.

3 Listen closely, Israel, and be careful to obey. Then all will go well with you, and you will have many children in the land flowing with milk and honey, just as the LORD, the God of your ancestors, promised you.

4 "Listen, O Israel! The LORD is our God, the LORD alone.

5 And you must love the LORD your God with all your heart, all your soul, and all your strength.

6 And you must commit yourselves wholeheartedly to these commands that I am giving you today.

7 Repeat them again and again to your children. Talk about them when you are at home and when you are on the road, when you are going to bed and when you are getting up.

8 Tie them to your hands and wear them on your forehead as reminders.

9 Write them on the doorposts of your house and on your gates.

6:20 "In the future your children will ask you, 'What is the meaning of these laws, decrees, and regulations that the LORD our God has commanded us to obey?'

21 "Then you must tell them, 'We were

statutes, and the judgments, which the LORD our God hath commanded you?

21 Then thou shalt say unto thy son, We were Pharaoh's bondmen in Egypt; and the LORD brought us out of Egypt with a mighty hand:

22 And the LORD shewed signs and wonders, great and sore, upon Egypt, upon Pharaoh, and upon all his household, before our eyes:

23 And he brought us out from thence, that he might bring us in, to give us the land which he sware unto our fathers.

24 And the LORD commanded us to do all these statutes, to fear the LORD our God, for our good always, that he might preserve us alive, as it is at this day.

Pharaoh's slaves in Egypt, but the LORD brought us out of Egypt with his strong hand.

22 The LORD did miraculous signs and wonders before our eyes, dealing terrifying blows against Egypt and Pharaoh and all his people.

23 He brought us out of Egypt so he could give us this land he had sworn to give our ancestors.

24 And the LORD our God commanded us to obey all these decrees and to fear him so he can continue to bless us and preserve our lives, as he has done to this day.

In Focus

Grandma Mabel was the matriarch of her family. She was a strong Christian woman, who upon the death of her husband of 12 years had raised their two sons and daughter in a middle income neighborhood in an inner city. She raised them with convictions and let them know that inspite of their great loss, they were going to be all right—they were going to make it; God would see to it.

Grandma Mabel taught them Christian values and lived those values before her children. On her nurse's salary and the insurance that her husband had left them, they were able to thrive and survive. Even more, with the Christian legacy that her husband had left the family and what Grandma Mabel had continued to teach and live, all three of her children went on to college and became successful. One was a social worker, the other an accountant, and her daughter became a teacher.

Often Grandma Mabel would remind her grown children, their spouses, and her grandchildren that it was prayer and obedience to God's Word that had brought her through her hard times. Prayer and obedience to God's commands had held her family together. Prayer and obedience to God's commands had helped her survive the lonely days, nights, and heartaches.

In today's study, Moses teaches the wilderness generation that, when they go over into the Promised Land (Canaan), God still expects them to follow His directives—His commands. They are to also teach them to their children, so that they can obey as well.

The People, Places, and Times

Moses. He was the leader, law-giver, and prophet of Israel whom God used to lead His people out of slavery in the land of Egypt. God gave the covenant laws, including the Ten Commandments, to Moses at Mount Sinai amidst smoke and flames (Exodus 19:18).

Canaan. It is a country west of the Jordan River. The name was also used in an extended sense to refer to all of Palestine west of the Jordan. Thus, Jerusalem was considered to be part of the land of Canaan.

Background

The book of Deuteronomy is generally considered by Christian and Jewish scholars to be the farewell address of Moses to the people of Israel. The setting of the address is in the plains of Moab, which was a high pastureland east of the Jordan River. Moses was speaking to a new generation of Israelites because the previous generation died off in the wilderness. Recall that as a result of their rebellion against God, the Israelites were forced to wander through the wilderness for forty years (Deuteronomy 1:26–2:1). Additionally, God barred Moses himself from entering into the Promised Land because of his own rebellion (Numbers 20:12). So on the plains of Moab, Moses was delivering a restatement of what God expected of this new generation of Israelites as they entered the Promised Land. Canaan was a land "flowing with milk and honey" (v. 3). It was also a land flowing with many different pagan gods. The Israelites were entering a polytheistic (many gods) culture and Moses was calling them to have allegiance to God alone.

Source:

Tigay, Jeffrey H. *The JPS Torah Commentary: Deuteronomy*. Philadelphia: The Jewish Publication Society/Jerusalem, 1996.

At-A-Glance

1. A Charge to Obey (Deuteronomy 6:1–4)
2. The Need for Love to Obey (v. 5)
3. The Methods for Remembering to Obey (vv. 6–9, 20–24)

In Depth

1. The Charge to Obey (Deuteronomy 6:1–4)

Verse 4 begins what is widely known among Jewish scholars as the *shama* (**shaw-MAH**), which is a Hebrew word meaning "hear." The Shama is a prayer that is recited daily by observant Jews to remind them of their call to remain loyal to Jehovah God. Given that the Israelites were about to enter a land whose inhabitants pledged allegiance to many gods, God found it important to remind them, through His prophet Moses, that their loyalty belonged to Him. The previous generation found it difficult to resist the allure of other gods (see Numbers 25:1–2, Deuteronomy 4:3–4). In Exodus 32:1 (NIV), for example, it says the people "gathered around Aaron and said, 'Come, make us gods who will go before us.'" This is the incident when Aaron made them a golden calf and the people partied and offered burnt offerings to the golden image. Moses had to plead with God not to wipe them out for this act of disobedience (Exodus 32:11–14)!

One very important reason for this command to loyalty is found in the first commandment, "I am the Lord your God, who brought you out of Egypt, out of the land of slavery. You shall have no other gods before me" (Deuteronomy 5:6–7). Loyalty was demanded because God was the one who acted on Israel's behalf in history. After all, it was He who brought the Israelites out of slavery in Egypt. Loyalty was the proper response to God's gracious act.

Thus, God gave the new generation this injunction—to hear that the Lord is God alone. He will contend with no rivals. God alone is worthy of devotion and worship. God knew that there would be many distractions in Canaan that could lead the Israelites astray into many vile and corrupt things. Believe it or not, that very thing is true of us today! We may not be in danger of making graven images and bowing down before them; but there are several idols to which we can give our loyalty. For instance, there's the allure of a bustling career, wealth, even popularity among our peers and coworkers. However, since He delivered us from the slavery of sin, loyalty to God is the appropriate response from us as well (Romans 6:18). Out of sheer gratitude for our emancipation, we should pledge our allegiance to Him.

2. The Need for Love to Obey (v. 5)

As we have seen above, loyalty was the appropriate response of the Israelites for God's gracious acts in their lives, and it is also the appropriate response of those of us whom God has acted graciously toward. Not only did Moses call the Israelites to remain loyal to God, he also gave them a command to love God. The command to love here is not just a command to have a certain feeling. Rather, it is a call to express love through action. The connection between love and action is seen throughout the book of Deuteronomy. For instance: "But it was because the LORD loved you and kept the oath he swore to your forefathers that he brought you out with a mighty hand and redeemed you from the land of slavery, from the power of Pharaoh king of Egypt" (Deuteronomy 7:8, NIV). Another is "He defends the cause of the fatherless and the widow, and loves the alien, giving him food and clothing" (Deuteronomy 10:18, NIV).

God expresses His love in tangible ways. Israel was expected to demonstrate its love for God by keeping His commands. And as a result of obeying God's commands, Moses said that the Israelites would enjoy long life (v. 2), things would "go well" with them (v. 3) and they would "increase greatly" (v. 3). God's commands were given to benefit the Israelites, not burden them unduly. The command to love God by obeying His commands is not peculiar to the Israelites. Jesus, when asked by the Pharisees what the greatest commandment was, pointed them to Deuteronomy 6:5. Also, it is written in 1 John 5:3, "This is love for God: to obey his commands." For those of us who say we love God, the test of whether it is true is determined by our obedience to His commands. As with the Israelites, God's commands are not overly burdensome for us. Jesus says, "For my yoke is easy and my burden is light" (Matthew 11:30, NIV). There is also a benefit for obedience. The writer of Hebrews says that the reward for obedience is "eternal salvation" (5:9, NIV).

Moses pointed out that this love is not to be partial. The command is to love God "with all your heart and with all your soul and with all you strength" (Deuteronomy 6:5). One commentator writes, "To do something with all the heart and soul means to do it with the totality of one's thoughts, feelings, intentions, and desires." The heart was considered to be the seat of thought, intention, and feeling while the soul was the seat of the emotions, passions, and desires. God was calling the Israelites to love Him with everything they had. As indicated by Jesus, we are called to this same kind of love (Mark 12:28–34).

3. The Methods for Remembering to Obey (vv. 6–9, 20–24)

Recall that earlier we discovered the Israelites were entering a place that had plenty of things to attract their attention away from God. Thus Moses admonishes them to keep God's commandments on their hearts (v. 6). According to Jewish commentator Moshe Weinfeld, the idea of putting words on one's heart was frequently found in the political loyalty oaths of the ancient Near East. The commentator gives an example of a Hittite treaty, "and the following word let it into the heart." God knew that the only way for the Israelites to resist distraction and remain obedient to Him was to let His commands into the heart. This was to be done by thinking and talking about the commands all the time (v. 7). The psalmist reiterates this sentiment, "Blessed is the man that walketh not in the counsel of the ungodly, nor standeth in the way of sinners, nor sitteth in the seat of the scornful. But his delight is in the law of the LORD; and in his law doth he meditate day and night" (Psalm 1:1–2). The way to remain loyal to God and love Him, through our actions, is to constantly have His Word on our minds. This will ensure that we are being guided by God's values and not the world's values.

The Israelites were also charged with teaching their children to obey God's commands (v. 7). This is the natural extension of the covenant promise God made to Abraham to be his God and the God of his descendants after him (Genesis 17:7). God demands the loyalty, love, and obedience of all of His people. And just as Moses was teaching them to observe God's commands, they were responsible for teaching the next generation the commands also. Verses 20–24 give the parents the reasons for continually passing on the commands. God's actions and God's promises to His people reveal clearly why the chosen people should always obey God and put Him first. The apostle Paul echoes this truth in his letter to the Ephesians: "bring them [children] up in the training and instruction of the Lord" (6:3, NIV). God not only requires that we obey His commands, but that we also teach our children to obey them.

Sources:

Dunn, James, and John W. Rogerson, eds. *Eerdmans Commentary on the Bible.* Grand Rapids, Mich.: Wm. B. Eerdmans Publishing Company, 2003.

Packer, J. I., and M. C. Tenney, eds. *Illustrated Manners and Customs of the Bible.* Nashville: Thomas Nelson Publishers, Inc., 1980.

Strong, James. *Strong's Exhaustive Concordance of the Bible.* Nashville: Thomas Nelson Publishers, Inc., 1990.

Weinfeld, Moshe. *The Anchor Bible: Deuteronomy 1–11: A New Translation with Introduction and Commentary, Volume 5.* New York: Doubleday, 1991.

Search the Scriptures

1. What were the benefits of obeying God's commandments (Deuteronomy 6:2–3)?

2. What does it mean to love the Lord with all your heart, soul, and strength (v. 5)?

3. Where are we supposed to talk about God's commandments (v. 7)?

4. What is the reason to be given to children when they ask why we follow God's commands (vv. 20–24)?

Discuss the Meaning

1. John 14:21 tells us that Jesus says, "Whoever has my commands and obeys them, he is the one who loves me." What are the commands He's talking about? Do we as Christians still have to obey the Ten Commandments?

2. Moses told the Israelites that their observance of God's commands affects not only themselves, but their children and grandchildren also (Deuteronomy 6:1–2). Why do you think this is so? Can you think of any examples of disobedience that has affected subsequent generations?

3. Traditionally, Jewish scholars have taken Deuteronomy 6:8–9 literally and called on the faithful to wear phylacteries with portions of Hebrew Scripture tucked inside, and to post words on their

doorposts. Do you think Moses intended for this verse to be taken literally? If not, what do you think he meant?

Lesson in Our Society

In our society, personal autonomy is a really big deal. The ability to rule oneself and decide what is right and wrong is considered to be an important right. How does this idea match up with God's call to obey His commandments—to allow Him to determine right and wrong?

Make It Happen

Take some time to examine your own heart this week. Determine whether you have been obeying God's commands or making your own rules. If you have children, ask yourself if you have been teaching them to observe God's commands faithfully.

Follow the Spirit

What God wants me to do:

____

____

Remember Your Thoughts

Special insights I have learned:

____

____

More Light on the Text

Deuteronomy 6:1–9, 20–24

In the preceding chapter (chapter 5), Moses rehearsed the Sinai law for the Children of Israel and the circumstances under which it was initially given. He urged them to always keep the law of God so that they could reap the benefit, which was long life in the land that Lord had promised them. The next nine verses define the law, how the people were to keep it, and to what extent they should keep it in order for them to reap the benefits that come with it. They were to preserve the law by teaching it to their generations to come. The portion under discussion constitutes the Shama of Israel's religion, and the basis for the Christian belief in the one eternal God.

1 Now these are the commandments, the statutes, and the judgments, which the LORD your God commanded to teach you, that ye might do them in the land whither ye go to possess it: 2 That thou mightest fear the LORD thy God, to keep all his statutes and his commandments, which I command thee, thou, and thy son, and thy son's son, all the days of thy life; and that thy days may be prolonged.

Using the conjunction "now these," or *wazo'th* (**va-ZOTHE**), from the word *zo'th'* (**ZOTHE**), which can also be translated as "this, or this . . . that, or here is," Moses continued his thoughts from Deuteronomy chapter 5. The phrase, "Now these are the commandments, the statutes, and the judgments," includes all the commandments Moses had rehearsed with them in the previous chapter and the ones that were soon to follow (6:1ff). The Lord, Moses says, had ordered him to teach them or to remind them of the law, which they would keep when they possessed the land. The purpose of this rehearsal of the law in their hearing was so that they would remember to obey and fear the Lord. The fear of the Lord, which means reverence in one's heart for God, is the most powerful force for obedience. Proverbs describes the fear of the Lord as "the beginning of wisdom: and the knowledge of the holy is understanding" (9:10). The kind of "fear," (*yare'*) (**yaw-RAY**) used here is not to be afraid of God as if he were a dreadful and vengeful being standing over people, ready to punish them for the smallest infraction of His law. It speaks of more of respecting or revering God as the Father who deserves to be honored and respected. It also teaches that we ought to learn to respect God both as the law-giver and as a just and righteous judge, bearing in mind His justice as well as His mercy and long-suffering.

Moses used two Hebrew words, which are synonymous, *choq* (**khoke**), translated "statutes," and *mishpat* (**mish-PAWT**) rendered "commandment," by the King James Version (KJV) and "decrees and commands" in the *New International Version* (NIV). These words emphasized the importance of keeping the law of God. The law was to be perpetuated throughout the history of Israel. The reward for keeping the law was that they, their children, and future generations would live long. To live long refers not necessarily to an individual long life, which probably was included, but rather to the long life of Israel as a nation. Here it means if they "keep all His statutes and His commandments," they would possess the land for a long time; conversely if they failed to fear the Lord and keep His commandments, they would disinherit the land. Israel's captivity by Persia and Judah's exile to Babylon are consequences of their failure to keep the law of the Lord. Therefore, as each generation remembered to obey the commandments, they would enjoy the benefits of the land, and their days would be prolonged. The law was intended for their well-being so that Israel could enjoy life to the full, for it is "given that it may go well with you" (5:33; cf. 6:18; 12:28).

3 Hear therefore, O Israel, and observe to do it; that it may be well with thee, and that ye may increase mightily, as the LORD God of thy fathers hath promised thee, in the land that floweth with milk and honey.

"Hear therefore," that is, in view of the benefits, Moses urges them, as if pleading with them, to listen (hear) and obey (observe) the law of the Lord. If they will endeavor to keep the commandments, things will go well with them; they will multiply numerically in keeping with the promise the Lord made to their fathers. That promise includes living in the land that flows with milk and honey, which describes the fertility and productivity of the land.

4 Hear, O Israel: The LORD our God is one LORD: 5 And thou shalt love the LORD thy God with all thine heart, and with all thy soul, and with all thy might.

Verses 4–9, with 11:1–21, and Numbers 13:37–41 constitute the Shama or creed of Israel in the Hebrew liturgy, which pious Jews recite twice daily in their worship. It expresses the heart of Israel's confession of faith, and confirms first the unity of God ("the Lord is one," NIV), and second the covenant relationship between Israel ("the Lord our God"). The word translated "one" is the Hebrew word *'echad* (**ekh-AWD**) from *achad* which means "to unify; collect; to be united as one" (Genesis 2:24; 3:22; 11:1, 6, etc). Here, Moses implicitly declared the uniqueness of God of Israel, namely that Yahweh is the one God, and He is not a pantheon of many gods that are worshiped by the surrounding nations. Moses began this declaration by calling for the whole congregation of the people of Israel "Hear, O Israel" (*Shama' yisra'el '*) to pay attention to this important information, namely the uniqueness of God, and their response to Him. Moses invited the people to give Yahweh their complete allegiance by loving Him with the totality of their being: "with all thine heart, and with all thy soul, and with all thy might." Yahweh was to be Israel's sole object of worship and affection, and not other gods.

Verse 4 has been regarded as the positive way of expressing the negative commands of the first commandments of the Decalogue (5:7–10; cf. Exodus 20:2–4). In the New Testament, Christ, responding to the inquiry of the young lawyer, added the phrase "with all your mind," and described these two verses (vv. 4–5) as "the first and great commandment" (Matthew 22:37–38; Mark 12:29–30; Luke 10:27). This type of love requires total surrender of the whole being to God, who has given Himself completely, without reservation, and unconditionally to love the people of Israel. He, therefore, deserved and expected them to reciprocate with the same unreserved and total love for Him. This command to love the Lord is found frequently in Deuteronomy and expresses the response God expects from His people (10:12; 11:1, 13, 22; 12:3; 19:9; 30:6, 16, 20 etc.); it is also found in the covenant renewal of Joshua (Joshua 22:5; 23:11). The Scripture often links the command to love with the command to obey. Jesus said to his disciples, "If ye love me, keep my commandments" (John 14:15); "He that hath my commandments, and keepeth them, he it is that loveth me: and he that loveth me shall be loved of my Father, and I will love him, and will manifest myself to him" (John 14:21); and "If a man love me, he will keep my words: and my Father will love him, and we will come unto him, and make our abode with him" (John 14:23).

6 And these words, which I command thee this day, shall be in thine heart: 7 And thou shalt teach them diligently unto thy children, and shalt talk of them when thou sittest in thine house, and when thou walkest by the way, and when thou liest down, and when thou risest up.

"And these words, which I command thee this day," includes all the commandments in the previous chapter, the declarations in this chapter, and the ones following. These commandments were to be stored in their hearts, where nothing could touch them. The word *heart* in Hebrew is *lebab* (**lay-BAWB**) and is used also in verse 5. It refers to the seat of understanding, intellect, and intention. It is where we do our thinking, and where our character is formed. The heart represents the nucleus of the human being, in which decisions and moral choices, both good and bad, are made. True love, worship, and holy principles emanate from within the heart, as do the evil issues of life (Mark 7:19–21). The heart is also the seat of consciousness, therefore, to store the commandment in our heart is to keep it in our consciousness as long as we live. In other words, God's commandments should become a part of our being, and we are to be conscious of them all the days our lives. This is made explicit in the command that parents teach the commandments to their children diligently. The phrase "thou shalt teach them diligently" translates the Hebrew word *shanan,* which has an idea of "to sharpen, or to pierce." Moses instructed them of their parental duties. They were to teach the children the law constantly and systematically, formally and informally, until these words of the commandments pierce through to (penetrate) their hearts.

The commandments should be the center of their daily life, in conversation at home, or on the road, at bedtime, and when they rise up. They should go to bed at night, and arise in the morning with the law of the Lord embedded in their hearts so that they would not forget it. The Lord commanded Joshua: "Do not let this Book of the Law depart from your mouth; meditate on it day and night, so that you may be careful to do everything written in it. Then you will be prosperous and successful" (Joshua 1:8, NIV). Should any thing happen to the written law, the Israelites were to teach the commandments to their children, not only to instruct them in the ways of the Lord at an early age (Proverbs 22:6); but also perhaps to help preserve the law and their heritage for generations (v. 20ff).

8 And thou shalt bind them for a sign upon thine hand, and they shall be as frontlets between thine eyes. 9 And thou shalt write them upon the posts of thy house, and on thy gates.

To make the law a visible and permanent part of their life, the Israelites were to bind them upon their hands as a constant reminder of their allegiance to Yahweh and the law, and post it on their forehead and on the lintels of their houses. Binding them on their hands is probably a figurative expression of how diligent their allegiance to the law should be. The imagery is also used in the Jewish rituals of the Passover (Exodus 13:9), in the sacrifice of the firstborn animals and the redemption of the firstborn sons (Exodus 13:16). The same idea is expressed in a number of the Proverbs, regarding mercy and truth (3:3), obedience to parental commandments (6:21), and keeping God's law (7:3). The Jews later interpreted it literally and enclosed some written portions of the law in small cases, called phylacteries (cf. Matthew 23:5), and bound them on their hands and foreheads. The significance of these instructions is well understood, and that is to keep them conscious of God, by a visible and constant reminder of the law.

6:20 And when thy son asketh thee in time to come, saying, What mean the testimonies, and the statutes, and the judgments, which the LORD our God hath commanded you? 21 Then thou shalt say unto thy son, We were Pharaoh's bondmen in Egypt; and the LORD brought us out of Egypt with a mighty hand: 22 And the LORD shewed signs and wonders, great and sore, upon Egypt, upon Pharaoh, and upon all his household, before our eyes: 23 And he brought us out from thence, that he might bring us in, to give us the land which he sware unto our fathers.

An African adage says that when an old man dies in a village or tribe, it is as if an entire library is burned or destroyed. A whole history or heritage of a village or family would be lost if it were not passed to the next generation. To preserve the legacy of the people, there is a need to tell stories to the children at a young age about the family, the village, or the tribe where they have been, and how they got to that moment of their journey of life. This was how the Africans preserved their history before the art of writing was introduced. This is the same instruction Moses gives in these verses. Apart from the formal teaching of the law to the new generation (v. 6), the parents have the obligation to tell stories about their heritage, the mighty deliverance God gave them from the land of Egypt and from the hand of Pharaoh, and how God led them through the wilderness into the land of promise.

Here are two methods of education: formal (didactic, v. 6) and informal, telling stories (inductive, v. 20ff) through question and answer. The children's questions offer opportunities for explanation and teaching. Such questions and opportunities are, of course, made possible if the parents themselves are clearly keeping the law so as to raise some curiosity in the minds of their children. The question "What mean the testimonies" can be reworded thus:

"What is the real significance of the law? Why do we have to keep the law?" By answering these questions, the father rehearses the historical basis of the law, how it originated, and the benefits of observing it. Rather than giving a simple answer, the Lord demands the parents to tell the full story of the acts of God in redemption from bondage, which is the basis of the law. This redemptive story of God's mighty deeds would instill a spirit of gratitude and loving obedience to the Lord; it would generate worship and reverence for God in the minds of the people. Keeping the law demonstrates our love for the Lord.

24 And the LORD commanded us to do all these statutes, to fear the LORD our God, for our good always, that he might preserve us alive, as it is at this day.

Added to the historical basis of the law in redemption (vv. 21–23), the reason for keeping the law is that they might fear (honor) the Lord and enjoy the blessings and benefits of redemption—"for our good always" (v. 24). It is also for their preservation in the land. It is not only necessary to keep or obey the law of God, it is also necessary, as Moses seems to intimate here, that the children know whole story behind what they do, why they worship the Lord and not the other gods. Therefore, the law would be meaningless and ineffective without the story behind it—the redemptive story from Egypt to the Promised Land. Likewise, the Christian life or the creed would have no meaning without the story behind it—the redemptive story of the death and resurrection of the Lord and Saviour Jesus Christ. Taking our children to church is not enough; we are to teach them diligently, and tell them constantly the story about the Saviour and significance of His death, and its benefit to us. We should always heed Peter's admonition, "sanctify the Lord God in your hearts: and be ready always to give an answer to every man that asketh you a reason of the hope that is in you with meekness and fear" (1 Peter 3:15).

Sources:

Packer, J. I., Merrill C. Tenney, and William White. *Nelson's Illustrated Encyclopedia of Bible Facts.* Nashville: Thomas Nelson Publishers, 1995.

Vine, W.E. *Vines Complete Expository Dictionary of Old and New Testament Words.* Edited by Merrill F. Unger and William White Jr. Nashville: Thomas Nelson Publishers, 1996.

Daily Bible Readings

M: Rewards of Obedience
Leviticus 26:3–13
T: Penalties of Disobedience
Leviticus 26:14–26
W: Consequences of Disobedience
1 Samuel 15:17–26
T: Disobeying the Son
John 3:31–36
F: Listening and Obeying
Psalm 81:11–16
S: Treasure God's Commands
Proverbs 2:1–11
S: Diligently Observing God's Law
Deuteronomy 6:1–9, 20–24

NOTES

TEACHING TIPS

August 30

Bible Study Guide 13

1. Words You Should Know

A. Return (Deuteronomy 30:2, 3) *shuwb* (Heb.)—To bring back, to restore.

B. Plenteous (v. 9) *yathar* (Heb.)—To be left over, to excel, show preeminence, to show excess, to have more than enough.

2. Teacher Preparation

Unifying Principle—The Promise of Life. Believers must always remember that God has called us to keep His commandments. We need to know and appreciate that our obedience to God's Word is essential to divine blessing. Consequently, we need to have a made-up mind to do His will. It is our decision—our choice. However, disobedience can bring grave consequences. Moses' life testifies to that.

A. Prepare for this lesson by reading the Focal Verses and the More Light on the Text section.

B. Answer the Search the Scriptures and Discuss the Meaning questions.

C. Pray that the Lord will guide you as you lead His people in the lesson.

3. Starting the Lesson

A. Pray that the Lord would use the class time to illuminate His Word in the hearts of His people.

B. Ask for a volunteer to read the In Focus section. Discuss.

C. Ask for another volunteer to read the Background section. Discuss.

4. Getting into the Lesson

A. Read Focal Verses aloud.

B. Now use the In Depth section to lead in discussion.

C. Answer the Search the Scriptures and Discuss the Meaning questions in class.

5. Relating the Lesson to Life

A. Have the class read the Lesson in Our Society section.

B. Give and discuss answers given to the question.

6. Arousing Action

A. Read the Make It Happen section.

B. Encourage the class to give to God those areas of their life where they are failing to follow Him.

C. Close the class in prayer.

Worship Guide

For the Superintendent or Teacher
Theme: God Calls for Decision
Theme Song: "I Will Follow Him"
Devotional Reading: Joshua 24:14–24
Prayer

GOD CALLS FOR DECISION

Bible Background • DEUTERONOMY 30
Printed Text • DEUTERONOMY 30:1–10 Devotional Reading • JOSHUA 24:14–24

AIM for Change

By the end of the lesson, we will:
EXPLORE Moses' promise that God will reward the Israelites' love and faithfulness with prosperity;
CONSIDER the importance of loving and obeying God; and
CHOOSE to obey God's call to obedience.

Keep in Mind

"And the LORD thy God will circumcise thine heart, and the heart of thy seed, to love the LORD thy God with all thine heart, and with all thy soul, that thou mayest live" (Deuteronomy 30:6).

Focal Verses

KJV **Deuteronomy 30:1** And it shall come to pass, when all these things are come upon thee, the blessing and the curse, which I have set before thee, and thou shalt call them to mind among all the nations, whither the LORD thy God hath driven thee,
2 And shalt return unto the LORD thy God, and shalt obey his voice according to all that I command thee this day, thou and thy children, with all thine heart, and with all thy soul;
3 That then the LORD thy God will turn thy captivity, and have compassion upon thee, and will return and gather thee from all the nations, whither the LORD thy God hath scattered thee.
4 If any of thine be driven out unto the outmost parts of heaven, from thence will the LORD thy God gather thee, and from thence will he fetch thee:
5 And the LORD thy God will bring thee into the land which thy fathers possessed, and thou shalt possess it; and he will do thee good, and multiply thee above thy fathers.
6 And the LORD thy God will circumcise thine heart, and the heart of thy seed, to love the LORD thy God with all thine heart, and with all thy soul, that thou mayest live.
7 And the LORD thy God will put all these curses upon thine enemies, and on them that hate thee, which persecuted thee.
8 And thou shalt return and obey the voice of the LORD, and do all his commandments which I command thee this day.
9 And the LORD thy God will make thee plenteous in every work of thine hand, in the fruit of thy

NLT **Deuteronomy 30:1** "In the future, when you experience all these blessings and curses I have listed for you, and when you are living among the nations to which the LORD your God has exiled you, take to heart all these instructions.
2 If at that time you and your children return to the LORD your God, and if you obey with all your heart and all your soul all the commands I have given you today,
3 then the LORD your God will restore your fortunes. He will have mercy on you and gather you back from all the nations where he has scattered you.
4 Even though you are banished to the ends of the earth, the LORD your God will gather you from there and bring you back again.
5 The LORD your God will return you to the land that belonged to your ancestors, and you will possess that land again. Then he will make you even more prosperous and numerous than your ancestors!
6 "The LORD your God will change your heart and the hearts of all your descendants, so that you will love him with all your heart and soul and so you may live!
7 The LORD your God will inflict all these curses on your enemies and on those who hate and persecute you.
8 Then you will again obey the LORD and keep all his commands that I am giving you today.
9 "The LORD your God will then make you successful in everything you do. He will give you many

body, and in the fruit of thy cattle, and in the fruit of thy land, for good: for the LORD will again rejoice over thee for good, as he rejoiced over thy fathers:

10 If thou shalt hearken unto the voice of the LORD thy God, to keep his commandments and his statutes which are written in this book of the law, and if thou turn unto the LORD thy God with all thine heart, and with all thy soul.

children and numerous livestock, and he will cause your fields to produce abundant harvests, for the LORD will again delight in being good to you as he was to your ancestors.

10 The LORD your God will delight in you if you obey his voice and keep the commands and decrees written in this Book of Instruction, and if you turn to the LORD your God with all your heart and soul.

In Focus 

As many African Americans over 40 look back over the annals of time, they can vividly recall a point in their lives when their parents had strict rules or laws of conduct to be followed outside the home. In fact, children were often given "the law" before they left the premises. The instructions usually went like this: (1) "Remember that you are representing our family when you go out, so don't embarrass us; (2) If I have to speak to you, you will get it when we get back home; (3) You'd better show your home training!"

Oftentimes these instructions were followed by the proverbial deadly, warning eye. That eye was just that, a "dangerous eye"—an eye of impending negative consequences. It could engender the fear of God in any rambunctious child. That eye often said, "You better give your soul to the Lord, because when you get home, your behind is going to be mine!"

In today's lesson, God is the caring parent and He is instructing Moses to tell the new generation of Israelites how to conduct themselves once they go over into the Promised Land. He knew that the Israelites could take on the ungodly behaviors of the people who already possessed the land. Therefore, the Israelites are to obey God's commands and be blessed or disobey and suffer the negative consequences. God calls the new generation to decision.

The People, Places, and Times

God's Law. God kept His word and fulfilled His promises to Abraham, Isaac, and Jacob to bring the Israelites out of Egypt (see Exodus). However, at Sinai, God made a covenant (an agreement) with them in which He set out obligations that have often been understood as "laws." These laws were among Israel's most precious possessions. In fact, their keeping these laws distinguished them as a people from the heathen nations around them. These laws covered all aspects of life and regulated relationships and dealings in both personal and economic matters. They laid down critical guidelines for the way Israel should conduct itself with other nations. More importantly, these laws regulated the sacrifices through which the Israelites related to Almighty God, and by which their sins could and would be forgiven.

Source:
Alexander, T. Desmond, et. al., eds. *New Dictionary of Biblical Theology.* Downers Grove, Ill.: InterVarsity Press, 2000.

Background

In today's passage, Moses prophetically speaks of what will occur if the Israelites break God's covenant. The people would be scattered over the face of the earth and live in exile from God and the Promised Land. However, he aims to comfort their hearts by speaking of the new covenant God will make with those who return to Him.

Source:
Tigay, Jeffrey H. *The JPS Torah Commentary: Deuteronomy.* Philadelphia: The Jewish Publication Society /Jerusalem, 1996.

At A Glance

1. Repentance and Restoration (Deuteronomy 30:1–5)
2. Circumcision of the Heart (v. 6)
3. Promise of Prosperity (vv. 7–10)

In Depth

1. Repentance and Restoration (Deuteronomy 30:1–5)

This chapter continues the discussion Moses began in previous chapters. Verse 1 begins, "And it shall come to pass, when all these things are come upon thee, the blessing and the curse, which I have set before thee…." The phrase "these things" refers to the punishment God would hand down after Israel's foretold breaking of His covenant, as recorded in chapter 29. Moses painted a dire picture, "The whole land will be a burning waste of salt and sulfur—nothing planted, nothing sprouting, no vegetation growing on it. It will be like the destruction of Sodom and Gomorrah, Admah and Zeboiim, which the LORD overthrew in fierce anger. All the nations will ask: 'Why has the LORD done this to this land? Why this fierce, burning anger?'" (Deuteronomy 29:23–24, NIV). Even though this gloomy state of affairs would result from Israel's rebellion, Moses said there was still hope. He said that when they "return unto the LORD thy God" (v. 2) and "obey his voice" (v. 2) then God would "have compassion upon thee, and will return and gather thee from all the nations, whither the LORD thy God hath scattered thee" (v. 3). Moses presented the promise of restoration conditioned upon Israel's repentance.

God seeks the humility and submission of His people. When we've turned from His ways to our own, He seeks our return. The chronicler records, "if my people, who are called by my name, will humble themselves and pray and seek my face and turn from their wicked ways, then will I hear from heaven and will forgive their sin and will heal their land" (2 Chronicles 7:14, NIV). When we repent of our sins and turn back to God, He graciously restores us and the joy of His salvation (Psalm 51:12).

2. Circumcision of the Heart (v. 6)

Not only does God promise restoration for fallen Israel but He promises something more. Moses indicated that the "LORD thy God will circumcise thine heart, and the heart of thy seed" (v. 6). This verse is thought to point to the new covenant God would make with His people, "'This is the covenant I will make with the house of Israel after that time,' declares the LORD. 'I will put my law in their minds and write it on their hearts. I will be their God, and they will be my people'" (Jeremiah 31:33, NIV). God promised to circumcise the hearts of His people "so that you will love the LORD your God with all your heart and with all your soul, that you may live" (v. 6, ESV).

The reference to circumcision is an analogy with the Old Testament practice of cutting away the foreskin. It was a purification ritual, symbolizing cleansing from sin and sanctification for God's purposes. Concerning the circumcision of the heart, Meredith Kline insightfully notes, "What had been externally symbolized in circumcision, the Old Testament sacrament of consecration, would be spiritually actualized by the power of God (cf. 10:16; Jeremiah 31:33 ff.; 32:39 ff.; Ezekiel 11:19; 36:26–27)." The promise Moses delivered tells us that not only will God restore the repentant but also He will give them the power to live faithfully before Him.

Of course this promise is fulfilled in the New Testament with the descending of the Holy Spirit at Pentecost. Before ascending into heaven to sit on the right-hand side of the Father, Jesus told His disciples, "But you will receive power when the Holy Spirit has come upon you" (Acts 1:8, ESV). The apostle Paul elaborated on this power: "But I say, walk by the Spirit, and you will not gratify the desires of the flesh" (Galatians 5:16, ESV). The Holy Spirit is integral to a life of obedience. He gives us the power to keep God's commands. If we are to be successful in our walk, we must rely heavily on the power of the Holy Spirit.

3. Promise of Prosperity (vv. 7–10)

Finally, after Israel's repentance, restoration, and the circumcision of their hearts, God promised to prosper them. God would prosper Israel's industry, give them many children, and ensure bumper crop returns in its agriculture.

It is important to note that Moses was not addressing the Israelites individually, but Israel as a whole. When they returned to Him, God aimed to prosper His people as a whole. We can see that this is so by noticing how Israel ended up exiled from their prosperous land. In chapter 28, Moses wrote, "If you are not careful to do all the words of this law that are written in this book…then the Lord will bring on you and your offspring extraordinary afflictions, afflictions severe and lasting, and sicknesses grievous and lasting" (Deuteronomy 28:58–59, ESV). Disobedience to God's law not only meant affliction for the generation that initially broke the covenant, but lasting effects for their progeny as well. Thus it follows that God would also restore and prosper the returning generation and its future generations, too.

What does this mean for us today? Again turning to Meredith Kline, "The restored theocratic kingdom in Canaan is used as a typical figure for the anti-typical reality, the eternal kingdom of God in the renewed universe. That will be secured by a divine judgment, for while the people of God are to inherit the earth, their enemies will be plagued with every curse (v. 7). The Messianic salvation is, thus, a new exodus and conquest, a renewal of the covenant mediated through Moses and Joshua, first at Sinai and afterwards in Moab and at Ebal and Gerizim." God's temporal blessing of ethnic Israel was but a shadow of what He intended to do. The covenant promise made to Abraham was that in him "all the families of the earth shall be blessed" (Genesis 12:3, ESV). From the beginning, it was God's plan to have "a people for his own possession" that would "proclaim the excellencies of him who called you out of darkness into his marvelous light" (1 Peter 2:9, ESV). When we accept Christ, we become members of the one body (Ephesians 4:4) and share in the prosperity God has promised for His people (Galatians 3:29).

Sources:

James Dunn and John W. Rogerson, eds. *Eerdmans Commentary on the Bible.* Grand Rapids, Mich./Cambridge, U. K.: William B. Eerdmans Publishing Co., 2003.

Packer, J. I., Merrill C. Tenney, and William White. *Nelson's Illustrated Encyclopedia of Bible Facts.* Nashville: Thomas Nelson Publishers, 1995.

Tigay, Jeffrey H. *The JPS Torah Commentary: Deuteronomy.* Philadelphia/Jerusalem: The Jewish Publication Society, 1996.

Tokkunboh Adeyemo, ed. *Africa Bible Commentary.* Nairobi, Kenya: WordAlive Publishers, 2006.

Weinfeld, Moshe. *The Anchor Bible: Deuteronomy 1–11: A New Translation with Introduction and Commentary, Volume 5.* New York: Doubleday, 1991.

Search the Scriptures

1. What were the conditions Moses said must be fulfilled in order for Israel to experience restoration (vv. 1–2)?

2. Who has to return and obey the Lord for restoration to take place (v. 2)?

3. To whom is the promise of the circumcision of the heart made (v. 6)?

4. In what ways does the Lord promise to prosper Israel (v. 9)?

Discuss the Meaning

1. Chapter 30 has Moses addressing Israel in the present moment about a future event. Why do you think he still says things like "when all these things come upon you" and "the LORD your God will restore your fortunes," instead of using the pronouns "they" and "theirs" (vv. 1, 3)? What does this imply about your relation with other believers?

2. What do you think Moses meant when he said that God would "circumcise thine heart, and the heart of thy seed" (v. 6)? What role does the baptism of the Holy Spirit play in this circumcision, if any?

3. How do you understand the promise of prosperity in verse 9? Does it mean that God will make each individual "abundantly prosperous"? What does Moses mean by prosperity (money, real estate, power)?

Lesson in Our Society

In his book *City of God,* St. Augustine distinguished two contrasting ways of life, the city of man versus the city of God. The values and ideals of the city of God are far superior to those of the city of man. This was to be evidenced by the higher quality of life lived by the inhabitants of the city of God. In Deuteronomy, we see God setting up Israel as the example of how life is supposed to be. When they rebelled, they took the template for godly living away from the watching world. In what ways do you think the contemporary church has taken away the template for godly living from the watching world? Where have we missed our opportunities?

Make It Happen

Examine your own life and the life of your family. Are you obeying the Lord's voice with all your heart and soul? If not, return to the Lord today and experience the forgiveness and restoration He promises to those who do.

Follow the Spirit

What God wants me to do:

____

____

Remember Your Thoughts

Special insights I have learned:

____

____

More Light on the Text

Deuteronomy 30:1–10

1 And it shall come to pass, when all these things are come upon thee, the blessing and the curse, which I have set before thee, and thou shalt call them to mind among all the nations, whither the LORD thy God hath driven thee,

"And the LORD thy God will circumcise thine heart, and the heart of thy seed, to love the LORD thy God with all thine heart, and with all thy soul, that thou mayest live" (Deuteronomy 30:6).

The sons and daughters of the new generation of Israelites, God's chosen people, were on the east side of the Jordan River, in view of the Promised Land—Canaan. While camped there, Moses wanted to prepare these offspring to possess the land promised to their forefathers, Abraham, Isaac, and Jacob. Therefore, he reminded them of what God had done for their forefathers and them, and also encouraged this generation to rededicate their lives to the one true God. He did not want them to follow in the footsteps of the faithless, thankless, murmuring, and complaining generation before them. Consequently, while making his third address to the new generation in which he reviews or spells out the terms of God's laws, Moses calls them to commitment.

It had been 40 years since God and Israel made their covenant (contract) (Exodus 19–20). In essence this contract stated that God promised to bless the Israelites by making them the nation through whom the rest of the world could know an Almighty, Holy God—the creator of the universe. However, in return, in order to receive physical and spiritual blessings; they were to love and obey the Lord, their God. They were to keep His laws—His commandments. This is what Moses reviewed with the new generation. He wanted them to obey the terms of the covenant or contract so that they would be blessed in all that they did. After reviewing God's laws for the people, the legal contract between God and the Israelites had to be renewed. After all, this was a new generation. Moses then reinstated the covenant.

The phrase "And it shall come to pass, when all these things" in the Hebrew is *hayah* (**haw-yaw**), and means "occurrences, sayings, utterances." Moses was prophetically looking into the future. He saw the plight of the Israelites. He saw their disobedience to the one true God. Therefore, he told them, when all the before-mentioned blessings and curses had come upon them, they were to meditate on them in the land to which their God would exile or drive them. Upon meditating on all these things, if they would then make a decision to obey God and keep His commands, God would restore their fortunes.

God wanted to forgive the Israelites for their sins and return them unto Himself. He was waiting for them to keep their part of the covenant. He always kept His.

2 And shalt return unto the LORD thy God, and shalt obey his voice according to all that I command thee this day, thou and thy children, with all thine heart, and with all thy soul;

The word "return" in the Hebrew is *shuwb* (**shoob**), and it means "to turn back, to restore, repent." God desired that His people would repent of their many sins, in which they broke their agreement with Him. Moses therefore called them to commitment, a renewed commitment to obey the living God. The phrase, "and shalt obey" in Hebrew is *shama'* (**shaw-MAH**), and it means "listen to, yield to." God wanted this new generation, as He did the old, to listen to His commands and yield to them—follow them to the letter in their everyday living. In other words, the Lord was reminding the Israelites that they must choose to obey Him—they must choose the path of obedience. Not only must the parents choose, but they must teach His laws to their children through ritual, instruction, and memorization to make sure that the next generations followed His edicts as well.

The anonymous writer of Psalm 1 tells us "Blessed is the man that walketh not in the counsel of the ungodly, nor standeth in the way of sinners, nor sitteth in the seat of the scornful, but his delight is in the law of the LORD; and in his law doth he meditate day and night" (vv. 1–2). Clearly, blessing would come from delighting in God's laws, meditating on them, and obeying them. God wanted His chosen people and their seed to receive His blessings, so He told Moses to tell the parents what they needed to do and how to instruct their children so future generations would be blessed as well.

3 That then the LORD thy God will turn thy captivity, and have compassion upon thee, and will return and gather thee from all the nations, whither the LORD thy God hath scattered thee.

God made a promise that if they would repent and turn to their God, He would have compassion upon them and free them from their captivity—the captivity in which He would put them. Note that He reminded them that He would gather them from all the nations where He would scatter them because of their disobedience. Make no mistake; if they disobeyed Him, He wanted them to know just who would drive them from the Promised Land. It would not be Satan, not their enemies, but it would be the Lord, their God. Not only would He drive them from the Promised Land, but He would do it with a strong, mighty hand. He would use their enemies to carry them off into captivity (see the books of the prophets).

The phrase "hath scattered" in the Hebrew is *puwts* (**poots**), and it means "to be dispersed, dashed to pieces." God let the Israelites know in no uncertain terms that He would bring much suffering on them for their disobedience. There would be dire consequences to sin—to breaking their binding covenant or contract with Him. Romans 6:23 says, "For the wages of sin is death; but the gift of God is eternal life through Jesus Christ our Lord." The Israelites' disobedience would bring them death. Their obedience would bring blessings and life.

4 If any of thine be driven out unto the outmost parts of heaven, from thence will the LORD thy God gather thee, and from thence will he fetch thee:

When they obeyed and renewed commitment to Him, God promised to get them or gather them wherever they might be in captivity. The phrase, "unto the outmost" in Hebrew is *qatseh* (**kaw-TSEH**), and it means "end, extremity, outskirts." In other words, no matter where they might be on the earth that God has created, He would personally gather them back together as a nation. This imagery portrays God as the loving parent He is. He had Moses tell His sheep that if they obeyed Him, He would go and get them, wherever they might be.

This should bless every believer! It tells us, too,

that because we are His people, no matter what hell we may find ourselves in, God will bring us out (either in this life or the eternal life to come). He will be there to help us. All He asks is that we obey His commands, that we do His will. Can you picture the creator of the universe, the great I Am running to meet His wayward, prodigal children? Because they have repented and turned back to Him, He wants to restore them—give back what they lost because of their disobedience.

5 And the LORD thy God will bring thee into the land which thy fathers possessed, and thou shalt possess it; and he will do thee good, and multiply thee above thy fathers.

The phrase "thou shalt possess" in Hebrew is *yarash* (**yaw-RASH**) and it means "seize, inherit, take possession." God used Moses to continue to spell out the promises in the contract or covenant. Not only would He bring them back into the land their fathers possessed, but He would make sure that they possessed Canaan as well. This was their inheritance and no one but God Himself could take it from them. Anyone trying to take it would experience the wrath of almighty God.

6 And the LORD thy God will circumcise thine heart, and the heart of thy seed, to love the LORD thy God with all thine heart, and with all thy soul, that thou mayest live.

God told the new generation that He would circumcise not only their hearts, but the hearts of their children as well. The phrase "will circumcise," in Hebrew, is *muwl* (**mool**), and it means "to be cut off, cut down." The word "heart" in Hebrew is *lebab* (**lay-BAWB**) and means "inner man, mind, will, soul, understanding." To circumcise the heart means "to open oneself to God" (Leviticus 26:41). In other words, God would put His laws in their hearts so that they would not sin against their God. They would be open to their God. They would obey their God. He, now, is the agent of their circumcision. Previously, it was Israel, itself, who was to circumcise their hearts. Deuteronomy 10:16 (NRSV) says, "Circumcise, then, the foreskin of your heart, and do not be stubborn any longer." Now, God, Himself, would cut away the flesh or that old "sin nature" that constantly caused them to disobey the Lord.

John 4:14 tells us that "But whosoever drinketh of the water that I shall give him shall never thirst; but the water that I shall give him shall be in him a well of water springing into everlasting life." This water or living water is God's Spirit, given to believers at Pentecost.

God wants His children to follow Him, to follow His edicts. Obeying Him will lead to everlasting life. In this church age or age of grace, He has given His children His indwelling Spirit so that we will not sin against God. Isaiah 44:3 says, "For I will pour water upon him that is thirsty, and floods upon the dry ground: I will pour my spirit upon thy seed, and my blessing upon thine offspring." Paul says in Romans 8:9, "But ye are not in the flesh, but in the Spirit, if so be that the Spirit of God dwell in you. Now if any man have not the Spirit of Christ, he is none of his." Therefore, God has given believers a helper (His Holy Spirit) to assist us in obeying His commands. Believers, however, must choose to follow the Spirit's leading in everyday living.

7 And the LORD thy God will put all these curses upon thine enemies, and on them that hate thee, which persecuted thee.

If the new generation would repent—turn back to the Lord—He would put the curses He had promised to put on Israel for their disobedience, on their enemies instead. The phrase "thee, which persecuted" in Hebrew is *radaph* (**raw-daf**) and means "to pursue, put to flight, chase." An all-knowing God knew that Israel would have many enemies chasing them down and putting them in captivity, because they were not going to obey God's laws. He was going to use some of them to chastise Israel for its disobedience. Once God used their enemies for His purpose, He then vowed to punish these enemies by putting curses on them. In other words, God would use ungodly people to punish His chosen people for their disobedience. Afterward, He would punish the ungodly people. God always has a plan and He works His plan.

8 And thou shalt return and obey the voice of the LORD, and do all his commandments which I command thee this day. 9 And the LORD thy God will make thee plenteous in every work of thine hand, in the fruit of thy body, and in the fruit of thy cattle, and in the fruit of thy land, for good: for the LORD will again rejoice over thee for good, as he rejoiced over thy fathers:

Obedience to God' commands brings untold

blessing, either in this life or the life to come. God reassured the new generation of restoration in this life. He gave the tenets of how He would restore and bless them if they would return to Him and obey His edicts, and do all his commandments—not just some of them. He told them if they would again obey Him by repenting and asking for divine forgiveness, He would restore their fortunes. He promised to once again take delight in His chosen people—people who were to show the rest of the world how to walk and how not to walk with a holy God. He promised to make them plenteous in every work of their hand. The phrase "will make thee plenteous" in the Hebrew is *yathar* (**yaw-THAR**), and means "to excel, show preeminence, to show excess, have more than enough, have an excess." God promised the nation as a whole abundance in the fruit of their hands. He would give them excess, more than enough in their offspring, cattle, and crops.

10 If thou shalt hearken unto the voice of the LORD thy God, to keep his commandments and his statutes which are written in this book of the law, and if thou turn unto the LORD thy God with all thine heart, and with all thy soul.

God stipulated how the new generation of Israelites was to repent and turn to Him. He specified that they were to do so with all their heart. The phrase, "if thou shalt hearken" in the Hebrew is *shama'* (**shaw-MAH**), and it means "to hear with intentions of interest, to listen to, to consent, to obey." Not only were they to hear the voice of the Lord, through His Word; they were to consent to obey the tenets of His edicts. Then, they were to turn unto God with all their hearts. The phrase, "of the law" in the Hebrew is *towrah,* (**to-RAW**), and it means "the Deuteronomic or Mosaic Law." "With all thine heart," in Hebrew, is *lebab* (**lay-BAWB**), and it means "mind, knowledge, thinking, reflection, memory, conscience, as seat of emotions and passions, as seat of courage." The phrase "with all thine soul" in Hebrew is *nephesh* (**NEH-fesh**), and it means "seat of emotions and passions, activity of mind, activity of the will, activity of the character." In other words, they are to turn to the Lord with their whole being; they are to honor God and His Word. As they walk in His ways, they are to be "red-hot" for Him and not "lukewarm." God addressed this grave problem of believers being lukewarm when He told the apostle John to tell the church of the Laodiceans, "I know thy works, that thou art neither cold nor hot: I would thou wert cold or hot. So then because thou art lukewarm, and neither cold nor hot, I will spue thee out of my mouth" (Revelation 3:15–16). The new generation, therefore, was to walk with God, in God's way. They were to choose life and not death! "He that hath an ear, let him hear what the Spirit saith unto the churches" (Revelation 3:22).

Sources:

Geoffrey W. Bromiley, ed. *International Standard Bible Encyclopedia.* Grand Rapids, Mich.: William B. Eerdmans, 1979.

Enns, John *The Moody Handbook of Theology.* Chicago: Moody Press, 1989.

Erickson, Millard J. *Christian Theology.* Grand Rapids, Mich.: Baker Books, 1998.

The New Oxford Annotated Bible. New York: Oxford University Press, Inc., 2000.

Daily Bible Readings

M: Observe God's Laws
Psalm 105:37–45
T: Obey Christ's Commands
Matthew 28:16–20
W: A Gracious and Merciful God
Nehemiah 9:16–20
T: A Pledge of Obedience
Joshua 24:14–24
F: To Love God Is to Obey
1 John 5:1–5
S: I Love You, O Lord
Psalm 18:1–6
S: Return to the Lord
Deuteronomy 30:1–10

NOTES

Vinny Boriello (516) cell 312-4950
(516) 921-2284

BERNARD (1.15.09) EX 33 JA 1:12 et al
misinterpretation & EXTREMES AVOIDED by Knowing the WORD
Spirits MUST be TESTED @ the WORD.

- Blasphemy -vs- H.S. (MT 12:31)
- SUICIDES Judas (MT 27:5); Saul (1SA 31:1-6); Samson (Jdg 16:30)
- Umbrageous (um brā jes) [umbra= shade or shadow, dark central part of a sunspot] (umbrageux, shy, suspicious orig shady)
  - giving shade; shady; easy offended.